Frommer's®
Caribbean

Our Caribbean

by Darwin Porter & Danforth Prince

THINK CARIBBEAN, AND SWAYING PALM TREES, WHITE-SAND BEACHES, turquoise waters, and a steel band playing in the background are likely to spring to mind. A fantasy? Sure, but in the Caribbean it can also be a reality.

Each island has its own distinct heritage, but all offer hedonistic pleasures and the promise of romance. Of course, issues like drugs, crime, and poverty plague some of the larger cities, but you won't have trouble discovering your own little slice of paradise. In our many years traveling the Caribbean, we've collected a vast storehouse of memories. Here, and in the photos that follow, are some of our personal favorites:

Sitting in a rustic restaurant with a pink-hued tropical punch listening to the sound of a *coquí* (a tiny tree frog). Jumping into a swimming hole fed by a rushing waterfall in Puerto Rico's tropical rainforest, El Yunque. Delaying breakfast at Anguilla's *luxe* Moorish Cap Juluca hotel for an early morning dip in cool, clear, blue water. Diving solo on Grand Cayman and discovering a sunken British merchant ship that last saw daylight in 1794. Shopping the bustling open-air market at St. George's in Grenada for nutmeg and mace to use back in our own kitchen. Lounging under a towering palm in Barbados as the azure waters of Bottom Bay Beach beckon.

© Doug Scott/AGE Fotostock

The French port of **MARIGOT (left)** on the island of St. Martin is a sleepy backwater, but it's also the capital of this tiny island nation (the other part of the island, known as Sint Maarten, is governed by the Netherlands). This section of the port, where fishermen still set out early in the morning in pursuit of the day's catch, lies between Baie de Marigot and Simpson Bay Lagoon. From ramshackle houses comes the aroma of West Indian spices and French croissants baking in the morning. Right around the bend is another Marigot, a port of cruise ships and multimillion-dollar yachts.

The living is easy among the sheltering palms at **BOTTOM BAY BEACH (above)** in Barbados, a tropical strip of brilliant white sand washed by the aquamarine waters of the sometimes turbulent Atlantic. Far removed from the glitter and glamour of Barbados' golden western coast, Bottom Bay lies in the south-eastern corner of the island, just north of the island's most famous landmark, Sam Lord's Castle.

HANDELSKADE (above), the main quay of Willemstad, capital of the Dutch island of Curaçao, is a storybook setting—rows of pastel-colored buildings trimmed with elaborate dormers, cupolas, and curving gables. These buildings front one of the world's busiest ports.

Much beloved by photographers, the fabled **CHATTEL HOUSES OF BARBADOS (right)** come in vivid colors like peppermint stripe, fire-engine red, and shocking pink. These small makeshift homes, built by rural people, were hastily assembled on plantations in need of workers, and then moved elsewhere as labor requirements demanded.

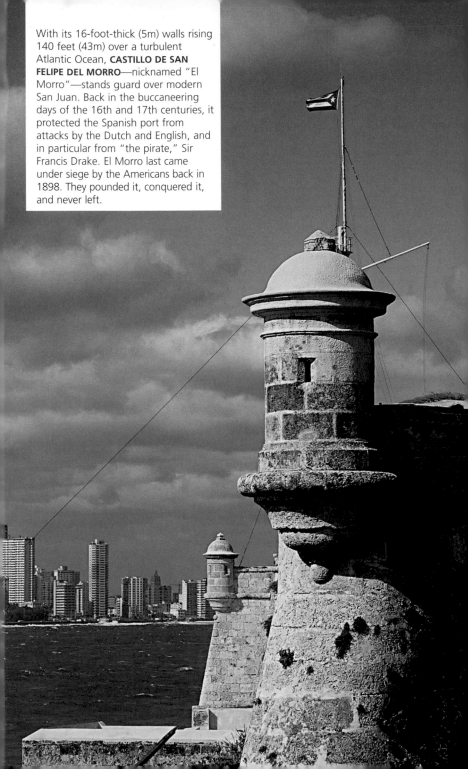

With its 16-foot-thick (5m) walls rising 140 feet (43m) over a turbulent Atlantic Ocean, **CASTILLO DE SAN FELIPE DEL MORRO**—nicknamed "El Morro"—stands guard over modern San Juan. Back in the buccaneering days of the 16th and 17th centuries, it protected the Spanish port from attacks by the Dutch and English, and in particular from "the pirate," Sir Francis Drake. El Morro last came under siege by the Americans back in 1898. They pounded it, conquered it, and never left.

Anguilla is known for chic and super-expensive hotels, but also for **LOBSTERMEN (left)**. Fishing off the coastline here turns up the Caribbean's richest catch of spiny lobster. Like the ancient Arawak Indians before them, Anguilla fishermen set out in handcrafted boats in pursuit of this white-fleshed delicacy.

The strains of **MUSIC (below)** can be heard anywhere and everywhere in the West Indies: while riding an overcrowded bus with chickens going to market, while drinking beer in a beachfront dive, and especially at carnival time when islanders dance in the streets. The people of the Caribbean can use almost anything to make music, but their most famous instruments are the steel drums created from discarded oil drums. The rhythms of reggae and soca (a soul-calypso blend) have spread across the globe. Aficionados claim reggae makes you think, and soca makes you dance.

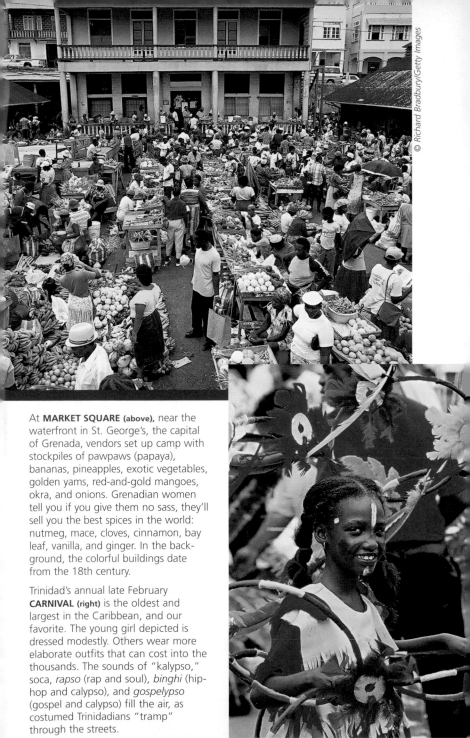

At **MARKET SQUARE (above),** near the waterfront in St. George's, the capital of Grenada, vendors set up camp with stockpiles of pawpaws (papaya), bananas, pineapples, exotic vegetables, golden yams, red-and-gold mangoes, okra, and onions. Grenadian women tell you if you give them no sass, they'll sell you the best spices in the world: nutmeg, mace, cloves, cinnamon, bay leaf, vanilla, and ginger. In the background, the colorful buildings date from the 18th century.

Trinidad's annual late February **CARNIVAL (right)** is the oldest and largest in the Caribbean, and our favorite. The young girl depicted is dressed modestly. Others wear more elaborate outfits that can cost into the thousands. The sounds of "kalypso," soca, *rapso* (rap and soul), *binghi* (hip-hop and calypso), and *gospelypso* (gospel and calypso) fill the air, as costumed Trinidadians "tramp" through the streets.

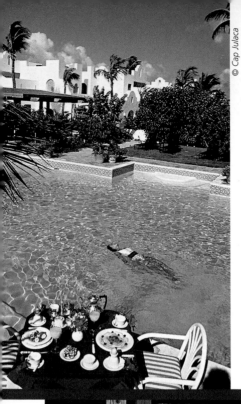

© Cap Juluca

Decadent **CAP JULUCA (left)**, on the island of Anguilla, rises from the beach like a Moorish village of whitewashed one- and two-story villas. While floating in the pool, you can enjoy the intoxicating scents of jasmine and frangipani wafting from the gardens. The South Caribbean's most photographed view—the twin Pitons set in a lush valley over a sun-glinted sea at St. Lucia—is yours and yours alone when you stay in one of the octagonal cottages clinging to a hillside on the landscaped grounds of **ANSE CHASTANET (below)**. The exclusive **BIRAS CREEK RESORT (above right)**, on Virgin Gorda in the British Virgin Islands, is a perfect hideaway for those seeking seclusion. If you're bored with the view you can always wander around the surrounding nature preserve, feeding hibiscus blossoms to the 3-foot-long (1m) iguanas. Set on 300 rolling, green-covered acres (121 hectares) of St. Croix, the deluxe **BUCCANEER (below right)**, the island's best resort, opens onto three coves of white sandy beaches set against a backdrop of coconut palms.

© Anse Chastenet Resort

A **DIVER (above)** has a close encounter with a gray angelfish on the left and a fat, speckled Nassau grouper on the right. These fish are among the friendlier denizens of the deep off the coastline of Provo, site of the main tourist development in the little island nation of Turks and Caicos.

The **"WRECK OF THE TEN SAILS" (right)** sank at what is now Gun Bar. On February 8, 1794, 10 England-bound merchant vessels ran aground off the treacherous reefs of Grand Cayman, today the Caribbean's top scuba-diving destination.

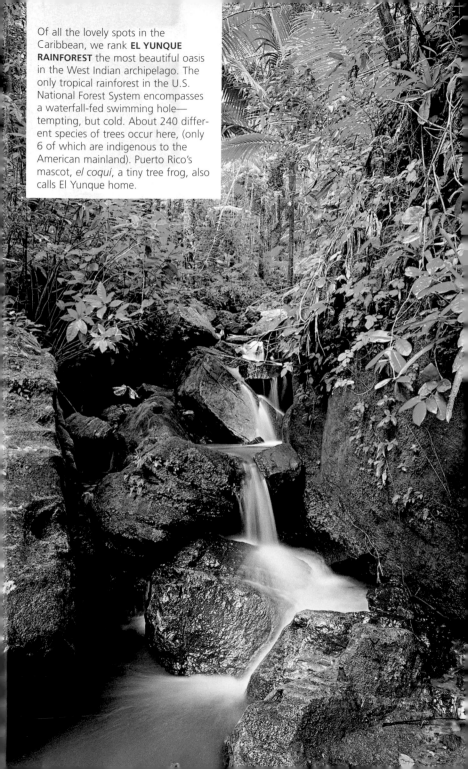

Of all the lovely spots in the Caribbean, we rank **EL YUNQUE RAINFOREST** the most beautiful oasis in the West Indian archipelago. The only tropical rainforest in the U.S. National Forest System encompasses a waterfall-fed swimming hole—tempting, but cold. About 240 different species of trees occur here, (only 6 of which are indigenous to the American mainland). Puerto Rico's mascot, *el coquí*, a tiny tree frog, also calls El Yunque home.

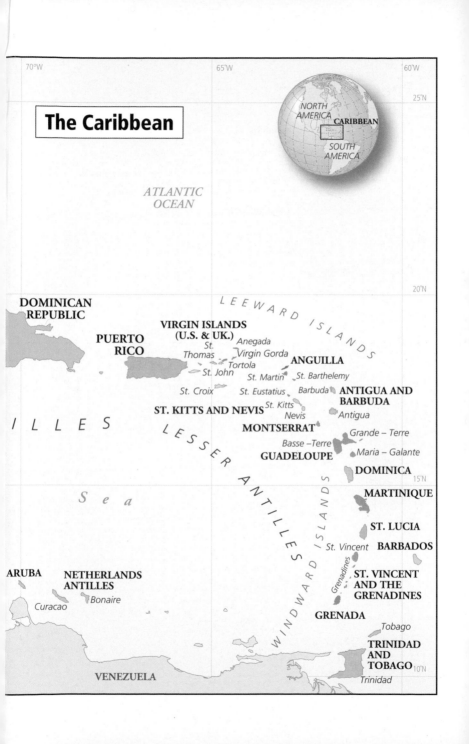

The Caribbean

70°W · 65°W · 60°W

25°N

NORTH
AMERICA
CARIBBEAN
SOUTH
AMERICA

ATLANTIC
OCEAN

20°N

DOMINICAN
REPUBLIC

LEEWARD ISLANDS

PUERTO
RICO

VIRGIN ISLANDS
(U.S. & UK.)
St.
Thomas
Anegada
Virgin Gorda
Tortola
St. John
St. Martin
St. Barthelemy

ANGUILLA

St. Croix
St. Eustatius
Barbuda

ANTIGUA AND
BARBUDA

ST. KITTS AND NEVIS
St. Kitts
Nevis
Antigua

I L L E S

MONTSERRAT
Basse –Terre
GUADELOUPE
Grande – Terre
Maria – Galante

DOMINICA

15°N

S e a

MARTINIQUE

ST. LUCIA

St. Vincent
BARBADOS

ARUBA
NETHERLANDS
ANTILLES
Bonaire
Curacao

Grenadines

ST. VINCENT
AND THE
GRENADINES

GRENADA

Tobago

TRINIDAD
AND
TOBAGO

10°N

VENEZUELA

Trinidad

Old San Juan

ATLANTIC OCEAN

Castillo San Felipe del Morro

Cemeterio de San Juan

Murallas de San Juan

EL CAMPO DEL MORRO

Calle del Morro

Murallas de San Juan

Fort San Cristobal

Norzgaray

Plaza Colón

Calle O'Donell

C. Tamarindo

C. Capilla

C.J.J. Acosta

Calle Tanca

Calle Sol

Calle Luna

Calle San Sebastián

Calle San Justo

Calle Cruz

Calle San José

Del Cristo

Norzgaray

Plaza San José

Calle San Francisco

Plaza de Armas

Calle Fortaleza

Calle Tetuan

Parque de las Palomas

Paseo Princesa

Calle Recinto

Calle Puntillo

El Arsenal

La Puntilla

Calle Presidio

Av. Munoz Rivera

Paseo de Covadonga

Calle San Augustin

C. de Muelle

Calle de Contreras

Calle Allen

Calle Marina

Marina

Calle Harding

Calle Gen. Pershing

Calle Braumbaugh

1

25

38

25

0   1/10 Mile

0   100 Meters

Frommer's®

Caribbean

2008

by Darwin Porter & Danforth Prince

Here's what the critics say about Frommer's:

"Amazingly easy to use. Very portable, very complete."
—*Booklist*

"Detailed, accurate, and easy-to-read information for all price ranges."
—*Glamour Magazine*

"Hotel information is close to encyclopedic."
—*Des Moines Sunday Register*

"Frommer's Guides have a way of giving you a real feel for a place."
—*Knight Ridder Newspapers*

Wiley Publishing, Inc.

About the Authors

As a team of veteran travel writers, **Darwin Porter** and **Danforth Prince** have produced titles for Frommer's, including guides to Italy, France, the Caribbean, England, and Germany. A film critic, columnist, and broadcaster, Porter is also a Hollywood biographer. His most recent releases are *Brando Unzipped,* documenting the private life of Marlon Brando, and *Jacko: His Rise and Fall,* the first complete biography ever written on the tumultuous life of Michael Jackson. Prince was formerly employed by the Paris bureau of the *New York Times* and is today the president of Blood Moon Productions and other media-related firms.

Published by:

Wiley Publishing, Inc.

111 River St.
Hoboken, NJ 07030-5774

ISBN: 978-0-470-14563-0

Editor: William Travis
Production Editor: Jana M. Stefanciosa
Cartographer: Roberta Stockwell
Photo Editor: Richard Fox
Anniversary Logo Design: Richard Pacifico
Production by Wiley Indianapolis Composition Services

Front cover photo: Woman reclining in hammock, seen from behind
Back cover photo: Martinique: Fort-de-France: Woman selling spices at the market

For information on our other products and services or to obtain technical support, please contact our Customer Care Department within the U.S. at 800/762-2974, outside the U.S. at 317/572-3993 or fax 317/572-4002.

Wiley also publishes its books in a variety of electronic formats. Some content that appears in print may not be available in electronic formats.

Manufactured in the United States of America

5 4 3 2 1

Contents

27 The U.S. Virgin Islands   698

Index   760

List of Maps

An Invitation to the Reader

In researching this book, we discovered many wonderful places—hotels, restaurants, shops, and more. We're sure you'll find others. Please tell us about them, so we can share the information with your fellow travelers in upcoming editions. If you were disappointed with a recommendation, we'd love to know that, too. Please write to:

Frommer's Caribbean 2008
Wiley Publishing, Inc. • 111 River St. • Hoboken, NJ 07030-5774

An Additional Note

Please be advised that travel information is subject to change at any time—and this is especially true of prices. We therefore suggest that you write or call ahead for confirmation when making your travel plans. The authors, editors, and publisher cannot be held responsible for the experiences of readers while traveling. Your safety is important to us, however, so we encourage you to stay alert and be aware of your surroundings. Keep a close eye on cameras, purses, and wallets, all favorite targets of thieves and pickpockets.

Other Great Guides for Your Trip:

Frommer's Caribbean Cruises & Ports of Call
Frommer's Caribbean Ports of Call
Frommer's Jamaica
Frommer's Puerto Rico
Frommer's Virgin Islands
Frommer's Portable Turks & Caicos
Frommer's Portable Dominican Republic

Frommer's Star Ratings, Icons & Abbreviations

Every hotel, restaurant, and attraction listing in this guide has been ranked for quality, value, service, amenities, and special features using a **star-rating system.** In country, state, and regional guides, we also rate towns and regions to help you narrow down your choices and budget your time accordingly. Hotels and restaurants are rated on a scale of zero (recommended) to three stars (exceptional). Attractions, shopping, nightlife, towns, and regions are rated according to the following scale: zero stars (recommended), one star (highly recommended), two stars (very highly recommended), and three stars (must-see).

In addition to the star-rating system, we also use **eight feature icons** that point you to the great deals, in-the-know advice, and unique experiences that separate travelers from tourists. Throughout the book, look for:

Finds	Special finds—those places only insiders know about
Fun Fact	Fun facts—details that make travelers more informed and their trips more fun
Kids	Best bets for kids and advice for the whole family
Moments	Special moments—those experiences that memories are made of
Overrated	Places or experiences not worth your time or money
Tips	Insider tips—great ways to save time and money
Value	Great values—where to get the best deals
Warning	Warning—traveler's advisories are usually in effect

The following **abbreviations** are used for credit cards:

AE	American Express	DISC	Discover	V	Visa
DC	Diners Club	MC	MasterCard		

Frommers.com

Now that you have this guidebook to help you plan a great trip, visit our website at **www.frommers.com** for additional travel information on more than 3,500 destinations. We update features regularly to give you instant access to the most current trip-planning information available. At Frommers.com, you'll find scoops on the best airfares, lodging rates, and car rental bargains. You can even book your travel online through our reliable travel booking partners. Other popular features include:

- Online updates of our most popular guidebooks
- Vacation sweepstakes and contest giveaways
- Newsletters highlighting the hottest travel trends
- Online travel message boards with featured travel discussions

What's New in the Caribbean

ANGUILLA Evoking the minimalist cool of South Beach, **Kú,** Shoal Bay East (✆ **264/497-2011**), has become the choice boutique hotel of the island. Suites, in five one to three story buildings, are among the finest on the island. See chapter 3.

ANTIGUA In the Barrymore Beach Hotel, **Julian's Alfresco,** Runaway Bay (✆ **268/562-1545**), set in tropical gardens off the beach, puts a creative flair on fusion cuisine, flavoring otherwise ordinary dishes with exotic spices. See chapter 4.

ARUBA One of the major resort hotels of Aruba has reopened as the **Occidental Grand Aruba,** J.E. Irausquin Blvd. 83 (✆ **800/858-2258** or 297/586-4500), rising over Palm Beach. Massively renovated and improved, the hotel provides the widest range of drinking and dining facilities in Aruba.

The old Wyndham has blossomed into the vastly improved **Westin Aruba Resort and Spa,** J.E. Irausquin Blvd., 77 (✆ **877/822-2222** or 297/586-4466), also on Palm Beach. Each of its rooms, scattered across 18 floors, opens onto a balcony. It also has the best steakhouse on the island. See chapter 5.

BARBADOS After a long closure for rebuilding, the **Hilton Barbados,** Needham's Point, Aquatic Gap (✆ **800/445-8667** or 246/426-0200), has bounced back and is better than ever. Standing on lush tropical acres, it lies at the southern ridge of Bridgetown (the capital) and is as modern as tomorrow, with jutting balconies and wide expanses of glass. See chapter 6.

CAYMAN ISLANDS After a massive rebuilding in the wake of Hurricane Ivan, many new restaurants have opened and old ones reopened. Chief among these is the **Cracked Conch/MacaBuca Oceanside Tiki Bar and Grill,** West Bay Rd. (✆ **345/945-5217**), which serves some of the island's best seafood. On the island's more isolated north coast, **Kaibo Bar & Grill,** in the Kaibo Yacht Club, Cayman Kai (✆ **345/947-9975**) serves juicy burgers, fresh salads, and fresh seafood along with steaks and pastas. See chapter 9.

CURACAO The **Avila Beach Hotel,** Penstraat 130-134 at Willemstad (✆ **800/747-8162** or 599/9-461-4377), long an island favorite, opened a new annex, Octagon Wing, in 2006, with 68 desirable suites. See chapter 10.

DOMINICA Posh is not a word you normally associate with the rugged adventure island of Dominica. That changed with the opening of **Silks,** a posh luxury boutique inn at Hatton Garden at Marigot (✆ 767/445-8856). Surrounded by tropical vegetation, it lies between two freshwater rivers and offers rooms in a wide variety of styles, even an African décor. Johnny Depp and Orlando Bloom chose to stay here during the shooting of *Pirates of the Caribbean: Dead Man's Chest.* See chapter 11.

DOMINICAN REPUBLIC A new north coast entry is **Casa Colonial,** Playa Dorado (© **809/571-9727**), a boutique hotel with lavish oceanfront master suites and a full-service spa. At the fast-emerging resort of Punta Cana, the **Paradiscus Palma Reale,** Playa de Bavaro (© **809/ 688-5000**), gives all competitors a run for their money. This is our favorite all-inclusive along the coast, with a stylish, sophisticated décor and a lot of upmarket luxuries such as a deluxe spa. See chapter 12.

GUADELOUPE After a complete renovation, the island's **Club Med La Caravelle,** Ste-Anne (© **800/CLUB-MED** or 590/85-49-50) delivers larger, better accommodations and an increase in the number of suites. The place is more kid friendly than ever with the introduction of expanded facilities for them, including a day camp. See chapter 14.

MARTINIQUE One of the hottest new addresses for dining is **Havana Cafe,** Havana Plage at Grand Anse (© **596/ 69-07-38**). Surprisingly, it doesn't serve a Cuban cuisine but tasty French cuisine, with the famous crepes of Brittany among other delights. You can drop in at almost any time of the day or night for platters of mussels or meats from the grill. A much posher choice is **Le Peche,** Anse Mitan (© **596/66-02-99**), housed in a flamboyant painted building on the sea. The chefs here prepare a fusion of French and Caribbean specialties. The results are evocative of the French Alps, the origins of the creative team who run this chic new rendezvous. See chapter 16.

PUERTO RICO Delta (© **800/ 221-1212**) has made it easier for New Yorkers or residents of Orlando to reach San Juan. From New York's JFK, the airline flies three times daily or else two times daily from Orlando.

In San Juan, the expansion at the **Caribe Hilton,** Calle Los Rosales (© **800/ HILTON** or 787/721-0303) continues.

Next to the main hotel, a cluster of luxurious Condado Lagoon Villas has been completed at the newly named **Paseo Caribe.** The addition of these rooms makes the Hilton the largest hotel in the Greater San Juan area. See chapter 17.

ST. BARTS La Plage, Le Tom Beach Hotel, Plage St-Jean (© **590/27-53-13**), is a beachfront restaurant that made a lot of "waves" in the winter of 2006 and 2007, with its fantasy Caribbean colors. Live bands in the evening keep the restaurant pulsating, while the ever-changing menu explodes with flair. See chapter 19.

ST. CROIX Until a few months ago the Cormorant Beach Club was the most famous gay hotel in the Caribbean. Not so anymore. Taken over by new management, it's now **The Palms at Pelican Cove,** 4126 La Grande Princesse (© **800/ 548-4460** or 340/778-8920). It's still gay friendly, but its clientele is now more diverse. See chapter 27.

ST. LUCIA There are now nonstop flights from the United States to this island aboard **Delta** (© **800/221-1212**), flying in every Friday to Tuesday from Atlanta. **American** (© **800/433-7300**) now flies daily from Miami to St. Lucia. Once you land on island, head for **Jacques Waterfront Dining,** Vigie Marina (© **758/458-1900**) for some of the best seafood and Caribbean dishes. Chef Jacky Rioux even smokes his own fish and meat. See chapter 22.

ST. MARTIN One of the island's most charming boutique hotels, the oceanfront **Alamanda Resort,** Baie Orientale (© **800/622-7836** or 590/52-87-40) presents a cluster of Creole houses that surround a lushly landscaped outdoor pool. See chapter 23.

ST. THOMAS The deluxe and very expensive **Ritz-Carlton St. Thomas,** 6900 Great Bay (© **800/241-3333** or 340/775-3333), just got even better following a $40 million renovation. Its most dramatic new feature is a key-activated Club Lounge with 55 new bedrooms, 16 executive suites, and 2 exclusive villas. Both the landscaping and the public rooms have also been considerably upgraded. See chapter 27.

TRINIDAD   Caribbean   Airlines (℃ 800/538-2942) has become a major player in carrying passengers to the southern Caribbean, stopping at Port-of-Spain, the capital of Trinidad. The airline offers service from New York, Miami, and Philadelphia, and also flies in from Toronto or London.

In Trinidad, **Coblentz Inn,** 44C Coblentz Ave. (℃ 868/621-0541), a little boutique hotel, lures visitors away from the Port-of-Spain with its moderate prices, comfort, and one of the town's best restaurants. See chapter 25.

TURKS AND CAICOS Spirit Airlines (℃ 800/772-7117) is now flying in from Fort Lauderdale to Provo on weekends. Spirit offers one flight a week to Grand Turk as well. At Provo, one of the best and most expensive hotels, part of the Sandals chain, is **Beaches Turks & Caicos Resort & Spa,** Lower Bight Rd. (℃ 800/232-2437 or 649/946-8000). A recent $70 million expansion and improvement resulted in upgraded family suites, and the addition of a water park, a gigantic swimming pool, and an "Italian Village." See chapter 26.

1

The Best of the Caribbean: Choosing the Perfect Island

In the Caribbean, you can hike through national parks and scuba dive along underwater mountains. But perhaps your idea of the perfect island vacation is to plunk yourself down on the sands with a frosted drink in hand. Whether you want a veranda with a view of the sea or a plantation house set in a field of sugar cane, this chapter will help you choose the vacation that best suits your needs.

For a thumbnail portrait of each island, see "The Islands in Brief," in chapter 2.

1 The Best Beaches

Good beaches with soul-warming sun, crystal-clear waters, and fragrant sea air can be found on virtually every island of the Caribbean, with the possible exceptions of Saba (which has rocky shores) and Dominica (where the few beaches have dramatically black sands that absorb the hot sun).

- **Shoal Bay** (Anguilla): This luscious stretch of silvery sand helped put Anguilla on the world-tourism map. Snorkelers are drawn to the schools of iridescent fish that dart among the coral gardens offshore. You can take the trail walk from Old Ta to little-known Katouche Beach, which provides perfect snorkeling and is also a prime site for a beach picnic under shade trees. See chapter 3.
- **The Beaches of Antigua:** Legend has it that there is a beach here for every day of the year, though we haven't bothered to confirm that by counting. Antiguans claim, with justifiable pride, that their two best beaches are Dickenson Bay, in the northwest corner of the island, and Half Moon

Bay, which stretches for a white-sandy mile along the eastern coast. Most major hotels open directly onto a good beach, so chances are good yours will be built on or near a strip of white sand. See chapter 4.

- **Palm Beach** (Aruba): This superb white-sand beach put Aruba on the tourist map. Several publications, including *Condé Nast Traveler,* have hailed it as one of the 12 best beaches in the *world*. It's likely to be crowded in winter, but for swimming, sailing, or fishing, it's idyllic. See chapter 5.
- **The Gold Coast** (Barbados): Some of the finest beaches in the Caribbean lie along the so-called Gold Coast of Barbados, site of some of the swankiest deluxe hotels in the Northern Hemisphere. Our favorites include Paynes Bay, Brandon's Beach, Paradise Beach, and Brighton Beach, all open to the public. See chapter 6.
- **Cane Garden Bay** (Tortola, British Virgin Islands): One of the Caribbean's most spectacular stretches, Cane Garden Bay has 2km (1¼ miles) of

white sand and is a jogger's favorite. It's a much better choice than more obvious (and more crowded) Magens Bay beach on neighboring St. Thomas. See chapter 8.

- **Seven Mile Beach** (Grand Cayman, Cayman Islands): It's really about 9km (5½ miles) long, but who's counting? Lined with condos and plush resorts, this beach is known for its array of watersports and its translucent aquamarine waters. Australian pines dot the background, and the average winter temperature of the water is a perfect 80°F (27°C). See chapter 9.

- **The Beaches of the Dominican Republic:** There are two great options here: the beaches of resort-riddled Punta Cana at the easternmost tip of the island, or those at Playa Dorada along the northern coast, which fronts the Atlantic. Punta Cana is a 30km (20-mile) strip of oyster-white sands set against a backdrop of palm trees, and Playa Dorada is filled with beaches of white or beige sands. See chapter 12.

- **Grand Anse Beach** (Grenada): This 3km (2-mile) beach is reason enough to go to Grenada. Although the island has some 45 beaches, most with white sand, this is the fabled one, and rightly so. There's enough space and so few visitors that you'll probably find a spot just for yourself. The sugary sands of Grand Anse extend into deep waters far offshore. Most of the island's best hotels are within walking distance of this beach strip. See chapter 13.

- **Seven Mile Beach** (Negril, Jamaica): In the northwestern section of the island, this beach stretches for 11km (6¾ miles) along the sea, and is backed by some of the most hedonistic resorts in the Caribbean. Not for the conservative, the beach also contains some nudist sections along with bare-all Booby Cay offshore. See chapter 15.

- **Diamond Beach** (Martinique): This bright, white-sandy beach stretches for about 10km (6¼ miles), much of it developed. It faces a rocky offshore island, Diamond Rock, which has uninhabited shores. See chapter 16.

- **Luquillo Beach** (Puerto Rico): This crescent-shaped public beach, about 50km (30 miles) east of San Juan, is the local favorite. Much photographed because of its white sands and coconut palms, it also has tent sites and picnic facilities. The often-fierce waters of the Atlantic are subdued by the coral reefs protecting the crystal-clear lagoon. See chapter 17.

- **St-Jean Beach** (St. Barthélemy): A somewhat narrow, golden sandy beach, St-Jean is the gem of the island, reminiscent of the French Riviera (though you're supposed to keep your top on). Reefs protect the beach, making it ideal for swimming. See chapter 19.

- **The Beaches of St. Maarten/St. Martin:** Take your pick. This island, divided about equally between France and the Netherlands, has 39 white-sandy beaches. Our favorites include Dawn Beach, Mullet Bay Beach, Maho Bay Beach, and Great Bay Beach on the Dutch side. Orient Beach is another standout—not because of its sands but because of the nudists. See chapter 23.

- **Canouan** (The Grenadines): Most of the other beaches recommended in this section have been discovered and may be crowded in winter. But if you're looking for an idyllic, secluded stretch of perfect white sand, head for the remote and tiny island of Canouan, one of the pearls of The Grenadines, a string of islands lying south of its parent, St. Vincent. You'll

The Caribbean Islands

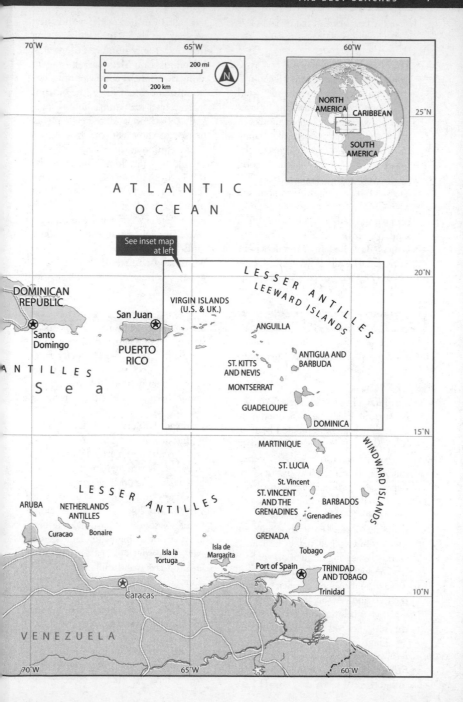

have the beaches and the crystal-clear waters to yourself, even in winter. See chapter 24.

- **The Beaches of Tobago:** For your Robinson Crusoe holiday in the southern Caribbean, head to the little island of Tobago. Even Trinidadians fly over here on weekends to enjoy the beach life. It doesn't get any better than a long coral beach called Pigeon Point on the northwestern coast. Other good beaches on Tobago include Back Bay (site of an old coconut plantation) and Man-O-War Bay, known for its beautiful natural harbor and long stretch of sand. See chapter 25.

- **Grace Bay Beach** (Providenciales, Turks and Caicos Islands): These 20km (12 miles) of pale sands are the pride of Provo; *Condé Nast Traveler*

has called this one of the world's best beaches. It's such a spectacular setting that increasing numbers of resorts, including Club Med, have sprung up along the shore. A couple of miles out from the northern shore, the beach is fringed by a reef with fabulous snorkeling. Back on land, there are plenty of places where you can rent water-sports equipment. See chapter 26.

- **Trunk Bay** (St. John): Protected by the U.S. National Park Service, this beach is one of the Caribbean's most popular. A favorite with cruise-ship passengers, it's known for its underwater snorkeling trail, where markers guide you along the reef just off the white sands; you're sure to see a gorgeous rainbow of tropical fish. See chapter 27.

2 The Best Snorkeling

The Virgin Islands offer some particularly outstanding sites, but there are many other great places for snorkeling in the Caribbean.

- **Antigua:** This is a snorkeler's dream. Most of its lovely beaches open onto clear, calm waters populated by rainbow-hued tropical fish. The marine life offshore is particularly dense, including colorful sea anemones. The rich types of different elk and brain coral make snorkeling particularly rewarding. See chapter 4.

- **Bonaire Marine Park** (Bonaire): All the attributes that make Bonaire a world-class diving destination apply to its snorkeling, too. Snorkelers can wade from the shores off their hotels to the reefs and view an array of coral and a range of colorful fish. In particular, the reefs just off Klein Bonaire and Washington-Slagbaai National Park receive rave reviews. See chapter 7.

- **Stingray City** (Grand Cayman): Stingray City is an easy 4m (13-ft.)

diving site that can also be seen while snorkeling. It's an extraordinary experience to meet the dozens of tame, gentle stingrays that glide around you in the warm, crystal-clear waters. See chapter 9.

- **Curaçao Underwater Marine Park** (Curaçao): In contrast to Curaçao's arid terrain, the marine life that rings the island is rich and spectacular. The best-known snorkeling sites, in the Curaçao Underwater Marine Park, stretch for 20km (12 miles) along Curaçao's southern coastline, and there are many other highly desirable sites as well. Sunken ships, gardens of hard and soft coral, and millions of fish are a snorkeler's treat. See chapter 10.

- **St. Martin:** The best snorkeling on the island lies on the French side, where the government religiously protects the calm waters, which are populated with schools of brilliantly colored fish. Find a tiny cove and explore the shallow reefs along its shores, especially in the northeastern underwater nature reserve. See chapter 23.

- **The Grenadines:** Every island offers great snorkeling possibilities right off magnificent white-sandy beaches. In most places you'll have the waters to yourself. A reef stretching for 1.5km (1 mile) along the island of Canouan invites snorkelers, and the waters are filled with beautiful brain coral and rainbow-hued fish. The snorkeling is also good at Palm Island and Petit St. Vincent. See chapter 24.

- **Tobago:** Enormous colonies of marine life inhabit the shallow, sun-dappled waters off the coastline facing Venezuela. Buccoo Reef on Tobago is especially noteworthy, and many local entrepreneurs offer snorkeling cruises. See chapter 25.

- **Provo** (Turks and Caicos): Although this island is known primarily as one of the world's best dive sites, it also provides a number of snorkeling possibilities. The government has established snorkel trails at Smith's Reef and Bight Reef, right off of Provo's spectacular Grace Bay Beach. These reefs are right off the shoreline, and they provide easy access into the fragile but stunningly beautiful world of coral gardens, the most dramatic in the vast area immediately south of The Bahamas. See chapter 26.

- **Coki Point Beach** (St. Thomas): On the north shore of St. Thomas, this beach offers excellent snorkeling,

especially around the coral ledges near Coral World's underwater tower, a favorite with cruise-ship passengers. See chapter 27.

- **Buck Island** (St. Croix): More than 250 species of fish, as well as a variety of sponges, corals, and crustaceans, have been found at this 340-hectare (840-acre) island and reef system, 3km (2 miles) off St. Croix's north shore. The reef is strictly protected by the National Park Service. See chapter 27.

- **Cane Bay** (St. Croix): One of the best diving and snorkeling sites on St. Croix is off this breezy north-shore beach. On a clear day, you can swim out 140m (450 ft.) and see the Cane Bay Wall that drops off dramatically to deep waters below. Multicolored fish and elkhorn and brain coral abound. See chapter 27.

- **Trunk Bay** (St. John): Trunk Bay's self-guided 205m-long (670-ft.) trail has large underwater signs that identify species of coral and other items of interest. The beach has showers, changing rooms, equipment rentals, and a lifeguard. See chapter 27.

- **Haulover Bay** (St. John): A favorite with locals, this small bay is rougher than Leinster and is often deserted. The snorkeling is dramatic, with ledges, walls, nooks, and sandy areas set close together. At this spot, only about 180m (600 ft.) of land separates the Atlantic Ocean from the Caribbean Sea. See chapter 27.

3 The Best Diving

All the major islands offer diving trips, lessons, and equipment, but here are the top picks.

- **Bonaire:** The highly accessible reefs that surround Bonaire have never suffered from poaching or pollution, and the island's environmentally conscious diving industry ensures they never will. Created from volcanic

eruptions, the island is an underwater mountain, with fringe reefs right off the beach of every hotel on any part of the island. See chapter 7.

- **Virgin Gorda:** Many divers plan their entire vacations around exploring the famed wreck of the HMS *Rhone,* off Salt Island. This royal mail steamer, which went down in 1867, is the most celebrated diving site in the Caribbean. See chapter 8.

- **Grand Cayman:** This is a world-class diving destination. There are 34 dive operators on Grand Cayman (with five more on Little Cayman, plus three on Cayman Brac). A full range of professional diving services is available, including equipment sales, rentals, and repairs; instruction at all levels; underwater photography; and video schools. See chapter 9.

- **Saba:** Islanders can't brag about its beaches, but Saba is blessed with some of the Caribbean's richest marine life. It's one of the premier diving locations in the Caribbean, with 38 official diving sites. The unusual setting includes underwater lava flows, black sand, large strands of black coral, millions of fish, and underwater mountaintops submerged under 27m (90 ft.) of water. See chapter 18.

- **Turks and Caicos Islands:** These islands provide a rich assortment of relatively unexplored underwater sites, including sea lanes where boaters and divers often spot whales from January to March. A collection of unusual underwater wrecks includes the HMS *Endymion,* which sank during a storm in 1790. Miles of reefs house myriad kinds of colorful marine life. Right off Grand Turk, experienced divers love the many miles of "drop-off" diving, where the sea walls plunge into the uncharted depths of blue holes more than 2,100m (6,900 ft.) below sea level. As you descend you'll see colonies of black coral, rare forms of anemone, purple sponges, stunning gorgonian, endless forms of coral, and thousands of fish. See chapter 26.

- **St. Croix:** Increasingly known as a top diving destination, St. Croix hasn't yet overtaken Grand Cayman, but has a lot going for it. Beach dives, reef dives, wreck dives, nighttime dives, wall dives—they're all here. The highlight is the underwater trails of the national park at Buck Island, off St. Croix's mainland. Other desirable sites include the drop-offs and coral canyons at Cane Bay and Salt River. Davis Bay is the location of the 3,600m-deep (12,000-ft.) Puerto Rico Trench, the fifth-deepest body of water on earth. See chapter 27.

4 The Best Sailing

Virtually every large-scale hotel in the Caribbean provides small sailboats (most often Sunfish, Sailfish, and small, one-masted catamarans) for its guests. If you're looking for larger craft, the almost-ideal sailing conditions in the Virgin Islands and The Grenadines come instantly to mind. These two regions offer many options for dropping anchor at secluded coves surrounded by relatively calm waters. Both areas are spectacular, but whereas the Virgin Islands have more dramatic, mountainous terrain, The Grenadines offer insights into island cultures little touched by the modern world.

Other places to sail in the Caribbean include Antigua, Barbados, St. Martin, and the French-speaking islands. But if you plan on doing a lot of sailing, know that the strongest currents and biggest waves are usually on the northern and eastern sides of most islands—the Atlantic (as opposed to the Caribbean) side.

- **The Grenadines:** Boating is a way of life in The Grenadines, partly because access to many of the tiny remote islands is difficult or impossible by airplane. One of the most prominent local charter agents is **Nicholson**

Yacht Charters (✆ 800/662-6066 in the U.S.), headquartered in nearby St. Vincent. On Bequia, Mustique, Petit St. Vincent, and Union Island, all the hotels can put you in touch with local entrepreneurs who rent sailing craft. See chapter 24 for more details.

- **The Virgin Islands:** Perhaps because of their well-developed marina facilities (and those of the nearby United States), the Virgin Islands receive the lion's share of devoted yachties. The reigning capital for sailing is Tortola, the largest island of the British Virgins. On-site are about 300 well-maintained sailing craft available for bareboat rentals and perhaps 100 charter yachts.

  The largest of the Caribbean's yacht chartering services is **The Moorings** (✆ 888/535-7289 in the U.S. and Canada, or 284/494-2331 in the British Virgin Islands; www.moorings.com). This yachting charter center is described more fully in chapter 8, as are the other outfits in this paragraph. On the island of Virgin Gorda, in the British Virgin Islands, the best bet for both boat rentals and accommodations, as well as for a range of instruction, is the **Bitter End Yacht Club** (✆ 800/872-2392 in the U.S., or 284/494-2746; www.beyc.com).

  Some of the biggest charter business in the Caribbean is conducted on St. Thomas, especially at **American Yacht Harbor,** Red Hook (✆ 340/775-6454), which offers bareboat and fully crewed charters. Other reliable rental agents include **Charteryacht League,** at Flagship (✆ 800/524-2061 in the U.S., or 340/774-3944; www.vicl.org). The U.S. Virgin Islands are covered in chapter 27.

  On St. Croix, boating is less essential to the local economy than it is on St. Thomas or in the British Virgins, so if you're taking a Virgin Islands sailing trip, plan accordingly.

5 The Best Golf Courses

Some of the world's most famous golf architects, including Robert Trent Jones (both Jr. and Sr.), Pete Dye, and Gary Player, have designed challenging courses in the Caribbean.

- **Tierra del Sol Golf Course** (Aruba; ✆ 297/58-67800; www.tierradelsol.com): Robert Trent Jones, Jr., has designed an 18-hole, par-71, 6,811-yard course that is one of the grandest in the southern Caribbean. On the northwest coast of this arid, cactus-studded island, the course takes in Aruba's indigenous flora, including the divi-divi tree. See p. 120.

- **Teeth of the Dog** and **The Links,** both at Casa de Campo (Dominican Republic; ✆ 809/523-3333, ext. 3187): Teeth of the Dog is one of designer Pete Dye's masterpieces.

Seven holes are set adjacent to the sea, whereas the other 11 are confoundedly labyrinthine. The resort also has a second golf course, The Links, which some claim is even more difficult. See p. 278.

- **Golf de St-François** (Guadeloupe; ✆ 590/88-41-87): Six of its 18 holes are ringed with water traps, the winds are devilishly unpredictable, and the par is a sweat-inducing 71. This fearsome course displays the wit and skill of its designer, Robert Trent Jones, Sr. Most of the staff is multilingual, and because the course is owned by the local municipality, it's a lot less snobby than you might expect. See p 351.

- **The Tryall Club** (Montego Bay, Jamaica; ✆ 876/956-5660): This is the finest golf course on an island known for its tricky breezes. The site occupied by The Tryall Club was once the home of one of Jamaica's best-known sugar plantations, the only remnant of which is a ruined water-wheel. The promoters of Johnnie Walker Scotch, who know a lot about golfing, use this place for their most prestigious competition. In winter, the course is usually open only to guests of The Tryall Club. See p. 379.

- **Cinnamon Hill Ocean Course** (Rose Hall, Jamaica; © 866/831-1313): This is one of the top five courses in the world, even though it faces tough competition in Montego Bay. The signature hole is 8, which doglegs onto a promontory and a green that thrusts about 180m (600 ft.) into the sea. The back nine, however, are the most

scenic and most challenging, rising into steep slopes and deep ravines on Mount Zion. See p. 379.

- **Four Seasons Resort Nevis** (Nevis; © 869/469-1111): We consider this our personal favorite in all of the Caribbean, and so do readers of *Caribbean Travel & Life*. It was carved out of a coconut plantation and tropical rainforest in the 1980s, and its undulating beauty is virtually unequaled. Designed by Robert Trent Jones, Jr., the course begins at sea level, rises to a point midway up the slopes of Mount Nevis, and then slants gracefully back down near the beachfront clubhouse. Electric carts carry golfers through a labyrinth of well-groomed paths, some of which skirt steep ravines. See p. 554.

6 The Best Tennis Facilities

- **Curtain Bluff** (Antigua; © 888/289-9898 in the U.S., or 268/462-8400): Small, select, and carefully run by people who love tennis, this is also the annual site of a well-known spring tournament. The courts are set in a low-lying valley. See p. 78.

- **Casa de Campo** (Dominican Republic; © 800/877-3643 or 809/523-8698): The facilities here include 13 clay courts (10 are lit, and 2 are ringed with stadium seating), 4 all-weather Laykold courts, a resident pro, ball machines, and tennis pros who are usually available to play with guests. During midwinter, residents and clients of Casa de Campo have first crack at court times. See p. 276.

- **Half Moon Rose Hall** (Montego Bay, Jamaica; © 876/953-2211): This resort sprawls over hundreds of acres, with about a dozen tennis courts and at least four squash and/or racquetball courts. Jamaica has a strong, British-based affinity for

tennis, and Half Moon keeps the tradition alive. See p. 367.

- **El Conquistador Resort & Golden Door Spa** (Puerto Rico; © 800/468-5228 or 787/863-1000): Facilities at this megaresort include 7 Har-Tru tennis courts, a resident pro, and a clubhouse with its own bar. If you're looking for a partner, the hotel will find one for you. Only guests of the hotel can use the courts, some of which are illuminated for night play. See p. 497.

- **Wyndham Sugar Bay Beach Resort & Spa** (St. Thomas; © 800/996-3426 in the U.S., or 340/777-7100; www.wyndham.com): The resort offers the first stadium tennis court in the U.S. Virgin Islands, with a capacity of 220 spectators. In addition, it has four Laykold courts, each of which is lit for night play. There's an on-site pro shop, and lessons are available. See p. 705.

- **The Buccaneer** (St. Croix; ✆ **800/ 255-3881** in the U.S., or 340/ 773-2100; www.thebuccaneer.com): Hailed as having the best tennis facilities in the Virgin Islands, this resort hosts several tournaments every year. There are eight all-weather Laykold courts, two of which are illuminated at night; there's also a pro shop. Nonguests can play here for a fee. See p. 726.

7 The Best Places to Honeymoon

More and more couples are exchanging their vows in the Caribbean. Many resorts will arrange everything from the preacher to the flowers, so we've included in the following list some outfits that provide wedding services. For more information about the various options and the legal requirements for marriages on some of the more popular Caribbean islands, see chapter 2.

- **Cap Juluca** (Anguilla; ✆ **888/858-5822** in the U.S., or 264/497-6779; www.capjuluca.com): A unique postmodern design and a thrillingly beautiful beach are the highlights of this resort. It resembles a Saharan Casbah, with domed villas that seem to float against the scrubland and azure sky. It's an extremely stylish setting for romance. More than any other resort on Anguilla, Cap Juluca affords privacy with its 72 hectares (180 acres). In a secluded villa, honeymooners can enjoy private pools and huge tubs for two. You can join other guests for meals and/or retreat into total seclusion. See p. 60.

- **St. James's Club** (Antigua; ✆ **800/ 858-4618** in the U.S., or 268/460-5000; www.eliteislandresorts.com): There are enough diversions at this very posh, British-style resort to keep a honeymooning couple up and about for weeks. Breakfast, lunch, and dinner are included, along with unlimited drinks. Among the perks is a private, candlelit dinner for two in a romantic setting. Honeymooners are greeted with a bottle of champagne and freshly cut bougainvillea in their rooms, which can be private villas, suites, or, for complete isolation, a hillside home. Unlike Cap Juluca, which promotes seclusion, this is for honeymooners who prefer an active lifestyle, gambling at the casino, taking in the beach, or enjoying the widest array of dining and drinking options of any hotel on the island. See p. 80.

- **Biras Creek Estate** (Virgin Gorda, B.V.I.; ✆ **800/223-1108** in the U.S., or 310/440-4225; www.biras.com): If you're eager to escape your in-laws and bridesmaids after a wedding ceremony, this is the place. It's a quintessential mariner's hideaway that can be reached only via a several-mile boat ride across the open sea. Perched on a narrow promontory jutting into the Caribbean, it's an intensely private retreat set on 60 hectares (150 acres) with a crisscrossing network of signposted nature trails. Spacious, open-air, walled showers are provided in each bathroom. Honeymooners come here not to be pampered, but to be left alone to do their thing. Entertainment and dancing enliven some evenings, but for the most part you'll enjoy utter tranquility. Its king-size beds are the best on the island. Don't come here for a lot of activities. See p. 192.

- **Peter Island Resort** (Peter Island, B.V.I.; ✆ **800/346-4451** or 284/ 495-2000; www.peterisland.com): Romantics appreciate the isolation of this resort, on a 720-hectare (1,780-acre) private island south of Tortola and east of St. John. Reaching it requires a 30-minute waterborne transfer, which many urban refugees consider part of the fun. It's very laid-back—bring your new spouse and a good book, and enjoy the comings and goings of yachts at the island's private marina while you recover from the stress of your wedding. See p. 201.

- **Hyatt Regency Grand Cayman** (Grand Cayman; ℂ **800/233-1234** in the U.S., or 345/949-1234; www.hyatt.com): Hands down, this is the most glamorous and best-land-scaped resort in the Cayman Islands. Honeymooners can buy a package that includes champagne and wine, a room with an oversize bed, a 1-day jeep rental, a romantic sundowner sail on a 12m (39-ft.) catamaran, and discounts at clothing stores, the resort's restaurants, and a golf course. They'll even present you with a honeymoon memento for your home. See p. 209.

- **Sandals Royal Caribbean** (Jamaica; ℂ **800/726-3257** in the U.S., or 876/953-2232; www.sandals.com): There are a handful of members of this resort chain in Jamaica alone (plus three others on St. Lucia, one in Turks and Caicos, and yet another one on the island of Antigua that is far less grand). Each prides itself on providing an all-inclusive (cash-free) environment where meals are provided in abundance. Enthusiastic members of the staff bring heroic amounts of community spirit to ceremonies celebrated on-site. Sandals provides everything from a preacher to petunias (as well as champagne, a cake, and all the legalities) for you to get hitched here. Any of these resorts can provide a suitable setting, but one of the most appealing is **Sandals Royal Caribbean,** outside Montego Bay, Jamaica. See p. 371.

- **El Conquistador Resort & Golden Door Spa** (Puerto Rico; ℂ **800/ 468-5228** or 787/863-1000): A complex of hotels set on a forested bluff overlooking the sea, this is one of the most lavish resorts ever built in the Caribbean. The architecture incorporates Moorish gardens and Andalusian fortresses. You can relax on hammocks for two on the resort's offshore private island, or soak in one of the dozen private Jacuzzis artfully concealed by vegetation throughout the grounds. See p. 497.

- **The Horned Dorset Primavera** (Puerto Rico; ℂ **800/633-1857** or 787/823-4030; www.horneddorset. com): This is the most elegant, inti-mate, secluded, romantic inn in Puerto Rico. It has private plunge pools; a cantilevered porch over the sea perfect for champagne at sunset; a fabulous candlelit restaurant; vast, well-equipped bathrooms with tubs big enough for two; sea-view bal-conies; romantic four-poster beds; and a discreet, helpful staff that doesn't interfere with honeymooners who want to be alone. See p. 488.

- **Golden Lemon Inn & Villas** (St. Kitts; ℂ **800/633-7411** in the U.S., or 869/465-7260): It started its life as a French manor house during the 17th century, but by the time its present owners began restoring it, the Golden Lemon was decidedly less glamorous. It required the refined tastes of Arthur Leaman, a former edi-tor at *House & Garden,* to bring it to its full potential. Today the Golden Lemon is an authentic Antillean retreat—luxurious, laid-back, and romantic—set in an isolated fishing village loaded with charm. See p. 543.

- **Four Seasons Resort Nevis** (Nevis; ℂ **800/332-3442** in the U.S., 800/ 268-6282 in Canada, or 869/469-1111): Though not as historic as some of the island's plantation-style inns, the Four Seasons rules without peer as the most deluxe hotel on the island, with the most extensive facilities. Set in a palm grove adjacent to the island's finest beach, it has the atmosphere of a supremely indulgent country club. The Four Seasons offers a 4-day wedding package with a choice of ceremony styles (in a church or on a beach, with a judge or with a civil magistrate). The resort's pastry chef designs each wedding cake individually, and the staff can arrange music, photographs, flowers, legalities, and virtually anything else you want. See p. 554.

- **Anse Chastanet** (St. Lucia; © **800/ 223-1108** in the U.S., or 758/ 459-7000; www.ansechastanet.com): Offering panoramic views of mountains and jungle, this intimate hotel is a winner with romantics. With its small size, it provides a lot of privacy and rustic charm. Its wedding package includes all legal processing, a wedding cake, and champagne, and add-ons cover everything from photography to a post-wedding sunset sail. See p. 572.
- **Petit St. Vincent Resort** (The Grenadines; © **954/963-7401**): If your idea of a honeymoon is to run away from everybody except your new spouse, this is the place. It takes about three planes and a boat to reach it, but the effort to get here is worth it, if you want total isolation and

privacy. Even the staff doesn't bother you unless you raise a flag for room service. If the honeymoon's going well, you may never have to leave your stone cottage by the beach. The artfully built clubhouses and bungalows were crafted from tropical woods and local stone. The results are simultaneously rustic and lavish. See p. 645.

- **Le Grand Courlan Resort & Spa** (Tobago; © **868/639-9667**): This is the favorite honeymoon retreat on Tobago. If you want to be fussed over, you and your new spouse can attend the spa for relaxing massages, or you can be left entirely alone to enjoy the bay outside your window or the sandy beach at your doorstep. From Guyanan hardwood to Italian porcelain, the decor is refined and elegant. See p. 665.
- **The Buccaneer** (St. Croix; © **800/ 255-3881** in the U.S., or 340/773-2100; www.thebuccanneer.com): Posh and discreet, this resort has some of the most extensive vacation facilities on St. Croix—three beaches, eight tennis courts, a spa and fitness center, an 18-hole golf course, and 3km (2 miles) of carefully maintained jogging trails. The accommodations include beachside rooms with fieldstone terraces leading toward the sea. The resort's stone sugar mill (originally built in 1658) is one of the most popular sites for weddings and visiting honeymooners on the island. See p. 726.

8 The Best Places to Get Away from It All

In addition to the choices below, see also the listings under "The Best Places to Honeymoon," above for information on Peter Island Resort in the British Virgin Islands, and Petit St. Vincent Resort and The Cotton House, both in The Grenadines.

- **Biras Creek Estate** (Virgin Gorda, B.V.I.; © **800/223-1108** in the U.S., or 310/440-4225; www.biras.com): The only access to this resort is by private launch. The sea air and the views over islets, cays, and deep blue waters will relax you in your charming guest room. The nautical atmosphere will quickly remove all thoughts of the 9-to-5 job you left behind.

- **Guana Island Club** (Guana Island, B.V.I.; ℂ **800/544-8262** in the U.S., or 284/494-2354; www.guana.com): One of the most secluded hideaways in the entire Caribbean, this resort occupies a privately owned 340-hectare (840-acre) bird sanctuary with nature trails. Head here for views of rare plant and animal life and for several excellent uncrowded beaches. See p. 202.

- **Little Cayman Beach Resort** (Cayman Islands; ℂ **800/327-3835** in the U.S. and Canada, or 345/948-1033; www.littlecayman.com): The only practical way to reach the 26-sq.-km (10-sq.-mile) island where this resort is located is by airplane.

Snorkelers will marvel at some of the most spectacular and colorful marine life in the Caribbean. The resort has the most complete watersports facilities on the island, and bikes are available for exploring. See p. 230.

- **Rawlins Plantation Inn** (St. Kitts; ℂ **800/346-5358** in the U.S., or 869/465-6221): Surrounded by 5 hectares (12 acres) of carefully manicured lawns and tropical shrubbery, and set on a panoramic hillock about 100m (330 ft.) above sea level, this hotel with its rugs of locally woven rushes and carved four-poster beds evokes a 19th-century plantation. You'll be separated from the rest of the island by hundreds of acres of sugar cane, and there are few phones and no televisions. See p. 544.

9 The Best Family Vacations

- **Hyatt Regency Aruba Resort & Casino** (Aruba; ℂ **800/233-1234** in the U.S. and Canada, or 297/58-61234; www.hyatt.com): Designed like a luxurious hacienda, with award-winning gardens, this resort is the most upscale on Aruba. Supervised activities for children 3 to 12 include games and contests such as crab races and hula-hoop competitions. See p. 108.

- **Sandy Beach Island Resort** (Barbados; ℂ **800/448-8355** in the U.S., or 246/435-8000): Set amid lots of fast-food and family-style restaurants on the southwest coast, this family-oriented hotel provides one- and two-bedroom suites. Each unit has a kitchen, so you can cook for yourself and save money. The beach is a few steps away, and the ambience is informal. If you bring the kids, they'll have plenty of playmates. See p. 140.

- **Hyatt Regency Grand Cayman** (Grand Cayman Island; ℂ **800/233-1234** in the U.S., or 345/949-1234; www.hyatt.com): Safe and serene, Grand Cayman Island, with its 11km (6¾-mile) sandy beach, seems designed for families with children. No one coddles children as much as the Hyatt people, who offer not only babysitting but also Camp Hyatt, with an activity-filled agenda, for children 3 to 12. See p. 209.

- **Breezes Curaçao** (Curaçao; ℂ **599/9-736-7888**; www.breezes.com): One of the most welcoming resorts for families is Breezes Curaçao, which has the best kiddie programs on island in its on-site Camp Breezes. Making it even more fun for children, the inclusive resort lies next to both the Undersea National Park and the Sea Aquarium and opens onto one of Curaçao's most beautiful and longest beaches. See p. 237.

- **Sunset at the Palms Resort & Spa** (Negril, Jamaica; ℂ **800/234-1707** in the U.S., or 876/957-5350; www.sunsetatthepalms.com): Rising on stilts, these wooden cottages with private decks add a sense of adventure to a beach vacation. Surrounded by tropical vegetation, families are only steps from the beach. Features for kids include a playground, computer games, arts-and-crafts lessons, and even storytelling sessions. Children under 2 stay free if they share a room with their parent; children 2 to 12 are $25 extra. See p. 388.

- **FDR** (Runaway Bay, Jamaica; ℂ **888/337-5437** in the U.S., or 876/973-4592; www.fdrholidays.com): FDR gives you a suite with its own kitchen, and a "vacation nanny" whose duties include babysitting. Neither its beach nor its pool is the most appealing on Jamaica, but the price is right, and the babysitting is part of the all-inclusive deal. Programs for children include dress-up parties, donkey rides, basketball, tennis, and snorkeling. See p. 373.

- **El Conquistador Resort & Golden Door Spa** (Puerto Rico; ℂ **800/468-5228** or 787/863-1000): Children aren't forgotten amid the glamour and hoopla of this fabulous resort. Camp Coquí provides day care daily

from 9am to 3pm for children 3 to 12, at a price of $40 per child per day. Activities include fishing, sailing, arts and crafts, and nature treks. Babysitting services are available, and children 15 and under stay free in a room with a parent. See p. 497.

- **Four Seasons Resort Nevis** (Nevis; ℂ **800/332-3442** in the U.S., 800/268-6282 in Canada, or 869/469-1111): The staff of the Kids for All Seasons day camp are kindly, matronly souls who work well with children. During the adult cocktail hour, when parents might opt for a romantic sundowner, kids attend a supervised children's hour that resembles a really good birthday bash. Other kid-friendly activities include tennis lessons, watersports, and storytelling. See p. 554.

- **The Buccaneer** (St. Croix; ℂ **800/255-3881** in the U.S., or 340/773-2100; www.thebuccaneer.com): Posh, upscale, with extremely good service, this hotel is a longtime favorite that occupies a 96-hectare (240-acre) former sugar estate. Its kids' programs (ages 2–12) include a half-day sailing excursion to Buck Island Reef and guided nature walks that let kids touch, smell, and taste tropical fruit. See p. 726.

10 The Best Inns

- **Admiral's Inn** (Antigua; ℂ **268/460-1027**; www.admiralsantigua.com): The most historically evocative corner of Antigua is Nelson's Dockyard, which was originally built in the 1700s to repair His Majesty's ships. The brick-and-stone inn that flourishes here today was once a warehouse for turpentine and pitch. In the late 1960s it was transformed into a well-designed and very charming hotel. *Note:* If you're sensitive to

noise, you might be bothered by the sometimes raucous bar and restaurant. See p. 83.

- **Avila Beach Hotel** (Curaçao; ℂ **800/747-8162** or 599/9-461-4377): This hotel's historic core, built in 1780 as the "country house" of the island's governor, retains its dignity and simplicity. Although it's been a hotel since the end of World War II, 40 bedrooms in motel-like outbuildings and upgraded the sports and dining facilities were added in the early 1990s. Today the Avila provides a sandy beach and easy access to the shops and distractions of nearby Willemstad. See p. 237.

- **Spice Island Beach Resort** (Grenada; ℰ **846/628-1701** in the U.S., or 473/444-4258;www.spicebeachresort.com): Each of this hotel's 66 units is a suite (with Jacuzzi) either beside the beach (one of Grenada's best) or near a swimming pool. Friday night features live music from the island's most popular bands. See p. 315.

- **François Plantation** (St. Barthélemy; ℰ **590/29-80-22**): At this inn, about a dozen pastel-colored bungalows are scattered among the lushest gardens on St. Barts. The mood is discreet, permissive, and fun. The food is French-inspired and served on a wide veranda decorated in a whimsical colonial style. See p. 517.

- **Ottley's Plantation Inn** (St. Kitts; ℰ **800/772-3039** in the U.S., or 869/465-7234): As you approach, the inn's dignified verandas appear majestically at the crest of 14 hectares (35 acres) of impeccably maintained lawns and gardens. It's one of the most charming plantation-house inns anywhere in the world, maintained with style and humor by its expatriate U.S. owners. The food is the best on the island, and the setting will soothe your tired nerves within a few hours after you arrive. See p. 543.

- **Montpelier Plantation Inn** (Nevis; ℰ **869/469-3462**): Style and grace are the hallmarks of this former 18th-century plantation, now converted to an inn and set on a 40-hectare (100-acre) estate. Guests have included the late Princess of Wales. Cottage rooms are spread across 4 hectares (10 acres) of ornamental gardens. Swimming, horseback riding, windsurfing, a private beach, and "eco-rambles" fill the agenda. See p. 556.

- **The Hermitage Beach Club** (Nevis; ℰ **800/682-4025** in the U.S., or 869/469-3477): Guests stay in clapboard-sided cottages separated by carefully maintained bougainvillea and grasslands. The beach is a short drive away, but this slice of 19th-century plantation life (complete with candlelit dinners amid the antiques and polished silver of the main house) is decidedly romantic. See p. 556.

- **The Frangipani** (Bequia, The Grenadines; ℰ **784/458-3255;** www.frangipanibequia.com): This is the century-old homestead of the Mitchell family, whose most famous scion later became prime minister of St. Vincent. Today, it's a small, very relaxed inn. It's fun to watch the yachts setting out to sea from the nearby marina. See p. 635.

11 The Best Destinations for Serious Shoppers

Because the U.S. government allows its citizens to take (or send) home more duty-free goods from the U.S. Virgins than from other ports of call, the U.S. Virgin Islands remain the shopping bazaar of the Caribbean. U.S. citizens may carry home $1,400 worth of goods untaxed, as opposed to only $400 to $600 worth of goods from most other islands in the Caribbean. (The only exception to this rule is Puerto Rico, where any purchase, regardless of the amount, can be carried tax free back to the U.S. mainland.) St. Maarten/St. Martin, which is ruled jointly by France and the Netherlands, gives the Virgins some serious shopping competition. It is virtually a shopper's mall, especially on the Dutch side. Although the U.S. doesn't grant the generous customs allowances on

St. Maarten/St. Martin that it does to its own islands, the island doesn't have duty so you still can find some lovely bargains.

- **Aruba:** The wisest shoppers on Aruba are cost-conscious souls who have carefully checked the prices of comparable goods before leaving home. Duty is relatively low (only 3.3%). Much of the European china, jewelry, perfumes, and watches has a disconcerting habit of reappearing in every shopping mall and hotel boutique on the island, so after you determine exactly which brand of watch or china you want, you can comparison shop. See chapter 5.

- **Barbados:** Local shops seem to specialize in all things English. Merchandise includes bone china from British and Irish manufacturers, watches, jewelry, and perfumes. Bridgetown's Broad Street is the shopping headquarters of the island, although some of the stores here maintain boutiques (with similar prices but a less extensive range of merchandise) at many of the island's hotels and in malls along the congested southwestern coast. Except for cigarettes and tobacco, duty-free items can be hauled off by any buyer as soon as they're paid for. Duty-free status is extended to anyone showing a passport or ID and an airline ticket with a date of departure from Barbados. See chapter 6.

- **The Cayman Islands:** Goods are sold tax free from a daunting collection of malls and minimalls throughout Grand Cayman. Most of these are along the highway that parallels Seven Mile Beach; you'll need a car to shop around. There are also lots of stores in George Town, which you can explore on foot, poking in and out of some large emporiums in your search for bargains. See chapter 9.

- **Curaçao:** In the island's capital, tidy and prosperous Willemstad, hundreds of merchants are only too happy to cater to your needs. A handful of malls lies on Willemstad's outskirts, but most shops are clustered within a few blocks of the center of town. During seasonal sales, goods might be up to 50% less than comparable prices in the United States; most of the year, you'll find luxury items (porcelain, crystal, watches, and gemstones) priced at about 25% less than in the U.S. Technically, you'll pay import duties on virtually everything you buy, but rates are so low you may not even notice. See chapter 10.

- **The Dominican Republic:** The island's best buys include handicrafts, amber from Dominican mines, and the distinctive pale-blue semiprecious gemstone known as larimar. The amber sold by street vendors may be nothing more than orange-colored, transparent plastic; buy only from well-established shops if your investment is a large one. Other charming souvenirs might include a Dominican rocking chair (JFK used to sit in one), which is sold boxed, in ready-to-assemble pieces. Malls and souvenir stands abound in Santo Domingo, in Puerto Plata, and along the country's northern coast. See chapter 12.

- **Jamaica:** The shopping was better in the good old days, before taxes added a 10% surcharge. Despite that, Jamaica offers a wealth of desirable goods, including flavored rums, Jamaican coffees, handicrafts (such as woodcarvings, woven baskets, and sandals), original paintings and sculpture, and cameras, watches, and DVD players. Unless you're a glutton for handmade souvenirs (which are available on virtually every beach and street corner), you'd be wise to limit most of your purchases to bona fide merchants and stores. See chapter 15.

- **Puerto Rico:** For U.S. citizens, there's no duty on anything bought in Puerto Rico. That doesn't guarantee that prices will be particularly low, however. You can find lots of jewelry and watches, often at competitive prices, especially in the island's best-stocked area, Old San Juan. Also of interest are such Puerto Rican handicrafts as charming folkloric papier-mâché carnival masks and *santos,* carved wooden figures depicting saints. See chapter 17.

- **St. Maarten/St. Martin:** Because of the massive influx of cruise ships, shopping in Dutch St. Maarten is now about the finest in the Caribbean, though you may have to fight the crowds. Because there's no duty, prices can be 30% to 50% lower than in the U.S. Forget about local crafts and concentrate on leather goods, electronics, cameras, designer fashions, watches, and crystal, along with linens and jewelry. Philipsburg, capital of the island's Dutch side, is the best place to shop. Although it can't compete with Dutch St. Maarten, French St. Martin is becoming a more popular shopping destination, especially for goods such as fashion or perfumes imported from France. See chapter 23.

- **St. Thomas:** Many of its busiest shops are in restored warehouses that were originally built in the 1700s. Charlotte Amalie, the capital, is a shopper's town, with a staggering number of stores stocked with more merchandise than anywhere else in the entire Caribbean. However, despite all the fanfare, real bargains are hard to come by. Regardless, the island attracts hordes of cruise-ship passengers on a sometimes-frantic hunt for bargains, real or imagined. Look for two local publications, *This Week* and *Best Buys;* either might steer you to the type of merchandise you're seeking. If at all possible, try to avoid shopping when more than one cruise ship is in port—the shopping district is a madhouse on those days. See chapter 27.

- **St. Croix:** This island doesn't have the massive shopping development of St. Thomas, but its merchandise has never been more wide-ranging than it is today. Even though most cruise ships call at Frederiksted, with its urban mall, our favorite shops are in Christiansted, which has many one-of-a-kind boutiques and a lot of special finds. Prices are about the same here as on St. Thomas. See chapter 27.

12 The Best Nightlife

Nighttime is sleep time on the British Virgins, Montserrat, Nevis, Anguilla, St. Eustatius, Saba, St. Barts, Dominica, Bonaire, St. Vincent, and all of The Grenadines. The serious partier will probably want to choose one of the following destinations.

- **Aruba:** This island has 10 casinos, each with its own unique decor and each with a following of devoted gamblers. Some offer their own cabarets and comedy shows, dance floors with live or recorded music,

restaurants of all degrees of formality, and bars. The casinos are big, splashy, colorful, and, yes, people even occasionally win. Drinks are usually free while you play. The legal tender in most of Aruba's casinos is the U.S. dollar. See chapter 5.

- **Barbados:** Bridgetown is home to at least two boats (the *Bajan Queen* and the *Jolly Roger*) that embark at sundown for rum-and-reggae cruises, as well as oversize music bars like Harbour Lights. Otherwise, a host of bars,

British-style pubs, dozens of restaurants, and dance clubs (both within and outside large hotels) beckon from St. Lawrence Gap or the crowded southwest coast. See chapter 6.

- **Curaçao:** Although outdistanced by Aruba, the action spinning around the island's casinos make this one of the southern Caribbean's hot spots for gamblers. Salinja, a sector of Willemstad, has lively bars where locals and visitors drink and party until the wee hours, and live jazz often fills the air. See chapter 10.

- **The Dominican Republic:** Large resort hotels in the Dominican Republic evoke a Latino version of Las Vegas. If cabaret shows aren't your thing, there are enough dance clubs in the major towns and resorts to keep nightclubbers busy for weeks. The tourist areas of Puerto Plata and Santo Domingo are sprinkled with casinos, and the island's ever-developing north shore contains its share of jingle-jangle, too. Our favorite is the casino in the Renaissance Jaragua Hotel & Casino in Santo Domingo, which offers floor shows, live merengue concerts, a wraparound bar, and at least five different restaurants. See chapter 12.

- **Jamaica:** Many visitors are drawn here by a love for the island's distinct musical forms. Foremost among these are reggae and soca, both of which are performed at hotels, resorts, and raffish dives all over the island. Hotels often stage folkloric shows that include entertainers who sing, dance, swallow torches, and walk on broken glass. There are also plenty of indoor/outdoor bars where you might actually be able to talk to people. See chapter 15.

- **Puerto Rico:** Puerto Rico contains all the raw ingredients for great nightlife, including casinos, endless rows of bars and taverns, cabaret shows with girls and glitter, and dance clubs that feature everything from New York imports to some of the best salsa and merengue anywhere. The country's gaming headquarters lies along the Condado in San Juan, although there are also casinos in megaresorts scattered throughout the island. The casinos here are the most fun in the Caribbean. Each contains lots of sideshows (restaurants, merengue bars, art galleries, piano bars, and shops) that can distract you from the roulette and slots. Puerto Ricans take pride in dressing well at their local casinos, which enhances an evening's glamour. (*Note:* You can't drink at the tables.) If you're a really serious partyer, you'll have lots of company in Puerto Rico. Be prepared to stay out very late; you can recover from your Bacardi hangover on a palm-fringed beach the next day. See chapter 17.

- **St. Maarten/St. Martin:** This island has a rather cosmopolitan nightlife and contains the densest concentration of restaurants in the Caribbean, each with its own bar. Dance clubs are often indoor/outdoor affairs. Hotel casinos abound on the Dutch side, and if you're addicted to the jingle of slot machines and roulette wheels, you won't lack for company. The casinos tend to be low-key, which might appeal to you if you dislike high-stakes tables with lots of intensity. See chapter 23.

- **St. Thomas:** The Virgin Islands' most active nightlife is found here. Don't expect glitzy shows like those in San Juan's Condado area, and don't expect any kind of casino. But you can find plenty of fun at the beach bars, restaurants, concerts, clubs, and folklore and reggae shows. See chapter 27.

2

Planning Your Trip
to the Caribbean

Golden beaches shaded by palm trees and crystalline waters teeming with colorful tropical fish—it's all just a few hours' flight from the East Coast of the United States. Dubbed the "Eighth Continent of the World," the Caribbean islands have an amazing variety of terrain that ranges from thick rainforests to haunting volcanoes, from white- to black-sand beaches. Spicy food, spicier music, and a gentle, leisurely lifestyle draw millions of visitors each year, all of whom are searching for that perfect place in the sun. In this chapter, we'll help you choose the right destination and the right time to go, and we'll explore the best strategies for getting a good airfare or package deal.

1 The Islands in Brief

ANGUILLA Although it's developing rapidly as vacationers discover its 19km (12 miles) of arid but spectacular beaches, Anguilla (rhymes with *vanilla*) is still quiet, sleepy, and relatively free of racial tensions. A flat, coral island, it maintains a maritime tradition of proud fisherfolk, many of whom still make a living from the sea, catching lobsters and selling them at high prices to expensive resorts and restaurants. Although there's a handful of moderately priced accommodations, Anguilla is a very expensive destination, with small and rather exclusive resorts. It's as posh as St. Barts, but without all the snobbery. There are no casinos (and that's the way most of the locals want it). In fact, there's not much to do here except lie in the sun, bask in luxury, and enjoy fine dining.

ANTIGUA Antigua is famous for having a different beach for each day of the year, but it lacks the lushness of such islands as Dominica and Jamaica. Some British traditions (including a passion for

cricket) linger, even though the nation became independent in 1981. The island has a population of 80,000, mostly descended from the African slaves of plantation owners. Antigua's resorts are isolated and conservative but very glamorous; its highways are horribly maintained; and its historic naval sites are interesting. Antigua is politically linked to the sparsely inhabited and largely undeveloped island of Barbuda, about 50km (30 miles) north. In spite of its small size, Barbuda has two posh, pricey resorts.

ARUBA Until its beaches were "discovered" in the late 1970s, Aruba, with its desertlike terrain and lunarlike interior landscapes, was an almost-forgotten outpost of Holland, valued mostly for its oil refineries and salt factories. Today, vacationers come for the dependable sunshine (it rains less here than literally anywhere else in the Caribbean), the spectacular beaches, and an almost total lack of racial tensions despite an amazingly culturally diverse population. The high-rise hotels of Aruba are within walking distance of each other along a strip of fabulous beach. You don't stay in old, converted, family-run sugar mills here, and you don't come for history. You come here if you're interested in gambling and splashy high-rise resorts.

BARBADOS Originally founded on a plantation economy that made its aristocracy rich on the backs of slave laborers, this Atlantic outpost was a staunchly loyal member of the British Commonwealth for generations. Barbados is the Caribbean's easternmost island, a great coral reef floating in the mid-Atlantic and ringed with glorious beige-sand beaches. Cosmopolitan Barbados has the densest population of any island in the Caribbean, with few racial tensions despite its history of slavery. A loyal group of return visitors appreciates its stylish, medium-size hotels (many of which carry a hefty price tag). Service is usually extremely good, a byproduct of the British mores that have flourished here for a century. Topography varies from rolling hills and savage waves on the eastern (Atlantic) coast to densely populated flatlands, rows of hotels and apartments, and sheltered beaches in the southwest. If you're looking for a Las Vegas–type atmosphere and fine beaches, go to Aruba. If you want history (there are lots of great houses and old churches to explore), a quiet, conservative atmosphere, and fine beaches, come here.

BONAIRE Its strongest historical and cultural links are to Holland, and although it has always been a poor relation of nearby Curaçao, Bonaire has better scuba diving and better bird life than any of its larger and richer neighbors. The terrain is as dry and inhospitable as anything you'll find in the Caribbean, a sparse desert landscape offset by a wealth of marine life that thrives along miles of offshore reefs. The island isn't overly blessed with natural resources. But those coral reefs around most of the island attract divers and snorkelers from all over the world. The casino and party crowd should head for Aruba instead.

THE BRITISH VIRGIN ISLANDS (B.V.I.) Still a British Crown Colony, this lushly forested chain consists of about 50 small, mountainous islands (depending on how many rocks, cays, and uninhabited islets you want to include). Superb for sailors, the B.V.I. are less populated, less developed, and have fewer social problems than the U.S. Virgin Islands. **Tortola** is the main island, followed by **Virgin Gorda,** where you'll find some of the poshest hotels in the West Indies. **Anegada,** a coral atoll geologically different from the other members of the B.V.I., mainly attracts the yachting set. Come here for the laid-back lifestyle, the lovely sandy beaches, the friendly people, and the small, intimate inns.

THE CAYMAN ISLANDS This trio of islands is set near the southern coast of Cuba. It's a prosperous, tiny nation dependent on Britain for its economic survival and attracting millionaire expatriates from all over the world by means of some very lenient tax and banking laws. Relatively flat and unattractive, these islands are covered with scrubland and swamp, but they have more than their share of expensive private homes and condominiums. Until the millennium, **Grand Cayman** enjoyed one of the most closely knit societies in the Caribbean, although recent prosperity has created some socioeconomic divisions. The warm, crystal-clear waters and the colorful marine life in the offshore reefs surrounding the island attract scuba divers and snorkelers. Many hotels line the luscious sands of Seven Mile Beach.

CURAÇAO Because much of the island's surface is an arid desert that grows only cactus, its canny Dutch settlers ruled out farming and made Curaçao (Coo-ra-*sow*) into one of the Dutch Empire's busiest trading posts. Until the post–World War II collapse of the oil refineries, Curaçao was a thriving mercantile society with a capital (Willemstad) that somewhat resembled Amsterdam and a population with a curious mixture of bloodlines, including African, Dutch, Venezuelan, and Pakistani. The main language here is Papiamento, a mixture of African and European dialects, though Dutch, Spanish, and English are also spoken. Tourism began to develop during the 1980s, and many new hotels have been built since then. The island has a few interesting historic sights, and Willemstad is one of the most charming towns in the Caribbean. If you're choosing among the Dutch ABC islands, go to Aruba for beaches and gambling, Bonaire for scuba diving, and Curaçao for little cove beaches, shopping, history, and its distinctive "Dutch-in-the-Caribbean" culture.

DOMINICA An English-speaking island set midway between Guadeloupe and Martinique, Dominica (Doh-mi-*nee*-kah), the largest and most mountainous island of the Windward Islands, is not to be confused with the Dominican Republic (see below). A mysterious, little-visited land of waterfalls, rushing streams, and rainforests, it has only a few beaches, most of which are lined with black volcanic sand. But if you like the offbeat and unusual, you may find this lush island the most fascinating in the Caribbean. Some 82,000 people live here, including 2,000 descendants of the Carib Indians. Roseau, one of the smallest capitals in the Caribbean, is more like an overgrown Creole village than a city. Dominica is one of the poorest islands in the Caribbean, and it has the misfortune of lying directly in the hurricane belt.

THE DOMINICAN REPUBLIC Occupying the eastern two-thirds of Hispaniola, the island it shares with Haiti, the mountainous Dominican Republic is the second-largest country of the Caribbean. Long a victim of various military dictatorships, it now has a more favorable political climate and is one of the most affordable destinations in the Caribbean. Its crowded capital is Santo Domingo, with a population of two million. The island offers lots of Latin color, zesty merengue music, and many opportunities to dance, drink, and party. Unfortunately, the contrast between the wealth of foreign tourists and the poverty of locals is particularly conspicuous, and it's not the safest island. For fun in the sun and good beaches, head for La Romana in the southeast, Punta Cana on the easternmost shore, Puerto Plata in the northwest, or any resorts along the Amber Coast in the north.

GRENADA The southernmost nation of the Windward Islands, Grenada (Gre-*nay*-dah) is one of the lushest islands in the Caribbean. With its gentle climate and extravagantly fertile volcanic soil, it's one of the largest producers of spices in the Western Hemisphere. There's a lot of very appealing local color on Grenada, particularly since the political troubles of the 1980s seem, at least for the moment, to have ended. There are beautiful white-sand beaches, and the populace (a mixture of English expatriates and islanders of African descent) is friendly. Once a British Crown Colony but now independent, the island nation also incorporates two smaller islands: Carriacou and Petit Martinique, neither of which has many tourist facilities. Grenada's capital, St. George's, is one of the most charming towns in the Caribbean.

GUADELOUPE Although it isn't as sophisticated or cosmopolitan as the two outlying islands over which it holds administrative authority—St. Barthélemy and the French section of St. Martin—there's a lot of natural beauty in this *département* of mainland France. With a relatively low population density (only 440,000 people live here, mostly along the coast), butterfly-shaped Guadeloupe is actually two distinctly different volcanic islands separated by a narrow saltwater strait, the Rivière Salée. It's ideal for scenic drives and Creole color, offering an unusual insight into the French colonial world. The island has a lot of good beaches, each one different, and a vast national park (a huge tropical forest with everything from wild orchids to coffee and vanilla plants). It's life *à la française* in the Tropics, but we'd give the nod to Martinique (see below) if you can visit only one French island.

JAMAICA   A favorite of North American honeymooners, Jamaica is a mountainous island that rises abruptly from the sea 145km (90 miles) south of Cuba and about 160km (100 miles) west of Haiti. One of the most densely populated nations in the Caribbean, with a vivid sense of its own identity, Jamaica has a history rooted in the plantation economy and some of the most turbulent and impassioned politics in the Western Hemisphere. In spite of its economic and social problems, Jamaica is one of the most successful black democracies in the world. The island is large enough to allow the more or less peaceful coexistence of all kinds of people within its beach-lined borders—everyone from expatriate English aristocrats to dyed-in-the-wool Rastafarians. Its tourist industry has been plagued by the island's reputation for aggressive vendors and racial tension, but it is taking steps to improve the situation. Overall, and despite its long history of social unrest, increasing crime, and poverty, Jamaica is a fascinating island. It offers excellent beaches, golf, eco-tourism adventures, and fine hotels in all price brackets, making it one of the most popular destinations in the Caribbean, especially since you can find package deals galore.

MARTINIQUE   One of the most exotic French-speaking destinations in the Caribbean, Martinique was the site of a settlement demolished by volcanic activity (St. Pierre, now only a pale shadow of a once-thriving city). Like Guadeloupe and St. Barts, Martinique is legally and culturally French (certainly many islanders drive with a Gallic panache—read: very badly), although many Creole customs and traditions continue to flourish. The beaches are beautiful, the Creole cuisine is full of flavor and flair, and the island has lots of tropical charm. Even more than Guadeloupe, this is the social and cultural center of the French Antilles. If you'd like to visit a charmingly beautiful island with elegant people, the Martiniquaise will wish you *bonjour.*

PUERTO RICO   Home to 3.9 million people whose primary language is Spanish (though English is widely spoken, too), the Commonwealth of Puerto Rico is under the jurisdiction of the United States and has a more-or-less comfortable mix of Latin culture with imports from the U.S. mainland. It's the most urban island of the Caribbean, with lots of traffic and relatively high crime, though it compensates with great beaches, glittering casinos, a range of hotels in all price brackets, sports and eco-tourism offerings, good hearty food, and sizzling salsa clubs. The island's interior is filled with rainforests and ancient volcanic mountains; the coastline is ringed with gorgeous sandy beaches. The commonwealth also includes a trio of small offshore islands: Culebra, Mona, and Vieques (the last has the most tourist facilities). San Juan, the island's 16th-century capital, has some of the most extensive and best-preserved Spanish colonial neighborhoods in the New World, with historic sites and lots of things to see and do, and a steady flow of cruise-ship passengers who keep the stores and casinos filled throughout much of the year. You can usually find great package deals through Puerto Rico's hotels and resorts.

SABA   Saba is a cone-shaped extinct volcano that rises abruptly and steeply from the watery depths of the Caribbean. There are no beaches or historic sights to speak of, and the local Dutch- and English-speaking populace has traditionally made a living from fishing, trade, and needlework, rather than tourism. Hotel choices are limited. Saba's thrifty, seafaring folk can offer insights into the old-fashioned lifestyle of the Netherlands Antilles. There's only one road on the island, and unless you opt to hike away from its edges, you'll have to follow the traffic along its narrow, winding route. Basically, you come here if you want to hang out at your hotel pool, climb up to a rainforest, go diving, and perhaps make a day trip to one of the nearby islands. Saba's a place to visit if you like to collect untouristy islands. You may want to come just for the afternoon—you can do this by plane or trimaran.

ST. BARTHÉLEMY (ALSO CALLED ST. BARTS OR ST. BARTHS)   Part of the French *département* of Guadeloupe, lying 24km (15 miles) from St. Martin, St. Barts is a small, hilly island with a population of 6,500 people who live on 34 sq. km (13 sq. miles) of verdant terrain ringed by pleasant white-sand beaches. A small number of African descendants live harmoniously on this chic Caribbean island with descendants of Norman and Breton mariners and a colony of more recent expatriates from Europe. An expensive and exclusive stomping ground of the rich and famous, with a distinctive seafaring tradition and a decidedly French flavor, St. Barts has a lovely "storybook" capital in Gustavia. For sophistication and luxury living, St. Barts is equaled in the Caribbean only by Anguilla, and the price tag isn't cheap. It's a place to visit if you want to wind down from a stressful life.

ST. EUSTATIUS (ALSO CALLED STATIA)   Statia is part of the Netherlands Antilles and the Leeward Islands, lying to the west of Dutch Sint Maarten. During the 1700s, this Dutch-controlled island ("The Golden Rock") was one of the most important trading posts in the Caribbean. During the U.S. War of Independence, a brisk arms trade helped to bolster the local economy, but the glamour ended in 1781, when British Admiral Romney sacked the port, hauled off most of the island's wealth, and propelled St. Eustatius onto a path of obscurity—where it remained for almost 200 years, until the advent of tourism. Today, the island is among the poorest in the Caribbean, with 21 sq. km (8 sq. miles) of arid landscape, beaches with strong and sometimes dangerous undertows, a population of around 2,900 people, and a sleepy capital, Oranjestad. Out of desperation, the island is very committed to maintaining its political and fiscal links to the Netherlands. This is a destination for people who are interested in American Revolution–era history and who like hanging out around a pool at a friendly, informal local inn. Most people will want to make a day trip to see the historic sites, have lunch, and leave.

ST. KITTS & NEVIS   The first English settlement in the Leeward Islands, St. Kitts has a rich sense of British maritime history. With 176 sq. km (69 sq. miles) of land, St. Kitts enjoyed one of the richest sugar-cane economies of the plantation age. This island lies somewhat off the beaten tourist track and has a very appealing, intimate charm. A lush, fertile mountain island with a rainforest and waterfalls, it is crowned by the 1,138m (3,733-ft.) Mount Liamuiga—a crater that thankfully has remained dormant (unlike the one at Montserrat). St. Kitts is home to some 38,000 people and Brimstone Hill, the Caribbean's most impressive fortress. Come here for the beaches and the history, for lush natural scenery, and to stay at a restored plantation home that's been turned into a charming inn. Lots of sporting activities, ranging from mountain climbing to horseback riding, are also available.

Many Nevisians feel strongly about eventually breaking away from St. Kitts, from which Nevis is separated by 3km (2 miles) of water. Nevis was spotted by Columbus in 1493 on his second voyage to the New World. He called it Nieves—Spanish for snows—when he saw the cloud-crowned volcanic isle that evoked for him the snow-capped peaks of the Pyrenees. Known for its long beaches of both black and white sand, Nevis, more than any other island in the Caribbean, has turned its former great houses, built during the plantation era, into some of the most charming and atmospheric inns in the West Indies. It also has the Four Seasons Resort for those who want world-class elegance and service. The capital city of Charlestown looks like a real Caribbean backwater, though it is home to hundreds of worldwide businesses that are drawn to Nevis for its tax laws and bank secrecy.

ST. LUCIA   St. Lucia (*Loo*-sha), 39km (24 miles) south of Martinique, is the second largest of the Windward Islands, with a population of around 162,000. Although in 1803 Britain eventually won control of the island, French influence is still evident in the Creole dialect spoken here. A volcanic island with lots of rainfall and great natural beauty, it has white- and black-sand beaches, bubbling sulfur springs, and beautiful mountain scenery. Most tourism is concentrated on the island's northwestern tip, near the capital (Castries), but the arrival of up to 200,000 visitors a year has definitely altered the old agrarian lifestyle throughout the island. Come here for the posh resorts and the gorgeous beaches, the rainforests, and the lush tropical foliage.

SAINT MAARTEN/ST. MARTIN Lying 232km (144 miles) east of Puerto Rico, this scrub-covered island has been divided between the Dutch (Sint Maarten) and the French (Saint Martin) since 1648. Regardless of how you spell its name, it's the same island on both sides of the unguarded border—though the two halves are quite different. The Dutch side contains the island's major airport, more shops, and more tourist facilities, and the French side has some of the poshest hotels and superior food. Both sides are modern, urbanized, and cosmopolitan. And both suffer from traffic jams, a lack of parking space in the capitals, tourist-industry burnout (especially on the Dutch side), and a disturbing increase in crime. In spite of the drawbacks, there's a lot to attract you here—great beaches, the shopping (some of the Caribbean's best), the gambling, the self-contained resorts, the nonstop flights from the U.S., the nightlife, and some of the best restaurants in the Caribbean. From here, you can fly over for a day trip to St. Eustatius or Saba.

ST. VINCENT & THE GRENADINES The natural beauty of this miniarchipelago has long been known to divers and the yachting set, who consider its north-to-south string of cays and coral islets one of the loveliest sailing regions in the world. The nation's population is only about 116,000 (of mostly African descent). **St. Vincent** (29km/18 miles long and 18km/11 miles wide) is by far the largest and most fertile island in the country. Its capital is the sleepy, somewhat dilapidated town of Kingstown (not to be confused with Kingston, Jamaica). **The Grenadines,** some 32 neighboring islands, stretch like a pearl necklace to the south of St. Vincent. These include the charming boat-building communities of

Bequia and Mustique, where the late Princess Margaret had a home. Less densely populated islands in the chain include the tiny outposts of Mayreau, Canouan, Palm Island, and Petit St. Vincent, which was mostly covered with scrub until hotel owners planted much-needed groves of palm and hardwood trees and opened resorts.

TRINIDAD & TOBAGO

The southernmost of the West Indies, this two-island nation lies just 11km (6¾ miles) off the coast of Venezuela. Both islands once had sugar-plantation economies and enjoyed fantastic wealth during the 18th century. Trinidad is the most industrialized island in the Caribbean, with oil deposits and a polyglot population from India, Pakistan, Venezuela, Africa, and Europe. Known for its calypso music and carnival celebrations, it is also one of the most culturally distinctive nations in the Caribbean, with a rich artistic tradition. In its 4,662 sq. km (1,818 sq. miles), you'll find a bustling capital (Port-of-Spain), wildlife sanctuaries, and an impressive variety of exotic flora and fauna. What you won't necessarily find are beaches. While Trinidad has some excellent ones, they are far removed from the capital and hard to find.

For beach life, head for Tobago, which is about 30km (20 miles) northeast of Trinidad. Tiny Tobago (14km/8¾ miles wide and 42km/26 miles long) is calmer and less heavily forested, with a rather dull capital (Scarborough) and an impressive array of white-sand beaches. While Trinidad seems to consider tourism only one of many viable industries, Tobago is absolutely dependent on it. Life is sleepy on Tobago, unlike bustling Trinidad. Tobago has coral reefs ideal for scuba diving, rainforests, powdery sands, shoreline drives, lanes of coconut palms, and a soothing get-away-from-it-all atmosphere—we hope it stays that way.

TURKS & CAICOS

Although these islands are actually part of the Bahamian archipelago—they are to the east of the southernmost islands of The Bahamas, directly north of Haiti and the Dominican Republic—they are governed separately.

Home of Cockburn Town, the capital of Turks and Caicos (Kayk-us), Grand Turk nevertheless has a small-town atmosphere. The farthest island from Florida, it totals 23 sq. km (9 sq. miles). Although Grand Turk is ringed by abundant marine life, most of the island's surface is flat, rocky, and dry. The diving here is world-class—the main draw for most visitors. Grand Turk has a relatively undeveloped tourist infrastructure, although it offers a scattering of inns and hotels.

One of the larger islands of the Turks and Caicos, Providenciales, or "Provo," is green but arid, with miles of scrubland and stunted trees covering the island's low, undulating hills. Whatever the Turks and Caicos have to offer in organized sports is found here, including the nation's only golf course, boat tours, and diving excursions. The 19km (12-mile) beach and pristine coastline of Provo were a tourist development waiting to happen. In the late 1970s, hotel megaliths such as Club Med poured money into increasingly popular low-rise eco-conscious resorts. Now Provo's tourist infrastructure far surpasses anything on Grand Turk. The island also has the best cuisine and the finest entertainment in the Turks and Caicos, but it's still much, much sleepier than the big developments of Aruba.

THE U.S. VIRGIN ISLANDS

Formerly Danish possessions, these islands became part of the United States in 1917. Originally based on a plantation economy, St. Croix is the largest and flattest of the U.S. Virgins, and St. Thomas and St. John are more mountainous.

All three islands offer stunning beaches, great snorkeling, sailing, and lovely scenery, but they are, unfortunately, rather expensive destinations. If you want great shopping and lots of diversions, facilities, bars, restaurants, and modern resort hotels, go to overbuilt **St. Thomas,** sometimes referred to as the shopping mall of the Caribbean. Cruise-ship passengers pass through constantly. **St. Croix** also has good facilities, though not as many as St. Thomas. It's more laid-back, a better place to escape for peace and quiet. **St. John** is most often visited on a day trip from St. Thomas. Much of this island is devoted to a national park, a gift from Laurance Rockefeller to the national park system. Petty crime is on the increase, however—an unfortunate fly in the ointment of this otherwise soothing corner of paradise. 2 Visitor InformationAll the major islands have tourist representatives who will supply information before you go; we list each one in the "Fast Facts" section of the individual island chapters.

The **Caribbean Tourism Organization,** 80 Broad St., 32nd Floor, New York, NY 10004 (© **212/635-9530;** fax 212/635-9511; www.onecaribbean.org or www.doitcaribbean.com), can also provide general information.

SIGHTSEEING: INFO ON THE WEB

The Internet is a great source of current travel information. Whenever possible throughout this book, we've included Web addresses along with phone numbers and addresses for attractions, outfitters, and other companies. We've also given each hotel and resort's website, so you can see pictures of a property before you make your reservation.

2 Entry Requirements

PASSPORTS

All travelers coming from the Caribbean, including Americans, are now required to have a passport to enter or re-enter the United States. You'll certainly need identification at some point, and a passport is the best form of ID for speeding through Customs and Immigration. Driver's licenses are not acceptable as a sole form of ID.

Note: Children are required to present a passport when reentering the United States at airports. More information on obtaining a passport for a minor can be found at http://travel.state.gov.

VISAS

Visas are usually not required, but some countries may require you to fill out a tourist card. (See the individual island chapters for details.)

CUSTOMS

Each island has specific guidelines on what you can bring in with you; these are detailed in the destination chapters that follow. Generally, you're permitted to bring in items intended for your personal use, including tobacco, cameras, film, and a limited supply of liquor—usually 40 ounces.

Just before you leave home, check with your country's Customs or Foreign Affairs department for the latest guidelines—including information on items that are not allowed to be brought into your home country—since the rules are subject to change and often contain some surprising oddities.

U.S. Customs and Border Protection allows $1,600 worth of duty-free imports every 30 days from the U.S. Virgin Islands; if you go over this amount, you're taxed at 1.5% rather than the usual 3%. The duty-free limit is $800 for other Caribbean Basin destinations. If you visit only Puerto Rico, you don't have to go through Customs at all, since the island is a U.S. commonwealth.

Tips   New Passport Requirements

New regulations issued by the Homeland Security Department now require virtually every air traveler entering the U.S. to show a passport—and future regulations will cover land and sea entry as well. As of January 23, 2007, all persons, including U.S. citizens, traveling by air between the United States and Canada, Mexico, Central and South America, the Caribbean, and Bermuda are required to present a valid passport. Similar regulations for those traveling by land or sea (including ferries) are expected as early as January 1, 2008.

Joint Customs declarations are possible for members of a family traveling together. For instance, if you are a husband and wife with two children, your purchases in the U.S. Virgin Islands become duty-free up to $6,400! Unsolicited gifts can be sent to friends and relatives at the rate of $200 per day from the U.S. Virgin Islands and $50 a day from the other islands. U.S. citizens, or returning residents at least 21 years of age, traveling directly or indirectly from the U.S. Virgin Islands, are allowed to bring in free of duty 1,000 cigarettes, 5 liters of alcohol, and 100 cigars (but not Cuban cigars). Duty-free limitations on articles from other countries are generally 1 liter of alcohol, 200 cigarettes, and 200 cigars.

You should collect receipts for all purchases made abroad. You must also declare on your Customs form the nature and value of all gifts received during your stay abroad. It's prudent to carry proof that you purchased expensive cameras or jewelry on the U.S. mainland. If you purchased such an item during an earlier trip abroad, you should carry proof that you have previously paid Customs duty on the item.

Sometimes merchants suggest a false receipt to undervalue your purchase. *Beware:* You could be involved in a sting operation—the merchant might be an informer to U.S. Customs.

If you use any medication that contains controlled substances or requires injection, carry an original prescription or note from your doctor.

For specifics on what you can bring back, download the invaluable free pamphlet *Know Before You Go* online at **www.cbp.gov**. (Click on "Travel," and then click on "Know Before You Go! Online Brochure.") Or contact the **U.S. Customs & Border Protection (CBP)**, 1300 Pennsylvania Ave., NW, Washington, DC 20229 (© **877/287-8667**) and request the pamphlet.

U.K. citizens should contact **HM Revenue & Customs** at © **0845/010-9000** (© 02920/501-261 from outside the U.K.), or consult their website at www.hmrc.gov.uk.

For a clear summary of **Canadian** rules, write for the booklet *I Declare,* issued by the **Canada Border Services Agency** (© **800/461-9999** in Canada, or 204/983-3500; www.cbsa-asfc.gc.ca).

Citizens of **Australia** should request a helpful brochure available from Australian consulates or Customs offices, *Know Before You Go.* For more information, call the **Australian Customs Service** at © **1300/363-263,** or log on to www.customs.gov.au.

For **New Zealand** Customs information, contact the **New Zealand Customs Service** at © **04/473-6099** or 0800/428-786, or log on to www.customs.govt.nz.

3 When to Go

THE WEATHER

The temperature variations in the Caribbean are surprisingly slight, averaging between 75°F and 85°F (24°C–29°C) in both winter and summer. It can get really chilly, however, especially in the early morning and at night. The Caribbean winter is usually like a perpetual May. Overall, temperatures in the mid-80s (high 20s Celsius) prevail throughout most of the region, and trade winds make for comfortable days and nights, even without air-conditioning.

The humidity and bugs can be a problem here year-round. However, more mosquitoes come out during the rainy season, which usually occurs in autumn.

If you come in the summer, be prepared for really broiling sun in the midafternoon.

Brochures make people feel that it's literally always sunny in the Caribbean, and that isn't necessarily the case. Different islands get different amounts of rain. On Aruba, it hardly ever rains; on other islands, you can have overcast skies your entire vacation. Winter is generally the driest season, but even then, it can be wet in mountainous areas, and you can expect brief afternoon showers, especially in December and January, on Martinique, Guadeloupe, Dominica, St. Lucia, on the north coast of the Dominican Republic, and in northeast Jamaica.

If you want to know how to pack just before you go, check the Weather Channel's online 5-day forecast at **www. weather.com** for the latest information.

HURRICANES   The curse of Caribbean weather, the hurricane season lasts—officially, at least—from June 1 to November 30. But there's no cause for panic: Satellite forecasts give enough warning that precautions can be taken.

To get a weather report before you go, call the nearest branch of the **National Weather Service,** listed in your phone directory under the "U.S. Department of Commerce." You can also check the **Weather Channel** on the Web at **www. weather.com**.

THE HIGH SEASON & THE OFF SEASON

The Caribbean has become a year-round destination. The "season" runs roughly from mid-December to mid-April, which is generally the driest time of year in the Caribbean and the most miserable time of year in the U.S. Northeast and Midwest and in Canada. Hotels charge their highest prices during the peak winter period, and you'll have to make your reservations well in advance—months in advance if you want to travel over Christmas or in the depths of February, especially around U.S. President's Day weekend.

The off season in the Caribbean—roughly from mid-April to mid-December (although this varies from hotel to hotel)—is one big summer sale, though it's become more popular in recent years. In most cases, hotels, inns, and condos slash 20% to 50% off their winter rates.

Dollar for dollar, you'll spend less money by renting a summer house or self-sufficient unit in the Caribbean than you would on Cape Cod, Fire Island, or Laguna Beach. You just have to be able to tolerate strong sun if you're considering coming in the summer.

Off season, the beaches are less crowded, and you can get good deals. But restaurants close and hotels offer fewer facilities and may even use the off season for construction—make sure to ask what work is going on. If you decide to go anyway, ask for a room far away from the noise. If you're single and going off season, ask for the hotel's occupancy rate. You want crowds!

Because there's such a drastic difference in high-season and off-season rates at most hotels, we've included both on every property we review. You'll see the incredible savings you can enjoy if your schedule allows you to wait a couple of months for your fun in the sun.

4 Getting There

BY PLANE

American Airlines (© 800/433-7300; www.aa.com) is the major carrier throughout the region. Other airlines serving the islands include **Air Canada** (© 888/247-2262 in the U.S. and Canada; www.aircanada.ca); **Air Jamaica** (© 800/523-5585; www.airjamaica. com); **British Airways** (© 800/247-9297 in the U.S., or 0870/850-9850 in the U.K.; www.britishairways.com); **Caribbean Airlines** (© 800/920-4225; www.caribbean-airlines.com); **Cayman Airways** (© 800/422-9626; www.cayman airways.com); **Continental** (© 800/231-0856; www.continental.com); **Delta** (© 800/221-1212; www.delta.com); **LIAT** (© 888/844-5428 in most of the Caribbean, or 268/480-4601 elsewhere; www.liatairline.com); **Northwest/KLM** (© 800/225-2525; www.nwa.com); **United** (© 800/241-6522; www.united. com), and **AmericaWest/US Airways** (© 800/428-4322; www.usairways.com), plus some smaller regional carriers. In each of the island chapters that follow, we'll list details on which airlines fly the various routes.

FLYING FOR LESS: TIPS FOR GETTING THE BEST AIRFARE

- Passengers who can book their ticket either **long in advance or at the last minute,** or who **fly midweek** or **at less-trafficked hours** may pay a fraction of the full fare. If your schedule is flexible, say so, and ask if you can secure a cheaper fare by changing your flight plans.
- Search **the Internet** for cheap fares. The most popular online travel agencies are **Travelocity.com** (www. travelocity.co.uk); **Expedia.com**(www. expedia.co.uk and www.expedia.ca); and **Orbitz.com**. In the U.K., go to **Travelsupermarket** (© 0845/345-5708; www.travelsupermarket.com), a flight search engine that offers flight comparisons for the budget airlines whose seats often end up in bucket-shop sales. Other websites for booking airline tickets online include **Cheap flights.com,   SmarterTravel.com, Priceline.com,** and **Opodo** (www. opodo.co.uk). Meta search sites (which find and then direct you to airline and hotel websites for booking) include **Sidestep.com** and **Kayak. com**—the latter includes fares for budget carriers like Jet Blue and Spirit as well as the major airlines. **Site59.com** is a great source for last-minute flights and getaways. In addition, most **airlines** offer online-only fares that even their phone agents know nothing about. British travelers should check **Flights International** (© 0800/0187050; www.flights-international.com) for deals on flights all over the world.
- Keep an eye on local newspapers for **promotional specials** or **fare wars,** when airlines lower prices on their most popular routes.
- **Consolidators,** also known as bucket shops, are wholesale brokers in the airline-ticket game. Consolidators buy deeply discounted tickets ("distressed" inventories of unsold seats) from airlines and sell them to online ticket agencies, travel agents, tour operators, corporations, and, to a

Tips   Getting Through the Airport

- Arrive at the airport at least 1 hour before a domestic flight and 2 hours before an international flight. You can check the average wait times at your airport by going to the TSA **Security Checkpoint Wait Times** site (waittime/tsa.dhs.gov).
- Know what you can carry on and what you can't. For the latest updates on items you are prohibited to bring in carryon luggage, go to **www.tsa. gov/travelers/airtravel.**
- Beat the ticket-counter lines by using the self-service electronic ticket kiosks at the airport or even printing out your boarding pass at home from the airline website. Using curbside check-in is also a smart way to avoid lines.
- Help speed up security before you're screened. Remove jackets, shoes, belt buckles, heavy jewelry, and watches and place them either in your carryon luggage or the security bins provided. Place keys, coins, cellphones, and pagers in a security bin. If you have metallic body parts, carry a note from your doctor. When possible, keep packing liquids in checked baggage.
- Use a TSA-approved lock for your checked luggage. Look for Travel Sentry certified locks at luggage or travel shops and Brookstone stores (or online at www.brookstone.com).

lesser degree, the general public. Consolidators advertise in Sunday newspaper travel sections (often in small ads with tiny type), both in the U.S. and the U.K. They can be great sources for cheap international tickets. On the down side, bucket shop tickets are often rigged with restrictions, such as stiff cancellation penalties (as high as 50% to 75% of the ticket price). And keep in mind that most of what you see advertised is of limited availability. Several reliable consolidators are worldwide and available online. **STA Travel** (www. statravel.com) has been the world's leading consolidator for students since purchasing Council Travel, but their fares are competitive for travelers of all ages. **Flights.com** (© **800/ TRAV-800;** www.flights.com) has excellent fares worldwide, particularly to Europe. They also have "local"

websites in 12 countries. **FlyCheap** (© 800/FLY-CHEAP; www.1800 flycheap.com) has especially good fares to sunny destinations. **Air Tickets Direct** (© 800/778-3447; www. airticketsdirect.com) is based in Montreal and leverages the currently weak Canadian dollar for low fares; they also book trips to places that U.S. travel agents won't touch, such as Cuba.

- Join frequent-flier clubs. Frequent-flier membership doesn't cost a cent, but it does entitle you to free tickets or upgrades when you amass the airline's required number of frequent-flier points. You don't even have to fly to earn points; frequent-flier credit cards can earn you thousands of miles for doing your everyday shopping. But keep in mind that award seats are limited, seats on popular routes are hard to snag, and more and more

---

Tips **Don't Stow It—Ship It**

Though pricey, it's sometimes worthwhile to travel luggage-free, particularly if you're toting sports equipment, meeting materials, or baby equipment. Specialists in door-to-door luggage delivery include **Virtual Bellhop** (www. virtualbellhop.com); **SkyCap International** (www.skycapinternational.com); **Luggage Express** (www.usxpluggageexpress.com); and **Sports Express** (www. sportsexpress.com).

---

major airlines are cutting their expiration periods for mileage points—so check your airline's frequent-flier program so you don't lose your miles before you use them. *Inside tip:* Award seats are offered almost a year in advance, but seats also open up at the last minute, so if your travel plans are flexible, you may strike gold. To play the frequent-flier game to your best advantage, consult the community bulletin boards on FlyerTalk (www.flyertalk.com) or go to Randy Petersen's Inside Flyer (www.inside flyer.com). Petersen and friends review all the programs in detail and post regular updates on changes in policies and trends.

LONG-HAUL FLIGHTS: HOW TO STAY COMFORTABLE

- Your choice of airline and airplane will definitely affect your leg room. Find more details about U.S. airlines at **www.seatguru.com**. For international airlines, the research firm Skytrax has posted a list of average seat pitches at **www.airlinequality.com.**
- Emergency exit seats and bulkhead seats typically have the most legroom. Emergency exit seats are usually left unassigned until the day of a flight (to ensure that someone able-bodied fills the seats); it's worth getting to the ticket counter early to snag one of these spots for a long flight. Many passengers find that bulkhead seating (the row facing the wall at the front

of the cabin) offers more legroom, but keep in mind that bulkhead seats have no storage space on the floor in front of you.
- To have two seats for yourself in a three-seat row, try for an aisle seat in a center section toward the back of coach. If you're traveling with a companion, book an aisle and a window seat. Middle seats are usually booked last, so chances are good you'll end up with three seats to yourselves. And in the event that a third passenger is assigned the middle seat, he or she will probably be more than happy to trade for a window or an aisle.
- Ask about entertainment options. Many airlines offer seatback video systems where you get to choose your movies or play video games—but only on some of their planes. (Boeing 777s are your best bet.)
- To sleep, avoid the last row of any section or the row in front of an emergency exit, as these seats are the least likely to recline. Avoid seats near highly trafficked toilet areas. Avoid seats in the back of many jets—these can be narrower than those in the rest of coach. Or reserve a window seat so you can rest your head and avoid being bumped in the aisle.
- Drink water before, during, and after your flight to combat the lack of humidity in airplane cabins. Avoid alcohol, which will dehydrate you.

- If you're flying with kids, don't forget to carry on toys, books, pacifiers, and snacks and chewing gum to help them relieve ear pressure buildup during ascent and descent.

5 Money & Costs

It's always advisable to bring money in a variety of forms on a vacation: a mix of cash, credit cards, and traveler's checks. You should also exchange enough petty cash to cover airport incidentals, tipping, and transportation to your hotel before you leave home, or withdraw money upon arrival at an airport ATM.

In many international destinations, ATMs offer the best exchange rates. Avoid exchanging money at commercial exchange bureaus and hotels, which often have the highest transaction fees.

CURRENCY

Widely accepted on many of the islands, the U.S. dollar is the legal currency of the U.S. Virgin Islands, the British Virgin Islands, and Puerto Rico. Many islands use the Eastern Caribbean dollar, but will probably present your hotel bill in U.S. dollars. For details, see "Fast Facts" in the individual island chapters.

ATMs

The easiest and best way to get cash away from home is from an ATM (automated teller machine), sometimes referred to as a "cash machine," or a "cashpoint." The **Cirrus** (© **800/424-7787**; www.master card.com) and **PLUS** (© **800/843-7587**; www.visa.com) networks span the globe. Go to your bank card's website to find ATM locations at your destination. Be sure you know your daily withdrawal limit before you depart. *Note:* Many banks impose a fee every time you use a card at another bank's ATM, and that fee can be higher for international transactions (up to $5 or more) than for domestic ones (where they're rarely more than $2). In addition, the bank from which you withdraw cash may charge its own fee. For international withdrawal fees, ask your bank.

Note: Banks that are members of the **Global ATM Alliance** charge no transaction fees for cash withdrawals at other Alliance member ATMs; these include Bank of America, Scotiabank (Canada, Caribbean & Mexico), Barclays (U.K. and parts of Africa), Deutsche Bank (Germany, Poland, Spain, and Italy), and BNP Paribas (France).

CREDIT CARDS

Credit cards are another safe way to carry money. They also provide a convenient record of all your expenses, and they generally offer relatively good exchange rates. You can withdraw cash advances from your credit cards at banks or ATMs but high fees make credit-card cash advances a pricey way to get cash. Keep in mind that you'll pay interest from the moment of your withdrawal, even if you pay your monthly bills on time. Also, note that many banks now assess a 1% to 3% "transaction fee" on **all** charges you incur abroad (whether you're using the local currency or your native currency).

It's highly recommended that you travel with at least one major credit card. You must have a credit card to rent a car, and hotels and airlines usually require a credit card imprint as a deposit against expenses.

TRAVELER'S CHECKS

You can buy traveler's checks at most banks. They are offered in denominations of $20, $50, $100, $500, and sometimes $1000. Generally, you'll pay a service charge ranging from 1% to 4%.

The most popular traveler's checks are offered by **American Express** (© **800/807-6233** or © **800/221-7282** for card

Tips Small Change

When you change money, ask for some small bills or loose change. Petty cash will come in handy for tipping and public transportation. Consider keeping the change separate from your larger bills, so that it's readily accessible and you'll be less of a target for theft. U.S. dollars are accepted nearly everywhere, and in some countries, such as Jamaica, most locals prefer their tips to be in U.S. dollars.

holders—this number accepts collect calls, offers service in several foreign languages, and exempts Amex gold and platinum cardholders from the 1% fee.); **Visa** (© 800/732-1322)—AAA members can obtain Visa checks for a $9.95 fee (for checks up to $1,500) at most AAA offices or by calling © 866/339-3378; and **MasterCard** (© 800/223-9920).

Be sure to keep a record of the traveler's checks serial numbers separate from your checks in the event that they are stolen or lost. You'll get a refund faster if you know the numbers.

American Express, Thomas Cook, Visa, and **MasterCard** offer **foreign currency traveler's checks**, useful if you're traveling to one country or to the Euro zone; they're accepted at locations where dollar checks may not be.

Another option is the new prepaid traveler's check cards, reloadable cards that work much like debit cards but aren't linked to your checking account. The **American Express Travelers Cheque Card,** for example, requires a minimum deposit, sets a maximum balance, and has a one-time issuance fee of $14.95. You can withdraw money from an ATM (for a fee of $2.50 per transaction, not including bank fees), and the funds can be purchased in dollars, euros, or pounds. If you lose the card, your available funds will be refunded within 24 hours.

6 Travel Insurance

The cost of travel insurance varies widely, depending on the destination, the cost and length of your trip, your age and health, and the type of trip you're taking, but expect to pay between 5% and 8% of the vacation itself. You can get estimates from various providers through **InsureMyTrip. com**. Enter your trip cost and dates, your age, and other information, for prices from more than a dozen companies.

U.K. citizens and their families who make more than one trip abroad per year may find an annual travel insurance policy works out cheaper. Check **www.money supermarket.com**, which compares prices across a wide range of providers for single- and multi-trip policies.

Most big travel agents offer their own insurance and will probably try to sell you their package when you book a holiday. Think before you sign. **Britain's Consumers' Association** recommends that you insist on seeing the policy and reading the fine print before buying travel insurance. **The Association of British Insurers** (© 020/7600-3333; www.abi.org.uk) gives advice by phone and publishes *Holiday Insurance*, a free guide to policy provisions and prices. You might also shop around for better deals: Try **Columbus Direct** (© 0870/033-9988; www. columbusdirect.net).

TRIP-CANCELLATION INSURANCE

Trip-cancellation insurance will help retrieve your money if you have to back out of a trip or depart early, or if your travel supplier goes bankrupt. Trip cancellation traditionally covers such events as sickness, natural disasters, and State Department advisories. The latest news in trip-cancellation insurance is the availability of **expanded hurricane coverage** and the **"any-reason"** cancellation coverage—which costs more but covers cancellations made for any reason. You won't get back 100% of your prepaid trip cost, but you'll be refunded a substantial portion. **TravelSafe** (© **888/885-7233;** www.travelsafe.com) offers both types of coverage. Expedia also offers any-reason cancellation coverage for its air-hotel packages.

For details, contact one of the following recommended insurers: **Access America** (© 866/807-3982; www.accessamerica. com); **Travel Guard International** (© 800/826-4919; www.travelguard. com); **Travel Insured International** (© 800/243-3174; www.travelinsured. com); and **Travelex Insurance Services** (© 888/457-4602; www.travelex-insurance.com).

MEDICAL INSURANCE

For travel overseas, most U.S. health plans (including Medicare and Medicaid) do not provide coverage, and the ones that do often require you to pay for services upfront and reimburse you only after you return home.

As a safety net, you may want to buy travel medical insurance, particularly if you're traveling to a remote or high-risk area where emergency evacuation might be necessary. If you require additional medical insurance, try **MEDEX Assistance** (© 410/453-6300; www.medex assist.com) or **Travel Assistance International** (© **800/821-2828;** www.travel assistance.com; for general information on services, call the company's **Worldwide Assistance Services, Inc.**, at © 800/ 777-8710).

Canadians should check with their provincial health plan offices or call **Health Canada** (© **866/225-0709;** www.hc-sc. gc.ca) to find out the extent of their coverage and what documentation and receipts they must take home in case they are treated overseas.

LOST-LUGGAGE INSURANCE

On international flights (including U.S. portions of international trips), baggage coverage is limited to approximately $9.07 per pound, up to approximately $635 per checked bag. If you plan to check items more valuable than what's covered by the standard liability, see if your homeowner's policy covers your valuables, get baggage insurance as part of your comprehensive travel-insurance package, or buy Travel Guard's "BagTrak" product.

If your luggage is lost, immediately file a lost-luggage claim at the airport, detailing the luggage contents. Most airlines require that you report delayed, damaged, or lost baggage within 4 hours of arrival. The airlines are required to deliver luggage, once found, directly to your house or destination free of charge.

7 Health

STAYING HEALTHY

Keep the following suggestions in mind:

- On some islands, it's best to drink bottled water during your trip. (See "Fast Facts" in the individual island chapters for details.)
- If you experience diarrhea, moderate your eating habits and drink only

bottled water until you recover. If symptoms persist, consult a doctor.

- The Caribbean sun can be brutal. Wear sunglasses and a hat and use sunscreen liberally. Limit your time on the beach the first day. If you do overexpose yourself, stay out of the sun until you recover. If your exposure is followed by fever or chills, a headache, or a feeling of nausea or dizziness, see a doctor.

- One of the biggest menaces is the "no-see-ums," which emerge mainly in the early evening. You can't see these gnats, but you sure can "feel-um." Window screens can't keep these critters out, so carry bug repellent.

- Mosquitoes are a nuisance. Malaria-carrying mosquitoes in the Caribbean are confined largely to Haiti and the Dominican Republic. If you're visiting either, consult your doctor for preventive medicine at least 8 weeks before you leave. Dengue fever is prevalent in the islands, most prominently on Antigua, St. Kitts, Dominica, and the Dominican Republic. To date, no satisfactory treatment has been developed; visitors are advised to avoid mosquito bites—as if that were possible.

- Infectious hepatitis has been reported on islands such as Dominica and Haiti. Unless you have been immunized for both hepatitis A and B, consult your doctor about the advisability of getting a gamma-globulin shot before you leave. The United States **Centers for Disease Control and Prevention** (© **800/394-1945;** www.cdc.gov) provides up-to-date information on necessary vaccines and health hazards by region or country.

- Pack prescription medications in your carry-on luggage. Carry written prescriptions in generic, not brand-name, form, and dispense all prescription medications from their original labeled vials. Many people try to slip drugs such as cocaine into the Caribbean (or pick them up there). Drugs are often placed into a container for prescription medication after the legal medications have been removed. Customs officials are well aware of this type of smuggling and often check medications if they suspect a passenger is bringing illegal drugs into or out of a country.

- If you wear contact lenses, pack an extra pair in case you lose one.

WHAT TO DO IF YOU GET SICK AWAY FROM HOME

Finding a good doctor in the Caribbean is not a problem, and most speak English. See the "Fast Facts" section in each chapter for specific names and addresses on each individual island.

If you worry about getting sick away from home, you might want to consider medical travel insurance (see the section on travel insurance above). In most cases, however, your existing health plan will provide all the coverage you need. Be sure to carry your identification card in your wallet.

If you suffer from a chronic illness, consult your doctor before your departure. For conditions like epilepsy, diabetes, or heart problems, wear a **MedicAlert identification tag** (© **888/633-4298;** www.medic alert.org), which will immediately alert doctors to your condition and give them access to your records through MedicAlert's 24-hour hot line.

Contact the International Association for Medical Assistance to Travelers (IAMAT; © 716/754-4883 or, in Canada, 416/652-0137; www.iamat.org) for tips on travel and health concerns in the islands you're visiting, and for lists of local, English-speaking doctors. The United States Centers for Disease Control and Prevention (© 800/311-3435; www.cdc.gov) provides up-to-date information on health hazards by region or country and offers tips on food safety. Travel Health Online (www.tripprep.com), sponsored by a consortium of travel medicine practitioners, may also offer helpful advice on traveling abroad. You can find listings of reliable medical clinics overseas at the International Society of Travel Medicine (www.istm.org).

8 Specialized Travel Resources

TRAVELERS WITH DISABILITIES

Most disabilities shouldn't stop anyone from traveling. There are more options and resources out there than ever before.

In general, the Caribbean is not easy for persons with disabilities. Attractions and sights, for the most part, don't have elevators, ramps, or wheelchair-accessible toilets. Nor are most hotels constructed for accessibility. If you are contemplating a holiday in the sun, consider the islands of Puerto Rico or one of the U.S. Virgins—St. Thomas, St. Croix, or St. John. As part of U.S. territories, these islands must abide by the Americans with Disabilities Act. Even so, getting around can still be difficult. Transportation is woefully inadequate and many Caribbean hotels lie in hilly or mountainous regions. However, some resorts have ground-floor bedrooms with wide doors and accessible bathrooms. We've indicated this in the amenities section of the hotel reviews.

Organizations that offer a vast range of resources and assistance to disabled travelers include **MossRehab** (© 800/CALL-MOSS; www.mossresourcenet.org); the **American Foundation for the Blind** (AFB; © 800/232-5463; www.afb.org); and **SATH** (**Society for Accessible Travel & Hospitality**; © 212/447-7284; www.sath.org). **AirAmbulanceCard.com** is now partnered with SATH and allows you to preselect top-notch hospitals in case of an emergency.

Access-Able Travel Source (© 303/232-2979; www.access-able.com) offers a comprehensive database on travel agents from around the world with experience in accessible travel; destination-specific access information; and links to such resources as service animals, equipment rentals, and access guides.

Many travel agencies offer customized tours and itineraries for travelers with disabilities. Among them are **Flying Wheels Travel** (© 507/451-5005; www.flying wheelstravel.com); and **Accessible Journeys** (© 800/846-4537 or 610/521-0339; www.disabilitytravel.com).

Flying with Disability (www.flying-with-disability.org) is a comprehensive information source on airplane travel. **Avis Rent a Car** (© 888/879-4273) has an "Avis Access" program that offers services for customers with special travel needs. These include specially outfitted vehicles with swivel seats, spinner knobs, and hand controls; mobility scooter rentals; and accessible bus service. Be sure to reserve well in advance.

Also check out the quarterly magazine *Emerging Horizons* (www.emerging horizons.com), available by subscription ($16.95 year U.S.; $21.95 outside U.S).

The "Accessible Travel" link at **Mobility-Advisor.com** (www.mobility-advisor.com) offers a variety of travel resources to disabled persons.

British travelers should contact **Holiday Care** (© 0845/124-9971 in UK only; www.holidaycare.org.uk) to access a wide range of travel information and resources for disabled and elderly people.

GAY & LESBIAN TRAVELERS

The most gay-friendly Caribbean islands are the U.S. possessions, most notably Puerto Rico, which is hailed as the "gay capital of the Caribbean" and offers gay guesthouses, nightclubs, bars, and dance clubs. To a lesser extent, the U.S. Virgin Islands are welcoming, too.

The French islands—St. Barts, St. Martin, Guadeloupe, and Martinique—are technically an extension of mainland France, and the French have always regarded homosexuality with a certain blasé tolerance. However, don't let your guard down. One gay man was so viciously attacked in 2005 that he suffered brain damage.

The Dutch islands of Aruba and Bonaire are quite conservative, so discretion is suggested. But in a surprise move in 2005, their sister island of Curaçao became the first in the Caribbean to publicly announce that it was embracing the gay and lesbian community, urging such travelers to visit their island as a gay-friendly destination, and such hotels as Kura Hulanda have joined the Gay & Lesbian Travel Association. Even certain nightclubs in Willemstad have proclaimed their "gay friendly" atmosphere in an attempt to attract patrons from this community of travelers.

Gay life is fairly secretive in many of the sleepy islands of the Caribbean. Some islands even have repressive antihomosexual laws. Homosexuality is actively discouraged in places like the Cayman Islands, but as a result of pressure from gay advocacy groups, past homophobia is slowly giving way to tolerance. In Barbados, homosexuality is illegal, and there is often a lack of tolerance in spite of the large number of gay residents and visitors on the island.

Jamaica is the most homophobic island in the Caribbean, with harsh antigay laws, even though there is a large local gay population. The famous all-inclusive **Sandals** of Jamaica had until 2004 a discriminatory policy of admitting only male-female couples. However, under pressure they were forced to rescind the ban and admit same-sex couples.

The International Gay and Lesbian Travel Association (IGLTA; © **800/448-8550** or 954/776-2626; www.iglta.org) is the trade association for the gay and lesbian travel industry, and offers an online directory of gay- and lesbian-friendly travel businesses and tour operators.

Many agencies offer tours and travel itineraries specifically for gay and lesbian travelers. **Above and Beyond Tours** (© **800/397-2681**; www.abovebeyond tours.com) are gay Australia tour specialists. San Francisco–based **Now, Voyager**

(© **800/255-6951**; www.nowvoyager. com) offers worldwide trips and cruises, and **Olivia** (© **800/631-6277**; www. olivia.com) offers lesbian cruises and resort vacations.

Gay.com Travel (© **800/929-2268** or 415/644-8044; www.gay.com/travel or www.outandabout.com) is an excellent online successor to the popular *Out & About* print magazine. It provides regularly updated information about gay-owned, gay-oriented, and gay-friendly lodging, dining, sightseeing, nightlife, and shopping establishments in every important destination worldwide. British travelers should click on the "Travel" link at **www.uk.gay.com** for advice and gay-friendly trip ideas.

The Canadian website **GayTraveler (gaytraveler.ca)** offers ideas and advice for gay travel all over the world.

The following travel guides are available at many bookstores, or you can order them from any online bookseller: *Spartacus International Gay Guide, 35th Edition* (Bruno Gmünder Verlag; www.spartacus world.com/gayguide); *Odysseus: The International Gay Travel Planner, 17th Edition* (www.odyusa.com); and the *Damron* guides (www.damron.com), with separate, annual books for gay men and lesbians.

SENIOR TRAVEL

Mention that you're a senior when you make your travel reservations. Although all of the major U.S. airlines except America West have canceled their senior-discount and coupon-book programs, many hotels still offer discounts for seniors. In most cities, people over the age of 60 qualify for reduced admission to theaters, museums, and other attractions, as well as discounted fares on public transportation.

Members of **AARP,** 601 E St. NW, Washington, DC 20049 (© **888/687-2277**; www.aarp.org), get discounts on hotels, airfares, and car rentals. AARP offers members a wide range of benefits, including *AARP: The Magazine* and a monthly newsletter. Anyone over 50 can join.

The **U.S. National Park Service** offers a **Golden Age Passport** that gives seniors 62 years or older lifetime entrance to all properties administered by the National Park Service—national parks, monuments, historic sites, recreation areas, and national wildlife refuges—for a one-time processing fee of $10, which must be purchased in person at any NPS facility that charges an entrance fee. Besides free entry, a Golden Age Passport also offers a 50% discount on federal-use fees charged for such facilities as camping, swimming, parking, boat launching, and tours. For more information, go to www.nps.gov/fees_passes.htm or call © **888/467-2757.**

Many reliable agencies and organizations target the 50-plus market. **Elderhostel** (© **800/454-5768;** www.elderhostel.org) arranges worldwide study programs for those aged 55 and over. **ElderTreks** (© **800/741-7956** or 416/558-5000 outside North America; www.eldertreks.com) offers small-group tours to off-the-beaten-path or adventure-travel locations, restricted to travelers 50 and older.

Recommended publications offering travel resources and discounts for seniors include: the quarterly magazine *Travel 50 & Beyond* (www.travel50andbeyond.com) and the bestselling paperback *Unbelievably Good Deals and Great Adventures That You Absolutely Can't Get Unless You're Over 50 2005–2006, 16th Edition* (McGraw-Hill), by Joann Rattner Heilman.

FAMILY TRAVEL

To locate accommodations, restaurants, and attractions that are particularly kid-friendly, refer to the "Kids" icon throughout this guide.

Recommended family travel websites include **Family Travel Forum** (www.familytravelforum.com), a comprehensive site that offers customized trip planning; **Family Travel Network** (www.familytravelnetwork.com), an online magazine providing travel tips; and **TravelWith YourKids.com** (www.travelwithyourkids.com), a comprehensive site written by parents for parents offering sound advice for long-distance and international travel with children

WOMEN TRAVELERS

Check out the award-winning website **Journeywoman** (www.journeywoman.com), a "real life" women's travel-information network where you can sign up for a free e-mail newsletter and get advice on everything from etiquette and dress to safety. The travel guide *Safety and Security for Women Who Travel* by Sheila Swan and Peter Laufer (Travelers' Tales Guides), offering common-sense tips on safe travel, was updated in 2004.

AFRICAN-AMERICAN TRAVELERS

Black Travel Online (www.blacktravelonline.com) posts news on upcoming events and includes links to articles and travel-booking sites. **Soul of America** (www.soulofamerica.com) is a comprehensive website, with travel tips, event and family-reunion postings, and sections on historically black beach resorts and active vacations.

Agencies and organizations that provide resources for black travelers include: **Rodgers Travel** (© **800/825-1775;** www.rodgerstravel.com); the **African American Association of Innkeepers International** (© **877/422-5777;** www.africanamericaninns.com); and **Henderson Travel & Tours** (© **800/327-2309** or 301/650-5700; www.hendersontravel.com), which has specialized in trips to Africa since 1957.

Go Girl: The Black Woman's Guide to Travel & Adventure (Eighth Mountain Press) is a compilation of travel essays by writers including Jill Nelson and

Audre Lorde. *The African-American Travel Guide* by Wayne C. Robinson (Hunter Publishing; www.hunterpublishing.com) was published in 1997, so it may be somewhat dated. *Travel and Enjoy Magazine* (© 866/266-6211; www.travelandenjoy.com) is a travel magazine and guide. The well-done *Pathfinders Magazine* (© 877/977-PATH; www.pathfinderstravel.com) includes articles on everything from Rio de Janeiro to Ghana to upcoming ski, diving, golf, and tennis trips.

STUDENT TRAVEL

The International Student Travel Confederation (ISTC; www.istc.org) was formed in 1949 to make travel around the world more affordable for students. Check out its website for comprehensive travel services information and details on how to get an International Student Identity Card (ISIC), which qualifies students

for substantial savings on rail passes, plane tickets, entrance fees, and more. It also provides students with basic health and life insurance and a 24-hour helpline. The card is valid for a maximum of 18 months. You can apply for the card online or in person at STA Travel (© 800/781-4040 in North America; www.statravel.com), the biggest student travel agency in the world; check out the website to locate STA Travel offices worldwide. If you're no longer a student but are still under 26, you can get an International Youth Travel Card (IYTC) from the same people. It entitles you to some discounts. Travel CUTS (© 800/592-2887; www.travelcuts.com) offers similar services for both Canadians and U.S. residents. Irish students may prefer to turn to USIT (© 01/602-1904; www.usit.ie), an Ireland-based specialist in student, youth, and independent travel.

9 Sustainable Tourism/Ecotourism

Some of the best wildlife cruises are packaged by **Oceanic Society Expeditions** (© 800/326-7491; www.oceanic-society.org). Whale-watching jaunts and some research-oriented trips are also featured. You can swim with humpback whales in the Dominican Republic, for example.

Puerto Rico's varied and often hard-to-reach natural treasures have been conveniently packaged into a series of affordable eco-tours. **Hillbilly Tours,** Route 181, Km 13.4, San Juan (© 787/760-5618; www.hillbillytours.com), specializes in nature-based and countryside tours in Puerto Rico's rainforest. **AdvenTours,** El Yunque (© 787/889-0251; www.adventourspr.com), features customized private tours with activities like bird-watching, hiking, camping, visits to coffee plantations, and kayaking. **Aventuras Tierra Adentro,** 268 Piñero Ave., San Juan (© 787/766-0470; www.aventuraspr.com), specializes in rock climbing,

body rafting, caving, and canyoning, among other activities. **Eco Xcursion Aquatica,** Road 191, Km 1.7, Rio Grande, Fajardo (© 787/888-2887), offers some of the best rainforest hikes and mountain-bike tours.

Machias Adventures (© 888/427-3497 or 203/227-7337; www.machiasadventures.com) arranges adventure tours to St. Vincent, including hiking up a volcano, a day sailing with a crew, seeking out the huge variety of bird life, and hiking up a river canyon to a dramatic water pool—a perfect pool for swimming. The cost of these 7-day jaunts is $2,450 per person, based on double occupancy.

Although one could argue that any vacation that includes an airplane flight can't be truly "green," you can go on holiday and still contribute positively to the environment. You can offset carbon emissions from your flight in other ways.

Frommers.com: The Complete Travel Resource

It should go without saying, but we highly recommend **Frommers.com**, voted Best Travel Site by *PC Magazine*. We think you'll find our expert advice and tips; independent reviews of hotels, restaurants, attractions, and preferred shopping and nightlife venues; vacation giveaways; and an online booking tool indispensable before, during, and after your travels. We publish the complete contents of over 128 travel guides in our **Destinations** section covering nearly 3,800 places worldwide to help you plan your trip. Each weekday, we publish original articles reporting on **Deals and News** via our free **Frommers.com Newsletter** to help you save time and money and travel smarter. We're betting you'll find our new **Events** listings (http://events. frommers.com) an invaluable resource; it's an up-to-the-minute roster of what's happening in cities everywhere—including concerts, festivals, lectures, and more. We've also added weekly **Podcasts, interactive maps,** and hundreds of new images across the site. Check out our **Travel Talk** area featuring **Message Boards** where you can join in conversations with thousands of fellow Frommer's travelers and post your trip report once you return.

Choose forward-looking companies that embrace responsible development practices, helping preserve destinations for the future by working alongside local people. An increasing number of sustainable tourism initiatives can help you plan a family trip and leave as small a "footprint" as possible on the places you visit.

Responsible Travel (www.responsible travel.com) contains a great source of sustainable travel ideas and is run by a spokesperson for responsible tourism in the travel industry. **Sustainable Travel International** (www.sustainabletravel international.org) promotes responsible tourism practices and issues an annual Green Gear & Gift Guide.

You can find eco-friendly travel tips, statistics, and touring companies and associations—listed by destination under "Travel Choice"—at the TIES website, www.ecotourism.org. Also check out **Conservation International** (www. conservation.org)—which, with *National Geographic Traveler,* annually presents **World Legacy Awards** (www.wlaward.

org)˙ to those travel tour operators, businesses, organizations, and places that have made a significant contribution to sustainable tourism. **Ecotravel.com** is part online magazine and part ecodirectory that lets you search for touring companies in several categories (water-based, land-based, spiritually oriented, and so on).

In the U.K., **Tourism Concern** (www. tourismconcern.org.uk) works to reduce social and environmental problems connected to tourism and find ways of improving tourism so that local benefits are increased.

The **Association of British Travel Agents** (ABTA; www.abtamembers.org/ responsibletourism) acts as a focal point for the U.K. travel industry and is one of the leading groups spearheading responsible tourism.

The **Association of Independent Tour Operators** (AITO; www.aito.co. uk) is a group of interesting specialist operators leading the field in making holidays sustainable.

For information about the ethics of swimming with dolphins and other outdoor activities, visit the **Whale** **and Dolphin Conservation Society** (www.wdcs.org) and **Tread Lightly** (www.treadlightly.org).

10 Staying Connected

TELEPHONES

Generally, hotel surcharges on long-distance and local calls are astronomical, so you're better off using your **cellphone**. Many public pay phones at airports now accept American Express, MasterCard, and Visa credit cards.

CELLPHONES

The three letters that define much of the world's wireless capabilities are **GSM** (Global System for Mobile Communications), a big, seamless network that makes for easy cross-border cellphone use throughout Europe and dozens of other countries worldwide. In the U.S., T-Mobile, AT&T Wireless, and Cingular use this quasi-universal system; in Canada, Microcell and some Rogers customers are GSM, and all Europeans and most Australians use GSM. GSM phones function with a removable plastic SIM card, encoded with your phone number and account information. If your cellphone is on a GSM system, and you have a world-capable multiband phone such as many Sony Ericsson, Motorola, or Samsung models, you can make and receive calls across civilized areas around much of the globe. Just call your wireless operator and ask for "international roaming" to be activated on your account.

For many, **renting** a phone is a good idea. While you can rent a phone from any number of overseas sites, including kiosks at airports and at car-rental agencies, we suggest renting the phone before you leave home. North Americans can rent one before leaving home from **InTouch USA** (© 800/872-7626; www. intouchglobal.com) or **RoadPost** (© 888/ 290-1606 or 905/272-5665; www.road

post.com). InTouch will also, for free, advise you on whether your existing phone will work overseas; simply call © **703/222-7161** between 9am and 4pm EST, or go to **http://intouchglobal. com/travel.htm**.

Buying a phone can be economically attractive, as many nations have cheap prepaid phone systems. Once you arrive at your destination, stop by a local cellphone shop and get the cheapest package; you'll probably pay less than $100 for a phone and a starter calling card. Local calls may be as low as 10¢ per minute, and in many countries incoming calls are free.

INTERNET/E-MAIL WITHOUT YOUR OWN COMPUTER

Most major airports have **Internet kiosks** that provide basic Web access for a per-minute fee.

WITH YOUR OWN COMPUTER

More and more hotels, resorts, airports, cafes, and retailers are going **Wi-Fi** (wireless fidelity), becoming "hotspots" that offer free high-speed Wi-Fi access or charge a small fee for usage. Most laptops sold today have built-in wireless capability. To find public Wi-Fi hotspots at your destination, go to **www.jiwire.com**; its Hotspot Finder holds the world's largest directory of public wireless hotspots.

Wherever you go, bring a connection kit of the right power and phone adapters, a spare phone cord, and a spare Ethernet network cable—or find out whether your hotel supplies them to guests.

Online Traveler's Toolbox

Veteran travelers usually carry some essential items to make their trips easier. Following is a selection of handy online tools to bookmark and use.

- **Airplane Food** (www.airlinemeals.net)
- **Airplane Seating** (www.seatguru.com; and www.airlinequality.com)
- **Foreign Languages for Travelers** (www.travlang.com)
- **Maps** (www.mapquest.com)
- **Subway Navigator** (www.subwaynavigator.com)
- **Time and Date** (www.timeanddate.com)
- **Travel Warnings** (http://travel.state.gov, www.fco.gov.uk/travel, www.voyage.gc.ca, or www.dfat.gov.au/consular/advice)
- **Universal Currency Converter** (www.xe.com/ucc)
- **Visa ATM Locator** (www.visa.com), **MasterCard ATM Locator** (www.mastercard.com)
- **Weather** (www.intellicast.com; and www.weather.com)

11 Packages for the Independent Traveler

Package tours are simply a way to buy the airfare, accommodations, and other elements of your trip (such as car rentals, airport transfers, and sometimes even activities) at the same time and often at discounted prices.

Especially in the Caribbean, package tours are *not* the same thing as escorted tours. You'll be on your own, but in most cases, a package to the Caribbean will include airfare, hotel, and transportation to and from the airport—and it'll cost you less than just the hotel alone if you booked it yourself. A package deal might not be for you if you want to stay in a more intimate inn or guesthouse, but if you like resorts, read on.

You can find an amazing array of packages to popular Caribbean destinations. Some packages offer a better class of hotels than others. Some offer the same hotels for lower prices. Some offer scheduled flights on airlines, and others book charters. Remember to comparison shop among at least three different operators, and always compare apples to apples.

Many land-and-sea packages include meals, and you might find yourself locked into your hotel dining room every night if your meals are prepaid. If you're seeking a more varied dining experience, avoid **AP (American Plan),** which means full board, and opt for **MAP (Modified American Plan),** meaning breakfast and either lunch or dinner. That way, you'll at least be free for one main meal of the day and can sample a variety of an island's regional fare.

One good source of package deals is the airlines themselves. Most major airlines offer air/land packages, including **American Airlines Vacations** (© 800/321-2121; www.aavacations.com), **Delta Vacations** (© 800/654-6559; www.deltavacations.com), **Continental Airlines Vacations** (© 800/301-3800; www.covacations.com), and **United Vacations** (© 888/854-3899; www.unitedvacations.com). Several big **online travel agencies—**Expedia, Travelocity, Orbitz, Site59, and Lastminute.com—also do a brisk business in packages.

The biggest hotel chains, casinos, and resorts also offer package deals. If you already know where you want to stay, call the resort itself and ask if it offers land/air packages.

To save time comparing the prices and value of all the package tours out there, contact **TourScan, Inc.** (© **800/962-2080** or 203/655-8091; www.tourscan.com). Every season, the company computerizes the contents of travel brochures that contain about 10,000 different vacations at 1,600 hotels in the Caribbean, the Bahamas, and Bermuda. TourScan selects the best-value vacation at each hotel and condo.

Other tour operators include the following:

- **Club Med** (© **888/932-2582;** www.clubmed.com) has various all-inclusive options throughout the Caribbean and the Bahamas, as does **Sandals** (© **888/726-3257;** www.sandals.com).
- **SuperClubs** (© **877/467-8737;** www.superclubs.com) has a wide variety of all-inclusive resorts in Jamaica, Curaçao, and the Dominican Republic.

Travel packages are also listed in the travel section of your local Sunday newspaper. Or check ads in national travel magazines such as *Arthur Frommer's Budget Travel Magazine, Travel & Leisure, National Geographic Traveler,* and *Condé Nast Traveler.*

12 Special-Interest Trips

BIKING The Dominican Republic is the best mountain-bike destination in the Caribbean. *Bicycling Magazine* said the island defies all stereotype, "with its towering mountains and miles of single track." The best-organized trips are offered by **Iguana Mama Mountain Bike,** Cabarete (© **800/849-4720** in the U.S., or 809/571-0908; www.iguanamama.com).

BIRD-WATCHING Victor Emanuel Nature Tours (© **800/328-8368** or 512/328-5221; www.ventbird.com) offers 10-day bird-watching trips led by a biologist in Trinidad and Tobago. Each trip costs approximately $3,075 per person, and trips are based at the **Asa Wright Nature Centre** (© **800/426-7781;** www.asawright.org), where you can see 150 of the more than 400 species of birds found in Trinidad. Field trips and discussions on the symbiosis between plant and bird life are available. The agency also offers a 14-day birding tour to the Dominican Republic, costing $2,595 per person, and 8-day nature tours to Jamaica, costing $2,675 per person.

HIKING Unlike many of its neighboring islands, Jamaica's mountain peaks climb to 2,220m (7,282 ft.). The flora, fauna, waterfalls, and panoramas of those peaks have attracted increasing numbers of hikers determined to experience the natural beauty of the island firsthand. Because of the dangers involved, it's often best to go on an organized tour. Good ones are offered by **Sunventure Tours,** 30 Balmoral Ave., Kingston 10, Jamaica, W.I. (© **876/960-6685;** www.sunventuretours.com). For more information, refer to the section "The Blue Mountains," in chapter 15.

SCUBA TRIPS A number of outfitters offer scuba packages and cruises. **Aqua Hut** (© 610/642-3483; www.aquahut.net) specializes in diving trips throughout the Caribbean for individuals, couples, and families. Its destinations range from the British Virgin Islands to Bonaire. **Island Dreams Tours & Travel** (© **800/346-6116** or 713/973-9300; www.divetrip.com) also offers trips, including itineraries in the Cayman Islands, Bonaire, and Turks and Caicos.

> ### Tips   Websites for Divers
>
> For useful information on scuba diving in the Caribbean, check out the website of the **Professional Association of Diving Instructors (PADI)** at **www.padi.com**. This site provides descriptions of dive destinations throughout the Caribbean and a directory of PADI-certified dive operators. *Scuba Diving Magazine* also has a helpful website at **www.scubadiving.com**. Both sites list dive package specials and display gorgeous color photos of some of the most beautiful dive spots in the world.

Explorer Ventures (℡ 800/322-3577 or 903/887-8521; www.explorerventures.com) takes divers on its *Caribbean Explorer II* to excursions in the waters of St. Kitts, Turks and Caicos, and Saba. Trips usually last a week.

Another specialist in this field is **Caradonna Caribbean Tours** (℡ 800/328-2288 or 407/774-9000; www.caradonna.com), which offers adventurous scuba-cruise packages to Bonaire, St. Croix, and St. Kitts, among other islands.

SEA KAYAKING   The only outfitter in the Virgin Islands that offers sea-kayaking/island-camping excursions is Arawak Expeditions, based in Cruz Bay, St. John (℡ 800/238-8687 in the U.S., or 340/693-8312; www.arawakexp.com). It provides kayaking gear, healthy meals, camping equipment, and two experienced guides. Multiday excursions range from $1,095 to $1,195.

13 Tips on Accommodations

SURFING FOR HOTELS

In addition to the online travel booking sites **Travelocity, Expedia, Orbitz, Priceline,** and **Hotwire,** you can book hotels through **Hotels.com, Quikbook** (www.quikbook.com), and **Travelaxe** (www.travelaxe.net).

HotelChatter.com is a daily webzine offering smart coverage and critiques of hotels worldwide. Go to **TripAdvisor.com** or **HotelShark.com** for helpful independent consumer reviews of hotels and resort properties.

It's a good idea to **get a confirmation number** and **make a printout** of any online booking transaction.

SAVING ON YOUR HOTEL ROOM

WATCH OUT FOR THOSE EXTRAS!
Nearly all islands charge a government tax on hotel rooms, usually 7½% to 9%, but that rate varies from island to island. When booking a room, make sure you understand whether the price you've been quoted includes the tax. That will avoid an unpleasant surprise when it comes time to pay the bill. Sometimes the room tax depends on the quality of the hotel— it might be relatively low for a guesthouse but steeper for a first-class resort.

Furthermore, most hotels routinely add 10% to 12% for "service," even if you didn't see much evidence of it. That means that with tax and service, some bills are 17% or even 25% higher than the price that was originally quoted to you! Naturally, you need to determine just how much the hotel, guesthouse, or inn plans to add to your bill at the end of your stay, and whether it's included in the initial price.

That's not all. Some hotels slip in little hidden extras that mount quickly. For example, it's common for many places to quote rates that include a continental breakfast. Should you prefer ham and eggs, you will pay extra charges. If you request special privileges, like extra towels for the beach or laundry done in a hurry, surcharges may mount. It pays to watch those extras and to ask questions before you commit.

WHAT THE ABBREVIATIONS MEAN

Rate sheets often have these classifications:

- **MAP (Modified American Plan)** usually means room, breakfast, and dinner, unless the room rate has been quoted separately, and then it means only breakfast and dinner.
- **CP (Continental Plan)** includes room and a light breakfast.
- **EP (European Plan)** means room only.
- **AP (American Plan)** includes your room plus three meals a day.

HOTELS & RESORTS Many budget travelers assume they can't afford the big hotels and resorts. But there are so many packages out there (see the section "Packages for the Independent Traveler," earlier in this chapter) and so many frequent sales, even in winter, that you might be pleasantly surprised.

Some hotels are often quite flexible about their rates, and many offer discounts and upgrades whenever they have a big block of rooms to fill and few reservations. The smaller hotels and inns are not as likely to be generous with discounts, much less upgrades.

ALL-INCLUSIVE RESORTS The promises are persuasive: "Forget your cash, put your plastic away." Presumably, everything's all paid for in advance at an "all-inclusive" resort. But is it?

The all-inclusives have a reputation for being expensive, and many of them are, especially the giant **SuperClubs** of Jamaica or even the **Sandals** properties

(unless you book in a slow period or off season).

In the 1990s, so many competitors entered the all-inclusive game that the term now means different things to the various resorts that use this marketing strategy. The ideal all-inclusive is just that—a place where everything, even drinks and watersports, is included. But in the narrowest sense, it means a room and three meals a day, with extra charges for drinks, sports, whatever. When you book, it's important to ask and to understand exactly what's included in your so-called all-inclusive. Watersports programs vary greatly at the various resorts. Extras might include horseback riding or sightseeing.

The all-inclusive market is geared to the active traveler who likes organized entertainment, a lot of sports and workouts at fitness centers, and who also likes a lot of food and drink.

If you're single or gay, avoid Sandals. If you have children, stay away from Hedonism II in Negril, Jamaica, which lives up to its name. Some Club Meds are targeted more for singles and couples, other aggressively pursue the family market. Some Club Meds have Mini Clubs, Baby Clubs, and Teen Clubs at some of their properties, at least during holiday and summer seasons.

The trick is to look for that special deal and to travel in off-peak periods, which doesn't always mean just from mid-April to mid-December. Discounts are often granted for hotels during certain slow periods, called "windows," most often after the New Year's holiday. If you want a winter vacation at an all-inclusive, choose the month of January—not February or the Christmas holidays, when prices are at their all-year high.

One good deal might be **Club Med's "Wild Card,"** geared to singles and couples. You must be 18 or over, and reservations must be made 2 or more weeks before departure. One week before departure,

Club Med tells you which "village" on which island you're going to visit. If this uncertainty doesn't bother you, you can save $150 to $300 per weekly package. Deals like this can change constantly, so check to see exactly how "wild" this card is to play. Each package includes round-trip air transportation from New York, double-occupancy accommodations, all meals with complimentary wine and beer, use of all sports facilities except scuba gear (extra charges), nightly entertainment, and other recreational activities such as boat rides, snorkeling expeditions, and picnics. For more information, call ✆ **888/932-2582.**

GUESTHOUSES   An entirely different type of accommodations is the guesthouse, where most of the Antilleans themselves stay when they travel. In the Caribbean, the term "guesthouse" can mean anything. Sometimes so-called guesthouses are really like simple motels built around swimming pools. Others are small individual cottages, with their own kitchenettes, constructed around a main building in which you'll often find a bar and a restaurant that serves local food. Some are surprisingly comfortable, often with private baths and swimming pools. You may or may not have air-conditioning.

For value, the guesthouse can't be topped. You can always journey over to a big beach resort and use its seaside facilities for only a small charge, perhaps no more than $5. Although they don't have any frills, the guesthouses we've recommended are clean and safe for families or single women. The cheapest ones are not places where you'd want to spend a lot of time, because of their simple, modest furnishings.

RENTING A CONDO, VILLA, OR COTTAGE   Particularly if you're a family or a group of friends, a "housekeeping holiday" can be one of the least expensive ways to vacation in the Caribbean, and if you like privacy and independence, it's a good way to go. Accommodations with kitchens are now available on nearly all the islands. Some are individual cottages, others are condo complexes with swimming pools, and some are private homes that owners rent out while they're away. Many (though not all) places include maid service, and you're given fresh linens as well.

In the simpler rentals, doing your own cooking and laundry or even your own maid service may not be your idea of a good time in the sun, but it saves money—a lot of money. The savings, especially for a family of three to six people, or two or three couples, can range from 50% to 60% of what a hotel would cost. Groceries are sometimes priced 35% to 60% higher than on the U.S. mainland, as nearly all foodstuffs have to be imported, but even so, preparing your own food will be a lot cheaper than dining at restaurants.

There are also quite lavish homes for rent, where you can spend a lot and stay in the lap of luxury in a prime beachfront setting.

Many villas have a staff, or at least a maid who comes in a few days a week, and they also provide the essentials for home life, including linens and housewares. Condos usually come with a reception desk and are often comparable to a suite in a big resort hotel. Nearly all condo complexes have pools (some more than one). Like condos, villas range widely in price and may begin at $700 per week for a modest one and go over $50,000 a week for a luxurious one. More likely, the prices will be somewhere in between.

You'll have to approach these rental properties with a certain sense of independence. There may or may not be a front desk to answer your questions, and you'll have to plan your own watersports.

For a list of agencies that arrange rentals, refer to the accommodations sections of the individual island chapters.

You can also ask each island's tourist office for good suggestions. Make your reservations well in advance.

Here are a few agencies renting throughout the Caribbean:

- **Villas of Distinction** (© **800/289-0900** in the U.S.; www.villasof distinction.com) offers upscale private villas with one to six bedrooms and a pool. Domestic help is often included. They have offerings on St. Martin, Anguilla, Mustique, Barbados, the U.S. and British Virgins, the Cayman Islands, St. Lucia, Nevis, Turks and Caicos, St. Barts, and Jamaica. Descriptions, rates, and photos are available online.

- **At Home Abroad** (© **212/421-9165;** fax 212/533-0095; www.at homeabroadinc.com) has private upscale homes for rent on Antigua, Barbados, Dominican Republic, Grenada, Jamaica, Mustique, St. John, St. Croix, St. Martin, St. Thomas, Tortola, and Virgin Gorda, most with maid service included.

- **Caribbean Connection Plus Ltd.** (© **888/255-6889;** fax 203/202-3145; www.islandhoppingexperts. com) has many apartments, cottages, and villas in the Caribbean, especially on St. Kitts and Nevis, but also on some of the more obscure islands such as St. Eustatius, Tobago, St. Vincent, and Dominica. Caribbean Connection specializes in island hopping with InterIsland Air, and offers especially attractive deals for U.S. West Coast travelers. This is one of the few reservations services staffed by people who have actually been on the islands, so patrons can talk to people who really know the Caribbean.

- **Hideaways International** (© **800/843-4433** in the U.S., or 603/430-4433; www.hideaways.com) publishes *Hideaways Guide,* a pictorial directory of home rentals throughout the world, including the Caribbean, especially the British Virgin Islands, the Cayman Islands, Jamaica, and St. Lucia, with full descriptions so you know what you're renting. Rentals range from cottages to staffed villas to whole islands! Other services include yacht charters, cruises, airline ticketing, car rentals, and hotel reservations. Annual membership is $185. Membership information, listings, and photos are available online.

- **Heart of the Caribbean Ltd.** (© **800/231-5303** or 262/783-5303; www. hotcarib.com) is a villa wholesale company offering travelers a wide range of private villas and condos on several islands, including St. Maarten/St. Martin, Barbados, and St. Lucia. Accommodations range from one to six bedrooms, and from modest villas and condos to palatial estates. Homes have complete kitchens and maid service. Catering and car rentals can also be provided. Rates, listings, and photos are available online.

LANDING THE BEST ROOM

Somebody has to get the best room in the house. It might as well be you. You can start by joining the hotel's frequent-guest program, which may make you eligible for upgrades. A hotel-branded credit card usually gives its owner "silver" or "gold" status in frequent-guest programs for free. Always ask about a corner room. They're often larger and quieter, with more windows and light, and they often cost the same as standard rooms. When you make your reservation, ask if the hotel is renovating; if it is, request a room away from the construction. Ask about nonsmoking rooms and rooms with views. Be sure to request your choice of twin, queen- or king-size beds. If you're a light sleeper, ask for a quiet room away from vending or ice machines, elevators, restaurants, bars, and discos. Ask for a room that has been recently renovated or refurbished.

If you aren't happy with your room when you arrive, ask for another one. Most lodgings will be willing to accommodate you.

In resort areas, particularly in warm climates, ask the following questions before you book a room:

- What's the view like? Cost-conscious travelers may be willing to pay less for a back room facing the parking lot, especially if they don't plan to spend much time in their room.

- Does the room have air-conditioning or ceiling fans? Do the windows open? If they do, and the nighttime entertainment takes place alfresco, you may want to find out when show time is over.

- What's included in the price? Your room may be moderately priced, but if you're charged for beach chairs, towels, sports equipment, and other amenities, you could end up spending more than you bargained for.

- How far is the room from the beach and other amenities? If it's far, is there transportation to and from the beach, and is it free?

14 Getting Married in the Caribbean

See also "The Best Places to Honeymoon," in chapter 1, for information on specific resorts that offer wedding and honeymoon packages. **Club Med** (© 888/932-2582; www.clubmed.com), **Sandals** (© 888/726-3257; www.sandals.com), and **SuperClubs** (© 877/467-8737; www.superclubs.com) are three chains that have married many couples.

If you yearn to take the plunge in the Caribbean, you need to know the requirements on the different islands.

ANGUILLA Couples need to file a license application on Anguilla, which takes approximately 48 hours to process. You'll need to present a passport, and, if applicable, proof of divorce or the death certificate of a deceased spouse. The fee for the license US$244 and stamp duty is US$270. For further information, contact the **Registrar of Births, Deaths, and Marriages,** Judicial Department, The Valley, Anguilla, B.W.I. (© 264/497-2377).

ANTIGUA & BARBUDA There's a 24-hour waiting period for marriages on Antigua. The registration fee of $40 must be paid at the Courthouse located in the new government buildings on Queen Elizabeth Highway. A couple appears at the Ministry of Justice in the capital of St. John to complete and sign a declaration before a marriage coordinator and pays a $150 license fee. The coordinator will arrange for a marriage officer to perform a civil ceremony at any of Antigua's hotels or another place the couple selects. The fee for the marriage officer is $50. Several hotels and resorts offer wedding/honeymoon packages. For more information on civil or religious wedding ceremonies, contact the **Antigua and Barbuda Department of Tourism,** 305 E. 47th St., Suite 6A, New York, NY 10017 (© 888/268-4227 or 212/541-4117; www.antigua-barbuda.org).

ARUBA In 2004 it became possible for civil marriages by nonresidents to take place in Aruba. A number of requirements are called for, however, including birth certificates with a raised seal, photo ID, and proof that one is indeed both single and eligible to marry. It's best to review requirements with the Office of Civil Registry, Schoolstraat 2 in Oranjestad (© 297/583-4400).

BARBADOS Couples can now marry the same day they arrive on Barbados, but they must first obtain a marriage license from the **Ministry of Home Affairs** (© 246/228-8950). Bring either a passport or a birth certificate and photo ID,

US$100 (BD$200) cash, and US$28 (BD$55) for the revenue stamp which you can obtain at the local post office, a letter from the authorized officiant who will perform the service, plus proof, if applicable, of pertinent deaths or divorces from any former spouse(s). A Roman Catholic wedding on Barbados has additional requirements. For more information, contact the **Barbados Tourism Authority,** 800 Second Ave., New York, NY 10017 (© **800/ 221-9831** in the U.S., or 212/986-6516; www.barbados.org).

BONAIRE   The bride and/or groom must have a temporary residency permit, obtained by writing a letter to the governor of the **Island Territory of Bonaire,** Kaya Grandi na 2, Kralendijk, Bonaire, N.A. (© **599/717-8322**). The letter, submitted at least 4 weeks in advance of departure for Bonaire, should request permission to marry on Bonaire and to apply for temporary residency. You'll also need to inform the governor of your arrival and departure dates and the date you wish to marry. The partner who applies for residency must be on the island for 7 days before the wedding. A special dispensation must be issued by the governor if there is less than a 10-day time period between the announcement of the marriage and the ceremony. In addition, send two passport photos, copies of the bride's and groom's passports, birth certificates, and, if applicable, proof of divorce or the death certificate of a deceased spouse.

If you desire, you can arrange your wedding on Bonaire · through **Multro Travel and Tours,** Muller Light House Beach Resort no. 22 (P.O. Box 237), Bonaire, N.A. (© **599/717-8334;** fax 599/ 717-8834; www.bonaireweddings.com), or check with the hotel where you're planning to stay. Some hotels arrange weddings on special request. For further information, contact the **Bonaire Government Tourist Office,** 80 Broad St.,

Suite 3202, New York, NY 10020 (© **800/ 266-2473** or 212/956-5912; www.info bonaire.com).

THE BRITISH VIRGIN ISLANDS Island residency is not required, but a couple must apply for a marriage license at the attorney general's office and must stay in the B.V.I. for 3 days while the application is processed. Present a passport or original birth certificate and photo identification, plus certified proof of your marital status and, if applicable, proof of divorce or the death certificate of a deceased spouse. Two witnesses must be present. The fee is $35 if the ceremony is in office or $100 for a ceremony performed elsewhere. Marriages can be performed by the local registrar or by the officiant of your choice. You are also required to buy $110 worth of stamps if you are in the territory less than 15 days or $50 if you are in the B.V.I. more than 15 days. Contact the **Registrar's Office,** P.O. Box 418, Road Town, Tortola, B.V.I. (© **617/475-2646** in the U.S. or 284/ 494-2930 in BVI; www.britishvirgin islands.com).

THE CAYMAN ISLANDS   Visitors have to call ahead and arrange for an authorized person to marry them. The name of the "marriage officer," as it is called, has to appear on the application for a marriage license. The application for a marriage license costs $200 and can be obtained from the **Deputy Chief Secretary's Office,** 3rd Floor, Government Administration Building, George Town (© **345/244-2222**). There is no waiting period. Present a birth certificate, the embarkation/disembarkation cards issued by the island's immigration authorities, and, if applicable, divorce decrees or proof of a spouse's death. Complete wedding services and packages are offered by **Cayman Weddings of Grand Cayman,** which is owned and operated by Caymanian marriage officers Vernon and

Francine Jackson. For more information, contact them at P.O. Box 678, Grand Cayman (© 345/949-8677; fax 345/949-8237; www.caymanweddings.com.ky). A brochure, *Getting Married in the Cayman Islands*, is available from **Government Information Services,** Broadcasting House, Grand Cayman (© 345/949-8092; fax 345/949-5936).

CURAÇAO   Couples must be on island 3 days before applying for a marriage license, for which there is a 14-day waiting period. Passport, birth certificate, return ticket, and, if applicable, proof of divorce or the death certificate of a deceased spouse are required. The $225 fee is subject to change, so check in advance. For further information, call the **Curaçao Tourist Board,** 5810 Biscayne Blvd., Miami, FL 33137 (© 800/287-2226 or 305/285-0511; fax 305/285-0535; www.ctb.an).

JAMAICA   In high season, some Jamaican resorts witness several weddings a day. Many of the larger resorts have wedding coordinators on staff who can arrange for an officiant, a photographer, and even the wedding cake and champagne. Some resorts even throw in your wedding with the cost of your honeymoon at the hotel. Both the Jamaican Tourist Board and your hotel will assist you with the paperwork. Participants must reside on Jamaica for 24 hours before the ceremony. Bring birth certificates and affidavits saying you've never been married before. If you've been divorced or widowed, bring copies of your divorce papers or a copy of the deceased spouse's death certificate. The license and stamp duty cost US$75-US$80. Or you can apply in person at the **Ministry of National Security,** 12 Ocean Blvd., Kingston, Jamaica (© 876/906-4908).

PUERTO RICO   There are no residency requirements for getting married in Puerto Rico. For U.S. citizens, blood tests are required, although a test conducted on the U.S. mainland within 10 days of the ceremony will suffice. A doctor in Puerto Rico must sign the license after conducting an examination of the bride and groom. For complete details, contact the **Commonwealth of Puerto Rico Health Department,** Demographic Registry, P.O. Box 11854, Fernandez, Juncos Station, San Juan, PR 00910 (© 787/728-7980).

ST. LUCIA   Both parties must be on the island for 4 days before the ceremony. Present your passport or birth certificate, plus, if applicable, proof of divorce or the death certificate of a deceased spouse. It usually takes about 2 days before the ceremony to process all the paperwork. Fees run around EC$303 (US$112) for a lawyer (one is usually needed for the application to the governor-general), EC$135 (US$50) for the registrar to perform the ceremony, and EC$130 (US$480) for the stamp duty, notary, certificates, and the license. Some resorts also offer wedding packages that include all the necessary arrangements for a single fee. For more information, contact the **St. Lucia Tourist Board,** 800 Second Ave., Suite 910, New York, NY 10017 (© 800/456-3984 or 212/867-2950; fax 212/867-2795; www.stlucia.org).

TURKS & CAICOS   You need the usual documents here, including passport, original birth certificate, proof of status (if single, a sworn affidavit), and a divorce decree, plus a $50 license fee. You must be on island for 24 hours to establish residency. For more details, contact the **Registrars of Marriages** on Front Street at © 649/926-2800 in Provo.

THE U.S. VIRGIN ISLANDS   No blood tests or physical examinations are necessary, but there is a $50 notarized application and a $50 license fee, and an 8-day waiting period, which is sometimes waived depending on circumstances.

Civil ceremonies before a judge of the territorial court cost $250 each; religious ceremonies performed by clergy are equally valid. Fees and schedules for church weddings must be negotiated directly with the officiant. More information is available from the **U.S. Virgin Islands Division of Tourism,** 1270 Ave. of the Americas, New York, NY 10020 (℃ **800/372-8784** or 212/332-2222; www.usvitourism.vi).

The U.S. Virgin Islands tourism offices distribute the guide *Getting Married in the U.S. Virgin Islands,* which gives information on all three islands, including wedding planners, places of worship, florists, and limousine services. The guide also provides a listing of island accommodations that offer in-house wedding services.

Couples can apply for a marriage license for **St. Thomas** or **St. John** by contacting the **Territorial Court of the Virgin Islands,** P.O. Box 70, St. Thomas, U.S.V.I. 00804 (℃ **340/774-6680**). You can apply for weddings on **St. Croix** by contacting the **Territorial Court of the Virgin Islands,** Family Division, P.O. Box 929, Christiansted, St. Croix, U.S.V.I. 00821 (℃ **340/778-9750**).

15 Chartering Your Own Boat

For detailed information on the cruise lines serving the Caribbean, pick up a copy of *Frommer's Caribbean Cruises & Ports of Call* (Wiley Publishing, Inc.).

Experienced sailors and navigators can charter "bareboat," a fully equipped rental boat with no captain or crew. You're on your own, and you'll have to prove your qualifications before you're allowed to rent one. Even an experienced skipper may want to take along someone familiar with local waters, which may be tricky in some places.

You can also charter a boat with a skipper and crew. Charter yachts, ranging from 15 to 30m (50–100 ft.), can accommodate 4 to 12 people.

Most yachts are rented on a weekly basis, with a fully stocked bar and equipment for fishing and watersports. The average charter carries four to six passengers, and usually is reserved for 1 week.

The Moorings (℃ **888/952-8420** in the U.S. and Canada; www.moorings. com) operates the largest charter yacht fleet in the Caribbean. Its main branch is located in the British Virgin Islands, but it has outposts in St. Martin, Guadeloupe, Martinique, St. Lucia, and Grenada, to name a few. Each location has a regatta of yachts available for chartering. Depending on their size, yachts are rented to as many as four couples at a time. You can arrange to rent bareboat (for qualified sailors only) or rent yachts with a full crew and cook. Depending on circumstances, the vessels come equipped with a barbecue, snorkeling gear, a dinghy, and linens. The boats are serviced by an experienced staff of mechanics, electricians, riggers, and cleaners. If you're going out on your own, you'll get a thorough briefing on Caribbean waters, reefs, and anchorages. Seven-night combined hotel-and-crewed-yacht packages start at $1,900 per person in Tortola.

Nicholson Yacht Charters (℃ **800/ 662-6066** in the U.S., or 617/661-0555; fax 617/661-0554; www.yachtvacations. com) is one of the best in the business, handling charter yachts for use throughout the Caribbean basin, particularly the route between St. Maarten and Grenada and the routes around the U.S. Virgin Islands, British Virgin Islands, and Puerto Rico. Featuring boats of all sizes, the company rents motorized vessels or sailing yachts up to 89m (292 ft.) long. Sometimes groups of friends rent two or more yachts (each sleeping eight guests in four double cabins) to race each other from island to island during the day and anchor near each other in secluded coves at night. The price for renting a yacht or motor yacht depends on the number in your party, the size of the vessel, and the time of the year. Weekly rates range from $6,000 up to $175,000 plus. You can get a small but comfortable vessel for two starting at $4,000. A 22m (72-ft.) yacht for six can go for $11,000 and up.

Sunsail (© **888/350-3568** in the U.S.; www.sunsail.com) specializes in yacht chartering from its bases in the British Virgin Islands, Antigua, St. Vincent, St. Martin, and Martinique. More than 150 bareboat and crewed yachts, between 9 and 16m (30 and 52 ft.), are available for cruising these waters. Programs include Caribbean racing and regattas, flotilla sailing, skippered sailing, and one-way or stay-and-sail bareboat cruises. Weekly rentals of bareboats begin at $1,350, with yacht charters beginning at $12,000 per week. The company usually requires a deposit of 25% of the total rental fee; arrangements should be made months in advance. Sunsail also offers charter flights from the United States to the Virgin Islands.

3

Anguilla

Anguilla (rhymes with *vanilla*) used to tout itself as the Caribbean's best-kept secret. Small, serene, and secluded, visitors could enjoy the privacy of small-island life and still be close to St. Maarten/St. Martin, with its gambling, shopping, and nightlife. However, the island's secret was let out in the 1990s when the opening of some superdeluxe (and superexpensive) hotels attracted a sophisticated jet set. Now one of the Caribbean's most chic destinations—rivaling even St. Barts (a prettier island and just as luxurious)—Anguilla has nonetheless remained tranquil. If you're looking to rest, unwind, and be pampered, this is the place for you.

The post-millennium opening of some moderately priced hotels means that even more visitors can enjoy Anguilla's standards of tropical luxury. However, note that except for a handful of large-scale hotels, operations on Anguilla tend to be small and informal, as the island has tried to control development and conserve natural beauty and resources. And with good reason: The coastline has some of the finest white-sand beaches in the Caribbean. More than 30 beaches dot the island, shaded by sea-grape trees.

The northernmost of the British Leeward Islands in the eastern Caribbean, 8km (5 miles) north of St. Maarten, Anguilla is only 26km (16 miles) long, with 91 sq. km (35 sq. miles) in land area. The little island has a population of approximately 9,000 people. Most are of African descent, though many are European, predominantly Irish. Anguilla's scant rainfall makes for unproductive soil that supports mainly low foliage and sparse scrub vegetation. The locals work primarily in the tourist industry or fish for lobster.

Once part of the federation with St. Kitts and Nevis, Anguilla gained its independence in 1980 and has since been a self-governing British possession. In 1996, however, London issued a policy statement that locals have viewed as a move to push them toward independence. Many Anguillians believe that Britain has now reduced its global ambitions and wants to relinquish colonies that have become too expensive to maintain. Though islanders may fear going it alone as a nation, they know that to retain Britain's protection, they would also have to abide by British laws—including its liberal position on gay rights. For the most part, islanders remain archly conservative and often homophobic.

Anguilla Great House Beach Resort **8**
Arawak Beach Inn **11**
Blue Waters Beach Apartment **1**
Cap Juluca **3**
Covecastles Villa Resort **2**
CusinArt Resort & Spa **4**
Easy Corner Villas **9**
Frangipani Beach Club **6**
Kú **10**
La Sirena **5**
Malliouhana **7**

1 Essentials

VISITOR INFORMATION

The **Anguilla Tourist Board,** Coronation Avenue, The Valley, Anguilla, B.W.I. (© 264/497-2759; fax 264/497-2710), is open Monday to Friday from 8am to 5pm.

In the United States, contact Ms. Marie Walker, 246 Central Ave., White Plains, NY 10606 (© 914/287-2400; fax 914/287-2404) or log onto www.anguilla-vacation.com.

In the United Kingdom, contact the **Anguilla Tourist Board,** 7A Crealock St., London SW182BS (© 208/871-0012).

GETTING THERE

BY PLANE   More than 50 flights into Anguilla are scheduled each week, not counting various charter flights. There are no nonstop flights from mainland North America, however, so visitors usually transfer through San Juan, Puerto Rico, or nearby St. Maarten. Some visitors also come from St. Kitts, Antigua, or St. Thomas.

Anguilla's most reliable carrier, **American Eagle** (© 800/433-7300 in the U.S. and Canada; www.aa.com), the commuter partner of American Airlines, has two nonstop daily flights to Anguilla from American's hub in San Juan. In the off season, flights are reduced to one each day during the week and two on weekends. Flights leave at different times based on the seasons and carry 44 to 46 passengers. Schedules are subject to change, so check with the airline or your travel agent.

From Dutch St. Maarten, **Winair** (Windward Islands Airways International; © **866/ 466-0410** in the U.S. and Canada; www.fly-winair.com) has four daily flights to Anguilla. The small airline also has Anguilla links to the islands of Saba, St. Eustatius, St. Barts, St. Kitts, and Nevis.

LIAT (© **888/844-LIAT** in the U.S. and Canada, or 264/497-5002; www.liatairline. com) offers flights Friday through Wednesday to Anguilla from Antigua via St. Kitts. It's not the most punctual airline.

A small airline, **Caribbean Star** (© **866/864-6272** in the U.S. and Canada, or 264/497-8690; www.flycaribbeanstar.com) wings in from St. Kitts and Antigua on Thursday, Friday, and Sunday. Schedules are likely to change, so it's always best to call and confirm before planning any trip.

BY FERRY   Ferries run between the ports of Marigot Bay, French St. Martin, and Blowing Point, Anguilla, every 30 to 45 minutes. The trip takes 20 to 25 minutes, making it easy for visitors on one island to do a day trip to the other. The first ferry leaves St. Martin at 8am and the last at 7pm; from Blowing Point, the first ferry leaves at 7:30am and the last at 6:15pm. The one-way fare is US$12 to US$15 (£6.25– £7.80) plus a US$3 (£1.55) departure tax. No reservations are necessary; schedules and fares, of course, are always subject to change. Ferries vary in size, and none take passenger vehicles.

GETTING AROUND

BY RENTAL CAR   To explore the island in any depth, it's best to rent a car, though be prepared for badly paved roads. Four-wheel-drive vehicles aren't necessary, however. Several rental agencies on the island can issue the mandatory Anguillian driver's license, which is valid for 3 months. You can also get a license at police headquarters in the island's administrative center, The Valley, and at ports of entry. You'll need to present a valid driver's license from your home country and pay a one-time fee of US$20 (£10). *Remember:* Drive on the left side of the road!

Most visitors take a taxi from the airport to their hotel and arrange, at no extra charge, for a rental agency to deliver a car there the following day. All rental companies offer small discounts for rentals of 7 days or more.

There's a branch of **Avis** at The Quarter (© **800/331-1212** in the U.S. and Canada, or 264/497-2642; www.avis.com), which offers regular cars and some four-wheel-drive vehicles. Local firms include **Connor's Car Rental,** c/o Maurice Connor,

---

Fun Fact A Special Celebration

Anguilla's most colorful annual festival is **Carnival,** held jointly under the auspices of the Ministries of Culture and Tourism. Boat races are Anguilla's national sport, and they make up much of the Carnival celebration. The festival begins on Thursday before the first Monday in August and lasts a week. Carnival harks back to Emancipation Day, or "August Monday," in 1834, when all enslaved Africans were freed.

South Hill (℡ **264/497-6433**), **Triple K Car Rental,** Airport Road (℡ **264/497-5934**), and **Island Car Rentals,** Airport Road (℡ **264/497-2723**).

BY TAXI   Typical taxi fares are US$24 (£12) from the airport to Cap Juluca, US$16 (£8.30) to the Fountain Beach Hotel, and US$22 (£11) to the Malliouhana hotel. Most rides take 15 to 20 minutes. For a cab, call **Airport Taxi Stand** at ℡ **264/497-5054.**

FAST FACTS: Anguilla

Banks Banks with ATMs are open Monday to Thursday 8am to 3pm, Friday 8am to 5pm. The most reliable is **Scotiabank,** The Valley, Fairplay Commercial Complex (℡ **264/497-3333**).

Currency The **Eastern Caribbean dollar (EC$)** is the official currency of Anguilla, although U.S. dollars are the actual "coin of the realm." The exchange rate is permanently fixed at EC$2.70 to each US$1 (EC$1 = US37¢/50p). *Unless otherwise specified, prices in this chapter are quoted in U.S. dollars and British pounds.*

Customs Even for tourists, duties are levied on imported goods at varying rates: from 5% on foodstuffs to 30% on luxury goods, wines, and liquors.

Documents All visitors must have an onward or return ticket. U.S., British, and Canadian citizens must have a valid passport.

Electricity The electricity is 110-volt AC (60 cycles), so no transformers or adapters are necessary to use U.S. appliances.

Hospitals For medical services, consult the **Princess Alexandra Hospital,** Stoney Ground (℡ **264/497-2551** or **2552**), or one of several district clinics.

Language English is spoken here.

Liquor Laws Beer, wine, and liquor are sold 7 days a week during regular business hours. It's legal to have an open container on the beach.

Pharmacies Go to the **Health Authority** at the Princess Alexandra Hospital, Stoney Ground (℡ **264/497-2551** or **2552**), open Monday to Friday from 8am to 5pm and Saturday from 10am to noon.

Police You can reach the police at their headquarters in The Valley (℡ **264/497-2333**) or the substation at Sandy Ground (℡ **264/497-2354**). In an emergency, dial ℡ **911.**

Post Office The main post office is on Wallblake Road, The Valley (℡ **264/497-2528**). Collectors consider Anguilla's stamps valuable, and the post office also operates a philatelic bureau, open Monday to Thursday from 8am to 3:30pm, Friday 8am to 5pm. Airmail postcards and letters cost US$1.50 (80p) to the U.S., Canada, and the United Kingdom.

Safety Although crime is rare here, secure your valuables; never leave them in a parked car or unguarded on the beach. Anguilla is one of the safest destinations in the Caribbean, but you should still take standard precautions.

Taxes The government collects a 10% tax on rooms and a departure tax of US$20 (£10) if you leave the island by air, US$3 (£1.55) if you leave by boat.

Telephone Telephone, cable, and Telex services are offered by **Cable & Wireless Ltd.,** Wallblake Road, The Valley (© **264/497-3100**), open Monday to Friday 8am to 5pm. To call the United States from Anguilla, dial **1**, the area code, and the seven-digit number.

Time Anguilla is on Atlantic Standard Time year-round, which means it's usually 1 hour ahead of the U.S. East Coast—except when the U.S. is on daylight saving time, when the clocks are the same.

Weather The hottest months in Anguilla are July to October; the coolest, December to February. The mean monthly temperature is about 80°F (27°C).

2 Accommodations

VERY EXPENSIVE

Cap Juluca ✶✶✶   This is one of the most boldly conceived, luxurious oases in the Caribbean, fronting one of the island's best white-sand beaches. Overlooking Maundays Bay on a rolling 72-hectare (179-acre) site, Cap Juluca caters to Hollywood stars and financial barons and offers serious pampering. You're welcomed with a bottle of chilled champagne, and sorbet is served on the beach. This is the only resort on the island to match the classy Malliouhana (see below). Malliouhana has superior dining and service, but Cap Juluca fronts a better beach, and its accommodations are plusher.

Most of the villa-style accommodations have soaring domes, walled courtyards, labyrinthine staircases, and concealed swimming pools ringed with thick walls so you can take it all off. Inside, a mixture of elegantly comfortable wicker furniture is offset with Moroccan accessories. Rooms are spacious, with luxurious beds and Italian-tile floors. If money is no object, opt for the extravagant suites with their own plunge pools. Large marble and mirrored baths are luxuriously appointed, with tub/shower combinations. Although the cuisine at this hotel has never been better—the chefs have been called "the dream team"—it still doesn't equal Malliouhana. At the elegant Pimms (© **264/497-6666** for reservations), you can count on imaginative seafood-based dishes with Asian accents.

Maundays Bay (P.O. Box 240), Anguilla, B.W.I. © **888/858-5822** in the U.S., or 264/497-6779. Fax 264/497-6617. www.capjuluca.com. 98 units, 18 villas. Winter/spring US$825–US$1,670 (£429–£868) double, from US$2,590 (£1,347) suite; off season US$440–US$1,145 (£229–£595) double, from US$1,245 (£647) suite. AE, MC, V. **Amenities:** 3 restaurants; 2 bars; outdoor pool; driving range; 3 tennis courts; fitness center; spa; kayaks; scuba diving; snorkeling; waterskiing; windsurfing; children's programs (in summer only); rental cars; business center; room service (7:30am–10pm); massage; babysitting; laundry service; dry cleaning. *In room:* A/C, dataport, minibar, hair dryer, safe, Wi-Fi.

Covecastles Villa Resort ✶✶   A cross between a collection of private homes and a monumental yet minimalist resort on a white-sand beach, this is a wonderful (if shockingly expensive) small resort, with an attentive staff. Designed by award-winning architect Myron Goldfinger in 1985 and enlarged in 1998, Covecastles combines elements from North Africa, the Caribbean, and the futuristic theories of Le Corbusier. The units include an interconnected row of town house–style beach structures that accommodate two to four persons, and a handful of larger, fully detached villas that house up to six. Each building has views of the sea, amid the dunes and scrublands of the southwestern coast. The most spectacular place to stay is the five-bedroom grand villa that opens directly on the beach—one of the most fabulous accommodations in the Caribbean. This place offers even more privacy than Cap Juluca.

Large bedrooms have twin or king-size beds with hand-embroidered linens and deluxe mattresses, and bathrooms are large and stylish with tub/shower combinations. Guest rooms have louvered doors and windows crafted from Brazilian walnut; terracotta tiles; comfortably oversize rattan furniture; a fully equipped, state-of-the-art kitchen; and a hammock.

The resort's French chef pampers guests with candlelit dinners of impeccable quality, in an intimate private dining room that overlooks the beach or en suite.

Shoal Bay West (P.O. Box 248), Anguilla, B.W.I. © **800/223-1108** in the U.S., or 264/497-6801. Fax 264/497-6051. www.covecastles.com. 15 units. Winter US$895–US$1,095 (£465–£569) beach house, US$1,395–US$4,295 (£725–£2,233) villa; off season US$595–US$695 (£309–£361) beach house, US$895–US$2,895 (£465–£1,505) villa. AE, MC, V. Closed mid-Aug to mid-Oct. **Amenities:** Restaurant; tennis court; aerobics; deep-sea fishing; glass-bottom boat excursions; kayaks; scuba diving; snorkeling; Sunfish sailboats; windsurfing; bicycles; car rental; secretarial service; room service (8am–9pm); massage; babysitting; laundry service. *In room:* Ceiling fan, TV, dataport, full kitchen, beverage maker, hair dryer, iron, safe, Wi-Fi.

CuisinArt Resort & Spa 𝕬𝕬𝕬

Yes, it's owned by CuisinArt, and, yes, it fronts a powdery beach of white sand (assuming that this is your next question). Evoking the architecture of nearby Cap Juluca, this is Anguilla's latest word in luxury. For privacy and seclusion, CuisinArt challenges Covecastles. A complex of whitewashed villas crowned by blue domes and surrounded by lush tropical foliage, it seems straight out of Mykonos. The resort offers the first-ever hydroponic farm and the only full-service resort spa in Anguilla. (Their milk-and-honey-almond scrub is the most fantastic we've experienced.) It also features an herb garden, an orchid solarium, and a rare plant house. Italian upholsteries, Haitian cottons, dark-wood furniture, and large tub/shower combination bathrooms in soft-toned Italian marble characterize the well-furnished accommodations.

The Hydroponic Café's daily lunch features the US$1-million, .6-hectare (1½-acre) hydroponic farm's fresh vegetables in salads and other light fare. The Santorini Restaurant is the fine-dining choice, with a French rotisserie on-site. Expect brawny, lusty dishes infused with the flamboyant flavors and spices of the Caribbean.

Rendezvous Bay (P.O. Box 2000), Anguilla, B.W.I. © **800/943-3210** or 264/498-2000. Fax 264/498-2010. www.cuisinart resort.com. 93 units. Winter US$685–US$850 (£356–£442) double, US$950–US$1,385 (£494–£720) suite; off season US$400–US$625 (£208–£325) double, US$550–US$1,015 (£286–£527) suite. AE, MC, V. Closed Sept–Oct. **Amenities:** 3 restaurants; 3 bars; outdoor pool; 3 tennis courts; fitness center; spa; Jacuzzi; deep-sea fishing; kayaks; sailing; scuba diving; snorkeling; windsurfing; mountain bikes; horseback riding; salon; limited room service; babysitting; laundry service; dry cleaning; nonsmoking rooms; rooms for those w/limited mobility. *In room:* A/C, TV, dataport, minibar, hair dryer, iron, safe, Wi-Fi.

Frangipani Beach Club 𝕬

Set on 1.5km (1 mile) of luscious white sand, this flamingo-pink condo complex, which underwent extensive renovations in 2006, feels like a villa along the Spanish Mediterranean, with wrought-iron railings and red-tile roofs. Its major competition is La Sirena, but La Sirena is more of a resort, with better facilities, including dining, whereas Frangipani attracts self-catering types who want to have their own condos in Anguilla. Accommodations are light and airy, done in soft pastels with natural rattan furnishings; they're very comfortable, with king-size beds. All units also have marble bathrooms with tub/shower combinations, along with private terraces or balconies. Many of the more expensive rooms have full kitchens, and two- or three-bedroom units work for families or friends traveling together.

Meads Bay (P.O. Box 1378), Anguilla, B.W.I. © **866/780-5165** in the U.S., or 264/497-6442. Fax 264/497-6440. www.frangipaniresort.com. 17 units. Winter US$400–US$500 (£208–£260) double, from US$800 (£416) suite; off season US$250–US$350 (£130–£182) double, from US$450 (£234) suite. AE, MC, V. Closed Sept–Nov. **Amenities:** Restaurant; 2 bars; outdoor pool; tennis court; fishing; kayaks; snorkeling; limited room service; laundry service; dry cleaning. *In room:* TV, dataport, beverage maker, hair dryer, iron, Wi-Fi.

Malliouhana (★(★★★ (Kids   The Caribbean's ultrachic hotel, this cliff-side retreat conjures up images of Positano in the Tropics. It's even more spectacular than Cap Juluca—opulent and lavishly decorated, and situated on a rocky bluff between two white-sand beaches. In fact, it outdazzles Cap Juluca in every way except for that resort's fabulous beach and glitzier digs. Malliouhana's 10 hectares (25 acres) are lushly landscaped with terraces, banks of flowers, pools, and fountains. Thick walls and shrubbery provide seclusion. A 224-member staff attends to 55 units; their motto is "Your wish is my command."

Haitian art and decorations are so splendid that you might not spot Gwyneth Paltrow sitting among the palms. Spacious bedrooms and suites are distributed among the main buildings and outlying villas. Each room has tropical furnishings and wide private verandas; the villas can be rented as a single unit or subdivided into three. Three of the suites have private Jacuzzis, and one unit has a private pool. Some accommodations open onto garden views, and others front Meads Bay Beach or Turtle Cove. Many rooms have luxurious four-poster beds, plus spacious Italian marble bathrooms with tubs and shower stalls. If you're traveling with a child, this is a kid-friendly oasis, complete with a water park and faux pirate ship.

Meads Bay (P.O. Box 173), Anguilla, B.W.I. © **800/835-0796** in the U.S., or 264/497-6111. Fax 264/497-6011. www. malliouhana.com. 55 units. Winter US$880–US$940 (£458–£489) double, US$1,095–US$1,285 (£569–£668) suite; off season US$465–US$695 (£242–£361) double, from US$825–US$875 (£429–£455) suite. AE, MC, V. Closed Sept–Oct. **Amenities:** 2 restaurants; 2 bars; 3 outdoor pools; 4 tennis courts; gym; spa; Jacuzzi; boat trips; fishing; sailing; snorkeling; water-skiing; windsurfing; children's play area; library; salon; room service (7am–10:30pm); massage (spa only); babysitting; laundry service; dry cleaning; TV room. *In room:* A/C, ceiling fan, dataport, minibar, hair dryer, safe.

EXPENSIVE

Kú (★ (Value   Is it Anguilla or the minimalist cool of South Beach? This all-suite hotel opens onto lovely Shoal Bay East fronting 2 miles (3.2km) of white sands, among the finest in the world. The folks at the swanky Cap Juluca run this sensuous enclave named for what the Arawaks called a sacred place. It's a casual yet chic resort, designed to attract well-heeled young professionals. It's a sort of dine-barefoot-under-the-stars kind of hedonistic retreat. Its 75-foot-long (23m) bar and hip French/Caribbean restaurant, where a DJ spins the tunes, set the tone for this ultra-plush enclave. The 775-square-foot, white-on-white suites are among the island's finest, each with a fully equipped kitchen and an exceedingly stylish bathroom. The suites lie in five one- to three-story buildings, and each unit features an oceanfront or oceanview balcony. A small spa offers massages, facials, and other treatments.

Shoal Bay East, B.W.I. © **800/869-5827** or 264/497-2011. Fax 264/497-3355. www.kuanguilla.com. 27 units. Winter US$295–US$395 (£153–£205) double; off-season US$160–US$200 (£83–£104). AE, DC, MC, V. **Amenities:** Restaurant; bar; outdoor pool; gym; spa; dive shop; laundry service. *In room:* A/C, TV, kitchen, hair dryer, safe, Wi-Fi.

La Sirena (★   Built in 1989 on 1 hectare (2½ acres) of sandy soil, a 4-minute walk from a clean white beach, this Swiss-owned resort is inviting, intimate, and low-key. At least 80% of its clientele comes from Switzerland or Germany. Accommodations, arranged in two-story bougainvillea-draped wings, are large and airy, with fine rattan and wicker furnishings. Some have air-conditioning; all have ceiling fans. Rooms have large double, queen-, or king-size beds with fine linens. Bathrooms are spacious, with tub/shower combinations. To reach the beach, guests walk down through the garden and a sandy footpath. Beach hats, umbrellas, and lounge chairs await on the sand. If possible, request rooms away from the second-floor Top of the Palms restaurant to avoid the kitchen's noise and fumes.

The Top of the Palms is open to cool ocean breezes and offers views over Meads Bay and the surrounding treetops. A well-trained local chef prepares specialties ranging from alpine fondues to West Indian favorites.

Meads Bay (P.O. Box 200), Anguilla, B.W.I. (*C*) 800/331-9358 in the U.S., or 264/497-6827. Fax 264/497-6829. www. sirenaresort.com. 29 units. Winter US$285–US$350 (£148–£182) double, US$400–US$470 (£208–£244) suite; off season US$160–US$200 (£83–£104) double, US$240–US$270 (£125–£140) suite. MAP (breakfast and dinner) US$52 (£27) per person extra. AE, MC, V. **Amenities:** Restaurant; bar; 2 outdoor pools; tennis court (nearby); dive center; snorkeling; windsurfing; car rental; limited room service; babysitting; laundry service. *In room:* A/C (in some), ceiling fan, dataport, minibar, hair dryer, safe.

MODERATE

Anguilla Great House Beach Resort
On Rendezvous Bay, with its 4km (2½ miles) of white sand, this bungalow colony features cottages of gingerbread trim that sit in landscaped gardens. Each bungalow contains a number of well-furnished bedrooms, which can be rented in various configurations depending on your needs. You also get an offering of different beds here, including both king- and queen-size, or else two double beds. We particularly like the private porches opening onto water views. Rooms can be opened to capture trade winds, though they are also equipped with air-conditioning and ceiling fans. Bathrooms are small, tidily kept, and contain showers. The beachside amenities are good and include lounge chairs, umbrellas, kayaks, Sunfish sailboats, windsurfers, and both snorkeling and fishing gear.

Rendezvous Bay, Anguilla, B.W.I. (*C*) 264/497-6061. Fax 264/497-6019. www.anguillagreathouse.com. 35 units. Winter US$230 (£120) 1-bedroom, US$290 (£151) 2-bedroom, US$560 (£291) 3-bedroom; off-season US$165 (£86) 1-bedroom, US$228 (£119) 2-bedroom, US$360 (£187) 3-bedroom. AE, MC, V. **Amenities:** Restaurant; bar; outdoor pool; fishing; kayaks; snorkeling; Sunfish sailboats; windsurfing; limited room service; laundry service; nonsmoking rooms. *In room:* A/C, ceiling fan, hair dryer, iron.

Arawak Beach Inn *(Value)*
Built on the site of an ancient Arawak village and only minutes from beautiful Shoal Bay Beach, this comfortable and inviting family-run hotel is a good value (for pricey Anguilla, anyway), especially during the summer months. It opens onto views of Scilly Cay and Captains Ridge. It offers studios and one-bedroom suites in octagonal-shaped buildings. Beachfront units are built in the style of a re-created Amerindian village and are equipped with wet bars and beverage makers, plus large balconies or terraces. Furnishings are comfortable and include king-size beds, plus small bathrooms, each with a shower.

The rather formal restaurant serves good Continental and Caribbean cuisine.

Island Harbour (P.O. Box 1403, The Valley), Anguilla, B.W.I. (*C*) 877/427-2925 or 264/497-4888. Fax 264/497-4889. www.arawakbeach.com. 17 units. Winter US$225–US$275 (£117–£143) double; off season US$125–US$185 (£65–£96) double. Children under 12 stay free in parent's room. MC, V. **Amenities:** Restaurant; beach bar; outdoor pool; canoeing; windsurfing; bike rental; car rental; limited room service; babysitting; laundry service. *In room:* Ceiling fan, TV (in some), fridge, hair dryer (in some), safe, Wi-Fi, no phone.

Blue Waters Beach Apartments *(Kids)*
Fronting .8km (½ mile) of white-sand beachfront, this tranquil resort has a vaguely Moorish look. It offers well-designed and immaculately kept one-bedroom units and two-bedroom apartments, each opening directly onto the beach and cooled by a ceiling fan. The family-friendly apartments attract the self-sufficient traveler: Each unit has a complete kitchen, ample closets, and

comfortable furnishings such as king-size beds. Bathrooms are immaculately white, very Calvin Klein, each with a shower stall. Rooms have terraces or balconies.

Shoal Bay West (P.O. Box 69), Anguilla, B.W.I. © **264/497-6292.** Fax 264/497-6982. www.bluewatersbeach.com. 9 units. Winter US$305 (£159) 1-bedroom apt, US$430 (£224) 2-bedroom apt; off season US$154 (£80) 1-bedroom apt, US$215 (£112) 2-bedroom apt. AE, MC, V. **Amenities:** Bar. *In room:* Ceiling fan, TV, kitchen, safe.

INEXPENSIVE

Easy Corner Villas   On a bluff overlooking Road Bay, this modest villa complex is located a 5-minute drive from a good beach. On the main road west of the airport, Easy Corner Villas is owned by Maurice E. Connor, the same entrepreneur who rents many of the cars on the island. His one-, two-, and three-bedroom apartments are simply furnished and set on landscaped grounds with beach views from their private porches. Each comes equipped with a kitchen, combination living and dining room, a ceiling fan and air-conditioning, good beds, and large, airy living areas, plus small bathrooms with shower stalls. Maid service is available for an extra charge, except on Sunday.

South Hill (P.O. Box 65), Anguilla, B.W.I. © **264/497-6433.** Fax 264/497-6410. www.caribbean-inns.com. 12 units. Winter US$110 (£57) studio, US$160 (£83) 1-bedroom villa, US$195 (£101) 2-bedroom villa, US$240 (£125) 3-bedroom villa; off season US$90 (£47) studio, US$125 (£65) 1-bedroom villa, US$155 (£81) 2-bedroom villa, US$195 (£101) 3-bedroom villa. AE, MC, V. **Amenities:** Laundry service; car rental. *In room:* A/C, ceiling fan, TV, kitchen, beverage maker.

3 Dining

VERY EXPENSIVE

Malliouhana Restaurant FRENCH/CARIBBEAN   Even better than the restaurant at Cap Juluca, Malliouhana Restaurant, with the Caribbean's most ambitious French menu, offers fluidly choreographed service, fine food, a 25,000-bottle wine cellar, and a glamorous clientele. You'll dine in an open-sided pavilion on a rocky promontory over the sea. At night your candlelit table will be set with French crystal, Limoges china, and Christofle silver. There are well-spaced tables, an ocean view, and a splashing fountain.

The hors d'oeuvres selection is the finest on island, including delectable concoctions of fresh Anguillian lobster prepared in various ways. You are likely to savor such main courses as baked filet of mahi-mahi with roasted tomatoes and a green onion sauce or else golden crisp cooked duck with mango chutney and a Jamaican peppercorn sauce. Dessert might be an old-fashioned slice of French-style apple tart.

Meads Bay. © **264/497-6111.** Reservations required. Main courses US$34–US$48 (£18–£25). AE, MC, V. Daily 7–11am, 12:30–3pm, and 7:30–10:30pm.

EXPENSIVE

Blanchards INTERNATIONAL   Bob and Melinda Blanchard are the masterminds behind this elegantly casual, intensely fashionable restaurant on a garden-swathed pavilion beside the sea, next to the Malliouhana's beach. The cuisine is the most creative on island, and Blanchards has attracted a sprinkling of celebs (say hi to Robert De Niro or Janet Jackson if you see them). Blanchards' 3,000-bottle wine cellar is one of the finest in the Caribbean.

Behind tall teal shutters (which can be opened to the sea breezes), you can savor sophisticated food with a Caribbean flair, enhanced with spices from Spain, Asia, California, and the American Southwest. Dishes change according to the inspiration of chef Melinda but are likely to include such delights as lobster cakes with mixed greens and a tomato-flavored tartar sauce. Here the famous Anguillian lobster is grilled with a honey glaze or a Cajun spicy sauce. Prepared with faultless technique is the tuna, seared on the outside and served rare inside along with Israeli couscous. For a real island dessert, opt for the cracked coconut with coconut ice cream accompanied by a rum-custard sauce in a chocolate-crusted shell.

Meads Bay. ℭ 264/497-6100. www.blanchardrestaurant.com. Reservations required. Main courses US$34–US$58 (£18–£30). AE, MC, V. Mon–Sat 6:30–10pm. Closed Sept–Oct and Mon in off season.

Hibernia 🐾🐾 *Finds* FRENCH/INDOCHINESE   Following Blanchards' lead closely, this is another little stunner of creativity. Chef Raoul Rodriguez and his wife, hostess Mary Pat O'Hanlon, have converted a lovely West Indian cottage into a charming restaurant with a French- and Indonesian-inspired decor that's a nice change of pace. When you taste Chef Raoul's creative dishes, you'll know why he was voted chef of the year in 1997. He's as good now as he was then—maybe better. Start with Asian mushroom soup, or a selection of finely sliced, smoked West Indian fish. Main courses are likely to include Caribbean fish filets in a spicy Thai broth or crayfish sautéed with shiitake mushrooms and flavored with a tangy ginger sauce. French duck magret is a stunning choice, its light honey glaze the perfect touch.

Island Harbour. ℭ 264/497-4290. www.hiberniarestaurant.com. Reservations recommended. Main courses US$28–US$41 (£15–£21). AE, MC, V. Tues–Sat noon–2pm and 7–9pm; Sun 7–9pm. Closed Aug–Sept, and Mon–Tues during low season.

Koal Keel 🐾🐾 INTERNATIONAL/CARIBBEAN   This romantic French/Caribbean restaurant is housed in one of the island's most historic homes, a former sugar plantation Great House from the 1790s. (Across the road you can see the oldest dwelling on the island, originally a building sheltering slaves.) Koal Keel has a type of 18th-century oven slaves built for their Dutch masters. Two French chefs (one of whom worked with the legendary Joel Robuchon in Paris), along with another chef from Punjab, turn out first-rate international dishes. Launch your meal with such delights as pan-seared duck foie gras with cinnamon-poached pears, going on to such mains as snapper tandoori with coconut rice or grilled chicken breast with lemongrass in an orange sauce. Most of the dishes are reasonably priced except for the fresh lobster, which is always expensive and depends on the market quotations of the day.

The Valley. ℭ 264/497-2930. www.koalkeel.com. Reservations required. Main courses US$24–US$75 (£13–£39). AE, MC, V. Mon–Sat 6:30–8:30pm.

Mango's 🐾 AMERICAN/CARIBBEAN   In a pavilion a few steps from the edge of the sea, on the northwestern part of the island, Mango's serves healthier cuisine than the island's other top restaurants. The fresh fish, meat, and produce are grilled with a minimum of added fats or calories. All the breads and desserts, including ice cream and sorbet, are made fresh daily on the premises. You might start with delectable lobster cakes and homemade tartar sauce, or creamy conch chowder. Grilled local lobster and spicy whole snapper are featured main courses, but the best main dish is the simple grilled fish with lemon-and-herb butter.

Seaside Grill, Barnes Bay. ℭ 264/497-6479. www.mangos.ai. Reservations required. Main courses US$26–US$42 (£14–£22). AE, MC, V. Wed–Mon 7–9:30pm. Closed Aug–Oct.

Overlook 🐾🐾 CARIBBEAN   Perched on a cliff overlooking Sandy Ground Bay, you get fine dining and a panoramic view at chef Deon Thomas's laid-back place.

Each dish seems imbued with the chef's creative Caribbean flair. Island art adorns the walls of the dining room here, or else you can eat on the veranda. The restaurant serves only in winter; in summer the staff decamps for Martha's Vineyard. Start with such delights as a chilled gazpacho with roasted coconut shavings or else a fish sampler with a tamarind aioli and fruit salsa. Main courses are prepared with skill and a solid technique, ranging from a roasted whole triggerfish to the garlic-crusted snapper with a champagne *buerre blanc* and pink peppercorns. For dessert, try the "decadent" chocolate rum cake with Grand Marnier chocolate soup. When you're also presented with a mango key lime pie or a rum raisin rice pudding, the choice becomes difficult.

South Hill. ⓒ 264/497-4488. Reservations required. Main courses US$28–US$35 (£15–£18). AE, MC, V. Mon–Sat 1–3pm and 7–10pm. Closed May–Oct.

Straw Hat ⍟ ASIAN/CARIBBEAN   The panoramic setting by the sea and the distant vistas of French St. Martin more than match the superb cuisine. A plain wooden structure, the restaurant stands on pilings overlooking a virtual aquarium of fish below. On a hot day, the cold cucumber-and-dill soup is refreshing, as is the cilantro-infused ceviche of local red snapper with plantain chips. Some dishes, like the jerk pork tenderloin, are traditional favorites; others are more eclectic, like the seared Anguillian red snapper with a lime, ginger, and saffron sauce or the grilled loin of tuna with Asian noodles and a compote of caramelized onions. A cilantro, lime, and pecan pesto pasta can be served with your choice of grilled chicken, tuna, or red snapper. For dessert, order the chocolate indulgence—three types of chocolate in one cake.

Forest Bay. ⓒ 264/497-8300. www.strawhat.com. Reservations recommended. Main courses US$24–US$39 (£13–£20). AE, DISC, MC, V. Mon–Sat 6:30–9:30pm. Closed Sept–Oct.

MODERATE

Cedar Grove Café ⍟ CARIBBEAN   In the olden days, if you wanted to eat at this beachfront, you had to dine with the chickens in someone's backyard. No more: Cedar Grove continues the restaurant explosion on Anguilla. It's one of the hottest dining tickets on the island. In a setting evocative of *Casablanca,* you can enjoy a series of ever-changing specialties, based on the best and freshest ingredients. Signature dishes include lobster cakes with slivers of fresh ginger and a dash of curry-cream sauce. Try the coconut-crusted shrimp in a mango-ginger sauce, or the rice-paper red snapper, which is genuinely delicious.

Rendezvous Bay. ⓒ 264/497-6549. Breakfast US$8–US$15 (£4.15–£7.80); main courses US$16–US$45 (£8.30–£23) at lunch or dinner. AE, MC, V. Daily 7am–11pm. Closed Sept to mid-Oct.

Trattoria Tramonto ⍟ *Finds* NORTHERN ITALIAN   One of the island's best, this breeze-swept restaurant lies between Blue Waters Beach Apartments and Covecastles. The chef, Valter Belli, hails from Emilia Romanga in northern Italy. The tables lie near the water with distant views of St. Martin. The "sundowners" here are the best on island, including a peachy Bellini as good as that served at Harry's Bar in Venice. Other champagne drinks are mixed with fruits like mango, passion fruit, or guava. The chef takes special care with his appetizers, including a *zuppa di pesce* (fish soup with porcini mushrooms) and spicy hot penne with a garlic, tomato, and red-pepper sauce. All the entrees are superb and prepared with care, including a delectable red snapper with a caper-laced fresh tomato sauce or, our favorite and the house specialty, lobster-filled ravioli in a truffle-cream sauce. "It's of the gods," we heard a diner at the next table say.

Gwen, Reggae & Barbecue

Want to spend a lazy day on Upper Shoal Bay, which arguably has the whitest sand in the Caribbean? Drop in at **Gwen's Reggae Grill** (© 264/497-2120), which has a full bar and features Gwen Webster's barbecue. Open Monday to Saturday 10am to 5pm, it is best on a Sunday when it showcases live reggae performances. The bar closes at 7pm on Sunday. Gwen's piña coladas are the best on Anguilla, as is her special slaw. Try her shrimp salad or fish sandwiches. Off the beach there is easy snorkeling. The palm grove here is about the only naturally shady spot on island, and it comes with a fleet of hammocks.

Shoal Bay West. © 264/497-8819. www.trattoriatramonto.com. Reservations required. Main courses lunch US$8–US$28 (£4.15–£15), dinner US$22–US$42 (£11–£22). MC, V. Tues–Sun noon–3pm and 6:30–9pm. Closed Aug–Oct.

Zara's Restaurant ✪ ITALIAN/CARIBBEAN   Award-winning master chef Shamash Brooks presides at this casually elegant place, which opened in 1996. Since then it has won many fans who visit every time they return to Anguilla. The chef—known island wide for his pasta dishes—uses excellent ingredients, which are prepared to order. His fish dishes, especially the crusted snapper, are delightful, and he does veal, chicken, and steak equally well. Try his Bahamian cracked conch, and look for various daily specials. A few items are costly, but most dishes are in the moderate range.

Allamanda Beach Club, Upper Shoal Bay East. © 264/497-3229. Reservations required. Main courses US$14–US$38 (£7.30–£20). DISC, MC, V. Daily 6:30–9pm.

INEXPENSIVE

Good, affordable food is served in a festive atmosphere at **Johnno's Beach Bar,** Road Bay, Sandy Ground (© 264/497-2728), and at **Pumphouse Bar & Grill,** Sandy Ground (© 264/497-5154). See "Anguilla After Dark," below, for details. Johnno's is open for lunch and dinner; the Pumphouse is open only for dinner.

Ferryboat Inn _Value_ CARIBBEAN/FRENCH   Established by English-born John McClean and his Anguillian wife, Marjorie, this place is one of the best deals on the island. On the beach, a short walk from the Blowing Point ferry pier, it features French onion soup, black-bean soup, some of the best lobster thermidor on the island, and scallop of veal Savoyard. Unless you order expensive shellfish, most dishes are reasonably priced.

The McCleans also rent six one-bedroom apartments and a two-bedroom beach house. In winter, apartments cost US$176 to US$198 (£92–£103), and the beach house is US$308 (£160). Off season, an apartment is US$99 to US$115 (£52–£60), and the beach house is US$195 (£101).

Cul de Sac Rd., Blowing Point. © 264/497-6613. www.ferryboatinn.ai. Reservations recommended. Main courses US$16–US$37 (£8.30–£19). AE, MC, V. Tues–Sat noon–3pm, daily 7–10pm. Turn right just before the Blowing Point Ferry Terminal and travel 140m (450 ft.) before making a left turn.

Ripples CARIBBEAN/INTERNATIONAL   This restaurant is earthier and more British than most others in Sandy Ground, which has the biggest cluster of bars and restaurants on Anguilla. Its cheerful staff and long, busy bar will make you feel as though you're on the set of _Cheers_. Set in a restored clapboard house, it has a raised deck, a casual West Indian decor, and a crowd of regulars. Local fish—mahimahi, snapper, tuna, and grouper—are prepared any way you like. The coconut-shrimp house special, puffy brie in beer batter, and Creole-style conch are the reasons we keep coming back. Only a few dishes are at the high end of the price scale.

Sandy Ground. ✆ **264/497-3380.** Reservations recommended. Main courses US$18–US$30 (£9.35–£16). MC, V. Daily 11:30am–midnight.

4 Beaches

Superb beaches put Anguilla on the tourist map. There are dozens of them, plus another handful on the outer cays. The island's interior may be barren, but there's no denying the beauty of its shores. Miles and miles of pristine, powdery-soft sands open onto crystal-clear waters. Many of the beaches are reached via bone-jarring dirt paths that ultimately give way to sand and sea. All the beaches are open to the public, but you may have to walk through the lobby of a deluxe hotel to reach one.

The best beaches are on the west end of the island, site of the most expensive hotels. **Rendezvous Bay** is the island's most famous, a long curving ribbon of pale gold sand that stretches along the bay for 4km (2½ miles). It's calmer, warmer, and shallower than Shoal Bay, which is on the Atlantic side. With an alfresco beach bar, it attracts all kinds, from families to romantic couples.

Our favorite is 3km (2-mile) **Shoal Bay** ★★ in the northeast, one of the best beaches in the Caribbean. With silver-white, powder-soft sands, it also has some of Anguilla's best coral gardens, home to hundreds of tiny iridescent fish, making it great for snorkeling. Umbrellas, beach chairs, and other equipment are available here so you can enjoy the backdrop of coconut palms and sea-grape trees. This beach is often called Shoal Bay East to distinguish it from Shoal Bay West (see below). The waters are usually luminous, transparent, and brilliantly blue. At noon the sands are blindingly white, but at sunrise and sunset they turn a pink to rival any beach in Bermuda. You'll hear music from the terraces of the Hardbroke Cafe and Uncle Ernie's. The Upper Shoal Bar serves first-rate tropical drinks, and souvenir shops hawk T-shirts and suntan lotion on the beach. For a little more tranquility, you can also take the trail walk from Old Ta to little-known **Katouche Beach,** which offers perfect snorkeling and is also a prime site for a beach picnic under shade trees.

Shoal Bay West, next to Maundays Bay, has pristine white sands opening onto the southwest coast. You'll find deluxe accommodations, including Covecastles, on these shores.

Moments Grilled Lobster on a Remote Cay

At Island Harbor, just wave your arms, and a boatman will pick you up and transport you across the water to **Scilly Cay,** pronounced "silly key." You wouldn't really call this place an island; it's more like a spit of sand 150m (500 ft.) off the coast of the main island's northeastern shoreline. At a little cafe and bar here, you can select a fabulous fresh lobster. Grilled while you wait, the lobster is marinated in a sauce of honey-laced orange juice, orange marmalade, roasted peanuts, virgin olive oil, curry, and tarragon. Chicken is prepared here the same way. Lunch is served Tuesday to Sunday from noon to 3pm.

Adjoining Shoal Bay West, and site of Cap Juluca, is 1.5km-long (1-mile), white-sand **Maundays Bay Beach,** justifiably one of the island's most popular shorelines, with good snorkeling and swimming. Though the waters are luminescent and usually calm, sometimes the wind blows enough to attract windsurfers and sailboats. On a clear day you can see St. Martin across the way.

Sandy Isle, on the northwest coast, is a tiny islet with a few palms surrounded by a coral reef. It lies offshore from Road Bay. Once here, you'll find a beach bar and restaurant, and a place to rent snorkeling gear and buy underwater cameras. During the day a small ferry heads here every hour from Sandy Ground.

The northwest coast has a number of other beaches worth seeking out, notably **Barnes Bay Beach,** filled with powdery white sand and opening onto clear blue waters. You can relax in the shade of the chalky hillside or a beach umbrella or join the windsurfers and snorkelers. It's usually less crowded after lunch.

Almost never crowded, **Little Bay Beach** is one of the most dramatic in Anguilla, set against steep cliffs. Here the sands are grayish, but snorkelers and scuba divers don't seem to mind. The beach also attracts bird-watchers and picnickers. Local weddings are sometimes performed here.

Road Bay Beach, also on the northwest coast, is known for spectacular sunsets and clear blue waters, often filled with yachts coming from St. Martin. A watersports center here on the beach will set you up with gear. You can also watch lobstermen set out in their boats.

The beaches along the northeast coast are the stuff of fantasies—especially if you've got a four-wheel-drive. Calm and tranquil, the incredibly blue waters of **Island Harbour Beach** attract both locals and the odd visitor or two. For centuries Anguillians have set out from these shores to haul in Anguillian lobster. There are a few beach bars and alfresco dining rooms here, so you can make a day of it—or take a 3-minute boat ride over to Scilly Cay.

Chances are you'll have **Captain's Bay's Beach** all to yourself. Near Junk's Hole, it's better for enjoying the sun and sand than it is for swimming. The undertow is dangerous, though the setting is dramatic and appealing.

5 Sports & Other Outdoor Pursuits

CRUISES & BOATING   A great way to have fun on Anguilla is to cruise to a secluded beach on an offshore cay for a picnic and some snorkeling, whether on your own or with a group. Several outfitters on the island rent vessels, including **Anguillian Divers**(© **264/497-4750;** www.anguilliandivers.com), offering a 10m (31-ft.) motorboat.

FISHING   Your hotel can arrange for you to cast your line with a local guide, but you should bring your own tackle. Agree on the cost before setting out, however, to avoid the "misunderstandings" that are commonly reported.

Malliouhana, Meads Bay (© **264/497-6111**), has a 12m (40-ft.) fishing cruiser, *Dakota,* which holds up to 12 passengers. You can charter it for fishing parties for US$400 (£208) for up to 4 hours. All fishing gear and a snack basket are included. **Garfield Richardson** (© **264/497-2956**) rents his *Gotcha* for fishing excursions at the rate of US$500 (£260) for 4 hours or US$900 (£468) for an 8-hour day. For this rate, four fishermen are taken out, the fee including snacks and equipment.

GOLF   Anguilla's first golf course, created by golf legend Greg Norman, opened in 2006 as part of the 111-hectare (274 acre) St. Regis Resort, which is not scheduled for completion until the winter of 2008. The **Temenos Golf Club** ✹✹✹, Anguilla Merrywing West End (© **264/222-8200**), is an 18-hole, par-72, 7,100-yard course, featuring 14 oceanview holes. Greens fees are US$415 (£216) per person, including cart, caddies, and locker room access, one of the highest such fees in the Caribbean. Club rental costs an additional US$65 (£34). Bob and Melinda Blanchard, owners of the famous Blanchard's Restaurant (see above), have opened Zurra's restaurant on the golf course grounds next to the club house.

SCUBA DIVING & SNORKELING   Most of the coastline of Anguilla is fringed by coral reefs, and the island's waters are rich in marine life, with sunken coral gardens, brilliantly colored fish, caves, and stingrays offshore. Conditions for scuba diving and snorkeling on the island are ideal. In addition, the government of Anguilla has artificially enlarged the existing reef system, a first for the Caribbean. Battered and outmoded ships, deliberately sunk in carefully designated places, act as nurseries for fish and lobster populations and provide new dive sites. At **Stoney Bay Marine Park** off the northeast coast, you can explore the ruins of a Spanish ship that sank in the 1700s.

   Anguillian Divers, Meads Bay (© **264/497-4750**), is a one-stop dive shop that answers most diving needs. PADI instructors are on hand, with a two-tank dive costing US$70 (£36), plus another US$10 (£5.20) for equipment. Another good choice is **Shoal Bay Scuba & Water Sports** (© **264/497-4371**), with one of the best-designed dive boats in the area. (It was custom built.) A two-tank dive costs US$80 (£42), plus US$10 (£5.20) for equipment.

   It's easy to find places to rent snorkeling gear on the island's most popular beaches, if your hotel doesn't provide it. The snorkeling's great at Shoal Bay, Maundays Bay, Barnes Bay, Little Bay, and Road Bay.

TENNIS   Most of the resorts have their own tennis courts. (See "Accommodations," earlier in this chapter.) **Malliouhana,** Meads Bay (© **264/497-6111**), has a pro shop and four championship Laykold tennis courts. All courts are lit for night games.

6 Exploring Anguilla

The best way to get an overview of the island is on a **taxi tour.** In about 2½ hours, a local driver (all of them are guides) will show you everything for about US$50 (£26). The driver will also arrange to let you off at your favorite beach after a look around, and then pick you up and return you to your hotel or the airport. Call **Airport Taxi Stand** at © **264/497-5054** or **Blowing Point Ferry Taxi Stand** at © **264/497-6089.** If you want more organized sightseeing, call **Bennie's Tours** at Blowing Point (© **264/497-2788**). This is the island's most reliable tour operator.

   Boat trips can sometimes be arranged to **Sombrero Island,** 61km (38 miles) northwest of Anguilla. This mysterious island, with its lone lighthouse, is 360m (1,200 ft.) wide at its broadest point and 1.2km (¾ mile) in length. Phosphate miners abandoned it in 1890, and limestone rocks, now eroded, rise in cliffs around the island. The treeless, waterless terrain evokes a moonscape. Ask at your hotel desk if you can be hooked up with a vessel sailing over to the island.

   For that rare rainy day, there is the **Heritage Museum Collection,** East End at Pond Ground (© **264/497-4092**), open Monday to Saturday 10am to 5pm, charging US$5

(£2.60) admission. Artifacts on display range from the golden age of the Arawak Indians to the British "invasion" of the island in 1969. In addition to artifacts, photographs also tell the story, including those documenting a visit from Queen Elizabeth II in 1964.

One of Anguilla's most festive, and certainly most colorful, annual festivals is **Carnival,** held jointly under the auspices of the Ministries of Culture and of Tourism. Boat races are Anguilla's national sport, and during Carnival they form 60% of the celebration, in which the island's people display their culture, drama, creativity, and love of their land. The festival begins on the first Monday in August and continues for 1 week. Carnival harks back to Emancipation Day, or "August Monday" as it's called, when all enslaved Africans were freed.

7 Shopping

For serious shopping, it's best to take the ferry (see earlier in this chapter) and visit the big stores in Marigot on French St. Martin. Little branch shops of some of the bigger stores are also found on Anguilla, but the better merchandise and the larger selection can be found just a ferryboat ride away.

On Anguilla itself, the most fun shopping is at **World Art & Antiques Gallery,** West End Road, The Valley (© 264/497-5950), where Nik and Christie Douglas have assembled a fascinating array of collectibles from around the world. Treasures include Chinese bronzes and jades, exotic jewelry, tribal and pre-Columbian sculptures and masks, and antiques and paintings.

What you can't get in St. Martin is local arts and crafts from Anguilla. The best of these are on display at the **Savannah Gallery,** Coronation Street, Lower Valley (© 264/497-2263), on the road to Crocus Bay, and the **Devonish Art Gallery,** West End Road (© 264/497-2949). Courtney Devonish is a well-known potter and sculptor. You can also preview original paintings by local artists at **Loblolly Gallery,** in Rose Cottage, Crocus Hill Road (© 264/497-6006).

8 Anguilla After Dark

Nightlife on Anguilla centers mainly on the various hotels, especially in winter, when they host barbecues, West Indian parties, and singers and other musicians. The hotels hire calypso combo groups and other bands, both local and imported.

Open-air **Johnno's Beach Bar,** Road Bay, Sandy Ground (© 264/497-2728), is a favorite of Hollywood types when they visit Anguilla. The club serves Beck's beer on the beach, along with barbecued spareribs, grilled chicken, and fresh fish for lunch and dinner. Live entertainment takes place Wednesday 7pm to 1am and Friday 10pm to 2am. A weekly Sunday barbecue begins at noon, with live light jazz music starting midafternoon in winter. Try the Johnno Special (similar to a piña colada, but made with rum and guava berries).

A restaurant-cum-beach-bar, **Palm Grove Bar & Grill,** Junk's Hole Bay (© 264/497-4224), offers a long stretch of uncrowded white sand and offshore reefs full of eels, squid, and manta rays. Nat Richardson, the owner, is waiting to boil or grill fresh-caught lobster, crayfish, or shrimp for you. *Bon Appétit* liked his johnnycakes so much it stole the recipe and published it. Hours are usually 11am to around 6:30pm daily, but they can vary greatly depending on when the owner feels like getting there, and whenever clients decide to show up.

Pumphouse Bar & Grill, Sandy Ground (© 264/497-5154), is the island's latest hot spot, featuring 30 different rums. The food is good, too, served in a funky dining room with an uneven concrete slab floor that was originally designed as a repair station for heavy trucks. Standard but satisfying menu items include platters of fish or chicken, steaks, and a Caesar salad with slices of jerk chicken. Go any time from 6pm to 2am, except Sunday, when it's closed. Reggae lovers should show up on Wednesday and Saturday nights; Thursday nights are often devoted to merengue.

There are some other little nighttime joints on Anguilla that seem to close with irritating irregularity. Most of these dives are active only on the weekend, including **Dune Preserve** at Rendezvous Bay (© 264/497-2660), where the best-known singer on island, "Bankie" Banx, performs. You might also check out another weekend hot spot, **The Red Dragon Disco,** The Valley (© 264/497-2687), where dancers gyrate to the latest recorded music.

Cigar aficionados flock to **Elio's** in The Valley at Bedney's Plaza, off West and Main roads (© 264/497-7822). Elio's features a walk-in humidor with some 200 exotic brands of cigars, including the fabled Cuban Cohiba Robustos (illegal in the U.S.). The best rum on island is also sold here, including 15-year-old bottles of Ron Varadero, also from Cuba. While you smoke and drink, you can listen to an array of tapes including Cubano and general Latino recordings. The bar is small but choice with only six stools at the counter and five tables outside.

Antigua & Barbuda

Antiguans say that they have a different beach for every day of the year. That may be an exaggeration, but the beaches here are certainly spectacular: most are protected by coral reefs, and the sand is often sugar white.

Antigua, Barbuda, and Redonda form the independent nation of Antigua and Barbuda, within the Commonwealth of Nations. Redonda is an uninhabited rocky islet of less than a square mile, located 32km (20 miles) southwest of Antigua. Barbuda, which lies 42km (26 miles) to the north of Antigua, is covered at the end of this chapter.

Antigua (An-*tee*-gah) may be an independent nation, but it is still British in many of its traditions. Economically, it has transformed itself from a poverty-stricken island of sugar plantations to a modern-day vacation haven. The landscape of rolling, rustic Antigua is dotted with stone towers that were once sugar mills.

The inland scenery isn't as dramatic as what you'll find on St. Kitts, but, oh, those beaches! If you want high rises and glittering gambling and nightlife, head elsewhere, perhaps to Puerto Rico. Antigua does have some casinos, but they're hardly a reason to visit, and most of its hotels are intimate one- or two-story inns rather than glitzy, sprawling resorts. In general, the dining and shopping of Antigua are comparable to those of St. Kitts but don't hold up to those of St. Maarten/St. Martin or the U.S. Virgin Islands.

Most locals will treat you with respect if you show them respect, but Antigua is hardly the friendliest of islands in the Caribbean—too much unemployment, too great a gap between rich and poor.

Most hotels, restaurants, beach bars, and watersports facilities lie north of the capital of **St. John's,** in the northwest. St. John's is a large, neatly laid-out town 10km (6¼ miles) from the airport and less than a mile from Deep Water Harbour Terminal. This port city is the focal point of commerce and industry and the seat of government and shopping. Protected within a narrow bay, St. John's is charming, with cobblestone sidewalks and weather-beaten wooden houses with corrugated iron roofs and louvered Caribbean verandas. Trade winds keep the wide streets cool. Since all the major resorts are on good beaches, most visitors tend to stay put, going into St. John's for a day's shopping jaunt or to English Harbour for some history.

Before volcanic ash covered much of Antigua's neighbor, **Montserrat,** that little island was a destination in its own right. It was once a haven for many American expatriates, mostly retired couples, and at one time was the Caribbean island of choice for music stars like Paul McCartney, who came here to write and record songs.

Montserrat is slowly bouncing back, hoping to recapture the tourism it used to enjoy. Until the volcanic dust settles, however, it is most often visited as a day trip from Antigua, mainly by curiosity or adventure seekers.

1 Essentials

VISITOR INFORMATION

You can contact the **Antigua and Barbuda Department of Tourism** at 305 E. 47th St., 6A, New York, NY 10017 (© **212/541-4117;** fax 212/541-4789; www.antigua-barbuda.org); or 25 SE Second Ave., Suite 300, Miami, FL 33131 (© **305/381-6762;** fax 305/381-7908). A toll-free number also gives information: © **888/268-4227.** Operators are available Monday to Friday 9am to 5pm Eastern Time.

In Canada, contact the **Antigua and Barbuda Department of Tourism and Trade,** 60 St. Claire Ave. E., Suite 304, Toronto, ON M4T 1N5 (© **416/961-3085;** fax 416/961-7218). In England the tourist office is at 45 Crawford Pl., London W1H 4LP (© **020/7258-0700).**

On the island, the **Antigua and Barbuda Department of Tourism,** at the corner of Nevis Street and Friendly Alley (© **268/462-0480;** fax 268/462-2483), is open Monday to Thursday 8am to 4:30pm and Friday 8am to 3pm.

GETTING THERE

Before you book your flight, read "Packages for the Independent Traveler" in chapter 2—it could save you a bundle. Even if you don't book a package, you should check that chapter's tips on finding the best airfare.

The major airline that flies to Antigua's V. C. Bird Airport is **American Airlines** (© **800/433-7300** in the U.S. and Canada; www.aa.com), which offers four daily nonstop flights to Antigua from its hub in San Juan, Puerto Rico. A flight takes about 1½ hours, and each departs late enough in the day to allow easy transfers.

Continental (© **800/231-0856** in the U.S. and Canada; www.continental.com) has flights 3 days a week out of Newark, New Jersey.

British Airways (© **800/247-9297** in the U.S. and Canada; www.britishairways.com) flies daily from London's Gatwick Airport. **Virgin Atlantic Airways** (© **077/0574-7747** in the U.K., 800/821-5438 in the U.S. or Canada; www.virgin-atlantic.com) also offers nonstop flights from London.

Air Canada (© **888/247-2262** in the U.S. and Canada, or 268/462-1147; www.aircanada.ca) has regularly scheduled flights from Toronto to Antigua on Saturdays.

BWIA (© **800/538-2942** in the U.S. and Canada; www.bwee.com) is increasingly popular. Each week, flights depart for Antigua—one from Toronto; five from Kingston, Jamaica; two from New York; and two from London.

US Airways (© **800/428-4322** in the U.S. and Canada, or 268/480-5700; www.usairways.com) offers nonstop flights from Philadelphia and Baltimore.

The **Caribbean Star** (© **866/864-6272** in the U.S. and Canada, or 268/480-2591; www.flycaribbeanstar.com), based in Antigua, flies from Miami and San Juan, as well as from some other islands.

Fun Fact Special Events

The week before the first Tuesday in August, summer **Carnival** brings exotic costumes that recall Antiguans' African heritage. Festivities include a beauty competition, and calypso- and steel-band competitions. The big event in spring is **Sailing Week** in late April or early May.

Antigua

ATLANTIC OCEAN

Airport ✈
Beach 🏖
Mountain ▲

Hodges Bay
Dutchman's Bay
Prickly Pear Island
Long Island
Dickenson Bay 2
Cedar Grove
Runaway Beach 3
Coolidge
1
Deep Water Harbour
Fort James
V. C. Bird Airport
Guiana Island
Deep Bay
St. John's
Hawksbill Beaches 4
Parham
Five Islands 5
Pineapple Beach
Long Bay
Indian Town Point
Pares
Devil's Bridge
Darkwood Beach 6
Jennings
All Saints
Betty's Hope
Willikie's
Jolly Harbour
Bolans
Megaliths
15
Potworks Dam
Freetown
Driftwood Beach
Boggy Peak
Fig Tree Dr.
Falmouth
10
Half Moon Bay
Johnson's Point
Urlings
Falmouth Bay
11
Willoughby Bay
Morris Bay
Old Road
9
English Harbour
Turner's Beach 7 8
Pigeon Point
12
14
Mamora Bay
Carlisle Bay 13
Shirley Heights
Nelson's Dockyard National Park

Caribbean Sea

Admiral's Inn **13**
Carlisle Bay **8**
The Catamaran Hotel & Marina **9**
CocoBay Resort **6**
The Copper and Lumber Store Hotel **10**
Curtain Bluff **7**
Galley Bay **5**
Harmony Hall **15**
Hawksbill by Rex Resorts **4**
The Inn at English Harbour **12**
Jumby Bay Resort **1**
Ocean Inn **11**
St. James's Club **14**
Sandals Grande Antigua Resort & Spa **2**
Siboney Beach Club **3**

PUERTO RICO
BRITISH VIRGIN ISLANDS
ATLANTIC OCEAN
ANGUILLA
LESSER ANTILLES LEEWARD ISLANDS
U.S. VIRGIN ISLANDS
ANTIGUA AND BARBUDA
ST. KITTS AND NEVIS
Antigua
MONTSERRAT
Caribbean Sea
GUADELOUPE
DOMINICA

GETTING AROUND

BY TAXI   Taxis meet every airplane, and drivers wait outside the major hotels. If you're going to spend a few days here, a particular driver may try to "adopt" you. The typical one-way fare from the airport to St. John's is US$11 (£5.70), but to English Harbour it's US$31 (£16) and up. The government of Antigua fixes rates, and taxis are meterless.

Taxis aren't cheap, but they're the best way to see Antigua, as the drivers also act as guides. Most taxi tours go from the St. John's area to English Harbour. Drivers generally charge a flat rate of US$24 for three or four passengers and often wait 30 minutes or more while you sightsee around English Harbour. If you split the cost with another couple, these tours become more affordable.

To call a taxi in St. John's, dial ⓒ **268/460-8300.**

BY RENTAL CAR   To drive on island, you must obtain an Antiguan license, which costs US$12 (£6.25) and requires a valid driver's license from home. Most car-rental firms can issue you an Antiguan license, which they usually do without a surcharge. *Remember:* Drive on the left.

It's best to stick with the major U.S. rental companies rather than using a local agency. Try **Avis** (*©* **800/331-1212** in the U.S. and Canada, or 268/462-2847; www. avis.com) or **Hertz** (*©* **800/654-3131** in the U.S. and Canada, or 268/462-4114; www.hertz.com) for service at the airport. Another agency to try is **Dollar** on Factory Road, St. John's (*©* **800/800-4000** in the U.S. and Canada, or 268/462-0362; www.dollarcar.com).

BY BUS   Although buses are a cheap option, we don't recommend them for the average visitor. Service is erratic and undependable, and roads are impossibly bumpy. In theory buses operate between St. John's and the villages daily from 5:30am to 6pm, but don't count on it. In St. John's, buses leave from two different "stations"—on Market Street near the Central Market, and on Independence Avenue adjacent to the Botanical Gardens. Most fares are US$1 (50p). There is no central information bureau to call for schedules.

FAST FACTS: Antigua

Banks   Banks are usually open Monday to Thursday 8am to 3pm and on Friday 8am to 1pm and 3 to 5pm. Try **Royal Bank** at High and Market streets in St. John's (*©* **268/480-1150**). You'll find several ATMs here.

Currency   These islands use the **Eastern Caribbean dollar (EC$)**. Nearly all hotels bill in U.S. dollars, however, and only certain tiny restaurants present their prices in EC$. When you inquire about a price, make sure you know the type of dollars quoted. The EC dollar is worth about 37¢ in U.S. currency (EC$2.70 = US$1). *Unless otherwise specified, prices in this chapter are quoted in U.S. dollars and British pounds.*

Customs   Arriving visitors are allowed to bring in 200 cigarettes or 50 cigars, 1 quart of liquor, and 6 ounces of perfume.

Documents   A valid passport is required from U.S., British, and Canadian nationals. All arriving visitors must have a departing ticket.

Electricity   Most of the island's electricity is 220-volt AC (60 cycles), which means that U.S. appliances require transformers. The Hodges Bay area and some hotels, however, are supplied with 110-volt AC (60 cycles).

Emergencies   In an emergency, contact the police (*©* **268/462-0125**), the fire department (*©* **268/462-0044**), or an ambulance (*©* **268/462-0251**). You can also call *©* **911** or *©* **999** for any type of emergency.

Hospital   The principal medical facility on Antigua is **Holberton Hospital**, on Hospital Road, St. John's (*©* **268/462-0251**).

Language   The official language is English.

Liquor Laws   Beer and liquor are sold in many stores, 7 days a week. It's legal to have an open container on the beach.

Safety Antigua is generally safe, but that doesn't mean you should wander alone at night on St. John's near-deserted streets. Don't leave valuables unguarded on the beach, either.

Taxes & Service Charges Visitors must pay a departure tax of US$20 (£10) and an 8.5% government tax on hotel bills. Most hotels also add a service charge of between 10% and 15%.

Telephone Telephone calls can be made from hotels or the office of **Cable & Wireless,** on Long Street in St. John's (© **268/462-0840**). You can also send faxes and telegrams from Cable & Wireless. To call Antigua from the United States, dial **1268,** and then the number. To call the United States from Antigua, dial **1,** the area code, and then the number. You might want to purchase a phone card, which you can use to connect with an American long-distance company. You can reach **MCI** at © **800/888-8000** and **Sprint** at © **800/829-0965.**

Time Antigua is on Atlantic Standard Time year-round, so it's 1 hour ahead of U.S. Eastern Standard Time (EST). When daylight saving time takes over in the U.S., then Antigua's time is the same as the eastern United States.

Water Tap water is generally safe to drink here, but many visitors prefer to drink only bottled water.

Weather The average year-round temperature ranges from 75°F to 85°F (24°C–29°C).

2 Accommodations

Antigua's hotels are generally small, and many are closed during the summer. Owners may decide to shut down early if business isn't good. Air-conditioning is uncommon except in first-class hotels, and be warned: Antigua at midday can be quite steamy and uncomfortable.

An 8.5% government tax and a service charge of between 10% and 15%, depending on your hotel, are added to your hotel bill, which makes quite a difference in your final tab.

Antigua has lots of shockingly expensive hotels and resorts, but there are ways you can bring down the prices. Consider booking a package if you're interested in one of those pricey places. Refer to the section "Packages for the Independent Traveler," in chapter 2.

Because getting around the island is difficult, your choice of where to stay is crucial. (The hotels are all plotted on the island map on p. 75.) Those who prefer high winds, breaking waves, and dramatic scenery should stay on the northwest side, north of the capital of St. John's. This is an area of middle-bracket resorts such as Sandals. If you want to spend most of your vacation at one resort, venturing out only occasionally, and can afford it, try one of the superexclusive places such as Curtain Bluff or St. James's Club on the remote southern coast. History buffs interested in atmospheric B&Bs should try either Admiral's Inn or the Inn at English Harbour, unless a good beach is crucial. If it is, then head for one of the big resorts, all of which are on sandy beaches.

In addition to the choices listed in this section, Chez Pascal (see "Dining," later in this chapter) also offers accommodations.

VERY EXPENSIVE

Carlisle Bay ⭐⭐⭐ *Kids*   Giving every first-class resort in the Caribbean a serious run for its money is this stunner from the owner of London's über-boutique hotel One Aldwych. The resort's entire collection of furniture, all dark Indonesian teak and creamy Italian upholstery, is custom-made. Set on a picture-perfect bay, the resort offers every luxe amenity from a world-class spa to tennis pros to serious food in two restaurants. Kids even have their own movie theater. Each of the 80 suites opens into a sea view. The Beach Suites are steps away from the water; the Ocean Suites have an extra perk—you can pour yourself into a hot bath in the spacious tub and gaze out a big picture window onto the mangrove lagoon behind the resort—a wild, freshwater environment that can, blessedly, never be developed. The Carlisle Suites are the biggest units, with three bedrooms, a sitting room, and a kitchen. The resort's well-stocked library has a cool, contemporary look, but at night it seems to glow from within, an old-fashioned beacon for book lovers. No question: Carlisle Bay offers swimming, sailing, and diving as well as tennis and yoga, but this is a resort for true relaxation. Service is top-notch.

Old Rd., St. Mary's, Antigua, W.I. © 800/628-8929 or 268/484-0002. Fax 268/484-0003. www.carlisle-bay.com. 80 suites. Winter US$990–US$1,140 (£515–£593) double; off-season US$725–US$790 (£377–£411) double. Special packages available. AE, DC, MC, V. **Amenities:** 2 restaurants; 3 bars; outdoor pool; 9 lighted tennis courts; fitness gym; full-service spa; boat excursions; dive center; children's programs; movie theater; library; shopping; 24-hr. room service; 1-hr. pressing and dry-cleaning service; afternoon tea. *In room:* A/C, minibar, safe.

Curtain Bluff ⭐⭐⭐ *Kids*   This serene oasis is the island's premier resort, with a price tag to match and enough ambience and class to make St. James's Club (see below) look like a glorified Holiday Inn. Twenty-four kilometers (15 miles) from the airport on the southwest shore, the hotel occupies the most lushly tropical section of the island, in the village of Old Road, and sits on two beautiful beaches (one turbulent, the other calm). This place is for a mature old-money crowd, who like the clubby feel and the good service.

The beautifully furnished accommodations include deluxe units with king-size beds; a terrace room with a king-size, four-poster bed; and spacious suites with two balconies. The roomy bathrooms have beautiful tiles, deluxe toiletries, tubs and showers, dual vanities, and bidets. Accommodations in the newer units are more spacious, with upgraded furnishings and two double beds. The two-story suites are among the most luxurious in the Caribbean. Although at times in the midday heat you may wish for air-conditioning, ceiling fans and trade winds generally keep the rooms cool. Some guests come primarily for the superb food. French-born Christophe Blatz keeps his Continental menu limited, so he can freshly prepare and artistically arrange everything. Curtain Bluff restaurant has the Caribbean's most extensive wine selection. Although it's not a requirement, men are encouraged to wear jackets during the dinner hour in high season.

P.O. Box 288, Antigua, W.I. © 888/289-9898 in the U.S., or 268/462-8400. Fax 268/462-8409. www.curtainbluff. com. 72 units. Winter US$995–US$1,395 (£517–£725) double, from US$2,245 (£1,167) suite; off season US$645–US$875 (£335–£455) double, from US$1,120 (£582) suite. Rates are all-inclusive. AE, MC, V. **Amenities:** 2 restaurants; 2 bars; outdoor pool; putting green; 4 tennis courts; fitness center; aerobics; boccie court; croquet; squash court; yoga; deep-sea fishing; dive shop; kayaks; sailing; scuba diving; snorkeling; water-skiing; windsurfing; children's programs; access to computer facilities; room service (10am–11pm); massage; babysitting; laundry service; dry cleaning; TV room. *In room:* Ceiling fan, dataport, safe, sauna (in suites).

Galley Bay 🐚🐚 This is still the best place to chill out in luxury, even after being taken over by Elite Island resorts and turned into an all-inclusive. It has none of that toga-party hysteria associated by such lesser all-inclusives as Sandals. Though movie stars are no longer photographed topless on the hotel beach (as Greta Garbo once was), the resort still has an aura of exclusivity. The Gauguin-inspired Tahitian-style rentals are laid-back, but classically elegant. These intimate rooms open onto 16 secluded hectares (40 acres) of beachfront gardens, a bird sanctuary, and a lagoon, with the biggest draw, of course, being 1.2km (¾ mile) of white-sand beach. Choose among beachfront bungalows, the more romantic Gauguin rondavels (tikilike huts) with thatch roofs, or deluxe accommodations and suites in the two-story wings. The Italian marble bathrooms with shower are part of the allure. Dining is among the best on the island either in the Sea Grape or the Gauguin Restaurant, the latter more intimate and casual, located at the beach.

Five Islands (P.O. Box 305), St. John's, Antigua, W.I. ⓒ **800/858-4618** or 268/462-0302. Fax 268/462-4551. www. eliteislandresorts.com. 69 units. Winter US$925–US$1,100 (£481–£572) double, US$1,150–US$1,250 (£598–£650) suite. Off season US$725–US$900 (£377–£468) double, US$1,000–US$1,050 (£520–£546) suite. Rates are all-inclusive. AE, DISC, MC, V. Children under 16 not allowed except during holiday season. 5-night minimum stay required in winter except Feb (7-night minimum); 8-night minimum during holiday season. **Amenities:** 2 restaurants; 2 bars; outdoor pool; tennis court; gym; fitness center; kayaks; sailing; scuba diving; snorkeling; windsurfing; bike rentals; game room; limited room service; laundry service/dry cleaning; walking trails; rooms for those w/limited mobility. *In room:* A/C, TV, dataport, minifridge, beverage maker, hair dryer, safe.

Hawksbill by Rex Resorts 🐚 *(Kids)* Named after an offshore rock that resembles a hawksbill turtle, this 15-hectare (37-acre) all-inclusive resort is about 15km (10 miles) west of the airport and 6km (3¾ miles) southwest of St. John's. Set on four beaches (one reserved for those who want to go home sans tan lines), it caters to active types and is popular for weddings and honeymoons. This resort draws families and happy couples who like its informality and might feel uncomfortable in the atmosphere of pretension and social climbing that you get at Curtain Bluff. The hotel revolves around an open-air, breezy central core. Bedrooms are small and comfortably furnished, with tubs and showers. The least expensive accommodations open onto a garden; there are more secluded beachfront units available as well. The West Indian great house has three bedrooms for three to six occupants, with king-size beds and kitchenettes. *Note:* Rooms have neither TVs nor air-conditioning, but the atmosphere is usually lively, with some live music in season.

Five Islands Village (P.O. Box 108), St. John's, Antigua, W.I. ⓒ **268/462-0301.** Fax 268/462-1515. www.hawksbill. com. For reservations call ⓒ **305/471-6170.** 111 units. Winter US$350–US$400 (£182–£208) double, US$460–US$510 (£239–£265) triple; off season US$270–US$330 (£140–£172) double, US$385–US$440 (£200–£229) triple. Rates are all-inclusive. AE, MC, V. **Amenities:** 2 restaurants; 2 bars; tennis court; wellness center; snorkeling; Sunfish sailboats; water-skiing; windsurfing; nonsmoking rooms. *In room:* Ceiling fan, fridge, beverage maker, iron, safe.

Jumby Bay Resort 🐚🐚🐚 This sybaritic retreat has a celebrity-and-CEO crowd that can afford its expensive rates. It occupies a 132-hectare (326-acre) offshore island. Boats depart from the Antiguan "mainland" every hour from 7am to midnight daily. You can preregister for the 3km (2-mile) ride on the Antiguan side. With secluded white-sand beaches along a coastline protected by coral reefs, the grounds have been handsomely planted with loblolly and white cedar.

Guests are coddled and pampered in a way that only Curtain Bluff tops. A haven for naturalists, the resort features Pasture Bay Beach on the island's windward side, home to endangered species of turtles, rare birds, and sheep. All the accommodations are frequently refurbished, including a 12-unit Mediterranean-style complex, two-and three-bedroom luxury villas, and several spacious private manor houses. Following a US$5.6-million renovation, completed in 2006, the resort is looking fresher than ever, with upgraded rooms and suites. Beds are luxurious, as are the spacious marble-and-tile bathrooms with tubs. Only the bedrooms within the suites are air-conditioned. In light of the constant trade winds, no one seems to mind.

For breakfast and lunch, it's casual fare at the open-air Beach Pavilion. Dinner is at the Veranda Restaurant, the signature restaurant in the 230-year-old English plantation manor. Dinner Sunday night is an upscale beachfront barbecue. Imaginative and well-prepared dishes are inspired by Europe, America, and the Caribbean.

Long Island (P.O. Box 243), St. John's, Antigua, W.I. © 268/462-6000. Fax 268/462-6020. www.jumbybayresort.com. 51 units. Winter US$1,200–US$1,350 (£624–£702) double, from US$1,550–US$3,000 (£806–£1,560) suite; off season US$775–US$875 (£403–£455) double, from US$975–US$1,950 (£507–£1,014) suite. Rates are all-inclusive. AE, DC, MC, V. **Amenities:** 2 restaurants; 3 bars; golf arranged; 3 tennis courts; fitness center; snorkeling; Sunfish sailboats; water-skiing; windsurfing; bicycles; 24-hr. room service; babysitting. *In room:* A/C, ceiling fan, dataport, kitchenette, minibar, beverage maker, hair dryer, safe.

St. James's Club ★★ (Kids)

This remote, 40-hectare (99-acre) resort on Mamora Bay on two sand beaches tries for glamour, but it falls far behind Curtain Bluff and Jumby Bay, and it doesn't have the state-of-the-art maintenance of those properties, either. (To be fair, although it's very expensive, at least it hasn't jacked up its prices to the shocking levels of those two places.) Midrange package tours from Britain and America continue to fill many of the rooms on occasions. The sports facilities are among the Caribbean's best.

Some of the rooms are standard and medium-size, but others are spacious. The resort has never been able to escape the architectural curse of its former existence as a somewhat banal-looking Holiday Inn. Despite that, all units have excellent beds, combination bathrooms (tub/shower), commodious vanities, dual basins, and sliding-glass doors that open onto private balconies or patios. Pricey two-bedroom villas and hillside homes are also available.

If you're looking into a package all-inclusive deal, be aware that the cuisine is merely average. You can relax in the Rainbow Garden Dining Room, or dine alfresco by candlelight at the Docksider Restaurant overlooking Mamora Bay. Piccolo Mondo serves Italian and international food, and simple lunches are available at the Coco Beach Barbecue. Sometimes the setting is more exciting than the cuisine. Guests can top off the evening at the Jacaranda nightclub. Many enjoy gambling in the glamorous but small European-style casino.

Mamora Bay (P.O. Box 63), St. John's, Antigua, W.I. © 800/858-4618 in the U.S., or 268/460-5000. Fax 268/460-3015. www.eliteislandresorts.com. 257 units, including 73 villas. Winter US$360–US$620 (£187–£322) double from US$580–US$1,310 (£302–£681) suite; off season US$265–US$310 (£138–£161) double, from US$480–US$1,210 (£250–£629) suite. Children age 2 and under stay free in parent's room. AE, MC, V. **Amenities:** 4 restaurants; 5 bars; 4 outdoor pools; casino; 6 tennis courts; fitness center; spa facilities, Jacuzzi; sauna; aqua bikes; deep-sea fishing; kayaking; marina; pedal boats; sailboards; sailing; scuba diving; snorkeling; water-skiing; playground and playhouse for children; salon; room service (7am–11pm); massage; babysitting; laundry service; dry cleaning dance club; nonsmoking rooms. *In room:* A/C, ceiling fan, TV, dataport, hair dryer, safe.

Sandals Grande Antigua Resort & Spa ★

If you like a resort where everything's paid in advance and you virtually live in a walled compound with lots of organized activities, this might be for you. After years of refusing to admit homosexual couples, Sandals is now open to all, regardless of sexual preference. On one of the island's best beaches, the resort offers eight different room categories, most of which are medium-size. Some of the more romantic ones offer four-poster beds and ocean views. Typical amenities include small patios and plush mattresses. If you want honeymoon privacy, opt for a cottage suite (because of its octagonal shape, the staff calls it a rondavel) opening directly onto Dickenson Beach.

A quintet of bars and restaurants serve everything from Tex-Mex to sushi. Il Palio's Italian specialties are particularly good, and the beachfront restaurant is another excellent spot for meals.

Dickenson Bay (P.O. Box 147), St. John's, Antigua, W.I. © **888/726-3257** or 268/462-0267. Fax 268/462-4135. www. sandals.com. 193 units. Winter US$380–US$420 (£198–£218) per person double, from US$995 (£517) per person suite; off season US$395–US$420 (£205–£218) per person double, from US$955 (£497) per person suite. Rates are all-inclusive. AE, DC, MC, V. **Amenities:** 5 restaurants; 5 bars; 5 outdoor pools; 5 whirlpools; 2 tennis courts; fitness center; spa (spa services not included in all-inclusive rate); watersports; laundry service; rooms for those w/limited mobility. *In room:* A/C, TV, dataport, hair dryer, beverage maker, iron, safe.

EXPENSIVE

CocoBay Resort ⨂   Set near three beaches, this hillside compound of colorful wood-sided, tin-roofed cottages lies on 4 headland hectares (10 acres). When this all-inclusive opened in 2000, it gave Sandals some real competition. Understated elegance and West Indian charm combine in this cliff-side setting on the "sunset side" of the island.

Accommodations are unpretentious, modeled on local architecture raised on stilts, with hand-carved furnishings and island art providing both comfort and color. It attracts a hip clientele who'd never patronize one of the stuffier resorts like Curtain Bluff. Guests stay in cottages or in one of four "plantation houses," suitable for up to four occupants, on the hill. Each cottage has a four-poster king-size bed, a private porch, and wooden louvered windows, plus a bathroom with a shower. Bathrooms in the plantation house have full-size tubs. Children 14 and older are welcome.

Valley Church (P.O. Box 431), St. John's, Antigua, W.I. © **800/816-7587** in the U.S., or 268/562-2400. Fax 268/562-2424. www.cocobayresort.com. 41 units. Winter US$175–US$205 (£91–£107) per person double, US$830 (£432) plantation house for up to 4; off season US$140–US$170 (£73–£88) per person double, US$690 plantation house for up to 4. Rates include all meals and watersports. AE, MC, V. **Amenities:** 2 restaurants; 2 bars; outdoor pool; gym; spa; kayaks; sailing; snorkeling; massage; laundry service; dry cleaning; nonsmoking rooms. *In room:* Ceiling fan, fridge, beverage maker, hair dryer, safe, no phone.

The Copper and Lumber Store Hotel ⨂   Forget a pool. Forget a beach. This is the "museum hotel" of English Harbour, with more atmosphere than even The Inn at English Harbour and Admiral's Inn (see below). As its name suggests, this charming, 18th-century building was originally a store that sold wood and copper for repairing British sailing ships. The store and its adjacent harbor structures are built of brick that once was used as ships' ballast. Each of the period units is brick-lined, uniquely designed, and filled with fine Chippendale and Queen Anne reproductions, antiques, brass chandeliers, hardwood paneling, and hand-stenciled floors. The showers look as if they belong in a sailing vessel, with thick mahogany panels and polished brass fittings. All suites have kitchens with aging equipment, private bathrooms (with showers only), and ceiling fans. All the mattresses are first-rate. The downside is the stream of visitors who view it as a museum rather than an inn. Although the English expatriates who founded the hotel in the 1980s did so with great imagination, today the Antiguan government runs it with less flair.

A traditional English pub serves standard food daily, and the Wardroom serves a solid Continental dinner nightly. You may want to skip both of these for fish and chips and Bass on tap at the jumping **Mainbrace Pub** next door.

Nelson's Dockyard, English Harbour (P.O. Box 1283), St. John's, Antigua, W.I. © **268/460-1058.** Fax 268/460-1529. www.copperandlumberhotel.com. 14 units. Winter US$195–US$275 (£101–£143) double, US$275–US$325 (£143–£169) suite; off season US$135–US$195 (£70–£101) double, US$145–US$275 (£75–£143) suite. MAP (breakfast and dinner) US$50–US$60 (£26–£31) per person extra. MC, V. From St. John's, follow the signs southeast to English Harbour. **Amenities:** Restaurant; pub; babysitting; laundry service; ferry service to Galleon Beach. *In room:* A/C, kitchen, beverage maker, hair dryer, iron.

The Inn at English Harbour 🐝

This small inn occupies one of the finest sites on Antigua, 4 hectares (10 acres) that directly flank a beach, with views over Nelson's Dockyard and English Harbour. Better run than its closest competitor, the Copper and Lumber Store Hotel (see above), more elegant than nearby Admiral's Inn (see below), The Inn at English Harbour is tranquil, informal, and very unpretentious. Its old-fashioned, historic charm continues to appeal despite the availability of more glamorous places on the island. The late actor Richard Burton liked it so well he spent two of his honeymoons here. Of course, that was a long time ago and many of the main guest rooms are showing their age these days. You can take a free water taxi to finer beaches along English Harbour. White-tile floors, screened plantation shutters, balconies, and excellent beds invite you to linger. The least expensive units are farthest from the beach, on a hillside. Six suites are decorated with a scattering of British and Caribbean antiques.

The inn is known for high-quality cooking. Lunch is served both at the beach house and in the main dining room. Have a drink before dinner in the old-style English Bar with stone walls and low overhead beams. Live entertainment is provided in winter.

English Harbour (P.O. Box 187), St. John's, Antigua, W.I. © **800/970-2123** in the U.S., or 268/460-1014. Fax 268/ 460-1603. www.theinn.ag. 34 units. Winter US$334–US$458 (£174–£238) double, from US$608–US$666 (£316– £346) suite; off season US$178–US$229 (£93–119) double, from US$275–US$314 (£143–£163) suite. MAP (breakfast and dinner) US$60 (£31) per person extra. AE, MC, V. From St. John's, head south, through All Saints and Liberta, until you reach the south coast. **Amenities:** 2 restaurants; 2 bars; outdoor pool; 2 tennis courts; health club; day sailing; deep-sea fishing; scuba diving; water-skiing; bike rental; horseback riding; car rental; room service (7am–9pm); babysitting; laundry service; nonsmoking rooms; water taxi to Nelson's Dockyard. *In room:* Ceiling fan, TV, fridge, hair dryer, safe.

Siboney Beach Club 🐝

Owned by Aussie Tony Johnson and his wife, Ann, the Siboney Beach Club is named for the Amerindian tribe who predated the Arawaks. Set north of St. John's on .4 hectares (1 acre) of thickly foliated land fronting the 1.5km-long (1-mile) white-sand beach of Dickenson Bay, the resort is shielded on the inland side by a tall, verdant hedge. The club's social center is the Coconut Grove restaurant (see "Dining," below). The comfortable suites are in a three-story balconied building draped with bougainvillea and other vines. The suites have louvered windows for natural ventilation, and TVs are available. All units have separate bedrooms, living rooms, and balconies or patios, plus tiny kitchens behind moveable shutters. Each comes with a small, immaculately kept private bathroom with shower. There's also a tree house: a single room with a king-size bed and jungle decor perched high in a *Ficus benjamina* tree.

Dickenson Bay (P.O. Box 222), St. John's, Antigua, W.I. © **800/533-0234** in the U.S., or 268/462-0806. Fax 268/462-3356. www.siboneybeachclub.com. 12 suites. Winter US$190–US$325 (£99–£169) double; off season US$150–US$205 (£78–£107) double. AE, MC, V. **Amenities:** Restaurant; bar; outdoor pool; babysitting; laundry service; dry cleaning. *In room:* A/C, TV (on request), dataport, kitchenette, beverage maker, hair dryer, iron, safe.

MODERATE

Admiral's Inn 🕊🕊   Though down in third position when stacked against its competitors, The Inn at English Harbour and the Copper and Lumber Store Hotel (see above), this place is full of character and atmosphere. Designed in 1785, the year Nelson sailed into the harbor as captain of the HMS *Boreas,* and completed in 1788, the building here once housed British officers stationed at the dockyards, with a ground floor devoted to the storage of tar and boat-repair supplies. Loaded with West Indian charm, this place in the heart of Nelson's Dockyard is constructed of weathered brick that was brought from England to be used as ships' ballast. Stay here if you want to experience Caribbean history, especially if you're an Anglophile and don't mind commuting to the beach.

There are three types of accommodations. The most expensive are the ground-floor rooms in a tiny brick building across the courtyard from the main structure. Each of these spacious units has a little patio, a garden entry, and air-conditioning. The front rooms on the first floor of the main building, with views of the lawn and harbor, are also more expensive. The back rooms on this floor are less pricey, and all have air-conditioning. With dormer-window views over the yacht-filled harbor, the least expensive rooms on the top floor are smaller and quiet, but they can get warm on summer afternoons. Not all rooms have air-conditioning.

For details on the inn's restaurant, see "Dining," below.

English Harbour (P.O. Box 713), St. John's, Antigua, W.I. © 268/460-1027. Fax 268/460-1153. www.admirals antigua.com. 14 units. Winter US$145–US$180 (£75–£94) double, US$400 (£208) apt for 4; off season US$90–US$120 (£47–£62) double, US$270 (£140) apt for 4. Extra person US$30 (£16). MAP (breakfast and dinner) US$55 (£29) per person extra. AE, MC, V. Closed Sept to mid-Oct. Take the road southeast from St. John's, following the signs to English Harbour. **Amenities:** Restaurant; bar; snorkeling; free transport to beaches; room service (7:30am–9pm); laundry service; dry cleaning. *In room:* A/C (in most), ceiling fan, no phone (in some).

Harmony Hall 🕊 *Finds*   These are about the only accommodations in Antigua that could qualify as one of the little plantation inns so common on many other islands. This art gallery and restaurant-cum-hotel was constructed around a former sugar mill. Standing on 2.5 hectares (6½ acres) of land, Harmony Hall opens onto Brown's Bay, part of the greater body of water, Nonsuch Bay. It is secluded and tranquil. Its Neapolitan owners have restored two separate villas, carving each into six large bedrooms with high ceilings and installing Italian marble and tiles for the bathrooms. It's not on the beach, but some good sands are just down the hill and there's also an on-site swimming pool. Complimentary boat trips are arranged to the uninhabited Green Island, with its lovely beaches and idyllic snorkeling conditions.

Brown's Bay Mill (P.O. Box 1558, St. John's), near Freetown, Antigua, W.I. © 268/460-4120. Fax 268/460-4406. www.harmonyhall.com. 12 units. Winter US$420 (£218) double; off season US$352 (£183) double. Rates include breakfast. AE, DISC, MC, V. Closed mid-May to Nov. **Amenities:** Restaurant (lunch daily, dinner Fri–Sat); bar; outdoor pool; tennis court; room service (dinner only, Sun–Thurs); babysitting; laundry service. *In room:* A/C, ceiling fan, minibar, beverage maker.

INEXPENSIVE

The Catamaran Hotel & Marina   A favorite since the 1970s, the Catamaran opens onto a palm-lined beach at Falmouth Harbour, a 3km (2-mile) drive from English Harbour. Peace, tranquility, and lots of bougainvillea plants prevail. There's an Internet cafe inside the hotel where you can use computers for US$30 (£16) for the first hour, US$10 (£5.20) each additional hour.

On the second floor, each of eight self-contained, motel-style rooms has a comfortable bed (in many cases, a four-poster), a queen-size mattress, and a balcony overlooking the water. The Captain's Cabin is the most luxurious. The ground-floor rooms are small but comfortable. Additional units are within a waterside annex. All but two of the units have kitchens, and each is furnished with a tiled, shower-only bathroom.

Boaters will like the hotel's location at the 30-slip Catamaran Marina. You can purchase supplies at a nearby grocery store.

Falmouth Harbour (P.O. Box 958), St. John's, Antigua, W.I. © **268/460-1036.** Fax 268/460-1339. www.catamaran-antigua.com. 14 units. Winter US$150–US$200 (£78–£104) double, Captain's Cabin US$210 (£109); off season US$115–US$165 (£60–£86) double, Captain's Cabin US$170 (£88). Extra person US$25 (£13). Children under 10 stay free in parent's room. DISC, MC, V. **Amenities:** 2 restaurants; bar; outdoor pool; sport-fishing; Internet cafe; babysitting; laundry service; dry cleaning. *In room:* A/C (in 2 units), TV, ceiling fan, kitchenette (in most), beverage maker, hair dryer, no phone (prepaid cellphones can be rented).

Ocean Inn ✮ *Finds*   This is Antigua's premier B&B, just a 10-minute walk from some golden sandy beaches. It's a special place, with the coziest and most homelike decor on the island and a welcoming ambience that's due to the friendly owners, Sandra and Eustace Potter. Accommodations are either in the main building or in one of the cottages on the grounds; each comes with a little deck opening onto the marina. Most rooms are equipped with a small, tiled bathroom with shower, and everything is beautifully kept. The garden of the hotel overlooks the historic dockyard. Guests share the communal swimming pool, or meet for drinks in the Tree Trunk Bar. The most popular night here is Thursday, when there's an open-air barbecue. This is a delightful place to stay in Antigua if you enjoy B&Bs.

P.O. Box 838, English Harbour, Antigua, W.I. © **268/463-7950.** Fax 268/460-1263. www.theoceaninn.com. 12 units. Winter US$85–US$150 (£44–£78) double; US$150 (£78) double room in cottage; off season US$65–US$85 (£34–£44) double, US$85 (£44) double room in cottage. Rates include continental breakfast. AE, MC, V. **Amenities:** Restaurant (breakfast only); bar; outdoor pool; exercise room; babysitting; laundry service; dry cleaning. *In room:* A/C, TV (in most), beverage maker, hair dryer, no phone.

3 Dining

Although the Eastern Caribbean dollar (EC$) is used on these islands, only certain tiny restaurants present their prices in the local currency. When you inquire about a price, make sure you know which type of dollar is being quoted.

IN ST. JOHN'S

Big Banana-Pizzas in Paradise ✮ *Kids* PIZZA/SUBS/SALADS   In former slave quarters, this family-friendly place serves up some of the best pizza and grilled chicken sandwiches in the eastern Caribbean. It stands amid the most stylish shopping and dining emporiums in town, a few steps from the Heritage Quay Jetty. The frothy drinks, coconut or banana crush, are practically desserts. You can also order overstuffed baked potatoes and fresh-fruit or lobster salad. On Thursday a reggae band entertains from 9pm to 1am.

Redcliffe Quay, St. John's. © **268/480-6985.** www.bigbanana-antigua.com. Pizzas, sandwiches, and salads US$4–US$15 (£2–£8). AE, MC, V. Mon–Sat 8am–11pm.

George ✮ *Finds* CARIBBEAN   Antiguan hospitality, a finely honed cuisine, and a laid-back atmosphere cause a never-ending stream of foodies to head to the home of owner Philip George-John. In his restored Georgian family manse, the host will feed you well and show you a good time. Many of the daily specials are based on long-standing

Antiguan recipes. The ingredients are fresh, and everything is prepared with loving care. The best time to go for an authentic experience is on Saturday, when island specialties are served, including "goat water," souse, "conch water," and pepperpot stew. To finish off, try the creamy rice pudding. Antiguans take their ribs seriously and George-John prepares the best on island. The ribs are slow roasted with a caramelized passion-fruit and pineapple glaze.

Market and Redcliffe Sts., St. John's. © 268/562-4866. Reservations required. Main courses US$14–US$28 (£7–£15). AE, MC, V. Daily 9am–10pm.

Papa Zouk *(Finds)* SEAFOOD   If you like seafood, zouk (French Creole music with strong African influences), and rum, you've come to the right place. This dive is known for its extensive collection of rums. Its signature tropical fruit drink is called Ti-punch, and is well worth a try. To the strains of zouk music, you can have a New Orleans–type Creole party in the Caribbean. To start, try the stuffed clams baked with cheese or a selection of tapas. For dinner, you might order the savory bouillabaisse or a delectable pan-fried red snapper. The house special is the Carnival Platter, a medley of seafood such as mussels, scallops, and shrimp. The service is among the friendliest in town.

Hilda Davis Dr., St. John's. © 268/464-6044. Reservations recommended. Main courses US$9.50–US$22 (£4.95–£11). No credit cards. Tues–Sat 7–10pm.

ELSEWHERE AROUND THE ISLAND

Admiral's Inn *(G)* AMERICAN/CREOLE   Enjoy lobster, seafood, and steaks in this 17th-century hotel (see "Accommodations," earlier in this chapter), and make sure to try our favorite appetizer, the pumpkin soup. The chefs use quality ingredients to create four or five main courses daily. Though the atmosphere is sometimes more exciting than the cuisine, the service is agreeable. Before dinner, order a drink in the bar and read the names of sailors carved into the wood 100 years ago.

In Nelson's Dockyard, English Harbour. © 268/460-1027. Reservations recommended, especially for dinner in high season. Main courses lunch US$10–US$20 (£5.20–£10), dinner US$20–US$30 (£10–£16). AE, MC, V. Daily 8am–10pm. Closed Sept to mid-Oct.

Bay House INTERNATIONAL   This is the charming and intimate dining room associated with a 45-unit family-owned hotel set in a garden on a hillside, a 10-minute walk uphill from the beach at Dickenson Bay. Surrounded by lattices and potted plants in the open-sided dining room, you can take in westward-facing views sweeping out over the hillside and down to the jagged coastline—genuinely fabulous at sunset. Lunch consists of simple salads, stuffed baguette sandwiches, and grills. The kitchen's culinary flair is more obvious at nighttime, when meals might begin with a salad of baby shrimp with grapefruit segments and truffle oil, or fresh chicken livers flambéed with brandy and served with shallots. Main dinner courses feature grilled fish; fresh local lobster that's either grilled and served with lime-and-garlic sauce, or prepared thermidor style. Steaks are served in a light soy sauce with braised Chinese cabbage. For vegetarians there's a platter piled high with grilled Provençal vegetables and served with mixed salads. The most popular dessert is an Antiguan pineapple flambéed in rum and served with rum-raisin ice cream.

In the Tradewinds Hotel, Dickenson Bay. © 268/462-1223. Reservations recommended. Main courses lunch US$16–US$25 (£8.30–£13), dinner US$35–US$70 (£18–£36). AE, MC, V. Daily 6am–10:30pm.

Chez Pascal 🍴 FRENCH   This Gallic-inspired bistro is like a small corner of France in Antigua—except here its gardens bloom with tropical vegetation. On the west coast of the island atop a hilly plateau, near the Royal Antiguan and Galley Bay Hotels, it features well-prepared cuisine, served on an open-air terrace around an illuminated swimming pool.

French colonial trappings include copper pots, rough-textured ceramics, dark-stained wicker and rattan, and tropically inspired fabric designs. The chef, Pascal Milliat, inherited generations of cooking skills in his former home, Lyon. Assisted by his Brittany-born wife, Florence, he prepares and serves classic French dishes with sublime sauces and seasonings. Fine cookery showcases a chicken-liver mousse with basil-flavored butter sauce, lobster bisque en croûte, sea scallops on a bed of leeks, roasted rack of lamb with herbes de Provence (prepared for only two diners at a time), and grouper with beurre blanc sauce.

On the premises are four very large bedrooms. Each unit has a whirlpool tub, air-conditioning, fridge, rattan furniture, sea views, and color schemes inspired by the sand and sky. With breakfast included, singles or doubles range from US$225 (£117) in winter and US$175 (£91) in low season.

Galley Bay Hill, Five Islands. ℂ **268/462-3232.** Reservations recommended. Main courses EC$65–EC$135 (US$24–US$50/£13–£27). AE, DC, MC, V. Tues–Sat 11am–3:30pm and 6:30–11pm. Closed Sept.

Coconut Grove 🍴🍴 INTERNATIONAL/SEAFOOD   North of St. John's in a coconut grove right on the beach, simple tables on a flagstone floor beneath a thatch roof are cooled by sea breezes. This is most visitors' dream of what a Caribbean restaurant should be. And it's one of the island's best. Soup is prepared fresh daily from local ingredients like ginger, carrot, and pumpkin. Lobster and shrimp dishes figure prominently, along with a catch of the day and a daily vegetarian special. Lunch fare is lighter. During happy hour at the bar (4–7pm), all drinks are half price.

In the Siboney Beach Club, Dickenson Bay. ℂ **268/462-1538.** Reservations required. Main courses lunch US$12–US$23 (£6–£12), dinner US$23–US$31 (£12–£16). AE, MC, V. Daily 7am–11:30pm.

Coco's CARIBBEAN/INTERNATIONAL   If you opt to dine here, the loudest noise you'll hear—other than the clinking of porcelain and glassware—is the sound of splashing waves. That's because part of the restaurant is built on pilings sunk into the beachfront, granting diners an unimpeded view over the Caribbean and Antigua's westward-facing headlands, including Indian Mountain. Because it's within an all-inclusive resort, management urges diners who aren't staying at the hotel to phone in advance of their arrival. Diners eat at tables sheathed in azure-colored tiles. Lunches are simpler than dinners, focusing on salads, burgers, sandwiches, and pastas. The best dinner items are usually the grilled catch of the day, marinated and covered with butter. Also recommended is grilled mahimahi prepared in puff pastry like a beef Wellington and served with a slow-simmered Creole sauce of fresh tomatoes, sweet garden peppers, and onions.

Mount Prospect, Jolly Bay. ℂ **268/462-9700.** Reservations required. Main courses EC$90–EC$150 (US$33–US$56/£18–£30). AE, MC, V. Daily 7:30–10am and noon–2:30pm and 7–9pm.

Julian's Alfresco 🍴🍴 *Finds* INTERNATIONAL   For romantic dining, this bright, airy, and colorful restaurant is set in tropical gardens just steps from the beach at Runaway Bay. Chef Julian Waterer wanders the world for his inspiration, stopping off at Asian ports, South American countries, and most definitely European kitchens. Talk about fusion cuisine. His cooking is creative and wonderfully delicate. His specialties such as fish cakes (with lots of crab) seasoned with Asian curries and a sweet red chili sauce are impressive. His Black angus grills and "sizzlers" will delight the meat eater. We like the way he uses exotic sauces and spices to wake up what might be ordinary dishes—take the guava peppercorn coulis, for example, or the pineapple and coriander salsa. Desserts are equally yummy. Since its opening, this has become one of Antigua's favorite restaurants, a real discovery.

Barrymore Beach Hotel, Runaway Bay. ℂ 268/562-1545. Reservations required. Main courses US$14–US$28 (£7–£15). AE, DC, MC, V. Tues–Sun 6:30–10pm.

Le Bistro ☆ FRENCH   Less than a kilometer (½ mile) inland from the coast of Hodges Bay, this restaurant occupies a stone-sided structure built as a clubhouse for a now-defunct golf course. Sporting informal charm, it's Antigua's oldest continuously operated restaurant (since 1981). The owners are English-born Philippa Esposito and her husband, Raffaele, from Capri. Perfectly prepared with a dash of flair are such appetizers as grilled calamari salad with shrimp in balsamic vinaigrette or spinach salad with sautéed portobello mushrooms with tomato and strips of mozzarella. The chef takes justifiable pride in such dishes as fresh blackened salmon in a tomato-and-pineapple sauce and the grilled mahimahi on a bed of spinach with glazed beets and a lime-and-butter sauce.

Hodges Bay. ℂ 268/462-3881. www.lebistro-antigua.com. Reservations recommended. Main courses EC$50–EC$100 (US$19–US$37/£10–£20). AE, MC, V. Tues–Sun 6:30–10:30pm.

Sticky Wicket ☆ INTERNATIONAL/CARIBBEAN   Lying next to a cricket field, this restaurant allows you to watch a match while you eat. It's one of the island's most popular sports-oriented gathering spots, but its lounge decorated with cricket memorabilia and the courtyard overlooking the sports arena are more posh than you might expect, and the food is certainly far better than at most sports bars. The creations are sometimes simple, sometimes complex, but almost always satisfying, as exemplified by the West Indian pork rib plate or the grilled lamb souvlakia. You might launch your repast with a chile-flavored tomato dipping sauce or tasty shrimp and seafood fritters with a rémoulade. The soups and salads are always fresh and homemade, including Antiguan lobster bisque or an East Indian curried chicken salad mixed with toasted coconut and fresh fruit. Nothing quite tops the Key lime cheesecake for dessert.

Pavilion Dr., Coolidge. ℂ 268/481-7000. www.thestickywicket.com. Reservations recommended. Main courses EC$30–EC$90 (US$11–US$33/£6–£18). AE, MC, V. Daily 11am–midnight.

4 Beaches

There's a lovely white-sand beach on **Pigeon Point** at Falmouth Harbour, about a 4-minute drive from Admiral's Inn (p. 83). With calm waters and pristine sands, this is the best beach near English Harbour, but it's often crowded, especially when a cruise ship is in port. It's ideal for snorkelers and swimmers of most ages and abilities.

Dickenson Bay ☆☆ in the northwest, directly north of St. John's, is one of the island's finest beaches, with its wide strip of powder-soft sand and blissfully calm turquoise waters. This safe beach attracts families with small children. You can rent watersports equipment at the **Halcyon Cove Hotel** (ℂ 268/462-0256; fax 268/462-0271). Refreshments are available at the hotel, or mosey over to the casual bars and restaurants nearby.

On the north side of Dickenson Bay, you'll find more secluded beaches and some ideal snorkeling areas along the fan-shaped northern crown of Antigua. For a fee, locals will sometimes take beachcombers to one of the uninhabited offshore islets, such as **Prickly Pear Island,** surrounded by beautiful coral gardens. One of the island's best snorkeling spots is **Paradise Reef,** a 1.5km-long (1-mile) coral garden of stunning beauty north of Dickenson Bay (see "Scuba Diving, Snorkeling & Other Watersports," in "Sports & Other Outdoor Pursuits," below).

If you're seeking solitude, flee to **Johnson's Point.** Between the hamlets of Johnson's Point and Urlings at Antigua's southwestern tip below Jolly Harbour, this beach opens onto the tranquil Caribbean Sea. There are no facilities, but the sand is dazzling white, and the waters, usually clear and calm, are populated with schools of rainbow-hued tropical fish.

Near Johnson's Point on the southwest coast, **Turner's Beach** is idyllic. This is one of the best places to lie out in the tropical sun, cooled by trade winds. The beach has fine white sand and gin-clear waters. If the day is clear (as it usually is), you can see the volcanic island of Montserrat.

If you head east of Urlings and go past the hamlet of Old Road, you'll reach **Carlisle Bay,** site of one of the island's most celebrated shores. Against a backdrop of coconut groves, two long beaches extend from the spot where Curtain Bluff, the island's most deluxe hotel, sits atop a bluff. Here, where the calm Caribbean meets the more turbulent Atlantic, the water is impossibly blue.

South of Jolly Harbour, **Driftwood Beach** is directly north of Johnson's Point, in the southwest. The white sands and calm, clear waters are delightful. It is close to all the villas at Jolly Harbour Beach Resort Marina, however, and can be overcrowded.

In the same vicinity is **Darkwood Beach,** a 5-minute drive south of Jolly Harbour Marina and the Jolly Harbour Golf Club. Here the shimmering waters are almost crystal blue. The snorkeling is great, and you can bet that gentle trade winds will keep you cool. Located in a tourist zone, it is likely to be crowded—almost unbearably so when cruise ships are in port.

If you continue north toward St. John's and cut west at the turnoff for Five Islands, you'll reach the four secluded **Hawksbill Beaches** on the Five Islands peninsula. The beaches here have white sands, dazzling blue-and-green waters, and coral reefs ideal for snorkeling. On one of them, you can sunbathe and swim in the buff. The Five Islands peninsula is the site of major hotel developments. Though it's secluded, the beaches are sometimes crowded.

Perhaps Antigua's most beautiful beach, **Half Moon Bay** 🌴🌴 stretches for nearly 1.5km (1 mile) on the southeastern coast, a 5-minute drive from Freetown village. The Atlantic surf is liable to be rough, but that doesn't stop a never-ending stream of windsurfers, who head out beyond the reef, which shelters protected waters for snorkeling. The beach is now a public park and ideal for a family outing. Half Moon Bay lies east of English Harbour near Mill Reef.

Directly north of Half Moon Bay, east of the village of Willikies, **Long Bay** fronts the Atlantic on the far eastern coast of Antigua. Guests of the Long Bay Hotel and the Pineapple Beach Club usually populate this sandy strip. The shallow waters are home to stunning coral reefs and offer great snorkeling.

In the same vicinity, **Pineapple Beach** is a 5-minute drive heading northeast from Willikies. It opens onto **Long Bay** and the west coast (Atlantic side) of Antigua. Crystal-blue waters make it ideal for snorkeling. Most beach buffs come here just to sun on nearly perfect white sands.

5 Sports & Other Outdoor Pursuits

BOATING & YACHT CHARTERS   If you're contemplating serious yachting around Antigua, as many well-heeled visitors do, make arrangements through **Nicholson Yacht Charters** (© **800/662-6066** in the U.S. and Canada, or 268/460-1530) well in advance of your trip. It offers boats of all sizes.

Once on Antigua, if you plan only minor sailing such as in a Sunfish or small catamaran like Hobie Waves, or windsurfing, contact **Sea Sports,** on the beach in front of the Halcyon Cove Hotel at Dickenson Bay (© **268/462-3355**). This outfitter also gives 3-hour eco-tours for US$50 (£26) per person, including snorkeling gear and lunch.

CRUISES   All the major hotel desks can book boat cruises. You can also call **Tropical Adventures** (© **268/480-1225**), which offers day trips to neighboring Barbuda aboard a motorized catamaran, the *Excellence,* that's suitable for up to 70 passengers at a time. Departures are every Friday and Sunday at 9:30am, returning the same day around 4:30pm. The price is US$100 (£52) per person (no children under 8 allowed), which includes lunch, use of snorkeling equipment, and a visit to Barbuda's bird sanctuary. **Barbuda-bound cruises** depart from **Tony's Water Sports** at Dickenson Bay. For information and reservations, call © **268/462-6326;** fax 268/462-2065.

FISHING   Many anglers visit Antigua just for the big-game fishing offshore, where wahoo, tuna, and marlin abound. The *Obsession* (© **268/464-3174**) is a 15m (50-ft.) Hatteras Sportfisherman with excellent equipment. You can battle the big ones in a featured "fighting chair." For the day, the *Obsession* charges from US$850 (£442), a fee that is shared by all the passengers (usually at least nine). A competitor of similar size, the *Nimrod* (© **268/460-1568**) is captained by Terry Bowen, who knows where to find the best catches. In addition to fishing charters, you can arrange for the *Nimrod* to circle the island or go on sunset cruises. A full around-the-island tour costs US$1,300 (£676), with a half-day going for US$775 (£403). This price is usually divided among at least 10 passengers. The best deep-sea fishing charter is *Overdraft* (© **268/464-4954;** www.antiguafishing.com), a large 12m (40-ft.) fiberglass boat that goes in hunt of dolphin (the fish), shark, barracuda, wahoo, and other creatures of the deep. Captain Frank Hart knows his fishing grounds. Up to six fishermen are accommodated at one time; a 4-hour charter costs US$495 (£257), and an 8-hour charter goes for US$790 (£411).

GOLF   Antigua's golf facilities are not on par with some of the other islands', but its premier course, the 18-hole, par-70 **Cedar Valley Golf Club,** Friar's Hill Road (© **268/462-0161**), is good. This course was designed by the late Richard Aldridge and is 5km (3 miles) east of St. John's, near the airport. It has panoramic views of Antigua's northern coast. Daily greens fees are US$35 (£18) for 18 holes. Cart rentals cost US$30 (£16) for 18 holes, and club rentals cost US$20 (£10).

HIKING   The best hiking tours in Antigua are given by **Tropikelly Trails** (© **268/461-0383**). The trail leads from the hamlet of Wallens Estate, in the tropical rainforest on the south side of Antigua, and climbs to the top of Signal Hill. Tours cost US$40 (£21) per person, and last for about 3 hours each; however, they're only conducted with a minimum of four participants.

PARASAILING   Parasailing is gaining popularity on Antigua. Facilities are available during the day, Monday to Saturday, on the beach at Dickenson Bay.

SCUBA DIVING, SNORKELING & OTHER WATERSPORTS   The reefs that fringe Antigua are home to beautiful, brilliantly colored fish. Many of the island's beaches (see "Beaches," above) have clear, pure, calm waters that make for great snorkeling. The most popular, such as Dickenson Bay, have concessions where you can rent snorkel gear and other equipment if it isn't available from your hotel.

Scuba diving is best arranged through **Dive Antigua,** at the Rex Halcyon Cove, Dickenson Bay (© **268/462-3483**). A resort course is US$85 (£44), which includes a shallow dive; a two-tank dive costs US$79 (£41). A five-dive package goes for US$360 (£187), and open-water certification costs US$493 (£256). Prices do not include equipment, an additional US$21 (£11).

Splish Splash (© **268/462-3483**) regularly conducts 2-hour snorkeling jaunts over to Paradise Reef for US$35 (£18) per person. Departures are daily at 11am and again at 1pm.

TENNIS   Well-off tennis buffs check into **Curtain Bluff** (see "Accommodations," earlier in this chapter). Its courts are the finest on the island. Most of the major hotels have courts as well, and some are lit for night games. (We don't recommend playing tennis at midday—it's just too hot!) Hotel guests usually play for free; if you're not a guest, you'll have to book a court and pay charges that vary from place to place.

WINDSURFING   Most of the major resorts along the beach rent windsurfing equipment. The best outfitters are **Sea Sports** (© **268/462-3355**) at Dickenson Bay, charging US$50 (£26) per hour, or **Sunsail Club Colonna** (© **268/462-6263;** Hodges Bay), which rents equipment for US$120 (£62) per day.

6 Exploring the Island

IN ST. JOHN'S

The most colorful sight of St. John's is the **Saturday morning market,** when many islanders come into the capital to hawk everything from birds and luscious fruits to beautiful flowers and handicrafts. The sights, sounds, and smells of Antigua are at their photographic best here from 8am to noon. However, don't snap a picture of any market person without asking permission first. Most of them will want you to tip them for the privilege of photographing them. The public market lies on Market Street at the southern end of St. John's, at the point where it intersects with All Saints Rd. and Valley Rd.

St. John's Cathedral, the Anglican church between Long and Newgate streets at Church Lane (© **268/462-4686**), has resurrected itself time and again—it's been destroyed by earthquakes and rebuilt on the same site at least three times since it was first constructed in 1683. The present structure dates from 1845. Exhibits at the **Museum of Antigua & Barbuda,** at Market and Long streets (© **268/462-1469**), are within one of Antigua's oldest buildings, built by English colonials in 1750 as a courthouse. The museum covers the island's history, from prehistoric days up to its independence from Britain in 1981. Exhibitions include examples of each of the semiprecious stones (especially jade) you can find on Antigua, as well as models of sugar plantations, steam engines, paintings, and historical prints. It's open Monday through Friday from 8:30am to 3pm and on Saturday from 10am to 2pm. There is a US$3 (£1.55) suggested donation.

AROUND THE ISLAND

Eighteen kilometers (11 miles) southeast of St. John's is **Nelson's Dockyard National Park** ✿✿✿ (© 268/460-1379), one of the eastern Caribbean's biggest attractions. English ships took refuge from the hurricanes in this harbor as early as 1671. The park's centerpiece is the restored Georgian naval dockyard, which was used by admirals Nelson, Rodney, and Hood, and was the home of the British fleet during the Napoleonic Wars. From 1784 to 1787, Nelson commanded the British navy in the Leeward Islands and made his headquarters at English Harbour. The dockyard museum recaptures the 18th-century era of privateers, pirates, and battles at sea. Its colonial naval buildings remain as they were when Nelson was here. Although Nelson never lived at **Admiral House** (© 268/460-8181)—it was built in 1855—his telescope and tea caddy are on display, along with other nautical memorabilia.

The park itself has sandy beaches and tropical vegetation, with various species of cactus and mangroves. A migrating colony of African cattle egrets shelters in the mangroves. Archaeological sites here predate Christ. Nature trails, with coastal views, lead you through the flora. Tours of the dockyard last 15 to 20 minutes; nature walks along the trails can last anywhere from 30 minutes to 5 hours. The dockyard and all the buildings noted in this section are open daily from 9am to 5pm. Children 12 and under are admitted free. The admission price of US$5 (£2.60) includes admission to Admiral House, Clarence House, and Dow's Hill Interpretation Center (see below).

The best **nature trail** on Antigua, a well-tended footpath, goes up the hill from English Harbour to **Shirley Heights** ✿, beginning at the Galleon Beach Hotel. Follow the sign that points to the lookout. The trail is marked with tape on the branches of trees. Eventually you reach a summit of nearly 150m (490 ft.), where you're rewarded with a panoramic view. If you'd like to get more information about the walk, you can pick up a free brochure at the dockyard at the office of the National Parks Authority. This walk is easy; it takes less than an hour to reach the peak.

Another major attraction is the **Dow's Hill Interpretation Center** (© 268/481-5045), just 4km (2½ miles) southeast of the dockyard. The only one of its kind in the Caribbean, the center presents multimedia presentations that cover six periods of the island's history, including the era of Amerindian hunters, the era of the British military, and the struggles connected with slavery. A belvedere opens onto a panoramic view of the park. Admission to the center, including the multimedia show, is included in the price of admission to the dockyards. Hours are daily from 9am to 5pm.

Tips Forts & Photo Ops

In the 1700s Antigua's coastline was ringed with British forts. Although they're in ruins today, the views from these former military strongholds are among the most panoramic in the Caribbean—and you can visit them for free. You can begin at St. John's harbor (the capital), which was once guarded by **Fort Barrington** on the south and **Fort James** on the north. Later you can head down to **Fort James Bay,** where you'll find a couple of bars right on the sand, including **Russell's Beach Bar,** which is most active on Sunday afternoon. It's an ideal place to unwind with a beer. In the south, near English Harbour, check out the view from **Shirley Heights.**

On the way back, take **Fig Tree Drive** ⭐, a 32km (20-mile) circular drive across the main mountain range. It passes through lush tropical hills and fishing villages along the southern coast. You can pick up the road just outside Liberta, north of Falmouth. Winding through a rainforest, it passes thatched villages, every one with a church and lots of goats and children running about. But don't expect fig trees: *Fig* is an Antiguan name for bananas.

Betty's Hope (© 268/462-1469), a picturesque ruin just outside the village of Pares on the eastbound route to Long Bay, was Antigua's first sugar plantation (from 1650). You can tour it Tuesday to Saturday from 10am to 4pm (US$2/£1.05 for adults, free for children). Exhibits in the visitor's center trace the sugar era, and you can also see the full restoration of one of the original plantation's two windmills. If you visit, you may see the local masons, who are sporadically involved in the restoration of the curing and boiling plant, where sugar cane used to be processed into sugar, rum, and molasses.

Indian Town is one of Antigua's national parks, on the island's northeastern point. Over the centuries, Atlantic breakers have lashed the rocks and carved a natural bridge known as **Devil's Bridge.** It's surrounded by numerous blowholes spouting surf, a dramatic sight. An environmentally protected area, Indian Town Point lies at the tip of a deep cove, Indian Town Creek. The park fronts the Atlantic at Long Bay, just west of Indian Town Creek at the eastern side of Antigua. Birders flock here to see some 36 different species. The park is blanketed mainly by the acacia tree, a dry shrub locally known as "cassie." A large, meadowed headland around Devil's Bridge makes a great spot for a **picnic.** Arm yourself with directions and a good map before you start out. The main highway ends at Long Bay, but several **hiking trails** lead to the coastline. Our favorite hike is to Indian Town Point at a distance of 2km (1½ miles). This is the most scenic walk in the park, passing through a protected area of exceptional natural beauty. Long Bay is great for snorkeling, but you'll need to bring your gear.

7 Shopping

Most of Antigua's shops are clustered on **St. Mary's Street** or **High Street** in St. John's. Some stores are open Monday to Saturday from 8:30am to noon and 1 to 4pm, but this varies greatly from place to place—Antiguan shopkeepers are an independent lot. Many of them close at noon on Thursday.

Duty-free items include English woolens and linens. You can also purchase Antiguan goods: local pottery, straw work, rum, floppy foldable hats, shell curios, and hand-printed fabrics.

If you're in St. John's on a Saturday morning, visit the **fruit and vegetable market** at the south end of Market Street. The juicy Antiguan black pineapple alone is worth the trip.

One prime hunting ground in St. John's is the **Redcliffe Quay** waterfront on the southern edge of town, where nearly three-dozen boutiques are housed in former warehouses set around tree-shaded, landscaped courtyards. Our favorite is **A Thousand Flowers** (© 268/462-4264), which sells linens, all-natural fiber, rayon, and other fabrics.

At the **Gazebo** (© 268/460-2776), expect a little bit of everything, from a mass of south-of-the-border pottery to Indonesian wood items, and (our favorite) stunning blue-glaze plates. Additional Redcliffe Quay shops include **Isis** (© 268/462-4602) for unique Egyptian jewelry, cotton gowns, and handicrafts; and **The Goldsmitty** (© 268/462-4601), where precious stones are set in unique, exquisite creations of 14- and 18-karat gold.

Noreen Phillips, Redcliffe Quay (© 268/462-3127), is one of the island's major fashion outlets. Cruise-ship passengers beeline here for both casual wear and beaded glitzy dress clothes. **Exotic Antigua,** Radcliffe Quay, St. Mary's Street (© 268/562-1288), specializes in Caribbean-made gifts and clothing, including T-shirts and casual wear, and handicrafts.

At **Lipstick,** Heritage Quay (© 268/562-1133), you can browse a daunting array of cosmetics and perfumes, some of them locally made, many of the others imported from the U.S., Britain, and France. **Shoul's Chief Store,** St. Mary's Street at Market Street (© 268/462-1140), is an all-purpose department store selling fabric, appliances, souvenirs (more than 300 kinds), and general merchandise.

Heritage Quay, Antigua's first shopping-and-entertainment complex, features some 40 duty-free shops and an arcade for local artists and craftspeople. Its restaurants and food court offer a range of cuisines and views of St. John's Harbour. Many shops are open all day, Monday through Saturday.

At the foot of St. Mary's Street, stop in at **The Camera Shop** (© 268/562-4738), a Kodak distributor and photofinisher selling film and brand-name cameras. **Fashiondock** (© 268/462-9672) is known for its duty-free Prada, Moshino, and Gucci accessories, plus other Italian styles. **Sunseekers** (© 268/462-4523) carries the largest collection of duty-free swimwear in the Caribbean. **Colombian Emeralds** (© 268/462-2342) is the world's biggest retailer of these gemstones. **Albert's Jewelry** (© 268/462-3108) sells the best selection of watches on Antigua, plus china and crystal. Nick Maley, a makeup artist who worked on *Star Wars* and *The Empire Strikes Back,* founded **Island Arts,** upstairs at Heritage Quay (© 268/462-2787). You can purchase his own fine-art reproductions or browse through everything from low-cost prints to works by artists exhibited at the Museum of Modern Art in New York.

Rain Boutique, Lower St. Mary's (© 268/462-0118), sells casual clothes, formal wear, hats, scarves, shoes, jewelry, and handbags.

At Falmouth Harbour, **Seahorse Studios & Gift Shop** (© 268/469-1457) specializes in batiks, T-shirts, signs, and table linens. Their affiliated branch at English Harbour, **Seahorse Art Gallery** (© 268/469-1457), sells paintings, engravings, and watercolors, with lots of emphasis on seascapes.

The best for last: Head for **Harmony Hall** ⚔, in Brown's Bay Mill, near Freetown (© 268/460-4120), following the signs along the road to Freetown and Half Moon Bay. This restored 1843 plantation house and sugar mill overlooking Nonsuch Bay is ideal for a lunch stopover, a shopping expedition, even an overnight (see "Accommodations," earlier in this chapter). It displays an excellent selection of Caribbean arts and crafts. Lunch is served daily from noon to 3:30pm, featuring Green Island lobster, flying fish, and other specialties. Sunday is barbecue day.

8 Antigua After Dark

Antigua has some of the best steel bands in the Caribbean. Most nightlife revolves around the hotels. If you want to roam Antigua at night looking for that hot local club, arrange to have a taxi pick you up, so you're not stranded in the wilds somewhere.

The best gambling joint on island is **Grand Princess Casino,** Jolly Harbour (© 268/562-9900), spread across three floors, offering a lot more than gambling. You can dine in the first-class Bellagio Restaurant, patronize an Internet cafe, get down in a dance club, enjoy flashy Las Vegas entertainment in a lounge, or even work out at the rooftop fitness center. The most glamorous place to go is the **St. James's Club** at Mamora Bay (© 268/460-5000), which has the island's most flamboyant gambling palace. Other action is found at **King's Casino** on Heritage Quay (© 268/462-1727), the only casino in St. John's proper. Entrance is free and no ID is required. You must be 18 to play.

Steel bands, limbo dancers, calypso singers, folkloric groups—there's always something happening by night on Antigua. Your hotel can probably tell you where to go on any given night. The following clubs are reliable hot spots.

The best place to be on island on Sunday afternoon is **Shirley Heights Lookout** at Shirley Heights (© 268/460-1785). Beginning at 4pm, a barbecue is offered here, followed by a reggae and steel-pan band for dancing later in the evening. Celebrities such as Chuck Norris and Whitney Houston have joined in the fun. Many locals arrive on any late afternoon, grab a sundowner, and head for the patio in the rear to watch Antigua's most spectacular sunset. Sunday's EC$15 (US$5.55/£3) cover charge includes the first drink.

18 Carat, Lower Church St., St. John's (© 268/562-1858), opened in 2002 and rose instantly to the status of most popular and sought-after dance club and night bar on the island. Expect a cover charge, ranging from EC$10 to EC$20 (US$3.70–US$7.40/£2–£4) per person, an indoor-outdoor format that's open to a view of the night air of downtown St. John's, and a barrage of music that includes lots of reggae and soca. It's open Friday to Sunday 8pm to 1am.

Stop in at the **Bay House,** Tradewinds Hotel, Marble Hill (© 268/462-1223) for the island's best mix of singles (both straight and—to a much lesser degree—gay). **Lashings,** Runaway Bay (© 268/462-4438), is the hangout of local cricketers, and always attracts a fun-loving bevy of patrons who dance the night away after ordering Tex-Mex fare.

Live nightly entertainment takes place right on the beach at **Millers by the Sea,** at Runaway Beach (© 268/462-9414). Its happy hour is the best in town.

At English Harbour, action centers on the **Admiral's Inn** (© 268/460-1027), a barefoot-friendly kind of place. You can always play a game of darts and there's live music Thursday and Saturday nights, usually a local 14-piece steel band. Try one of Norman's daiquiris (the island's best), and ask the bartender about the famous guests he's served, from Richard Burton to Prince Charles. Another much-frequented English Harbour watering hole is **The Life Bar,** Nelson's Dockyard, VHF #68 (© 268/562-2353), the most popular spot for visitors arriving aboard yachts. We like its nautical atmosphere and the wooden pier that the action centers on. On occasion, it's West Indian party time, with live groups performing. The most authentic British pub at Nelson's Dockyard is **Mainbrace** (© 268/460-1058), with darts, of course, and fish and chips, and on some nights live jazz. The pub is part of The Copper and Lumber Store Hotel (see "Accommodations," earlier in this chapter).

9 Barbuda

Barbuda is part of the independent nation of Antigua and Barbuda. It's the Caribbean's last frontier, even though it is home to two of the region's most expensive and exclusive resorts. (See below for a review of the K-Club. The other property is the Coco Point Beach Resort, which we don't recommend because we think it has an exclusive, snobby atmosphere.) Charted by Columbus in 1493, the island is 42km (26 miles) north of Antigua. Twenty-four kilometers (15 miles) long by 8km (5 miles) wide, it has a population of only 1,200 hardy souls, most of whom live around the unattractive village of Codrington. There's no lush tropical scenery, no paved roads, few hotels, and only a handful of restaurants.

So what's the attraction? The island's 27km (17 miles) of pink- and white-sand beaches—almost like those of Bermuda. (We prefer the sands north of Palmetto Point.) Barrier reefs protect the island and keep most of the waters tranquil. Beaches on the southwestern shore stretch uninterrupted for 15km (10 miles); these are the best for swimming. The beaches on the island's eastern shore fronting the Atlantic are somewhat rougher, but they're good for beachcombing and shell collecting. The temperature seldom falls below the average of 75°F (24°C).

Visitors gravitate to Barbuda to see fallow deer, guinea fowl, pigeons, and wild pigs. Anglers can also negotiate with small-boat owners to fish for bonefish and tarpon.

Day visitors usually head for **Wa'Omoni Beach Park** to visit the frigate bird sanctuary, snorkel for lobster, and eat barbecue. The frigate bird sanctuary is one of the world's largest and a very impressive sight. You can see the birds, *Fregata magnificens,* sitting on their eggs in the mangrove bushes, which stretch for miles in a long lagoon accessible only by small motorboat. Various hotels and resorts on Antigua arrange tours to the sanctuary. The island attracts about 150 other species of birds, including pelicans, herons, and tropical mockingbirds.

While you're here, look into the **"Dividing Wall,"** which once separated the imperial Codrington family from the African islanders. Also visit the **Martello Tower,** which predates the known history of the island. Purportedly the Spanish erected it before the British occupied the island. Several tours explore interesting **underground caves** on Barbuda. Stamp collectors might want to stop in at the **Philatelic Bureau** in Codrington (no phone).

ESSENTIALS

GETTING THERE The island is a 15-minute flight from Antigua's Byrd Airport. Barbuda has two airfields: one at Codrington and the other a private facility, the Coco Point Airstrip, which is some 13km (8 miles) from Codrington at the Coco Point Lodge.

To reach Barbuda from Antigua, you can contact **Carib Aviation** (✆ **268/462-3147**), a carrier loosely associated with LIAT, the national airline of Antigua and Barbuda. It operates two daily flights from Antigua's Byrd Airport to Barbuda's Codrington Airport. Planes hold 19 passengers each for a ride that takes between 15 and 20 minutes one-way. Round-trip passage costs from EC$188 (US$70/£38) per person, depending on restrictions.

GETTING AROUND Many locals rent small four-wheel-drive Suzukis, which are the best way to get around the island. They meet incoming flights at Codrington Airport, and prices are negotiable. You'll need an Antiguan driver's license (p. 76) if you plan to drive.

ACCOMMODATIONS & DINING

The Beach House ✸✸✸ *Finds* This is the perfect sanctuary, an idyllic retreat from an overcrowded world. Opening onto a 29km (18-mile) arc of pink sand, laced with crushed pink coral, this is the place to take Nicole Kidman (or Tom Cruise, depending on your taste) for an off-the-record weekend. With a minimalist decor and generous use of white, this is a superstylish house, with purple heartwood floors and white Italian cotton slipcovers used throughout. A night sleeping in one of the four-posters, with their silky Italian sheets, is bliss. Bedrooms are spacious and inviting, each with a sumptuous bathroom with tub and shower. At times the bedrooms are so pure and white they are almost hospital antiseptic. The unobtrusive staff, the island's best, doesn't bother you unless you need something, and then they seem to materialize from nowhere. Sightseeing tours of the island can be arranged, including a visit to the frigate bird sanctuary or to caves and blue lagoons.

Many guests prefer to dine on a terrace covered by sailcloth, the tables overlooking the water. The dishes are a perfect blend of Caribbean and Mediterranean, featuring freshly caught, local fish.

Palmetto Point, Barbuda, Antigua, W.I. ✆ **888/776-0333** in the U.S., or 631/537-1352. www.thebeachbarbuda.com. 21 units. Winter US$1,020 (£530) junior suite, US$1,264 (£657) 1-bedroom suite; off season US$750–US$795 (£390–£413) junior suite, US$975–US$995 (£507–£517) 1-bedroom suite. Rates include breakfast. AE, MC, V. **Amenities:** Restaurant; bar; outdoor pool; spa; scuba diving; horseback riding; 24-hr. room service; laundry service. *In room:* A/C.

K-Club ✸✸ The most costly hotel to open in the Caribbean in recent years, the beachfront K-Club brings a chic Italian panache to one of the most far-flung backwaters of the Antilles. The resort opened in 1990, when a planeload of glitterati headed for Barbuda en masse. The K-Club is the "temple in the desert" of Italy's Krizia Mariuccia Mandelli, whose sports and evening wear empire has grossed a fortune. On site is a boutique stocked with the designer's latest fashions. The resort is set on more than 80 hectares (200 acres), adjacent to the Beach House (see above). Conceived by Italian architect Gianni Gamondi, the cottages and main clubhouse have roofs supported by a forest of white columns. Accommodations come in a huge range of styles and shapes; a hip island vibe predominates throughout. The Caribbean rattan furnishings include sumptuous beds. Bathrooms have two sinks, a bidet and adjacent shower, and a basket of deluxe toiletries. Rooms also have plenty of space for luggage.

The cuisine is Mediterranean, with an emphasis on Italian specialties and fresh pasta. The chef passionately believes in fresh ingredients, and his food is not only the finest on Barbuda but also tops anything on Antigua.

Barbuda, Antigua, W.I. © 268/460-0304. Fax 268/460-0305. www.kclubbarbuda.com. 29 units. Winter US$1,400 (£728) cottage for 2, US$2,000 (£1,040) suite, US$3,300 (£1,716) villa; off season US$950 (£494) cottage for 2, US$1,400 (£728) suite, US$2,400 (£1,248) villa. Rates include all meals, but no drinks. AE, DC, MC, V. Closed Sept to mid-Nov. No children under 12. **Amenities:** Restaurant; bar; outdoor pool; 2 tennis courts; wellness center; Jacuzzi; deep-sea fishing; snorkeling; Sunfish sailing; water-skiing; windsurfing; transportation from Codrington Airport; limited room service; massage; laundry service; dry cleaning. *In room:* A/C, ceiling fan, TV, dataport, minibar, fridge, beverage maker, hair dryer, safe.

10 Montserrat

Adventurous or eco-minded visitors are returning to the partially destroyed island of Montserrat. Known as "the Emerald Isle of the Caribbean," partly because of its verdant vegetation and partly because of its historic links to Ireland, Montserrat is 19km (12 miles) long and 11km (6¾ miles) wide, about the size of Manhattan. Two-thirds of the population of 12,000 had to be evacuated in 1995 and 1996 after the island's volcano, Chance's Peak, blew its top, smothering the southern two-thirds of the island with pyroclastic flows of hot gases and boiling hot ash, sometimes traveling downhill at hurricane velocity. In the aftermath, much of the island's southern tier—including the island's only airport—was burnt, buried, or rendered uninhabitable.

Although the biggest blast occurred on June 25, 1997, Mount Chance and other peaks in the Soufrière Hills had been rumbling for generations. Since the explosions, only about one-third of the original population has stayed on island, the others having been evacuated, or emigrating of their own volition, to the U.K. or, less frequently, to such neighboring islands as Antigua. Today, thanks to enormous investment of time and energy from local and international geologists, the path of future pyroclastic flows can more or less be predicted. That has allowed tourism to return to the island, albeit in very small volumes. In fact, the volcanic eruptions have defined Montserrat as one of the most haunting natural and geological spectacles in the Caribbean.

The last major eruption occurred on July 12, 2003, when almost two-thirds of the Soufrière Hills volcanic dome collapsed, sending ash and rocky debris as much as 50,000 feet into the sky over Montserrat. In the aftermath, some islanders found themselves shoveling 5-foot "drifts" of volcanic debris off their verandas and out from the bottom of their swimming pools. Today, a visit to Montserrat can solicit hundreds of stories about heroism, endurance, sacrifice, and backbreaking labor.

Since the destruction of Plymouth, the island's historic and once-charming capital, Montserrat's new commercial center and gerrymandered capital is a rapidly growing strip of land between Brades and Little Bay, on the island's north coast. Overall, you'll get the sense of a small community galvanized into new forms of self-reliance and cooperation, with lots of emphasis on somewhat gritty business-related visits from construction crews and British and international relief agencies.

Pear-shaped and mountainous, and most definitely volcanic in origin, Montserrat lies 43km (27 miles) southwest of Antigua, about midway between Nevis and Guadeloupe. Before the volcanic eruptions, Montserrat was known as the place where such musicians as Elton John, Paul McCartney, Sting, and Stevie Wonder had studios. They, along with much of the rest of Montserrat's glitterati, moved long ago to safer, and more convenient, sites.

English is the island's official language, although it's spoken with a faint Irish brogue, a holdover from the island's early Irish settlers. The Eastern Caribbean dollar is the official unit of currency, although U.S. dollars are widely accepted. By international agreement each EC dollar is permanently fixed—at the time of this writing—at 37¢ (20p). There is no local representative of American Express (you'll have to go to Antigua for that), but the island's biggest and most comprehensive travel agency is **Runaway Travel,** P.O. Box 54, Sweeneys, Montserrat, B.W.I. (© **664/491-2800**). They'll arrange access to Federal Express shipments, sell a limited roster of airline tickets, and perform a limited array of financial services, including foreign exchange.

A valid passport is required for everyone.

ESSENTIALS

INFORMATION   Contact the **Montserrat Tourist Board,** 7 Farara Plaza, Brades, Montserrat, B.W.I. (© **664/491-2230;** www.visitmontserrat.com). For up-to-the-minute information specifically related to the island's volcanic activity, check out www.mvo.ms.

GETTING THERE   Montserrat is most easily reached from Antigua. The $20 million Gerald's Airport opened in 2005 near a hamlet on the north side of the island. **Winair** (© **664/491-2362** or 664/491-2533; www.fly-winair.com) wings in several times daily on the 20-minute flight from Antigua, using 19-seat Twin Otters.

Less expensive are the ferryboats that depart twice a day, every Monday to Saturday, from Antigua, carrying passengers who pay between EC$140 to EC$200 (US$52–US$74/£28–£40) round-trip each, depending on the day of the week they travel. In most cases, their departure point is Heritage Quay in St. John's, although whenever that port is clogged because of cruise-ship activities, they'll depart from Deepwater Harbour, a very short walk from Heritage Quay. It takes about an hour to reach Montserrat's Little Bay. One-way ferryboat passage costs EC$102 (US$38/£20) per person. There is a departure tax of US$21 (£11) per person leaving Montserrat.

Ferryboat seats don't require advance bookings.

GETTING AROUND   **By Taxi & Bus**   Although the island has about 25km (15 miles) of surfaced roads, most of the island's vehicular traffic is limited to the route between Jack Boy Hill, on the island's northeasterly tip, and the village of Fleming, incorporating the island's heliport and most points within the designated "northern safety zone" en route. The typical taxi fare from the heliport to any of the hotels in the northern tier, including Tropical Mansion Suites and the Vue Pointe Lodge, ranges from EC$20 to EC$60 (US$7.40–US$22/£4–£12). Sightseeing tours in a local taxi, when viable, cost between EC$80 to EC$120 (US$30–US$44/£16–£24) per hour, depending on how many hours you want to spend touring.

The only regular **buses** are those running from Salem near the island's southernmost tip to Lookout on the island's northern end, passing through hamlets that include Brades, Sweeney's, and St. John's en route. Sweeney's is the site of a newly built, government-funded residential community on the island's northern tip. The fare is EC$2 (75¢/40p) between any two points along this route. Don't expect the conventional buses you find in large North American cities. These are usually 15-seater minivans, each individually painted. If you want the bus to make a reasonable detour from the designated route, the driver will usually do it for an additional, negotiable fee, pending the approval of the other passengers.

By Rental Car   None of the major U.S.-based car-rental companies operates on Montserrat, although you can find a handful of privately owned agencies. You are required to buy a local Montserrat driver's license for EC$50 (US$19/£10), which should accompany your own valid license. Rarely are these available directly from the rental agency. More often you'll need to purchase a license from the immigration office at either the heliport or the ferryboat terminal, or from the island's **Police Traffic Department** in Salem (© **664/491-2555**), which is open 24 hours a day.

Most island car-rental agencies stock a battered roster of Toyota Corollas, Toyota RAV4s, Suzuki jeeps, or Mazdas, which rent for EC$120 (US$44/£24) and up a day, or from EC$575 (US$213/£115) per week, depending on their make and model, and the duration of your rental. A collision-damage waiver costs from EC$24 to EC$30 (US$8.90–US$11/£4.80–£6) per day. Even if you buy it, you'll still be liable for the cost of some of the repairs to your vehicle if you damage it, for any reason, during your tenure.

Be-Beeps Car Rentals (© **664/491-3787**) is in the hamlet of Olveston, near Salem, close to the Vue Pointe Hotel, recommended below. **M.S. Osborne,** Brades (© **664/491-2494**) has a virtual monopoly on supplying most of the Nissans and Suzukis, including some SUVs, on the island.

Before you begin driving here, be aware: You must drive on the left and you should be careful of the steep, winding roads, which can be treacherous. In addition, volcanic ash on the roads can make for slippery driving conditions.

ACCOMMODATIONS

Accommodations are extremely limited. The island's finest accommodations are in the **Vue Pointe Hotel,** Old Road Bay (© **664/491-5210;** fax 664/491-4813; www.vue pointe.com) in the hamlet of Old Towne. In 2003, after the Herculean effort of hauling away 2,500 truckloads of volcanic debris, the freshly repainted hotel opened for business. Once loaded with sun-loving tourists, it has, since the crisis, evolved into the island's premier lodging for scientists and volcanologists. With tennis courts, a restaurant and bar, an outdoor pool, salon, library, gift shop, and a brightly painted collection of cottages that dot the verdant hillside that rolls gently downhill to the sea, it's a charming and pleasant place that has become especially cost-effective since its owners, Carol and Cedric Osborne, lowered their rates for doubles to US$119 (£62) for units without kitchens and US$120 (£62) for units with kitchens. MasterCard and Visa are accepted.

Vue Pointe's direct competitor, catering mostly to business travelers, is the well-conceived **Tropical Mansions Suites** (© **664/491-8767;** fax 664/491-8275; www.tropical mansion.com), within the hamlet of Sweeney's and with its own outdoor pool and restaurant. At this 18-room motel, a double room with breakfast included costs US$119 to US$150 (£62–£78) per night. MasterCard and Visa are accepted.

Grand View Bed & Breakfast ✯ *Value*, Baker Hill (© **664/491-2284**; fax 664/ 491-6876; www.grandviewmni.com), is for those who like a homelike place to stay with one of the island's best hosts, Theresa Silcott, who will also prepare you a great dinner if you make a reservation. Overlooking Little Bay, the B&B has 6 units (including 3 suites), which are simple but well maintained and comfortable. In lieu of air conditioning, you get fresh mountain air. Each of these spacious rooms come with TV and phone. Ham radio enthusiasts stay here, enjoying the flat roof which is ideal for antennae. Double rooms with private bath cost US$90 (£47), with suites going for US$120 (£62) during the day. Theresa not only tends to her guests but tends to her botanical herb garden as well.

RENTING A HOUSE ON MONTSERRAT

Montserrat real estate, thanks to the recent volcanic explosions, has disappointed more real estate investors than virtually any other island in the Caribbean. But what that means for you is now you can select from a pool of affordable buildings (at least 100) of all sizes, shapes, and degrees of comfort and maintenance that can be rented for anywhere from a few days to a season or more. We firmly believe that if you're tempted to rent a house for a Caribbean holiday, you should stay for the first time on island within a conventional hotel, and then—for a second- or third-time holiday—consider renting from a reputable agent. Three of the best agencies include **West Indies Real Estate, Ltd.,** P.O. Box 355, Brades (© **664/491-8666;** fax 664/491-8668; www. wirealest.com); **Trade Winds Real Estate,** P.O. Box 365, Olveston (© **664/491-2004;** fax 664/491-6229; www.tradewindsmontserrat.com); and **Montserrat Enterprises, Ltd.,** P.O. Box 58, Old Towne (© **664/491-2431;** fax 664/491-4660; www.montserrat enterprises.com).

DINING

JJ's Cuisine CARIBBEAN   Dominica-born Zephrina Jnofinn owns and operates this popular restaurant, in a building that's within a 5-minute drive from the airport. Inside the simple dining room you can order lobster, a worthy version of mountain chicken (frogs' legs) sautéed in garlic and butter, sandwiches, and excellent burgers that Zephrina concocts herself with a few secret ingredients.

St. John's Main Rd., Sweeney's Center. © **664/491-9024.** Reservations required. Burgers and sandwiches EC$6.50– EC$15 (US$2.40–US$5.55/£1.30–£3); platters EC$18–EC$65 (US$6.65–US$24/£3.60–£13). No credit cards. Mon–Sat 8am–midnight.

Oriel Café CARIBBEAN   The cafe shares the white-and-green building it occupies with the island's tourist board and several other government entities. Opened in 2003, it serves casual fare, such as sandwiches, salads, and burgers, plus pork chop platters, grilled fish, and steaks, and daily specials. Gregarious and friendly, the restaurant employs a hardworking staff whose uniforms match the coloring (yellow and black) of Montserrat's national bird, the Oriel.

Brades Main Rd. © **664/491-7144.** Reservations required. Main courses EC$13–EC$18 (US$4.80–US$6.65/ £2.60–£3.60) at lunch, EC$21–EC$27 (US$7.75–US$10/£4.20–£5.40) at dinner. No credit cards. Daily 7am–8pm.

Restaurant at Vue Pointe Hotel ✯ CARIBBEAN   This restaurant serves the island's best food. Freshly caught seafood is a specialty. Expect well-prepared cuisine supervised by the creative and hardworking owners, Carol and Cedric Osborne, and served by a young staff of enthusiastic trainees. Dishes include chicken, steak, fresh fish, suckling pig, and salads.

⟨Tips⟩ Beaches

Montserrat isn't known for its white-sand beaches. Most of its beaches have black volcanic sand, and they lie on the northern rim of the island, the part not threatened by volcanic activity. And many observers have noted that the beaches have actually improved, becoming bigger, sandier, and wider since the volcano deposited millions of tons of sand, ash, and debris upon them. The best beach on the island—and the only one with white sand—is **Rendezvous Bay**, which is only accessible via water taxis that depart from both Little Bay and the nearly adjacent Carr's Bay, or after a half-hour's hike. If you want to walk, the routes to Rendezvous Bay are especially convenient from either Little Bay or from the hamlet of Drummond's, adjacent to the airport. More readily accessible but less popular and hotter on bare feet are the dark-sand (a slate-gray color) beaches at **Carr's Bay, Woodlands Beach, Lime Kiln Bay, Little Bay** (near the arrival of the ferryboats from Antigua), and **Bunkum Bay**. The staff at **Tropical Mansions Suites** (✆ 664/491-8767) or the **Vue Pointe Hotel** (✆ 664/491-5210) can arrange day sails to these beaches.

At Vue Pointe Hotel, Old Road Bay. ✆ 664/491-5210. Reservations required for dinner. Main courses EC$27–EC$75 (US$10–US$28/£5.40–£15). MC, V. Daily noon–2:30pm and 7–9pm.

Tina's Restaurant CARIBBEAN   Set within a green-and-white Antillean house, this place is less than a 5-minute drive uphill from the ferryboat terminal. Tina Farrell established it in 1998 after she was evacuated from her home on Montserrat's southern tier. Expect a cozy, down-home Caribbean feel, with savory portions of chicken or beef, as well as grilled-chicken salads or lobster salads, and whatever fresh fish was hauled in by local fishermen that day.

Brades Main Rd. ✆ 664/491-3538. Reservations recommended. Lunch main courses EC$20–EC$25 (US$7.40–US$9.25/£4–£5); set lunch menu EC$45 (US$17/£9); set dinner menu and dinner main courses EC$45–EC$65 (US$17–US$24/£9–£13). MC, V. Mon–Sat 8am–midnight.

AROUND THE ISLAND

SCUBA DIVING   Montserrat offers 30 excellent dive sites, each with a rich assortment of marine life, including spotted drums and copper sweepers, and perhaps a large sea turtle. At the rim of the island's marine shelf, where relatively shallow waters suddenly drop off to great depths, divers can plunge into 21m-deep (69-ft.) waters to see mammoth sponges along with large star and brain coral reefs. Bryan Cunningham and his lovely wife, Tish, own the **SeaWolf Diving School** (✆ 664/496-7807; www.seawolfdivingschool.com). One-tank dives cost US$55 (£29), two-tank dives cost US$88 (£46), and night dives cost US$60 (£31). Snorkeling equipment can be rented for US$10 (£5.20).

SIGHTS   An active volcano can itself be a point of interest. The **Soufrière Hills Volcano** in the still-restricted southern part of the island is eerily fascinating, but by no means should any novice visitor to Montserrat venture into this region without a trained guide. Armed with clear instructions from geologists about where and where *not* to visit, taxi drivers and tour operators (see below) can sometimes show you the island's southern tier, but conditions, of course, are subject to change at any moment.

You can see mudslides, layers of volcanic ash, and from a safe distance, the ghostly remains of the partially destroyed former capital of Plymouth. (The only deaths suffered during the island's volcanic explosions occurred on June 25, 1997, when 19 people were farming in an area that had been declared an exclusion zone.)

The government discourages anyone from remaining within the southern two-thirds of the island from 6pm until 6am the following day, and some areas, including the former capital of Plymouth, are completely off-limits. Not only does the southern zone lack electricity and running water, but the government also wishes to prevent squatters from settling on land abandoned by the many homeowners who evacuated the island.

A good place to learn about the volcanic catastrophe is the **Montserrat Volcano Observatory** ✛ (© **664/491-5647;** www.mvo.ms), which is in Flemings, above the village of Salem, on the island's north coast. The observatory is about a 25-minute drive from the ferry terminal and about a 30-minute drive from the airport. Depending on how busy the staff is recording seismic phenomena on the day of your arrival, tours may or may not be available. No reservations are necessary, and the cost is EC$10 (US$3.70/£2) per person. The tour consists of a 30-minute talk about the observatory's goals and objectives, and an introduction to its activity over the past few years. There's an opportunity to look at a number of informative exhibits, including the instruments that constantly monitor the volcano's pulse and power.

TOURS   One of the best tour operators, and especially appealing if you're based in Antigua, is **Jenny's Montserrat Day Tours** (© **268/461-9361** in Antigua, no local phone in Montserrat). Operated by Montserrat native Jennifer Burke from a base in Antigua, it charges around US$130 (£68) per person, depending on the day of the week. Advance reservations are necessary and there are no tours on Sunday. Tours begin and end at the Deep Water Harbor at St. John's in Antigua. The price includes ferryboat transit to Montserrat, breakfast and lunch, and a detailed tour of between 6 and 7 hours, with English-language commentary from a trained guide and driver.

Aruba

The most popular island in the Dutch Caribbean, Aruba draws droves of visitors, from honeymooners and sun worshippers to snorkelers, sailors, and weekend gamblers. When you lie back along the 11km (6¾-mile) stretch of white-sand beach, you can enjoy an average 82°F (28°C) daytime temperature, trade winds, and very low humidity. Moreover, peddlers won't harass you, the island is relatively safe, and you won't feel racial tensions.

Don't come for local culture and history—you're here to enjoy fantastic sandy Palm Beach, one of the best beaches in the world, and evenings of dining and drinking, moonlit strolls, and gambling in the glittery casinos. The main resort area is a row of comfortable but familiar high-rise hotels along a gorgeous shoreline, like a beach strip in Florida.

The smallest of the ABC Islands (Aruba, Bonaire, and Curaçao), Aruba is 32km (20 miles) long and 10km (6¼ miles) wide, with a landmass of 298 sq. km (116 sq. miles). Its coastline on the leeward side is smooth and serene, with white-sand beaches; but on the eastern coast, the windward Atlantic side, it looks rugged and wild. Dry and sunny almost year-round, Aruba has clean, exhilarating air, like in the desert of Palm Springs, California. Forget lush vegetation. Aruba lies outside the hurricane belt and gets less rain than virtually any other popular island in the Caribbean.

Though it is still a Dutch protectorate, Aruba became a nation unto itself in 1986. Some visitors have called Oranjestad, Aruba's capital, a "Holland-meets-Disney fantasia" because of its step-gabled Dutch architecture painted with a Caribbean palette of bright pastels. With more than a dozen resort hotels populating its once-uninhabited beaches, it is now one of the Caribbean's most popular destinations. A post-millenium moratorium on hotel construction, however, has halted the building of new resorts—so for now, Aruba remains safe from rampant overdeveloping.

1 Essentials

VISITOR INFORMATION

Before you leave home, contact the **Aruba Tourism Authority** at the following locations: 1200 Harbor Blvd., Weehawken, NJ 07086 (© **201/330-0800;** fax 201/330-8757; ata.newjersey@aruba.com); One Financial Plaza, Suite 2508, Fort Lauderdale, FL 33394 (© **954/767-6477;** fax 954/767-0432); 10655 Six Pines Dr., Suite 145, Woodland, TX 77380 (© **281/362-1616;** fax 281/362-1644); and in the U.K., The Copperfields, 25 Copperfield St., London SE1 0EN (© **020/7928-1600;** fax 020/7928-1700; geoff@saltmarshpr.co.uk).

Information is available on the Web at **www.aruba.com** or by calling © **800/ TOARUBA.**

Once on the island, you can go to the **Aruba Tourism Authority** at L. G. Smith Blvd. 172, Oranjestad (© 297/582-3777), for information.

GETTING THERE

Before you book your flight, read "Packages for the Independent Traveler" in chapter 2—it could save you a bundle. Even if you don't book a package, you should check that chapter's tips on finding the best airfare.

On **American Airlines** (© 800/433-7300 in the U.S. and Canada; www.aa.com), Aruba-bound passengers can catch a daily nonstop 4½-hour flight from New York's JFK Airport. American also flies nonstop from Boston, Miami, and San Juan, Puerto Rico. American has lots of great-value packages to Aruba, as well, including a selection of several resorts. Ask for the tour department, or talk to a travel agent.

US Airways (© 800/428-4322 in the U.S. and Canada; www.usairways.com) flies nonstop from Charlotte, North Carolina, and Philadelphia several days a week.

Continental Airlines (© 800/231-0856 in the U.S. and Canada; www.continental.com) flies to Aruba via nonstop flights from Newark, New Jersey, and also from Houston three times a week.

United Airlines (© 800/864-8331 in the U.S. and Canada; www.united.com) has daily service from Chicago.

Delta (© 800/221-1212 in the U.S. and Canada; www.delta.com) flies to Aruba from its hub in Atlanta, taking 4¾ hours. The airline also offers Saturday-only flights from New York's JFK Airport.

Air Canada (© 888/247-2262 in the U.S. and Canada; www.aircanada.com) has connections from Quebec City and Toronto to Aruba.

GETTING AROUND

BY RENTAL CAR   It's easy to rent a car in Aruba. Excellent roads connect major tourist attractions, and all the major rental companies accept valid U.S. or Canadian driver's licenses. Major U.S. car-rental companies maintain offices on Aruba at the airport and at major hotels. No taxes are imposed on car rentals on Aruba, but insurance can be tricky. Even when you purchase a collision-damage waiver, you are still responsible for the first $300 to $500 (£156–£260) worth of damage. (Avis doesn't even offer this waiver. In the event of an accident, you would be liable for up to the full value of damage to your car unless you have private insurance.) Rental rates range between $40 and $90 (£21–£47) per day.

Try **Budget Rent-a-Car,** at Queen Beatrix Airport (© 800/527-0700 in the U.S. and Canada, or 297/58-28600; www.budget.com); **Hertz,** Sabana Blanca 35 (© 800/654-3131 in the U.S. and Canada, or 297/58-21845; www.hertz.com); **Thrifty Car Rental,** L. G. Smith Blvd. 9 (© 800/847-4389 in the U.S. and Canada, or 297/58-35600; www.thrifty.com); and **Avis,** Queen Beatrix Airport (© 800/331-1212 in

---

⌜Fun Fact **Carnival**

Many visitors come here for the annual pre-Lenten Carnival, a month-long festival held in January, February, or March, with events day and night. The music, dancing, parades, costumes, and "jump-ups" (Caribbean hoedowns) make Carnival the highlight of Aruba's winter season. For more information, contact the tourist office.

Aruba

Map legend (top left):
- ✈ Airport
- Beach
- Cruise Ship Dock
- Lighthouse

LESSER ANTILLES
ARUBA
NETHERLANDS ANTILLES
Curaçao   Bonaire
VENEZUELA
0   200 mi
Caracas

Scale:
0   3 mi
0   3 km
N

**Map labels:**
California Point
California Lighthouse
1
Malmok Beach
Hadicurari (Fishermen's Huts)
2   2A
2B
4   3
5
Palm Beach
6
10
11   1A
12   1B
8   9
13
Eagle Beach
Manchebo Beach
14
Druif Beach
Alto Vista Chapel
Noord
3B
3A
2A   2B
4B
4A
6B
6A
Bushiribana
Natural Bridge
Caribbean Sea
15
Hooiberg
Santa Cruz
7B
7A
ARIKOK
Queen Beatrix Airport
16   1B
7A   7B
7A
Caves of Canashito
Spanish Lagoon
NATIONAL
Boca Prins Sand Dunes
Jamanota   PARK
Fontein Cave
Quadirikiri Cave
Savaneta
1B
7A
7B
1A
San Nicolas
Boca Grandi
Caribbean Sea
Rodger's Beach
Baby Beach
Seroe Colorado
Colorado Point

Hotel list (bottom left):
Amsterdam Manor Beach Resort **11**
Aruba Marriott Resort & Stellaris Casino **6**
Aruba Millenium Resort **9**
The Arubian Inn **13**
The Boardwalk Vacation Retreat **5**
Bucuti Beach Resort Aruba **14**
Coconut Inn **8**
Hyatt Regency Aruba Resort & Casino **10**
La Cabana All-Suites Beach Resort& Casino **12**
The Mill Resort & Suites **7**
Occidental Grand Aruba **3**
Radisson Aruba Resort & Casino **2**
Renaissance Aruba Beach Resort & Casino **15**
Tierra del Sol Aruba Resort Spa & Country Club **1**
The Vistalmar **16**
Westin Aruba Resort & Spa **4**

the U.S. and Canada, or 297/58-28617; www.avis.com). Car rentals are also available at **Dollar Rent-a-Car,** whose branch is at the Queen Beatrix Airport (© 800/800-4000 in the U.S. and Canada, or 297/58-30101; www.dollar.com). **National** (© 800/227-7368 in the U.S. and Canada; www.nationalcar.com) has branches at Oranjestad, Holiday Inn (© 297/58-63768), and at the Queen Beatrix Airport (© 297/58-25451).

BY BUS   Aruba has excellent bus service, with regular daily service from 6am to midnight. Round-trip fare between the beach hotels and Oranjestad is $2 (£1.05). Bus schedules are available at the **Arubus Office** at the central bus station on Zoutmanstraat. Your hotel reception desk will know when the buses pass by. Try to have the exact change. For schedules and information, call Arubus Co. (© **297/58-82300;** www.arubus.com).

BY TAXI   Taxis are unmetered but rates are fixed, so tell the driver your destination and ask the fare before you get in. The main office is near Palm Beach between Eagle Bowling Center and Taco Bell. A dispatch office is located at the Bosabao (② 297/ 58-22116). A ride from the airport to most of the hotels, including those at Palm Beach, costs about $22 (£11) per car, with a four-passenger maximum. Some locals don't tip, but we suggest you do, especially if the driver has helped you with luggage. On some parts of the island, it's next to impossible to locate a taxi and you'll have to call. If you're going to a remote location, it's a good idea to ask the driver to return for you at a certain time.

The English-speaking drivers are usually willing tour guides. Most seem well informed and eager to share their knowledge with you. A 1-hour tour (you don't need much more than that) costs from $40 (£21) for a maximum of four passengers.

BY MOTORCYCLE & MOPED   Because Aruba's roads are good and the terrain is flat, many visitors like to rent mopeds and motorcycles. You can find rentals at **Semver Cycle Rental,** Noord 22 (② 297/58-66851), where scooters begin at $28 (£15) per day.

FAST FACTS: Aruba

Banks   Banks are open Monday to Friday from 8am to noon and 1:30 to 4pm. The most centrally located bank is **Aruba Bank** at Caya Betico Croes 12 (② 297/ 58-21550). It's not hard to find an ATM (including one at the airport).

Currency   The currency is the **Aruba florin (AFl),** which is divided into 100 cents. Silver coins are in denominations of 5¢, 10¢, 25¢, and 50¢, and 1 and 2½ florins. The 50-cent piece, the square *yotin,* is Aruba's best-known coin. The exchange rate, fairly consistent over the years, was 1.77 AFl to US$1 (1 AFl is worth about US56¢). (Just before you leave home, you can check the current exchange rates on the Web at **www.xe.com**.) U.S. dollars, traveler's checks, and major credit cards are widely accepted on the island. *Unless otherwise specified, prices in this chapter are quoted in U.S. dollars and British pounds.*

Documents   To enter Aruba, U.S. and Canadian citizens and British subjects may submit a valid passport or an original birth certificate with an embossed seal, along with photo ID. We always recommend carrying your passport whenever you visit a foreign country.

Electricity   The electricity is 110-volt AC (60 cycles), the same as in the United States.

Emergencies   For the police or fire department, dial ② 911. In a medical emergency, dial ② 58-74300.

Hospital   For medical care, go to the **Horacio Oduber Hospital** on L. G. Smith Boulevard (② 58-74300; this is also the number to call in case of a medical emergency). This modern building near Eagle Beach has excellent medical facilities. Hotels also have medical doctors on call, and there are good dental facilities as well (appointments can be made through your hotel).

Language   The official language is Dutch, but nearly everybody speaks English. Spanish is also widely spoken, as is the local dialect, Papiamento.

Liquor Laws Liquor is sold on any day of the week throughout the island in most stores, including grocery stores and delis. By law (which doesn't seem to be strictly enforced), you can have an open container on the beach only if the liquor is purchased at one of the bars of the resort hotels lining the beachfront.

Safety Aruba is one of the Caribbean's safest destinations, in spite of its numerous hotels and casinos. Pickpockets and purse-snatchers are around, of course, but they're rare. Still, it's wise to guard your valuables. Never leave them unattended on the beach or even in a locked car. (See the box below for more on safety.)

Taxes & Service Charges The government of Aruba imposes a 6% room tax and a $36 (£19) airport departure tax. Your hotel will add a 15% to 20% service charge for room, food, and beverages.

Telephone To call Aruba from the United States, dial ℂ **011** (the international access code), then **297** (the country code for Aruba), then **58** (the area code) and the five-digit local number. If you're in Aruba, you have to dial **58** followed by the five-digit local number.

Time Aruba is on Atlantic Standard Time year-round; most of the year, Aruba is 1 hour ahead of Eastern Standard Time (when it's 10am in Aruba, it's 9am in New York). When daylight saving time is in effect in the United States, clocks in New York and Aruba show the same time.

Water The water, which comes from the world's second-largest desalination plant, is pure.

Weather The island lies far outside the hurricane belt, so there is no threat of tropical storms. The average annual temperature is 82°F (28°C).

2 Accommodations

Most of Aruba's hotels are bustling, self-contained resorts. There's a dearth of family or budget hotels. Guesthouses are also rare and tend to fill up early in winter with faithful return visitors.

In season, it's imperative to make reservations well in advance. Don't ever arrive expecting to find a room on the spot. You must give Immigration the address where you'll be staying when you arrive.

Don't forget to ask if the 6% room tax and 15% to 20% service charge (see above) are included in the rates quoted when you make your reservation.

Before you try to book your hotel on your own, read the section "Packages for the Independent Traveler," in chapter 2. Lots of the big resorts in Aruba are frequently featured in packages, which can bring their rates down dramatically.

In lieu of renting an actual house or villa, which you can do on some islands, your best bet here is to rent an apartment or condo. Amsterdam Manor Beach Resort (p. 111) is a good place for such rentals.

VERY EXPENSIVE

Aruba Marriott Resort & Stellaris Casino 🎁🎁 *(Kids)* Although it's no Hyatt (see below), this eight-story luxury high rise lies at a far extension of Palm Beach, forming a U around a large courtyard with lush landscaping. When you walk in, the waterfalls, streams, and fountains evoke a tropical garden. Known also for its casino and health spa, the hotel offers spacious and vividly decorated bedrooms, with large balconies opening onto prime views of the ocean. Each room is loaded with amenities, including a walk-in closet, dual sinks, and in-room movies.

Lunch can be poolside or else at Waves on the beach. La Vista offers Continental fare in a casual atmosphere. For more elegant dining, head for Tuscany's Ristorante, which has a northern Italian menu. The spa is state-of-the-art, with great massages and body wraps evocative of Indonesia.

L. G. Smith Blvd. 101, Palm Beach, Aruba. © **800/223-6388** in the U.S., or 297/58-69000. Fax 297/58-60649. www. marriott.com. 413 units. Winter $619–$700 (£322–£364) double, $769–$1,549 (£400–£805) suite; off season $209–$390 (£109–£203) double, $389–$569 (£202–£296) suite. AE, DC, MC, V. **Amenities:** 5 restaurants; 4 bars; outdoor pool; casino; 2 tennis courts; health club; deluxe Mandara Spa; Jacuzzi; sauna; dive shop; jet skis; kayaks; parasailing; sailing; snorkeling; water-skiing; children's programs; game room; room service; massage; babysitting; laundry service; dry cleaning; nonsmoking rooms; rooms for those w/limited mobility. *In room:* A/C, TV, minibar, beverage maker, hair dryer, iron, safe, Wi-Fi.

Hyatt Regency Aruba Resort & Casino 🏖🏖🏖 *(Kids)*

The most glamorous resort on Aruba—even more so than the Radisson (see below)—lies on 5 landscaped beachfront hectares (12 acres) 3km (2 miles) north of Oranjestad. Built in the early 1990s for more than $57 million, the nine-story resort offers a series of public rooms reminiscent of a large-scale Latin American hacienda. Its gardens, Aruba's finest, are dotted with waterfalls and reflecting pools. The bedrooms are luxurious, with many extras, including original artwork commissioned from around the Americas. The rooms are not as large, however, as those at the Marriott (see above). Extras include a king-size or two double beds, and big bathrooms with combo tub/showers and tile floors. Guests in the hotel's 18 Regency Club rooms enjoy a private concierge, upgraded linens, and other amenities.

In general, the Hyatt has better restaurants than any other hotel in Aruba. You can choose among four restaurants and lounges, including the lovely indoor/outdoor Ruinas del Mar restaurant, with Mediterranean food. The Casino Copacabana offers entertainment and gaming tables.

A $2.5-million multilevel pool complex and lagoon (with waterfalls, tropical gardens, and slides) is the showcase of the resort.

J. E. Irausquin Blvd. 85, Palm Beach, Aruba. © **800/233-1234** in the U.S. and Canada, or 297/58-61234. Fax 297/ 58-61682. www.hyatt.com. 360 units. Winter $545–$645 (£283–£335) double, $730–$2,230 (£380–£1,160) suite; off season $315–$375 (£164–£195) double, $570–$1,825 (£296–£949) suite. MAP (breakfast and dinner) $72 (£37) per person extra. AE, DC, DISC, MC, V. **Amenities:** 4 restaurants; 4 bars; ice-cream and coffee shop; 3-level outdoor pool/lagoon complex; casino; 2 lit tennis courts; health club; spa; Jacuzzi; canoes; dive shop; scuba diving; snorkeling; horseback riding; children's center and programs; game room; car rental; business center; room service; massage; babysitting; laundry service; dry cleaning; nonsmoking rooms; rooms for those w/limited mobility. *In room:* A/C, ceiling fan, TV, minibar, beverage maker, hair dryer, iron, safe.

Occidental Grand Aruba 🏖 *(Kids)*

Rising high above Palm Beach, this hotel, calls itself "a cruise ship on land." To stay at this all-inclusive is to feel part of an ongoing house party with a lot of action and organized activities. Guests have direct access to one of the island's best beaches. The hotel consists of a pair of nine-story interconnected towers in a landscaped garden with a lagoon-shaped swimming pool in the center. The well-managed resort attracts families, repeat guests, and international tour groups. The resort reopened in 2006 following massive renovations, and it's now better than ever in its history. Rooms are wide ranging but all feature elegant tile and marble floors with private balconies. All of the bathrooms are now state of the art, with a full tub-and-shower combo. The hotel also has one of the widest ranges of drinking and dining facilities on island, including Mexican, Pan-Asian, Caribbean fusion, and, our favorite, L'Olio, with a finely tuned Italian cuisine and an impressive wine list.

J. E. Irausquin Blvd. 83 (P.O. Box 218), Palm Beach, Aruba. ✆ **800/858-2258** in the U.S., or 297/58-64500. Fax 297/58-63191. www.occidentalhotels.com. 391 units. Winter $565–$875 (£294–£455) double, $875–$1,102 (£455–£573) suite; off season $450–$714 (£234–£371) double, $714–$944 (£371–£491) suite. Rates are all-inclusive. AE, MC, V. **Amenities:** 6 restaurants; deli; 6 bars (1 swim-up); outdoor pool; casino; 2 lit tennis courts; fitness center; Jacuzzi; boating; dive shop; snorkeling; windsurfing; children's club; drugstore; salon; room service; massage; babysitting; laundry service; dry cleaning; nonsmoking rooms. *In room:* A/C, minibar, hair dryer, iron, safe.

Radisson Aruba Resort & Casino ✦✦✦ *Kids*
One of the 10 most luxurious resorts in the southern Caribbean, this eight-floor hotel occupies 6 choice hectares (15 acres) along Palm Beach. Its high points are cascading waterfalls and the Aruba Tower, from whose rooms guests enjoy panoramic views of the Caribbean. Pampering sets the tone—everything from spacious balconies with teak patio furniture, full-size marble bathrooms with tub/shower combinations, to the most elaborate package of toiletries in the Caribbean. Spacious guest rooms are in a Colonial/West Indian style, with mahogany four-poster beds, oversize mirrors, and plantation shutters. The private accommodations here are even more stylishly inviting than those at Hyatt and Marriott, especially if you book the concierge floor, which has extra amenities.

J. E. Irausquin Blvd. 81, Palm Beach, Aruba. ✆ **800/333-3333** in the U.S., or 297/58-66555. Fax 297/58-63260. www.radisson.com. 358 units. Winter $460–$575 (£239–£299) double, $700–$900 (£364–£468) suite; off season $265–$430 (£138–£224) double, from $475 (£247) suite. AE, DC, DISC, MC, V. **Amenities:** 4 restaurants; 2 bars; 2 outdoor pools; casino; golf privileges; 2 tennis courts; fitness center; spa; canoes; dive shop; sailing; water-skiing; windsurfing; children's center; business center; room service; babysitting; laundry service; dry cleaning; rooms for those w/limited mobility. *In room:* A/C, TV, minibar, beverage maker, hair dryer, iron, safe, Wi-Fi.

Tierra del Sol Aruba Resort Spa & Country Club ✦✦
This is the number-one choice for golfers in the southern Caribbean. Luxurious villa living is combined with a state-of-the-art fitness center and spa on 240 hectares (590 acres) of landscaping that includes one of the Caribbean's best 18-hole golf courses, the creation of Robert Trent Jones, Jr. The vast complex sprawls across a cactus-studded landscape on the north coast, evocative of parts of Arizona. Your choices are two- or three-bedroom condos or free-standing villas that also come with two or three bedrooms, ideal for families or friends traveling together. A great deal of Aruba's "only planned community" is owned by second homers, so expect a widely varied decor. We have, however, found the furnishings tasteful and tropical, very Caribbean in their breezy motif. Rooms come with king-size and queen-size beds, or twins and private tiled bathrooms with tubs and showers. Accommodations open onto covered terraces with tables and chairs and a view of the golf course or ocean.

Malmokweg, Aruba. ✆ **800/992-2015** or 297/58-67800. Fax 297/58-64970. www.tierradelsol.com. 112 units. Winter $650 (£338) 2-bedroom condo, $765 (£398) 2-bedroom villa, $700 (£364) 3-bedroom condo, $895 (£465) 3-bedroom villa; off season $395 (£205) 2-bedroom condo, $425 (£221) 2-bedroom villa, $425 (£221) 3-bedroom condo, $525 (£273) 3-bedroom villa. AE, DISC, MC, V. **Amenities:** 2 restaurants; 3 bars; outdoor pool; golf; 2 tennis courts; fitness center; spa; business center. *In room:* A/C, TV, kitchen, washer/dryer, iron, safe.

Westin Aruba Resort & Spa ✦✦✦
The Wyndham has given way to the Westin people, and the upgrade and improvements are remarkable in this latest reincarnation. Built in 1975, the deluxe hotel has been renovated to such an extent that it's now among the leaders opening onto the sands of Palm Beach. Everything from body

wraps at its spa to windsurfing and scuba diving is offered here. The beautifully furnished bedrooms are spacious and tasteful in dark rattan and cherrywood, and the large bathrooms are among the best in Aruba, complete with tub/shower combos and even phones. The hotel rises 18 floors, each room opening onto a balcony. Among the many choices of restaurants, the most romantic is Azull where master chefs prepare gourmet four-course dinners with the finest market-fresh ingredients. Pago Pago is one of the best steakhouses on island. (Are you up for a 24-ounce rib-eye?) Cabaret Royale is one of the island's best night clubs, and Casablanca Casino is one of Aruba's liveliest and most dramatic in décor.

J.E. Irausquin Blvd. 77, Palm Beach, Aruba. © 877/822-2222 in the U.S. or 297/58-64466. Fax 297/58-68217. www.arubaresortspa.com. 478 units. Winter $419–$469 (£218–£244) double; off-season $259–$359 (£135–£187) double; year-round from $559 (£291) suite. AE, MC, V. **Amenities:** 7 restaurants; 4 bars; outdoor pool; casino; 2 tennis courts; health club; spa; watersports; children's program; car-rental desk; room service; babysitting; laundry service; dry cleaning; nonsmoking rooms; rooms for those w/limited mobility. *In room:* A/C, TV, minibar, coffeemaker, hair dryer, iron, safe, Wi-Fi.

EXPENSIVE

Bucuti Beach Resort Aruba ★★ *Finds*   At little three-story Bucuti, you get personal service, European charm, and lush landscaping on a lovely 6-hectare (15-acre) stretch of one of the Caribbean's best beaches, the most secluded part of Eagle Beach. What this hotel has that those above don't is intimacy, a personal approach to inn keeping, and a sense of seclusion. It's a top choice for honeymooners. Each spacious, well-furnished, bright bedroom is on the beach and has two queen-size beds or one king-size bed and sleeper sofa. The most expensive units have two queen-size beds and an oceanfront balcony or terrace. The oceanfront Tara Wing, with beautiful, elegant bedrooms and a first-class spa, opened in 2004. All rooms have well-maintained bathrooms with tub/shower combos.

Across from the Alhambra Bazaar and Casino, the hotel operates the oceanfront Pirates' Nest Restaurant, a replica of a 17th-century Dutch galleon that specializes in good steaks, fresh seafood, and theme nights.

Eagle Beach, Aruba. © 297/58-31100. Fax 297/58-25272. www.bucuti.com. 102 units. Winter $325–$365 (£169–£190) double, $420 (£218) bungalow or junior suite; off season $210–$240 (£109–£125) double, $295 (£153) bungalow or junior suite. MAP (breakfast and dinner) $33 (£17) per person extra. AE, DISC, MC, V. **Amenities:** Restaurant; 2 bars; outdoor pool; open-air health club; spa; tour desk; 24-hr. business center; babysitting; laundry service; coin-operated laundry; dry cleaning. *In room:* A/C, TV, minibar, fridge, beverage maker, hair dryer, iron, safe, microwave, Wi-Fi.

La Cabana All-Suite Beach Resort & Casino ★★ *Kids*   This is megaresort city. As one of the Caribbean's largest hotel complexes, La Cabana dwarfs anything else on the island. If an intimate West Indian inn is your dream, flee the premises. Otherwise join in the communal fun, which has been ongoing here since 1991. Couples of all ages and persuasions, honeymooners, and families with very active kids live harmoniously on acres of landscaped grounds in self-contained "villages" across the street from Eagle Beach. Spacious, well-furnished suites come in widely varied combinations, and range from studios for one or two adults, to one-, two-, or three-bedroom suites. Ground-floor rooms afford less privacy, and suites come with well-equipped kitchens, patios, or verandas.

J. E. Irausquin Blvd. 250, Oranjestad, Aruba. © 800/835-7193 in the U.S. or Canada, or 297/58-79000. Fax 297/58-78680. www.lacabanavillas.com. 811 units. Winter $379 (£197) studio, $399 (£207) 1-bedroom, $639 (£332) 2-bedroom, $959–$1,089 (£499–£566) 3-bedroom; off season $189–$289 (£98–£150) studio, $219–$319 (£114–£166)

1-bedroom, $349–$549 (£181–£285) 2-bedroom, $529–$799 (£275–£415) 3-bedroom. Children under 12 stay free in parent's room (limit 2). Various packages offered. AE, DC, MC, V. **Amenities:** 6 restaurants; 5 bars; 3 outdoor pools; casino; 5 tennis courts; health club; spa; children's center; business center; babysitting; coin-operated laundry; non-smoking rooms. *In room:* A/C, ceiling fan, TV, kitchenette, beverage maker, hair dryer, safe.

Renaissance Aruba Beach Resort & Casino 🌟🌟🌟 Unlike the properties reviewed above, the Renaissance is not on Palm Beach; however, it has a lot of other attractions. Located in the Seaport Village Complex, the island's largest shopping and entertainment facility, this sprawling, bustling place is two resorts in one. Next to two marinas and a recreational park, it's the only major resort at Oranjestad Harbor and the only resort on Aruba that has a 16-hectare (40-acre) private island, six beaches, and a round-the-clock casino. The first resort (with 290 units) is adjacent to the Sea-port Mall and has an outdoor pool and terrace. The second resort (with 251 one-bed-room suites) is a timeshare resort that caters to yachties; rooms are rented out when timeshare owners are not present. Each of the one-bedroom suites opens onto the beach. Each unit has a kitchenette, blond rattan furniture with floral pastel prints, and a small balcony, plush carpeting, and either a king- or two queen-size beds. Bathrooms offer deluxe toiletries and a tub/shower combo.

You have a choice of more than a dozen restaurants spread out between the hotel and the mall complex.

L. G. Smith Blvd. 82, Oranjestad, Aruba. © 800/421-8188 in the U.S. and Canada, or 297/58-36000. Fax 297/58-25317. www.marriott.com. 541 units in 2 resorts. Winter $285–$330 (£148–£172) double, from $415 (£216) suite; off season $191–$255 (£99–£133) double, from $310 (£161) suite. Extra person $50 (£26). Children 12 and under stay free in parent's room. Breakfast and dinner plans available. AE, DC, DISC, MC, V. **Amenities:** 4 restaurants; 4 bars; 2 outdoor pools; 2 casinos; tennis court; exercise room; spa; fishing; scuba diving; water-skiing; windsurfing; children's programs; room service; babysitting; laundry service; coin-operated laundry; nonsmoking rooms; rooms for those w/limited mobility. *In room:* A/C, TV, dataport, minibar, beverage maker, hair dryer, iron, safe, Wi-Fi.

MODERATE

Amsterdam Manor Beach Resort 🌟🌟 *(Kids)* Inspired by the canal-front row houses in Amsterdam, this hotel sports a Dutch gingerbread facade. In an arid land-scape across the street from Eagle Beach, where there's good snorkeling and swim-ming, it has a series of inner courtyards.

Even the accommodations are Dutch colonial in style, with pine furniture and country-rustic blues, soft reds, and greens. In some cases, high ceilings lead to gable-capped peaks. Both studios and one- or two-bedroom apartments have fully equipped kitchens. This is a good choice for families, with babysitting, use of washer/dryers, and a children's playground. Units are small but well maintained and inviting, with ceil-ing fans, balconies or terraces (often with a sea view), white-tile floors, and textured walls. The small bathrooms have tubs and showers.

J. E. Irausquin Blvd. 252 (P.O. Box 1302), Oranjestad, Aruba. © 800/932-6509 in the U.S., or 297/52-71100. Fax 297/52-71112. www.amsterdammanor.com. 72 units. Winter $235–$255 (£122–£133) studio, $325–$440 (£169–£229) suite; off season $149–$169 (£77–£88) studio, $209–$249 (£109–£129) suite. AE, DC, MC, V. **Amenities:** Restaurant; bar; outdoor pool; kiddie pool; fitness center; playground; concierge; car rental; business center; laundry service; coin-operated laundry; dry cleaning; nonsmoking rooms; rooms for those w/limited mobility. *In room:* A/C, TV, dataport, kitchenette, fridge, beverage maker, hair dryer, iron, safe.

The Boardwalk Vacation Retreat This charming island-style hotel is special, offering several one- or two-bedroom casitas and lying only 135m (443 ft.) from the island's best swimming and beach area, Palm Beach. Units are spacious, with large pri-vate patios amidst lush gardens and near a swimming pool. Personalized service and privacy are the hallmarks. Bedrooms are decorated with floral paintings on the walls, tile floors, and tropical rattan pieces. The location is only a short walk from high-rise hotels, casinos, and watersports facilities. Private hammocks are a special feature, and each casita's living room adjoins a small kitchen.

Bakval 20, Aruba. ℂ 297/58-66654. Fax 297/58-61836. www.arubaboardwalk.com. 13 units. Winter $211–$301 (£110–£157) double; off season $156–$221 (£81–£115) double. Diving, windsurfing, and tennis packages available. Extra person $15 (£7.80). Children under 12 stay free in parent's room. AE, DISC, MC, V. **Amenities:** Outdoor pool; babysitting; laundry service. *In room:* A/C, ceiling fan, TV, dataport, kitchen, beverage maker, hair dryer, safe, Wi-Fi.

The Mill Resort & Suites 𝒦 *Finds*   This complex of two-story concrete buildings with red roofs is set in an arid, rather dusty location. It's adjacent to a large, modern re-creation of a Dutch windmill, a kitschy Aruban landmark. Units ring a large swimming pool, and glorious Palm Beach lies across the highway, a 5-minute walk away. The room decor is tropical, with white rattan furniture and carpeting or white floor tiles; many units have king-size beds and Jacuzzi-style tubs. This hotel is best for independent travelers who don't mind venturing out to find their own dining and fun.

J. E. Irausquin Blvd. 330, Palm Beach, Aruba. ℂ 800/992-2015 or 297/58-67700. Fax 297/58-67271. www.mill resort.com. 200 units. Winter $215–$225 (£112–£117) double, $245 (£127) junior suite, $375 (£195) 1-bedroom suite, $530 (£275) 2-bedroom suite; off season $90–$110 (£47–£57) double, $115–$145 (£60–£75) junior suite, $185–$230 (£96–£120) 1-bedroom suite, $270 (£140) 2-bedroom suite. Extra person $15 (£7.80) in summer; $20 (£10) in winter. Children under 14 stay free in parent's room. AE, DC, DISC, MC, V. **Amenities:** Restaurant; bar; 2 outdoor pools (one for kids); 2 tennis courts; fitness center; sauna; children's programs; salon; massage; babysitting; laundry service; dry cleaning; nonsmoking rooms; rooms for those w/limited mobility. *In room:* A/C, TV, beverage maker, hair dryer, safe.

INEXPENSIVE

Aruba Millennium Resort *Value*   This is a roadside motel evocative of Florida that is similar to the Arubiana Inn (see below), except it rises two stories and is a short walk from the white sands of Palm Beach and six casinos. Many of the island's best restaurants are also within a walk of the complex. Accommodations are studios or one-bedroom suites with complete kitchen facilities and a private balcony. Furnishings are very Caribbean, with pastel fabrics and walls and white wicker and bamboo furnishings. Rooms are coated in white tile, each with a small but efficiently organized private bathroom with shower.

Palm Beach 33, Palm Beach, Aruba. ℂ 297/58-61120. Fax 297/58-62506. www.arubamillenniumresort.com. 22 units. Winter $130–$172 (£68–£89) double; off season $60–$95 (£31–£49) double. Children under 12 $10 (£5.20) extra. MC, V. **Amenities:** Outdoor pool; 4 whirlpools. *In room:* A/C, TV, coffeemaker, kitchenette, fridge, beverage maker, iron, safe.

The Arubiana Inn *Value*   Lying only a 15-minute walk from Eagle Beach, one of the island's finest, this small and intimate inn is for those wishing to avoid the megaresorts along the beach. The place is really like a motel you might encounter along the Florida Keys, not dramatic or spectacular in any way, but offering decent, well-maintained accommodations. The cacti-studded landscape may make you think you've landed in Scottsdale. Built of coral stone with much use of a russet-brown terra cotta, the complex encloses a communal section with a pool and chaise longues. Rooms are comfortable but rather basic, very West Indian in motif with light pastels, tiles, wicker, and rattan, along with tiny bathrooms with tub/shower combinations. Each unit also comes with a small living room area.

Bubali 74, Noord, Aruba. ⓒ **297/58-77700.** Fax 297/58-71770. www.arubianainn.com. 16 units. Winter $85 (£44) double; off season $70 (£36) double. Children under 12 stay free in parent's room. AE, MC, V. **Amenities:** Bar; outdoor pool; babysitting; rooms for those w/limited mobility; minimarket. *In room:* A/C, TV, fridge, safe, microwave.

The Vistalmar   An affordable and intimate place to stay on Aruba, this property is on a dead-end street in a residential neighborhood, and features a sun deck that's built directly over the water. The swimming is off a beach with a mix of sand and rocks. It's quite a bargain, however, for in addition to your accommodations you will have complimentary use of bikes, picnic coolers, snorkeling equipment, beach towels, and an outdoor grill. The complex of apartments is in two similar buildings, each with a balcony or courtyard offering water views. A little more stylish than some of the more bare-bones apartment units rented on the island, the accommodations here are spacious and furnished for comfort. Your hosts, among the island's more personable, have a wealth of island information. They even stock your refrigerator with food for your first night here.

Each apartment has a king-size bed with a well-maintained bathroom with a tub and shower, a separate dressing area, a fully equipped kitchen, and a living room with a sleeper sofa. There's also a second sleeping room and a sun porch.

Bucutiweg 28, Aruba. ⓒ **297/58-28579.** Fax 297/58-22200. www.arubavistalmar.com. 8 units. Winter $115–$165 (£60–£86) apt; off season $85–$115 (£44–£60) apt. No credit cards. **Amenities:** Snorkeling; bicycles; coin-operated laundry; 1 room for those w/limited mobility. *In room:* A/C, kitchenette, fridge, beverage maker, iron, safe.

3 Dining

Sometimes—at least on off-season package deals—visitors on the Modified American Plan (breakfast and dinner) are allowed to dine around on an exchange plan with other hotels. Ask your hotel for details.

IN ORANJESTAD
EXPENSIVE

Chez Mathilde ⓖⓖ FUSION/FRENCH   Oranjestad's French restaurant is expensive, but most satisfied customers agree that it's worth the price. The chef's savory kettle of bouillabaisse contains more than a dozen different sea creatures. Our favorite, the delectable rack of lamb chops with fine French herbs and filet of red snapper arrives with a lightly peppered crust and lemon dressing. You get not only distinguished food and service, but an elegant setting as well. In this carefully preserved 19th-century building, dining rooms are intimate, tables are beautifully set, and the decor is restrained but romantic. Live piano music enhances the total experience. The restaurant is near the Renaissance hotel complex, a 5-minute drive north of the airport.

Havenstraat 23. ⓒ **297/58-34968.** www.chezmathilde.com. Reservations recommended. Main courses $29–$45 (£15–£23). AE, DISC, MC, V. Daily 11:30am–2:30pm and 6–11pm.

Driftwood ⓖ *(Finds* SEAFOOD/ARUBAN   The married partners who run this restaurant have an unusual setup: Herbert Merryweather spends the day on the high seas catching the fish served that night in the restaurant, while Francine Merryweather stays on-site, directing the sometimes busy traffic in the dining room. The setting is an Aruban-style antique house in the center of Oranjestad, with interior walls covered with (guess what) irregular pieces of driftwood. The menu items that are always available include Argentine filet mignon served with a bacon-flavored mushroom sauce; boneless breast of chicken with Parmesan and linguine; stewed conch; and shrimp in

Creole sauce. But the composition of the fish menu varies according to the day's catch. It might include mahimahi, wahoo, kingfish, grouper, or lobster. These will be prepared after a consultation with a staff member, usually Francine, who will propose any of several methods of preparation, either blackened, meunière, fried, or baked, along with appropriate garnishes and sauces.

Klipstraat 12. ℂ 297/58-32515. www.driftwoodaruba.com. Reservations recommended. Main courses $17–$36 (£8.85–£19). AE, MC, V. Wed–Mon 5:30–10:30pm (last order).

Gasparito ✦ *Finds* ARUBAN/SEAFOOD   This bright, upbeat restaurant is set in a traditional *cunugu* (Aruban-style house) with yellow walls and local artwork. The atmosphere is lively and the food varied. Diners can enjoy baked chicken stuffed with a peach, filet mignon served with either sautéed mushrooms or black-pepper sauce, or *keshi yena*—Dutch cheese stuffed with a choice of beef, chicken, or seafood. The menu also features an array of fresh seafood, including lobster served with a garlic-butter sauce or sautéed with onions, green peppers, tomatoes, and a multitude of spices.

Gasparito 3. ℂ 297/58-67044. www.gasparito.com. Reservations recommended. Main courses $18–$38 (£9.35–£20). AE, DC, DISC, MC, V. Daily 5:30–11pm.

Le Dôme ✦ BELGIAN/FRENCH   Owners from Belgium operate this elegant restaurant on Eagle Beach where some 12,000 bricks were shipped from Belgium to create an "Antwerp atmosphere." The menu is sumptuous and excellently prepared, beginning with bold cold and hot appetizers. Delights are duck liver mousse served with a blueberry compote or a lobster-based vegetable soup. The chef's signature dishes are his game specialties, including breast of pheasant with cranberry compote or a venison-sirloin chop pan fried and glazed with a Poivrade sauce. One of the delights of dining in Aruba is to partake of the four-course "once in a lifetime" game menu served here. You can order other main courses as well, including *le passion du jour,* your platter depending on whatever the local fishermen caught that day.

J. E. Irausquin Blvd. 224. ℂ 297/58-71517. www.ledome-aruba.com. Reservations recommended. Main courses $22–$44 (£11–£23). AE, DC, DISC, MC, V. Daily noon–3pm and 6pm–midnight.

L.G. Smith Steak & Chophouse ✦✦ STEAK/SEAFOOD   The dining choices at the Renaissance Aruba Resort & Casino are vast, but nothing quite tops this chophouse which, in spite of its name, is no ordinary steak joint. Hip and sophisticated, it looks like one of the elegant sets from *Miami Vice,* with its wood paneling, waterfall wall, quartzite-stone columns, black furniture with white leatherette cushions, and a panoramic view of the Oranjestad marina. Located next to the upper level of the casino entrance, the restaurant doesn't survive on its trendy décor alone, but serves one of the best selections, perhaps the best, of meat in Aruba, ranging from porterhouse to New York strip. Naturally, you expect surf and turf on the menu, but the chef goes far beyond the routine, offering such dishes as locally caught tuna with a cilantro-laced mango salsa or free-range chicken with a red-pepper laced cranberry juice. Grouper is regularly featured, with a superb sauce resting on a bed of fresh spinach. If you passed on the thick chocolate cake, you might opt for the carrot cake resting under a carrot topping glace with a layer of carrot jelly.

In the Renaissance Aruba Resort & Casino, L.G. Smith Blvd. 82, Oranjestad. ℂ 297/58-36000. Reservations recommended. Main courses $28–$58 (£15–£30). AE, DISC, MC, V. Mon–Sat 6–11pm.

Marandi ✦ INTERNATIONAL   Because it offers dining with a view, the Marandi is often referred to as Aruba's sunset restaurant. Next to the Havana nightclub, it is an elegantly casual place, noted for its tranquil atmosphere, good service, and well-prepared food. A lot of wood and bamboo are used for the decor. Appetizers range from stir-fried shrimp with green asparagus to lasagna with cherry tomatoes, mussels, and calamari. Main courses vary widely in their inspiration, from the Mediterranean flavors of the tapenade (olives, anchovies, fresh basil, and a tomato-garlic sauce) served with the grilled catch of the day, to the Japanese-influenced tuna steak in teriyaki sauce with tempura vegetables.

L. G. Smith Blvd. © 297/58-20157. www.marandiaruba.com. Reservations required. Main courses $19–$38 (£9.90–£20). AE, DISC, MC, V. Daily 5:30–10:30pm.

MODERATE

Cuba's Cookin' ★ *Finds* CUBAN   One of the oldest buildings on Aruba, constructed as a private home in 1877, is the setting for a restaurant where Batista-era Havana seems to come back to life. The most popular drink at its bar is a mint, rum, and sugar-laced *mojito*. There's a main dining room, plus three smaller areas, each lined with paintings inspired by the urban life in the Tropics and, in some cases, imported from Cuba. Lunch is simple, usually heaping platters of fish, chicken, or steak garnished with salad and vegetables. Dinners are more elaborate, and more representative of old-time Cuban cuisine. Try *ropa vieja* (shredded skirt steak fried with green peppers, tomatoes, and onions) or a succulent version of *picadillo de res* (ground beef garnished with olives and raisins). Cuban or Dominican cigars are available at the end of the meal. Every Monday to Saturday night this downtown Oranjestad place is mobbed with islanders coming for the live merengue, salsa, and Cuban jazz that goes from 7:30pm until at least 1am.

Wilhelminastraat 27 (across from the police station). © 297/58-80627. www.cubascookin.com. Reservations recommended. Main courses $15–$33 (£7.80–£17). AE, DC, MC, V. Mon–Sat noon–2:30pm and 5:30–11pm.

Hostaria da' Vittorio ★ ITALIAN   Chef Vittorio Muscariello dazzles with specialties he learned cooking in the Mediterranean. His open kitchen exposes his secrets, which keeps some of his local fans returning again and again. There's a casual trattoria feel to the place, with bright linen tablecloths and the use of wood and earth tones. Even if the ingredients are imported, the chef seems to make everything taste fresh. The menu showcases consistently well-prepared fare that might include such starters as a seafood soup swimming with grouper, shrimp, mussels, clams, squid, and baby octopus or baked-fresh baby artichokes, tantalizingly flavored with garlic and herbs and served with black olives. The U.S. beef tenderloin is baked in puff pastry with porcini mushrooms, and the U.S. veal shank is delectably braised in a dry white wine with fresh herbs and spices. Our favorite pasta is the cheese ravioli cooked in a walnut sauce.

L. G. Smith Blvd. 380 (across from the Hyatt Regency), Palm Beach. © 297/58-63838. Reservations recommended. Main courses $18–$39 (£9.10–£20); pizzas $12–$15 (£6–£7.55). AE, DISC, MC, V. Daily 11am–3pm and 6–11pm.

La Dolce Vita ★ NORTHERN ITALIAN   This restaurant is the most acclaimed Italian dining spot on Aruba, recognized by the food and wine critics at *Gourmet* magazine in 2002. It may not be as elegant as Valentino's (p. 117), but the food is better. The creative menu contains a few unusual dishes in addition to traditional favorites. A meal might include slices of veal served either Parmesan style, *cordon bleu* style, with Marsala sauce, a la Florio (with artichokes), or a la Bartolucci (with ricotta, spinach, and mozzarella). Snapper comes four ways: simmered with clams and mussels, broiled with lemon or with wine, or stuffed with pulverized shrimp. We salivate over the stewpot of fish, served with linguine in red or white clam sauce.

Sasaky Hwy., Italiaastraat 46, Eagle Beach. © 297/58-85592. www.ladolcevitaaruba.com. Reservations recommended, especially in winter. Main courses $15–$40 (£7.80–£21). AE, DISC, MC, V. Daily 5:30–11pm.

INEXPENSIVE

The Paddock INTERNATIONAL   In the heart of Oranjestad, this cafe and bistro overlooks the harbor, a short walk from virtually every shop in town. Much of the staff is hip and European. No one will mind whether you opt for a drink, a cup of tea or coffee, a snack of sliced sausage and Gouda cheese, or a full-fledged meal. The menu offers crab, salmon, shrimp, and tuna sandwiches; salads; pita-bread sandwiches stuffed with chicken and a garlic sauce with plenty of tang; fresh poached or sautéed fish; and a glazed tenderloin of pork.

L. G. Smith Blvd. 13. © 297/58-32334. www.paddock-aruba.com. Sandwiches, snacks, and salads $2–$8 (£1.05–£4.15); main courses $16–$30 (£8.30–£16). MC, V. Daily 10am–2am.

NEAR PALM BEACH
EXPENSIVE

Chalet Suisse 🐾 SWISS/INTERNATIONAL   Set beside the highway near La Cabana Hotel, this alpine-chalet restaurant feels like an old-fashioned Swiss dining room. In deliberate contrast to the arid scrublands that surround it, the restaurant is an air-conditioned refuge of thick plaster walls, pinewood panels, and a sense of *gemutlichkeit* (comfort). Tempting menu items include a lobster bisque, Dutch pea soup, beef stroganoff, a pasta of the day, Wiener schnitzel, roast duckling with orange sauce, red snapper with Creole sauce, and an array of high-calorie desserts. The chefs claim they serve the best rack of lamb in the Southern Hemisphere. We can't vouch for that, but it's really good. The hearty Swiss fare is good, if a bit heavy for the Tropics. Finish off with a smooth chocolate fondue or the eternal favorite, Swiss apple strudel. Most dishes are at the lower end of the price scale.

J. E. Irausquin Blvd. 246. © 297/58-75054. www.chaletsuisse-aruba.com. Reservations recommended. Main courses $23–$54 (£12–£28). AE, DC, DISC, MC, V. Mon–Sat 5:30–10:30pm.

MODERATE

Madame Janette 🐾🐾 *Finds* ARUBAN/CARIBBEAN/INTERNATIONAL   In a low-slung Aruban-style house, a short ride from Palm Beach, this local dive exudes island atmosphere, attracting windsurfers and a casual, laid-back crowd to its tables set in a "desert courtyard." Karsten Gesing, a European chef, has created a buzz among local foodies with his imaginative menu and clever blending of ingredients. We recommend Madame's Hot Shrimps, succulent prawns baked in a well-flavored marinara sauce topped with Gouda and Gorgonzola. Even though the delicate texture of the seafood is overpowered, the taste is still delightful. Or try the West Indian rock lobster in a velvety cream sauce laced with cognac, or the toasted almond grouper in a light cream sauce flavored with fresh spinach. The rack of lamb is the chef's masterpiece, with a family-secret marinade. Finish off with such desserts as bourbon vanilla ice cream with blueberry sauce or a Swiss-chocolate truffle mousse. Mama Jamaica is a fresh pineapple marinated in old Appleton rum and served with vanilla ice cream topped with roasted coconut flakes.

Cunuco Abao 37 (next to the Blue Village Villas). © 297/58-70184. Reservations required. Main courses $22–$32 (£11–£17). AE, MC, V. Wed–Mon 6–11pm.

I don't speak sign language.

A hotel can close for all kinds of reasons.
Our Guarantee ensures that if your hotel's undergoing construction, we'll let you know in advance. In fact, we cover your entire travel experience. See www.travelocity.com/guarantee for details.

travelocity®
You'll never roam alone.

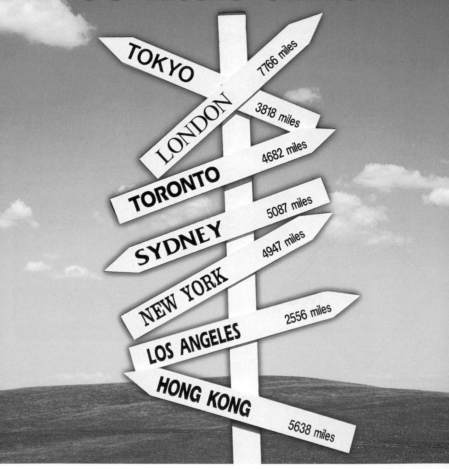

IN OR NEAR NOORD

Buccaneer ✿ SEAFOOD/INTERNATIONAL   In a rustic building near the hamlet of Noord, close to many of the island's biggest high-rise hotels, the Buccaneer is one of Aruba's most popular seafood restaurants. Inside, you'll find a nautical decor and a dozen bubbling aquariums. There are a number of tempting appetizers, such as crabmeat cocktail or a savory plate of escargots with an infusion of Pernod. Lobster thermidor appears on the menu, or you can try the land-and-sea platter with fresh fish, shrimp, and tender beef tenderloin. The food is hearty and delicious. A spacious bar area is a good place to linger over drinks.

Gasparito 11-C, Noord. ✆ 297/58-66172. Reservations not accepted. Main courses $14–$26 (£7–£14). AE, DC, DISC, MC, V. Mon–Sat 5:30–10pm.

Lekker Brasserie CHINESE/DUTCH   Set within a 10-minute drive north of Oranjestad, this is one of Aruba's most evocative restaurants. (*Lekker* means "tasty" in Dutch.) There's a semicircular bar area and a tropical dining room filled with rattan and bamboo furniture. The chefs prepare many Chinese favorites, along with the kind of Indonesian dishes that evoke nostalgia in Dutch visitors on holiday in Aruba. Dishes include *papapankan,* a Dutch version of slow-cooked pork; *nasi goreng* (fried rice with vegetables and meat); *bami goreng* (fried noodles with vegetables and meat); satay (skewers of grilled chicken or beef served with a peanut sauce); egg foo yong; chow mein; and curried chicken in the style of Bali.

Noord 39. ✆ 297/58-62770. Reservations recommended. Main courses $10–$16 (£5.20–£8.30). DC, DISC, MC, V. Sun–Thurs 4pm–3am, Fri–Sat 4pm–5am.

The Old Cunucu House ✿ ARUBAN/INTERNATIONAL   When originally constructed as a private house in the 1920s, this was the only building in the neighborhood. Today it retains its original decor of very thick, plaster-coated walls, ultrasimple furniture, and tile floors. Many visitors start with a cocktail under a shed-style roof in front, where chairs and tables overlook a well-kept garden studded with desert plants. The restaurant maintains a warm, traditional feeling, and focuses on local and international recipes including fish soup, fried squid, and coconut fried shrimp. Several dishes are served with *funchi* (Caribbean polenta) and *pan bati* (a local pancake). The skilled chef knows how to embellish a traditional repertoire with first-class ingredients.

Palm Beach 150, Noord. ✆ 297/58-61666. Reservations recommended. Main courses $19–$46 (£9.90–£24). AE, DISC, MC, V. Daily 11:30am–3pm and 5–11pm.

Valentino's ✿ NORTHERN ITALIAN   This is the most elegant Italian restaurant on Aruba, even if La Dolce Vita's (p. 115) food is somewhat better. In the central courtyard of an upscale condominium complex, guests enjoy cocktails near the entrance, and then climb a flight of stairs to the peak-ceilinged dining room. Here you can check out the glassed-in, well-designed kitchen, and bask in the attention of the well-trained staff. It's a cozy, comfortable place with views over the palms and pools of the condominium complex. The prices are somewhat high, but you'll forget that when you taste the food. The fish dishes are your best bet; also excellent are the chicken Parmesan, veal scaloppine, tenderloin pepper steak, and rack of lamb in rosemary sauce with mint jelly.

In the Caribbean Palm Village, Noord 43-E. ✆ 297/58-62700. Reservations recommended. Main courses $26–$50 (£14–£26). AE, MC, V. Mon–Sat 6–11pm.

AT TIERRA DEL SOL/NORTH ARUBA

La Trattoria "El Faro Blanco" ✿ ITALIAN   Charming and authentically Italian, this restaurant, built in 1914, was originally the local lighthouse keeper's home. It's now managed by the same people who maintain the nearby golf course. The staff is mostly European, and the head chef studied in Italy. Views sweep out over the sea, the island's northern coastline, and the island's largest golf course. The menu covers a full range of Italian cuisine, with a heavy dose of aromatic Neapolitan specialties. The best examples include heaping platters of fish and vegetable antipasti; linguine with shrimp, octopus, scallops, clams, and tomatoes (wins our vote for the island's best pasta); red snapper cooked in a potato crust with olive oil and rosemary; and *osso buco* (veal shank) served with Parmesan-laced risotto Milanese. The desserts are excellent; we recommend tiramisu or pears poached in red wine served with ice cream. The bar is a favorite stop for golfers.

At the California Lighthouse, North Aruba. ✆ **297/58-60787**. Reservations required. Main courses $23–$36 (£12–£19). AE, DISC, MC, V. Daily 5–11pm.

EAST OF ORANJESTAD

Charlie's Bar and Restaurant SEAFOOD/ARUBAN   Charlie's is the best reason to visit San Nicolas—but come for the good times and the brew, not the food. The bar dates from 1941 and is the most overly decorated joint in the West Indies, sporting an array of memorabilia and local souvenirs. Where roustabouts and roughnecks once brawled, you'll now find tables filled with visitors admiring thousands of pennants, banners, and trophies dangling from the high ceiling. Two-fisted drinks are still served, but the menu has improved since the good old days, when San Nicolas was one of the toughest towns in the Caribbean. You can now enjoy freshly made soup, grilled scampi, Creole-style squid, and churrasco. Sirloin steak and red snapper are usually featured.

Main St., San Nicolas (a 25-min. drive east of Oranjestad). ✆ **297/58-45086**. Soup $7 (£3.65); main courses $22–$38 (£11–£20). AE, DISC, MC, V. Mon–Sat 11:30am–9:30pm (bar to 10pm).

4 Beaches

The western and southern shores of Aruba are called the Turquoise Coast. Along this stretch, Palm Beach and Eagle Beach (the latter closer to Oranjestad) are the best. No hotel along the strip owns these beaches, all of which are open to the public. (If you use any of the hotel's facilities, however, you'll be charged.)

The major resort hotels are built on the southwestern and more tranquil strip of Aruba. These beaches open onto calm waters that are ideal for swimming. The beaches on the northern side of Aruba, although quite beautiful, face choppy waters with stronger waves.

Palm Beach ✿✿✿ is a superb stretch of wide white sand that fronts hotels. It's great for swimming, sunbathing, sailing, fishing, and snorkeling. Unfortunately, it's crowded in the winter. The waters off this beach are incredibly blue and teeming with neon-yellow fish and flame-bright coral reefs. Billowing rainbow-colored sails complete the picture. Along Palm Beach, all the resorts are set in flowering gardens. Of course, a river of water keeps these gardens blooming in this otherwise arid landscape, but the gardens take on a special beauty precisely because the island is so dry. As you walk along the beach, you can wander through garden after garden, watching the native bird life. The tropical mockingbird feeds on juicy local fruits, and the black-faced grassquit and the

⎛Moments Sunset at Bubali Pond

The **Bubali Pond** bird sanctuary lies on the north side of Eagle Beach at Post Chikito, south of De Olde Molen (a 19th-century windmill-turned-restaurant, Aruba's most famous landmark). Flocks of birds cluster at this freshwater pond, particularly at sunset, which makes for a memorable sight. You can see pelicans galore; black olivaceous cormorants; the black-crowned night herons; great egrets with long, black legs and yellow bills; and spotted sandpipers. Even the large wood stork and the glossy scarlet ibis sometimes fly in from Venezuela.

---

green-throated carib hover around the flowers and flowering shrubs. If you stop to have a drink at one of the hotels' open-air bars, chances are you'll be joined by a bananaquit hoping to steal some sugar from you.

Also worth seeking out is **Hadikurari (Fisherman's Huts),** where swimming conditions, in very shallow water, are excellent. The only drawback to this white-powder-sand beach is some pebbles and stones at the water's edge. This beach is known for some of the finest windsurfing on island and is the site of the annual **Hi-Winds Pro-Am Windsurfing Competition.** Facilities include picnic tables.

Quite similar to Palm Beach, **Eagle Beach** ⋳ is next door on the west coast, fronting a number of timeshare units. With gentle surf along miles of white-powder sand, swimming conditions here are excellent. Hotels along the strip organize watersports and beach activities.

The white-powder sands of **Punta Brabo,** also called **Manchebo Beach,** are a favorite among topless sunbathers. Actually, Manchebo is part of the greater Eagle Beach (see above), and the Manchebo Beach Resort is a good place to stop, as it offers a dive shop and rents snorkeling gear. It's also set amid 40 hectares (100 acres) of gardens, filled with everything from cacti to bougainvillea.

Practically every visitor winds up on Eagle Beach and Palm Beach. If you'd like something more private, head for **Baby Beach** ⋳ on the eastern end of Aruba. The beach has white-powder sand and tranquil, shallow waters, making it ideal for swimming, and it's the best place on the island for beach-based snorkeling. There are no facilities other than a refreshment stand and shaded areas. You'll spot the Arubans themselves here on weekends. (Our local friends love this beach and may be furious at us for telling you about it!) Baby Beach opens onto a vast lagoon shielded by coral rocks that rise from the water. Bring your own towels and snorkeling gear.

Next to Baby Beach on the eastern tip of the island, **Rodger's Beach** also has white-powder sand and excellent swimming conditions. The backdrop, however, is an oil refinery at the far side of the bay. But the waters remain unpolluted, and you can admire both large and small multicolored fish and strange coral formations. The trade winds will keep you cool.

5 Sports & Other Outdoor Pursuits

CRUISES   For a boat ride and a few hours of snorkeling, contact **De Palm Tours,** which has offices in eight of the island's hotels. Its main office is at L. G. Smith Blvd. 142, in Oranjestad (✆ **800/766-6016** in the U.S. and Canada, or 297/58-24400). De Palm Tours offers a 4-hour cruise that visits two coral reefs and the German shipwreck *Antilla* on Sunday to Friday. The cost is $62 (£32) per person.

DEEP-SEA FISHING   In the deep waters off the coast of Aruba you can test your skill and wits against the big ones—wahoo, marlin, tuna, bonito, and sailfish. **De Palm Tours** (see above) takes a maximum of six people (four can fish at the same time) on one of its five boats, which range in length from 8 to 12m (26–39 ft.). Half-day tours, with all equipment included, begin at $300 (£156) for up to four people. The price for a full-day trip is $600 (£312). Boats leave from the docks in Oranjestad. De Palm maintains 13 branches, most of which are located in Aruba's major hotels.

GOLF   Aruba's **Tierra del Sol Golf Course** (© 297/58-67800), designed by Robert Trent Jones, Jr., is on the northwest coast near the California Lighthouse. The 18-hole, par-71, 6,811-yard course combines lush greens with the beauty of the island's indigenous flora, such as the swaying divi-divi tree. Facilities include a restaurant and lounge in the clubhouse, plus a swimming pool. Golf Hyatt manages the course. In winter, greens fees are a whopping $145 (£75), including golf cart, or $88 (£46) after 3pm. Off-season greens fees are $98 to $118 (£51–£61), or $78 to $88 (£41–£46) after 2pm. The course is open daily from 7am to 7pm.

A less pricey alternative is the **Aruba Golf Club,** Golfweg 82 (© 297/58-42006), near San Nicolas on the southeastern end of the island. Although it has only 10 greens, you play them from different tees to simulate 18-hole play. Twenty-five different sand traps add an extra challenge. Greens fees are $10 (£5.20) for 9 holes. The course is open Tuesday to Sunday from 7:30am to 5pm. You can rent golf carts and clubs in the on-site pro shop. On the premises, you'll find an air-conditioned restaurant and changing rooms with showers.

HORSEBACK RIDING   **De Palm Tours,** L. G. Smith Blvd. 142 (© **800/766-6016** in the U.S. and Canada, or 297/58-24400), will make arrangements for you to ride at **Rancho Del Campo** (© **297/58-50290;** www.ranchodelcampo.com). You can also book directly through their website. Two daily rides last 2½ hours each and cut through a park to a natural pool, where you can dismount and cool off with a swim. The price is $60 to $100 (£31–£52) per person, and the minimum age is 10 years.

TENNIS   Most of the island's beachfront hotels have tennis courts, often cooled by trade winds, and some have top pros on hand to give instruction. Many of the courts can also be lit for night games. We don't advise playing in Aruba's hot noonday sun. Some hotels allow only guests on their courts.

The best tennis is at the **Aruba Racquet Club** (© 297/58-60215), the island's first world-class tennis facility, which has eight courts, an exhibition center court, a swimming pool, a bar, a small restaurant, an aerobics center, and a fitness center. The club is open Monday through Friday 6am to 9pm, Saturday 8:30am to 5pm, and Sunday 10am to 4pm. Rates are $10 (£5.20) per hour per court if they are busy, but a $10 (£5.20) day pass can be purchased during off season, and lessons are available by appointment only. The location is Rooisanto 21 on Aruba's northwest coast, near the California Lighthouse.

WATERSPORTS   You can snorkel in shallow waters, and scuba divers find stunning marine life with endless varieties of coral and tropical fish in myriad hues; at some points visibility extends up to 30m (90 ft.). Most divers set out for the German freighter *Antilla,* which was scuttled in the early years of World War II off the northwestern tip of Aruba, not too far from Palm Beach.

Red Sail Sports, Palm Beach (© **297/58-61603;** www.redsailaruba.com), is the island's best watersports center. The activities include sailing and scuba diving. Red Sail dive packages include shipwreck dives and marine-reef explorations. Guests first receive a poolside dive-safety course from Red Sail's certified instructors. Those who wish to become certified can achieve full PADI certification in 3 days for $350 (£182). One-tank dives cost $45 (£23), and two-tank dives are $70 (£36). Night dives are $49 (£25).

6 Seeing the Sights

IN ORANJESTAD ⊛

Aruba's capital, Oranjestad, attracts more shoppers than sightseers. The bustling city has a very Caribbean flavor, with part-Spanish, part-Dutch architecture. The main thoroughfare, L. G. Smith Boulevard, cuts in from the airport along the waterfront and on to Palm Beach, changing its name along the way to J. E. Irausquin Boulevard. Most visitors cross it to head for **Caya G. F. Betico Croes** and the best duty-free shopping.

After a shopping trip, you might return to the harbor where fishing boats and schooners, many from Venezuela, are moored. Nearly all newcomers to Aruba like to photograph the **Schooner Harbor.** Colorful boats dock along the quay, and boat people display their wares in open stalls. The local patois predominates. A little farther along, at the **fish market,** fresh fish is sold directly from the boats. **Wilhelmina Park,** named after Queen Wilhelmina of the Netherlands, is on the sea side of Oranjestad. The park features a tropical garden along the water and a sculpture of the Queen Mother.

AN UNDERWATER JOURNEY

One of the island's most fun activities is an underwater journey on one of the world's few passenger submarines, operated by **Atlantis Submarines** ⊛, Seaport Village Marina (opposite the Sonesta), Oranjestad (© **866/546-7820** in the U.S. and Canada, or 297/58-86881). Even nondivers can witness a coral reef firsthand without risking the obstacles and dangers of a scuba expedition. Carrying 46 passengers to a depth of up to 45m (150 ft.), the ride provides all the thrills of an underwater dive—but keeps you dry. In 1995, an old Danish fishing vessel was sunk to create a fascinating view for divers and submariners.

There are four departures from the Oranjestad harbor front Monday to Sunday from 10am to 1pm. Each tour includes a 15-minute catamaran ride to Barcadera Reef, 3km (2 miles) southeast of Aruba—a site chosen for the huge variety of its underwater flora and fauna. At the reef, participants are transferred to the submarine for a 1-hour underwater lecture and tour.

Allow 2 hours for the complete experience. The cost is $84 (£44) for adults and $37 (£19) for children age 4 to 16 (children under age 4 are not admitted). Advance reservations are essential. A staff member will ask for a credit card number (and give you a confirmation number) to hold the booking for you.

IN THE COUNTRYSIDE

If you can lift yourself from the sands for an afternoon, you might enjoy driving into the *cunucu,* which in Papiamento means "the countryside." Here Arubans live in modest, colorful, pastel-washed houses, decorated with tropical plants that require expensive desalinated water. Visitors who venture into the center of Aruba will want to see the strange **divi-divi tree,** with its trade wind-blown coiffure.

You probably will want to visit Aruba's best-known man-made landmark, **Hooiberg,** affectionately known as "The Haystack." From Oranjestad, take Caya G. F. Croes (7A) toward Santa Cruz. Anybody with the stamina can climb steps to the top of this 160m-high (525-ft.) hill. On a clear day, you can see Venezuela from here.

Aruba is studded with massive boulders. You can see the most impressive ones at **Ayo** and **Casibari,** northeast of Hooiberg. Diorite boulders stack up as high as urban buildings. The rocks weigh several thousand tons and their peculiar shapes puzzle geologists. Ancient Amerindian drawings appear on the rocks at Ayo. At Casibari, you can climb to the top for a panoramic view of the island or a close look at rocks that nature has carved into seats or prehistoric birds and animals. Pay special attention to the island's unusual species of lizards and cacti. Casibari is open daily from 9am to 5pm, with no admission charge. There's a lodge at Casibari where you can buy souvenirs, snacks, soft drinks, and beer.

Guides can also point out drawings on the walls and ceiling of the **Caves of Canashito,** south of Hooiberg. You may see some giant green parakeets here, too.

NEAR SAN NICOLAS

As you drive along the highway toward the island's southernmost section, you may want to stop at the **Spaans Lagoen (Spanish Lagoon),** where pirates hid and waited to plunder rich cargo ships in the Caribbean. Today it's an ideal place for snorkeling, and you can picnic at tables under the mangrove trees.

To the east, you'll pass an area called **Savaneta,** where some of the oldest traces of human habitation on Aruba have been unearthed. You'll also find the oil tanks that marked the position of the **El Paso Oil & Transport Company,** the Exxon subsidiary around which the town of San Nicolas developed. San Nicolas was a company town until 1985, when the refinery curtailed operations. Nineteen kilometers (12 miles) from Oranjestad, it is now called the Aruba Sunrise Side, and tourism has become its main economic engine.

Boca Grandi, on the windward side of the island, is a favorite windsurfing location; if you prefer quieter waters, try Baby Beach and Rodgers Beach, on Aruba's leeward side. Seroe Colorado (Colorado Point) overlooks the two beaches. From here, you can see the Venezuelan coastline and the pounding surf on the windward side. If you climb down the cliffs, you're likely to spot an iguana; protected by law, the once-endangered saurians now proliferate in peace.

You can see cave-wall drawings at the **Guadarikiri Cave** and **Fontein Cave.** At the **Huliba** and **Tunnel of Love** caves, guides and refreshment stands await visitors. The Tunnel of Love cave requires some physical stamina to explore. It is filled with steep climbs, and its steps are illuminated only by hand-held lamps. Wear sturdy shoes and watch your step.

7 Shopping

Aruba manages to offer goods from six continents along the .8km-long (½-mile) **Caya G. F. Betico Croes,** Oranjestad's main shopping street. Technically this is not a free port, but the duty is so low (3.3%) that prices are attractive—and Aruba has no sales tax. You can find the usual array of Swiss watches; German and Japanese cameras; jewelry; liquor; English bone china and porcelain; Dutch, Swedish, and Danish silver and pewter; French perfume; British woolens; Indonesian specialties; and Madeira embroidery. Delft blue pottery is an especially good buy. Other good buys include Dutch cheese (Edam and Gouda), Dutch chocolate, and English cigarettes in the airport departure area.

Alhambra, J. E. Irausquin Blvd. 47 (© **297/58-89000**), is a complex of buildings and courtyards designed like an 18th-century Dutch village. About a dozen shops here sell souvenirs, leather goods, jewelry, and beachwear. From the outside, the complex looks Moorish, with serpentine mahogany columns, arches, and domes.

8 Aruba After Dark

CASINOS: LET THE GOOD TIMES ROLL 🕸🕸

The casinos in the big hotels along Palm Beach are the liveliest nighttime destinations. Most stay open into the wee hours. In plush gaming parlors, guests try their luck at roulette, craps, blackjack, and, of course, the one-armed bandits. Limits and odds are about the same as in the United States.

Casablanca Casino, at the Westin Aruba Resort & Spa, J.E. Irausquin Blvd. 77, Palm Beach (© **297/58-64466**), offers a design theme inspired by the cult classic of the 40s, *Casablanca,* with Bogie and Ingrid Bergman. In honor of that classic, there's even a Moroccan-style Rick's Café. A variety of live bands is often brought in to entertain. Blackjack, poker, craps, roulette, all the games of chance are here. Specialty drinks are a feature at the Casablanca Casino Bar, along with sports broadcasts on multiple TV screens.

Excelsior Casino, J. E. Irausquin Blvd. 230 (© **297/58-67777;** www.excelsiorcasino. com), wins the prize for all-around action. Its casino doors are open from 8am to 4am. The **Aruba Grand,** J. E. Irausquin Blvd. 79 (© **297/58-63900**), is open from noon to 2am. **Casino Masquerade,** at the Radisson Aruba Resort & Casino, J. E. Irausquin Blvd. 81, Palm Beach (© **297/58-66555**), is one of the newer casinos on Aruba. On the lower-level lobby of the hotel, it's open from noon to 3am daily. Table games start at 4pm. It offers blackjack, single deck, roulette, Caribbean stud, craps, and Let It Ride.

One of the island's best is the **Crystal Casino** at the Renaissance Aruba Beach Resort & Casino at Seaport Village (© **297/58-36000**), open daily 24 hours. The 1,260-sq.-m (13,560-sq.-ft.) casino has 10 blackjack tables, 405 slot machines, 5 roulette tables, 4 Caribbean stud-poker tables, 1 craps table, and 1 minibaccarat table. New games of chance are added regularly. This place has luxurious furnishings, ornate moldings, marble, and crystal chandeliers.

One of the largest and splashiest casinos is found at the **Hyatt Regency Aruba,** J. E. Irausquin Blvd. 85 (© **297/58-61234**).

A busy casino on the premises of **Alhambra,** J. E. Irausquin Blvd. 47 (© **297/ 58-35000**), is open from 10am until very early in the morning, usually 4am. **Aladdin Theatre** adjoins the casino. Shows feature gymnasts, dancers, singers, and magicians, but don't have the professionalism and appeal of the big hotel revues recommended below.

The **Occidental Grand Aruba Casino,** J. E. Irausquin Blvd. 83 (© **297/58-69039**), is known for its Caribbean stud poker at the tables, and also for games of blackjack, roulette, baccarat, and craps. Its slot machines open for action at noon, and tables and other games open at 5pm. Another choice, the **Stellaris Casino,** at Marriott's Aruba Ocean Club, L. G. Smith Blvd. 1012, Palm Beach (© **297/58-69000**), is a large casino that starts to get busy daily at 2pm, when gamblers arrive to play roulette, craps, and Caribbean stud poker.

BIG STAGE REVUES

Aruba stages more Las Vegas–type spectacles than any other island in the Caribbean. These shows are most often at hotels but are open to nonguests who reserve a table. Some of the best shows are staged at the **Seaport's Crystal Theatre,** in the Renaissance Aruba Beach Resort & Casino, L. G. Smith Blvd. 82, in Oranjestad (© 297/ 58-36000). "Let's Go Latin," its current and long-running revue, has been attracting audiences from around the world with its nearly 200 lavish costumes, and some two dozen performers. Exquisite bods strut the stage in this ooh-la-la extravaganza. The talent comes from Cuba where, as one performer told us, "rhythm is in our blood."

Tickets for just the show cost $44 (£23), or $22 (£11) for children under 12. A dinner-show package costs $75 (£39) per person. Show times are Monday to Saturday at 9pm.

The biggest stage shows in Aruba are at **Las Palmas Ballroom,** in the Occidental Grand Aruba, J. E. Irausquin Blvd. 83, Palm Beach (© 297/58-64500, ext. 387). Six different spectacles a week are staged every Monday to Saturday, starting at 9pm. The cost is $53 (£28) per person, including dinner and one show. Dinner is from 6:30 to 9pm. The show is different every night—a revue of Latin rhythms one night, Broadway tunes the next night, or a "fantasy" on another night.

You'll think you've arrived in Havana when you attend performances at the **Cabaret Royal Showroom,** Westin Aruba Beach Resort & Spa, J. E. Irausquin Blvd. 77, Palm Beach (© 297/58-64466). It stages hot Cuban revues, with dancing and salsa music. Nearly all of the performers—music makers, dancers, and singers—come from Cuba. It's a high-energy revue with Latin and American classic songs, ballads, and Broadway favorites. The dinner show includes a three-course menu for $59 (£31) per person, but for only $20 (£10) you can enjoy the "cocktail show." Dinner show seatings are at 7pm, the revue beginning at 8:30pm. There are no shows Sunday or Monday.

THE CLUB & BAR SCENE

We like to begin our Aruban nights at **Salt 'n Pepper,** J. E. Irausquin Blvd. 368A (© 297/58-63280), where we can order the island's best tapas. Three or four of these appetizers are large enough to make a meal. If you bring in a set of original salt and pepper shakers for the owners to keep, you get your first glass of wine free with your dinner. *Note:* Sets can't be "borrowed" from local restaurants and hotels. Sangria, consumed in an alfresco courtyard, is the usual drink of choice, and the bar stays open until 1am.

Mambo Jumbo, in the Royal Plaza Mall, L. G. Smith Boulevard (© 297/58-33632), is sultry and relaxing. Expect a cosmopolitan blend of Dutch and Latino visitors, and lots of Latin rhythms. The volume is kept at a tolerable level for anyone who wants to have a conversation. There's an array of specialty drinks; imagine coconut shells, very colorful straws, and large fruit. Hours are 10pm to 2am, Monday to Friday, depending on the night of the week.

Iguana Joe's Caribbean Bar & Grill, Royal Plaza Mall, L. G. Smith Boulevard (© 297/58-39373), enjoys an equal vogue among visitors and islanders. It's known for its huge array of specialty drinks, including Pink Iguana, Grandma Joe's Pink Lemonade, and the aptly named Lethal Lizard, packing four shots of liquor in a half-liter carafe. Line your stomach with fresh salads, pastas, fresh mahimahi, sizzling fajitas, and rich homemade desserts. Hours are Monday through Saturday 11am to midnight, and Sunday 5pm to midnight.

Aruba's most popular nighttime attraction is a 1957 Chevy, **Kukoo Kunuku** (© **297/58-62010**), a psychedelically painted party bus that hits half a dozen of the island's hottest bars. The carousing begins at "sundowner" time at 6pm and goes on until around midnight, Monday to Saturday. Every reveler gets maracas for this pub-crawl on wheels. The cost of $59 (£31) per person includes dinner, champagne toast on the beach, a free drink at the three bars, and a pickup at your hotel.

If you're young and like a party atmosphere, head for the aptly named **La Fiesta,** Aventura Mall, in Oranjestad (© **297/58-38000**). This popular bar rocks all night.

Carlos 'N Charlie's Aruba, Westraat 3A (© **297/58-20355**), in the heart of Oranjestad, is a great place to party. It offers such cornpone fun as dancing in the conga line with the crazy waiters. Part of a rapidly growing chain, the bar/restaurant appeals to singles, families, cruise-ship passengers—you name it. After 10pm, there's "dirty dancing." Mexican dishes are the staple, but the kitchen will also whip you up a "gringo burger," even some "tequila fish" fired in butter and garlic. Lunch main dishes go from $10 to $15 (£5.20–£7.80), with dinner courses costing $20 to $25 (£10–£13). Hours are daily 11am to 1am, and a $5 (£2.60) cover is imposed on Friday and Saturday nights.

6

Barbados

Endless pink- and white-sand beaches and a rich West Indian tradition are what put Barbados (Bar-*bay*-dose) on the map. Barbados is easily reached from the United States and has a grand array of hotels (many of them super expensive). Although it doesn't offer casinos, it has more than just beach life. It's a terrific destination for travelers interested in learning about West Indian culture, and it has more sightseeing attractions than most Caribbean islands.

After morning mists burn off to expose panoramas of valley and ocean, the Bajan landscape is one of the most majestic in the southern Caribbean. It's an ideal place to go on lovely driving tours to take in all the little seaside villages, plantations, gardens, and English country churches, some dating from the 17th century.

Barbados is known as "Little England" in the Caribbean. Afternoon tea remains a tradition in many places, cricket is still the national sport, and many Bajans speak with a British accent. Despite this legacy, islanders are weighing the possibility of a divorce from the mother country.

Don't rule out Barbados if you're seeking a peaceful island getaway. Although the south coast is known for its nightlife and the west-coast beach strip is completely built up, some of the island remains undeveloped. The east coast is fairly tranquil, and you can often be alone here (but because it faces the Atlantic, the waters aren't as calm as they are on the Caribbean side). Many escapists, especially Canadians seeking a low-cost place to stay in winter, don't seem to mind the Atlantic waters at all. Not only does the Atlantic Coast have Bathsheba Beach going for it, but it is also home to some of the most visited attractions on the island. These include Andromeda Botanical Garden, Farley Hill National Park, Barbados Wildlife Reserve, and Harrison's Cave.

Although crime has been on the rise in recent years, Barbados is still a relatively safe destination. The difference between the haves and the have-nots doesn't result in the violence seen on other islands like Jamaica. Bajans have a long history of welcoming foreign visitors, and that tradition of hospitality is still ingrained in most locals.

1 Essentials

VISITOR INFORMATION

In the United States, you can contact the following offices of the **Barbados Tourism Authority:** 800 Second Ave., New York, NY 10017 (© **800/221-9831**); 3440 Wilshire Blvd., Suite 1215, Los Angeles, CA 90010 (© **213/380-2198**); or 150 Alhambra Circle, Suite 1000, Miami, FL 33134 (© **305/442-7471**).

The Canadian office is at 105 Adelaide St. West, Suite 1010, Toronto, Ontario M5H 1P9 (© **800/268-9122** in the U.S. and Canada, or 416/214-9880). In the United

Kingdom, contact the Barbados Tourism Authority at 263 Tottenham Court Rd., London W1T 7LA (© 020/7636-9448 or 020/7636-9449).

On the Internet, go to **www.barbados.org**. The tourism office may be able to help you track down condo and villa rentals.

On the island, the local **Barbados Tourism Authority** office is on Harbour Road (P.O. Box 242), Bridgetown (© 246/427-2623).

GETTING THERE

Before you book your flight, be sure to read the section "Packages for the Independent Traveler," in chapter 2; it can save you a bundle. Even if you don't book a package, see that chapter's tips on finding the best airfare.

More than 20 flights arrive on Barbados from all over the world every day. **Grant-ley Adams International Airport** (© 246/428-7101) is on Highway 7, on the southern tip of the island at Long Bay, between Oistins and a village called The Crane. From North America, the four major gateways to Barbados are New York, Miami, Toronto, and San Juan, Puerto Rico. Flying time to Barbados is 4½ hours from New York, 3½ hours from Miami, 5 hours from Toronto, and 1½ hours from San Juan.

Virgin Atlantic Airways (© 800/862-8621 in the U.S. and Canada; www.virgin-atlantic.com) flies daily from London's Gatwick Airport to Barbados.

American Airlines (© 800/433-7300 in the U.S. and Canada; www.aa.com) has dozens of connections passing through San Juan, plus daily nonstop flights to Barbados from Miami. **BWIA** (© 800/538-2942 in the U.S. and Canada; www.bwee. com), the national airline of Trinidad and Tobago, flies daily from New York and Miami, and offers many flights from Trinidad. **US Airways** (© 800/428-4322 in the U.S. and Canada; www.usairways.com) flies daily from New York's LaGuardia to Philadelphia, Washington, or Baltimore, then on to Barbados. There are no nonstop flights on US Airways from New York to Barbados.

All flights are nonstop from Toronto to Barbados. **Air Canada** (© 888/247-2262 in the U.S. and Canada; www.aircanada.com) has daily flights from Toronto in winter. From Montréal connections are made through Toronto.

Barbados is a major hub of the Caribbean-based airline **LIAT** (© 888/844-5428 in most of the Caribbean, 268/480-5601 for reservations, or 246/428-0986 at the Barbados airport; www.liatairline.com), which provides generally poor service to Barbados from a handful of neighboring islands, including St. Vincent and The Grenadines, Antigua, and Dominica.

Air Jamaica (© 800/523-5585 in the U.S. and Canada; www.airjamaica.com) offers daily flights that link Barbados to Atlanta, Baltimore, Boston, Chicago, and Miami through the airline's Montego Bay hub. Air Jamaica also flies between Los Angeles and Barbados on Monday and Wednesday (but it requires an overnight stay in Montego Bay). Nonstop flights from New York to Barbados are available at least 4 days a week (Mon, Wed, Fri, and Sun).

Cayman Airways and **Air Jamaica** have joined forces to provide an air link from Grand Cayman to Barbados and Trinidad, via Kingston in Jamaica. Flights wing out of Grand Cayman Sunday, Monday, Thursday, and Friday, linking up in Kingston with continuing flights to Barbados and Port-of-Spain, with daily return flights. For reservations and information, call Air Jamaica at © 800/523-5585.

British Airways (© 800/247-9297 in the U.S. and Canada; www.britishairways. com) flies nonstop daily to Barbados from London's Gatwick Airport.

Barbados

MARTINIQUE

ST. LUCIA

ST. VINCENT
AND THE
GRENADINES

GRENADA

BARBADOS

WINDWARD ISLANDS

VENEZUELA

TRINIDAD
AND TOBAGO

*ATLANTIC
OCEAN*

Martin's Bay
Congor Rocks
Consett Bay

JOHN

*CULPEPPER
ISLAND*

Ragged Point
Lighthouse

Three Houses

Kitridge Point

Bushy Park

Sunbury
Plantation
House

Sandford

Bottom Bay

ST. PHILIP

5

Long Bay

Heritage Park
& Rum Factory

Marchfield

Beachy Head

Crane Beach

7

21

Grantley Adams
Int'l Airport

Long Bay

Accra Beach Hotel & Resort **13**
Allamanda Beach Hotel **12**
Amaryllis Beach Resort **12**
Cobblers Cove Hotel **1**
Coral Reef Club **2**
The Crane **21**
Divi Southwinds Beach Resort **17**
Fairholme **18**
Hilton Barbados **11**
The House **6**
Little Arches **19**
Peach & Quiet **20**
Sandpiper **4**
Sandy Beach Island Resort **14**
Sandy Lane Hotel & Golf Club **6**
The Savannah **10**
Sea-U Guest House **8**
Southern Palms **15**
Tamarind Cove **7**
Traveller's Palm **5**
Turtle Beach Resort **16**
Villa Nova **9**

Finds **Special Events**

One of the hottest jazz festivals in the Caribbean is the **Barbados Jazz Festival.** Also known as "Paint It Jazz," it takes place in mid-January. International artists appear along with the best in local jazz talent. For tickets and further details, contact festival organizers at www.barbadosjazzfestival.com.

In mid-February, the **Holetown Festival** at St. James is a weeklong event commemorating the landing of the first European settlers at Holetown in 1627. Highlights include street fairs, police band concerts, a music festival in the parish church, and a road race.

During the first week of April, the **Oistins Fish Festival** commemorates the signing of the charter of Barbados with fishing, boat racing, fish-boning competitions, a Coast Guard exhibition, food stalls, arts and crafts, dancing, singing, and road races.

Beginning in mid-July and lasting until the first week of August, the **Crop Over Festival** is the island's major national festival, celebrating the completion of the sugar-cane harvest and recognizing the hardworking men and women in the sugar industry. Communities all over the island participate in fairs, concerts, calypso competitions, car parades, and other cultural events. The climax of the festival occurs at **Kadooment Day,** a national holiday on the first Monday in August, which becomes the biggest party of the year in Barbados.

GETTING AROUND

BY RENTAL CAR   If you don't mind **driving on the left,** you may find a rental car ideal on Barbados. You'll need a temporary permit if you don't have an international driver's license. The rental agencies listed below can all issue this visitor's permit, or you can go to the police desk upon your arrival at the airport. You must have a license from home and pay a registration fee of BD$10 (US$5). The speed limit is 32kmph (20 mph) inside city limits, 72kmph (45 mph) elsewhere on the island. Due to frequent delays at airport counters, we suggest taking a taxi from the airport to your hotel, and then calling to have your rental car delivered. No taxes apply to car rentals on Barbados.

None of the major U.S.-based car-rental agencies operates on Barbados, but a host of local companies rent vehicles. Except in the peak midwinter season, cars are usually readily available without prior reservations. Be forewarned that many local companies continue to draw serious complaints from readers, both for overcharging and for the poor conditions of their vehicles. Proceed very carefully with rentals on this island. Check the insurance and liability issues carefully when you rent.

The island's most frequently recommended agency is **National Car Rentals,** Lower Carlton, St. James (© **246/426-0603**), which has a wide selection of Japanese cars. (Note that it's *not* affiliated with the U.S. chain of the same name.) National is 15km (10 miles) north of Bridgetown, near the main highway (Hwy. 1); it delivers cars to almost any location on the island, and the driver who delivers it will carry the necessary forms for the Bajan driver's license.

Other comparable companies include **Sunny Isle Motors,** Dayton, Worthing Main Road, Christ Church (✆ **246/435-7979**), and **P&S Car Rentals,** Pleasant View, Cave Hill, St. Michael (✆ **246/424-2052**).

BY TAXI   Taxis aren't metered, but rates are fixed by the government; one cab can carry up to four passengers for the same fare. Taxis are plentiful and easily identifiable by the letter *Z* on their license plates. Drivers will produce a list of standard rates (BD$50–BD$60/US$25–US$30 per hour, subject to change). To call a taxi, contact one of the following services: **Paramount Taxi Service** (✆ **246/429-3718**), **Royal Pavilion Taxi Service** (✆ **246/422-1260**), or **Lyndhurst Taxi Service** (✆ **246/436-2639**). A typical taxi ride from the airport to Bridgetown costs BD$30 to BD$45 (US$15–US$23); to Holetown along the western Gold Coast, BD$45 to BD$60 (US$23–US$30); and to St. Lawrence Gap, site of many of the less expensive hotels, BD$25 (US$13).

BY BUS   Take a bus only as a last resort, as the service is unreliable, in spite of the fact that many Bajans depend on this service to get to and from work. The nationally owned buses of Barbados are blue with yellow stripes. They're not numbered, but their destinations are marked on the front. On most major routes, buses run every 30 minutes or so. Wherever you go, the fare is BD$1.50 (US75¢), exact Barbados change required. Departures are from Bridgetown, leaving from Fairchild Street for the south and east, and from Lower Green and the Princess Alice Highway for the north going along the west coast. Call the **Barbados Tourism Authority** (✆ **246/427-2623**) for schedules and information.

Privately operated **minibuses** run shorter distances and travel more frequently. They are bright yellow with blue stripes, with their destinations displayed on the bottom-left corner of the windshield. Minibuses in Bridgetown are boarded at River Road, Temple Yard, and Probyn Street. The fare is BD$1.50 (US75¢).

FAST FACTS: Barbados

American Express   The island's affiliate is **Going Places Travel,** Suite 27, Becklith Mall, Nile Street (✆ **246/431-2423**), in Bridgetown.

Banks   Most banks are open Monday to Thursday 8am to 5pm, and Friday 8am to 3pm. The major banks of Barbados, **all with ATMs,** are found along Broad Street in Bridgetown, including branches of First Caribbean Bank (formerly Barclays), the Barbados National Bank, and the Bank of Nova Scotia. These banks also have branch offices in Holetown, Speightstown, and along the St. Lawrence Gap south of Bridgetown. There are ATMs at the airport as well, plus at bank branches throughout the island.

Consulates & High Commissions   The **Embassy of the United States** is on Broad Street, Bridgetown (✆ **246/436-4950**), and the **Canadian High Commission** at Lower Bishop's Court, Pine Road, Bridgetown (✆ **246/429-3550**). The **British High Commission** is found at Lower Collymore Rock, St. Michael (✆ **246/430-7880**).

Currency   The **Barbados dollar (BD$)** is the official currency, available in $5, $10, $20, and $100 notes, as well as 10¢, 25¢, and $1 silver coins, plus 1¢ and 5¢ copper coins. The Barbados dollar is permanently fixed because of an international agreement at the rate of approximately 50¢ in U.S. currency. In contrast, the value of the British pound is not permanently fixed, and as such, it floats freely, going up or down in relation to a wide range of political and economic factors that change from day to day. At presstime for this edition £1 equaled approximately BD$3.90. Most stores take traveler's checks or U.S. dollars. However, it's best to convert your money at banks and pay in Barbados dollars. *Unless otherwise specified, prices in this chapter are quoted in U.S. dollars and British pounds.*

Customs Most items for personal use (within reason, of course) are allowed into Barbados, except agricultural products and firearms. You can bring in perfume for your use if it's not for sale. You're also allowed a carton of cigarettes and a liter of liquor.

Documents Citizens of all countries need a passport to enter Barbados, including those from the United States and Canada. Cruise-ship passengers need only the ship's magnetic identification card. However, if a cruise begins and ends in Barbados, a passport is required.

Electricity The electricity is 110-volt AC (50 cycles), so you can use your U.S.-made appliances.

Emergencies In an emergency, dial the police at ℂ **211**, the fire department at ℂ **311**, and an ambulance at ℂ **511**.

Hospitals The **Queen Elizabeth Hospital** is located on Martinsdale Road in St. Michael (ℂ **246/436-6450**). Of the several private clinics, one of the most expensive and best recommended is the **Bayview Hospital**, St. Paul's Avenue, Bayville, St. Michael (ℂ **246/436-5446**).

Language The Bajans speak English, but with their own island lilt.

Liquor Laws Liquor, beer, and wine are sold throughout the island at every outlet from grocery stores to convenience stores on any day the stores are open. Open containers are illegal on the beach.

Safety Crimes against visitors used to be rare, but there are today reports of pickpocketing, armed robbery, and even sexual assault. Avoid leaving cash or valuables in your hotel room; beware of purse snatchers when walking, exercise caution on the beach or at attractions; and be wary of driving in isolated areas.

Taxes A 7½% government sales tax is tacked on to hotel bills. A 15% VAT (value-added tax) is levied on all meals. (For example, if your hotel costs US$200 per night, and you are charged US$50 per person for a MAP, you'll have to pay a 7½% government tax plus the 10% additional service charge for the US$200 room rate, and then an additional 15% VAT on the MAP rate.) Some visitors view these additional charges as "larcenous." They certainly won't make you happy when you go to pay your final bill. There's a departure tax of BD$25 (US$13) which is payable in either U.S. dollars or Barbadian currency.

Telephone To call Barbados from the United States, dial **1**, then **246** (the area code for Barbados) and the local number. Once on Barbados, to call another number on the island, only the local number is necessary.

Time Barbados is on Atlantic Standard Time year-round, so it's 1 hour ahead of New York except during daylight saving time, when Barbados's time is the same as the eastern United States.

Tipping Most hotels and restaurants add at least a 10% service charge to your bill. If service is extremely good, you may want to supplement that. If it has not been included, you may want to tip your waiter 10% to 15%. Taxi drivers expect a 10% tip.

Water Barbados has a pure water supply. It's pumped from underground sources in the coral rock that covers most of the island, and it's safe to drink.

Weather Daytime temperatures are in the 75°F to 85°F (24°C–29°C) range throughout the year.

2 Accommodations

Barbados has some of the best hotels in the Caribbean, many of which are small and personally run.

Most of our recommendations are on fashionable St. James Beach, which is the entire strip of beachfront bordering the parish of St. James. Although hotels are scattered around Barbados, most of them lie on the tranquil west coast as opposed to opening onto the turbulent Atlantic in the east. If you're in Barbados on business, you may want a hotel in Bridgetown, the capital. If you're into the grand life, head for one of the fashionable resorts north of Bridgetown, all of which open onto sandy beaches. Otherwise, if you want something more informal and less expensive, go to the lower south coast, especially around the busy strip of St. Lawrence Gap, where you can find the most reasonably priced nightlife, restaurants, and local bars. This area also has beaches, although they're not as fabulous as those claimed by the pricey resorts north of Bridgetown. The prices of many of Barbados' hotels are among the most celestial in the Caribbean, rivaled only by Anguilla and St. Barts. Just when you think a hotelier won't dare raise prices any more than they already are, he adds another US$200 or so to your daily room cost.

If you want a holiday in the southern Caribbean, but haven't come into your inheritance, consider such neighboring islands as St. Vincent or Grenada.

To rent your own villa, cottage, or house on Barbados, contact **Jennifer Alleyne Ltd.,** Molyneux Plantation, St. James, Barbados, W.I. (© **246/432-1159;** www.jal barbados.com), which has properties in a wide range of prices.

ON THE WEST COAST
VERY EXPENSIVE
Cobblers Cove Hotel ☆☆☆   This former mansion on a white-sand beach is built in a mock-medieval style on the site of a former British fort. A member of Relais & Châteaux, the hotel is a favorite honeymoon retreat. Elegant suites are housed in 10 Iberian-style villas, situated throughout lush gardens. Each unit has a spacious living room and bathroom, a private balcony or patio, and a wet bar. To keep the property in top-notch condition, nine bedrooms are completely redecorated each year. Two of the most exclusive accommodations on the entire island are the Camelot and Colleton suites, on the rooftop of the original mansion; they're beautifully decorated and offer

panoramic views of both the beach and the garden. Both have their own pool. For their lethal prices, refer to the high end of the prices given below; other units are at the low end of the price scale.

The Terrace Restaurant, with its open-air dining room overlooking the sea, creates generally lighter and more refined fare than the heavier French food served at some of its competitors along the Gold Coast.

Road View, Speightstown, St. Peter, Barbados, W.I. © **800/890-6060** in the U.S., 020/8350-1001 in London, or 246/422-2291. Fax 246/422-1460. www.cobblerscove.com. 40 units. Winter US$730–US$1,050 (£380–£546) double, US$2,100–US$2,450 (£1,092–£1,274) Camelot or Colleton suite; off season US$430–US$970 (£224–£504) double, US$915–US$1,200 (£476–£624) Camelot or Colleton suite. Rates include American breakfast. AE, MC, V. Closed Sept to mid-Oct. No children under 12 allowed Jan–Mar. **Amenities:** Restaurant; bar; outdoor pool; lit tennis court; gym; snorkeling; Sunfish sailboats; water-skiing; windsurfing; tour desk; car rental; room service; babysitting; laundry service; dry cleaning. *In room:* A/C, minibar, beverage maker, hair dryer, iron, safe.

Coral Reef Club ☆☆

This family-owned and -managed luxury hotel is one of the best and most respected establishments on the island, set on elegantly landscaped grounds beside a white-sand beach that's ideal for swimming. A collection of veranda-fronted private units is scattered about the main building and clubhouse on 5 hectares (12 acres), fronting the ocean. Rental units, housed in cottages, the main building, or in small, coral-stone wings in the gardens, can vary greatly, but each has a luxurious bed (a king-size, twins, or a four-poster) and a tiled bathroom, with a combination tub/shower. All units have private patios, and some have separate dressing rooms.

You can lunch in an open-air area, take afternoon tea, and then enjoy a first-rate dinner in a room with three sides open to ocean views. There's a folklore show and barbecue every Thursday, plus a Monday Bajan buffet featuring an array of food (including whole baked fish) and local entertainment.

Hwy. 1, St. James Beach, Barbados, W.I. © **800/223-1108** in the U.S., or 246/422-2372. Fax 246/422-1776. www.coral reefbarbados.com. 88 units. Winter US$610–US$910 (£317–£473) double, US$1,060–US$2,510 (£551–£1,305) suite; off season US$245–$420 (£127–£218) double, US$550–US$1,310 (£286–£681) suite. AE, MC, V. Drive 5 min. north of Holetown on Hwy. 1. No children under 12 allowed Jan–Mar. **Amenities:** Restaurant; bar; 2 outdoor pools; 2 tennis courts; fitness room; dive shop; salon; room service; massage; babysitting; laundry service; dry cleaning; rooms for those w/limited mobility. *In room:* A/C, minibar, hair dryer, safe.

The House ☆☆☆ *(Finds)*

The House is a sanctuary of tranquility and privacy, with the most personal service in Barbados. This exclusive retreat doesn't even call itself a hotel but "a concept." At the moment you arrive an "ambassador," clad in white linen, materializes to serve you during your stay. The approach to the complex sets the tone, as you go over a wooden bridge across a lake studded with water lilies, passing along blossoming bougainvillea. Each unit is a luxuriously furnished suite containing many thoughtful extras such as Evian water and fresh fruit. All the bedrooms contain tubs and showers, and the most desirable accommodations overlook the golden sands at Paynes Bay, a 30-minute drive north of the airport. Two suites even have their own indoor pools.

Next door is Daphne's, the ultimate in island dining with an eclectic Italian menu inspired by its famous London counterpart. Ever had a delectable dish like marinated white anchovies with roast beets and linguine with spicy crab?

Hwy. 1, Paynes Bay, St. James, Barbados, W.I. © **246/432-5525.** Fax 246/432-5255. www.thehousebarbados.com. 33 units. Winter US$1,100–US$1,780 (£572–£926) double; off season US$680–US$1,490 (£354–£775) double. Rates include full breakfast. AE, DC, MC, V. No children under 12 allowed. **Amenities:** Restaurant; bar; outdoor pool; Jacuzzi; kayaks; sailing; snorkeling; water-skiing; airport limousine; room service; massage; laundry service; dry cleaning. *In room:* A/C, TV, beverage maker, hair dryer, iron, safe, Wi-Fi.

Lone Star Hotel ⓕ *Finds*   Talk about recycling old buildings. This chic restaurant and hotel was converted from a dreary garage built in the 1940s. Today the gas jockeys and grease monkeys are long gone and you're more likely to see Monaco's Prince Albert running around the joint, or perhaps Mariah Carey or John Cleese. The Lone Star offers four sumptuous suites—two on a good beach and the others on the upper level. Each is individually named to commemorate the building's former function. You can book into the Buick, Lincoln, Cord, or Studebaker suites, where you will find spacious bedrooms, beautiful furnishings, and opulent modern bathrooms with Philip Starck fittings. Upper suites open onto large furnished balconies. The building has had a long and colorful history, and during World War II a coral stone cave was carved out as a hideaway in case German bombs rained down. Today it is the wine cellar for the restaurant.

Hwy. 1, Mount Standfast, St. James, Barbados, W.I. ⓒ 246/419-0599. Fax 246/419-0597. www.thelonestar.com. 4 units. Winter US$550–US$850 (£286–£442) double; off season US$300–US$400 (£156–£208) double. Extra person US$80 (£42). Rates include full breakfast. Children under 14 stay free in parent's room. AE, MC, V. **Amenities:** Restaurant; bar; room service; babysitting; laundry service; dry cleaning. *In room:* A/C, TV, minibar, beverage maker, hair dryer, iron, safe.

Sandpiper ⓕ   The Coral Reef Club (see above) does it better, but if it's full, try this South Seas resort on a white-sand beach. Completely overhauled in 2005, it's a self-contained, intimate resort, set in a small grove of coconut palms and flowering trees. A cluster of rustic-chic units surrounds the pool; some have fine sea views. The rooms open onto little terraces that stretch along the second story, where you can order drinks or have breakfast. Accommodations are large, consisting of superior rooms and one- or two-bedroom suites beautifully furnished with tropical pieces. Each has a private terrace, luxurious bed, and small fridge. The medium-size bathrooms are equipped with combination tub/showers.

The refined cuisine is both Continental and West Indian; weekly buffets are offered in winter. The menu is varied and based on the best of seasonal products, so you can dine here every night without getting bored.

Holetown (a 3-min. walk north of town), St. James, Barbados, W.I. ⓒ 800/223-1108 in the U.S., 800/567-5327 in Canada, or 246/422-2251. Fax 246/422-0900. www.sandpiperbarbados.com. 45 units. Winter US$765–US$1,190 (£398–£619) double, US$845–US$2,510 (£439–£1,305) suite; off season US$365–US$745 (£190–£387) double, US$830–US$1,310 (£432–£681) suite. AE, MC, V. No children under 12 allowed Jan–Mar. **Amenities:** Restaurant; 2 bars; outdoor pool; 2 tennis courts; fitness center; children's programs; room service; babysitting; laundry service; dry cleaning. *In room:* A/C, fridge, beverage maker, hair dryer, safe.

Sandy Lane Hotel & Golf Club ⓕⓕⓕ   Sandy Lane is one of the most luxurious places to stay in the southern Caribbean, as its horrifying prices and high-flying clientele will attest. Tiger Woods rented the whole place out for his 2004 wedding, and other celeb guests include Beyoncé and Jay-Z, Jerry Seinfeld, and Cindy Crawford. Ronald Tree, an heir to the Marshall Field's department store fortune, built Shady Lane in the 1960s. After falling into neglect, it was rescued in 1997 by Irish investors, who poured US$350 million into its reconstruction. Fortunately, its pristine beach set against a backdrop of swaying palms needed no such rehabilitation.

The Palladian-style Sandy Lane is practically identical to its first incarnation, with the addition of a mammoth spa, better restaurants, and a trio of golf courses. You'll feel like royalty when checking in—especially when your valet unpacks your suitcase. On request, you can be picked up at the airport in the hotel's Bentley.

The rooms are furnished grandly, with lots of extras not found at any of its competitors—such as a motion-sensor alarm to alert maids you're in the room, and a marble shower with seven adjustable nozzles. Accommodations are decorated mostly with redwood furnishings, each with a king-size bed or two twins. The bathrooms are the most luxurious on the island, and in addition to the shower, also contain oversize tubs and a bidet.

Four on-site restaurants offer the finest hotel dining on Barbados and serve mostly a French or Mediterranean cuisine. There's also the Spa Cafe for the weight conscious.

Hwy. 1, Paynes Bay, St. James, Barbados, W.I. ℭ **246/444-2000**. Fax 246/444-2222. www.sandylane.com. 112 units. Winter US$2,800–US$3,700 (£1,456–£1,924) double, US$4,000–US$9,200 (£2,080–£4,784) suite; off season US$900–US$1,500 (£468–£780) double, US$2,900–US$7,000 (£1,508–£3,640) suite. AE, DC, MC, V. **Amenities:** 4 restaurants; 5 bars; outdoor pool; 3 golf courses; 9 tennis courts; fitness center; health spa; kayaks; sailing; water-skiing; children's program; concierge; salon; room service; massage; nonsmoking rooms. *In room:* A/C, TV, minibar, beverage maker (on request), hair dryer, safe.

Tamarind Cove ⚲ On 240m (790 ft.) of prime beachfront, this flagship of a British-based hotel chain (St. James Properties) is a major challenger to the Coral Reef Club and Sandpiper properties (see above), attracting the same upscale clientele. The Croal Reef still has a slight edge in luxury, but Tamarind is the equal of the Sandpiper in style and comfort.

Designed in an Iberian style, with pastel-colored walls and red terra-cotta roofs, the hotel occupies a desirable location on St. James Beach, 2km (1¼ miles) south of Holetown. The chic and comfortable rooms are in a series of hacienda-style buildings interspersed with vegetation. Many units have a patio or balcony overlooking the gardens or ocean. The well-appointed bathrooms come with dual basins, spacious Roman tubs, stall showers, and long marble counters. Nearly a dozen oceanfront suites come with four-poster beds, evoking a plantation house atmosphere. Families with one or two kids often book one of the smaller suites. Many units have a patio or private balcony overlooking either the gardens of the ocean.

The Caribbean and international food served here is among the finest of the resorts along the Gold Coast. There's some kind of musical entertainment nearly every night.

Hwy. 1, Paynes Bay, St. James Beach (P.O. Box 429), Bridgetown, Barbados, W.I. ℭ **800/326-6898** in the U.S. or Canada, or 246/432-1332. Fax 246/432-6317. www.tamarindcovehotel.com. 110 units. Winter US$573–US$836 (£298–£435) double; off season US$408–US$728 (£212–£379) double. Rates include breakfast and dinner. AE, MC, V. **Amenities:** 2 restaurants; bar; 3 outdoor pools; golf privileges; 2 nearby tennis courts; exercise room; water-skiing; windsurfing; nearby horseback riding; children's programs; concierge; business center; 3 boutiques; salon; room service; babysitting; massage; laundry service. *In room:* A/C, TV, minibar, beverage maker, hair dryer, iron, safe.

INEXPENSIVE

Allamanda Beach Hotel *Kids* *Value* This complex is one of the best bargains on Barbados and is ideal for families. Directly on a rocky shoreline 4km (2½ miles) southeast of Bridgetown, the hotel is in the heart of the village of Hastings. The U-shaped complex is built around a pool terrace overlooking the sea. Functional and minimalist in decor, the accommodations are clean and comfortable, with tiny but fully equipped kitchenettes. You face a choice of a regular hotel room, a studio, or a one-bedroom suite. All have balconies or decks, and some units have air-conditioning. Each unit has a small bathroom with a shower stall; only three occupants are allowed in a double room.

Although some athletic guests attempt to swim off the nearby rocks, most walk 5 minutes to the white sands of nearby Rockley (Accra) Beach. A small restaurant on the property serves very average American and Bajan fare.

Hastings, Christ Church, Barbados, W.I. ⓒ 246/438-1000. Fax 246/435-9211. www.allamandabeach.com. 50 units. Winter US$170 (£88) double, US$197 (£102) studio, US$250 (£130) suite; off season US$120 (£62) double, US$137 (£71) studio, US$171 (£89) suite. Extra person US$38 (£20). AE, MC, V. **Amenities:** Restaurant; bar; outdoor pool; room service; babysitting; laundry service; dry cleaning. *In room:* A/C, ceiling fan, TV, kitchenette, fridge, beverage maker, hair dryer, iron, safe.

Traveller's Palm   Within a 10-minute walk of a good beach, this is for self-suffi-cient types who are not too demanding and want to save money. There's a choice of simply furnished, one-bedroom apartments with fully equipped kitchens and well-maintained bathrooms with shower units. They're simple, slightly worn apartments, with bright but fading colors, but they're quite a deal in this high-rent district. The apartments have living and dining areas, as well as patios where you can have break-fast or a candlelit dinner you've prepared yourself (no meals are served here). To run the in-room air-conditioners you must purchase tokens.

265 Palm Ave., Sunset Crest, St. James, Barbados, W.I. ⓒ 246/432-6750. Fax 246/432-7229. www.sunsetcrest resort.com. 16 units. Winter US$165 (£86) apt for 2; off season US$125 (£65) apt for 2. MC, V. **Amenities:** Snack bar; bar; outdoor pool; babysitting; laundry service; dry cleaning. *In room:* Token-operated A/C, kitchenette.

SOUTH OF BRIDGETOWN/THE SOUTH COAST
VERY EXPENSIVE
Little Arches ⭑⭑ *Finds*   A real discovery, this family-owned boutique hotel overlooks white-sand Enterprise Beach on the south coast. It's a little charmer for those who seek out personalized hotels. The ocean-view bedrooms are individually styled with four-poster king-size beds, along with such extras as private Jacuzzi sun decks. Italian fabrics and well-chosen furnishings grace the bedrooms. The colorful rooms look like an arranged set waiting for the *House & Garden* photographers. The extras make this place really thrive: a roof-deck swimming pool, a holistic massage therapist, an alfresco restaurant run by an international chef, and free use of mountain bikes. The location is a short walk from the village of Oistins at a point 6.5km (4 miles) from St. Lawrence Gap and 13km (8 miles) from the airport. Children under 16 are not welcome.

Enterprise Coast Rd., Christ Church, Barbados, W.I. ⓒ 800/860-8013 in the U.S., or 246/420-4689. Fax 246/418-0207. www.littlearches.com. 10 units. Winter US$399–US$552 (£208–£287) double; off season US$244–US$336 (£127–£174) double. AE, MC, V. No children under 16 allowed. **Amenities:** Restaurant; bar; outdoor pool; yacht; mountain bikes; room service; massage; laundry service. *In room:* A/C, TV, kitchenette (in 3 units), beverage maker, hair dryer, iron, safe.

The Savannah ⭑ *Finds*   Blending traditional with the contemporary, this hotel on the beach offers some of the most luxurious bedrooms on the south coast. Sections of this complex, like the original plantation house for example, have been standing here for 2 centuries. Today, two newly built extensions reach toward the sea on the well-landscaped grounds of tropical foliage. The waterfalls cascading into the lagoon-style pool are particularly lovely.

Opening onto views of the pool, garden, or ocean, bedrooms are elegantly furnished with mahogany four-poster beds and modern amenities like high-speed Internet access. Rooms also open onto spacious patios or balconies. Extras range from nightly enter-tainment to beauty treatments, including a Swedish massage. The Savannah is a 10-minute drive from Bridgetown and about a 25-minute ride from the airport.

Garrison Main Rd., Hastings, Christ Church, Barbados, W.I. ⓒ 800/868-9429 in the U.S., or 246/435-9473. Fax 246/435-8822. www.gemsbarbados.com. 98 units. Winter US$330–US$660 (£172–£343) double; off season US$265–US$530 (£138–£276) double. Children under 12 stay free in parent's room. Rates include continental breakfast. AE, MC, V. **Amenities:** 2 restaurants; 2 bars (1 swim-up); 2 outdoor pools; fitness center; spa services; children's programs;

salon; room service; babysitting; laundry service; dry cleaning; nonsmoking rooms. *In room:* A/C, ceiling fan, TV, beverage maker, hair dryer, iron, safe.

Turtle Beach Resort ☆☆ *Kids*   Opening onto 450m (1,480 ft.) of white-sand beach, this posh south-coast resort opened in 1998 and was named after the turtles that sometimes nest on the nearby sands. It's an all-inclusive property, drawing families, couples, and honeymooners. An open-air lobby opens onto the beach. All midsize rooms have ocean views, wicker furniture, ceiling fans, and voice mail. Beds have fine linens, and each one-bedroom suite offers both a queen-size bed and a sofa bed. If needed, free rollaway beds are provided. Bathrooms are luxurious, with tubs and showers.

The open-air restaurant, Chelonia, serves international, nouvelle dishes that are—especially for Barbados—rather artfully experimental. The casually elegant Waterfront serves informal food such as design-your-own pizzas. Casual Asiago serves pleasant Italian fare. For diversity, Turtle Beach offers a dine-around program with its other tony properties, including Crystal Cove and Coconut Creek. There's also nightly entertainment—calypso, jazz, cabaret, and more.

Dover, near St. Lawrence Gap, Barbados, W.I. *ⓒ* 800/326-6898 in the U.S., or 246/428-7131. Fax 246/428-6089. www.turtlebeachresortbarbados.com. 164 units. Winter US$906–US$1,200 (£471–£624) suite for 2; off season US$434–US$714 (£226–£371) suite for 2. Rates are all-inclusive. AE, DC, MC, V. **Amenities:** 3 restaurants; 3 bars; 3 outdoor pools; golf privileges; 2 lit tennis courts; gym; Jacuzzi; kayaks; sailing; snorkeling; windsurfing; children's club and playground; tour desk; car rental; room service; massage (in room); babysitting; laundry service; dry cleaning. *In room:* A/C, ceiling fan, TV, fridge, coffeemaker, hair dryer, iron, safe.

EXPENSIVE

Accra Beach Hotel & Resort ☆   This hotel, totally rebuilt in 1996, lies on the prettiest beach on the south coast, only 10 minutes from the airport, with Bridgetown about 3km (2 miles) to the west.

In a West Indian "megastyle," the three-story property is tastefully laid out, and offers spacious rooms opening onto a view of the pool or ocean. The units have large balconies and wooden shutters, plus full-size bathrooms with showers and tubs. The look is a bit sterile, more corporate hotel than island escape. Steer clear of units marked "island view," as the panorama is of the parking lot. The variety in dining is particularly noteworthy, ranging from The Fig Tree's pizzas in a garden setting to Wytukai, the only Polynesian restaurant on island. A barbecue and floor show on every Thursday is a highlight. *Note:* Much of the hotel is open air (including a dance floor), and the mosquitoes appreciate that fact.

Hwy. 7, Accra Beach, Rockley, Christ Church, Barbados, W.I. *ⓒ* 246/435-8920. Fax 246/435-6794. www.accrabeach hotel.com. 146 units. Winter US$286–US$406 (£149–£211) double, US$457–US$1,200 (£238–£624) suite; off season US$160–US$291 (£83–£151) double, US$286–US$910 (£149–£473) suite. AE, MC, V. **Amenities:** 3 restaurants; 2 bars (1 swim-up); outdoor pool; nearby golf; fitness center; squash court; snorkeling; car rental; business center; room service; babysitting; laundry service; dry cleaning; nonsmoking rooms; rooms for those w/limited mobility; open-air dance floor. *In room:* A/C, ceiling fan, TV, beverage maker, hair dryer, iron, safe.

Amaryllis Beach Resort *Kids*   Recycled from an older resort, this complex on the south coast is a more affordable option than some of the gold-plated properties farther north. Right on the beach in the historic Garrison area, the Amaryllis Beach Resort has very appealing tropical gardens and a deluxe pool.

Bedrooms are midsize to spacious and furnished in a tasteful Caribbean motif. You have various accommodation options, ranging from regular hotel rooms to studios, or even one- or two-bedroom suites for families or groups. Each of the tiled and well-maintained bathrooms comes with tub or shower. Bedrooms open onto balconies or patios, with views of the landscaped grounds or the ocean. Because of the wide range of drinking and dining facilities, you can dine under the stars and enjoy live Bajan entertainment without leaving the grounds at night.

Palm Beach, Hastings, Barbados, W.I. © 246/438-8000. Fax 246/426-9566. www.amaryllisbeachresort.com. 150 units. Winter US$270–US$290 (£140–£151) double, US$290–US$345 (£151–£179) studio, US$400–US$570 (£208–£296) suite; off season US$255–US$275 (£133–£143) double, US$275–US$330 (£143–£172) studio, US$385–US$555 (£200–£289) suite. AE, MC, V. **Amenities:** 4 restaurants; beach bar; outdoor pool; children's pool; tennis court; fitness center; kids' club; Internet cafe; business center; self-service laundry; rooms for those w/limited mobility. *In room:* A/C, TV, kitchenette (in some), hair dryer, iron, safe (in some).

Divi Southwinds Beach Resort 🌟 *Kids*   Midway between Bridgetown and Oistins on a .8km (½ mile) sandy beach, this resort was created when two distinctly different complexes were combined. The present resort consists of buildings scattered over 20 hectares (50 acres) of sandy flatlands. The showpiece is the newer (inland) complex, housing one- and two-bedroom suites with full kitchens—perfect for small families. These units look like a connected series of town houses, with wooden balconies and views of a large L-shaped pool. From here, you need only cross through two groves of palm trees and a narrow lane to reach the beach. The more modestly furnished older units lie directly on the beachfront, ringed with palm trees, near an oval pool. Each unit contains a full-size bathroom with tub and shower.

The Aquarius Restaurant serves decent food, and there's another casual spot for drinks and snacks by the beach.

St. Lawrence Gap, Christ Church, Barbados, W.I. © 800/367-3484 in the U.S., or 246/428-7181. Fax 246/428-4674. www.diviresorts.com. 160 units. Winter US$329–US$339 (£171–£176) double, US$419 (£218) suite; off season US$215–US$229 (£112–£119) double, US$278 (£145) suite. Children under 12 stay free in parent's room. AE, DC, MC, V. **Amenities:** 2 restaurants; 2 bars; beach snack bar; 3 outdoor pools; 2 tennis courts; fitness room; sailboat rentals; scuba diving; snorkeling; poolside activities for kids; salon; coin-operated laundry. *In room:* A/C, TV, kitchen, beverage maker, safe.

Hilton Barbados 🌟🌟 *Kids*   In 1650 Charles Fort was built on this site followed by a lighthouse. But today a completely rebuilt Hilton rises at this point on more than 14 acres of land at the southern edge of Bridgetown near a very good white sandy beach, but also near some oil tanks. The hotel's architecture on the rugged peninsula incorporates jutting balconies and wide expanses of glass. Bedrooms are arranged around a central courtyard filled with tropical gardens. Each of the well-furnished units has a view of Carlisle bay on the north side or the Atlantic on the south. Guests staying on the Executive Floor enjoy access to a luxurious lounge overlooking the bay. An oceanview spa has been installed on the 6th floor opening onto panoramic views. Warning: Rates below are only approximate, as the hotel is rather cagey about quoting tariffs in advance, as if wanting to give itself flexibility on a month-by-month basis when they see what the demand is. Whatever your final bill is, expect a 17.45% tax and service charge added as well.

Needham's Point, Aquatic Gap, St. Michael. © 800/445-8667 in the U.S., or 246/426-0200. Fax 246/228-7730. www.hiltoncaribbean.com. 317 units. Winter US$585–US$645 (£304–£335) double, from US$820 (£426) 1-bedroom suite. Off-season US$430–US$490 (£224–£255) double, US$820 (£426) 1-bedroom suite. **Amenities:** 3 restaurants; 2 bars; spa; children's programs; laundry service; health club; 3 tennis courts. *In room:* A/C, TV, minibar, safe, beverage maker, iron, Wi-Fi.

Southern Palms   A seafront club on 300m (990 ft.) of sand, with a distinct personality, Southern Palms lies on the Pink Pearl Beach of Barbados, midway between the airport and Bridgetown. The core of the resort is a pink-and-white manor house

built in the Dutch style, with a garden-level colonnade of arches. Spread along the sands are arched two- and three-story buildings, with Italian fountains and statues creating a Mediterranean feel. In its more modern block, an eclectic mixture of rooms includes some with kitchenettes, some facing the ocean, others opening onto the garden, and some with penthouse luxury. Each unit has a small bathroom containing a shower stall. A cluster of straw-roofed buildings, housing the drinking and dining facilities, links the accommodations.

The Garden Terrace Restaurant serves both West Indian and Continental cuisine. The Khus-Khus bar provides burgers, fish cakes, and light snacks. In general, the local Bajan dishes are the best. A local band often entertains with merengue, calypso, and steel-band music.

St. Lawrence, Christ Church, Barbados, W.I. ℂ 800/223-6510 in the U.S., or 246/428-7171. Fax 246/428-7175. www.southernpalms.net. 92 units. Winter US$230–US$270 (£120–£140) double, US$330 (£172) suite; off season US$136–US$165 (£71–£86) double, US$193 (£100) suite. MAP (breakfast and dinner) US$45 (£23) per person extra in winter, US$25 (£13) per person extra off season. AE, DC, MC, V. **Amenities:** Restaurant; bar; 2 outdoor pools; 2 tennis courts; exercise room; scuba lessons; windsurfing; salon; room service; babysitting; laundry service; coin-operated laundry; dry cleaning. *In room:* A/C, TV, kitchenette (in suites), fridge, beverage maker (in some), hair dryer, iron, safe.

INEXPENSIVE

Fairholme Lying a 5-minute walk from a good beach, this converted plantation house has been enlarged over the past 20 years or so with a handful of connected annexes. The main house and its original gardens are just off a major road, 10km (6¼ miles) southeast of Bridgetown. The older section has 10 double rooms, each with a living-room area and a patio overlooking an orchard and a pool. The best units are the 20 Spanish-style studio apartments, which have cathedral ceilings, dark beams, traditional furnishings, and balconies or patios. All units have neatly kept bathrooms with shower units. Air-conditioning is available only in the studios, while the older doubles have ceiling fans.

The restaurant here has a reputation for home cooking—wholesome and nothing fancy, but the ingredients are fresh. Guests may also use the waterfront cafe and bar at Fairholme's neighbor, the Sea Breeze.

Maxwell, Christ Church, Barbados, W.I. ℂ 246/428-9425. Fax 246/420-2389. 30 units. Winter US$45 (£23) double, US$60 (£31) studio apt; off season US$40 (£20) double, US$55 (£28) studio apt. DC, MC, V. **Amenities:** Restaurant; outdoor pool; breakfast-only room service. *In room:* A/C (in some), ceiling fan, kitchenettes (in some), fridge (in some).

Peach & Quiet 🌟 *Finds* The name alone attracted us to this little hideaway, an oceanfront property lying in 1.5 hectares (4 acres) of gardens at the southern tip of Barbados. Peach and Quiet is about a 15-minute drive from the restaurants and bars at St. Lawrence Gap. Guests can walk to the beaches in about 5 minutes, and they are also drawn to a rock pool which attracts some 100 species of rainbow-hued fish. All the spacious units are suites, each furnished in a style evocative of a Greek island. Your fan-cooled bedroom comes with a king-size bed, a double, or else two doubles along with a minimum of furnishings (although it's very comfortable). The bathrooms are equipped with showers, and each room opens onto a terrace or private balcony.

Inch Marlow Main Rd., Inch Marlow, Christ Church, Barbados, W.I. ℂ 246/428-5682. Fax 246/428-2467. www.peachandquiet.com. 22 units. Year-round US$99–US$109 (£52–£57) double. MC, V. **Amenities:** Restaurant; bar; outdoor pool. *In room:* Ceiling fan, fridge, beverage maker, safe.

Sandy Beach Island Resort 🌟🌟 *Kids* Definitely not to be confused with Sandy Lane, this hotel, originally established in 1980 and renovated in 2001, is a simple but thoroughly reliable choice, resting on .8 hectares (2 acres) of beachfront land, 6km (3¾ miles) southeast of Bridgetown. The Bajan-owned property rises around its architectural centerpiece, a soaring, cone-shaped structure known as a *palapa*. Great for families, the resort contains standard motel-like double rooms, and one- and two-bedroom suites. All the simply decorated and spacious units have fully equipped kitchenettes, private balconies or patios, and locally made furniture, plus small bathrooms containing shower units. Facilities for travelers with disabilities are available in some of the ground-floor suites.

Kolors, serving average seafood and steaks, is situated under the *palapa* and opens onto a view of the sea and pool. Every Monday, when nonguests are welcome, the resort sponsors a rum-punch party and a Bajan buffet. Entertainment is offered 3 nights a week in winter.

Worthing, Christ Church, Barbados, W.I. © **800/448-8355** in the U.S., or 246/435-8000. Fax 246/435-8053. 127 units. Winter US$158 (£82) double, US$315 (£164) 1-bedroom suite, US$365 (£190) 2-bedroom suite; off season US$99 (£52) double, US$162 (£84) 1-bedroom suite, US$245 (£127) 2-bedroom suite. Extra person US$28 (£15). MAP (breakfast and dinner) US$45 (£23) per person extra. Children under 13 stay free in parent's room. AE, DC, DISC, MC, V. **Amenities:** Restaurant; bar; outdoor pool; boating; scuba lessons; snorkeling; windsurfing; children's center; room service; babysitting; laundry service; dry cleaning; rooms for those w/limited mobility. *In room:* A/C, TV, kitchenettes (in suites), fridge, beverage maker, hair dryer, safe.

ON THE EAST COAST
VERY EXPENSIVE

The Crane ⊕ It's so old it's new again. Opened in 1887, this is arguably the Caribbean's first resort hotel. Near the easternmost end of the island, 23km (14 miles) east of Bridgetown, the hotel has bounced back for a new lease on life. What hasn't changed is Crane Beach, called by many the most beautiful spot on earth. It's spectacular with powder-soft white sand that can look pink in certain lights.

In the main house are 18 rooms with hardwood floors, resting under 3.5m (11-ft.) ceilings. These are graced with antiques and four-poster beds. Some of these accommodations offer wraparound balconies. We prefer these units, but you can also book into one of the three modern buildings with a series of one-, two-, and three-bedroom rooms. These, too, have such lovely features as Jacuzzis, Asian carpets, plunge pools, and handcrafted furnishings.

Crane Bay, St. Philip, Barbados, W.I. © **800/223-9815** in the U.S., or 246/423-6220. Fax 246/423-5343. www.the crane.com. 98 units. Winter US$347–US$1,210 (£180–£629)double, US$529–US$2,280 (£275–£1,185) suite; off season US$165–$552 (£86–£287) double, US$253–US$1,034 (£132–£538) suite. MAP (breakfast and dinner) US$75 (£39) per person extra. AE, MC, V. **Amenities:** Restaurant; 2 bars; outdoor pool; exercise room; room service; babysitting; laundry facilities. *In room:* A/C, TV, kitchenette in 1 suite, minibar, beverage maker, hair dryer, iron, safe.

Villa Nova ⊕⊕⊕ *(Finds)* This is one of the last of the island's great houses. Once it was a sightseeing attraction open to the public. Built in 1834 as a sugar plantation, it's furnished with period antiques and Barbadian mahogany and surrounded by 6 walled hectares (15 acres) of tropical forest and lush gardens. Its most famous association was with Sir Anthony Eden, former prime minister of Great Britain, who purchased the estate from the government in 1965. In 1966, Eden, the earl of Avon, and his wife, the countess, entertained Queen Elizabeth II and Prince Philip at Villa Nova. Sir Winston Churchill also holidayed here.

Today, in the midst of sugar, banana, and mango plantations, it's been turned into an exclusive hotel, following a multimillion-dollar refurbishment. Although the hotel has a very large swimming pool and terraces, you'll have to drive about 20 minutes to dip your toes into the surf. Rooms are beautifully furnished and spacious, each with its own private terrace. Every suite comes with a spacious bathroom with Victorian claw-footed tubs and walk-in showers. Decorator Nina Campbell designed each of the suites individually. Its food is among the finest of all the hotels, using regional organic produce whenever possible. Nearby are the golf courses of Sandy Lane and Royal Westmoreland.

Villa Nova, Venture, St. John, Barbados, W.I. ⓒ 246/433-1524. Fax 246/433-6363. www.villanovabarbados.com. 27 units. Winter US$700 (£364) double, US$850–US$1,500 (£442–£780) suite; off season US$450 (£234) double, US$600–US$950 (£312–£494) suite. Rates include continental or a la carte breakfast. AE, MC, V. **Amenities:** Restaurant; 2 bars; pool; golf privileges; 2 tennis courts; gym; spa; nearby watersports; nearby horseback riding; library; room service; laundry service; dry cleaning; nonsmoking rooms. *In room:* A/C, TV, hair dryer, safe.

INEXPENSIVE

Sea-U Guest House   Far from the so-called Platinum Coast, this undiscovered guesthouse is a retreat from the world. It's the lazy life here. Your biggest challenge will be to lie in a hammock strung between palms, taking in the view of the nearby waves or checking out the monkeys scampering about. This East Coast hideaway looks much older but is built in the traditional two-story Bajan plantation style. In lieu of air conditioning, the comfortably furnished and rather traditional bedrooms are cooled by sea breezes. The spacious accommodations are either studio apartments or guest cottages. The studios come with kitchenettes and each has a private bathroom with tub or shower. The guest cottages are air conditioned. At night a 3-course dinner is offered family style, costing US$23 per person. Your host and owner is Uschi Wetzels, a German travel writer.

Tent Bay, Bathsheba, St. Joseph, Barbados, W.I. ⓒ 246/433-9450. Fax 246/433-9210. www.seaubarbados.com. 7 units. Winter US$135–US$160 (£70–£83) double, US$160–US$190 (£83–£99) cottage for 2, US$335 (£174) cottage for 4; off season US$110–US$135 (£57–£70) double, US$135–US$165 (£70–£86) cottage for 2, US$285 (£148) cottage for 4. MC, V. **Amenities:** Restaurant; bar; natural dipping pools. *In room:* AC (in cottages), ceiling fan, kitchenettes.

3 Dining

ON THE WEST COAST
VERY EXPENSIVE

The Cliff ⓡⓡ INTERNATIONAL/THAI   Built atop a 3m (10-ft.) coral cliff, this open-air restaurant features a three-level dining room crafted with terra-cotta tiles and coral stone. Though it's not exclusive or even particularly formal, it has attracted Prince Andrew and other titled and bejeweled guests from nearby upscale hotels. The culinary technique is impeccably sharp, and the chefs select only the finest cuts of beef, the freshest seafood, and the choicest vegetables. The best items are grilled snapper drizzled with three types of coriander sauce (cream-based, oil-based, and vinaigrette style), accompanied with garlic mashed potatoes and Thai-style curried shrimp. For sheer innovation, dishes such as this put The Cliff near the top. Also try the fresh sushi when available. As you dine, watch for stingrays, which glide through the illuminated waters below; a sighting is considered good luck.

Hwy. 1, Derrick, St. James. ⓒ 246/432-1922. Reservations required in winter. Prix fixe menu BD$185 (US$93/£48). AE, MC, V. Daily 6:30–midnight.

EXPENSIVE

Carambola ⓡⓡ FRENCH/CARIBBEAN/ASIAN   Built beside the road that runs along the island's western coastline, this restaurant sits atop a 6m (20-ft.) seaside cliff and offers gorgeous, panoramic views from its dining terrace. Not only does the

Carambola have Barbados' most romantic setting, but its food is also in the same league as The Cliff (see above). The prizewinning cuisine is creative, with modern, French-nouvelle touches, but Caribbean flair and flavor. Try the chef's rich, frothy lobster cappuccino, or his stir-fry of shrimp and scallops in roasted peanut sauce. Another spectacular dish is rack of lamb with a honey-mustard crust, or you might try a favorite of ours, oven-roasted breast of duckling with anise seed and a bitter-orange marmalade. Save room for one of the luscious desserts, such as lime mousse. The impressive wine list features mostly French vintages. Lunch is not served, so go for an early dinner to best appreciate the views.

Hwy. 1, Derricks, St. James. ℂ **246/432-0832.** Reservations required. Main courses BD$64–BD$130 (US$33–US$65/£17–£34). AE, MC, V. Mon–Sat 6:30–9pm. Closed Aug. 2km (1¼ miles) south of Holetown on Hwy. 1.

Daphne's 👭 MODERN ITALIAN The owners of The House hotel (recommended earlier in this chapter) operate this sexy, intimate outpost of the fabled London eatery. The service is flawless, and the setting on the beach idyllic. The coconut-shell lampshades and Indonesian batiks evoke Bali. For greater privacy, silk curtains surround the tables. Chef Marco Festini is a whiz, turning out memorable dishes based on fresh ingredients, either local or imported. The pasta dishes get raves, especially the linguine with seafood and the *pappardella* (wide ribbon noodles) with rabbit ragout and black olives. The chef's most successful main dishes are grilled mahimahi with Marsala, *peperonata,* and zucchini; or the sesame-seed-encrusted tuna with arugula and tomatoes. We've also enjoyed the grilled tiger shrimp with Mediterranean salsa and couscous.

Paynes Bay, St. James. ℂ **246/432-2731.** Reservations required. Main courses lunch BD$55–BD$72 (US$28–US$36/£14–£19), dinner BD$70–BD$140 (US$35–US$70/£18–£36). AE, MC, V. Daily 12:30–3pm and 6:30–10:30pm. Closed Mon off season.

The Fish Pot 👭 *Finds* SEAFOOD/INTERNATIONAL Just minutes north of the port of St. Charles, this restaurant lies in a little fishing community called Shermans. The restaurant is in a family-run oceanfront hotel but is so special that even nonguests should visit. The complex was constructed on the site of a 17th-century fort that later was used to store sugar. The food is intensely flavored and produced with finesse. The appetizers are among the most imaginative on the coast, everything from Canadian scallops seared with chutney spices and cilantro oil to baked king prawns with a garnish of tomato. Other delights include cracker-crusted tuna and grilled swordfish along with a seafood platter for two and raised lamb shanks.

You may fall in love with the place and want to stay here in its one-, two-, or three-bedroom chattel-styled cottages, each furnished to a high standard with a living room and a spacious covered dining terrace off a fully equipped kitchen. Winter rates for two begin at US$380 (£198) for a double, but are lowered to US$237 (£123) in off season.

In Little Good Harbour, Shermans, St. Peter. ℂ **246/439-3000.** Fax 246/439-2020. www.littlegoodharbour barbados.com. Main courses lunch US$11–US$42 (£5.70–£22), dinner US$22–US$70 (£12–£36). MC, V. Daily 8:30–10am, noon–3pm, and 6:30–9pm.

La Mer 👭 INTERNATIONAL Intricately associated, architecturally and socially, with the upscale Port St. Charles Condo and Marina complex in which it's located, this is a stylish and breezy restaurant with a prominent bar, a terrace that overlooks some of the most expensive yachts in the Caribbean, and a clientele made up of local homeowners and well-heeled foreign visitors. After dark, powerful spotlights illuminate the schools of fish swimming around the moored boats nearby. The decor features big glass windows with a view of the lagoon, lots of flowers and flickering candles, and artfully designed lighting from overhead spotlights. Menu items include the kind of hearty mariners' fare that goes beautifully with the fresh salt air. Begin with duck-liver pâté or shrimp in a sweet-and-sour rum sauce. Main courses include Angus steak or fish of the day—mahimahi, swordfish, or tuna—often grilled and served with a lime-flavored butter sauce. Dessert usually includes caramelized banana crepes with rum-raisin ice cream, the kind of thing that's worth ruining your diet for. The bar is stylish but rarely raucous, and usually closes by 11pm.

In the Port St. Charles Condo and Marina complex, Speightstown, St. Peter. ℃ **246/419-2000.** Reservations required. Main courses US$20–US$48 (£10–£25); Sun lunch buffet US$65 (£34) per person. AE, DC, MC, V. Sun noon–3pm; Tues–Sat 6:30–9:30pm.

Lone Star Restaurant 𝖌 *Finds* BAJAN/INTERNATIONAL/SEAFOOD This restaurant fronting the beach has a casual atmosphere during the day, which becomes more elegant in the evening. When you're appreciating the dining room's muslin curtains, polished wood floors, and an open-to-view kitchen, it's hard to believe this space was once a garage. Top chefs cooking for a discerning international clientele turn out Caribbean fish pie (especially delectable with its cheesy mashed potatoes), blackened dolphin, and such fusion dishes as a Thai green king-prawn curry. Downstairs Mediterranean and modern European dishes, along with Barbadian specialties, are the focus, whereas the culinary delights of Southeast Asia are served upstairs—mainly Thai, Vietnamese, and Chinese dishes. You can even get Japanese dishes such as sushi and sashimi. Such *fruits de mer* as king prawns, crab legs, pure Iranian caviar, and fresh oysters add to the utterly delightful but frighteningly expensive seafood selections.

Hwy. 1, Mount Standfast, St. James. ℃ **246/419-0599.** Reservations required. Main courses US$30–US$120 (£16–£63). AE, MC, V. Daily 11:30am–3:30pm and 6:30–10:30pm.

Mango's by the Sea 𝖌𝖌 INTERNATIONAL/SEAFOOD This restaurant and bar overlooking the water is best known for its seafood: The owners, Montreal natives Gail and Pierre Spenard, buy the catch of the day directly from the fishermen's boats. The food is exceedingly good, and the seasonings aren't as overpowering as they are at many Bajan restaurants. Appetizers might be anything from smoked salmon to pumpkin soup. If you don't want fish, opt for the 8-ounce U.S. tenderloin steak cooked to perfection or the fall-off-the-bone barbecued baby back ribs. Top off your meal with passion fruit cheesecake or star fruit torte. There's live entertainment on some nights. Next door is an art gallery under the same management, which features the silk-screen prints of artist Michael Adams.

2 West End, Queen St., Speightstown, St. Peter. ℃ **246/422-0704.** Reservations required. Main courses BD$48–BD$68 (US$24–US$34/£13–£18). AE, MC, V. Daily 6–9:30pm.

The Tides 𝖌 INTERNATIONAL/CARIBBEAN This former beachfront villa is now occupied by a charming and graceful restaurant that serves fine food. The chef and owner, Guy Beasley, fine-tuned his culinary skills with the Roux brothers in England—arguably the top chefs there. Today, he's moved to Barbados, attracting notables like Andrew Lloyd Weber and Tommy Hilfiger to his elegant precincts, where trees grow right through the ceiling.

Nearly 100 people can eat here at any given time, each enjoying a sea view. The atmosphere at night is romantically candlelit, the restaurant set in the midst of lush gardens. The chef specializes in seafood but also offers finely honed meat, poultry, and vegetarian dishes. When not appreciating the art collection displayed on the wall, you can enjoy crab cakes with a Thai sauce or the homemade Caribbean seafood chowder for starters. Follow with the fresh catch of the day—grilled, blackened, pan-fried, or poached. Other dishes to which we'd award a star include honey-and-mustard-coated roast of lamb with bacon-scented scalloped potatoes and the chargrilled filet of pork with Mexican rice, citrus juice, and a tangy orange salsa.

Holetown, St. James. ℂ 246/432-8356. Reservations required. Main courses lunch BD$45–BD$70 (US$23–US$35/£12–£18), dinner BD$65–BD$100 (US$33–US$50/£17–£26). MC, V. Mon–Fri noon–2:30pm; Mon–Sat 6:30–10:30pm.

MODERATE

Angry Annie's Restaurant & Bar ☆ *Value* INTERNATIONAL
Don't ask Annie why she's angry—she might tell you! Annie and Paul Matthews, both from the United Kingdom, run this friendly, cozy, 34-seat joint. It's decorated in tropical colors with a circular bar, and rock classics play on the excellent sound system. The dishes are tasty with lots of local flavor. The place is known for its "famous" ribs, the most savory on the island. We like the garlic-cream potatoes and the fresh local vegetables. Annie also turns out fresh fish and excellent pasta dishes. Get your meal to go if you'd like to dine back in your room.

First St., Holetown, St. James. ℂ 246/432-2119. Main courses US$12–US$45 (£6.25–£23). MC, V. Daily 5–10pm.

Il Tempio ☆☆ ITALIAN
Even the great opera singer Luciano Pavarotti thinks this restaurant at the southern end of the western coast serves the best Italian food in Barbados. Many of the specialties are evocative of owners Anna Pirrelli's and Leo Valente's hometown in Bari; others are inspired by Sardinia, home to chef Alesso Dotto. The chef's light touch is ideal for tropical dining. The homemade pastas are a delight, including his fettuccine alla carbonara. The lasagna *del Vesuvio* comes with a tantalizing meat sauce, and the main dishes are equally delectable, especially the veal medallions with onion and black grapes in a chardonnay-wine sauce. Mouthwatering desserts are prepared fresh nightly, and happy hour is Tuesday to Sunday 4 to 6pm.

Fitts Village, St. James. ℂ 246/417-0057. Reservations required. Main courses BD$45–BD$92 (US$23–US$46/£12–£24). MC, V. Tues–Sun noon–2:30pm and 6:30–10pm. Closed Aug-Sept.

Ragamuffin's ☆ *Value* CARIBBEAN
This is a real discovery: an affordable, lively place that serves authentic island cuisine. It's the only restaurant in Barbados in a traditional chattel house. The broiled T-bones are juicy and perfectly flavored; there's always an offering of fresh fish; and vegetarians can enjoy stir-fried vegetables with noodles. Other highlights include blackened fish, the local version of a spicy West Indian curry, and a zesty jerk chicken salad.

First St., Holetown, St. James. ℂ 246/432-1295. Reservations recommended. Main courses US$15–US$27 (£7.80–£14). AE, MC, V. Daily 6:30–10pm (sometimes until midnight).

BRIDGETOWN

Waterfront Café INTERNATIONAL/BAJAN
This is your best bet if you're in Bridgetown shopping or sightseeing. In an historic warehouse originally built to store bananas and freeze fish, this cafe serves international fare with a strong emphasis on Bajan specialties. Try the fresh catch of the day prepared Creole style, or pan-seared steak. For vegetarians the menu features such dishes as three-mushroom pasta, vegetable soup, and usually a special of the day. Both diners and drinkers are welcome

here for Creole food with lots of stir-fried dishes, including a version made with fish. Tuesday nights bring live steel-band music and a Bajan buffet. To see the Thursday-night Dixieland bands, reserve about a week in advance. There's jazz on Wednesday, Friday, and Saturday.

Cavans Lane, the Carenage, Bridgetown. ℭ 246/427-0093. Reservations required. Main courses lunch BD$32–BD$74 (US$16–US$37/£8.30–£19), dinner BD$38–BD$85 (US$19–US$43/£9.90–£22). AE, DC, MC, V. Mon–Sat 10am–10pm.

ON THE SOUTH COAST
MODERATE
David's Place ℛ BAJAN   Owner/operators David and Darla Trotman promise you'll sample "Barbadian dining at its best"—and they deliver on that promise at a reasonable price. The restaurant is on top of the St. Lawrence Water Gap, in an old-fashioned seaside house on St. Lawrence Bay. The tables are positioned so that diners enjoy a view of the Caribbean. Pumpkin or cucumber soup or the pickled chicken wings are good starters. For a main course, fish steaks (mahimahi, kingfish, barracuda, shark, or red snapper) served in a white-wine sauce or deep-fried Bajan style are the best choice on the menu. Also recommended are the Baxters Road chicken marinated in lime, salt, and herbs, then deep-fried, and the hot-and-spicy pepper pot, with beef, salt pork, chicken, and lamb. Top off your meal with one of the old-fashioned desserts: a banana split, coconut cream pie, or carrot cake in rum sauce.

St. Lawrence Main Rd., Worthing, Christ Church. ℭ 246/435-9755. Reservations recommended. Main courses BD$50–BD$85 (US$25–US$43/£13–£22). AE, DISC, MC, V. Tues–Sun 6–10pm.

Pisces ℛ BAJAN/SEAFOOD   This beautiful restaurant with a tropical decor offers alfresco dining at the water's edge. Begin with one of the soups, perhaps Pisces fish chowder or lobster bisque, or a savory appetizer like flying fish Florentine. Seafood fanciers enjoy such dishes as pan-fried filet of salmon with a crisp herb crust and a light passion fruit sauce laced with citrus juice, or else the potato-crusted filet of Atlantic salmon, a seared filet with a crisp potato crust served with a champagne beurre blanc. You might also be drawn to the seasonal Caribbean fish, which can be broiled, blackened, or pan-fried, and then served with lime-herb butter. A limited but good selection of poultry and meat is offered, including marinated chicken breast served in Bajan curry with jasmine rice and seasonal vegetables.

St. Lawrence Gap, Christ Church. ℭ 246/435-6564. Reservations recommended. Main courses BD$45–BD$125 (US$23–US$63/£12–£33). AE, DC, MC, V. Daily 6–10:30pm (last order). From Bridgetown, take Coast Rd. south about 6km (¾ miles); turn right at the sign toward St. Lawrence Gap.

ON THE EAST COAST
MODERATE
Atlantis Hotel ℛ *Finds* BAJAN   Harking back to the Barbados of many years ago, the sunny, breeze-filled restaurant, with its sweeping view of the turbulent ocean, is often filled with both Bajans and visitors. It's located between Cattlewash-on-Sea and Tent Bay on the east (Atlantic) coast. The copious buffets are one of the best values on the island. You can sample such Bajan foods as pumpkin fritters, peas and rice, macaroni and cheese, *souse* (pigs' feet marinated in lime juice), and Bajan pepper pot. No one ever leaves hungry.

Bathsheba, St. Joseph. ℭ 246/433-9445. Reservations required for Sun buffet and 7pm dinner, recommended at all other times. 3-course fixed-price lunch BD$45 (US$23/£12); 3-course prix-fixe dinner BD$50 (US$25/£13); Sun buffet BD$54 (US$27/£14). AE, MC, V. Daily 8–10am, 12:30–3pm, and 6–8pm.

Finds **The Island's Freshest Fish**

Savvy locals can guide you to the historic **Oistins Fish Market,** southeast of Bridgetown and past the settlements of Hastings and Worthing. This is where Bajan fishermen unload their daily catch and sell it directly to the customer— ideal if you have accommodations with a kitchen. If not, you can find nearly a dozen shacks selling fresh-cooked fish: Flying fish is in the fryer and fish steaks like wahoo are on the grill. On Friday night, the local vendors sponsor live bands and a medley of food stalls from 6 to 10:30pm.

Round House Inn Restaurant & Bar INTERNATIONAL/BAJAN Built in 1832, this restaurant lies on the rugged east coast of Barbados with its dramatic view of the Atlantic Ocean. The owners, Robert and Gail Manley, will usher you to a table perched atop a rocky ledge opening onto the Bathsheba "Soup Bowl," the best surfing beach in Barbados. You can also come here for dinner under the moonlight, as the place lies only a half-hour drive from Bridgetown.

The freshest of ingredients go into the wholesome, good-tasting food, which is made all the more delightful by a reggae band on Saturday nights or a guitarist on Sunday. Tuck into such appetizers as flying fish pâté or brie baked in a light-rum-and-walnut sauce. For your main course, you'd do well with either the oven-baked dolphin steak or the blackened catch of the day resting on your plate. The chef will always whip you up a traditional grilled sirloin with sautéed onions as well.

Bathsheba, St. Joseph. © 246/433-9678. Reservations required on Sun, recommended at all other times. Main courses BD$28–BD$42 (US$14–US$21/£7.28–£11). MC, V. Mon–Sat 8:30–10am, 11:30am–3:30pm, and 6–9pm; Sun 8–10am and 11:30am–5pm.

4 Beaches

The island's beaches are all open to the public—even those in front of the big resort hotels and private homes—and the government requires that there be access to all beaches, via roads along the property line or through hotel entrances. The beaches on the west coast—also known as the **Gold Coast** 🏖🏖—are the most popular.

ON THE WEST (GOLD) COAST The waters are calm here. Major beaches include **Paynes Bay,** which is accessed from the Coach House, south of Holetown, and has a parking area. This is a good choice for watersports, especially snorkeling. The beach can get rather crowded, but the beautiful bay is worth the effort. Directly south of Payne's Bay, at Fresh Water Bay, are three of the best west-coast beaches: **Brighton Beach, Brandon's Beach,** and **Paradise Beach.**

We also recommend **Mullins Beach,** where the glassy-blue waters attract snorkelers. There's parking on the main road and some shady areas. At the Mullins Beach Bar, you can order that rum drink you've been craving.

ON THE SOUTH COAST **Casuarina Beach** is accessed from Maxwell Coast Road, going across the property of the Casuarina Beach Hotel. This is one of Barbados' wider beaches, and it's cooled by trade winds even on the hottest August days. Windsurfers are especially fond of this one. Food and drinks can be ordered at the hotel.

Silver Sands Beach, to the east of Oistins, is near the southernmost point of Barbados, directly east of South Point Lighthouse and near the Silver Rock Hotel. This white-sand beach is a favorite with many Bajans (who probably want to keep it a secret from tourists as much as possible). The Silver Rock Bar sells drinks.

Sandy Beach, accessible via the parking lot on the Worthing main road, has tranquil waters opening onto a lagoon. It's a family favorite, and especially boisterous on weekends. Food and drinks are available.

ON THE SOUTHEAST COAST   The southeast coast is the site of big waves, especially at **Crane Beach,** the white-sand strip set against a backdrop of palms that you've probably seen in travel magazines. The beach is spectacular, and Prince Andrew, who has a house overlooking it, might agree. It offers excellent bodysurfing, but at times the waters may be too rough for all but the strongest swimmers; take appropriate precautions. The beach is set against cliffs, and Crane Beach Hotel towers above.

Bottom Bay 𝕱, north of Sam Lord's Castle Resort, is one of our all-time Bajan favorites. Park on the top of a cliff, then walk down the steps to this much-photographed tropical beach with its grove of coconut palms; there's even a cave. The sand is brilliantly white against the aquamarine sea, a picture-postcard perfect beach paradise.

ON THE EAST (ATLANTIC) COAST   The miles and miles of uncrowded beaches on the rougher Atlantic side are ideal for strolling, but swimming can be dangerous. Waves are extremely high, and the bottom tends to be rocky. The currents are also unpredictable. Many travelers enjoy the rugged grandeur of these beaches, especially those in the **Bathsheba/Cattlewash** areas.

5 Sports & Other Outdoor Pursuits

GOLF   Open to all is the Tom Fazio 18-hole championship golf course of **Sandy Lane Hotel,** St. James (© **246/444-2000**), on the west coast. Greens fees for 18 holes are US$220 (£114) for nonguests and US$185 (£96) for guests in winter, and US$175 (£91) for nonguests and US$140 (£73) for guests in summer. For its famed "Old Nine" holes, which wind through the estate grounds, US$95 (£50) for nonguests and US$85 (£44) for guests in winter, and US$90 (£47) for nonguests and US$80 (£42) for guests in summer. Carts and caddies are available for US$30 (£16).

The **Royal Westmoreland Golf and Country Club,** Westmoreland, St. James (© **246/422-4653**), has become the island's premier golf course. Designed by Robert Trent Jones, Jr., this US$30-million, 18-hole course is spread across 200 hectares (500 acres) overlooking the Gold Coast. It is part of a private residential community and can be played only by guests of the Royal Pavilion, Glitter Bay, Colony Club, Tamarind Cove, Coral Reef, Crystal Cove, Cobblers Cove, Sandpiper Inn, and Sandy Lane. It costs BD$175 (US$88/£46) for 9 holes year-round and BD$350 (US$175/£91) for 18 holes in winter, including a cart. Fees in off season with a cart are BD$100 (US$50/£26).

Barbados Golf Club, Durants, Christ Church (© **246/428-8463;** fax 256/420-8205; www.barbadosgolfclub.com), on the south coast, opened as Barbados's first public championship golf course in 2000. The 6,800-yard, par-72 course, designed by Ron Kirby, hosted the PGA Seniors Tournament in 2003. Greens fees for 18 holes are US$135 (£70) in winter and US$90 (£47) off season. A 3-day unlimited golf pass during winter is US$330 (£172), and US$210 (£109) off season.

HIKING   The **Barbados National Trust** (© **246/426-2421**) gives Sunday-morning hikes throughout the year. Led by young Bajans and members of the National Trust, the popular hikes cover a different area of the island each week. The guides give brief talks on subjects such as geography, history, geology, and agriculture. The hikes, free and open to all ages, are divided into fast, medium, and slow categories, with groups of no more than 10. Hikes leave promptly at 6am, and take about 3 hours to complete. There are also hikes at 3:30 and 5:30pm, the latter conducted only on moonlit nights. For more information, contact the Barbados National Trust.

In 1998, Barbados created a trail that explores the natural history and heritage of Speightstown, once a major sugar port and even today a fishing town with old houses and a bustling waterfront. The **Arbib Nature & Heritage Trail** takes you through town, the mysterious gully known as "the Whim," and the surrounding districts. The first marked trail is an 8km (5-mile) trek, which begins outside St. Peter's Church in Speightstown, traverses the Whim, crosses one of the last working plantations in Barbados (Warleight), and leads to historic 18th-century Dover Fort, following along white-sand beaches at Heywoods before ending up back in town. For information and reservations, call the Barbados National Trust, and ask for a trail map at the tourist office.

The rugged, dramatic **east coast** stretches about 25km (15 miles) from the lighthouse at Ragged Point, the easternmost point of Barbados, north along the Atlantic coast to Bathsheba and Pico Teneriffe. This is the island's most panoramic hiking area. Some hardy souls do the entire coast; if your time is limited, try our favorite walk, the 6km (3¾-mile) stretch from Ragged Point to Consett Bay, along a rough, stony trail that requires only moderate endurance. Allow at least 2½ hours. A small picnic facility just north of Bathsheba is a popular spot for Bajan families, especially on Sundays. As for information, you're pretty much on your own, although if you stick to the coastline, you won't get lost.

HORSEBACK RIDING   A different view of Barbados is provided by **Caribbean International Riding Centre,** St. Andrew, Sarely Hill (© **246/422-7433**). With nearly 40 horses, Mrs. Roachford and her daughters offer a variety of trail rides for all levels of experience, ranging from a 1½-hour jaunt for US$60 (£31) to a 2½-hour trek for US$90 (£47). You'll ride through some of the most panoramic parts of Barbados, including the hilly terrain of the Scotland district. Along the way, you can see wild ducks and water lilies, with the rhythm of the Atlantic as background music.

SCUBA DIVING & SNORKELING   The clear waters off Barbados have a visibility of more than 30m (100 ft.) most of the year. More than 50 varieties of fish are found on the shallow inside reefs, and there's an unusually high concentration of hawksbill turtles. On night dives, you can spot sleeping fish, night anemones, lobsters, moray eels, and octopuses. Diving is concentrated on the leeward west and south coasts, where hard corals grow thick along the crest of the reef, and orange elephant ear, barrel sponge, and rope sponge cascade down the drop-off of the outer reef.

On a 2km-long (1¼-mile) coral reef 2 minutes by boat from **Sandy Beach,** sea fans, corals, gorgonians, and reef fish are plentiful. *J.R.,* a dredge barge sunk as an artificial reef in 1983, is popular with beginners for its coral, fish life, and 6m (20-ft.) depth. The *Berwyn,* a coral-encrusted tugboat that sank in Carlisle Bay in 1916, attracts photographers for its variety of reef fish, shallow depth, good light, and visibility.

Asta Reef, with a drop of 24m (79 ft.), has coral, sea fans, and reef fish in abundance. It's the site of a Barbados wreck that was sunk in 1986 as an artificial reef. **Dottins,** the most beautiful reef on the west coast, stretches 8km (5 miles) from Holetown to Bridgetown and has numerous dive sites at an average depth of 12m (39 ft.) and drop-offs of 30m (100 ft.). The SS *Stavronikita,* a Greek freighter, is a popular site for advanced divers. Crippled by fire in 1976, the 108m (354-ft.) freighter was sunk .4km (¼ mile) off the west coast to become an artificial reef in **Folkestone Underwater**

Park, north of Holetown. The mast is at 12m (39 ft.), the deck at 24m (79 ft.), and the keel at 36m (118 ft.). While you explore the site, you might spot barracuda, moray eels, and a vibrant coat of bright yellow tube sponge, delicate pink rope sponge, and crimson encrusting sponge. The park has an underwater snorkel trail, plus glass-bottom boat rides, making it a family favorite.

The **Dive Shop,** Pebbles Beach, Aquatic Gap, St. Michael (© **246/426-9947**), offers some of the best scuba diving on Barbados, charging US$55 (£29) for a one-tank dive and US$80 (£42) for a two-tank dive, including equipment. Every day, three dive trips go out to the nearby reefs and wrecks; snorkeling trips and equipment rentals are also available. Visitors with reasonable swimming skills who have never dived before can sign up for a resort course. Priced at US$70 (£36), these include pool training, safety instructions, and a one-tank open-water dive. The establishment is NAUI- and PADI-certified, and is open Sunday to Friday from 8:30am to 4:30pm. Other dive shops in Barbados that rent or sell snorkeling equipment include **Hazel's Water World,** Bridgetown, St. Michael (© **246/426-4043**).

Several companies also operate snorkeling cruises that take you to particularly picturesque areas; see "Tours & Cruises" under "Seeing the Sights," below.

TENNIS   The big hotels have tennis courts that can be reserved even if you're not a guest. In Barbados, most tennis players still wear traditional whites. **Folkestone Park,** Holetown (© **246/422-2314**), is a free public tennis court. Courts at the **Barbados Squash Club,** Marine House, Christ Church (© **246/427-7913**), can be reserved for BD$35 (US$18/£9.10) for 45 minutes.

WINDSURFING   Experts say the windsurfing off Barbados is as good as any this side of Hawaii. Windsurfing on Barbados has turned into a very big business between November and April, attracting thousands of windsurfers from as far away as Finland, Argentina, and Japan. The shifting of the trade winds between November and May and the shallow offshore reef of **Silver Sands** create unique conditions of wind and wave swells. This allows windsurfers to reach speeds of up to 50 knots and do complete loops off the waves. Silver Sands is rated the best spot in the Caribbean for advanced windsurfing (skill rating of 5–6).

Club Mistral Windsurfing Club, with two branches on the island, can get you started. Beginners and intermediates usually opt for the branch in Oistins (© **246/428-7277**), where winds are constant but the sea is generally flat and calm. Advanced intermediates and experts usually go to the branch adjacent to the Silver Sands Hotel, in Christ Church (© **246/428-6001**), where stronger winds and higher waves allow surfers to combine aspects of windsurfing and conventional Hawaiian-style surfing. Both branches use boards and equipment provided by the Germany-based Club Mistral. Equipment rents for US$55 (£29) per half-day or US$75 (£39) for a full day at Oistins, depending on where and what you rent; rates are more expensive at the Christ Church branch.

6 Seeing the Sights

TOURS & CRUISES

Barbados is worth exploring, either in a rental car or with a taxi-driver guide. Unlike many Caribbean islands, Barbados has fair roads. They are, however, poorly signposted, and newcomers invariably get lost—not only once, but several times. If you lose your way, you can generally find people in the countryside helpful.

ORGANIZED TOURS   **Bajan Tours,** Shak-Shak Complex, no. 4 Frere Pilgrim, Christ Church (© **246/228-6000**), is a locally owned and operated company. The best bet for the first-timer is the Exclusive Island Tour, departing Monday to Friday between 8 and 8:30am and returning between 2:30 and 3pm. It covers all the island's highlights, including the Barbados Wildlife Reserve, the Chalky Mount Potteries, and the rugged east coast. All tours cost BD$120 (US$60/£31) per person and include a full buffet lunch.

CRUISES   Most popular and fun are the *Jolly Roger* **"Pirate" Cruises** run by Jolly Roger Cruises (© **246/430-0900**), operating from Bridgetown Harbour at Shallow Draught. *Jolly Roger* is an ersatz, Disneyesque replica of an 18th-century pirate galleon. Departures are from one of two distinctly different berths within Bridgetown Harbour; ask at the time of your reservation which it will be. Passengers can rope swing, swim, snorkel, and suntan on the top deck. Even mock weddings are staged. A buffet lunch with rum punch is available Sunday from 11am to 3pm. Lunch cruises cost BD$105 (US$53/£27) per person.

Catamaran lunch cruises are offered by **Tall Ships** (© **246/430-0900**), located at Shallow Draught near Bridgetown Harbour. The 4-hour-long catamaran lunch cruises are offered daily beginning at 10am.

Part cruise ship, part nightclub, the **MV *Harbour Master Blockbuster*** (© **246/430-0900**) is a 30m (100-ft.), three-story vessel with theme decks, a modern galley, and two bars. It has a dance floor, and also offers formal buffets on its Calypso Deck. On the Harbour Master Deck, there's a bank of TVs for sports buffs. The showpiece of the vessel is an onboard semisubmersible, which is lowered hydraulically to 2m (6½ ft.) beneath the ship. This is, in effect, a "boat in a boat," with 30 seats. Lunch and dinner cruises cost BD$140 (US$70/£36) and BD$150 (US$75/£39) per person; the semisubmersible experience costs another BD$25 (US$13/£6.50). This cruise is offered on Wednesday 11am to 4pm.

SUBMERGED SIGHTSEEING   You no longer have to be an experienced diver to see what lives 45m (150 ft.) below the surface of the sea; you can simply sail aboard one of the vessels operated by **Atlantis Submarines,** Shallow Draught, Bridgetown (© **246/436-8929**). The air-conditioned sightseeing submarines seat 28 to 48 passengers and make several dives daily from 9am to 1pm Monday, Tuesday, Thursday, and Friday, and 9am to 4pm on Wednesday. Passengers are transported aboard a ferryboat from the Carenage in downtown Bridgetown to the submarine site, about 2km (1¼ miles) from the west coast of Barbados. The ride offers a view of the west coast of the island. The submarine, *Atlantic III,* features viewing ports that allow you to see a rainbow of colors, tropical fish, plants, and even a shipwreck that lies upright and intact below the surface. The cost is US$89 (£46) for adults, US$57 (£30) for children 13 to 17, and US$45 (£23) for children 12 and under. In addition, you can take a tour aboard a Rhino Rider, an inflatable motorized craft that goes up the West Coast on a tour lasting 2 hours for US$83 (£43). There's a 30-minute stop for a snorkeling adventure at a nearby shipwreck where you can feed the fish, and also a beach stop. Tours are run Monday, Tuesday, Thursday, and Friday from 9am to 1pm, and on Wednesday from 9am to 4pm. Children 14 and under are not permitted.

HELICOPTER TOURS   There is now a new and fascinating way to sightsee Barbados. **Bajan Helicopters,** Bridgetown heliport, St. Michaels (© **246/431-0069;** fax 246/431-0086; www.funbarbados.com), offers a tour that involves soaring in an air-conditioned jet 50km (30 miles) over either saw-toothed cliffs and animal-shaped rocks or ultramarine boats floating on serene beaches, depending on which coast you are touring. The helicopter seats up to five people and tours last 20 to 30 minutes. We recommend bringing cameras and camcorders so you can share this experience with friends. The cost is US$140 to US$180 (£73–£94) per person.

EXPLORING BRIDGETOWN

Often hot and clogged with traffic, the capital, Bridgetown, merits a morning's shopping jaunt (see "Shopping," below), plus a visit to some of its major sights.

Since about half a million visitors arrive on Barbados by cruise ship each year, the government has opened a US$6-million **cruise-ship terminal** with 20 duty-free shops, 13 local retail stores, and scads of vendors. Cruise passengers can choose from a range of products, including the arts and crafts of Barbados, jewelry, liquor, china, crystal, electronics, perfume, and leather goods. The interior was designed to re-create an island street scene; some storefronts appear as traditional chattel houses in brilliant island colors, complete with streetlights, tropical landscaping, benches, and pushcarts.

Begin your tour at the waterfront, called the **Carenage** (French for "turning vessels on their side for cleaning"). This was a haven for clipper ships, and even though today it doesn't have the color of yesteryear, it's still worth exploring.

At **Trafalgar Square,** the long tradition of British colonization is immortalized. The monument here, honoring Lord Nelson, was executed by Sir Richard Westmacott and erected in 1813. The great gray Victorian/Gothic **Public Buildings** on the square look like ones you might find in London. The east wing contains the meeting halls of the Senate and the House of Assembly, with some stained-glass windows representing the sovereigns of England. Look for the "Great Protector" himself, Oliver Cromwell.

Behind the Financial Building, **St. Michael's Cathedral,** east of Trafalgar Square, is the symbol of the Church of England. This Anglican church was built in 1655 but was completely destroyed in a 1780 hurricane. Reconstructed in 1789, it was again damaged by a hurricane in 1831. George Washington supposedly worshiped here on his visit to Barbados.

The **Synagogue,** Synagogue Lane (© 246/426-5792), is one of the oldest synagogues in the Western Hemisphere and is surrounded by a burial ground of early Jewish settlers. The present building dates from 1833. It was constructed on the site of an even older synagogue, erected by Jews from Brazil in 1654. It's now part of the National Trust of Barbados—and a synagogue once again. It's open Monday to Friday from 9am to 3pm; a donation is appreciated.

First made popular in 1870, **cricket** is the national pastime on Barbados. Matches can last from 1 to 5 days. If you'd like to see one, watch for announcements in the newspapers or ask at the **Barbados Cricket Association,** at Kensington oval (© 246/436-1397).

From Bridgetown you can take a taxi to **Garrison Savannah,** just south of the capital, a venue for horse races.

Barbados Museum, St. Ann's Garrison, St. Michael (© 246/427-0201), is in a former military prison. Extensive collections show the island's development from prehistoric to modern times and give fascinating glimpses into the natural environment and fine examples of West Indian maps. The museum sells a variety of quality publications, reproductions, and handicrafts. Hours are Monday to Saturday from 9am to

Bridgetown

BARBADOS

⊛ Bridgetown

American Express **1**
Barbados Museum **9**
Carenage **2**
Garrison Savannah **7**
Public Buildings **4**
St. Ann's Fort **8**
St. Michael's Cathedral **6**
Synagogue **5**
Trafalgar Square **3**

✝ Church
ⓘ Information
⊠ Post Office

5pm, Sunday from 2 to 6pm. Admission is BD$12 (US$6/£3.10) for adults, BD$5.75 (US$2.90/£1.50) for children.

Nearby, the russet-red **St. Ann's Fort,** on the fringe of the savanna, garrisoned British soldiers in 1694. The fort wasn't completed until 1703. The **Clock House** survived the hurricane of 1831.

SEEING THE INLAND SIGHTS
IN THE CENTER OF THE ISLAND 🔆🔆

Many visitors stay on those fabulous west-coast beaches, but the island's true beauty is its lush interior. If you have the time, we highly recommend a hike, drive, or tour through such rarely visited parishes as St. Thomas and St. George (both are land-locked) and the wild Atlantic coast parishes of St. Andrews, St. Joseph, and St. John.

Flower Forest 🔆   This former sugar plantation stands 255m (836 ft.) above sea level near the western edge of the Scotland district, 2km (1¼ miles) from Harrison's Cave. Set in one of the most scenic parts of Barbados, it's more than just a botanical garden; it's where people and nature unite to create something beautiful. After viewing the grounds, visitors can purchase handicrafts at Best of Barbados.

Richmond Plantation, St. Joseph. ℂ 246/433-8152. Admission BD$18 (US$9/£4.70) adults, BD$8 (US$4/£2.10) children 6–14, free for children 5 and under. Daily 9am–5pm.

Francia Plantation 🔆   A fine family home, the Francia Plantation stands on a wooded hillside overlooking the St. George Valley and is still owned and occupied by descendants of the original owner. Built in 1913, the house blends West Indian and European architectural influences. You can explore several rooms, including the dining room with its family silver and an 18th-century James McCabe bracket clock. On the walls are antique maps and prints, including a map of the West Indies printed in 1522.

Gun Hill, St. George, Barbados. ℂ 246/429-0474. Admission US$6 (£3.10). Mon–Fri 10am–4pm. On the ABC Hwy., turn east onto Hwy. 4 at the Norman Niles Roundabout (follow the signs to Gun Hill); after going .8km (½ mile), turn left onto Hwy. X (follow the signs to Gun Hill); after 2km (1¼ miles), turn right at the Shell gas station and follow Hwy. X past St. George's Parish Church and up the hill for 2km (1¼ miles), turning left at the sign to Francia.

Harrison's Cave 🔆🔆 *Kids*   The underground world here, the number-one tourist attraction of Barbados, is viewed from aboard an electric tram and trailer. You'll see bubbling streams, tumbling cascades, and subtly lit deep pools, while all around stalactites hang overhead like icicles, and stalagmites rise from the floor. Visitors may disembark and get a closer look at this natural phenomenon at the Rotunda Room and the Cascade Pool. Although it's interesting, it may not impress those who have been to the far more spectacular Carlsbad or Luray Caverns.

Welchman Hall, St. Thomas. ℂ 246/438-6640. Admission BD$40 (US$20/£10). Daily 9am–4pm. Closed Good Friday, Easter Sunday, and Christmas.

⸜Tips⸝ The Great Tour

From mid-January through the first week of April, you can tour a different great house every Wednesday afternoon from 2:30 to 5:30pm, many rarely seen by the public. You'll see a great array of plantation antiques and get a feeling for the elegant colonial lifestyle once commonplace on Barbados. For more information, call ℂ 246/426-2421.

Welchman Hall Gully 🐵   The Barbados National Trust owns this lush tropical garden, which contains specimens of plants—many of them labeled—that were here before the English settlers landed in 1627, and later imports that include cocoa bushes, and trees from which both cloves and nutmeg are produced. Occasionally you'll spot a wild monkey amidst the flora. You can also see breadfruit trees that are supposedly descendants of the seedlings brought ashore by Captain Bligh, of *Bounty* fame.

Welchman Hall, St. Thomas. ✆ 246/438-6671. Admission BD$12 (US$6/£3.10) adults, BD$5.75 (US$2.90/£1.50) children 6–12, free for children 5 and under. Daily 9am–5pm. Take Hwy. 2 from Bridgetown.

SIGHTS ALONG THE WEST COAST
Folkestone Marine Park & Visitor Centre *Kids*   Set beside a shimmering stretch of coral sand beach, this is a "water park," lying just north of Holetown. It combines a museum and aquarium to illustrate the rich marine life of Barbados. An underwater snorkeling trail goes around a reef, and you can see the same sights in a glass-bottom boat. A number of beachfront restaurants and bars are nearby, and there is an on-site gift shop open Monday to Friday 9am to 5pm.

Church Point, Holetown, St. James. ✆ 246/422-2314. Free admission. Snorkeling with equipment $10(£5.20). Museum US$1.15 (60p) adults, 50¢ (25p) children. Mon–Fri 9am–5pm.

The Malibu Beach Club & Visitor Center   Lying to the north of Bridgetown, this manufacturer of white rum has been going strong since 1897. The distillery is known for producing a very popular island drink, coconut rum. To make this tour even more enticing, the center is constructed on an idyllic stretch of white-sand beach set against a backdrop of sea-grape and almond trees. Also on-site is a beachside grill where lunch and rum punches are served. The price of the tour includes a rum drink and the use of a beach chair. In contrast to the sunny beach, the distillery is dark with a lot of old equipment, including a century-old copper-pot still.

Black Rock, Brighton, St. Michael. ✆ 246/425-9393. Admission BD$20 (US$10/£5.20), or BD$65 (US$33/£17) with lunch and transportation from your hotel. Mon–Fri 9am–5pm.

The Mount Gay Rum Tour & Gift Shop   On the northern edge of Bridgetown, you can learn the story of island rum, produced here virtually since the British first settled on the island in 1627. By 1655 Barbados was producing some 900,000 gallons of rum annually. The actual distillery is in St. Lucy Parish to the north, but at this center you can see both old and contemporary equipment used in rum making, along with rows and rows of barrels. First you view a video about Mount Gay's history, followed by a 15-minute crash course in rum making. The tour concludes with a rum tasting. Rum, along with gift items, is for sale in the on-site shop. You can make a reservation for an admission-free tour of the actual Mount Gay refinery by calling ✆ **246/425-8757.**

Spring Garden Hwy., Brandons, St. Michael. ✆ 246/425-8757. Admission BD$12 (US$6/£3.10), or BD$65 (US$33/£17) including lunch and transportation from your hotel; free for children under 12. Mon–Fri 9:30am–3:30pm.

IN THE SOUTHEAST (ST. PHILIP)
Heritage Park & Rum Factory   After driving through cane fields, you'll arrive at the first rum distillery to be launched on the island since the 19th century. Inaugurated in 1996, this factory is located on a former molasses and sugar plantation dating back some 350 years. Produced on-site is ESA Field, a white rum praised by connoisseurs. Adjacent is an admission-free park where Barbadian handicrafts are displayed. You'll also find an array of shops and carts selling food, handicrafts, and products.

Foursquare Plantation, St. Philip. ✆ 246/420-1977. Free admission. Mon–Fri 9am–4:30pm.

Moments A Beautiful Picnic Spot

Farley Hill National Park surrounds what used to be one of the greatest houses of Barbados, Farley Hill, a mansion in ruins. The park lies to the north of the parish of St. Peter, directly across the road leading into the Barbados Wildlife Reserve. You can bring in a picnic and wander in the park, overlooking the turbulent waters of the Atlantic. You can enter the park for free if you're walking, but it costs US$2 (£1.05) to bring a car in. Hours are daily 8:30am to 5pm.

Sunbury Plantation House 𝒜 If you have time to visit only one plantation or great house in Barbados, make it this one. It's the only great house on Barbados where all the rooms are open for viewing. The 300-year-old plantation house is steeped in history, featuring mahogany antiques, old prints, and a unique collection of horse-drawn carriages. Take the informative tour, then stop in the Courtyard Restaurant and Bar for a meal or drinks; there's also a gift shop. A candlelight dinner is offered at least once a week; this five-course meal, served at a 200-year-old mahogany table, costs BD$188 (US$94) per person.

6 Cross Rd., St. Philip. ✆ **246/423-6270.** Admission BD$15 (US$7.50/£3.90) adults, BD$7.50 (US$3.75/£1.95) children 5–12. Daily 9am–4:30pm (last tour).

IN THE NORTHEAST
Andromeda Botanic Gardens 𝒜 On a cliff overlooking the town of Bathsheba on the rugged east coast, limestone boulders make for a natural 3-hectare (7½-acre) rock-garden setting. Thousands of orchids, hundreds of hibiscus and heliconia, and many varieties of ferns, begonias, palms, and other species grow here in splendid profusion. You'll occasionally see toads, frogs, herons, lizards, hummingbirds, and sometimes a mongoose or a monkey.

Bathsheba, St. Joseph. ✆ **246/433-9384.** Admission BD$18 (US$9/£4.70) adults, BD$9 (US$4.50/£2.35) children 6–12, free for children 5 and under. Daily 9am–5pm.

St. Nicholas Abbey Surrounded by sugar-cane fields, this Jacobean plantation great house has been around since about 1650. It was never actually an abbey—around 1820 an ambitious owner simply christened it as such. More than 80 hectares (200 acres) are still cultivated each year. The house, characterized by its curved gables, is believed to be one of three Jacobean houses in the Western Hemisphere. Only the ground floor of the structure is open to the public.

On Cherry Tree Hill, Hwy. 1, St. Peter. ✆ **246/422-8725.** Admission BD$25 (US$13/£6.50) adults, BD$15 (US$7.50/£3.90) children 11 and under. Daily 10am–3:30pm.

7 Shopping

You may find duty-free merchandise here at prices 20% to 40% lower than in the United States and Canada—but you've got to be a smart shopper to spot bargains, and you should be familiar with prices back in your hometown. Duty-free shops have two prices listed on items of merchandise: the local retail price and the local retail price less the government-imposed tax.

Some of the best duty-free buys include cameras, watches, crystal, gold jewelry, bone china, cosmetics and perfumes, and liquor (including locally produced Barbados rum and liqueurs), along with tobacco products and cashmere sweaters, tweeds, and sportswear from Britain. If you purchase items made on Barbados, you don't have to pay duty.

The quintessential Barbados handicrafts are black-coral jewelry and clay pottery. The latter originates at **Highland Pottery, Inc.** (© 246/422-9818), which is worth a visit. Potters turn out different products, some based on designs that are centuries old. The potteries (which are signposted) are north of Bathsheba on the east coast, in St. Joseph Parish near Barclay's Park. In shops across the island, you'll also find a selection of locally made vases, pots, pottery mugs, glazed plates, and ornaments.

Island artisans weave wall hangings from local grasses and dried flowers, and also turn out straw mats, baskets, and bags with raffia embroidery. Leatherwork, particularly handbags, belts, and sandals, is also found on Barbados.

IN BRIDGETOWN Cruise passengers generally head for the **cruise-ship terminal** at Bridgetown Harbour, which has some 20 duty-free shops, 13 local shops, and many vendors (see "Exploring Bridgetown" under "Seeing the Sights," above).

At **Articrafts,** Norman Center Mall, Broad Street (© 246/427-5767), John and Roslyn Watson have assembled an impressive display of Bajan arts and crafts. Roslyn's distinctive wall hangings are decorated with objects from the island, including sea fans and coral. The unique **Colours of De Caribbean,** the Waterfront Marina (next to the Waterfront Café, on the Carenage; © 246/436-8522), carries a limited selection of original hand-painted and batik clothing, all made in the West Indies, plus jewelry and decorative objects.

Cave Shepherd, Broad Street (© 246/431-2121), is the largest department store on the island and the best place for duty-free merchandise. There are branches at Sunset Crest in Holetown, Da Costas Mall, Grantley Adams Airport, and the Bridgetown cruise-ship terminal, but if your time is limited, try this outlet, as it has the widest selection. The store sells perfumes, cosmetics, fine crystal and bone china, cameras, jewelry, swimwear, leather goods, men's designer clothing, handicrafts, liquor, and souvenirs. You can take a break in the cool comfort of the Balcony, overlooking Broad Street, which serves vegetarian dishes and has a salad bar and beer garden.

Harrison's, 10–14 Broad St. (© 246/431-5500), has six branch stores, all selling a wide variety of duty-free merchandise, including china, crystal, jewelry, watches, liquor, and perfumes—all at fair prices. Also for sale are some fine leather products handcrafted in Colombia.

Little Switzerland, in the Da Costas Mall, Broad Street (© 246/431-0030), offers a wide selection of watches, fine jewelry, and an array of goodies from Waterford, Lalique, Swarovski, Baccarat, and others.

Pelican Crafts Centre, Harbour Road (© 246/426-4391), is rather an overpriced tourist trap, hawking craft items. In Bridgetown, go down Princess Alice Highway to the city's Deep Water Harbour, where you'll find this tiny colony of thatch-roofed shops. Most of the shops here are gimmicky, but a few interesting items can be found if you search hard enough. Sometimes you can see craftspeople at work.

ELSEWHERE ON THE ISLAND **The Watering Hole,** Highway 7, St. Lawrence Gap (© 246/435-6375), is not only the best place to purchase bottles of Bajan rum at duty-free prices, but is also a great dive for hanging out. A small bottle of rum (about 6 oz.) sells for around US$7. Some locals as well as savvy visitors come here and make an evening of it, sampling the various rum drinks. Of course, you may need someone to carry you back to your hotel as these punches are lethal. Opening times vary—call to be sure—but we've seen this place going strong at 3am. One of the most interesting shopping jaunts in Barbados is to **Tyrol Cot Heritage Village,** Codrington Hill, St. Michael (© 246/424-2074), the former home of the Bajan national hero, Sir Grantley Adams. On the grounds of the former prime minister's estate is a colony of artisans, who turn out an array of articles for sale ranging from paintings to pottery, from baskets to handmade figurines.

Earthworks Pottery/On the Wall Gallery, Edgehill Heights 2, St. Thomas (© 246/425-0223), is one of the artistic highlights of Barbados. Deep in the island's central highlands, Canadian-born Goldie Spieler and her son, David, create whimsical ceramics in the colors of the sea and sky; many are decorated with Antillean-inspired swirls and zigzags. On the premises are a studio and a showroom that sells the output of at least half a dozen other island potters. Purchases can be shipped.

The **Shell Gallery "Contentment,"** Gibbes Hill, St. Peter (© 246/422-2593), has the best collection of shells in the West Indies. Also offered are shell jewelry, and local pottery and ceramics.

Greenwich House Antiques, Greenwich Village, Trents Hill, St. James (© 246/432-1169), a 25-minute drive from Bridgetown, feels like a genteel private home where the objects for sale seem to have come from the attic of your slightly dotty great aunt. Dozens of objects fill every available inch of display space, including Barbados mahogany furniture.

8 Barbados After Dark

ON THE WEST COAST   A lot of the evening entertainment around here revolves around the big resorts, many of which have lovely bars, some of which host bands and beach parties in the evening. See "Accommodations," earlier in this chapter.

Some say the green-and-white **Coach House,** Paynes Bay, St. James (on the main Bridgetown-Holetown road, just south of Sandy Lane, about 10km/6¼ miles north of Bridgetown; © 246/432-1163), is 200 years old. Attracting mostly visitors, this is a Bajan version of an English pub, with an outdoor garden bar. From 6 to 10pm you can order bar meals, including flying-fish burgers, priced at BD$12 (US$6/£3.10) and up. A lunchtime buffet is offered Monday to Friday BD$35 (US$18/£9.10), and there is also a well-attended Saturday night buffet costing BD$50 (US$25/£13).

John Moore Bar, on the waterfront, Weston, St. James (© 246/422-2258), is the most atmospheric and least pretentious bar on Barbados. Open to the sea breezes, and much weather-beaten, it's the nerve center of this waterfront town, filled day and night with a congenial group of neighborhood residents, and a scattering of tourists. Most visitors opt for a rum punch or beer, but you can order up a plate of local fish if you don't mind waiting.

One of our favorite bars in Barbados is **Olives Bar & Bistro,** Second Street at the corner of Highway 1, in Holetown (© 246/432-2112). Not only is it a fine restaurant but it's also a good place to spend 2 or 3 hours before or after dinner—maybe both. Found upstairs in a *Casablanca*-like setting of potted palms and whirling fans, it draws a convivial international crowd, mostly ex-pats, Americans, and English visitors in their 30s and 40s.

IN BRIDGETOWN   For the most authentic Bajan evening possible, head for **Baxters Road** in Bridgetown, where there's always something cooking Friday and Saturday nights after 11pm. In fact, if you stick around until dawn, you'll find the party's still going strong. Some old-time visitors have compared Baxters Road to the back streets of New Orleans in the 1930s. If you fall in love with the place, you can "caf crawl" up and down the street, where nearly every bar is run by a Bajan mama.

The most popular "caf" on Baxters Road is **Enid's** (she has a phone, "but it doesn't work"), a little ramshackle establishment where Bajans come to devour fried chicken at 3 in the morning. This place is open daily from 8:30pm to 8:30am, when the last satisfied customer departs into the blazing morning sun and the employees go home to get some sleep. Stop in for a Banks beer.

Boatyard Bar & South Deck Grill, Bay Street in Bridgetown (© 246/436-2622), is one of the busiest and most animated of the youth-oriented bars in Bridgetown occupying an outdoor, beach-fronting building whose interior is lavishly decorated in Creole colors of bright yellow, blue, and pink. If you want food, the menu features simple platters of fish, chicken, or burgers. If you want to go swimming, the beach lies almost directly adjacent to the foundations of this place. Expect a 5-minute trek from central Bridgetown, hordes of dancers jiving to the DJ every Tuesday, Wednesday, Friday, and Saturday, and lots of local gossip. Open daily 9am to sometimes as late as 3am, depending on business.

Harbour Lights, Marine's Villa, Lower Bay Street, 2km (1¼ miles) southeast of Bridgetown (© 246/436-7225; www.harbourlightsbarbados.com), is the most popular weekend spot for dancing, drinking, and flirting on all of Barbados. In a modern seafront building with an oceanfront patio (which gives dancers a chance to cool off), the place plays reggae, soca, and whatever else is popular until the wee hours nightly. The barbecue pit/kiosk serves up hot dogs, chicken sandwiches, fish, and hamburgers on Monday, Wednesday, and Friday. Monday is beach party night; the BD$98 (US$49/£26) charge includes transportation to and from your hotel, a barbecue buffet, drinks, and a live band. On Wednesday and Friday, the cover is BD$35 (US$18/£9.10). The place attracts a large local following, with a few foreign visitors showing up.

ON THE SOUTH COAST   The bustling activity at **Cafe Sol,** St. Lawrence Gap, Christ Church (© 246/435-9531), attracts a very convivial crowd. As a specialty of the house, the bartender rubs the margarita glasses with Bajan sugar instead of the usual salt.

Plantation Restaurant and Garden Theatre, Main Road (Hwy. 7), St. Lawrence, Christ Church (© 246/428-5048), is the island's main showcase for evening dinner theater and Caribbean cabaret. It's completely touristy, but enjoyable nonetheless. Every Wednesday and Friday, dinner is served at 6:30pm, followed by a show, *Bajan Roots and Rhythm,* at 8pm. Expect elaborate costumes and lots of reggae, calypso, and limbo. For US$85 (£44), you get dinner, the show, and transportation to and from your hotel; the show alone costs US$50 (£26). Reserve in advance.

The Ship Inn, St. Lawrence Gap, Christ Church (© 246/435-6961), is among the leading entertainment centers on the south coast. The pub is the hot spot: Top local bands perform most nights, offering reggae, calypso, and pop music. The entrance fee ranges from free (if you're eating dinner) to US$10. The place draws an equal number of visitors and locals.

The best sports bar, without equal, is **Bubba's Sports Bar,** Rockley Main Road, Worthing, Christ Church (© 246/435-6217), which offers a couple of satellite dishes, a 3m (10-ft.) video screen, and a dozen TVs. Wash a Bubba burger down with a Banks beer.

Bonaire

Unspoiled Bonaire is only gently touched by development. Although your options range from bird-watching to doing nothing, Bonaire is foremost a scuba diver's delight and also offers some of the Caribbean's best snorkeling. This sleepy island doesn't attract crowds and has none of Aruba's glitzy diversions except for a few small casinos with minor action. Instead, turquoise waters beckon travelers to discover colorful clouds of tropical fish. Come here for the diving, not the beaches.

Bonaire is also a bird-watcher's haven, where flamingos nearly outnumber the sparse human population. There are about 200 different species of birds—not only the flamingo, but also the big-billed pelican, parrots, snipes, terns, parakeets, herons, and hummingbirds. A pair of binoculars is an absolute necessity.

Bonaireans zealously protect their precious environment. Even though they eagerly seek tourism, they aren't interested in creating another Aruba, with its high-rise hotel blocks. Spearfishing isn't allowed in its waters, nor is the taking or destruction of any coral or other living animal from the sea. Unlike some islands, Bonaire isn't just surrounded by coral reefs—it *is* the reef, sitting on the dry, sunny top of an underwater mountain.

Boomerang-shaped Bonaire is close to the coast of Latin America, just 81km (50 miles) north of Venezuela. Part of the Netherlands Antilles (an autonomous part of the Netherlands), Bonaire has a population of about 10,000 and an area of about 290 sq. km (113 sq. miles). The capital is **Kralendijk** (*Kroll*-en-dike). It's most often reached from its neighbor island of Curaçao, 48km (30 miles) to the west; like Curaçao, Bonaire is desertlike, with a dry and brilliant atmosphere. Often it's visited by day-trippers, who rush through in pursuit of the shy, elusive flamingo. Its northern sector is hilly, tapering up to Mount Brandaris, all of 236m (774 ft.). However, the southern half, flat as a pancake, is given over to bays, reefs, beaches, and a salt lake that attracts the flamingos.

1 Essentials

VISITOR INFORMATION

Before you go, contact the **Bonaire Government Tourist Office** at Adams Unlimited, 10 Rockefeller Plaza, Suite 900, New York, NY 10020 (© **800/BONAIRE** in the U.S., or 212/956-5912) or **www.infobonaire.com** for information.

On the island, the **Bonaire Government Tourist Bureau**, Kaya Grandid 2 (© 599/717-8322) is open Monday to Friday from 7:30am to noon and 1:30 to 5pm.

GETTING THERE

American Airlines (© **800/433-7300** in the U.S. and Canada; www.aa.com) offers three round-trip flights per week between San Juan, Puerto Rico and Bonaire. In

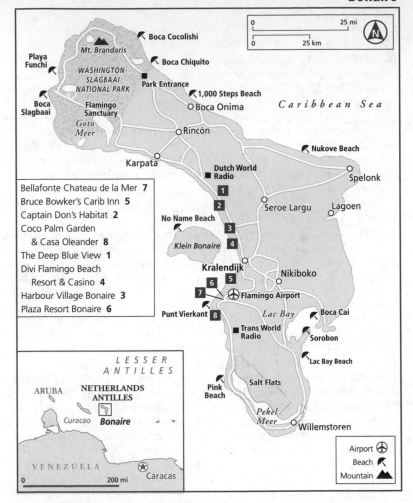

Hotels (listed in box):

- Bellafonte Chateau de la Mer **7**
- Bruce Bowker's Carib Inn **5**
- Captain Don's Habitat **2**
- Coco Palm Garden
  & Casa Oleander **8**
- The Deep Blue View **1**
- Divi Flamingo Beach
  Resort & Casino **4**
- Harbour Village Bonaire **3**
- Plaza Resort Bonaire **6**

addition to that, it provides one-stop service to Bonaire from many U.S. gateway cities such as New York.

An airline based in Bonaire, **BonairExpress** (© **599/717-3471**) has 12 flights per day between Bonaire and Curaçao and six flights per day between Bonaire and Aruba. On these flights, BonairExpress uses 46-seat ATR42 turboprop planes.

Air Jamaica (© **800/523-5585** in the U.S. and Canada; www.airjamaica.com) flies to Bonaire on Wednesday, Thursday, Saturday, and Sunday from its hub in Montego Bay. Air Jamaica also operates nonstop flights to Bonaire from Atlanta, Baltimore/Washington, Boston, Chicago, Los Angeles, Miami, Newark, New York (JFK), Orlando, and Philadelphia via its Montego Bay hub. Additionally, the airline's code share agreement with Delta Air Lines, and its joint fare arrangements and compatible schedules with United Air Lines and other U.S. carriers, extends its access to more than 150 cities within the continental U.S.

GETTING AROUND

Even though most of the island is flat and renting a moped or motor scooter is fun, be prepared for some unpaved, pitted, and rocky roads.

BY RENTAL CAR   Consider renting a four-wheel-drive vehicle, especially from October to January, when it can be muddy.

Avis (© **800/331-1212** in the U.S. and Canada; www.avis.com) is at Flamingo Airport. Weekly arrangements are cheaper, but daily rates range from US$40 to US$50 (£21–£26), with unlimited mileage. Also at the airport, **Total Car Rental** (© **599/717-7424;** www.totalcarrentalbonaire.com) rents such vehicles as cars and pickup trucks. Some automatic, air-conditioned four-door sedans are available. **Island Car Rentals,** Flamingo Airport #12 (© **599/717-2100;** www.islandcarrentalbonaire.com), rents soft-top jeeps for US$40 (£21) a day. It pays to shop around: Sometimes—but not always—you can make a better deal with a local agency.

Your valid U.S., British (you must have had it for 2 years), or Canadian driver's license is acceptable for driving on Bonaire. Drive on the right on Bonaire.

BY TAXI   Taxis are unmetered, but the government has established rates. All taxis carry a license plate with the letters **TX.** Each driver must produce a price list upon request. As many as four passengers can go along for the ride, unless there's too much luggage. A trip from the airport to your hotel should cost about US$8 to US$25 (£4.15–£13). From 7pm to midnight, fares are increased by 20%; from midnight to 7am, they go up by 50%.

Most taxi drivers can take you on a tour of the island, but you'll have to negotiate a price according to how long a trip you want and what you want to see. For more information, call **Taxi Central Dispatch** (© **599/717-8100**).

BY BICYCLE   If you're in good shape, you might consider renting a bike, although you'll have to contend with the hot sun and powerful trade winds. Nevertheless, much of the island is flat, and if you follow the main road, you'll go along the water's edge. The best deals are at **Cycle Bonaire,** Kaya L. D. Gerjharts (© **599/717-7558**), where you can rent a 21-speed 830 Trek for US$15 to US$20 (£7.80–£10) per day. Rental includes a water bottle, lock, helmet, repair kit, and first-aid kits. A map is provided for free.

FAST FACTS: Bonaire

Banks Banks are usually open Monday to Friday from 8am to 3:30pm. **RBTT Bank,** Kaya Korona 15 (© **599/717-4500**), is the most convenient facility for visitors, and it has an ATM. There's also an ATM at the airport.

Currency Bonaire's coin of the realm is the **Netherlands Antillean florin (NAf),** sometimes called a guilder. The official rate is 1.77 NAf to USUS$1 (1 NAf = US56¢). However, U.S. dollars are widely accepted. *Unless otherwise specified, prices in this chapter are quoted in U.S. dollars and British pounds.*

Customs Besides articles for personal use, visitors over 15 are allowed 400 cigarettes, 50 cigars, 250 grams of tobacco, 2 liters of distilled beverages, and 2 liters of wine.

Documents U.S. and Canadian citizens need proof of citizenship; a passport or certified birth certificate with a photo I.D. is required. All others require a valid passport. A return or continuing ticket is also required along with sufficient means to support yourself during your stay. (Maximum stay is 14 days with the possibility of extending the visit to 90 days.)

Electricity The electricity on Bonaire is slightly different from that used in North America—110 to130 volts/50 cycles, as opposed to U.S. and Canadian voltages of 110 volts/60 cycles. Adapters and transformers are not necessary for North American appliances, but because of the erratic current, you should still proceed with caution when using any appliance and try to avoid usage if at all possible. *Warning:* Electrical current used to feed or recharge finely calibrated diving equipment should be stabilized with a specially engineered electrical stabilizer. Every diving operation on the island has one of these as part of its standard equipment for visiting divers.

Emergencies Call ℂ **911** in case of fire or for the police or ambulance.

Hospital The **St. Franciscus Hospital** is located at Kaya Soeur Bartola 2 in Kralendijk (ℂ **599/717-8900**). A plane on standby at the airport takes seriously ill patients to Curaçao for treatment.

Language English is widely spoken, but you'll hear Dutch, Spanish, and Papiamento, the local dialect, as well.

Liquor Laws Beer, wine, and liquor are sold in all kinds of stores 7 days a week. It's legal to have an open container on the beach.

Safety Bonaire is quite a safe haven in this crime-infested world. But remember, any place that attracts tourists also attracts people who prey on them. Safeguard your valuables.

Taxes The government requires a US$6.50- (£3.40) per-person daily room tax on all hotel rooms. Upon leaving Bonaire, you'll be charged an airport departure tax of US$20 (£10), so don't spend every penny. There's also an inter-island departure tax of US$5.75 (£3) if you are flying to Curaçao.

Telephone To call Bonaire from the United States, dial **011** (the international access code), then **599** (the area code for Bonaire), and then **717** (the exchange) and the four-digit local number. Once on Bonaire, to call another number on the island, only the four-digit local number is necessary. You can access **AT&T Direct** on the island by dialing ℂ **001-800/872-2881**. It's often difficult to make international calls from Bonaire; phone service here lags far behind that on Aruba and Curaçao. Once you're connected to your party, the line isn't always crystal clear. Many hotel rooms don't have private phones. If you want to place an important international call, it's better to go to **TELBO,** the central phone company for the island. It's at Kaya Libertador Simon Bolivar, next to the tourist office.

Time Bonaire is on Atlantic Standard Time year-round, 1 hour ahead of Eastern Standard Time. (When it's noon on Bonaire, it's 11am in Miami.) When daylight saving time is in effect in the United States, clocks in Miami and Bonaire show the same time.

Tipping Most hotels and guesthouses add a 10% service charge in lieu of tipping. Restaurants generally add a service charge of 15% to the bill. Taxi drivers expect a 10% tip.

Water Drinking water comes from distilled seawater and is safe.

Weather Bonaire is known for its warm climate, with temperatures hovering around 82°F (28°C). The water temperature averages 80°F (27°C). It's warmest in August and September, coolest in January and February. The average rainfall is 22 inches, and December to March are the rainiest months. Like all the Dutch ABC (Aruba, Bonaire, and Curaçao) islands, Bonaire lies outside the hurricane belt, which comes as a relief to many visitors planning to visit the Caribbean during the hurricane season.

2 Accommodations

Hotels, all facing the sea, and in many cases opening onto beaches, are low-key, personally run operations where everybody gets to know everybody else in no time. They are concentrated on the west coast of the island immediately north or immediately south of the capital of Kralendijk.

Remember that taxes and service charges are seldom included in the prices you're quoted, so ask about them when making your reservations. Be sure to read the section "Packages for the Independent Traveler" in chapter 2 before you book a hotel on your own.

Your best deal at one of the dive resorts, such as Captain Don's Habitat, is to book a package deal, often for a week. Depending on the house count, more limited bookings can be accommodated if rooms are available.

VERY EXPENSIVE

Harbour Village Bonaire 𝄢𝄢𝄢 Conceived by one of the largest land developers in Venezuela, this exclusive complex, the most stylish on the island, is designed like an Iberian village, opening onto a sandy beach. It's upscale and well managed, offering services and resort amenities to well-heeled divers who don't want the more laid-back atmosphere of Captain Don's Habitat (see below). Accommodations are in a cluster of Dutch Caribbean–style villas painted in pastels, with red-tile roofs and terraced balconies. Guest rooms have tropical decor, four-poster beds, white-tile floors, natural-wood furniture, island-style ceiling fans as well as air-conditioning, and marble bathrooms, with deluxe toiletries, shower stalls, and robes.

A wide array of very good food awaits you. Our favorite restaurant is La Balandra Beach Bar and Restaurant, a gazebo-like structure set beside a massive pier; an octagonal bar area flanked by an open grill and salad bar is open to the sea view and breezes. The marina-front Lighthouse Restaurant at Harbour Village serves seafood specialties in a cozy nautical decor.

Kaya Gobernador N. Debrot 17, Playa Lechi (P.O. Box 312), Bonaire, N.A. © 800/424-0004 in the U.S. and Canada, or 599/717-7500. Fax 599/717-7507. www.harbourvillage.com. 30 units. Winter US$365–US$395 (£190–£205) double, US$565–US$615 (£294–£320) 1-bedroom suite, US$805–US$855 (£419–£445) 2-bedroom suite; off season US$265–US$285 (£138–£148) double, US$460 (£239) 1-bedroom suite, US$645 (£335) 2-bedroom suite. Children under 16 stay free in parent's room. AE, DC, DISC, MC, V. **Amenities:** Restaurant; 2 bars; outdoor pool; 4 tennis courts; fitness center; spa; dive center; marina; bikes; airport pickup; room service; babysitting; laundry service. *In room:* A/C, ceiling fan, TV, kitchenette (in suites), hair dryer, safe.

EXPENSIVE

Captain Don's Habitat ☆ Built on a coral bluff overlooking the sea and a tiny beach about 5 minutes north of Kralendijk, this divers' resort, with an air of congenial informality, is for those whose souls belong to the sea. Habitat and its accompanying dive shop are the creation of Captain Don Stewart, Caribbean pioneer and "caretaker of the reefs," a former Californian who sailed his schooner from San Francisco through the Panama Canal, arriving on a reef in Bonaire in 1962—he's been here ever since. Known on the island as the "godfather of diving," Captain Don was instrumental in the formation of the Bonaire Marine Park, whereby the entire island became a protected reef.

More than 90% of the guests here opt for a package, which incorporates a variable number of dives with accommodations ranging from standard doubles to villas with full kitchens and ocean-view verandas. Each unit has a bathroom with tub/shower combinations. The most popular is the 8-day/7-night package. This resort has an oceanfront restaurant and two seaside bars. A casual, laid-back crowd gathers for meals at Rum Runners, the social hub. Theme nights are staged weekly, which divert guests from the rather standard fare served here.

Kaya Gobernador N. Debrot 103, Pier 7, Bonaire, N.A. ☎ 599/717-8290. Fax 599/717-8240. For reservations and business arrangements, contact Captain Don's Habitat, 10800 Biscaye Blvd., Suite 320, Miami, FL 33161 (☎ 800/327-6709; fax 305/981-9397). www.habitatdiveresorts.com. 72 units. Winter US$236–US$259 (£123–£135) double, from US$265 (£138) suite; off season US$197–US$216 (£102–£112) double, from US$240 (£125) suite. AE, MC, V. **Amenities:** Restaurant; 2 bars; outdoor pool; dive program; babysitting; laundry service; dry cleaning; rooms for those w/limited mobility. *In room:* A/C, TV, kitchenette (in some), fridge, beverage maker, safe, no phone (in some).

The Deep Blue View ☆☆ *Finds* Staying here is like being in your own private villa. This small, intimate retreat in the Santa Barbara Heights district is informally luxurious, and our favorite on the island. Luxuriant foliage envelops the villa, which attracts honeymooners, families, and romantic couples, among others. Each of the beautifully furnished guest rooms comes with a large patio and pool area. All accommodations have vaulted ceilings and tiled floors. Bathrooms are small and rather functional looking, each with a shower. (Only one contains a complete bath with tub and shower.) The little extras make the difference here. The staff will even "brown bag" your breakfast if you've got an early flight, and when you head to the beach they give you thick towels, packed lunches, and cold drinks in coolers for an additional charge. From the villa's tiled patio, you experience a 180-degree vista of the Caribbean, whose color led to the name of the villa. As the sun goes down, you can enjoy happy hour or barbecue by the pool. Menneo de Bree, a dive instructor, will give you valuable diving tips.

Santa Barbara Heights, Kaya Diamanta 50, Bonaire, N.A. ☎ 599/717-8073. Fax 599/717-8073. www.deepblue view.com. 5 units. Year-round US$165–US$195 (£86–£101) per week double. Rates include breakfast. AE, MC, V. No children under 12. **Amenities:** Laundry service; dry cleaning. *In room:* A/C, ceiling fan, hair dryer, iron, no phone.

Plaza Resort Bonaire ☆ This luxury resort lies a short drive from the airport, on a strip of land midway between a saltwater lagoon and a sandy stretch of Caribbean beachfront. Designed in 1995 by a team of Italian architects, it resembles a white-sided village along the coast of southern Portugal, thanks to terra-cotta roofs and a pair of bridges that traverse the lagoon for easy access to the 5 hectares (12 acres) of grounds. It's an extremely large property for Bonaire, where most hotels are more intimate. Some units are privately owned. Rooms are quite large, though be aware that what management here refers to as suites are actually very large bedrooms, without interior dividers. The one- and two-bedroom villas contain kitchenettes, ceiling fans, and simple, summery furnishings. Most units are large and airy, with private balconies, and queen-size beds. Bathrooms are roomy and luxurious, with showers and deep tubs.

J. A. Abraham Blvd. 80, Bonaire, N.A. © **800/766-6016** in the U.S., or 599/717-2500. Fax 599/717-7133. www.plaza resortbonaire.com. 200 units. Winter US$250–US$280 (£130–£146) suite, US$310 (£161) 1-bedroom villa, US$380 (£198) 2-bedroom villa; off season US$170–US$250 (£88–£130) suite, US$210–US$280 (£109–£146) 1-bedroom villa, US$280–US$350 (£146–£182) 2-bedroom villa. Extra person US$30 (£16). AE, MC, V. **Amenities:** 3 restaurants; bar; outdoor pool; 4 tennis courts; health club; spa; boats; dive shop; marina; sailing; windsurfing; bikes; children's programs; car rental; salon; room service; babysitting; laundry service. *In room:* A/C, TV, kitchenette (in some), fridge, beverage maker, hair dryer, safe.

MODERATE

Bellafonte Chateau de la Mer �“ *Finds*   This hotel, styled like a palazzo, offers the most elegant and personalized living on island. Except for its pool, it lacks the amenities of the larger resorts, but is a bastion of comfort, style, and grace in all other respects. Its personalized service—the staff even dispenses savvy advice—makes it extra special. The rooms are decorated not only with taste but also a sense of glamour in its use of such trendy decor as teak wood or stainless steel. The private balconies that come with the accommodations make them all the more desirable. The pool and Jacuzzi seem to "hang out" over the water. The small resort also caters to divers and surfers, with safe storage of equipment and "sweet water" showers.

E.E.G. Boulevard 10, Belnem, N.A. © **599/717-3333**. Fax 599/717-8581. www.bellafontebonaire.com. 20 units. Winter US$130–US$270 (£68–£140) double, US$270–US$310 (£140–£161) 2-bedroom suites; off season US$95–US$195 (£50–£101) double, US$225–US$255 (£117–£133) 2-bedroom suites. AE, MC, V. **Amenities:** Outdoor pool; dive shop, laundry service; 2 private piers. *In room:* A/C, TV, kitchens (in some), safe.

Divi Flamingo Beach Resort & Casino �“ *Kids*   Divi is the comeback kid, having reinvented itself after a massive restoration that began at the beginning of the millennium. Modern furnishings, paint, tiles, and rejuvenated air-conditioning have made this once-tired waterfront hostelry more comfortable than it's been in years. Originally a seedy cluster of flimsy wooden bungalows used to intern German prisoners in World War II, today the resort consists of individual cottages and seafront rooms with private balconies. These accommodations rest on piers above the surf so you can stand on your balcony and watch rainbow-hued tropical fish in the waters below. The resort's original rooms are supplemented timeshare units, forming Club Flamingo. These are the best accommodations, and each can be rented by the day or week. The timeshare units are clustered in a neo Victorian pavilion facing a curving pool, and each comes with a kitchenette with carved cupboards and cabinets of pickled hardwoods. All units have well-kept bathrooms with tub/shower combinations. Chibi-Chibi and Calabas provide satisfying, straightforward meals featuring fresh local seafood and Continental specialties.

J. A. Abraham Blvd., Bonaire, N.A. © **800/367-3484** in the U.S., or 599/717-8285. Fax 599/717-8238. www.divi flamingo.com. 130 units. Winter US$203–US$242 (£106–£126) double, from US$267 (£139) studio; off season US$153–US$184 (£80–£96) double, from US$200 (£104) studio. Rates about 10% higher between Christmas and New Year's. MAP (breakfast and dinner) US$45 (£23) per person extra. Several inclusive packages offered. AE, DC, MC, V. **Amenities:** 2 restaurants; bar; 2 outdoor pools; casino; fitness center; spa services; dive shop; snorkeling; children's programs; car rental; salon; room service; babysitting; laundry service; rooms for those w/limited mobility. *In room:* A/C, TV, beverage maker, iron, safe.

INEXPENSIVE

Bruce Bowker's Carib Inn 🗚 *Value*   On a sliver of a beach, this inn, owned and managed by American diver Bruce Bowker, is occupied by dedicated scuba divers drawn to its five-star PADI dive facility. This is the most intimate little diving resort

on Bonaire and remains one of the island's best values. All rooms have kitchenettes; larger units have a full kitchen, and maid service is provided daily. The accommodations are furnished with tropical rattan, and every year management devotes time and money to paint, repair, and spruce them up. Each of the bathrooms has a shower stall, but not a bathtub, although the many repeat guests, who book this place far in advance every winter, don't seem to care. The hotel will not book through travel agents.

J. A. Abraham Blvd. 46 (P.O. Box 68), Kralendijk, Bonaire, N.A. © 599/717-8819. Fax 599/717-5295. www.caribinn.com. 10 units. Year-round US$119 (£62) studio efficiency apt (maximum 2 people); US$139 (£72) 1-bedroom apt (maximum 2 people); US$159 (£83) 2-bedroom apt (up to 4 people); US$189 (£98) 3-bedroom house (up to 4 people). Extra person US$10 (£5.20). DISC, MC, V. **Amenities:** Outdoor pool; scuba diving. *In room:* A/C, TV, kitchenette, no phone.

Coco Palm Garden & Casa Oleander *Value*   In the tranquil residential area of Belnem, south of the airport and Kralendijk, these vacation homes are a real discovery. Two friendly neighbors, Brigitte and Marin, combined their two properties into a cohesive whole and opened their affordable guesthouses to the world, drawing divers and windsurfers or anyone wanting to get away from the bigger resort hotels. Their accommodations consist of a series of little houses, studios, and apartments. A typical studio comes with one queen-size bed, a kitchen, a porch with tables and chairs, and a small garden with hammock and sun bed. Rooms are well furnished and have small bathrooms with showers. Even though each of the accommodations is self-sufficient, there are public areas, including a terrace for sunning, a pool, and a restaurant and bar for guests only. The cuisine consists mainly of Asian dishes.

Kaya van Eps 9, Belnem, Bonaire, N.A. © 599/717-2108. Fax 599/717-8193. www.cocopalmgarden.org. 22 units. Year-round US$66–US$86 (£34–£45) double; US$89–US$105 (£46–£55) house for 2. Extra person US$16 (£8.05). Children under 12 US$10 (£5.20) extra in parent's room. AE, DISC, MC, V. **Amenities:** Restaurant; bar; outdoor pool; babysitting. *In room:* A/C, kitchen, beverage maker, no phone.

3 Dining

EXPENSIVE

Donna & Giorgio ITALIAN   Lying directly to the north of Kralendijk, this restaurant specializes in authentic Italian dishes. Donna and her Sardinian husband, Giorgio, bring a taste of Italy to Bonaire, and they do so better than anybody else on island. From his home country, Giorgio brought his family recipes and his flair for cooking them. Pizza, homemade pasta, and daily specials lure diners to this restaurant decorated with local art and its adjacent sidewalk cafe. Daily specials are displayed on a blackboard, and they invariably feature freshly caught lobster. Tagliatelle lobster is a specialty. In the same vein, you can also order jumbo shrimp. It's all here, from tapas to tiramisu. The food is appealing and generous, and Giorgio imbues every dish with flavor.

Kaya Grandi 60. © 599/717-3799. Reservations recommended. Main courses US$17–US$36 (£8.85–£19). MC, V. Restaurant daily 6:30–11pm, bar daily 5:30–11pm. Closed Sept.

La Guernica TAPAS/INTERNATIONAL   In a 150-year-old building, this restaurant and lounge bar serves the island's finest tapas. The interior is decorated like a hacienda in Mexico with tiles and artifacts, and outdoor seating overlooks the harbor. The tapas always delight, and can be ordered as starters or main courses. Your table can share tapas that include a carpaccio of beef with fresh Parmesan cheese, smoked salmon with red onions, or fried and marinated calamari rings with Greek tzatziki dressing.

Some of the best main courses on a recent menu included coconut shrimp in a creamy ginger sauce, sashimi of tuna with fried vegetables, or the catch of the day served on a potato stuffed with a julienne of vegetables. Lobster is the house specialty and it's prepared in several different ways. For a different taste, we recently enjoyed it cooked in vanilla oil with a risotto of vegetables. For something really Caribbean, finish your meal with bananas fried in a rum sauce and served with vanilla ice cream.

Kaya Bonaire 4C. ℂ **599/717-5022.** Reservations recommended. Main courses US$16–US$23 (£8.30–£12). AE, MC, V. Daily 11am–10pm.

Mona Lisa 🐸 FRENCH/INTERNATIONAL A local favorite on the main street of town, this is one of the best places for food that tastes homemade. The prices are more than reasonable, considering the quality of the food and the generous portions. Although many regulars come just to patronize the Dutch bar and catch up on the latest gossip, the old-fashioned dining room deserves serious attention. Guests enjoy the fresh fish of the day (often wahoo) or such meat dishes as a leg of lamb filet, tournedos, and sirloin steak. The most popular appetizers are onion soup, Bonairean fish and vegetable soup, and shrimp cocktail. Mona Lisa is known for serving fresh vegetables on an island where nearly everything is imported.

Kaya Grandi 15. ℂ **599/717-8718.** Reservations recommended. Main courses US$18–US$32 (£9.35–£17); fixed-price menu US$40 (£21). MC, V. Restaurant Mon–Sat 6–10pm, bar Mon–Sat 4pm–2am.

MODERATE

Blue Moon INTERNATIONAL This seafront bistro near the Divi Flamingo is in one of the island's oldest houses. Intimate tables and candlelight create a romantic ambience in the main restaurant, although you can dine less formally outside on the terrace overlooking the harbor. The menu always features the catch of the day as well as steak dishes. Sample a delectable stuffed chicken breast with pear or apple, or jumbo shrimp pesto, followed by one of the homemade desserts. Finish off with one of the rich, Cuban-style coffees. Flavors are precisely defined, although nearly all ingredients have to be imported. Specials change daily.

Kaya Hellmund 5. ℂ **599/717-8617.** Reservations recommended. Main courses US$13–US$23 (£6.75–£12). MC, V. Thurs–Tues 5–10pm.

Le Flamboyant INTERNATIONAL Offering a creative menu and patio dining, along with good food, this restaurant is installed in an old house. Flamboyant colors, such as red and orange, adorn the interior. Fresh fish, based on the catch of the day, is the specialty. Seafood can be cooked more or less to your specifications. A number of well-prepared international dishes, including meat and chicken, are also on the menu, depending on what's best in any season and the shopping at the market that day. The sumptuous desserts are made fresh daily.

Kaya Grand 12. ℂ **599/717-3919.** Reservations recommended. Main courses US$8.50–US$23 (£4.40–£12). AE, DC, MC, V. Mon–Sat noon–3pm and 6–10pm.

Richard's Waterfront Dining 🐸🐸 STEAK/SEAFOOD We've had some of our best meals on Bonaire here. On the airport side of Kralendijk, within walking distance of the Divi Flamingo Beach Resort, this restaurant, with its large covered terrace, was once a private home. Reasonable in price, it's the favorite of many locals who have sampled every restaurant on the island. Boston-born Richard Beady and his Aruban partner, Mario, operate a welcoming oasis with a happy hour at 5:30pm. Gathered around the coral bar, guests peruse the chalkboard menu listing the offerings for the night: grilled wahoo or the fresh catch of the day, filet mignon béarnaise, U.S. sirloin with green-peppercorn sauce, scampi, or pasta. If it's on the menu, start with the fish soup. The menu is kept small so that each night's entrees can be given the attention they deserve. The kitchen focuses on bringing out the natural flavors of a dish without overwhelming it with sauces or too many seasonings. You'll be welcomed warmly. The most recent addition is a Kon-Tiki hut at the end of the pier, which is most often booked by honeymooners, who are given their own serving staff.

J. A. Abraham Blvd. 60. (𝄐 599/717-5263. Reservations recommended for groups of 6 or more. Main courses US$15–US$23 (£7.80–£12). DISC, MC, V. Tues–Sun 6–10pm.

Zeezicht Restaurant INTERNATIONAL/JAPANESE   This is the best place in the capital to see the sunset. Join the old salts or the people who live on boats to watch the sun go down, and try to see the "green flash" that Hemingway wrote about. Zeezicht (pronounced *Zay*-zict and meaning "sea view") has long been popular for its excellent local cooking. It serves a small Indonesian *rijstafel* (rice served with numerous accompaniments), as well as fresh fish from the nearby fish market, plus lobster and steak. The restaurant runs a sushi bar that also features other Japanese dishes.

Kaya Cachi-Craane 12. (𝄐 599/717-8434. Main courses US$12–US$23 (£6.25–£12); fixed menu US$33–US$55 (£17–£29). DISC, MC, V. Daily 8am–11pm.

4 Beaches

For the most part, the beaches are full of coral and feel gritty to bare feet. Those on the leeward side (the more tranquil side of the island) are often narrow strips. To compensate, some hotels have shipped in extra sand for their guests.

Pink Beach, south of Kralendijk, out past Salt Pier, is the best, despite its narrow strip of sand, shallow water, and lack of shade. It's aptly named: The beach really is a deep pink color, from the corals that have been pulverized into sand by the waves. Bring your own cooler and towels, as there are no refreshment stands or equipment rentals to mar the panoramic setting. It's also wise to bring along some sun protection, as the few palm trees bordering the dunes offer little shade. Enter the water at the southern end of this beach, as the northern tier has some exposed rock. Many Bonaireans flock here on weekends, but during the week you'll have the beach to yourself. The ideal place to watch the sunset and the flamingos fly south to Venezuela, Pink Beach attracts families, couples, and singles looking for a quiet place to relax and take in some sun.

Bonaire's offshore island, tiny, uninhabited **Klein Bonaire,** just 1.5km (1 mile) offshore, has some pristine beaches. Popular for snorkeling, scuba diving, and picnicking, **No Name Beach,** on the north side of Klein Bonaire, features a 273m (895-ft.) white-sand beach. Snorkelers can see a rainbow of colorful fish darting through stunning formations of elkhorn coral. Accessible only by boat, Klein Bonaire is home to sea turtles and other indigenous wildlife. Ask at your hotel if arrangements can be made for a trip to the island.

Playa Funchi, within Washington Slagbaai National Park, is good for snorkeling. Regrettably, it has almost no sand and no facilities, and the area surrounding the beach is a bit smelly. On one side of the beach, there's a lagoon where flamingos nest; the other side is good for snorkeling. Also within the park, the more appealing **Boca Slagbaai** draws snorkelers and picnickers. You can spot flamingos nearby. A 19th-century building houses decent toilets and showers; drinks and snacks are also available. Don't venture into the waters barefoot, as the coral beach can be quite rough. A final beach at the national park is **Boca Cocolishi,** a black-sand strip on the northern coast. This is the windiest beach on Bonaire; you'll certainly stay cool as the trade winds whip the surf up. The waters are too rough for swimming, but it's a good picnic spot.

Many of Bonaire's beaches are along the east coast. The best spot for windsurfers is **Lac Bay Beach,** on the southern shore of Lac Bay. There are mangroves at the north end of the bay. A couple of windsurfing concessions usually operate here, and food and drink are available. One unusual spot is **Nukove Beach,** a minicave in a limestone cliff with a small white-sand channel, which cuts through the dense wall of elkhorn coral near the shore, giving divers and snorkelers easy access to the water. Farther north is **1,000 Steps Beach,** where 67 steps (although it can feel like 1,000 on the way back up) carved out of the limestone cliff lead to the white-sand beach. This beach offers good snorkeling and diving, a unique location and view, and nearly perfect solitude.

5 Diving & Snorkeling ✶✶✶

Much of Bonaire's allure is based on its teeming offshore reefs and dive sites. Its true beauty is under the sea, where visibility is 30m (100 ft.), 365 days of the year, and the water temperatures range from 78°F to 82°F (26°C–28°C). One of the richest reef communities in the entire West Indies, Bonaire has plunging walls that descend to a sand bottom at 40m or so (130 ft.). The reefs are home to various coral formations that grow at different depths, ranging from the knobby brain coral at .9m (3 ft.) to staghorn and elkhorn up to about 3m (10 ft.) deeper, and gorgonians, giant brain, and others. Swarms of rainbow-hued tropical fish inhabit the reefs, and the deep reef slope is home to a range of basket sponges, groupers, and moray eels. Most of the diving is done on the leeward side, where the ocean is lake flat. There are more than 40 dive sites on sharply sloping reefs. Divers from around the world leave with a sense of awe about how good the diving really is.

Bonaire Marine Park ✶✶ was created to protect the coral-reef ecosystem off Bonaire. The park incorporates the entire coastline of Bonaire and neighboring **Klein Bonaire.** The park is policed, and services and facilities include a visitor information center at the **Karpata Ecological Center,** lectures, slide presentations, films, and permanent dive-site moorings.

Visitors are asked to respect the marine environment and to refrain from activities that may damage it, including sitting or walking on the coral. All marine life is completely protected. This means there's no fishing or collecting fish, shells, or corals—dead or alive. Spearfishing is forbidden, as is anchoring; all craft must use permanent moorings, except for emergency stops. (Boats shorter than 4m/13 ft. may use a stone anchor.) Most recreational activity in the marine park takes place on the island's leeward side and among the reefs surrounding Klein Bonaire.

The major hotels offer personalized, close-up encounters with the island's fish and other marine life under the expertise of Bonaire's dive guides. **Divi Dive Bonaire,** on the beachfront of the Divi Flamingo Beach Resort & Casino, J. A. Abraham Boulevard, north of Kralendijk (© **599/717-8285**), is among the island's most complete scuba facilities. It's open daily from 8am to 12:30pm and 1:30 to 5pm. It operates out of a well-stocked beachfront building, renting diving equipment and offering expeditions. A resort course for first-time divers costs US$80 (£42); for experienced divers, a one-tank dive goes for US$42 (£22), a two-tank dive for US$63 (£33).

Captain Don's Habitat Dive Shop, Kaya Gobernador N. Debrot 103 (© 599/ 717-8290), is a PADI five-star training facility. The open-air, full-service dive shop includes a classroom, photo/video lab, camera-rental facility, equipment repair, and compressor rooms. Habitat's slogan is "Diving Freedom": Divers can take their tanks and dive anywhere, day or night. Most head for "The Pike," .8km (½ mile) of protected reef right in front of the property. The highly qualified staff is here to assist and advise, but not to police or dictate dive plans. Diving packages include boat dives, unlimited offshore diving (24-hr. a day), unlimited air tanks, weights, and belts. Some dive packages also include accommodations and meals (see "Accommodations," earlier in this chapter). If you're not staying at the hotel as part of a dive package, you can visit for a beach dive, costing US$26 (£14). If you want to rent snorkeling equipment, the charge is US$13 (£6.75) a day. A boat dive, with all equipment, goes for US$49 (£26).

Bonaire Dive and Adventures, adjacent to the Sand Dollar Condominium Retreat, Kaya Gobernador N. Debrot (© 599/717-2229), is open daily from 8:30am to 4:30pm. It offers dive packages, PADI and NAUI (National Association of Underwater Instructors) instruction, and equipment rental and repairs; boat and shore trips with an instructor are available by appointment. A beginning course, including two dives, costs US$105 (£55) per person. The photo shop offers underwater photo and video shoots, PADI specialty courses by appointment, E-6 slide processing, print developing, and equipment rental and repair.

Bonaire's coral reefs are also an underwater paradise for snorkelers. They start in just inches of water and therefore have dense coral formations in very shallow surf. Most snorkeling on the island is conducted in 5m (16 ft.) of water or less, and there's plenty to see even at this depth. As you travel around the island, particularly in the northern area, you'll see evidence of prehistoric reefs now 12 to 30m (39–98 ft.) above sea level, having lived submerged for hundreds of thousands of years and then uplifted as the island slowly rose.

Snorkeling equipment can be rented at the **Carib Inn,** J. A. Abraham Boulevard (© 599/717-8819); **Bonaire Dive and Adventures,** Kaya Gobernador N. Debrot (© 599/717-2229); and **Captain Don's Habitat Dive Shop,** Kaya Gobernador N. Debrot 103 (© 599/717-8290). A full day's rental of mask, fins, and snorkel costs US$7 (£3.65). Most snorkelers swim out to reefs from points directly offshore, but most of the dive operators will also allow snorkelers to ride out to dive sites with scuba divers for US$12 (£6.25), plus the equipment rental cost.

6 Sports & Other Outdoor Pursuits

Bonaire is most striking underwater, but the sailing and birding are great, too.

BIRD-WATCHING   Bonaire is home to about 200 species of birds, 80 of which are indigenous to the island. Most famous are its flamingos, which can number 15,000 during the mating season. For great places to bring your binoculars, see "Exploring the Island," below.

FISHING   Bonaire's offshore fishing grounds has some of the best fishing in the Caribbean, and the Bonaire Marine Park allows line fishing. A good day's catch might include mackerel, tuna, wahoo, dolphin (mahimahi), blue marlin, amberjack, grouper, sailfish, or snapper. Bonaire is also one of the best-kept secrets of bonefishing enthusiasts.

Your best bet is Chris Morkos of **Piscatur Fishing Supplies,** Kaya Herman 4, Playa Pabao (© **599/717-8774;** www.piscatur.com). A native Bonairean, he has been fishing all his life. A maximum of six people are taken out on a 13m (43-ft.) boat with a guide and captain, at a cost of US$400 (£208) for a half-day, US$475 (£247) for ¾ day, or US$550 (£286) for a whole day, including all tackle and bait. Reef fishing is another popular sport, in boats averaging 5 to 6m (16–20 ft.). A maximum of two people can go out for a half-day at US$275 (£143). A maximum of two people can fish for bonefish and tarpon on the island's large salt flats for US$250 (£130) for a half-day.

HIKING   **Washington Slagbaai National Park** (see "Exploring the Island," below) has a varied terrain; those ambitious enough to climb some of its steep hills are rewarded with panoramic views. The hiking possibilities are seemingly endless. Small hidden beaches with crashing waters by the cliffs provide ideal spots for picnics.

MOUNTAIN BIKING   Biking is an ideal way to see Bonaire's hidden beauty; you can explore more than 300km (186 miles) of trails and dirt roads, venturing off the beaten path to enjoy the scenery. Ask at the tourist office for a trail map that outlines the most scenic routes. You can check with your hotel about arranging a trip, or call **Cycle Bonaire,** Kaya Gobernador N. Debrot 79 (© **599/717-2227**), an outfit that maintains an inventory of 24-speed mountain bikes, each of which rents for a price of US$15 (£7.80) per day.

SAILING   At **Bonaire Boating,** at Harbour Village (© **599/790-1228**), you can rent small boats for between US$80 (£42) for a half-day and US$120 (£62) for a full day, without crew, but you'll first have to demonstrate that you're versed in sailing techniques.

SEA KAYAKING   Paddle the protected waters of Lac Bay, or head for the miles of flats and mangroves in the south (the island's nursery), where you can see baby fish and wildlife. Kayak rentals are available at **Jibe City,** Lac Bay (© **599/717-5233;** www.jibecity.com), for US$25 (£13) per half-day or US$35 (£18) for a full day.

TENNIS   There are two courts, lit for night play, at the **Sand Dollar Condominium Retreat,** Kaya L.D. Gerjharts 11D (© **800/288-4773**). If the courts aren't in use by residents, nonresidents pay a fee (subject to change) of US$13 (£6.75) per hour.

WINDSURFING   Lac Bay's consistent conditions and shallow, calm waters are suitable for windsurfers with a wide range of skill levels. Call **Bonaire Windsurfing** (© **599/717-2288**) for details. A half-day costs US$40 (£21).

7 Exploring the Island

Bonaire Sightseeing Tours (© 599/717-8778) will show you the island, both north and south, taking in the flamingos, slave huts, conch shells, Goto Lake, the Amerindian inscriptions, and other sights. You can take a half-day City and Country Tour, lasting 3 hours and costing from US$26 (£14) per person, which allows you to see the entire northern section and the southern part as far as the slave huts.

KRALENDIJK

Locals call Kralendijk *Playa,* Spanish for "beach." A dollhouse town of some 2,500 residents, Kralendijk is small, neat, pretty, Dutch-clean, and just a bit dull. Its stucco buildings are painted pink and orange, with an occasional lime green. The capital's jetty is lined with island sloops and fishing boats.

Kralendijk nestles in a bay on the west coast, opposite **Klein Bonaire,** or Little Bonaire, an uninhabited, low-lying islet that's a 10-minute boat ride away.

The main street of town leads along the beachfront on the harbor. A Protestant church was built in 1834, and **St. Bernard's Roman Catholic Church** has some interesting stained-glass windows.

At **Fort Oranje,** you'll see a lone cannon dating from the days of Napoleon.

THE TOUR NORTH

The road north is one of the most beautiful stretches in the Antilles, with turquoise waters on your left and coral cliffs on your right. You can stop at several points along this road, where there are paved paths for strolling or bicycling.

After leaving Kralendijk and passing the Sunset Beach Hotel and the desalination plant, you'll come to **Radio Nederland Wereld Omroep (Dutch World Radio).** It's a 13-tower, 300,000-watter. Opposite the transmitting station is a lovers' promenade. Built by nature, it's an ideal spot for a picnic.

Continuing, you'll pass the storage tanks of the Bonaire Petroleum Corporation, the road heading to **Goto Meer,** the island's inland sector, with a saltwater lake. Several flamingos prefer this spot to the salt flats in the south.

Down the hill, the road leads to a section called **Dos Pos** ("two wells"); the palm trees and vegetation here are a contrast to the rest of the island, where only the drought-resistant kibraacha and divi-divi trees, tilted before the constant wind, can grow, along with forests of cacti.

Bonaire's oldest village is **Rincón.** Slaves who used to work in the salt flats in the south once lived here. The Rincón Ice Cream Parlour makes homemade ice cream in a variety of interesting flavors; there are also a couple of bars here. Above the bright roofs of the village is the crest of a hill called **Para Mira,** which means "stop and look."

A side path outside Rincón takes you to some **Arawak inscriptions** supposedly 500 years old. The petroglyph designs are in pink-red dye. At nearby **Boca Onima,** you'll find grotesque grottoes of coral.

Before going back to the capital, you might take a short bypass to **Seroe Largu,** which has a good view of Kralendijk and the sea. Lovers frequent the spot at night.

THE NATIONAL PARK

Washington Slagbaai National Park ★★ (© 599/785-0017; www.washingtonpark bonaire.org) has varied terrain that includes desertlike areas, secluded beaches, caverns, a visitor center, and a bird sanctuary. Occupying 6,000 hectares (14,820 acres) of Bonaire's northwesternmost territory, the park was once plantation land, producing divi-divi, aloe, and charcoal; today it functions as a wildlife preserve.

You can see the park in a few hours, although it takes days to appreciate it fully. If you want to drive through the park, you must use a four-wheel-drive vehicle. Even so, you may want to reconsider going if it's rained recently as the roads quickly become deeply mired in mud and difficult to navigate—even in a four-wheel drive. There are two routes: a 24km (15-mile) "short" route, marked by green arrows, and a 35km (22-mile) "long" route, marked by yellow arrows. The roads are well marked and safe, but somewhat rugged, although improvements are ongoing. For those wanting a closer look, the hiking possibilities are nearly endless. The entrance fee is US$10 (£5.20) for adults and US$5 (£2.60) for children age 12 and under. The park is open daily except holidays from 8am to 5pm. You must enter before 2:45pm.

Whichever route you take, there are a few important stops you shouldn't miss. Just past the gate is **Salina Mathijs,** a salt flat that's home to flamingos during the rainy season. Beyond the salt flat on the road to the right is **Boca Chiquito,** a white-sand beach and bay. A few miles up the beach lies **Boca Cocolishi,** a two-part black-sand beach. Many a couple has raved about their romantic memories of this beach, perfect for a secluded picnic. A ridge of calcareous algae separates its deep, rough seaward side and calm, shallow basin. The basin and the beach were formed by small pieces of coral and mollusk shells (*cocolishi* means "shells"), thus the black sand. The basin itself has no current, so it's perfect for snorkeling close to shore.

The main road leads to **Boca Bartol,** a bay full of living and dead elkhorn coral, sea fans, and reef fish. A popular watering hole good for bird-watching is **Poosdi Mangel. Wajaca** is a remote reef, perfect for divers and home to the island's most exciting sea creatures, including turtles, octopuses, and triggerfish. Immediately inland is **Mount Brandaris;** at 236m (774 ft.) it's Bonaire's highest peak. At its foot is **Bronswinkel Well,** a watering spot for pigeons and parakeets. More than 200 species of birds live in the park, many with such exotic names as bananaquit and black-faced grassquit. Bonaire has few mammals, but you'll see goats and donkeys, perhaps even a wild bull.

In 2005 it became possible to spend the night in one of the park buildings; it costs US$57 (£30) per person. However, the park cannot be used as a hotel, and all overnight visitors also have to be registered at a hotel on the island. In essence, this means you'll be paying for two sleeping quarters on the same night. The park stopover is viewed as "an extra activity." To book a stay in the park, call © **599/785-8444.** The website is www.washingtonparkbonaire.org.

HEADING SOUTH

Leaving the capital again, you pass the **Trans World Radio antennae,** towering 150m (492 ft.) in the air, transmitting with 810,000 watts. This is one of the hemisphere's most powerful medium-wave radio stations, the loudest voice in Christendom, and the most powerful nongovernmental broadcast station in the world. It sends out inter-denominational Gospel messages and hymns in 20 languages to places as far away as Eastern Europe and the Middle East.

You then come to the **salt flats** ☞, where the brilliantly colored pink flamingos live. Bonaire shelters the largest accessible nesting and breeding grounds in the world. The flamingos build high mud mounds to hold their eggs. The best time to see the birds is in spring, when they're nesting and tending their young. Slaves once worked the salt flats, and the government has rebuilt some primitive stone huts, bare shelters little more than waist high. The slaves slept in these huts, and returned to their homes in Rincón in the north on weekends. The centuries-old salt pans have been reactivated by the International Salt Company. Near the salt pans, you'll see some 9m (30-ft.) obelisks in white, blue, and orange, built in 1838 to help mariners locate their proper anchorages.

Farther down the coast is the island's oldest lighthouse, **Willemstoren,** built in 1837. Still farther along, **Sorobon Beach, Lac Bay Beach,** and **Boca Cai** come into view. They're at landlocked Lac Bay, which is ideal for swimming and snorkeling. Conch shells are stacked up on the beach. The water here is so vivid and clear, you can see coral 20m to 36m (66–118 ft.) down in the reef-protected waters.

8 Shopping

Walk along **Kaya Grandi** in Kralendijk to see an assortment of goods, including gemstone jewelry, wood, leather, sterling, ceramics, liquors, and tobacco, priced 25% to 50% less than in the United States and Canada. Prices are quoted in U.S. dollars, and major credit cards and traveler's checks are accepted.

Benetton, Kaya Grandi 29 (© 599/717-5107), claims to offer its brightly colored merchandise at prices about one-quarter less than most U.S. outlets.

Littman Jewelers, Kaya Grandi 33 (© 599/717-8160), sells Tag Heuer dive watches and also carries Daum French crystal and Lladró Spanish porcelain. Next door is **Littman's Gifts,** selling standard and hand-painted T-shirts, plus sandals, hats, Gottex swimsuits, gift items, costume jewelry, and toys.

Although hardly great, other stores you might want to visit include **Best Buddies,** Kaya Grandi 32 (© 599/717-7570), which is known for its *pareos* or beach wraps and its batiks from Indonesia. Nearby at **Island Fashions,** Kaya Grandi 5 (© 599/717-7565), you can pick up the latest clothes and gifts.

9 Bonaire After Dark

Underwater **slide shows** provide entertainment for both divers and nondivers. The best shows are at **Captain Don's Habitat** (© 599/717-8290; see "Accommodations," earlier in this chapter). Shows are presented in the hotel bar, Rum Runners, Friday night from 7 to 9pm.

Divi Flamingo Beach Resort & Casino, J. A. Abraham Boulevard (© 599/717-8285), promoted as "The World's First Barefoot Casino," offers blackjack, roulette, poker, wheel of fortune, video games, and slot machines. Entrance is free; hours are Monday to Saturday from 8pm to 2am.

Karel's Beach Bar, on the waterfront (© 599/717-8434), is almost Tahitian in its high-ceilinged, Tiki-hut design. This popular place perches above the sea on stilts. In Bogie's Casablanca, everybody came to Rick's. In Bonaire, everybody goes to Karel's: divers, sunset seekers, boaters, off-the-record couples—you name it. Zeezicht's full menu (p. 169) is also available to patrons of Karel's. Johan Visser also owns the restaurant. You can sit at the long rectangular bar with many of the island's dive and boating professionals, or select a table near the balustrades overlooking the illuminated surf. A sushi bar has been added. Wednesday is karaoke, with cocktailed crooners singing from 10pm; Friday and Saturday live bands, including reggae and pan, are brought in. Otherwise, a DJ spins discs as you drink the night away. Drinks are half price and beer costs US$2.50 (£1.30) during happy hour, 5 to 7pm.

We nominate the **City Cafe,** Kaya Grandi 7 (© 599/717-8286), as the island's funkiest bar. Painted in screaming shades of electric blue, scarlet magenta, and banana, it's a popular local hangout with a no-holds-barred vibe.

8

The British Virgin Islands

With their small bays and hidden coves, the British Virgin Islands (B.V.I.) are among the world's loveliest sailing grounds. Strung over the northeastern corner of the Caribbean, about 100km (60 miles) east of Puerto Rico, are some 40 islands (although that figure includes small, uninhabited cays or spits of land). Only three of the British Virgins are of any significant size: Tortola (which means "Dove of Peace"), Virgin Gorda ("Fat Virgin"), and Jost Van Dyke. Remote Norman Island is said to have been the inspiration for Robert Louis Stevenson's *Treasure Island*. On Deadman's Bay, a rocky cay, Blackbeard marooned 15 pirates and a bottle of rum, which gave rise to the ditty.

Columbus came this way in 1493, but the British Virgins apparently made little impression on him. Although the Spanish and Dutch protested, the English officially annexed Tortola in 1672. Today these islands are a British colony, with

their own elected government and a population of about 17,000.

The vegetation is varied and depends on the rainfall. In some parts, palms and mangos grow in profusion, whereas other places are arid and studded with cactus.

There are predictions that mass tourism is on the way, but so far the British Virgins are among the most laid-back islands in the Caribbean, a paradise for those who want to get away from it all in a peaceful, stunningly beautiful setting. Except for a few deluxe hotels on Virgin Gorda, the inns of the B.V.I. represent life the way the Caribbean used to be before the advent of high-rise condos, McDonald's, and fleets of cruise ships. If you want an array of shops, restaurants, hotels, and nightlife, head for the U.S.V.I. But if you want an unhurried way of life, where you often provide your own amusement, seek the peace and tranquility of the B.V.I.

1 Essentials

VISITOR INFORMATION

Before you go, contact the **British Virgin Islands Tourist Board,** 1270 Broadway, Suite 705, New York, NY 10001 (© **800/835-8530** or 212/696-0400). Other branches of the **British Virgin Islands Information Office** are located at 3450 Wilshire Blvd., Suite 1202, Los Angeles, CA 90010 (© **213/736-8931**), and at 1275 Shiloh Rd., Suite 2930, Kennesaw, GA 30144 (© **770/874-5951**). In the United Kingdom, contact the **B.V.I. Information Office,** 15 Upper Grosvenor St., London W1K 7PJ (© **207/355-9585**).

The tourist board's official website is **www.bvitourism.com**.

The British Virgin Islands

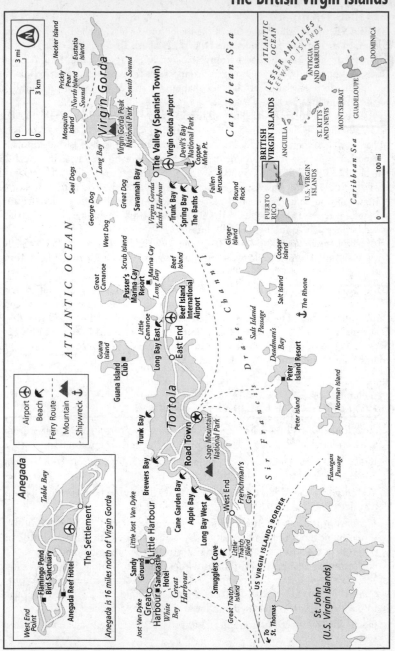

GETTING THERE

BY PLANE   **Beef Island,** the site of the major airport serving the British Virgins, is connected to Tortola by the one-lane **Queen Elizabeth Bridge.**

There are no nonstop flights from New York, Chicago, Miami, or L.A. to the British Virgin Islands, but you can make connections from San Juan, Puerto Rico, and St. Thomas to Beef Island/Tortola. (See chapters 17 and 27 for information on flying to these islands.)

Your best bet to reach Beef Island/Tortola is to take **American Eagle** (© **800/ 433-7300** in the U.S. and Canada; www.aa.com), which has dozens of flights to its hub in San Juan, and then at least four daily trips from San Juan to Beef Island/Tortola.

Another choice, if you're on one of Tortola's neighboring islands, is the much less reliable **LIAT** (© **888/844-5428** in the U.S. and Canada, or 284/495-1187; www.liatairline.com). This Caribbean carrier makes the short hop to Tortola from Antigua and St. Maarten in small planes not known for their frequency or careful scheduling. Reservations are made through travel agents or through the larger U.S.-based airlines that connect with LIAT hubs.

Air Sunshine (© **800/327-8900** in the U.S. and Canada, or 284/495-8900; www.airsunshine.com) flies between San Juan or St. Thomas to Beef Island/Tortola and Virgin Gorda.

BY FERRY   You can travel from Charlotte Amalie, St. Thomas, by public ferry to West End and Road Town on Tortola, a 45-minute voyage along Drake's Channel through the islands. The trip costs $25 to $28 one-way, and $45 to $49 round-trip. Boats making this run include **Native Son** (© **284/495-4617**) and **Smith's Ferry Service** (© **284/495-4495**). **Inter-Island Boat Services** (© **284/495-4166**) has routes from St. John to the West End on Tortola.

FAST FACTS: The British Virgin Islands

American Express   There are local representatives on Tortola and Virgin Gorda. See individual island "Fast Facts" later in this chapter for information.

Banks   Banks are generally open Monday through Thursday from 8am to 3pm, Friday from 9am to 5pm. Most banks have ATMs.

Currency   The U.S. dollar is the legal currency, much to the surprise of British travelers. *Prices in this chapter are quoted in U.S. dollars.*

Customs   You can bring items intended for your personal use into the British Virgin Islands, but only in discreet amounts. In other words, yes to a bottle of perfume or even two, but no to two suitcases filled with unopened fragrances. For returning U.S. residents, the duty-free allowance is only $800, providing you have been out of the country for 48 hours. You can send unsolicited gifts home if they total less than $100 per day to any single address. You don't have to pay duty on items classified as handicrafts, art, or antiques.

Electricity   The electrical current is 110-volt AC (60 cycles), as in the United States.

Emergencies   Dial © **999** in the event of an emergency.

Entry Requirements U.S. citizens and Canadians, plus others, need a valid passport.

Language The official language is English.

Liquor Laws Alcoholic beverages can be sold any day of the week, including Sunday. You can have an open container on the beach, but be careful not to litter, or you will be fined.

Mail Postal rates in the British Virgin Islands are 35¢ for a postcard (airmail) to the United States or Canada; 50¢ for a first-class airmail letter (½ oz.) to the United States and Canada.

Maps The best map of the British Virgin Islands is published by Vigilate and is sold at most bookstores in Road Town.

Medical Assistance The B.V.I.'s major hospital is **Peebles Hospital** in Road Town on Tortola; the island has more than a dozen doctors. If you need medical help, your hotel will put you in touch with the islands' medical staff.

Newspapers & Magazines The B.V.I. has no daily newspaper, but the *Island Sun*, published Wednesday and Friday, is a good source of information on local entertainment, as is the *BVI Beacon*, published on Thursday. *Standpoint* is another helpful publication that comes out on Monday and Saturday.

Safety Crime is rare here; in fact, the British Virgin Islands are among the safest places in the Caribbean. Still, you should take all the usual precautions you would anywhere, and don't leave items unattended on the beach.

Taxes There is no sales tax. A government tax of 7% is imposed on all hotel rooms. A $20 departure tax is collected from everyone leaving by air, $5 for those departing by ferry, or $7 if departing by cruise ship.

Telephone You can call the British Virgins from the United States by just dialing **1**, the area code **284**, and the number. From all public phones and from some hotels, you can access **MCI** by dialing ✆ **800/888-8000**. You can reach **Sprint** at ✆ **800/877-4646** and **AT&T** at ✆ **800/225-5288**.

Time The islands operate on Atlantic Standard Time year-round. In the peak winter season, when it's 10am in the British Virgins, it's 9am on the U.S. East Coast (EST). However, when the U.S. goes on daylight saving time, EST is the same as B.V.I. time.

Tipping & Service Charges Most hotels add on a 5% to 15% service charge; ask if it's already included when you're initially quoted a price. A 10% service charge is often (but not always) added on to restaurant bills; you can leave another 5% if you thought the service was unusually good. You usually don't need to tip taxi drivers, since most own their own cabs, but you can tip 10% if they've been unusually helpful.

Water The tap water in the British Virgin Islands is safe to drink.

Weather During the winter, temperatures in the British Virgin Islands range between 72°F and 82°F (22°C–28°C). September is the warmest month, with temperatures averaging 90°F (32°C). Temperatures rarely drop below 77°F (25°C) in winter or rise above 90°F (32°C) in summer.

2 Tortola ★★

Most visitors head to Virgin Gorda if they want to check into one of the posh, secluded inns and stay there, barely leaving the grounds. On Tortola, however, you have more shopping, restaurants, attractions, nightlife, and other diversions to occupy your time. Here you can sample more of the local life, ranging from visiting colorful markets to sailing. Tortola has one of the great beaches of the Caribbean, **Cane Garden Bay.** Here you also have a larger selection of accommodations from which to choose, with many at more moderate prices.

On the southern shore of this 62-sq.-km (24-sq.-mile) island is **Road Town,** the capital of the British Virgin Islands. It has the seat of Government House and other administrative buildings, but it feels more like a small village than a town. The landfill at Wickham's Cay, a 28-hectare (69-acre) town center development and marina in the harbor, has lured a massive yacht-chartering business here and has transformed the sleepy capital into more of a bustling center.

Rugged mountain peaks characterize the entire southern coast, including Road Town. On the northern coast are white-sand beaches, banana trees, mangos, and clusters of palms.

Close to Tortola's eastern end, **Beef Island** is the site of the main airport for passengers arriving in the British Virgins. The tiny island is connected to Tortola by the one-lane Queen Elizabeth Bridge, which the queen dedicated in 1966. On the north shore of Beef Island is Long Bay Beach.

ESSENTIALS

VISITOR INFORMATION   A **B.V.I. Tourist Board Office,** at the center of Road Town near the ferry dock (© **284/494-3134**), has information about hotels, restaurants, tours, and more. Pick up a copy of *The Welcome Tourist Guide,* which has a useful map of the island.

GETTING THERE   Because Tortola is the gateway to the British Virgin Islands, the information on how to get here is covered in the above "Essentials" section.

GETTING AROUND   **Taxis** meet every arriving flight. Government regulations prohibit anyone from renting a car at the airport, so you'll have to take a taxi to your hotel. Fares are set by the government, and taxis are unmetered. The fare from the Beef Island airport to Road Town is $24 each for one to three passengers. A **taxi tour** lasting 2½ hours costs $55 for one to three people. To call a taxi in Road Town, dial © **284/494-2322;** on Beef Island, © **284/495-1982.**

A handful of local companies and U.S.-based chains rent cars. **Itgo** (© **284/494-5150**) is located at 1 Wickham's Cay, Road Town; **Avis** (© **800/331-1212** in the U.S. and Canada, or 284/494-3322; www.avis.com) maintains offices opposite police headquarters in Road Town; and **Hertz** (© **800/654-3131** in the U.S. and Canada, or 284/495-4405; www.hertz.com) has offices outside Road Town, on the island's West End, near the ferryboat landing dock. Rental companies will usually deliver your car to your hotel. All three companies require a valid driver's license and a temporary B.V.I. driver's license, which the car-rental agency can sell you for $10; it's valid for 3 months. Because of the volume of tourism to Tortola, you should reserve a car in advance, especially in winter.

Tortola

Cooper Island Beach Club **1**
Lambert Beach Resort **4**
Long Bay Beach Resort & Villas **2**
Sebastian's on the Beach **3**
The Sugar Mill **3**

Airport
Beach
Mountain

ATLANTIC OCEAN

Rough Point
Shark Bay
Brewers Bay
Mount Healthy National Park
Larimers Bay
Trunk Bay
Cooper Bay
Rogue Bay Point
Josiah's Bay
Wesley Will
Belle Vue Rd.

Cane Garden Bay
Carrot Bay
Skyworld
Cane Garden Bay Rd.
Joe's Hill Rd.
Fahia Hill
Wickham's Cay
Road Harbour

Apple Bay
Zion Hill Rd.
Long Bay West
Belmont Point
Long Bay **2**
Belmont Pond
Smugglers Cove
Steele Point
Soper's Hole
Frenchman's Cay
Little Thatch Island
To Jost Van Dyke
To St. Thomas

West End
Freshwater Pond
Fort Recovery
Sage Mountain 1,780 ft.
Sage Mountain National Park
Ridge Rd.
Drake's Highway

Hannah
Sea Cow Bay
Nanny Cay
Road Town
To Peter Island

Parham Town **4**
East End
Elizabeth Beach
Long Bay East
Beef Island Int'l Airport
Beef Island Rd.
Trellis
Beef Island
Bluff Bay
The Bluff
To Virgin Gorda

Fat Hogs Bay
Buck Island
Whelk Point
Paraquita Bay
Brandy Wine Bay
Blackburn HWY
Lambert Rd.
Baughter's Bay

Caribbean Sea

BRITISH VIRGIN ISLANDS
Anegada
Virgin Gorda
Tortola
U.S. VIRGIN ISLANDS
Jost Van Dyke
PUERTO RICO
ANGUILLA
ST. KITTS AND NEVIS
Caribbean Sea
0   100 mi

N

0   2 mi
0   2 km

Remember: Drive on the left. Roads are pretty well paved, but they're often narrow, windy, and poorly lit, and they have few, if any, lines, so driving at night can be tricky. It's a good idea to rent a taxi to take you to that difficult-to-find beach, restaurant, or bar.

FAST FACTS The local **American Express** representative is Travel Plan, Waterfront Drive (© **284/494-4000**).

Local bank branches include the **Bank of Nova Scotia** (Scotia Bank), Wickham's Cay (© **284/494-2526**), or **First Caribbean National Bank,** Wickham's Cay (© **284/494-2171**), both near Road Town. There's also a branch of **First Bank** at Road Town on Wickham's Cay I (© **284/494-2662**). Each has its own ATM.

The best place for camera supplies on Tortola is **Bolos Department Store,** Wickham's Cay (© **284/494-2867**).

For dental emergencies, contact **Dental Surgery** (© **284/494-3274**), in Road Town, behind the Skeleton Building and next to the *BVI Beacon,* the local newspaper.

Peebles Hospital, Porter Road, Road Town (© **284/494-3497**), has X-ray, emergency, and laboratory facilities. The best pharmacy is **Medicure Pharmacy,** Road Town (© **284/494-6189**).

The main **police headquarters** is on Waterfront Drive near the ferry docks on Sir Olva Georges Plaza, with a branch office in Road Town in the town center (© **284/494-3822**).

ACCOMMODATIONS

None of the island's hotels is as big or splashy as the hotels in the U.S. Virgin Islands, and that's just fine with most of Tortola's repeat visitors. All rates are subject to between a 10% and 16% service charge, depending on the hotel, and a 7% government tax on the room. Be sure to read the section "Packages for the Independent Traveler" in chapter 2 before you book your hotel on your own.

VERY EXPENSIVE

Long Bay Beach Resort & Villas ⚘ This resort lies on a 2km-long (1¼-mile) sandy beach. In a setting on the north shore, about 10 minutes from West End, it's the only full-service resort on the island, a low-rise complex set in a 21-hectare (52-acre) estate. Unfortunately, complaints about service and maintenance have marred its once stellar reputation. The accommodations include hillside rooms and studios; the smallest and most basic have simple furnishings while the deluxe beachfront rooms and cabanas have either balconies or patios that overlook the ocean. The resort also offers two- and three-bedroom villas complete with a kitchen, living area, and large deck with a gas grill. If you're not staying right on the beach, you can still enjoy an ocean view from any of the other accommodations. All units have one four-poster king-size or two queen-size beds, plus large bathrooms with tiled showers.

The Beach Café is in the ruins of an old sugar mill. The Garden Restaurant offers dinner by reservation only and serves a variety of local and international dishes in an elegant, alfresco setting. The cuisine is among the finest of any hotel on the island, especially the fresh fish, and the wine list is extensive.

P.O. Box 433, Road Town, Tortola, B.V.I. © **800/345-0356** in the U.S. and Canada, or 284/495-4252. Fax 284/495-4677. www.longbay.com. 152 units. Winter $510 double, $580 junior suite, $800–$1,050 2-bedroom villa; off season $285 double, $330 junior suite, $590 2-bedroom villa. AE, DISC, MC, V. **Amenities:** 3 restaurants; 3 bars; outdoor pool; 2 tennis courts; health club; spa; sauna; snorkeling; horseback riding; car-rental desk; babysitting; laundry service; dry cleaning; nonsmoking rooms. *In room:* A/C, TV, dataport, kitchen (in villas), beverage maker, hair dryer, safe, wet bar.

The Sugar Mill ⓕ   Set in a lush tropical garden on the site of a 300-year-old sugar mill on the north side of Tortola, this secluded cottage colony sweeps down the hillside to its own little beach, with vibrant flowers and fruits brightening the grounds. The accommodations are contemporary and well designed, ranging from suites and cottages to studios, all self-contained with kitchenettes and private terraces with views. Rooms have twin or king-size beds, plus well-maintained private bathrooms with showers. Four of the units are suitable for families of four. The latest addition, the Plantation House suites, evokes traditional Caribbean architecture, with fine stonework, breezy porches, and lacy gingerbread. Just steps from the beach, a pair of two-bedroom air-conditioned suites has tropical decor and sea views. Each has a king-size bed and a large bathroom with double sinks.

Lunch is served down by the beach at Islands, which features Caribbean specialties like jerk ribs or stuffed crab, plus burgers and salads. Dinner is offered at the Sugar Mill Restaurant (see "Dining," below).

Apple Bay (P.O. Box 425), Road Town, Tortola, B.V.I. ⓒ 800/462-8834 in the U.S., or 284/495-4355. Fax 284/495-4696. www.sugarmillhotel.com. 23 units. Winter $340 double, $355 triple, $370 quad, $695 2-bedroom villa; off season $255–$275 double, $270–$290 triple, $285–$305 quad, $535–$585 2-bedroom villa. MAP (breakfast and dinner) $70 per person extra. AE, MC, V. Closed Aug–Sept. From Road Town, drive west 11km (6¾ miles), turn right (north) over Zion Hill, and turn right at the T-junction opposite Sebastian's; Sugar Mill is .8km (½ mile) down the road. Children 12 and under not accepted in winter. **Amenities:** 2 restaurants; 2 bars; outdoor pool; scuba diving; snorkeling; windsurfing; concierge; car rental; babysitting; laundry service; dry cleaning; 1 room for those w/limited mobility. In room: A/C, ceiling fan, TV (in villa and master suite), dataport, kitchenette (in some), fridge, hair dryer, iron.

EXPENSIVE

Lambert Beach Resort ⓕ Finds   On the remote northeastern section of the island, this is the place for escapists who want isolation. Perched in an amphitheater sloping to the water, the resort opens onto a .8km (½-mile) beach of white sand set against a backdrop of palm trees. To reach the resort, you'll need to rent a car or take a taxi; it's about a 15-minute car ride from Road Town. Once here, you'll find some of the B.V.I.'s best white-sand cove beaches, along with a large swimming pool. Playground facilities for children make this a family favorite.

The Mediterranean-style cottage cluster is spread across eight one-floor structures, each containing a combination of suites with a living room, veranda, and bedrooms. The preferred rooms open onto the beach, while the others front tropical gardens. Bedrooms are spacious and feature sand-hued walls, stained wood, ceramic tiled floors, and tropical motifs. Each unit comes with a private bathroom with tub or shower.

The food here is Caribbean cuisine with Italian, French, and international overtones. Dishes, boasting market-fresh ingredients, are well made.

Lambert Bay, East End, Tortola, B.V.I. ⓒ 284/495-2877. Fax 284/495-2876. www.lambertbeachresortbvi.com. 38 units. Winter $190–$260 double, $220–$450 suite; off season $165–$215 double, $190–$385 suite. AE, DC, MC, V. **Amenities:** Restaurant; bar; outdoor pool; tennis court; watersports equipment; reef fishing; limited room service. In room: A/C, minibar.

MODERATE

Cooper Island Beach Club ⓕ Finds   This ultimate escapist's retreat is far from luxurious, but is the perfect place for those who want to experience simplicity. This one-of-a-kind hotel lies on a hilly island on the southern tier of the Sir Francis Drake Channel, about 8km (5 miles) south of Tortola. There are no roads on the island, shopping centers, nightclubs, or other diversions. This spot is for those who like do nothing except sun, swim, and relax.

The midsize units come with a bedroom, a living room, and a kitchen, plus a balcony and a bathroom with a shower that is almost outdoors. The property is powered by a generator, which only runs at night. Thus, lighting and ceiling fans are powered by 12-volt DC, and there is one 110-volt outlet in each room, which can be used to recharge batteries at night. The freshwater supply comes from rain, and is stored in a cistern under each room. Each building uses a solar heater, and all toilets are flushed with sea water. The on-site Sail Caribbean Divers offers snorkeling, kayaks, dinghy rentals, and full scuba services.

Manchioneel Bay, Road Town, Tortola, B.V.I. ℭ 800/542-4624 or 413/863-3162 in the U.S., or 284/495-9084. Fax 413/863-3662. www.cooper-island.com. 11 units. Winter $195 double; off season $105–$135 double. Extra person $25. No credit cards. **Amenities:** 2 restaurants; bar; watersports equipment rental; dive shop. *In room:* Kitchenette, no phone.

Sebastian's on the Beach   This hotel is located at Little Apple Bay, about a 15-minute drive from Road Town, on a long beach that has some of the best surfing in the British Virgin Islands. The rooms are housed in three buildings, with only one on the beach. All come with Indonesian furniture and balconies or porches. You should be careful here about room selection, as accommodations vary considerably. Most sought after are the beachfront rooms, only steps from the surf; they have an airy tropical vibe, with tile floors, balconies, patios, and screened jalousies. The rear accommodations on the beach side are less desirable—not only do they lack views, but they're also subject to traffic noise. Also, avoid the two noisy bedrooms above the commissary. The dozen less expensive, rather Spartan rooms in the back of the main building lack views, but they're only a short walk from the beach.

Little Apple Bay (P.O. Box 441), West End, Tortola, B.V.I. ℭ 800/336-4870 in the U.S., or 284/495-4212. Fax 284/495-4466. www.sebastiansbvi.com. 30 units. Winter $135–$285 double; off season $85–$180 double. Breakfast and dinner $45 per person extra. AE, DISC, MC, V. **Amenities:** Restaurant; bar. *In room:* A/C, TV, fridge, beverage maker, no phone (in some units).

DINING
EXPENSIVE

Brandywine Bay Restaurant 𝄐𝄐 ITALIAN/INTERNATIONAL   Set on a cobblestone garden terrace along the south shore overlooking Sir Francis Drake Channel, this is one of Tortola's most elegant, romantic restaurants. Davide Pugliese, the chef, and his wife, Cele, have earned a reputation for their outstanding Florentine fare. Davide changes his menu daily, based on the availability of fresh produce. The best dishes include beef carpaccio, roast duck, homemade pasta, his own special calf-liver dish (the recipe is a secret), and homemade mozzarella with fresh basil and tomatoes. The skillful cooking ranges from classic to inspired.

Brandywine Estate, Sir Francis Drake Hwy. ℭ 284/495-2301. www.brandywinebay.com. Reservations required. Appropriate dress required. Main courses $29–$39. AE, MC, V. Mon–Sat 6:30–9:30pm. Closed Aug–Oct. Drive 5km (3 miles) east of Road Town (toward the airport) on South Shore Rd.

Skyworld 𝄐𝄐 INTERNATIONAL   Skyworld continues to be all the rage, one of the best restaurants on the island. On one of Tortola's loftiest peaks, at a breezy 400m (1,312 ft.), it offers views of both the U.S. Virgin Islands and the British Virgin Islands. The restaurant is divided into two sections—a main dining room and a bar. Both sections offer the same menu.

The fresh fish chowder is an island favorite, as are other, oft-changing soups, including one with peaches and coconuts, and another of champagne, coconut, and melons. The fresh fish of the day is your best main course bet. We've enjoyed the oven-baked yellow-fin tuna with a pistachio and sesame-seed crust. Try the island's best Key lime pie or the heavenly cheesecake for dessert.

Ridge Rd., Road Town. ℂ 284/494-3567. Reservations recommended. Main courses $26–$31. AE, MC, V. Daily 10am–2:30pm and 5–11pm. Closed Christmas Day.

Sugar Mill Restaurant ⭐ CALIFORNIA/CARIBBEAN Transformed from a 3-century-old sugar mill (see "Accommodations," above), this is a romantic spot for dining. Colorful works by Haitian painters hang on the old stone walls, and big copper basins have been planted with tropical flowers. Before going to the dining room, once part of the old boiling house, visit the open-air bar on a deck that overlooks the sea.

Your hosts, the Morgans, know a lot about food and wine. One of their most popular creations, published in *Bon Appétit*, is curried banana soup. You might also begin with the roasted pepper salad or the especially tasty wild mushroom soup. For a main course, we'd recommend such dishes as pan-roasted duck breast served with Asian coleslaw and soba noodles or grilled fresh fish with a pineapple pepper salsa.

Apple Bay. ℂ 284/495-4355. Reservations required. Main courses $26–$35. AE, MC, V. Daily 8–10am, noon–2pm, and 7–9pm. Closed Aug–Sept. From Road Town, drive west 11km (6¾ miles), turn right (north) over Zion Hill, and turn right at the T-junction opposite Sebastian's; Sugar Mill is .8km (½ mile) down the road.

MODERATE

Gourmet picnic, anyone? **Gourmet Chandler,** Nanny Cay (ℂ 284/494-2894), offers fabulous fixings, including cheeses, snacks, groceries, wines, beer, breads, and fine chocolates. Open Monday to Saturday 8am to 5pm; Sunday 8am to 3pm.

Capriccio di Mare ⭐ ITALIAN Created in a moment of whimsy by the more upscale Brandywine Bay Restaurant (see above), this place is small, casual, laid-back, and a local favorite. It's the most authentic-looking Italian cafe in the Virgin Islands. At breakfast time, many locals stop in for a refreshing Italian pastry and a cup of cappuccino, or else a full breakfast. If it's evening, you might try the mango Bellini, a variation of the famous cocktail served at Harry's Bar in Venice. Begin with such appetizers as *piedini* (flour tortillas with various toppings), then move on to fresh pastas with succulent sauces, the best pizza on the island (our favorite is the one topped with grilled eggplant), or even well-stuffed sandwiches. If you arrive on the right night, you might even be treated to stuffed Cornish hen with scalloped potatoes. Also try one of the freshly made salads: We like the *insalata mista* with large, leafy greens and slices of fresh Parmesan.

Waterfront Dr., Road Town. ℂ 284/494-5369. Main courses $6.50–$15. MC, V. Mon–Sat 8am–9pm.

The Pub INTERNATIONAL This establishment is housed in a low-slung timbered building on a narrow strip of land between the coastal road and the southern edge of Road Town's harbor. It has a barnlike interior and a rambling veranda built on piers over the water. The pub attracts many of the island's yachties, as well as the local sports teams, who celebrate here after their games. More than 25 different kinds of beer are available. If you're here for a meal, some of the best options include Bahamian fritters, Caesar or Greek salads, pastas, four kinds of steaks, and burgers. Locals who frequent this place are especially fond of the chef's jerk chicken and his combo platter of spareribs, chicken, and fried shrimp. The chef also prepares a catch of the day. Happy hour brings discounted drinks daily from 5 to 7pm and on Friday, when hot wings and raw vegetable platters are offered.

Fort Burt Marina, Harbour Rd. ℂ 284/494-2608. Reservations recommended. Main courses $15–$35. AE, MC, V. Mon–Sat 6am–10pm; Sun 5pm–midnight.

Pusser's Landing CARIBBEAN   This location in West End, which opens onto the water, is nicer than the original location on the waterfront across from the ferry dock. In this nautical setting, you can enjoy fresh grilled fish of the day cooked to your requirements. Begin with a hearty soup, perhaps pumpkin or freshly made seafood chowder. Many of the main courses, most of which are moderate in price, have real island flavor, the most justifiably popular being jerk chicken Jamaican style, or the grilled chicken breast with fresh pineapple salsa. A classic is the curried shrimp over rice. Mud pie remains the choice dessert here, but the Key lime pie and mango soufflé are also appealing. Happy hour is daily from 5 to 7pm.

Frenchman's Cay, West End. © **284/495-4554.** Reservations required. Main courses $20–$36. AE, MC, V. Daily 11am–10pm.

HITTING THE BEACH

Beaches are rarely crowded on Tortola unless a cruise ship is in port. You can rent a car or a jeep to reach them, or take a taxi (but arrange for a time to be picked up).

Tortola's finest beach is **Cane Garden Bay** 🌴🌴🌴, on Cane Garden Bay Road directly west of Road Town. You'll have to navigate some roller-coaster hills to get there, but these fine white sands with sheltering palm trees are among the most popular in the B.V.I., and the lovely bay is beloved by yachties. Outfitters here rent Hobie Cats, kayaks, and sailboards. Windsurfing is possible as well. This is one beach that may get crowded, especially during high season. There are several places to eat, along with a handful of bars. **Rhymer's** (© **284/495-4639**) is our favorite, dispensing cold beer and refreshing rum drinks. If you're hungry, try the conch or lobster, black-bean gazpacho, or barbecued spareribs. The beach bar and restaurant is open daily from 8am to 9pm. Ice and freshwater showers are available and you can rent towels. Ask about renting Sunfish sailboats and windsurfers next door.

Surfers like **Apple Bay,** west of Cane Garden Bay, along North Shore Road. The beach isn't very big, but that doesn't diminish activity when the surf's up. Conditions are best in January and February. After enjoying the white sands here, stop for a drink at Bomba's Surfside Shack, a classic dive of a beach bar at the water's edge (see "Tortola After Dark," below).

Smugglers Cove, known for its tranquility and beautiful sands, lies at the extreme western end of Tortola, opposite the offshore island of Great Thatch and just north of St. John. It's a lovely crescent of white sand, with calm turquoise waters. A favorite local beach, it's at the end of bumpy Belmont Road. Once you get here, a little worse for wear, we think you'll agree that the crystal-clear water and the beautiful palm trees are worth the effort. Snorkelers like this beach, which is sometimes called "Lower Belmont Bay." It's especially good for beginners, since the reef is close to shore and easily reached. You'll see parrotfish, sea fans, sponges, and elkhorn and brain corals.

East of Cane Garden Bay and site of a campground, **Brewers Bay,** accessed from long, steep Brewers Bay Road, is ideal for snorkelers and surfers. This clean, white-sand beach is a great place to enjoy walks in the early morning or at sunset. Sip a rum punch from the beach bar, and watch the world go by.

The 2km-long (1¼-mile) white-sand beach at **Long Bay West,** reached along Long Bay Road, is one of the most beautiful in the B.V.I. Joggers run along the water's edge, and spectacular sunsets make it perfect for romantic strolls. The Long Bay Beach Resort stands on the northeast side of the beach; many visitors like to book a table at the resort's restaurant overlooking the water.

At the very east end of the island, **Long Bay East,** reached along Beef Island Road, is a great spot for swimming. Cross Queen Elizabeth Bridge to reach this 2km-long (1¼-mile) beach with great views and white sands.

EXPLORING THE ISLAND

Travel Plan Tours, Romasco Place, Harbour House (P.O. Box 437), Road Town (© 284/494-4000; www.aroundthebvi.com), offers a 3½-hour tour that touches on the panoramic highlights of Tortola (a minimum of four participants is required). The cost is $47 per person. The company also runs 3-hour **snorkeling tours** for $64 per person (with snacks included). A full-day **sailing tour** aboard a catamaran that goes from Tortola to either Peter Island or Norman Island costs $165 per person; a full-day tour, which goes as far afield as The Baths at Virgin Gorda and includes lunch, costs $125 per person. And if **deep-sea fishing** appeals to you, you can go for a half-day excursion, with equipment, for four fishermen and up to two "nonfishing observers" for $850 or the full day for $1,260.

A **taxi tour** costs $55 for two passengers for 2 hours, or $70 for 3 hours. To call a taxi in Road Town, dial © 284/494-2322; on Beef Island, © 284/495-1982.

J. R. O'Neal Botanic Gardens , Botanic Station, Road Town (no phone), fills up a 1.6-hectare (4-acre) site of lush tropical growth. Wander at leisure, taking in the pergola walk, a waterfall, a lily pond, tropical birdhouses, and miniature "rainforests." Of course, you can also enjoy the rich plant life that ranges here from exotic orchids to gardens of medicinal herbs. Admission is free; the gardens are open Monday to Saturday 9am to 4:30pm.

No visit to Tortola is complete without a trip to **Sage Mountain National Park** , rising to an elevation of 534m (1,752 ft.). Here you'll find traces of a primeval rainforest, and you can enjoy a picnic while overlooking neighboring islets and cays. Go west from Road Town to reach the mountain. Before you head out, stop by the tourist office and pick up the brochure *Sage Mountain National Park.* It has a location map, directions to the forest and parking, and an outline of the main trails through the park. Covering 37 hectares (91 acres), the park protects the remnants of Tortola's original forests not burned or cleared during the island's plantation era. From the parking lot, a trail leads to the main park entrance. The two main trails are the Rainforest Trail and the Mahogany Forest Trail.

Shadow's Ranch, Todman's Estate (© 284/494-2262), gives horseback rides through the national park or down to the shores of Brewers Bay. Call for details, daily from 9am to 4pm. The cost is from $100 per hour.

THE WRECK OF THE *RHONE* & OTHER TOP DIVE SITES

The one site in the British Virgin Islands that lures divers over from St. Thomas is the wreck of the **HMS *Rhone*** , which sank in 1867 near the western point of Salt Island. *Skin Diver* magazine called it "the world's most fantastic shipwreck dive." It teems with marine life and coral formations and was featured in the 1977 movie *The Deep.*

Although it's no *Rhone,* **Chikuzen** is another intriguing dive site off Tortola. It's an 81m (266-ft.) steel-hulled refrigerator ship, which sank off the island's east end in 1981. The hull, still intact under about 24m (79 ft.) of water, is now home to a vast array of tropical fish, including yellowtail, barracuda, black-tip sharks, octopus, and drum fish.

South of Ginger Island, **Alice's Wonderland** is a deep-dive site with a wall that begins at around 3.6m (12 ft.) and slopes gently to 30m (98 ft.). It abounds with marine life such as lobsters, crabs, rainbow-hued fan coral and mammoth mushroom-shaped coral. **Spyglass Wall** is another offshore dive site dropping to a sandy bottom and filled with sea fans and large coral heads. The drop is from 3 to 18m (10–59 ft.). Divers here seek out tarpon, eagle rays, and stingrays.

Blue Waters Divers, Nanny Call Marina, Road Town (© **284/494-2847;** www.bluewaterdiversbvi.com), is a PADI outfitter, offering various dive packages, including to the wreck of the *Rhone.* A resort course costs $105, a PADI open-water certification $370.

YACHT CHARTERS

Tortola boasts the largest fleet of bareboat sailing charters in the world. The best place to get outfitted is **The Moorings,** Wickham's Cay (© **888/535-7289** in the U.S. and Canada, or 284/494-2331; www.moorings.com). This outfit, along with a handful of others, makes the British Virgins the cruising capital of the world. You can choose from a fleet of sailing yachts, which can accommodate up to six couples in comfort and style. Depending on your nautical knowledge and skills, you can arrange a bareboat rental (with no crew) or a fully crewed rental with a skipper, a staff, and a cook. Boats come equipped with a portable barbecue, snorkeling gear, dinghy, linens, and galley equipment. The Moorings has an experienced staff of mechanics, electricians, riggers, and cleaners. If you're going out on your own, you'll get a thorough briefing session on Virgin Island waters and anchorages.

If you'd like sailing lessons, consider **Steve Colgate's Offshore Sailing School** (© **800/221-4326** in the U.S.), which offers courses in seamanship year-round.

SHOPPING

Most of Tortola's shops are on Road Town's Main Street. Unfortunately, the British Virgins have no duty-free shopping. British goods are imported without duty, and you can find some good buys among these imported items, especially in English china. In general, store hours are Monday to Saturday from 9am to 4pm.

You might start your shopping expedition at **Crafts Alive,** an open-air market lying in the center of Road Town and impossible to miss. It consists of a series of old-fashioned West Indian–style buildings that are stocked with local crafts and locally made goods, ranging from Caribbean dolls to straw hats, from crocheted doilies to pottery, plus, of course, the inevitable B.V.I. T-shirts.

Sunny Caribbee Herb and Spice Company, Main Street, Road Town (© **284/ 494-2178;** www.sunnycaribbee.com), in an old West Indian building, was the first hotel on Tortola. It's now a shop specializing in Caribbean spices, seasonings, teas, condiments, and handicrafts. With an aroma of spices permeating the air, this factory is an attraction in itself. You can buy two famous specialties here: the West Indian hangover cure and the Arawak love potion. A Caribbean cosmetics collection, Sunsations, includes herbal bath gels, island perfume, and sunscreens. There's a daily sampling of island products—perhaps tea, coffee, sauces, or dips.

Samarkand Jewelers, 94 Main St., Road Town (© **284/494-6415**), evokes an exotic land, but is actually an unusually good bet for jewelry and other items. Look for an intriguing selection of bracelets, pins, pendants in both silver and gold, and pierced earrings. Caribbean motifs such as palms and sea birds often appear in the designs of the jewelry.

Pusser's Company Store, Main Street and Waterfront Road, Road Town (© 284/494-2467), sells gourmet food items including meats, spices, fish, and a nice selection of wines. Pusser's Rum is one of the best-selling items here.

Arawak Boutique & Gift Shop, Nanny Cay Marina (© 284/494-5240), is known for its household furnishings such as placemats and candleholders, but it also sells sporty clothing for adults and kids, along with a selection of gifts and souvenirs.

Flamboyance, Waterfront Drive (© 284/494-4099), is the best place to shop for perfume and upscale cosmetics.

If you've rented a villa or condo, or even if your accommodations have a kitchenette, consider a visit to **Ample Hamper,** Inner Harbour Marina, Wickham's Cay I, Road Town (© 284/494-2494; www.amplehamper.com). This outlet stocks some of the best-packaged food and bottled wines on the island. It also has fresh fruit and a tasty selection of cheeses.

Philatelists from all over the world flock to the **British Virgin Islands Post Office,** Main Street, Road Town (© 284/494-3701, ext. 4996), for its exquisite, unusual stamps in beautiful designs. Even though the stamps carry U.S. monetary designations, they can only be used in the B.V.I. Most stamp collectors, however, collect the stamps rather than actually using them.

TORTOLA AFTER DARK

Ask around to find out which hotel might have entertainment on any given evening. Steel bands and fungi or scratch bands (African Caribbean musicians who improvise on locally available instruments) appear regularly, and nonresidents are usually welcome. Pick up a copy of *Limin' Times,* an entertainment magazine listing what's happening locally; it's usually available at hotels.

Bomba's Surfside Shack, Cappoon's Bay (© 284/495-4148), is the oldest, most memorable, and most uninhibited hangout on the island. Sitting on the beach near the West End, it's covered with Day-Glo graffiti and odds and ends of plywood, driftwood, and abandoned rubber tires. Despite its makeshift appearance, the shack has the sound system to create a really great party. Every month (dates vary), Bomba's stages a full-moon party, with free house tea spiked with hallucinogenic mushrooms. (The tea is free because it's illegal to sell it.) The place is also wild on Wednesday and Sunday nights, when there's live music and a $10 all-you-can-eat barbecue. It's open daily from 10am to midnight (or later, depending on business).

The bar at **The Moorings/Mariner Inn,** Wickham's Cay (© 284/494-2333), is the preferred watering hole for upscale yacht owners, but drink prices are low. Open to a view of its own marina, and bathed in a dim and flattering light, the place is relaxed.

Other places worth a stop on a barhopping jaunt include **The Jolly Roger Inn,** West End (© 284/495-4559; www.jollyrogerbvi.com), where you can hear local or sometimes American bands playing everything from reggae to blues. In the same area, visit **Stanley's Welcome Bar,** Cane Garden Bay (© 284/495-9424), where a rowdy frat-boy crowd gathers to drink, talk, and drink some more. Finally, check out **Sebastian's,** Apple Bay (© 284/495-4212), especially on Sunday, when you can dance to live music under the stars, at least in winter.

Rhymer's, on the popular stretch of beach at Cane Garden Bay (© 284/495-4639), serves up cold beer or tropical rum concoctions, along with a casual menu of ribs, conch chowder, and more. The beach bar and restaurant is open daily from 8am to 9pm.

3 Virgin Gorda ★★★

Virgin Gorda is where you come to relax and escape, at some of the poshest and most self-contained inns in the Caribbean, if you can afford them. Life here is much slower paced than on Tortola, without much shopping or nightlife. The island gets far less rain, making some sections of it quite arid. Goats wander among a landscape of cactus and scrub brush.

In 1493, on his second voyage to the New World, Columbus named this island Virgin Gorda, or "fat virgin" (from a distance, the island looks like a reclining woman with a protruding stomach). The second-largest island in the cluster of British Virgin Islands, Virgin Gorda is about 15km (10 miles) long and 3km (2 miles) wide, with a population of some 1,400. It's 19km (12 miles) east of Road Town and 42km (26 miles) from St. Thomas.

The island was a fairly desolate agricultural community until Laurance S. Rockefeller established the Little Dix Bay Hotel here in the early 1960s, following his success with the Caneel Bay resort on St. John in the 1950s. He envisioned a "wilderness beach," where privacy and solitude would reign. In 1971, the Virgin Gorda Yacht Harbour opened, turning the island into a world class destination for yachties. Operated by the Little Dix Bay Hotel, it accommodates 120 yachts today.

Try to visit Virgin Gorda, if only for the day, to see **The Baths,** gigantic rocks and boulders shaped by volcanic pressures millions of years ago. The beach at The Baths is simply spectacular. Virgin Gorda is also quite mountainous; if you're tired of flat Caribbean islands, you'll love the gorgeous, dramatic scenery here.

ESSENTIALS

GETTING THERE **Speedy's Fantasy** (© 284/495-5240) runs a ferry service between Road Town and Virgin Gorda. Monday to Saturday, at least four ferries a day leave from Road Town, three per day on Sunday. The cost is $15 one-way or $25 round-trip. From St. Thomas to Virgin Gorda, it offers service three times a week (on Tues, Thurs, and Sat), costing $35 one-way or $60 round-trip.

Most of the luxurious resorts have their own boats to take you from the airport on Beef Island to Virgin Gorda.

GETTING AROUND Independently operated open-sided **safari buses** run along the main road. Holding up to 22 passengers, these buses charge upwards from $3 to $4 per person to transport a passenger, say, from The Valley to The Baths. Additional taxi service is provided by **African Pride Taxi Service** in The Valley (© 284/495-6091), and by **Mahogany Rentals & Taxi Service** in The Valley (© 284/495-5539).

If you'd like to rent a car, try one of the local firms, including **Mahogany Rentals,** The Valley, Spanish Town (© 284/495-5469), across from the yacht harbor. This company is the least expensive on the island, beginning at around $55 daily for a Suzuki Sidekick. Road conditions on Virgin Gorda range from good to extremely poor; you're probably better off renting a 4WD vehicle. *Remember:* Drive on the left.

FAST FACTS You can reach the **police station** by calling © 284/495-7584. **First Caribbean International Bank** (© 284/495-5217) is located in Spanish Town at the Virgin Gorda Shopping Centre. It has an ATM.

Virgin Gorda

British Virgin Islands
- ANGUILLA
- ST. KITTS AND NEVIS
- Virgin Gorda
- Tortola
- Anegada
- U.S. VIRGIN ISLANDS
- Jost Van Dyke
- PUERTO RICO
- *Caribbean Sea*
- 100 mi

Legend:
- Airport
- Beach
- Ferry
- Mountain

Parjaros Point
Oil Nut Bay
Deep Bay
Berchers Bay
Berchers Bluff
John O Point
Biras Creek
Caribbean Sea
Prickly Pear Island
North Sound
Robin Bay
Joe Bay
Gun Creek
Leverick Bay
South Sound
South Sound Bluff
Little Bay
Blunder Bay
Mosquito Island
Gorda Peak
VIRGIN GORDA PEAK NATIONAL PARK
No Sound Rd
Mountain Point
Long Bay
Nail Bay Point
Plum Tree Bay
Mahoe Bay
Pond Bay
Savannah Bay
Handsome Bay
Little Dix Bay
St Thomas Bay
Virgin Gorda Yacht Harbour
Virgin Gorda Airport
Copper Mine Bay
Copper Mine Point
Copper Mine
Crook's Bay
Sir Francis Drake Channel
The Valley (Spanish Town)
Devil's Bay National Park
Trunk Bay
Spring Bay
The Baths
← To Tortola

N

3/4 mi
0.75 km

Legend:
- Biras Creek Estate **1**
- Bitter End Yacht Club **2**
- Fischer's Cove Beach Hotel **6**
- Guavaberry Spring Bay Vacation Homes **7**
- Little Dix Bay Hotel **5**
- Mango Bay Resort **4**
- Nail Bay Resort **3**

ACCOMMODATIONS
VERY EXPENSIVE

Biras Creek Resort ✺✺✺　Stay at this sophisticated and relaxing hideaway if you want to retreat from the world. This private, romantic resort is the classiest place on the island—Bitter End is more family-oriented, and Little Dix Bay more conventional. It stands at the northern end of Virgin Gorda like a hilltop fortress, opening onto the ocean. On a 60-hectare (140-acre) estate with its own marina, it occupies a narrow neck of land flanked by the sea on three sides. In fall 2006, the resort changed owners and underwent a name change and a new focus on making it more eco-friendly. From the Donghia furniture in the restaurant to an upgraded fitness center and the addition of new sports equipment such as Boston Whalers, the resort has been considerably improved. All the attractive, tropically decorated units have well-furnished bedrooms and private patios. Some have king-size beds, plus spacious bathrooms with inviting garden showers. There are no TVs in the rooms, but you get such luxuries as oceanview verandas. You get your own bikes while you're there, plus you have lots of hiking trails near the property to explore.

The food has won high praise; the wine list is also excellent. The hotel restaurant and open-air bar are quietly elegant, and there's always a table with a view. A barbecued lunch is often served on the beach.

North Sound (P.O. Box 54), Virgin Gorda, B.V.I. ✆ **800/223-1108** or 310/440-4225 in the U.S. Fax 310/440-4220. www.biras.com. 33 units. Winter $980–$1,500 double, $1,950 suite for 4; off season $675–$1,200 double, $1,550 suite for 4. Rates include all meals (no drinks). Ask about packages. AE, MC, V. Take the private motor launch from the Beef Island airport, $160 per person round-trip. No children under age 8. **Amenities:** Restaurant; bar; outdoor pool; 2 lit tennis courts; fitness center; Hobie Cats; kayaks; snorkeling; Sunfish sailboats; bikes; free beach trips; taxi service to launch; massage; babysitting; laundry service; dry cleaning; nonsmoking rooms. *In room:* A/C, ceiling fan, dataport, fridge, beverage maker, hair dryer, iron, safe.

Bitter End Yacht Club ✺✺✺　This is the liveliest of the B.V.I. resorts and even better equipped than the more exclusive Biras Creek. It's the best sailing and diving complex in the British chain. It opens onto one of the most unspoiled and secluded deep-water harbors in the Caribbean. Guests have unlimited use of the resort's million-dollar fleet and a complimentary introductory course at the Nick Trotter Sailing and Windsurfing School. The Bitter End offers an informal yet elegant experience in either a hillside chalet or a well-appointed beachfront overlooking the sound. Most units have varnished hardwood floors, sliding-glass doors, and wicker furnishings. All villas have two twins, two queen-size, or a king-size bed, plus a large dressing area and a shower with sea views.

For something novel, you can stay aboard one of the 9m (30-ft.) yachts, yours to sail, with dockage and daily maid service, meals in the Yacht Club dining room, and overnight provisions. Each yacht has a shower and can accommodate four comfortably.

First-rate meals are available in the Clubhouse Steak and Seafood Grille, the English Carvery, or the Pub, which also provides entertainment by a steel drum or reggae band.

John O Point, North Sound (P.O. Box 46), Virgin Gorda, B.V.I. ✆ **800/872-2392** in the U.S. for reservations, or 284/494-2746. Fax 284/494-4756. www.beyc.com. 85 units, 5 yachts. Winter (double occupancy) $830–$850 beachfront villa, suite, yacht, or hillside villa; off season (double occupancy) $590–$650 all units. Rates include all meals. AE, MC, V. Take the private ferry from the Beef Island airport, $30 per person one-way. **Amenities:** 3 restaurants; pub; outdoor pool; fitness center; boat trips to nearby cays; Boston whalers; scuba diving; snorkeling; sport-fishing; Sunfish sailing; windsurfing; babysitting; laundry service; dry cleaning. *In room:* A/C (in some), ceiling fan (in some), TV (available upon request), fridge, beverage maker.

Little Dix Bay Hotel ✦✦   Full of low-key luxury, along a curving white-sand beach, Little Dix Bay Hotel is a resort discreetly scattered along a .8km (½-mile) crescent-shaped private bay on a 200-hectare (490-acre) preserve. Many guests find this resort too pricey and stuffy; we ourselves prefer the more casual elegance of Biras Creek and the Bitter End Yacht Club, though Little Dix Bay does have an undeniably lovely setting, fine service, and a quiet elegance.

All rooms, built in the woods, have private terraces with views of the sea or gardens. Units come with ceiling fans and air-conditioning, and louvers and screens let in sea breezes. Some units are two-story rondavels (like Tiki huts) raised on stilts to form their own breezeways. Accommodations are roomy, airy, and decorated with tropical flair, each with a smart private bathroom with shower stall. Furnishings and fabrics evoke a Southeast Asian style with beautiful wicker or reed furniture, bamboo beds, Balinese boxes and baskets, and ceramic objets d'art.

1km (⅔ mile) north of Spanish Town (P.O. Box 70), Virgin Gorda, B.V.I. © **888/767-3966** in the U.S., or 284/495-5555. Fax 284/495-5661. www.littledixbay.com. 100 units. Winter $675–$895 double, from $2,000 suite; off season $395–$625 double, from $1,025 suite. MAP (breakfast and dinner) $90 per person extra. Extra person $75. AE, DISC, MC, V. Take the private ferry from the Beef Island airport, $90 per person round-trip. **Amenities:** 3 restaurants; 2 bars; 7 tennis courts; fitness center; sauna; deep-sea fishing; kayaks; scuba diving; snorkeling; Sunfish sailboats; water-skiing; children's programs; island tours; jeep rental; limited room service; massage; babysitting; laundry service. In room: A/C, ceiling fan, fridge, iron/ironing board, safe, robes.

EXPENSIVE

Guavaberry Spring Bay Vacation Homes ✦   Staying in one of these hexagonal, white-roofed redwood houses built on stilts is like living in a tree house. Screened and louvered walls let in sea breezes and The Baths, with its excellent sandy beach, is nearby. Each unique home, available for daily or weekly rental, has one or two bedrooms; all have private bathrooms with showers, full kitchens, and dining areas. And each has an elevated sun deck overlooking Sir Francis Drake Passage. The cottage colony is close to both the beach at Spring Bay and the Yacht Harbour Shopping Centre.

Spring Bay (P.O. Box 20), Virgin Gorda, B.V.I. © **284/495-5227.** Fax 284/495-5283. www.guavaberryspringbay.com. 18 units. Winter $215 1-bedroom house, $280 2-bedroom house; off season $140 1-bedroom house, $190 2-bedroom house. Extra person $17–$22. No credit cards. **Amenities:** Boats; fishing; sailing; scuba diving; snorkeling; jeep rental; commissary; babysitting. In room: Ceiling fan, kitchen, fridge, beverage maker, no phone.

Nail Bay Resort ✦   Near Gorda Peak National Park, and a short walk from a trio of usually deserted beaches, this resort enjoys an idyllic position. From its 60-hectare (150-acre) site, you can take in some of the best sunset views of Sir Francis Drake Channel and the Dog Islands. All the well-furnished units, each of which has a bathroom containing a shower stall, are comfortable and tasteful. Accommodations are wide ranging, including deluxe bedrooms, suites, apartments, and villas. This villa community has a core of a dozen units in two structures on a hillside, with sitting areas amid old sugar-mill ruins. The most modest units are hotel-style bedrooms in the main building. The best accommodations are the four estate villas—Sunset Watch, Mystic Water, Island Spice, and Island Dream.

At night, Nail Bay's landscaping is highlighted by illuminated stone walkways. One devotee told us that when she found the resort, it had the "exclusivity of Mustique, without that island's elitism."

Nail Bay (P.O. Box 69), Virgin Gorda, B.V.I. © **800/871-3551** in the U.S., 800/487-1839 in Canada, or 284/494-8000. Fax 284/495-5875. www.nailbay.com. 45 units. Winter $200–$250 double; off season $155–$180 double. AE, DISC, MC, V. **Amenities:** Restaurant; swim-up bar; outdoor pool; lit tennis court; Jacuzzi; kayaks; snorkeling; babysitting; laundry service; dry cleaning; nonsmoking rooms. In room: A/C, TV, dataport, kitchen, beverage maker, hair dryer, iron/ironing board, safe.

MODERATE

Fischer's Cove Beach Hotel   Swim from your doorstep in this group of units nestled near the sandy beach of St. Thomas Bay. Erected of native stone, each of the eight cottages is self-contained, with one or two bedrooms and a combination living/dining room with a kitchenette, plus a small bathroom with shower stall. You can stock up on provisions at a food store near the grounds. There are also 12 pleasant but simple rooms with views of Drake Channel. Each has its own private shower-only bathroom and private balcony.

The Valley (P.O. Box 60), Virgin Gorda, B.V.I. ℂ 284/495-5252. Fax 284/495-5820. www.fischerscove.com. 20 units. Winter $160–$165 double, $190–$315 studio cottage; off season $100 double, $125–$205 studio cottage. MAP (breakfast and dinner) $40 per person extra. AE, MC, V. **Amenities:** Restaurant; bar; watersports; bike rental; children's playground; jeep rental; babysitting; nonsmoking rooms. *In room:* A/C (in some), ceiling fans (in some), TV, dataport (in some), kitchenettes (in cottages), fridge, beverage maker, no phone (in cottages).

Mango Bay Resort ℛ *Value*   This well-designed compound of eight white-sided villas is set on lushly landscaped grounds overlooking the scattered islets of Drake's Channel on the island's western shore. It's a good value for your money. The accommodations are the most adaptable on the island—doors can be locked or unlocked to divide each villa into as many as four independent units. Costs vary with the proximity of your unit to the nearby beach. Interiors are stylish yet simple, often dominated by the same turquoise as that of the seascape in front of you. All of the units have an outside shower, and all have a bathroom with tub and shower. (The two-bedroom villas have two bathrooms with tub and shower.) Daily maid service is included. You can cook in, or dine on-site at Giorgio's Table (see "Dining," below), which is quite good and serves three meals a day.

Mahoe Bay (P.O. Box 1062), Virgin Gorda, B.V.I. ℂ 800/223-6510 in the U.S., 800/424-5500 in Canada, or 284/495-5672. Fax 284/495-5674. www.mangobayresort.com. 26 units. Winter $275 studio, $245–$490 1-bedroom unit, $350–$830 2-bedroom unit, $490 beachfront suite, $680 2-bedroom beachfront villa; off season $197 studio, $170–$315 1-bedroom unit, $240–$510 2-bedroom unit, $370 beachfront suite, $510 2-bedroom beachfront villa. MC, V. **Amenities:** Restaurant; bar; kayaks; sailing; snorkeling. *In room:* A/C, kitchen.

DINING

EXPENSIVE

Biras Creek Resort ℛℛ INTERNATIONAL   With even better cuisine than that of Little Dix Bay Pavilion (see below), this hilltop restaurant is our longtime island favorite, and for good reason. The resort hires the island's finest chefs, who turn out superb cuisine based on quality ingredients. The menu changes every night, but the panoramic view of North Sound doesn't. A recent sampling of the appetizers turned up such delights as five-spice duck salad for starters, followed by such well-prepared main courses as pan-seared salmon wrapped in Parma ham in a lentil-cream sauce or grilled grouper with an herby couscous. The chef's special grilled lobster is featured Sunday and Wednesday nights. Desserts are likely to range from a chilled green apple parfait to a choice of sorbets served with a chilled cantaloupe soup.

In Biras Creek, North Sound. ℂ 284/494-3555. Reservations required. Fixed-price dinner $85. AE, MC, V. Seatings daily 7–8:45pm.

Chez Bamboo ℛ *Finds* CAJUN/CREOLE   The closest approximation to a New Orleans supper club you're likely to find in Virgin Gorda is here, in a building with a big veranda and a location that's within a 5-minute walk north of the yacht club. Inside, are bamboo artifacts and a wraparound mural showing a jazz band playing within a forest of bamboo. Owner Rose Giacinto and Chef Joyce Rodriguez concoct superb versions of conch gumbo, Nassau grouper *en papillote,* and a New Orleans–style strip steak that's covered with creamy Worcestershire sauce. Desserts such as apple *crostini* and crème brûlée are among the very best of their ilk on the island. Live music, usually blues or jazz, is presented every Friday night on the terrace.

Next to the Virgin Gorda Yacht Harbour, Spanish Town. ℂ **284/495-5752.** Reservations recommended. Main courses $25–$45. AE, MC, V. Daily 5:30–10pm.

Little Dix Bay Pavilion ★ INTERNATIONAL   The most romantic of the dining spots on Virgin Gorda, this pavilion is our preferred choice at this deluxe resort, which also operates Sugar Mill Restaurant. At the Pavilion the guests (most middle-aged and well heeled) sit under a large thatched roof with the doors open to the trade winds. The chefs change the menu daily. Although many of the ingredients are shipped in frozen, especially meats and some seafood, there is much that is fresh and good. The most expensive items on the menu are the rack of lamb and grilled salmon. Many vegetables evoke the Pacific Rim, and the seafood keeps us returning again and again.

In the Little Dix Bay Hotel, 1km (⅔ mile) north of Spanish Town. ℂ **284/495-5555.** Reservations required. Main courses $36–$42. AE, MC, V. Daily 8–10:30am, noon–2:30pm, and 6–9:30pm.

MODERATE
The Flying Iguana   MEDITERRANEAN/FRENCH/WEST INDIAN   The owner of this place, Puck (aka Orlington Baptiste), studied his craft in Kansas City with the Hilton Group, before setting up this amiable restaurant overlooking the airport's landing strip and the sea. Potted hibiscus and many stuffed and carved iguanas ornament a room that's a celebration of West Indian mystique. The house drink is the Iguana Sunset, a concoction whose secret ingredients change according to the whim of the bartender. Whatever the recipe, it usually produces a lightheaded effect that goes well with the carefully conceived cuisine. The finest examples include fresh fish and all kinds of shellfish, including calamari, shrimp, scallops, and conch, often served in combination. Steak, chicken, and lamb, are seasoned in a way that evokes both the Caribbean and the Mediterranean. Happy hour is from 4 to 6pm daily.

The Valley, at the airport. ℂ **284/495-5277.** www.flyingiguanabvi.com. Reservations recommended. Main courses $6.50–$15 breakfast, $8.50–$20 lunch, $12–$36 dinner. MC, V. Daily 6:30am–9pm (last order).

Giorgio's Table ★ *Finds* ITALIAN   This is the only authentic Italian restaurant on the island. The chefs are flown in for the season from Venice, Milan, and Florence. A 15-minute drive north of Spanish Town, the restaurant opens onto a big covered terrace, although its varnished interior evokes a yacht. We like to sit out here at night, "star-struck," gazing up at the heavens with the sounds of the surf nearby. The chef says he cooks Italian instead of "American Italian," and the food is good, despite its reliance on a lot of imported ingredients. Fresh locally caught fish is generally the best bet, although you can order an array of succulent pastas and standard Italian staples like veal scaloppine. Pizzas and sandwiches will fill you at lunch. Looking at this place, we decided its owner, Giorgio, has an appropriate last name—Paradisio.

Mahoe Bay. ℂ **284/495-5684.** Reservations recommended. Main courses $17–$38 lunch, $17–$42 dinner. AE, MC, V. Daily 12:30–2:30pm and 6–9pm.

Rock Café CARIBBEAN/ITALIAN   Although the name suggests otherwise, this is not some island clone of the ubiquitous Hard Rock Cafe. You can stop for a drink in the special tequila bar upstairs before heading for a table later. The setting is amidst boulders like the ones at The Baths, the number-one sightseeing attraction on Virgin

Gorda. The recessed lighting and boardwalks add to the theatrical allure at night. Fortunately, the chefs don't depend just on the setting. The menu is wisely balanced, the dishes well prepared and consumed with affordable wine from a respectable list whose vintages range from Italy to California. Freshly caught red snapper comes in a tangy marinade, and we're especially fond of the chicken piccata. Live entertainment, usually a local band, is featured on Friday night.

The Valley. © **284/495-5482.** Reservations recommended. Main courses $19–$44. AE, MC, V. Daily 4pm–1am.

INEXPENSIVE

The Bath & Turtle INTERNATIONAL   At the end of the waterfront shopping plaza in Spanish Town sits the most popular pub on Virgin Gorda; it's packed with locals during the 4:30 to 6:30pm happy hour. Even if you don't care about food, you can join the regulars over midmorning mango coladas or peach daiquiris. There's live music every Wednesday and Friday night. From its handful of indoor and courtyard tables, you can order fried fish fingers, tamarind-ginger wings, very spicy chili, pizzas, fresh pasta, barbecue chicken, steak, lobster, and daily seafood specials such as conch fritters from the simple menu here.

Virgin Gorda Yacht Harbour, Spanish Town. © **284/495-5239.** Reservations required. Breakfast $5–$10; main courses $17–$23 lunch, $17–$35 dinner. AE, MC, V. Daily 7am–11pm.

The Restaurant at Leverick Bay *Kids* CONTINENTAL   A combined restaurant and beach bar, this is today's version of the old Pusser's, which now operates only a store here. During the day, you can enjoy all sorts of light meals, including croissant sandwiches, burgers, fried snapper, and pizza. There's also a children's menu. At night, the menu is more ambitious, featuring such intriguing appetizers as roasted pumpkin soup made with island-grown pumpkins and a splash of truffle oil. The chicken satay served with a spicy peanut dipping sauce is also enticing. The chef's main dish specialty is a tender and slow-roasted prime rib of beef with mashed potatoes and fresh vegetables. The fresh ahi tuna with a tangy wasabi and sweet soy sauce is full of aromatic flavor. If it's featured, you might also opt for the grilled wahoo, caught in local waters, marinated in lime, and served with West Indian rice and fresh vegetables.

Leverick Bay, North Sound. © **284/495-7154.** www.therestaurantatleverickbay.com. Reservations recommended. Main courses $28–$45; lunch $9–$19; pizzas from $10. MC, V. Daily 8am–10pm.

Top of The Baths CARIBBEAN   This aptly named green-and-white restaurant has a patio with a swimming pool. Locals gather here to enjoy the food they grew up on. At lunch, you can order an array of appetizers, sandwiches, and salad plates. You're invited to swim in the pool either before or after dining. At night, the kitchen turns out good home-style cookery, including fresh fish, lobster, chicken, and steaks. Look for one of the daily specials. And save room for a piece of that rum cake! Live steel bands perform on Sunday.

The Valley. © **284/495-5497.** Dinner $15–$28; sandwiches and salads $11–$18. AE, MC, V. Daily 8:30am–10pm.

EXPLORING THE ISLAND

The northern side of Virgin Gorda is mountainous, with Gorda Peak at 411m (1,348 ft.), the highest spot on the island. However, the southern half of the island is flat, with large boulders at every turn.

The best way to see the island if you're over for a day trip is to call **Andy Flax** at the Fischers Cove Beach Hotel. He runs the **Virgin Gorda Tours Association**

(© 284/495-5252), which will give you a tour for $45 per person. You can get picked up at the ferry dock if you give 24-hours notice.

HITTING THE BEACH   The best beaches are at **The Baths** ✪✪, where giant boulders form a series of tranquil pools and grottoes flooded with seawater. (Nearby snorkeling is excellent, and you can rent gear on the beach.) Scientists think volcanic activity brought these boulders to the surface eons ago.

Devil's Bay National Park can be reached by a trail from The Baths. The walk to the secluded coral-sand beach takes about 15 minutes through boulders and dry coastal vegetation.

The Baths and surrounding areas are part of a proposed system of parks and protected areas in the B.V.I. The protected area encompasses 273 hectares (674 acres) of land and includes sites at Little Fort, Spring Bay, The Baths, and Devil's Bay on the east coast.

Neighboring The Baths is **Spring Bay,** one of the best of the island's beaches, with white sand, clear water, and good snorkeling. **Trunk Bay** is a wide sandy beach reachable by boat or along a rough path from Spring Bay.

Savannah Bay is a sandy beach north of the yacht harbor, and **Mahoe Bay,** at the Mango Bay Resort, has a gently curving beach with neon-blue water.

DIVING   **Kilbrides Sunchaser Scuba** is located at the Bitter End Yacht Club North Sound (© **800/932-4286** in the U.S., or 284/495-9638). Kilbrides offers the best diving in the British Virgin Islands, at 15 to 20 dive sites, including the wreck of the ill-fated HMS *Rhone*. Prices range from $95 to $105 for a two-tank dive on one of the coral reefs. A one-tank dive in the afternoon costs $70. Equipment, except wet suits, is supplied at no charge. Hours are 7:45am to 5:30pm daily.

HIKING   Consider a trek up the stairs and hiking paths that crisscross Virgin Gorda's largest stretch of undeveloped land, **Virgin Gorda Peak National Park.** To reach the best departure point for your uphill trek, drive north of The Valley on the only road leading to North Sound for about 15 very hilly minutes. (Using a 4WD vehicle is a good idea.) Stop at the base of the stairway leading steeply uphill. There's a sign pointing to Virgin Gorda Peak National Park.

Depending on your climbing speed, it takes between 25 and 40 minutes to reach the summit of Gorda Peak, the highest point on the island. You'll be rewarded with sweeping views of the many scattered islets of the Virgin archipelago. There's a tower at the summit, which you can climb for enhanced views. Admire the flora and the fauna (birds, lizards, nonpoisonous snakes) that you're likely to run across en route. Be sure to bring sunscreen, and consider taking a picnic, as tables are scattered along the hiking trails.

VIRGIN GORDA AFTER DARK

There isn't a lot of action at night, unless you want to make some of your own. **The Bath & Turtle** pub, at Yacht Harbour (© **284/495-5239**), brings in local bands for dancing in the summer on Wednesday and Friday at 8:30pm. The **Bitter End Yacht Club** (© **284/494-2745**) has live music on Fridays. Reached only by boat, this is the best bar on the island. With its dark wood, it evokes an English pub and even serves British brews. Call to see what's happening at the time of your visit.

Andy's Chateau de Pirate, at the Fischer's Cove Beach Hotel, The Valley (© **284/495-5252**), is a sprawling, sparsely furnished local hangout. It has a simple stage, a very long bar, and huge oceanfront windows that almost never close.

4 Jost Van Dyke

About 150 people live on the 10 sq. km (4 sq. miles) of this mountainous island, off the west side of Tortola. On the south shore, **White Bay** and **Great Harbour** are good beaches. Although there are only a handful of places to stay, there are several dining choices, as the island is a popular stop for the yachting set and many cruise ships, including Cunard (and often some all-gay cruises). The peace and tranquility often disappear unless you're here when the cruise ships aren't.

In the 1700s, a Quaker colony settled here to develop sugar-cane plantations. One of the colonists, William Thornton, won the worldwide competition to design the U.S. Capitol in Washington, D.C. Smaller islands surround the place, including Little Jost Van Dyke, the birthplace of Dr. John Lettsome, founder of the London Medical Society.

ESSENTIALS

GETTING THERE   Take the ferry to White Bay on Jost Van Dyke from either St. Thomas or Tortola. (*Be warned:* Departure times can vary widely throughout the year, and often don't adhere very closely to the printed timetables.) Ferries from St. Thomas depart from Red Hook 3 days a week (Fri, Sat, and Sun), usually twice daily. More convenient (and more frequent) are the daily ferryboat shuttles from Tortola's isolated West End. The latter departs five times a day for the 25-minute trip, and costs $20 for adults round-trip, $10 for children 12 and under round-trip. Call the **Paradise New Horizons Ferry Service** (© 284/495-9278; www.jostvandykeferry.com) for information about departures from any of the above-mentioned points. If all else fails, carefully negotiate a transportation fee with one of the handful of privately operated water taxis.

EMERGENCIES   In the unlikely event that you need the police, call © 284/495-9345.

ACCOMMODATIONS

Sandcastle Hotel   A retreat for escapists who want few neighbors and absolutely nothing to do, these six cottages are surrounded by flowering shrubbery and bougainvillea, have panoramic views, and open onto a white-sand beach. Bedrooms are spacious, light, and airy, furnished in a tropical motif, with tile floors, local art, rattan furnishings, day beds, and king-size beds. Some units have enclosed showers, outside off the bathroom. At beachside bar, the Soggy Dollar, you mix your own drinks and keep your own tab. Visiting boaters often drop in to enjoy the beachside informality and order a drink called The Painkiller. A line in the guest book sums it up: "I thought places like this only existed in the movies."

White Bay, Jost Van Dyke, B.V.I. © 284/495-9888. Fax 284/495-9999. www.sandcastle-bvi.com. 6 units. Winter $245–$295 double; off season $160–$220 double. Extra person $35–$45. 3-night minimum. Children under 16 not permitted. MC, V. **Amenities:** Restaurant; bar; diving; fishing trips; sailing. *In room:* A/C (in 2 rooms), ceiling fan, no phone.

Sandy Ground   These self-sufficient apartments are along the edge of a beach on a 7-hectare (17-acre) hill site on the eastern part of Jost Van Dyke. The complex rents two- and three-bedroom villas. One of our favorites was built on a cliff that seems to hang about 25m (80 ft.) over the beach. The airy villas, each privately owned, are fully equipped with refrigerators and stoves. The interiors vary widely, from rather fashionable to bare bones. The living space is generous, and extras include private balconies or terraces. Most rooms have showers only.

The managers help guests with boat rentals and watersports. Diving, day sails, and other activities can also be arranged, and there are dinghies available. Snorkeling and hiking are among the more popular activities.

P.O. Box 594, West End, Tortola, B.V.I. ℂ 284/494-3391. Fax 284/495-9379. www.sandyground.com. 7 units. Weekly rates: winter $1,950 villa for 2; off season $1,400 villa for 2. Extra person $300 per week in winter, $200 off season. MC, V. Take a private water taxi from Tortola or St. Thomas. **Amenities:** Day sails; dinghies; diving; snorkeling. *In room:* Ceiling fan, fridge, beverage maker, no phone.

DINING

Abe's by the Sea WEST INDIAN   In this local bar and restaurant, sailors are satisfied with a menu of fish, lobster, conch, ribs, and chicken. Prices are low, too, and it's money well spent. With each main course you also get peas, rice, and coleslaw.

Little Harbour. ℂ 284/495-9329. Reservations required for groups of 5 or more. Dinner $20–$45; nightly barbecue $24. MC, V. Daily 7am–10pm.

Foxy's Tamarind Bar ✰✰ WEST INDIAN   Arguably the most famous bar in the B.V.I., this mecca of yachties and other boat people is built entirely around sixth-generation Jost Van Dyke native, Philicianno "Foxy" Callwood. He opened the place in the late 1960s, and guests have been coming back ever since. A songwriter and entertainer, Foxy is part of the draw. He creates impromptu calypso—almost in the Jamaican tradition—around his guests. If you're singled out, he'll embarrass you, but it's all in good fun. He also plays the guitar and takes a profound interest in preserving the environment of his native island.

Thursday through Saturday nights, a live band entertains. On other evenings, it's rock 'n' roll, reggae, or soca. The food and drink aren't neglected, either—try Foxy's Painkiller Punch. During the day, flying-fish sandwiches, *rotis* (Caribbean burritos), and the usual burgers are served, but evenings might bring freshly caught lobster, spicy steamed shrimp, or even grilled fish, depending on the catch of the day.

Great Harbour. ℂ 284/495-9258. www.foxysbar.com. Reservations recommended. Lunch $10–$15; dinner $18–$40. AE, MC, V. Daily 9:30am "until."

Sandcastle INTERNATIONAL/CARIBBEAN   This hotel restaurant often serves food that has been frozen, but, even so, the flavors remain consistently good. Lunch is served in the open-air dining room, while lighter fare and snacks are available at the Soggy Dollar Bar. Dinner is by candlelight, featuring four courses, including such dishes as mahimahi Martinique (marinated in orange-lemon-lime juice and cooked with fennel, onions, and dill). Sandcastle hen is another specialty likely to appear on the menu: It's a grilled Cornish hen that's been marinated in rum, honey, lime, and garlic. But we'd skip all that for the sesame snapper, if available. Meals are served with seasonal vegetables and fresh pasta, along with a variety of salads and homemade desserts. Those desserts are luscious, and include Key lime pie, Irish whiskey cheesecake, and mango mousse.

At the Sandcastle Hotel, White Bay. ℂ 284/495-9888. Reservations required for dinner by 4pm. Lunch main courses $6–$12; fixed-price dinner $40–$45. MC, V. Daily 9am–3pm and 1 seating at 7pm.

5 Anegada

The most northerly and isolated of the British Virgins, 48km (30 miles) east of Tortola, Anegada has a population of about 250, none of whom has found the legendary treasure from the more than 500 wrecks lying off its notorious Horseshoe Reef. It's different from the other British Virgins in that it's a coral-and-limestone atoll, flat, with a 750m (2,500-ft.) airstrip. Its highest point reaches 8m (26 ft.), and it hardly appears on the horizon if you're sailing to it.

At the northern and western ends of the island are some good white-sand beaches, which might be your only reason for coming here. This is a remote little corner of the Caribbean: Don't expect a single frill, and be prepared to put up with some hardships, such as mosquitoes. Most of the island has been declared off-limits to settlement and reserved for birds and other wildlife. The B.V.I. National Parks Trust has established a flamingo colony in a bird sanctuary, which is also the protected home of several different varieties of heron as well as ospreys and terns. It has also designated much of the interior of the island as a preserved habitat for Anegada's animal population of some 2,000 wild goats, donkeys, and cattle. Among the endangered species being given a new lease on life here is the rock iguana, a fierce-looking but quite harmless reptile that can grow to a length of 2m (6½ ft.). Although rarely seen, these creatures have called Anegada home for thousands of years.

ESSENTIALS

GETTING THERE Fly BVI (© 284/495-1747; www.fly-bvi.com) operates a charter/sightseeing service between Anegada and Beef Island off Tortola. The one-way cost is $125 for two to three passengers.

GETTING AROUND Limited taxi service is available on the island—not that you'll have many places to go. **Tony's Taxis,** which you'll easily spot when you arrive, will take you around the island. It's also possible to rent **bicycles;** ask around.

ACCOMMODATIONS

The Anegada Reef Hotel is the only major accommodations on the island. Neptune's Treasure (see "Dining," below) rents tents and basic rooms.

Anegada Reef Hotel ⓡ The only major hotel on the island is 5km (3 miles) west of the airport, right on the beachfront. It's one of the most remote places covered in this guide—guests who stay here are, in effect, hiding out. It's a favorite of the yachting set, who enjoy the hospitality. The hotel offers motel-like, very basic rooms with private porches, with either a garden or ocean view. Bathrooms are cramped with shower stalls. Come here for tranquility, not for pampering.

You can arrange to go inshore fishing, deep-sea fishing, or bonefishing (there's also a tackle shop); you can also set up snorkeling excursions and secure taxi service and jeep rentals.

There's a beach barbecue nightly; the house specialty is lobster, and many attendees arrive by boat. Reservations for the 7:30pm dinner must be made by 4pm. If you're visiting just for the day, you can use the hotel as a base. Call and they'll have a van meet you at the airport.

Setting Point, Anegada, B.V.I. © 284/495-8002. Fax 284/495-9362. www.anegadareef.com. 16 units. Winter $250–$375 double; off season $215–$325 double. Rates include all meals. MC, V. **Amenities:** Restaurant; bar; babysitting. *In room:* A/C, beverage maker, no phone.

DINING

Cow Wreck Beach Bar & Grill ⓡ *Finds* WEST INDIAN This laid-back, family-run, and definitely funky joint is a coveted address among yachties anchoring at Anegada. Ice-cold beer and the best lobster in the B.V.I. keep the patrons coming back. The crustaceans are kept in a cage under the water, waiting their "death summons" to the grill. Under a straw roof, diners sit at rough-hewn wooden tables placed outside on a terrace with a view of the water. If you go for lunch you can tie in a visit with a snorkel trip. At night this is the most popular place on the island for a sundowner. Other standard dishes appear on the menu, but we've never known a guest to order anything but lobster for a main course.

Lower Cow Wreck Beach. Ⓒ 284/495-8047. Reservations required for dinner. Main courses $18–$46. MC, V. Daily 7am–midnight, dinner seatings 6pm. Closing time for bar "when the last customer departs."

Neptune's Treasure *(Finds* INTERNATIONAL   Set near its own 24-slip marina, near the southern tip of the island in the same cluster of buildings that includes the more high-priced Anegada Reef Hotel, this funky bar and restaurant usually hosts a mix of yacht owners and local residents. Dining is in a spacious indoor area whose focal point is a bar and lots of nautical memorabilia. The drink of choice is a Dark and Stormy, composed of ginger beer and rum. The Soares family and their staff serve platters of swordfish, lobster, fish fingers, chicken, steaks, and ribs; dispense information about local snorkeling sites; and generally maintain order and something approaching a (low-key) party atmosphere.

They also offer nine simple bedrooms with air-conditioning. Depending on the season, rooms with a private bathroom rent for $70 to $110 double. Discounts are offered for stays of a week or more.

Between Pomato and Saltheap points, Anegada, B.V.I. Ⓒ 284/495-9439, or shortwave channel 16. Fax 284/495-8060. www.neptunetreasure.com. Reservations for dinner must be made by 4pm. Breakfast $8; lunch main courses $6–$24; dinner $18–$45. MC, V. Daily 8am–10pm.

6 Peter Island Ⓕ

Half of this island, which has a good marina and docking facilities, is devoted to the yacht club. The other part is deserted. Beach facilities are found at palm-fringed Deadman's Bay, which faces the Atlantic but is protected by a reef. All goods and services are at the one resort (see below). The island is so private that except for an occasional mason at work, about the only company you'll encounter will be an iguana or a feral cat whose ancestors were abandoned generations ago by shippers. (The cats are said to have virtually eliminated the island's rodent population.)

A complimentary, hotel-operated ferry, **Peter Island Ferry** (Ⓒ **284/495-2000**), departs Tortola from the pier at Trellis Bay, near the airport. Other boats depart six or seven times a day from Baugher's Bay in Road Town. Passengers must notify the hotel 2 weeks before their arrival so transportation can be arranged.

ACCOMMODATIONS

Peter Island Resort ⒻⒻⒻ   This 720-hectare (1,800-acre) tropical island is solely dedicated to Peter Island Resort guests and yacht owners who moor their crafts here. The island's tropical gardens and hillside are bordered by five gorgeous private beaches, including Deadman's Beach (in spite of its name, it's often voted one of the world's most romantic beaches in travel-magazine reader polls).

The resort contains 32 rooms facing Sprat Bay and Sir Francis Drake Channel (oceanview rooms), and 20 larger rooms on Deadman's Bay Beach (beachfront). Designed with a casual elegance, each has a balcony or terrace. The least desirable rooms are also the smallest and housed in two-story, A-frame structures next to the harbor. Bathrooms with tub/shower combinations range from standard motel-unit types to spectacular luxurious ones, depending on your room assignment. The Crow's

Nest, a luxurious four-bedroom villa, overlooks the harbor and Deadman's Bay and features a private swimming pool. The Hawk's Nest villas are three-bedroom villas set on a tropical hillside.

Peter Island (P.O. Box 211), Road Town, Tortola, B.V.I. © **800/346-4451** in the U.S., or 284/495-2000. Fax 284/495-2500. www.peterisland.com. 56 units. Winter $900–$1,070 double, $4,200 3-bedroom villa, $8,800 4-bedroom villa; off season $560–$660 double, $2,900–$3,360 3-bedroom villa, $5,900–$7,550 4-bedroom villa. Rates include all meals and transportation from the Tortola airport. AE, MC, V. **Amenities:** 2 restaurants; 2 bars; outdoor pool; 4 tennis courts; fitness center; gym; spa; deep-sea fishing; scuba diving; sea kayaks; snorkeling gear; Sunfish sailboats; water-skiing; windsurfing; bikes; limited room service; massage; babysitting; laundry service; dry cleaning; nonsmoking rooms. *In room:* A/C, minibar, hair dryer, iron, safe.

7 Guana Island ✶

This 340-hectare (840-acre) island, a nature preserve and wildlife sanctuary, is one of the most private hideaways in the Caribbean. Don't come here looking for action; rather, consider vacationing here if you want to retreat from the world. This small island right off the coast of Tortola offers seven virgin beaches and nature trails ideal for hiking; it abounds in unusual species of plant and animal life. Arawak relics have been found here. You can climb 242m (794-ft.) Sugarloaf Mountain for a panoramic view. It's said that the name of the island came from a jutting rock that resembled the head of an iguana.

The Guana Island Club will send a boat to meet arriving guests at the Beef Island airport (trip time is 10 min.).

ACCOMMODATIONS & DINING

Guana Island Club 🐾🐾   The sixth- or seventh-largest of the British Virgin Islands, Guana Island was bought in 1974 by Henry and Gloria Jarecki, dedicated conservationists who run this resort as a nature preserve and wildlife sanctuary. Upon your arrival on the island, a Land Rover will meet you and transport you up one of the most scenic hills in the region, in the northeast of Guana.

The cluster of white cottages was built as a private club in the 1930s on the foundations of a Quaker homestead. The stone cottages hold no more than 30 guests and have only two phones. Because the dwellings are staggered along a flower-dotted ridge overlooking the Caribbean and the Atlantic, the sense of privacy is almost absolute. Groups of up to 30 can rent the entire island. Although water is scarce, each of the airy accommodations has a shower. The decor is rattan and wicker, and each unit has a ceiling fan. Renting North Beach cottage, the most luxurious of the accommodations, is like renting a private home. The panoramic sweep from the terraces is spectacular, particularly at sunset. There are seven beaches, some of which require a boat to reach.

Guests will find a convivial atmosphere at the rattan-furnished clubhouse. Casually elegant dinners by candlelight are served on the veranda, with menus that include homegrown vegetables and Continental and U.S. specialties.

P.O. Box 32, Road Town, Tortola, B.V.I. © **800/544-8262** in the U.S. or 284/494-2354. Fax 284/442-2050. (For reservations, write or call the Guana Island Club Reservations Office, 10 Timber Trail, Rye, NY 10580; © **800/544-8262** in the U.S., or 914/967-6050; fax 914/967-8048.) www.guana.com. 15 units. Winter $775–$1,085 double, $1,450–$1,990 cottage; off season $695–$775 double, $1,390–$1,450 cottage. Rent the island for $18,500–$25,500 (per day!). Rates include all meals and drinks served with meals. MC, V. Closed Sept–Oct. Warning: Call ahead to see if children are being accepted. **Amenities:** Restaurant; self-service bar; 2 tennis courts; fishing; kayaks; sailboats; snorkeling; water-skiing; windsurfing; complimentary transport; massage; babysitting; laundry service; dry cleaning; nature trails. *In room:* Ceiling fan, wireless Internet, no phone.

9

The Cayman Islands

Although Grand Cayman is a major tourism destination, don't expect fast-paced excitement. Island life focuses on the sea. Snorkelers will find a paradise, beach lovers will relish the powdery sands of Seven Mile Beach, but party-hungry travelers in search of urban thrills might be disappointed. Come here to slow down and relax.

The Caymans, 773km (479 miles) due south of Miami, consist of three islands: **Grand Cayman, Cayman Brac,** and **Little Cayman.** Despite its name, Grand Cayman is only 35km (22 miles) long and 13km (8 miles) across at its widest point. The other islands are considerably smaller, of course, and contain very limited tourist facilities, in contrast to well-developed Grand Cayman. George Town on Grand Cayman is the capital and is therefore the hub of government, banking, and shopping.

English is the official language of the islands, although it's often spoken with an English slur mixed with an American southern drawl and a lilting Welsh accent.

1 Essentials

VISITOR INFORMATION

The **Cayman Islands Department of Tourism** (© 800/263-5805) has the following offices in the United States: Doral Centre, 8300 NW 53rd St., Suite 103, Miami, FL 33166 (© **305/599-9033;** fax 305/599-3766); One Lincoln Centre, 18 W. 140 Butterfield Rd., Suite 920, Oakbrook Terrace, IL 60181 (© **630/705-0650;** fax 630/705-1383); Two Memorial City Plaza, 820 Gessner, Suite 1335, Houston, TX 77024 (© **713/461-1317;** fax 713/461-7409); and 3 Park Ave., 39th Floor, New York, NY 10016 (© **212/889-9009;** fax 212/889-9125).

In Canada, contact Earl B. Smith, **Travel Marketing Consultants,** 234 Eglinton Ave. E., Suite 306, Toronto, ON M4P 1K5 (© **416/485-1550;** fax 416/485-7578).

In the United Kingdom, the contact is **Cayman Islands Department of Tourism,** 6 Arlington St., London SW1 1RE (© **020/7491-7771;** fax 020/7409-7773).

Two websites that describe the Cayman Islands include **www.caymanislands.ky** and **www.divecayman.ky.**

GETTING THERE

The Cayman Islands are easily accessible. Flying time from Miami is 1 hour, 10 minutes; from Houston, 2 hours, 45 minutes; from Tampa, 1 hour, 40 minutes; and from Atlanta, 3 hours, 35 minutes. Only a handful of nonstop flights are available from the U.S. Midwest, so most visitors use Miami as their gateway..

Cayman Airways (© **800/422-9626** in the U.S. and Canada, or 345/949-2311; www.caymanairways.com) has the most frequent service to Grand Cayman, with three daily flights from Miami, four flights a week from Tampa, and occasional nonstop flights from Houston. Depending on bookings and the season, they also fly

Fun Fact **Ahoy, Matey!**

Cayman Islands Pirates' Week is held during a 10-day period every year during early November. It's a national festival in which cutlass-bearing pirates and sassy wenches storm George Town, capture the governor, throng the streets, and stage a costume parade. The celebration, which is held throughout the Caymans, pays tribute to the nation's past and its cultural heritage. For the exact dates, contact the **Pirates Week Festival Office** (© **345/949-5859**; www. piratesweekfestival.com)

to Fort Lauderdale, Boston, Kingston (Jamaica), and Havana (Cuba). They're also the only airline with regularly scheduled service between Grand Cayman and the sister islands of Cayman Brac and Little Cayman.

Many visitors also fly to Grand Cayman on **American Airlines** (© **800/433-7300** in the U.S. and Canada; www.aa.com), which flies once a day from Miami. **Northwest Airlines** (© **800/447-4747** in the U.S. and Canada; www.nwa.com) flies, during winter only, several times a week from Detroit to Grand Cayman. **US Airways** (© **800/428-4322** in the U.S. and Canada; www.usairways.com) flies nonstop daily from Charlotte, N.C. **Delta** (© **800/221-1212** in the U.S. and Canada; www.delta.com) flies daily into Grand Cayman from its hub in Atlanta. **Continental Airlines** (© **800/231-0856** in the U.S. and Canada; www.continental.com) offers service between its Houston hub and Grand Cayman on Wednesday, Friday, Saturday, and Sunday. **Air Canada** (© **888/247-2262** in the U.S. and Canada; www.air-canada.ca) flies biweekly nonstop from Toronto on Sunday (in winter only) and Wednesday year-round, and **British Airways** (© **800/247-9297** in the U.S. and Canada, or 0870/850-9850 in the U.K.; www.britishairways.com) offers between three and four weekly flights, depending on the season, from London's Gatwick Airport with a stopover in Nassau.

FAST FACTS: The Cayman Islands

Business Hours Normally, banks are open Monday to Thursday from 9am to 4pm, and Friday 9am to 4:30pm. Shops are usually open Monday to Saturday from 9am to 5pm.

Currency The legal tender is the Cayman Islands dollar (**CI$**), currently valued at US$1.25 (CI80¢ equal US$1/60p). Canadian, U.S., and British currencies are accepted throughout the Cayman Islands, but you'll save money if you exchange your U.S. dollars for Cayman Islands dollars. The Cayman dollar breaks down into 100 cents. Coins come in 1¢, 5¢, 10¢, and 25¢ denominations. Bills come in denominations of CI$1, CI$5, CI$10, CI$25, CI$50, and CI$100 (there is no CI$20 bill). Most hotels quote rates in U.S. dollars. However, many restaurants quote prices in Cayman Islands dollars, which might lead you to think that food is much cheaper than it is. *Unless otherwise specified, prices in this chapter are quoted in U.S. dollars and British pounds.*

The cost of living in the Cayman Islands is about 20% higher than in the United States.

Documents Citizens of the United States should carry a valid passport, both for the purposes of entering the Cayman Islands, and also for ease in returning to the U.S. at the end of their trip. Citizens of the United Kingdom and Canada should have at least a certified birth certificate with a raised seal and a photo ID, although a passport is preferred. All visitors need a return or ongoing ticket.

Electricity It's 110-volt AC (60 cycles), so U.S. and Canadian appliances will not need adapters or transformers.

Emergencies For medical, police, or fire-related emergencies, dial © **911.**

Hospital There's a hospital on Grand Cayman and another small one on Cayman Brac. Seriously ill cases, or cases associated with a genuinely serious accident on Little Cayman are usually transported by plane or helicopter to Grand Cayman. On Grand Cayman, the **Cayman Islands Hospital** is at 1 Hospital Road (© **345/949-8600**); on Cayman Brac, the **Faith Hospital** is at Stake Bay (© **345/948-2243**); and on Little Cay, the **Little Cayman Clinic** (© **345/948-0072**) lies adjacent to the airport. You can summon emergency help on all three of the islands by dialing 911.

Language English is the official language of the islands.

Liquor Laws Beer, wine, and liquor are sold at most grocery and convenience stores Monday to Saturday (not on Sun). It is legal to have an open container on the beach.

Taxes A government tourist tax of 10% is added to your hotel bill. A departure tax of CI$20 (US$25/£12) is collected when you leave the Caymans, usually in the form of a fee that's automatically included in the price of your airplane ticket. There are no taxes on goods and services.

Telephone To call the Cayman Islands from the United States, dial **1**, then the **345** area code, and the local number. Once you're on the island, to charge a long-distance call to a calling card, here are some access numbers: **AT&T** at © **800/872-2881, Sprint** at © **888/366-4663,** and **MCI** at © **800/624-1000.** In lieu of any of these three carriers (some smaller hotels might not accept them), the access code for a local telephone carrier (Blue Skies) is **800/534-9718.**

Time U.S. Eastern Standard Time is in effect year-round; daylight saving time is not observed.

Tipping Virtually every restaurant in the Cayman Islands adds a 10% to 15% service charge in lieu of tipping, so check your bill carefully. Hotels also often add a 10% service charge to your bill. Taxi drivers expect a 10% to 15% tip.

Water According to most official statements, the water in the Cayman Islands is safe to drink directly from the tap, but we've found that many local residents opt, instead, for bottled water whenever possible, using tap water only for cooking and cleaning.

Weather The temperature in the Cayman Islands seldom goes lower than 70°F (21°C) or higher than 90°F (32°C). The daily average is between 77°F (25°C) and 84°F (29°C).

Women's Resources If you have questions, or want guidance, about anything related to women's issues (including abortions, rape, or domestic abuse), contact the Women's Resource Center, Elizabethan Square, George Town, Grand Cayman (© **345/949-0006**).

Ivan the Terrible

In September 2004, the eye of Hurricane Ivan passed directly over Grand Cayman, pounding the island for hours with devastating 320-kmph/200-mph winds. Although no deaths were reported, the island was massively damaged, with many hotels, restaurants, tourism facilities, and private homes sustaining major damage. Many buildings were reduced to splintered wood or left without roofs. Thousands of islanders were left homeless. Naturally, the tourism infrastructure took a direct hit, and most of the island was not directly operational throughout the course of 2005. Demands for workers were great all over the island in 2005 and part of 2006, as crews from Jamaica, the United States, and in some cases as far away as India arrived to rebuild Grand Cayman. The smaller islands of Cayman Brac and Little Cayman were less ravaged and businesses were up and running much more quickly. Some investors, disillusioned with island life even before the hurricane, used the disaster as the incentive they needed to pull up stakes and move back to the U.S., Canada, or the U.K., making room for other, newly committed entrepreneurs to manage things in their wake.

By January of 2007, however, most of the island's infrastructure was fully operational, much of it restored to conditions that are better and more up-to-date than they were before the hurricane. A good example is Grand Cayman's Turtle Farm, which used Hurricane Ivan as the incentive it needed to massively improve and expand its facilities.

2 Grand Cayman ★★

The largest of the three islands and a real diving mecca, Grand Cayman survives and flourishes thanks to a unique blend of tourism, financial services, low crime, conservatism, and political stability. Home to the branch offices of more than 500 banks and dozens of insurance companies, its capital, George Town, is the offshore banking center of the Caribbean. (No problems finding an ATM here!) Retirees are drawn to the peace and tranquility of this British Crown Colony, site of many large-scale real estate and condominium developments. The overwhelming majority of the Cayman Islands' population of 52,000 lives on Grand Cayman. The manners and presuppositions of the locals reflect their British heritage.

ESSENTIALS

GETTING THERE   See the information at the beginning of this chapter.

VISITOR INFORMATION   The **Department of Tourism** is temporarily housed in the Regatta Office Park, Leeward 2, West Bay Road, P.O. Box 67, Grand Cayman KY1-1102 (© **345/949-0623;** fax 345/949-4053). A move is expected soon, but at the time of writing, a new address wasn't yet known. Even after the move, government spokespersons define the organization's ongoing hours as Monday to Friday 8:30am to 5pm.

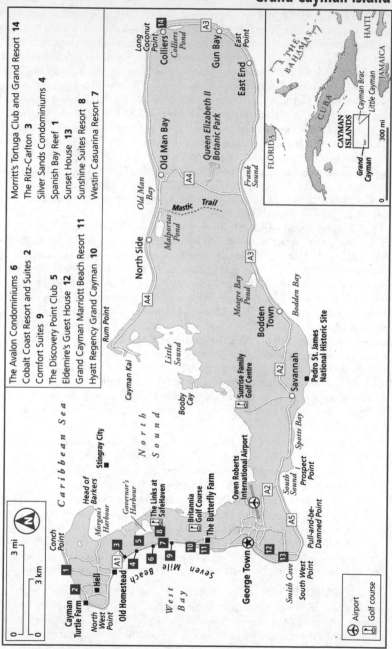

Grand Cayman Island

The Avalon Condominiums **6**
Cobalt Coast Resort and Suites **2**
Comfort Suites **9**
The Discovery Point Club **5**
Eldemire's Guest House **12**
Grand Cayman Marriott Beach Resort **11**
Hyatt Regency Grand Cayman **10**

Morritt's Tortuga Club and Grand Resort **14**
The Ritz-Carlton **3**
Silver Sands Condominiums **4**
Spanish Bay Reef **1**
Sunset House **13**
Sunshine Suites Resort **8**
Westin Casuarina Resort **7**

GETTING AROUND   All arriving flights are met by taxis. The fares are fixed by the director of civil aviation (© **345/949-7811**); typical one-way taxi fares from the airport to Seven Mile Beach for between 1 to 3 passengers and their luggage range from US$15 to US$20 (£7.80–£10). Cabs are legally required to carry a printed version of the official rates established by the Caymanian government, usually inside the cab drivers' notebooks.

Taxis (which can hold a maximum of five people) can also take visitors on around-the-island tours. **Cayman Cab Team** (© **345/926-8294**) offers 24-hour service. You can also call **A.A. Transportation** at © **345/949-7222.**

The island has limited **bus service,** with approximately 38 minibuses operated by 24 licensed operators, serving eight routes daily from 6am to midnight. The bus terminal lies adjacent to the public library on Edward Street in George Town. The one-way per person fare from George Town to points within George Town and along most of Seven Mile Beach is CI$2 (US$2.50/£1.20). Fares from George Town to far-distance points of Grand Cayman, say, to the most distant tip of the East End, can go as high as CI$3.50 (US$4.40/£2.10) each way.

If you can safely and responsibly drive on the left, consider renting a car. Several car-rental companies operate on the island, including **Avis,** through Avis Cisco (© **800/ 331-1212** in the U.S. and Canada, or 345/949-2468; www.aviscayman.com); **Budget** (© **800/527-0700** in the U.S. and Canada, or 345/949-5605; www.budgetcayman. com); **Hertz,** through a local franchise, Ace Rent-a-Car (© **800/654-3131** or 345/949-2280; www.hertzcaribbean.com); or **Andy's Rent-a-Car,** a well-respected local car rental company (© **345/949-8111;** www.andys.ky). Each will issue the mandatory Cayman Islands driving permit for an additional US$7.50 (£3.90). All four require that you make reservations between 6 and 36 hours before pickup. Government regulations demand that drivers be at least 21 years old to rent a car, and some require that drivers be at least 25. Each of the outfits maintain rental kiosks and inventories of available cars within walking distance of the airport, although most visitors find it easier to take a taxi to their hotels and then arrange for the cars to be brought to them.

Remember to drive on the left and to reserve your car as far in advance as possible, especially in midwinter.

FAST FACTS   The only full-service hospital is the **Cayman Islands Hospital** (also known as the George Town Hospital), 1 Hospital Road (© **345/949-8600**). The largest pharmacy is **Island Pharmacy,** West Shore Centre, Seven Mile Beach (© **345/949-8987**), open Monday to Saturday from 9am to 6pm.

In George Town, the main branch of the **post office** and Philatelic Bureau is located on Edward Street (© **345/949-2474**). It's open Monday to Friday from 8:30am to 5pm. There are branch offices on Cayman Brac and Little Cayman, and a total of at least nine additional branch post offices on Grand Cayman as well, including branches at the airport, along Seven Mile Beach, and in the barren-looking, rock-studded neighborhood known as "Hell," each maintaining the same hours as the main branch.

ACCOMMODATIONS

Nearly all the hotels are lined up along Seven Mile Beach. Hotels, unlike many Caymanian restaurants, generally quote prices in U.S. dollars. When choosing a hotel, keep in mind that the quoted rates do not include the 10% government tax or the hotel service tax, which varies between 6% and 10%, depending on the hotel.

Consider booking a package tour to make those expensive resorts more affordable. See the sections "Packages for the Independent Traveler" and "Tips on Accommodations" in chapter 2 before you book.

VERY EXPENSIVE

The Avalon Condominiums ★★

One of Grand Cayman's best condo complexes is The Avalon, which occupies prime real estate on a stretch of Seven Mile Beach that was actually widened by sand deposits left in the wake of Hurricane Ivan. Painted a distinctive shade of blue-violet (the staff refers to it as "orchid"), it consists of 27 oceanfront three-bedroom/three-bathroom units, 19 of which can be rented. Only a short distance from restaurants, about a 10-minute drive from George Town, it's well-maintained, extremely pleasant, and stylish. Children under 12 are allowed on-site, but overall, they're rather carefully "policed" for misbehavior and loud noises, a policy that contributes to a sense of calm and sedate well-being that the residents and investors work hard to maintain. The well-appointed, spacious units have an English colonial motif, durable, flowered or pastel-colored upholsteries, plus king-size or twin beds. Each condo has a fully equipped open-sided kitchen (upgraded in 2006), and a large, screened lanai that overlooks a stretch of the beach.

West Bay Rd. (P.O. Box 31236), Grand Cayman, B.W.I. © 345/945-4171. Fax 345/945-4189. www.cayman.org/avalon. 27 units. Winter US$740 (£385) apt for 4, US$815 (£424) apt for 6; off season US$515 (£268) apt for 4, US$580 (£302) apt for 6. Surcharges of up to 10% apply during Christmas, Thanksgiving, and Easter. AE, MC, V. **Amenities:** Outdoor pool; tennis court; fitness center; Jacuzzi; sauna; nonsmoking rooms. *In room:* A/C, TV, dataport, kitchen, beverage maker, iron, safe, washer/dryer, cribs, private garage.

Hyatt Regency Grand Cayman Beach Suites ★★

Despite the fact that it's stylish, elegant, well-maintained, and sought-after as a highly desirable address, no other deluxe resort in the Cayman Islands carries as many memories of Hurricane Ivan. Set directly on the sands of Seven Mile Beach, this property originated in the 1980s as a small part of the sprawling 36-hectare (89-acre) Britannia Resort development, a resort that reigned for several years as the largest and most stylish hotel in the Cayman Islands. In 2004, to the amazement of virtually everyone, Hurricane Ivan demolished the part of the resort that lay inland from the beach, and spared these "beach suites," which lay (and still do) directly beside the sea. What used to be the showcase and centerpiece of the Hyatt Regency, the former site of around 230 very upscale accommodations still languishes, hidden from view of the average passerby, in a state of disrepair, pending settlement of an insurance dispute.

Despite this, the beach suites—originally conceived as an afterthought to the larger resort—are some of the most sought-after accommodations on Grand Cayman. And although the land on which the truncated resort sits is relatively compact, the owners have placed lots of distractions and diversions on site, including two restaurants, Hemingway's and the Bamboo Bar (see below), a health club and spa, the island's largest branch of Red Sail Watersports, and direct access to Seven Mile Beach. Rooms, each configured as a compact but artfully designed suite, are well-upholstered, luxurious and have private verandas with views of the sea. Each has a king-size bed or two double beds, a spacious bathroom with a tub made of Italian marble, bright colors, and cherrywood furniture.

George Town, Seven Mile Beach (P.O. Box 1588), Grand Cayman, B.W.I. © 800/233-1234 in the U.S., or 345/949-1234. Fax 345/949-8528. www.hyattregencygrandcayman.com. 53 suites. Winter US$700 (£364) 1-bedroom suite, US$1,800–US$2,300 (£936–£1,196) 2-bedroom suite; off season US$295–US$480 (£153–£250) 1-bedroom suite, US$610–US$1,180 (£317–£614) 2-bedroom suite. AE, DC, DISC, MC, V. **Amenities:** 3 restaurants; 4 bars; 2 pools (1 with swim-up bar); 9-hole golf course; health club; spa; Jacuzzi; room service (7am–11pm); babysitting; laundry service; nonsmoking rooms; rooms for those w/limited mobility. *In room:* A/C, cable TV, fridge, toaster-oven, microwave, beverage maker, hair dryer, iron, safe, Wi-Fi.

The Ritz-Carlton ⭐⭐⭐ *Kids*   With amenities and a service level that's rivaled only by the Westin, the Ritz-Carlton is the largest, plushest, most prestigious, most spectacular, and most awe-inspiring resort in the Cayman Islands. With a size and in a league and a class of its own, it defies comparison to virtually everything else on Grand Cayman. And unless you make a concentrated effort to explore other parts of the island, it's very easy, once you've checked in, to never venture beyond its boundaries.

Straddling both sides of the boulevard that parallels Seven Mile Beach, the hotel is divided into two regal and very large but distinctly separate buildings, each painted the color of sand. Binding the components together is a soundproofed, climate-controlled catwalk that stretches above the sometimes congested rush-hour traffic of West Bay Street. From inside the catwalk, thanks to a changing array of artwork, elaborate soundproofing, and the fact that the windows are inset with frosted glass, you'll have absolutely no sense of the workaday world outside. Everything is climate controlled, meticulously manicured, and covered with marble, stone, expensive hardwoods, or ultraplush wall-to-wall carpeting. No other hotel in the Cayman Islands so effectively evokes Europe in the tropics. At its best, this is a richly decorated, sedate, and very expensive architectural fantasy that's run with a bright, hardworking, and polite staff.

The Ritz covers 58 hectares (144 acres), the entire width of the island, from Seven Mile Beach to North Sands, including a Greg Norman designed golf course, children's programs designed by Jean-Michel Cousteau, and the world's first spa inspired by La Prairie's Silver Rain. All the rooms are blissful, but the especially luxurious ones are available at The Reserve, a collection of two dozen oceanfront condos with large living and dining areas and wide terraces (units can be booked as one, two, or three bedrooms).

The bigger of its two swimming pools is a curvy, beachfront affair that's the largest body of fresh water in the country. The best of its five restaurants (Blue, which is separately recommended in "Where to Dine") is the most expensive, with the most prestigious celebrity chef in the country.

West Bay Rd., Grand Cayman, B.W.I. ℂ **800/241-3333** or 345/943-9000. Fax 345/943-9001. www.ritzcarlton.com. 365 units. Winter from US$649 (£337) double, from US$1,300 (£676) suite. Off-season from US$249 (£129) double, from US$599 (£311) suite. AE, DC, MC, V. **Amenities:** 5 restaurants; 2 bars; outdoor pool; golf course; spa; children's programs; 24-hr. room service; babysitting; laundry/dry cleaning; nonsmoking rooms; rooms for those w/limited mobility. *In room:* A/C, TV, dataport, hair dryer, minibar, safe.

Silver Sands Condominiums ⭐ *Kids*   A good choice for families, this modern eight-building complex is arranged horseshoe-fashion on the relatively low-density stretch of sandy beachfront, 11km (7 miles) north of George Town. The well-maintained apartments are grouped around a rectangular freshwater pool. The eight three-story apartment blocks, each painted pale blue, were solidly built to high standards in the late 1970s, in ways more substantial than newer buildings. Each is configured as either a two-bedroom/two-bathroom or three-bedroom/three-bathroom unit. The two-bedroom units can hold up to six people, and the three-bedroom units can house up to eight. Each apartment comes with a balcony, a fully equipped kitchen, and a small bathroom with shower. In all, this is a smoothly run operation, which, in spite of its high costs, satisfies most guests.

West Bay Rd., Seven Mile Beach (P.O. Box 752WB), Grand Cayman, B.W.I. ℂ **345/949-3343.** Fax 345/949-1223. www.silversandscondos.com. 42 units. Winter US$486–US$507 (£253–£264) 2-bedroom apt, US$586–US$686 (£305–£357) 3-bedroom apt; off season US$314–US$328 (£163–£171) 2-bedroom apt, US$386–US$478 (£201–£249) 3-bedroom apt. Additional person US$25 (£13) extra. Children 12 and under stay free in parent's room. Minimum stay 7 nights in winter, 3 nights in off season. AE, MC, V. **Amenities:** 2 tennis courts; laundry facilities; nonsmoking rooms. *In room:* A/C, ceiling fans, cable TV, kitchen, beverage maker, iron, safe, cribs.

Spanish Bay Reef Resort ☆ This is a small, intimate, all-inclusive resort set in an isolated location amid the scrublands of the northwestern tip of Grand Cayman. Rather informally run, and radically rebuilt and completely operational in the wake of the hurricane devastation of 2004, the electric-pink, one- and two-story stucco units are favorites with divers. There's great snorkeling and diving right offshore from the jagged and rocky seafront. (Don't expect a sandy beachfront here: Swimmers lower themselves into the surf using an interconnected series of metal steps. Thanks to the fantastic marine life offshore, no one seems to mind.) But if you're seeking resort-style accommodations, a sense of plush, and lots of extras, this place may not appeal to you. The accommodations, which are rather simple, have balconies or patios with garden or ocean views. Beds are comfortable, but bathrooms are a bit cramped, containing tub/shower combos. The casual furnishings are in a Caribbean motif.

Rates include all meals and beverages, island sightseeing, entertainment, use of bicycles, introductory scuba and snorkeling lessons, unlimited snorkeling, an unlimited number of dives from the shore (including tanks and weight belt), round-trip transfers, taxes, and service. If you're a diver, ask about certified diver's packages when making your reservations. Guests lounge around Calico Jack's Poolside Bar and later enjoy an expansive menu (with lots of fish) in the Spanish Main Restaurant

Spanish Bay Reef Resort, 167 Conch Point Road, West Bay (P.O. Box 903GT), Grand Cayman, B.W.I. ☎ 800/48-2DIVE in the U.S., or 345/949-3765. Fax 345/949-1842. www.caymanresortsonline.com. 64 units. Winter US$265–US$290 (£138–£151) per person double, US$315–US$325 (£164–£169) per person 1-bedroom condo; off season US$175–US$185 (£91–£96) per person double, US$265–US$290 (£138–£151) per person 1-bedroom condo. Children under 17 pay US$35–US$100 (£18–£52) each per night, depending on their age, in parent's room. Rates are all-inclusive. Ask about dive packages. AE, MC, V. **Amenities:** Restaurant; 1 bar; outdoor pool; Jacuzzi; dive shop; scuba diving; snorkeling; bikes; babysitting; laundry service. *In room:* A/C, ceiling fan, cable TV, dataport.

Westin Casuarina Resort ☆☆☆ After the Ritz Carlton, this is the best-accessorized, most elegant, and plushest resort in the Cayman Islands. Set directly astride the sands of Seven Mile Beach, and painted an eye-catching tone of dark gray with a turquoise-colored roof, it has artfully landscaped gardens and grounds, plenty of facilities, and a beautiful oval-shaped swimming pool which, until it was surpassed in size by one of the swimming pools at the nearby Ritz-Carlton, was the largest on Grand Cayman. Most of the bedrooms have French doors that open onto private balconies and conservative, comfortable furnishings. Units are a bit small for such a luxury hotel but are well equipped and comfortable, having been upgraded in 2005 and 2006. Bathrooms are a bit less upscale than you might have thought, considering the overall elegance of the hotel, but each has an oversized tub. Thanks to the building's layout in the form of a giant "U," about 2/3 of the accommodations have sea views, a higher percentage than those within the Ritz-Carlton: The others simply look out on the parking lot and West Bay Road, so ask questions when you reserve.

The most upscale of the restaurants is the very charming four-star, deluxe Casa Havana, a dinner-only restaurant that evokes the glitter and glamour of pre-Castro Cuba.

West Bay Road, Seven Mile Beach (P.O. Box 30620), Grand Cayman, B.W.I. ☎ 800/937-8461 in the U.S., or 345/945-3800. Fax 345/949-5825. www.westincasuarina.com. 343 units. Winter US$345–US$749 (£179–£389) double, US$1,050–US$3,150 (£546–£1,638) suite; off season US$264–US$560 (£137–£291) double, US$735–US$1,390 (£382–£723) suite. AE, MC, V. **Amenities:** 3 restaurants; 3 bars; outdoor pool; golf; exercise room; spa; sauna; dive shop; children's programs; 24-hr. room service; dry cleaning; nonsmoking rooms; rooms for those w/limited mobility. *In room:* A/C, cable TV, dataport, refrigerator, minibar, beverage maker, hair dryer, iron, safe.

EXPENSIVE

The Discovery Point Club ⚡ *Kids*   Located at the far end of the northern stretch of Seven Mile Beach, in West Bay (10km/6 miles from George Town), this tranquil and relatively isolated group of beige-painted condos is entirely composed of ocean-bordering suites. The venue here is local, West Indian, and rural—if you're looking for big-city ways, forget it—and staff members are thoroughly steeped in local mores and mannerisms. Some of the best snorkeling along the beach is found just off the shores here. When you tire of snorkeling, you can retreat to the club's freshwater pool or heated Jacuzzi. The accommodations here are comfortable and well-maintained, and in some cases, better than those offered by some nearby competitors. Condos feature tasteful furnishings, well-maintained private bathrooms with tubs and showers and a screened-in patio. Each renovated unit is decorated by the individual owner, and all come with fully equipped kitchens. Children under 6 stay free, and cribs and roll-aways are available. Each condo receives daily maid service. Between December and March, management here will agree to subdivide any two-bedroom suite into studios and one-bedroom suites by locking doors within each individual unit.

West Bay Rd., West Bay (P.O. Box 439), Grand Cayman, B.W.I. ⓒ **345/945-4724.** Fax 345/945-5051. www.discovery pointclub.com. 45 units. Winter, US$650 (£338) 2-bedroom apt for 4; off season US$210 (£109) studio for 2, US$300 (£156) 1-bedroom apt for 2, US$345 (£179) 2-bedroom apt for 4. AE, DISC, MC, V. **Amenities:** Outdoor pool; 2 tennis courts; Jacuzzi; laundry services; coin-op washers and dryers. *In room:* A/C, cable TV, kitchen, dataport, hair dryer, safe.

Grand Cayman Marriott Beach Resort ⚡   Way down in the pecking order from the Ritz-Carlton and the Westin Casuarina, this five-story choice on Seven Mile Beach is still among the top-ranked hotels on the island. A favorite with large package-tour groups and conventions, it's a 5-minute drive north of George Town. The resort has watersports facilities and there's good snorkeling 15m (50 ft.) offshore. Its ochre-colored, vaguely Hispanic design contains roofed-over loggias that open onto views of the sea, a verdantly landscaped interior courtyard, or the sides of the hotel, overlooking neighboring structures close by on either side. Regrettably, it sits astride a relatively narrow portion of Seven Mile Beach, a fact that contributes to a densely populated strip of sand in front, and just a bit too much congestion around the edges of the swimming pool, but there's lots to do at this family-friendly resort, with lots of emphasis on organized activities. The accommodations were all remodeled and are among the most spacious on the island. Each contains modern art, dark-grained wood furniture that includes an armoire, pastel walls, tropical-patterned fabrics, large closets, and private balconies. Bathrooms are spacious, with tub/shower combos.

389 West Bay Rd., Seven Mile Beach (P.O. Box 30371), Grand Cayman, B.W.I. ⓒ **800/228-9290** in the U.S., or 345/949-0088. Fax 345/949-0288. www.marriott.com/gcmgc. 305 units. Winter US$380 (£198) double, US$645–US$1,030 (£335–536) junior suite, US$1,600 (£832) suite; off season US$184–US$246 (£96–£128) double, US$310–US$485 (£161–£252) junior suite, US$500–US$780 (£260–£406) 1-bedroom suite, US$760–US$1,200 (£395–£624) 2-bedroom suite; 10% surcharge applies over Christmas. AE, DISC, MC, V. **Amenities:** 2 restaurants; 2 bars; outdoor pool; health club; Jacuzzi; sauna; dive shop; supervised children's programs (Camp Coconuts); 24-hour room service; laundry service; dry cleaning; nonsmoking rooms; rooms for those w/limited mobility. *In room:* A/C, cable TV, refrigerator, beverage maker, hair dryer, iron, safe.

MODERATE

Cobalt Coast Resort and Suites ⚡⚡ *Finds*   Fans of this resort liken it to a contemporary, European bed-and-breakfast where most of the clients are deeply involved with diving. It's one of the best resorts for divers on Grand Cayman, thanks to the on-site presence of a full-service dive operation (Divetech), and the presence, a short distance offshore, of a deep drop-off (the North Wall) that's loaded with many different types of marine life. Don't expect a sand beach: The coastline is entirely composed of jagged rocks, with ladders and metal steps by which you'll lower yourself into the surf. There are also very few links, or even very many reminders, of the glittery tourist scene of Seven Mile Beach, whose extreme northern terminus lies 5km (3 miles) to the south. Ironically, this was the only hotel on Grand Cayman that suffered very little damage from the hurricane of 2004, but despite that, management spent some money in 2005 upgrading the accommodations. These include both oceanfront suites and standard rooms, which are roomy, modern, cozy, and soothing, with Marimekko fabrics from Finland and European plumbing fixtures. On-site is a well-managed, well-run restaurant, Duppies, which serves platters of local food, sandwiches, salads, and well-prepared light fare.

18 Seafan Dr., West Bay, Grand Cayman, B.W.I. *Ⓒ* 888/946-5656 in the U.S., or 345/946-5656 for hotel or 345/946-5658 for Divetech dive center. Fax 345/946-5657 for hotel or 345/946-5659 for dive center. www.cobaltcoast.com or www.divetech.com. 18 units. Winter US$260 (£135) double, US$325 (£169) 1-bedroom suite for 2, US$495 (£257) 2-bedroom suite or villa for 4; off-season US$230 (£120) double, US$275 (£143) 1-bedroom suite for 2, US$455 (£237) 2-bedroom suite or villa for 4. Many dive packages available. AE, DC, MC, V. **Amenities:** Restaurant; bar; outdoor pool; Jacuzzi; watersports equipment rentals. *In room:* A/C, cable TV, fridge, beverage maker, hair dryer, safe, Wi-Fi.

Morritt's Tortuga Club and Grand Resort *ℛ*

On 3 beachfront hectares (7½ acres) on the east end of the island, this resort offers some of the island's best windsurfing and some of its best diving. Tortuga Divers (p. 223), which runs a branch on the premises, focuses on the busy dive trade and, to a lesser extent, the busy windsurfing trade that has developed offshore from this isolated but surprisingly busy hotel.

About a 40km (25-mile) drive from the airport, the club is composed of clusters of three-story beachfront condos opening onto the water. At the time of writing, about 80% of this hotel had been repaired after the hurricane damages of 2004, although some visible damage remained in 2007. Each was built in the Antillean plantation style from the wreckage of a former hotel. And each is part of either the Tortuga Club or the Grand Resort. There's a bit more space within units at the Grand Resort, whose rooms are between 10% and 15% more from the rates noted below, and kitchens are a bit upgraded from those within the Tortuga Club. Many are rented as time-share units, often to visiting British and Canadian residents who appreciate the calm of this resort's isolated position on Grand Cayman's distant east end. Each of the comfortably furnished apartments has a fully equipped kitchen, although many guests opt for meals in the complex's simple restaurant. Each unit has a small bathroom containing a shower.

East End (P.O. Box 496GT), Grand Cayman, B.W.I. *Ⓒ* 800/447-0309 in the U.S., or 345/947-7449. Fax 345/947-7669. www.morritts.com. 160 units. Winter US$230–US$250 (£120–£130) studio, US$320–US$360 (£166–£187) 1-bedroom apt, US$440–US$475 (£229–£247) 2-bedroom apt; off season US$185–US$200 (£96–£104) studio, US$240–US$285 (£125–£148) 1-bedroom apt, US$330–US$370 (£172–£192) 2-bedroom apt. AE, DISC, MC, V. **Amenities:** Restaurant; 4 bars; 3 outdoor pools; exercise room; watersports; babysitting; laundry room; nonsmoking rooms; rooms for those w/limited mobility. *In room:* A/C, cable TV, kitchenette, beverage maker, iron, safe.

Sunshine Suites Resort

Built in 1998 on a flat-as-a-pancake stretch of scrubland that requires a 5-minute trek across the busy traffic of West Bay Street before reaching the sands of Seven Mile Beach, this is a well-designed resort compound which is usually acknowledged as being the least expensive lodgings on Seven Mile Beach. Resembling a decent but somewhat anonymous and uncluttered apartment complex on the outskirts of, say Washington D.C., it evokes a private country club, including a relatively small swimming pool. Both inside and out, the design reflects British colonial architecture. Each of the units has its own kitchen, so many guests prepare their meals on-site, avoiding the high cost of many of the nearby restaurants, and contributing to a hands-off laissez-faire dynamic which suits many of the guests here just fine. Each of the accommodations is equipped with a midsize private bathroom with tub and shower. Nestled in the compound's center are a handful of gazebos and the resort's simple restaurant, the Sunshine Grill, which is known for the quality of its burgers.

112 West Bay Rd., Grand Cayman, B.W.I. (C) **877/786-1110** in the U.S., or 345/949-3000. Fax 345/949-1200. www.sunshinesuites.com. 132 units. Winter US$200–US$220 (£104–£114) double, US$245–US$265 (£127–£138) 1-bedroom suite for 2 or 4; off-season US$170–US$190 (£88–£99) double, US$215–US$235 (£112–£122) 1-bedroom suite for 2 to 4. Rates include continental breakfast. AE, DISC, MC, V. **Amenities:** Restaurant; bar; outdoor pool; free use of nearby fitness center; watersports equipment rentals; business center; coin-op washers and dryers. *In room:* A/C, TV, dataport, kitchen, Wi-Fi.

Sunset House   Set on a coastal road about 1.2km (¾ mile) south of George Town, this is a well-recommended middle-bracket hotel whose rooms are divided among a quartet of two-story pink-sided outbuildings. Accommodations are no-nonsense and relatively comfortable. This place is favored by divers and snorkelers, who appreciate the jagged, mostly rock shoreline (site of excellent snorkeling possibilities) and the extensive diving programs. You're given a number of options for accommodations here, ranging from the cheapest (a unit opening onto the courtyard) to the most expensive (a roomy suite that contains extras such as private balconies, two double beds, a full kitchen, and a living room). The midrange standard bedrooms open onto views of the sea and contain more space than the courtyard units.

Don't expect to swim here off sand: You must lower yourself via ladders directly into the sea. Two good reasons for staying here are direct access to the hotel's much-praised restaurant, Seaharvest, and its sprawling bar, which is especially busy every Friday night. About 80% of the guests staying at the hotel here are scuba enthusiasts, and about 80% of the clients at the hotel's bar and restaurant are full-time island residents.

390 S. Church St., PO Box 479, George Town, Grand Cayman, KY1-1106. (C) **345/949-7111.** Fax 345/949-7101. www.sunsethouse.com. 59 units. Winter US$165–US$210 (£86–£109) double, US$255 (£133) suite, US$300 (£156) apt; off season US$130–US$180 (£68–£94) double, US$200 (£104) suite, US$220 (£114) apt. AE, DISC, MC, V. **Amenities:** Restaurant; bar; outdoor pool; Jacuzzi; on-site dive shop (Sunset Divers) offering watersports equipment rentals. *In room:* A/C, TV, Wi-Fi, kitchen in apts, fridge in suites.

INEXPENSIVE

Eldemire's Guest House   Set within a quiet and completely unpretentious residential neighborhood on the landward side of South Church Road, 1.5km (1 mile) south of downtown George Town, this is one of only two bed-and-breakfast inns on Grand Cayman. Basic and completely free of glitter, it's run with a relaxed sense of humor by Carol "Tootie" Eldemire Huddleston, the congenial but outspoken and no-nonsense Jamaica-born entrepreneur ("a helluva matriarch") who lives just across the street. Accommodations lie within either the main house or within a handful of outbuildings. Each of the rooms is a simple, sparsely furnished affair, with well-worn furniture and few frills. Each has a private bathroom with shower, and about half contain a tub-shower combo. Smith Cove Beach lies within a 5-minute walk. Residents of the double rooms have access to the house's communal kitchen, and each of the suites and apartments contains a simple kitchenette. Ms. Huddleston advises us that sometime during the course of 2007, a full-time dive operation will relocate itself to a point on-site.

18 Pebbles Way, George Town, Grand Cayman, B.W.I. (C) **345/916-8369.** Fax 345/949-4595. www.eldemire.com. 13 units. Winter US$109 (£57) double, US$149 (£78) 1-bedroom apt, US$229 (£119) 2-bedroom apt; off season US$85 (£44) double, US$110 (£57) 1-bedroom apt, US$115 (£60) 2-bedroom apt. **Amenities:** Outdoor pool; bike rental; coin-op washers and dryers. *In room:* A/C, TV, kitchenettes (in suites and apts).

DINING

Make sure you understand which currency the menu is printed in. If it's not written on the menu, ask the waiter if the prices are in U.S. dollars or Cayman Island dollars. It will make a big difference when you get your final bill. See "Currency" under "Fast Facts."

Because virtually everything must be shipped in, Cayman Islands restaurants are among the most expensive in the Caribbean. For the best value, opt instead for West Indian fare like conch and grouper, which are invariably less expensive. Fewer and fewer restaurants offer turtle these days, although traditionally it's been a culinary star in the Caymans. Today, if it's served, it will appear most often as turtle steak, but sometimes in soups or stews.

EXPENSIVE

The Brasserie 🍴🍴 CARIBBEAN/CONTINENTAL   Elegant and stylish, and favored by members of Grand Cayman's investment community, this restaurant seems very far removed from the tourist hubbub of Seven Mile Beach and other tourist-geared areas. It was built in the mid-1990s as part of a glistening office compound that is one of the most architecturally avant-garde in the Cayman Islands, with a low-slung pavilion surrounded by soaring branches of, among others, the Canadian National Bank.

Expect a Caribbean colonial decor with high ceilings, artfully carved teakwood and mahogany furniture, spinning ceiling fans, and a cool, breezy layout that might evoke an upscale private club in a long-gone British colonial empire. Lunches focus on upscale and upbeat salads such as a fresh yellowfin tuna tataki with pine nuts, feta cheese, and sweet basil vinaigrette, and pastas such as gnocchi with langoustine and prosciutto. Dinners are more formal and more expensive, with main courses that include roasted loin of Colorado lamb with braised endive and Pernod-chorizo broth. Greg Vassos is the talented chef, something of a celebrity on island in his own right.

Cricket Sq., Elgin Ave. ⓒ 345/945-1815. Reservations recommended, especially at lunch. Lunch salads and platters CI$15–CI$30 (US$19–US$38/£9–£18); dinner main courses CI$20–CI$38 (US$25–US$48/£12–£23); tapas CI$4–CI$8 (US$5–US$10/£2.40–£4.80). AE, DC, MC, V. Mon–Fri 11:30am–2:30pm; tapas menu daily 4:30–7pm; dinner daily 6–10pm.

Calypso Grill 🍴🍴 *Finds* SEAFOOD/INTERNATIONAL   At first glance you might think this is little more than a waterfront shack. But when you enter, you'll find a charming, funky, and slightly psychedelic bar and restaurant that absolutely drips with Creole colors, a sense of whimsy, and even a bold and creative sense of elegance. If the wind isn't too brisk, you can sit on a wooden deck directly above the water, watching workaday fishing craft depositing their loads at West Bay's busiest fishing port. The venue is very authentic with a clientele that derives from many walks of Caymanian life, from the monied to the bohemian—all of it a far cry from the congestion and glitter of Seven Mile Beach. Perch at the rectangular bar here for a cocktail or any of about a dozen kinds of wine by the glass, or, if a table isn't likely to become available, opt for a full meal. The best menu items include marinated conch; a creamy version of lobster bisque; Cuban-style shrimp with sherry-flavored cream sauce; fresh fish (ask the waiter what's available) that can be blackened, grilled, or sautéed; veal chops with chanterelles; and a garlic-laced version of shrimp linguine. Favorite desserts include mango crêpes and sticky toffee pudding.

Morgan's Harbour, West Bay. ⓒ 345/949-3948. Reservations required for dinner. Main courses CI$24–CI$33 (US$30–US$41/£14–£20). AE, DC, MC, V. Tues–Sat 11:30am–2:30pm, Sun 12:30–2:30pm, and Tues–Sun 6–10pm.

The Cracked Conch/MacaBuca Oceanside Tiki Bar & Grill 🌟🌟 SEAFOOD/ INTERNATIONAL   This place reopened with fanfare in 2006 and immediately became the focus of recommendations across Grand Cayman. Nestled into the jagged rocks of West Bay, on the seacoast near the northern terminus of Seven Mile Beach, across the road from the Turtle Farm, it serves some of the island's freshest seafood. It's also a dining and drinking destination in its own right, a magnet for young, attractive residents of Grand Cayman. The best way to appreciate this place involves drinks and perhaps a focus on the big-screen TVs at the MacaBuca Tiki Bar, and then a migration to a table on the open-sided veranda at the Cracked Conch. As a whole, the experience involves views of flickering torches and the sound of surf crashing against the jagged rocks nearby, hallucinatory rum punches and martinis, and very good food.

Informal menu items available throughout the day and evening at MacaBuca and at lunch at The Cracked Conch, include salads, fried calamari, breaded and fried conch steaks, and beef, chicken, or conch burgers. More formal and elaborate dishes, available for dinner at The Cracked Conch, feature steamed conch and snapper coconut casserole, and a skillfully prepared roulade of conch and turtle steak. Sunday brunches here are festive, with buffet stations set up within the establishment's gleaming stainless-steel kitchen. There's also an elegant indoor bar here as well.

West Bay Rd., near Turtle Bay Farm. ⓒ 345/945-5217. Reservations required. At MacaBuca, platters, sandwiches, and salads CI$17–CI$21 (US$21–US$26/£10–£13); at Cracked Conch, dinner main courses CI$14–CI$36 (US$18–US$45/£8.40–£22). All-you-can-eat buffet-style Sun brunch CI$26 (US$33/£16). AE, MC, V. Cracked Conch daily 11am–3pm and 5:30–10pm; MacaBuca Tiki Bar open daily 10am to at least midnight.

Grand Old House 🌟🌟 AMERICAN/CARIBBEAN/PACIFIC RIM   The Grand Old House is the island's premier caterer and hosts everything from lavish weddings and political functions to informal family celebrations. This former plantation house lies amid venerable trees 2km (1¼ miles) south of George Town, past Jackson Point. Built on bedrock near the edge of the sea, it stands on 129 ironwood posts that support the main house and a bevy of gazebos.

For appetizers, we recommend the roasted lobster Napoleon or the marinated conch Cayman Island–style with tomato, cilantro, and Key lime flavorings. Also worthwhile is the tequila-infused snow crab and lobster laid on a mango gazpacho with spicy cucumber noodles. A signature main course is a platter of baked shrimp and scallops gratin in white wine, or the Cayman-style turtle steak in a tomato and white-wine sauce. Among fish dishes, we like the fire-roasted Chilean sea bass in balsamic syrup on a sweet-potato mash with a candied lemon and mango beurre blanc.

Petra Plantation, 648 S. Church St. ⓒ 345/949-9333. Reservations required. Main courses CI$23–CI$34 (US$29–US$43/£14–£20). AE, DISC, MC, V. Daily 11am–3pm (Nov–Apr only) and year-round 5:30–10pm.

Hemingway's 🌟🌟 SEAFOOD/INTERNATIONAL   Some of the best seafood on the island can be found 3km (2 miles) north of George Town at the premier restaurant of the Hyatt Regency Beach Suites. It occupies a rambling, single-story annex of the hotel that contains it, in a spot shoehorned between the beach and a pair of swimming pools. There's a rather plush bar inside, a favorite after-work hangout that's favored by managers of competing, non-affiliated restaurants nearby; a big-windowed, air-conditioned dining room; and tables set outside, on a shaded colonnade near trails of bougainvillea and spinning overhead fans. The menu is among the most imaginative on the island and has won acclaim from *Gourmet* magazine. Appetizers include a tasty coconut shrimp with a mango marmalade accent, Cuban-style barbecued turtle steak, well-spiced crab cakes, paella, and an absolutely fantastic deep-fried version of a whole red snapper that's de-boned and artfully presented like a piece of sculpture with pickled onions, bell peppers, and garlic-laced mashed potatoes. There's also catch of the day, prepared any way you want it, including blackened, and citrus-and-cumin-marinated tenderloin of pork.

In the Hyatt Regency Grand Cayman Beach Suites, West Bay Rd. © **345/949-1234**. Reservations required. Lunch main courses CI$10–CI$16 (US$13–US$20/£6–£9.60); Dinner main courses CI$22–CI$35 (US$28–US$44/£13–£21). AE, DC, DISC, MC, V. Daily 11:30am–2:30pm and 6–10pm.

Lighthouse at Breakers ☆ CARIBBEAN/ITALIAN/SEAFOOD

On the south shore of the island, this cozy, elegant, and nautically decorated landmark lies about a 30-minute drive east from George Town. Its creative menu mainly features fresh local seafood. A well-trained chef, backed up by a skilled staff, offers well-prepared meals, attracting both locals and visitors. Put yourself in the hands of the mostly European staff and sit back to enjoy such tempting appetizers as penne pasta with shrimp, asparagus, tomatoes, and pesto; or tuna sushi rolled in sesame seeds. For your main course, opt for the mixed grill of Caribbean seafood, lobster with gnocchi and shrimp, filet mignon with brandy-flavored cream sauce, or a veal chop topped with Gorgonzola and pancetta ham. The restaurant has one of the best wine cellars on the island. Immediately adjacent to the restaurant is a towering life-sized replica of a lighthouse, its trademark and signature, that's visible for many miles out to sea

Breakers. © **345/947-2047**. Reservations recommended. Lunch main courses CI$11–CI$16 (US$14–US$20/£6.60–£9.60); Dinner main courses CI$16–CI$42 (US$20–US$53/£9.60–£25). AE, DISC, MC, V. Daily 11:30am–3:30pm and 5:30–10pm.

Lobster Pot ☆ SEAFOOD/INTERNATIONAL

Folksy and charming, but not quite as good and as polished as Hemingway's, Lobster Pot is still an island favorite. It overlooks the water from its second-floor perch at the northern perimeter of George Town, directly beside the road that funnels traffic into the capital from Seven Mile Beach. As its name suggests, it serves lobster prepared in many different ways: Cayman style, broiled in its shell, as lobster bisque, and as a mouth-watering salad. Braised jerk chicken, turtle steak, and stuffed Chilean salmon are also on the menu. Most dishes are right on the mark. A house specialty is the "Cayman Trio," consisting of portions of broiled lobster tail, garlic-sautéed shrimp, and grilled fresh local fish, all piled onto the same platter. The place is also known for its succulent steaks. For lunch, you might opt for English-style fish and chips or perhaps lobster quesadillas or lobster-studded pasta. The Lobster Pot's wine bar is a pleasant place for a drink.

245 N. Church St. © **345/949-2736**. Reservations recommended in winter. Main courses lunch CI$8–CI$26 (US$10–US$33/£4.80–£16); dinner CI$19-CI$35 (US$24–US$44/£12–£21). AE, DISC, MC, V. Mon–Fri 11:30am–2:30pm; daily 5–10pm.

Portofino Wreckview Restaurant ☆ ITALIAN/INTERNATIONAL/CARIBBEAN

In 1962 an American cargo ship, the *Liberty,* sank during a storm on a reef close to Grand Cayman's eastern shore. Today, split into three thoroughly rusted separate sections that rest in shallow water, it provides a focal point for the panoramas that open before you from the terrace of this restaurant. The most popular independent restaurant on Grand Cayman's East End, it draws clients from the hotel and resort complexes nearby.

You might begin a meal here with a satay of beef or chicken, served with a cucumber-and-peanut sauce, then follow with a savory version of *zuppa di pesce* (fish soup); breaded conch steak served in traditional East End style; turtle steak; any of several kinds of pasta; and the house specialty, baked seafood Portofino, which delectably combines lobster, tiger shrimp, scallops, and mousseline potatoes au gratin. Lunches are simpler than dinners, focusing on salads, sandwiches, pastas, and grilled fish.

In Colliers, East End. © 345/947-2700. Reservations recommended. Lunch platters CI$10–CI$21 (US$13–US$26/£6–£13); dinner main courses CI$15–CI$30 (US$19–US$38/£9–£18). AE, DISC, MC, V. Daily 11:30am–10pm.

The Reef Grill at Royal Palms 🕉🕉🕉 SEAFOOD

This is one of the island's finest, and one of our favorite, restaurants on Grand Cayman, a site that manages to be chic, savvy, elegant, hip, and fun all at the same time. It's positioned on a strategic plot of land in the heart of the Seven Mile Beach "golden strip." The savvy entrepreneurs who rent the space maintain a compound of one- and two-story buildings that include a beachfront bar and grill, a nightclub, and a classy citadel of gourmet cuisine. To fully appreciate the place, we recommend a brisk walk-through as a means of determining which corner of the place you'd most like to occupy. Let's just say that the inland, "landlocked" bar and dining area is elegant, red, and evocative of an upscale corner of Europe, and the seafront bar offers dance-floor views of Grand Cayman's most nubile and flirtatious chatterboxes.

Favorites here include Maytag blue cheese salad with chopped Granny Smith apples and spiced pecans; conch fritters with jerk-flavored mayonnaise; a melt-in-your-mouth honey and soy-glazed sea bass with Thai-style curried vinaigrette; and jumbo scallops with smoked bacon and a fricassee of corn, accompanied by mashed potatoes garnished with chunks of lobster tail. If you opt to dine under the stars, and if it's a Friday or Saturday, you'll hear some of the most talented local musicians playing soca and calypso in the bar pavilion about a hundred paces away. One of the helpful, experienced staff members will guide you through one of the Cayman's best wine lists.

In the Royal Palms Beach Club, Seven Mile Beach. © 345/945-6358. Reservations recommended. Main courses lunch CI$8–CI$11 (US$10–US$14/£4.80–£6.60), dinner CI$21–CI$32 (US$26–US$40/£13–£19). AE, MC, V. Daily 11am–3pm and 5:30–10pm. Closed Sun night between May and Dec.

Ristorante Pappagallo 🕉 NORTHERN ITALIAN/SEAFOOD

One of the island's most memorable restaurants lies on a 6-hectare (15-acre) bird sanctuary overlooking a natural lagoon, 15 minutes north of George Town. Its designers incorporated Caymanian and Aztec weaving techniques in its thatched roof. Glass doors, black marble, and polished brass mix a kind of Edwardian opulence with a Tahitian decor. Inside, you'll see some of the most beautiful (caged) parrots on the island, separated from the dining and drinking area (for sanitary reasons) by plate-glass windows. The lobster-and-scallop bisque in coconut cream and the carpaccio of raw beef with arugula are appealing appetizers. Pastas are full of flavor, especially the fettuccine with lemon-grilled chicken and sun-dried tomatoes and the penne with homemade sausage. Fish and shellfish are well prepared, or you can opt for either the peppered West Indian pork tenderloin in an apple-bourbon sauce, or a combination of lobster and shrimp, prepared in the style of the chef, with pepper, garlic, diced tomatoes, mushrooms, and a flaming brandy and tarragon-flavored cream sauce.

Close to the Villas Pappagallo, Conch Point Road, Barkers, in West Bay (near the northern terminus of West Bay Rd., 13km/8 miles north of George Town). © 345/949-1119. Reservations recommended. Main courses CI$18–CI$34 (US$23–US$43/£11–£20). AE, MC, V. Daily 6–10:30pm.

The Wharf 🕉 CARIBBEAN/CONTINENTAL

On the northern fringe of George Town, at the southernmost edge of Seven Mile Beach, this is a dining, drinking, and nightlife emporium that's fun, tropical, artfully illuminated, and sometimes sought after by trend-conscious hipsters of Grand Cayman Island. More than half of the place is built on wharves and piers that jut seaward, allowing fish to swim under your dining table as you eat, and even to make appearances in an open area that's the target of a plethora of spotlights that catch their every silvery movement. (The feeding of the tarpon, something approaching an underwater frenzy, occurs every night at 9pm.) The restaurant is decorated in tones of turquoise and blue, and offers dining within an air conditioned interior, or outside on either an elevated veranda or on a waterside terrace. The sound of the surf mingles with chatter from the Ports of Call Bar and music from the strolling Paraguayan harpist, Eugenio Leon.

Many diners begin with the blue crab-and-shrimp salad with cucumber and mango or the golden fried Caribbean lobster cake with a roasted corn relish. Main dishes are a delight, especially the basil and pistachio-crusted sea bass in a creamy champagne sauce or the grilled turtle-and-lobster pie with rice and vegetables. A local favorite is the pork tenderloin Tortuga baked between sugar cane and served with a dark-rum sauce. Fresh fish can be prepared any way you want: blackened, almondine, grilled, or "island-style." The kitchen makes a laudable effort to break away from typical, dull menu items, and for the most part they succeed.

43 West Bay Rd., Seven Mile Beach. ✆ 345/949-2231. Reservations recommended. Main courses CI$22–CI$37 (US$28–US$46/£13–£22). AE, MC, V. Daily, year-round, 6–10pm.

MODERATE

Chicken! Chicken! *Kids* *Value* AMERICAN   This venue completely lacks glamour, but within its cheerful and unpretentious premises (it looks like the interior of a brightly painted Creole cottage), you can feed an entire family for less money than at virtually any other restaurant on Grand Cayman. The specialty here, and the only available main course, is tender, richly seasoned, perfectly cooked chicken. As many as 32 chickens at a time rotate enticingly in the glare of the island's biggest and most theatrical rotisserie, prominently positioned near the restaurant's entrance. Each chicken is flavored with herbs and a touch of garlic. After placing your order at the stand-up counter, you can opt to dine in the restaurant, or you can haul your chicken away for consumption somewhere else. The chicken (breast, thigh, or whole roasted birds, depending on your order) is accompanied by corn bread and your choice of coleslaw, rice, or beans.

In the West Shore Shopping Plaza, West Bay Rd. ✆ 345/945-2290. Lunch CI$7–CI$8 (US$8.75–US$10/ £4.20–£4.80); dinner CI$9–CI$11 (US$11–US$14/£5.40–£6.60). AE, MC, V. Daily 11am–10pm.

KaiboBar & Grill INTERNATIONAL   Isolated on Grand Cayman's Northern Coast, in a location that's adjacent to a busy marina, this place offers good food and an irreverent and gregarious atmosphere. Some aspects of the place evoke a beach compound in Polynesia, thanks to flaming torches, multi-level terraces, and cabanas roofed in palm thatch. Menu items focus on juicy burgers, fresh salads, seafood prepared any way you want, steaks, and pastas, any of which can be accompanied by sunset-colored drinks that tend to get the party roaring.

In the Kaibo Yacht Club, Cayman Kai, North Side. ✆ 345/947-9975. Reservations not necessary. Lunchtime platters, salads, and sandwiches CI$8–CI$11 (US$10–US$14/£4.80–£6.60); dinner main courses CI$18–CI$25 (US$23–US$31/£11–£15). AE, MC, V. Daily 11am–11pm; bar remains open nightly till 1am.

Mezza's INTERNATIONAL   Hip, breezy, Europeanized, and urban, this restaurant sits one floor above a landmark liquor store (Big Daddy's), immediately adjacent to the Treasure Island Hotel. This is a venue that you might expect to encounter in

South Beach, Miami. Lunches are simple, featuring steak sandwiches, burgers, Caesar salads, and seafood pasta. The dinner menu is more artful, with dishes that include bacon-wrapped mahi-mahi; basil-encrusted salmon steaks; sautéed shrimp with wine sauce and asparagus; steak au poivre with pommes frites; and fettuccine with jerk chicken. Caramel pecan fudge cake, or the crème brûlée, make for enticing desserts.

233 West Bay Rd., above Big Daddy's Liquor Store. ✆ 345/946-3992. Reservations recommended. Main courses CI$21–CI$32 (US$26–US$40/£13–£19), Wines by the glass CI$7–CI$19 (US$8.75–US$24/£4.20–£11). AE, DC, MC, V. Sun–Fri noon–4pm, daily 6–11pm.

Rackham's Pub & Restaurant AMERICAN/CARIBBEAN   If you're interested in an extensive menu and open-air dining with a beautiful view, then you should try this place. In the morning you can watch boats coming to port, and in the evening you can see their lights as they head back out to sea. Your best bets here are the Caribbean shrimp, fish and chips, grilled mahimahi marinated in jerk sauce, Caesar salad, pan-fried grouper with rice and beans, and a wide array of curries and pastas.

93 N. Church St., George Town. ✆ 345/945-3860. Reservations recommended for parties of 6 or more. Main courses CI$9–CI$30 (US$11–US$38/£5.40–£18). AE, MC, V. Kitchen open daily 10:30am–11pm; bar open Mon–Fri 9am–1am; Sat 10am–midnight; Sun 10:30am–midnight.

HITTING THE BEACH

One of the finest beaches in the Caribbean, Grand Cayman's **Seven Mile Beach** 🌟🌟🌟, which begins north of George Town, has sparkling white sands rimmed with Australian pines and palms. (Technically, it's called West Bay Beach, but everybody just says Seven Mile Beach.) Although it's not actually as long as its name claims, it is still a honey: 9km (5½ miles) of white, white sands stretching all the way to George Town. It tends to be crowded near the big resorts, but the beach is so big you can always find some room to spread out your towel. There are no peddlers to hassle you, and the beach is for the most part kelp-free and beautifully maintained.

Because the beach is on a relatively tranquil side of Grand Cayman, there is no great tide and the water is generally placid and inviting, ideal for families, even those with small children. A sandy bottom slopes gently to deep water. The water's so clear that you can usually see what's swimming in it. It's great for snorkelers and swimmers of most ages and abilities.

From one end of the beach to the other, most immediately adjacent to their neighbors, there are hotels and condos, many with beachside bars that you can visit. Originally, only buildings with three stories or less were allowed on the beach; but that changed in the 1990s with the construction of several six- and even seven-story towers. The increased "population density" has added greater numbers of people to the sands during periods of high occupancy, which you may or may not like, depending on your values, your aesthetics, and your lifestyle. All sorts of watersports concessions can be found along this beach, including kiosks that rent snorkel gear, boats, windsurfers, WaveRunners, paddlecats, and aqua trikes. Parasailing and water-skiing are also available. Two hotels, particularly well accessorized as water sports headquarters, include the Hyatt Regency Grand Cayman Beach Suites and the Marriott. But even if you're staying in a relatively obscure guesthouse or condominium, most watersports outfits, including members of the well-respected Red Sail group, will shuttle-bus you from any point along Seven Mile Beach to the departure point for your particular excursion.

Grand Cayman also has a number of minor beaches, although their allures pale in comparison to Seven Mile Beach. Visit these if you want to escape the crowds. Many beaches on the east and north coasts of Grand Cayman are relatively desirable, layered in many cases with pale sand and protected in some cases by offshore barrier reefs, so waters are generally tranquil. The best windsurfing on Grand Cayman is off the eastern shore, with particularly good conditions on the beaches adjacent to the separately recommended Morritt's resorts.

One of our favorites is on the north coast, bordering **Cayman Kai.** This beach is a Caribbean cliché of charm, with palm trees and beautiful sands, along with changing facilities. You can snorkel along the reef to Rum Point. The beach is also ideal as a Sunday-afternoon picnic spot. **Red Sail Sports** at Rum Point offers windsurfers, WaveRunners, sailboats, water-skiing, and even glass-bottom boat tours to see the stingrays offshore. It also offers scuba diving.

SPORTS & OTHER OUTDOOR PURSUITS

What they lack in nightlife, the Caymans make up for in watersports—the fishing, swimming, water-skiing, snorkeling, and especially diving are among the finest in the Caribbean. Coral reefs and coral formations encircle the islands and are filled with lots of marine life (which scuba divers and snorkelers are forbidden to disturb, by the way).

It's easy to dive close to shore, so boats aren't necessary, but there are plenty of boats and scuba facilities available. On certain excursions, we recommend a trip with a qualified dive master. There are many dive rental shops, but they won't rent you scuba gear or supply air unless you have a card from one of the national diving schools, such as NAUI or PADI. Hotels also rent diving equipment to their guests, as well as arrange snorkeling and scuba-diving trips.

Universally regarded as the most up-to-date and best-equipped watersports facility in the Cayman Islands, **Red Sail Sports** maintains its administrative headquarters at Coconut Place (P.O. Box #31473, Grand Cayman KY1-1206; © **877/REDSAIL** in the US or 345/945-5965; www.redsailcayman.com) and its largest, best-accessorized branch at the Hyatt Regency Grand Cayman Beach Suites, West Bay Road (© **345/ 949-8745**). Other locations are at the Westin Casuarina (© **345/949-8732**); at Rum Point (© **345/947-9203**); at the Marriott Beach Resort (© **345/949-6343**); at the Courtyard by Marriott (© **345/946-5481**); and at Morritt's Tortuga Club (© **345/ 947-2097**). Red Sail has a wide range of offerings, from deep-sea fishing to sailing, windsurfing, diving, and more. Red Sail can also arrange water-skiing for US$75 (£39) per half-hour (the cost can be divided among several people) and parasailing at US$70 (£36) for a ride that will keep you aloft for between 8 and 12 giddy and vertiginous minutes.

The following are the best options for a gamut of outdoor activities.

CRUISES **Red Sail Sports** (see above) has a number of inexpensive ways you can go sailing in Cayman waters, including a glass-bottom boat ride costing US$30 (£16) without snorkeling equipment or US$40 (£21) with snorkeling equipment. It also offers sunset cruises costing US$35 (£18), as well as a 9am-to-1:15pm sail to Stingray City, with snorkeling equipment and lunch included in the price of US$80 (£42) per person. Children under 12 pay half price.

FISHING Grouper and snapper are most plentiful for those who bottom-fish along the reef. Deeper waters turn up barracuda and bonito. Sport-fishers from all over the world come to the Caymans for the big ones: tuna, wahoo, and marlin. Most hotels can make arrangements for charter boats; experienced guides are also available. **Bayside Water Sports**, from a base at the Morgan's Harbour Marina (© **345/949-3200**),

Tips Into the Deep: Submarine Dives

So scuba diving's not enough for you? You want to see the real undiscovered depths of the ocean? On Grand Cayman, you can take the *Atlantis* reef dive. It's expensive, and in some participants can induce severe feelings of claustrophobia, but it's a unique way to go underwater—and one of the island's most popular attractions.

The *Atlantis XI*, Harbour Avenue (© 345/949-7700), is a submersible that's 20m (66-ft.) long, weighs 80 tons, and was built to carry 48 passengers. You can view the reefs and colorful tropical fish through the 26 large viewpoints .6m (2 ft.) in diameter, as it cruises at a depth of 30m (100 ft.) through the maze of coral gardens at a speed of 1½ knots; a guide keeps you informed.

On the *Atlantis* Expedition dive, operated both day and night, you'll experience the reef and see the famous Cayman Wall; the dive lasts 55 minutes and costs US$84 (£44). Children 4 to 12 are charged US$49 (£25). *Atlantis XI* dives between 5 and 9 times a day, depending on the number of cruise ships moored offshore on any particular day. Advance reservations are recommended at least 2 days in advance.

offers deep-sea-fishing excursions in search of tuna, marlin, and wahoo on a variety of air-conditioned vessels with an experienced crew. Tours depart at 7am and noon, last half a day, and cost around US$800 (£416; a full day costs US$1,100/£572). The fee can be split among four to six people.

GOLF   As of this writing, only two golf courses were up and operational. Of those two, the 9-hole **Blue Tip** (© 345/943-9015) course is reserved only for residents of that organization's hotel or condo units. A third course, the Links at Safehaven, wasn't open as of early 2007, and plans on restricting access to members only. If you're a golfer, that leaves only the **Britannia Golf Club** (© 345/745-4653), a well-respected, open-to-the-public 9-hole golf course that's positioned across the avenue from the Hyatt Regency Grand Cayman Beach Suites. Designed by Jack Nicklaus, it charges greens fees of US$100 (£52) for 9 holes, or US$150 (£78) if you opt to play the course twice, thereby playing 18 holes. Cart rentals are included, but club rentals cost US$20 (£10) for 9 holes or US$40 (£21) for 18 holes. The **Britannia Bar and Grill** (© 345/745-4653), open daily for lunch and dinner, offers a view of the lake.

HIKING   The **Mastic Trail** is a restored 200-year-old footpath through a 2-million-year-old woodland area in the heart of the island. The trail lies west of Frank Sound Road, about a 45-minute drive from the heart of George Town, and showcases the reserve's natural attractions, including a native mangrove swamp, traditional agriculture, and an ancient woodland area—home to the largest variety of native plant and animal life found in the Cayman Islands.

Although the trail is supervised and maintained, during periods of heavy rain the southern end is likely to be flooded. The government therefore recommends hikers approach the trail from the northern end, off Further Road, as opposed to via the southern end, off Frank Sound Road.

Guided tours of the trail, organized by the **Cayman Islands National Trust**, are scheduled every Wednesday at 9am, and every fourth Saturday, also at 9am. Tours last 2 to 3 hours each, and are limited to a maximum of 15 participants. Reservations are strongly recommended, and the cost is US$25 (£13) per person. The hike is not recommended for children under 6, seniors, or persons with physical disabilities. Wear comfortable, sturdy shoes and carry water and insect repellent. For reservations, call The National Trust © **345/949-0121.** If the scheduled departure time for these organized tours isn't practical or convenient, you can stop into the headquarters of the National Trust, on South Church Street (© **345/949-0121**), Monday to Friday from 9am to 5pm for a self-guided walking tour/map of the trail. The guidebook/map, which describes the botanical and geological features you're likely to see en route, costs CI$5 (US$6.25/£3).

SCUBA DIVING & SNORKELING   **Red Sail Sports** (see above) offers beginners' scuba diving as well as excursions for the experienced. A two-tank morning dive includes exploration of two different dive sites at depths ranging from 15 to 30m (50–100 ft.), and costs US$110 (£57). Beginners can take a daily course that costs US$150 (£78) per person. See also "Cruises," above, for information on Red Sail Sports snorkel cruises.

The offshore waters of Grand Cayman are home to one of the most unusual underwater attractions in the world, **Stingray City** ☆☆. Set in the sun-flooded, 4m-deep (13-ft.) waters of North Sound, about 3km (2 miles) east of the island's northwestern tip, the site originated in the mid-1980s when local fishers cleaned their catch and dumped the offal overboard. They quickly noticed scores of stingrays (which usually eat marine crabs) feeding on the debris, a phenomenon that quickly attracted local divers and marine zoologists. Today, between 30 and 50 relatively tame stingrays hover in the waters around the site for daily handouts of squid and ballyhoo from increasing hordes of snorkelers and divers. To capitalize on the phenomenon, about half a dozen entrepreneurs lead expeditions from points along Seven Mile Beach, traveling around the landmass of Conch Point to the feeding grounds. The previously recommended **Red Sail Sports** offers one-tank scuba dives to Stingray City, priced at US$70 (£36), plus equipment, and snorkeling excursions to the site as well. Snorkel excursions cost between US$30 (£16) and US$80 (£42), depending on the time you intend to spend there, the distance the shuttle bus will have to travel to retrieve you at your hotel, and whether or not lunch is included as part of the experience. *Warning:* Stingrays possess deeply penetrating and viciously barbed stingers capable of inflicting painful damage to anyone who mistreats them. If you encounter one, be alert, and don't make any fast moves. (The rays can panic, we're told.) And above all, as the divers say, never try to grab one by the tail.

Despite the potential dangers, divers and snorkelers seem amazingly adept at feeding, petting, and stroking the velvet surfaces of these batlike creatures while avoiding unpleasant incidents.

You'll find plenty of concessions offering snorkel gear for rent along Seven Mile Beach. The snorkeling is great in the clear, warm waters here. Other popular sites are Parrot's Reef and Smith's Cove, south of George Town. Lush reefs abound with parrotfish, coral, sea fans, and sponges. Also great for snorkelers is Turtle Farm Reef, a short swim from shore, with a miniwall rising from a sandy bottom.

Another good dive outfit, **Tortuga Divers** (© **345/947-7449**), operates out of Morritt's Tortuga Club and Resort at East End, site of what's described as the best windsurfing conditions in the Cayman Islands, with easy access to the rich marine life. This outfitter caters to both experienced and novice divers, offering dives, whenever business justifies it, at 9am and 2pm. Half-day or full-day snorkeling adventures can also be arranged at the same time, and all types of gear are available for rent. The morning two-tank scuba dive costs US$110 (£57), the afternoon one-tank dive goes for US$75 (£39). A half-day's snorkeling costs US$50 (£26), going up to US$75 (£39) for a full day, the price including lunch.

TENNIS   A total of nine tennis courts are available to the public at the **Cayman Islands Tennis Club,** Ann Bonney Crescent, South Sound (© **345/949-9469**). The fee for up to 2 hours use of either asphalt or "classic clay" surfaced courts is CI$10 (US$13/£6) per person. Hours can vary, according to the season and the weather, so call ahead before coming here.

WINDSURFING   The best place for windsurfing on the island is the beachfront resort of **Morritt's Tortuga Club & Resort** at the East End (© **345/947-7449**). There, Tortuga Divers, an outfit that's associated with Red Sail Sports, charges US$35 (£18) for 1 hour, US$85 (£44) for 3 hours, and US$135 (£70) for 5 hours. A 1-hour lesson can be arranged for US$55 (£29), which is followed by a 1-hour practice session that's included in the price. The favorable windsurfing conditions here result from nearly constant winds blowing in from offshore, and an offshore reef that protects the waters of the lagoon in most cases from unpredictable waves.

EXPLORING THE ISLAND

The capital, **George Town,** can easily be explored in an afternoon; stop by for its restaurants and shops (and banks!)—not sights. The town does have a clock monument to King George V and the post office on Edward Street is the oldest government building in use in the Caymans. Stamps sold here are collected avidly.

Even as late as January of 2007, the island's premier museum, the **Cayman Islands National Museum,** Harbor Drive, in George Town (© **345/949-8368**), still remains closed after serious hurricane damage in 2004. It occupies an antique building directly on the water. During the emergency construction following the devastation of the hurricane, rehabilitation of this museum was "de-prioritized," so check its status before heading here.

The veranda-fronted building once served as the island's courthouse. Today the formal exhibits include a collection of Caymanian artifacts collected by Ira Thompson beginning in the 1930s, and the museum incorporates a gift shop, theater, cafe, and more than 2,000 items portraying the natural, social, and cultural history of the Caymans. You might also go to **Hell!** At the north end of West Bay Beach is a jagged piece of rock named Hell by a former commissioner. There the postmistress will stamp "Hell, Grand Cayman" on your postcard to send back to the U.S.

Cayman Turtle Farm ⟨, at Boatswain's Beach, Northwest Point (© **345/ 949-3894**), in the heart of the West Bay district, about a 25-minute drive north of George Town, is the only green-sea-turtle farm of its kind in the world. Once the islands had a multitude of turtles in the surrounding waters (which is why Columbus called the islands "Las Tortugas"), but today these creatures are sadly few in number, and the green sea turtle has been designated an endangered species. (You cannot bring turtle products into the United States.) The turtle farm was radically upgraded and enlarged in the wake of hurricane damage in 2004, having reopened in September 2006 in new premises across the road from its previous location. Its main function involves providing the local market with edible turtle meat (preventing the need to hunt turtles in the wild) and to replenish the waters with hatchling and yearling turtles. Visitors today can observe about a hundred circular concrete tanks in which these sea creatures exist in every stage of development; the hope is that one day their population in the sea will regain its former status. Turtles here range in size from 6 ounces to 600 pounds. At a snack bar and restaurant, you can sample turtle dishes. There's a well-stocked gift shop on site. The turtle farm is open daily from 8am to 5:30pm (last admission is at 4:30pm).

Admission, which includes the tour, costs US$50 (£26) for adults, US$25 (£13) for children ages 2 to 12, free for children under 2.

If you're driving, you might want to go along **South Sound Road,** which is lined with pines and, in places, old wooden Caymanian houses. After leaving the houses behind, you'll find good spots for a picnic.

Pedro St. James National Historic Site, Savannah (*©* **345/947-3329**), is a restored great house dating from 1780, when only 400 people lived on the island. It lasted until 1970 when it was destroyed by fire. Now rebuilt, it is the centerpiece of a new heritage park with a visitor center and an audiovisual theater with a laser light show. Because of its size, the great house was called "the Castle" by generations of Caymanians. Its primary historic importance dates from December 5, 1831, when residents met here to elect Cayman's first legislative assembly. The great house sits atop a limestone bluff with a panoramic view of the sea. Guests enter via a US$1.5-million visitor center with a landscaped courtyard, a gift shop, and a cafe. Self-guided tours are possible. You can explore the house's wide verandas, rough-hewn timber beams, gabled framework, mahogany floors and staircases, and wide-beam wooden ceilings. Guides in 18th-century costumes are on hand to answer questions. Admission is US$10 (£5.20) for adults, and free for those 12 and under. Hours are daily from 9am to 5pm. A video, which describes the site's role within the history of the nation and the labor expended to restore it, is screened every hour on the hour, daily from 10am to 4pm.

On the road again, you reach **Bodden Town,** once the largest settlement on the island. At Gun Square, two cannons commanded the channel through the reef. They are now stuck muzzle-first into the ground.

On the way to **East End,** just before Old Isaac Village, you'll see the onshore sprays of water shooting up like geysers. These are called blowholes, and they sound like the roar of a lion.

Later, you'll spot the fluke of an anchor sticking up from the ocean floor. As the story goes, this is a relic of the famous "Wreck of the Ten Sails" in 1788. A more recent wreck can also be seen—the *Ridgefield,* a 7,500-ton Liberty ship from New England, which struck the reef in 1943.

Old Man Bay is reached by a road that opened in 1983. From here you can travel along the north shore of the island to **Rum Point,** which has a good beach and is a fine place to end your island tour. Rum Point got its name from barrels of rum that once washed ashore here after a shipwreck. Today, it is dreamy and quaint, surrounded by towering casuarina trees blowing in the trade winds. Most of these trees have hammocks hanging from their trunks, inviting you to partake of the leisurely life. With its cays, reefs, mangroves, and shallows, Rum Point is a refuge that extends west and south for 11km (7 miles). It divides the two "arms" of Grand Cayman. The sound's many spits of land and its plentiful lagoons are ideal for snorkeling, swimming, wading, and birding. It you get hungry, drop in to the Wreck Bar for a juicy burger. After visiting Rum Point, you can head back toward **Old Man Village,** where you can go south along a cross-island road through savanna country that will eventually lead you west to George Town.

On 24 hectares (59 acres) of rugged wooded land off Frank Sound Road, North Side, a 45-minute drive east from Georgetown, the **Queen Elizabeth II Botanic Park** (*© 345/947-9462*) offers visitors a short walk through a tract that includes wetland, swamp, dry thicket, mahogany trees, orchids, and bromeliads. Hurricane Ivan destroyed some of the vegetation, but since then, the park has grown back. The walking trail is 1km (.6 mile) long. You'll probably see chickatees, which are freshwater turtles found only on the Caymans and in Cuba. Occasionally you'll spot the rare Grand Cayman parrot, or perhaps the anole lizard, with its cobalt-blue throat pouch. Even rarer is the endangered blue iguana. The park is open daily April to September 9am to 6:30pm; October to March 9am to 5:30pm. The last ticket is sold an hour before closing. Admission is CI$6 (US$7.50/£3.60) for adults, CI$4 (US$5/£2.40) for children, and free for children 5 and under. There's a visitor center with changing exhibitions, plus a canteen for food and refreshments. It's set adjacent to the woodland trail and includes a heritage garden with a re-creation of a traditional Cayman home, garden, and farm; a floral garden with .6 hectares (1½ acres) of flowering plants; and a .8-hectare (2-acre) lake with three islands, home to many native birds.

GRAND CAYMAN AFTER DARK

Lone Star Bar & Grill, West Bay Road (*© 345/945-5175*), across the road from the Hyatt Regency Grand Cayman Beach Suites, is a transplanted corner of the Texas Panhandle. You can enjoy burgers in the dining room or head immediately for the bar in back. Here, beneath murals of Lone Star beauties, you can sip lime and strawberry margaritas and watch several sports events simultaneously on 14 different TV screens. Monday and Thursday are all-you-can-eat fajita nights, costing CI$13 (US$16/£7.80), and Tuesday is all-you-can-eat spicy tacos, for CI$10 (US$13/£6); Wednesday is all-you-can-eat surf and turf, priced at CI$27 (US$34/£16). Classier and in its own way more intriguing is the Reef Grill and the **Royal Palms Beach Club,** West Bay Road (*© 345/945-6358*), with a beachfront bar that's open to the trade winds where you can dance the night away in the moonlight. Local bands play here every Friday night beginning at 9pm, and every Thursday and Saturday night beginning at 8pm.

My Bar, on the grounds of the Sunset House Hotel, 390 S. Church St., on the southern periphery of George Town (*© 345/949-7111*), is a place that's very far removed from Seven Mile Beach. It attracts the local dive shop staff and lots of lawyers, especially on Fridays. It has the highest Polynesian-style thatch roof on Grand Cayman, and some of the stiffest drinks. Open Monday to Thursday and Saturday from 9am to midnight, Friday 9am to 1am.

Fidel Murphy's, in the Queen's Court Shopping Center, West Bay Road (*© 345/949-5189*), is the unofficial Irish capital on Grand Cayman, with a wood-paneled premises that would have made James Joyce feel at home and foaming mugsful of every imaginable kind of beer and "spirits." Open Monday to Friday from 10:30am to 1am, Saturday and Sunday from 10:30am to midnight.

The Bamboo Lounge, on the ground floor of the Hyatt Regency Grand Cayman Beach Suites, West Bay Road (*© 345/947-8744*), is about as urban and trendy a venue as you'll find on island, with a red-black-and-high-octane décor that's as pan-Asian and fusion as its cuisine.

An earthier and more down-to-earth alternative is the bar at **Morgan's Harbour Marina,** Morgan's Harbour (② **345/946-7049**). Thanks to the raffish charm of its Austria-born owner, Richard Schweiger, it's developed a fast reputation for throwing into the same workaday setting millionaires from New York with local roustabouts and marina crew members in ways that can lead to unexpectedly surreal dialogues. Shoehorned between gas pumps at the nearby marina and stocks of provisions for outfitting boats, there's a battered bar area serving stiff drinks, fresh lobster, and unassuming platters of burgers, salads, and steaks, priced at CI$5 to CI$26 (US$6.25–US$33/ £3–£16). It's open daily from 7am to 1am.

3 Cayman Brac ⟨★⟩

The "middle" island of the Caymans was given the name *Brac* (Gaelic for "bluff") by 17th-century Scottish fishers who settled here. The bluff for which the 19km-long (12-mile) island was named is a towering limestone plateau rising 42m (138 ft.) above the sea, covering the eastern half of Cayman Brac. Caymanians refer to the island simply as Brac, and its 1,400 inhabitants, a hospitable bunch, are known as Brackers. In the early 18th century the Caymans were occupied by pirates, and Edward Teach, the infamous Blackbeard, is supposed to have spent quite a bit of time around Cayman Brac. The island is about 145km (90 miles) east of Grand Cayman.

There are more than 170 caves honeycombing the limestone heights of the island. Some of the caves are at the bluff's foot; others can be reached only by climbing over jagged limestone rock. One of the biggest is Great Cave, which has a number of chambers. Harmless fruit bats cling to the roofs of the caverns.

On the south side of the bluff you won't see many people, and the only sounds are the sea crashing against the lavalike shore. The island's herons, wild green parrots, and a wide diversity of other bird species can be seen here. Most of the Brackers live on the north side, many in traditional wooden seaside cottages, some built by the island's pioneers. Given the variety of flowers, shrubs, and fruit trees in many of the yards, the islanders must all have green thumbs. You'll see poinciana trees, bougainvillea, Cayman orchids, croton, hibiscus, aloe, sea grapes, cactus, and coconut and cabbage palms. Gardeners grow cassava, pumpkins, breadfruit, yams, and sweet potatoes.

There are no actual towns, only settlements, such as Stake Bay (the "capital"), Spot Bay, the Creek, Tibbitts Turn, the Bight, and West End, where the airport is.

ESSENTIALS

GETTING THERE   Flights from Grand Cayman to Cayman Brac are operated by **Cayman Airways** and its affiliate, **Cayman Express** (② **800/422-9626** in the U.S. and Canada, or 345/949-8200; www.caymanairways.com). Between the two companies, there are between four and seven flights a day, depending on the day of the week, between Grand Cayman and Cayman Brac. The cost of a round-trip ticket is around US$132 (£69) per person. Note in advance that the larger planes (such as the 737s, with 122 seats) flying this route allow twice the luggage allotment per passenger, without payment of additional supplements of the 18-seaters, so if you have a lot of luggage, it's wise to opt for a flight on one of the 737s. An outfit that charters flights within the Cayman Islands is **Island Air Flight Charters** (② **345/949-5252;** www.islandaircayman.com).

VISITOR INFORMATION   A little office, the **Cayman Brac Tourist Office,** has opened at West End Community Park (② **345/948-1649**). If you're stopping in, call first to see if anybody's going to be there.

EMERGENCIES   There's a small hospital, the 18-bed **Faith Hospital** at Stake Bay (© **345/948-2243**). For emergencies of any kind on Cayman Brac, dial © 911.

ACCOMMODATIONS

Brac Caribbean Beach Resort ⊛

The largest condo structure on the island offers 16 bright, spacious two-bedroom/two-bathroom or two-bedroom/three-bathroom condos on a white sandy beach, along with a pool and scuba-diving program. Each unit has a full-size refrigerator with an icemaker and a microwave, and 12 units open onto private balconies. A variety of items, including breakfast food, are stocked before your arrival. The master bedroom is furnished with a queen-size bed, the guest bedrooms with twin beds. Bathrooms are medium in size, each with a tub/shower combination. The units are rather simply furnished in a Caribbean tropical motif. The hotel offers some of the best dining on the island, at the Captain's Table (see below).

Stake Bay (P.O. Box 4), Cayman Brac, B.W.I. © **345/948-2265.** Fax 345/948-1111. www.866thebrac.com. 16 units. Winter US$185 (£96) apt for 2, US$245 (£127) apt for 4 and weekly US$1,100 (£572) apt for 2, US$1,600 (£832) apt for 4; off season US$139 (£72) apt for 2, US$184 (£96) apt for 4 and weekly US$825 (£429) apt for 2, US$1,200 (£624) apt for 4. Dive packages from US$888 (£462) per person double occupancy, including 7 nights stay and 5 days of 2-tank dives. AE, MC, V. **Amenities:** Restaurant; bar; outdoor pool; scuba diving; snorkeling; coin-operated laundry; nonsmoking rooms. *In room:* A/C, ceiling fans, TV, kitchen, beverage maker.

Brac Reef Beach Resort ⊛

On a sandy plot of land on the south shore 3km (2 miles) east of the airport, near some of the best snorkeling in the region, this family-friendly, family-run resort contains motel-style units comfortably furnished with carpeting, ceiling fans, air-conditioning, and tub/shower combination bathrooms. Durable and resilient, it's the most visible hotel on Cayman Brac. Once the location was little more than a maze of sea grapes, a few of whose venerable trunks still rise amid the picnic tables, hammocks, and boardwalks. There are still lots of nature trails surrounding the resort, good for bird-watching. Don't expect grandeur or anything approaching urban style or posh: It simply isn't part of the equation here.

Lunches are informal affairs, and dinners are most often served buffet style under the stars.

P.O. Box 56, KY2-2001 Cayman Brac, B.W.I. © **800/594-0843** or 727/369-2507 for reservations in the U.S. and Canada, or 345/948-1323. www.bracreef.com. 40 units. Winter US$195–US$245 (£101–£127) double; off season US$140–US$190 (£73–£99) double. Dive and FAP packages available. AE, MC, V. **Amenities:** Restaurant; bar; pool; tennis court; day spa; Jacuzzi; dive shop; reef fishing; snorkeling; babysitting; laundry service; nonsmoking rooms. *In room:* A/C, ceiling fans, cable TV, hair dryer.

Walton's Mango Manor ⊛⊛

Unique on Cayman Brac, this is a personalized, intimate B&B that's more richly decorated, more elegant, and more appealing than you might have thought possible in such a remote place. Originally the home of a sea captain, it was moved to a less exposed location and rebuilt from salvaged materials shortly after the disastrous hurricane of 1932. Set on 1.6 hectares (4 acres) on the island's north shore, within a lush garden, it contains intriguing touches such as a banister salvaged from the mast of a 19th-century schooner. The best accommodations are on the upper floor and have narrow balconies with sea views. Each room has a small bathroom equipped with a shower stall. There is also a two-bedroom, two-bathroom luxury villa, the perfect getaway for two to four guests. The villa contains a kitchen, washer/dryer, phone, TV, and both air-conditioning and ceiling fans. Your hosts are Brooklyn-born Lynne Walton and her husband, George, a former USAF major who retired to his native Cayman Brac.

Stake Bay (P.O. Box 56), Cayman Brac, KY2-2101 Cayman Islands. ©/fax **345/948-0518**. www.waltonsmango manor.com. 6 units. Winter US$115–US$130 (£60–£68) double; off season US$100–US$115 (£52–£59) double; year-round villa US$185 (£96) daily or US$1,200 (£624) weekly for 1-2 persons; US$210 (£109) per night or US$1,400 (£728) per week for 3-4 persons. Rates for doubles include full breakfast. MC, V. *In room:* A/C, no phone.

DINING

Biggie's AMERICAN/CONTINENTAL   It's the newest restaurant on the island, the kind of place that generated a lot of buzz when it first opened, and a place whose staff and owner (Kent Rankin) work hard to keep clients happy. It faces a traffic roundabout on the island's West End, occupying a peachy-white painted dining room with clean white napery and glass-topped tables. Lunches focus on an all-you-can-eat American-style buffet of salads and hot foods; dinners are more elaborate, more formal, and permeated with continental flair, with lots of emphasis on seafood, chicken, beef, and pastas, some of them all-vegetarian.

West End. © **345/948-2449**. Reservations recommended. Lunch buffet CI$15 (US$19/£8.95); dinner main courses CI$13–CI$45 (US$16–US$56/£7.80–£27). MC, V. Daily 11am–2:30pm and 5:30–9pm.

Captain's Table AMERICAN   The decor here is vaguely nautical, with oars over and around the bar and pieces of boats forming the restaurant's entryway. The restaurant offers both indoor, air-conditioned seating and outdoor, poolside dining. Every Saturday night, its karaoke party draws in more business than any other bar on the island. Begin a meal here with shrimp and lobster cocktail or a conch fritter, and then try one of the soups, such as black bean or a tomato-based conch chowder. Main dishes include everything from the catch of the day, often served pan-fried, to barbecue ribs. Lunch features burgers, salads, and sandwiches.

In Brac Caribbean Beach Village, Stake Bay. © **345/948-1418**. Reservations recommended. Dinner main courses CI$15–CI$30 (US$19–US$38/£9–£18); lunch main courses from CI$6–CI$10 (US$7.50–US$13/£3.60–£6). AE, MC, V. Daily 11am–3pm and 6–9:30pm; bar open daily 11:30am–midnight.

FUN ON & OFF THE BEACH

The biggest lure on Cayman Brac is the variety of **watersports**—swimming, fishing, snorkeling, and some of the world's best diving. There are undersea walls on both the north and south sides of the island, with stunning specimens lining their sides. The big attraction for divers is the **MV *Tibbetts*,** a 99m-long (325-ft.) Russian frigate resting in 30m (100 ft.) of water, a relic of the Cold War sunk in September 1996.

Hatches into the ship have been barred off to promote diver safety. Over the years, marine life has become more and more pronounced on this relic. For information on diving in Cayman Brac, click on www.divecayman.ky.

History buffs might check out the **Cayman Brac Museum,** in the former Government Administration Building, Stake Bay (© **345/948-2622**), which has an interesting collection of Caymanian antiques, including pieces rescued from shipwrecks and items from the 18th century. Hours are Monday to Friday from 9am to noon and 1 to 4pm, Saturday from 9am to noon. Admission is free, but donations are accepted.

4 Little Cayman ★

The smallest of the Cayman Islands, cigar-shaped Little Cayman has only about 170 permanent inhabitants. About 15km (10 miles) long and 2km (1¼ miles) across at its widest point, it lies about 120km (75 miles) northeast of Grand Cayman and some 8km (5 miles) from Cayman Brac. The entire island is coral and sand.

The islands of the Caymans are mountaintops of the long-submerged Sierra Maestra Range, which runs north and into Cuba. Coral formed layers over the underwater peaks, eventually creating the islands. Beneath Little Cayman's Bloody Bay is one of the mountain's walls—a stunning sight for snorkelers and divers.

This is a near-perfect place for diving and fishing. The late Jacques Cousteau hailed the waters around the little island as one of the three finest diving spots in the world. The flats on Little Cayman are said to offer the best bonefishing in the world, and a brackish inland pool can be fished for tarpon. Even if you don't dive or fish, you can row 182m (597 ft.) off Little Cayman to isolated and uninhabited Owen Island, where you can swim at the sandy beach and picnic by a blue lagoon.

There may still be pirate treasure buried on the island, but it's thought to be in the dense interior of what is now the largest bird sanctuary in the Caribbean. In addition to having the largest population of rock iguanas in the entire Caribbean, which are easy to spot, Little Cayman is also home to one of the oldest species of reptiles in the New World—the tree-climbing *Anulis maynardi* (which is known by no other name). This rare lizard is difficult to spot because the females are green, the males brown, and both blend into local vegetation.

Blossom Village, the island's "capital," is on the southwest coast.

Most visitors fly from Grand Cayman to Little Cayman aboard any of the several daily flights operated by Cayman Express, a subdivision of **Cayman Airways** (© **800/422-9626** in the U.S. and Canada, or 345/949-8200; www.caymanairways.com), the national carrier. The cost of round-trip passage aboard any of its 18-seater planes is US$131 (£68). Since luggage is limited, without payment of an additional surcharge, to two suitcases per person, totaling no more than 55 pounds for both bags, it's wise to pack lightly. Airplanes only land and take off on Little Cayman during daylight hours.

ACCOMMODATIONS

Little Cayman Beach Resort ★★   Lying on the south coast, this resort was built in 1991 and enlarged and renovated in 2005. It's close to many of the island's diving and sporting attractions, including the South Hole Sound Lagoon's bonefishing. It's popular with anglers, divers, bird-watchers, and adventurous types. The hotel, owned by Michael Tibbetts, lies only 1.5km (1 mile) from the Edward Bodden Airport and it has a white-sand beach fringing a shallow, reef-protected bay. It is divided into three

Little Cayman

pastel, coral-colored, two-story buildings with gingerbread trim. The most desirable units are the 12 oceanfront rooms. Each unit has a ceiling fan, a color scheme of creams and tones of green, and each has an inviting, airy atmosphere. Each unit has one king-size or two double beds, plus a combination bathroom (tub/shower).

Blossom Village, Little Cayman, Cayman Islands, B.W.I. © **800/327-3835** in the U.S. and Canada, or 345/948-1033. Fax 345/948-1040. www.littlecayman.com. 40 units. Winter US$169–US$242 (£88–£126) double; off season US$149–US$230 (£77–£120) double. MAP (breakfast and dinner) costs US$55 (£29) extra per person per day. Dive packages available. AE, MC, V. **Amenities:** Restaurant; bar; outdoor pool; tennis court; health club; spa; Jacuzzi; sauna; watersports; free use of bicycles; babysitting; laundry service; nonsmoking rooms. *In room:* A/C, ceiling fan, TV, kitchenette, beverage maker, hair dryer, no phone.

Pirates Point Resort, Ltd.   For watersports or just relaxing, this resort near West End Point offers a family environment with gourmet cuisine, although it's a notch down from Little Cayman Beach Resort. The place has remodeled rooms, and a non-air-conditioned family cottage with two large rooms. In addition, it has four seaside cottages, with balconies overlooking Preston Bay. The bathrooms are well maintained, with shower stalls.

The resort's packages include a room, three excellent meals per day with appropriate wines and all alcoholic beverages, and two-tank boat dives daily, featuring tours of the Bloody Bay Wall and Jackson Reef. Other activities include snorkeling, bird-watching, and exploring.

The food is excellent. The owner and manager, Texas-born Gladys Howard, is an award-winning cookbook author and a graduate of Cordon Bleu in Paris. She has studied with such stars as the late Julia Child, Jacques Pepin, and James Beard. She uses fresh fruits and vegetables grown locally, as well as local seafood.

Preston Bay, Little Cayman, Cayman Islands, B.W.I. © **345/948-1010.** Fax 345/948-1011. www.piratespointresort.com. 10 units. Winter US$675 (£351) nondiver, US$870 (£452) diver; off-season US$597 (£310) nondiver, US$780 (£406) diver. Rates include 3 meals a day for 3 days, plus 3 days of diving at the higher rate. Children 5–12 free in parent's room. MC, V. No children under 5. **Amenities:** Restaurant; bar; outdoor pool; Jacuzzi; sauna; bonefishing; diving; snorkeling; tarpon fishing; coin-operated laundry; off-island picnics; rooms for those w/limited mobility. *In room:* A/C (in some), no phone.

DINING

Birds of Paradise AMERICAN/CONTINENTAL   This spot caters primarily to Little Cayman Beach Resort guests but welcomes anyone. The specialty is buffet-style dinners—the kind your parents might have enjoyed back in the 1950s or 1960s. Saturday night features the island's most generous barbecue spread—all the ribs, fish, and Jamaican-style jerk chicken you'd want. On other nights, try the prime rib, fresh fish

Caribbean style (your best bet), or chicken (either Kiev or *cordon bleu*). There's a freshly made salad bar, and homemade desserts are yummy, especially the Key lime pie. At night, opt for an outdoor table under the stars.

At Little Cayman Beach Resort. ℂ **345/948-1033.** Reservations recommended for dinner for nonguests. Breakfast CI$12 (US$15/£7.20); lunch CI$17 (US$21/£10); dinner CI$35 (US$44/£21). AE, MC, V. Daily 7–8:30am, 12:30–1:30pm, and 6:30–8pm.

The Hungry Iguana AMERICAN/CARIBBEAN At the beach, you'll spot the mammoth iguana mural that marks this place immediately. The island's tastiest dishes are served here, a winning combination of standard American fare and some zesty flavors from islands to the south. It's the rowdiest place on Little Cayman, especially the sports bar with its satellite TV in the corner, a sort of TGI Friday's atmosphere. Lunch is the usual burgers and fries along with some well-stuffed sandwiches. We prefer the grilled chicken salad. Dinner gets a little more elaborate—there's usually a special meat dish of the day, depending on the market (supplies are shipped in once a week by barge). The chef always seems willing to prepare a steak as you like it. Marinated conch with homemade chips is another tasty choice.

Paradise Resort. ℂ **345/948-0007.** Reservations recommended. Lunch main courses CI$7–CI$16 (US$8.75–US$20/ £4.20–£9.60); dinner main courses CI$15–CI$40 (US$19–US$50/£9–£24). AE, MC, V. Daily noon–2:30pm and 5:30–9pm; bar Mon–Fri noon–1am, Sat–Sun noon–midnight.

SPORTS & OTHER OUTDOOR PURSUITS

The **Governor Gore Bird Sanctuary** ☆ is home to some 5,000 pairs of red-footed boobies. As far as it is known, this is the largest colony of such birds in the Western Hemisphere. The sanctuary, which is near the small airport, is also home to dramatic colonies of snowy egrets and black frigates. Many bird-watchers from the U.S. fly into Little Cayman just to see these bird colonies.

The best **fishing** is at Bloody Bay, lying off the island's north coast. It is especially noted for its bonefishing and tarpon catches. For fishing, contact **Sam McCoy's Diving and Fishing Lodge** (ℂ **345/948-0026**).

The **Bloody Bay Wall** ☆☆, the best dive site on island and one of the great dive spots in the Caymans, lies just 20 minutes offshore by boat. The drop here begins at only 6m (20 ft.) but plunges to more than 360m (1,180 ft.). For more information about how to enjoy it, click on www.divecayman.ky or call **Paradise Divers** at ℂ **877/ 322-9626** in the U.S., or 345/948-0001; fax 345/948-0002.

10

Curaçao

Curaçao (Coo-ra-*sow*), together with Bonaire, St. Eustatius, St. Maarten, and Saba, is in the Kingdom of the Netherlands as part of the Netherlands Antilles. Just 56km (35 miles) north of the coast of Venezuela, Curaçao, the "C" of the Caribbean's Dutch ABC (Aruba, Bonaire, and Curaçao) islands, is the most populous of the Netherlands Antilles. Visitors come for its distinctive culture, warm people, duty-free shopping, lively casinos, and watersports. Fleets of tankers head out from its harbor to bring refined oil to all parts of the world. If you want grand high-rise resorts on spectacular beaches, head for Aruba (see chapter 5). Curaçao has a few middle-bracket resorts on the beach, mostly along the island's southern coast, but we've always found the shopping and cultural experiences here more appealing than the beaches.

Alonso de Ojeda and Amerigo Vespucci spotted Curaçao in 1499. The Spaniards exterminated all but 75 members of a branch of the peaceful Arawaks. However, they in turn were ousted by the Dutch in 1634, who also had to fight off French and English invasions.

The Dutch made the island a tropical Holland in miniature. Peter Stuyvesant ruled Curaçao in 1644. The island was turned into a Dutch Gibraltar, bristling with forts. Thick ramparts guarded the harbor's narrow entrance; the hilltop forts (many now converted into restaurants) protected the coastal approaches.

In the 20th century, Curaçao remained sleepy until 1915, when the Royal Dutch/Shell Company built one of the world's largest oil refineries here to process crude oil from Venezuela. Workers from some 50 countries poured onto the island, turning Curaçao into a multicultural, cosmopolitan community of about 171,000. Curaçao has its own governmental authority, relying on the Netherlands only for defense and foreign affairs.

The largest of the Netherlands Antilles, Curaçao is 60km long (37 miles) and 11km (6¾ miles) across at its widest point. Because of all that early Dutch building, Curaçao is the most important island architecturally in the entire West Indies, with more European flavor than anywhere else. After leaving the capital, **Willemstad,** you plunge into a strange, desertlike countryside evocative of the U.S. Southwest. The relatively arid landscape is studded with three-pronged cactus, spiny-leafed aloe, and divi-divi trees, with their windblown foliage. Classic Dutch-style windmills are scattered in and around Willemstad and in parts of the countryside.

1 Essentials

VISITOR INFORMATION

In the United States, contact the **Curaçao Tourist Board** at 3361 SW 3rd Ave., Suite 102, Plantation, FL 33145 (© **800/3-CURACAO**). You can also point your Web browser to **www.curacao-tourism.com**.

> *Fun Fact* **Special Events**
>
> The big event of the year is the **Curaçao Carnival,** which starts on New Year's Day, with various festivities extending until the day before Ash Wednesday. The schedule is available at the tourism office. The most fun events, similar to hoe-downs, are called "jump-ups." The highlight of carnival is the **Festival di Tumba,** the second week in February, in which the island's musicians vie for prizes in a hot contest. Other carnival events include the crowning of a queen and king, street parades, concerts, and even a children's carnival.

Once you're on the island, go to the **Curaçao Tourist Board,** Pietermaai 19 (© 599/9-434-8200).

GETTING THERE

The air routes to **Curaçao International Airport,** Plaza Margareth Abraham (© 599/9-839-3100), are firmly linked to those leading to nearby Aruba. In recent years, however, some airlines have initiated nonstop routings into Curaçao from such international hubs as Miami.

American Airlines (© 800/433-7300 in the U.S. and Canada; www.aa.com) flies daily to Curaçao from Miami; it departs late enough in the day to permit easy connections from cities all over the northeastern U.S. American also offers flights to neighboring Aruba, from New York, Miami, and San Juan, Puerto Rico. American Airlines also offers discounted hotel/airfare packages. The regional affiliate of American Airlines, **American Eagle,** flies from San Juan to Curaçao.

GETTING AROUND

BY RENTAL CAR   Because all points of interest on Curaçao are easily accessible via paved roads, you may want to rent a car. U.S., British, and Canadian visitors can use their own licenses, if valid. *Note:* Traffic moves on the right. International road signs are observed.

Avis (© 800/331-1212 in the U.S. and Canada, or 599/9-868-1163; www.avis.com) and **Budget** (© 800/527-0700 in the U.S. and Canada, or 599/9-868-3420; www.budgetrentacar.com) offer some of the lowest rates. Budget usually offers the best deal if it has compact cars with manual transmissions in stock. **Hertz** (© 800/654-3131 in the U.S. and Canada, or 599/9-888-0088; www.hertz.com) is also on island. Rentals are cheaper if you reserve from North America at least a week before your departure, and rates vary depending on the various times of the year and seasonal promotions.

Local car-rental firms include **Rent a Yellow,** Cascoreweg 33 (© 599/9-767-3777). The lowest rates are for vehicles without air-conditioning, costing from $21 (£11) daily. Rates include tax and insurance.

BY TAXI   Taxis are unmetered, so ask your driver to quote a price before you get in. Drivers are supposed to carry an official rate sheet, which they'll produce upon request. Charges go up by 25% after 11pm. Tipping isn't customary among islanders, but from tourists, drivers will appreciate a discretionary 10% tip, especially if they've helped with your luggage. The fare from the airport to Willemstad is about $20 (£10),

Avila Beach Hotel **7**
Breezes Curaçao **9**
Chogogo Resort **11**
Curaçao Marriott Beach Resort
 & Emerald Casino **3**
Floris Suite Hotel **4**
Habitat Curaçao **1**
Hilton Curaçao Resort **5**
Hotel Holland **2**
Kurá Hulanda Spa and Casino **6**
Lions Dive & Beach Resort **10**
Plaza Hotel Curaçao **8**

and the cost can be split among four passengers. If a piece of luggage is so big that the trunk lid won't close, you'll be assessed a surcharge of $1 (50p).

In town, the best place to get a taxi is on the Otrabanda side of the floating bridge. To summon a cab, call ☏ **599/9-869-0752.** Cabbies will usually give you a tour of the island for around $30 (£16) per hour for up to four passengers.

BY BUS Some hotels operate a free shuttle that takes you from the suburbs to the shopping district of Willemstad. A fleet of DAF yellow buses operates from Wilhelmina Plein, near the shopping center, to most parts of Curaçao. Some limousines function as buses. If you see one listing your destination, you can hail it at any of the designated bus stops.

FAST FACTS: Curaçao

Banks Normal bank hours are Monday to Friday from 8am to 3:30pm. The **Banco Popular** and the **Bank of America** remain open during the lunch hour (noon–1pm), doing business Monday to Friday from 9am to 3pm. Banks and ATMs can be found in Willemstad.

Currency While Canadian and U.S. dollars are accepted for purchases on the island, the official currency is the **Netherlands Antillean florin (NAf),** also called a **guilder,** which is divided into 100 NA (Netherlands Antillean) cents. The exchange rate as of this writing is US$1 to 1.77 NAf (1 NAf = US56¢). Shops, hotels, and restaurants usually accept most major U.S. and Canadian credit cards. *Unless otherwise specified, prices in this chapter are quoted in U.S. dollars and British pounds.*

Documents To enter Curaçao, U.S. or Canadian citizens need proof of citizenship, such as a birth certificate or a passport, along with a return or continuing airline ticket out of the country and photo ID. (We recommend that you bring a passport.) British subjects need a valid passport.

Electricity The electricity is 110- to 130-volt AC (50 cycles), the same as in North America, although many hotels have transformers for European appliances.

Emergencies For **police,** call ⓒ **911.** For **ambulance,** call ⓒ **912.** For **fire,** call ⓒ **115.**

Hospital The **St. Elisabeth Hospital,** Breedestraat 193 (ⓒ **599/9-462-4900**), near Otrabanda in Willemstad, is one of the most up-to-date facilities in the Caribbean.

Language Dutch, Spanish, and English are spoken on Curaçao, along with Papiamento, a patois that combines the three major tongues with Amerindian and African dialects. Most people in the tourism industry speak English, but you can always thank them by saying *masha danki* (*mas*-ha-dank).

Safety Although Curaçao is not plagued with crime, it's wise to safeguard your valuables.

Taxes Curaçao levies a room tax of 12% on accommodations and a $3 (£1.55) daily (per room) energy tax on all hotels. There's a departure tax of $22 (£11).

Telephone To call Curaçao from the United States, dial **011** (the international access code), then **599** (the country code for Curaçao), and then **9** (the area code) and the local number. Once on Curaçao, to call another number on the island, only the local seven-digit number is necessary; to make calls to an off-island destination, dial **021** and then the area code and number. You can reach **AT&T Direct** on the island by dialing ⓒ **800/225-5288.**

Time Curaçao is on Atlantic Standard Time year-round, 1 hour ahead of Eastern Standard Time and the same as eastern daylight saving time.

Water The water comes from a modern desalination plant and is safe to drink.

Weather Curaçao has an average temperature of 81°F (27°C); trade winds keep the island quite comfortable. It's flat and arid, with an average rainfall of only 22 inches per year.

2 Accommodations

Most hotels are in the capital of Willemstad or in one of the suburbs, which lie only 10 to 15 minutes from the shopping center. The bigger hotels often have free shuttle buses running into town, and most have their own beaches and pools.

Curaçao is a bustling commercial center, and the downtown hotels often fill up fast with business travelers as well as visitors from neighboring countries such as Venezuela. It's important to reserve well in advance.

When making reservations, ask if the room tax and service charge are included in the price you're quoted. Be sure to take a look at the section "Packages for the Independent Traveler" in chapter 2 for money-saving tips.

EXPENSIVE

Avila Beach Hotel 𝒦 Set on a beach, this hotel has more charm, atmosphere, and personality than the resorts described below. It consists of a beautifully restored 200-year-old mansion and a large extension, called La Belle Alliance. In 2006 it opened a new annex, the Octagon Wing, containing 68 suites, the most desirable of the accommodations found here. The mansion was converted into a hotel in 1949, and today attracts the royals of the Netherlands. Each of the rooms in the newer Blues Wing has a balcony with an ocean view; some also contain kitchenettes. The rooms in the main mansion, though rather basic and small, still have charm. Most units have a king-size bed or full-size beds. The newer units have combination tub/showers, whereas some of the smaller rentals are shower only. The hotel lies on the shore road leading east out of the city from the shopping center.

The romantic, open-air Belle Terrace, shaded by huge trees, features a full a la carte menu of well-prepared international food. Blues, an elevated restaurant/bar at the end of the pier, caters to small, informal parties with a taste for jazz, swing, and, of course, blues (see "Dining," below). Antillean nights feature local cuisine and live music, and there are barbecues Saturday night.

Penstraat 130–134 (P.O. Box 791), Willemstad, Curaçao, N.A. ℭ **800/747-8162** in the U.S., or 599/9-461-4377. Fax 599/9-461-1493. www.avilahotel.com. 137 units. Winter $250–$410 (£130–£213) double, $360–$1,200 (£187–£624) suite; off season $200–$340 (£104–£177) double, $290–$1,100 (£151–£572) suite. Extra person $20 (£10). AE, DC, MC, V. From the airport, follow signs to Punda; turn left after the 2nd traffic light in town; stay on the right side of the Plaza Smeets road and go straight. The hotel is on the right. **Amenities:** 3 restaurants; 4 bars; outdoor swimming pool; tennis court; spa; room service; babysitting; laundry service. *In room:* A/C, TV, kitchenette (in some), minibar, beverage maker, hair dryer, safe, Jacuzzi (in some).

Breezes Curaçao 𝒦𝒦 *Kids* Adjacent to both the Undersea National Park and Sea Aquarium, this big all-inclusive resort—a member of SuperClubs—opens onto one of Curaçao's most beautiful and longest beaches, with good snorkeling offshore. Although it caters to couples and singles, the resort also welcomes families, and its Camp Breezes has the best kiddies program on island. For those who like to gamble, it also has Curaçao's largest casino.

Bedrooms and suites come in a wide configuration of rooms, including the most desirable, those overlooking the ocean; others front the hotel's gardens. Bathrooms come with either showers or complete tub/shower combinations, and all open onto private patios or balconies. If the food isn't always gourmet, there is at least plenty of it. It's a real all-you-can-eat type of place, from breakfast buffets in the morning to lavish dinner feasts at night. Cuisine choices range from Italian to island specialties to Japanese, plus there's a beach grill. It also has an active entertainment program, complete with guest and staff talent shows.

Dr. Martin Luther King Blvd. 78, Willemstad, Curaçao, N.A. © 599/9-736-7888. Fax 599/9-461-7205. www.breezes.com. 341 units. Winter $255–$300 (£133–£156) per person double, $350–$390 (£182–£203) per person suite; off season $225 (£117) per person double, from $268–$310 (£139–£161) per person suite. Rates are all-inclusive. AE, DC, MC, V. **Amenities:** 3 restaurants; 5 bars; 3 outdoor pools; casino; 2 tennis courts; fitness center; spa; Jacuzzi; deep-sea fishing; dive shop; snorkeling; windsurfing; children's program (kids' snack bar, playground); babysitting; laundry service; nonsmoking rooms; rooms for those w/limited mobility; dance club. *In room:* A/C, TV, beverage maker, hair dryer, iron, safe.

Curaçao Marriott Beach Resort & Emerald Casino ★★ *Kids*   This is the most glamorous and most prominent hotel on the island, set beside the largest and most popular beach on Curaçao. It's 10 minutes from both the airport and Willemstad. The hotel is a cluster of three-story buildings whose distinctive shape and ocher color were adapted from traditional Dutch colonial architecture. The open-sided lobby was designed for optimum views of the beach and the hotel's many fountains. Scattered throughout the property are unusual, often monumental, artworks by local and international artists, and a collection of unfussy, overstuffed furniture.

Most of the colorful rooms have a view of the ocean and one king-size or two double beds, plus a spacious bathroom with a combination tub/shower.

Although never rising to any great imagination or flair, the food here is consistently good, with quality ingredients. There's also a big casino.

Piscadera Bay (P.O. Box 6003), Willemstad, Curaçao, N.A. © 888/236-2427 in the U.S., or 599/9-736-8800. Fax 599/9-462-7502. www.marriott.com. 237 units. Winter $289–$389 (£150–£202) double, from $539 (£280) suite; off season $179–$279 (£93–£145) double, from $429 (£223) suite. AE, DC, DISC, MC, V. **Amenities:** 4 restaurants; 2 bars; outdoor pool; casino; 2 tennis courts; Jacuzzi; sauna; diving; jet skis; kayaks; sailing; snorkeling; water-skiing; children's programs; car rental; business center; room service; massage; babysitting; laundry service; nonsmoking rooms; rooms for those w/limited mobility. *In room:* A/C, TV, minibar, hair dryer, iron, safe, Wi-Fi.

Floris Suite Hotel ★★★ *Finds*   The Dutch millionaire philanthropist and architect Dr. Jacob Gelt Dekker created this gem of a boutique hotel in the vicinity of the Curaçao World Trade Center. Unlike any hotel on island, the all-suite hotel blends aspects of European colonial with West Indian architecture. Natural stone tiles are wedded with solid mahogany doors and windows. The compound is enveloped by a tropical garden whose focal point is a swimming pool. A good private sandy beach is just across the street.

The standard of luxury differs from suite to suite. For example, the Royal Suites offer a separate bedroom with one king-size bed. In the living area is yet another queen-size sleeper sofa, and a fully equipped kitchen with a large covered porch or balcony. Everything is designed for comfort and convenience. A spa center is within walking distance, and a dive headquarters is just across from the hotel.

John F. Kennedy Blvd., Piscadera Bay, Curaçao, N.A. © 599/9-462-6111. Fax 599/9-462-6211. www.florissuitehotel.com. 71 units. Winter $215–$345 (£112–£179) double; off season $170–$295 (£88–£153) double. AE, MC, V. **Amenities:** Restaurant; bar; outdoor pool; tennis court; fitness center; spa; room service; babysitting; laundry service; coin-operated laundry; nonsmoking rooms. *In room:* A/C, TV, kitchenette, minibar, beverage maker, hair dryer, safe.

Kurá Hulanda Spa and Casino ★★ *Finds*   The island's most imaginative and unusual hotel opens onto St. Anna Bay in Otrabanda near the Queen Emma Bridge. If you'd like to escape impersonal modern hotel blocks, head here and immerse yourself in the Dutch colonial architecture of the 18th and 19th centuries. The property is the creation of Dr. Jacob Gelt Dekker, who also created the Museum Kurá Hulanda

(p. 249), on the same grounds. Bedrooms are beautifully furnished with Indian marble bathrooms with tub and shower, all the modern amenities, and elegant beds and furnishings. Some accommodations also have kitchenettes. You're not on a beach, but if you're seeking West Indian inns or hotels with character, this is your best bet in the ABC islands.

Langestraat 8, Willemstad, Curaçao, N.A. © 877/264-3106 in the U.S., or 599/9-434-7700. Fax 599/9-434-7701. www.kurahulanda.com. 100 units. Winter $210–$410 (£109–£213) double, $460–$1,000 (£239–£520) suite; off season $200–$240 (£104–£125) double, from $275–$650 (£143–£338) suite. AE, DC, MC, V. **Amenities:** 4 restaurants; bar; 2 outdoor pools; casino; fitness center; business services; room service; babysitting; laundry service; nonsmoking rooms. *In room:* A/C, ceiling fans, TV, kitchenette (in some), hair dryer, safe.

MODERATE

Habitat Curaçao *&*   Opening onto a private beach, this is Curaçao's best choice for divers. About 20 minutes from Willemstad, on the uncrowded southwest coast, this oceanfront resort provides environmentally sensitive diving vacations. Facilities include a PADI five-star instruction center offering diving courses from novice to instructor levels. The resort is set in manicured gardens. Accommodations include junior suites tastefully furnished with two queen-size beds, a fully equipped kitchenette, a large balcony or patio, and a full bathroom. Villas each have two bedrooms, a living room, an outdoor kitchen, a bathroom, and a large patio. All bathrooms contain tub/shower combos.

Rif St. Marie, Curaçao, N.A. © 800/327-6709 in the U.S., or 599/9-864-8304. Fax 599/9-864-8464. www.habitat curacaoresort.com. 70 units. Winter $154–$196 (£80–£102) double; off season $140–$180 (£73–£94) double. Dive packages available. AE, MC, V. **Amenities:** Restaurant; bar; outdoor pool; exercise room; diving; sailing; snorkeling; windsurfing; babysitting; laundry service; nonsmoking rooms; rooms for those w/limited mobility. *In room:* A/C, TV, kitchenette, hair dryer, safe.

Hilton Curaçao Resort *&& Kids*   Although this hotel was built in 1965, it has a new lease on life following renovations and improvements when the people from Hilton took it over. Today, it rises five floors above the northern perimeter of Willemstad, amid rocky bluffs. Glass-enclosed elevators cling to the outside walls of the hotel, offering a panoramic view as you're whisked to your room. Each of the midsize accommodations has a view of either the ocean or the garden. Outfitted in pastel colors, the rooms contain traditional furnishings, private balconies, and generously proportioned bathrooms with tubs and showers. Rooms on the executive floor are somewhat better furnished and offer amenities like fax machines. The hotel opens onto two private sandy beaches.

The food isn't great, but it's varied—everything from Italian trattoria favorites to fresh seafood. A social director organizes theme nights based on Mexican or Antillean food and dance music. There's a casino on-site.

John F. Kennedy Blvd. (P.O. Box 2133), Piscadera Bay, Willemstad, Curaçao, N.A. © 800/774-1500 in the U.S. and Canada, or 599/9-462-5000. Fax 599/9-462-5846. www.hilton.com. 196 units. Winter $240–$310 (£125–£161) double, from $330 (£172) suite; off season $170–$240 (£88–£125) double, from $260 (£135) suite. AE, DC, DISC, MC, V. **Amenities:** 2 restaurants; 2 bars; outdoor pool; children's pool; casino; 2 tennis courts; fitness center; spa; boating; dive shop; sailing; children's center; car rental; free shuttle to town; room service; babysitting; laundry service; nonsmoking rooms; rooms for those w/limited mobility. *In room:* A/C, TV, beverage maker, hair dryer, iron, safe.

Lions Dive & Beach Resort   On the island's largest white-sand beach, this hotel vies for the divers' trade with Habitat Curaçao (see above), which has better diving facilities. The hotel lies a 30-minute taxi ride southeast of the airport. This complete dive resort features programs supervised by the Underwater Curaçao staff. Each of its

comfortable though standard accommodations has a sea and/or garden view, a balcony or terrace, two double beds, and a shower-only bath.

Bapor Kibrá, Willemstad, Curaçao, N.A. ℂ 599/9-434-8888. Fax 599/9-434-8889. www.lionsdive.com. 105 units. Winter $360–$532 (£187–£277) per person for 3 nights; off season $258–$402 (£134–£209) per person for 3 nights. Dive packages available. AE, MC, V. **Amenities:** Restaurant; beach bar; outdoor pool; health club; dive shop; sailing; massage; babysitting; laundry service; rooms for those w/limited mobility. *In room:* A/C, TV, kitchenettes (in some), fridge, safe.

Plaza Hotel Curaçao   Standing guard over the Punda side of St. Anna Bay, right in the heart of Willemstad, the 14-story Plaza is nestled in the ramparts of an 18th-century waterside fort on the eastern tip of the harbor entrance, a 30-minute drive south of the airport. In fact, it's one of the harbor's two "lighthouses." (The hotel has to carry marine collision insurance, the only accommodations in the Caribbean with that distinction.) The original part of the hotel was built in 1954, long before mass tourism swept the island, and followed the style of the arcaded fort. However, now there's a tower of rooms stacked 15 stories high. Each of the smallish bedrooms is comfortably furnished and contains a small tub/shower combo.

The pool, with a bar and suntanning area, is inches away from the parapet of the fort. The Waterfort Restaurant serves standard American and Continental dishes.

Plaza Piar (P.O. Box 813), Willemstad, Curaçao, N.A. ℂ 599/9-461-2500. Fax 599/9-461-6543. www.plazahotel curacao.com. 252 units. Winter $145–$180 (£75–£94) double, $200–$325 (£104–£169) suite; off season $85–$125 (£44–£65) double, $130–$159 (£68–£83) suite. All-inclusive plan $20 (£10) per person extra. AE, MC, V. **Amenities:** 2 restaurants; 3 bars; outdoor pool; casino; Sunset sailboats; car rental; room service; laundry service; nonsmoking rooms; rooms for those w/limited mobility. *In room:* A/C, TV, kitchenette (in some), hair dryer, safe.

INEXPENSIVE

The Landhuis Daniel (see "Dining," below) is one of the best accommodations values on the island.

Chogogo Resort   Lying on Curaçao's east end, a 2-minute walk from Jan Thiel Beach, this resort is for visitors seeking an apartment or a bungalow. It is named after a species of local flamingo and set within an arid landscape between the oceanfront beaches and a shallow saltwater bay southeast of Willemstad. One- and two-story buildings dot the grounds; these contain the guest bungalows, studios, and apartments, each with a kitchenette, airy, unpretentious furniture, and a compact shower-only bathroom.

Jan Thiel Bay, Curaçao, N.A. ℂ 599/9-747-2844. Fax 599/9-747-2424. www.chogogo.com. 120 units. Winter $110 (£57) studio for 3, $120 (£62) apt for 2, $185 (£96) bungalow for 2, $205 (£107) bungalow for 4; off season $100 (£52) studio for 3 $112 (£58) apt for 2, $152 (£79) bungalow for 2, $172 (£89) bungalow for 4. AE, MC, V. **Amenities:** Restaurant; bar; outdoor pool; children's wading pool; coin-operated laundry. *In room:* A/C, TV, kitchenette, beverage maker, safe.

Hotel Holland   A 2-minute drive from the airport, Hotel Holland contains the Flying Dutchman Bar, a popular gathering place, plus a casino. You can see airplanes landing from your perch at the edge of the poolside terrace.

This property is the domain of former Navy frogman Hans Vrolijk and his family. Hans still retains his interest in scuba and arranges dive packages for his guests. The comfortably furnished accommodations have VCRs, fridges, tub/shower combination bathrooms, and balconies. It's a 30-minute drive to the nearest good beach, so you definitely need a rental car if you stay here.

F. D. Rooseveltweg 524, Curaçao, N.A. ℂ 599/9-868-8044 or 599/9-868-8014. 45 units. Year-round $85–$100 (£44–£52) double; from $125 (£65) suite. AE, DC, MC, V. **Amenities:** Restaurant; bar; outdoor pool; casino; laundry service. *In room:* A/C, TV/VCR, fridge (in some), beverage maker (in some).

3 Dining

EXPENSIVE

Astrolab Observatory Restaurant 🐦🐦 CONTINENTAL/SEAFOOD   In the Kurá Hulanda compound (see above), this world-class restaurant is adjacent to the Indian Marble Garden, all part of the restored 18th-century village of Otrobanda. This is the best of the many restaurants located within this shopping and dining compound. The restaurant is named for the collection of astrolabes on display nearby. The chefs here create a finely honed modern Continental cuisine, which is served both indoors and outdoors on a terrace under a mammoth ficus tree.

Start with the lump-crab cake with a caper rémoulade sauce or the pumpkin-cream soup with ground nutmeg. The best main dishes include a pan-fried filet of pompano in a lemon-butter sauce with red polenta, and green seafood stew, the kettle brimming with Caribbean lobster, shrimp, black mussels, and the fresh catch of the day. The poached sea bass and sautéed salmon served with lentil ragout and a pumpkin-flavored pesto is a marvelous combination of flavors and textures.

Kurá Hulanda, Langestraat 8, Otrobanda, Willemstad. ℂ 599/9-434-7700. Reservations recommended. Main courses $21–$38 (£11–£20). AE, DC, MC, V. Tues–Sun 7–11pm.

Belle Terrace 🐦 INTERNATIONAL/DANISH   This open-air restaurant, in a 200-year-old mansion on the beachfront of Willemstad, offers superb dining in a relaxed and informal atmosphere. The beachfront Schooner Bar, where you can enjoy rum punch, is shaped like a weather-beaten ship's prow looking out to sea. The restaurant, sheltered by an arbor of flamboyant branches, serves such specialties as pickled herring, smoked salmon, and a Danish lunch platter. Local dishes, such as *keshi yena* (baked Gouda cheese with a spicy chicken filling), are also on the menu. On Saturday night there's a mixed grill and a serve-yourself salad bar, all accompanied by live music. The fish is always fresh, and the chef prepares it to perfection, whether grilled, poached, or meunière.

In the Avila Beach Hotel, Penstraat 130, Willemstad. ℂ 599/9-461-4377. Reservations required. Main courses $17–$25 (£8.85–£13); 3-course fixed-price meal $29 (£15); Sat barbecue $33 (£17). AE, MC, V. Daily noon–2:30pm and 7–10pm. From the center of town, drive east along the Pieter Maai Weg (which becomes Pennstraat) for about 1.5km (1 mile).

Bistro Le Clochard 🐦 FRENCH/SWISS   This restaurant fits snugly into the northwestern corner of the grim ramparts of Fort Rif, at the gateway to the harbor. We think that Fort Nassau (see below) is better, but Bistro Le Clochard finishes a close second. Its entrance is marked with a canopy leading to a series of rooms, each built under the 19th-century vaulting of the old Dutch fort. This appealingly formal restaurant has several seating options, including a greenhouse-style glassed-in dining room near the entrance and an outdoor terrace. Appetizers like snails marinated in cognac or crepes stuffed with a seafood ragout with a hollandaise sauce seem more appropriate to a Paris bistro than a tropical island. The kitchen staff is at its best when preparing beef dishes; the tenderloin with assorted mushrooms in a cream sauce is especially recommended. The catch of the day always appears on the menu with a lemon-butter sauce.

In Riffort Village (a condominium complex), on the Otrabanda side of the pontoon bridge. ℂ 599/9-462-5666. Reservations recommended. Main courses $35–$46 (£18–£24). AE, DC, DISC, MC, V. Daily noon–2pm and 6:30–10:45pm (Harborside Terrace bar daily noon–11pm).

Fort Nassau 🍴🍴 INTERNATIONAL/SEAFOOD   This restored restaurant and bar is built on a hilltop overlooking Willemstad in the ruins of a buttressed fort dating from 1796. Inside, Fort Nassau has retained an 18th-century decor; outside, from the Battery Terrace, a 360-degree panorama of the sea, the harbor, and Willemstad unfolds. You can stop by the chic bar just to enjoy a drink and watch the sunset.

Queen Beatrix and Crown Prince Claus of the Netherlands have dined here, and rumor has it they were more captivated by the view than by the food. We are impressed with the perfectly prepared filet of grouper. Watch out for the cream of mustard (yes, that's right) soup—an acquired taste. Opt for the pan-fried filet of red snapper, or even a well-prepared steak with garlic-infused mashed potatoes. Also good are oven-roasted rack of lamb with pickled red onions and almond potatoes, and the caramelized filet of salmon on a bed of creamy leeks with fried polenta and plantain.

Schottegatweg 82, near Point Juliana, a 5-min. drive from Willemstad. ⓒ 599/9-461-3081 or 599/9-461-3450. Reservations required. Main courses $24–$29 (£13–£15). AE, DC, MC, V. Daily 6:30–11pm.

La Pergola 🍴 ITALIAN   This is one of the five restaurants nestled into the weather-beaten core of the island's oldest fort, and it's thrived here for more than a decade. As the name implies, a replica of a Renaissance-style pergola enhances the decor. The kitchen and one of the three dining areas are in the cellar; two others benefit from streaming sunlight and a view over the seafront. Menu items change virtually every day, and all use truly authentic recipes. The best examples include gnocchi of chicken, fettuccine Giulio Cesare (with ham, cream, and mushrooms), a succulent version of *grigliata mista* (mixed grill), and a top-notch preparation of exotic mushrooms, in season, garnished with Parmesan cheese and parsley. The red snapper in extra virgin olive oil and garlic is a palate pleaser. Looking for something a little different? Ask for *maltagliata* (pasta cut at random angles and lengths) served with either Gorgonzola sauce or Genoan-style pesto. The lobster dishes, including lobster with olive oil and garlic and black pasta with lobster and squid, are among the best on island. In addition, a dozen pizzas are available.

In the Waterfront Arches, Waterfort Straat, Willemstad. ⓒ 599/9-461-3482. Reservations recommended. Main courses $17–$32 (£8.85–£17). AE, MC, V. Mon–Sat noon–11pm; Sun 5–11pm.

The Wine Cellar 🍴 INTERNATIONAL   Opposite the cathedral in the center of town is the domain of Nico and Angela Cornelisse and their son, Daniel, who offer one of the most extensive wine lists on the island. The atmosphere is reminiscent of an old-fashioned Dutch home. The kitchen turns out an excellent lobster salad and a sole meunière in a butter-and-herb sauce. You might also try fresh red snapper in garlic sauce, filet mignon from Argentina, or the rack of lamb with rosemary-port sauce. Game dishes, imported throughout the year from Holland, usually include venison roasted with mushrooms, hare, and roast goose. After years of dining here, we have found the food commendable in every way—dishes are hearty and full of flavor, and there are selections for lighter appetites as well. Of course, as good as the food is, it never matches the impressive wine list.

Intersection of Ooststraat and Concordiastraat, Willemstad. ⓒ 599/9-461-2178. Reservations required. Main courses $20–$37 (£10–£19). AE, MC, V. Mon–Fri noon–2pm and 6:30–11pm; Sat 6:30–11pm.

MODERATE

Avalon 🍴 INTERNATIONAL/SUSHI   The Art Deco look and lively atmosphere evokes a restaurant on South Beach in Miami, and an imaginative menu and specialty drinks draw an endless stream of diners. Our favorite meal here just happens to be the signature dish: crispy red devil snapper. Other favorites are adobo-crusted hanger steak and a vegetarian choice, the Thai red curry bowl. Intricately prepared sushi rolls are also available. After dinner, many visitors and locals drop in to sample the martini menu and Cuban cigars.

Caracasbaaiweg 8. ℂ 599/9-465-6375. Reservations recommended. Main courses $21–$25 (£11–£13). AE, MC, V. Mon–Sat noon–3pm; Mon–Thurs 6–11pm; Fri–Sat 6–11:30pm.

Blues SEAFOOD/INTERNATIONAL As you dine here on a pier jutting far out from the beachfront of the Avila Beach Hotel, water ripples beneath your seat and heaping platters of fresh seafood challenge even the heartiest of appetites. You might enjoy blue mussels cooked in wine sauce with shallots and herbs, or lobster with a lime-and-orange beurre blanc. An especially impressive dish is the seafood special, compiled from three different types of fish, depending on the catch of the day. If after all this hearty fare from Neptune you still have room left, the chef makes great desserts, including one of our favorites, a chocolate tart.

In the Avila Beach Hotel, Penstraat 130, Willemstad. ℂ 599/9-461-4377. Reservations recommended. Main courses $22–$33 (£11–£17); 3-course fixed-price menu $35 (£18). AE, MC, V. Daily 7–11pm. From the center of town, drive east along the Pieter Maai Weg (which becomes Pennstraat) for about 1.5km (1 mile).

Joanchi's Restaurant ✦ *Finds* SEAFOOD/CREOLE The proprietor of this establishment is likely to greet you himself and inform you that his iguana soup is the best on island. We've not made a survey but he's very persuasive. On island, iguana is reputed to have the same aphrodisiac properties as the legendary oyster in America. In a rustic country-style setting with antiques and oak walls, diners are treated to a savory local cuisine. The fish is among the freshest on island. Our recent sampling of the grilled wahoo was perfection itself. You can also order delectable garlic shrimp or else stewed goat for meat eaters. Most visitors drop in for lunch. Locals swear by this place, but it also welcomes visitors from abroad.

Westpunt 15, Westpunt. ℂ 599/9-864-0126. Reservations required for dinner. Main courses $14–$20 (£7.30–£10). Daily noon–11pm.

Landhuis Daniel ✦ *Finds* NOUVELLE CREOLE CUISINE Surrounded by arid scrubland about 3km (2 miles) south of Westpunt, near the island's most northwesterly tip, this place was originally built in 1711 as an inn and tavern. Today, its mustard-colored facade, white columns, terra-cotta roof, and old-fashioned green-and-yellow dining room are carefully preserved and historically authentic. Menu items are cooked slowly, to order, in a setting of sea breezes and sunlight streaming in the big windows. Launch your repast with a spicy Caribbean seafood bisque. We generally order the main catch of the day, often requesting it with a basil-cream sauce and pine nuts; however, another favorite is the Argentine beef tenderloin with spicy pumpkin sauce or the baked swordfish with shrimp sauce.

Renting for $60 (£31) a night year-round each, eight very simple but comfortable bedrooms are one floor above the restaurant. They are tidily maintained and have small private bathrooms with shower units. Only five are air-conditioned, but all have ceiling fans—or you can rely on the trade winds to keep cool.

In the Landhuis Daniel Inn, Wegnaar, Westpunt. ℂ 599/9-864-8400. Reservations recommended. Main courses lunch $10–$18 (£5.20–£9.35), dinner $15–$26 (£7.80–£14). AE, DC, MC, V. Daily 8am–2pm and 5–11pm.

Rijsttafel Restaurant Indonesia and Holland Club Bar ✦ *Value* INDONESIAN This is the best place on the island to sample Indonesian *rijstafel*, the traditional rice table served here with 16, 20, or 25 zesty side dishes. The spicy food is a good change of pace when you tire of seafood and steak. Warming trays are placed on your table; the service is buffet style. You can season your plate with peppers rated hot, very hot, and palate-melting. It's best to go with a party so that all of you can share in the feast, although at lunchtime, the selection of dishes is more modest.

Mercuriusstraat 13, Salinja. (©) 599/9-461-2606. Reservations recommended. Main courses $18–$32 (£9.35–£17); *rijsttafel* $24 (£13) for 16 dishes, $28 (£15) for 20 dishes, $50 (£26) for 25 dishes; vegetarian *rijsttafel* $27 (£14) for 16 dishes. AE, MC, V. Mon–Sat noon–2pm and 6–9:30pm; Sun 6–10pm. Take a taxi to this villa in the suburbs near Salinja, near Breezes Curaçao southeast of Willemstad.

4 Beaches

Its beaches (called *playas* or *bocas*) aren't the best in the Dutch Leewards, but Curaçao does have nearly 40 of them, ranging from hotel sands to secluded coves. *Playas* are the larger, classic sandy beaches, and *bocas* are small inlets between two large rock formations. The northwest coast is generally rugged and difficult for swimming, but the more tranquil waters of the west coast are filled with sheltered bays, offering excellent swimming and snorkeling.

Seaquarium Beach, just to the east of the center of Willemstad, charges a fee of $3 (£1.30) for access to its complete facilities, including two bars, two restaurants, a watersports shop, beach-chair rentals, changing facilities, and showers. The calm waters make this beach ideal for swimming.

Just northwest of Willemstad, **Blauwbaai (Blue Bay)** is the largest and most popular beach on Curaçao, with enough white sand for everybody. Along with showers and changing facilities, there are plenty of shady places to retreat from the noonday sun. To get here, follow the road that goes past the Holiday Beach Hotel, heading in the direction of Juliandorp. Follow the sign that tells you to bear left for Blauwbaai and the fishing village of San Michiel.

Farther up the west coast, about 30 minutes from Willemstad in the Willibrordus area on the west side of Curaçao, **Daaibooi** is a good beach, though there are no showers or changing rooms. Wooden umbrellas provide shade. Snorkelers are attracted to the sides of the bay, as the cliffs rise out of the surf. Small rainbow-hued fish are commonplace, and many varying corals cover the rocks. This beach gets very crowded with locals on Sunday.

A beach popular with families and a base for fishing boats, **Playa Lagun** lies well concealed in the corner of the village of Lagun as you approach from Santa Cruz. The narrow cove is excellent for swimming because of the tranquil, shallow water. Rainbow-hued fish appear everywhere, so the beach is also a favorite with snorkelers. Some concrete huts provide shelter from the scorching sun; a snack bar is open on weekends.

Knip Bay, just north of Playa Lagun, has white sands, rocky sides, and beautiful turquoise waters, making it suitable for snorkeling, swimming, and sunbathing. The

---

Tips A Word of Caution to Swimmers

Beware of stepping on the spines of the sea urchins that sometimes abound in these waters. To give temporary first aid for an embedded urchin's spine, try the local remedies of vinegar or lime juice. Locals advise a burning match if you're tough. Although the urchin spines are not dangerous, they can give you several days of real discomfort.

beach tends to be crowded on weekends, often with locals. Changing facilities and refreshments are available. **Warning:** Manchineel trees provide some shade, but their fruit is poisonous; never seek shelter under the trees when it rains, as drops falling off the leaves will cause major skin irritation.

Playa Abao, with crystal turquoise waters, is at the northern tip of the island. One of Curaçao's most popular strands, this is often called Playa Grandi ("Big Beach"). It can get very, very hot at midday, but thatched shade umbrellas provide some protection. A stairway and ramp lead down to the excellent white sands. There's a snack bar in the parking lot. Near the large cove at Playa Abao is **Playa Kenepa** ✸, which is much smaller but gets our nod as one of the island's most beautiful strips. Partially shaded by trees, it's a good place for sunbathing, swimming, and shore diving. A 10-minute swim from the beach leads to a reef where visibility is frequently 30m (100 ft.). Baby sea turtles are often spotted here. A snack bar is open on weekends.

Westpunt, a public beach on the northwestern tip of the island, is known for the Sunday divers who jump from its gigantic cliffs into the ocean below. You can spot little, rainbow-hued boats and fishermen's nets hanging out to dry here. There are no facilities at this beach, which tends to be exceptionally hot and has no shade trees (bring lots of sunscreen). The calm waters offer excellent swimming, though they're not good for snorkeling.

South of Willemstad is **Santa Barbara Beach.** It's between the open sea and the island's primary watersports and recreational area known as Spanish Water. A mining company owns this land, which also contains Table Mountain, a remarkable landmark, and an old phosphate mine. The natural beach has pure-white sand and calm water. A buoy line protects swimmers from boats. Facilities include restrooms, changing rooms, a snack bar, and a terrace; water bicycles and small motorboats are available for rent. The beach, open daily from 8am to 6pm, has access to the Curaçao Underwater Marine Park.

5 Sports & Other Outdoor Pursuits

CRUISES   Taber Tours, Dokweg (© **599/9-737-6637;** www.tabertours.com), offers a handful of seagoing options, such as a 5-hour sunset and snorkeling cruise to a beach on Wednesday and Friday; the excursion costs $35 to $50 (£18–£26) for adults, including gear and one cocktail. Children pay half price. Charter cruises are also available.

Travelers looking for an experience similar to the sailing days of yore should book a trip on the **Insulinde,** Handelskade (© **599/9-560-1340** [note that this is a cellular phone and the connection may be poor]; fax 599/9-461-1538; www.insulinde.com). The 36m (118-ft.) traditionally rigged sail clipper is available for day trips and chartering. A daily tour on Wednesday and Friday leaves at 7am and returns at 6:30pm, taking passengers to a sunken tugboat for snorkeling and a swim at Santa Barbara Beach. The cost is $38 (£20) per person (half price for kids), with free use of snorkel gear. Other tours, including some dinner buffets, are available, providing that a minimum of 20 people sign up. Call for more information about what might be offered at the time of your visit. Advance reservations are required for all trips.

Like a ghost ship from ancient times, a dual-masted, five-sailed wooden schooner cruises silently through the waters of Curaçao. It carries a name steeped in legend— the **Bounty** (© **599/9-560-1887;** www.bountyadventures.com)—though it's not a replica of its famous namesake. Sailing and snorkeling trips depart Wednesday, Friday, and Sunday at 10am from Spanish Water, making a stop at Caracas Bay for great snorkeling before a return at 2:30pm. The price is $59 (£31) for adults or $30 (£16) for children ages 3 to 12. Prices include a barbecue buffet, dessert, salad bar, drinks, and use of snorkeling gear.

GOLF The **Curaçao Golf and Squash Club,** Wilhelminalaan, in Emmastad (© 599/9-737-3590), is your best bet. Greens fees are $30 (£16), and both clubs and trolleys can be rented. The 10-hole course (the only one on the island) is open daily from 7:30am to sundown.

An 18-hole course lies at **Blue Bay Golf Course,** a par-72 course at Landhuis Blauw, on the road to Bullenbaai (© 599/9-868-1755). This challenging course, designed by Rocky Roquemore, takes advantage of Curaçao's seaside terrain and views of the Caribbean. Some shots are over water. Depending on the time of year, greens fees range from $58 to $100 (£30–£52), plus $15 (£7.80) to rent a cart. Hours are daily from 7am to 5pm.

HORSEBACK RIDING At Christoffel National Park, **Rancho Alfin** (© 599/9-864-0535) specializes in private trips along unspoiled trails, riding smooth-gaited "paseo" horses suitable even for nonriders. The ride, which lasts about 2 hours, costs $40 (£21). Departures are Monday to Saturday at 8:30am. Call for reservations daily between 8am and 4pm.

TENNIS Most of the deluxe hotels have tennis courts. Another option is the **Santa Catherine Sports Complex,** Koraal Tabac (© 599/9-767-7030), where court costs are $10 to $20 (£5.20–£10) per hour.

WATERSPORTS Most hotels offer their own watersports programs. If your hotel isn't equipped, we suggest heading for one of the most complete watersports facilities on Curaçao, **Seascape Dive and Watersports,** at the Hilton Hotel Curaçao (© 599/9-462-5000; www.seascapecuracao.com). Specializing in snorkeling and scuba diving to reefs and underwater wrecks, it operates from a hexagonal kiosk set on stilts above the water, just offshore from the hotel's beach.

Open from 8am to 5pm daily, the company provides snorkeling excursions for $45 (£23) per person in an underwater park offshore from the hotel, and jet-ski rentals for $60 (£31) per half-hour. An introductory scuba lesson, conducted by a competent dive instructor with PADI certification, goes for $70 (£36); four-dive packages cost $136 (£71).

Seascape can also arrange deep-sea fishing for $450 (£234) for a half-day tour carrying a maximum of six people, $560 (£291) for a full-day tour. Drinks and equipment are included, but you'll have to get your hotel to pack your lunch. The full-day tour does not include lunch.

Ocean Encounters, in Bapor Kibrá (© 599/9-461-8131; www.oceanencounters.com), has a complete PADI-accredited underwater sports program. A fully stocked modern dive shop provides retail and rental equipment. Individual dives and dive packages are offered, costing $26 (£14) per dive for guided shore dives. An introductory dive for novices is priced at $75 (£39), and a snorkel trip costs $25 to $45 (£13–£23), including equipment, but is only offered on Sunday and Thursday. Shop hours are daily 8am to 5pm. Scuba divers and snorkelers can expect spectacular scenery in waters with visibility often exceeding 30m (100 ft.) at the **Curaçao Underwater Marine Park** 🐠🐠, which stretches along 20km (12 miles) of Curaçao's southern coastline. Although the park technically begins at Breezes Curaçao and extends all the way to East Point, the island's most southeasterly tip, some scuba aficionados and island dive operators are aware of other excellent dive sites outside the official boundaries of this park. Lying beneath the surface of the water are steep walls, at least two shallow wrecks, gardens of soft coral, and more than 30 species of hard coral. Although access from shore is possible at Jan Thiel Bay and Santa Barbara Beach, most people visit the park by boat. For easy and safe mooring, there are 16 mooring buoys, placed at the best dive and snorkel sites. A snorkeling trail with underwater interpretive markers is laid out just east of Breezes Curaçao and is accessible from shore. Spearfishing, anchoring in the coral, or taking anything from the reefs, except photographs, is strictly prohibited.

6 Exploring the Island

Most cruise-ship passengers see only Willemstad—or, more accurately, its shops—but you may want to get out into the *cunucu,* or countryside, and explore the towering cacti and rolling hills topped by *landhuizen* (plantation houses) built more than 3 centuries ago.

WILLEMSTAD ✺✺

Willemstad was originally founded as Santa Ana by the Spanish in the 1500s. Dutch traders found a vast natural harbor, a perfect hideaway along the Spanish Main, and they renamed it Willemstad in the 17th century. Not only is Willemstad the capital of Curaçao, but it's also the seat of government for the Netherlands Antilles. Today rows of pastel-colored, red-roofed town houses adorn the downtown area. After 10 years of restoration, the historic center of Willemstad and the island's natural harbor, Schottegat, were inscribed on UNESCO's World Heritage List.

The easiest way to go exploring is to take a 1¼-hour **trolley tour,** visiting the highlights of the city. The open-sided cars, pulled by a silent "locomotive," make several trips each week. Tours leave at 10 or 11am. The tour begins at Fort Amsterdam near the Queen Emma Pontoon Bridge. The cost is $22 (£11) for adults, $16 (£8.30) for children 2 to 12. Call ✆ **599/9-461-0011** for more information (Mon only).

The city developed on both sides of the canal. It's divided into **Punda** (Old World Dutch ambience and the best shopping) and **Otrabanda** ("the other side," the contemporary side). A pedestrian walkway, the **Queen Emma Pontoon Bridge,** connects both sections. Powered by a diesel engine, it swings open many times a day to let ships from all over the globe pass in and out of the harbor.

From the bridge, there's a view of the old **gabled houses** in harmonized pastel shades. The bright colors, according to legend, are a holdover from the time when one of the island's early governors had eye trouble, and flat white gave him headaches. The colonial-style architecture, reflecting the Dutch influence, gives the town a storybook look. The houses, built three or four stories high, are crowned by steep gables and roofed with orange Spanish tiles. Hemmed in by the sea, a tiny canal, and an inlet, the streets are narrow, and they're crosshatched by still narrower alleyways.

Except for the pastel colors, Willemstad may remind you of old Amsterdam. It has one of the most intriguing townscapes in the Caribbean. But don't let the colors deceive you: Up close, the city can be rather dirty.

A **statue of Pedro Luis Brion** dominates the square known as Brionplein right at the Otrabanda end of the pontoon bridge. Born in Curaçao in 1782, Brion became the island's favorite son and best-known war hero. Under Simon Bolivar, he was an admiral of the fleet and fought for the independence of Venezuela and Colombia.

Moments **The Floating Market**

A few minutes' walk from the pontoon bridge, at the north end of Handelskade, is the **Floating Market** ⚓, where scores of schooners tie up alongside the canal, a few yards from the main shopping area. Boats arrive from Venezuela and Colombia, as well as other West Indian islands, to dock here and sell tropical fruits and vegetables—a little bit of everything, in fact, including handicrafts. The modern market under its vast concrete cap has not replaced this unique shopping expedition, which is fun to watch. Hours are daily 6am to 6pm—arrive early or stay late.

In addition to the pontoon bridge, the **Queen Juliana Bridge** opened to vehicular traffic in 1973. Spanning the harbor, it rises 59m (194 ft.), which makes it the highest bridge in the Caribbean and one of the tallest in the world.

The Waterfront originally guarded the mouth of the canal on the eastern or Punda side, but now it has been incorporated into the Plaza Hotel. The task of standing guard has been taken over by **Fort Amsterdam,** site of the Governor's Palace and the 1769 Dutch Reformed church. The church still has a British cannonball embedded in it. The arches leading to the fort were tunneled under the official residence of the governor.

A corner of Fort Amsterdam stands at the intersection of Breedestraat and Handelskade, the starting point for a plunge into the island's major **shopping district.**

At some point, visit the **Waterfort Arches,** which stretch for .4km (¼ mile). They rise 9m (30-ft.) high and are built of barrel-vaulted 17th-century stone set against the sea. At Waterfort, you can explore boutiques, develop film, cash a traveler's check, or purchase fruit-flavored ice cream. You can walk through to a breezy terrace on the sea for a local Amstel beer or a choice of restaurants. The grand buildings and cobbled walkways are illuminated at night.

Between the I. H. (Sha) Capriles Kade and Fort Amsterdam, at Hanechi di Snoa 29, stands the **Mikve Israel-Emanuel Synagogue** (© 599/9-461-1067), the oldest extant synagogue in the Western Hemisphere. Consecrated on the eve of Passover in 1732, it houses the oldest Jewish congregation in the New World. Joaño d'Illan led the first Jewish settlers (13 families) to the island in 1651, almost half a century after their expulsion from Portugal by the Inquisition. The settlers came via Amsterdam to Curaçao. This synagogue, a fine example of Dutch colonial architecture, covers about a square block in the heart of Willemstad; it was built in a Spanish-style walled courtyard, with four large portals. Following a Portuguese Sephardic custom, sand covers the sanctuary floor, representing the desert where Israelites camped when the Jews passed from slavery to freedom. The highlight of the east wall is the Holy Ark, rising 5m (16 ft.); a raised *banca* (balustraded dais), canopied in mahogany, is on the north wall.

Adjacent to the synagogue courtyard is the **Jewish Cultural Historical Museum,** Hanechi di Snoa 29 (© 599/9-461-1633), housed in two buildings dating from 1728. They were originally the rabbi's residence and the bathhouse. The 250-year-old *mikvah* (a bath for religious purification purposes) was in constant use until around 1850, when the buildings were sold. They have since been reacquired through the Foundation for the Preservation of Historic Monuments and turned into the present museum. On display are ritual, ceremonial, and cultural objects, many of which date from the 17th and 18th centuries and are still used by the congregation for holidays and events.

The synagogue and museum are open to visitors Monday through Friday from 9 to 11:45am and 2:30 to 4:45pm, and, if there's a cruise ship in port, Sunday from 9am to 4:30pm. Services are Friday at 6:30pm and Saturday at 10am. Visitors are welcome, with appropriate dress required. There's a $5 (£2.60) museum entrance fee for adults (includes synagogue); it's free for children under 15.

Museum Kurá Hulanda, Kipstraat 9 (© 599/9-434-7765), is one of the most unusual—and one of the largest—museums in the Caribbean, housed in once-dilapidated 1800s buildings rescued from oblivion. The exhibits reflect the passion of Dr. Jacob Gelt Dekker, a Dutchman who resides next door. He has spent a great deal of his life devoted to the history and culture of Africa, and he has roamed that continent in search of cultural artifacts. At Otrabanda he has assembled his prize collection, including its most interesting exhibit, a life-size reconstruction of a slave ship that once sailed from the Ivory Coast carrying captured slaves into bondage and often death in the West. One exhibit, "Origin of Man," has a series of intriguing fossils. You can hear African music as you study the grotesque wood masks, and look at everything from fertility dolls to sculptures from shona stone, along with such musical instruments as the djembe or the ballaphone. Much of the museum is devoted to objects that evoke the cultures of the former empires of West Africa. Hours are daily 10am to 5pm; admission is $6 (£3.10) for adults and $3 (£1.55) for children.

You can walk to the tiny **Curaçao Museum,** Van Leeuwenhoekstraat (© 599/9-462-3873), from the Queen Emma Pontoon Bridge. Built in 1853 by the Royal Dutch Army Corps of Engineers as a military quarantine hospital, the building was carefully restored from 1946 to 1948 and is a fine example of 19th-century Dutch architecture, now housing paintings, objets d'art, and furniture crafted in the 19th century by local cabinetmakers. There's also a large collection from the Caiquetio tribes, the early inhabitants described by Amerigo Vespucci as 2m-tall (6½-ft.) giants, and a reconstruction of a traditional music pavilion in the garden, where Curaçao musicians give regular performances. It's open Monday to Friday 9am to noon and 2 to 5pm; Sunday 10am to 4pm. Admission is $3 (£1.55) for adults, $1.75 (90p) for children 13 and under.

Maritime Museum, Van De Brandhof Straat 7 (© 599/9-465-2327), is in the historic Scharloo neighborhood of Willemstad, just off the old harbor of St. Anna Bay. More than 40 permanent displays trace the story of Curaçao, beginning with the arrival of the island's original inhabitants in 600 B.C. Video presentations cover the development of Curaçao's harbor and the role of the island as one of the largest slave depots in the Caribbean. There are also five oral histories (one from a 97-year-old Curaçaoan who served on the cargo vessel *Normandie*), antique miniatures, 17th-century ship models, and a collection of maps. Admission is $10 (£5.20) for adults, $7 (£3.65) for children 12 to 16; free for children under 12. Hours are Tuesday to Sunday 10am to 4pm.

WEST OF WILLEMSTAD

On Schottegatweg West, northwest of Willemstad, past the oil refineries, lies the **Beth Haim Cemetery,** the oldest Caucasian burial site still in use in the Western Hemisphere. Meaning "House of Life," the cemetery was consecrated before 1659. There are some 2,500 graves on about 1 hectare (2½ acres) here. The carving on some of the 17th- and 18th-century tombstones is exceptional.

Country House Museum, 19km (12 miles) west of Willemstad at Doktorstuin 27 (© 599/9-864-2742), is a small-scale restoration of a 19th-century manor house that has thick stone walls, a thatched roof, and artifacts that represent the old-fashioned methods of agriculture and fishing. It's open Monday to Friday from 9am to 5pm, Saturday and Sunday from 9am to 6pm. Admission is $2 (£1).

En route to Westpunt, you'll come across a seaside cavern known as **Boca Tabla,** one of many such grottoes on this rugged, uninhabited northwest coast. In the Westpunt area, a 45-minute ride from Punda in Willemstad, **Playa Forti** is a stark region characterized by soaring hills and towering cacti, along with 200-year-old Dutch land houses, the former mansions that housed slave owners.

Out toward the western tip of Curaçao, a high-wire fence surrounds the entrance to the 1,800-hectare (4,446-acre) **Christoffel National Park** ✦✦ in Savonet (℃ **599/ 9-864-0363**), about a 45-minute drive from the capital. A macadam road gives way to dirt, surrounded on all sides by abundant cactus and bromeliads. In the higher regions you can spot rare orchids. Rising from flat, arid countryside, 369m-high (1,210-ft.) **St. Christoffelberg** is the highest point in the Dutch Leewards. Donkeys, wild goats, iguanas, the Curaçao deer, and many species of birds thrive in this preserve, and there are some Arawak paintings on a coral cliff near the two caves. The park has 32km (20 miles) of one-way trail-like roads, with lots of flora and fauna along the way. The shortest trail is about 8km long (5 miles) and, because of the rough terrain, takes about 40 minutes to drive through. There are also various walking trails; one takes you to the top of St. Christoffelberg in about 1[bf]½ hours. (Come early in the morning, when it isn't too hot.) The park is open Monday to Saturday from 7:30am to 4pm, Sunday from 6am to 3pm. The entrance fee is $10 (£5.20) per person and includes admission to the museum.

Next door, the park has opened the **National Park Shete Boka (Seven Inlets;** ℃ **599/9-864-0363**). This turtle sanctuary contains a cave with pounding waves off the choppy north coast. Admission to this park is $2.50 (£1.30) per person.

NORTH & EAST OF WILLEMSTAD

Just northeast of the capital, **Fort Nassau** was completed in 1797 and christened Fort Republic by the Dutch. Built high on a hill overlooking the harbor entrance to the south and St. Anna Bay to the north, it was fortified as a second line of defense in case the waterfront gave way. When the British invaded in 1807, they renamed it Fort George in honor of their own king. Later, when the Dutch regained control, they renamed it Orange Nassau in honor of the Dutch royal family. Today, diners have replaced soldiers (see "Dining," earlier in this chapter).

Curaçao Liqueur Distillery, Landhuis Chobolobo, Saliña a Arriba (℃ **599/9-461- 3526**), offers a chance to visit and taste at Chobolobo, the 17th-century *landhuis* where the famous Curaçao liqueur is made. The cordial is a distillate of dried peel of a particular strain of orange found only on Curaçao. Several herbs are added to give it an aromatic bouquet. One of the rewards of a visit here is a free snifter of the liqueur, offered Monday to Friday from 8am to noon and 1 to 5pm.

Curaçao Seaquarium, off Dr. Martin Luther King Boulevard at a site called Bapor Kibrá (℃ **599/9-461-6666;** www.curacao-sea-aquarium.com), has more than 400 species of fish, crabs, anemones, sponges, and coral on display in a natural environment. Located a few minutes' walk along the rocky coast from the Breezes Curaçao Resort, the Seaquarium is open daily from 8:30am to 5:30pm. Admission is $15 (£7.80) for adults, $7.50 (£3.90) for children 5 to 12.

Special features of the aquarium are sea lion and dolphin encounters, costing $58 to $179 (£30–£93) for divers or $34 to $154 (£18–£80) for snorkelers. Divers, snorkelers, and experienced swimmers can feed, film, and photograph sharks, which are separated from them by a large window with feeding holes. In the animal-encounters section, you can swim among stingrays, grouper, sea turtles, and other marine life, feeding and photographing these creatures in a controlled environment where safety is always a consideration. The Seaquarium is also the site of Curaçao's only full-facility, palm-shaded, white-sand beach. There is also a 3-D slide presentation in the minitheater.

Seaworld Explorer ✪ is a semisubmersible submarine that departs the Seaquarium daily in the mornings (times vary) on hour-long journeys into the deep. You're taken on a tour of submerged wrecks off the shores of Curaçao and treated to close encounters of coral reefs with rainbow-hued tropical fish. The *Explorer* has a barge top that submerges only 2 or so meters (6½ ft.) under the water, but the submerged section has wide glass windows allowing passengers underwater views, which can extend 33m (108 ft.). Reservations must be made a day in advance by calling © **599/9-461-0011.** It costs $40 (£21) for adults, $25 (£13) for children 11 and under.

Curaçao Underwater Marine Park ✪✪ (© **599/9-462-4242**), established in 1983 with the financial aid of the World Wildlife Fund, stretches from the Breezes Curaçao Resort to the east point of the island, a strip of about 20km (13 miles) of untouched coral reefs. For information on snorkeling, scuba diving, and trips in a glass-bottom boat to view the park, see "Sports & Other Outdoor Pursuits," earlier in this chapter.

The **Hato Caves,** F. D. Rooseveltweg (© **599/9-868-0379**), have been called mystical. Every hour, guides take visitors through this world of stalagmites and stalactites, found in the highest limestone terrace of the island. Actually, they were once old coral reefs, and were formed when the ocean water fell and the landmass was lifted up over the years. Over thousands of years, limestone formations were created, some mirrored in an underground lake. After crossing the lake, you enter the Cathedral, an underground cavern. The largest hall of the cave is called La Ventana ("The Window"). Also on display are samples of ancient Indian petroglyph drawings. The caves are open daily from 10am to 4pm; admission is $7 (£3.65) for adults and $5 (£2.60) for children under 13.

7 Shopping ✪✪

Curaçao is a shopper's paradise. Some 200 shops line the major shopping streets such as Heerenstraat and Breedestraat. Right in the heart of Willemstad is the 5-block **Punda** shopping district. Most stores are open Monday through Saturday from 8am to noon and 2 to 6pm (some 8am–6pm). When cruise ships are in port, stores are also open for a few hours on Sunday and holidays. To avoid the cruise-ship crowds, do your shopping in the morning.

Look for good buys on French perfumes, Dutch Delft blue souvenirs, finely woven Italian silks, Japanese and German cameras, jewelry, silver, Swiss watches, linens, leather goods, liquor, and island-made rum and liqueurs, especially Curaçao liqueur, some of which has a distinctive blue color. The island is famous for its 5-pound wheels of Gouda and Edam cheeses. You'll also see wooden shoes, although we're not sure what you'd do with them. Some of the stores also stock some deals on intricate lacework imported from Portugal, China, and everywhere in between. If you're a street shopper and want something colorful, consider one of the woodcarvings or flamboyant paintings from Haiti or the Dominican Republic. Both are hawked by street vendors at any of the main plazas.

Incidentally, Curaçao is not technically a free port, but its prices are often inexpensive because of its low import duty.

Every garment sold in **Bamali,** Breedestraat Punda 2 (© **599/9-461-2258**), is designed and, in many cases, crafted by the store owners. Influenced largely by Indonesian patterns, the airy attire includes V-neck cotton pullovers perfect for a casual, hot-weather climate, as well as linen shifts, often in batik prints, appropriate for a glamorous cocktail party. Most pieces here are for women; all are made from all-natural materials, such as cotton, silk, and linen, and there's also a limited array of sandals, hats, scarves, and leather bags. **Benetton,** Schottegatweg-Oost 148 Salinas (© **599/9-461-4619**), has invaded Curaçao with all its many colors. Some items are marked down by about 20% below U.S. prices (this is done to get rid of surplus stock from the previous season); in-season clothing is available as well.

Bert Knubben Black Koral Art Studio, in the Breezes Curaçao Resort, Dr. Martin Luther King Boulevard (© **599/9-465-2122**), is synonymous with craftsmanship and quality. Although it's illegal to collect black coral here, an exception was made for Bert, a diver who has been harvesting corals and fashioning them into fine jewelry and objets d'art for more than 35 years. Collectors avidly seek out this type of coral, not only for the quality of its craftsmanship, but also because it's becoming increasingly rare and may one day not be offered for sale at all.

Gandelman Jewelers, Breedestraat 35, Punda (© **599/9-461-1854**), is the island's best and most reliable source for jewelry, often exquisitely designed and set with diamonds, rubies, emeralds, sapphires, and other gemstones. You can also find watches and the unique line of Prima Classe leather goods embossed with the world map.

Little Holland, Braedestraat 37, Punda (© **599/9-461-1768**), specializes in silk neckties, Panama hats, Nautica shorts and shirts, Swiss Army knives, and, most important, a sophisticated array of cigars. Crafted in Cuba, the Dominican Republic, and Brazil, they include some of the most prestigious names in smoke, including Montecristos, Cohiba, and Churchills. *Remember:* It's still illegal to bring Cuban cigars into the United States; smoke them here.

Electronics are a good buy on Curaçao, as they can be sold duty-free; we recommend the very reliable **Boolchand's,** Freedome Blokd 1, Punda (© **599/9-461-2262**), in business since 1930. If you can't find what you're looking for, try **Palais Hindu,** Heerenstraat 17 (© **599/9-461-6897**), which sells a wide range of video and cassette recorders, TVs, speakers, minidisc players, photographic equipment, and watches.

Penha & Sons, Heerenstraat 1 (© **599/9-461-2266**), in the oldest building in town (1708), has a history dating from 1865. It has long been known for its fine selection of perfumes, cosmetics, and designer clothing (for both men and women). It distributes such names as Calvin Klein, Yves Saint Laurent, Elizabeth Arden, Clarins, and Estée Lauder, among others.

La Casa Amarilla (The Yellow House), Breedestraat 46 (© **599/9-461-3222**), operating since 1887 in a yellow-and-white 19th-century building, sells an intriguing collection of perfume and cosmetics from all over the world and is an agent of Christian Dior, Guerlain, Cartier, and Van Cleef & Arpels.

At **Landhuis Groot Santa Martha,** Santa Martha (© **599/9-864-1559**), craftspeople with disabilities fashion unusual handicrafts, some evoking those found in South America.

There are a lot more stores to check out, including **New Amsterdam,** Gomerzpein 14 (© **599/9-461-2437**), a long-established store known for its Hummel figurines and hand-embroidered tablecloths, among other items. For novelties and souvenirs, head for **Warenhaus Van Der Ree,** Breedestraat 5, Punda (© **599/9-461-1645**).

8 Curaçao After Dark (★(★

Most of the action spins around the island's **casinos:** the **Marriott Beach Resort,** Piscadera Bay (© 599/9-736-8800); **Holiday Beach Hotel & Casino,** Otrabanda, Pater Euwensweg 31 (© 599/9-462-5409); **Plaza Hotel & Casino,** Plaza Piar, in Willemstad (© 599/9-461-2500); and **Breezes Curaçao Resort,** Dr. Martin Luther King Blvd. 8 (© 599/9-736-7888).

Emerald Casino at the Marriott is especially popular, designed to resemble an open-air courtyard. It features 143 slot machines, 6 blackjack tables, 2 roulette wheels, 2 Caribbean stud poker tables, a craps table, a baccarat table, and a minibaccarat table. The casino at the Breezes Curaçao is the liveliest on the island. These hotel gaming houses usually start their action at 2pm, and some of them remain open until 4am.

The landlocked, flat, and somewhat dusty neighborhood of **Salinja** is now the nightlife capital of Curaçao. **Club Zen/K-Oz Bar,** 129 Salinjastraat (© 599/9-461-4443 or 599/9-696-7145), is one of the hottest clubs in Curaçao, drawing the bump-and-grind after midnight crowd. On most nights you pay a $10 (£5.20) cover to enter. On Thursday and Saturday nights, techno prevails at Zen. On Friday, the action switches upstairs to the stylish rooftop retreat K-Oz, where DJs rule the night. Among the other venues is **Blues,** in the Avila Beach Hotel, Penstraat 130 (© 599/9-461-4377), a restaurant with a hopping bar that's packed every night except Mondays. Live jazz is offered Thursday from 7 to 10pm and Saturday from 9pm to midnight, with no cover.

Club Façade, Lindbergh 32 (© 599/9-461-4640), in the Salinja district, is one of the most popular dance clubs on the island. Spread over several different levels of a modern building, it has a huge bar, three dance floors, and live music nightly. It's open Thursday and Friday from 8pm to 3am. The cover is $5 to $10 (£2.60–£5.20).

On Monday, Friday, and Saturday nights the place to be is **Ole! Ole!,** Salinja (© 599/9-461-7707), offering live jazz music. If you like to party on the beach, head for **Hook's Hut,** Piscadera Bay (© 599/9-462-6575). Jazz is a regular feature here, and it's also known to book the best local music on the island.

A pontoon boat, *Mi Dushi,* Baya Beach at the end of Caracas Bai St. (© 599/9-747-4489), is a floating club with a dance floor, three bars, and a full barbecue. *Mi Dushi* sails every Monday, Thursday, and Saturday 1 to 5pm, costing $60 (£31) for adults and $20 (£10) for children 12 and under.

11

Dominica

The beaches aren't worth the effort to get here, but the landscape and rivers, as well as increasingly renowned scuba diving, are. Nature lovers who visit Dominica (Dom-in-*ee*-ka) experience a wild, rugged Caribbean setting, as well as the rural life that has largely disappeared on the more developed islands. Dominica is, after all, one of the poorest and least developed islands in the Caribbean. There are no casinos and no megaresorts—and hardly any road signs. It's also one of the less expensive islands in the Caribbean, and probably the only one that Columbus would still recognize.

Hiking and mountain climbing are good reasons to visit Dominica; its flora is made unbelievably lush by frequent rainfall. Covered by a dense tropical rainforest that blankets its mountain slopes, including cloud-wreathed Morne Diablotin at 1,424m (4,671 ft.), it has vegetation unique in the West Indies. The mountainous island is 47km (29 miles) long and 26km (16 miles) wide, with a total land area of 751 sq. km (293 sq. miles), much of which has never been seen by explorers. Should you visit, you'll find clear rivers, waterfalls, hot springs, and boiling lakes.

With a population of 71,000, Dominica lies in the eastern Caribbean, between Guadeloupe to the north and Martinique to the south. The Caribs, indigenous people of the Caribbean, whose numbers have dwindled to 3,000, live as a community on the northeast of the island and still practice the art of traditional basketry.

Clothing is casual, including light summer wear for most of the year. However, take along walking shoes for those trips into the mountains and a sweater for cooler evenings. Locals, who are rather conservative, do not allow bikinis and swimwear to be worn on the streets of the capital city, **Roseau,** or in the villages.

1 Essentials

VISITOR INFORMATION

Before you go, you can contact the **Dominica Tourist Office** at 110-64 Queens Blvd. (Box 427), Forest Hills, NY 11375 (© **888/645-5637** or 718/261-9615; fax 718/261-0702).

In England, information is available from **Morris Kevan International,** Mitre House, 66 Abbey Rd., Bush Hill Park Enfield, Middlesex (© **0181/3500-1000;** fax 0181/3500-1011).

You can also get information on the Web at **www.dominica.dm**.

On the island, the **Dominica Tourist Information Office** is on the Old Market Plaza, Roseau, with administrative offices at the National Development Corporation offices, Valley Road (© **767/448-2045;** fax 767/448-5840); it's open Tuesday to Friday 8am to 4pm, Monday from 8am to 5pm.

There are also information bureaus at **Melville Hall Airport** (© **767/445-7051**) and **Canefield Airport** (© **767/449-1199**).

Dominica

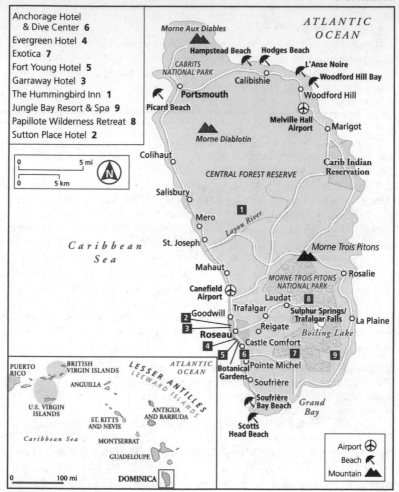

Anchorage Hotel
   & Dive Center **6**
Evergreen Hotel **4**
Exotica **7**
Fort Young Hotel **5**
Garraway Hotel **3**
The Hummingbird Inn **1**
Jungle Bay Resort & Spa **9**
Papillote Wilderness Retreat **8**
Sutton Place Hotel **2**

Airport
Beach
Mountain

GETTING THERE

BY PLANE   Neither of the two airports on Dominica is large enough to handle a jet, so there are no nonstop flights from the U.S. or Canada. The **Melville Hall Airport** (© 767/445-7100) is on the northeastern coast, a 1½-hour taxi ride from Roseau on the southwestern coast. The drive takes you across the island through the forest and coastal villages; the fare is EC$52 (US$19/£10) per person when there are four passengers. On your own, the fare could be EC$135 (US$50/£26).

The more modern **Canefield Airport** (© 767/449-1199) is about a 15-minute taxi ride north of Roseau. The 600m (2,000-ft.) airstrip accommodates smaller planes than those that can land at Melville Hall. From here, the typical taxi fare into town is EC$46 (US$17/£8.85). There's also a public bus (with an *H* that precedes the number on the license plate) that costs only EC$22 (US$8.15/£4.25) per person; buses come every 20 minutes and hold between 15 and 18 passengers.

> **Fun Fact** **National Day**
>
> National Day celebrations on November 3 commemorate both Columbus's 1493 discovery of the island and its independence, in 1978. Cultural celebrations of Dominica's traditional dance, music, song, and storytelling begin in mid-October and continue to Community Day, November 4, when people undertake community-based projects.

For many from the U.S., the easiest way to reach Dominica is via the daily **American Eagle** (© **800/433-7300** in the U.S. and Canada; www.aa.com) flight from American's hub in San Juan, Puerto Rico.

If you're already in the Caribbean, you can fly to Dominica from several other islands aboard **Caribbean Star** (© **800/723-1111** in the U.S. and Canada, 800/744-7827 in the Caribbean, or 268/480-2561 in Antigua; www.flycaribbeanstar.com). The little airline offers two daily nonstop flights from St. Lucia, three flights daily from Antigua, and two flights daily from Barbados. There is one flight daily but with a stopover from the islands of St. Kitts, St. Maarten, St. Vincent, Tortola (B.V.I.), and Trinidad.

BY BOAT   The *L'Express* (© **767/448-2181**), sailing from the French West Indies, runs between Guadeloupe in the north to Martinique in the south; Dominica is a port of call along the way. Departures are 6 days a week; call for exact schedules.

For schedule information, contact **White Church Travel,** 5 Great Marlborough St., Roseau (© **767/448-2181**). A one-way fare costs EC$195 (US$72/£37).

GETTING AROUND

BY RENTAL CAR   If you rent a car, there's a fee of EC$30 (US$11/£5.70) to obtain a driver's license, which is available at the airports. The island has 500km (310 miles) of paved roads, and only in a few areas is a four-wheel-drive vehicle necessary. *Note:* Driving is on the left.

There are a handful of small, usually family-owned car-rental companies, the condition and price of whose vehicles vary widely. They include **Valley Rent-a-Car,** Goodwill Road, Roseau (© **767/448-3233**); and **Best Deal Rent-A-Car,** 15 Hanover St., Roseau (© **767/449-9204**).

BY TAXI   You can hire a taxi at either the Melville Hall or Canefield airports. Prices are regulated by the government (see "Getting There," above, for airport fares). If you want to see the island by taxi, the driver will charge from EC$194 to EC$250 (US$72–US$93/£37–£48) for a tour that lasts between 4 and 5 hours. Rates are usually valid for between one and four passengers. After 6pm, taxis may be hard to find, so call ahead.

BY MINIBUS   The public transportation system consists of private minibus service between Roseau and the rest of Dominica. These flamboyantly painted minibuses are filled mainly with schoolchildren, workers, and country people who need to come into Roseau. On most Caribbean islands we don't recommend buses, but on Dominica they afford terrific insights into local life. Taxis may be a more reliable means of transport for visitors, but there are hotels at which buses call during the course of the day. You can also just hail a bus when you see it, and tell the driver where you want to go. Fares range from EC$1.50 to EC$10 (55¢–$3.80)/30p–£3). Buses are identified by the letter **H** that precedes their license numbers.

FAST FACTS: Dominica

Banks Banks are open Monday to Thursday from 8am to 2pm, Friday from 8am to 5pm. There are several major bank branches in Roseau, complete with ATMs that dispense EC dollars.

Currency Dominica uses the **Eastern Caribbean dollar (EC$),** worth about EC$2.70 to US$1 (EC$1 = US37¢). U.S. dollars are readily accepted, though you'll usually get change in EC dollars. *Unless otherwise specified, prices in this chapter are quoted in U.S. dollars and British pounds.*

Customs Dominica is lenient, allowing you to bring personal and household effects, plus 200 cigarettes, 50 cigars, and 40 ounces of liquor or wine per person.

Documents To enter, U.S. and Canadian citizens must have a passport. In addition, an ongoing or return ticket must be shown. British visitors should have a valid passport.

Electricity The electricity is 220–240-volt AC (50 cycles), so both adapters and transformers are necessary for U.S.-made appliances. It's smart to bring a flashlight with you, in case of power outages.

Emergencies To call the police, report a fire, or summon an ambulance, dial ⓒ **999.**

Hospital There's **Princess Margaret Hospital,** Federation Drive, Goodwill (ⓒ **767/ 448-2231),** but those with serious medical conditions may want to forego a visit to the hospital in Dominica, as island medical facilities are often inadequate.

Language English is the official language. Locals often speak a Creole-French patois.

Pharmacies The island's best-stocked drugstore is **Jolly's Pharmacy,** in Roseau at 37 Great George St., and 12 King George V St. Both branches share the same phone number and hours (ⓒ **767/448-3388).** They're open Monday to Friday from 8am to 5pm, and Saturday from 8am to 2pm.

Safety Although crime is rare here, you should still safeguard your valuables. Never leave them unattended on the beach or in a locked car.

Taxes A 10% government room tax is added on accommodations, and a 5% tax applies to   alcoholic drinks and food items. Anyone who remains on Dominica for more than 24 hours must pay an EC$55 ($20/£11) departure tax.

Telephone To call Dominica from the United States, dial **1,** then **767** (the country code for Dominica) and the local number. To call Dominica from another island within the Caribbean, just dial **767,** plus the seven-digit local number. International direct dialing is available on Dominica, as well as U.S. direct service through AT&T. You can contact **AT&T** in Dominica by dialing ⓒ **800/ 872-2881.** Most hotel telephone operators throw up their hands at even placing a long-distance call for a resident. Instead, they connect their clients to the island's long-distance phone operator, who dials the call for a client, and then calls are billed directly to a client's room.

Time Dominica is on Atlantic Standard Time, 1 hour ahead of Eastern Standard Time in the United States. Dominica does not observe daylight saving time, so when the United States changes to daylight saving time, clocks in Dominica and the U.S. East Coast tell the same time.

Tipping Most hotels and restaurants add a 10% service charge to bills; check carefully to see if it's been added. If this charge has not been included, tipping is up to you, though an additional 15% for particularly good service is always welcome.

Water Tap water is generally considered safe to drink, but because it's different from what you're used to, it still might cause a stomach disorder. Better stick to bottled water to be on the safe side.

Weather Daytime temperatures average between 70° and 85°F (21°C–29°C). Nights are much cooler, especially in the mountains. The rainy season is June to October, when there can be hurricane activity. Dominica lies in the hurricane belt, and fierce storms have taken their toll on the island over the years.

2 Accommodations

The government imposes a 10% tax on hotel rooms and a 5% tax on beverages and food, which will be added to your hotel bill. On top of that most hotels add a 10% service charge.

If you don't want to rent a car, it's best to stay in Roseau, where you can get around better. But if you'd like to experience nature, head for one of the remote inns in exotic tropical settings.

IN ROSEAU & CASTLE COMFORT

Anchorage Hotel & Dive Center   The Anchorage, established in 1971, is at Castle Comfort, .8km (½ mile) south of Roseau. For the active traveler, there is no better choice, as scuba diving, whale-watching, hiking, fishing, and bird-watching are emphasized. The Armour family provides small rooms with balconies overlooking a pool. The best open onto a view of the Caribbean and contain two double beds. The others are more standard, each with comfortable twins beds or one double. Bathrooms are adequate, with showers and decent shelf space. Although it's at the shore, there's little or no sandy beach available, so guests spend their days around the pool. However, the hotel has its own jetty, you can swim off the pebble beach, and there's a squash court.

The hotel's French and Caribbean cuisine is simple, with an emphasis on fresh fish and vegetables. A West Indian band plays music once a week for dancing.

Castle Comfort (P.O. Box 34), Roseau, Dominica, W.I. © 767/448-2638. Fax 767/448-5680. www.anchorage hotel.dm. 32 units. Year-round US$66–US$84 (£34–£18) double. Rates include breakfast. Children 11 and under 50% deduction on meals. AE, MC, V. **Amenities:** Restaurant; bar; outdoor pool; sailing; scuba diving; snorkeling; room service; babysitting; laundry service. *In room:* A/C, TV, fridge (in some), beverage maker, iron, Wi-Fi.

Evergreen Hotel   This seafront, family-run hotel looks a bit like a Swiss chalet from the outside, but inside there's an open-air restaurant with bright jungle prints, crystal teardrop chandeliers, and an Art Deco bar. It lies 1.5 km (1 mile) south of Roseau. A more modern-looking annex, though sterile, has better rooms than the main building. A few units have wraparound tile-floored verandas; all have stone accents. Accommodations are bright and airy, with most rooms having two double beds and ample storage space; bathrooms have showers only. The nicest is the Honeymoon Hut, an exotic and charming retreat for either honeymooners or off-the-record weekenders. A stony beach is visible a few steps beyond the garden. Inside and out, the airy, comfortably modern place is trimmed with local gommier wood.

Castle Comfort (P.O. Box 309), Roseau, Dominica, W.I. © 767/448-3288 or -3276. Fax 767/448-6800. www.avirtual dominica.com/evergreen. 16 units. Year-round US$127–US$169 (£66–£34) double. Children under 12 stay free in parent's room. Rates include full breakfast. AE, MC, V. **Amenities:** Restaurant; bar; pool; scuba diving; snorkeling; horseback riding; room service; babysitting; laundry service. *In room:* A/C, TV, hair dryer, safe, Wi-Fi.

Fort Young Hotel ⚓   Occupying a cliff-side setting, this modern hotel grew from the ruins of the 1770 Fort Young, once the island's major military installation. Traces of its former historic role remain, including cannons at the entrance. It's always attracted business travelers, but now more and more tourists are drawn to the comfortable bedrooms with ceiling fans and balconies. Here you are elevated far above the "mosquito line," so you can actually sit out and enjoy the balmy Caribbean air without being attacked. The hotel has 18 oceanfront guest rooms and three one-bedroom suites at the base of a cliff below the existing fort; it's worth the extra money to ask for one of these suites, which have direct ocean views, a sitting area, bathrooms with whirlpool tub/shower combinations, and two king-size beds. There's no beach, but there's a swimming pool.

Waterfront Restaurant is in a candlelit room with stone walls and wooden rafters. The Jamaican chef draws on his homeland for inspiration and is also an expert at regional dishes. Much of his repertoire has a Continental flair.

Victoria St. (P.O. Box 519), Roseau, Dominica, W.I. © 767/448-5000. Fax 767/448-5006. www.fortyounghotel.com. 70 units. Year-round US$85–US$170 (£44–£88) double; from US$200 (£104) suite. AE, MC, V. **Amenities:** 2 restaurants; bar; outdoor pool; health club; spa; Jacuzzi; sauna; dive center; mooring facilities; whale-watching; island tours; room service; laundry service. *In room:* A/C, ceiling fan, TV, kitchenette (in some), minibar (in some), beverage maker, hair dryer, safe (in some), Wi-Fi.

Garraway Hotel   This is the best inn for those who want to be in the capital and plan to rely on public transportation—usually business travelers, although it's a perfectly acceptable choice for vacationers, too. Of course, it's nowhere near a beach. This hotel is adjacent to the home of its owners, the Garraway family, and is the closest thing to a Ramada Inn on the island. Most of the spacious guest rooms have vistas stretching all the way to Dominica's southernmost tip. Each is outfitted with rattan furniture and pastel floral-print fabrics, one king-size or two double beds, and a combination tub/shower bathroom. Public rooms are given an authentic island touch with artwork and locally made vetiver-grass mats. On the premises is the Balisier restaurant (see "Dining," below).

Place Heritage, The Bayfront (P.O. Box 789), Roseau, Dominica, W.I. © 767/449-8800. Fax 767/449-8807. www. garrawayhotel.com. 30 units. Year-round US$90 (£47) double; US$120–US$150 (£62–£78) suite. Children under 12 stay free in parent's room. AE, DC, MC, V. **Amenities:** Restaurant; bar; room service; laundry service; nonsmoking rooms. *In room:* A/C, TV, hair dryer, iron.

Tips **Mosquito Alert**

At night you are likely to be plagued with mosquitoes. If that's a real problem for you, check into the Fort Young Hotel (see below), which is above the "mosquito line." Most hotels offer mosquito netting. Remember, you came to Dominica for unspoiled nature, right?

Sutton Place Hotel 🐟🐟 This small, historic property stands in the center of town and was once a 1930s guesthouse run by "Mother" Harris, a matriarch who became a local legend. Destroyed by Hurricane David in 1979, the new Sutton Place was rebuilt in a traditional Caribbean style by the same Harris family, which continues the old traditions but with far greater style. Rooms are tastefully furnished with antiques, including four-poster beds, brass desk lamps, and teak furnishings in the shower-only bathrooms. Suites contain fully equipped kitchenettes. The staircase and floors of the suites are laid with a fine hardwood, tauroniro, from South America. Stylized floral arrangements, exotic prints, and luxurious fabrics contribute to the upscale style.

The restaurant, The Sutton Grill, is now one of the choice places to dine in Roseau, with a Creole/international menu that also embraces some dishes from Italy, China, and India. The nearest beach is about 2km (1¼ mile) away.

25 Old St. (P.O. Box 2333), Roseau, Dominica, W.I. ✆ **767/449-8700.** Fax 767/448-3045. www.suttonplacehotel dominica.com. 8 units. Year-round US$95 (£49) double; US$135 (£70) suite. Extra person US$30 (£16). Rates include breakfast. AE, DISC, MC, V. **Amenities:** Restaurant; bar; business center; room service; laundry service. *In room:* A/C, ceiling fan, TV, kitchenette (in suites), beverage maker, hair dryer, Wi-Fi.

IN THE RAINFOREST

Papillote Wilderness Retreat 🐟 *Finds* This eco-inn is run by the Jean-Baptiste family: Cuthbert, who handles the restaurant, and his wife, Anne Grey, a marine scientist. Their unique resort, 6km (3¾ miles) east of Roseau, stands right in the middle of Papillote Forest, at the foothills of Morne Macaque. In this remote setting, you're surrounded by exotic fruits, flowers, and herb gardens. The rooms provide modern comforts like up-to-date bathrooms with plenty of hot water. They are most inviting with their hardwood floors, jungle-painted walls, floral quilts, and fresh flowers.

Don't expect constantly sunny weather, since this part of the jungle is known for its downpours; however, that's what keeps the orchids, begonias, and brilliantly colored bromeliads lush. The 5 hectares (12 acres) of sloping and forested land have a labyrinth of stone walls and trails, beside which flow freshwater streams, a few of which originate in hot mineral springs. Natural hot mineral baths are available, and you'll be directed to a secluded waterfall where you can swim in the river. The Jean-Baptistes also run a boutique that sells Dominican products, including appliquéd quilts made by local artisans. Even if you don't stay here, it's an experience to dine on the thatch-roofed terrace.

Trafalgar Falls Rd. (P.O. Box 2287), Roseau, Dominica, W.I. ✆ **767/448-2287.** Fax 767/448-2285. www.papillote.dm. 7 units. Year-round US$110 (£57) double; US$115–US$125 (£60–£65) suite. MAP (breakfast and dinner) US$35 (£18) per person extra. AE, DISC, MC, V. Closed Sept 1–Oct 15. **Amenities:** Restaurant; bar; 3 hot mineral pools; room service; laundry service. *In room:* Ceiling fan, Wi-Fi, no phone.

AT MORNE ANGLAIS

Exotica 🐟 *Finds* This tropical setting is home to what's called an "agro-eco" resort, with some 38 different flowers and fruit trees growing on the 2-hectare (5-acre) organic farm. When you finally reach the place after a harrowing ride, you can enjoy the cool mountain breezes 480m (1,580 ft.) above sea level, at a point some 8km (5 miles) from Roseau. In 1995, Fae and Altherton Martin built this cluster of cottages on the western slope of Mount Anglais in the southern half of the island. The resort's cottages are constructed from hardwoods, cured pine, and stone. Accommodations are comfortable and tastefully furnished, each with a private porch, spacious living room, kitchen, large bedroom with two double beds, and private bathrooms with tub/shower combos. All are nonsmoking. You can go wading in a nearby stream, a 5-minute walk away.

You can prepare your own meals or dine at the Sugar Apple Cafe, enjoying such delights as steamed local fish or apricot-glazed chicken with savory rice.

Morne Anglais (P.O. Box 109), Roseau, Dominica, W.I. © 767/448-8839. Fax 767/448-8829. www.exotica-cottages.com. 6 units. Winter US$140 (£73) double; off season US$109 (£57) double. Extra person US$20 (£10). Children under 12 stay free in parent's room. MAP (breakfast and dinner) US$35 (£18) per person extra. AE, DISC, MC, V. **Amenities:** Cafe; laundry service; rooms for those w/limited mobility. *In room:* Ceiling fan, kitchen, beverage maker, hair dryer, iron.

AT POINT MULATRE

Jungle Bay Resort & Spa ★ *Finds*   This is a so-called "wellness" and adventure retreat, one of the finest on this eco-friendly island. Opening in 2005, the resort is a holistic health spa with a mammoth "yoga terrace." In all, there are 35 rustically outfitted cottages with wood furnishings perched like birds nests on the hillside. The structures were made from volcanic stone and tropical hardwoods. The resort also features the Spa du Soleil, yoga studios, two restaurants serving health food, and hiking trails shooting out in all directions. Hikes cover a 23-hectare (57-acre) sanctuary, filled with tropical birds and an array of exotic plant life. A spring-fed stream cascades along the valley below the hotel. Cottages are accessed through a series of stone stairways and footpaths. At your semi-outdoor shower, your body communes with nature, or so they say. Organized activities include a full range of spa treatments, yoga classes, and even cultural activities such as live entertainment and dancing.

Point Mulatre, Dominica. © 767/446-1789. Fax 767/446-1090. www.junglebaydominica.com. 35 units. Winter US$189 (£98) double; off-season US$159 (£83) double. 7-night honeymoon and eco-adventure packages available. MC, V. **Amenities:** 2 restaurants; beach bar; outdoor pool; spa; fitness classes. *In room:* Ceiling fan, no phone.

AT MORNE DANIEL

The Hummingbird Inn ★ *Value*   A 3km (2-mile) drive from Roseau and the Canefield Airport and a 2-minute walk to the beach, this hilltop retreat is a great little bargain. Opening onto panoramic views, the rooms are in two bungalows and have louvered windows and doors to capture the breezes in lieu of air-conditioning. Ceilings fans hum day and night, and you can also retreat to terraces with hammocks. Each of the accommodations has bedside tables and reading lamps (not always a guarantee on Dominica). All rooms are nonsmoking. The handmade quilts on the beds, which have excellent mattresses, add a homey touch. One four-poster bed, a mammoth wooden affair, is 250 years old. Bathrooms are small but well maintained, and each has a shower. This is a friendly, family-style place, and there are lovely gardens with exotic plants that attract both hummingbirds and iguanas. The local cook is one of the best on the island, and she'll pack a picnic lunch for you.

Morne Daniel (P.O. Box 1901), Roseau, Dominica, W.I. ©/fax 767/449-1042. www.thehummingbirdinn.com. 10 units. Winter US$99 (£52) double, US$136 (£71) suite; off season US$85 (£44) double, US$120 (£62) suite. Extra person US$20 (£10). Children under 12 stay free in parent's room. AE, DC, DISC, MC, V. **Amenities:** Restaurant; bar; room service; babysitting; laundry service. *In room:* Ceiling fan, safe.

AT HATTON GARDEN/MARIGOT

Silks ★★★   This is the poshest luxury boutique on island, housed in a villa and former rum distillery dating from the 1600s. During the shooting of *Pirates of the Caribbean—Dead Man's Chest,* actors Johnny Depp and Orlando Bloom slept here. The hotel lies on the east coast of Dominica near the Atlantic and is surrounded by two acres of landscaped gardens between two freshwater rivers. Rooms are regally decorated, the style ranging from Creole plantation to African. The Rum Mango room is independent from the main building, with its own garden and terrace. All the accommodations are spacious and beautifully furnished, and you sleep under mosquito nets on wooden floors. Many guests request the tower of Josephine, with its antique four-poster (said to have once been occupied by Josephine before she married Napoleon). Fine food and wine are served at the on-site restaurant, using fresh ingredients, often from the kitchen's own garden. Tables overlook the Pagua River.

Hatton Garden, Marigot, Dominica, W.I. ✆ 767/445-8846. Fax 767/445-8092. www.silks-hotel.com. 5 units. US$300–US$330 (£156–£171) double. Rates include breakfast. MC, V. **Amenities:** Restaurant; Internet; babysitting; business facilities; car rentals; laundry service. *In room:* Ceiling fans, hair dryer, no phone.

3 Dining

If you're going out in the evening, always call to make sure the restaurant you want to visit is actually open. You'll also have to arrange transportation there and back; you probably don't want to drive yourself because of the bad lighting, hairpin turns, and blind corners.

Dominica is a lush island like Grenada and grows a lot of its own foodstuff, but fish and meats are generally shipped in frozen.

IN ROSEAU

Balisier ☆ CREOLE/INTERNATIONAL   Named after a small red flower that thrives in the jungles of Dominica, this restaurant was designed to maximize the views over Roseau's harbor. We highly recommend the food, which might include blackened tuna; chicken Garraway (breast of chicken stuffed with plantain and sweet corn); loin of pork with pineapple, mushrooms, and onions; and a choice of steak, vegetarian, or lobster entrees. Crab backs are a favorite local dish. End your meal with a slice of homemade coconut-cream pie. Lunches might feature West Indian curries, fish Creole, or several kinds of salads.

In the Garraway Hotel, Place Heritage, The Bayfront. ✆ 767/449-8800. Reservations recommended. Main courses lunch EC$40–EC$80 (US$15–US$30/£7.80–£16), dinner EC$30–EC$80 (US$11–US$30/£5.70–£16); Fri lunch buffet EC$40 (US$15/£7.80). AE, MC, V. Daily 8am–2:30pm and 7–10pm.

Guiyave CREOLE   This airy restaurant occupies a wood-frame West Indian house. Rows of tables almost completely fill the narrow balcony overlooking the street outside. You can enjoy a drink at the stand-up bar on the second floor. Specialties include various Creole grills and different preparations of conch, octopus, lobster, spareribs, chicken, and pork chops. On Saturday, *rotis* (Caribbean burritos) and "goat water" (a local goat stew) are available. The place is known for refreshing juices like soursop, tamarind, sorrel, cherry, and strawberry. There's also a patisserie specializing in local pastries. The lunch buffet is served only on weekdays, not on Saturday.

15 Cork St. ✆ 767/448-2930. Reservations recommended. Main courses EC$18–EC$60 (US$6.65–US$22/£3.45–£12); lunch buffet EC$34 (US$13/£6.55). AE, MC, V. Daily 8am-3pm and Thurs-Mon 6:30-10pm.

La Robe Creole ☆☆ WEST INDIAN/CREOLE   The best independent restaurant in the capital, La Robe Creole sits on the second floor of a colonial house, beside a sunny plaza on a slope above the sea. The staff, dressed in madras Creole costumes, serves food in a long, narrow dining room capped with heavy beams and filled with 19th-century relics. You can enjoy pumpkin-pimento soup, callaloo with cream of coconut soup, crab backs (in season), and shrimp in coconut with garlic sauce. For dessert, try banana or coconut cake or ice cream.

A street-level section of the restaurant, **The Mouse Hole** (Monday to Saturday 7:30am to 4pm), is a good place for food on the go. You can buy freshly made sandwiches, salads, and light meals. They make good Trinidad-inspired *rotis* (Caribbean burritos).

3 Victoria St. ℂ **767/448-2896.** Main courses EC$27–EC$76 (US$10–US$28/£5.20–£15). AE, MC, V. Mon–Sat 11am–11pm.

Pearl's Cuisine 𝔎 *Finds* CARIBBEAN   Come to this restored Creole house with a veranda for a true taste of Dominica: Chef Pearl's island delicacies are renowned locally. Begin with one of her tropical fruit juices, followed by perhaps freshly caught crayfish as an appetizer. Whenever lobster is available, it's served at dinner any way you want it. She also makes some mean pork chops, and her curried goat will put hair on your chest. Try the potato salad and spareribs or the codfish and plantains if you want to really go local.

50 King George V St. ℂ **767/448-8707.** Lunch EC$6–EC$35 (US$2.20–US$13/£1.15–£6.75). DC, MC, V. Mon–Sat 9:30am–6pm.

World of Food Restaurant and Bar 𝔎 *Finds* CREOLE   This is one of Roseau's most charming Creole restaurants; some even call its owner, Vena McDougal, the best Creole cook in town. We more or less agree, but the competition is stiff. You can have a drink at the stone-walled building at the far end of the garden (in the 1930s the garden belonged to novelist Jean Rhys, author of *Wide Sargasso Sea*), but many guests select one of the tables in the shadow of a large mango tree. Specialties include steamed fish or fish steak, pork chops, chicken-filled *roti*, black pudding, breadfruit puffs, conch, and *tee-tee-ree* (fried fish cakes). Vena also makes the best rum punches on the island.

In Vena's Hotel, 48 Cork St. (with another entrance on Field's Lane). ℂ **767/448-3286.** Main courses EC$25–EC$54 (US$9.25–US$20/£4.80–£10). AE, MC, V. Daily 7:30am–10pm.

IN THE RAINFOREST

Papillote Wilderness Retreat 𝔎 *Finds* CREOLE/CARIBBEAN   Even if you're not staying here, come by taxi for lunch; it's only 6km (3¾ miles) east of Roseau. For dinner, you'll need to make reservations. Amid exotic flowers, century-old trees, and filtered sunlight, you'll dine overlooking a gorgeous vista of rivers and mountains. The array of healthful food includes flying fish and truly delectable freshwater prawns known as *bookh*. Freshly caught kingfish is also a tasty treat. Breadfruit or dasheen puffs merit a try if you've never had them, and the tropical salads—we recommend the green papaya chicken salad—are filled with flavor.

Trafalgar Falls Rd. ℂ **767/448-2287.** Reservations recommended for lunch, required for dinner. Main courses EC$30–EC$60 (US$11–US$22/£5.75–£12). AE, DC, DISC, MC, V. Daily 7am–10:30pm (dinner served at 7:30pm).

4 Sports & Other Outdoor Pursuits

BEACHES   If you really want a great beach, you should choose another island. Dominica has some of the worst beaches in the Caribbean; most are rocky and have gray-black volcanic sand. But some beaches, even though they don't have great sand or shade, are still good for diving or snorkeling in the turquoise waters.

The best beach on the island lies on the northwest coast. **Picard Beach** stretches for about 3km (2 miles), a strip of grayish sand with palm trees as a backdrop. It's ideal for snorkeling or windsurfing. You can drop in for food or a drink at one of the hotels along the beach.

On the northeast coast, four beaches—**Hampstead Beach, Hodges Beach, L'Anse Noire,** and **Woodford Hill Bay**—are among the island's most beautiful, although none are great for swimming. Divers and snorkelers often come here, even though the water can be rough. Watch out for the strong currents.

The southwest coast also has some beaches, but the sand here is black and rock-studded. Nonetheless, snorkelers and scuba divers flock to **Soufrière Bay Beach** and **Scotts Head Beach** for the clear waters and the stunning underwater walls.

HIKING   Wild and untamed Dominica offers hikers some of the most bizarre geological oddities in the Caribbean. Sights include scalding lava covered with a hot, thin, and not-very-stable crust; a boiling lake where mountain streams turn to vapor as they come into contact with superheated volcanic fissures; and a barren wasteland known as the "Valley of Desolation."

All these attractions are in the heavily forested 6,800 hectares (16,800 acres) of the **Morne Trois Pitons National Park** ⚔, in the island's south-central region. You should go with a guide—there are plenty of them waiting for your business in the village of Laudat. Few markers appear en route, but the trek, which includes a real assortment of geological oddities, stretches 10km (6¼ miles) in both directions from Laudat to the Boiling Lake. Ferns, orchids, trees, and epiphytes create a tangle of underbrush; insect, bird, and reptilian life is profuse.

The hill treks of Dominica have been described as "sometimes easy, sometimes hellish," and if it should happen to rain during your climb (and it rains very frequently on Dominica), the paths are likely to become very slippery. But botanists, geologists, and experienced hikers all agree that climbs through the jungles of Dominica are the most rewarding in the Caribbean. Hikers should walk cautiously, particularly in areas peppered with bubbling hot springs. Regardless of where you turn, you'll run into streams and waterfalls, the inevitable result of an island that receives up to 400 inches of rainfall a year. Winds on the summits are strong enough to have pushed one recreational climber to her death several years ago, so be careful.

An adventure only for the most serious and experienced hiker is to **Boiling Lake** and the **Titou Gorge,** a deep and very narrow ravine whose depths were created as lava flows cooled and contracted. En route, you might spot rare Sisserou and Jacquot parrots, monkeys, and vines whose growth seems to increase visibly on an hourly basis. The lake itself lies 10km (6¼ miles) east of Roseau, but reaching it requires about 4 hours of hiking, some of it strenuous. Go only with a guide, which can be arranged through the tourist office. (See "Visitor Information," earlier in this chapter, and the "Tips" box below.)

Taking the Wotton Waven Road, you branch off in the direction of **Sulphur Springs,** volcanic hot springs that are evidence of Dominica's turbulent past. Jeeps and Land Rovers can get quite close. This bubbling pool of gray mud sometimes belches smelly sulfurous fumes. The trail begins at the **Titou Gorge,** where you can go for a cooling swim in a pool or enjoy the hot spring waters alongside the pool. A 5-minute swim will take you up the gorge to a small cave with a beautiful waterfall. After the gorge the marked trail goes through the appropriately named **"Valley of Desolation"** and comes out at Boiling Lake on the far side, a trek of 2 to 3 hours one-way. Sulfuric fumes in the area have destroyed much of the once-flourishing vegetation in the region.

Boiling Lake is the world's second-largest solfatara lake, measuring 63m (207 ft.) across. It is a bubbling cauldron with vapor clouds rising above blue-gray water. The

> ⓣ Tips **Getting a Guide**
>
> Locals warn that to proceed along the island's badly marked trails into danger-
> ous areas is not a good idea; climbing alone or even in pairs is not advised.
> Guides should be used for all unmarked trails. You can arrange for a guide at
> the office of the **Dominica National Park,** in the Botanical Gardens in Roseau
> (ⓒ **767/448-2401**), or the Dominica Tourist Board. Forestry officials recommend
> **Ken's Hinterland Adventure Tours & Taxi Service,** Fort Young Hotel on Victoria
> Street, Roseau (ⓒ **767/448-4850**). You can also call **NBC** (ⓒ **767/448-2045** or
> **4272**) to arrange a tour. Depending on the destination and the attractions,
> treks cost US$140 to US$240 (£73–£125) per person for up to four participants
> and require 4 to 8 hours round-trip. Minivan transportation from Roseau to the
> starting point of your hill climb is usually included in the price.

depth of the lake is not known. The water temperature in the lake averages around 190°F (88°C). The lake is not the crater of a former volcano but a flooded fumarole. Getting here is extremely difficult and even hazardous. Some visitors have even stum-bled and fallen to their deaths into the boiling waters. The trail is most often very slip-pery because of rainfall. You'll encounter few visitors along this trail and, if you do, will likely be glad for the company, especially if a hiker is returning from the area where you're heading. He or she can give you advance reports of the conditions ahead of you.

See "Exploring the Island," below, for details on gorgeous **Cabrits National Park.**

KAYAKING 🐵🐵 Dominica is probably the best place in all the Caribbean for kayaking. Depending on the size, you can rent a kayak for US$26 to US$50 (£14–£26) for a half-day, then go on a unique adventure around the rivers and coast-line of the lushest island in the West Indies. **Nature Island Dive,** in Roseau (ⓒ **767/ 449-8181**), offers rentals and gives the best advice. You can combine bird-watching, swimming, and snorkeling as you glide along. Consider Soufrière Bay, a marine reserve in southwest Dominica. Off the west coast, you will discover tranquil Caribbean waters with rainbow-hued fish along the beaches in Mero, Salisbury, and in the region of the Layou and Macoucherie rivers.

SCUBA DIVING Diving has taken off on Dominica. The underwater terrain is spectacular. Most of the diving is on the southwestern end of the island, with its dra-matic drop-offs, walls, and pinnacles. These volcanic formations are interwoven with cuts, arches, ledges, and overhangs, home to sponges, gorgonians, and corals. An abundance of invertebrates, reef fish, and unusual sea creatures such as sea horses, frogfish, batfish, and flying gunards attract underwater photographers.

Dive Dominica, in the **Castle Comfort Diving Lodge** (P.O. Box 2253, Roseau), Castle Comfort, Dominica, W.I. (ⓒ **767/448-2188**), gives open-water certification (both NAUI and PADI) and instruction. Two diving catamarans and a handful of smaller boats get you to the dive sites in relative comfort. The dive outfit is part of a hotel, a 15-room lodge where at least 90% of the clientele checks in as part of a dive package. A 7-night dive package, double occupancy, begins at US$1,099 (£572) per person, including breakfasts and dinners, five two-tank dives, and one night dive. A single tank dive for nonguests goes for US$50 (£26), a two-tank dive for US$80

(£42), and a night dive for US$55. All rooms in the lodge are air-conditioned, and have TVs, phones, and Wi-Fi. On the premises are a bar (for residents and their guests only) and a Jacuzzi.

Divers from all over the world come to the **Dive Centre**, at the Anchorage Hotel in Castle Comfort (© **767/448-2638**). With a pool, classrooms, a private dock, a miniflotilla of dive boats, and a fully qualified PADI staff, this is the most complete dive resort on Dominica. A single-tank dive costs US$60 (£31); a double-tank dive, US$79 (£41); and a one-tank night dive, US$65 (£34). A whale- and dolphin-watch from 2pm to sunset is popular and costs US$50 (£26) per person. There is an additional US$4 (£2) charge for use of the marine park for two people. Rum punch is served.

SNORKELING   Snorkeling sites are never far away, regardless of where you are on Dominica. In all, there are some 30 first-rate snorkeling areas immediately off the coast. The western side of the island, where nearly all of the snorkeling takes place, is the lee side, meaning the waters are tranquil. You can explore the underwater hot springs at Champagne and Toucari, the Coral Gardens off Salisbury, and the southern shoreline of Scotts Head Beach, with more than 190 species of flamboyantly colored fish. The closeness of the reefs to shore makes snorkeling here some of the best in the Caribbean. Your hotel or one of the dive shops can set you up with gear.

SWIMMING   The beaches may be lousy, but Dominica has some of the best river swimming in the Caribbean. Some say the little island has 365 rivers, one for every day of the year. The best places for swimming are the refreshing ponds at the base of a waterfall, of which there are dozens on the island. Your best bets are on the west coast at the **Picard** or the **Machoucherie rivers.** On the east coast, the finest spot is **White River,** near the hamlet of La Plaine. Consider also the **Layou River** and its gorges. Layou is the island's largest river, ranging from tranquil beach-lined pools ideal for swimming to deep gorges and turbulent rapids. All the rivers are pristine and make nice spots for a little sunbathing or perhaps a picnic lunch along their banks.

The staff at the tourist office (see "Visitor Information," earlier in this chapter) knows the island intimately and will help you map out a place for a picnic and a swim during your tour of the island, depending on where you're going. They'll also arm you with a good map and directions if you're heading out on your own.

Our favorite place for a dip is the **Emerald Pool Trail,** which lies in the Morne Trois Pitons National Park. You reach it northeast of Pont Casse, going for 6km (3¾ miles) along an unmarked road taking you north to Castle Bruce. Eventually you reach a sign pointing to the Emerald Pool Trail, the most accessible trail in this lush national park. A 30-minute hike takes you to a stunning cascade of water dropping 6m (20 ft.). This is Emerald Falls, where you can go for a cooling swim. Chances are, you'll have it all to yourself.

5 Exploring the Island

Those making day trips to Dominica from other Caribbean islands will want to see the **Carib Indian Reservation** ⚑, in the northeast. In 1903, Britain got the surviving Caribs to agree to live on 1,480 hectares (3,656 acres) of land. Today, this reservation is the last remaining turf of the once-hostile tribe for whom the Caribbean was named. Today they survive by fishing, growing food, and weaving baskets and vetiver-grass mats, which they sell to the outside world. The baskets sold at roadside stands make especially good buys. Once you get here there isn't a lot to do, although watching the Caribs making traditional dugout canoes is interesting.

It's like going back in time when you explore **Morne Trois Pitons National Park** ✦✦, a primordial rainforest. Mists rise gently over lush, dark-green growth, drifting up to blue-green peaks that have earned Dominica the nickname "Switzerland of the Caribbean." Framed by banks of giant ferns, rivers rush, and tum ble, trees sprout orchids, green sunlight filters down through trees, and roaring waterfalls create a blue mist. One of the best starting points for a visit to the park is the village of **Laudat,** 11km (6¾ miles) from Roseau. (See also "Hiking," above.)

The best tour is the **Rain Forest Aerial Tram,** at the corner of Old Street and Great George Street in Laudat (✆ 767/448-8775), but it's open only when cruise ships are in port. For US$55 (£29) per person you're taken on a 90-minute tour that starts at the village of Laudat, "sailing" over the rainforest through the Morne Trois Pitons National Park. Along the way you're treated to exotic bird life, beautiful waterfalls, and much tropical flora.

Eight kilometers (5 miles) up from the **Roseau River Valley,** in the south-central sector of Dominica, **Trafalgar Falls** is reached after driving through the village of Trafalgar. Shortly beyond the hamlet of Trafalgar and up a short hill, there's a little kiosk where you can hire a guide to take you on the short walk to the actual falls. In all, allow about 1½ hours for the trip from Trafalgar to the falls. This is the only road or pathway into the falls, and you'll have to approach on foot, as the slopes are too steep for vehicles. After a 20-minute walk past ginger plants and vanilla orchids, you arrive at the base, where a trio of falls converges in a rock-strewn pool.

For another great way to spend half a day, head for the **Papillote Wilderness Retreat** (see previous recommendations in "Accommodations" and "Dining," earlier). The botanical garden alone is worth the trip, as are the views of mountains and lush valleys. Near the main dining terrace is a Jacuzzi-size pool, which is filled with the mineral-rich waters of a nearby hot spring. Nonguests can use the pool for EC$11 (US$4.05/£2.10). Bring sturdy walking shoes in addition to a bathing suit.

On the northwestern coast, **Portsmouth** is Dominica's second-largest settlement. Here you can row up the Indian River in native canoes, visit the ruins of old Fort Shirley in Cabrits National Park, and bathe at Sandy Beach on Douglas Bay and Prince Rupert Bay.

Cabrits National Park ✦✦ (no phone), on Dominica's northwestern coast, immediately adjacent to Douglas Bay, is a 525-hectare (1,300-acre) protected site, only about 25% of which is devoted to dry land. Here are low-rising hills, tropical forests,

---

Moments Searching for Moby Dick

You'll see more sperm whales, pilot whales, killer whales, and dolphins during **whale- and dolphin-watching trips** ✦ off Dominica than off any other island in the Caribbean. A pod of sperm whales can often be spotted just yards from your boat, since there are no laws here regarding the distance you must keep from the whales. The **Anchorage Hotel,** at Castle Comfort (✆ 767/448-2638), offers the best tours. A 4-hour trip costs US$50 (£26), but children under 12 pay half price. The vessels leave the dock every Wednesday and Sunday at 2pm (call ahead for availability).

swampland, volcanic-sand beaches, coral reefs, and the sprawling ruins of a fortified, 18th-century garrison of British, then French, construction. This is one of the area's great natural attractions, and if your time is limited, you may want to head here even if you skip everything else in Dominica. The park's land extends over a panoramic promontory formed by the low-rising twin peaks of extinct volcanoes (known as East Cabrit and West Cabrit) overlooking beaches, with Douglas Bay on one side and Prince Rupert Bay across the headland. The marine section of the park extends over the teeming marine life of the shallow waters of Douglas Bay.

If you want to explore the park underwater, we strongly encourage you to take one of the scuba or snorkeling trips organized by the officially designated dive operator for the park, **Cabrit's Dive Center,** Picard Estate, Portsmouth (© 767/445-3010). If you're interested in hiking, you'll find about 3km (2 miles) of trails, each clearly marked with brown-and-yellow signs, pointing out the geological and architectural highlights of the park. Foremost among these is **Fort Shirley,** a forbidding-looking hulk that was last used as a military post in 1854. The park's **Welcome Center** (no phone) contains a small on-site **museum** (open daily 9am–5pm; free admission) that highlights the natural and historic aspects of the park. The staff will make suggestions about the trails you might want to follow, but since the surface of the park is relatively limited in scope, it's hard to get lost. Signs point from the welcome center to the ruins of Fort Shirley, and to the low summits of the East and West Cabrit hills, neither of which rises more than about 150m (490 ft.) above sea level.

6 Shopping

Store hours are usually Monday to Friday from 8am to 5pm and Saturday from 9am to 1pm.

In Roseau, the **Old Market Plaza,** of historical significance as a former slave-trading market and more recently the site of a Wednesday-, Friday-, and Saturday-morning vegetable market, now houses three craft shops, each specializing in coconut, straw, and Carib craft products.

The handmade Dominican vetiver-grass mats sold at **Tropicrafts Island Mats,** 41 Queen Mary St. and Turkey Lane (© 767/448-2747), are known throughout the world, and you can watch the weaving process during store hours. They also sell dolls, shopping bags, and place mats, all appliquéd by hand.

Outlets for crafts include **Dominica Pottery,** Bayfront Street at Kennedy Avenue, Roseau (no phone), run by a local priest. An array of pottery made from local clays is on sale, as well as other handicrafts. **Ego Boutique,** 9 Hillsborough St., Roseau (© 767/448-2336), has the best selection of clothing, much of it in the classic West Indian style, along with some locally made crafts and home accessories.

Crazy Banana, Leopold Building on the waterfront (© 767/449-8091), offers a little preview of some of the best items for which the Caribbean is known, including handicrafts, handmade jewelry, bottles of rum, cigars, and regional paintings.

7 Dominica After Dark

It's not very lively, but there is some evening activity. A couple of the major hotels, such as the **Fort Young Hotel,** Victoria Street (© 767/448-5000), have entertainment on weekends, usually a combo or "jing ping" (traditional local music). The clubs and bars in these hotels attract mainly foreign visitors, so if you'd like to go where the locals go, head for one of the following.

The Warehouse, Checkhall Estate (© 767/448-5451), a 5-minute drive north of Roseau, adjacent to Canefield Airport, is the island's major dance club, and packed every Saturday. Recorded disco, reggae, and other music is played from 10pm to 5am in this 200-year-old stone building, once used to store rum. The cover is EC$12 (US$4.45/£2.30).

Check out **Krazy Terrace,** 16 King George V (© 767/440-0180), if late-night dancing is your thing.

Other hot spots include **Symes Zee's,** 34 King George V St., Roseau (© 767/448-2494), the domain of Symes Zee, the island's best blues man. A local band entertains with blues, jazz, and reggae. Here's your chance to smoke a reasonably priced Cuban cigar.

12

The Dominican Republic

Sugar-white beaches, inexpensive resorts, and rich natural beauty have long drawn visitors to the Dominican Republic, while at the same time, a not-so-fair reputation for high crime, poverty, and social unrest has scared away many others. Which is it, a poverty-stricken country rife with pickpockets and muggers, or a burgeoning destination of beautiful beach bargains?

The answer is a little of both. The people of the Dominican Republic are among the friendliest in the Caribbean, and the hospitality here seems more genuine than in more commercialized Puerto Rico. The weather is nearly perfect year-round. And the Dominican Republic's white-sand beaches are among the finest in the Caribbean. Punta Cana/Bávaro, for example, is the longest strip of white sand in the entire region.

Safety is still a concern in the Dominican Republic, but it shouldn't dissuade you from planning a vacation here. Crime consists primarily of theft, robberies, and muggings, and most of it is limited to Santo Domingo (although the north coast resorts around Puerto Plata and Playa Dorada are not as safe as they should be). There is a low incidence of violent crime against tourists, however. Follow some simple common-sense rules, and you'll be fine. (See "Fast Facts," below, for details.)

The combination of low prices and beautiful terrain has made the Dominican Republic one of the fastest-growing destinations in the Caribbean. Bargain-hunting Canadians, in particular, flock here in droves. Don't expect the lavish, spectacular resorts that you'll find on Puerto Rico or Jamaica, but do expect your vacation to be that much less expensive.

Often mistakenly referred to as "just a poor man's Puerto Rico," the Dominican Republic has its own distinct cuisine and cultural heritage. Its Latin flavor is a sharp contrast to the character of many nearby islands, especially the British- and French-influenced ones.

Columbus sighted its coral-edged Caribbean coastline on his first voyage to the New World and pronounced: "There is no more beautiful island in the world." The first permanent European settlement in the New World was on November 7, 1493, and its ruins still remain near Montecristi in the northeast part of the island.

In the heart of the Caribbean archipelago—nestled amid Cuba, Jamaica, and Puerto Rico—the island of Hispaniola (Little Spain) is divided between Haiti, on the westernmost third of the island, and the Dominican Republic, which has a lush landmass about the size of Vermont and New Hampshire combined. In the Dominican interior, the fertile Valley of Cibao (rich sugar-cane country) ends its upward sweep at Pico Duarte, the highest mountain peak in the West Indies, which soars to 3,125m (10,250 ft.).

Much of what Columbus first sighted still remains in a natural, unspoiled condition. One-third of the Dominican Republic's 1,401km (869-mile) coastline is devoted to beaches. The best are in Puerto Plata and La Romana, although

Puerto Plata and other beaches on the Atlantic side of the island have dangerously strong currents at times.

Almost from its inception, the country was steeped in misery and bloodshed, climaxing with the infamous reign of dictator Rafael Trujillo (1930–61) and the ensuing civil wars (1960–66). But the country has been politically stable since then, and is building and expanding rapidly. The economic growth hasn't benefited everybody, though. The country is still poor, even by Caribbean standards.

The greatest threat to the Dominican Republic these days comes from hurricanes, which periodically flatten entire towns. The major resorts have become adept at getting back on their feet quickly after a hurricane, but if a hurricane hits the country before your trip, you might want to call ahead and make sure your room is still standing.

1 Essentials

VISITOR INFORMATION

In the United States, you can contact the **Dominican Republic Tourist Information Center** at 136 E. 57th St., Suite 803, New York, NY 10022 (© **888/374-6361** or 212/588-1012); or at 348 Brickell Ave., Suite 405, Miami, FL 33131 (© **305/358-2899;** fax 305/358-4185). In Canada, try the office at 208 Crescent St., Montréal, PQ H3G 2B8 (© **800/563-1611** or 514/499-1918; fax 514/499-1393), or at 26 Wellington St., Suite 201, Toronto, ON M53 1S2 (© **800/494-5050;** fax 416/361-2130). Don't expect too much specific information.

In England, there's an office at 20 Hand Court, High Holborn, WC1 (© **020/7242-7778**).

On the Web, check out **www.dominicanrepublic.com**.

GETTING THERE

Before you book your airline tickets, read the section "Packages for the Independent Traveler" in chapter 2—it could save you a bundle. Even if you don't book a package, see that chapter's tips on finding the best airfare.

American Airlines (© **800/433-7300** in the U.S. and Canada; www.aa.com) has the most frequent service, offering at least a dozen flights daily from cities throughout North America to either Santo Domingo or Puerto Plata. Flights from hubs like New York, Miami, or San Juan, Puerto Rico, are usually nonstop. American also offers some good package deals.

If you're heading to one of the Dominican Republic's smaller airports, your best bet is to catch a connecting flight with **American Eagle,** American's local commuter carrier. Its small planes depart every day from San Juan, Puerto Rico, for airports throughout the Dominican Republic, including Santo Domingo, Puerto Plata, La Romana, and Punta Cana.

Continental Airlines (© **800/231-0856** in the U.S. and Canada; www.continental.com) flies daily between Newark, New Jersey, and Santo Domingo.

JetBlue Airlines (© **800/538-2583** in the U.S. and Canada; www.jetblue.com) flies from New York to the Dominican Republic, and **US Airways** (© **800/428-4322** in the U.S. and Canada; www.usairways.com) also flies from New York to the island. In addition, **Delta Airlines** (© **800/221-1212** in the U.S. and Canada; www.delta.com) flies from both New York and Miami to the Dominican Republic.

Other airlines servicing the area include **Air Transat** (© **866/847-1118** in the U.S. and Canada) which flies to Santo Domingo from Toronto, Vancouver, and Montréal.

Iberia (© **800/772-4642** in the U.S. and Canada; www.iberia.com) flies daily from Madrid to Santo Domingo, making a brief stop in San Juan.

For information on flights into Casa de Campo/La Romana, see the section "La Romana & Altos de Chavón," below.

Be warned: Arriving at Santo Domingo's Las Américas International Airport is confusing and chaotic. Customs officials, who tend to be rude and overworked, may give you a very thorough check. Stolen luggage is not uncommon here; beware of "porters" who offer to help with your bags. Arrival at La Unión International Airport, 37km (23 miles) east of Puerto Plata on the north coast, is generally much smoother and safer, but you should still be cautious.

GETTING AROUND

Getting around the Dominican Republic is not always easy if your hotel is in a remote location. The most convenient modes of transport are shuttle flights, taxis, rental cars, *públicos* (multipassenger taxis), and *guaguas* (public buses).

BY PLANE   The quickest and easiest way to get across a difficult landscape is on one of the shuttle flights offered by **Air Santo Domingo** (© **809/261-5222**), flying from Santo Domingo to Punta Cana and La Romana, among other towns. A one-way fare from Santo Domingo to Punta Cana costs US$85 (£44).

BY RENTAL CAR   The best way to see the Dominican Republic is to drive. Motorists drive on the right here. Although major highways are relatively smooth, the country's secondary roads, especially those in the east, are riddled with potholes and ruts. Roads also tend to be badly lit and poorly marked in both the city and the countryside. Drive carefully and give yourself plenty of time when traveling between island destinations. Watch out for policemen who may flag you down and accuse you (often wrongly) of some infraction. Many locals give these low-paid policemen a US$5 (£3) *regalo,* or gift "for your children," and are then free to go.

The high accident and theft rate in recent years has helped to raise car-rental rates here. Prices vary, so call around for last-minute quotes. Make sure you understand your insurance coverage (or lack thereof) before you leave home. Your credit card issuer may already provide you with insurance; call to find out.

For reservations and more information, call the rental companies at least a week before your departure: **Avis** (© **800/331-1212** in the U.S. and Canada, or 809/535-7191; www.avis.com), **Budget** (© **800/527-0700** in the U.S. and Canada, or 809/549-0351; www.budget.com), and **Hertz** (© **800/654-3131** in the U.S. and Canada, or 809/221-5333; www.hertz.com) all operate in the Dominican Republic. All three have offices at the Santo Domingo and Puerto Plata airports, as well as in downtown Santo Domingo. Avis and Hertz also have offices in La Romana and in Punta Cana.

Although the cars may be not as well maintained as the big three above, you can often get a cheaper deal at one of the local firms, notably **McAuto Rental Cars** (© **809/688-6518**). If you want a car with seat belts, you must ask. Your Canadian or American driver's license is suitable documentation, along with a valid credit card or a substantial cash deposit.

BY TAXI   Taxis aren't metered, and determining the fare in advance (which you should do) may be difficult if you and your driver have a language problem. You can easily hail a taxi at the airport and at most major hotels. *Warning:* Don't get into an unmarked street taxi. Many visitors, particularly in Santo Domingo, have been assaulted and robbed by doing just that. The minimum fare within Santo Domingo

Dominican Republic

Azurro Club (Azurro Club Estrella and Azurro Club Cabarete) **8**
Barceló Bávaro Beach, Golf & Casino Resort **1**
Bávaro Princess **18**
Casa de Campo **16**
Casa Colonial **1**
Francés Sofitel **12**
Gran Ventana Beach Resort **3**
Hilton Santo Domingo **10**
Hostal Nicolás Nader **11**
Hotel Santo Domingo **13**

Iberostar Costa Dorada **4**
La Puntilla de Piergiorgio **6**
Marien Coral Puerto Plata **1**
Meliá Caribe Tropical Resort **19**
Natura Cabañas & the Attabeyra Spa **7**
Occidental Gran Flamenco **5**
Paradise Beach Resort & Casino **2**
Paradisus Palma Real **17**
Renaissance Jaragua Hotel & Casino **14**
Sofitel Nicolas de Ovando **9**
Sosúa Bay Hotel **6**
Sunscape Casa del Mar **15**

---

is RD$95 (US$2.85/£1.45). In Santo Domingo, the most reliable taxi company is **Tecni-Taxi** (© 809/567-2010). In Puerto Plata, call **Tecni-Taxi** at © 809/320-7621.

BY PUBLIC TRANSPORTATION *Públicos* are unmetered multipassenger taxis that travel along main thoroughfares, stopping often to pick up people waving from the side of the street. A *público* is marked by a white seal on the front door. You must tell the driver your destination when you're picked up to make sure the *público* is going there. A ride is usually RD$5 (15¢/8p). The minimum fare is RD$3 (10¢/5p).

Public buses, often in the form of minivans or panel trucks, are called *guaguas* (pronounced *gwa-gwas*). For about the same price, they provide the same service as *públicos,* but they're generally more crowded. Larger buses provide service outside the towns. Beware of pickpockets on board.

FAST FACTS: The Dominican Republic

Banks Most banks are open Monday to Friday 8:30am to 4:30pm. **ATMs** are found at all branches of **Banco Popular**. Banks at the malls stay open until 6pm.

Currency The Dominican monetary unit is the **peso (RD$)**, made up of 100 centavos. Coin denominations are 1, 5, 10, 25, and 50 centavos, 1 peso, and 5 pesos. Bill denominations are RD$5, RD$10, RD$20, RD$50, RD$100, RD$500, RD$1,000, and RD$2,000. Price quotations in this chapter sometimes appear in U.S. and sometimes in Dominican currency, depending on the policy of the establishment. *Unless otherwise specified, prices in this chapter are quoted in U.S. dollars and British pounds.* The use of any currency other than Dominican pesos is technically illegal, but few seem to heed this mandate. At the time of writing, the exchange rate was about RD$32 to US$1 (meaning that centavos are practically worthless). Stated differently, RD$1 equals US.03¢. Bank booths at the international airports and major hotels will change your currency at the prevailing free-market rate.

Customs Visitors are allowed to bring in 200 cigarettes, 1 liter of alcohol, and gifts not exceeding a value of US$100 (£52). Anything over that will be subjected to import taxes.

Documents To enter the Dominican Republic, citizens of the United States, Canada, the United Kingdom, Australia, New Zealand, and other countries need a valid passport. Upon your arrival at the airport in the Dominican Republic, you must purchase a tourist card for US$10 (£5.20). You can avoid waiting in line by purchasing this card when checking in for your flight to the island.

Electricity The country generally uses 110-volt AC (60 cycles), so adapters and transformers are usually not necessary for U.S. appliances. To be safe, ask when booking your hotel.

Embassies All embassies are in Santo Domingo, the capital. The **U.S. Embassy** is on Calle Cesar Nicholas Penson at the corner of Máximo Gomez (✆ **809/ 221-2171**). The embassy of the **United Kingdom** is located at Av. 27 de Febrero, No. 233 Edificio Corominas Pepin (✆ **809/472-7111**). The embassy of **Canada** is found at Calle Capitán Eugenio de Marchena 39 (✆ **809/685-1136**).

Emergencies Call ✆ **911**.

Language The official language is Spanish; many people also speak some English.

Safety The Dominican Republic has more than its fair share of crime. (See "Getting There," above, for a warning about crime at airports.) Avoid unmarked street taxis, especially in Santo Domingo; you could be targeted for assault and robbery. While strolling around the city, beware of hustlers selling various wares; pickpockets and muggers are common here, and visitors are easy targets. Don't walk in Santo Domingo at night. Locals like to offer their services as guides, and it is often difficult to decline. Hiring an official guide from the tourist office is your best bet. Lock valuables in your hotel safe, carry only a reasonable amount of cash or (better yet) one or two credit cards, and avoid dark deserted places just like you would at home. (*One note:* The single male will find more solicitations from prostitutes [*putas* in Spanish] here than anywhere else in the Caribbean. *Putas* are at their most visible and aggressive in such relatively unmonitored tourist zones as Cabarete, and within the bars and lounges of most of the deluxe hotels of Santo Domingo, especially the Jaragua.)

Taxes A departure tax of US$20 (£10) is assessed and must be paid in U.S. currency. The government imposes a 16% tax on hotel rooms, which is usually topped by an automatic 10% service charge, bringing the total tax to staggering heights.

Telephone The area code for the Dominican Republic is **809.** You place calls to or from the Dominican Republic just as you would from any other area code in North America. You can access **AT&T Direct** by dialing ℂ **800/222-0300.** You can reach **MCI** at ℂ **800/888-8000** and **Sprint** at ℂ **800/877-7746.**

Time Atlantic Standard Time is observed year-round. Between November and March, when it's noon in New York and Miami, it's 1pm in Santo Domingo. However, during U.S. daylight saving time, it's the same time in the Dominican Republic and the U.S. East Coast.

Tipping Most restaurants and hotels add a 10% service charge to your check. Most people usually add 5% to 10% more, especially if the service has been good.

Water Stick to bottled water.

Weather The average temperature is 77°F (25°C). August is the warmest month, and January the coolest month, although even then it's warm enough to swim.

2 La Romana ⊕ & Altos de Chavón ⊕⊕⊕

On the southeast coast of the Dominican Republic, La Romana was once a sleepy sugar-cane town that specialized in cattle raising. Visitors didn't come near the place until Gulf + Western Industries opened a luxurious tropical paradise resort, the Casa de Campo, about 2km (1¼ mile) east of town. It's the finest resort in the Dominican Republic, and especially popular among golfers.

Just east of Casa de Campo is Altos de Chavón, a charming and whimsical copy of what might have been a fortified medieval village in Spain, southern France, or Italy. It's the country's leading attraction.

ESSENTIALS

VISITOR INFORMATION The government maintains **La Romana Tourist Office** at Teniente Amado García 22 (ℂ **809/550-6922**), open Monday to Friday 8am to 6pm. The staff is earnest and hardworking, but don't expect to come away with a wealth of information.

GETTING THERE By Plane American Airlines (ℂ **800/433-7300** in the U.S.; www.aa.com) flies once a day to the Casa de Campo airport (its international code is LRM) from Miami, with a travel time of about 2½ hours each way. (Yes, it's a slow plane.) **American Eagle** (same phone number) operates at least two (and in busy seasons, at least three) daily nonstop flights to Casa de Campo/La Romana airport (LRM) from San Juan, Puerto Rico. The flight takes about 45 minutes, and it departs late enough in the day to permit transfers from other flights. US Airways (© **800/ 622-1015**) offers nonstop weekly service, usually on Saturday, from Charlotte, North Carolina.

BY CAR   You can drive here in about an hour and 20 minutes from Santo Domingo's international airport (SDQ), along Las Américas Highway. (Allow another hour if you're in the center of the city.) Of course, everything depends on traffic conditions. (Watch for speed traps—low-paid police officers openly solicit bribes, whether you're speeding or not.)

GETTING AROUND   Most visitors don't rent a car but rely on local transportation, which is very haphazard and operated by independent drivers. You'll find both taxis and *motoconchos* (motorized scooters) at the northeast corner of Parque Central in the heart of La Romana. A typical ride almost anywhere within town costs less than RD$75 (US$2.25/£1.15), with the average taxi ride costing less than RD$150 (US$4.50/£2.25). Prices are always to be negotiated, of course.

LA ROMANA
ACCOMMODATIONS

Casa de Campo ⭐⭐⭐   Translated as "country house," Casa de Campo, on its own beach, functioned for many years as the most visible, most alluring, and most glamorous resort in the Dominican Republic. And although its pre-eminence has been challenged by newer, more cutting-edge resorts, it still exerts a powerful hold on the imagination of the country's image of itself as a tourist destination. There's a staggering variety of accommodations you can rent here, from a conventional but very comfortable hotel room to an entire house. Decor tends to be reasonably consistent throughout: Tiles, craft objects, and mahogany furniture mostly built in the D.R., mahogany louvered doors, and neutral-toned fabrics, usually white, adorn the interior of both the public areas and the accommodations. And thanks to the vast acreage associated with this place, your lodgings might, according to your preference, be either near the beach or near one of the resort's four golf courses. In addition to the conventional hotel rooms, only about 150 of the resort's total of 1,400 private homes are available for rent. Some are clustered in a semiprivate hilltop compound with views overlooking the meadows, the sugar cane, and the fairways down to the distant sea.

La Romana, Dominican Republic. © **800/877-3643** in the U.S., or 809/523-8698. Fax 809/523-8394. www.casade-campo.com.do. 279 units. Winter US$353–US$385 (£184–£200) double, US$664 (£345) suite; off season US$224–US$250 (£117–£130) double, US$434 (£226) suite. All-inclusive plans are extra. AE, DC, MC, V. **Amenities:** 8 restaurants; 5 bars; 2 outdoor pools; 20 semi-private pools; 4 18-hole golf courses; 13 tennis courts (10 lit); health club; aerobics; watersports equipment; bikes; horseback riding; polo; children's center (ages 3–12); theater; limited room service; massage; babysitting; laundry service. *In room:* A/C, TV, minibar, hair dryer, iron/ironing board, safe.

Sunscape Casa del Mar ⭐ *Kids*   This contender on a spectacular beach is giving the grand dame of Casa de Campo a run for the money. The golf and tennis facilities here aren't as elaborate as those at Casa de Campo, and there are no polo grounds, but the resort is beautifully landscaped, and the beach is palm fringed. Accommodations are within a well-designed series of three-story buildings with yellow walls and blue-tiled roofs. Decor inside features lots of tile, varnished hardwood, wicker, and rattan, plus a neatly appointed shower-only bathroom. There's an overall cheerfulness about the place and lots of emphasis on merengue music that helps keep the good times rolling. Everything served in all of the resort's restaurants is covered by the all-inclusive price. Da Mario serves Italian food, Chinese is on the menu at Asia, and the

Seaside Grill serves beachfront barbecues and grills, Dominican style. There's also a buffet restaurant and a disco. This is one of the very rare all-inclusive resorts that offers the availability of a day pass, priced at US$50(£26) per person per day, allowing up close and personal access to the facilities.

Bayahibe Beach, La Romana, Dominican Republic. © 866/786-7227 in the U.S., or 809/221-8880. Fax 809/221-2776. www.sunscaperesorts.com. 851 units. Winter US$150–US$167 (£78–£87) per person double, US$184 (£96) per person suite; off season US$60–US$95 (£31–£49) per person double, US$72–US$120 (£37–£62) per person suite. A day pass for non-residents costs US$50 (£26) per person. Rates are all-inclusive. AE, MC, V. **Amenities:** 5 restaurants; 6 bars; 2 outdoor pools; disco; 4 tennis courts (each lit for night play); health club; Jacuzzi; sauna; watersports equipment; bikes; horseback riding; children's programs; room service; babysitting. *In room:* A/C, TV, minibar, hair dryer, iron, safe.

DINING

La Casita ✿ ITALIAN/INTERNATIONAL   This is the most elegant and substantial restaurant in downtown La Romana, a stylish and well-managed enclave of chic that's the regular dining choice of some the homeowners from nearby Casa de Campo. Established in the late 1980s, and outfitted like a country tavern in the countryside of Italy, it has lined its walls with handpainted porcelain collected during the owners' travels in Italy and Spain. We'd urge you to seek out the tiny corner bar of this place before or after your meal, where walls are lined with the sophisticated caricatures and cartoons of Dominican artist/architect Roberto Copa, the designer of Altos de Chavon. If you opt for a meal here, you'll be in rather upscale company: Menu items include lobster thermidor, filet of sea bass *meunière*, grilled salmon with white wine and herbs, and all manner of pastas.

Calle Francisco Richiez 57. © 809/556-5932. Reservations recommended. Main courses RD$250–RD$1,200 (US$7.50–US$36/£3.75–£18). AE, DC, MC, V. 11am–11pm daily.

Shish Kabab MIDDLE EASTERN/INTERNATIONAL/DOMINICAN   Few local residents can even imagine La Romana without the Shish Kabab, an informal, well-managed restaurant with a polite and hardworking staff. Set within a few blocks of the Parque Central Duarte (La Romana's most central square), the restaurant serves Middle Eastern and international cuisine that's a wholehearted change of pace from Dominican fare. Naturally, the chefs specialize in kababs, but there are many other Middle Eastern specialties as well, notably *baba ghanoush*, with mashed eggplant studded with fresh parsley, fresh garlic, lemon juice, olive oil, and sesame paste. The beef kababs are tastily grilled, and there's even a shish kabab pizza. Skewered grouper is yet another worthy specialty. Don't overlook the wall of this place that's covered, edge-to-edge, with frame photographs of the baseball stars, meringue singers, and politicians who have dined here.

Calle Francisco del Castillo Marquez 32. © 809/556-2737. Pizzas RD$320–RD$450 (US$9.60–US$14/£4.80–£6.75); Main courses RD$180–RD$390 (US$5.40–US$12/£2.70–£5.85). AE, DC, MC, V. Tues–Sun 10am–midnight.

HITTING THE BEACH

La Minitas, Casa de Campo's main beach and site of a series of bars and restaurants, is a small but immaculate beach and lagoon that requires a 10-minute shuttle-bus ride from the resort's central core. Bus transportation is provided, or you can rent an electric golf cart. A bit farther afield (a 30-min. bus ride, but only a 20-min. boat ride), **Bayahibe** is a large, palm-fringed sandy crescent on a point jutting out from the shoreline. Finally, **Catalina** is a fine beach on a deserted island, surrounded by turquoise waters; it's just 45 minutes away by motorboat. Unfortunately, many other visitors from Casa de Campo have learned of the glories of this latter retreat, so you're not likely to have the sands to yourself.

SPORTS & OTHER OUTDOOR PURSUITS

Casa de Campo is headquarters for just about any sporting activity or outdoor pursuit in the area. Call the resort's guest services staff at © **809/523-3333** for more information. **Casa del Mar** weighs in with a heavy array of outdoor activities ranging from horseback riding to banana boating. Call **809/221-8880** for more details.

FISHING   You can arrange **freshwater river–fishing trips** through Casa de Campo. Some of the biggest snook ever recorded have been caught around here. A 3-hour tour costs RD$868 (US$31/£16) per person, and includes tackle, bait, and soft drinks. A 4-hour deep-sea fishing trip costs RD$15,372 to RD$20,496 (US$549–US$732/£286–£381) per boat, with 8 hours going for RD$22,204 to RD$30,744 (US$793–US$1,098/£412–£571).

GOLF   *Golf* magazine declared Casa de Campo (© **809/523-3333,** ext. 3187) "the finest golf resort in the world." The **Teeth of the Dog** ✦✦✦ course has been called "a thing of almighty beauty," and it is. The ruggedly natural terrain has seven holes skirting the ocean. Opened in 1977, **The Links** ✦✦✦ is an inland course modeled after some of the seaside courses of Scotland. In the late 1990s, the resort added a third golf course to its repertoire, **La Romana Country Club,** which tends to be used almost exclusively by residents of the surrounding countryside rather than by guests of Casa de Campo.

   The cost for 18 holes of golf is RD$4,480 (US$160 (£83) at the Links and RD$5,544 (US$198/£103) at Teeth of the Dog and the La Romana Country Club. (Some golf privileges may be included in packages to Casa de Campo.) You can also buy a 3-day membership, which lets you play all courses for RD$7,056 (US$252/£131) per person (for Casa de Campo guests only). A 7-day membership costs RD$14,056 (US$502/£261). You can hire caddies for RD$700 (US$25/£13); electric golf-cart rentals cost RD$560 (US$20/£11) per person per round. Each course is open 7:30am to 5:30pm daily. Call far in advance to reserve a tee time if you're not staying at the resort.

HORSEBACK RIDING   Trail rides at Casa de Campo or Casa del Mar cost RD$700 (US$25/£13) per person for 1 hour, RD$1,120 (US$40/£21) for 2 hours. The stables shelter 250 horses, although only about 40 of them are available for trail rides. For more information, call **Casa del Campo** at © **809/523-3333,** ext. 5249, or **Casa del Mar** at © **809/221-8880.**

SNORKELING   **Casa de Campo** has one of the most complete watersports facilities in the Dominican Republic. You can charter a boat for snorkeling, with a minimum of eight people (The resort maintains eight charter vessels.) Full-day snorkeling trips to Isla Catalina cost RD$980 (US$35/£18) per snorkeler. Rental of fins and masks cost RD$140 (US$5/£2.60) per day; guests on all-inclusive plans use gear for free. Snorkeling is also included in the all-inclusive rates at **Casa del Mar** (© **809/221-8880**).

TENNIS   **Casa de Campo'**s 13 clay courts are available from 7am to 9pm. (They're lit at night.) Charges are RD$672 (US$24/£13) per court per hour during the day or RD$840 (US$30/£16) at night. Lessons are RD$1,708 (US$61/£32) per hour with a tennis pro, and RD$1,372 (US$49/£26) with an assistant pro. Call far in advance to reserve a court if you're not staying at the resort. The four courts at **Casa del Mar** (© **809/221-8880**) are reserved for the resort's all-inclusive guests.

ALTOS DE CHAVON: AN ARTISTS' COLONY

In 1976 a plateau about 150km (100 miles) east of Santo Domingo was selected by Charles G. Bluhdorn, then chairman of Gulf + Western Industries, as the site for a remarkable project. Dominican stonecutters, woodworkers, and ironsmiths began the task that would produce **Altos de Chavón,** a flourishing Caribbean art center set above the canyon of the Río Chavón and the Caribbean Sea.

A walk down one of the cobblestone paths of Altos de Chavón reveals architecture reminiscent of another era at every turn. Coral block and terra-cotta brick buildings house artists' studios, craft workshops, galleries, stores, and restaurants. Mosaics of black river pebbles, sun-bleached coral, and red sandstone spread out to the plazas. The **Church of St. Stanislaus** is the central attraction on the main plaza, with its fountain of the four lions, colonnade of obelisks, and panoramic views. Mass is held every Saturday and Sunday at 5pm.

The **galleries** (© **809/523-8470**) at Altos de Chavón offer an engaging mix of exhibits. In three distinct spaces—the Principal Gallery, the Rincón Gallery, and the Loggia—the work of well-known and emerging Dominican and international artists is showcased. The gallery has a consignment space where finely crafted silk-screen and other works are sold. Exhibits change about every month.

Altos de Chavón's *talleres* are craft ateliers, where local artisans produce ceramic, silk-screen, and woven-fiber products. From the clay apothecary jars with carnival devil lids to the colored tapestries of Dominican houses, the rich island folklore is much in evidence. The posters, note cards, and printed T-shirts that come from the silk-screen workshops are among the most sophisticated in the Caribbean. All the products of Altos de Chavón's *talleres* are sold at **La Tienda** (© **809/523-3333,** ext. 5398), the foundation village store.

The Altos de Chavón **Regional Museum of Archaeology** (© **809/523-8554**) houses the objects of Samuel Pion, an amateur archaeologist and collector of treasures from the vanished Taíno tribes, the island's first settlers. The timeless quality of some of the museum's objects makes them seem strangely contemporary in design—one discovers sculptural forms that recall the work of Brancusi or Arp. The museum is open Tuesday to Sunday from 9am to 8pm; entrance is free.

At the heart of the village's performing-arts complex is the 5,000-seat open-air **amphitheater.** Since its inauguration by the late Frank Sinatra and Carlos Santana, the amphitheater has hosted concerts (by Julio Iglesias and Gloria Estefan, among others), symphonies, theater, and festivals. The annual Heineken Jazz Festival has brought together such diverse talents as Dizzy Gillespie, Toots Thielmans, Randy Brecker, Shakira, Carlos Ponce, Carlo Vives, and Jon Secada.

The creations at **Everett Designs** (© **809/523-8554**) are so original that many visitors mistake this place for a museum. Each piece of jewelry is handcrafted by Bill Everett in a minifactory at the rear of the shop.

DINING

El Sombrero MEXICAN   In this thick-walled, colonial-style building, within the upper altitudes of Altos de Chavon, near the village church, jutting timbers and roughly textured plaster evoke a corner of Old Mexico. There's a scattering of rattan furniture and an occasional example of Mexican weaving, but the main draw is the spicy cuisine. Red snapper in garlic sauce is usually very good as are the beef and chicken fajitas. Most guests dine outside on the covered patio, within earshot of a group of wandering minstrels. Chances are you've had better versions of the standard nachos, enchiladas, tortillas with shrimp, black-bean soup, pork chops, grilled steaks marinated in tequila, and brochettes served here, but a margarita or two will make it a fun night out anyway.

Altos de Chavón. **©** **809/523-3333.** Reservations recommended. Main courses RD$400–RD$1,000 (US$12–US$30/£6–£15). AE, MC, V. Daily 6–11pm.

Giacosa ITALIAN/INTERNATIONAL   This is one of the few restaurants within Altos de Chavón that's not owned and operated by Casa de Campo. Within a two-story stone Tuscan-style building whose windows open onto a spectacular view over the Chavon river's chasm, you can try Mediterranean dishes such as seafood soup studded with lobster and shrimp; eggplant filled with goat cheese, pine nuts, and prosciutto; and black angus filet with wine sauce and truffles.

Altos de Chavón. **©** **809/523-8466.** Reservations recommended. Main courses RD$450–RD$1,450 (US$14–US$44/£6.75–£22). Six-course tasting menu RD$1,700 (US$51/£26). AE, MC, V. Daily noon–midnight.

La Piazzetta ITALIAN   Much of the allure of this place derives from the way its outdoor tables are positioned on a stone terrace that showcases a spectacular view over the river valley of the Chavon. But if you prefer indoor dining, this restaurant offers an air-conditioned replica of an antique stone-sided farmhouse, the kind you'd have expected in Tuscany or perhaps Andalusía. Our favorites are the *gnocchi* stuffed with three kinds of cheeses; risotto flavored with pumpkin and shrimp; grilled chicken; filet of hake with local greens and sautéed potatoes; and lasagna Bolognese.

In Altos de Chavon, near the church. **©** **809/523-8698.** Reservations recommended. Main courses RD$400–RD$990 (US$12–US$30/£6–£15). AE, DC, MC, V. Daily 6–11pm.

3 Punta Cana ⭑

On the easternmost tip of the island is Punta Cana, site of several major vacation developments with more scheduled to arrive in the near future. Known for its spectacular beaches and clear waters, Punta Cana is an escapist's dream. Its 32km (20 miles) of white sands, set against a backdrop of swaying palm trees, are unrivaled in the Caribbean, and that's the chief and perhaps only reason to come here.

Many Europeans (especially Spaniards) rushed to take advantage of Punta Cana's desirable climate—within one of the most arid landscapes in the Caribbean, it rarely rains during daylight hours. Capitalizing on cheap land and the virtually insatiable desire of Europeans for sunny holidays during the depths of winter, a half-dozen European hotel chains participated in something akin to a land rush, acquiring large tracts of sugar-cane plantations and pastureland. Today, at least a dozen megahotels, most with no fewer than 500 rooms, some with even more, attract a clientele that's about 70% European or Latin American. The hotel designs here range from the not particularly inspired to low-rise megacomplexes designed by the most prominent Spanish architects.

Some of them have some of the most lavish beach and pool facilities in the Caribbean, spectacular gardens, and relatively new concepts in architecture (focusing on postmodern interplays between indoor and outdoor spaces).

Don't expect a real town here. Although the mailing address for most hotels is the dusty and distinctly unmemorable Higüey, very few guests ever spend time there. Most remain on the premises of their all-inclusive hotels.

If you choose to vacation in Punta Cana, you won't be alone, as increasing numbers of Latino celebrities are making inroads, usually renting private villas within private compounds. Julio Iglesias has been a fixture here for a while. And one of the most widely publicized feuds in the Dominican Republic swirled a few years ago around celebrity designer Oscar de la Renta, who abandoned his familiar haunts at Casa de Campo for palm-studded new digs at Punta Cana.

Above all, don't expect a particularly North American vacation. The Europeans were here first, and many of them still have a sense of possessiveness about their secret hideaway. For the most part, the ambience is Europe in the Tropics, as seen through a Dominican filter. You'll find, for example, more formal dress codes, greater interest in soccer matches than in the big football game, and red wine rather than scotch and soda at dinner. Hotels are aware of the cultural differences between their North American and European guests, and sometimes strain to soften the differences that arise between them.

ESSENTIALS

GETTING THERE   **American Eagle** (© **800/433-7300** in the U.S. and Canada; www.aa.com) offers two to six daily nonstop flights to Punta Cana from San Juan, Puerto Rico; flying time is about an hour. You can also opt for one of American Eagle's two or three (depending on the season) daily flights from San Juan to La Romana and then make the 90-minute drive to Punta Cana.

GETTING AROUND   Most **taxi fares,** including those connecting the airport with most of the major hotels, range from RD$800 (US$24/£12) for up to four passengers. Your hotel can summon a cab for you. If you want to tour along the coast, you can **rent a car** on-site at the car-rental desks of all the major resorts.

ACCOMMODATIONS

Barceló Bávaro Beach, Golf & Casino Resort 𝒦𝒦   This huge complex of low-rise luxury hotels opens onto one of the most desirable of the many white-sand beaches along the 32km (20-mile) coast known as Bávaro Beach. Until it was surpassed by equally ambitious developments early in the millennium, this was defined, at least for a while, as the most ambitious resort colony in the Dominican Republic, a project whose scope hadn't been equaled since the early days of Casa de Campo. There's even a church on the premises for weddings, and a reputation for good, and in some cases, extremely good, food. Built in postmodern Spanish style, it occupies almost 12 sq. km (4¾ sq. miles) of land, including some of the best seafront property on the island.

The resort consists of five separate hotels: Bávaro Beach Hotel, Bávaro Caribe Hotel, Bávaro Golf Hotel, Bávaro Casino Hotel, and the latest contender, the Bávaro Palace Hotel. Arranged within a massive park, and connected via a labyrinth of roadways and bike trails, all but one is parallel to the beachfront. (The Bávaro Casino Hotel faces the golf course.) Neither the decor nor the gardens are as well-conceived and stylish as those within, say, the Paradisus group or the Meliá Caribe Tropical (see below), but the effect is nonetheless comfortable and pleasant. Accommodations in all five hotels are roughly equivalent and are outfitted in tropical furniture, with private verandas or terraces, plus an attractively tiled bathroom with tub and shower. (The Bávaro Palace's rooms are bigger and somewhat more comfortable than the others.) Bedrooms have tile floors, Dominican-made furniture, and colorful upholsteries and fabrics.

Each of the restaurants within this megahotel is interconnected by minivan service, and each will cheerfully accept diners from even the most far-flung corners of the compound. The most upscale and "gastronomic" of the lot is Chez Palace, serving French cuisine, some of whose main dishes require that all-inclusive guests pay a reasonable supplement for their meal. Other, slightly less pretentious eateries include Bohio and La Piña for Dominican food; Los Piños for Italian cuisine; the Coral Steakhouse for two-fisted slabs of grilled beef, chicken, and veal; Mexico Lindo for Mexican food; and an absolutely vast buffet setup within the open-to-the-breezes Ambar.

Apdo. Postal 3177, Punta Cana, Higüey, Dominican Republic. (C) **800/227-2356** in the U.S., or 809/686-5797. Fax 809/656-5859. www.barcelo.com. 1,921 units. Winter US$209 (£109) per person double in Palace, rooms in any of the other 4 hotels US$258 (£134) per person; off season US$157 (£82) per person double in Palace, doubles in any of the other 4 hotels US$154 (£80) per person. Prices are all-inclusive. Discounts of 45%–65% for children 2–12 staying in parent's room. AE, DC, MC, V. **Amenities:** 12 restaurants; 13 bars; 6 outdoor pools; whirlpools big enough for 30 people; casino; 3 discos; 18-hole golf course; 9 tennis courts; health club; aerobics; watersports equipment; horseback riding; 3 theaters; salon; limited room service; massage; babysitting; laundry service; dry cleaning; nonsmoking rooms; rooms for those w/limited mobility. *In room:* A/C, TV, minibar, hair dryer, iron, safe.

Bávaro Princess 🐟
Drawing some of its architectural inspiration from Bali, this hotel opens onto a 2km-long (1¼-mile) white-sand private beach. The Spanish-born architect Alvaro Sanz retained most of the palms and mangrove clusters on the property and installed freshwater reservoirs, creating an oasis not only for vacationers, but also for the many species of birds that call the resort home. All accommodations lie within low-slung bungalows. The split-level suites contain refrigerators and king-size or twin beds, each fitted with comfortable furnishings. The small bathrooms have combination tub/showers and marble counters.

Playa Arena Gorda, Punta Cana, Higüey, Dominican Republic. (C) **809/221-2311.** Fax 809/686-5427. 768 units. Year-round US$100–US$200 (£52–£104) double. Rates are all-inclusive. AE, MC, V. **Amenities:** 7 restaurants; 10 bars; 2 outdoor pools; 4 lit tennis courts; health club; kayaks; Sunfish sailboats; windsurfing; scooter rental; horseback riding; concierge; car rental; shopping arcade; room service; babysitting; laundry service; dry cleaning; dance club. *In room:* A/C, ceiling fans, TV, beverage maker, minibar, hair dryer, iron, safe.

Meliá Caribe Tropical Resort 🐟 (Kids)
The Meliá complex is less upscale than the Bávaro, but we prefer its innovative design. A series of bungalows is scattered within a spectacular garden, with palm trees, fountains, and real flamingos. When you tire of the grounds (if ever!), a little train will transport you over to the beach where topless sunbathing is commonplace. The lobby sets a fashionable tone with its lagoons, boardwalks, sculptures, and bubbling fountains. There's even a richly paneled, well-ventilated hideaway outfitted with poker tables, a bar, and an impressive inventory of Dominican cigars where patrons can puff away for hours. The spa is the best in the area, offering special features such as aromatherapy massages.

Accommodations are clustered into four distinct parcels of land, two of them adjacent to the beach and the most dramatic swimming pools in the Dominican Republic. The other two lie about .2km (200 yards) inland, adjacent to lobby/reception areas and a cluster of dance clubs, cabaret stages, gift shops, and restaurants. Spacious bedrooms are among the best in Punta Cana, with intricately crafted tile and stonework, private terraces or verandas, and roomy bathrooms with tiled showers.

On-site are 11 different **eateries,** including a trio of large-scale dining rooms (Los Atabales, El Turey, and La Alambra) with an ongoing roster of buffets; two **restaurants** with mostly a la carte French food (Le Gourmet and Ma Maison); a Mexican restaurant (Los Panchos) with a mixture of a la carte and buffet service; a pasta and pizza joint (Gondola); a Pan-Asian restaurant (Pagoda); a Japanese sushi bar (Hokkaido); and a seafood restaurant (Capri), which is open only for dinner. Know before you go that during periods when the hotel isn't fully booked, not all of these are likely to be open.

Playa Bávaro, Altagracia, Punta Cana, Dominican Republic. © **800/336-3542** in the U.S., or 809/221-1290. Fax 809/221-6638. www.solmelia.com. 1,144 units. Year-round US$343–US$530 (£178–£276) per person. Rates are all-inclusive. AE, DC, MC, V. **Amenities:** 11 restaurants; 20 bars; 7 outdoor pools; casino; 27-hole golf course; 8 lighted tennis courts; health club; 2 spas; snorkeling; windsurfing; children's programs; business center; laundry service; non-smoking rooms; rooms for those w/limited mobility; dance club. *In room:* A/C, ceiling fans, TV, minibar, hair dryer, safe.

Paradisus Palma Real 🎖🎖 (Kids) This is our favorite all-inclusive hotel in Punta Cana. It's one of the newest hotels at the resort, one of only four members of the same Spain-based hotels, and the kind of place where the kinks and errors of earlier, less sophisticated hotels have been ironed out and corrected. It's also the beneficiary of one of the most sophisticated designs in Punta Cana, permeated with stylish hints at Iberian antecedents that absolutely reek of the best aspects of creative contemporary design. The hotel's architecture seems to ripple and undulate from its entrance, past multiple and highly theatrical staircases, five different restaurants, one of which remains open through the long Caribbean night. The pools are spectacular, as is the beach. A complicated structure of add-on luxuries (spa packages, additional attention from the concierge staff, upgraded children's diversions) are available, and usually come with occupancy of somewhat upgraded accommodations.

The Paradisus Palma Real, after its inauguration in 2005, surpassed the glamour and allure of its slightly older (ca. 1996, 542-unit) sibling, the **Paradisus Punta Cana**, which lies about two miles away. Although both of the Paradisus hotels are desirable, we prefer the Paradisus Palma Real. In both hotels, most rooms have garden views, although some choice units open onto the ocean. Each comes with a tiled bathroom with tub or shower. Both hotels also offer more dining choices than any other along the coast—every cuisine from French to Chinese, from Mexican to Japanese, along with international, Dominican, and American food specialties. Entertainment is diverse, ranging from a karaoke disco to an aqua bar to bars that often serve Dominican cigars with their drinks. Theme parties are big here, and there are live shows nightly.

Paradisus Palma Real: Playas de Bávaro, Higüey, Dominican Republic. © **809/688-5000.** Fax 809/688-5800. www.solmelia.com. 685 units. Year-round US$178–US$950 (£93–£494) double. Children 2–12 pay 50% of adult rate. AE, DC, MC, V. Rates are all-inclusive. Free parking. **Amenities:** 5 restaurants; 6 bars; 2 pools; casino; nearby 18-hole golf; 3 tennis courts; health club; spa; sauna; watersports equipment; deep-sea fishing; horseback riding; children's center; room service; laundry service; dry cleaning; archery; bike and walking tours; karaoke disco; nightly entertainment. *In room:* A/C, TV, minibar, coffeemaker, hair dryer, iron, safe.

DINING

Given the wealth of restaurants in the hotels listed above, many guests never leave the premises for meals. But the following are worth a special trip.

Capitán Cook 🎖 SEAFOOD Set between the beachfront and the main street of Cortecito, this is the most enduringly popular local dive in town. Don't expect elaborate food, fancy sauces, or social prestige: In fact, when you approach the outdoor vestibule that prefaces the place, you might think you've entered the forecourt to a garage. The allure here is the ultrafresh seafood that's simply but superbly grilled to order from a chalkboard menu. A battery of outdoor grills lies near the entrance to a dining area whose tables are positioned beneath palm-frond gazebos overlooking a crowded stretch of rather narrow beach. Additional seating is upstairs, within an air-conditioned dining room that resembles a log cabin perched on stilts above Main Street. Some guests don't bother to consult the menu, but order their meal based on whatever is sputtering over coals or displayed on ice as they enter. Platters of grilled fish, freshwater crab, or lobster will be accompanied by lime-flavored butter sauce, salad, and your choice of baked potatoes or french fries. As an alternative, try the paella, spaghetti with shellfish, creole-style beefsteak, fish brochettes "Captain Cook," and/or a combination platter of grilled shrimp and calamari. Beer is often the accompaniment for anything served here, perhaps preceded by a rum-based cocktail.

Note: If you phone this place the day of your intended visit, the staff will probably offer to send a motorboat to pick you up at whatever suitable pier lies closest to your hotel, without any additional charge. (A US$5 (£2.60) tip to the boat attendants, however, would be appreciated.)

Playa El Cortecito, Marina El Cortecito. © 809/552-0645. Reservations recommended for dinner. Main courses RD$250–RD$1,300 (US$7.50–US$39/£3.75–£20). AE, DC, MC, V. Daily noon–midnight.

Chez Palace ☞ INTERNATIONAL   This is the showcase restaurant of one of the biggest resort complexes in the Dominican Republic. If you're not staying at one of the Barcelo hotels, you'll have to make reservations in advance. The decor is cool and stylish, as if it were imported from a chic resort in the south of Spain. A formally dressed staff serves superb dishes that include salmon mousse in a prawn sauce, tartar of tenderloin, grilled red snapper, grouper with mustard sauce, and filet mignon with truffles and foie gras. The prix-fixe menu offers many different choices.

In the Bávaro Palace Hotel, within the Barcelo Bávaro Beach, Golf & Casino Resort. © 809/686-5797. Reservations required. Prix-fixe dinner US$25 (£13). AE, DC, MC, V. Daily 7–11pm.

BEACHES

One of the Caribbean's great beaches stretches along the **Costa del Coco,** or Coconut Coast, covering more than 32km (20 miles) of brilliant white sand. Flanked by the all-inclusives, the major beaches here include Playa Macao, Playa Cortecito, Playa Bávaro, Playa Punta Cana, and Playa Punta Juanillo. The upmarket all-inclusives have staked out the best beachfront properties, so everything is done for you here, including unlimited access to food and drinks and watersports concessions at each hotel. For facilities, bars, and restaurants, you can use the hotel at which you are a guest. This beachfront is the stuff of travel magazines, with perfect sand and lots of coconut palms. Under an almost constant blue sky during the day, European, American, and Canadian guests frolic at the gin-clear waters.

The beaches at **Punta Cana** are wide, gorgeous, and safe to swim offshore throughout the year. An improvised series of barricades run parallel to some stretches of the coastal road, prohibiting access to the various beaches fronting the hotels. Entrances guarded by security forces prevent nonguests from entering, since once inside you're entitled to unlimited food and drink.

Activities abound, not only scuba diving but snorkeling, windsurfing, kayaking, water biking, sailing, beach volleyball or soccer, even water polo, along with aqua aerobics and tons of children's activities.

HORSEBACK RIDING

Within Punta Cana, the guest services staff at your hotel can arrange horseback riding for you, but if they can't, consider an equestrian jaunt at the region's biggest stables. These are headquartered at **Rancho RN-23,** Arena Gorda (© 809/747-7356 or 7538). It supervises as many as 125 horses that are stabled at three separate "ranches," each within a reasonable distance of one another. For RD$1,800 (US$54/£27) an hour, you'll be guided on equestrian tours through groves of coconut palms near the beach and, in most cases, onto the beach itself. To reach it, you'll follow some clearly marked signs 3km (2 miles) through some of the wildest terrain left in Punta Cana, down winding sandy paths to a series of palm groves, to the site of these stables. *Note:* Many potential riders who think that a two-hour equestrian excursion will be easy often find it more tiring, with more mosquitoes and horseflies then they might have expected.

GOLF

The Bávaro Golf Course, at **Barcelo Bávaro Beach, Golf & Casino Resort,** Bávaro Beach (© **809/686-5797**), is the best golf course on this end of the island, and bears the honor of being the golf course whose allure helped open the eastern DR to the tourist boom. Greens fees are RD$1,920 ($60/£31) for 18 holes, with cart rentals going for RD$1,440 (US$45/£23). Guests of the hotel pay only 50% of greens fees. Open daily 7am to 5pm.

Punta Cana Golf Club, near the Punta Cana Resort and Club (© **809/ 959-4653**), is the best and most sought-after of the four golf courses now flourishing in Punta Cana. Fronting the sea, it was designed by P. B. Dye of the famous golfing family. Fourteen of its holes open onto panoramic views of the Caribbean Sea, and four play along the ocean itself. For 18 holes, hotel guests pay RD$3,520 (US$110/£57), and nonguests are charged RD$4,800 (US$150/£78). In summer, greens fees are reduced to RD$2,144 (US$67/bp]34) for hotel guests, RD$2,944 (US$92/£46) for nonguests.

PUNTA CANA AFTER DARK

Bávaro Disco, on the grounds of the Barcelo Bávaro Beach, Golf & Casino Resort (© **809/686-5797**), has emerged as the hottest, most popular, and sexiest dance club in Punta Cana, thanks to a superb sound system. The venue is more European than North American, thanks to a heavy concentration of clients from Italy, Spain, and Holland. If you've been tempted to dress provocatively but never had the courage, the permissive and sexually charged ambience at this enormous club will give you the confidence to try. Painted black, with simulated stars overhead and lots of mirrors, the place is open nightly from 11pm to 5am. Entrance is free for residents of the Barcelo Hotel complex; nonguests pay RD$1,200 (US$36/£18).

4 Puerto Plata ⭐⭐

Columbus wanted to establish a city at Puerto Plata and name it La Isabela. Unfortunately, a tempest detained him, so it wasn't until 1502 that Nicolás de Ovando founded Puerto Plata ("port of silver"), 209km (130 miles) northwest of Santo Domingo. The port became the last stop for ships going back to Europe, their holds laden with treasures taken from the New World.

Puerto Plata appeals to a mass-market crowd that prefers less-expensive all-inclusives. More accommodations of this kind continue to pop up on this coast, and yet many are still booked solid almost year-round. An unfortunate byproduct of the all-inclusive trend is that several excellent restaurants have been forced to close; in fact, the most popular dining choice along the coast now is Pizza Hut.

Most of the hotels are not actually in Puerto Plata itself but in a tourist zone called Playa Dorada, which consists of major hotels, a scattering of secluded condominiums and villas, a Robert Trent Jones, Jr.–designed golf course, and a riding stable.

Although this was the first custom-built tourist haven in the Dominican Republic, the beaches are not the greatest. They're relatively narrow, and subject—as most beaches are—to the vagaries of hurricane erosion. Don't expect Robinson Crusoe–style isolation either; you'll never be alone on a stretch of beach in Puerto Plata, since the beach is shared with the residents of at least nine hotels, all jostling for position. However, if you enjoy beige sand that's rarely too hot to walk on, and a never-ending array of watersports kiosks, chaise lounges, and loudspeakers projecting merengue music, you'll be happy here. *One important note:* It rains a lot in Puerto Plata during the winter. If you want guaranteed sun, go to Punta Cana or the beaches on the southern coast.

ESSENTIALS

GETTING THERE   The international airport is east of Playa Dorado on the road to Sosúa. **American Eagle** (© **800/433-7300** in the U.S. and Canada; www.aa.com) has daily 2-hour flights from San Juan, Puerto Rico, to Puerto Plata. Flights cost from RD$5,600 to RD$11,760 (US$168–US$353/£84–£176) per person round trip from San Juan to Puerto Plata. American Airlines also flies daily from Miami (2 hr., 10 min) and from New York (3 hr., 30 min). Most of the Puerto Plata resorts are about a 40-minute drive from the airport.

From Santo Domingo, the 3½-hour drive directly north on Autopista Duarte passes through the lush Cibao Valley, home of the tobacco industry and Bermudez rum, and through Santiago de los Caballeros, the second-largest city in the country, 145km (90 miles) north of Santo Domingo.

GETTING AROUND   **Avis** (© **800/331-1212** in the U.S. and Canada, or 809/586-0214; www.avis.com), **Budget** (© **800/472-3325** in the U.S. and Canada, or 809/586-0413; www.budget.com), and **Hertz** (© **800/654-3131** in the U.S. and Canada, or 809/586-0200; www.hertz.com) all have offices at the airport.

You probably won't need to rent a car, however, if you're staying at one of the all-inclusive resorts. You might just like to get around Puerto Plata by **motor scooter,** although the roads are potholed. You can rent a scooter at the guest services kiosk at just about any large hotel in Puerto Plata.

Minivans are another means of transport, especially if you're traveling outside town. They leave from Puerto Plata's Central Park and will take you all the way to Sosúa. Determine the fare before getting in. Usually a shared ride between Puerto Plata and Sosúa costs RD$45–RD$60 (US$1.35–US$1.80/70p–95p) per person. Service is daily from 6am to 9pm.

If you take a **taxi,** agree with the driver on the fare before your trip starts, as cabs are not metered. You'll find taxis on Central Park in Puerto Plata. At night, it's wise to rent your cab for a round-trip. If you go in the daytime by taxi to any of the other beach resorts or villages, check on reserving a vehicle for your return trip. A taxi from Puerto Plata to Sosúa will cost around RD$580 (US$17/£8.70) each way (for up to four occupants).

VISITOR INFORMATION   There's an **Office of Tourism** on Calle José del Carmen Ariza 45 (© **809/586-3676**). Hours are Monday to Friday 8am to 3pm.

FAST FACTS   Round-the-clock **drugstore** service is offered by **Farmacia Deleyte,** Calle John F. Kennedy 89 (© **809/586-2583**). Emergency medical service is provided by **Clínica Dr. Brugal,** Calle José del Carmen Ariza 15 (© **809/586-2519**). To summon the **police** in Puerto Plata, Calle Luis Ginêbra, call © **809/586-2331**.

ACCOMMODATIONS

Casa Colonial 𝕲𝕲𝕲 This is the most sophisticated, most intimate, and most socially prestigious hotel in the Dominican Republic, a relatively recent architectural gem that successfully functions as the crown jewel of a respected local hotel chain, VH. It was the first hotel in the country to join the Small Luxury Hotels of the World marketing group, and as an à la carte boutique hotel, it is distinctly and definitely never included within the roster of Puerto Plata's mass market all-inclusives. Baronial and aristocratic-looking, it evokes a combination of a Greek Orthodox church and a Palladian-style Renaissance villa, with hints of Andalusia and a definite sense of Spanish colonial chic. Its central core contains two deluxe restaurants, and its annex artfully combines lush gardens and a view of a primal-looking mangrove lagoon immediately adjacent to a stretch of highly desirable beachfront. The on-site full-service spa, the Bagua, reeks of *haute* California hip.

Bedrooms are all-white retreats that are high-ceilinged, large, and in some cases, very large. Other than the Presidential suite, the best accommodations are the lavish oceanfront master suites with private entrances. This is a very adult, and appealingly indulgent kind of place, where the presence of children under 12 is not encouraged.

Playa Dorado (P.O. Box 22), Puerto Plata, Dominican Republic. ⓒ 809/571-9727. Fax 809/320-4017. www.vhhr.com. 50 units. US$260–US$420 (£135–£218) junior suites for 2, US$420–US$670 (£218–£348) specialty suites for 2. AE, DC, MC, V. **Amenities:** 2 restaurants; 3 bars; outdoor pool; golf privileges; health club; spa; room service; babysitting; laundry service; nonsmoking rooms; rooms for those w/limited mobility. *In room:* A/C, TV, minibar, beverage maker, hair dryer, iron, safe.

Gran Ventana Beach Resort 𝕲 *Kids* This is the largest of three nearly adjacent hotels that are each administered by the VH chain. Of the three, this has the most whimsical and least formal décor; a discreetly glamorous place that doesn't take itself too seriously. It occupies 100 landscaped hectares (247 acres) of ocean front that's divided into three distinctly defined clusters. The quietest and calmest of the three is the Beata Wing, which is just a bit removed but easily accessible, on foot, to the more animated Catalina and Saona clusters. You'll find a higher percentage of children here than at many other of Playa Dorada's resorts, thanks to a Kid's Klub, a glorified daycare center with its own mini-disco for adolescents and lots of good-natured attendants. The resort is composed of a series of three-story buildings, softened with landscaping, that are each trimmed with latticework and vaguely-Victorian-inspired fretwork; each unit has mahogany furniture, ceiling fans, a balcony or patio, and, in many cases, views of the sea. Bedrooms are compact but efficiently designed. Bathrooms are a bit small but have up-to-date plumbing with tub/shower combos. The gardens and lawns surrounding the site are dotted with gazebos, flowering shrubs, and tropical plants and palms.

The all-inclusive plan limits a guest to 1 hour per day for each of the following: snorkeling, windsurfing, sailing, horseback riding, kayaks, and scuba diving. It limits dining at the exclusive Octopus (an octagonally-shaped "gourmet" dining room with the most elaborate cuisine) to guests who reserve in advance. Some kind of live entertainment is presented here almost every night.

Playa Dorada (Apdo. Postal 22), Puerto Plata, Dominican Republic. ⓒ 809/320-2111. Fax 809/320-2112. www.vhhr.com. 506 units. Year-round US$80–US$150 (£42–£78) double; US$115–US$175 (£60–£91) junior suites; US$130–US$270 (£68–£140) suites. Rates are per person, double occupancy, and all-inclusive. AE, DC, MC, V. **Amenities:** 5 restaurants; 7 bars; 3 outdoor pools; tennis court; health club; sauna; watersports equipment; horseback riding; children's center; salon; room service; massage; babysitting; laundry service; dry cleaning; 1 room for those w/limited mobility. *In room:* A/C, TV, minibar, hair dryer, safe.

Iberostar Costa Dorada 🐸 *(Kids)*   With easy access to the beach, this hotel is owned and operated by a sophisticated Madrid-based chain, Iberostar. Elegant and striking, it has one of the most exciting designs of any hotel in Puerto Plata, with some of the most intricate stone, tile, and mosaic work, and a rambling combination of Taíno, Andalusian, and Moorish architecture. Several roofs of this hotel are covered with woven palm fronds, noteworthy for a hotel of this scale, sheltering a design that opens onto views of arcades, hidden courtyards, and fountains. A day or night pass, which entitles you to a meal, a round of drinks, and a view of the unusual design, costs US$40 (£21) per adult (either 6pm–2am or 10am–6pm), or half price per child under age 12.

Rooms are cool and airy, with tilework floors, earth tones, brightly colored upholsteries, wall weavings inspired by Taíno designs, and big windows. Each has a compact, shower-only bathroom, and the staff seems more alert and hip to the expectations of an international clientele.

Costa Dorada, Carretera Luperón, Km 4, Marapicá, Puerto Plata, Dominican Republic. ✆ **809/320-1000.** Fax 809/320-2023. www.iberostar.com. 516 units. Year-round US$105–US$177 (£55–£92) per person double; US$115–US$187 (£60–£97) per person junior suite. Rates are all-inclusive. AE, MC, V. **Amenities:** 4 restaurants; 5 bars; large pool; kayaks; sailing; windsurfing; children's activities. *In room:* A/C, TV, minibar, hair dryer, iron, safe.

Marien Coral Puerto Plata 🐸 *(Kids)*   This is an artfully designed compound, which we like almost as much as the Iberostar, which sits immediately next door. Couples seeking privacy at this all-inclusive resort will find it here, but those wanting around-the-clock activities will also be rewarded. Decor inside is stylish and more cutting edge than what you'll find within some other, older resorts, such as the Paradise Beach in neighboring Playa Dorada. A lagoon-shaped swimming pool and a series of three-story pastel-colored buildings radiate outward from an artful, Taíno-inspired central core, all of it set against a backdrop of sandy beach. A tobacco-leaf theme predominates, including replicas of broad leaves inlaid in ceramic tiles, upholstery fabrics, artwork, and even in the handmade iron headboards in the bedrooms. On site is a theater where concerts and meringue shows are presented for up to 750 people at a time.

The bedrooms are midsize to spacious, each well furnished and containing a balcony or ground-floor patio. A tropical decor prevails, with terra-cotta tile floors and sand-colored walls. Bathrooms are beautifully maintained with tub/shower combo. Restaurants are colorful enough, and the food is varied enough, so that you shouldn't become bored with the full-board arrangement. All-you-can-eat dinners, Caribbean seafood, barbecue nights, and both Mexican and Dominican specialties are some of the choices awaiting you.

Costa Dorada, Puerto Plata, Dominican Republic. ✆ **877/464-4586** in the U.S., or 809/320-1515. Fax 809/320-1414. www.coralhotel.com. 325 units. Year-round US$105–US$125 (£55–£65) per person. Rates all-inclusive. AE, DC, MC, V. **Amenities:** 4 restaurants, including an all-night snackbar; 4 bars; outdoor swimming pool (also children's pool); fitness room; state-of-the-art spa; sauna; Jacuzzi, children's club; babysitting; nonsmoking rooms; 1 room for those w/limited mobility. *In room:* A/C, TV, beverage maker, hair dryer, safe.

Occidental Gran Flamenco 🐸 *(Kids)*   Opening onto a tranquil stretch of Las Papas Beach, this is one of the most consistently reliable hotels in Puerto Plata, exuding Iberian flair and a low-key classiness that some of its competitors lack. Operated by the Spain-based Occidental chain, and radically renovated, it has a tasteful, discreetly elegant lobby outfitted with flowers and reproductions of Taíno statues. Accommodations are set within clusters of three-story buildings with white walls and red terra-cotta roofs. Throughout the accommodations there's a sense of Iberian dignity, with strong contrasts of dark paneling with white walls, and blue-and-white tile work.

More expensive rooms, in the Club Miguel Ange, are somewhat larger and have upgraded amenities and round-the-clock access to a concierge. Each bathroom has a tub/shower combo.

Dining options range from hot dogs, burgers, and pizza, to an array of international cuisine including seafood and a sampling of Mediterranean dishes. Our favorite is the grill restaurant, Las Reses.

Complejo Playa Dorada (P.O. Box 547), Puerto Plata, Dominican Republic. ⓒ **809/320-5084.** Fax 809/320-6319. www.occidental-hoteles.com. 582 units. Year-round US$130–US$150 (£68–£78) double. Rates are all-inclusive. AE, MC, V. **Amenities:** 8 restaurants; 6 bars; 2 outdoor pools; disco; golf course; tennis courts; aerobics; Jacuzzi; watersports equipment; horseback riding; children's center; travel agency; salon; babysitting; laundry service. *In room:* A/C, TV, minibar (in suite), safe.

DINING

Hemingway's Café INTERNATIONAL/MEXICAN   The rough-hewn character of this place stands in stark contrast to the manicured exterior of the shopping center that contains it. Inside, you'll find a dark and shadowy plank-sheathed bar and grill, dotted with accessories you might have found on a pier in Key West. The menu lists pastas, fajitas, quesadillas, meal-size salads, burgers, and generously portioned steaks. After around 9pm, a karaoke machine cranks out romantic or rock 'n' roll favorites.

Playa Dorada Plaza. ⓒ **809/320-2230.** Main-course platters RD$330–RD$1,050 (US$9.90–US$32/£4.95–£16). AE, MC, V. Daily noon–2am.

Jardín Suizo Malecón INTERNATIONAL   Simple, well-scrubbed, and unpretentious, a tradition here since 1990, this restaurant sits directly astride the Malecón's most easterly end, and because of a rather small sign, is a bit difficult to spot. Some things about it might remind you of a trattoria in southern Europe, thanks to tiles, cloth-draped tables set close together, and views out over the seafront promenade. Sliding windows are pulled back to take in views of the ocean. The food is fresh and well prepared, although some of the dishes might be a little heavy for the tropics. You can order such dishes as sliced filet of pork in a mushroom-flavored cream sauce, or three different medallions of meat in a wine sauce. The best item we enjoyed on the menu is the freshly caught fish filet of the day in garlic sauce. Many international dishes are offered as well, including tasty shish kabob, chicken curries, and a thick beef stroganoff.

Ave. Circunvalación Norte 13A, at the corner of Calle Paul Harris. ⓒ **809/586-9564.** Main courses RD$220–RD$480 (US$6.60–US$14/£3.30–£7). AE, DC, MC, V. Mon–Sat 11am–11pm. Closed 3 weeks in July.

La Verandah/Lucia ✦✦✦ CARIBBEAN/CONTINENTAL/ASIAN FUSION Set within different areas of Puerto Plata's most upscale hotel, these are the two most elegant and sophisticated restaurants along the north shore of the Dominican Republic. Much of their allure derives from Chef Rafael Vasquez, whose earthy but elegant culinary style has earned him the justifiable title of the country's most celebrated chef. Both restaurants emanate high-design, cutting edge charm, although their respective colors and decors are carefully calibrated for view in streaming sunlight (La Verandah) or within the shadows of the evening (Lucia).

La Verandah, beside the beach, is a study in angular lines and cool tones of aqua and turquoise; Lucia, with its acres of white linen, evokes the high-ceilinged, candle-lit, intensely Europeanized dining room of a land baron on a colonial plantation. The menu might include grilled red snapper with grilled pineapple and slices of lobster tail prepared tempura-style and served with avocados. Delectable desserts include mango tacos with pistachio ice cream. An even more decadent dessert choice is known as a "volcano." Combining in sculptural elegance a deep-fried pyramid of semi-melted chocolate with ice cream, it tastes even better than it looks.

In the Casa Colonial. In La Verandah, main courses US$8–US$24 (£4.15–£13); in Lucia, main courses US$12–US$35 (£6.25–£18). AE, DC, MC, V. La Verandah, daily 11:30am–5pm; Lucia, daily 6pm–midnight.

Le Papillon CARIBBEAN/CONTINENTAL   This is an unusual but charming restaurant set on a hillside in a residential neighborhood about 5km (3 miles) south-west of Puerto Plata. The expatriate German owner, Thomas Ackermann, manages to combine aspects of the Black Forest with merengue music. The best way to start a meal here is with a *caipirinha* (a Brazilian cocktail) at the bar beneath the cane-frond ceiling. Later, within an open-sided pavilion overlooking a forest, you'll be presented with a menu that's divided into categories that feature different preparations of pork, chicken, beef, seafood, rabbit, and even vegetarian offerings. Enduring favorites include fettuccine with lobster; "pirate" kabobs with shrimp, tenderloin of beef, and vegetables; an especially worthy chicken stuffed with shrimp and served with saffron sauce; and a four-fisted version of chateaubriand that's only prepared for two. Some savvy locals have complained that this restaurant can get just a bit pricier than it should, but in light of its cultural oddities, it's probably worth it.

Villas Cofresi, in Cofresi © 809/970-7640. Reservations recommended. Main courses RD$400–RD$800 (US$13–US$26/£7–13.50). AE, MC, V. Tues–Sun 6–10:30pm. From the center of Puerto Plata, drive 5km (3 miles) south, following the signs to Santiago. Turn left at the signs to Villas Cofresi.

Sam's Bar & Grill STEAKHOUSE   The *gringo* and *gringa* expats have made Sam's their favorite dive since way back in 1970, when it was first established. In the center of town, only a block and a half from Central Park and the Malecón, it lies in a Vic-torian building from 1896. Marilyn Monroe photographs and caricatures by local artists form the decor. Here is where you can order a plate of meatloaf like your mama made or, the eternal favorite, steak and eggs. The cook does a tasty filet of beefsteak and more ambitious dishes, such as chicken *cordon bleu*. Come here for the memories, the good times, and, of course, the good-tasting food. You can start your day with fluffy pancakes, and later enjoy freshly made soups, salads, and sandwiches for lunch along with hot dishes.

Calle José del Carmen Ariza 34, Castilla Hotel. © 809/586-7267. Main courses RD$180–RD$250 (US$5.40–US$7.50/£2.70–£3.75). No credit cards. Daily 8am–10pm.

HITTING THE BEACH

Although they face the sometimes-turbulent waters of the Atlantic, and it rains a lot in winter, it's the beaches that put the north coast on the tourist map. The beaches at **Playa Dorada** are known collectively as the "Amber Coast" for the deposits of amber that have been discovered here. Playa Dorada has one of the highest concentrations of hotels on the north coast, so the beaches here, though good, are almost always crowded, both with tourists and locals. The beaches have lovely white or powdery beige sand and the waters are very popular with water-skiers and windsurfers. Many concession stands along the beach rent equipment.

Another good choice in the area, **Luperón Beach** lies about an 80-minute drive to the west of Puerto Plata. This is a wide stretch of powdery white sand, set amid palm trees that provide wonderful shade when the noonday sun grows too fierce. It's better for windsurfing, scuba diving, and snorkeling than swimming. Various watersports concessions are found here, along with several snack bars.

SPORTS & OTHER OUTDOOR PURSUITS

The north coast is a watersports scene, although the sea tends to be rough. Snorkeling is popular, and the windsurfing is among the best in the Caribbean.

GOLF   Robert Trent Jones, Jr., designed the 18-hole **Playa Dorada** championship golf course (© **809/320-4262**), which surrounds the resorts and runs along the coast. Even nongolfers can stop at the clubhouse for a drink or a snack to enjoy the views. Greens fees are RD$1,820 (US$55/£27) for 18 holes; RD$1,260 (US$38/£19) for 9 holes; a caddy costs RD$336 (US$10/£5.05). It's best to make arrangements at the activities desk of your hotel.

The 4,888-yard **Playa Grande Golf Course,** at Playa Grande, Km 9, Carretera Rio San Juan-Cabrera (© **800/858-2258** in the U.S. and Canada, or 809/582-0860), is generating a lot of excitement. Some pros have already hailed it as one of the best courses in the Caribbean. Its design consultant was Robert Trent Jones, Jr. Ten of its holes border the Atlantic, and many of these are also set atop dramatic cliffs overlooking the turbulent waters of Playa Grande Beach. Greens fees are RD$3,360 (US$101/£50) in winter, RD$1,400 to RD$1,820 (US$42–US$55/£21–£27) off season.

TENNIS   Nearly all the major resort hotels in this area have tennis courts.

WATERSPORTS   Your watersports options in Puerto Plata are numerous. Most of the kiosks on the beaches here are ultimately run by the same company and prices don't vary among them. If there isn't one close to your hotel, try **Playa NACO Centro de Deportes Acuaticos** (© **809/320-2567**), a rustic clapboard-sided hut on the beachfront of the Dorado NACO Hotel. Prices are as follows: bana-boat rides, RD$280 (US$8.40/£4.20) for a 10- to 12-minute ride; water skiing, RD$560 (US$17/£8.40) for a 10- to 15-minute ride; sea kayak and Sunfish sailboat rental, RD$560 (US$17/£8.40) per hour; sailboards, RD$560 (US$17/£8.40) a day; and paragliding, RD$1,400 (US$42/£21) for a 10-minute ride.

There are watersports kiosks about every 100m (330 ft.) along the beach, any of which will rent you snorkeling gear and tell you the best spots for seeing fish. Puerto Plata isn't great for snorkeling, but you can take a boat trip to some decent sites.

SEEING THE SIGHTS

Ocean World 𝒦𝒦 (Kids), Calle Principale 3 at Cofresi (© **809/291-1111;** www.ocean world.net), is the largest entertainment complex in the country, lying 5km (3 miles) west of Puerto Plata. It combines a plush casino and a world-class marina with such mass market venues as a kiddie park and an aquarium for marine life. There is a series of watery "pens" and habitats for the care, feeding, and display of dolphins, sea lions, sharks, stingrays, piranhas, and other denizens of the Amazon rainforest. A number of close encounters with these nautical creatures, especially dolphins, is offered, but these encounters are not cheap, ranging from US$70 to US$250 (£36–£130) per person, depending on your age and the length of exposure you opt for. Supervision of these encounters is carefully monitored by trainers, and reservations are recommended. For those 13 and up, admission is US$55 (£29), lowered to US$40 (£21) for ages 4 to 12. Free 3 and under.

Fort San Felipe, the oldest fort in the New World, is a popular attraction (© **809/ 261-6043**). Philip II of Spain ordered its construction in 1564, a task that took 33 years to complete. Built with 2m-thick (6½-ft.) walls, the fort was virtually impenetrable, and the moat surrounding it was treacherous—the Spaniards sharpened swords and embedded them in coral below the surface of the water. The doors of the fort are only 1m (3¼ ft.) high, another deterrent to swift passage. During Trujillo's rule, Fort San Felipe was used as a prison. Standing at the end of the Malecón, the fort was restored in the early 1970s. Admission is RD$20 (60¢/30p), free for children under 12. It's open daily 9am to 4:45pm.

Isabel de Torres (© **809/970-0501**), an observation tower that was heavily fortified during the reign of Trujillo, affords a panoramic view of the Amber Coast from a point near the top, 780m (2,555 ft.) above sea level. You reach the observation point by *teleférico* (cable car), a 10-minute ascent. Once here, you're also treated to 3 hectares (7½ acres) of botanical gardens. The round-trip costs RD$200 (US$6/£3) for adults, RD$100 (US$3/£1.50) for children age 12 and under. The aerial ride runs Thursday to Tuesday 8:30am to 5pm. There's often a long wait in line for the cable car, and at certain times it's closed for repairs, so check at your hotel before you head out.

You can see a collection of rare amber specimens at the **Museo de Ambar Dominicano (Museum of Dominican Amber),** Calle Duarte 61 (© **809/586-2848**), near Puerto Plata's Central Park. It's open Monday to Friday 8am to 6pm, Saturday 9am to 5pm. Guided tours in English are offered. Admission is RD$40 (US$1.20/60p) or RD$7 (20¢/10p) for children.

SHOPPING

The neoclassical house sheltering the Museo de Ambar Dominicano (see above) also contains the densest collection of **boutiques** in Puerto Plata. Many of the paintings here are from neighboring Haiti, but the amber, larimar, and mahogany woodcarvings are local.

Plaza Turisol Complex, the largest shopping center on the north coast, has about 80 different outlets and the most upscale and tasteful merchandise. Make this your first stop if you want to get an idea of what's available in Puerto Plata—make it your only stop if you don't have time to visit all the shopping centers. It's about 5 minutes from Puerto Plata and Playa Dorada, on the main road heading east. Nearby is a smaller shopping center, **Centro Commercial Playa Dorada** (© **809/320-6645**), with about 80 shops selling handicrafts, clothing, souvenirs, and gifts. Both it and the Plaza Turisol are open daily 9am to 9pm.

Plaza Isabela, in Playa Dorada about 450m (1,500 ft.) from the entrance to the Playa Dorada Hotel complex, is a collection of small specialty shops constructed in Victorian gingerbread style, although much of its inventory has a Spanish inspiration or flair. Here you'll find the main branch of the Dominican Republic's premier jeweler, **Harrison's** (© **809/586-3933**), a specialist in platinum work. Madonna, Michael Jackson, and Keith Richards have all been spotted wearing Harrison's jewelry. The store has a special clearance area; tours are available. There's another branch in the Centro Comercial Playa Dorada (© **809/320-2219**) in the Playa Dorada Hotel complex.

PUERTO PLATA, PLAYA DORADO, & COSTA DORADA AFTER DARK

Casino action dominates the night. Newest with the most imaginative décor is the **Casino at Ocean World** 🐟🐟, Calle Principale 3 at Cofresi (© **809/291-1111**). Its cabaret show staged here, with gorgeous dancers, is the best in the D.R., rivaling some of the spectaculars in Las Vegas. A well-recommended way to experience the charms of this place involves booking a place on the "Ocean World Magical Nights." For US$69(£36) per person, you'll get round-trip transfers by minivan from most of Puerto Plata's hotels, unlimited access to a well-stocked dinner buffet, access to a dolphin night show, and a sea lion night show, access to the casino and the location's many bars, and access to a Las Vegas-style review, replete with views of performers artfully outfitted in a minimalist style. Your hotel desk can usually book such tours for you.

Less modern, but within the Playa Dorado hotel complex, is the sprawling, block-buster-style casino at the **Holiday Village Golden Beach** (Playa Dorado, ℂ 809/ 320-3800). The Playa Dorada Hotel complex itself contains about 14 hotels, some of which have **discos** that welcome anyone, guest or not, into their confines. These after-dark diversions tend to be filled mainly with foreign visitors, although they occasionally attract locals looking to hook up with tourists. None charge a cover, and the almost-universal drink of choice, Presidente Beer, costs RD$110 (US$3.30/£1.65) a bottle.

At least three discos pulse out dance music every night of the week within the Playa Dorada complex beginning at 10pm. The wildest, most animated, and most raucous is **Mangú,** Playa Dorado (ℂ 809/320-3800). Its designers positioned it adjacent to the Holiday Village Golden Beach Resort, but with separate entrances. You'll find an attractive blend of both local residents, many eager to score with an off-island visitor, and holiday makers, who merge and mix in an animated blend of hot bodies and hot meringue. Entrance is free for residents of the Holiday Village, but around RD$100 (US$3/£1.50) for non-residents. Expect flashing lights, hundreds of writhing bodies, and a skin, glitter, and feathers show that begins at 11:30pm.

Mangu's most visible competitor is the **Roadway Western Bar and Mix Grill,** in the Playa Dorada Plaza (ℂ 809/320-4502). Set within a simulated recreation of a log cabin, on the back side of the resort's busiest shopping center, its walls are outfitted with Gringo/Gringa slogans like "Gringas are forever." There's no cover charge, but a Presidente beer goes for RD$120 (US$3.60/£1.80).

A final contender for the nightlife circuit in Puerto Plata is **Crazy Moon,** adjacent to the lobby of the Paradise Hotel (ℂ 809/320-3663). Though not as sweepingly popular as either Mangu or the Roadway Bar, it can be a lot of fun, and the music is always danceable.

5 Sosúa ★

About 24km (15 miles) east of Puerto Plata is one of the finest beaches in the Dominican Republic, **Sosúa Beach.** A strip of soft, white sand more than .8km (½ mile) wide, it's tucked in a cove sheltered by coral cliffs and has crystal-clear water. The beach connects two strikingly disparate communities, which together make up the town known as Sosúa. As increasing numbers of visitors flock to Sosúa, mainly for its beach life, it is beginning to rival Puerto Plata. You won't find the superdeluxe resorts that are commonplace in Puerto Plata, but prices in Sosúa are half what they are at the big resorts and the beaches are just as lovely.

At one end of the beach is **El Batey,** an area with residential streets, gardens, restaurants, shops, and hotels. Real-estate transactions have been booming in this area and many villas have been constructed, fronted by newly paved streets.

At the other end of Sosúa Beach lies the typical village community of **Los Charamicos,** a sharp contrast to El Batey. Here you'll find tin-roofed shacks, vegetable stands, chickens scrabbling in the rubbish, and warm, friendly people.

Sosúa was founded in 1940 by European Jews seeking refuge from Hitler. Trujillo invited 100,000 of them to settle in his country on a banana plantation, but only 600 or so Jews were actually allowed to immigrate, and of those, only about a dozen or so remained on the plantation. There are some 20 Jewish families living in Sosúa today, and for the most part they are engaged in the dairy and smoked-meat industries, which the refugees began during the war. Biweekly services are held in the local one-room synagogue. Many of the Jews intermarried with Dominicans, and the town has taken on an increasingly Spanish flavor; women of the town are often seen wearing both the Star of David and the Virgin de Altagracia, the patron saint of the Dominicans. Nowadays many German expatriates are also found in the town.

GETTING THERE   To get here from Puerto Plata, take the autopista (Rte. 5) east for about 30 minutes. If you venture off the main highway, anticipate enormous potholes. Taxis, charter buses, and *públicos* from Puerto Plata and Playa Dorada let passengers off at the stairs leading down from the highway to Sosúa beach. Most rides cost RD$60 to RD$100 (US$1.80–US$3/90p–£1.50).

ACCOMMODATIONS

La Puntilla de Piergiorgio ⭐ *Value*   This hotel lies in a residential neighborhood, within a 10-minute walk from the bustling commercial center of Sosúa. Built on a rocky promontory high above the beach, it has a neo-Victorian design that includes lots of enticing gingerbread, lattices, and whimsical grace. Accommodations are bright, large, well maintained, and outfitted with white-tile floors, flowered chintz upholsteries, and a semicircular veranda with views of either the garden or the ocean. Each accommodation comes with a small but neatly arranged tiled private bathroom with shower stall.

Calle La Puntilla 1, El Batey, Sosúa, Dominican Republic. © 809/571-2215. Fax 809/571-2786. 51 units. Year-round US$75–US$110 (£39–£57) double. Rates include breakfast. AE, MC, V. **Amenities:** Restaurant; bar; outdoor pool; room service; babysitting; laundry service; dry cleaning. *In room:* A/C, TV, hair dryer, safe.

Sosúa Bay Hotel ⭐⭐   Launched in 2002, this handsome colonial-style hotel is all-inclusive, with some of the consistently best food at the resort, and a view that opens directly onto the tranquil waters of Sosúa Bay. This is one of Sosúa's attempts to attract more upscale clients who might normally patronize Playa Dorada. The pillared lobby is the most impressive at the resort. It's the pampered life here. You can start your breakfast with a mimosa and be wined and dined throughout the day, staying up late dancing to the sound of merengue. The midsize bedrooms, scattered across a three-floor building, are decorated with colonial-style wood furnishings and colorful bedspreads and draperies. Each comes with a tiled bathroom with tub and shower. If available, choose one of the superior doubles with ocean view; others open onto lushly planted gardens. Your choice is of one king-size bed or else two double beds; most accommodations come with private balconies.

The cuisine is varied and among the best at the resort. Breakfast and lunch buffets are lavish. At night you can dine more formally—and much better—at various venues that feature the likes of Italian or international cuisine. The resort also has some of the best entertainment at Sosúa, and offers one of the most diversified activities programs.

Dr. Alejo Martínez 1, Sosúa, Dominican Republic. © **809/571-4000.** Fax 809/571-4545. www.starzresorts.com. 243 units. Year-round US$95–US$180 (£49–£94) per person, per night double. Children 4–11 50% discount. Rates are all-inclusive. AE, MC, V. Free parking. **Amenities:** 3 restaurants; 2 bars; 2 outdoor pools (1 for children); health club; aerobics; yoga; watersports equipment; bikes; laundry service; dry cleaning. *In room:* A/C, TV, fridge, safe.

DINING

Morua Mai INTERNATIONAL   This is the most visible, and most deeply entrenched, restaurant in downtown Sosúa. Established by German entrepreneurs in the 1970s, and set at the town's busiest intersection, it manages to remain somewhat aloof from Sosua's burgeoning sex industry, thanks to a location in a neighborhood that's a few blocks removed from the densest concentration of putanas and their pimps. It was designed of timbers and palm thatch like an enormous Taíno teepee, under which ceiling fans slowly spin, and wicker and wooden furniture help create an ambience conducive to the leisurely consumption of tropical drinks and well-prepared food. Steaks and seafood are staples here. Depending on the arrival of fresh supplies that day, the menu might also include four different preparations of lobster; several kinds of shrimp, including a version with spicy tomato sauce and fresh vegetables; four different preparations of sea bass, including a version flavored with Chablis; orange-flavored chicken spiced with ginger; steak Diana, flavored with bacon; and pork in mustard-flavored cream sauce. An excellent version of paella contains chunks of lobster and fresh shrimp.

Pedro Clisante 5, El Batey. (℃ 809/571-2966. Breakfast RD$75-RD$85 (US$2.25–US$2.55/£1.15–£1.30); pizzas and pastas RD$175–RD$225 (US$5.25–US$6.75/£2.65–£3.40); main courses RD$100–RD$1,275 (US$3–US$38/£1.50–£19). AE, MC, V. Daily 8am–midnight.

On the Waterfront 😼😼 INTERNATIONAL/SEAFOOD   The memory of Marlon Brando's Oscar-winning 1954 movie, *On the Waterfront*, is perpetuated here. This informal yet elegant restaurant sits on a cliffside, serving the finest cuisine among the independent restaurants of Sosúa. To everyone's delight, especially the owners, in 2005, ocean currents and tides unexpectedly deposited vast amounts of sand at the base of this restaurant, creating an "instant beach" which has added considerably to its allure. As you peruse the menu, take in sweeping views before deciding on the best of the catch of the day, which might feature fresh lobster, sea bass, conch, calamari, or red snapper, the latter tasting delectable when perfectly grilled as it is here. If you don't want fish, try a tender steak in pepper sauce or some lamb chops grilled with aromatic herbs. Other menu highlights include filet of sole in a tangy orange sauce or fettuccine primavera.

Calle Dr. Rosendo 1. (℃ 809/571-2670. Reservations recommended. Main courses RD$540–RD$1,200 (US$16–US$36/£8.10–£18). AE, MC, V. Daily 7am–10pm.

SPORTS & OTHER OUTDOOR PURSUITS

There are watersports kiosks about every 90m (300 ft.) along the beach, any of which will rent you snorkeling gear and tell you the best spots for seeing fish. You can also rent sailboats, windsurfers, and other watersports gear at any of the kiosks.

Gipsy Ranch, Carretera Sosúa-Cabarete, opposite the Coconut Palm Resort (℃ 809/571-1373), is the region's largest and best-recommended **riding stable,** home to about 20 horses, which can be hired for equestrian treks of between 1 and 4 hours. You'll begin your experience at the stone corral about 7km (4½ miles) from Sosúa and 5km (3 miles) from Cabarete. A ½-hour jaunt goes for RD$448 (US$13/£6.70); a 4-hour excursion through forests and along beaches costs RD$1,596 (US$48/£24). Reservations are strongly recommended.

Many divers are attracted to the waters off Sosúa. In town the best outfitter is **Northern Coast Diving,** Calle Pedro Clisante 8 (℃ 809/571-1028; www.northern coastdiving.com). There are more than a dozen diving sites off the coast, including a wreck, a canyon dive, and a wall dive. Northern Coast offers PADI-certified divemasters or instructors, featuring a two-tank boat dive for RD$1,960 (US$59/£29) with equipment, RD$1,680 (US$50/£25) without. For RD$9,800 (US$294/£147) you get 3 days of diving and certification training. The outfitter also offers 3-hour snorkeling excursions for RD$1,120 (US$34/£17) per person.

Several adventure tours are offered by **El Tour Tours,** corner of Calle Dr. Alejo Martínez and Calle Duarte (© **809/571-4195;** www.eltour.net), founded in 1999. River rafting is an exciting pastime costing RD$1,820 (US$55/£27). They can also arrange horseback riding for RD$896 (US$27/£13) and catamaran sailing for RD$2,100 (US$63/£32).

SHOPPING

Patrick's Silversmithy, Calle Pedro Clisante 3 (© **809/571-2121**), was established by British expatriate Patrick Fagg in 1973 as a showcase for his unusual jewelry designs. At least half of the inventory here is made within his studios, and each incorporates such local stones as larimar, amber, and black coral. About 80% of the inventory is made from silver, making these one-of-a-kind creations affordable.

The best art gallery is **Viva,** Calle Dr. Alejo Martínez 10 (© **809/571-4222**), which sells local art and giftware. An excellent selection of Dominican masters is on sale; the giftware includes beautifully crafted wood sculptures in mahogany and *guayacán* (ironwood). Many ceramic "faceless" dolls are also for sale.

6 Cabarete

The winds that blow constantly southward off the Atlantic swept in a hip young crowd in the 1990s, as Cabarete emerged as the premier windsurfing site in the Caribbean. But only a small portion of the visitors who come here today are actually interested in the waves and jumping on a board. Many bask in the glory of the surfers by day and strut their stuff in the hyperhip town bars by night.

To service the needs of the growing number of visitors, the town has attracted some of the most aggressive prostitutes in the Dominican Republic; all ages, all skin tones, all degrees of blatancy. If you're a heterosexual male in Cabarete, you'll absolutely never, ever, lack for female companionship, paid or unpaid.

News of Cabarete's allure has spread among the 20-something populations of Europe. Especially prevalent are visitors from northern Europe; there are fewer North Americans here than you'd expect.

The big attraction is **Cabarete Beach,** with its white sands and ideal wind and surf conditions. Cabarete isn't particularly distinguished architecturally, consisting of a series of relatively small-scale hotels, restaurants, and gift shops lining either side of the highway that parallels the north coast. Virtually everything in town lies along this street (Calle Principal), with the exception of small-scale shops that are found on narrow alleyways that bisect the main street. But as word of the resort has spread, there have been increasing numbers of large all-inclusive hotels built on the outskirts of town.

GETTING THERE   To reach Cabarete from Sosúa, continue east along the autopista (Rte. 5) for about 13km (8 miles). Taxis and *públicos* from Sosúa will also take you here.

ACCOMMODATIONS

Azurro Club (Azurro Club Estrella and Azurro Club Cabarete) ⊕   One of Cabarete's more deeply entrenched resorts was built in the late 1990s in a stylish, avant-garde design. It has been bought, reconfigured, and expanded by the well-recommended Azurro chain of resorts. Today, you'll find slightly more upscale accommodations in the Azurro Cabarete, and lodgings that are just a notch less comfortable across the road, in the Azurro Estrella. With direct access to a wide sandy beach, on

---

(Tips) Serious Windsurfing

Cabarete hosts an annual weeklong windsurfing tournament every June. Only amateurs are allowed to participate. For more information, contact the **Happy Surf School,** Hotel Villa Taina, Calle Principal (© **809/571-0784**), or any staff member at the **Azurro Club** (© **809/571-0808**).

---

the outskirts of Cabarete's main commercial core, it's noted for a soaring network of steel girders, and an attempt on the part of the staff to keep its guests amused with a variety of organized although somewhat haphazard daily activities. Despite a slightly disorganized staff, this is one of our favorite large-scale hotels in Cabarete, thanks to its convenient location and sense of style. The respective buildings of this resort rise in four-story designs, usually around well-landscaped central courtyards. Bedrooms are well maintained, attractive, and airy, usually with white-tile floors and large bathrooms with tubs and showers.

Calle Principal, Cabarete, Dominican Republic. © **809/571-0808.** Fax 809/571-0904. www.starzresorts.com. 272 units. Winter US$175–US$240 (£91–£125) double; off season US$125–US$140 (£65–£73) double. Rates are all-inclusive. AE, MC, V. **Amenities:** 3 restaurants; 3 bars; 3 outdoor pools; gym; room service; babysitting; laundry service; dry cleaning; nonsmoking rooms; rooms for those w/limited mobility. *In room:* A/C, TV, hair dryer, iron, safe.

Natura Cabañas & the Attabeyra Spa ✿ *(Finds)* This is the ultimate eco-sensitive boutique hotel, perfect for those who enjoy a return to nature and an abandonment of the comforts that some travelers wouldn't want to do without. Located between Cabarete and Sosúa, the hotel occupies the site that was conceived as the owner's (a Chilean expatriate named Lole Sumar) private home. In 1990, she opted to improve her acreage with a series of artfully rustic wood and concrete structures for the shelter and amusement of like-minded new-age friends. Some are mushroom-shaped organic-looking structures, others are more functional structures of wood clapboards and thick beams. Regardless of the shelter you select, you'll get a sense of living on a sunny, not particularly stressful summer camp for adults and their children. None of the units has air conditioning, a TV, or telephone, but there are yoga classes conducted without charge for residents twice a week. Don't come here looking for upscale flair and urban style, since you really won't find it. Instead, you have an almost defiant sense that people are in Cabarete to get their lives back in order, read quietly in the sun, often in hammocks, and communicate with the great outdoors.

Meals cost RD$420–RD$860 (US$13–US$26/£6.30–£13) and are likely to include creole-style braised octopus; langoustines with mushroom sauce; grilled tuna steak with pistachio; and dorado with coconut. The on-site spa is new age-centered, small-scale, and personalized.

In the La Perla Marina Complex, Cabarete, Dominican Republic. © **809/571-1507.** www.naturacabana.com. 11 units. Year-round US$160 (£83) double; US$210 (£109) triple; US$240 (£125) quad. MC, V. **Amenities:** 2 restaurants; bar; outdoor pool; yoga classes; spa; massage; free use of mountain bikes; horseback riding; jeep rental facilities. *In room:* kitchen (in some), no phone.

DINING

Casa del Pescador ✿ SEAFOOD Since 1988, Casa del Pescador has served sophisticated seafood in an engagingly hip environment that's the domain of a Swiss expatriate. It's right on the beach, in the heart of town. To begin, sample the chef's flavor-filled fish consommé. He does very well with shrimp, too, either with pastis sauce or more zestily, with curry and fresh garlic. On a hot day, the seafood salads are a welcome relief and tasty, too, as are the grilled octopus in spicy Creole sauce and fresh lobster in garlic sauce. (Unless you love garlic, you might find the latter overpowering; ask for butter instead.) Although there's a full wine list, Presidente beer seems the best accompaniment to the fish, especially on hot, sultry nights.

Calle Principal. ℭ **809/571-0760.** Reservations recommended for dinner. Main courses US$8–US$23 (£4.15–£12). AE, DC, MC, V. Daily 10am–11pm.

SPORTS & OTHER OUTDOOR PURSUITS

Not surprisingly, Cabarete is home to one of the Caribbean's best **windsurfing schools, Carib Wind Center,** Playa Cabarete (ℭ **809/571-0640,** www.caribwind.com). It's devoted to teaching proper techniques and to renting state-of-the-art equipment. Equipment rental costs US$45 (£23) for 5 hours, and instruction is US$35 (£18) per hour. Clients who book a week or more in advance receive discounts of around 20%. A worthy competitor, located just a few doors away, is the **Fanatic Windsurfing Center,** Calle Principale, ℭ **809/571-0861;** www.fanatic-cabarete.com. Fanatic sometimes offers rates a bit less expensive than those at the Carib Wind Center.

Although windsurfing attracts more media attention than any other sport in Cabarete, conventional surfing is also big and getting bigger. Because of the prevailing tides and wind patterns, it's best undertaken at **Playa Encuentro,** a 2 km (1.2-mile) stretch of beachfront that's 4km (2.4 miles) west of Cabarete and 5km (3 miles) east of Sosúa. Here, surfboards are rented from a crowd of active aficionados at the Club M-Endy, Playa El Encuentro, Carretera Sosúa-Cabarete (ℭ **809/571-1625**). Renting a surfboard costs US$20 (£10) per day and lessons can be arranged for around US$35 (£18) an hour.

Iguana Mama at Cabarete (ℭ **800/849-4720** in the U.S., or 809/571-0908; www.iguanamama.com) offers the best **mountain biking** and **hiking.** Going strong since 1993, it features a trek to Mount Isabel de Torres with experienced guides that lasts a full day and costs US$65 (£34) per person. If enough people book, this tour is offered daily. Another trek involves a 900m (2,950-ft.) downhill cruise, costing US$40 (£21) per person and held only Monday, Wednesday, and Friday.

Finally, **Gipsy Ranch** (ℭ **809/571-1373**) is the most complete riding stable in the Dominican Republic; they'll take you **horseback riding** at a cost of US$20 (£10) per person for an hour or US$60 (£31) for a 4-hour ride.

CABARETE AFTER DARK

Las Brisas, Calle Principal Cabarete (ℭ **809/571-0614**), is the most popular nightlife venue in Cabarete. Arrive after 10:30pm when the dance club action begins. From 8am to 10:30pm daily, food is served. The dance floor is illuminated with strobe lights and lasers, and the bar is always busy. Many patrons arrive with dates of their own, but if you're a man flying solo, never fear, as a bevy of attractive working women are invariably on hand to provide companionship.

Hip nightlife is also found at the little bars—shanties, really—along the beach. There's live music every night after sunset. Tuesday nights it's salsa and merengue at **Onno's Bar** (ℭ **809/571-0461**). **The Bamboo Bar** is the place to be on Friday night, and on Saturday the new **Wave Bar** and **Tribal Café** (no phones) draw the most patrons. On virtually any night of the week, you can find dialogue and a sense of cosmopolitan hip at the **Café Pitu,** Calle Principal (ℭ **809/571-0861**). Set a few steps from the also-recommended Onno's Bar, and radically upgraded late in 2006, it's the bar that's almost always cited as a centerpiece of Cabarete nightlife. It also offers wireless internet access throughout its premises, thereby creating a sometimes studious venue of scantily clad athletes swigging rum punches and surfing the net. *Note:* Only some of these bars have phone numbers, and none bears an individual street number on the Calle Principale, but each of them is easy to spot as you walk up and down either the beach or the town's main street.

7 Santo Domingo ★★★

Santo Domingo is one of the Caribbean's most vibrant cities, with a 12-block Colonial Zone to rival that of Old San Juan in Puerto Rico. Come here to walk in the footsteps of Cortés, Ponce de León, and, of course, Columbus himself. Allow at least a day to capture some of the highlights of the old city such as its Alcazar and its Catedral Santa Maria la Menor.

Santo Domingo is also one of the grand shopping bazaars of the Caribbean, with such "hot" items as hand-wrapped cigars for sale virtually everywhere, along with local handicrafts. Jewelry made of larimar or amber is also much sought after. From gambling to merengue, Santo Domingo is also one of the liveliest cities in the Caribbean after dark. Be careful, however. Most of the Dominican Republic's crime is concentrated in Santo Domingo. Keep valuables in your hotel safe, carry a minimum of cash with you, don't wear flashy jewelry, and if in doubt, take a cab.

Bartholomeo Columbus, brother of Christopher, founded the city of New Isabella (later renamed Santo Domingo) on the southeastern Caribbean coast in 1496. It's the oldest city in the New World and the capital of the Dominican Republic. Santo Domingo has had a long, sometimes glorious, more often sad, history. At the peak of its power, Diego de Velázquez sailed from here to settle Cuba, Ponce de León went forth to conquer and settle Puerto Rico and Florida, and Cortés set out for Mexico. The city today still reflects its long history—French, Haitian, and especially Spanish.

ESSENTIALS

GETTING THERE See the beginning of this chapter for details on the airlines serving Santo Domingo.

FAST FACTS There's a **24-hour drugstore** called San Judas Tadeo, Ave. Independencia 57 (© **809/685-8165**). The best hospital in Santo Dominco, and the one recommended by the U.S. Embassy, is **Clinica Abreu,** Calle Beller 42 (© **809/688-4411**). Most of its English-speaking doctors trained in the United States, and it never closes. For the **police,** call © **911.**

VISITOR INFORMATION The **Tourist Office** is located at Avenida Mexico, Esquina Calle 30 de Marzo (© **809/221-4660;** www.godominicanrepublic.com), open Monday to Friday from 8am to 3pm.

ACCOMMODATIONS
EXPENSIVE

Hilton Santo Domingo ★★★ A soaring, artfully designed tower set directly on the seafront, this is the finest, tallest, and most desirable hotel in Santo Domingo. Its inauguration added the first new major hotel to the nation's capital in 15 years, and its location at the corner of the pivotal Maximo Gomez filled what had until then been a gaping dark hole on a key building site in one of the town's showplace neighborhoods. It was configured as part of the Malecón Center, a waterside development that includes three separate towers for condominiums, a 21-story hotel, the newest casino in town, and a small but choice shopping mall. We prefer its ultra-comfortable rooms to any others in town. This hotel is not, and doesn't even try to be, a full-service resort, but if you want to play tennis or golf, the concierge can set it up for you. Rooms, which begin on the eighth floor and go upward from there, are richly furnished and plush, with excellent beds and in most cases, views that stretch far out to sea. Visitors since the inauguration of this hotel have included South African archbishop Desmond Tutu and actors Robert De Niro, Jaime Fox, Colin Farrell, and Angelina Jolie and Brad Pitt.

Avda George Washington 500 at the NW corner of the Avda Maximo Gomez, Malecón Center, Santo Domingo, Dominican Republic. © 800/HILTONS in the U.S. or 809/685-0000. Fax 809/731-4143. www.hiltoncaribbean.com 228 units. US$115–US$215 (£60–£112) double; US$226–US$550 (£118–£286) suite. AE, DC, MC, V. **Amenities**: Restaurant; 2 bars; outdoor swimming pool; casino workout room; room service; laundry service/dry cleaning. *In room*: A/C, TV, minibar, coffeemaker, hair dryer, iron, safe, Wi-Fi.

Hotel Santo Domingo ✶✶✶   Run by Premier Resorts & Hotels, the Hotel Santo Domingo is tastefully extravagant without having the glitzy overtones of the Jaragua (see below). Those seeking local character in a home-grown hotel should check in here. This waterfront hotel sits on 6 tropical hectares (15 acres), 15 minutes from the downtown area, in the La Feria district.

Oscar de la Renta helped design the interior. Most of the rooms have views of the sea, though some face the garden. Accommodations have bright floral carpets, tasteful Caribbean fabrics, and mirrored closets along with firm double beds. Bathrooms are tiled with tub/shower combos and adequate shelf space. The superior Excel Club rooms offer sea-view balconies and other amenities. Excel guests also have access to a private lounge.

The cuisine is among the finest hotel food in the capital.

Av. Independencia (at the corner of Av. Abraham Lincoln), Santo Domingo, Dominican Republic. © 800/877-3643 in the U.S., or 809/221-1511. Fax 809/535-0876. www.hotelsantodomingo.com.do. 215 units. Year-round US$140–US$170 (£73–£88) double; US$270 (£140) Excel Club double; US$410 (£213) executive suite. Rates include American breakfast. AE, MC, V. **Amenities**: Restaurant; 2 bars; Olympic-size outdoor pool; 3 lit tennis courts; gym; sauna; business center; salon; room service; babysitting; laundry service; dry cleaning. *In room:* A/C, TV, minibar, beverage maker, hair dryer, safe.

Renaissance Jaragua Hotel & Casino ✶✶   A Las Vegas–style palace, this 10-story hotel lies on the 6-hectare (15-acre) site of the old Jaragua (Ha-*ra*-gwa) Hotel, which was popular in Trujillo's day. Open since 1988, it's a splashy, pink-colored waterfront palace that doesn't have the dignity and class of the Hotel Santo Domingo. For example, the casino and bars are often rife with prostitutes plying their trade. Located off the Malecón and convenient to the city's major attractions and shops, the hotel consists of two separate buildings: the 10-story Jaragua Tower and the two-level Jaragua Gardens Estate. Jaragua has the largest casino in the Caribbean, a 1,000-seat Vegas-style showroom, a cabaret theater, and a dance club. The luxurious rooms, the largest in Santo Domingo, feature multiple phones, refrigerators, and marble bathrooms with large makeup mirrors and tub/shower combinations.

The Jaragua features some of the best hotel dining in the city. You can enjoy tasty Dominican barbecue and some of Santo Domingo's best steaks.

Av. George Washington 367, Santo Domingo, Dominican Republic. © 800/331-2542 in the U.S. and Canada, or 809/221-2222. Fax 809/686-0528. www.renaissancehotels.com. 300 units. Year-round US$109–US$169 (£57–£88) double; US$320 (£166) junior suite; US$500–US$725 (£260–£377) suite. Valet parking US$2 (£1.05). AE, DC, MC, V.

Amenities: Restaurant; 2 bars; outdoor pool; casino; tennis center with 4 lit clay courts and pro shop; health club and spa; salon; room service; babysitting; laundry service; dry cleaning; nonsmoking rooms; dance club. *In room:* A/C, TV, kitchenettes (in some), minibar, fridge, hair dryer, iron, safe.

Sofitel Nicolas de Ovando 🐦🐦 In the heart of the colonial city, this 16th-century mansion has been restored and reopened as a hotel with all the modern amenities. For those seeking comfort among antiquity, this is an even better bet than the smaller Francés Sofitel (see below), another restoration. On the premises is a restaurant with a terrace facing a courtyard and two bars with a view of the pool. All the bedrooms are well furnished and handsomely maintained. The choice of accommodations ranges from standard doubles to spacious suites, which can also be used as family units. The classic architecture of the original mansion has been respected, although the property has been vastly enlarged.

Calle Las Damas, Santo Domingo, Dominican Republic. © **809/685-9955**. Fax 809/686-6590. www.sofitel.com. 104 units. Year-round US$160–US$200 (£83–£104) double; US$500 (£260) junior suite; US$650 (£338) suite. AE, DC, MC, V. **Amenities:** Restaurant; 2 bars; outdoor pool; gym; room service; laundry service; dry cleaning; nonsmoking rooms; rooms for those w/limited mobility; dance club. *In room:* A/C, TV, minibar, hair dryer, iron, safe.

INEXPENSIVE

Francés Sofitel ⭐   A favorite small hotel in the old city, this intimate inn lies within a stone-fronted town house dating from the 16th century. Arches surround an Iberian-style fountain, and columns reach up to the second-floor patios, with palms and tropical plants surrounding the rooms. You'll think you've arrived in Seville. A gracefully winding stone staircase leads to the high-ceilinged and thick-walled bedrooms outfitted in a somber, rather dark colonial style. Accommodations are simple but tasteful, with rugs resting on tile floors; each has a somewhat cramped but tidily kept bathroom with shower and tub.

Calle las Mercedes (corner of Calle Arzobispo Meriño), Santo Domingo, Dominican Republic. © **809/685-9331**. Fax 809/685-1289. www.sofitel.com. 19 units. Year-round US$159 (£83) double. Rates include breakfast. AE, MC, V. **Amenities:** Restaurant; bar; room service; laundry service/dry cleaning. *In room:* A/C, TV, minibar, hair dryer, iron, safe.

Hostal Nicolás Nader ⭐ *Finds*   This is a small, almost luxurious little hotel from the colonial era and also the former home of a former D.R. president, Ulises Heureaux. This 19th-century building has been sensitively restored. Many people in the area drop in during the day to check out the little art gallery in the courtyard or to patronize the on-site restaurant and bar. The bedrooms range from midsize to spacious, and each is comfortably furnished and comes with a bathroom with a tub/shower combo. The white paint in all the rooms gives the limestone-built mansion a real tropical flavor. You get quite a lot for your money here.

Calle General Luperón 151 at Calle Duarte, Santo Domingo, Dominican Republic. © **809/687-6674**. Fax 809/687-7887. www.naderenterprises.com. 10 units. Year-round US$80 (£42) double. Children 8 and under stay free in parent's room. AE, MC, V. **Amenities:** Restaurant; bar. *In room:* A/C, TV.

DINING

Most of Santo Domingo's restaurants stretch along the seaside, bordering Avenida George Washington, popularly known as the Malecón. Some of the best restaurants are in hotels. It's safest to take a taxi when dining out at night.

In most restaurants, casual dress is fine, although shorts are frowned upon at the fancier, more expensive spots. Many Dominicans prefer to dress up when dining out, especially in the capital.

EXPENSIVE

El Mesón de la Cava ⭐ DOMINICAN/INTERNATIONAL   At first we thought this was a gimmicky club—you descend a perilous iron stairway into an actual cave with stalactites and stalagmites—but the cuisine is among the finest in the capital. The quality ingredients are well prepared and beautifully flavored. Recorded merengue, Latin jazz, blues, and salsa give the place a festive ambience. Launch your repast with the small shrimp sautéed in a delicate sauce of garlic or white wine, perhaps a mixed seafood or "sexy" conch gratinée. The gazpacho is also an excellent beginning, as is the bubbling *sopa de pescado* (red snapper chowder). Follow it up with the grilled Caribbean rock lobster or the double French lamb chops, which are done to tender perfection.

Mirador del Sur 1. © **809/533-2818**. Reservations required. Main courses RD$350–RD$1,400 (US$11–US$42/ £5.25–£21). AE, DC, MC, V. Daily noon–midnight.

Lina Restaurant 👌👌 INTERNATIONAL/SPANISH This is one of the most prestigious restaurants in the Caribbean. Spanish-born Lina Aguado originally came to Santo Domingo as the personal chef of the dictator Trujillo, whom she served until opening her own restaurant. Today, four master chefs, whom Dona Lina entrusted with her secret recipes, rule the kitchen of this modern hotel restaurant. The cuisine is international, with an emphasis on Spanish dishes, and the service is first-rate. Try the paella Valenciana, the finest in the Dominican Republic. We're equally enticed by the sea bass flambé with brandy, and few can resist the mixed seafood medley doused with Pernod (it's cooked casserole style). Lina's cuisine even wins the approval of some hard-to-please Madrileños we know, who are a bit contemptuous of Spanish food served outside Spain.

In the Barcelo Gran Hotel Lina. Máximo Gómez and 27 de Febrero aves. (€ **809/563-5000**, ext. 7250. Reservations recommended. Main courses RD$260–RD$1,000 (US$7.80–US$30/£3.90–£15). AE, DC, DISC, MC, V. Daily noon–4pm and 6:30pm–midnight.

Vesuvio I 👌 ITALIAN Along the Malecón, the most famous Italian restaurant in the Dominican Republic draws crowds of visitors and local businesspeople in spite of its fading decor. What to order? That's always a problem, as the Neapolitan owners, the Bonarelli family, have worked since 1954 to perfect and enlarge the menu. As they claim: "We like to catch it ourselves, cook it from scratch, or even grow it if that's possible." Their homemade soups are excellent. Fresh red snapper, sea bass, and oysters are prepared in enticing ways. Specialties include Dominican crayfish *a la Vesuvio* (topped with garlic and bacon). Recent menu additions feature *pappardelle al Bosque* (noodles with porcini mushrooms, rosemary, and garlic), and black tallarini with shrimp *a la crema*.

The owner claims to be the pioneer of pizza in the Dominican Republic. At **Trattoria Vesuvio** next door (€ **809/221-3000**), he makes a unique .9m-long (3-ft.) pizza! There's also **Vesuvio II** at Av. Tiradentes 17 (€ **809/562-6060**).

Av. George Washington 521. (€ **809/221-3333**. Reservations recommended. Main courses RD$350–RD$850 (US$11–US$26/£5.25–£13). AE, MC, V. Daily 11am–midnight.

INEXPENSIVE
La Briciola 👌👌 ITALIAN/INTERNATIONAL This place has a touch of class, offering an elegant setting in two restored colonial palaces from the 16th century. Tables are romantically candlelit at night. In the Colonial Zone, it stands in front of Plazoleta Park. The menu reflects a commitment to prime ingredients and a determination not to let style overrule substance. The dishes here hardly test the creative culinary limits of the chefs but are tried-and-true favorites, beginning with many different pastas and sauces—all made fresh daily. Our favorite is the delectable linguini with "fruits of the sea." Sometimes you're in the mood just for a good steak, and the chefs oblige with a perfectly grilled T-bone cooked to your specifications. This is also a good place at which to order fresh fish. Dominican rice accompanies all the meat and fish courses. A piano bar overlooks a courtyard.

Calle Arzobispo Meriño 152-A. (€ **809/688-5055**. Reservations required. Main courses RD$300–RD$550 (US$9–US$17/£4.50–£8.25). AE, DC, DISC, MC, V. Mon–Sat noon–3pm and 7pm–midnight. Closed Dec 24, 25, 31, and Jan 1.

La Résidence 👌 *Finds* CONTINENTAL/CARIBBEAN It isn't particularly animated, but the food is surprisingly lavish at this showcase of the France-based Sofitel chain. The setting is historic (a ca. 1502 mansion transformed into a hotel), and if you happen to be within the historic zone, it's an excellent and easy-to-find dining choice. This is one of the few upscale restaurants in town offering spit-roasted lamb (rubbed with spices and served with bacon, garlic, and vinegar sauce) and rabbit (a boned saddle stuffed with bacon and mushrooms). Dominican-inspired dishes include roast lobster with wok-fried vegetables; a fricassee of pork chops with local spices; and braised "Dominican-style" red snapper. There's even a frequently changing array of vegetarian dishes.

In the Sofitel Nicolas de Ovando, Calle Las Damas. ℂ **809/685-9955.** Reservations not necessary. Main courses RD$325–RD$890 (US$9.75–US$27/£5.10–£14). AE, DC, MC, V. Daily 7am–midnight.

Pata é Palo ⓕ INTERNATIONAL   Part of Pata é Palo's charm derives from its location, overlooking Plaza Colón, the graceful arcades of the Alcazar de Colón, where amiable clusters of Dominican families promenade every night at dusk. During the 1500s, the building was a bistro under the supervision of a mysterious Dutch buccaneer known as Peg-Leg (Paté Palo), who's credited with establishing the first tavern in the New World.

In the late 1990s, another Dutchman and his four partners transformed the place into a gregarious and engaging bistro that on weekends is one of the most crowded and popular singles bars in the country. Tables are thick-topped wooden affairs, set either on the plaza outside or within the antique walls of the dark and shadowy interior. The food is some of the best in the capital, and is usually accompanied by live guitar music every Thursday to Sunday from 6 to 10pm. Having dined here many times, we can highly recommend the sautéed shrimp in coconut-curry sauce. On festive occasions, ask for the brochette of mixed meats; the meat has been marinated in fresh spices and herbs and is artfully flambéed at your table. The sea bass with white-wine sauce is perfectly prepared, although the fancy Continental dishes such as charbroiled steak with onion sauce and a grilled rack of lamb might be more suited for the cold Alps.

La Atarazana 21, Zona Colonial. ℂ **809/687-8089.** Burgers and salads RD$425–RD$475 (US$13–US$14/£6.60–£7.40); main courses RD$550–RD$1,200 (US$17–US$36/£8.25–£18). AE, MC, V. Mon–Fri 4pm–1:30am; Sat–Sun noon–1:30am.

SPORTS & OTHER OUTDOOR PURSUITS

BEACHES   The Dominican Republic has some great beaches, but they aren't in Santo Domingo. The principal beach resort near the capital is at **Boca Chica,** less than 3km (2 miles) east of the airport and about 31km (19 miles) from the center of Santo Domingo. Here you'll find clear, shallow blue water, a white-sand beach, and a natural coral reef. The east side of the beach, known as "St. Tropez," is popular with Europeans. In recent years, the backdrop of the beach has become rather tacky, with an array of pizza and fast-food stands, beach cottages, chaise lounges, watersports concessions, and plastic beach tables.

Slightly better maintained is the narrow white-sand beach of **Playa Juan Dolio** or **Playa Esmeralda,** a 20-minute drive east of Boca Chica. Several resorts have recently located here. With all the hotels lining this beach, it's likely to be as crowded as Boca Chica any day of the week.

HORSE RACING   Santo Domingo's racetrack, **Galapagos Hipódromo V Centenario,** on Avenida Las Américas, Km 14.5 (ℂ **809/687-6060**), schedules races Tuesday, Thursday, and Saturday at 2pm. You can spend the day here and have lunch at the track's restaurant. Admission is free.

TENNIS   You can often play on the courts at the major resorts if you ask your hotel desk to call in advance for you and make arrangements.

Moments Uno, Dos, Tres Strikes You're Out

Dominicans were crazy about baseball long before their countryman Sammy Sosa set the United States on fire with his home-run race against Mark Mc-Gwire. Almost every Major League baseball team has at least one player from the Dominican Republic on its roster these days. Pedro Martinez, Manny Ramirez, and Alphonso Soriano are just a few of the all-star team of players who hail from the Dominican Republic.

If you're here between October and January, you might want to catch a game in the Dominican Republic's Professional Winter League. The **Liga de Beisbol stadium** (*©* 809/567-6371) is in Santo Domingo; check local newspapers for game times, or ask at your hotel. There are also games at the Tetelo Vargas Stadium in San Pedro de Macoris, known to die-hard sports fans as the "land of shortstops" for the multitude of infielders that call this tiny town home.

SEEING THE SIGHTS

Prieto Tours, Av. Francia 125 (*©* **809/685-0102**), one of the capital's leading tour operators, offers a 3-hour tour of the **Colonial Zone,** leaving most mornings at 9am and again at 3pm if there's sufficient demand; it costs US$25 (£13). A 6-hour tour visits the Colonial Zone, the **Columbus Lighthouse,** the **Aquarium,** and the city's modern neighborhoods; the US$35 (£18) fee includes lunch and entrance to several well-known museums and monuments. About an hour of the tour is devoted to shopping.

THE RELICS OF COLUMBUS & THE COLONIAL ERA

Santo Domingo—a treasure trove of historic, sometimes crumbling, buildings—is undergoing a major government-sponsored restoration. The old town is still partially enclosed by remnants of its original city wall. The narrow streets, old stone buildings, and forts are like nothing else in the Caribbean, except perhaps Old San Juan. The only thing missing is the clank of the conquistadors' armor.

Ancient and modern Santo Domingo meet at the **Parque Independencia,** a big city square whose most prominent feature is its **Altar de la Patria**—a national pantheon dedicated to the nation's heroes, Duarte, Sanchez, and Mella, who are buried here. These men led the country's fight for freedom from Haiti in 1844. As in provincial Spanish cities, the square is a popular family gathering place on Sunday afternoon. At the entrance to the plaza is **El Conde Gate,** named for El Conde (the count) de Penalva, the governor who resisted the forces of Admiral Penn, the leader of a British invasion. It was also the site of the March for Independence in 1844, and holds a special place in the hearts of Dominicans.

In the shadow of the Alcázar, **La Atarazana** is a fully restored section of one of the New World's finest arsenals. It extends for a city block, holding within it a catacomb of shops, art galleries, boutiques, and some good regional and international restaurants.

Just behind river moorings is the oldest street in the New World, **Calle Las Damas (Street of the Ladies),** named not because it was the red-light district, but for the elegant ladies of the viceregal court who used to promenade here in the evening. It's lined with colonial buildings.

Just north is the chapel of **Our Lady of Remedies,** where the first inhabitants of the city attended Mass before the cathedral was erected.

Try to see the **Puerta de la Misericordia** (Calle Palo Hincado just north of Calle Arzobispo Portes). Part of the original city wall, this "Gate of Mercy" was once a refuge for colonists fleeing hurricanes and earthquakes.

The **Monastery of San Francisco** is a mere ruin, lit at night. That any part of it is still standing is a miracle; it was hit by earthquakes, pillaged by Drake, and bombarded by French artillery. To get here, go along Calle Hostos and across Calle Emiliano Tejera; continue up the hill, and about midway along you'll see the ruins.

You'll see a microcosm of Dominican life as you head east along **Calle El Conde** from Parque Independencia to **Plaza de Colón (Columbus Square),** which has a large bronze statue honoring the discoverer, made in 1882 by a French sculptor, and the **Catedral de Santa Maria la Menor** (see below).

Alcázar de Colón 🐾

The most outstanding structure in the old city is the Alcázar, a palace built for Columbus's son, Diego, and his wife, who was also niece to Ferdinand, king of Spain. Diego became the colony's governor in 1509, and Santo Domingo rose as the hub of Spanish commerce and culture in America. For more than 60 years, this coral limestone structure on the bluffs of the Ozama River was the center of the Spanish court, entertaining such distinguished visitors as Cortés, Ponce de León, and Balboa. The nearly two dozen rooms and open-air loggias are decorated with paintings, period tapestries, and 16th-century antiques.

Calle La Atarazana (at the foot of Calle Las Damas). ✆ 809/682-4750. Admission RD$50 (US$1.50/70p). Tues–Sat 9am–5pm; Sun 9am–4pm.

Catedral de Santa Maria la Menor 🐾

The oldest cathedral in the Americas was begun in 1514 and completed in 1540. Fronted with a golden-tinted coral limestone facade, the church combines elements of both Gothic and baroque with some lavish plateresque styles as exemplified by the high altar chiseled out of silver. The treasury has an excellent art collection of ancient woodcarvings, furnishings, funerary monuments, silver, and jewelry.

Calle Arzobispo Meriño (on the south side of Plaza de Colón). ✆ 809/689-1920. Admission RD$30 (90¢/45p). Cathedral Mon–Sat 9am–4:30pm, Sun Masses begin at noon; treasury Mon–Sat 9am–4pm.

El Faro a Colón (Columbus Lighthouse)

Built in the shape of a cross, the towering 206m-tall (676-ft.) El Faro a Colón monument is both a sightseeing attraction and a cultural center. In the heart of the structure is a chapel containing the Columbus tomb, and, some say, his mortal remains. The "bones" of Columbus were moved here from the Cathedral de Santa Maria la Menor (see above). (Other locations, including the Cathedral of Seville, also claim to possess the explorer's remains.) The most outstanding and unique feature is the lighting system composed of 149 searchlights and a 70-kilowatt beam that circles out for nearly 70km (44 miles). When illuminated, the lights project a gigantic cross in the sky that can be seen as far away as Puerto Rico.

Although the concept of the memorial is 140 years old, the first stones were not laid until 1986, following the design submitted in 1929 by J. L. Gleave, the winner of the worldwide contest held to choose the architect. The monumental lighthouse was inaugurated on October 6, 1992, the day Columbus's "remains" were transferred from the cathedral.

Av. España (on the water side of Los Tres Ojos, near the airport in the Sans Souci district). ✆ 809/591-1492. Admission RD$65 (US$1.95/£1) adults, RD$5 (15¢/8p) children 11 and under. Tues–Sun 9am–5:30pm.

Museo de las Casas Reales (Museum of the Royal Houses)   Through artifacts, tapestries, maps, and re-created halls, including a courtroom, this museum traces Santo Domingo's history from 1492 to 1821. Gilded furniture, arms and armor, and other colonial artifacts make it the most interesting museum of Old Santo Domingo. It contains replicas of the *Niña,* the *Pinta,* and the *Santa Maria,* and one exhibit is said to hold some of Columbus's ashes. In addition to pre-Columbian art you can see the main artifacts of two galleons sunk in 1724 on their way from Spain to Mexico, along with remnants of another 18th-century Spanish ship, the *Concepción.*

Calle Las Damas (at corner Las Mercedes). (*©* 809/682-4202. Admission RD$30 (90¢/45p), RD$5 (15¢/8p). Tues–Sun 9am–5pm.

SHOPPING

The best buys in Santo Domingo are handcrafted native items, especially amber jewelry.

Ever since the Dominicans presented John F. Kennedy with what became his favorite rocker, visitors have wanted to take home a **rocking chair.** These rockers are often sold unassembled, for easy shipping. Other good buys include Dominican rum, hand-knit articles, macramé, ceramics, and crafts in native mahogany.

The best shopping streets are **El Conde,** the oldest and most traditional shop-flanked avenue, and **Avenida Mella.** In the colonial section, **La Atarazana** is filled with galleries and gift and jewelry stores, charging inflated prices. Duty-free shops are found at the airport, in the capital at the **Centro de los Héroes,** and at both the Hotel Santo Domingo and the Hotel Embajador. Shopping hours are generally Monday to Saturday from 9am to 12:30pm and 2 to 5pm.

Head first for the National Market, **El Mercado Modelo,** Avenida Mella, filled with stall after stall of crafts, spices, and produce; you can easily get lost in the crush. The merchants are eager to sell, so remember to bargain. You'll see a lot of tortoise-shell work, but exercise caution, since many species, especially the hawksbill turtle, are on the endangered-species list and could be impounded by U.S. Customs if discovered in your luggage. Also for sale are rockers, mahogany, sandals, baskets, hats, and clay braziers for grilling fish.

Amber World Museum, Arzobispo Meriño 452 (*©* **809/686-5700**), lives up to its name. Many visitors flock here to see plants, insects, and even scorpions fossilized in resin millions of years ago. Although some of the displays are not for sale, in an adjoining salon you can watch craftspeople at work, polishing and shaping raw bits of ancient amber for sale. To visit the museum costs adults RD$50 (US$1.50/75p) and children up to age 12 enter free. Open Monday to Saturday 8:30am to 6pm and Sunday 9am to 1pm.

Another reliable source for stunning amber, as well as coral, is **Ambar Nacional,** Calle Arzobispo Meriño (*©* **809/686-5700**). This is also the best source for purchasing larimar jewelry. In general, prices here are a bit less expensive than those at the more prestigious Amber World Museum nearby.

Tips **You Call That a Bargain?**

Always haggle over the price of handicrafts, particularly in the open-air markets. No stall-keeper expects you to pay the first price asked. Remember the Spanish words for too expensive: *muy caro.*

In the center of the most history-laden section of town is the well-known **Galería de Arte Nader,** Rafael Augusto Sanchez 22 (© **809/544-0878**), which displays so many Latin paintings that they're sometimes stacked in rows against the walls. The works of the country's best-known painters and most promising newcomers are displayed here (though to be honest, the Dominican Republic is short on painters with international reputations). There is also a lot of tourist junk, shipped in by the truckload from Haiti. In the ancient courtyard in back, you can get a glimpse of how things looked in the Spanish colonies hundreds of years ago.

Nuebo, Fantino Falco 36, Naco (© **809/562-3333**), is patronized by some of the capital's most upscale buyers. This shop sells a carefully chosen assortment of art objects, lamps, and furnishings. With some persuasion, anything you buy here can be shipped.

Columbus Plaza (Decla, S.A.), Calle Arzobispo Meriño 206 (© **809/689-0565**), is one of the largest, supermarket-style gift and artifacts stores in the country. Well-organized and imaginative, with a helpful English-speaking staff, it sprawls over three floors of a modern building divided into boutiques specializing in amber, larimar, gold and silver jewelry, cigars, paintings and sculpture, plus craft items.

Cigars are big sellers in Santo Domingo. The best selection is at **Cigar King,** Calle Conde 208, Baguero Building (© **809/686-4987**), in the colonial city. Its selection of Dominican and Cuban cigars in a temperature-controlled room is wide ranging.

SANTO DOMINGO AFTER DARK
DANCE CLUBS

Local young people flock to the dance clubs in droves after dinner. Even the hotel dance clubs cater to locals as well as tourists. Great dancers abound, so go and watch even if you don't feel like dancing.

La Guácara Taína, Avenida Mirador del Sur, in Parque Mirador del Sur (© **809/533-1051**), is the best *discoteca* in the country, drawing equal numbers of locals and visitors. Set in an underground cave within a verdant park, the specialty is merengue, salsa, and other forms of Latin music. There are three bars, two dance floors, and banquettes and chairs nestled into the rocky walls. The cover is RD$300 (US$9/£4.50), includes one drink. It's open Wednesday to Sunday from 9pm; closing time varies.

Fantasy Disco, Avenida Heroes de Luperón 29, La Feria (© **809/535-5581**), is one of the capital's most popular dance clubs, about a block inland from the Malecón. Once you get past the vigilant security staff, you'll find lots of intimate nooks and crannies, a small dance floor, and one of the country's best-chosen medleys of nonstop merengue music. Entrance is free, and beer costs RD$75 to RD$100 (US$2.25–US$3/£1.15–£1.50) a bottle. The place is open daily from 6pm to 4am.

Jet Set, Centro Comercial El Portal, Avenida Independencia (© **809/533-9707**), is one of the capital's most formal and elaborate nightclubs, admitting couples only, and nobody who is too rowdy. Most of the tables and chairs slope down toward an amphitheater-style dance floor, giving the place the feel of a bullfighting arena. The collection of live orchestras that play here are better than anywhere else in town. Entrance costs between RD$300 to RD$1,200 (US$9–US$36/£4.50–£18), depending on the artist. The Jet Set takes off at 9pm and flies until the early morning.

ROLLING THE DICE

Santo Domingo has several major casinos, all of which are open nightly until 4 or 5am. Gambling here is a very minor attraction and the odds are pretty much against you. If gambling is your raison d'être, you'd do better to plan a holiday in Puerto Rico.

The **Majestic Casino** in the Malecón Center, Avda. George Washington 500 (© 809/687-4853), is the newest casino in town. Managing to be somehow glittery but tasteful at the same time, it isn't the most animated casino in the capital, and on quiet nights it can be a bit staid, but you'll quickly get the feeling that it's deep into the process of finding a clientele of its own. Open daily 4pm to 4am.

The **Renaissance Jaragua Hotel & Casino,** Av. George Washington 367 (© 809/535-9292) has the most razzmatazz, and it's where Las Vegas style gamblers converge to lose big bucks. You can't miss the brightly flashing sign; it's the most dazzling light along the Malecón. You can wager on blackjack, baccarat, roulette, and slot machines in either Dominican pesos or U.S. dollars. Open daily 4pm to 4am.

Another casino is at the **Hispaniola Hotel,** Avenida Independencia (© 809/221-7111), open daily noon to 5am. One of the most stylish choices is the **Casino Diamante,** in the Meliá Santo Domingo Hotel & Casino, Av. George Washington 361 (© 809/682-2102). Its bilingual staff will help you play blackjack, craps, baccarat, and keno, among other games. There's also a piano bar. The casino is open daily noon to 6am.

13

Grenada

This sleepy island has friendly people, a lush interior that includes Grant Etang National Park, and the lovely and popular white sands of Grand Anse Beach. Crisscrossed by nature trails and filled with dozens of secluded coves and sandy beaches, Grenada has moved beyond the turbulence of the 1980s. It's not necessarily for the serious party person and definitely not for those seeking action at the casino. Instead, it attracts visitors who like snorkeling, sailing, fishing, and doing nothing more invigorating than lolling on a beach under the sun.

The "Spice Island," Grenada is an independent, three-island nation (the other two islands are Carriacou, the largest of the Grenadines, and Petite Martinique). Grenada has more spices per square mile than any other place in the world: cloves, cinnamon, mace, cocoa, tonka beans, ginger, and a third of the world's supply of nutmeg. "Drop a few seeds anywhere," the locals will tell you, "and you have an instant garden." The interior is like a jungle of palms, oleander, bougainvillea, purple and red hibiscus, crimson anthurium, bananas, breadfruit, ferns, and palms.

1 Essentials

VISITOR INFORMATION

In the United States, the **Grenada Tourist Office** is at 305 Madison Ave., Suite 2145, New York, NY 10165 (© 212/687-9554).

In London, contact the **Grenada Board of Tourism,** 11 Blades Court, 121 Deodar Rd., London SW15 2NU (© 020/8877-4516).

On the island, pick up maps, guides, and general information at the **Grenada Board of Tourism,** the Bums Point, in St. George's (© 473/440-2279), open Monday to Friday from 8am to 4pm.

You can find information on the Web at **www.grenadagrenadines.com.**

GETTING THERE

Point Salines International Airport lies at the southwestern toe of Grenada. The airport is a 5- to 15-minute taxi ride from most of the major hotels.

American Airlines (© 800/433-7300 in the U.S. and Canada, or 473/444-2222; www.aa.com) flies daily to Grenada from New York and Miami. **US Airways** (© 800/428-4322 in the U.S. and Canada, or 473/439-0681; www.usairways.com) has weekly flights from Philadelphia.

British Airways (© 800/247-9297 in the U.S. and Canada; www.britishairways.com) flies to Grenada every Tuesday and Friday from London's Gatwick Airport, making a single stop at Antigua en route.

Air Jamaica (© 800/523-5585 in the U.S. and Canada; www.airjamaica.com) offers nonstop flights from New York to Grenada two to three times a week.

Allamanda Beach Resort **2**
Bel Air Plantation **13**
Blue Horizons Garden Resort **7**
Calabash **11**
Coyaba **4**
The Flamboyant Hotel **3**
Gem Holiday Resort **5**
Grenada Grand Beach Resort **5**
Grenadian by Rex Resorts **10**
Laluna **9**
La Sagesse **14**
Spice Island Beach Resort **6**
True Blue Bay Resort **1**
Twelve Degrees North **12**

Caribbean Star (© **866/864-6272** in the U.S. and Canada; or 800/723-1111 in Grenada; www.flycaribbeanstar.com) flies daily from Antigua via Dominica, St. Vincent, St. Lucia, and Trinidad. **SVG Air** (© **800/624-1843** in the U.S. and Canada; www.svgair.com) flies from Carriacou and Union Island to Grenada, and **LIAT** (© **473/440-3967;** www.liatairline.com) flies between Grenada and several neighboring islands in the southern Caribbean. Finally, **Virgin Atlantic Airways** (© **800/821-5438** in the U.S. and Canada, or 800/744-7477 in Grenada; www.virgin-atlantic.com) flies nonstop once a week from London's Heathrow Airport.

GETTING AROUND

BY TAXI Taxi rates are set by the government. Most arriving visitors take a cab at the airport to one of the hotels near St. George's, at a cost of US$15 (£7.80). Add US$4 (£2.80) to the fare from 6pm to 6am. You can also use most taxi drivers as a guide for a day of sightseeing; negotiate a price beforehand.

BY RENTAL CAR *Remember:* Drive on the left. A U.S., British, or Canadian driver's license is valid on Grenada; however, you must obtain a local permit, costing EC$30 (US$11/£6). These permits can be bought either from the car-rental company or from the traffic department at the Carenage in St. George's. The Carenage is both

Fun Fact **Carnival on Grenada**

The second weekend of August brings colorful Carnival parades, music, and dancing. The festivities begin on Friday, continuing practically nonstop through Tuesday. Steel bands and calypso groups perform at Queen's Park. **Jouvert,** one of the highlights of the festival, begins at 5am on Monday with a parade of Djab Djab/Djab Molassi, devil-costumed figures daubed with molasses. (*Be warned:* Don't wear nice clothes to attend this event—you may get sticky from close body contact.) The Carnival finale, a gigantic "jump-up" (like a hoedown), ends with a parade of bands from Tanteen through the Carenage into town.

the walkway and the road that loops around the horseshoe-shaped St. George's Harbour. It is the capital's principal thoroughfare.

Try **Dollar Rent-a-Car,** at the airport (© **800/800-4000** in the U.S. and Canada, or 473/444-4786; www.dollar.com). You can also find a branch of **Avis** (© **800/331-1212** in the U.S.; www.avis.com) at the airport, as well as an office for **Thrifty** (© **800/847-4389** in the U.S., or 473/847-4984; www.thrifty.com).

A word of warning about local drivers: There's such a thing as Grenadian driving machismo; the drivers take blind corners with abandon. An extraordinary number of accidents are reported in the lively local paper. Gird yourself with nerves of steel, and be on the lookout for children and pedestrians when driving at night. Many foreign visitors, in fact, find any night driving hazardous.

BY BUS   Minivans, charging EC$1.50–EC$6.50 (55¢–US$2.40/30p–£1.30), are the cheapest way to get around. The most popular run is between St. George's and Grand Anse Beach. Most minivans depart from Market Square or from the Esplanade area of St. George's.

FAST FACTS: Grenada

Banks Banks in St. George's, the capital, include **First Caribbean International Bank,** at Church and Halifax streets (© **473/440-3232**); **Scotiabank,** on Halifax Street (© **473/440-3274**); the **Public Bank of Grenada,** at Halifax and Hillsborough streets (© **473/440-3566**); the **Royal Bank of Trinidad & Tobago (RBTT),** at Halifax and Cross streets (© **473/440-3521**); and the **Grenada Cooperative Bank,** on Church Street (© **473/440-2111**). Most have ATMs. Hours are usually Monday through Thursday from 8am to 3pm and Friday from 8am to 5pm.

Currency The official currency is the **Eastern Caribbean dollar (EC$),** approximately EC$2.70 to US$1 (EC$1 = US37¢/20p). Always determine which dollars, EC or U.S., you're talking about when someone on Grenada quotes you a price. *Unless otherwise specified, prices in this chapter are quoted in U.S. dollars and British pounds.*

Documents A valid passport is required of U.S., British, and Canadian citizens entering Grenada, plus a return or ongoing ticket.

Electricity Electricity is 220–240-volt AC (50 cycles), so transformers and adapters will be needed for U.S.-made appliances.

Embassies & High Commissions The **U.S. Embassy** is located at L'Anse aux Epines Salines, St. George's (© 473/444-1173). The **British High Commission** is on Church Street, St. George's (© 473/440-3536).

Emergencies Dial © **911** for police, fire, or an ambulance.

Hospital **St. George's General Hospital** located on Grandetang Road, St. George's (© 473/440-2051), has an X-ray department and operating room. Private doctors and nurses are available on call.

Language English is commonly spoken. Creole English, a mixture of several African dialects, English, and French, is spoken informally by most.

Pharmacies Try **Gittens Pharmacy,** Halifax Street, St. George's (© 473/440-2165), open weekdays from 8am to 6pm (Thurs until 5pm), and Saturday from 8am to 3pm.

Post Office The general post office, at the Pier, St. George's, is open Monday to Friday from 8am to 4pm.

Safety Street crime occurs here, tourists have been victims of armed robbery in isolated areas, and thieves frequently steal U.S. passports and alien registration cards in addition to money. Muggings, purse snatchings, and other robberies occur in areas near hotels, beaches, and restaurants, particularly after dark. Don't leave valuables unattended at the beach. Be cautious when walking after dark, or take a taxi. Report a stolen or lost passport immediately to the local police and the embassy.

Taxes A 10% VAT (value-added tax) is imposed on food and beverages, and there's an 8% room tax. You'll pay a departure tax of US$20 (£10) when you leave.

Telephone The area code for all of Grenada is **473**. You can call to or from Grenada as you would to or from any other area code in North America. Public phone and fax services are available at the Carenage offices of **Grenada Cable & Wireless** in St. George's (© 473/440-1000 for all offices). The office is open Monday to Thursday from 8am to 5pm, and Friday from 8am to 4pm.

Time Grenada is on Atlantic Standard Time year-round, which means it's usually 1 hour ahead of the U.S. East Coast—except during daylight saving time, when the clocks are the same.

Tipping A 10% service charge is added to most restaurant and hotel bills. No additional tip is expected.

Water Stick to bottled water.

Weather Grenada has two distinct seasons: dry and rainy. The dry season is from January to May; the rest of the year is the rainy season, although the rainfall doesn't last long. The average temperature is 80°F (27°C). Because of constant trade winds, there's little humidity.

2 Accommodations

Whether you're looking for a kitchenette apartment, a small, intimate inn, or a major resort, you'll find it waiting for you in Grenada, which has some of the best and most varied accommodations in the southern Caribbean. Unless you want to stay in an atmospheric inn tucked away somewhere, opt for a hotel lined up along Grand Anse Beach. All you'll have to do is walk out the door and head for the ocean.

Your hotel or inn will probably add a service charge of 10% to your bill—ask about this in advance.

VERY EXPENSIVE

Bel Air Plantation 𝕬𝕬𝕬 *Finds*   A secluded hideaway and one of the most dramatic of the island accommodations stands on a 7-hectare (18-acre) tract of lush land on the southwestern side of the island. Beautifully integrated into the almost junglelike terraced waterfront landscape, this is a coterie of vibrantly colored gingerbread cottages built up and down the hillside overlooking St. David's Harbour. Surrounded by tropical gardens, each of the airy, spacious accommodations offers privacy and old-world charm, but also modern amenities. Each unit is furnished with its own character and personality, everything centering on a "waterfront village," complete with a restaurant, bar, grocery, deli, cafe, art gallery, and gift shop. Even the simplest accommodations here, the cottages, are handsomely furnished. You can live higher on the hog by renting one of the two-bedroom villas with spacious master bedrooms and living rooms furnished in wicker and teak. All the bathrooms are well maintained, but the cottages have small, rather functional bathrooms with showers only, whereas the villas have much larger facilities with whirlpool baths.

St. David's Point, St. George's, Grenada, W.I. ℂ 473/444-6305. www.belairplantation.com. 11 units. Winter US$270–US$325 (£140–£169) cottage, US$350–US$425 (£182–£221) 1-bedroom villa, US$475–US$595 (£247–£309) 2-bedroom villa; off season US$250–US$270 (£130–£140) cottage, US$325–US$350 (£169–£182) 1-bedroom villa, US$425–US$475 (£221–£247) 2-bedroom villa. AE, MC, V. **Amenities:** Restaurant; bar; outdoor pool; kayaks; snorkeling; room service (8am–10:30pm); laundry service; dry cleaning. *In room:* A/C, ceiling fan, TV, kitchens (in some), fridge, beverage maker, hair dryer, safe.

Calabash 𝕬𝕬𝕬   On a landscaped 3-hectare (7½-acre) beach, the Calabash is today the leading hotel on Grenada. Of all the upmarket inns on the island, it is the smallest and most posh, drawing a devoted repeat clientele, especially among its British clients. Everything is refined and low-key—nothing splashy. Eight kilometers (5 miles) south of St. George's and only minutes from the airport, it occupies an isolated section of L'Anse aux Epines (Prickly Bay). Foremost among the multitude of shrubs here are the scores of beautiful *calabashes* (gourds) for which the resort was named. The eight private plunge-pool suites and 22 whirlpool-bath suites all have verandas and either one king-size bed or two double beds. Bathrooms are very spacious, with big stall showers, oversize tubs, and bidets.

The restaurant, Rhodes, serves excellent food (p. 320), and entertainment, ranging from piano music to steel bands, is provided 4 or 5 nights a week.

L'Anse aux Epines (P.O. Box 382), St. George's, Grenada, W.I. ℂ 473/444-4334. Fax 473/444-5050. www.calabashhotel. com. 30 units. Winter US$570–US$1,000 (£296–£520) suite for 2; off season US$295–US$760 (£153–£395) suite for 2. Extra person winter US$250 (£130); off season US$150 (£78). Children under 12 stay free in parent's room. Dinner US$60 (£31) per person extra. Rate includes breakfast. AE, MC, V. Children 12 and under not permitted Jan to mid-Mar. **Amenities:** 2 restaurants; 2 bars; outdoor pool; golf privileges; tennis court; exercise room; sailboat rentals; snorkeling; room service (10am–10pm); babysitting; laundry service; rooms for those w/limited mobility. *In room:* A/C, ceiling fan, TV, minibar, beverage maker, hair dryer, iron, safe.

Laluna 𝕬𝕬𝕬   One of Grenada's best hotels lies on an isolated, beautiful beach at Quarantine Point, near the extreme southern tip of the island. Designed along architectural lines you might expect in Indonesia, the resort consists of 16 thatch-covered, wood-and-stone-sided cottages, each with a small pool, artwork, and fabric-swathed four-poster beds imported from Bali. Bathrooms are light, airy, tropical affairs, often open to the breezes and each containing a shower stall. Scattered up and down a hillside, about 1.5km (1 mile) north of the Port Salines airport, they lie within a 2-minute walk from the beach. The resort's social and architectural centerpiece is a clubhouse larger than the cottages, the site of big verandas, a restaurant, a good-looking bar area, and check-in facilities.

With clients that have included *Sports Illustrated* swimsuit models and Mick Jagger's ex-wife Jerry Hall, it is a glittery, hedonistic niche with an appealing ironic edge. The restaurant (p. 319), which is open to nonresidents who phone in advance, is less than 12m (40 ft.) from the beach, and separated from the airy bar by a communal swimming pool.

Morne Rouge (P.O. Box 1500), St. George's, Grenada, W.I. ℂ **866/452-5862** in the U.S., or 473/439-0001. Fax 473/439-0600. www.laluna.com. 16 cottages. Winter US$505–US$990 (£263–£515) cottages and suites for 1–2 people, US$995–US$1,420 (£517–£738) cottages for 1–4 people; off season US$360–US$785 (£187–£408) cottages and suites for 1–2 people, US$720–US$995 (£374–£517) cottages for 1–4 people. MAP (breakfast and dinner) US$80 (£42) per person extra. AE, MC, V. **Amenities:** Restaurant; bar; outdoor pool; exercise room; kayaks; sailing; snorkeling; windsurfing; bikes; limited room service; massage facilities; laundry service. *In room:* A/C, ceiling fan, TV, minibar, beverage maker, hair dryer, safe, Wi-Fi, plunge pools (in some).

Spice Island Beach Resort 🌟🌟🌟   This is *the* classic beach resort, where you can run from your bungalow onto the island's most perfect stretch of white sand. It's not the most romantic or atmospheric hotel on the island, but its location along a 360m (1,600 ft.) expanse of Grand Anse Beach is unequaled. The main house, reserved for dining and dancing, has a tropical feel and lots of tasteful touches. Of the accommodations, we prefer the beach suites for their location. In the wake of Hurricane Ivan's destruction, management upgraded the property to the tune of US$10 million. Beachfront rooms—more than half the resort's total room count—were torn down and reconstructed with greater space than before. Second-floor suites have terraces overlooking the ocean and the garden; 17 units have their own private plunge pools. In the refurbishing, room decor was considerably upgraded, with Philippe Starck fixtures, flat-screen TVs, DVD players, frette linens, and Molton Brown amenities. The bathrooms are the largest and most luxurious on Grenada, with showers and Jacuzzis.

Well-crafted international cuisine is served at Oliver's Restaurant, an open-air pavilion on the beach.

Grand Anse Beach (P.O. Box 6), St. George's, Grenada, W.I. ℂ **473/444-4258.** Fax 473/444-4807. www.spicebeach resort.com. 66 units. Winter US$765–US$785 (£398–£408) double, US$1,020–US$1,520 (£530–£790) suite; off season US$635–US$665 (£330–£346) double, US$815–US$1,210 (£424–£629) suite. Rates are all-inclusive. Children under 5 free. AE, MC, V. **Amenities:** Restaurant; bar; outdoor pool; complimentary greens fees at Grenada Golf Course; tennis court; fitness center; spa; Jacuzzi; sauna; kayaks; sailing; snorkeling; limited room service; laundry service. *In room:* A/C, ceiling fan, TV, dataport, minibar, beverage maker, hair dryer, iron, safe.

EXPENSIVE
Blue Horizons Garden Resort 🌟   Lying 8km (5 miles) south of Point Salines Airport, this is an eco-tourist resort, with energy-saving toilets and solar heaters. A short walk from Grand Anse Beach, the resort attracts both scuba divers and nature enthusiasts. All the well-furnished units come with private terraces and small kitchenettes. Rentals are in two configurations—one with a king-size bed and pullout bed settee, the other with two queen beds plus a pullout. Trees and tropical plantings are spread across the handsomely landscaped 2.5 hectare (6 acres) grounds. It is estimated that nearly two dozen species of birds call the property home.

Grand Anse, Grenada, W.I. © **473/444-4316**. Fax 473/444-2815. www.grenadabluehorizons.com. 32 units. Winter US$220 (£114) double; off season US$155 (£81) double. Extra person winter US$55 (£29); off season US$40 (£21). AE, DC, MC, V. **Amenities:** Restaurant; 2 bars; outdoor pool; recreation room; babysitting; laundry service. *In room:* A/C, TV, kitchenette, hair dryer, iron, safe.

Coyaba 🕊

On a 2-hectare (5-acre) site on Grand Anse Beach, this resort, whose name means "heaven" in Arawak, is 10km (6¼ miles) from St. George's and 5km (3 miles) north of the airport. The hotel has views of town and of St. George's Harbour. All units have double beds, verandas or patios, and spacious bathrooms with tiled tub/shower combos. For persons with disabilities, the widened doorways, ramps, and three wheelchair-accessible guest rooms here make it the best choice on the island.

Breakfast and lunch are served under the palm-thatch-covered roof of the Arawak Cabana, adjacent to the swimming pool. Dinners are served at the Carpet and are usually based on themes that change nightly, including Italian night, steak and barbecue night, and seafood night.

Grand Anse Beach (P.O. Box 336), St. George's, Grenada, W.I. © **473/444-4129**. Fax 473/444-4808. www.coyaba.com. 80 units. Winter US$310 (£161) double; off season US$205 (£107) double. Extra person winter US$50 (£26), off season US$25 (£13). MAP (breakfast and dinner) US$60 (£31). AE, DC, MC, V. **Amenities:** 2 open-air restaurants; 2 bars (1 swim-up); outdoor pool; tennis court; golf; canoes; sailing; snorkeling; limited room service; laundry service; nonsmoking rooms; rooms for those w/limited mobility. *In room:* A/C, TV, hair dryer.

Grenada Grand Beach Resort 🕊

On 8 hectares (20 acres) of lush ground, this hotel stands on a desirable stretch of white-sandy beachfront, across from the Grand Anse Shopping Centre. Guests are ushered between a pair of manicured formal gardens to their (often small) rooms, which are tiled and furnished with mahogany pieces. Each has a balcony or patio and a well-kept bathroom equipped with a tub/shower combo. The beach-view rooms are the most desirable, naturally. You can dine indoors or out at the Waterfront Restaurant, which has passable international cuisine.

Grand Anse Beach (P.O. Box 441), Grenada, W.I. © **473/444-4371**. Fax 473/444-4800. www.grenadagrand.com. 240 units. Winter US$210–US$275 (£109–£143) double, US$825–US$1,350 (£429–£702) suite; off season US$162–US$227 (£84–£118) double, US$470–US$900 (£244–£468) suite. Children 16 and under stay free in parent's room. AE, DISC, MC, V. **Amenities:** Restaurant; 2 bars (1 swim-up); 2 pools; golf; 2 tennis courts; fitness center; 2 Jacuzzis; diving; snorkeling; car rental; salon; limited room service; massage; babysitting; laundry service; nonsmoking rooms; rooms for those w/limited mobility. *In room:* A/C, TV, dataport, beverage maker (in some), hair dryer.

Grenadian by Rex Resorts 🕊 *Kids*

This is the largest and most bustling hotel on the island, though not the best. It's a convention-group favorite, set on 14 rocky, partially forested hectares (35 acres) that slope steeply down to a pair of white-sand beaches. Each of the cream-and-pale-blue units is uniquely configured, and each is outfitted in rattan, wicker, and muted tropical fabrics. Eighty-four units offer ocean views and are all air-conditioned. The more expensive rooms contain tub/shower combos. The bathrooms in other units are more compact and have shower units. Adjacent to the accommodations is a .8-hectare (2-acre) artificial lake strewn with islands that are connected to the "mainland" with footbridges.

The International features buffets with foods from around the world, but The Oriental's Asian cuisine is far better. A bit more casual, Spicers serves local dishes for lunch. The Tamarind Lounge offers cabaret singing and dance music.

Tamarind Bay, Point Salines (P.O. Box 893), St. George's, Grenada, W.I. © **473/444-3333**. Fax 473/444-1111. www.rexcaribbean.com. 212 units. Winter US$280–US$335 (£146–£174) double, from US$400 (£208) suite; off season US$210–US$400 (£109–£208) double, from US$350 (£182) suite. AE, DC, MC, V. **Amenities:** 3 restaurants; 3

bars; 2 tennis courts; fitness center; dive shop; sailing; snorkeling; water-skiing; windsurfing; children's club; tour desk; limited room service; babysitting; laundry service; nonsmoking rooms; rooms for those w/limited mobility. *In room:* A/C, TV (in some), minibar (in some), hair dryer (in some).

Twelve Degrees North 🐸🐸 On a very private beach, this cluster of spotlessly clean efficiency apartments is owned and operated by Joseph and Patricia Gaylord, who personally greet visitors on the front lawn. Many staff members have been with Mr. Gaylord since he opened the place years ago. They'll cook breakfast, prepare lunch (perhaps pumpkin soup and flying fish), do the cleaning and laundry, and fix regional specialties for dinner (which you can heat up for yourself later). A housekeeper/cook, assigned to each unit, arrives as early as 8am (you determine the exact time) to perform the thousand small kindnesses that make Twelve Degrees North a favorite lair for repeat guests. All units are equipped with kitchens, large beds, and shower-only bathrooms with robes.

L'Anse aux Epines (P.O. Box 241), St. George's, Grenada, W.I. ©/fax **473/444-4580** (call collect to make reservations). www.twelvedegreesnorth.com. 8 units. Winter US$225 (£117) 1-bedroom apt for 2, US$350 (£182) 2-bedroom apt for 4; off season US$150 (£78) 1-bedroom apt for 2, US$265 (£138) 2-bedroom apt for 4. Extra person US$60–US$70 (£31–£36). MC, V. No children under 15 accepted. **Amenities:** Beach bar; outdoor pool; tennis court; snorkeling; Sunfish sailboats; tandem kayak. *In room:* Ceiling fan, beverage maker, hair dryer, no phone.

MODERATE

Allamanda Beach Resort 🐸 Opening onto a wide stretch of Grand Anse Beach, this is one of the best full-service operations on the island, with everything from a watersports center to a spa. Accommodations open onto views of the water. Units come with either a little terrace or a balcony, and some are suitable for persons with disabilities. The decor is light and airy in a Caribbean tropical motif, with tile floors, well-kept bathrooms with tub/shower combos, and, in some cases, whirlpool baths in the tiled bathrooms.

The DeSoleil Restaurant, set within an open-sided pavilion directly on the beach, serves international and Caribbean cuisine.

Grand Anse Beach (P.O. Box 27), St. George's, Grenada, W.I. © **473/444-0095.** Fax 473/444-0126. www.allamanda resort.com. 50 units. Year-round US$125–US$155 (£65–£81) double, US$270–US$325 (£140–£169) suite. MC, V. **Amenities:** Restaurant; bar; tennis court; gym; spa; snorkeling; outdoor pool; limited room service; massage; laundry service; rooms for those w/limited mobility. *In room:* A/C, TV, kitchenettes (in some), fridge, hair dryer, iron, safe.

The Flamboyant Hotel A well-established standby, this hotel occupies a hillside that slopes down to Grand Anse Beach, in a neighborhood peppered with other resorts. It was designed as a complex of modern, red-roofed buildings punctuated with an outdoor swimming pool. The management arranges parties, crab races, barbecues, dinner dances, and live reggae music several nights a week. Each medium-size unit has a loggia-style balcony overlooking the beach, tile floors, good beds, and floral-patterned curtains and upholsteries. The apartments contain kitchenettes. The somewhat-cramped bathrooms have tub/shower combos and are well maintained. The restaurant serves international and Caribbean meals and faces the sea.

Grand Anse Beach (P.O. Box 214), St. George's, Grenada, W.I. © **473/444-4247.** Fax 473/444-1234. www.flamboyant. com. 63 units. Winter US$170–US$190 (£88–£99) double, US$400–US$550 (£208–£286) 2-bedroom apt for 4; off-season US$130–US$140 (£68–£73) double, from US$305 (£159) suite. Extra person US$30–US$50 (£16–£26). AE, DC, DISC, MC, V. **Amenities:** Restaurant; bar; outdoor pool; dive shop; kayaks; snorkeling equipment; game room; car and jeep rental; business center; minimart; limited room service; babysitting; laundry service; nonsmoking rooms. *In room:* A/C, TV, dataport, kitchenettes (in some), minibar, beverage maker (in some), hair dryer, iron, safe.

True Blue Bay Resort This family-run resort takes its name from an old indigo plantation that once stood here, but panoramic views of Prickly Bay's blue waters make the name appropriate today as well. You can select one-bedroom apartments with verandas overlooking the bay, or two-bedroom cottages nestled in tropical gardens. The accommodations are tastefully furnished in pastels and tropical rattan pieces, with excellent beds, either king-size or twin. Each unit has a fully equipped kitchen and a tiled, shower-only bathroom.

Lunches and evening snacks are served in a raffish-looking beachfront grill called Stuart's Bar. Dinner at the True Blue Bay Restaurant is more formal. Also facing the water, it focuses on Caribbean and international dishes.

Old Mill Rd., True Blue (P.O. Box 1414), St. George's, Grenada, W.I. © 473/443-8783. Fax 473/444-5929. www.true bluebay.com. 31 units. Winter US$224–US$849 (£117–£442) double; off season US$153–US$377 (£80–£196) double. Extra person US$25–US$35 (£13–£18). AE, MC, V. **Amenities:** Restaurant; 2 bars; 2 outdoor pools; exercise room; dive shop; yacht charter; limited room service; rooms for those w/limited mobility. In room: A/C (in some), ceiling fan, TV, kitchenette, beverage maker, hair dryer, safe.

INEXPENSIVE

Gem Holiday Resort (Kids) Opening onto Morne Rouge Beach, this complex of self-catering apartments is family friendly. It's owned and operated by the Beadeau family, which welcomes guests to its one- and two-bedroom apartments. The units are a bit small, but they are fully equipped, with a kitchenette, good beds, mahogany furnishings, shower-only bathrooms, and a private terrace opening onto the beach. There is an on-site dance club, Fantazia 2001 (see "Grenada After Dark," later in this chapter).

Morne Rouge Bay (P.O. Box 58), St. George's, Grenada, W.I. © 473/444-4224. Fax 473/444-1189. www.gembeach resort.com. 18 units. Winter US$126–US$207 (£66–£108) double; off season US$75–US$148 (£39–£77) double. Extra person US$20 (£10). AE, DC, DISC, MC, V. **Amenities:** Restaurant; bar; minimart; babysitting; laundry service; dry cleaning; dance club. In room: A/C, TV, kitchen, fridge, beverage maker, hair dryer, iron/ironing board.

La Sagesse (Finds) On a sandy, tree-lined beach 15km (10 miles) from the airport, La Sagesse consists of a seaside guesthouse, a simple, open-air restaurant serving Caribbean-style meals, a bar, and an art gallery, with watersports available. Nearby are trails for hiking and exploring, a haven for wading and shore birds, hummingbirds, hawks, and ducks. Rivers, mangroves, and a salt pond sanctuary enhance the natural beauty of the place. The original great house of what was once La Sagesse plantation contains two apartments, each with high ceilings and comfortable beds, plus shower-only bathrooms. Guests also have a choice of a two-bedroom beach cottage, with comfortable furnishings and a wraparound porch. The least desirable accommodations are two small, economy-priced bedrooms in back of the inn's patio restaurant.

St. David's (P.O. Box 44), St. George's, Grenada, W.I. © 473/444-6458. Fax 473/444-6458. www.lasagesse.com. 12 units. Winter US$150–US$195 (£78–£101) double; off-season US$80 US$100 (£42–£52) double. Extra person US$20 (£10). MC, V. **Amenities:** Restaurant; bar; snorkeling; babysitting; laundry services; rooms for those w/limited mobility. In room: A/C (1 room), ceiling fan, beverage maker, hair dryer, no phone.

3 Dining

EXPENSIVE

Banana's CARRIBEAN/INTERNATIONAL With a monkey-themed decor, this restaurant enjoys a loyal local following with a smattering of visitors. Some tables have panoramic views of Prickly Bay. Although dishes are international in scope, we prefer the Caribbean specialties such as Creole *lambi* (conch). A tantalizing array of seafood kabobs is offered, along with a popular, perfectly grilled steak and succulent Italian-style pastas. Main dishes are served with generous helpings of rice, freshly made salads, and fresh vegetables.

In True Blue Bay Rd., St. George's. © **473/444-4662.** Reservations recommended. Main courses EC$35–EC$60 (US$13–US$22/£7–£12). MC, V. Mon and Wed–Fri 10am–11pm, Tues and Sat–Sun 4–11pm.

Coconut Beach Restaurant ⊛ FRENCH/CREOLE This informal restaurant occupies a green clapboard house set directly on the beach. From the dining room, you can watch the staff working in the exposed kitchen. They'll definitely be working on callaloo soup, made with local herbs and blended to a creamy smoothness. The kitchen specializes in various kinds of lobster, including the classic served with garlic butter, and an imaginative stir-fry with ginger chile. Fish dominates, including a catch of the day served with mango chutney. Almost anything prepared with fresh conch is terrific, but we also like the chicken breast cooked in local herbs and lime juice.

Warning: Because the restaurant is close to several major hotels, many people have opted to walk along the beach to reach it. Don't! Tourists have been robbed and had their lives threatened by machete-carrying thugs. Even if it's a short ride, take a taxi.

Grand Anse Beach (about .8km/½ mile north of St. George's). © **473/444-4644.** Reservations recommended. Lunch platters EC$19–EC$85 (US$7.05–US$31/£3.80–£17); main courses EC$37–EC$90 (US$14–US$33/£7.40–£18). AE, MC, V. Wed–Mon 12:30–9:30pm.

La Belle Creole ⊛⊛ WEST INDIAN The inspired Creole cuisine and its romantic setting make this restored restaurant one of the island leaders. It's run by the Hopkins family who still use recipes from the founding matriarch who for years was hailed as the island's finest chef, especially in her use of homegrown products. Set in the lush tropical gardens of the Blue Horizons resort, the restaurant offers both elegant surroundings and good service. Begin with the green banana soup (the finest version of this we've ever had). Another soup that has a distinct West Indian flavor is the chilled Christophine soup (similar to squash). Lobster can be prepared as you like it, and there are such other delights as a pork tenderloin with a spicy peanut sauce or fish mousse. Want to start with Grenada's version of caviar? It's the roe of a sea urchin. Lunch is taken at poolside.

Grand Anse. © **473/444-4316.** Reservations recommended. Breakfast or lunch US$6–US$12 (£3.10–£6.25); dinner main courses US$19–US$35 (£13–£18) Daily 7:30–10am, 12:30–2:30pm, and 7–9pm.

Laluna ITALIAN/INTERNATIONAL This is the restaurant that feeds, nourishes, and entertains the sometimes-hedonistic international clientele of one of Grenada's newest and quietly stylish cottage compounds. And it does so exceedingly well. You'll dine in a thatch-covered setting, adjacent to the sea and a swimming pool, enjoying the cooking of a Sicily-born chef with wide-ranging experience in Asia. The best dishes include seafood gnocchi; sushi; pasta *a l'amatriciana* (with salami, ham, tomatoes, capers, and olives); and seafood Benedetto, a medley of wine-and-tomato-soaked seafood served over rice. A perfectly grilled steak or lobster almost invariably appears on the menu.

In the Laluna Resort, Morne Rouge (P.O. Box 1500). © **473/439-0001.** Reservations required. Main courses EC$65–EC$99 (US$24–US$37/£13–£20). AE, MC, V. Daily 7:30am–11pm.

Oliver's Restaurant ⊛ CREOLE/SEAFOOD Want to dine on an uncrowded beachfront protected from sudden tropical showers? The parapet here, built of imported pine and cedar, looks like a Le Corbusier rooftop. The view is of one of the finest beaches in the Caribbean—miles of white sand sprouting an occasional grove of sea-grape or almond trees. Some of the best hotel food on the island is served in this winning setting. You can even eat your lunch in a swimsuit. Local seafood is featured on the constantly changing menu. The most generous buffet on the island, a real Grenadian spread, is served on Friday, along with live entertainment.

Spice Island Beach Resort, Grand Anse Beach. ℂ 473/444-4258. Reservations required for nonguests. Full breakfast US$30 (£16), continental breakfast US$20 (£10). Lunch main courses US$10–US$25 (£5.20–£13). 6-course fixed-price dinner US$75 (£39). AE, DC, DISC, MC, V. Daily 7:30–10am, 12:30–3:00pm, and 7–9:30pm.

The Red Crab ✦ WEST INDIAN/INTERNATIONAL
The food at The Red Crab isn't as good as that at the restaurants recommended above, but it's a fun, lively place to be at night. Only a short taxi ride from the major hotels, The Red Crab attracts visitors and locals alike and is especially popular with students from the medical college. Patrons can dine inside or out under the starry sky. The beefsteaks, especially the pepper steak, are among Grenada's finest. Other offerings include local lobster tail; *lambi* (conch); and locally caught fish such as snapper, dolphin (mahimahi), and grouper, though other island chefs prepare better versions of these seafood dishes. If you weren't old enough to have dined in the '50s, you can at least experience that decade's popular cuisine and order beef stroganoff, veal *cordon bleu,* or lobster Newburg.

L'Anse aux Epines. ℂ 473/444-4424. Reservations required. Main courses EC$35–EC$90 (US$13–US$33/£7–£18). AE, MC, V. Mon–Sat 11am–2pm and 6–11pm.

Rhodes ✦✦✦ INTERNATIONAL/SEAFOOD
One of London's most exciting chefs, Gary Rhodes, has invaded Grenada. Opened in 2004, the chic restaurant is the finest place to eat on the island, and the atmosphere is so cozy one diner compared it to being wrapped in a "sybaritic cocoon." Rhodes came to Grenada to acquaint himself with its local produce and many spices. He then designed the menu around these same flavors, and trained local chefs in his cooking style. The actual recipes change daily but feature seafood. In London, Rhodes is known for his daring twists and creative flavors, so expect some delightful surprises if you show up here.

In the Calabash Hotel, L'anse Aux Epines. ℂ 473/444-4334. Reservations required. Main courses EC$40–EC$90 (US$15–US$33/£8–£18). AE, MC, V. Daily 7–9:30pm.

MODERATE
Aquarium Beach Club & Restaurant SEAFOOD
This beachfront club near the airport changes personality depending on the time of day. You can rent snorkeling equipment or ocean kayaks in the morning and return in the afternoon for a good seafood lunch. In the evening, the convivial bar fills up, often with locals. On Sunday afternoons there's always something happening, like the lobster barbecue.

At dinner the place becomes slightly more formal, and a full menu is offered. Your best bet is the fresh fish of the day, prepared as you like it. Lots of other good dishes emerge from the kitchen as well, including two specialties: a tender and well-flavored pepper steak, and a spinachlike callaloo cannelloni, a uniquely Caribbean concoction. Most of the main courses are inexpensive; only the barbecued lobster will tax your wallet.

Point Salines. ℂ 473/444-1410. Reservations required. Main courses EC$43–EC$95 (US$16–US$35/£8.60–£19). AE, MC, V. Tues–Sun 10am–midnight.

La Boulangerie FRENCH/ITALIAN   Don't be deterred by the shopping center location. This French coffee shop and bakery is an ideal spot for a good breakfast or light lunch (served throughout the afternoon). And prices at dinner are very reasonable. In the early morning, visitors throng here for the freshly brewed coffee, pastries, and croissants. The afternoon crowd devours well-stuffed baguettes, sandwiches, and pizzas.

Le Marquis Shopping Complex, Grand Anse Beach. ℂ **473/444-1131.** Sandwiches and pizzas EC$27–EC$39 (US$10–US$14/£5.40–£7.80); dinner main courses EC$25–EC$65 (US$9.25–US$24/£5–£13). No credit cards. Daily 8:30am–9:30pm.

The Nutmeg SEAFOOD/CREOLE   Right on the harbor, The Nutmeg is a rendezvous point for the yachting set. Its informal atmosphere is suitable for a snack or full-fledged dinner. The drinks are especially good; try one of the Grenadian rum punches made with Angostura bitters, grated nutmeg, rum, lime juice, and syrup. There's always fresh fish, and usually callaloo or pumpkin soup. *Lambi* (the ubiquitous conch) is done very well here. A small wine list has some California, German, and Italian selections, and you can drop in just for a beer to enjoy the sea view. Sometimes, however, you'll be asked to share a table.

The Carenage, St. George's. ℂ **473/440-2539.** Main courses EC$35–EC$73 (US$13–US$27/£7–£15). AE, MC, V. Mon–Sat 8am–11pm; Sun 4–11pm.

INEXPENSIVE

Deyna's Tasty Food ⋆ *Finds* GRENADIAN   This little eatery is a closely guarded secret among locals. It's reached by heading up Melville Street to a modest three-story building overlooking the sea. The chef, Deyna Hercules, resembles her namesake. Her savory stuffed crabs are the island's best, and you'll see her other specialties scribbled on a countertop chalkboard. She's known for her "fix up"—a sampling of the best food of the day, perhaps stewed fish, green plantains, and curried goat. She also serves Grenada's national dish, an "oil down," made with salted meat and breadfruit cooked in coconut milk. And where else could you get a tasty batch of *titiri*, minnow-size fish just plucked from the Caribbean? Wash them down with "bush tea" steeped from black sage leaves. Adventurous diners opt for one of the gamey specialties such as *manicou* (a cross between an opossum and a large rat).

Melville St., St. George's. ℂ **473/440-6795.** Reservations recommended. Main courses EC$22–EC$28 (US$8.15–US$10/£4.40–£5.60). MC, V. Mon–Sat 8am–7pm; Sun 10am–4pm.

La Sagesse ⋆ CARIBBEAN/CONTINENTAL   Opening onto a sandy beach, this romantic open-air spot is one of the quirkiest places to dine on island. Although it is casually run, it serves good food based on fresh ingredients. The seafood served here is some of the island's finest. You can order freshly made salads and well-stuffed sandwiches throughout the day. The *lambi* (conch) is an excellent choice, but on most nights, you can choose from a full range of fish, including dolphin (mahimahi) and grouper. In the evening several Continental dishes appear. The restaurant also caters to vegetarians.

In the La Sagesse nature center, south of St. David's. ℂ **473/444-6458.** Reservations not required. Main courses EC$35–EC$75 (US$13–US$28/£7–£15). MC, V. Daily 8am–10:30pm.

Morne Fendue ⋆ *Finds* CREOLE   This plantation house is the ancestral home of the late owner, Betty Mascoll. It was built in 1912 of carefully chiseled river rocks held together with a mixture of lime and molasses. Miss Mascoll died in 1998, but her loyal staff, including Kathleen McQueen, carries on her tradition. They need time to prepare food for your arrival, so it's imperative to give them a call to let them know you're coming by. Lunch is likely to include yam-and-sweet-potato casserole, curried chicken with lots of hot spices, and a hot pot of pork and oxtail. Because this is very much a private home, tipping should be done tactfully. Nonetheless, the hardworking cook and maid seem genuinely appreciative of a gratuity.

St. Patrick's (40km/25 miles north of St. George's). © 473/442-9330. Reservations required. Fixed-price lunch EC$45 (US$17/£9). No credit cards. Daily 12:30–4pm. Dinner served upon request. Follow the coastal road north out of St. George's; after you pass through Nonpareil, turn inland (east) and continue through Sauteurs and follow the signs to Morne Fendue.

4 Beaches

The best of Grenada's 45 beaches are in the southwestern part of the island. The granddaddy of them all is **Grand Anse Beach** ����, 3km (2 miles) of sugar-white sand fronting a sheltered bay. This beach is really the stuff of dreams—it's no surprise that many of the major resort hotels are here. A lot of visitors never leave this part of the island. Protected from strong winds and currents, the waters here are relatively safe, making Grand Anse a family favorite. The clear, gentle waters are populated with schools of rainbow-hued fish. Palms and sea-grape trees offer shade. Watersports concessions include water-skiing, parasailing, windsurfing, and scuba diving; vendors peddle coral jewelry, local crafts, and the inevitable T-shirts.

The beach at **Morne Rouge Bay** � is less popular but just as nice, with white sands bordering clear waters. Morne Rouge is noted for its calm waters and some of the best snorkeling in Grenada. It's about 2km (1¼ miles) south of Grand Anse Bay.

Pink Gin Beach lies near the airport at Point Salinas, bordering the resort, LaSource and Rex Grenadian. This is also a white-sand beach with clear waters, ideal for swimming and snorkeling. (No one seems to know why it's called Pink Gin Beach.) You can find a restaurant and kayak rentals here.

Also on Grenada's southern coast, **La Sagesse Beach** is part of La Sagesse nature center. This especially powdery strip of white sand is a lovely, tranquil area; in between time spent on the beach, you can go for nature walks in most directions. A small restaurant opens onto the beach.

If you like your waters more turbulent, visit the dramatic **Pearl's Beach,** north of Grenville on the Atlantic coast. The light-gray sand stretches for miles and is lined with palm trees. You'll practically have the beach to yourself.

Part of Levera National Park, **Levera Beach,** at the northeastern tip of the island, is one of the most beautiful on Grenada. Its sands front the Atlantic, which usually means rough waters. Many locals come here for Sunday picnics.

5 Sports & Other Outdoor Pursuits

DEEP-SEA FISHING   Fishers visit from November to March in pursuit of both blue and white marlin, yellowfin tuna, wahoo, sailfish, and more. Most of the bigger hotels have a sports desk that arranges fishing trips. The **Annual Game Fishing Tournament,** held in January, attracts a number of regional and international participants. For more information, call Robert Miller at (© **473/444-2220**).

GOLF   At the **Grenada Golf Course and Country Club,** Woodlands (© **473/444-4128**), you can tee off on a 9-hole course with views of both the Caribbean Sea and the Atlantic. Greens fees are only US$25 (£13) for 9 holes, or US$40 (£21) if you want to play it twice (to get 18 holes). Hours are Monday to Saturday 10am to 6pm.

HIKING   Grenada's lushness and beauty make it one of the best Caribbean islands for hiking. If you have time for only one hike here, take it in the **Grand Etang National Park and Forest Preserve** ⊛ (✆ 473/440-6160). Its sheer scenic beauty makes the **Lake Circle Trail** our number-one choice on the island. The trail makes a 30-minute circuit along Grand Etang Lake, the crater of an extinct volcano, amidst a forest preserve and bird sanctuary. You're likely to see the yellow-billed cuckoo and the emerald-throated hummingbird. The park is also a playground for Mona monkeys. Another easy hike, the **Morne LeBaye Trail,** begins at the park's center and affords a view of the 710m (2,329-ft.) Mount Sinai and the east coast. Of course, you can also take longer hikes, perhaps to the peak of **Mount Qua Qua** at 712m (2,335 ft.). Carry plenty of water and remember that trails can be slippery after a rainfall (especially June–Nov), so wear good hiking shoes.

You can hike the shorter trails independently, but you might wish to hire a guide for the ascent to Mount Qua Qua or the even more demanding hike to Mount Catherine, at 827m (2,713 ft.). The former costs US$25 (£13) per person for a 4-hour hike, while the latter is US$90 (£47). For information, call **Telfor Bedeau Hiking Tours** (✆ 473/442-6200). Good hiking trails can also be found at **Levera National Park** (see "A Spectacular Rainforest & More," below).

SAILING   Two large party boats, designed for 120 and 250 passengers, operate out of St. George's Harbour. The **Rhum Runner** and **Rhum Runner II,** c/o Best of Grenada, P.O. Box 188, St. George's, Grenada, W.I. (✆ 473/440-4386), make three trips daily, with lots of emphasis on strong liquor, steel-band music, and good times. Three-hour tours, conducted every morning and afternoon, coincide with the arrival of cruise ships, but will carry independent travelers if space is available. Evening tours on Friday and Saturday from 7:30pm to midnight are much more frequently attended by island locals, and are more bare-boned, louder, and usually less restrained. The cost is EC$25 (US$9.25/£5) per person.

SCUBA DIVING & SNORKELING   Grenada provides divers with an underwater world rich in submarine gardens, exotic fish, and coral formations, sometimes with visibility stretching to 36m (120 ft.). Off the coast is the wreck of the ocean liner *Bianca C,* which is nearly 180m long (590 ft.). Novice divers can stick to the west coast of Grenada, while more experienced divers might search out sights along the rougher Atlantic side.

Aquanuts, in the True Blue Bay, Grand Anse Beach (✆ 473/444-1126), has night dives or two-tank dives for US$79 to US$95 (£41–£50) respectively; PADI instructors offer an open-water certification program for US$420 (£218) per person. They also offer **snorkeling trips** (1½–2 hr.) for US$30 (£16). You can rent snorkel gear as well, even if you don't take the boat ride.

Giving Aquanuts serious competition is affable **Eco-Dive,** at the Coyaba Beach Resort on Grand Anse Beach (✆ 473/444-7777 or 473/444-4129). There's a PADI instructor on-site and the dive boat is well equipped with well-maintained gear. Both scuba diving and snorkeling jaunts to panoramic reefs and shipwrecks teeming with marine life are offered. A single dive costs US$48 (£25); a 6-dive package US$240 (£125). A **snorkeling trip** can be arranged for US$32 (£17). Diving instruction, including a resort course, is available.

If you'd rather strike out on your own, take a drive to Woburn and negotiate with a fisher for a ride to **Glovers Island,** an old whaling station, and snorkel away. Glovers

Island is an uninhabited rock spit a few hundred yards offshore from the hamlet of Woburn.

TENNIS   Most big resorts have tennis courts. There are public courts, as well, both at Grand Anse and in Tanteen in St. George's.

6 Exploring the Island

ST. GEORGE'S & VICINITY

The capital city of Grenada, **St. George's** ᏜᏜ is the prettiest harbor town in the West Indies. Its landlocked inner harbor is actually the deep crater of a long-dead volcano— or so one is told. In the town, you can see some of the most charming Georgian colonial buildings in the Caribbean, still standing despite a devastating hurricane in 1955. The steep, narrow hillside streets are filled with houses of ballast bricks, wrought-iron balconies, and sloping, red-tile roofs. Many of the pastel warehouses date from the 18th century. Frangipani and flamboyant trees add to the palette of color.

The port, which some compare to Portofino, Italy, is flanked by old forts and bold headlands. Among the town's attractions are an 18th-century pink **Anglican church,** on Church Street, and the **Market Square,** where colorfully attired farm women offer even more colorful produce for sale. **Fort George,** on Church Street, built by the French, stands at the entrance to the bay, with subterranean passageways and old guardrooms and cells.

Everyone strolls along the waterfront of the **Carenage** Ꮬ on the inner harbor, or relaxes on its pedestrian plaza, with seats and hanging planters providing shade from the sun. The best place to sit and have a drink is **The Nutmeg** (see "Dining," above). From its large open windows you'll have great views of the harbor activity. The hamburgers and rum drinks are great, too.

On this side of town, the **Grenada National Museum,** at the corner of Young and Monckton streets (© **473/440-3725**), is set in the foundations of an old French army barracks and prison built in 1704. Small but interesting, it houses finds from archaeological digs, petroglyphs, native fauna, the first telegraph installed on the island, a rum still, and memorabilia depicting Grenada's history. The most comprehensive exhibit traces the native culture of Grenada. Hours are Monday through Friday from 9am to 4:30pm, Saturday from 10am to 1pm. Admission is US$2.50 (£1.30).

You can take a drive up to Richmond Hill and **Fort Frederick,** begun by the French in 1779 and completed by the English in 1791. From its battlements, you'll have a superb view of the harbor and of the yacht marina.

An afternoon tour of St. George's and its environs might take you into the mountains north of the capital. A 15-minute drive delivers you to **Annandale Falls** Ꮬ, a tropical wonderland, with a cascade about 15m (50 ft.) high. You can enjoy a picnic surrounded by liana vines, elephant ears, and other tropical flora and spices. The **Annandale Falls Centre** (© **473/440-2452**) offers gift items, handicrafts, and samples of the indigenous spices of Grenada. Nearby, an improved trail leads to the falls where you can enjoy a refreshing swim. Swimmers can use the changing cubicles at the falls for free. The center is open daily from 8am to 4pm.

A SPECTACULAR RAINFOREST & MORE

If you head north out of St. George's along the western coast, you can take in beaches, spice plantations, and the fishing villages that are so typical of Grenada.

You'll pass through **Gouyave,** a spice town that's the center of the nutmeg and mace industry. At the **Grenada Cooperative Nutmeg Association** (© 473/444-8337), near the entrance to Gouyave, huge quantities of the spice are aged, graded, and processed. This is the best place to see spices being readied for market. Workers sit on stools in the natural light from the open windows of the aging factory, and laboriously sort the raw nutmeg and its byproduct, mace, into different baskets for grinding, peeling, and aging. Jams, jellies, syrups, and more are sold. Hours are Monday to Friday 8am to 4pm; admission is US$1 (50p).

In the northeast corner of the island (just east of Sauteurs) is palm-lined **Levera Beach,** an idyll of sand where the Atlantic meets the Caribbean. This is a great spot for a picnic lunch, but swimming can sometimes be dangerous. On the distant horizon you'll see some of the Grenadines.

Opened in 1994, the 180-hectare (445-acre) **Levera National Park** ⊕ has several white-sand beaches for swimming and snorkeling, although the surf is rough here where the Atlantic meets the Caribbean. It's also a **hiker's paradise,** although you should go hiking here only after you've hiked Grand Etang National Park and Forest Preserve (see "Hiking," above), which is lusher and of far greater interest. Levera Park contains a mangrove swamp, a lake, and a bird sanctuary, where you might see a rare tropical parrot. Offshore are coral reefs and sea-grass beds.

Heading down the east coast of Grenada, you reach **Grenville,** the island's second city. If you pass through on a Saturday morning, you can enjoy the hubbub of the native produce market. There's also a fish market along the waterfront. A nutmeg factory here welcomes visitors. From Grenville, you can cut inland into the heart of Grenada. Here you're in a world of luxuriant foliage, and you pass along nutmeg, banana, and cocoa plantations.

In the center of the island, reached along the major interior road between Grenville and St. George's, is **Grand Etang National Park** ⊕ (© 473/440-6160), containing the island's spectacular rainforest. For information about hikes in the park, see "Hiking," above.

On your descent from the mountains, you'll pass hanging carpets of mountain ferns. Going through the tiny hamlets of Snug Corner and Beaulieu, you eventually come back to the capital.

7 Shopping

Everybody who visits Grenada goes home with a basket of **spices,** better than any you're likely to find in your local supermarket. Vendors will besiege you wherever you go. Their hand-woven panniers of palm leaf or straw are full of items grown on the island, including the inevitable nutmeg, as well as mace, cloves, cinnamon, bay leaf, vanilla, and ginger. Grenada is no grand merchandise mart of the Caribbean like St. Thomas or St. Maarten, but you may find some local handicrafts, gifts, and even art.

If you like to attend Caribbean markets as much as we do, head for **Market Square** at the foot of Young Street in St. George's. The market is at its liveliest on Saturday morning, but is also open Monday to Friday. It's best to go between 8am and noon. An array of handicrafts is for sale, but fresh spices are more plentiful.

For something really special, visit **Arawak Islands Ltd.,** Upper Belmont Road, in St. George's (© 473/444-3577; www.arawak-islands.com), founded in 1986 by Angelia Clements, a German woman. From the raw materials of Grenada, especially nutmeg and cinnamon, she manufactures delectable tropical perfumes and toiletries.

The company is committed to natural products and minimal processing, and sells some items purchased from island companies and packaged here at the on-site workshop.

8 Grenada After Dark

Regular evening entertainment is provided by the resort hotels and includes steel bands, calypso, reggae, folk dancing, and limbo—even crab racing. Ask at your hotel desk to find out what's happening at the time of your visit.

The island's most popular nightspot is **Fantazia 2001,** Morne Rouge Beach (© 473/ 444-2288). It's air-conditioned, with state-of-the-art equipment, good acoustics, and fantastic lights, and plays the best in regional and international sounds. There are live shows Saturday. The cover ranges from US$5 to US$8 (£2.60–£4.15).

You can also try **Club Banana,** True Blue, St. George's (© 473/444-4662), down by the marina. Every Friday and Saturday night it operates a disco from 10pm to 2am, charging a cover of EC$35 to EC$40 (US$13–US$15/£7–£8).

The **Beachside Terrace** at the Flamboyant Hotel, Grand Anse (© 473/444-4247), is a laid-back spot featuring a steel band on Wednesday and Saturday, and, our favorite, a beach barbecue with live calypso music and limbo dancing on Sunday.

One of our favorite bars is **Aquarium Beach Club & Restaurant** at Point Salines (© 473/444-1410), which also serves delectable food (see "Dining," earlier in this chapter). From the sprawl of decks open to the trade winds, you can enjoy the lights of St. George's Harbour here at night.

For those seeking culture, the 250-seat **Marryshow Folk Theatre,** Herbert Blaize Street near Bain Alley, St. George's (© 473/440-2451), offers performances of Grenadian, American, and European folk music, drama, and West Indian interpretative folk dance. Check with the theater or the tourist office to see what's on. Tickets usually cost EC$25 (US$9.25/£5).

14

Guadeloupe

Guadeloupe gives travelers a taste of France in the Tropics. In addition to its Gallic flair and fine Creole cuisine (among the best in the Caribbean), it offers some excellent beaches and mountainous, lush terrain full of gorgeous scenery. The resorts are not as spectacular and plush as those on, say, Anguilla or Jamaica, though there are some large beachfront properties; but you can have a real island experience at small inns where locally prepared food and tranquility will be highlights of your stay.

Guadeloupe is part of the Lesser Antilles, about 320km (200 miles) north of Martinique. It actually comprises two different islands, separated by a narrow seawater channel known as the Rivière Salée. **Grande-Terre,** the eastern island, is full of rolling hills and sugar plantations. **Basse-Terre,** to the west, is a rugged mountainous island, dominated by the 1,440m (4,723-ft.) volcano, La Soufrière, which is still alive and dotted with banana plantations. Guadeloupe's mountains are covered with tropical forests, impenetrable in many places. Beautiful white-sand beaches ring its islands. In the unlikely event that you should grow bored on Guadeloupe, you can hop over to really remote islands offshore, including **Iles des Saintes** and **Marie-Galante.**

1 Essentials

VISITOR INFORMATION

For information before you go, contact the **French Government Tourist Office** (© 202/ 659-7779; www.francetourism.com). There are offices at 444 Madison Ave., New York, NY 10022 (© **212/838-7800**); 9454 Wilshire Blvd., Suite 715, Beverly Hills, CA 90212 (© **310/271-6665**); or 676 N. Michigan Ave., Suite 3360, Chicago, IL 60611 (© **312/751-7800**).

GETTING THERE

To get to Guadeloupe, most U.S. travelers will have to fly elsewhere in the Caribbean and transfer. You can take an **American Airlines** (© 800/433-7300 in the U.S. and Canada; www.aa.com) flight to its hub in San Juan, Puerto Rico, and then get one **American Eagle** flight daily on to Guadeloupe. There are also connections available through Martinique (see chapter 16).

Air Canada (© **888/247-2262** in the U.S. and Canada, or 590/21-12-77; www.aircanada.ca) flies between Montreal and Guadeloupe every Saturday year-round. Between December and April only, they also maintain an additional flight from Montreal and Guadeloupe, every Wednesday. Passengers can also fly from Toronto on one of the daily nonstop flights to Barbados. From there, passengers can transfer onto other carriers (usually LIAT), making the ongoing journey to points within the French West Indies.

Air France (© **800/237-2747** in the U.S. and Canada; www.airfrance.com) flies into Guadeloupe every day from Paris, with efficient connections from Britain and the rest of Europe. Air France also maintains direct service to Guadeloupe from Miami, via Port-au-Prince, Haiti, three days per week.

If you're already on the islands, you can wing into Guadeloupe on **LIAT** (© **888/844-5428** in the U.S., or 268/480-5601; www.liatairline.com), which flies here from Antigua, St. Maarten, St. Croix, St. Lucia, Martinique, Barbados, Grenada, Trinidad, and Dominica. **Air Caraïbes** (© **877/772-1005** in the U.S. and Canada, or 590/82-47-00; www.aircaraibes.com) operates about a half-dozen flights a day into Guadeloupe from Martinique, as well as at least one flight a day from both St. Barts and French St. Martin, and a daily flight from Cayenne in French Guyana.

Consider arriving in Guadeloupe as many of the locals do, on one of the daily **ferry-boats** operated by **Express des Iles** (© **590/83-04-43**), whose vessels originate every day in Fort-de-France, Martinique, at 2pm, make a 30-minute stopover in Dominica en route (departing from Dominica around 4pm), and then dock at the quays of Pointe-à-Pitre sometime around 5:45pm, depending on weather, tides, and the vagaries of island life.

One-way passage to Pointe-à-Pitre from Dominica costs 65€ ($84) per person each way; one-way passage to Guadeloupe from Martinique is 66€ ($85) and round-trip 100€ ($130), partly the result of government subsidies. For timetables and more information in Guadeloupe, call **Agence Penchard** (the local representative of Express des Iles) at © **590/83-04-43.** For timetables and information in Martinique, contact Express des Iles directly at © **596/63-05-45**; www.express-des-iles.com.

GETTING AROUND

BY RENTAL CAR　You may want to rent a car on Guadeloupe so you can explore Basse-Terre; the loop around the island is one of the most scenic drives in the Caribbean. Car-rental kiosks at the airport are open to meet international flights. Rental rates at local companies might appear lower, but several readers have complained of mechanical problems, billing irregularities, and difficulties in resolving insurance disputes in the event of accidents. Therefore, we recommend reserving a car in advance through one of North America's largest car-rental companies: **Hertz** (© **800/654-3131** in the U.S. and Canada, or 590/82-00-14; www.hertz.com) or **Avis** (© **800/331-1212** in the U.S. and Canada, or 590/21-13-54; www.avis.com), both of which are headquartered at the airport. Many of the major hotels also have car-rental desks. You'll have to pay a one-time airport surcharge of 20€ ($26) and VAT (value-added tax) of 8.5%. Prices are usually 20% to 25% lower between March and early December, excepting July and August.

Driving is on the right-hand side of the road, and there are several gas stations along the island's main routes. Because of the distance between gas stations in outlying regions, try not to let your gas gauge fall below the halfway mark when driving outside of the capital.

BY TAXI　You'll find taxis when you arrive at the airport, but no limousines or buses. From 7pm until 6am, cabbies are legally entitled to charge you 40% more than the regular fare. Some, but not all, taxis in Guadeloupe have meters, although the driver will either activate them or not, depending on a complicated set of parameters involving the time of day, your destination, and his or her whim, even though fares are technically regulated by the French government. If the taxi you're about to enter doesn't have a working meter, always agree on a price before getting in. Approximate fares are

Guadeloupe

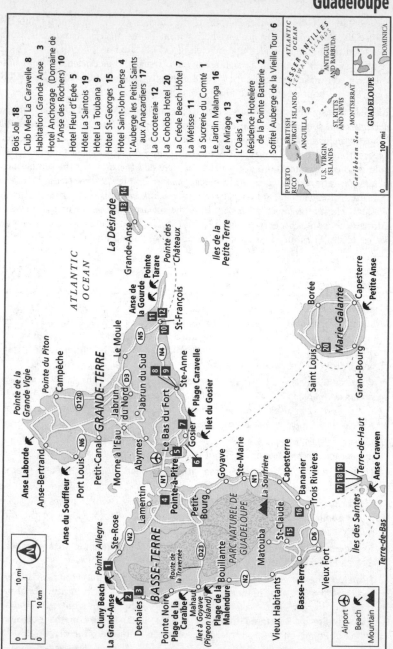

Bois Joli **18**
Club Med La Caravelle **8**
Habitation Grande Anse **3**
Hotel Anchorage (Domaine de l'Anse des Rochers) **10**
Hotel Fleur d'Épée **5**
Hôtel La Saintois **19**
Hôtel La Toubana **9**
Hôtel St-Georges **15**
Hôtel Saint-John Perse **4**
L'Auberge les Petits Saints aux Anacardiers **17**
La Cocoteraie **12**
La Cohoba Hotel **20**
La Créole Beach Hôtel **7**
La Métisse **11**
La Sucrerie du Comté **1**
Le Jardin Malanga **16**
Le Mirage **13**
L'Oasis **14**
Résidence Hotelière de la Pointe Batterie **2**
Sofitel Auberge de la Vieille Tour **6**

20€ to 25€ ($26–$33) from the airport to the hotels of Gosier; or about 11€ to 15€ ($14–$20) from the airport to anywhere within Pointe-à-Pitre. Radio taxis can be contacted throughout Guadeloupe by calling **C.D.L. Taxi** at ✆ **590/20-74-74.** It's possible, but very expensive, to sightsee by taxi. Usually, the concierge at your hotel will help you make arrangements. Fares are usually around 160€ to 170€ ($208–$221) for a 7-hour day for up to four passengers.

BY BUS   Small buses link almost every hamlet to Pointe-à-Pitre. However, you may need to know some French to use the system. In Pointe-à-Pitre, you can catch a bus from the following departure points: If you're going anywhere in Basse-Terre you'll depart from the Gare Routière de Bergevin. If the northern half of Grande-Terre is your destination, catch a bus at the Gare Routière de Mortenol. For the southern end of Grande-Terre, the buses depart from the *prolongement* (extension) of the Marché de la Darse. Infrequent and somewhat erratic service is available daily from 5:30am to 7:30pm. There is no direct bus service from the airport to Pointe-à-Pitre. To travel the entire island would cost between 4€ and 5€ ($5.20–$6.50). Many visitors find it easier, especially when they first arrive on Guadeloupe, to take a taxi.

FAST FACTS: Guadeloupe

Banks   Banks on Guadeloupe are usually open Monday to Friday 9am to 3pm, but in recent years, some, but not all, as a means of coordinating their hours with those of their clients, have begun operating Monday to Friday 8am to noon, and 2 to 3:30pm. There are about a dozen banks in Pointe-à-Pitre, most with ATMs (they're called *distributeurs des billets*).

Currency   Because the territory of Guadeloupe falls under the same monetary system as mainland France, the island uses the **euro (€)** as its mode of exchange. The current rate of exchange is 1€ equals US$1.30. *Prices in this chapter are quoted in U.S. dollars and euros.*

Customs   Items for personal use, such as tobacco, cameras, and film, are admitted without formalities or tax if not in excessive quantity.

Documents   U.S., British, or Canadian residents need a passport, plus a return or ongoing plane ticket.

Electricity   The local electricity is 220-volt AC (50 cycles), which means that U.S.-made appliances will need a transformer and an adapter. Some of the big resorts may lend these to guests, but don't count on it.

Emergencies   Call the **police** at ✆ **17.** To report a **fire** or summon an **ambulance,** dial ✆ **18.** For **medical emergencies** dial ✆ **15.**

Hospitals   There are five modern hospitals on Guadeloupe, plus about two dozen clinics. Hotels and the Guadeloupe tourist office can assist in locating English-speaking doctors. There's a 24-hour emergency room at the **Centre Hôpitalier Universitaire de Pointe-à-Pitre,** Abymes (✆ **590/89-10-10**), on the northern fringe of Pointe-à-Pitre. For emergency services at this hospital, dial ✆ **15.**

Language   The official language is French; Creole is the unofficial second language. English is spoken only in the major tourist centers, rarely in the countryside.

Liquor Laws Liquor is sold in grocery and liquor stores on any day of the week. It's legal to have an open container, though the authorities are very strict about littering, disorderly behavior, and drunk driving.

Pharmacies The pharmacies carry French medicines, and most over-the-counter U.S. drugs have French equivalents. Prescribed medicines can be purchased if you have the prescription with you. At least one drugstore is always open; the tourist office can tell you what pharmacies are open at what time.

Police In an emergency, call ℂ **17**. Otherwise, call ℂ **590/89-77-17**.

Safety Guadeloupe is relatively free of serious crime. But don't go wandering alone at night on the streets of Pointe-à-Pitre; by nightfall they are relatively deserted and might be dangerous. Purse snatching by fast-riding motorcyclists has been reported, so exercise caution.

Taxes A departure tax, required on scheduled flights, is included in the air-fares. Hotel taxes are included in all room rates.

Telephone To call Guadeloupe from the United States, dial **011** (the interna-tional access code), then **590** (the country code for Guadeloupe), then **590** again, and the rest of the local number, which will be six digits. If you want to call another island of the French Antilles, be aware that St. Barts, French St. Martin, and offshore dependencies of Guadeloupe such as Ile des Saints or La Désirade are all directly linked to the phone network of Guadeloupe. Conse-quently, no telephone prefix is required, and you can dial any of those islands simply by dialing the six-digit local phone number. But if you're on Guadeloupe and want to dial someone in Martinique, you'll have to punch in the prefix for Martinique **(0596)**, followed by the six-digit local number.

Time Guadeloupe is on Atlantic Standard Time year-round, 1 hour ahead of Eastern Standard Time (when it's 6am in New York, it's 7am on Guadeloupe). When daylight saving time is in effect in the U.S., clocks in New York and Guadeloupe show the same time.

Tipping Hotels usually add a 10% to 15% service charge. Restaurants always add a 15% service charge, and no additional tip is needed. Most taxi drivers who own their own cars do not expect a tip; if they've been especially helpful with your luggage, you might give them an additional 10%.

Water While on Guadeloupe, stick to bottled water only.

Weather The average temperature in Guadeloupe is 82°F (28°C) in summer, dropping to an average of 76°F (24°C) in winter. The rainiest months are between June and October.

2 Pointe-à-Pitre

The port and chief city of Guadeloupe, Pointe-à-Pitre, lies on Grande-Terre. Unfor-tunately, it doesn't have the old-world charm of Fort-de-France on Martinique, and what beauty it does possess is often hidden behind closed doors.

Having been burned and rebuilt so many times, the port now lacks character. Mod-ern apartments and condominiums form a high-rise backdrop over jerry-built shacks and industrial suburbs. The rather narrow streets are jammed during the day with a colorful crowd that creates a permanent traffic jam. However, at sunset the town becomes quiet again and almost deserted. The only charm left is around the waterfront, where you half expect to see Bogie sipping rum at a cafe table.

Most visitors just drop in to Pointe-à-Pitre for **shopping.** It's best to visit the town in the morning (you can easily cover it in half a day), taking in the waterfront and outdoor market (the latter is livelier in the early hours).

The town center is **place de la Victoire,** a park shaded by palm trees and poincianas. Here you'll see some old sandbox trees said to have been planted by Victor Hugues, the mulatto who organized a revolutionary army of both whites and blacks to establish a dictatorship. In this square he kept a guillotine busy, and the death-dealing instrument stood here until modern times.

With the completion of the **Centre Saint-John-Perse,** the waterfront of Pointe-à-Pitre has been transformed from a bastion of old warehouses and cruise-terminal buildings into an architectural complex comprising a hotel, three restaurants, 80 shops and boutiques, a bank, and the expanded headquarters of Guadeloupe's Port Authority. Named for Saint-John Perse, the 20th-century poet and Nobel Laureate who was born just a few blocks away, the center is designed in contemporary French Caribbean style, which blends with the traditional architecture of Pointe-à-Pitre. On the island, go to the local tourist office, the **Comité du Tourisme des Iles de la Guadeloupe,** Square de la Banque 5 (© **590/82-09-30;** www.lesilesdeguadeloupe.com), for maps, information, and advice.

ACCOMMODATIONS

Hôtel Saint-John Perse   Stay here only if you have business in town or need to be here for an early morning flight (it's 15 min. from the airport). This hotel rises four stories above the harbor front, near the quays. The small rooms are clean, simple, and furnished with locally crafted mahogany pieces. Very few have views of the sea. Bathrooms are small with no frills; about half have tub/shower combos. Once you check in, the laissez-faire staff will probably leave you alone until the end of your stay.

There's a simple coffee shop/cafe on street level. To reach a beach, you'll have to travel 3km (2 miles) to the east to Le Bas du Fort and the Gosier area (see below).

Centre Saint-John-Perse, quai de Croisières (at the harbor front), 97110 Pointe-à-Pitre, Guadeloupe, F.W.I. © **590/82-51-57.** Fax 590/82-52-61. www.saint-john-perse.com. 44 units. Winter 100€ ($130) double; off-season 90€ ($117) double. Rates include continental breakfast. AE, MC, V. **Amenities:** Coffee shop; laundry service; dry cleaning. *In room:* A/C, TV, safe.

DINING

Côté Jardin ᡧ FRENCH   This is one of the finest, most upscale independent restaurants in Guadeloupe, with an allegiance to the tenets of French cooking that you might expect on the French mainland. Because of its fine food and its sense of Gallic style, no one really cares that there isn't a water view. Surrounded by potted flowers and shrubs, with a view over palm trees and reproductions of paintings by Miró and Matisse, you'll dine in a white-and-green room with a hint of Provence. Menu items focus on fresh shellfish, much of which comes from fish tanks near the restaurant's entrance. Scallops with a Noilly Prat vermouth sauce, sweetbreads and morels in puff pastry, and several different preparations of foie gras (including a succulent version that's fried and served with a reduction of sweet Banyuls wine) make a flavorful beginning. This restaurant is particularly proud of specific European menu items which include *boeuf charolais* imported from France, usually served with pepper sauce.

La Marina, Pointe-à-Pitre. ℂ **590/90-91-28.** Reservations recommended. Main courses 26€–36€ ($34–$47); prix-fixe menus 36€–42€ ($47–$55). AE, MC, V. Mon–Fri noon–2:30pm; Mon–Sat 7:30–10pm.

Restaurant Sucré-Salé TRADITIONAL FRENCH   In the heart of Pointe-à-Pitre, adjacent to an Air France office and near several banks, this restaurant is always filled at lunchtime with dealmakers and office workers. The decorative theme revolves around jazz, with portraits of Louis Armstrong, Billie Holliday, and Miles Davis. A covered terrace overlooking the busy boulevard serves as an animated singles bar on Friday and Saturday nights. The charming Marius Pheron, the Guadeloupe-born owner who did an 18-year stint in Paris, offers filets of snapper served with pommes soufflés and black pepper or marmalade of onions, meal-size salads, entrecôte steaks, and an impressive medley of grilled fish. The restaurant hosts a jazz concert once a month; posters announcing the event appear all over town.

Blvd. Légitimus, Pointe-à-Pitre. ℂ **590/21-22-55.** Reservations recommended. Main courses 15€–28€ ($20–$36). MC, V. Mon–Fri noon–3pm; Tues–Sat 7–9:30pm.

SHOPPING

We suggest that you skip a shopping tour of Pointe-à-Pitre if you're going to Fort-de-France on Martinique, as you'll find far more merchandise there, and perhaps friendlier service. If you're not, however, we recommend the following shops, some of which line rue Frébault.

Your best buys will be anything French—perfumes from Chanel, silk scarves from Hermès, cosmetics from Dior, crystal from Lalique and Baccarat. Though they're still expensive, we've found some of these items discounted (but not often) as much as 30% below U.S. or Canadian prices. Most shops will accept U.S. dollars, but they'll give these discounts only for purchases made by traveler's check. Purchases are duty-free if brought directly from store to plane. In addition to the places below, there are also two duty-free shops at **Raizet Airport** (ℂ **590/21-14-66**) selling liquor, rums, perfumes, crystal, and cigarettes.

Most shops open at 8:30am, close at 1pm, and then reopen between 3 and 5:30pm. They're closed on Saturday afternoons, Sundays, and holidays. When the cruise ships are in port, many shopkeepers stay open longer and on weekends, and sometimes remain open throughout the midday closing.

One of the best places to buy French perfumes, at prices often lower than those charged in Paris, is **Phoenicia,** 8 rue Frébault (ℂ **590/83-50-36**), which has a good selection of imported cosmetics as well. Another leading perfume shop is **Au Bonheur des Dames,** 49 rue Frébault (ℂ **590/82-00-30**), also known for its skin-care products.

If you're adventurous, you may want to seek out some native goods in little shops along the back streets of Pointe-à-Pitre. Look for the straw hats, or *salacos,* made in Les Saintes islands, usually created from split bamboo. Native **doudou dolls** are also popular gift items.

Moments **The Essence of Guadeloupe**

At some point as you stroll through the market, order a glass of rum from one of the local vendors, and ask for *rhum agricole,* a pure form of the drink that's fermented from sugar-cane juice. Savvy locals claim that the rum (whose brand name is Rhum Damoiseau) is the only kind you can drink without a hangover the next morning.

Open-air stalls surround the **Marché Couvert (covered market)** at the corner of rue Frébault and rue Peynier. Here you can discover the many fruits, spices, and vegetables that are fun to look at as well as to taste. In madras turbans, local Creole women make deals over their strings of fire-red pimientos. The bright fabrics they wear compete with the rich colors of oranges, papayas, bananas, mangos, and pineapples. Best times to visit are Monday to Saturday 8am to 2pm.

3 Le Bas du Fort

Just 3km (2 miles) east of Pointe-à-Pitre is the tourist area of Le Bas du Fort, near Gosier. This is the best place to stay if you'd like to be near (but not in) the capital and if you'd like a location near the international airport. Although it has some good sandy beaches, there are far better ones farther out from the center. One drawback is that the area is rather built up and you may not find the tranquility here you'll enjoy in other parts of Guadeloupe.

Aquarium de la Guadeloupe, place Créole, Marina Gosier (© 590/90-92-38), is one of the largest and most modern aquariums in the Caribbean. Just off the highway near Le Bas du Fort Marina, the aquarium is home to tropical fish, coral, underwater plants, huge sharks, and other sea creatures. Hours are daily from 9am to 7pm. Admission is 8.50€ ($11) for adults, 5€ ($6.50) for children 5 to 12, and free for kids under 5.

ACCOMMODATIONS

Fleur d'Été *Kids* Few other hotels on Guadeloupe have been reconfigured and regrouped as often and as radically as this one. Originally built as a member of the chain-hotel Novotel in the mid-1970s, it was combined with neighboring structures into a larger resort, partly the result of devastating hurricanes, all traces of which have been eradicated. That mega-resort was carved up early in the millennium into condo units (now independent and positioned across the boulevard). Fleur d'Eté isn't the most stylish hotel on Guadeloupe, but its owners have spruced up the design (basically a chain-motel boxy look) with bright colors, especially tones of blue. Most units have tailed floors, an efficiently designed floor plan, and in most cases, either a private terrace or a veranda. It sits directly beside a coastline dotted with a pair of crescent-shaped bays and a short, white-sand beach. The staff is laid-back and cooperative, and the clientele includes a relatively young-ish group of mainland French who turn up here in bikini-clad droves, and who seem to appreciate the hotel's holiday village format.

Le Bas du Fort, 97100 Gosier. © 590/90-40-00. Fax 590/90-99-07. www.blue-season-hotels.com. 190 units. Winter 224€–240€ ($291–$312) double; off season 150€–180€ ($195–$234) double. Rates include breakfast. AE, DC, MC, V. **Amenities:** 2 restaurants; 1 bar; outdoor pool; tennis court; fitness center; free use of snorkeling equipment; children's programs; salon; massage; laundry service/dry cleaning; rooms for those w/limited mobility. *In room:* A/C, TV, hair dryer, safe.

DINING

Rosini *Kids* NORTHERN ITALIAN/VENETIAN This is the best Italian restaurant in the French West Indies, thanks to the sophisticated father-in-law/son-in-law team of Venice-born Luciano Rosini and Christophe Giraud, from Provence. It's contained within two air-conditioned dining rooms on the ground floor of an upscale condo complex across from the Fleur d'Eté in Le Bas du Fort. Recorded opera music sets the mood for succulent versions of tournedos layered with foie gras, *osso buco* (veal shanks), and freshwater prawns served *diavolo* style in a spicy tomato, garlic, and parsley sauce with freshly made fettuccine. Ravioli comes stuffed either with veal and herbs or with lobster. At least 10 types of pizza are available for kids. English is readily understood here.

La Porte des Caraïbes, Le Bas du Fort Gosier. © 590/90-87-81. Reservations recommended. Main courses 15€–38€ ($20–$49). AE, MC, V. Daily noon–2:30pm and 7–11pm.

4 Gosier

Gosier is where some of the best beachfront in Guadeloupe begins, and it has become one of the island's major resort centers, since it has nearly 8km (5 miles) of sandy but narrow beach, stretching east from Pointe-à-Pitre. All the hotels below are close to the sands. We like the funky charm of the town, which evokes a little resort along the French Riviera. Unlike many parts of the Caribbean, this area attracts mainly French visitors, so you'll feel as though you're on a Mediterranean holiday. Gosier also has some of the island's best dining and nightlife, plus a casino.

You can take a 15-minute climb to the 18th-century ruins of **Fort Fleur-d'Epée.** Its dungeons and battlements are testaments to the ferocious fighting between the French and British armies in 1794. The ruins command the crown of a hill, which affords good views over the bay of Pointe-à-Pitre in a gardenlike setting. If the visibility is good, you can see the neighboring offshore islands of Marie-Galante and Iles des Saintes.

ACCOMMODATIONS

La Créole Beach Hôtel
This is one of the largest resorts on Guadeloupe, but because it's divided into four distinct sections, you'll get a sense of isolation and privacy. It's alongside two sandy beaches within a lush setting of lawns, trees, hibiscus, and bougainvillea, and it has a strong French Creole flavor.

The most upscale section is Les Palmes, which was completed in 2002 and has the best furnishings and the most spacious rooms. Second is Le Creole, a three-story building with verandas influenced by French colonial architecture. Slightly less desirable is Le Mahogany, a comfortable compound with oceanfront rooms (most without kitchens). The most basic, Le Yucca, houses the family units with kitchens. Most rooms are spacious and contain two queen-size beds. All units contain a private bathroom, most with a shower (one-fourth of them feature a tub/shower combination).

La Route des Epices serves excellent local specials and an international cuisine. Le Zawag lies just on the rocks by the sea, offering fresh fish and seafood.

Pointe de la Verdure, B.P. 61, 97190 Gosier, Guadeloupe, F.W.I. © 590/90-46-46. Fax 590/90-46-66. www.deshotels etdesiles.com. 345 units. Winter 131€–226€ ($170–$294) double, 264€ ($343) junior suite; off season 100€–162€ ($130–$211) double, 212€ ($276) junior suite. Children under 12 stay free in parent's room. Rates include continental breakfast. AE, DC, MC, V. **Amenities:** 2 restaurants; bar; snack bar; outdoor pool; deep-sea fishing; sailboat rentals; scuba diving; water-skiing; windsurfing; room service; babysitting; laundry service; dry cleaning; nonsmoking rooms; rooms for those w/limited mobility. *In room:* A/C, TV, kitchenette (in some), minibar, fridge, hair dryer, safe (in some).

Sofitel Auberge de la Vieille Tour
Though today it's a Sofitel, this place was once a family inn built around the shadow of an old sugar mill. Set on a 3-hectare (7½-acre) bluff, the property encompasses a small private beach.

The older guest rooms are relatively short on charm. The better maintained units are usually within La Résidence, a series of town house–style accommodations set near the pool. Their desirability is rivaled only by units referred to as "luxury-class," set close to the water near the beach. Rooms have comfortable furnishings and compact bathrooms with shower stalls or tub/shower combinations.

The restaurants La Vieille Tour and Le Zagaya serve excellent French and Creole food, respectively, in relatively elegant, semiformal settings. L'Ajoupa is a grill-style indoor-outdoor affair.

Montauban, 97190 Gosier, Guadeloupe, F.W.I. © 800/221-4542 in the U.S., or 590/84-23-23. Fax 590/84-33-43. www.sofitel.com. 180 units. Winter 240€–410€ ($312–$533) double; off season 218€–290€ ($283–$377) double; year-round 650€ ($845) suite. Rates include continental breakfast. AE, MC, V. **Amenities:** 3 restaurants; 2 bars; outdoor pool; 2 tennis courts; scuba diving; snorkeling; room service (6am–10pm); laundry service; dry cleaning; nonsmoking rooms. In room: A/C, TV, minibar, beverage maker, hair dryer, safe.

DINING

Le Bananier CREOLE   Locals flock to this restaurant where some of the most imaginative dishes in the Creole repertoire are handled with finesse and charm. Within an air-conditioned, 60-year-old clapboard-sided cottage, you'll enjoy old-fashioned staples such as stuffed crab backs and *accras* (beignets) of codfish. Much more appealing, however, are dishes like filet mignon served with black pepper and papaya sauce; a *clafoutis* (gratinéed medley) of shellfish; and a *tourtière d'oeufs aux crabes* (an omelet with breaded and baked crabmeat, fresh tomatoes, and reduction of callaloo leaves). The menu's most appealing dessert is banana flambéed in Schrubb, an obscure island liqueur made from fermented orange peels and prized by the owners' grandparents.

Rue Principale de Gosier, Montauban. © 590/84-34-85. Reservations recommended. Main courses 12€–28€ ($16–$36). AE, DC, MC, V. Tues–Sun noon–2pm and 7–10pm.

5 Ste-Anne

About 14km (8¾ miles) east of Gosier, little Ste-Anne is a sugar town and a resort with many fine beaches and lodgings. In many ways, it's the most charming village of Guadeloupe, with its pastel-colored town hall, its church, and its principal square, **Place de la Victoire,** which features a statue of French abolitionist Victor Schoelcher.

ACCOMMODATIONS & DINING

Club Med La Caravelle 🏖 Kids   This all-inclusive chain resort, covering 18 hectares (44 acres) along a peninsula dotted with palm trees, opens onto one of the finest beaches in the French West Indies. The renovated guest rooms tend to be small, but have good beds. (All but 10 units have twin beds; the others have queen-size beds.) Tiled and shower-only bathrooms are compact and short on amenities. The building known as Marie-Galante contains the resort's largest and most comfortable rooms (each with a terrace or veranda). This resort was closed for a full nine months in 2006 for a radical renovation of the premises, wherein walls were demolished that had previously separated some of the smaller, boxier rooms, leading to the creation of fewer, but larger, units, and an increase in the percentage of suites.

Children are welcome here, and their numbers are particular visible during periods of school holidays on the French mainland. Consequently, there's been a recent upgrade in the children's facilities here, with a "Mini-Club" with child-minding and day-camp facilities, which keep young children and teenagers amused and diverted when their parents are either at rest or at play. Despite that, however, this resort tends to attract lots of adult couples and singles. The resort has an annex containing only single rooms, a boon for solo travelers. The meals here are nothing if not generous. The breakfast and lunch buffet tables groan with French, Continental, and Creole food. Dinner is served in the main dining room or in the candlelit, more romantic

Moments Begin the Beguine

The folkloric dance troupe **Les Ballets Guadeloupéans** makes frequent appearances at the big hotels, whirling and moving to the rhythms of island music in colorful costumes and well-choreographed routines. Some resorts, including the Club Med La Caravelle, use their visit to set the theme for the evening, serving up a banquet of traditional island dishes to accompany the dance, music, and costumes.

Ask at your hotel where the Ballets Guadeloupéans will be appearing during your stay. Schedules vary widely according to the season and the touring agenda of the Ballets (part of their year is spent touring, usually in Europe or aboard some of the larger cruise ships), but you can usually catch them as they rotate through the Kalenda Resort, the Club Med La Caravelle, and—depending on a wide set of circumstances—the Creole Beach and/or the Novotel Coralia. On the night of any of these performances, you can order a drink at the bar and catch the show, or join in the hotel buffet for a flat price. Buffets usually start around 7:30pm, with the show beginning at 9:30pm.

---

annex restaurant beside the sea. There's live entertainment several nights a week, sometimes a Brazil-inspired samba band, and once a week, usually on Monday, the Guadeloupe folklore ballet, Les Ballets Guadeloupéans.

97180 Ste-Anne, Guadeloupe, F.W.I. © **800/CLUB-MED** in the U.S., or 590/85-49-50. Fax 590/85-49-70. www.club med.com. 297 units. Winter 150€–300€ ($195–$390) double, 300€–400€ ($390–$520) suite; off season 120€–250€ ($156–$325) weekly, 240€–400€ ($312–$520) suite. Rates are per person based on double occupancy. Rates are all-inclusive. Children age 4–12 are charged 80% of the adult rate. Single supplement 10%–50% above the per-person double rate. AE, MC, V. **Amenities:** 2 restaurants; 2 bars; outdoor pool; 4 tennis courts; gym; aerobics; archery; basketball; fitness center; volleyball; kayaks; snorkeling; scuba diving; windsurfing; children's program; laundry service; dry cleaning; rooms for those w/limited mobility; night club. *In room:* A/C, TV, beverage maker, hair dryer, iron, safe.

Hôtel La Toubana *G*   Built on 2 hectares (5 acres) of sloping land close to the beach (a 5-min. walk on a path carved into the cliff side), La Toubana is centered around a low-lying stone building on a rocky cliff overlooking the bay and Ste-Anne Beach. Many guests come here just for the panoramic view, which on a clear day encompasses Marie-Galante, Dominica, La Désirade, and the Iles des Saintes, but you'll quickly learn that there's far more to this place than just a panorama. The redroofed bungalows lie scattered among the tropical shrubs along the adjacent hillsides (*toubana* means "small house" in Arawak); there are 10 garden units and 12 more upscale ocean-view units. Each has a kitchenette, comfortable French furnishings, a terrace, a rather compact tub/shower combination bathroom, and either two twin beds or one king-size bed. Cots for kids are available on request.

Le Baobab offers both indoor and alfresco dining of fine quality in a site overlooking the pool. It serves the best lobster on the island. The beachfront bar serves tropical drinks and occasionally hosts live entertainment.

Durivage (B.P. 63), 97180 Ste-Anne, Guadeloupe, F.W.I. © **800/451-3734** in the U.S., or 590/88-25-78. Fax 590/88-38-90. 32 units. Winter 212€–252€ ($276–$328) double; off season 144€–170€ ($187–$221) double. Rates include continental breakfast. AE, MC, V. **Amenities:** Restaurant; bar; outdoor pool; tennis court; deep-sea fishing; snorkeling; scooters; babysitting. *In room:* A/C, kitchenette, hair dryer.

6 St-François ⟨⋆

Continuing east from Ste-Anne, you'll notice many old round towers named for Father Labat, the Dominican founder of the sugar-cane industry. These towers were once used as mills to grind the cane. St-François, 40km (25 miles) east of Pointe-à-Pitre, used to be a sleepy fishing village. Then Air France discovered it and opened a Meridien hotel with a casino. That was followed by the promotional activities of J. F. Rozan, a native who invested heavily to make St-François a jet-set resort. Now the once sleepy village has first-class accommodations, as well as an airport available to private jets, a golf course (it's the golfing center of the island), and a marina, where there's a casino (see "Guadeloupe After Dark," near the end of this chapter). It also has some good beaches and is known for its Creole restaurants.

ACCOMMODATIONS

Hotel Anchorage (Domaine de l'Anse des Rochers)   The largest hotel on Guadeloupe sprawls across 8 hectares (20 acres) of sloping land in St-François and has an attractive sandy beach. Accommodations are housed in either a half-dozen multi-leveled, hotel-style buildings, each of which contains 39 units, or 32 bungalows (4 units per bungalow). The decor is airy, summery, and uncluttered. Bedrooms are fairly routine, usually small, each with a tiled, shower-only bathroom. Despite the size of the resort, guests still feel a sense of isolation and intimacy, thanks to the way the place is configured into smaller blocks. Expect lots of young families with children, honeymooners, and European package-tour groups.

There are four dining choices here, ranging from formal Le Sucrier, serving European cuisine to a deli-style outlet for takeout. You can catch live entertainment at the resort's two bars.

Domaine de l'Anse des Rochers, 97118 St-François, Guadeloupe, F.W.I. ⟨ **590/93-90-31.** Fax 590/88-43-21. www.hotelsanchorage.fr. 356 units. Winter 170€–178€ ($221–$231) double; off season 66€–83€ ($86–$107) double. AE, MC, V. **Amenities:** 4 restaurants; 2 bars; outdoor pool; beach volleyball; jet skis; scuba diving; snorkeling; archery; car rental; laundry service; dry cleaning; rooms for those w/limited mobility. *In room:* A/C, TV (in some), dataport, kitchenette, hair dryer (in some), safe.

La Cocoteraie ⟨⋆⟨⋆   This is a plush, suites-only resort, the island's finest choice for a luxury holiday. It opens onto a lagoon with two private but small white-sand beaches. The hotel hides behind a colonial plantation-style facade, flanked by a series of buildings, also in the colonial style. Twenty of the units are more desirable because they open right onto the beach. Across from the hotel lies the Robert Trent Jones, Sr., golf course. Each unit comes with a spacious patio or a balcony overlooking the water or else one of the largest hotel pools on Guadeloupe. Some of the accommodations are equipped with a duo of tub-only baths; others have tub/shower combos.

Meals are served in a well-designed, open-sided pavilion, La Varangue (see "Dining" below). Lunch menus are relatively simple. Evenings are more romantic, with flickering candles and a wider choice of (mostly French) food.

Ave. De l'Europe, 97118 St-François, Guadeloupe, F.W.I. ⟨ **800/322-2223** in the U.S., or 590/88-79-81. Fax 590/88-78-33. www.la-cocoteraie.com. 50 suites. Winter 395€–540€ ($520–$710) suite; off season 251€–388€ ($330–$510) suite. AE, DC, MC, V. Closed Aug 24–Oct 21. **Amenities:** Restaurant; bar; outdoor pool; golf; 2 tennis courts; fitness center; car rental; limited room service; babysitting; laundry service; dry cleaning; rooms for those w/limited mobility. *In room:* A/C, TV, minibar, hair dryer, safe.

La Métisse ⟨⋆ *Value*   The French call this place a *hotel de charme*. Built around a pool with a raised hot tub, it is a pink stucco hotel with personalized service and tasteful, comfortable accommodations. Built on a hill, the property's grounds are cooled by trade winds. It's not on the beach, but there is an artificially illuminated swimming pool. The owners will transport you to the beach or give you a ride into town or even to the nearby golf course. Doors can be opened to connect some of the units, which is a plus for families. The gardens are attractively planted with jasmine, gardenia, palms, hibiscus, and frangipani. The bar is noted for its fresh fruit cocktails, including the cocktail Métisse (a blend of coconut, banana, maracudja, and cinnamon). Bedrooms are furnished with white cane pieces and immaculately kept. Your room opens onto a poolside terrace where a tropical breakfast is served.

66 Les Hauts de Saint François, 97118 St-François, Guadeloupe, F.W.I. ℂ 590/88-70-00. Fax 590/90-88-59. www. im-caraibes.com/metisse. 7 units. Winter 149€ ($194) double; off season 126€ ($164) double. Rates include continental breakfast. AE, MC, V. **Amenities:** Bar; outdoor pool; babysitting; laundry service; rooms for those w/limited mobility. *In room:* A/C, TV, minibar, hair dryer, safe.

DINING

La Varangue ☆ FRENCH   Named after the figureheads that used to grace the prows of pirate ships, this is the culinary showcase (and the only restaurant) within Le Meridien La Cocoteraie hotel. In many ways, it functions as the social and decorative showcase of the hotel as well, positioned as it is adjacent to a low bridge that traverses the resort's swimming pool, near the reception desk of the hotel, within full view of the beach and the hotel gardens. Menu items at lunch revolve around fresh salads, pastas, and relatively simple versions of grilled fish and meats. Dinners are more elaborate, more leisurely, and more romantic, with flickering candles and such dishes as a crabmeat tart with exotic mushrooms; cream of shellfish soup; a confit of dorado (mahimahi) with tandoori spices and coconut milk; and an elegant version of lobster salad. And for any die-hard lover of Gallic food, there's even foie gras flash-seared in butter, similar to something you'd find on the French mainland.

In Le Meridien La Cocoteraie, Ave. de l'Europe, St-François. ℂ 590/88-79-81. Reservations recommended for non-residents of the hotel. Lunch platters 17€–32€ ($22–$42); dinner main courses 19€–39€ ($25–$51). AE, DC, MC, V. Daily 12:30–2:30pm and 7:30–10pm.

7 Pointe des Châteaux

Eleven kilometers (6¾ miles) east of St-François is the rocky headland of Pointe des Châteaux, the easternmost tip of Grand-Terre, where the Atlantic meets the Caribbean. Here, where crashing waves sound around you, you'll see a cliff sculpted by the sea into dramatic castlelike formations, the erosion typical of France's Brittany coast. The view from here is panoramic. At the top is a cross erected in the 19th century.

You might want to walk to **Pointe des Colibris,** the extreme end of Guadeloupe. From here you'll have a view of the northeastern sector of the island, and to the east a look at La Désirade, an island that has the appearance of a huge vessel anchored far away. (See the section "Side Trips from Guadeloupe," later in this chapter.)

Pointe des Châteaux has miles of coved white-sand beaches. Most of these are safe for swimming, except at the point where the waves of the turbulent Atlantic encounter the tranquil Caribbean Sea, churning up the waters. Since there are no hotels here, you can come just for the day to enjoy the beaches.

DINING

Iguane Café ☆ *Finds* FRENCH/INTERNATIONAL   This bistro/cafe is one of the best dining choices on the island, just as good as the stellar Le Château de Feuilles (see

(Moments Nude Trysting

This part of Guadeloupe is studded with wind-carved coves. At **Anse Tarare,** the Caribbean Sea meets the Atlantic Ocean. From the signposted parking lot along the Route de la Pointe des Châteaux, you'll see a narrow pathway leading through scrub to the sea and Anse Tarare. If you want, you (and your loved one) can strip down here. Of course, it's wise to bring the makings of a French beachside picnic—a bottle of chilled rosé, a wheel of Brie, and a freshly baked baguette.

below). Owners Marie and Sylvan Serrouart serve their creative cuisine at a point on the road connecting St.-François with Pointe des Châteaux. The restaurant has a colorful West Indian decor, an open-air kitchen, and English-language menus. Don't come here in a rush, as food is cooked to order and the service is, well, relaxed. Mellow out at the bar, with its selection of nearly two dozen rum punches, including one flavored with cinnamon. A novelty drink comes from a large jar of rum with several hibiscus flowers floating inside. On the creative and varied menu, begin with a delectable sheep's cheese appetizer, battered in a crust with zesty Creole spices. You might also opt for the goose-liver pâté or a Napoleon of sweet breads and lobster. We always gravitate to the fresh fish of the day, perhaps snapper, aromatically cooked in a puff pastry, or John Dory with Indian spices. Also good is caramelized chicken cooked in coconut milk and steamed fish flavored with five spices, the sweetbreads, and shrimp in saffron sauce. For dessert, try the lemon-and-lime soufflé, or the coconut crisps served with chocolate sauce.

Route de la Pointe des Châteaux, St. François. (590/88-61-37. Reservations recommended. Main courses 23€– 30€ ($30–$39). AE, MC, V. Wed–Mon 7:30–10:30pm; Sun 12:30–2:30pm. Closed Sept 10–Oct 10.

A STOP IN LE MOULE

To go back to Pointe-à-Pitre from Pointe des Châteaux, you can use an alternative route, the N5 from St-François. After a 14km (8¾-mile) drive, you'll reach the village of **Le Moule,** which was founded at the end of the 17th century and known long before Pointe-à-Pitre. It used to be a major shipping port for sugar, but was devastated in the hurricane of 1928 and never regained its importance. Now it's a tiny coastal fishing village. Because it offers more than 15km (10 miles) of crescent-shaped beach, it's developing as a destination.

Specialties of this Guadeloupean village are *palourdes,* the clams that thrive in the semisalty mouths of freshwater rivers. Known for being more tender and less rubbery than saltwater clams, they often, even when fresh, have a distinct sulfur taste not unlike that of overpoached eggs. Local gastronomes prepare them with saffron and aged rum or cognac.

To return to Pointe-à-Pitre, we suggest that you use Route D3 toward Abymes. The road winds around as you plunge deeply into Grand-Terre. About halfway along the way a road is signposted to **Jabrun du Nord** and **Jabrun du Sud.** These two villages are inhabited by Caucasians with blond hair, said to be survivors of aristocrats slaughtered during the Revolution. Those who escaped found safety by hiding out in Les Grands Fonds. The most important family here is named Matignon, and they gave their name to the colony known as "les Blancs Matignon." These citizens are said to be related to the late Prince Rainier of Monaco. Pointe-à-Pitre lies only 16km (10 miles) from Les Grand Fonds.

8 The North Coast of Grande-Terre ⭑⭑

From Pointe-à-Pitre, head northeast toward Abymes, passing next through Morne à l'Eau; you'll reach the small but not insignificant settlement of **Petit Canal** after 21km (13 miles). This is Guadeloupe's sugar-cane country, and a sweet smell fills the air.

PORT LOUIS

Continuing northwest along the coast from Petit Canal, you come to Port Louis, well known for its beautiful beach, **Anse du Souffleur,** which lacks facilities. We like it best in spring, when the brilliant white sand is effectively shown off against the flaming red poinciana. During the week, the beach is an especially quiet spot. The little port town has some good restaurants.

DINING

Le Poisson d'Or ⭑ *Finds* CREOLE   You enter this white-sided Antillean house by walking down a narrow corridor and emerging into a rustic dining room lined with varnished pine. Despite the simple setting, the food is well prepared and satisfying. You might begin with rillettes of marlin or stuffed crabs, followed by a heaping platter of raw shellfish, grilled lobster, or local fish, either grilled or prepared as a savory *court bouillon*. If you're in the mood for something French inspired, consider a wine-flavored boeuf bourguignon, or an *entrecôte maître d'hotel* (grilled steak with butter and fresh herbs). Dessert might be a flambéed banana or a scoop of coconut-flavored ice cream. Don't even think of coming here at night without an advance reservation—you might find the place locked up and empty.

2 rue Sadi-Carnot, Port Louis. ⓒ **590/22-88-63.** Reservations required for dinner. Main courses 12€–25€ ($16–$33); fixed-price menus 16€–35€ ($21–$46). AE, MC, V. Daily 11am–4pm. Closed Sept. Drive northwest from Petit-Canal along the coastal road.

ANSE-BERTRAND

About 8km (5 miles) from Port Louis is Anse-Bertrand, the northernmost village of Guadeloupe. What is now a fishing village was the last refuge of the Carib tribes, and a reserve was once created here. Everything now, however, is sleepy.

DINING

Le Château de Feuilles ⭑⭑ FRENCH/CARIBBEAN   We've had some of our finest meals on Guadeloupe here. Set inland from the sea, amid 3 rolling hectares (7½ acres) of greenery and blossoming flowers, this hideaway is owned and run by a Norman-born couple, Jean-Pierre and Martine Dubost, who moved here to escape civilization. To reach their place, which is 14km (8¾ miles) from Le Moule, near the eastern tip of Grande-Terre, you drive past the ruins of La Mahaudière, an 18th-century sugar mill. A gifted chef who makes maximum use of local ingredients, Monsieur Dubost prepares pâté of warm sea urchins; sautéed conch with Creole sauce; a cassoulet of land crabs; a parcel of beef served with a sauce that's made from red wine, bone marrow, and a coulis of tomatoes; daurade with callalou leaves; a seafood sauerkraut served in a scooped-out green papaya; and a Caribbean adaptation of a classic French recipe, magret of duckling with fresh sugar cane. Two especially unusual dishes are a *pave de tazar* (a local fish), served with a garlic-flavored cream sauce, and a dish we've never seen anywhere else, green papaya stuffed with a fricassee of *lambi* (conch), scallops, and flying fish, all of it encased in puff pastry.

Campêche, Anse-Bertrand. © **590/22-30-30.** Reservations required, especially in summer when meals are prepared only in anticipation of your arrival. Main courses 20€–30€ ($26–$39). MC, V. Oct–Aug Tues–Sun 11:30am–4pm.

CONTINUING AROUND THE NORTHERN TIP

From Anse-Bertrand, you can drive along a gravel road heading for **Pointe de la Grande Vigie** ⊙, the northernmost tip of the island, which you'll reach after 6km (3¾ miles) of what we hope will be cautious driving. Park your car and walk carefully along a narrow lane that will bring you to the northernmost rock of Guadeloupe. The view of the sweeping Atlantic from the top of rocky cliffs is remarkable—you stand about 85m (280 ft.) above the sea.

Afterward, a 6km (3¾-mile) drive south on a good road will bring you to the **Porte d'Enfer,** or "Gateway to Hell," where the sea rushes violently against two narrow cliffs.

After seeing this remote part of the island, you can head back, going either to **Morne à l'Eau** or **Le Moule** before connecting to the road taking you back to Pointe-à-Pitre.

9 Around Basse-Terre ⊙⊙⊙

Leaving Pointe-à-Pitre by Route N1, you can explore the western coast and the island of Basse-Terre. Here you'll find views as panoramic as those along the corniche along the French Riviera, but without the heavy traffic and crowds. After 2km (1¼ miles) you cross the Rivière Salée at Pont de la Gabarre. This narrow strait separates the two islands that form Guadeloupe. For the next 6km (3¾ miles) the road runs straight through sugar-cane fields.

At the sign, on a main crossing, turn right on Route N2 toward **Baie Mahault.** (Don't confuse this with the town of Mahault on Basse-Terre's westernmost coast.) Head northwest to **Lamentin,** a village settled by *corsairs* at the beginning of the 18th century. Scattered about are some colonial mansions, but neither of these villages merits a stopover.

STE-ROSE

From Lamentin, you can drive for 10km (6¼ miles) to Ste-Rose, where you'll find several good **beaches.** On your left, a small road leads in a few minutes to **Sofaia,** from which you'll have a panoramic view over the coast and forest preserve. You can easily skip this, however, if you're rushed for time.

Your main reason to stop here is La Sucrerie du Comté, one of the island's most atmospheric inns, set on the ruins of a sugar factory with gardens. The nearest beach is only a 10-minute stroll away. You might also stop in Ste-Rose for lunch at one of Basse-Terre's best restaurants, Restaurant Clara (see below).

ACCOMMODATIONS

La Sucrerie du Comté ⊙   Although you'll see the ruins of a 19th-century sugar factory (including a rusting locomotive) on this hotel's 5 hectares (12 acres) of forested land overlooking the sea, most of the resort is modern. The medium-size accommodations are in 26 pale pink or green-toned bungalows. Each cozy bungalow has chunky and rustic handmade furniture and a bay window overlooking either the sea or a garden. (Each bungalow contains two units, both with ceiling fans; none has a

TV or phone.) Shower-only bathrooms are tiny but tidy. The nearest major beach is La Grand-Anse, a 10- to 15-minute drive from the hotel. There's a small and narrow beach (Plage des Amandiers) within a 5-minute walk from the hotel, although the swimming here isn't very good.

Comté de Loheac, 97115 Ste-Rose, Guadeloupe, F.W.I. ℂ 590/28-60-17. Fax 590/28-65-63. www.prime-invest.com. 52 units. Winter 75€–93€ ($98–$121) double; off season 53€–60€ ($69–$78) double. Rates include breakfast. AE, DC, MC, V. Closed Sept 1–Oct 5. **Amenities:** Restaurant; bar; outdoor pool; fishing; scuba diving; snorkeling; car rental; babysitting; laundry service; dry cleaning; rooms for those w/limited mobility. *In room:* A/C, ceiling fan, mini-bar, beverage maker, hair dryer, safe, no phone.

DINING
Restaurant Clara ⚑ CREOLE   On the waterfront near the center of town is the culinary statement of Clara Lesueur. Clara lived for 12 years in Paris as a member of an experimental jazz dance troupe, but years ago she returned to Guadeloupe, her home, to set up this breezy restaurant. Try for a table on the open patio, where palm trees complement the color scheme.

Clara artfully melds the classic French style of fine dining with authentic Creole flavors. Specialties include skate fish with rice and curry sauce, poached crayfish with Creole sauce and vegetables, brochette of swordfish and/or tuna, several different preparations of conch, *salade de coffre* (made from a local fish whose name translates as "trunkfish"), and braised chicken thighs stuffed with pulverized conch or stuffed crab with avocado. The "sauce chien" that's served with many of the dishes is a blend of hot peppers, garlic, lime juice, and "secret things." The house drink is made with six local fruits and ample quantities of rum.

Blvd. Maritime, Ste-Rose. ℂ **590/28-72-99.** Reservations recommended. Main courses 10€–30€ ($13–$39). MC, V. Mon–Tues and Thurs–Sat noon–2:30pm and 7–10pm; Sun noon–2:30pm.

DESHAIES/LA GRAND-ANSE
A few miles farther along, you reach Pointe Allegre, the northernmost point of Basse-Terre. **Cluny Beach** is where the first settler landed on Guadeloupe, and it's a great place to break up your drive with a swim, although the waters are sometimes rough and there are no beach facilities.

Three kilometers (2 miles) farther will bring you to **La Grand-Anse** ⚑, one of the best beaches on Guadeloupe. It is very large and still secluded, sheltered by many tropical trees, especially palms. The place is ideal either for a swim or a picnic, although, again, there are no facilities.

At **Deshaies,** immediately to the south, snorkeling and fishing are popular, but you must bring your own equipment. The narrow road alongside the beach winds up and down and has a corniche look to it, with the blue sea underneath, and the view of green mountains studded with colorful villages.

Fourteen kilometers (8¾ miles) from Deshaies, **Pointe Noire** comes into view; its name comes from the black volcanic rocks. Look for the odd polychrome cenotaph in town, the only reason to stop over.

ACCOMMODATIONS
Habitation Grande Anse ⚑   Lying across the coastal road from one of the island's best beaches, Grande-Anse, this somewhat battered assemblage of bungalows and studio apartments, each with natural-grained wood trim, is evocative of a Mediterranean village. All units have kitchenettes and contain rattan furniture, white walls, and a simple, summery decor that's well suited to life close to the beach. All the accommodations

have small private bathrooms with showers. Don't expect too many activities here— the focus is on sunbathing surrounded by the tropical landscaping beside the beach. The on-site restaurant is, in theory, open for breakfast and dinner, but because the hotel does not have a full-time chef and because business is often slow, it may not be running when you visit. But since most guests are devoted to preparing their own meals, no one really seems to care.

Localité Ziotte, 97126 Deshaies, Guadeloupe, F.W.I. © **590/28-45-36.** Fax 590/28-51-17. www.hotelhga.com. 50 units. Winter 102€–152€ ($133–$198) double studio with kitchen, 220€–350€ ($286–$455) two-bedroom apt w/kitchen for up to 6. Off season 102€ ($133) double studio w/kitchen, 220€ ($286) two-bedroom apt w/kitchen for up to 6. AE, DC, MC, V. **Amenities:** Bar; outdoor pool; watersports; car rental. *In room:* A/C, TV, minibar, kitchen, safe.

Résidence Hoteliére de la Pointe Batterie
Built in 1996 on steeply sloping land near the edge of both the rainforest and the sea, these all-wood villas each contain a veranda, a kitchen, ceiling fans, good beds, and summery furniture made from rattan, local hardwoods, and wicker. All units have at least a tub/shower combo; the two-bedroom villas have an additional shower unit. The nearest beach, La Grand-Anse, is a 3-minute drive, or a long uphill walk, away. In addition to the communal pool, some of the villas have their own private pools.

Le Canon de la Baie specializes in Creole food from atop a wooden deck whose pilings are sunk directly into the seabed.

97126 Pointe Batterie, Deshaies, Guadeloupe, F.W.I. © **800/322-2223** in the U.S., or 590/28-57-03. Fax 590/28-57-28. www.pointe-batterie.com. 19 villas. Winter 261€ ($339) 2-bedroom villa w/pool (for up to 6), 209€ ($272) 1-bedroom villa w/pool (for up to 4), 119€ ($155) 1-bedroom suite without pool (for up to 4); off season 146€ ($190) 2-bedroom villa w/pool (for up to 6), 125€ ($163) 1-bedroom villa w/pool (for up to 4), 63€ ($82) 1-bedroom suite without pool (for up to 4). MC, V. **Amenities:** Restaurant; bar; outdoor pool; tennis court (nearby); spa; rooms for those w/limited mobility. *In room:* A/C, ceiling fans, TV, dataport, kitchen.

DINING
La Caféière Beauséjour ⊀ (Finds) CREOLE
A meal here could be the most memorable one you have in the French West Indies. In the green Pointe-Noire Valley on the site of a coffee plantation, this restaurant is one of Guadeloupe's dining secrets. It is the domain of Bernadette Hayot-Beauzelin, who grows the produce and herbs used in many of her nouvelle Creole dishes. Ms. Hayot-Beauzelin welcomes you into her home, which was constructed in 1764, years after Louis XIV sent the first coffee plant to Guadeloupe in 1721. (Ms. Hayot-Beauzelin is called a *bèkè*—that's a white Creole whose family came here from France some 3 centuries ago to colonize the French West Indies.)

Don't expect a menu—you'll be told what the kitchen prepared that day. Starting in the early morning, Ms. Hayot-Beauzelin gathers the fresh fruits and vegetables that make her meals so special—everything from tomatoes and bananas to passion fruit and avocados. We still remember the quiche made with fresh leeks and papaya. Your main course might be a delectable smoked duck served with some Pan-Asian sauce that tastes of ginger, with side dishes of fries (cut like french fries) from the breadfruit tree and pumpkin purée. Ms. Hayot-Beauzelin's coffee is the island's best. Always call for a reservation first, and get good directions.

Acomat Pointe Noire. © **590/98-10-09.** Reservations required. Main courses 16€–28€ ($21–$36). Fixed-price menu 40€–48€ ($52–$62). MC, V. Tues–Sun noon–2:30pm. Dinner available for groups only. Closed Sept 1–Oct 15.

Les Gommiers CREOLE
Named after the large rubber trees that grow nearby, this popular restaurant serves up well-flavored dishes in a dining room lined with plants.

You can order such Creole staples as *accras de morue* (codfish beignets), *boudin Créole* (blood pudding), fricassee of freshwater crayfish, seafood paella, and a custardlike dessert known as *flan coco*. Dishes inspired by France include goat-meat stew, grilled steaks, and veal scallops. We return year after year, and have never detected any lessening of quality. One chef told us, "We are not technically perfect, but we cook from the heart."

Rue Baudot, Pointe Noire. © 590/98-01-79. Main courses 12€–16€ ($16–$21); fixed-price menu 11€–25€ ($14–$33). MC, V. Daily 11:30am–3pm; Wed–Sat 7–10pm.

PARC NATUREL DE GUADELOUPE: A TROPICAL FOREST 🌟🌟

Six kilometers (3¾ miles) from Pointe Noire, you reach **Mahault.** On your left is the **Route de la Traversée** 🌟🌟, the Transcoastal Highway. This is the best way to explore the scenic wonders of **Parc Naturel de Guadeloupe,** passing through a tropical forest as you travel between the capital, Basse-Terre, and Pointe-à-Pitre.

To preserve Parc Naturel, Guadeloupe has set aside 30,000 hectares (74,000 acres), about one-fifth of its entire terrain. Easily accessible via modern roads, this is a huge tract of mountains, tropical forests, and gorgeous scenery, and one of the largest and most spectacular parks in the Caribbean.

The park is home to a variety of tame animals, including *titi* (a raccoon, adopted as the park's official mascot) and such birds as the wood pigeon, turtledove, and thrush. Small exhibition huts, devoted to the volcano, the forest, or to coffee, sugar cane, and rum, are scattered throughout the park. Parc Naturel has no gates, no opening or closing hours, and no admission fee.

You can hike for a mere 15 minutes or stretch out your adventure for an entire day. The 290km (180 miles) of trails here take in rainforests and the wooded slopes of the 1,444m-high (4,736-ft.) Soufrière volcano, and pass by hot springs, rugged gorges, and rushing streams. (See also "Hiking" under "Sports & Other Outdoor Pursuits," later in this chapter.)

From Mahault, you drive slowly in a setting of giant ferns and luxuriant vegetation. Six kilometers (3¾ miles) after the fork, you reach **Les Deux Mamelles (The Two Breasts),** where you can park your car and go for a hike. Some of the trails are for experts only; others, such as the **Pigeon Trail,** will bring you to a summit of about 780m (2,560 ft.), where the view is impressive. Expect to spend at least 3 hours going each way. Halfway along the trail you can stop at **Forest House;** from that point, many lanes, all signposted, branch off on trails that will take anywhere from 20 minutes to 2 hours.

The most enthralling walk in the park is to the **Chute de l'Ecrevisse** 🌟, the "Crayfish Waterfall," a little pond of very cold water at the end of a .4km (¼-mile) path. This spot in the tropical forest is one of the most beautiful spots on the island. The pool found at the base of the falls is an ideal place for a cooling swim. In just 10 minutes you can reach this signposted attraction from the Corossol River Picnic Area. To the left of the Route de la Traversée, a short trail parallels the Corossol River, ending at the crayfish falls.

After the hike, the main road descends toward **Versailles,** a village about 8km (5 miles) from Pointe-à-Pitre.

BOUILLANTE

If you don't take the Route de la Traversée at this time but want to continue exploring the west coast, you can head south from Mahault until you reach the village of

Bouillante, which is exciting for only one reason: You might encounter the former French film star and part-time resident, Brigitte Bardot.

DINING

Chez Loulouse ✿ CREOLE   This good choice for lunch offers plenty of offhanded charm, and it stands on the well-known beach opposite Pigeon Island. Many guests prefer their rum punches on the lovely veranda, overlooking loaded boats preparing to depart and merchants hawking their wares. The colorful dining room has a ceiling of palm fronds, wraparound Creole murals, and reggae music emanating from the bar. The charming Mme. Loulouse Paisley-Carbon holds court here, assisted by her nieces, nephews, and children. She offers house-style Caribbean lobster, spicy versions of conch, octopus, *accras de morue* (codfish beignets), gratin of *christophene* (Caribbean squash), and savory *colombos* (curries) of chicken or pork.

Malendure Plage. ☎ 590/98-70-34. Reservations required for dinner. Main courses 12€–28€ ($16–$36); fixed-price menu 18€–40€ ($23–$52). AE, MC, V. Daily noon–3:30pm and 7–10pm.

Le Rocher de Malendure FRENCH/CREOLE   On a rocky peninsula 9m (30 ft.) above the rich offshore reefs near Pigeon Island, this restaurant offers gorgeous views. Each table is sheltered from direct sunlight (and rain) by a shed-style roof, which also affords a greater sense of privacy. Much of the cuisine served here is seafood caught in offshore waters: grilled red snapper, fondues of fish, marinated marlin steaks, and different preparations of crayfish and conch. There's a special emphasis here on marlin, with several creative adaptations that feature it as the main ingredient. Examples include rillettes of marlin, marlin sushi, brochettes of marlin, and fried scallops of marlin. There's also a well-prepared version of dorado (mahimahi) with vanilla sauce, and a mousse of wahoo that's usually an excellent starter. Meat dishes include veal in raspberry vinaigrette and filet of beef with any of three different sauces.

The restaurant also operates a small hotel on-site, **Le Jardin Tropical** (☎ **590/98-77-23**), renting 10 bungalows, which cost 64€ ($83) per night, single or double occupancy. Each small unit has a sea view, air-conditioning, a ceiling fan, a tiny bathroom with shower, and a simple kitchenette, where many visitors cook most of their meals. Amenities include a pool, laundry service, and a bar.

Malendure Pigeon, 97125 Bouillante. ☎ **590/98-70-84.** Fax 590/98-89-92. Reservations recommended. Main courses 14€–39€ ($18–$51). AE, V. Thurs–Tues noon–4pm and 7–10:30pm. Closed Sept.

BASSE-TERRE ✿

The winding coastal road brings you to **Vieux Habitants (Old Settlers),** one of the oldest villages on the island, founded in 1636. The name comes from the people who settled it: After serving in the employment of the West Indies Company, they retired here, but they preferred to call themselves inhabitants, so as not to be confused with slaves.

Another 15km (10 miles) of winding roads bring you to **Basse-Terre,** the capital of Guadeloupe. This sleepy town of some 15,000 inhabitants lies between the water and La Soufrière, the volcano. Founded in the 1640s, it's the oldest town on the island and still has a lot of charm. Tamarind and palm trees shade its market squares. Although there are many modern buildings, some grand old colonial structures are still standing.

The town suffered heavy damages at the hands of British troops in 1691 and again in 1702. It was also the center of fierce fighting during the French Revolution, when the political changes that swept across Europe caused explosive tensions on Guadeloupe.

As it did in France, the guillotine claimed many lives on the island during the infamous Reign of Terror.

In spite of the town's history, there isn't much to see in Basse-Terre except for a 17th-century **cathedral** and **Fort St-Charles,** which has guarded the city (not always well) since it was established. Much modernized and reconstructed over the years, the cathedral is only of passing interest. On the narrow streets, you can still see old clapboard buildings, upper floors of shingle-wood tiles, and wrought-iron balconies. For the most interesting views, seek out the **Place du Champ d'Arbaud** and the **Jardin Pichon.** At the harbor on the southern tier of town, you can see **Fort Delgrès,** which once protected the island from the English. There are acres of ramparts to be walked with panoramic vistas in all directions.

Originally selected as Guadeloupe's capital because of its prevailing breezes and location above the steaming lowlands of Pointe-à-Pitre, Basse-Terre is today a city that's curiously removed from the other parts of the French Antilles that it governs, and, when the business of the day is concluded, it's an oddly calm and quiet town. The neighboring municipality of **St-Claude,** in the cool heights above the capital, was always where the island's oldest families proudly maintained their ancestral homes and where they continue to live today. These families, direct descendants of the white, slave-owning former plantation owners who originally hailed from such major French Atlantic ports as Bordeaux and Nantes, tend to live quietly, discreetly, and separately from both the island's blacks and the French *métropolitains* whose tourist ventures have helped change the face of Guadeloupe.

ACCOMMODATIONS & DINING

Hôtel St-Georges   This tastefully modern inn, built in the late 1990s, is set on a hill with sweeping views over the town, the gardens, and from the upper floors, the sea. A series of three-story buildings centers on a large swimming pool. The medium-size bedrooms are outfitted, Creole style, with dark-grained and rattan furniture, tiled floors, and small bathrooms trimmed with touches of marble. Most accommodations come with a tub/shower combo, the rest with showers. Overall, this place has the feel of a business hotel. Le Lamasure specializes in French, Continental, and Creole cuisine, serving dinner only.

Rue Gratien, Parize, 97120 St-Claude, Guadeloupe, F.W.I. ✆ **590/80-10-10.** Fax 590/80-30-50. www.hotelstgeorges. com. 40 units. Year-round 110€ ($143) double; 135€ ($176) suite. Extra person 10€ ($13). AE, DC, MC, V. **Amenities:** Restaurant; snack bar; outdoor pool; fitness center; squash court; laundry service; dry cleaning; rooms for those w/limited mobility. *In room:* A/C, TV, minibar.

Le Jardin Malanga ℛ *Finds*   Clandestine lovers, honeymooners, and those passionate about nature view this as their secret hideaway in Guadeloupe. In a secluded location in the midst of a former banana plantation, it overlooks the Les Saintes archipelago. The nearest beach, La Plage de Trois Rivières, lies a 15-minute drive away. Wander in a secret garden of banana trees, birds of paradise flowers, rare orchids, hibiscus (the favorite food of iguanas), and flowering tropical foliage. Those who appreciate a place that looks like an outpost of French Guinea will gravitate to the main house of the inn, which was constructed in 1927 and contains a smattering of family antiques. Day trips can be made to Iles de Saintes, or to the nearby national park of Guadeloupe. You can also stay on-site, lounging at the swimming pool built into a cliff. Each of the bedrooms is comfortably and tastefully furnished, with bathrooms tiled in white. Some bathtubs open onto scenic views. The French Creole meals are often made with produce from the hotel's own gardens and are worth a detour.

Route de Hermitage, Trois Rivières 97114, Guadeloupe, F.W.I. (𝒞 **590/92-67-57.** Fax 590/92-67-58. 9 units. Year-round 245€ ($319) double in cottage; 336€ ($437) family unit in colonial house; 259€ ($337) triple. Rates include continental breakfast. AE, MC, V. **Amenities:** Restaurant; bar; outdoor pool; laundry service; nonsmoking rooms. *In room:* A/C, hair dryer, no phone.

AROUND LA SOUFRIERE 𝕣𝕣

The big attraction of Basse-Terre is the famous sulfur-puffing **La Soufrière** volcano, which is currently dormant. Rising to a height of some 1,444m (4,736 ft.), it's flanked by banana plantations and lush foliage.

After leaving the capital at Basse-Terre, you can drive to **St-Claude,** a suburb 6km (3¾ miles) up the mountainside at a height of 570m (1,870 ft.). It has a reputation for a perfect climate and various privately owned tropical gardens.

From St-Claude, you can begin the climb up the narrow, winding road the Guadeloupeans say leads to hell—that is, **La Soufrière.** The road ends at a parking area at La Savane à Mulets, at an altitude of 990m (3,247 ft.). At this point you have to leave your car and climb to the mouth of the volcano. Currently, the belching beast is quiet and it's presumed safe to climb to the summit at 1,444m (4,736 ft.), the tallest elevation in the Lesser Antilles. (Allow about 2 hr. for this climb.) In 1975, the appearance of ashes, mud, billowing smoke, and earthquakelike tremors proved that the old beast was still alive. In the resettlement process that followed the eruption, 75,000 inhabitants were relocated to safer terrain in Grande-Terre. No deaths were reported, but the inhabitants of Basse-Terre still keep a wary eye on this smoking giant.

Even in the parking lot, you can feel the heat of the volcano merely by touching the ground. Steam emerges from fumaroles and sulfurous fumes from the volcano's "burps." Of course, fumes come from its pit and mud cauldrons as well. Esoteric and technical information is available only with advance reservations, Fridays between 2 and 5pm, at a government-funded laboratory, **Observatoire Volcanologique le Houëlmont,** 97113 Gourbeyre (𝒞 **590/99-11-33**). Conceived as an observation post for seismic and volcanic activities, and staffed with geologists and volcanologists from the French mainland, it can be toured without charge by anyone who's interested in the technical aspects of this science. A visit here is best for children ages 10 and up.

DINING

Chez Paul de Matouba CREOLE/INTERNATIONAL   You'll find good food in this family-run restaurant, which sits beside the banks of the small Rivière Rouge (Red River). The dining room on the second floor is enclosed by windows, which allow you to take in the surrounding dark-green foliage of the mountains. The cooking is Creole, and the specialty is crayfish dishes, though well-prepared East Indian meals are also available. By all means, drink the mineral or spring water of Matouba. Hearty meals include perfectly executed stuffed crab, *colombo* (curry) of chicken, and an array of French, Creole, and Hindu specialties. You're likely to find the place overcrowded in winter with the tour-bus crowd.

Rivière Rouge. (𝒞 **590/80-01-77.** Main courses 8€–22€ ($10–$29); fixed-price menu 16€–18€ ($21–$23). No credit cards. Daily noon–3pm. Follow the clearly marked signs; it's beside a gully close to the center of the village.

THE WINDWARD COAST 𝕣𝕣

From Basse-Terre to Pointe-à-Pitre, the road N1 follows the east coast, called the Windward Coast. The country here is richer and greener than elsewhere on the island. There's no major sight or stopover along the way, so if your time is limited, you can simply savor the views along the coastal road, with the sea to your right and scenic landscapes to your left.

To reach the little town of **Trois Rivières** you have a choice of two routes: One goes along the coastline, coming eventually to Vieux Fort, from which you can see Les Saintes archipelago. The other heads across the hills, Monts Caraïbes.

Near the pier in Trois Rivières you'll see the pre-Columbian petroglyphs carved by the original inhabitants, the Arawaks. They're called merely **Roches Gravées,** or "carved rocks." In this **Parc Archéologique** at Bord de la Mer (© **590/92-91-88**), the rock engravings are of animal and human figures, probably dating from A.D. 300 or 400. You can also see specimens of plants, including cocoa, pimento, and banana, that the Arawaks cultivated long before the Europeans set foot on Guadeloupe. Hours are daily 8:30am to 5pm; admission is 2€ ($2.60) for adults, free for children under 12.

After leaving Trois Rivières, continue north on N1. Passing through the village of Bananier after a 15-minute drive, you turn to your left at Anse Saint-Sauveur to reach the famous **Les Chutes du Carbet** ⚘, a trio of waterfalls that are wonderful to behold year-round. If you have time for only one stopover along the route, make it this one. The road to two of them is a narrow, winding one, along many steep hills, passing through banana plantations as you move deeper into a tropical forest.

Les Chutes du Carbet are the tallest falls in the Caribbean. The waters pour down from La Soufrière at 240m (787 ft.) in a trio of stages on the eastern slopes of Guadeloupe. The upper cascade falls 123m (403 ft.) through a steep crevice. Drawing the most visitors and the easiest to reach is the middle falls at 108m (354 ft.), dropping into a bigger canyon than the upper cascade. The second cascade in the falls is likely to be overrun with tour groups. The lower cascades drop only 20m (66 ft.) and are less interesting.

You can hike to each cascade. To reach the dramatic second stage from the little town of Saint-Sauveur, head inland via the village of Habituée, going to the end of the road. From here, follow the signs for a 30-minute walk along a marked trailway to the foot of the falls. There is a picnic area nearby.

If you have plenty of time and are in good shape, you can also reach the upper falls from here. Follow a signposted trail but note that this level of hiking takes about 1½ hours and is very steep, difficult, and often slippery. *Warning:* On November 21, 2004, a minor earthquake in the region unleashed many tons of mud and to a lesser degree, rock, which poured down from the hills onto some of the hiking trails leading to Carbet Falls. The local government has committed itself to clearing the trails of mud and debris, but as a safety precaution, check with the island's tourist office before setting out on excursions in the region just to be sure.

After your hike, continue northeast on N1 to Capesterre. From there a 7km (4¼-mile) drive brings you to **Ste-Marie.** In the town square, you can see the statue of the first visitor who landed on Guadeloupe: Christopher Columbus, who anchored .4km (¼ mile) from Ste-Marie on November 4, 1493. If you'd like to see the same view that greeted Columbus, you can stop off here. The statue and that view are the only reasons to take a look.

After Ste-Marie, you pass through Goyave, then Petit-Bourg, seeing on your left the route de la Traversée before reaching Pointe-à-Pitre.

10 Beaches

Chances are your hotel will be right on a beach, or no more than 20 minutes from a good one. Plenty of natural beaches dot the island, from the surf-brushed dark strands of western Basse-Terre to the long stretches of white sand encircling Grande-Terre.

Public beaches are generally free, but some charge for parking. Unlike hotel beaches, they have few facilities. Hotels welcome nonguests, but charge for changing facilities, beach chairs, and towels.

Sunday is family day at the beach. Topless sunbathing is common at hotels, less so on village beaches.

Most of the best beaches lie between Gosier and St-François on Grande Terre. Visitors usually head for the hotel beaches at **Gosier.** Stone jetties were constructed here to protect the beaches from erosion. Since this area has the largest concentration of tourists, it's likely to be crowded.

These beaches are not peas in a pod. There's no shade at the **Creole Beach** fronting Creole Beach Hotel, although you can retreat to the bar there for a drink. A stone retaining wall blocks access to the water. Nearby, the **Salako Beach** has more sand and is set against a backdrop of palms that provide some shade. Part of this beach also leads up to a jetty. This is a fine sandy beach (although a little too crowded at times) and it also contains a snack bar.

Also nearby, **Arawak Beach** is a gorgeous spot, with plenty of swaying palm trees providing a bit of shade on the beige sands. It, too, is protected by jetties. Close at hand, **Callinago Beach** is smaller than Arawak, but still has a pleasant crescent of beige sand and palms.

Le Bas du Fort, 3km (2 miles) east of Pointe-à-Pitre and close to Gosier, is another popular area. Guests at the Hotels Fleu d'Eté and Marissol share its beaches, which are also protected by jetties. This is a picture-postcard tropical beach with tranquil waters, plenty of sand, and palms for shade. There are hotel bars as well as snack bars and vendors (some of whom are rather aggressive).

Some of Grande-Terre's best beaches are in the **Ste-Anne** area, site of Club Med La Caravelle. **Plage Caravelle** is heaped with white sand, attracting crowds of sunbathers; snorkelers, too, are drawn to the beach's reef-protected waters.

The French visitors here often like to go nude, and there is no finer nude beach than **Pointe Tarare,** a 45-minute drive from Gosier. This beach lies east of St-François at Pointe des Chateaux. It's one of the island's most pristine, tranquil beaches, but there's no shade to protect you from the fierce noonday sun. You can snorkel here if the water's not kicking up. There's a good restaurant by the car park. *Warning:* The tourist office doesn't recommend that women come here unaccompanied.

If you're not a nudist, you can enjoy the lovely strip of white sand at **Anse de la Gourde,** lying between St-François and Pointe des Chateaux. It has good sand, but it tends to become crowded on weekends.

The eastern coast of Grande-Terre is less desirable for swimming, as it fronts the more turbulent Atlantic. Nonetheless, the sands at **Le Moule** make for an idyllic beach because a reef protects the shoreline. There are also beach bars here—and the inevitable crowds, especially on weekends. You'll find a more secluded strip of sand north of here at **La Porte d'Enfer.**

There are two other excellent beaches on the northwestern coast: one at **Anse Laborde** just outside the village of Anse-Bertrand, the other called **Anse du Souffleur** at Port-Louis. We especially like the beach at Souffleur for its brilliant, flamboyant trees that bloom in the summer. There are no facilities here, but you can pick up provisions in the shops in the little village, then enjoy a picnic on the beach.

In Basse-Terre, a highly desirable beach is **La Grande-Anse,** just outside Deshaies, reached by heading west from Sainte Rose along the N2. You won't find any facilities here, but we think you'll like the powdery sands, tranquil waters, and palm trees. Another desirable beach is **Plage de la Malendure,** on the west coast (the more tranquil side) of Basse-Terre across from Pigeon Island. This is a major center for scuba diving, but the sand tends to be dark here.

If you want to escape the crowds, seek out the spurs and shoulders produced by the mountains of Basse-Terre. In the northwest is a string of fine sandy beaches. Although small, these are highly desirable enclaves for sunbathing. Favorites include **La Plage de Cluny** (near Pointe Allegre), **Plage de la Tillette,** and **Plage de la Perle.** *Warning:* The beaches on the north coast of Basse-Terre are exceedingly dangerous for swimming. **Plage de Cluny** is especially treacherous (with very large waves), and there have been several deaths by drowning.

South of Pointe Noire, also on the west coast, is **Plage des Caraïbes,** with its calm waters and sandy strip. This beach has picnic facilities, a shower, and toilets.

Other good beaches are found on the offshore islands, **Iles des Saintes** (see below) and **Marie-Galante** (see the end of this chapter).

11 Sports & Other Outdoor Pursuits

DEEP-SEA FISHING   Blue marlin, wahoo (known locally as *thazar*), and yellowfin tuna can be fished throughout the year; the season for dorado (mahimahi) is limited to November through May. Hotels can usually recommend a deep-sea outfitter or two. A well-recommended outfitter is **Michel's Deep Sea Fishing** (© 590/55-21-35), who's usually moored offshore the Plage de Malendure, but who moves his craft to various ports on Guadeloupe and its offshore dependencies, depending on the tides, the season, and business. For a "very full" half-day experience at big game fishing, with a departure at 7:30am and a return scheduled for around 3pm, he charges 120€ ($156) per person, with all equipment included, minimum three passengers. A competitor that we know less well, but with roughly the same deal, is **Le Manolo** (© 590/90-75-49).

GOLF   Guadeloupe's only golf course is the well-known **Golf de St-François** 𝕲𝕲, avenue de l'Europe, 97110 St-François (© 590/88-41-87), opposite the Le Kalenda Resort which will remain closed during the lifetime of this edition. The course runs alongside a 320-hectare (790-acre) lagoon where windsurfing, water-skiing, and sailing prevail. Designed by Robert Trent Jones, Sr., it's a challenging 6,755-yard, par-71 course, with water traps on 6 of the 18 holes, not to mention massive bunkers, prevailing trade winds, and a particularly fiendish 400-yard, par-4 9th hole. The par-5 6th is the toughest hole on the course; its 450 yards must be negotiated in the constant easterly winds. Greens fees are 40€ ($52) per day per person, which allows a full day of playing time. You can rent clubs for 15€ ($20) a day; an electric cart costs 36€ ($47) for 18 holes. Hours are daily from 7:30am to 6:30pm.

HIKING   The 30,000-hectare (74,100-acre) **Parc Naturel de Guadeloupe** (© 590/80-86-00) contains some of the best hiking trails in the Caribbean. The 290km (180 miles) of trails cut through the deep foliage of rainforest, passing waterfalls and cool mountain pools, hot springs, and rugged gorges along the way. The big excursion country, of course, is around the volcano, La Soufrière. Another highlight is Chutes du Carbet, one of the tallest waterfalls in the Caribbean, with a drop of 240m (787 ft.). More details are available in the touring notes on the Windward Coast near the end of the section "Around Basse-Terre," earlier in this chapter.

Hiking brochures are available from the tourist office. Hotel tour desks can make arrangements. For information about this and other hikes in the national park, contact **Organisation des Guides de Montagne de la Caraïbe,** Maison Forestière, Matouba (© **590/92-06-10**).

Warning: Hikers may experience heavy downpours. The annual precipitation on the higher slopes is 6.3m (248 in.) per year, so be prepared with rain gear.

SCUBA DIVING   Guadeloupe is more popular for scuba diving than any of the other French-speaking islands. The allure is the relatively calm seas and **La Réserve Cousteau,** a kind of French national park with many intriguing dive sites, where the underwater environment is rigidly protected. Jacques Cousteau once described the waters off Guadeloupe's Pigeon Island as "one of the world's 10 best diving spots." Sergeant majors become visible at a depth of 9m (30 ft.), spiny sea urchins and green parrotfish at 18m (59 ft.), and magnificent stands of finger, black, brain, and star coral at 24m (79 ft.).

The most popular dive sites include Aquarium, Piscine, Jardin de Corail, Pointe Carrangue, Pointe Barracuda, and Jardin Japonais. Although scattered around the periphery of the island, many are in the bay of Petit Cul-de-Sac Marin, south of Rivière Salée, the channel that separates the two halves of Guadeloupe. North of the Salée is another bay, Grand Cul-de-Sac Marin, where the small islets of Fajou and Caret also boast fine diving.

Reacting to the rich diversity of underwater flora and fauna, which thrive at relatively shallow—and relatively safe—depths, several entrepreneurs have set up shop. One of these is **Les Heures Saines,** Rocher de Malendure, Bouillante (© **590/98-86-63**), whose trio of dive boats departs three times a day at 10am, 12:30pm, and 3pm, for explorations of the waters within the reserve. With all equipment included, dives—depending on the level of expertise of the participants, and the intended destination—cost from 50€ ($65) each. Novices, at least for the very first time they engage in the sport, pay 58€ ($75) for what is referred to as a *baptême* (baptism).

Les Heures Saines maintains its own 13-unit hotel, **Le Paradis Creole** (© **590/98-71-62;** www.plongee-guadeloupe.com). Here, simple, motel-style accommodations rent for 75€ ($98) in winter and 53€ to 55€ ($69–$72) off season. All have either air-conditioning or ceiling fans, but no TV or phone, and very few frills. Many of them are occupied almost exclusively by avid divers, and to a lesser degree, hill climbers, on tour-group holiday from the French mainland.

This outfit's slightly larger competitor, located a short distance away, is **Centre International de la Plongée (C.I.P. Bouillante),** Lieu-Dit Poirier, Malendure Plage, Pigeon, 97125 Bouillante (© **590/98-81-72;** www.cip-guadeloupe.com). It's acknowledged as the most professional dive operation on the island. In a wood-sided house on Malendure Plage, close to a well-known restaurant, Chez Loulouse, it's well positioned at the edge of the Cousteau Underwater Reserve. Certified divers pay 35€ ($46) for a one-tank dive. A "resort course" for first-time divers costs 45€ ($59) and is conducted one-on-one with an instructor. Packages of 6 or 10 dives are offered for 181€ ($235) and 275€ ($358), respectively. PADI open-water certification costs 382€ ($497). It's usually awarded as part of a 6- or 7-day instruction ritual, but in a pinch, if its participants are extremely motivated, it can be passed in 3 days if you communicate your wishes and ambitions in advance.

TENNIS   If you're a guest at a large-scale hotel with courts of its own, tennis will usually be free, although there might be a small fee for nighttime illumination if it's available. If your hotel doesn't have a court of its own, and if you've called nearby hotels without any luck about using—even for a fee—one of their courts, try either of the two tennis courts at the **Tennis Club de St-François,** Plage des Raisins Claires, St-François (© **590/88-75-61**). Use of one of the courts costs around 10€ ($13) per hour.

WINDSURFING For an intensive immersion in the sport, within a context that includes lots of like-minded aficionados, consider enrolling in one of the windsurfing programs at **UCPA (Unino des Centres de Plein-Air),** 97118 St-François (© **590/88-54-84** or 590/88-64-80; www.ucpa.com). Here, you'll find a community devoted to outdoor warm-weather sports, replete with hotel-style lodgings in simple bunga-lows, each of them beach-fronting affairs built in 1986, set close to a swimming pool and dining hall. Each contains simple and durable furniture and a ceiling fan, but none has TV, phone, air-conditioning, or any other grace note. If you're already an experienced windsurfer, you can always drop in for a practice run—windsurfers rent for 30€ ($39) for a half-day rental—but participants are encouraged to remain on-site for between 5 and 7 days, buying sports packages whose arithmetic makes each individual session cost a lot less. With half-board included, per-person rates, double occupancy, cost from 280€ to 400€ ($364–$520) per week. Packages that build endurance and skill in windsurfing, surfing, kite surfing, and golf are readily available.

12 Guadeloupe After Dark

Guadeloupeans claim that *la biguine* was invented here, not on Martinique, and they dance it as if it truly was their own. Of course, there's also calypso, technically imported from points farther south such as Trinidad, merengue sounds from the Dominican Republic, salsa from Puerto Rico, and fusion jazz from Cuba, too—the islanders are known for their dancing.

Ask at your hotel for details on the folkloric **Ballets Guadeloupéans** performances (p. 337). This troupe makes frequent appearances at the big resorts.

The major casino, one of only two on the island, both administered by the same company, is **Casino Gosier-les-Bains,** 43 Pointe de la Verdure, Gosier (© **590/84-79-68**). A casually elegant spot, it's open daily from 10am until 4am, although the hottest games—those associated with the roulette, chemin de fer, and blackjack—don't open till 8:30pm. ID is requested. All areas of the casino are free of admission.

A smaller casino, with fewer slot machines but with the same opening hours and admission charge, is **Casino de St-François,** avenue de l'Europe (© **590/88-41-31**), near the Le Kalenda Resort in St-François.

If you don't like casino action, you can find other nighttime diversions in Guade-loupe, although these tend to be seasonal, with more offerings in the winter. Sheathed in wood, and open to the outdoor breezes, the **Zoo Rock Café** at La Marina in Gosier (© **590/90-77-77**) offers a revolving series of theme parties ("Midnight in Rio" and "Carnival in New Orleans") that might remind you of something in St-Tropez.

Cuban salsa and Latin dancing draw patrons to **Lollapalooza,** 122 Montauban, Gosier (© **590/84-58-58**), where pictures of dictator Fidel and the long-dead Che Guevara decorate the walls. If you get tired of this joint, try **Fanzy Bar,** Mathurin Poucette (© **590/84-41-34**), where musical styles might include 1980s-style French disco, Bob Marley reggae, and in an occasional orgy of nostalgia, Edith Piaf singing songs from the 1940s and '50s. **Zenith,** Bord de Mer, Bas-du-Fort (© **590/90-72-04**), goes in and out of fashion as a sought-after island nightclub and dance club. All these bars are free but the island's dance clubs charge a uniform fee of about 20€ ($26), which includes the cost of a first drink. After that, most cocktails are a pricey 10€ to 15€ ($13–$20).

The clientele and psychedelic colors of **Bar Americano,** sur la Plage in Ste-Anne (© **590/88-38-99**), might make you believe that the 1960s era of flower power is still alive and thriving. Set directly adjacent to the beach, and artfully grungy, it's the kind of hangout that might remind you of your college years. More animated, but open only Friday and Saturday nights, is **La Cascade,** in Gosier (© **590/20-36-59**), which rocks and rolls, often to salsa or other Latin beats, for an audience of locals and short-term holidaymakers.

13 Side Trips from Guadeloupe

ILES DES SAINTES ☆

A cluster of eight islands off the southern coast of Guadeloupe, the Iles des Saintes are certainly off the beaten track. The two main islands and six rocks are Terre-de-Haut, Terre-de-Bas, Ilet-à-Cabrit, La Coche, Les Augustins, Grand Ilet, Le Redonde, and Le Pâté. Only Terre-de-Haut ("land of high") and, to a lesser extent, Terre-de-Bas ("land below") attract visitors; **Terre-de-Haut** is the most interesting, and the only island with overnight accommodations.

Some claim that Iles des Saintes has one of the nicest bays in the world, a Lilliputian Rio de Janeiro with a sugarloaf. The isles, just 10km (6 miles) from the main island, were visited by Columbus on November 4, 1493, who named them "Los Santos."

The history of Iles des Saintes is very much the history of Guadeloupe itself. In years past, the islands have been heavily fortified, as they were Guadeloupe's Gibraltar. The climate is very dry, and until the desalination plant opened, water was often rationed.

The population of Terre-de-Haut is mainly Caucasian, all fisherfolk or sailors and their families who are descended from Breton *corsairs* (pirates). The very skilled sailors maneuver large boats called *saintois* and wear hats called *salacos,* which are shallow and white, with sun shades covered in cloth built on radiating ribs of thick bamboo. Frankly, the hats look like small parasols. If you want to take a photograph of these sailors, please make a polite request (in French, otherwise they won't know what you're talking about). Visitors often like to buy these hats (if they can find them) for use as beachwear.

Some visitors travel to the Iles des Saintes for the day just to go scuba diving. The island's two leading dive outfitters are **Dive-Bouteille** (© **590/99-54-25**); and **Pisquettes** (© **590/99-88-80**). Both charge competitive rates and have staffs well versed in the esoterica of the region's many dive sites. Rates are 46€ ($60) for the first dive, with a 3-dive package costing from 125€ ($163).

ESSENTIALS

GETTING THERE   From Pointe-à-Pitre, **flights** depart via **Air Caraïbes** (© **0820/ 825-825**) two or three times a day for the 15-minute ride to Terre-de-Haut, on the Iles des Saintes. One-way passage costs 72€ ($94); round-trip passage costs 135€ ($176). The airport is a truncated landing strip that accommodates nothing larger than small propeller planes such as a 20-seat Twin Otter.

Since air connections from Grande-Terre to Terre-de-Haut are scheduled only three days a week (see above), most islanders reach Terre-de-Haut by ferryboat, for which there are two distinctly different departure points. Every Monday and Thursday at 8am, boats leave Pointe-à-Pitre's Gare Maritime de Bergevin, Centreville, across the street from the city's biggest open-air market, arriving an hour later on Terre-de-Haut. Round-trip passage costs 33€ ($43) per person. Returns from Terre-de-Haut for Pointe-à-Pitre are scheduled those same days (Monday to Thursday) at 4pm. For transit information, contact **Exprès des Iles** at (© **590/91-52-15**).

Other ferryboats, operated by a different carrier, depart twice a day from Guadeloupe's port at Trois-Rivieres (near the southern of Basse-Terre) at 6:45am and 3:45pm, taking 25 or 30 minutes for the transit to the quays at Bourg, on Terre-de-Haut, for a price of 19€ ($25) roundtrip. Boats return to Trois-Rivieres from Terre-de-Haut every day at 8:30am and 6:30pm. For transit information, contact the **Compagnie des Iles du Sud** ((© **590/98-30-08**).

VISITOR INFORMATION   In the center of town and easy to spot is the **Office du Tourisme,** 39 rue de la Grand Anse, Bourg, 97137 Terre-de-Haut ((© **590/99-58-60**). Its information, for the most part, is in French, but a map of the island might come in handy.

GETTING AROUND   On an island that doesn't have a single car-rental agency, you get about by walking or riding a bike or motor scooter, which can be rented at hotels and in town near the pier. **Localizé,** at Route Aerodrome in Terre-de-Haut ((© **590/99-51-99**), rents both motorboats and scooters, costing from 15€ to 25€ ($20–$33) per day, depending on the model.

There are also minibuses called *taxis de l'Ile* (eight in all), which take six to eight passengers. A taxi from the airport to the port at Bourg costs 9€ ($12).

ACCOMMODATIONS ON TERRE-DE-HAUT

Bois Joli   Set on the western edge of the island, about 3km (2 miles) from the village of Bourg, this complex of pink-stucco buildings forms one of the most isolated resorts on the island. Known for housing families from the French mainland, it offers both conventional bedrooms within the main house, plus eight outlying bungalows set into palm groves near the beach. Two of the bungalows have kitchenettes, but don't cost more than the other units. Decor includes bold-patterned fabrics, comfortable chairs, and modern but blandly international furnishings, plus small bathrooms with a shower. The food served in the dining room emphasizes local Creole cuisine.

97137 Terre-de-Haut, Les Saintes, Guadeloupe, F.W.I. (© 590/99-50-38. Fax 590/99-55-05. www.hotelboisjoli.fr. 31 units. Winter 139€ ($181) double, 196€ ($255) bungalow for 2; off season 95€ ($124) double, 138€ ($179) bungalow for 2. Rates include breakfast. Half-board 29€ ($38) per person per day. MC, V. **Amenities:** Restaurant; bar; outdoor pool; laundry service; dry cleaning. *In room:* A/C, kitchen (in some), fridge.

L'Auberge les Petits Saints aux Anacardiers ✦   The choice place to stay—and also to dine—is this antiques-filled former mayor's house set on a hillside site with a view of the turquoise bay and the adjacent beach. Surrounded by a tropical garden, a 5-minute walk north of Bourg, this is a tranquil retreat with much colonial charm. The owners, Jean Foraste and Laurence Nonjoie, have filled the house with their collection of furnishings and objects from around the world. All bedrooms, except a one-bedroom bungalow and a separate guesthouse, have queen-size or twin beds. The guesthouse has five spacious rooms and is suitable for friends traveling together or families. All rooms have showers and toilets, but no bathtubs; corridor showers are also available.

Well-prepared food (French and Creole) on the island is served for dinner here—the restaurant is open to the public but you should call for a reservation.

La Savane, 97137 Terre-de-Haut, Les Saintes, Guadeloupe, F.W.I. ℂ **590/99-50-99.** Fax 590/99-54-51. www.petits saints.com. 10 units. Winter 140€ ($182) double, 180€–240€ ($234–$312) suite; off season 110€ ($143) double, 150€–180€ ($195–$234) suite. Rates include breakfast. AE, MC, V. **Amenities:** Restaurant; bar; outdoor pool. *In room:* A/C, TV, minibar, hair dryer.

DINING ON TERRE-DE-HAUT

La Saladerie FRENCH/SEAFOOD   With a decor of art painted on shipwreck parts, this restaurant serves the best and freshest fish on island. Naturally, most guests order the fish of the day, which can be simply grilled or else served in a delectable fondue with six homemade sauces. Begin perhaps with the local version of gazpacho, going on to such Creole-inspired dishes as shrimp cooked in coconut milk. You compose your own salad from a choice of ingredients. French music is played in the background if you want to linger, sipping Calvados imported from Normandy.

Anse Mire, Terre-de-Haut. ℂ **590/99-53-43.** Reservations recommended. Main courses 11€–18€ ($14–$23). DC, MC, V. Wed–Sun 11:45am–2pm and 6:45–9pm. Closed Sept 15–Oct 15.

Les Amandiers CREOLE   Across from the town hall on the main square of Bourg is the most traditional Creole bistro on Terre-de-Haut. Monsieur and Madame Charlot Brudey are your hosts in this blue-and-white building, with tables and chairs on the upper balconies for open-air dining. *Lambi* (conch) is prepared either in a fricassee or a *colombo,* a savory curry stew. Also offered are a court bouillon of fish, a *gâteau* (terrine) of fish, and a seemingly endless supply of grilled crayfish, a staple of the island. The catch of the day is also grilled the way you like it. You'll find an intriguing collection of stews, concocted from fish, bananas, and *christophene* (Caribbean squash). Knowledge of French is helpful around here.

Place de la Mairie. ℂ **590/99-51-77.** Reservations recommended. Main courses 7.50€–16€ ($9.75–$21); fixed-price menu 12€–16€ ($16–$21). AE, MC, V. Winter daily noon–2:30pm and 7–9pm; off season, closed Fri evening.

Quai des Artistes ⭐ FRENCH/CARIBBEAN   Opened in 2006 by a pair of talented expatriates from the French mainland, this spot is the best and most posh restaurant on Terre-de-Haut, with a suave sense of style that's head and shoulders above most of the competition. Its walls are covered with paintings by one of the talented owners, Didier Spindler, and at least some of its surfaces are accented with art objects he collected with the restaurant's co-owner, Jean-Paul Colas, during travels in, among other places, Thailand and Morocco. Menu items combine local ingredients with creative flair and precepts of classical French cuisine, such as tuna "Kurasawa" (sushi quality tuna lightly seared, raw in the center, served with spices and algae, and named in honor of the Japanese film director); a brochette of chicken with soya and curry; magret of duckling with passionfruit sauce; and smoked swordfish.

Place Débarcadères, Bourg. ℂ **0590/92-70-98.** Reservations recommended. Main courses 18€–25€ ($24–$33). MC, V. Thurs–Mon 9:30am–11:30pm.

DIVING OFF TERRE-DE-HAUT

Scuba diving is not limited to mainland Guadeloupe. The underwater world off Les Saintes has attracted deep-sea divers as renowned as Jacques Cousteau, but even the less experienced may explore its challenging depths and multicolored reefs. Intriguing

> ### *Finds* An Escape to Pristine Beaches
>
> There is no finer beach than **Plage de Pompierre,** which curves around the bay like a half moon, and is set against a backdrop of palms. The beach lies only a 15- to 20-minute walk from where the ferry from Basse-Terre docks. Unless a cruise ship is in port, the beach is generally uncrowded, filled with mainland French enjoying the powdery-white sand wearing next to nothing. If you want to bare all, head for **Anse Crawen** on the western coastline. It is the legal nudist beach, although people often go nude on the other beaches, too. The best snorkeling is on the southern coast at **Plage Figuier,** which, chances are, you'll have almost to yourself.

underwater grottoes can be found near Fort Napoléon on Terre-de-Haut. Two well-recommended dive outfitters include **La Dive Bouteille,** Fond-du-Curé (© **590/99-54-25**), and **Club Pisquette,** Le Mouillage, in Bourg (© **590/99-88-20**). A resort course designed for unlicensed scuba divers costs 58€ ($75) and a one-tank dive for already-certified divers goes for 46€ ($60), with all equipment included.

AFTER DARK   Seemingly everybody, both locals and visitors, heads to **Coconuts,** rue Benoit Cassin (© **590/99-53-02**). This old-style *lolo* ("food kiosk" in the local dialect) is called Chez Cécile by locals; it's named for its owner, Cécile Samson. The club is near the place where the fishermen rest between trips, and some of them often hit the bar with their congas and bongos to drum up some music.

MARIE-GALANTE

Come to Marie-Galante to see the Caribbean the way it used to be before the advent of high-rise hotels and casinos. In just 1 hour from Pointe-à-Pitre you can be transported to a world that time seems to have forgotten. This offshore dependency of Guadeloupe is an almost-perfect circle of about 155 sq. km (60 sq. miles). Almost exclusively French speaking, it lies about 30km (20 miles) south of Guadeloupe's Grand-Terre and is full of rustic charm.

Today, some 12,500 inhabitants live here, making their living from sugar and rum, the latter said to be the best in the Caribbean. The best distillery to visit is **Distillerie Bielle,** Section Bielle, 97112 Grand-Bourg (© **590/97-93-62**). The island's climate is rather dry, and there are many good beaches, some of the finest in Guadeloupe's archipelago. One of these stretches of brilliantly white sand covers at least 8km (5 miles). However, swimming can be dangerous in some places. **Grand-Bourg,** the main town, is dominated by an 1845 baroque church. The island's best beach lies almost immediately adjacent to Grand-Bourg, **Plage de la Feuillère,** a 2km (1¼-mile) stretch of white sand that's favored by swimmers and sunbathers. Equally appealing, and more isolated, are the **Plages du Nord,** stretching across the island's northern tier. They include the **Plage du Vieux-Fort,** a 1km (½-mile) stretch of open white sand, and the **Place de l'Anse Canot,** a semicircular bay whose white sands encompass waters that are ideal for small sailcraft, thanks to wave-sheltered waters that are relatively calm.

ESSENTIALS

GETTING THERE   **Express des Iles,** Gare Maritime, Bergevin, Pointe-à-Pitre (© **590/91-52-15**), operates boat service to the island with three daily round-trips between Point-à-Pitre and Grand-Bourg. The round-trip costs 33€ ($43). Monday to Saturday, ferryboats depart from Pointe-à-Pitre for Grand-Bourg on Marie Galante, at 8:15am, 12:30pm, and 5:15pm, with Sunday departures occurring at 8:15am, 5pm, and 7pm. Monday to Saturday, ferryboats to Pointe-à-Pitre depart from Marie-Galante at 6am, 9am, and 4pm, and on Sunday, ferryboats leave from Marie-Galante at 6am, 4pm, and 6pm.

VISITOR INFORMATION   The **Office de Tourisme** is at rue du Fort, BP 15, 97112 Grand-Bourg, Marie-Galante (© **590/97-56-51;** fax 590/97-56-54; www.ot-mariegalante.com).

GETTING AROUND   A limited number of **taxis** are available at the airport, but be sure to negotiate the price before you drive off. Should you wish to rent a car, go to **Hertz** in Grand-Bourg (© **800/654-3001** in the U.S., or 590/97-59-80; www.hertz.com), where rentals range from 25€ to 55€ ($33–$72) per day.

ACCOMMODATIONS

La Cohoba Hotel (*Value*)   On Folle Anse, an uncrowded white-sand beach, this hotel is a bargain and a comfortable nest. The beach is edged with sea-grape and mahogany trees. The hotel itself takes its name from the cohoba plant, known to the Caribs as a plant whose red pods have hallucinogenic powers. The hotel, the largest on Marie-Galante, has small, suitelike rooms decorated with white tile and ghost-white walls, along with bright Caribbean colors and tiny but efficient shower-only bathrooms. The superior rooms have kitchenettes.

Cocoyer, BP 59, 97112 Marie-Galante, Guadeloupe, F.W.I. © 800/322-2223 in the U.S., or 590/97-50-50. Fax 590/97-97-96. 100 units. Winter 138€–154€ ($179–$200) double; off season 82€–108€ ($107–$140) double. Rates include continental breakfast. AE, MC, V. **Amenities:** Restaurant; bar; outdoor pool; 2 tennis courts; babysitting. *In room:* A/C, TV, kitchenette (in some), beverage maker (in some), hair dryer, safe.

DINING

Le Touloulou   CREOLE   Adjacent to the beach, with a hardworking staff and a casual crowd, Le Touloulou specializes in shellfish and crayfish culled from local waters. If sea urchins or lobster are your passion, you'll find them here in abundance, prepared virtually any way you want. Other standbys include a savory, and highly ethnic, version of *bébélé* (cow tripe enhanced with breadfruit, dumplings, and plantains) and conch served either as fricassee or in puff pastry.

In the mid-1990s, the restaurant added five very basic, bungalow-style accommodations, each with air-conditioning and a small private bathroom. Year-round, double occupancy costs 55€ ($72), with or without a kitchenette. A two-bedroom bungalow, with kitchenette, suitable for up to four occupants, costs 110€ ($143) year-round. Staff here tends to be blasé, bordering on terminally lethargic, so come armed with a sense of humor. At night, the bar is transformed into the island's only dance club.

Petite Anse, Marie-Galante. © 590/97-32-63. Fax 590/97-33-59. Main courses 11€–25€ ($14–$33); set menu 14€–25€ ($18–$33). MC, V. Tues–Sun noon–3:30pm; Tues-Sat 7–10:30pm. Closed Sept 15–Oct 15.

LA DESIRADE

La Désirade is one of the few islands in the Caribbean that is not touched by tourism of any significance. Most visitors come just for the day to enjoy the uncrowded white-sandy beach or perhaps to tour the island's barren expanses.

Columbus spotted this *terre désirée,* or "sought-after land," after his Atlantic crossing in 1493. The island, just 8km (5 miles) off the eastern tip of Guadeloupe proper, is less than 11km (6¾ miles) long and about 2km (1¼ miles) wide, and it has a single potholed road running along its length.

The island has fewer than 1,700 inhabitants, including the descendants of Europeans exiled here by royal command. There are a handful of exceptionally simple guesthouses charging from 45€ ($59) for overnight accommodations for two. Don't expect anything grand.

The main village is **Grande-Anse,** which has a small church with a presbytery and flower garden. **Le Souffleur** is a boat-building community, and at **Baie Mahault,** you'll see the ruins of the old leper colony (including a barely recognizable chapel) from the early 18th century.

The best **beaches** on the island's south side are **Souffleur,** a tranquil oasis near the boat-building center, and **Baie Mahault,** a small, quintessentially Caribbean beach with white sand and palm trees.

ESSENTIALS

VISITOR INFORMATION   For tourist information on La Désirade, call ℂ **590/ 85-00-86.**

GETTING THERE   From Grand-Terre most passengers opt for transit to La Désirade by **ferry,** which leaves from the wharves at St-François every day at 8am. Returns from La Désirade for St-François include a daily departure at 4:45pm, allowing convenient access for day-trippers. Trip time is around 50 minutes each way, depending on conditions at sea. Round-trip passage on the ferryboat costs 22€ ($27). Call ℂ **590/ 20-05-03** for schedules, but only from 4 to 7pm daily.

GETTING AROUND   Three or four **minibuses** run between the dock and the towns. To get around, you might negotiate with a local driver. **Bicycles** are also available at the hotels.

ACCOMMODATIONS

Accommodations are available at **L'Oasis** (ℂ **590/20-01-00**) and **Le Mirage** (ℂ **590/ 20-01-08;** fax 590/20-07-45). Both are at Beauséjour, .8km (½ mile) from the airport. L'Oasis has four plain rooms and charges 50€ to 62€ ($65–$81) for a double, including breakfast. Built in 1990 of concrete, it's simple and boxy, but is a short walk from a good beach. Le Mirage offers seven rather drab rooms and charges 40€ ($52) for a double, including breakfast. Also built of concrete around the same time as L'Oasis, it offers a simple bar, and it lies a bit closer to the sands than its competitor.

15

Jamaica

Most visitors have a mental image of Jamaica before they arrive: boisterous reggae and Rastafarianism; white, sandy beaches; and jungles, rivers, mountains, and clear waterfalls. Now add some remarkable art and cuisine and you have a pretty accurate picture of this island nation.

Jamaica lies 145km (90 miles) south of Cuba and is the third-largest of the Caribbean islands, with some 11,396 sq. km (4,444 sq. miles) of lush green land, a mountain ridge peaking at 2,220m (7,282 ft.) above sea level, and, on the north coast, many white-sand beaches with clear blue waters.

It can be a tranquil and intriguing island, but there's no denying that it's plagued by crime, drugs, and muggings. There are also palpable racial tensions. But many visitors are untouched by these problems; they're escorted from the airport to their heavily patrolled hotel grounds and venture out only on expensive organized tours. Vacationers are largely sheltered from the more unpredictable and sometimes dangerous side of Jamaica, and this kind of trip can suit you just fine if all you want is to unwind on a beautiful beach. Those who want to see "the real Jamaica," or at least see the island in greater depth, had better be prepared for some hassle. Vendors on the beaches and in the markets can be particularly aggressive.

Should you go? Certainly. You'll want to be prudent and cautious, just as if you were visiting New York, Miami, or Los Angeles. But the island has fine hotels and cuisine. It's a good choice for couples getting married or honeymooning. As for sports, Jamaica has the best golf courses in the West Indies, and its landscape offers lots of outdoor activities, like rafting and serious hiking. The island has gorgeous beaches and some of the finest diving in the world.

CHOOSING WHERE TO STAY ON JAMAICA

Jamaica is such a large island that you have a wide range of choices.

The grand dame is **Montego Bay,** which has three of the leading and poshest resorts in the Caribbean (Half Moon, Round Hill, and Tryall), plus a very good selection of moderately priced hotels. The beaches are fabulous here, though often crowded in winter due to the hotel density. There are fine golf courses, and the shopping is excellent for Jamaica, but the nightlife is surprisingly lackluster.

Younger and hipper than Montego Bay, **Negril** is a sleepy town (with surprisingly little in the way of dining or nightlife) that has a freewheeling, sensual personality and a spectacular stretch of beach. A row of resorts, many of them lavish all-inclusives, has sprouted up along its shores. One visitor who flies in every year claims Negril is for "sand and sex," but not necessarily in that order.

To the west, **Ocho Rios** has some of the grandest and most traditional resorts in Jamaica as well as some of the leading Sandals properties. But it doesn't have the best beaches, shops, or scenic attractions, and it's frequently overrun with cruise-ship passengers. Nonetheless, if you like the sound of a particular resort there and just plan to stay put on your resort's beach, this might be for you.

Port Antonio is for the upscale traveler who wants to escape the mass package tours of Ocho Rios or even Montego Bay. Come here for some good beaches plus great river rafting, scuba diving, or snorkeling.

Most visitors go to **Kingston** for business reasons only. It does have interesting museums and historic sights, fine galleries, and a diverse nightlife scene. But all in all, it's a city with some serious urban problems, and probably not what you're looking for in an island vacation. You certainly wouldn't go to Kingston for beaches.

1 Essentials

VISITOR INFORMATION

Before you go, you can get information from the **Jamaica Tourist Board** at 5201 Blue Lagoon Dr., Suite 670, Miami, FL (© **800/233-4582** in the U.S., or 305/665-0557; fax 305/666-7239). In Canada contact the office in Toronto at 303 Eglinton Ave. E, Suite 200, Toronto, ON M4P IL3 (© **800/465-2624** in the U.S. and Canada). Brits can contact the London office at 1-2 Prince Consort Rd., SW7 2BZ (© **020/7225-9090**). The official website of the Jamaica Tourist Board is **www.visitjamaica.com**.

Once on the island, you can find tourist offices at 64 Knutsford Blvd., **Kingston** (© **876/929-9200**); and Cornwall Beach, St. James, **Montego Bay** (© **876/952-4425**).

GETTING THERE

Before you book your own airfare, read the section "Packages for the Independent Traveler," in chapter 2—you may save a bundle, because there are always lots of package deals available to Jamaica's resorts.

There are two **international airports** on Jamaica: **Donald Sangster Airport** in Montego Bay (© **876/952-3124**) and **Norman Manley Airport** in Kingston (© **876/924-8452**). The most popular flights to Jamaica are from New York and Miami. Flying time from Miami is 1¼ hours; from Atlanta, 2½ hours; from Dallas, 3 hours; from Chicago and New York, 3½ hours; from Toronto, 4 hours; and from Los Angeles, 5½ hours.

Some of the most convenient service to Jamaica is provided by **American Airlines** (© **800/433-7300** in the U.S. and Canada; www.aa.com) through its hubs in New York and Miami. Throughout the year, one daily nonstop flight departs from New York's JFK airport for Montego Bay, continuing on to Kingston. Return flights to New York usually depart from Montego Bay. From Miami, at least two daily flights depart for Kingston and three daily flights for Montego Bay.

US Airways (© **800/428-4322** in the U.S. and Canada; www.usairways.com) has two daily flights from New York, stopping in Charlotte or Philadelphia. One daily flight leaves out of Baltimore, stopping in either Charlotte or Philadelphia before continuing to Jamaica. **Northwest Airlines** (© **800/447-4747** in the U.S. and Canada; www.nwa.com) flies directly to Montego Bay from Detroit or Minneapolis.

In 2004 **Continental Airlines** (© **800/231-0856** in the U.S. and Canada; www.continental.com) launched service from its Houston hub at the George Bush Intercontinental Airport, flying to Montego Bay.

Air Jamaica (© **800/523-5585** in the U.S. and Canada; www.airjamaica.com) operates one or more flights daily to Montego Bay and Kingston from such cities as

Jamaica

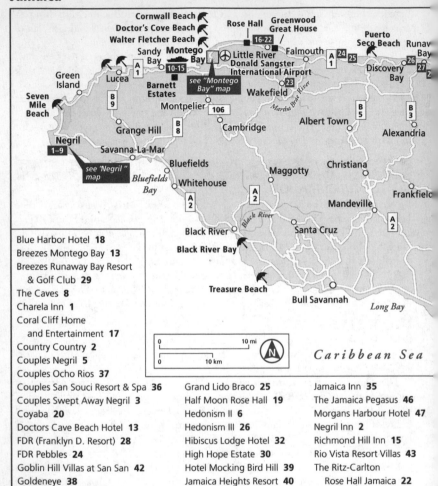

Blue Harbor Hotel **18**
Breezes Montego Bay **13**
Breezes Runaway Bay Resort
   & Golf Club **29**
The Caves **8**
Charela Inn **1**
Coral Cliff Home
   and Entertainment **17**
Country Country **2**
Couples Negril **5**
Couples Ocho Rios **37**

Couples San Souci Resort & Spa **36**
Couples Swept Away Negril **3**
Coyaba **20**
Doctors Cave Beach Hotel **13**
FDR (Franklyn D. Resort) **28**
FDR Pebbles **24**
Goblin Hill Villas at San San **42**
Goldeneye **38**

Grand Lido Braco **25**
Half Moon Rose Hall **19**
Hedonism II **6**
Hedonism III **26**
Hibiscus Lodge Hotel **32**
High Hope Estate **30**
Hotel Mocking Bird Hill **39**
Jamaica Heights Resort **40**

Jamaica Inn **35**
The Jamaica Pegasus **46**
Morgans Harbour Hotel **47**
Negril Inn **2**
Richmond Hill Inn **15**
Rio Vista Resort Villas **43**
The Ritz-Carlton
   Rose Hall Jamaica **22**

Miami, Fort Lauderdale, Orlando, Atlanta, Baltimore/Washington, D.C., Philadelphia, Chicago, Newark, Boston, Houston, Los Angeles, and New York. The airline has
connecting service within Jamaica through its reservation network to **International
Air Link** (see below).

   Air Canada (© **800/361-7585** in the U.S. and Canada; www.aircanada.com) flies
from Toronto to Jamaica daily. **British Airways** (© **800/247-9297**; www.britishairways.
com) has three nonstop flights weekly to Kingston from London's Gatwick Airport.

GETTING AROUND

Especially if you've booked a package at one of the big resorts, you're likely to have airport transfers from Montego Bay included. Many resorts send buses to pick up and
drop off their arriving and departing guests.

BY PLANE   Most travelers enter the country via Montego Bay. If you want to fly elsewhere, you'll need to use the island's domestic air service, which is provided by **International Air Link** (© **876/940-6660;** www.intlairlink.com), a subsidiary of Air Jamaica, whose planes usually hold between 10 and 17 passengers. The airline flies from the island's international airports at Montego Bay and Kingston to small airports around the island, including Boscobel (near Ocho Rios) and Tinson Pen (a tiny airport near Kingston for domestic flights only). For example, there are seven flights a day between Kingston and Montego Bay. In addition, there are two flights a day between Kingston and Ocho Rios and two flights between Montego Bay and Ocho Rios, each costing about US$70 (£36) one way. The only airports with car-rental facilities are the international airports at Kingston and Montego Bay.

Moments **A True Taste of Jamaica**

Wherever you go in Jamaica, you'll see ramshackle stands selling **jerk pork.** There is no more authentic local experience than to stop at one of these stands and order a lunch of jerk pork, preferably washed down with a Red Stripe beer. Jerk is a way of barbecuing spicy meats on slats of pimento wood, over a wood fire set in the ground. You can never be quite sure what goes into the seasoning, but the taste is definitely of peppers, pimento (allspice), and ginger. You can also order jerk chicken, sausage, fish, and even lobster. The cook will haul out a machete and chop the meat into bite-size pieces for you, then throw them into a paper bag.

BY TAXI Not all of Jamaica's taxis are metered; if yours is not, negotiate the price before you get in. In Kingston and on the rest of the island, special taxis and buses for visitors are operated by **JUTA** (Jamaica Union of Travelers Association; © **876/ 957-4620**) and have the union's emblem on the side of the vehicle. All prices are controlled, and any local JUTA office will supply a list of rates. JUTA drivers handle nearly all the ground transportation, and some offer sightseeing tours. A typical fare is US$15 (£7.80) per person for an airport transfer between Montego Bay and Negril, or US$80 (£42) for an airport transfer between Montego Bay and Ocho Rios. Rates are 25% higher after midnight.

BY RENTAL CAR Jamaica is big enough, and public transportation is unreliable enough, that a car is a necessity if you plan to do much independent sightseeing. You can also take an organized tour or a taxi tour to the major sights and spend the rest of the time on the beaches near your hotel.

Depending on road conditions, driving time for the 80km (50 miles) from Montego Bay to Negril is 1½ hours; from Montego Bay to Ocho Rios, 1½ hours; from Ocho Rios to Port Antonio, 2½ hours; and from Ocho Rios to Kingston, 2 hours.

Unfortunately, car-rental rates on Jamaica have skyrocketed recently, making it one of the most expensive rental scenes in the Caribbean. There's also a 15% government tax on rentals. Equally unfortunate are the unfavorable insurance policies that apply to virtually every car-rental agency on Jamaica.

Try **Budget Rent-a-Car** (© **800/472-3325** in the U.S. and Canada, 876/952-3838 at the Montego Bay Airport, or 876/924-8762 in Kingston; www.budget rentacar.com); with Budget, a daily collision-damage waiver is mandatory at US$15 (£7.80) per day. **Hertz** (© **800/654-3131** in the U.S. and Canada; www.hertz.com) operates branches at the airports at both Montego Bay (© **876/979-0438**) and Kingston (© **876/924-8028**). A typical rental might be a Mitsubishi Mirage for US$420 (£218) per week in winter, dropping to US$330 (£172) weekly off-season.

If you'd like to shop for a better deal with one of the local companies in Montego Bay, try **Jamaica Car Rental,** 23 Gloucester Ave. (© **876/952-5586**), with a branch at the Sangster International Airport at Montego Bay (© **876/952-9496**). Daily rates range from US$50 to US$60 (£26–£31). You can also try **United Car Rentals,** 49 Gloucester Ave. (© **876/952-3077**), which rents Toyotas and Hondas costing from US$64 (£33) per day for a four-door standard car with air-conditioning.

In Kingston, try **Island Car Rentals,** 17 Antigua Ave. (© **876/926-8012**), with a branch at Montego Bay's Sangster International Airport (© **876/952-7225**). It rents Hondas and Jimmys with rates beginning at US$76 (£40) daily in winter, US$58 (£30) in the off season.

Remember: Drive on the left, and exercise more than your usual caution here because of the unfamiliar terrain. Be especially cautious at night. Speed limits in town are 48kmph (30 mph), and 80kmph (50 mph) outside of town. Gas is measured in liters, and the charge is officially payable only in Jamaican dollars; some stations accept credit cards. Your own valid driver's license from back home is acceptable for short-term visits to Jamaica.

FAST FACTS: Jamaica

Banks Banks islandwide are open Monday to Friday from 9am to 5pm. You'll find **ATMs** in all the major resort areas and towns, including Port Antonio, Ocho Rios, and Kingston. There are several in Montego Bay, of course, and even one or two in sleepy Negril.

Currency The unit of currency on Jamaica is the **Jamaican dollar (J$),** and it uses the same symbol as the U.S. dollar ($). There is no fixed rate of exchange. Visitors to Jamaica can pay for most goods in U.S. dollars or with credit cards. Always check if prices are listed in U.S. dollars or Jamaican dollars.

In this guide we've generally followed the price-quotation policy of the establishment, whether in Jamaican dollars or U.S. dollars. The symbol J$ denotes prices in Jamaican dollars. *Unless otherwise specified, prices in this chapter are quoted in U.S. dollars and British pounds.*

Jamaican currency is issued in banknotes of J$50, J$100, J$500, and J$1,000. Coins are available in denominations of J$1, J$5, J$10, and J$20. At press time, but subject to change, 1 US dollar equaled approximately 67 Jamaican dollars, and 1 British pound equaled approximately 125 Jamaican dollars.

As this will probably fluctuate a bit during the lifetime of this edition, use these rates for general guidance only.

There are Bank of Jamaica exchange bureaus at both international airports (Montego Bay and Kingston), at cruise-ship piers, and in most hotels.

Customs Do *not* bring in or take out illegal drugs to or from Jamaica. Your luggage will be searched; marijuana-sniffing police dogs are stationed at the airport. You cannot bring fresh foodstuffs in the U.S.; however, you can bring in to Jamaica most items intended for personal use.

Documents U.S., British, and Canadian residents need a passport and a return or an ongoing ticket. Immigration cards, needed for bank transactions and currency exchange, are given to visitors at the airport arrival desks.

Electricity Most places have 110-volt AC (60 cycles), as in the United States. However, some establishments operate on 220-volt AC (50 cycles). If your hotel is on a different current from your U.S.-made appliance, ask for a transformer and an adapter.

Embassies, Consulates, & High Commissions Calling embassies or consulates in Jamaica is a challenge. Phones will ring and ring before being picked up, if they are answered at all. Extreme patience is needed to reach a live voice on the other end. The embassy of the **United States** is located at the Jamaica Mutual Life Bldg., 2 Oxford Rd., Kingston 5 (© 876/702-6000). The High Commission of **Canada** is situated at 3 West Kings House Rd., Kingston 10 (© 876/926-1500). The High Commission of the **United Kingdom** is found at 28 Trafalgar Rd., Kingston 10 (© 876/510-0700).

Emergencies For the **police**, dial © **119**; to report a **fire** or call an **ambulance,** dial © **110.**

Language Jamaicans speak English with a lovely lilt. Among themselves, they also speak patois, a fast-spoken blend of French, English, and a number of other languages.

Safety Major resorts have security guards who protect the grounds, so most vacationers don't have any real problems. It's not wise to accept an invitation to see "the real Jamaica" from some stranger you meet on the beach. Exercise caution when traveling around Jamaica. Safeguard your valuables, and never leave them unattended on a beach. Likewise, never leave luggage or other valuables in a car, or even the trunk of a car. The U.S. State Department has issued a travel advisory about crime rates in Kingston, so don't walk around alone at night. Caution is also advisable in many north-coast tourist areas, especially remote houses and isolated villas that can't afford security.

Taxes The government imposes between 10% and 15% room tax, depending on your category of hotel. You'll be charged US$27 (£14) departure tax at the airport, payable in either Jamaican or U.S. dollars. There's also a 20% government tax on rental cars and a 20% tax on all overseas phone calls.

Time Jamaica is on Eastern Standard Time year-round and doesn't follow daylight saving time. When the United States is on daylight saving time, at 6am in Miami it's 5am in Kingston.

Tipping A general 15% or 20% is expected in hotels and restaurants on occasions when you would normally tip. Some places add a service charge to the bill, so make sure you know whether or not it's already included. Tipping is not allowed in the all-inclusive hotels. Taxi drivers expect about 15%.

Water It's usually safe to drink piped-in water, islandwide, as it's filtered and chlorinated. However, it's prudent to drink bottled water if it's available.

Weather Expect temperatures around 77°F to 79°F (25°C–27°C) on the coast. Summer is a little warmer. In the mountains it can get as low as 40°F (4°C). There is generally a breeze, which in winter is noticeably cool. The rainy periods generally are October and November (although it can extend into Dec), and May and June. Normally rain comes in short, sharp showers; then the sun shines.

(**Warning**   **A Word on Marijuana**

You will almost certainly be approached by someone selling ganja (marijuana)—in fact, that's why many travelers come here. However, drugs, including marijuana, are illegal, and imprisonment is the penalty for possession. You don't want to experience the Jamaican penal system firsthand. Don't smoke pot openly in public. Of course, hundreds of visitors do and get away with it, but you may be the one who gets caught, and the person selling to you might even be a police informant. Above all, don't try to bring marijuana back into the United States. There are drug-sniffing dogs stationed at the Jamaican airports, and they will check your luggage. U.S. Customs agents, well aware of the drug situation on Jamaica, have arrested many tourists who have tried to bring some home.

---

2 Montego Bay ★★★

Situated on the northwestern coast of the island, Montego Bay (MoBay) first attracted tourists in the 1940s, when Doctor's Cave Beach became popular with wealthy vacationers who bathed in the warm water fed by mineral springs. It's now Jamaica's second-largest city.

Despite the large influx of visitors, Montego Bay still retains its identity as a thriving business and commercial center, and it functions as the market town for most of western Jamaica. It has cruise-ship piers and a growing industrial center.

Montego Bay has its own airport, so those who vacation here have little need to visit the capital, Kingston. MoBay is the most cosmopolitan of Jamaica's cities.

ESSENTIALS

MEDICAL FACILITIES   The **Cornwall Regional Hospital** is at Mount Salem (© **876/952-5100**). For medicines and prescriptions, try the **Overton Pharmacy,** 49 Union St., Overton Plaza (© **876/952-2699**).

ACCOMMODATIONS
VERY EXPENSIVE

Half Moon Rose Hall ★★★ *Kids*   Opening onto 160 hectares (395 acres) that take in a .8km (½-mile) stretch of white-sand beach, this is one of the Caribbean's grand hotels, without the snobbery of Round Hill or Tryall (see below). It also has far more activities, excitement, amenities, restaurants, and a better beach. About 13km (8 miles) east of Montego Bay's city center and 10km (6¼ miles) from the international airport, this is a classic_one of the top 25 tropical resorts, according to *Condé Nast Traveler.* It's a grand and appealing place, a true luxury hideaway with taste and style, and also highly acclaimed as an eco-sensitive resort.

Accommodations include conventional hotel rooms, suites, and a collection of superbly accessorized private villas (most villas have private pools and a full-time staff). Each unit is comfortably furnished with an English colonial/Caribbean motif and a private balcony or patio, plus a state-of-the-art bathroom with a tub/shower combo. Queen Anne–inspired furniture is set off by vibrant Jamaican paintings, and many units contain mahogany four-poster beds.

Montego Bay

ACCOMMODATIONS ■

Blue Harbour Hotel **14**
Breezes Montego Bay **10**
Coral Cliff Home and Enterainment **12**
Coyaba **9**
Doctors Cave Beach Hotel **8**
FDR Pebbles **2**
Half Moon Rose Hall **6**
Richmond Hill Inn **19**
Ritz-Carlton Rose Hall Jamaica **5**
Rose Hall Resort & Country Club **4**
Round Hill Hotel & Villas **20**
Sandals Royal Caribbean **3**
Starfish Trelawny **1**
Tryall Golf, Tennis & Beach Club **21**
Wexford Court Hotel **11**

For Tryall Club and
Round Hill Hotel & Villas,
see the "Jamaica" map.

Caribbean Sea

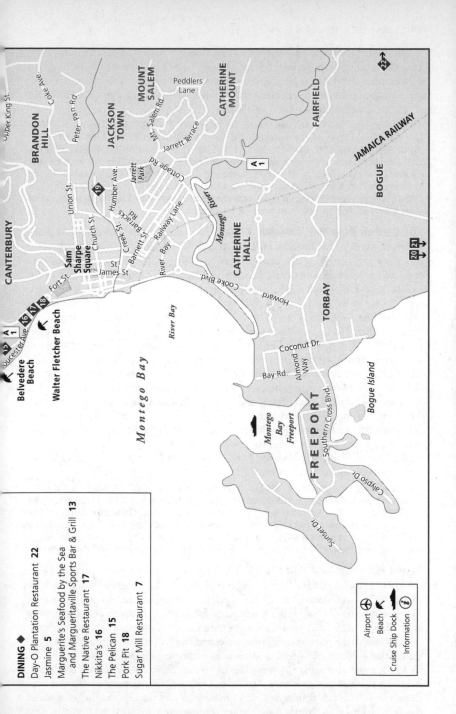

DINING ◆

Day-O Plantation Restaurant **22**

Jasmine **5**

Marguerite's Seafood by the Sea
and Margueritaville Sports Bar & Grill **13**

The Native Restaurant **17**

Nikkita's **16**

The Pelican **15**

Pork Pit **18**

Sugar Mill Restaurant **7**

Airport ✈

Beach ⚓

Cruise Ship Dock ⬆

Information ⓘ

CANTERBURY

BRANDON
HILL

Upper King St.

Coke Ave.

Union St.

Peter_pen Rd.

JACKSON
TOWN

MOUNT
SALEM

Peddlers
Lane

Mt. Salem Rd.

Jarrett Terrace

CATHERINE
MOUNT

FAIRFIELD

JAMAICA RAILWAY

BOGUE

Cottage Rd.

Jarrett
Park

Humber Ave.

Barracks
Rd.

Creek St.

Church St.

Barnett St.

Railway Lane

River Bay

Montego River

CATHERINE
HALL

A
1

Sam
Sharpe
Square

St.
James St.

Fort St.

Belvedere Beach

Walter Fletcher Beach

Gloucester Ave.

A
1

Montego Bay

River Bay

Cooke Blvd.

Howard

CATHERINE
HALL

TORBAY

FREEPORT

Montego
Bay
Freeport

Coconut Dr.

Bay Rd.

Almond
Way

Southern Cross Blvd.

Bogue Island

Calypso Dr.

Sunset Dr.

20 21

22

The Sugar Mill Restaurant, our favorite in Montego Bay, is beside a working water wheel from a bygone sugar estate. (See "Dining," later in this chapter.) The Seagrape Terrace offers delightful meals alfresco. Il Giardino, set within a convincing replica of a Renaissance palazzo, serves savory Italian cuisine. The resort also has a Pan-Asian restaurant, a steakhouse, and an English pub.

Half Moon Post Office, Rose Hall, St. James, Montego Bay, Jamaica, W.I. © **866/648-6951** in the U.S., or 876/953-2211. Fax 876/953-2731. www.halfmoon.com. 398 units. Winter US$400–US$620 (£208–£322) double, US$800–US$1,520 (£416–£790) suite; off season US$250–US$380 (£130–£198) double, US$580–US$1,060 (£302–£551) suite. Children under 12 stay free in parent's room. MAP (breakfast and dinner) US$85 (£44) per person extra. Ask about golf and spa packages. AE, DC, DISC, MC, V. **Amenities:** 6 restaurants; 7 bars; 4 outdoor pools; golf course; 13 tennis courts (9 lit); fitness club; squash; croquet; spa; Jacuzzi; 2 saunas; deep-sea fishing; dive shop; bike rental; children's activities; horseback riding; car rental; room service; Internet room; babysitting; laundry service; medical center. *In room:* A/C, TV, kitchenette (in some), minibar, hair dryer, iron, safe.

Ritz-Carlton Rose Hall Jamaica ★ *(Kids)*

The newest (2002) of the grand dame resorts of MoBay (that includes Half Moon and Round Hill), this blockbuster complex is big, bustling, upscale, and impressive, sprawling as it does across an adequately wide stretch of white-sand beach. (Clients seeking a better beach are shuttled to the nearby Rose Hall Beach Club, site of many motorized and nonmotorized watersports.) One of its major draws is the White Witch golf course, a 15-minute shuttle ride away. Its public areas try, at least, to duplicate the ambience of a traditional Jamaican Great House that's been updated and modernized into a big-time and oversized icon to "the good life." Come here if you're looking for a somewhat sanitized stopover in a big hotel saturated with international comforts, including a full-service spa. Frankly, this is not our favorite of the ultra-upscale resorts of Montego Bay—it lacks the sense of fantasy (gazebos, lavish gardens, bougainvillea burgeoning over lattices, and so forth) of Half Moon, and it utterly lacks the intimacy of Round Hill. This is not the most impressive in the Ritz-Carlton chain. For such a big and supposedly topnotch venue, the swimming pool isn't big enough. Accommodations, however, are appropriately luxurious, but with an upscale motif that could have been imported from virtually any luxury hotel in North America. Each features a deluxe bathroom with tub/shower combo.

Rose Hall, Montego Bay, Jamaica, W.I. © **800/241-3333** in the U.S. or Canada, or 876/953-2800. Fax 876/518-0110. www.ritzcarlton.com. 427 units. Winter US$699–US$999 (£363–£519) double, from US$2,500 (£1,300) suite; off season US$359–US$549 (£187–£285) double, from US$509 (£265) suite. Children under 12 stay free in parent's room. AE, DISC, MC, V. **Amenities:** 6 restaurants; 2 bars; outdoor pool; golf course; 2 tennis courts; health club; spa; Jacuzzi; nonmotorized watersports; children's activities; business center; room service; babysitting; laundry service; dry cleaning; nonsmoking rooms; rooms for those w/limited mobility. *In room:* A/C, TV, minibar, beverage maker, hair dryer, iron, safe.

Round Hill Hotel and Villas ★★★

Opened in 1953 on a small, private, white-sand beach, Round Hill is a legend, and the most prestigious address in Jamaica, even though it lacks the extensive facilities (and in some cases, the whimsical sense of romantic fantasy) of Half Moon. It originated as a small, clubby compound of private villas supervised by Lord Monson, on the grounds of a 44-hectare (110-acre) plantation devoted to the production of pineapples and allspice, attracting the aristocracy of Europe and some of the biggest media and entertainment moguls of the New World. By far the most spectacular accommodations here are those cloistered away on the surrounding hillsides, within white-sided villas. Decors of these luxurious villas are kept elegant and theatrical, thanks to acres of mahogany and marble, the skill of some of the best architects in North America and Europe, and frequent renovations. Less

---

Fun Fact **Catch a Fire: Jamaica's Reggae Festival**

For 4 days in July, Montego Bay comes alive with the pulsating sounds of reggae when a well-known festival is presented. **Reggae Sumfest** (www.reggae sumfest.com) takes place at Catharine Hall, a government-funded arts and entertainment development beside the Roseway Bypass in the MoBay industrial suburb of Freeport. Performers at this festival have included some of the biggest names in reggae, both from Jamaica and abroad—Ziggy Marley, Cocoa Tea, the Melody Makers, Barefoot Hammond, the Mystic Revelers, and others. Many local hotels are fully booked for the festival, so advance reservations are necessary. The Jamaican Tourist Board's U.S. and Canadian offices can give you information about packages and group rates for the festivals and fill you in on other events held throughout the year on Jamaica.

---

grand accommodations are within a rambling, two-story building (Pineapple House) set at the edge of the sea, overlooking a swimming pool that was enlarged early in 2006. Decor inside Pineapple House is all-white, light-hearted, and airy, with four-poster bamboo beds.

Breakfast is brought to your room or served on the dining terrace. Informal luncheons are held in an intimate straw hut with an open terrace in a little sandy bay. Standard Jamaican and Continental dishes are served on a candlelit terrace or in the Georgian colonial room overlooking the sea. Ralph Lauren decorated the cocktail area.

Rte. A1 (P.O. Box 64), Montego Bay, Jamaica, W.I. (C) **800/972-2159** in the U.S., or 876/956-7050. Fax 876/956-7505. www.roundhilljamaica.com. 74 units. Winter US$590–US$1,180 (£307–£614) double, from US$1,250 (£650) villa; off season US$350–US$600 (£182–£312) double, from US$780 (£406) villa. Extra person US$90 (£47). MAP (breakfast and dinner) US$90 (£47) per person extra. AE, DC, DISC, MC, V. **Amenities:** Restaurant; 3 bars; outdoor pool; 5 tennis courts (2 lit); health club; spa; dive shop; room service; babysitting; laundry service; nonsmoking rooms. *In room:* A/C, kitchen (in some), fridge, beverage maker, hair dryer, iron, safe.

Sandals Royal Caribbean 🏵🏵 This all-inclusive, couples-only (any combination) resort, with a tranquil atmosphere, lies on its own private beach. Some of the British colonial atmosphere remains (the formal tea in the afternoon), but there are modern touches as well, including a private, clothing-optional island reached by boat.

The spacious rooms range from standard to superior to deluxe. Best are the grand luxe beachfront rooms, with private patios or balconies. Each unit has a small but well-equipped private bathroom with a tub/shower combination. The cuisine is more varied here than at other MoBay Sandals, with, for example, Royal Thai, an Indonesian restaurant on an offshore island. The Regency and The Pavilion serve a rather good Jamaican-inspired cuisine, among other options. Children under 18 are not allowed at this resort.

Mahoe Bay (P.O. Box 167), Montego Bay, Jamaica, W.I. (C) **800/726-3257** in the U.S. and Canada, or 876/953-2232. Fax 876/953-2788. www.sandals.com. 181 units. Winter US$325–US$510 (£169–£265) double, from US$575 (£299) suite; off season US$295–US$485 (£153–£252) double, from US$550 (£286) suite. Rates are per couple and include all meals, drinks, and activities. 2-night minimum stay required. AE, DISC, MC, V. No one under 18 allowed. **Amenities:** 4 restaurants; 7 bars (2 swim-up); 4 outdoor pools; 5 whirlpools; 3 lit tennis courts; fitness center; sauna; canoes; kayaks; sailing; scuba diving; snorkeling; water-skiing; windsurfing; room service; massage; coin-operated laundry; dry cleaning; nonsmoking rooms; rooms for those w/limited mobility. *In room:* A/C, TV, beverage maker, hair dryer, iron, safe.

Tryall Golf, Tennis & Beach Club ★★★ *Kids* This is a top choice for vacationers who are serious about golf. With more spacious grounds than almost any other Jamaican hotel, this stylish and upscale resort sits 19km (12 miles) west of town on the site of an 880-hectare (2,175-acre) former sugar plantation. It has neither the fine beach of Half Moon, nor the elegant house-party atmosphere of Round Hill, but it's one of Jamaica's grandest resorts. The property lies along a 2km (1¼-mile) beachfront and is presided over by a 165-year-old Georgian-style great house.

The accommodations in luxurious villas are decorated in cool pastels with English colonial touches. All contain ceiling fans and some have air-conditioning, along with picture windows framing sea and mountain views. Bedrooms are exceedingly spacious, with luxurious beds, private patios or terraces, and tile floors. Bathrooms are roomy, with plenty of counter space and a tub/shower combination. The resort's villas are set amid lush foliage and are designed for privacy, each with a private pool. Nothing rents here for less than 5 days, and Tryall prefers weekly bookings. The most formal of the resort's dining areas is in the great house, but it's not the equal of the options available at Half Moon and the Ritz-Carlton. There's also a casual beach cafe, more for convenience than good food.

Many clients here are CEOs, so the hotel has opened an Internet room. On other fronts, Tryall is gaining recognition as one of the most eco-sensitive resorts in the Caribbean, winning acclaim as a "Green Globe Hotel."

St. James (P.O. Box 1206), Montego Bay, Jamaica, W.I. © 800/238-5290 in the U.S., or 876/956-5660. Fax 876/956-5673. www.tryallclub.com. 69 villas. Rates for 7 days: Winter US$3,080–US$3,850 (£1,602–£2,002) 1-bedroom villa, US$6,600 (£3,432) 2-bedroom villa; off season US$1,925–US$2,750 (£1,001–£1,430) 1-bedroom villa, US$2,310–US$3,300 (£1,201–£1,716) 2-bedroom villa. MAP (breakfast and dinner) US$85 (£44) per person extra. AE, DC, DISC, MC, V. **Amenities:** 2 restaurants; 4 bars (1 swim-up); outdoor pool; championship par-71 golf course; 9 Laykold tennis courts; fitness center; deep-sea fishing; snorkeling; windsurfing; horseback riding; children's programs; Internet room; salon; massage; babysitting; laundry service; nonsmoking rooms; rooms for those w/limited mobility. *In room:* A/C (in some), ceiling fan, TV, kitchen, fridge, beverage maker, hair dryer.

EXPENSIVE

Breezes Montego Bay ★★ A five-story complex, this SuperClub—called "a sandbox for your inner child"—is the only major hotel directly on the sands of Montego Bay's most popular public beach, Doctor's Cave. It's adult and indulgent, but without the raucous partying of Hedonism II (a member of the same chain). Bedrooms are tastefully furnished and breezy, overlooking either the beach or the garden that separates the hotel from the traffic of Montego Bay's main commercial boulevard, Gloucester Avenue. Rooms range from intimate cabins to lavish suites. The cabin rooms, 31 in all, are similar to a ship's cabin, with a queen-size bed. Slightly larger are the deluxe rooms, with twins or a king-size bed. The best are the deluxe oceanfront rooms, with king-size beds, and the oceanfront suites. All units have bathrooms with tub/shower combinations.

Informal but good meals are served at Jimmy's Buffet, a terrace overlooking the pool and the beach. More formal meals, with a more refined cuisine, are dished out at the candlelit Martino's, an Italian rooftop restaurant.

Gloucester Ave., Montego Bay, Jamaica, W.I. © 800/467-8737 in the U.S., or 876/940-1150. Fax 876/940-1160. www.superclubs.com. 124 units. Winter US$248–US$278 (£129–£145) double; off season US$268–US$298 (£139–£155) double. Rates include all meals, drinks, airport transfers, and most activities. AE, DC, DISC, MC, V. No children under 14 accepted. **Amenities:** 2 restaurants; 4 bars; outdoor pool; golf; 2 tennis courts; table tennis; billiards; fitness center; rooftop Jacuzzi; dive shop; kayaks; sailing; snorkeling; windsurfing; dance club. *In room:* A/C, TV, beverage maker, hair dryer, iron, safe.

Coyaba 𝄢𝄢 On a lovely strip of private beachfront, this small all-inclusive resort evokes a British colonial atmosphere. It was established in 1994 by American/ Jamaican/Chinese entrepreneurs, the Robertson family, and built from scratch at a cost of US$4 million. A 15-minute drive east of the center of Montego Bay, the resort is centered on an adaptation of an 18th-century great house.

Accommodations in the main building overlook the garden; those in the pair of three-story outbuildings lie closer to the beach and are somewhat more expensive. The decor is plantation style, with traditional prints, expensive chintz fabrics, French doors leading onto private patios or verandas, and mahogany furniture. Hand-carved bed-steads, often four-posters, are fitted with luxury coverings. The roomy bathrooms have combination tub/showers. Its bedrooms are modern and well maintained, and some units have been upgraded to junior suites with small refrigerators and a sleeper sofa. The hotel's main and most formal restaurant, the Vineyard, serves first-rate Jamaican and Continental dinners. Less upscale is Docks Caribbean Bar & Grill.

Little River, Montego Bay, Jamaica, W.I. ⓒ 877/232-3224 or 876/953-9150. Fax 876/953-2244. www.coyabajamaica. com. 50 units. Winter US$370–US$420 (£192–£218) double; off season US$210–US$260 (£109–£135) double. 2 children under 12 stay free in parent's room. AP (all meals) US$110 (£57) per person extra. Children 11 and under get a 50% discount on meals. AE, MC, V. **Amenities:** 3 restaurants; 3 bars; outdoor pool; lit tennis court w/free tennis clinic; health club; spa; Jacuzzi; kayaks; scuba; snorkeling; Sunfish sailboat; windsurfing; tour desk; car rental; room service; massage; nanny service; laundry service; nonsmoking rooms; rooms for those w/limited mobility. *In room:* A/C, ceiling fan, TV, beverage maker, hair dryer, iron, safe.

FDR Pebbles 𝄢 *Kids* No, it's not named after the U.S. president. This resort, which pioneered at Runaway Bay, invaded Montego Bay and quickly became the most family-friendly place in the area. It's even better than its parent outside Ocho Rios. FDR lies a 35-minute drive east of the airport, opening onto the waterfront and a beach. The resort is an all-inclusive property of cedarwood accommodations designed with real Jamaican flair, offering spacious living and bedroom areas, tub/shower combination bathrooms, plus generous balconies opening onto a view. It's most suited for families with two children, although a larger family can be very comfortable in adjoining units. Everything is geared towards family fun, with an array of activities including fishing and swimming in a nearby river and hiking along nature trails. Each family is assigned a "vacation nanny," who helps with housekeeping and babysitting.

In the restaurant, first-rate ingredients are fashioned into a rather standard repertoire of both Jamaican and American dishes. Portions are exceedingly generous.

Main St., Trelawny (P.O. Box 1933), Jamaica, W.I. ⓒ 888/FDR-KIDS in the U.S., or 876/617-2500. Fax 876/617-2512. www.fdrholidays.com. 96 units. Winter US$325–US$345 (£169–£179) per person double; off season US$180– US$290 (£93–£150) per person double. Children under 6 stay free in parent's room. Rates are all-inclusive. AE, DISC, MC, V. **Amenities:** 3 restaurants; 3 bars; outdoor pool; tennis court; volleyball; Jacuzzi; hiking; kayaks; scuba diving; snorkeling; Sunfish sailboats; biking; kids' club; teen center; Internet cafe; babysitting; dance club; nonsmoking rooms; rooms for those w/limited mobility. *In room:* A/C, TV.

Starfish Trelawny 𝄢 *Kids* Following a much-needed US$5-million renovation, this all-inclusive resort is one of the best value vacations on the island. Opening onto a stretch of powder-white, soft, sandy beach, it offers activities for both children and adults. The location is 37km (23 miles) east of MoBay airport. The most spacious rooms are the cottages at the rear of the hotel, which can house three adults and two children. For those who must have an ocean view, the resort rents some "superior" rooms, suitable for three adults and one child, with a balcony overlooking the beach. The least expensive units have a mountain or garden view, with a balcony, which can also accommodate three adults and a child. The wide range of sports and amenities make this an alluring choice. The food is fairly standard but there's a sushi bar with Teppanyaki tables and a pasta and pizza restaurant. Four-course gourmet dinners are served in the Casablanca Restaurant.

North Coast Hwy, Falmouth, Jamaica, W.I. ℂ 877/467-8737 in the U.S., or 876/954-2451. Fax 876/518-6356. www.starfishresorts.com. 350 units. Winter US$108–US$152 (£56–£79) per person double; off season US$88–US$140 (£46–£73)per person double. Rates are all-inclusive. AE, DC, MC, V. **Amenities:** 5 restaurants; 6 bars; 4 pools; minigolf; 4 lit tennis courts; fitness center; sauna; badminton; basketball; ice skating; rock climbing; trapeze; dive shop; sailing; snorkeling; windsurfing; children's center; Internet cafe; massage; babysitting; laundry service; dance club. In room: A/C, TV, minibar, hair dryer, iron, safe.

MODERATE

Coral Cliff Home and Entertainment ⟨R⟩ ⟨Value⟩   For good value, the Coral Cliff may be your best bet in Montego Bay, lying only a 2-minute walk from Doctor's Cave Beach. The hotel grew from a colonial-style building that was once the private home of Harry M. Doubleday (of the famous publishing family). It's located about 2km (1¼ miles) west of the center of town. Many of the light, airy, and spacious bedrooms open onto sea-view balconies. The rooms, as befits a former private house, come in a wide variety of shapes and sizes, most of them containing old colonial furniture, wicker, and rattan. Most units have twin beds. The bathrooms are small in the older bedrooms, but more spacious in the newer wing out back. Each is tidily maintained and has a combination tub/shower. Decent Jamaican and international dishes are served at Ma Loos restaurant.

165 Gloucester Ave. (P.O. Box 253), Montego Bay, Jamaica, W.I. ℂ 876/952-4130. Fax 876/952-6532. www.coral cliffjamaica.com. 12 units. Winter US$100–US$180 (£52–£94) double, US$120–US$200 (£62–£104) triple; off season US$80–US$140 (£42–£73) double, US$95–US$160 (£49–£83) triple. AE, MC, V. **Amenities:** 2 restaurants; bar; outdoor pool; casino; fitness center; spa; library; room service; babysitting; laundry service. In room: A/C, TV, safe.

Doctors Cave Beach Hotel ⟨R⟩ ⟨Value⟩   This three-story hotel offers great value and lies in the bustle of the town's commercial zone. It's across from Doctor's Cave Beach, the busiest and most crowded beach, but with the best sands, in the Montego Bay area. It has 2 hectares (5 acres) of tropical gardens. The well-maintained rooms are simply but comfortably furnished, and suites have kitchenettes. Rooms are rated standard or superior; the latter are more spacious and have balconies with a view. All units have tile floors, queen-size or twin beds (suites have king-size beds), and small but efficiently organized tiled bathrooms with combination tub/showers. The food is more authentic than at the resorts recommended above.

Gloucester Ave. (P.O. Box 94), Montego Bay, Jamaica, W.I. ℂ 876/952-4355. Fax 876/952-5204. www.doctorscave. com. 85 units. Winter US$155–US$175 (£81–£91) double, US$198 (£103) suite for 2; off season US$110–US$120 (£57–£62) double, US$130 (£68) suite for 2. Extra person US$25 (£13). MAP (breakfast and dinner) US$29 (£15) per person extra. AE, DC, MC, V. **Amenities:** Restaurant; bar; outdoor pool; fitness center; Jacuzzi; limited room service; babysitting; nonsmoking rooms; rooms for those w/limited mobility. In room: A/C, TV, kitchenette (in some).

Richmond Hill Inn ⟨R⟩ ⟨Finds⟩   If you're an avid beach lover, you should know in advance that the nearest beach is a 15-minute drive away from this hotel. It was built as the homestead of the Dewar family (the scions of scotch). Very little of the original villa remains, but what you'll find is a hilltop aerie ringed with urn-shaped concrete balustrades, a pool terrace suitable for sundowner cocktails, and comfortable, slightly fussy bedrooms done up in lace-trimmed curtains, homey bric-a-brac, and pastel colors. Each of the accommodations comes with a midsize bathroom with tub/shower combination. Both the bar and restaurant look out over Montego Bay.

Union St. (P.O. Box 362), Montego Bay, Jamaica, W.I. © **876/952-3859**. Fax 876/952-6106. www.richmond-hill-inn.com. 20 units. Winter US$115 (£60) double, US$189–US$450 (£98–£234) suite; off season US$70 (£36) double; US$140–US$375 (£7–£195) suite. MC, V. **Amenities:** Restaurant; bar; outdoor pool; room service (7am–10pm); babysitting. *In room:* A/C, TV, fridge (in some).

INEXPENSIVE

Blue Harbour Hotel On a hillside overlooking the harbor, midway between the airport and town off Route A1, this small 4-story hotel offers basic service in a friendly atmosphere. Rooms here are simple, and kitchenettes in the suites enable you to cook your own meals instead of dining out. If you do plan to dine out, the hotel offers a dine-around plan that includes 10 of Montego Bay's restaurants. (Transportation to and from the restaurants is provided.) Facilities include a swimming pool, air-conditioned lounge, and coffee shop serving breakfast and light lunch. Tennis courts are nearby, and arrangements can be made for golf, deep-sea fishing, scuba diving, and island tours. The hotel operates a shuttle once a day to Doctor's Cave Beach, leaving at 10am.

6 Sewell Ave. (P.O. Box 212), Montego Bay, Jamaica, W.I. © **876/952-5445**. Fax 876/952-8930. http://fly.to/jamaica. 25 units. Winter US$68 (£35) double, US$86 (£45) triple; off-season US$54 (£28) double, US$70 (£36) triple. Each additional person US$15 (£7.80). Children 11 and under stay free in parent's room. Rates include continental breakfast. AE, MC, V. **Amenities:** Coffee shop; lounge; outdoor pool; nearby sports such as golf and tennis; tour desk; limited room service; nonsmoking rooms; rooms for those w/limited mobility. *In room:* A/C, TV, kitchenette (in some), safe.

Wexford Court Hotel *Kids* Especially good for families on a budget, this hotel lies within a 5-minute walk of Doctor's Cave Beach. The apartments have living/dining areas and kitchenettes, so you can cook for yourself. All the rooms have patios shaded by gables and Swiss chalet–style roofs, and each has a tiled, shower-only bathroom. The restaurant serves some zesty Jamaican dishes in a setting that evokes a 1950s Howard Johnson.

39 Gloucester Ave. (P.O. Box 108), Montego Bay, Jamaica, W.I. © **888/790-5264** or 876/952-2854. Fax 876/952-3637. www.thewexfordhotel.com. 60 units. Winter US$115–US$120 (£60–£62) double, US$130 (£68) apt; off season US$105–US$110 (£55–£57) double, US$120 (£62) apt. Up to 2 children under 12 stay free in parent's room. MAP (breakfast and dinner) US$34 (£18) per person extra. AE, DISC, MC, V. **Amenities:** Restaurant; bar; outdoor pool; room service; babysitting; laundry service; rooms for those w/limited mobility. *In room:* A/C, TV, kitchenette (in some), safe.

DINING
EXPENSIVE

Jasmine *&&* INTERNATIONAL Small, boutique-y, and intimate, this is the most upscale and most fussed-over restaurant within the also-recommended Ritz-Carlton Rose Hall Resort. As such, non-residents (some of them hotel insiders themselves from competing hotels) have used a meal here as an excuse to check out the premises of Montego Bay's newest five-star hotel. To reach the dining room, depending on which access doors are open at the time, you might have to pass through the rambling length of a less-upscale restaurant, Horizons, next door. Jasmine's occupies a jewel-like circular room that, if you squint your eyes and if the illumination is by candlelight, you might almost imagine was transplanted directly from a château in France. Twelve intricately laid tables accent tones of blue-gray and white, and flickering candles set the mood. Additional seating is available on an outdoor veranda. What impresses here is the sense of intimacy, romance, and stylish internationalism. Delectable menu items include Asian spring rolls, a Napoleon of blue crabmeat, Jamaican

---

Finds   Going Native on the Street

MoBay has some of the finest and most expensive dining on the island. But if you're watching your wallet and have an adventurous streak, try the terrific street food. The densest concentration of street food in Montego Bay is available at the junction of Gloucester Avenue and Kent Road. (The .8km/½-mile strip of beach-fronting boulevard stretching along both sides of that junction is also known as Bottom Road or, less formally, as "The Hip Strip.") The Hip Strip is lined with bars, food stands, and shops catering to the beach trade. At any of these stands, you might try authentic jerk pork or seasoned spareribs, grilled over charcoal fires and sold with extra-hot sauce. To complete the experience, order a Red Stripe beer to go with it. Cooked shrimp are also sold on the streets of downtown MoBay, especially along St. James Street. They don't look it, but they're very spicy, so be warned. And if you have an efficiency unit with a kitchenette, you can buy fresh lobster or the catch of the day and make your own dinner.

---

pumpkin and carrot soup, Singapore-style lobster chili, spice-encrusted loin of lamb, Asian-style grilled filet mignon, and five-spice marinated pork loin.

In the Ritz-Carlton Rose Hall Hotel, Rose Hall, Montego Bay. ℂ 876/953-2800. Reservations recommended. Main courses US$36–US$48 (£19–£25). AE, DC, MC, V. Dinner only, daily 6:30–9:30pm.

Nikkita's ⭐⭐ MODERN JAMAICAN   In terms of cuisine, this is the most ambitious restaurant in Montego Bay. It occupies a prominent ochre-colored building along Montego Bay's "Hip Strip," in the heart of town. Inside, the decor is reminiscent of a stylish restaurant you might find in Miami, with dark wood trim and a floral, slightly Florentine twist. There are two distinctly different venues within this place that include a posh-looking and deliberately upscale bar and a restaurant. Here, menu items are carefully researched, more "fussed over" than anything within any other restaurant in the neighborhood, and artful. Examples include a country veal and pork pâté; a terrine of grilled vegetables; a "gateau" of smoked marlin and ackee (the national fruit) served with *bammy* (cassava) bread; a whole baked lobster that's removed from its shell, diced, and mixed with diced scallops, crabmeat, and shrimp and then put back into the lobster shell.

Gloucester Ave. ℂ 876/979-6373. Reservations recommended. Main courses US$30–US$60 (£16–£31). AE, DC, DISC, MC, V. Daily 6pm–midnight.

Sugar Mill Restaurant ⭐⭐ INTERNATIONAL/CARIBBEAN   After a drive through a rolling landscape, you'll come across this restaurant near the ruin of what used to be a water wheel for a sugar plantation. The lovely setting and exquisite cuisine make this place a perennial favorite. You can dine by candlelight either indoors or on an open terrace with a view of a pond, the water wheel, and plenty of greenery. Lunch can be a relatively simple affair—a daily a la carte offering is best preceded by Mama's pumpkin soup and followed with homemade rum-and-raisin ice cream. For dinner, try one of the chef's zesty versions of jerk pork, fish, or chicken. He also prepares the day's catch with considerable flair. Smoked north-coast marlin is a specialty. On any given day, you can ask the waiter what's cooking in the curry pot. Chances are it will be a Jamaican specialty such as goat, full of flavor and served with island chutney.

At Half Moon, Rose Hall. © 876/953-2314. Reservations required. Main courses US$24–US$46 (£13–£24). AE, MC, V. Daily 6:30–10pm. Private van transportation provided; ask when you reserve.

MODERATE

Day-O Plantation Restaurant ✭ *Finds* INTERNATIONAL/JAMAICAN Here's
your chance to wander back to Jamaica's plantation heyday. This place was originally built in the 1920s as the home of the overseer of one of the region's largest sugar producers, the Barnett Plantation. The restaurant occupies a long, indoor/outdoor dining room that's divided into two halves by a dance floor and a small stage. Here, owner Paul Hurlock performs as a one-man band, singing and entertaining the crowd while his wife, Jennifer, and their three children manage the dining room and kitchen.

Every dish is permeated with Jamaican spices. Try the chicken in plantation style, with red-wine sauce and herbs; the filet of red snapper in Day-O style, with olives, white wine, tomatoes, and peppers; or, even better, one of the best versions of jerked snapper in Jamaica. We also like the grilled rock lobster with garlic butter.

Day-O Plantation, Lot 1 Fairfield. © 876/952-1825. www.dayorestaurant.com. Reservations suggested. Main courses US$15–US$35 (£7.80–£18). AE, MC, V. Tues–Sun noon–11pm. 8-min. drive west of town off Rte. A1 toward Negril. Private van transportation provided; ask when you reserve.

Marguerite's Seafood by the Sea and Margueritaville Sports Bar & Grill
INTERNATIONAL/SEAFOOD This two-in-one restaurant across from the Coral Cliff Hotel serves its seafood on a breeze-swept terrace overlooking the sea. There's also an air-conditioned lounge with an adjoining "Secret Garden." The chef specializes in exhibition cookery at a flambé grill. Although the menu is mainly devoted to seafood and fresh fish, there are also numerous innovative pastas and rather standard meat dishes. The Cheeseburger in Paradise is the most popular item on the menu, but you can also order Jamaican jerk chili, jerk burgers, and Jamaican pizza, even such Rastafarian dishes as Rasta Roots served with rice and peas. The DJ lives in a lair in the mouth of a *faux* great shark, and, of course, plays more than just Jimmy Buffet tunes. The homemade dessert options change, and a reasonable selection of wines is served. The sports bar and grill features a 34m (112-ft.) waterslide, live music, satellite TV, watersports, a sun deck, and a straightforward menu of seafood, sandwiches, pasta, pizza, salads, and snacks—nothing fussy. Naturally, the bartenders specialize in margaritas, which come in 52 different flavors.

Gloucester Ave. © 876/952-4777. Reservations recommended for Marguerite's Seafood by the Sea. Main courses US$24–US$50 (£12–£26); snacks and platters from US$10–US$14 (£5.20–£7.30). AE, MC, V. Restaurant daily 6–10:30pm; sports bar daily 11am–10pm (club open until 3am).

The Native Restaurant ✭ *Finds* JAMAICAN/INTERNATIONAL Some of the
finest Jamaican dishes in the area are served at this casual, open-air restaurant. While taking in the panoramic views, try some of the appetizers including ackee and saltfish, jerk reggae chicken, and smoked marlin, which you can follow with steamed fish or jerk chicken. A more exotic specialty is Boonoonoonoos; billed as "a taste of Jamaica," it's a big platter with a little bit of everything—meats, fish, and vegetables.

29 Gloucester Ave. © 876/979-2769. Reservations recommended. Main courses US$13–US$32 (£6.75–£17). AE, DC, DISC, MC, V. Daily 7:30am–10:30pm.

The Pelican JAMAICAN   A Montego Bay landmark, the family-friendly Pelican has been serving good food at reasonable prices for more than a quarter century. Most of the dishes are at the lower end of the price scale, unless you order shellfish. Many diners come here at lunch for one of the well-stuffed sandwiches, juicy burgers, or barbecued chicken. You can also choose from a wide array of Jamaican dishes, including stewed peas and rice, curried goat, Caribbean fish, fried chicken, and curried lobster. A "meatless menu" is also featured. The soda fountain serves old-fashioned sundaes with real whipped cream.

Gloucester Ave. © 876/952-3171. Reservations recommended. Main courses US$14–US$24 (£7.30–£12). AE, MC, V. Daily 7am–11pm.

INEXPENSIVE

Pork Pit ✦ JAMAICAN   This joint—right in the heart of Montego Bay, near Walter Fletcher Beach—is the best place to go for Jamaica's famous jerk pork and jerk chicken. Many beachgoers desert their towels at noontime and head over here for a big, reasonably priced lunch. Picnic tables encircle the building, and everything is open-air and informal. A half-pound of jerk meat, served with a baked yam or baked potato and a bottle of Red Stripe, is usually enough for a meal. The menu also includes steamed roast fish.

27 Gloucester Ave. © 876/940-3008. 1 lb. of jerk pork US$11 (£5.70). MC, V. Daily 11am–11pm.

HITTING THE BEACH

Doctor's Cave Beach, on Gloucester Avenue (© 876/952-2566 for the beach club), is arguably the loveliest stretch of sand bordering Montego Bay. Its gentle surf, golden sands, and fresh turquoise water make it an inviting place to swim, and there's always a beach-party atmosphere. Placid and popular with families, it's the best all-around beach in Montego Bay. Sometimes schools of tropical fish weave in and out of the waters, but usually the crowds of frolicking people scare them away. Since it's almost always packed, especially in winter, you have to get there early to stake out a beach blanket-size spot. Admission is US$5 (£2.60) for adults, US$2.50 (£1.30) for children 12 and under; it's open daily 8:30am to sunset. The beach club here has well-kept changing rooms, showers, restrooms, a food court, a bar, a cybercafe, and a sundries shop. Beach chairs and umbrellas can be rented daily.

SPORTS & OTHER OUTDOOR PURSUITS

DEEP-SEA FISHING   **Seaworld Resorts,** whose main office is at the Cariblue Hotel, Rose Hall Main Road (© 876/953-2180; www.diveseaworld.com), operates flying-bridge cruisers, with deck lines and outriggers, for fishing expeditions. A half-day fishing trip costs US$400 (£208) for up to four participants.

DIVING, SNORKELING & OTHER WATERSPORTS   **Seaworld Resorts** (see above) also operates scuba-diving excursions, plus sailing, windsurfing, and more. Its dives plunge to offshore coral reefs, among the most spectacular in the Caribbean. There are three certified dive guides, one dive boat, and all the necessary equipment for both inexperienced and already-certified divers. One-tank dives cost US$40 (£21); night dives are US$75 (£39).

Doctor's Cave Beach is part of the **Montego Bay Marine Park,** which was established to protect the wide variety of marine life among the coral reefs right offshore from the popular beaches. You can rent snorkel gear from the beach club at Doctor's Cave, or from the beach clubs at any of the local beaches.

You might also like to head across the channel to check out **Coyaba Reef, Seaworld Reef,** and **Royal Reef,** which are full of barjacks, blue and brown chromis, yellow-headed wrasses, and spotlight parrotfish. You must have a guide here, as the currents are strong and the wind picks up in the afternoon. If you're not staying at a resort offering snorkeling expeditions, then Seaworld is your best bet. For about US$30 (£16) per hour, a guide swims with you and points out various fish.

GOLF   The **White Witch of Rose Hall Golf Course,** part of the Ritz-Carlton Rose Hall (© **876/518-0174**), is one of the most spectacular courses in the Caribbean, set on 80 hectares (200 acres) of lush greenery in Jamaica's old plantation country. The course is named after Annie Palmer, the notorious "White Witch" and mistress of Rose Hall nearby. Ten minutes from the deluxe resort by wheels, the course was created by Robert von Hagge, who designed the course to wind up and down the mountains, with panoramic vistas of the sea visible from 16 of the 18 holes. Greens fees are US$179 (£93) for hotel guests, US$199 (£103) for nonguests.

Cinnamon Hill Ocean Course 🌤🌤, Rose Hall (© **876/953-2650**), has a noted course with an unusual and challenging seaside and mountain layout. Its 8th hole skirts the water, then doglegs onto a promontory and a green thrusting 180m (600 ft.) into the sea. The back 9 are the most scenic and interesting, rising up steep slopes and falling into deep ravines on Mount Zion. The 10th fairway abuts the family burial grounds of the Barretts of Wimpole Street, and the 14th passes the former vacation home of late singer Johnny Cash. The 90m-high (300-ft.) 13th tee offers a rare panoramic view of the sea and the roof of the hotel, and the 15th green is next to a 12m (40-ft.) waterfall, once featured in a James Bond movie. Amenities include a fully stocked pro shop, a clubhouse, and a professional staff. Guests pay US$141 (£73) for 18 holes, or US$99 (£51) for 9 holes; nonguests pay US$160 (£83) for 18 holes and US$99 (£51) for 9 holes. Cart rental and the use of a caddy are included in the greens fees.

The excellent course at the **Tryall Club Jamaica** 🌤🌤🌤 (© **876/956-5660**), 20km (12 miles) from Montego Bay, is so regal that it's often the site of major tournaments. For 18 holes, guests of Tryall are charged US$85 (£44) in winter, US$40 (£21) the rest of the year. Nonguests pay US$125 (£65) year round.

Half Moon, at Rose Hall (© **876/953-2211**), features a championship course designed by Robert Trent Jones, Sr., with manicured and diversely shaped greens. Half Moon hotel guests pay US$85 (£44) for 18 holes including caddy and cart. Nonguests pay US$130 (£68) for 18 holes; carts cost US$35 (£18), and caddies (which are mandatory) are hired for US$20 (£10).

The **Superclubs Ironshore Golf Club,** Ironshore, St. James, Montego Bay (© **876/953-3681**), is another well-known 18-hole, par-72 course. Privately owned, it's open to all golfers. Greens fees for 18 holes are US$50 (£26), plus US$35 (£18) for a cart and US$16 (£8.30) for a caddy.

HORSEBACK RIDING   A good program is offered at the **Rocky Point Riding Stables,** at Half Moon, Rose Hall, Montego Bay (© **876/953-2286**). Housed in the most beautiful barn and stables in Jamaica, the stables have around 30 horses and a helpful staff. A 90-minute beach or mountain ride costs US$70 (£36).

RAFTING   Mountain Valley Rafting, P.O. Box 23, Montego Bay (© **876/956-4920**), gives somewhat tame and touristy excursions on the Great River, which depart from the Lethe Plantation, about 15km (10 miles) south of Montego Bay. For a little more adventure, skip that, and head over to Falmouth, 45km (28 miles) to the east, where you can raft on the **Martha Brae.** To reach the starting point from Falmouth, drive approximately 5km (3 miles) inland to **Martha Brae's Rafters Village** (© **876/ 952-0889**). The rafts are similar to those on the Rio Grande, near Port Antonio; you sit on a raised dais on bamboo logs. The cost is US$55 (£29), with two riders allowed on a raft, plus a small child if accompanied by an adult (but use caution). The trips last 1¼ hours and operate daily from 9am to 4pm. It's not necessary to wear swimsuits. Along the way, you can stop and order cool drinks or beer along the banks of the river. There's a bar, a restaurant, and two souvenir shops in the village.

TENNIS   Half Moon 🌟🌟🌟, outside Montego Bay (© **876/953-2211**), has the finest courts in the area. Its 13 state-of-the-art courts, seven of which are lit for night games, attract tennis players from around the world. Lessons cost US$30 (£16) per half-hour, US$55 to US$65 (£29 to £34) per hour. Residents play free, day or night. The pro shop, which accepts reservations for court times, is open daily from 7am to 9pm. If you want to play after those hours, you switch on the lights yourself. If you're not a hotel guest, you must purchase a day pass (US$40/£21 per person) at the front desk; it allows access to the resort's courts, gym, sauna, Jacuzzi, pools, and beach facilities.

Tryall Club Jamaica, St. James (© **876/956-5660**), offers nine hard-surface courts, three lit for night play. Day games are free for guests; nonguests pay US$30 (£16) per hour. There's a US$20 (£10) per hour charge to light the courts after dark. At least four on-site pros provide lessons for US$25 to US$35 (£13–£18) per half-hour, or US$45 to US$60 (£23–£31) per hour.

Rose Hall Resort & Country Club, Rose Hall (© **876/953-2650**), outside Montego Bay, is an outstanding tennis resort, though not the equal of Half Moon or Tryall. The hotel offers four hard-surface courts, each lit for night play. The resident pro charges US$50 (£26) per hour for lessons, US$35 (£18) for 45 minutes, or US$30 (£16) for 30 minutes.

Kids A Waterworld for Families

AquaSol Theme Park (aka Walter Fletcher Beach; © **876/979-9447** or 876/940-1344; www.aquasoljamaica.com): For years, this was a sunny, well-maintained beach, without too many improvements, positioned a short walk from the heart of Montego Bay. In 2004, a team of entrepreneurs added a compound of entertainment options, fenced everything in, and renamed it "The Aquasol Theme Park." Now, its sands bustle with scantily clad sunbathers and swimmers throughout the day. Then, beginning at around 8pm every Friday to Sunday, the site experiences a change of clientele when mobs of both Jamaicans and foreign visitors hang out in the moonlight, jamming and gossiping till the wee hours. The entrance fee allows access to a water sports kiosk; a pier where glass-bottomed boats are moored; a strip of sand; a beauty salon; a bar and grill-style restaurant; a gym/health club with a private local membership; and a dance club/bar with views of the sea, a collection of caged macaws, and surges of reggae and soca. Admission is US$5 (£2.60) for adults, US$3 (£1.55) for children under 12. Regardless of which of the facilities you opt to patronize, the entire compound is open Monday to Thursday 9am to 7pm, and 9am to at least midnight, and sometimes, later, depending on business, on Friday to Sunday.

Moments **Meeting Some Feathered Friends**

At the **Rocklands Wildlife Station,** about 2km (1¼ miles) outside Anchovy on the road from Montego Bay, St. James (© 876/952-2009), you can have a Jamaican doctor bird perch on your finger to drink syrup, feed small doves and finches millet from your hand, and watch dozens of other birds flying in for their evening meal. Don't take children age 5 and under to this sanctuary, as they tend to bother the birds. Admission is US$10 (£5.20); it's open daily from 9am to 5:30pm.

SEEING THE SIGHTS
TOURS & CRUISES

A **Hilton High Day Tour,** P.O. Box 162, Reading, St. James (© 876/952-3343; www.jamaicahiltontour.com) showcases the rich sociology of plantation life in the Jamaican hinterlands. Beginning at 8am every Tuesday, Wednesday, Friday, and Sunday, an air-conditioned minivan picks up participants at hotels in both Montego Bay and Negril, and returns them to their hotels the same day—at around 3pm to Montego Bay, and at around 4pm to Negril. Breakfast and a buffet lunch of Jamaican food (such as spit-roasted pork and a dozen different Jamaican vegetables) are included. Lunch, during which a local calypso band performs, takes place on the grounds of an 18th-century citrus farm, Hilton Plantation, reminiscent of the Jamaica of long ago.

During the tour, you can see the German-founded village of Seaford Town; the village of St. Leonard's; a local church and a local elementary school where schoolchildren, depending on the day's scheduling, might perform a short choral recital that includes the Jamaican national anthem; a dressmaking studio where simple garments can be made to order for pickup before the end of the day; and a sugar mill. As you reach altitudes above 600m (2,000 ft.), along the edge of Jamaica's scenic cockpit country, the scenery, sightseeing, and botany along the way changes radically from what you'd likely find along the Jamaican coast.

All-inclusive costs are US$64 (£33) per person for participants picked up at hotels in Montego Bay, US$75 (£39) for participants picked up in Negril. Advance reservations are required.

Day and evening cruises are offered aboard the *Calico,* a 17m (56-ft.) gaff-rigged wooden ketch that sails from Margaritaville on the Montego Bay waterfront. An additional vessel, *Calico B,* also carries another 40 passengers. For either cruise, transportation to and from your hotel can be arranged. The daily voyage departs at 10am and returns at 1pm and costs US$40 (£21); snorkeling (with equipment) is available. On the *Calico*'s evening voyage, which goes for US$25 (£13) and is offered daily from 5 to 7pm, cocktails and wine are served as you sail through the sunset. For information and reservations, call **Calico Pirate Cruises** (© 876/940-4465; www.calico piratecruises.com) a few days in advance.

THE GREAT HOUSES

Occupied by plantation owners, each great house of Jamaica was always built on high ground so that it overlooked the plantation itself and was in sight of the next house in the distance. It was the custom for the owners to offer hospitality to travelers crossing the island by road. While these homes are intriguing and beautiful, it's important to remember that they represent the sad legacy of slavery—they were built by slaves, and the lavish lifestyle of the original owners was supported by the profits of slave labor. The two great houses below can be toured in the same day.

Greenwood Great House 🐸   Some people find the 15-room Greenwood even more interesting than Rose Hall (see below), because it's undergone less restoration and has more literary associations. Erected between 1780 and 1800, the Georgian-style building was the residence of Richard Barrett, cousin of poet Elizabeth Barrett Browning. Elizabeth herself never visited Jamaica, but her family was one of the largest landholders here. An absentee planter who lived in England, her father once owned 33,600 hectares (82,992 acres) and some 3,000 slaves. On display is the original library of the Barrett family, with rare books dating from 1697, along with oil paintings of the family, Wedgwood china, rare musical instruments, and a collection of antique furniture.

On Rte. A1, 23km (14 miles) east of Montego Bay. (℃ 876/953-1077. Admission US$12 (£6.25) adults, US$6 (£3.10) children under 12. Daily 9am–6pm.

Rose Hall Great House 🐸   The legendary Rose Hall is the most famous great house on Jamaica. The subject of at least a dozen Gothic novels, it was immortalized in the H. G. de Lisser book, *White Witch of Rose Hall.* The house was built from 1778 to 1790 by John Palmer, a wealthy British planter. At its peak, this was a 2,640-hectare (6,521-acre) plantation, with more than 2,000 slaves. However, it was Annie Palmer, wife of the builder's grandnephew, who became the focal point of fiction and fact. Called "Infamous Annie," she was said to have dabbled in witchcraft. She took slaves as lovers and then killed them off when they bored her. Servants called her "the Obeah woman" (*Obeah* is Jamaican for voodoo). Annie was said to have murdered several of her husbands while they slept and eventually suffered the same fate herself. Long in ruins, the house has now been restored. Annie's Pub is on the ground floor.

Rose Hall Hwy., 15km (9¼ miles) east of Montego Bay. (℃ 888/910-7673. Admission US$20 (£10) adults, US$10 (£5.20) children 12 and under. Daily 9am–6pm. Last tour at 5:15pm.

SHOPPING 🐸🐸

Be prepared for aggressive vendors in Montego Bay, as in all of Jamaica. There's a feverish attempt to peddle goods to tourists, all of whom are viewed as rich. Therefore, prepare yourself for being pursued persistently.

Some so-called "duty-free" prices are lower than stateside prices, until the government hits you with a 10% "general consumption tax" on all purchases. But you can still find good duty-free items here, including Swiss watches, Irish crystal, Italian handbags, Indian silks, and liquors and liqueurs. Appleton's rums are an excellent value. Tia Maria, laced with coffee, and rum-based Rumona are among the best of the traditional liqueurs. Increasingly popular recent introductions to the liquor inventories of Jamaica include Smirnoff Black Ice, a light version of Red Stripe Beer, and delicious (and incredibly fattening) mudslides that are sold as individual servings in short brown bottles. Khus Khus is the most famous of the local perfumes. Jamaican arts and crafts are available in daunting quantities throughout the resorts, from vendors hawking goods on the beaches, and at the Crafts Market (see below).

The main shopping areas are at **Montego Freeport,** within easy walking distance of the pier; **City Centre,** where most of the duty-free shops are, aside from those at the large hotels; and the **Holiday Village Shopping Centre,** located across from the Holiday Inn, on Rose Hall Road, heading from Montego Bay toward Ocho Rios.

Moments **Rum, Reggae & an Escape**

When you want to escape, head for **Time 'n' Place**, just east of Falmouth (© 876/954-4371). On an almost deserted 3km (2-mile) beach sits this funky beach bar, built of driftwood. From Montego Bay, you can spot the sign by the side of the road before you reach Falmouth: IF YOU GOT THE TIME, THEN WE GOT THE PLACE. Sit back in this relaxed, friendly spot and listen to the reggae from the local stations. You can order daiquiris made from fresh local fruit, or stick around for peppery jerk chicken or lobster. Of course, Time 'n' Place isn't completely undiscovered—the fashion editors of *Vogue* occasionally use it as a backdrop for beach fashion shots.

If you have time for only one shopping complex, make it **Old Fort Craft Park,** as its handicrafts are more varied. It's grazing country for both souvenirs and more serious purchases. This shopping complex with 180 vendors (all licensed by the Jamaica Tourist Board) fronts Howard Cooke Boulevard (up from Gloucester Ave. in the heart of Montego Bay, on the site of Fort Montego). You can see wall hangings, handwoven straw items, and wood sculptures. You can even get your hair braided. Be aware that vendors can be very aggressive. If you want something, be prepared to bargain.

At the **Crafts Market,** near Harbour Street in downtown Montego Bay, you can find a good selection of handmade souvenirs of Jamaica, including straw hats and bags, wooden platters, straw baskets, musical instruments, beads, carved objects, and toys. That *jipijapa* (Panama-style) straw hat is important if you're out in the island sun.

One of the most intriguing places for shopping is an upscale mini-mall, **Half Moon Shopping Village,** on the coastal road about 13km (8 miles) east of the commercial center of Montego Bay. It caters to the guests of Half Moon, and the carefully selected merchandise is expensive. A bank, about 25 relatively upscale boutiques, a private hospital, and a private and well-respected prep school named in honor of the long-time manager of Half Moon, Heinz Simonowitz, are on the premises.

The best selection of native art is found at the **Gallery of West Indian Art,** 11 Fairfield Rd. (© 876/952-4547), with a wide selection of paintings not only from Haiti and Jamaica, but Cuba as well, along with Jamaican hand-carved wooden animals and even some painted hand-turned pottery.

MONTEGO BAY AFTER DARK

Nightlife is not guaranteed at Montego Bay's top hotels. In winter, the restaurants and bars of the Ritz-Carlton or Half Moon have the most diverse amusements. After dark it's sleepy at Round Hill and Tryall.

The following clubs attract mainly a crowd in their 20s to their 40s.

The number-one nightspot in MoBay is a two-in-one restaurant, **Marguerite's Seafood by the Sea** and **Margueritaville Sports Bar & Grill,** Gloucester Avenue (p. 377).

Cricket Club, at Rose Hall (© 876/953-2650), is more than just a sports bar; it's where people go to meet and mingle with an international crowd. Televised sports, karaoke singalongs, tournament darts, and backgammon are all part of the fun. It's open daily from 10pm to 2am; there's no cover.

The Brewery, Gloucester Avenue (© **876/940-2433**), is one of the city's most popular nightlife hangouts. It's a cross between an English pub and a Jamaican jerk-pork pit, but everyone is into Red Stripe and reggae. There's a woodsy looking bar, lots of neomedieval memorabilia, and a covered veranda in back overlooking busy Gloucester Avenue.

3 Negril (★(★(★

This once-sleepy village is now a tourist mecca, with visitors drawn to its beaches along three well-protected bays: Long Bay, Bloody Bay (aka Negril Harbour), and Orange Bay.

There are really two Negrils: The West End is the site of many little local restaurants and funky cottages that still take in visitors. This is the area to head to if you want to recapture some of the charm and freewheeling spirit first publicized here in the '60s, but don't expect a lot of creature comforts here. The other Negril is on the east end, the first area you approach on the road from Montego Bay. Here are the upscale hotels and some of the most gorgeous beachfronts. Come here if you want to experience Negril from the confines of a luxury resort, particularly an all-inclusive.

Negril became famous in the late 1960s, when it attracted American and Canadian hippies, who liked the idea of a place with no phones and no electricity; they rented modest digs on the West End where the local people extended their hospitality. But those days are long gone, and a strip of sophisticated hotels and all-inclusive resorts has sprouted along the sands of famous **Seven Mile Beach.**

Situated on the western tip of the island, Negril is 80km (50 miles) and about a 2-hour drive from Montego Bay's airport, along a winding road and past ruins of sugar estates and great houses.

ESSENTIALS

GETTING THERE   If you're going to Negril, you will fly into **Donald Sangster Airport** in Montego Bay. Some hotels, particularly the all-inclusive resorts, will arrange for airport transfers from that point. Be sure to ask when you book.

If your hotel doesn't provide transfers, you can fly to Negril's small airport, **International Air Link** (© **876/957-5924** in Negril, or 876/940-6660 in Montego Bay). The air fare for these scheduled charter flights—three passengers or more—can range from as low as US$60 (£31) to as high as US$95 (£49) per person, depending on the flight.

The ¼-hour **bus trip** costs US$21 (£11). We recommend **Tour Wise** (© **876/952-4943** or 876/952-0019 in Montego Bay, or 876/974-2323 in Ocho Rios). The bus will drop you off at your final destination once you reach Negril.

MEDICAL SERVICES   For a non-life-threatening emergency, try the **Negril Beach Medical Center,** Plaza Negril (© **876/957-4888**). **Negril Pharmacy,** Shop no. 14, in the Coral Seas Plaza (© **876/957-4076**), is open Monday to Saturday 9am to 7pm, and Sunday 10am to 4pm.

ACCOMMODATIONS
VERY EXPENSIVE

The Caves ⊛   Although the nearest beach is a 12-minute ride away, Negril's most atmospheric and elegant small inn still attracts international celebrities. In spite of its fame, however, there are drawbacks. There's a sense of snobbishness at this member of

Negril

ACCOMMODATIONS ■
The Caves **16**
Charela Inn **10**
Couples Negril **2**
Couples Swept Away Negril **5**
Country Country **9**
Hedonism II **3**
Negril Inn **11**
Rockhouse **14**
Sandals Negril Beach Resort & Spa **1**
Sunset at the Palms Resort & Spa **1**
Tensing Pen **17**

DINING ◆
Chicken Lavish **13**
Cosmo's Seafood Restaurant & Bar **6**
Da Gino's **12**
Margueritaville **8**
Norma's on the Beach at Seasplash **7**
Rick's Café **15**
Rockhouse Restaurant **14**

⊕ Airport
↖ Beach
ⓘ Information
⊠ Post Office

JAMAICA

Negril

Kingston

To Montego Bay

Bloody Bay

Booby Cay

Hedonism II Beach

Negril Airport

THE GREAT MORASS

A1

PARISH OF HANNOVER
PARISH OF WESTMORELAND

Long Bay

SEVEN MILE BEACH

Norman Manley Blvd.

Caribbean Sea

South Negril River

Crafts Market

Negril Yacht Club

Police Station

Plaza de Negril

Jamaica Tourist Board

Sheffield Rd.

Whitehall Rd.

WHITE HALL

West End Rd.

WEST END

0   1 mi
0   1 km

Chris Blackwell's Island Outpost hotels, generally the finest in the Caribbean, and the prices are very high compared to the competition. The hotel is on 1 hectare (2½ acres) of land that's perched above a honeycombed network of cliffs, 10km (33 ft.) above the surf on a point near Negril's lighthouse, close to Jamaica's westernmost tip. The setting, though lavishly publicized, is difficult to negotiate with its stairwells and catwalks.

Accommodations, well suited for groups of friends traveling together, are in breezy units within five cement and wood-sided cottages, each with a thatched roof and sturdy furniture. Matisse could have designed them. None has air-conditioning, and the windows are without screens. A TV and VCR can be brought in if you request them. Many of the units contain alfresco showers.

Sumptuous meals are prepared only for guests and are included, along with domestic Jamaican drinks from the bar, as part of the all-inclusive price.

P.O. Box 3113, Lighthouse Station, Negril, Jamaica, W.I. (✆ 800/688-7678 in the U.S. and Canada, or 876/957-0270. Fax 876/957-4930. www.islandoutpost.com. 10 units. Winter US$765–US$800 (£398–£416) double, US$1,265–US$1,444 (£658–£751) suite; off season US$515–US$535 (£268–£278). Rates include all meals and self-service bar. AE, MC, V. No children under 16 allowed. **Amenities:** 2 restaurants; bar; outdoor saltwater pool; spa; Jacuzzi; sauna; snorkeling; bikes; airport transfers; laundry service; nonsmoking rooms. *In room:* Ceiling fan, TV, minibar, beverage maker, hair dryer, safe, Wi-Fi.

EXPENSIVE

Couples Negril ⚘　If you're a loving male-female couple, you're welcomed at this romantic resort, lying on 300m (1,000 ft.) of white-sand beach, fronting Bloody Bay, 8km (5 miles) from the center of Negril. The formula worked in Ocho Rios (see later in this chapter), so it was repeated here. A rival of Sandals properties, this love nest is the site of many weddings and honeymoons. On 7 hectares (17 acres) facing crescent-shaped Negril Harbour, this resort caters to those who want back-to-back scheduled activities, ranging from tennis tournaments to fashion shows. Each good-size unit has a king-size bed and a CD player (bring your own tunes), plus a balcony or patio with a view of the bay or of the lush gardens. Furnishings, though standard, are comfortable, and everything is modern, including the tub/shower combo bathrooms. The best doubles are the deluxe beachfront suites, which have Jacuzzis and hammocks. No building in the complex is higher than the tallest coconut tree. On the east side of the property, nude sunbathing is permitted.

The food is good at all three restaurants here. Especially worth mentioning is Otaheite, which serves a Caribbean fusion cuisine. Mediterranean and Continental menus are also served. A resident band plays nightly and there's special entertainment planned throughout the week, including Caribbean dinner buffets with music.

Bloody Bay, Negril, Jamaica, W.I. (✆ 800/268-7537 in the U.S., or 876/957-5960. Fax 876/957-5858. www.couples. com. 234 units. Rates are per couple: winter US$699–US$806 (£363–£419) double, US$871–US$972 (£453–£505) suite for 2; off season US$578–US$669 (£300–£348) double, US$749–US$838 (£389–£436) suite for 2. Rates include all meals, drinks, and activities. AE, MC, V. No children under 18 allowed. **Amenities:** 3 restaurants; 4 bars (1 swim-up); 2 outdoor pools; golf; 14 tennis courts; fitness room; aerobics; basketball court; dive shop; glass-bottom boat trips; Sunfish sailing; game room; tour desk; limited room service; laundry service. *In room:* A/C, ceiling fan, TV, mini-bar (in some), beverage maker, hair dryer, iron, safe.

Couples Swept Away Negril ⚘⚘　This is one of the best beachside hotels in Negril—conscious of both sports and relaxation. All-inclusive, it caters to those eager for an ambience of all possible diversions available but absolutely no organized schedule and no pressure to participate if you just want to relax. Unlike the Couples above, this resort allows same-sex couples. As a staff member told us (privately, of course),

---

Fun Fact **The Naked Truth**

Nude bathing is allowed at a number of hotels, clubs, and beaches (especially in Negril), but only where there are signs stating SWIMSUITS OPTIONAL. Elsewhere, the law prohibits even topless sunbathing.

"We get the health-and-fitness nuts, and Sandals or Hedonism get the sex crazed." The resort occupies 8 flat and sandy hectares (20 acres), which straddle both sides of the highway leading in from Montego Bay.

The accommodations (the hotel calls them "veranda suites" because of their large balconies) are in 26 two-story villas clustered together and accented with flowering shrubs and vines, a few steps from Seven Mile Beach. Each lovely, airy, and spacious unit has a ceiling fan, a king-size bed, and (unless the vegetation obscures it) sea views. Wooden shutters let sunlight and breezes in. Units contain showers only.

The cuisine here is more health conscious and of better quality than that served at Sandals and Hedonism II. The resort's social center is its international restaurant, Feathers, which lies inland, across the road from the sea. There's also an informal beachfront restaurant and bar, plus a veggie bar serving fresh fruit, juices, pita sandwiches, salads, and vegetarian dishes.

Norman Manley Blvd. (P.O. Box 3077), Negril, Jamaica, W.I. (*C*) **800/268-7537** in the U.S. and Canada, or 876/957-4061. Fax 876/957-4060. www.couples.com. 212 units. Winter US$711–US$918 (£370–£477) double suite; off season US$565–US$820 (£294–£426) double suite. Rates are all-inclusive. Ask about spa packages. AE, MC, V. No children under 18 allowed. **Amenities:** 3 restaurants; 4 bars; 2 outdoor pools; 10 tennis courts; health club; racquetball; squash; spa; 2 Jacuzzis; sauna; glass-bottom boat trips; sailing; scuba diving; sea kayaks; snorkeling; water-skiing; windsurfing; bikes; tour desk; airport transfers; room service (breakfast only); laundry service. *In room:* A/C, ceiling fan, beverage maker, hair dryer, safe.

Hedonism II (*★*)   Devoted to the pursuit of sophomoric pleasure, and with less class than Couples Negril, Hedonism II packs the works into a one-package deal, including all the drinks and partying anyone could want. The complex lies at the northern end of Negril Beach. Of all the members of the SuperClubs chain, this is the most raucous. It's a meat market, deliberately inviting its mainly single guests to go wild for a week.

The rooms are stacked in dull two-story clusters dotted around a sloping 9-hectare (22-acre) site about 3km (2 miles) east of the town center. This is not a couples-only resort; singles are both accepted and encouraged. The hotel will find you a roommate if you'd like to book on the double-occupancy rate. Accommodations don't have balconies but are very spacious. Each has a king-size or twin beds, fitted with fine linen, with mirrors hanging over the beds. Each bathroom has a tub/shower combination.

On one section of this resort's beach, clothing is optional. It's called the "Nude" section; the other is known as the "Prude." The resort also has a secluded beach on nearby Booby Cay, where guests are taken twice a week for picnics.

There's nightly entertainment, along with a live band, a high-energy dance club, and a piano bar. International cuisine, a bit bland, is served in daily buffets. There's also a clothing-optional bar, a "prude" bar, and a grill.

Negril Beach Rd. (P.O. Box 25), Negril, Jamaica, W.I. (*C*) **800/859-7873** in the U.S., or 876/957-5070. Fax 876/957-5214. www.superclubs.com. 280 units. Winter US$500–US$589 (£260–£306) double; off season US$400–US$511 (£208–£266) double. Rates include all meals, drinks, and activities. AE, DC, DISC, MC, V. Children under 18 not accepted. **Amenities:** 4 restaurants; 5 bars (1 swim-up); 2 outdoor pools; 6 tennis courts; 2 indoor squash courts; fitness center; spa; glass-bottom Jacuzzi; sauna; aerobics; badminton; basketball court; rock climbing; trapeze; volleyball; dive shop; glass-bottom boat rides; kayaking; sailing; scuba diving; snorkeling; water-skiing; windsurfing; airport transfers; Internet cafe; massage; dance club; nonsmoking rooms; 1 room for those w/limited mobility. *In room:* A/C, TV, beverage maker, hair dryer, iron.

Sandals Negril Beach Resort & Spa 🏵

On 5 hectares (12 acres) of prime beach-front land a short drive east of the center of Negril, Sandals Negril is an all-inclusive, couples-only (straight and gay) resort that attracts a basically young, convivial, and unsophisticated audience. It's far more active and freewheeling than the more formal Sandals properties in Ocho Rios and Montego Bay. The casual, well-furnished rooms have a tropical motif, and come in a wide range of styles, but are generally spacious, each with a marble bathroom with a tub/shower combination. The best units open directly on the beach. Honeymooners usually end up in a Jamaican-built four-poster mahogany bed. For a balcony and sea view, you have to pay the top rates.

Rates include all meals; snacks; unlimited drinks, day and night, at one of four bars (including two swim-up pool bars); and nightly entertainment, including theme parties. Coconut Cove is the main dining room, but you can also eat at one of the specialty rooms. The Sundowner offers white-glove service and Jamaican cuisine, and low-calorie health food is served beside the beach. Kimono features Japanese cuisine. In the typical Sandals style, the food is rather standard, but there is great variety and no one goes hungry.

Norman Manley Blvd., Negril, Jamaica, W.I. © **800/726-3257** in the U.S. and Canada, or 876/957-5216. Fax 876/957-5338. www.sandals.com. 223 units. 2-night minimum stay. Winter US$370–US$480 (£192–£250) double, US$500–US$950 (£260–£494) suite; off season US$350–US$460 (£182–£239) double, US$465–US$950 (£242–£494) suite. Rates include all meals, drinks, and activities. AE, DISC, MC, V. No children under 16 allowed. **Amenities:** 6 restaurants; 5 bars (2 swim-up); 2 outdoor pools; 2 whirlpools; 4 tennis courts; fitness center; spa; sauna; aerobics; basketball; racquetball; shuffleboard; table tennis; volleyball; canoeing; kayaking; scuba diving; snorkeling; Sunfish sailboats; windsurfing; airport transfers; room service; massage; coin-operated laundry; dry cleaning; nonsmoking rooms. *In room:* A/C, TV, minibar (in some), beverage maker, hair dryer, iron, safe.

Sunset at the Palms Resort & Spa *Value* *Kids*

This place appeals to eco-travelers who want to get away from it all without spending a fortune; it's an especially good choice for families with kids. The wooden cabins (which have been featured in *Architectural Digest*) are in a forest, across the road from a beach called Bloody Bay. The 4 hectares (10 acres) of gardens are planted with royal palms, bull thatch, and a rare variety of mango tree.

The simple but stylish cabins are small timber cottages, none more than two stories high, rising on stilts. Each offers two spacious and comfortable bedrooms, plus a balcony and shower-only bathroom. Units were upgraded and improved in 2006, and all are brightened with vibrant Jamaican fabrics. The best are rented as "executive suites," with a sunken living and dining area, plus a pull-out queen-size sofa bed for small families. Simple but tasty Jamaican and international dishes are served.

Norman Manley Blvd. (P.O. Box 118), Negril, Jamaica, W.I. © **800/234-1707** in the U.S., or 876/957-5350. Fax 876/957-5381. www.sunsetatthepalms.com. 85 units. Winter US$475 (£247) double, US$650 (£338) suite; off season US$325 (£169) double, US$500 (£260) suite. Rates are all-inclusive. Children under 2 stay free in parent's room; children 2–12 US$75 (£39) extra. AE, MC, V. **Amenities:** 2 restaurants; 3 bars; outdoor pool; tennis court; fitness center; spa services; Jacuzzi; scuba diving; snorkeling; bike rental; car rental; room service; laundry service. *In room:* A/C, TV, beverage maker, hair dryer, iron (in executive suites).

MODERATE

Charela Inn ⚜   Simplicity, a sense of calm, a well-managed restaurant, and good value are the hallmarks of this seafront inn reminiscent of a Spanish hacienda. The inn sits on the main beach strip on 1 hectare (2½ acres) of landscaped grounds. The building's inner courtyard, with a tropical garden and a round, freshwater pool, opens onto one of the widest (75m/250 ft.) sandy beaches in Negril. Try for one of the 20 or so rooms with a view of the sea. Accommodations are generally spacious, often with a bit of Jamaican character with their wicker furnishings and ceiling fans. All have private patios or balconies. Most of the good-size bathrooms have tub/shower combinations, but some have showers only.

Le Vendôme, facing the sea and the garden, offers both an a la carte menu and a five-course fixed-price meal that changes daily. Several times a week in winter, the hotel offers some form of live entertainment.

Norman Manley Blvd. (P.O. Box 33), Negril, Jamaica, W.I. ⓒ 876/957-4277. Fax 876/957-4414. www.charela.com. 49 units. Winter US$166–US$221 (£86–£115) double; off season US$114–US$155 (£59–£81) double. MAP (breakfast and dinner) US$40 (£21) per person extra. 5-night minimum stay in winter. AE, MC, V. **Amenities:** Restaurant; bar; outdoor pool; kayaks; Sunfish sailboats; windsurfing; room service; laundry service; nonsmoking rooms; rooms for those w/limited mobility. *In room:* A/C, ceiling fan, TV, dataport, beverage maker, hair dryer.

Tensing Pen ⚜⚜ *Finds*   Our favorite nest in Negril lies on the western tip and has grown and evolved since its hippie era in the early 1970s. On a cliff, a 10-minute stroll from the landmark lighthouse, it is 6km (3¾ miles) south of the center of Negril. Hidden away from the world, the place is a little gem. Those aggressive beach vendors will never find you here, tucked behind a high wall. On 1 hectare (2½ acres) of grounds, you're surrounded by tropical planting. Laze in the hammocks or sunbathe on the terraces hewn out of rock. Sleep in a rustic stone cottage covered in thatch in a four-poster draped in mosquito netting, plantation house-style. Local tiles, tropical woods, bamboo rockers, ceiling fans, and louvered windows set the tone. Bathrooms with tub/shower combinations are a bit cramped. There's a communal kitchen where guests sometimes cook for each other. The only minor downfalls here are that the nearest beach is a 10- to 15-minute drive or a 30-minute walk and the staff tends to be disorganized.

Lighthouse Rd. (P.O. Box 3030), Negril, Jamaica, W.I. ⓒ 800/957-0387 in the U.S., or 876/957-0387. Fax 876/957-0161. www.tensingpen.com. 15 units. Winter US$170–US$539 (£88–£280) double; off season US$108–US$367 (£56–£191) double. Rates include breakfast. AE, MC, V. **Amenities:** Restaurant (dinner only); babysitting; laundry service; rooms for those w/limited mobility; communal kitchen. *In room:* A/C (in some), fridge, no phone.

INEXPENSIVE

Another low-budget option for lodging is found at Da Gino's (see "Dining," below).

Country Country ⚜   The owners of this intimate hotel were determined to outclass their competitors, so they turned to celebrity architect Ann Hodges, the creative force behind the gorgeous decor in many of the much more expensive Island Outpost properties. A narrow meandering path stretches from the coastal boulevard to the white-sand beach, where watersports await. Along the way is a collection of neo-Creole, clapboard-sided buildings that drip with elaborate gingerbread and cove moldings, each inspired by an idealized vision of vernacular Jamaican colonial architecture. The buildings are painted in a variety of peacock hues, highlighting their architectural features. Inside, concrete floors keep the spacious interiors cool. Each unit has a vaguely Victorian feel, with comfortable furnishings, plus a shower-only bathroom. There's a beachfront bar and grill.

Norman Manley Blvd. (P.O. Box 39), Negril, Jamaica, W.I. © **888/790-5264** in the U.S., or 876/957-4273. Fax 876/957-4342. www.countryjamaica.com. 17 units. Winter US$160–US$180 (£83–£94) double; off season US$125–US$140 (£65–£73) double. Rates include breakfast. AE, MC, V. **Amenities:** Restaurant; bar; limited room service; laundry service; nonsmoking rooms. *In room:* A/C, TV, fridge, beverage maker, hair dryer, safe.

Negril Inn 🐟   About 5km (3 miles) east of the town center in the heart of the Seven Mile Beach stretch, this is one of the smallest and most reasonably priced all-inclusive resorts in Negril. Because of its size, it's very low-key. The resort, not confined to couples only, offers very simple but comfortably furnished guest rooms with private balconies, in a series of two-story structures in a garden setting. Each unit has a small tiled bathroom with a tub/shower combination.

Included in the package are all meals, all alcoholic drinks (except champagne), and nightly entertainment. The restaurant is rather good.

Norman Manley Blvd. (P.O. Box 59), Negril, Jamaica, W.I. © **876/957-4209.** Fax 876/957-4365. www.negrilinn.com. 46 units. Winter US$180 (£94) double; US$225 (£117) triple. Off-season US$150 (£78) double, US$200 (£104) triple. Rates are all-inclusive. AE, MC, V. **Amenities:** Restaurant; bar; outdoor pool; 2 tennis courts; fitness center; Jacuzzi; room service. *In room:* A/C, hair dryer, iron, no phone.

Rockhouse 🐟   This funky boutique inn stands in stark contrast to hedonistic all-inclusive resorts like Sandals, and it offers very affordable rates. It's a cross between a South Seas island retreat and an African village, with thatched roofs capping stone-and-pine huts. A team of enterprising young Aussies restored and expanded this place, which was one of Negril's first hotels (the Rolling Stones hung out here in the 1970s). The rooms have ceiling fans, four-poster beds draped in mosquito netting, and open-air showers. All units contain queen-size beds, and four cottages have sleeping lofts with extra queen-size beds. Less than half a kilometer (¼ mile) from the beach, Rockhouse has a ladder down to a cove where you can swim and snorkel. After a refreshing dip in the cliff-side pool, you can dine in the open-sided restaurant pavilion serving excellent, spicy local fare three times a day.

West End Rd. (P.O. Box 3024), Negril, Jamaica, W.I. © **876/957-4373.** Fax 876/957-0557. www.rockhousehotel.com. 34 units. Winter US$150 (£78) studio, US$295 (£153) villa; off season US$125 (£65) studio, US$225 (£117) villa. No children under 12 allowed. AE, MC, V. **Amenities:** Restaurant; 2 bars; outdoor pool; sea kayaks; snorkeling; nonsmoking rooms. *In room:* A/C, minibar, hair dryer, safe.

DINING
EXPENSIVE
Norma's on the Beach at Seasplash 🐟🐟 INTERNATIONAL/JAMAICAN
The very durable matriarch, Norma Shirley, is hailed as the finest chef in Jamaica. Although it's unlikely that she'll appear on the premises at the time of your arrival, the chefs use her recipes for their inspiration—a cookery characterized by such regional products as callaloo (a spinachlike vegetable), papaya, and corn-fed free-range chicken. To reach the place, you have to proceed down a long, jungle-landscaped pathway from the parking lot (near the sea-hugging boulevard), through the gardens of the Sea Splash resort, to a pair of lattice-ringed wooden decks and pavilions beside a stretch of Seven Mile Beach. Pick your preferred dining venue—there are at least two, one of which lies at the top of a flight of wooden stairs. The menu is seasonally adjusted, with items that might include jerk pork or jerk chicken, stuffed chicken breasts, coconut chicken, Old Harbour (that is, spicy) shrimp, quesadillas, smoked marlin, and penne pasta dotted with jerk chicken. Lunches are invariably simpler, with burgers, coconut shrimp, fish burgers, and tuna melts.

In the Sea Splash Resort, Norman Manley Blvd. © **876/957-4041**. Reservations recommended. Breakfast US$4–US$8 (£2–£4.15); lunch main courses US$6–US$26 (£3.10–£14); dinner main courses US$13–US$26 (£6.75–£14). AE, DC, MC, V. Daily 7:30am–10:30pm.

Rick's Café ☆ SEAFOOD/STEAKS

At sundown, everybody in Negril heads toward the lighthouse along the West End strip to Rick's Café, whether they want a meal or not. Of course, the name was inspired by the old watering hole of Bogie's *Casablanca*. There was a real Rick (Richard Hershman), who first opened this bar back in 1974, but he's long gone. This laid-back cafe was made famous in the '70s as a hippie hangout, and ever since it's attracted the bronzed and the beautiful (and some who want to be). Management claims the sunset here is the most glorious in Negril, and after a few fresh-fruit daiquiris, you'll agree with them. (Actually, the sunset is just as spectacular at any of the waterfront hangouts in Negril, if nothing is blocking the view.) Casual dress is the order of the day, and the background music comprises reggae and rock. If you want dinner, you can order imported steaks along with a complete menu of blackened dishes, Cajun style. The fish (red snapper, fresh lobster, or grouper) is always fresh. The food is rather standard, and expensive for what you get, but that doesn't keep the touristy crowds away from the sunset party. You can also buy plastic bar tokens at the door, which you can use instead of money, a la Club Med. A bit tacky, we'd say. Bogie would never have tolerated this.

West End Rd. © **876/957-0380**. www.rickscafejamaica.com. Reservations accepted for parties of 6 or more. Main courses US$14–US$22 (£7.30–£12). AE, MC, V. Daily noon–10:30pm for food, till 2am for drinks.

Rockhouse Restaurant ☆ INTERNATIONAL

This is a gorgeous setting for enjoying some of the best food in Negril. Set on the premises of the previously recommended Rockhouse, it was developed by a team of Australian and Italian entrepreneurs who designed a bridgelike span, equivalent to a railway trestle, high above the surging tides of a rocky inlet on Negril's West End. You may get a touch of vertigo if you lean over the railing. This place attracts a hip international crowd. Enjoy a drink or two at the bar, which is built with glossy tropical hardwoods and coral stone, before your meal. Menu items, which are always supplemented with daily specials, might include a seasonal platter of smoked marlin or an upscale version of Jamaican peppered pork with yams.

In the Rockhouse, West End Rd. © **876/957-4373**. Reservations required for dinner in high season. Main courses US$9–US$23 (£4.70–£12). AE, MC, V. Daily 7am–10:30pm.

MODERATE

Da Gino's ITALIAN

Four octagonal, open-sided dining pavilions, separated from Negril's beachfront by a strip of trees, evolved as the escapist dream of Gino Travaini, the Italy-born owner. Pastas and bread are made fresh daily. The best chef's specialties feature linguine with lobster, filet of beef with peppercorns, various forms of scaloppini, and huge platters of grilled seafood.

On the premises are a dozen very simple huts, each octagonal, rustic, and camplike, that rent for between US$60 (£31) and US$120 (£62) each, double occupancy, depending on the season. Each has a TV, a very basic kitchenette, and a ceiling fan, but no air-conditioning.

In the Hotel Mariposa Hideaway, Norman Manley Blvd. © **876/957-4918**. Reservations recommended. Main courses US$10–US$28 (£5.20–£15). MC, V. Daily 7am–11pm.

Margueritaville AMERICAN/INTERNATIONAL   It's practically Disney gone Jamaican at this rowdy bar, restaurant, and entertainment complex. Thanks to the loaded buses that pull in for a field trip from some of Negril's all-inclusive hotels, it's a destination in its own right. People party here all day and night. There's an on-site art gallery where most of the works are by the very talented U.S.-born artist Geraldine Robbins, and at the gift shops you might actually be tempted to buy something. Every evening, beginning around 9pm, there's live music or perhaps karaoke. Permanently moored a few feet offshore is a pair of Jamaica's largest trampolines, whale-size floaters that feature high-jumping contests by any participant whose cocktails haven't affected them yet. Rock climbing is also available. Drinks are deceptively potent. In all this party atmosphere, you don't expect the food to be that good, but it might happily surprise, even though it consists of such fare as shrimp-and-tuna kabobs. You'll find Southern fried chicken, along with the standard club steaks and burgers.

Norman Manley Blvd. ℭ 876/957-4467. Burgers and sandwiches US$9–US$11 (£4.70–£5.70); main courses US$13–US$25 (£6.75–£13). MC, V. Daily 9am–10:30pm.

INEXPENSIVE

Chicken Lavish ⊛ *Finds* JAMAICAN   We've found that Chicken Lavish, whose name we love, is the best of the low-budget eateries. Just show up on the doorstep of this place along the West End beach strip, and see what's cooking. Curried goat is a specialty, as is fresh fried fish. The red snapper is caught in local waters. But the big draw is the restaurant's namesake, the chef's special Jamaican chicken. It's amazingly consistent, fried or served with curry or sweet-and-sour sauce. The chef will tell you, and you may agree, that it's the best on the island. Ironically, this utterly unpretentious restaurant has achieved something like cult status among counterculture travelers who have eaten here since the 1970s. You can dine on the roofed veranda or ask for takeout.

West End Rd. ℭ 876/957-4410. Main courses US$4–US$20 (£2–£10). AE, MC, V. Daily 10am–11pm.

Cosmo's Seafood Restaurant & Bar ⊛ *Finds* SEAFOOD/JAMAICAN   One of the best places to go for local seafood enters on a Polynesian thatched *bohio* (beach hut) open to the sea and bordering the main beachfront. In this rustic setting, Cosmo Brown entertains locals and visitors. You can order his famous conch soup, or conch in a number of other ways, including steamed or curried. He's also known for his savory kettle of curried goat, or you might prefer freshly caught seafood or fish, depending on what the catch turned up. Unless you order shellfish, most dishes are rather inexpensive.

Norman Manley Blvd. ℭ 876/957-4784. Main courses US$8–US$18 (£4.15–£9.35). MC, V. Daily 9am–10pm.

FUN ON & OFF THE BEACH

BEACHES   Beloved by the hippies of the 1960s, **Seven Mile Beach** ⊛⊛ is still going strong, but it's no longer the idyllic retreat it once was. Resorts attracting an international crowd now line this beach. Nudity, however, is just as prevalent as it's always been, especially along the stretch near Cosmo's. There's a carefree, laid-back vibe. On the western tip of the island, the white powdery sand stretches from Bloody Bay in Hanover to Negril Lighthouse in Westmoreland; clean, tranquil aquamarine waters, coral reefs, and a backdrop of palm trees add to the appeal. When you tire of the beach, you'll find all sorts of resorts, clubs, beach bars, open-air restaurants, and the like. Vendors will try to sell you everything from Red Stripe beer to ganja. Many of the big resorts have nude beaches as well. The hottest and most exotic is found at **Hedonism II,** although **Grand Lido** next door draws its fair share. Nude beaches at each of these resorts are in separate and "private" areas of the resort property. Total nudity is required for strolling the beach, and security guards keep peeping Toms at bay. Photography is not permitted. Most of the resorts also have nude bars, nude hot tubs, and nude swimming pools.

GOLF   Negril Hills Golf Club, Sheffield Road (© **876/957-4638;** www.negrilhills golfclub.com), is Negril's only golf course. It may not have the cachet of such Montego Bay courses as Tryall, but it's the only golf course in western Jamaica. Greens fees for this 18-hole, par-72 course are US$58 (£30), and club rental is US$18 (£9.36). Carts and caddies, which are not obligatory, cost US$35 (£18) and US$14 (£7.30), respectively. Anyone can play, but advance reservations are recommended before 7am.

HORSEBACK RIDING   Horseback riding, heretofore confined to the north shore, has come to Negril. For a close encounter with the natural beauty of this part of Jamaica, head for **Rhodes Hall Plantation,** signposted at the eastern edge of the resort (© **876/957-6883;** www.rhodesresort.com). It gives guided 2-hour excursions across the most scenic beauty spots on the outskirts of Negril. Along the way you'll pass some of the richest vegetation in the Caribbean, including breadfruit, guava, and even wild tobacco plants. Costs average US$60 (£31) per rider. There is a free pick-up service.

WATERSPORTS   Watersports equipment is easily available at any of at least seven associated kiosks that operate at strategic intervals along the sands of Seven Mile Beach. The best area for **snorkeling** is off the cliffs in the West End. The coral reef here is extremely lively, with marine life visible at a depth of about 3 to 5m (10–15 ft.). The waters are so clear and sparkling that just by wading in and looking down, you can see lots of marine life. The fish are small but extremely colorful.

Negril has the best and most challenging **scuba diving** in Jamaica. Unusual dive sites within an easy boat ride of Negril include **Shallow Plane,** the site of a Cessna aircraft that crashed in 15m (50 ft.) of water, and which is a diving attraction today; an underwater cave, **Throne Room,** which allows divers to enter at one end and ascend into the open air at the other; and two separate sites, each about 20m (65 ft.) underwater, known as **Shark's Reef** and **Snapper Drop.** Each of these is loaded with flora and fauna whose species change as the elevations change.

Negril Scuba Centre, in the Negril Beach Club Hotel, Norman Manley Boulevard (© **800/818-2963** in the U.S., or 876/957-9641), is the most modern, best-equipped scuba facility in Negril. A professional staff of internationally certified scuba instructors and dive masters teach and guide divers through Negril's colorful coral reefs. Beginners' dive lessons are offered daily, as well as multiple-dive packages for certified divers. Full scuba certifications and specialty courses are also available.

A resort course, designed for first-time divers with basic swimming abilities, costs US$75 (£39) and includes all instruction and equipment, a lecture on water and diving safety, and one open-water dive. A one-tank dive costs US$30 (£16) plus US$6 (£3.10) for equipment rental (not necessary if divers bring their own gear). More economical is a two-tank dive, which must be completed in 1 day. It costs US$55 (£29), plus the (optional) US$6 (£3.10) rental of all equipment. This organization is PADI-registered, although it accepts all recognized certification cards.

NEGRIL AFTER DARK 𝒢

Negril is not without nightspots, though you're likely to spend most evenings enjoying the entertainment in your own resort. Fun places are easy to find, as nearly *everything* is on Norman Manley Boulevard, the only major road in Negril.

See "Dining," above, for details on **Rick's Café** and **Margueritaville. The Jungle,** in Mariner's Negril Beach Club (© **876/957-4005;** www.junglenegril.com), is the most crowded, horny, exuberant, and famous dance club in Negril, with a penchant for attracting sports and music-industry celebrities. (Even trash-TV king Jerry Springer did a turn here.) Its slogan? "Unleash the Animal." The scene gets so mobbed during spring break that movie crews have actually flown in from the United States to film it. Most of the perspiration here is spilled on the ground level, where four bars and dance floors rock and roll with music that varies according to the night's individual theme. Head for the upper level for the much-needed "cool-downs" that, at least here, have developed into a laid-back art form all its own. Red Stripe and rum punches are the drinks of choice for a crowd that really seems to enjoy their estrogen and testosterone highs. Fortunately, security here at least appears to be tight, with a prominent sign in front that declares, "no prostitutes or gigolos, no drugs, no soliciting, no misconduct" and a forbidding-looking bar that locks the place up tighter than a jail during off-hours. The cover charge is US$9 (£4.70) for men (referred to on signs at the entrance as "Tarzans") and US$7 (£3.65) for women (referred to as "Janes"). The Jungle Arcade is a gaming room with around 100 slot machines. The club is open Wednesday to Saturday 8:30pm until the last patron staggers back to his or her hotel.

Alfred's Ocean Palace, Norman Manley Blvd. (© **876/957-4735;** www.alfreds. com), draws mainly locals but visitors are welcome; there's lots of intermingling. Set directly on the beach, it attracts primarily a young party crowd, but if you're 80, you'll still be warmly embraced, with your cold Red Stripe beer waiting. There's no cover, and in addition to grabbing a drink, you can order a bite to eat until midnight. Particularly interesting is the beach-party area, with a stage for live reggae and jazz acts. You can also boogie on the dance floor inside, shaking to hits you'll hear at clubs stateside.

Risky Business, Norman Manley Boulevard (© **876/957-3008;** www.riskybusinesses. com), sits a few feet from the waves. It can be sleepy or manic, depending on the music. In season, you can order burgers and sandwiches, and the Red Stripe is cheap all year round. It's mostly a young hangout with parties Monday, Thursday, and Saturday beginning at 9pm. There's no cover.

Mary's Bay Boat Bar & Grill, West End Road (© **876/454-2284**), the brainchild of a U.S. ex-pat, William H. Miller, lies just before Mi Yard Music Bar & the Love Boat, about a 10-minute walk west from the center of Negril. This popular bar opens onto a panoramic sweep of Negril's Seven Mile Beach. It offers a wide selection of drinks and serves an array of hot tasty Jamaican dishes. Live reggae music is presented on Tuesday night after 9pm. The bar is also a magnet during the day with showers and lockers, chaise longues, and an Internet cafe. Boat charter services—featuring fishing, snorkeling, and sunset cruises—also operate out of here.

4 Ocho Rios 𝒢

This north-coast resort is a 2-hour drive east of Montego Bay or west of Port Antonio. Ocho Rios was once a small banana and fishing port, but tourism became the leading industry long ago. Short on charm, it's now Jamaica's cruise-ship capital. The bay is dominated on one side by a bauxite-loading terminal and on the other by a range of hotels with sandy beaches fringed by palm trees.

Ocho Rios and neighboring Port Antonio have long been associated with Sir Noël Coward (who invited the world to his doorstep) and Ian Fleming, creator of James Bond. (See below for details about their homes here.)

Frankly, unless you're a cruise passenger, you may want to stay away from the major attractions when a ship is in port. The duty-free markets are overrun then, and the hustlers become more strident in pushing their crafts and junk souvenirs. Dunn's River Falls becomes almost impossible to visit at those times.

However, Ocho Rios has its own unique flavor and offers the usual range of sports, including a major fishing tournament every fall, in addition to a wide variety of accommodations.

In our view, you go to overrun Ocho Rios only if you want to stay put at one of the resorts here: It is home to some of the leading inns of the Caribbean as well as two stellar Sandals properties. When in the area, we prefer to stay away from the center of Ocho Rios itself, perhaps at a resort in Runaway Bay or something really special like Ian Fleming's Goldeneye.

ESSENTIALS

GETTING THERE   If you're going to Ocho Rios, you fly into the **Sangster Airport** in Montego Bay. Some hotels, particularly the larger resorts, will arrange for airport transfers from that point. Be sure to ask when you book.

By taxi, a typical one-way fare from Montego Bay to Ocho Rios is between US$88 to US$99 (£46–£52). Always negotiate and agree on a fare *before* getting into the cab.

If your hotel does not provide transfers, you can go by bus for a US$22 (£11) one-way fare. We recommend **Tour Wise** (© 876/952-0019 in Montego Bay, or 876/974-2323 in Ocho Rios). The bus will drop you off at your hotel; the trip takes 1 hour and 45 minutes.

You can rent a car for the 108km (67-mile) drive east along Route A1 (see "Getting Around" in the section "Essentials" at the beginning of this chapter).

VISITOR INFORMATION   The local office of the **Jamaica Tourist Board** is at Office #3 in the Ocean Villa Plaza on Main Street (© 876/974-2582). It is open Monday to Friday 8:30am to 4:30pm.

MEDICAL SERVICES   The nearest hospital is St. Ann's Bay Hospital (© 876/972-0150), 11km (6¾ miles) west. The most central pharmacy is **Ocho Rios Pharmacy,** Shop 67 in Ocean Village Plaza (© 876/974-2398), open Monday to Saturday 9am to 8pm and Sunday 9am to 7pm.

ACCOMMODATIONS
VERY EXPENSIVE

Couples Sans Souci Resort & Spa ✷✷✷   If a cookie-cutter Sandals is the last thing you want, head for this classier beachfront joint. Winner of four diamonds from AAA, this pink, cliff-side luxurious resort is 5km (3 miles) east of town on a forested plot of land abutting a good white-sand beach. There's a separate clothing-optional beach, a mineral bath big enough for an elephant, and a labyrinth of catwalks and bridges stretching over rocky chasms filled with surging water.

Each unit has a veranda or patio, copies of Chippendale furniture, plush upholstery, and subdued colonial elegance. Some contain Jacuzzis. Accommodations range from rather standard bedrooms to vast suites with large living and dining areas, plus kitchens. Deluxe touches include glazed-tile floors, luxurious beds, and marble bathrooms with whirlpool tubs. You'll enjoy the food at the elegant Casanova restaurant.

Rte. A3 (P.O. Box 103), Ocho Rios, Jamaica, W.I. © **800/268-7537** in the U.S., or 876/994-1206. Fax 876/994-1544. www.couples.com. 148 units. Winter US$725–US$833 (£377–£433) double; off season US$565–US$733 (£294–£381) double. Rates are all-inclusive. AE, DISC, MC, V. No children under 16 allowed. **Amenities:** 4 restaurants; 6 bars; 4 outdoor pools; golf; 2 lit tennis courts; health club; spa; 2 Jacuzzis; sauna; kayaks; sailing; scuba diving; snorkeling; water-skiing; windsurfing; room service; laundry service; dry cleaning; nonsmoking rooms; rooms for those w/limited mobility. *In room:* A/C, TV, minibar, beverage maker, hair dryer, iron, safe.

Goldeneye 🐠🐠 Few hotels in the world manage to be so luxurious and yet so appealingly informal as this intimate retreat. It surrounds the villa where the most famous secret agent in the world, James Bond (007), was created in 1952 by then-owner Ian Fleming. Fleming built the imposing but simple main house in 1946, and wrote each of the 13 original James Bond books there. In the early 1990s, music publisher–turned-hotelier Chris Blackwell bought and restored the by-then dilapidated property to its original modernist dignity. Fleming's original desk remains. The oversize Indonesian furniture is placed among memorabilia from what became the most famous spy movies in the world. The main house is usually only rented as a three-bedroom whole for extended house parties, often to rock stars and other celebs.

You're more likely to rent one of the four additional villas that were built in harmony with nature, on the surrounding property. Each evokes a tropical version of a billionaire's summer camp in Maine, thanks to a juxtaposition of indoor and outdoor spaces, sofas, and well-chosen decorative pieces. Each unit has a fully equipped kitchen. All drinks, food, and most activities are included in the price. The cuisine features some Jamaican favorites as well as international dishes.

There's a pool on the premises, but it's reserved for occupants of the main house. Masonry paths lead to a nearby beach.

Oracabessa, St. Mary, Jamaica, W.I. © **800/688-7678** in the U.S., or 876/975-3354. Fax 876/975-3620. www.island outpost.com. 5 villas. Winter US$950 (£494) 1-bedroom villa, US$1,150 (£598) 2-bedroom villa, US$1,350 (£702) 3-bedroom villa, US$3,800 (£1,976) Ian Fleming house; off season US$750 (£390) 1-bedroom villa, US$950 (£494) 2-bedroom villa, US$1,150 (£598) 3-bedroom villa, US$2,800 (£1,456) Ian Fleming house. Rates include all meals, drinks, and activities. AE, MC, V. **Amenities:** Outdoor pool (for Ian Fleming house guests); lit tennis court; jet skis; kayaks; snorkeling; windsurfing; room service; babysitting; laundry service. *In room:* A/C, TV, dataport, kitchenette, minibar, beverage maker, iron, safe.

Jamaica Inn 🐠🐠 Built in 1950, the gracious beachfront Jamaica Inn is a series of long, low buildings set in a U shape near the sea, 2km (1¼ miles) east of town. Noël Coward, arriving with Katharine Hepburn or Claudette Colbert, was a regular, and Errol Flynn and Ian Fleming used to drop in from time to time. It's an elegant anachronism, a true retro hotel, and has remained little changed in 4 decades, avoiding the glitter of all-inclusive resorts like Sandals.

Lovely patios open onto the lawns, and the bedrooms are reached along garden paths. Guest rooms are very spacious, with colonial two-poster beds, quality carved-wood period pieces, and balconies with balustrades that offer nice views. Bathrooms are elegant and roomy, gleaming with marble vanities, combination tub/showers, robes, and deluxe toiletries. The beach is a wide, champagne-colored strip; close to the shore, the sea is almost too clear to make snorkeling an adventure, but farther out it's rewarding. The European-trained chef prepares both refined international and Jamaican dishes. The emphasis is on cuisine that uses fresh local produce.

Main St. (P.O. Box 1), Ocho Rios, Jamaica, W.I. (C) **800/834-4608** in the U.S., or 876/974-2514. Fax 876/974-2449. www.jamaicainn.com. 47 units. Winter US$500–US$780 (£260–£406) double, US$600–US$815 (£312–£424) cottage; off-season US$280–US$425 (£146–£221) double, US$440–US$810 (£229–£421) cottage. Breakfast and dinner US$95 (£49.4) per person extra. AE, MC, V. Children 12 and under not accepted. **Amenities:** Restaurant; 2 bars; outdoor pool; fitness center; spa; kayaks; Sunfish sailboats; windsurfing; room service; babysitting; laundry service. *In room:* A/C, ceiling fan.

Royal Plantation Spa & Golf Resort 🦀🦀

This stately inn, a rival of the Jamaica Inn, has fallen under the Sandals umbrella and become the chain's most upmarket property in Jamaica. The hotel entrance evokes the antebellum South. At any moment, you expect Scarlett O'Hara to rush out to greet Rhett. You drive up a sweeping driveway and enter through a colonnaded portico. A complete renovation has brought major improvements to the rooms and public areas and added a full-service European spa. Accommodations are all suites, each opening onto the ocean views. Bedrooms are handsomely equipped with such extras as plush cotton robes, daily *New York Times,* fax service, Internet connections, CD players, and the like. Guests have full exchange privileges with the two other Sandals resorts in the area. The cuisine is far superior to that at the other Sandals properties, and the atmosphere less rowdy.

Main St., Ocho Rios, Jamaica, W.I. (C) **888/487-6925** in the U.S., or 876/974-5601. Fax 876/974-5912. www.royal plantation.com. 77 units. Winter US$520–US$1,870 (£270–£972) double; off season US$485–US$1,550 (£252–£806) double. Supplement of US$175 (£91) per person includes all meals, most drinks, all minibar fees, complimentary greens fees, airport transfers, and unlimited access to scuba diving and other water sports. AE, DISC, MC, V. No children under 18 allowed. **Amenities:** 4 restaurants; bar; golf at nearby Upton Golf & Country Club; 2 tennis courts; fitness center; billiards; croquet; spa; glass-bottom boat; scuba diving; room service; laundry service; dry cleaning. *In room:* A/C, TV, minibar, beverage maker, hair dryer, safe.

EXPENSIVE

Couples Ocho Rios 🦀

This is a couples-only resort. Most guests are married, and many are on their honeymoon. Everything is in pairs, even the chairs at night by the moon-drenched beach. Some guests slip away from the resort, which is an 18-minute drive (8km/5 miles) east of town, to Couples' private island to bask in the buff. (A shuttle boat transports visitors offshore to this beautiful little island with a fine sandy beach, a bar, and a pool. Security guards keep the gawkers from bothering guests here.)

In general, this is a classier operation than the more mass-market Sandals (at least the Dunn's River and the Ocho Rios versions). The bedrooms have a king-size bed or two doubles, pleasantly traditional furnishings, and a patio fronting either the sea or the mountains. Good-size bathrooms have a tub/shower combination. For a chain that's all-inclusive, the cuisine is above average.

Tower Isle, Rte. A3 (P.O. Box 330), Ocho Rios, Jamaica, W.I. (C) **800/268-7537** in the U.S., or 876/975-4271. Fax 876/ 975-4439. www.couples.com. 206 units. Winter US$635–US$673 (£330–£350) double, US$796–US$911 (£414– £474) suite; off season US$507–US$590 (£264–£306) double, US$673–US$835 (£350–£434) suite. Rates are per couple, per night, and include all meals, drinks, and activities. AE, DISC, MC, V. The hotel usually accepts bookings for a minimum of any 3 nights of the week, though most guests book by the week. No children under 18 allowed. **Amenities:** 5 restaurants; 4 bars; outdoor pool; golf; 4 tennis courts; health club; squash courts; yoga; spa; 4 Jacuzzis; sauna; kayaking; sailing; scuba diving; snorkeling; water-skiing; windsurfing; bike rental; horseback riding; Internet room; room service; nonsmoking rooms; rooms for those w/limited mobility. *In room:* A/C, TV, dataport, beverage maker, hair dryer, iron, safe.

Sandals Dunn's River Villagio Golf Resort & Spa 🦀

Located on a wide, sugary beach, this is the finest of the Sandals resorts, at least in the opinion of some guests who have sampled them all. Set on the beachfront between Ocho Rios and St. Ann's Bay, the resort is very sports oriented. It occupies 10 well-landscaped hectares (25 acres), offering attractively furnished and often quite spacious accommodations. Most rooms have an Italianate/Mediterranean motif. The elegant guest rooms are scattered among the six-story main building, two lanai buildings, and a five-story west wing. Extras include spacious balconies, walk-in closets, king-size beds, and tub/shower combinations. Before retreating to the dance club or enjoying the nightly entertainment, guests can choose among several dining options, selecting from an array of restaurants that attempt variety in lieu of first-rate cuisine. The International Room is elegant, with fabric-covered walls and rosewood furniture. The Windies Restaurant serves Caribbean specialties. D'Amoré offers Italian cuisine, and Restaurant Kimonos serves Chinese, Polynesian, and Japanese dishes.

Rte. A3 (P.O. Box 51), Ocho Rios, Jamaica, W.I. (© **800/726-3257** in the U.S. and Canada, or 876/972-1610. Fax 876/972-1611. www.sandals.com. 250 units. Winter US$370–US$440 (£192–£229) per person double, US$445–US$975 (£160–£507) per person suite; off season US$350–US$425 (£182–£221) per person double, US$445–US$975 (£160–£507) per person suite. Rates are all-inclusive. Minimum stay of 2 nights. AE, DISC, MC, V. No children under 18 allowed. **Amenities:** 4 restaurants; 5 bars (2 swim-up); 2 outdoor pools; 3 whirlpools; shuttle to 18-hole golf course; pitch-and-putt golf course; 4 tennis courts; health club; billiards; croquet; shuffleboard; volleyball; spa; 3 Jacuzzis; saunas; steam rooms; canoes; kayaks; sailboats; scuba diving; snorkeling; water-skiing; windsurfing; laundry service; dry cleaning; dance club; nonsmoking rooms; rooms for those w/limited mobility. *In room:* A/C, TV, beverage maker, hair dryer, iron, safe.

Sandals Grande Ocho Rios Beach & Villa Resort ⌖

This all-inclusive resort, which opened in 2004, is located 2km (1¼ mile) southeast of town, set on 18 hectares (44 acres) of tropical gardens on a private estate dotted with red-tile villas. A great house in the hills overlooks the Caribbean. Across from the imposing gate near the resort's entrance are the white sands of a private beach. This sprawling resort was created by merging Sandals Ocho Rios with Grande Sport Villa Golf Resort & Spa.

All but a handful of the accommodations are in one-, two-, or three-bedroom villas, each with a small pool, a fully equipped kitchen, and a shaded terrace. Honeymoon villas have their own whirlpools. Thirty-six units are traditional single or double rooms on the third floor of the great house. Accommodations are roomy, decorated in Caribbean colors, and have high ceilings. They're well furnished, with particularly fine beds, and the bathrooms with combination tub/showers are well maintained.

Main St. (P.O. Box 728), Ocho Rios, St. Ann, Jamaica, W.I. (© **800/726-3257** in the U.S. and Canada, or 876/974-1027. Fax 876/974-5700. www.sandals.com. 524 units. Per person: Winter US$300–US$390 (£156–£203) double, US$390–US$925 (£203–£481) suite; off-season US$290–US$380 (£151–£198) double; US$380–US$925 (£198–£481) suite. Rates are all-inclusive. 2-night minimum stay required. AE, MC, V. Children 15 and under not accepted. **Amenities:** 11 restaurants; 12 bars; 7 outdoor pools; 6 tennis courts; European-style spa; 5 Jacuzzis; 2 saunas; 2 steam rooms; scuba diving; laundry service; nonsmoking rooms; rooms for those w/limited mobility. *In room:* A/C, TV, kitchenette, minibar, beverage maker, hair dryer, iron, safe.

MODERATE

Hibiscus Lodge Hotel (Value)

This intimate little inn offers more value for your money than any other resort at Ocho Rios. Perched precariously on a cliff along the shore 3 blocks from the Ocho Rios Mall, the inn has character and charm. Mallards Bay Beach, shared by residents of some of the biggest hotels in Ocho Rios, lies within a 3- to 4-minute walk. All medium-size bedrooms, either doubles or triples, have small, shower-only bathrooms, ceiling fans, and verandas opening to the sea.

After a day spent in a pool suspended over the cliffs, or lounging on the large sun deck, guests can enjoy a drink in the unique bar with swinging chairs. The owners provide dining at the Almond Tree Restaurant (see "Dining," below).

83 Main St. (P.O. Box 52), Ocho Rios, St. Ann, Jamaica, W.I. © **876/974-2676**. Fax 876/974-1874. www.hibiscus jamaica.com. 26 units. Winter US$140 (£73) double, US$184 (£96) triple; off season US$129 (£67) double, US$165 (£86) triple. Rates include breakfast. AE, MC, V. **Amenities:** Restaurant; bar; outdoor pool; tennis court; Jacuzzi; limited room service. *In room:* A/C, ceiling fan, TV, hair dryer, iron, no phone.

High Hope Estate 🏨 Because this hotel is so intimate, whether you like it will depend on whether you click with the owner and the other guests. Basically, it's an upscale private home in the style of the British colonial world at its most rarefied that accepts paying guests. It was built for a socially prominent heiress, Kitty Spence, granddaughter of prairie-state populist William Jennings Bryan, and later served as the home and laboratory of a horticulturist who successfully bred 560 varieties of flowering hibiscus. The estate's 15 hectares (40 acres), set 165m (540 ft.) above the coast and 11km (6¾ miles) west of Ocho Rios, thrive with flowering plants as well as memories of such luminaries as Noël Coward, who used to play the grand piano that graces one of the public areas. There are absolutely no planned activities here. Bedrooms are a delight—spacious, well thought out, and exceedingly comfortable. The excellent bathrooms have tub/shower combinations. The staff is on hand to help supervise children, maintain the property, and prepare meals for anyone who gives advance notice.

The nearest beach is a 10-minute ride away. You could rent the entire villa with a group of friends, and you can purchase all-inclusive packages.

16 Top Rd. (P.O. Box 11), St. Ann's Bay, Jamaica, W.I. © **876/972-2277**. Fax 876/972-1607. www.highhopeestate. com. 5 units. Year-round US$95–US$165 (£49–£86) double. Rates include breakfast. MC, V. **Amenities:** Restaurant; outdoor pool; limited room service; babysitting; laundry service; nonsmoking rooms; rooms for those w/limited mobility. *In room:* Ceiling fan, minibar, beverage maker, hair dryer.

DINING
EXPENSIVE
The Dinner Terrace at The Jamaica Inn 🏨🏨 CONTINENTAL/CARIBBEAN
The timeless and discreetly upscale dining presentations at the Jamaica Inn seem to have endured better than many of this hotel's counterparts. There is, quite simply, nothing more upscale and dignified in town. Dinners, consequently, take on aspects of earlier, more graceful eras when guests actually gathered in the elegant, wood-paneled bar area, or on the moonlit terrace, for pre-dinner drinks before migrating into an open-sided (or, weather permitting, an open-air) dining room that's steeped in formal and undeniably upscale service rituals—the kind of venue where Sir Winston Churchill could (and frequently did) get in touch with colonial Jamaican posh. The menu changes nightly, and non-residents who opt to dine here are expected to reserve a table in advance. In 2004, age-old rules were modernized, allowing men to abandon their jackets and neckties in favor of well-groomed shirts with collars and long pants, during the dinner hour.

Main St. © **876/974-2514**. Reservations required. Set-price five-course menu US$53 (£28) without drinks. AE, MC, V. Daily 7:30–9pm.

MODERATE
Almond Tree Restaurant JAMAICAN/CONTINENTAL   The Almond Tree is a
two-tiered patio restaurant with a tree growing through the roof. Lobster thermidor is the tastiest item on the menu, but we also like the bouillabaisse (made with conch and lobster). Other excellent choices are the roast suckling pig, medallions of beef, and a fondue bourguignon. Jamaican plantation rice is a local specialty. The wine list offers

a variety of vintages, including Spanish and Jamaican. Have a cocktail in the unique "swinging bar"—with swinging chairs, that is.

In the Hibiscus Lodge Hotel, 83 Main St., St. Ann's Bay. © 876/974-2813. Reservations recommended. Main courses US$16–US$70 (£8.30–£36). AE, MC, V. Daily 7:30–10:30am, noon–2:30pm, and 6–9:30pm.

Evita's Italian Restaurant 🍴 ITALIAN   A 5-minute drive south of the commercial heart of Ocho Rios, in a hillside residential neighborhood that enjoys a panoramic view over the harbor and beachfronts, this is one of the most fun restaurants along the north coast of Jamaica. Its soul and artistic flair come from Eva Myers, the convivial former owner of some of the most legendary bars of Montego Bay, who established her culinary headquarters in this green-and-white gingerbread Jamaican house in 1990. An outdoor terrace adds additional seating and enhanced views. More than half the menu is devoted to pastas, including almost every variety known to northern and southern Italy. The fish dishes are excellent—especially the snapper stuffed with crabmeat and the lobster and scampi in a buttery white-cream sauce. Italian (or other) wines by the bottle might accompany your main course.

Eden Bower Rd. © 876/974-2333. Reservations recommended. Main courses US$12–US$23 (£6.25–£12). AE, MC, V. Daily 11am–11pm.

Little Pub Restaurant JAMAICAN/INTERNATIONAL   Located in a redbrick courtyard with a fishpond and waterfall in the center of town, this pub is the town's most popular. No one will mind if you just drop in for a drink at the bar. If you want dinner, proceed to one of the linen-covered tables topped with cut flowers and candles. We're fond of the barbecued chicken and grilled kingfish; you might also like the snapper or fresh lobster.

59 Main St. © 876/974-2324. Reservations recommended. Main courses US$8–US$20 (£4.15–£10). MC, V. Daily 10am–11pm.

INEXPENSIVE

BiBiBips INTERNATIONAL/JAMAICAN   Set in the main tourist strip of Ocho Rios, this restaurant (whose name is the owner's nickname) occupies a sprawling open-air compound of porches and verandas. Lots of single folks come just to hang out at the bar. Drinks and flirtations sometimes segue into dinner at the adjacent restaurant, where well-prepared menu items include Red Stripe shrimp, which is deep-fried in a beer-based batter; coconut-curried chicken; vegetarian Rasta Pasta; and a combination Creole-style seafood platter. Lunches are a bit simpler, focusing mostly on sandwiches, salads, and an especially delicious jerk chicken burger. Most dishes are at the low end of the price scale. There's live entertainment, usually some kind of rap or reggae band, on weekday afternoons or Saturday and Sunday nights.

93 Main St. © 876/974-6378. Main courses lunch US$10–US$25 (£5.20–£13), dinner US$25–US$35 (£13–£18). AE, MC, V. Daily 11am–2am.

Margaritaville at Ocho Rios 🧒 JAMAICAN   Lying in the new Island Village, a shopping and entertainment complex, this is one of the largest restaurants ever constructed on the north coast, seating 450 diners and drinkers. A high-energy bar and grill, Margaritaville provides all-day family fun with the entertainment continuing late at night. Attractions include a rooftop whirlpool tub, a 30m-long (98-ft.) waterslide, and a freshwater pool, along with three bars and a trading post. The decor is rustic West Indian with an Afro-Cuban aura. Of course, being a Jimmy Buffett dive, expect the world-famous tropical margaritas and those delectable Cheeseburgers in Paradise. There's dancing here—reggae-disco style—at night.

Turtle Beach Rd. (at the cruise-ship docks). ℭ 876/675-8976. Main courses US$12–US$22 (£6.25–£11); burgers and salads US$7–US$11 (£3.65–£5.70). AE, MC, V. Daily 8am–11pm for food; bar until 4:30am.

Ocho Rios Village Jerk Centre ⚑ *Finds* JAMAICAN   At this open-air restaurant, you can get the best jerk dishes along this part of the coast. When only a frosty Red Stripe beer can quench your thirst and your stomach is growling for the fiery taste of Jamaican jerk seasonings, head here—and don't dress up. The place isn't fancy; it's the food that counts. Fresh daily specials are posted on a chalkboard menu on the wall. The dishes are hot and spicy, but not *too* hot; hot spices are presented on the side for those who want to go truly Jamaican. The barbecue ribs are especially good, and fresh fish is a delight, perfectly grilled—try the red snapper. Vegetarian dishes are also available on request, and if you don't drink beer you can wash it all down with natural fruit juices.

Da Costa Dr. ℭ 876/974-2549. Jerk pork US$4 (£2) ¼ lb., US$10 (£5.20) 1 lb.; whole jerk chicken US$13 (£6.75). MC, V. Daily 10am–11pm.

HITTING THE BEACH

The most idyllic sands are at the often-overcrowded **Mallards Beach,** in the center of Ocho Rios and shared by hotel guests and cruise-ship passengers. Locals may steer you to the white sands of **Turtle Beach,** between the Renaissance Jamaica Grande and Club Jamaica. It's smaller, more desirable, and not as overcrowded as Mallards.

The most popular spot (stay away when cruise ships are in port!) is **Dunn's River Beach,** located below the famous falls. Another great spot is **Jamaica Grande's Beach,** which is open to the public. Parasailing is a favorite sport here.

Our favorite beach is at Goldeneye, writer Ian Fleming's former home, now a hotel. Follow the trail of 007 and head for **James Bond Beach** (ℭ **876/726-1630**), east of Ocho Rios at Oracabessa Beach. For US$5 (£2.60) adults, US$3 (£1.55) children, nonguests can enjoy its sand strip any day except Monday. There's a watersports rental center here as well.

You might also escape the crowds at Ocho Rios and head to the lovely beach at nearby Runaway Bay. (See the section "Runaway Bay," below.)

SPORTS & OTHER OUTDOOR PURSUITS

GOLF   **SuperClub's Runaway Golf Club,** at Runaway Bay near Ocho Rios on the north coast (ℭ **876/973-7319**), charges no fee to guests who stay at any of Jamaica's affiliated SuperClubs. For nonguests, the price is US$80 (£42) year-round. Any player can rent carts for US$35 (£18) for 18 holes; clubs are US$14 (£7.30) for 18 holes.

Sandals Golf & Country Club (ℭ **876/975-0119**), a 15-minute ride from the center of the resort, is a 6,500-yard course, known for its panoramic scenery some 210m (689 ft.) above sea level. (From the center of Ocho Rios, travel along the main bypass for 3km/2 miles until you reach Mile End Rd. A Texaco station is located at the corner of Mile End Rd. Turn right and drive for another 8km/5 miles until you come to the Sandals course on your right.) The 18-hole, par-71 course was designed by P. K. Saunders and opened in 1951 as the Upton Golf Club. Rolling terrain, lush vegetation, and flowers and fruit trees dominate the 48-hectare (119-acre) course. A putting green and driving range are available for those who wish to hone their skills first. Sandals guests play free; nonguests pay US$25 (£13) for 9 holes or US$45 (£23) for 18 holes.

TENNIS **Sandals Grand Ocho Rios Golf Resort & Spa,** Main Street, Ocho Rios (© 876/974-1027), focuses more on tennis than any other resort in the area. It offers three clay-surface and three hard-surface courts, all lit for night play. Guests play free, day or night, but nonguests must call and make arrangements with the manager. Nonguests can purchase a day pass for US$80 (£42) per person. The resort also sponsors twice-a-day clinics for both beginners and advanced players. Frequent guest tournaments are also staged, including handicapped doubles and mixed doubles.

EXPLORING THE AREA

A scenic drive south of Ocho Rios along Route A3 will take you inland through **Fern Gully** ✹, a lush gorge. This was originally a riverbed, but now the main road winds up some 210m (690 ft.) among a profusion of wild ferns, a tall rainforest, hardwood trees, and lianas. There are hundreds of varieties of ferns, and roadside stands offer fruits and vegetables, carved-wood souvenirs, and basketwork. The road runs for about 6km (3¾ miles). At Moneague, a small town, the A1 continues south into the interior of Jamaica, but it also heads back north along a route to the west of the southbound A3. If you take the A1 north, you'll come to the coast on the north shore at St. Ann's Bay.

Heading up A1 north, you'll pass the ruins of **Edinburgh Castle** lying 13km (8 miles) southwest of Claremont, the major town on the route back. These ruins—not worth a detour but of passing interest if you're driving by—are a local curiosity.

This 1763 lair was the former abode of one of Jamaica's most famous murderers, a Scot named Lewis Hutchinson, who used to shoot passersby and toss their bodies into a deep pit. At his so-called "castle," really a two-story house, Hutchinson invited his victims inside. There he would wine and dine them before murdering and then robbing them.

The authorities got wind of his activities. Although he tried to escape by canoe, Hutchinson was captured and hanged at Spanish Town on March 16, 1773. Evidently proud of his achievements (evidence of at least 43 bodies was found), he left 100 British pounds and instructions for a memorial to be built in his honor. It never was.

These castle ruins can be viewed on the northern outskirts of the village of Bensonton, near the Bensonton Health Club.

In **St. Ann's Bay,** the site of the first Spanish settlement on the island, you can see the **statue of Christopher Columbus,** cast in his hometown of Genoa and erected near St. Ann's Hospital on the west side of town, close to the coast road. There are a number of Georgian buildings in the town. We think that the **Courthouse** near the parish church, built in 1866, is the most interesting.

Brimmer Hall Estate Some 34km (21 miles) east of Ocho Rios, in the hills 3km (2 miles) from Port Maria, this 1817 estate is an ideal place to spend a day. You can swim in the pool and sample a wide variety of brews and concoctions. The Plantation Tour Eating House offers typical Jamaican dishes for lunch, and there's a souvenir shop with a good selection of ceramics, art, straw goods, woodcarvings, rums, liqueurs, and cigars. All this is on a working plantation where you're driven around in a tractor-drawn jitney to see the tropical fruit trees and coffee plants; the knowledgeable guides will explain the various processes necessary to produce the fine fruits of the island. This is a far more interesting experience than the trip to Croydon Plantation in Montego Bay, so if you're visiting both resorts and have time for only one plantation, make it Brimmer Hall.

Port Maria, St. Mary's. © **876/994-2309.** Tours US$18 (£9.35). Reservations required 3 days in advance. Tours Mon–Fri 9am–3pm.

Coyaba Gardens & Museum & Mahoe Falls

Two kilometers (1¼ miles) south of the center of Ocho Rios, at an elevation of 126m (413 ft.), this park and museum were built on the grounds of the former Shaw Park plantation. The word *coyaba* comes from the Arawak name for paradise. Coyaba is a Spanish-style museum with a river and gardens filled with native flora, a cut-stone courtyard, fountains, and a crafts shop and bar. The museum displays a collection of artifacts from the Arawak, Spanish, and English settlements in the area.

Shaw Park Rd. © **876/974-6235.** www.coyabagardens.com. Admission to the garden US$10 (£5.20); half-price for ages 12 and under. Daily 8am–6pm. Take the Fern Gully–Kingston Rd., turn left at St. John's Anglican Church, and follow the signs to Coyaba, just .4km (¼ mile) farther.

Dunn's River Falls *Overrated*

For a fee, you can relax on the beach or climb with a guide to the top of the falls. You can splash in the waters at the bottom of them or drop into the cool pools higher up between the cascades of water. A beach restaurant serves lackluster snacks and drinks, and dressing rooms are available. If you're planning to climb the falls, wear sneakers or sport sandals to protect your feet from the sharp rocks and to prevent slipping.

Climbing the falls with the crowds is a chance to experience some 180m (600 ft.) of cold but clear mountain water. In contrast to the heat swirling around you, the splashing water hitting your face and bare legs is cooling on a hot day. The problem here is slipping and falling, especially if you're joined to a chain of hands linking body to body. In spite of the slight danger, there seem to be few accidents. The falls aren't exactly a wilderness experience, with all the tour buses carrying cruise-ship passengers here. The place is always overrun.

Rte. A3. © **876/974-2857** or -5944. Admission US$6 (£3.10) adults, US$3 (£1.55) children 6–12, free for children under 6. Daily 8:30am–5pm. From the center of Ocho Rios, head west along Rte. A3.

Firefly ✸

This vacation retreat was the home of Sir Noël Coward and his longtime companion, Graham Payn, who, as executor of Coward's estate, donated it to the Jamaica National Heritage Trust. The recently restored house is more or less as it was on the day Sir Noël died in 1973. His Hawaiian-print shirts still hang in the closet of his austere bedroom, with its mahogany four-poster. The library contains a collection of his books, and the living room is warm and comfortable, with big armchairs and two grand pianos (where he composed several famous tunes). Guests stayed at Blue Harbour, a villa closer to Port Maria; they included Evelyn Waugh, Winston Churchill, Errol Flynn, Lord Laurence Olivier, Vivien Leigh, Claudette Colbert, Katharine Hepburn, Mary Martin, and the Queen Mother. Paintings by the noted playwright/actor/author/composer adorn the walls. An open patio looks out over the pool and the sea. Across the lawn, Sir Noël is buried under a simple white marble gravestone.

Grants Town, in St. Mary, 32km (20 miles) east of Ocho Rios above Port Maria. © **876/725-0920.** Admission US$10 (£5.20) adults, US$5 (£2.60) children under 12. Mon–Thurs and Sat 9am–5pm.

Harmony Hall

This was the centerpiece of a sugar plantation in the late 19th century. Today it has been restored and is the focal point of an art gallery and restaurant that showcases the painting and sculpture of Jamaican artists as well as a tasteful array of arts and crafts. Among the featured gift items are Sharon McConnell's Starfish Oils, which contain natural additives harvested in Jamaica. The gallery shop also carries the "Reggae to Wear" line of sportswear, designed and made on Jamaica, and Anabella boxes (for jewelry).

Tower Isles on Rte. A3, 6km (3¾ miles) east of Ocho Rios. © 876/975-4222. Free admission. Gallery daily 10am–6pm; restaurant Tues–Sun 10am–2:30pm and 6–11pm.

Island Village and Island Village Shopping Center ⊛

The 2002 opening of this exotic-looking playland represents one of the largest private investments of the past decade within the tourism infrastructure of Ocho Rios. Scattered over 2 hectares (5 acres) on a beachfront within a few steps of the city's cruise-ship terminal is a replica of an idealized Jamaican village, complete with elaborate gingerbread, hundreds of feet of boardwalk, and a medley of psychedelic colors that glow, rainbow-style, in the streaming sunlight. It's not without its own Disney-ish theme-park overtones—**sound stages** are strategically scattered within the sightlines of **bars** that serve the kind of high-octane cocktails that could fuel a heavily loaded jetliner from here to Kingston. Music and hotel impresario Christopher Blackwell, who takes credit for the "discovery" and marketing of Bob Marley, is half-owner of this venture—thus you won't find any shame here about emphasizing reggae as both a lifestyle and an artistic venue.

Within the compound you'll find about 35 **shops** selling clothing, books, souvenirs, "reggae wear," and Bob Marley memorabilia; and four or five restaurants and bars.

Small-scale reggae presentations occur spontaneously, often when a cruise ship is in port, and large-scale **blockbuster concerts** are scheduled about once a month, and are usually attended by hundreds, or even thousands. Except when there's a world-class concert—usually when there's no cruise ship in port—there's no admission charged for entrance to the compound, but an alert security staff ensures that "panhandlers, pickpockets, and lowlifes" (at least those residing in Jamaica) are kept off the premises. Access to the beachfront—with its own floating trampoline—costs US$5 (£2.60) per person.

Island Village, Turtle Beach Rd. No central switchboard—each establishment has its own phone. Free admission. Daily 9am–midnight.

Prospect Plantation

This working plantation adjoins the 18-hole Prospect Mini Golf Course. A visit to this property is an educational, relaxing, and enjoyable experience. On a leisurely tour by covered jitney through the scenic beauty of Prospect, you'll readily see why this section of Jamaica is called "the garden parish of the island." You can view the many trees planted by such visitors as Winston Churchill, Henry Kissinger, Charlie Chaplin, Pierre Trudeau, and Noël Coward. You'll learn about and see pimento (allspice), bananas, cassava, sugar cane, coffee, cocoa, coconut, pineapple, and the famous leucaena ("Tree of Life"). You can even sample some of the exotic fruit and drinks.

Horseback riding, costing US$58 (£30) per person for 1½ hours, is available for adults on three scenic trails at Prospect. Dolphin Cove Tours runs a jitney bus tour to the plantation from the center of Ocho Rios Monday to Saturday at 10:30am, 2pm, and 3:30pm.

Rte. A3, 5km (3 miles) east of Ocho Rios, in St. Ann. © 876/994-1058. Tours US$27 (£14) adults, US$15 (£7.80) for children 12 and under. Tours Mon–Sat at 10:30am, 2pm, and 3:30pm.

SHOPPING

For many, Ocho Rios provides an introduction to Jamaica-style shopping. After surviving the ordeal, some visitors may vow never to go shopping again. Literally hundreds of Jamaicans pour into Ocho Rios to peddle items to cruise-ship passengers and other visitors. Be prepared for aggressive vendors. Pandemonium greets many an unwary shopper, who must also be prepared for some fierce haggling. Every vendor asks too much at first, which gives them the leeway to "negotiate" until the price reaches a more realistic level. Is shopping fun in Ocho Rios? A resounding no. Do cruise-ship passengers and land visitors indulge in it anyway? A decided yes.

In general, the shopping is better in Montego Bay. If you're not going there, wander the Ocho Rios crafts markets, although much of the merchandise is repetitive.

SHOPPING CENTERS & MALLS   There are a number of shopping plazas in Ocho Rios. We've listed them because they're here, not because we heartily recommend them. Newer ones include the **New Ocho Rios Plaza,** in the center of town, with some 60 shops; opposite is the **Taj Mahal Mall,** with 26 duty-free stores. **Island Plaza** is another major shopping complex, as is the **Mutual Security Plaza** with some 30 shops.

Ocean Village Shopping Centre (© 876/974-2683) is one of the originals, with numerous boutiques, food stores, a bank, sundries purveyors, travel agencies, and service facilities. The **Ocho Rios Pharmacy** (© 876/974-2398) sells most proprietary brands, perfumes, and suntan lotions among its many wares. Nearby is the major competitor of Ocean Village, the **Coconut Grove Shopping Plaza,** which is linked by walkways and shrubs. The merchandise here consists mainly of local craft items, and this center is often overrun with cruise-ship passengers. Ocean Village is slightly bigger and more upscale—we prefer it.

Just east of Ocho Rios, the **Pineapple Place Shopping Centre** is a collection of shops in cedar-shingle-roofed cottages set amid tropical flowers.

The **Ocho Rios Craft Park** has 135 stalls. A vendor will weave a hat or a basket while you wait, or you can buy a ready-made hat, hamper, handbag, place mats, or lampshade. Other stands stock hand-embroidered goods and will make small items while you wait. Woodcarvers work on bowls, ashtrays, statues, and cups.

Island Plaza, right in the heart of Ocho Rios, has some of the best Jamaican art—all paintings are by local artists. You can also purchase local handmade crafts (be prepared to haggle), carvings, ceramics, kitchenware, and the inevitable souvenir T-shirts.

SPECIALTY SHOPS   **Swiss Stores,** in the Ocean Village Shopping Centre (© 876/974-2519), sells jewelry and all the big names in Swiss watches. The Rolex watches here are real, not those fakes touted by hustlers on the streets.

One of the best bets for shopping is **Soni's Plaza,** 50 Main St., which is the address of all the following recommended shops. **Casa de Oro** (© 876/974-5392) specializes in duty-free watches, fine jewelry, and classic perfumes. **Gem Palace** (© 876/974-2850) is the place to go for diamond solitaires, tennis bracelets, and 14-karat gold chains. **Mohan's** (© 876/974-9270) offers one of the best selections of 14-karat and 18-karat gold chains, rings, bracelets, and earrings. **Soni's** (© 876/974-2303) focuses strictly on souvenirs from coffee mugs to T-shirts. **Taj Gift Centre** (© 876/974-9268) has a little bit of everything: Blue Mountain coffee, film, cigars, and hand-embroidered linen tablecloths. **Diamonds Duty Free Fine Jewelry** (© 876/974-6455) beats most competition with its name-brand watches and jewelry.

OCHO RIOS AFTER DARK

Most evenings are devoted to some form of entertainment, often karaoke. Also see "Dining," earlier in this chapter, for a review of **BiBiBips,** where there's a hopping bar and live bands on Saturday and Sunday nights.

On other fronts, **Ocean's 11 Watering Hole,** Lot #6, Fisherman's Point Row (© **876/ 974-6896**), overlooks a boardwalk-style waterfront pier and is open daily from 8am until midnight. The club is liveliest on Tuesday night for karaoke from 9pm to 2am. **Strawberry's,** 6 James Ave. (© **876/898-1091**), is a three-tiered restaurant, bar, and night spot, where most of the money is generated from the street-level sports bar open daily noon to midnight. The upstairs dance club is open only Friday to Sunday 8pm to 2am.

5 Runaway Bay

Once a mere satellite of Ocho Rios, Runaway Bay, about 15km (10 miles) to the west, has become a destination in its own right, with white-sand beaches that are much less crowded than those in Ocho Rios.

Since you're so far removed from the action, such as it is, in Ocho Rios, you stay at Runaway Bay mainly if you're interested in hanging out at a particular resort. It is especially recommended for those who want to escape from the hordes descending on Ocho Rios, where cruise-ship crowds and aggressive vendors can intrude on your solitude.

This part of Jamaica's north coast has several distinctions: It was the first part of the island seen by Columbus, the site of the first Spanish settlement on the island, and the point of departure of the last Spaniards leaving Jamaica following their defeat by the British.

Most people who stay at Runaway Bay stay at one of the all-inclusives where meals are included. If you're not staying at such a resort, you can dine at **Runaway Heart Country Club,** which is open to nonguests; otherwise you can drive to Ocho Rios for meals.

ACCOMMODATIONS & DINING

Breezes Runaway Bay Resort & Golf Club ⭐   This stylish resort is all-inclusive. Passing through a park filled with tropical trees and shrubbery leads to the clubhouse. The lobby is the best re-creation of the South Seas on Jamaica, with hanging wicker chairs and totemic columns. There's a minijungle with hammocks and a nearby nude beach, in addition to the lovely stretch of sandy beach right out front. The resort lies 3km (2 miles) east of Paradise Beach and just next door to the town's second best beach, Cardiffall.

⸤Fun Fact Nude Nuptials

At Hedonism III Resort (p. 408), couples who want to see what they're getting before they tie the knot can be married in their birthday suits. Instead of a gown and a tuxedo, suntan lotion is recommended so that any body parts, already exposed, might not become overexposed, at least to the sun. After the "I do's" are said, the happy couple can head for the honeymoon suite at this adults-only all-inclusive.

Guest rooms are spacious, with a light, tropical motif. They're fitted with local woods, cool tile floors, and private balconies or patios. The most elegant are the suites, with Jamaican-made four-poster beds. The good-size bathrooms have combination tub/showers and generous marble counters.

Live music emanates from the stylish Terrace every evening at 7pm, and a nightclub offers live shows 6 nights a week at 10pm. Dine either in the beachside restaurant or in the more formal Italian restaurant, Martino's, which is the best. The resort's Starlight Grill has also expanded its menu to include a vegetarian cuisine. The club offers exchange and day-pass privileges with Hedonism III immediately next door.

P.O. Box 58 (10km/6¼ miles west of Ocho Rios), Runaway Bay, Jamaica, W.I. © 877/467-8737 in the U.S., or 876/973-4825. Fax 876/516-4155. www.superclubs.com. 234 units. Winter US$363–US$591 (£189–£307) double; off season US$256–US$525 (£133–£273) double. Rates include all meals, drinks, and activities. AE, DC, DISC, MC, V. No children under 14 allowed. **Amenities:** 4 restaurants; 4 bars; outdoor pool; golf; 4 tennis courts; fitness center; basketball; cricket; squash; 3 Jacuzzis; dive shop; kayaking; sailing; scuba diving; snorkeling; water-skiing; windsurfing; biking; room service; laundry service; nonsmoking rooms; rooms for those w/limited mobility. *In room:* A/C, TV, minibar (in some), beverage maker, hair dryer, iron, safe.

FDR (Franklyn D. Resort) *Kids*

Located on Route A1, 27km (17 miles) west of Ocho Rios, FDR is an all-inclusive that's the number-one choice if you're traveling with children. FDR lies 3km (2 miles) east of Paradise Beach and about .4km (¼ mile) east of Cardiffall. Its own no-name beach stretches for about 180m (600 ft.), a mixture of stone and sand. The resort, named after its Jamaican-born owner and developer, Franklyn David Rance, is on 2 hectares (5 acres) of flat, sandy land dotted with flowering shrubs and trees, on the main seaside highway. Each of the Mediterranean-inspired buildings has a terra-cotta roof, a loggia or an outdoor terrace, Spanish marble in the bathrooms, a kitchenette, and a personal attendant (called a vacation nanny), who cooks, cleans, and cares for children. Although neither the narrow beach nor the modest pools are the most desirable on the island, and most rooms lack a sea view, many visitors appreciate the spacious units and the resort's wholehearted concern for kids.

Two restaurants on the property serve free wine with lunch and dinner (and offer special children's meals), and a piano bar provides music every evening.

Main St. (P.O. Box 201), Runaway Bay, St. Ann, Jamaica, W.I. © 888/337-5437 in the U.S., or 876/973-4592. Fax 876/973-4600. www.fdrholidays.com. 76 units. Winter US$280–US$420 (£146–£218) double; off season US$240–US$270 (£125–£140) double. Rates are all-inclusive. Children 5 and under stay free in parent's suite; children 6–15 US$50 (£26) extra each. AE, MC, V. **Amenities:** 4 restaurants; 3 bars; 2 outdoor pools; tennis court; health club; Jacuzzi; dive shop; kayaks; scuba diving; snorkeling; windsurfing; bikes; children's center; Internet cafe; free babysitting (9:30am–4:45pm); laundry service; dance club; nonsmoking rooms. *In room:* A/C, ceiling fan, TV, kitchen.

Grand Lido Braco *G*

Established in 1995, this is one of the most historically evocative all-inclusive resorts in Jamaica, lying on a prime stretch of sandy, 320m (1,050-ft.) beachfront. Set on 34 hectares (84 acres) of land near Buena Vista, a 15-minute drive west of Runaway Bay, it's a re-creation of a 19th-century Jamaican Victorian village, with charming gingerbread architecture. A copy of a courthouse hosts entertainment, and benches line the borders of the town square, where artisans display their handiwork. The old Jamaica that's portrayed here is a rather sanitized, Disney version. Yet this is not a place for children; it is a primarily adult retreat.

Accommodations are in 12 blocks of three-story buildings, each trimmed in colonial-style gingerbread and filled with wicker furniture. All the spacious units have private patios or verandas and face the ocean; blocks one through six are closer to the beachfront, and blocks five and six face a strip of sand designated as a "clothing-optional" area. Beds are very comfortable, with fine linen; all rooms are equipped with CD players and radios; the bathrooms are well maintained and have showers.

Separate dining areas serve tasty Jamaican cuisine, pizza and pasta, and blander international fare; the Piacere Restaurant offers upscale dinners and has a dress code. For variety, Munasan serves Japanese sushi and Teppanyaki cuisine.

Rio Bueno, Trelawny, Jamaica. Ⓒ **877/467-8737** in the U.S., or 876/954-0000. Fax 876/518-6748. www.superclubs. com. 226 units. Winter US$595–US$1,100 (£309–£572) double; off season US$584–US$1,000 (£304–£520) double. Rates include all meals, drinks, airport transfers, and activities. AE, DC, DISC, MC, V. No children under 16 allowed. **Amenities:** 5 restaurants; 8 bars; 2 outdoor pools; 9-hole golf course; 3 tennis courts; squash; health club; spa; 4 Jacuzzis; sauna; steam room; kayaks; scuba diving; snorkeling; Sunfish sailboats; water-skiing; windsurfing; bikes; business center; room service; laundry service; dry cleaning; dance club. *In room:* A/C, TV, beverage maker, hair dryer, iron, safe.

Hedonism III ⒻᎨ   Following a chain format established in Negril, this latest beach-front Hedonism bills itself as a "truly active (and slightly wicked!) vacation." Though this branch of Hedonism isn't as rowdy and raunchy as the Negril branch—it's a little more serene and isolated from the action in town—it's still for the serious party person who likes to drink all night, hang out at the beach all day, and go wild at those toga parties. Set on 6 hectares (15 acres) of landscaped gardens on the eastern end of Runaway Bay, it features ocean views from all rooms and an all-inclusive package deal. Hedonism III has its own private, slightly rocky beach stretching for some 180m (600 ft.); a part of the beach is often nude. It lies a 15-minute drive east of Paradise Beach and a 10-minute walk west of Cardiffall.

Bedrooms are roomy and freshly decorated, with Jamaica's first-ever block of "swim-up" rooms. All swim-up rooms feature large marble tub/shower bathrooms with Jacuzzis and CD players. Single guests are paired up with a roommate of the same sex, or have to pay a single supplement.

Unique in Jamaica, the resort offers a circus workshop that features a flying trapeze, juggling, a trampoline "clinic," and various unicycle and bike-balancing acts. This workshop is offered Monday to Saturday.

The food here is quite decent—everything from Italian to Japanese to Jamaican. For nightlife, there's a dance club with a four-story water slide!

Runaway Bay, Jamaica, W.I. Ⓒ **877/467-8737** in the U.S., or 876/973-4100. Fax 876/973-5402. www.superclubs. com. 225 units. Winter US$358–US$560 (£186–£291) double; off season US$308–US$510 (£160–£265) double. Rates include all meals, drinks, and activities. AE, DC, DISC, MC, V. No children under 18 allowed. **Amenities:** 5 restaurants; 6 bars; 3 large pools; 3 tennis courts; fitness center; basketball court; ice skating rink; rock-climbing; volleyball; 3 Jacuzzis; sauna; kayaks; sailing; scuba diving; snorkeling; water-skiing; windsurfing; game room; room service; dance club; nonsmoking rooms; rooms for those w/limited mobility. *In room:* A/C, TV, dataport, beverage maker, hair dryer, iron, safe.

Runaway Bay H.E.A.R.T. Hotel ⒻᎨ *Value*   This place wins hands-down as the bargain of the north coast. One of Jamaica's few training and service institutions, the club and its adjacent academy are operated by the government to provide a high level of training for young Jamaicans interested in the hotel trade. The helpful staff of both professionals and trainees offers the finest service of any hotel in the area. Runaway lies a 30-minute drive east of Paradise Beach and a 5-minute drive to Cardiffall. Free shuttles are offered only to Cardiffall.

The good-size rooms are bright and airy. Bathrooms have generous shelf space and shower stalls. The accommodations open onto private balconies with views of well-manicured tropical gardens or vistas of the bay and golf course. Guests enjoy having a drink in the piano bar (ever had a cucumber daiquiri?) before heading for the dining room, the Cardiff Hall Restaurant, which serves superb Jamaican and Continental dishes.

Ricketts Ave. (P.O. Box 98), Runaway Bay, St. Ann, Jamaica, W.I. ℂ 876/973-6671. Fax 876/973-4704. 56 units. Winter US$100–US$105 (£52–£55) double, US$120–US$125 (£62–£65) triple, from US$200 (£104) suite; off-season US$90–US$95 (£47–£49) double, US$110–US$115 (£57–£60) triple, from US$180 (£94) suite. Rates include breakfast and dinner. AE, DISC, MC, V. **Amenities:** Restaurant; 3 bars; outdoor pool; gym; laundry service; rooms for those w/limited mobility. *In room:* A/C, TV.

BEACHES & OUTDOOR ACTIVITIES

The two best beaches at Runaway Bay are **Paradise Beach** and **Cardiffhall Lot Public Beach.** Both wide, white-sand strips are clean and well maintained—ideal spots for a picnic. If you're staying in Ocho Rios and want to escape the crowds, come here. There is a great natural beauty to this part of Jamaica, and many foreigners, especially Canadians, seek it out. You don't get a lot of facilities, however, so you'd better bring along whatever you need.

The waters are calm almost all year. Prevailing trade winds will keep you cool in the morning and late afternoon. Since there are no lifeguards, be careful, especially if you're with children.

Runaway Bay offers some of the best areas for **snorkeling** in Jamaica. The reefs are close to shore and swarming with marine life, including enormous schools of tropical fish such as blue chromis, triggerfish, small skate rays, and snapper. Since boats and fishing canoes can be a problem close to shore, go on a snorkeling excursion with the best diving facility at Runaway Bay: **Jamaqua Dive Center,** at Club Ambience (ℂ 876/973-4845; www.jamaqua.com), whose slogan is, "We Be Divin'." They take you to one of several protected reefs where the currents aren't dangerous, and where fishing boats are required to stay at least 180m (600 ft.) away from divers or snorkelers. The dive facility offers complete equipment rental and everything from one-tank dives to six-boat packages. A one-tank dive is US$42 (£22) and a two-tank dive costs US$75 (£39).

Jamaica's most complete **equestrian center** is the **Chukka Caribbean Adventures,** at Richmond Llandovery, St. Ann (ℂ 876/972-2506; www.chukkacaribbean.com), less than 6km (3¾ miles) east of Runaway Bay. A 1-hour trail ride costs US$60 (£31), while a 2-hour mountain ride goes for US$70 (£36). The most popular ride is a 3-hour beach jaunt for US$73 (£38) that involves riding over trails to the sea, then swimming in the surf. A more recent feature is a mountain and sea adventure on a bike (90% of which is downhill). The 2½-hour bike ride goes for US$60 (£31) and ends with a swim and some snorkeling.

SEEING THE SIGHTS

Columbus Park Museum, on Queens Highway, Discovery Bay (no phone), is a large, open area between the main coast road and the sea at Discovery Bay. Just pull off the road and walk among the fantastic collection of exhibits; admission is free. There's everything from a canoe made from a solid piece of cottonwood—the way Arawaks did it more than 5 centuries ago—to a stone cross that was originally placed on the Barrett Estate (14km/8¾ miles east of Montego Bay) by Edward Barrett, brother of poet Elizabeth Barrett Browning. You can see a tally, used to count bananas carried on men's heads from plantation to ship, as well as a planter's strongbox with a weighted lead base to prevent its theft. Other items are 18th-century cannons, a Spanish water cooler and calcifier, a fish pot made from bamboo, a corn husker, and a water wheel.

Pimento trees, which produce allspice, dominate the park, which is open Monday to Friday 8am to 4pm, Saturday 8am to noon.

You can also visit the **Seville Great House,** Heritage Park (© **876/972-2191**). Built in 1745 by the English, it contains a collection of artifacts once used by everybody from the Amerindians to African slaves. In all, you're treated to an exhibit of 5 centuries worth of Jamaican history. Modest for a great house, it has a wattle-and-daub construction. A small theater presents a 15-minute historical film about the house on request. It's open daily from 9am to 5pm; admission is US$4 (£2).

6 Port Antonio ⭑

Port Antonio, sometimes called the Jamaica of 100 years ago, is a verdant, somewhat bustling seaport on the northeast coast, 101km (63 miles) northeast of Kingston. It's a mecca of the titled and the wealthy, including European royalty and stars like Whoopi Goldberg and Peter O'Toole.

This small town is like many on the island: clean but cluttered, with sidewalks around a market filled with vendors, and tin-roofed shacks competing with old Georgian and modern brick and concrete buildings. At the market, you can browse for local craftwork, spices, and fruits.

Travelers used to arrive by banana boat and stay at the Titchfield Hotel (which burned down). Captain Bligh landed here in 1793 with the first breadfruit plants, and Port Antonio claims that the ones grown in this area are the best on the island. Visitors still arrive by water, but now it's in cruise ships that moor close to Navy Island, and the passengers come ashore just for the day.

Navy Island and the long-gone Titchfield Hotel were owned for a short time by Errol Flynn. The story is that after suffering damage to his yacht, he put into Kingston for repairs, visited Port Antonio by motorbike, fell in love with the area, and in due course acquired Navy Island (some say he won it in a bet). Later, he either lost or sold it and bought a nearby plantation, Comfort Castle. He was much loved and admired by the Jamaicans and was totally integrated into the community. They still talk of him in Port Antonio—his reputation for womanizing and drinking lives on.

We find Port Antonio one of the more relaxed retreats in Jamaica, certainly not as undiscovered as it was when William Randolph Hearst or J. P. Morgan visited, but a virtual Shangri-La compared to Ocho Rios or Montego Bay. It also has some of the finest beaches in Jamaica and has long been a center for some of the Caribbean's best deep-sea fishing. It's a good place to go to get away from it all.

ESSENTIALS

GETTING THERE   If you're going to Port Antonio, you can fly into the **Donald Sangster Airport** in Montego Bay or the **Norman Manley International Airport** in Kingston. Some hotels, particularly the larger resorts, will arrange for airport transfers from that point. Be sure to ask when you book. Port Antonio has its own small airfield. There are no regularly scheduled flights into the resort—only private charters.

You can rent a car for the 214km (133-mile) drive east along Route A1 (see "Getting Around" in the section "Essentials," at the beginning of this chapter), but we don't advise this 4-hour drive for safety's sake, regardless of which airport you fly into.

If you take a taxi, the typical one-way fare from Montego Bay is US$110 (£57), but always negotiate and agree upon a fare before you get into the cab.

MEDICAL FACILITIES   The **Port Antonio General Hospital** is at Naylor's Hill (© 876/993-2646).

ACCOMMODATIONS

Despite its charms, Port Antonio is suffering increasingly from a lack of business as travelers are drawn to the more famous Negril, Ocho Rios, and Montego Bay. Many of the hotels are forced to fill up empty rooms with low-cost tour groups hailing from everywhere from Italy to Canada. Because of this, we've found that some of the hotels in the area are showing signs of wear and deterioration.

MODERATE/EXPENSIVE

Goblin Hill Villas at San San ★   This green and sunny hillside—once said to shelter goblins—is now filled with Georgian-style vacation homes on San San Estate. The pool is surrounded by a vine-laced arbor, which lies just a stone's throw from an almost impenetrable forest. A long flight of steps leads down to the crescent-shaped sands of San San beach. This beach is now private, but guests of the hotel receive a pass. Everything has the aura of having last been fixed up in the 1970s, but the resort is still comfortable. The accommodations are town house-style; some have ceiling fans and king-size beds, some have twin beds, and none have phones. The generally roomy units are filled with handmade pine pieces, along with a split-level living and dining area with a fully equipped kitchen. All units have well-maintained bathrooms with tub/shower combinations. Housekeepers prepare and serve meals and attend to chores in the villas.

San San (P.O. Box 26), Port Antonio, Jamaica, W.I. © 800/472-1148 in the U.S., or 876/925-8108. Fax 876/925-6248. www.goblinhill.com. 28 units. Winter US$125–US$195 (£65–£101) 1-bedroom villa, US$205–US$265 (£107–£138) 2-bedroom villa; off season US$115–US$165 (£60–£86) 1-bedroom villa, US$170–US$195 (£88–£101) 2-bedroom villa. AE, MC, V. **Amenities:** Bar; outdoor pool; 2 tennis courts; car rental; room service; babysitting; laundry service; nonsmoking rooms. *In room:* A/C, ceiling fan, TV, kitchen, fridge, beverage maker (in some), no phone.

Hotel Mocking Bird Hill ★   A 10km (6-mile) drive east of Port Antonio, this charming, homey, and well maintained inn competes effectively with hotels and resorts that are larger, grander, and sometimes, much more pretentious. In 1993, two imaginative women transformed the place into a blue-and-white enclave of good taste, reasonable prices, and ecological consciousness. Set about 180m (590 ft.) above the coastline on a hillside laden with tropical plants, within a 5-minute drive from French-man's Cove Beach, the hotel attracts a clientele of mostly European visitors who revel in the artsy and ecologically alert setting. The accommodations are simple but tasteful and at their best, understatedly elegant, with neatly kept shower-only bathrooms, balconies or verandas, spinning ceiling fans, mosquito netting, and views that sweep over the rainforest down to the sea. Much of the establishment's interior, including its separately recommended restaurant (Mille Fleurs; see below), is decorated with artworks, many executed by Barbara Walker, one of the owners. There are massage options available on-site, as well as day hikes and classes in painting and drawing. If that doesn't tempt you, you can just relax and enjoy an herbal massage or the views that sweep out over the Blue Mountains and the Jamaican coastline.

Mocking Bird Hill, North Coast Hwy. (east of Port Antonio), Port Antonio, Jamaica, W.I. © 876/993-7267. Fax 876/993-7133. www.hotelmockingbirdhill.com. 10 units. Winter US$245–US$295 (£127–£153) double; off season US$165–US$220 (£86–£114) double. AE, MC, V. **Amenities:** Restaurant; bar; outdoor pool; Internet access; room service; laundry service; nonsmoking rooms; rooms for those w/limited mobility. *In room:* Ceiling fan, beverage maker, hair dryer, safe, no phone.

Trident Villas & Hotel 👫👫 This luxury hideaway is located on Allan Avenue, on the coast toward Frenchman's Cove. It sits regally above jagged coral cliffs with a sea-side panorama. The hotel's main building is furnished with antiques and cooled by sea breezes. Your accommodations will be a studio cottage or tower, reached by a path through the gardens. In the cottages, a large bedroom with ample sitting area opens onto a private patio with a sea view. All units have ceiling fans, plenty of storage space, and tasteful Jamaican antiques and colorful chintzes. Beds are most comfortable, and bathrooms have combination tub/showers. Trident has a horseshoe-shaped sandy beach cove at one end of its grounds, which is accessible by a path that meanders along a landscaped terrain. It's a strip of muddy-bottomed seafront that's not as appealing as a dip in the hotel pool, which is positioned near a graceful gazebo and sits above jagged rocks where the surf crashes and churns most of the day.

Rte. A4 (P.O. Box 119), Port Antonio, Jamaica, W.I. ⓒ 876/993-2602. Fax 876/993-2590. www.tridentjamaica.com. 27 units. Winter US$253–US$287 (£132–£149) double, US$488 (£254) 1-bedroom villa, US$976 (£508) 2-bedroom villa; off season US$120 (£62) double, US$280–US$292 (£146–£152) 1-bedroom villa, US$416 (£216) 2-bedroom villa. MAP (breakfast and dinner) US$48 (£25) extra per person per day. AE, MC, V. **Amenities:** Restaurant; bar; outdoor pool; croquet; deep-sea fishing; scuba diving; snorkeling; room service; massage; babysitting; laundry service; rooms for those w/limited mobility. *In room:* A/C, minibar, beverage maker, hair dryer, safe.

INEXPENSIVE

Jamaica Heights Resort 👫 *Finds* The funkiest, most amusing, and hippest guesthouse in town might be full of rock stars from Düsseldorf or up-and-coming filmmakers cranking out tomorrow's indie fave. The very worldly owner, Helmut Steiner, former professor of literature and philosophy in Berlin, and his wife, Charmaine, maintain this affordable but sophisticated retreat. It's set at the top of a rutted and very steep series of roads. The resort is not on a beach but provides transportation to two of the finest beach strips of sand at Port Antonio, Frenchman's Cove and San San.

Scattered amid the wedge-shaped 3-hectare (7½-acre) property are a half-dozen buildings, each white-walled with shutters, gazebos, climbing vines, and a pavilion for meditating over views of the forested terrain that cascades down to Port Antonio's harbor. The garden sports exotic palms, a stream with its own waterfalls, the most elegant Ping-Pong pavilion in the world, and dozens of botanical oddities from around the world. The minimalist accommodations are spotlessly clean. Each has a four-poster bed and funky lighting fixtures, plus tub/shower combination bathrooms. Doors can be opened or closed to create suites with between two and four bedrooms.

Spring Bank Rd., Port Antonio, Jamaica, W.I. ⓒ 876/993-3305. Fax 876/993-3563. www.jamaicaheights.net. 8 units. Year-round US$95–US$175 (£49–£91) double. No credit cards. **Amenities:** Restaurant; outdoor pool; watersports; laundry service; nonsmoking rooms. *In room:* Ceiling fan, beverage maker, no phone.

Rio Vista Resort Villas 👫👫 *Finds* Featured in *Condé Nast Traveler,* this place is ideal for a luxurious vacation, a honeymoon, or even an off-the-record weekend. Six kilometers (3¾ miles) west of Port Antonio (most of the luxe properties lie to the east), Rio Vista is only 3km (2 miles) from the little local airstrip, nestled between the Rio Grande River and the Caribbean Sea. On a 4-hectare (10-acre) estate planted with tropical fruits, it offers handsomely furnished one- and two-bedroom cottages, plus a honeymoon villa with a river view. The setting is a garden of flowers, spices, and sweet-smelling herbs. Rooms have vaulted wooden ceilings and well-maintained tiled bathrooms, each with a shower. A housekeeper services each cottage and can assist with meals. Candlelit dinners can be arranged. Air-conditioning in summer costs US$10 (£5.20) extra.

St. Margarets Bay (P.O. Box 4). © 876/993-5444. Fax 876/993-5445. www.riovistajamaica.com. 5 villas. Year-round US$135 (£70) 1-bedroom villa, US$165 (£86) 2-bedroom villa. Children 12 and under stay free in parent's room. MC, V. **Amenities:** Restaurant; bar; outdoor pool; rafting; limited room service; massage; laundry service; nonsmoking rooms. *In room:* A/C, TV, kitchen, beverage maker.

DINING

All hotel restaurants welcome nonguests for dinner, but reservations are required.

Mille Fleurs 🎖🎖 CARIBBEAN   This restaurant is terraced into a verdant hillside about 180m (590 ft.) above sea level with sweeping views over the Jamaican coastline and the faraway harbor of Port Antonio. Sheltered from the frequent rains, but open on the side for maximum access to cooling breezes, it features candlelit dinners, well-prepared food, and lots of New Age charm. Lunches include sandwiches, salads, grilled fish platters, and soups. At night, you might feast on fresh lobster or tender lamb and beef dishes, even savory rabbit or smoked marlin. The restaurant has been praised by *Gourmet* magazine for its dishes. You may want to try the coconut-and-garlic soup, and the fish with spicy mango-shrimp sauce is a specialty. Breads and most jams are made on the premises. Two dishes are vegetarian.

In the Hotel Mocking Bird Hill, North Coast Hwy. © 876/993-7267. Reservations recommended. Lunch platters US$9–US$35 (£4.70–£18); main courses US$21–US$40 (£11–£21). AE, MC, V. Daily 8:30–10:30am, noon–2pm, and 7–9:30pm.

Norma's at the Marina 🎖🎖 JAMAICAN/CONTINENTAL   Established in 2005, this is a branch of an upscale, Jamaica-wide restaurant chain made famous by a Jamaica-born, Florida-trained matriarch (Norma Shirley), who has been the subject of more publicity in the culinary press than any equivalent entrepreneur in Jamaica., The restaurant sprawls between two oversized gazebos that mark both ends of a brick-floored beachside terrace inside the fenced-in compound of the Port Antonio marina. Your meal might be served outdoors, on the above-mentioned terrace, or one floor above ground level, within a high-ceilinged, mahogany-trimmed dining room that's open to the breezes on two sides. Menu items are elegant and flavorful, representing the best of modern and creative Jamaican cuisine, and include crab back salad, elegant slices of smoked marlin, a "reggae salad" studded with sautéed shrimp, several different versions of grilled fish, teriyaki-flavored rib-eye steak, wood-smoked port riblets with a tamarind-flavored honey sauce; pan-seared butterfish filets, and grilled lobster with lime-flavored herb butter.

At the Port Antonio Marina. © 876/993-9510. Reservations recommended. Main courses US$10–US$25 (£5.20–£13). MC, V. Tues–Sat 10am–10pm; Sun noon–8pm.

Savannah Waterfront Restaurant 🎖 INTERNATIONAL/JAMAICAN   The elegant Trident Hotel Restaurant serves meals that evoke the Jamaica of the '50s. The cuisine is always prepared with first-class ingredients, though the setting and the white-glove service are generally more memorable than the food. The high-pitched wooden roof set on white stone walls holds several ceiling fans that gently stir the air. The antique tables are set with old china, English silver, and Port Royal pewter. The formally dressed waiters will help you choose your wine and whisper the name of each course as they serve it. The five-course dinner menu changes daily but might include a Jamaican salad, mahimahi with mayonnaise-and-mustard sauce, steak with broccoli and sautéed potatoes, and for dessert, peach Melba and Blue Mountain coffee with Tia Maria, a Jamaican liqueur.

In Trident Villas & Hotel, Rte. A4. © 876/993-2602. Reservations required. Jackets required for men. Main courses US$20–US$48 (£10–£25). AE, MC, V. Daily 7:30am–9:30pm. Head east on Allan Ave.

Moments **A Dip in the Blue Lagoon**

The young Brooke Shields made the film *The Blue Lagoon* in a calm, protected cove 15km (10 miles) east of Port Antonio. The water is so deep, nearly 6m (20 ft.) or so, that it turns a cobalt blue; there's almost no more scenic spot in all of Jamaica. The Blue Lagoon, with its small, intimate beach, is a great place for a picnic. (You can pick up jerk pork at various shacks along the Boston Beach area.)

HITTING THE BEACH

Port Antonio has several white-sand beaches, including the famous **San San Beach,** which has recently gone private. Guests of certain hotels are admitted with a pass; otherwise the fee is US$8 (£4.15).

Boston Beach is a free public beach, and it often has light surfing; there are picnic tables as well as a restaurant and snack bar. On your way here, stop and get the makings for a picnic lunch at the most famous area for peppery jerk pork and chicken on Jamaica. These rustic shacks also sell the much rarer jerk sausage. The beach is 18km (11 miles) east of Port Antonio and just east of the Blue Lagoon.

Also free is **Fairy Hill Beach** (Winnifred), but there are no changing rooms or showers here. **Frenchman's Cove Beach** attracts a chic crowd to its white-sand beach combined with a freshwater stream. Nonguests are charged US$3 (£1.55).

SPORTS & OTHER OUTDOOR PURSUITS

DEEP-SEA FISHING   Northern Jamaican waters are world renowned for their game fish, including mahimahi, wahoo, blue and white marlin, sailfish, tarpon, barracuda, and bonito. The **Jamaica International Fishing Tournament** and **Jamaica International Blue Marlin Team Tournament** run concurrently at Port Antonio every October. Most major hotels from Port Antonio to Montego Bay have deep-sea-fishing facilities, and there are many charter boats. Ask at your hotel.

RAFTING   Although it's not exactly adventurous (it's a tame and safe outing), the best—and the most fun—rafting experience on the island is here. Rafting started on the Rio Grande as a means of transporting bananas from the plantations to the waiting freighters. In 1871, a Yankee skipper, Lorenzo Dow Baker, decided that a seat on one of the rafts was better than walking, but it was not until Errol Flynn arrived that the rafts became popular as a tourist attraction. Flynn used to hire the crafts for his friends, and he encouraged the rafters to race down the Rio Grande, betting on the winners. Now that bananas are transported by road, the raft skipper makes one or maybe two trips a day down the waterway. If you want to take a trip, contact **Rio Grande Experience,** Berrydale (© **876/993-5778**).

The rafts, some 10m long (33 ft.) and only 2m wide (6½ ft.), are propelled by stout bamboo poles. There's a raised double seat about two-thirds of the way back. The skipper stands in the front, trousers rolled up to his knees, the water washing his feet, and guides the craft down the lively river, about 13km (8 miles) between steep hills covered with coconut palms, banana plantations, and flowers, through limestone cliffs pitted with caves, through the "Tunnel of Love," a narrow cleft in the rocks, then on to wider, gentler water.

Trips last 2 to 2½ hours and are offered from 9am to 5pm daily at a cost of US$50 (£26) per raft, which holds two passengers. A fully insured driver will take you in your rented car for a US$20 (£10) fee to the starting point at Berrydale or Grant's Level, where you board your raft. If you feel like it, take a picnic lunch, but bring enough for the skipper, too, who will regale you with lively stories of life on the river.

SNORKELING & SCUBA DIVING   The best outfitter is **Lady Godiva's Dive Shop** at Port Antonio Marina (© **876/428-3437**), 11km (6¾ miles) from Port Antonio. Full dive equipment is available. Technically, you can snorkel off most of the beaches in Port Antonio, but you're likely to see more if you venture farther offshore. The best spot is Winnifred on the far side of Dragon Bay. The reef is extremely active and full of a lot of exciting marine life. Lady Godiva offers two excursions daily to this spot for US$25 (£13) per person, including snorkeling equipment for the day.

PORT ANTONIO AFTER DARK

The **Tree Bar** draws a fashionable crowd to the grounds of Goblin Hill Villas at San San (© **876/925-8108**), high on a hill commanding a panoramic view of 5 hectares (12 acres). The aptly named bar is wrapped around huge ficus trees, whose mammoth aerial roots dangle over the drinking area. Giant-leafed pothos climb down the trunks. It's a sort of "Me Tarzan, You Jane" kind of place.

Go at your own risk to the infamous **Roof Club**, 11 West St. (© **876/715-5281**). The most crowded and animated nightclub in Port Antonio, it's one floor above street level in a boxy-looking industrial building in the heart of town. Inside, the venue is earthy, raunchy, crowded, and boozy, with enough secondhand ganja smoke to get virtually anyone high. Recorded (and, more rarely, live) reggae and soca music blares at high volumes. Expect a neopsychedelic decor of mirrors, UV lighting, and free-form Day-Glo artwork. A visit here is not for the squeamish or the faint-hearted, and it's a good idea to come with a friend and/or ally. Try to stay relatively sober, keep your wits about you, and enjoy the slow-moving gyrations of ordinary folks who—sometimes with the help of a spliff or two—get involved in the beat of the music and groove accordingly. Beers cost from US$2.25 (£1.15) each. It's open nightly from around 6pm, but most of the genuine hanging out happens after 11pm, especially from Thursday through Sunday.

7 Kingston & Vicinity

Kingston, the largest English-speaking city in the Caribbean, is the capital and cultural, industrial, and financial center of Jamaica. It's home to some 660,000 people, including those living on the plains between Blue Mountain and the sea.

The buildings here are a mixture of the modern, graceful, old, and just plain ramshackle. It's a busy city, as you might expect, with a natural harbor that's the seventh largest in the world. The University of the West Indies has its campus on the edge of the city.

Few other cities in the Caribbean carry as many negative connotations for North American travelers as Kingston, thanks to widely publicized, and sometimes exaggerated, reports of violent crime. Marry that with urban congestion, potholed roads, and difficult-to-decipher road signs that make it hard to navigate, and you've got a bad reputation.

But if you're an urban dweller who copes with everyday life in, say, New York, Atlanta, or Los Angeles, you know how to deal with city life, and Kingston doesn't have to be that scary. It offers resources and charms that can't be found anywhere else. It is here that Jamaica is at its most urban and confident, its most witty, its most exciting, and its most challenging. No other place in Jamaica offers as many singles bars, dance clubs, and cultural outlets—it's the nation's creative cauldron. If you're truly interested in Jamaican culture, Kingston can be very stimulating, as it's very far removed from the tourist-oriented economies of Negril, Ocho Rios, and Montego Bay.

We've carefully screened the recommendations contained within this guidebook, eliminating any that lie within the most dangerous neighborhoods. So keep an open mind about Kingston—it can be a lot of fun and very exciting.

ESSENTIALS

GETTING THERE See "Getting There," in section 1 of this chapter, for details on the airlines that serve Kingston's international airport.

GETTING AROUND Because Kingston is a rather confusing place to negotiate, many visitors rely on taxis.

MEDICAL FACILITIES The **University Hospital** is at Mona (© **876/927-1620**). **Moodie's Pharmacy** is in the New Kingston Shopping Centre (© **876/926-4174**).

ACCOMMODATIONS

The Jamaica Pegasus 🏨 A favorite with business travelers, the Jamaica Pegasus barely outclasses its nearest rival, the Hilton, in a close race. It's located in the banking area of Kingston, which is also a fine residential area. After a major renovation, the hotel is now better than ever and is the site of many conventions and social events. The hotel combines British style with Jamaican warmth, arranging watersports and sightseeing. Each of the well-furnished bedrooms is of moderate size and contains a bathroom with combination tub/shower and a balcony opening onto mountain, sea, or cityscape. The decorating, in dark tones, often brown, makes you yearn for the lighter pastel look of most Caribbean hotel bedrooms. Several floors of luxuriously appointed suites form the Knutsford Club, which offers special executive services.

The 4pm tea service is a bit of a social event among some residents. The premier restaurant is The Columbus. The Brasserie is the hotel's informal restaurant that opens onto the swimming pool, where a splashing fountain cools the air. It adjoins a circular bar near the pool, at which occasional barbecues are prepared.

81 Knutsford Blvd., Kingston 5, Jamaica, W.I. © 876/926-3690. Fax 876/929-5855. www.jamaicapegasus.com. 300 units. Year-round US$220–US$270 (£114–£140) double; US$350 (£182) junior suite; US$570 (£296) royal suite. AE, DC, DISC, MC, V. **Amenities:** 3 restaurants; 2 bars; outdoor pool; tennis courts; fitness center; jogging trail; business center; 24-hr. room service; laundry service; dry cleaning; nonsmoking rooms; rooms for those w/limited mobility. *In room:* A/C, TV, minibar, hair dryer, safe.

Terra Nova All Suite Hotel 🏨 *Finds* This house is on the western edge of New Kingston, near West Kings House Road. Built in 1924 for a young bride, it was converted into a hotel in 1959. It was the birthplace of the well-known hotelier and Island Records mogul, Chris Blackwell. Set in 1 hectare (2½ acres) of gardens with a backdrop of greenery and mountains, it's now one of the best small Jamaican hotels, although the rooms are rather basic and not at all suited for those who want a resort ambience. Most of the bedrooms are in a new wing. All units have neatly kept bathrooms with shower units. The Regency, with a marble floor and wide windows, serves local and international food.

17 Waterloo Rd., Kingston 10, Jamaica, W.I. © 876/926-2211. Fax 876/929-4933. www.terranovajamaica.com. 35 units. Year-round US$175–US$850 (£91–£442) double. AE, MC, V. **Amenities:** 2 restaurants; coffee shop; 2 bars; outdoor pool; fitness center; room service; nonsmoking rooms; rooms for those w/limited mobility. *In room:* A/C, TV, minibar (in some), beverage maker, hair dryer, iron, safe.

IN NEARBY PORT ROYAL

Morgans Harbour Hotel On the premises of this yachtie favorite is a 200-year-old redbrick building once used to melt pitch for His Majesty's navy, a swimming area defined by docks and buoys, and a series of wings whose eaves are accented with hints of gingerbread. Set on 9 hectares (22 acres) of flat and rocky seashore, the resort contains the largest marina in Kingston, plus a breezy waterfront restaurant and a popular bar (where ghost stories about the old Port Royal seem especially lurid as the liquor flows on Friday night). Longtime residents claim that the ghosts of soldiers killed by a long-ago earthquake are especially visible on hot and very calm days, when British formations seem to march out of the sea.

The well-furnished bedrooms are laid out in an 18th-century Chippendale-Jamaican style. Medium-size bathrooms are tidily maintained, each with a shower bath.

Port Royal, Kingston 1, Jamaica, W.I. ℭ **800/448-8355** in the U.S., or 876/967-8030. Fax 876/967-8061. 50 units. Year-round US$120–US$180 (£62–£94) double; US$190 (£99) suite. AE, MC, V. Take the public ferryboat that departs every 2 hr. from near Victoria Pier on Ocean Blvd.; many visitors arrive by car or taxi. **Amenities:** Restaurant; bar; 2 outdoor pools; room service; laundry service; nonsmoking rooms. *In room:* A/C, TV, minibar, beverage maker, hair dryer, iron.

DINING

Norma's on the Terrace ✦✦ JAMAICAN This is the creation of Jamaica's most famous businesswoman, Norma Shirley, purveyor of food to stylish audiences as far away as Miami. It's housed beneath the wide porticos of the gallery surrounding Kingston's most famous monument, Devon House. Ms. Shirley has taken the old, woefully dusty gardens and transformed them into something you'd find on a manicured English estate. Menus change with the season, but usually reflect Ms. Shirley's penchant for creative adaptations of her native Jamaican cuisine. Stellar examples include Jamaican chowder with crabmeat, shrimp, conch, and lobster; grilled whole red snapper encrusted with herbs and served with a thyme-and-caper sauce; and grilled smoked pork loin in a teriyaki/ginger sauce, served with caramelized apples. The hearty breakfast served here—of American and international dishes—is the best in town.

In Devon House, 26 Hope Rd. ℭ **876/968-5488.** Reservations recommended. Main courses US$20–US$60 (£10–£31). AE, DISC, MC, V. Mon–Sat 10am–10pm.

Redbones the Blues Café ✦✦ *(Finds)* JAMAICAN The name alone lured us to this elegant place, which is the only restaurant in Kingston with cuisine as good as Norma's on the Terrace. All aglow in yellow and peach hues, Redbones is in a former Spanish colonial house. You're greeted with pictures of jazz greats on the wall, everybody from Billie Holiday to Louis Armstrong. A cozy bar, its ceiling studded with records, is installed in someone's former bedroom. Owners Evan and Betsy Williams give standard Jamaican dishes a new twist. Ask for *bammy,* a cassava dish crowned with sautéed shrimp, or a platter of stuffed crab backs, a delectable selection on a tri-color salad. A spinach callaloo with cream cheese is encased in a divine strudel. Seafood pasta is laden with shrimp, lobster, and salmon in a creamy coconut sauce. The best item on the menu is spicy lamb chops in a guava glaze. Live jazz—or something—is always going on.

21 Braemar Ave. ℭ **876/978-6091.** Reservations required. Main courses US$17–US$35 (£8.80–£18). AE, MC, V. Mon–Fri noon–11pm; Sat 6–11pm.

HITTING THE BEACH

You don't really come to Kingston for beaches, but there are some here. To the southwest of the sprawling city are black-sandy **Hellshire Beach** and **Fort Clarence.** Both of these beaches are very popular with the locals on weekends. Both have changing rooms, heavy security, and numerous food stands. The reggae concerts at Fort Clarence are legendary on the island.

Just past Fort Clarence, the fisherman's beach at **Naggo Head** is an even hipper destination, or so Kingston beach buffs claim. After a swim in the refreshing waters, try out one of the food stands selling "fry fish" and *bammy* (cassava bread). The closest beach to the city (although it's not very good) is **Lime Cay,** a little island on the outskirts of Kingston Harbour, reached after a short boat ride from Morgan's Harbour at Port Royal.

SEEING THE SIGHTS

Even if you're staying at Ocho Rios or Port Antonio, you may want to visit Kingston for the sights or to make a trip to nearby Port Royal and Spanish Town.

From Kingston, you can make excursions into the Blue Mountains. See the section "The Blue Mountains," below.

IN TOWN

One of the major attractions, **Devon House,** 26 Hope Rd. (© **876/929-6602**), was built in 1881 by George Stiebel, a Jamaican who made his fortune mining in Latin America, becoming one of the first black millionaires in the Caribbean. A striking classical building, the house has been restored to its original beauty by the Jamaican National Trust. The grounds contain crafts shops, boutiques, two restaurants, shops that sell the best ice cream in Jamaica (in exotic fruit flavors), and a bakery and pastry shop with Jamaican puddings and desserts. The main house also displays furniture of various periods and styles. Admission to the main house is US$4.50 (£2.40); hours are Monday to Saturday from 9:30am to 4:30pm. Admission to the grounds (the shops and restaurants) is free.

Almost next door to Devon House are the sentried gates of **Jamaica House,** residence of the prime minister, a fine, white-columned building set well back from the road.

Continuing along Hope Road, at the crossroads of Lady Musgrave and King's House roads, turn left and you'll see a gate on the left with its own personal traffic light. This leads to **King's House,** the official residence of the governor-general of Jamaica, the queen's representative on the island. The outside and front lawn of the gracious residence, set in 80 hectares (200 acres) of well-tended parkland, is sometimes open for viewing Monday to Friday from 10am to 5pm. The secretarial offices are housed next door in an old wooden building set on brick arches. In front of the house is a gigantic banyan tree in whose roots, legend says, *duppies* (ghosts) take refuge when they're not living in the cotton trees.

National Library of Jamaica (formerly the West India Reference Library), Institute of Jamaica, 12 East St. (© **876/967-1526**), a storehouse of the history, culture, and traditions of Jamaica and the Caribbean, is the finest working library devoted to West Indian studies in the world. It has the most comprehensive, up-to-date, and balanced collection of materials on the region, including books, newspapers, photographs, maps, and prints. It's open Monday to Thursday from 9am to 5pm, Friday from 9am to 4pm.

Bob Marley Museum, 56 Hope Rd. (© 876/927-9152; www.bobmarley-foundation. com), is the most-visited sight in Kingston, but if you're not a Marley fan, it may not mean much to you. The clapboard house with its garden and high surrounding wall was the famous reggae singer's home and recording studio until his death on May 11, 1981. You can tour the house and view assorted Marley memorabilia, and you may even catch a glimpse of his children, who often frequent the grounds. Hours are Monday to Saturday from 9:30am to 4pm. Admission is US$7.50 (£4) for adults, J$200 (US$3/£1.60) children 13 to 18. It's reached by bus no. 70 or 75 from Halfway Tree, but take a cab to save yourself the hassle of dealing with Kingston public transport.

IN PORT ROYAL

From West Beach Dock in Kingston, a ferry ride of 20 to 30 minutes will take you to Port Royal, whose name in pirate lore conjures up visions of swashbuckling pirates led by Henry Morgan, swilling grog in harbor taverns. This was once one of the largest trading centers of the New World, with a reputation for being the wickedest city on earth. Blackbeard stopped here regularly on his Caribbean trips. But it all came to an end on June 7, 1692, when a third of the town disappeared underwater after a devastating earthquake. Nowadays, Port Royal, with its memories of the past, has been designated by the government for redevelopment as a tourist destination.

Today Port Royal is a small fishing village at the end of the Palisades strip. Some 2,000 residents live here with what many locals claim are a "lot of ghosts." Port Royal's seafaring traditions continue, and it's known for its seafood and ramshackle and much-battered architecture of yesterday. Once there were six forts here with a total of 145 guns, some of which can be seen today. Only Fort Charles still stands, however.

Fort Charles (© 876/967-8438), the only remaining fort of Port Royal's original six, has withstood attack, earthquake, fire, and hurricane. Built in 1656 and later strengthened by Morgan for his own purposes, the fort was expanded and further armed in the 1700s, until its firepower had more than 100 cannons, covering both the land and the sea approaches. In 1779, Britain's naval hero, Horatio Lord Nelson, was commander of the fort and trod the wooden walkway inside the western parapet as he kept watch for the French invasion fleet. Scale models of the fort and ships of past eras are on display. The fort is open daily from 9am to 5pm; admission is J$200 (US$3/ £1.60) for adults, J$100 (US$1.50/80p) for visitors under 18.

Part of the complex, **Giddy House,** once the Royal Artillery storehouse, is another example of what the earth's movements can do. Walking across the tilted floor is an eerie and strangely disorienting experience.

IN SPANISH TOWN

From 1662 to 1872, Spanish Town (19km/12 miles west of Kingston on A1) was the capital of the island. Originally founded by the Spaniards as Villa de la Vega, it was sacked by Cromwell's men in 1655, and all traces of Roman Catholicism were obliterated. The English cathedral, surprisingly retaining a Spanish name, **St. Jago de la Vega** (© 876/986-4405), was built in 1666 and rebuilt after being destroyed by a hurricane in 1712. As you drive into the town from Kingston, the ancient cathedral catches your eye with its brick tower and two-tiered wooden steeple, which was not added until 1831. Since the cathedral was built on the foundation and remains of the old Spanish church, it is half English and half Spanish, and displays two distinct styles: Romanesque and Gothic. Of cruciform design and built mostly of brick, it's one of the most interesting buildings on the island. The black-and-white marble stones of the aisles are interspersed with ancient tombstones, and the walls are heavy with marble memorials that almost chronicle Jamaica's history, dating back as far as 1662.

After visiting the cathedral, walk 3 blocks north along White Church Street to Constitution Street and the **Town Square.** This little square is surrounded by towering royal palms. On the west side is old **King's House,** gutted by fire in 1925, although the facade has been restored. This was the residence of Jamaica's British governors until 1872, when the capital was transferred to Kingston.

Beyond the house is the **Jamaica People's Museum of Craft & Technology,** Old King's House, Constitution Square (© 876/907-0322), open Monday to Thursday from 9:30am to 4:30pm and Friday 8:30am to 4pm. Admission is J$100 (US$1.50/80p) for adults, J$40 (60¢/30p) for children under 18. The garden contains examples of old farm machinery, an old water-mill wheel, a hand-turned sugar mill, a fire engine, and more. An outbuilding houses a museum of crafts and technology, together with a number of smaller agricultural implements. In the small archaeological museum are old prints, models, and maps of the town's grid layout from the 1700s.

The streets around the old Town Square contain many fine Georgian town houses intermixed with tin-roofed shacks. Nearby is the **market,** so busy in the morning that you may find it difficult, almost dangerous, to pass through. It provides, however, a bustling view of Jamaican life.

SHOPPING

Downtown Kingston, the old part of the town, is centered around **Sir William Grant Park,** formerly Victoria Park, a showpiece of lawns, lights, and fountains. Covered arcades lead off from King Street, and everywhere are teeming masses of people going about their business. There are some beggars and the inevitable hucksters who sidle up and offer "hot stuff, mon," frequently highly polished brass lightly dipped in gold and offered at prices as high as real gold.

For many years, the richly evocative paintings of Haiti were viewed as the most valuable contribution to Caribbean arts. There is on Jamaica, however, a rapidly growing perception of itself as one of the artistic leaders of the Third World. An articulate core of Caribbean critics is focusing the attention of the art world on the unusual, eclectic, and sometimes politically motivated paintings produced here.

Frame Centre Gallery, 10 Tangerine Place (© 876/926-4644), is one of the most important art galleries on Jamaica. Its founder and guiding force, Guy McIntosh, is widely respected today as a patron of the Jamaican arts. There are three viewing areas and a varied collection of more than 300 works.

Kingston Crafts Market, at the west end of Harbour Street (reached via Straw Ave., Drummer's Lane, or Cheapside), is a large, covered area of small stalls, selling all kinds of island crafts: wooden plates and bowls; pepper pots made from *mahoe* (the national wood of the island); straw hats, mats, and baskets; batik shirts; banners for wall decoration, inscribed with the Jamaican coat-of-arms; and wood masks with elaborately carved faces. You should bargain a bit, and vendors will take something off the price, but not very much.

The **Shops at Devon House,** 26 Hope Rd., ring the borders of a 200-year-old courtyard once used by slaves and servants. It's associated with one of the most beautiful and historic mansions on Jamaica, a building owned by the Jamaican National Trust. On-site is a mellow old restaurant and pub, **The Grog Shop** (© 876/960-9730). The most important shop is **Things Jamaican** (© 876/926-1961), showcasing the crafts of the country and carrying a food section that features island-made sauces and spices. **Wessi Art** (℃ **876/906-5016**) exhibits locally made ceramics, and **Jamaican Juice** (℃ **876/906-9424**) sells natural and organic juices made from island-grown fruits. **Cooyaa** (℃ **876/920-6167**) sells T-shirts and other memorabilia inspired by the career of Bob Marley and other reggae artists. The latest opening is an Internet cafe, which also offers a piano bar.

8 The Blue Mountains ★★★

Just a short drive north of Kingston is some of the most varied and unusual topography in the Caribbean, a beautiful mountain range laced with rough rivers, streams, and waterfalls. The 78,000-hectare (193,000-acre) **Blue Mountain–John Crow Mountain National Park** is maintained by the Jamaican government. The mountainsides are covered with coffee fields, producing a blended version that's among the leading exports of Jamaica. For the nature enthusiast, the mountains reveal a complex series of ecosystems that change radically as you climb from sea level into the fog-shrouded peaks.

The most popular, the most scenic, and our favorite climb begins at **Whitfield Hall** (℃ **876/927-0986**), a high-altitude hostel and coffee estate about 10km (6¼ miles) north of the hamlet of Mavis Bank. Reaching the **summit of Blue Mountain Peak** (900m/2,950 ft. above sea level) requires about 3½ hours, each way. Of course, there are much shorter variations if you don't want to see "everything." En route, hikers pass through acres of coffee plantations and forest, where temperatures are cooler than you might expect, and where high humidity encourages thick vegetation. Along the way, watch for an amazing array of bird life, including hummingbirds, many species of warblers, rufous-throated solitaires, yellow-bellied sapsuckers, and Greater Antillean pewees.

Dress in layers and bring bottled water. If you opt for a 2am departure in anticipation of watching the sunrise from atop the peak, carry a flashlight as well. Sneakers are usually adequate, although many climbers bring their hiking boots. Be aware that even during the "dry" season (Dec–Mar), rainfall is common. During the "rainy" season (the rest of the year), these peaks can get up to 3.8m (150 in.) of rainfall a year, and fogs and mists are frequent.

At no point do we recommend that you hike alone in the Blue Mountains, even if you're an experienced hiker. Weather conditions can change rapidly, and hiking maps are in general very poor. Since there are so few discernible landmarks, it is easy to lose your way.

Security is a major concern for an unaccompanied hiker, especially for those hiking on the Kingston side of the mountain. A guide will not only clear an overgrown path for you, but also may keep you out of harm's way. Bandits might rob you and then disappear into the vast wilderness of the Blue Mountains, where they are hard, if not impossible, to track down. If you appeal to local authorities, you will probably face indifference and a belated suggestion that "you should have used a guide." A better bet involves engaging one of Kingston's best-known specialists in eco-sensitive tours, **Sunventure Tours,** 30 Balmoral Ave., Kingston 10 (℃ **876/960-6685;** sunventuretours.com). The staff here can always arrange an individualized tour for you or your party, but offers a mainstream roster of choices as well. The **Blue Mountain Sunrise Tour** involves a camp-style overnight in one of the most remote and inaccessible areas of Jamaica. For US$60 to US$95 (£31–£49) per person, participants are picked up at their Kingston hotels, driven to an isolated ranger station, Wildflower Lodge, that's accessible only via four-wheel-drive vehicle, in anticipation of a two-stage hike that begins at 2pm. A simple mountaineer's supper is served at 6pm around a campfire at a ranger station near

Portland Gap. At 2am, climbers hike by moonlight and flashlight to a mountaintop aerie that was selected for its view of the 5am sunrise over the Blue Mountains. Climbers stay aloft until around noon that day, then head back down the mountain and return to their hotels by 4pm. A 4-hour trek, costing from US$45 to US$70 (£23–£36) per person, can also be arranged.

Another popular offering from the same company involves an excursion from Kingston **Y's Waterfall** on the Black River, in southern Jamaica's Elizabeth Parish. Participants meet in Kingston at 6:30am for a transfer to a raft and boating party near the hamlet of Lacovia, and an all-day waterborne excursion to a region of unusual ecological interest. Depending on the number of participants, fees range from US$80 to US$105 (£42–£55) per person, including lunch.

Blue Mountain Bike Tours (*©* **876/974-7075;** www.bmtoursja.com) offers all-downhill bike tours through the Blue Mountains—you peddle only about a half-dozen times on this several-mile trip. Visitors are driven to the highest navigable point in the Blue Mountains, where they are provided bikes and protective gear. Breakfast, lunch, snacks, and lots of information about coffee, local foliage, and history are provided. The cost is about US$93 (£48) per person. The tours run Monday to Saturday, departing at 9am and returning around 5pm.

ACCOMMODATIONS

Strawberry Hill *★★ Finds* Music-industry mogul turned hotelier extraordinaire Chris Blackwell worked here to re-create an idealized version of Jamaica that he remembered from his childhood. The setting is a former coffee plantation in the Blue Mountains, on precariously sloping rainforest terrain 930m (3,050 ft.) above the sea. Views from its terraces overlook the capital's twinkling lights. Eco-sensitive and fully contained, the resort has its own power and water-purification system, a small-scale spa, and elaborate botanical gardens. One former guest described this exclusive resort as a "home away from home for five-star Robinson Crusoes." Maps and/or guides are provided for tours of nearby coffee plantations, hiking and mountain biking through the Blue Mountains, and tours by night or by day of the urban attractions of nearby Kingston.

Accommodations are lavishly nostalgic, draped in bougainvillea and Victorian-inspired gingerbread, and outfitted with gracious mahogany furniture like that of a 19th-century Jamaican great house. Local craftspeople fashioned the cottages and furnished them with canopied four-poster beds and louvered mahogany windows. The elegant bathrooms, each designed in an artfully old-fashioned motif, come with tub/shower combinations. The food served in the hotel's glamorous restaurant is good enough to draw foodies from throughout eastern Jamaica.

Irish Town, Blue Mountains, Jamaica, W.I. *©* **800/688-7678** in the U.S., or 876/944-8400. Fax 876/944-8408. www.islandoutpost.com/strawberry-hill. 12 units. Year-round US$590 (£307) 1-bedroom suite or deluxe studio; US$790 (£411) deluxe villa; US$990 (£515) 2-bedroom villa. Rates include all meals. AE, DISC, MC, V. Guests are personally escorted to the hotel in a customized van or via a 7-min. helicopter ride. It's a 50-min. drive from the Kingston airport or 30 min. via mountain roads from the center of the city. **Amenities:** Restaurant; bar; outdoor pool; spa w/hydrotherapy facilities and massage; sauna; bike rental; room service; babysitting; laundry service; nonsmoking rooms; rooms for those w/limited mobility. *In room:* TV, kitchenette (in some), hair dryer, iron, safe.

16

Martinique

With beautiful white-sand beaches and a culture brimming with French flair, Martinique is part of the Lesser Antilles and lies in the semitropical zone; its western shore faces the Caribbean, and its eastern shore fronts the more turbulent Atlantic. The surface of the island is only 1,088 sq. km (424 sq. miles)—81km (50 miles) at its longest point and 34km (21 miles) at its widest point.

The terrain is mountainous, especially in the rainforested northern part, where the volcano Mount Pelée rises to a height of 1,397m (4,582 ft.). In the center of the island, the mountains are smaller, with Carbet Peak reaching a 1,188m (3,897-ft.) summit. The high hills rising among the peaks or mountains are called *mornes*. The southern part of Martinique has big hills that reach peaks of 350m (1,148 ft.) at Vauclin and 420m (1,378 ft.) at Diamant. The irregular coastline of the island has five bays, dozens of coves, and miles of sandy beaches. Almost a third of the island's year-round population of 360,000 lives in the capital and largest city, Fort-de-France.

The climate is relatively mild, with the average temperature in the 75°F to 85°F (24°C–29°C) range. At higher elevations, it's considerably cooler. The island is cooled by a wind the French called *alizé*, and rains are frequent but don't last very long. Late August to November is the rainy season. April through September are the hottest months.

The early Carib peoples, who gave Columbus such a hostile reception, called Martinique "the island of flowers," and indeed it has remained so. The lush vegetation includes hibiscus, poinsettias, bougainvillea, coconut palms, and mango trees. Almost any fruit can sprout from Martinique's soil, including pineapples, avocados, bananas, papayas, and custard apples.

Bird-watchers are often pleased at the number of hummingbirds, and visitors can also see mountain whistlers, blackbirds, and mongooses. Multicolored butterflies flit about, and after sunset, there's a concert of grasshoppers, frogs, and crickets.

1 Essentials

For advance information, contact the **French Government Tourist Office** in the U.S. at 444 Madison Ave., New York, NY 10022 (© **212/838-7800**). In Britain, contact 178 Piccadilly, London, W1J 9AL (© **0181/124-4123**). In Canada, write to 1981 McGill College Ave., Suite 490, Montréal, Québec H3A 2W9 (© **514/288-4264**). On the Web, go to **www.martinique.org**.

On the island, the **Martinique Tourist Office CMT** is on Immeuble Beaupré, Schoelcher (© **596/61-61-77**); it's open Monday to Friday from 8am to 12:30pm and 1:30 to 4:30pm. In addition to dispersing information about what to see and do in Martinique, the organization will reserve lodgings for clients in advance of their arrivals, without charge, through their **Service Loisirs Acceuil.** The information desk at Lamentin Airport is open daily until the last flight comes in.

GETTING THERE

BY PLANE Before you book your own airfare, read the section "Packages for the Independent Traveler" in chapter 2.

Lamentin International Airport (© 596/42-24-24) is outside the village of Lamentin, a 15-minute taxi ride east of Fort-de-France and a 40-minute taxi ride northeast of the island's densest concentration of resort hotels (Les Trois-Ilets peninsula). Most flights to Martinique require a transfer on a neighboring island—usually Puerto Rico, Antigua, or Barbados. From there another stopover or transfer in Guadeloupe is often required. Nonstop flights to any of the French islands from the U.S. mainland are rare.

You can fly on **American Airlines** (© 800/433-7300 in the U.S. and Canada; www.aa.com) from San Juan every Thursday, Friday, Sunday, and Monday. You can also fly on American to Santo Domingo in the Dominican Republic, then transfer onto **Air Caraïbes** (© 590/82-47-00; www.aircaraibes.com) to Martinique. Or you can fly to Miami, then transfer to **Air France** (© 800/237-2747 in the U.S. and Canada; www.airfrance.com) for the final lap of the flight to Martinique. From Miami passengers bound for Martinique transfer onto one or two daily **American Eagle** (same phone number as American Airlines) flights to Guadeloupe. From Guadeloupe, they transfer again onto one of up to 10 daily flights to Martinique on **Air Caraïbes** (formerly known as Air Guadeloupe).

Air France is the only airline with a direct connection from the United States to Martinique. Air France flies daily from Miami with a stopover in either Guadeloupe or Port-au-Prince. It operates separate nonstop flights from Paris to both Martinique and Guadeloupe. These depart at least once a day, and in some cases, depending on the season and the day of the week, twice a day. The airline also maintains three weekly flights from Port-au-Prince, Haiti, to Martinique, and three flights a week, depending on the season, between Cayenne, in French Guyana, and Martinique.

LIAT flies from St. Lucia, Antigua, and Barbados to both Martinique and Guadeloupe several times a day. Depending on the season, flights to the two islands are either separate or combined into a single flight, with touchdowns en route. Contact LIAT (Leeward Islands Air Transport) at © 888/844-LIAT within the Caribbean, or 866/549-5428 from Puerto Rico and U.S. Virgin Islands, or 1-268-480-5601/2 from other countries, including the U.S. and Canada. Note: Most visitors find it easier to book LIAT flights online at www.liatairline.com. St. Lucia, Antigua, and Barbados are important air-terminus links for such larger carriers as American Airlines (see above).

British Airways (© 800/247-9297 in the U.S. and Canada, or within the U.K. 0870/850-9850; www.britishairways.com) flies separately and daily to both Antigua and Barbados from Gatwick at London. From either of those islands, LIAT connects to either Guadeloupe or Martinique.

BY FERRY One particularly evocative means of travel between Martinique and Guadeloupe involves taking one of the motorized catamarans that are maintained by a local operator, **Exprèss des Iles.** Carrying between 395 and 495 passengers, depending on the boat, they require 3¾ hours of waterborne transit, which includes an intermediate stopover on either Dominica or Terre-de-Haut, in the Iles des Saintes. The

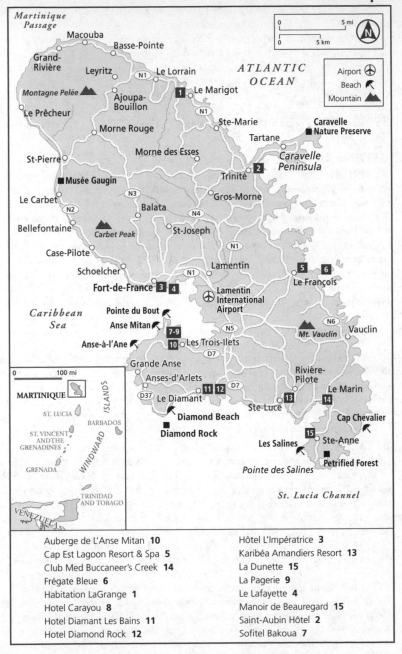

Martinique

Martinique Passage

Macouba
Basse-Pointe
Grand-Rivière
Leyritz
Le Lorrain
N1
Le Marigot **1**

ATLANTIC OCEAN

Montagne Pelée
Le Prêcheur
Ajoupa-Bouillon
N1
Ste-Marie
Tartane
Caravelle Nature Preserve

Morne Rouge
Morne des Esses
Caravelle Peninsula

St-Pierre
Musée Gaugin
Trinité **2**

Le Carbet
N3
Balata
Gros-Morne
N2
N4

Bellefontaine
Carbet Peak
St-Joseph

Case-Pilote
N1

Schoelcher
Lamentin
5 **6**
Le François

Fort-de-France **3** **4**
N1

Lamentin International Airport

Caribbean Sea
Pointe du Bout
N5
Mt. Vauclin
N6
Vauclin

Anse Mitan
7-9
Anse-à-l'Ane
10 Les Trois-Ilets
D7

Grande Anse
Rivière-Pilote
Anses-d'Arlets
D7
Le Marin

MARTINIQUE
D37
Le Diamant **11** **12**
13
Ste-Luce
14

0   100 mi

ST. LUCIA
BARBADOS
Diamond Beach
Cap Chevalier

ST. VINCENT AND THE GRENADINES
Diamond Rock
15 Ste-Anne
Les Salines

GRENADA
Petrified Forest

WINDWARD ISLANDS
Pointe des Salines

TRINIDAD AND TOBAGO
St. Lucia Channel

VENEZUELA

0   5 mi
0   5 km
N

Airport
Beach
Mountain

company usually operates three passages a week and sometimes more, between the two largest islands of the French West Indies.

Morning departures from Pointe-à-Pitre for Fort-de-France are usually at 8am (Sat at 11:30am, Sun at 10am), and departures from Fort-de-France for Pointe-à-Pitre are usually at 1pm, although the schedule can vary unexpectedly according to the season and the day of the week. Fares are 100€ ($130) round-trip or 65€ ($84) one-way. Children under 12 are granted reduced fares: 80€ ($104) round-trip or 50€ ($64) one way. For details and reservations, contact **Exprèss des Iles,** Gare Maritime, de Bergevin, 97110 Pointe-à-Pitre, Guadeloupe (© **590/91-52-15**), or **Terminal Inter-Iles,** Bassin de Radoub, 97200 Fort-de-France, Martinique (© **596/63-05-45**).

GETTING AROUND

BY RENTAL CAR   Unless you never plan to leave your hotel's beach, you probably want to rent a car to explore the island. Martinique has several local car-rental agencies, but clients have complained of mechanical difficulties and billing irregularities. We recommend renting from one of the U.S.-based firms. Driving in Martinique is on the right side of the road. *Note:* An international driver's license is required.

Budget has an office at 30 rue Ernest-Desproges, La Baie, Cruise Terminal, Fort-de-France, in addition to one at Lamentin (© **800/472-3325** in the U.S. and Canada, or 596/42-16-79 or 596/70-22-75; www.budgetrentacar.com). **Avis** is located at Lamentin Airport (© **800/331-1084** in the U.S. and Canada, or 596/66-04-27; www.avis.com), as is **Hertz** (© **800/654-3001** in the U.S. and Canada, or 596/51-01-01; www.hertz.com).

Regardless of which company you choose, you'll be hit with a value-added tax (VAT) of 8.5% on top of the final bill, plus either a charge of around 25€ ($33) if you ask the car to be delivered to your hotel, or an airport pickup charge of about 20€ ($26) if you retrieve your car at the airport. Collision damage waivers (CDWs), which eliminate some or all of your financial responsibility in the event of an accident, cost between 12€ and 25€ ($16–$33) per day at Budget and Hertz, and usually a bit more at Avis. Of these three car-rental companies, the rates at Budget tend to be the least expensive, although that depends on a wide array of seasonal variations.

BY TAXI   Local laws demand that any bona-fide Martiniquais cab must contain a working meter. For specific itineraries—wherein a passenger tells the driver where he or she wants to go—the meter must be "on" and functioning. **Radio Taxi** (© **596/63-63-62**), the island's largest dispatcher, advises us that if a taxi driver quotes a flat rate to a passenger instead of activating the meter, that you're being robbed, and you should immediately get out and find another cab. For an idea of prices, taxi rates between Fort-de-France and any hotel of La Pointe du Bout are 65€ ($85), but only 50€ ($65) from Lamentin Airport to any hotel of La Pointe du Bout. For a general tour of the island, prices are negotiable with the driver. Between 7pm and 6am, a 40% surcharge is assessed.

The rule about using a taxi's meter does not apply to passengers who want to hire a taxi for a **general tour** of the island. If that is your goal, expect to pay from 50€ ($65) per hour for up to four passengers, depending on the itinerary and routing you negotiate with the driver. Frankly, we find touring the island by taxi so expensive, and so easily corrupted by the whims of the individual driver, that we advise visitors to rent their own car for the day, driving themselves—armed with a good map—around the island's many rutted but often panoramic roads.

> *Fun Fact* **Carnival**
>
> If you like masquerades and dancing in the streets, you should be here to attend **Carnival,** or *Vaval,* as it's known here. Most of the celebrations associated with Carnival occur, depending on when Lent falls, for 5 days either in late February or early March, but there is also usually some form of celebration or contest conducted for the 6 Sundays prior. Most visible of these is the election of the **Carnival Queen,** a contest that's usually held the first Sunday before the actual week of Carnival itself. Each village prepares costumes and floats. Weekend after weekend, frenzied celebrations take place, reaching fever pitch just before Lent. Fort-de-France is the focal point for Carnival, but the spirit permeates the whole island. On Ash Wednesday, the streets of Fort-de-France are filled with *diablesses,* or she-devils (portrayed by members of both sexes). Costumed in black and white, they crowd the streets to form King Carnival's funeral procession. As devils cavort about and the rum flows, a funeral pyre is built at La Savane. When it's set on fire, the dancing of those she-devils becomes frantic (many are thoroughly drunk at this point). Long past dusk, the cortege takes the coffin to its burial, ending Carnival until next year.

BY BUS & TAXI COLLECTIF   There are two types of buses operating on Martinique. Regular buses, called *grands busses,* hold about 40 passengers and cost 2€ to 2.50€ ($2.60–$3.25) anywhere within the city limits of Fort-de-France. To travel beyond the city limits, nine-passenger *taxis collectifs* are used. These are privately owned minivans that traverse the island and bear the sign TC. Their routes are flexible and depend on passenger need. A one-way fare from Fort-de-France to Ste-Anne is about 10€ ($13). *Taxis collectifs* depart from the heart of Fort-de-France from the parking lot of Pointe Simon. There's no phone number to call for information about this unpredictable means of transport, and there are no set schedules. Traveling in a *taxi collectif* is for the adventurous visitor—these vehicles are crowded and not very comfortable.

BY FERRY   The least expensive—and most colorful—way to transfer between Fort-de-France and the hotel and tourist district of Pointe du Bout is via one of the *vedettes* (ferryboats) that depart from rue de la Liberté in Fort-de-France. Transit costs 3.80€ ($4.95) one-way or 6€ ($7.80) round-trip. Schedules for the ferryboats, at least 20 of which run at regular (usually 30-min.) intervals every day between 6:30am and 9pm, are printed in the free visitor's guide *Choubouloute,* in French and English, which is distributed by the tourist office. However, because the ferries are so frequent, most visitors dispense with attempting to understand the schedule altogether, and meander down to the waterfront to wait for the next boat.

There's a smaller ferryboat that runs between Fort-de-France and the unpretentious resorts of Anse Mitan and Anse-à-l'Ane, both across the bay and home to many two- and three-star hotels and modest Creole restaurants. The boat departs from rue de la Liberté in Fort-de-France at intervals of between 20 and 30 minutes every day from 7:30am to 6pm. The trip takes about 20 minutes. One-way and round-trip passage cost 3.80€ ($4.95) and 6€ ($7.80), respectively. If seas are extremely rough, or if there's a hurricane warning, all ferryboat services may be suspended.

For more information, call **Vedettes Madinina** (© **596/63-06-46**).

FAST FACTS: Martinique

Banks Most of the banks of Martinique maintain the following hours: Monday to Friday 7:30am to noon and 2:30 to 4pm. A few of them have opted to close on Wednesday afternoon. Others maintain a policy of remaining closed all day Monday, but opening their doors every Saturday morning between 7:30am and noon. There are about a dozen ATMs in Fort-de-France, at least three at Lamentin Airport, and a scattering of others throughout the island, usually in such touristed areas such as Pointe du Bout, Le Diamant, and Ste-Anne.

Currency Because Martinique falls under the same monetary system as mainland France, the island uses the **euro** as its mode of exchange. The current rate of exchange at press time was .77€ to the U.S. dollar or 1€ equals US$1.30. **Change Caraïbes** maintains full-service foreign currency divisions, as well as ATMs, at both Lamentin Airport (© **596/42-17-11**) and at 4 rue Ernest Desproges, in the center of Fort-de-France (© **596/60-28-40**). Banks give better exchange rates than hotels. *Prices in this chapter are quoted in U.S. dollars and euros.*

Customs Items for personal use, such as tobacco, cameras, and film, are admitted without formalities or tax if not in excessive quantity.

Documents U.S. and Canadian citizens need a valid passport. A return or ongoing ticket is also necessary. British citizens need only an identity card.

Electricity Electricity is 220-volt AC (50 cycles), the same as that used on the French mainland. However, check with your hotel to see if it has converted the electrical voltage and outlets in the bathrooms (some have). If it hasn't, bring your own transformer and adapter for U.S. appliances.

Emergencies Call the **police** at © **17**, report a **fire** by dialing © **18**, and summon an **ambulance** at © **17** or **18**. Ambulances can also be summoned by calling the island's emergency medical service (SAMU) at © **596/55-21-15** or 12 or 112.

Hospitals There are about 18 hospitals and clinics on the island, and there's a 24-hour emergency room at the island's largest, **Hôpital Pierre Zobda Quikman**, Châteauboeuf, 5km (3 miles) south from Fort-de-France (© **596/55-20-00**), on the road to Lamentin Airport.

Language French, the official language, is spoken by almost everyone. The local Creole patois uses words borrowed from France, England, Spain, and Africa. In the wake of increased tourism, English is occasionally spoken in the major hotels, restaurants, and tourist organizations—but don't count on driving around the countryside and asking for directions in English.

Liquor Laws Liquor is sold in grocery and liquor stores on any day of the week. It's legal to have an open container in public, though the authorities will be very strict with any littering, disorderly behavior, or drunk driving.

Pharmacies Try the **Pharmacie de la Paix,** at the corner of rue Perrinon and rue Victor-Schoelcher in Fort-de-France (© **596/71-94-83**), open Monday to Friday from 7:15am to 6:15pm and on Saturday from 7:45am to 1pm.

Safety Crime is hardly rampant on Martinique, yet there are still those who prey on unsuspecting tourists. Follow the usual precautions, especially in Fort-de-France and in the tourist-hotel belt of Pointe du Bout. It's wise to protect your valuables and never leave them unguarded on the beach.

Taxes & Service Charges Most hotels include a 10% service charge in the bill; all restaurants include a 15% service charge. Also added onto your hotel bill is a resort tax known locally as *une taxe hotelière*, which ranges from 2€ to 2.50€ ($2.60–$3.25) per person per night, depending on the hotel's rating and category.

Telephone To call Martinique from the United States, dial **011** (the international access code), then **596** (the country code for Martinique), and then, if it's a conventional (that is, noncellular) phone, dial 596 again, followed by the six-digit local number. If the number you're calling is a cellphone, dial 011, followed by 596, followed by 696, followed by the six-digit local number. To call the United States from Martinique, dial **19-1,** then the area code, then the seven-digit local number. To make a call within Martinique, only the six-digit local number is necessary.

Time Martinique is on Atlantic Standard Time year-round, 1 hour earlier than Eastern Standard Time except when daylight saving time is in effect in the U.S. Then, Martinique time is the same as on the East Coast of the United States.

Tipping Restaurants generally add a 15% service charge to all bills, which you can supplement if you think the service is outstanding. Some hotels also add a 10% service charge to your bill. Tip taxi drivers at least 15% of the fare.

Water The water is safe to drink throughout the island, but most residents stick to bottled water anyway.

Weather The climate is relatively mild—the average temperature is in the 75°F to 85°F (24°C–29°C) range.

2 Fort-de-France

With its iron-grille-work balconies overflowing with flowers, Fort-de-France, the largest town on Martinique, seems like a cross between New Orleans and a town on the French Riviera. It lies at the end of a large bay surrounded by green hills.

The proud people of Martinique are even more fascinating than the town of Fort-de-France, although today the Creole women are likely to be seen in jeans instead of their traditional turbans, Empress Joséphine–style gowns, and massive, jouncing earrings.

Narrow streets climb up the steep hills, where houses have been built to catch the overflow of the capital's more than 100,000 inhabitants.

ACCOMMODATIONS

Be sure to check out the "Packages for the Independent Traveler," section in chapter 2.

Don't stay in town if you want a hotel near a beach (see the hotels listed later in this chapter for beach resorts). If you do opt to stay in Fort-de-France, you'll have to take a ferryboat to reach the beaches at **Pointe du Bout** (see the section "Pointe du Bout & Les Trois-Ilets," below). The one exception is the Hôtel La Bâtelière, in the suburb of Schoelcher, which opens onto a small beach.

Hôtel L'Impératrice   Favored by businesspeople without unlimited expense accounts, this stucco-sided, five-story hotel faces a landscaped mall in the heart of town, near the water's edge. L'Impératrice was originally built in the 1950s and named in honor of one of Martinique's most famous exports, Joséphine. Its balconies overlook the traffic at the western edge of the sprawling promenade known as La Savane. The small- to medium-size guest rooms are modern and functional. The front rooms tend to be noisy, but they do offer a look into life along La Savane. Bathrooms are compact, with a combination tub/shower. Don't expect outstanding service. Almost no one speaks English, and many of the members of the staff seem a bit jaded. But despite the confusion in the very noisy lobby, and the unremarkable decor of the simple bedrooms, you might end up enjoying this hotel's unpretentiousness.

The hotel's restaurant, Le Joséphine, does a brisk business with local shoppers in town for the day.

Place de la Savane, 15 rue de la Liberté, 97200 Fort-de-France, Martinique, F.W.I. © 596/63-06-82. Fax 596/72-66-30. hotellimperatrice@wanadoo.fr. 24 units. Winter 72€–85€ ($94–$111) double; off season 65€–68€ ($85–$88) double. Rates include breakfast. AE, MC, V. **Amenities:** Restaurant; bar; laundry service; dry cleaning; rooms for those w/limited mobility. *In room:* A/C, TV.

Le Lafayette After 10pm, you'll enter this modest downtown hotel through its entrance on the rue Victor-Hugo; during daylight hours, you'll use a larger entrance that opens onto the rue de la Liberté, and climb a short flight of terra-cotta steps to reach the simple lobby. Don't expect grandeur; this hotel's snob appeal is practically nonexistent. The hotel was renovated, and its bedrooms are tidy and clean. Most units contain comfortable twin beds, with small, pure-white, shower-only bathrooms. The overall impression is neat but simple and unpretentious. The inn is the oldest continuously operating hotel on Martinique, originally built in the 1940s with quasi–Art Deco hints that are now slightly dowdy. There's a small restaurant on-site and several eateries are within a short walk.

5 rue de la Liberté, 97200 Fort-de-France, Martinique, F.W.I. © 596/73-80-50. Fax 596/60-97-75. www.lelafayette hotel.com. 22 units. 60€ ($78) double; extra bed 10€ ($13). AE, MC, V. **Amenities:** Restaurant; bar; laundry service; dry cleaning. *In room:* A/C, TV.

DINING

La Belle Epoque ★★ FRENCH   In a turn-of-the-20th-century house, this elegant choice features haute French cuisine. In the affluent suburb of Didier, this colonial-style restaurant stands high above the capital of Fort-de-France. The dining room is filled with crystal, silver, white linens, and beautiful tiles, the room opening onto a terrace with a view of the garden. Guests savor the inventive, superbly prepared cuisine. The fish dishes are the finest in the area, particularly filet of John Dory served with a lime butter and the roasted scallops served with spice butter. Some classic beef dishes are also offered; these are cooked to order and served with sauces that often contain foie gras and truffles. The best of these is filet of beef Périgourdine with foie gras and truffles. Smoked salmon appears on the plate with a vinaigrette of passion fruit, and magret de canard (duckling) is served with a foie gras and a Port wine sauce. Fresh lamb is flavored with thyme juice, and the chocolate fondant makes the perfect French dessert.

97 Route de Didier. © 596/64-41-19. Reservations required. Main courses 23€–37€ ($32–$48); fixed-price lunch 30€ ($39). MC, V. Tues–Fri noon–2pm; Mon–Sat 7:30–9:30pm.

Le Dôme ★★ *Finds* FRENCH/ANTILLEAN   Set on the uppermost (eighth) floor of a hotel in the Valmenière district, midway between Fort-de-France's commercial center and the airport—and far from the neighborhoods and haunts visited by the leisure-industry crowd—this establishment caters almost exclusively to a clientele of business travelers, many of whom come from the French mainland. Outfitted with a contemporary decor and hues of red, it boasts large bay windows, through which diners enjoy a view that sweeps along the island's coastline. Menu items blend traditional French cuisine with Antillean ingredients, sometimes in very creative ways. The best examples include a cream of *christophene* (Caribbean squash) soup with crayfish; ground rack of lamb served with a sauce made from cocoa powder and red wine; seawolf with coconut sauce; filet of John Dory with yellow bananas and anise; and braised breast of duckling served with a sauce based on Caribbean cherries.

In the Hôtel Valmenière, Ave. des Arawaks. (*C* 596/75-75-77. Reservations recommended. Main courses 22€–34€ ($29–$44). AE, DC, MC, V. Sun–Fri 12:30–2pm and Mon–Sat 7:30–10pm. Bus: 7.

SPORTS & OTHER OUTDOOR PURSUITS

If it's a beach you're looking for, take the ferry to **Pointe du Bout** (see the section "Pointe du Bout & Les Trois-Ilets," below). The island's only **golf course** is in Les Trois-Ilets, also discussed in the next section.

HIKING   Inexpensive guided hikes, sometimes within the boundaries of the **Parc Naturel Régional de la Martinique,** are organized year-round by the **CRRPM (Centre Régional des Randonnés Pedestres de la Martinique).** This organization also gives out maps of recommended hikes within Martinique, and offers advice about routings and access to departure points for walks and hill treks. You can write or call the park's administrative headquarters, BP 437, 97200 Fort-de-France (*C* **596/64-42-59**) for more information.

EXPLORING FORT-DE-FRANCE

At the heart of town is **La Savane,** a broad garden with many palms and mangos, playing fields, walks, and benches, plus shops and cafes lining its sides. In the middle of this grand square stands a statue of Joséphine, "Napoleon's little Creole," made of white marble by Vital Debray. The statue poses in a Regency gown and looks toward Les Trois-Ilets, where Joséphine was born. The statue was decapitated in 1991, probably because islanders felt she championed slavery. Near the harbor, at the edge of the park, you'll find vendors' stalls with handmade crafts, including baskets, beads, bangles, woodcarvings, and straw hats.

Your next stop could be the 1875 **Cathédrale St-Louis,** on rue Victor-Schoelcher. The religious centerpiece of the island, it's an extraordinary iron building, which has been likened to "a sort of Catholic railway station." A number of the island's former governors are buried beneath the choir loft.

A statue in front of the Palais de Justice is of the island's second main historical figure, **Victor Schoelcher,** who worked to free the slaves more than a century ago. **Bibliothèque Schoelcher,** 1 rue de la Liberté (*C* **596/70-26-67**), also honors this popular hero. Functioning today as the island's central government-funded library, the elaborate structure was first displayed at the Paris Exposition of 1889. The Romanesque portal, the Egyptian lotus-petal columns, even the turquoise tiles were imported piece by piece from Paris and reassembled here. It's open Monday 1 to 5:30pm, Tuesday to Friday 8:30am to 5:30pm, and Saturday 8:30am to noon.

Fort St-Louis, built in the Vauban style on a rocky promontory, guards the port. **Fort Tartenson** and **Fort Desaix** also stand on hills overlooking the port.

Musée Departemental d'Archeologie et de Prehistoire de la Martinique, 9 rue de la Liberté (*C* **596/71-57-05**), is the one place on Martinique that preserves its pre-Columbian past and has relics from the early settlers, the Arawaks and the Caribs. The museum has exhibits from the years from 3000 B.C. to A.D. 1635, but stops shortly after the arrival of the first French colonials on Martinique in the early 1600s. In other words, it's mostly an ethnological museum, which was enlarged and reorganized into a more dynamic and up-to-date place in 1997. The museum faces La Savane and is open Monday 1 to 5pm, Tuesday to Friday from 8am to 5pm, and on Saturday from 9am to noon; admission is 3.05€ ($3.95) for adults, 1.52€ ($2) for children 3 to 12 and students.

Musée Régional d'Histoire et d'Ethnographie, 10 Blvd. de Général-de-Gaulle, in Fort-de-France (© 596/72-81-87 or 596/63-85-55), is devoted to an illumination of the island's agrarian past (and the slave culture that made it possible). Expositions showcase the late-19th-century volcanic eruption that leveled St-Pierre, slavery and its effects on the island's society, and explorations of the sugar-cane industry. It's open Tuesday from 2 to 5pm, Saturday from 8:30am to noon, and Monday and Wednesday to Friday from 8:30am to 5pm. Entrance costs 3€ ($3.90) for adults, and .75€ ($1) for children under 12. Entrance is free for anyone who presents a valid student ID.

Sacré-Coeur de Balata Cathedral, at Balata, overlooking Fort-de-France, is a copy of the one looking down from Montmartre upon Paris—and this one is just as incongruous, maybe more so. It's reached by going along route de la Trace (Route N3). Balata is 10km (6¼ miles) northwest of Fort-de-France.

A few minutes away on Route N3, **Jardin de Balata** (© 596/64-48-73) is a tropical botanical park created by Jean-Philippe Thoze on land that the jungle was rapidly reclaiming around a Creole house that belonged to his grandmother. He has also restored the house, furnishing it with antiques and historic engravings. The garden contains a profusion of flowers, shrubs, and trees. It's open daily from 9am to 5pm. Admission is 6.50€ ($8.45) for adults, 2.50€ ($3.25) for children 7 to 12, and free for children 6 and under.

SHOPPING

Your best buys on Martinique are French luxury imports, such as perfumes, fashions, Vuitton luggage, Lalique crystal, and Limoges dinnerware. Sometimes (but don't count on it) prices are as much as 30% to 40% below those in the United States.

You're usually better off shopping in the smaller stores, where prices are 8% to 12% lower on comparable items, and paying in euros that you have exchanged at a local bank.

FORT-DE-FRANCE AFTER DARK

The most exciting after-dark activity is seeing a performance of the folkloric troupe **Les Grands Ballets Martiniquais** (see "Martinique's Traditional Dances," below).

The popularity of individual bars and dance clubs in Martinique rises and falls almost monthly. Many of them charge a cover between 10€ and 15€ ($13–$20), although that's often ignored if business is slow, and if you're a particularly appealing physical specimen. A nightclub and restaurant where anyone can be a star, at least for a few minutes, is **Le Karaoke Café California,** Immeuble Les Corneaux, Lamentin (© 596/50-07-71).

If you're on the party circuit around Martinique, you are likely to find the most action at **Crazy Nights,** Ste-Luce (© 596/68-56-68), a wild dance parlor that on weekends can attract hundreds of patrons, each bent on having one "crazy night." Jazz is showcased at the **Calebesse Café,** 19 bd. Allegre Le Marin (© 596/74-69-27),

Martinique's Traditional Dances

The sexy and rhythmic beguine was *not* an invention of Cole Porter. It's a dance of the islands—though exactly which island depends on whom you ask. Popular wisdom and the encyclopedia give the nod to Martinique, though Guadeloupeans claim it as their own, too.

Everybody who goes to Martinique wants to see the show performed by **Les Grands Ballets Martiniquais,** a troupe of about two dozen dancers, along with musicians, singers, and choreographers, who tour the island regularly. Their performances of the traditional dances of Martinique have been acclaimed in both Europe and the United States. With a swoosh of gaily striped skirts and clever acting, the dancers capture all the exuberance of the island's soul. The group has toured abroad with great success, but they perform best on their home ground, presenting tableaux that tell of jealous brides and faithless husbands, demanding overseers and toiling cane cutters. Dressed in traditional costumes, the island women and men dance the spirited mazurka, which was brought from the 18th- and 19th-century ballrooms of Europe, and, of course, the exotic beguine.

Les Grands Ballets Martiniquais usually perform Monday at the Hotel Diamond-Rock and Friday at the Sofitel Bakoua, but these schedules can vary, so check locally. The cost of dinner and the show is usually 46€ to 50€ ($60–$65). Most performances are at 8:30pm, with dinners at the hotels beginning at 7:30pm. The show is free for guests of the hotel where the troupe is performing. In addition, the troupe gives miniperformances aboard visiting cruise ships.

which sometimes features its own Billie Holiday clone. Meals are served, and the place is packed on Saturday nights. Live performances on Thursday around 10:30pm are a regular feature at **Les Soirees de l'Amphore,** Anse-Mitan (© **596/66-03-09**), a small restaurant and minibar. Funk, disco, and soul are all featured. Fort-de-France's most animated and busiest piano bar is **Le Club Piano-bar Privé,** 24 bd. Allègre (© **596/27-93-19**).

If you want to gamble, head for Martinique's major casino, **Casino Bâtelière Plaza,** at Schoelcher (© **596/61-73-23**), a 10-minute drive from the center of Fort-de-France. You'll need a passport and 11€ ($13) to enter the gaming rooms (men do not need a jacket and necktie). A special area reserved just for slot machines and their fans is open daily, without charge, from 10am to 3 or 4am. A more formal gambling area, with strip poker, roulette, and blackjack, is open daily from 8pm to 3am. This is the larger, newer, and more crowded of the two casinos in Martinique, with 140 slot machines, compared to the 40 slots at the Casino des Trois-Ilets in Pointe du Bout, which is described in "Pointe du Bout After Dark," later in this chapter. But that might change if and when the new casino at Trois-Ilets opens. There's a restaurant onsite, so you won't go hungry.

On a cultural note, **L'Atrium,** 6 rue Jacques Cazotte, Fort-de-France (© **596/60-78-78**), is the venue for major island cultural events, including dance and music. The theatrical presentations, of course, are in French. You can ask on island what might be happening at the time of your visit. For a not-always-up-to-date rundown on what's cooking entertainment-wise, click on **www.martiniquescoop.com**.

3 Pointe du Bout ⭐ & Les Trois-Ilets

Pointe du Bout is a narrow peninsula across the bay from the busy capital of Fort-de-France. It's the most developed resort area of Martinique, with at least four of the island's largest hotels, an impressive marina, about a dozen tennis courts, countless pools, facilities for horseback riding, and all kinds of watersports. There's also a handful of independent restaurants, a casino, boutiques, and in nearby Les Trois-Ilets, a Robert Trent Jones, Sr.–designed golf course. Except for the hillside that contains the Sofitel Bakoua Caralia, most of the district is flat and verdant, with gardens and rigidly monitored parking zones. All the hotels listed below are near the clean white-sand beaches of Pointe du Bout. Some of the smaller properties are close to the white-sand beaches of Anse Mitan. Les Trois-Ilets, the birthplace of Joséphine, the empress of France and wife of Napoleon Bonaparte, lies at the base of the peninsula on the bay.

GETTING THERE

If you're driving from Fort-de-France, take Route 1, which crosses the plain of Lamentin—the industrial area of Fort-de-France and the site of the international airport. Often the air is filled with the fragrance of caramel, from the large sugar-cane factories in the surrounding area. After about 30km (20 miles), you reach Les Trois-Ilets. Five kilometers (3 miles) farther on your right, take Route D38 to Pointe du Bout.

The **ferry service** runs all day long until midnight from the harbor front (rue de la Liberté) in downtown Fort-de-France. Round-trip fare is 8€ ($10). See "Getting Around" in section 1, earlier in this chapter, for details.

ACCOMMODATIONS
EXPENSIVE

Hotel Carayou ⭐ *Kids*   This hotel is popular with families because of its children's programs, and has always prided itself on its lush gardens and glamorous garden setting opening onto a small beach. The accommodations aren't the most attractive in the area, but they are housed in a series of three-story outbuildings, each encircled by large lawns dotted with coconut or palm trees and flowering shrubs. The seaside rooms are the best, and some of the units are air-conditioned. Against a setting of wood trim and whitewashed walls, the rooms are generally small but well maintained. Each bathroom is equipped with a tub/shower combination, a bidet, toiletries, and large mirrors.

Creole dishes, especially the seafood items, are prepared with flair at Le Boucault.

Pointe du Bout, 97229 Trois-Ilets, Martinique, F.W.I. ⓒ **596/66-04-04.** Fax 596/66-00-57. 201 units. Winter 230€–255€ ($299–$332) double; off season 160€ ($208) double. Rates include American buffet breakfast. AE, DC, MC, V. **Amenities:** 2 restaurants; bar; outdoor pool; tennis court; watersports; children's progam; laundry service; dry cleaning; nonsmoking rooms; rooms for those w/limited mobility. *In room:* A/C, TV, hair dryer, safe.

Sofitel Bakoua ⭐   Airline crews fill up many of the rooms at the Sofitel Bakoua, a hotel known for the beauty of its landscaping and its somewhat isolated hillside location. It consists of four low-rise buildings in the center of a garden. Built in 1967 and renovated several times since, accommodations come in a wide range of sizes, from small to spacious, and are comfortable albeit a bit battered, although a restoration of all units was scheduled for late in 2007. Rooms have balconies or patios, extra-comfortable beds, and small tiled bathrooms with showers and tubs.

There's a lunch restaurant, and evening meals are served in Le Châteaubriand, a formal but appealing French restaurant.

Pointe du Bout, 97229 Trois-Ilets, Martinique, F.W.I. ℂ 800/221-4542 in the U.S., or 596/66-02-02. Fax 596/66-00-41. www.sofitel.com. 139 units. Winter 410€–490€ ($533–$637) double, 980€ ($1,274) suite; off season 240€–380€ ($312–$494) double, 580€ ($754) suite. Rates include breakfast. MAP (breakfast and dinner) 48€ ($62) per person extra. AE, DC, MC, V. **Amenities:** 2 restaurants; 2 bars; outdoor pool; 2 tennis courts; deep-sea fishing; dive shop; scuba diving; snorkeling; windsurfing; limited room service; babysitting; laundry service; dry cleaning; rooms for those w/limited mobility. *In room:* A/C, TV, minibar, hair dryer, safe.

MODERATE

La Pagerie   The facilities here are relatively modest compared to those in some of the larger and more expensive hotels of Pointe du Bout, but guests can compensate by visiting the many restaurants, bars, and sports facilities in the area. Set close to the gardens of the Sofitel Bakoua (see above) and a 26km (16-mile) drive from the airport, this hotel offers comfortably modern bedrooms. Although the walls are thin, the units are neat and uncomplicated, with tile floors, small fridges, and balconies with views opening onto the bay. About two-thirds of the units contain tiny kitchenettes, at no extra charge. The accommodations are outfitted with floral prints, low-slung furnishings, and louvered closets. The tiled bathrooms have combination tub/showers, marble vanities, and wall-mounted showerheads. Guests usually walk 5 minutes to Hotel Carayou (see above) for watersports and access to the beach.

Pointe du Bout, 97229 Trois-Ilets, Martinique, F.W.I. ℂ 596/66-05-30. Fax 596/66-00-99. 93 units. Winter 135€ ($176) double; off season 78€ ($101) double. Rates include buffet breakfast. AE, MC, V. **Amenities:** Restaurant; bar; outdoor pool; laundry service; rooms for those w/limited mobility. *In room:* A/C, TV, kitchenette (in some), fridge.

INEXPENSIVE

Auberge de L'Anse Mitan   You don't get anything special here, but the price is right and many guests like this hotel's location at the isolated end of a road whose more commercial section is laden with restaurants and bustles at night. The hotel was built in 1930, but has been renovated several times, most recently in 2000, by the hospitable Athanase family. What you get today is a three-story concrete box-type structure. Six of the units are studios with kitchens and TVs; all have private showers. Rooms are boxy, but the beds are comfortable. Bathrooms are very small and cramped, but tidy.

35 rue des Anthuriums, L'Anse Mitan, 97229 Trois-Ilets, Martinique, F.W.I. ℂ 596/66-01-12. Fax 596/66-01-05. www.auberge-ansemitan.com. 21 units. Winter 70€ ($91) double, 65€ ($85) studio, 90€ ($117) triple; off season 55€ ($72) double, 50€ ($65) studio, 71€ ($92) triple. Rates include breakfast. *In room:* A/C, TV (in studios), kitchenette (in studios).

DINING

There isn't a great choice of restaurants, but here's the pick of the litter.

Au Poisson d'Or CREOLE   Its position near the entrance of the resort community of Pointe du Bout makes it easy to find. There's no view of the sea and the traffic runs close to the edge of the veranda and terrace, but the reasonable prices and the complete change of pace make up for that. The rustic dining room offers such classics as grilled fish, sometimes cooked in coconut milk; grilled conch scallops sautéed in white wine; poached local fish; and flan. These ordinary dishes are prepared with flair and served with style.

12 rue des Bougainvilliers, L'Anse Mitan. ✆ **596/66-01-80.** Reservations recommended. Main courses 12€–25€ ($16–$33); prix-fixe lunch 15€–23€ ($20–$30); and prix-fixe dinner 25€–33€ ($33–$43). AE, MC, V. Tues–Sun noon–2pm and 7–10pm. Closed July.

Havana Café FRENCH   Set in Pointe du Bout, amid the densest concentration of tourist hotels and leisure facilities of Martinique, this café evokes an idealized version of Cuba in its most decadent period, just before the rise to power of Fidel. Amid a color scheme of bright yellow and blue, and prefaced with a big American sedan, painted yellow, from the early 1960s, a mostly French-born staff serves stiff drinks as well as meal-sized salads, burgers, grilled cutlets, and heaping platters of mussels. There's a selection of raw tartars of fish, and a house cheeseburger called a "Havana Burger." And for anyone nostalgic for metropolitan France, there's a short list of the buckwheat crêpes endemic to Brittany (*des galettes*), stuffed, *Breton*-style, with savory or sweet fillings that include ham and cheese or ice cream with chocolate sauce. Some kind of music, either live or recorded, rocks and rolls the place every evening between 9:30pm and midnight, during which time it takes on the aura of a holiday-maker's singles bar. There's another beachside branch of this place, **Havana Plage,** at Grand Anse, Anse d'Arlets (✆ **596/69-07-38**), with the same menu items, prices, and hours, but this, Havana Café, is the more animated of the two.

In the Village Creole, Pointe du Bout. ✆ **596/66-15-93.** Main courses 7.50€–13€ ($9.75–$17). MC, V. Daily 9:30am–11:30pm.

La Villa Creole ☆ CREOLE/FRENCH   This restaurant, which lies a 3- or 4-minute drive from the hotels of Pointe du Bout, has thrived since the late 1970s, offering a colorful, small-scale respite from the island's high-rise resorts. Set within a simple but well-maintained Creole house, with no particular views other than the small garden that surrounds it, the restaurant serves fairly priced set-price menus of such staples as *accras de morue* (beignets of codfish), *boudin Créole* (blood sausage), and *feroce* (a local form of pâté concocted from fresh avocados, pulverized codfish, and manioc flour). A special delight is the red snapper prepared either with tomato sauce or grilled. If Creole food doesn't appeal to you, there's also a short list of dishes inspired by the traditional cuisine of mainland France, focusing on such Gallic staples as terrine of duck liver, a terrine of smoked salmon, and a confit of duckling with a purée of shallots. Owner Guy Bruère-Dawson, a singer and guitarist, entertains as you dine.

18 rue des Anthuriums, L'Anse Mitan. ✆ **596/66-05-53.** Reservations recommended. Main courses 12€–34€ ($16–$44); set-price menus 16€–40€ ($21–$52). AE, MC, V. Tues–Sat noon–2pm; Mon–Sat 7–10:30pm.

Le Pacha ☆ FRENCH/CARIBBEAN   Le Pacha opened in October 2006, within a sea-fronting building that's virtually hidden from the landward side by a thick screen of palm trees and vegetation. Inside, in an environment painted in tones of pink, orange, and variations of green, you'll find a dedication to creative cuisine that's directly affected by the French Alps origins of the creative team who run the place. The same menu is offered at both lunch and dinner. Alongside pizzas and salads, the menu includes such elaborate creations as a duet of fish (Atlantic mackerel and Caribbean *balahou*) served with orange sauce; a cassolette of freshwater crayfish with foie gras; and a roasted half-lobster served with fresh tomatoes, tarragon, and pistou. A deeply upholstered leather sofa near the entrance functions as a kind of throne at this place, supposedly allowing any Jean, Philippe, or Pierre to feel like a pacha, or sultan, in his own right. Le Pacha is a short walk from the departure point for the ferryboats heading to and from Fort-de-France.

Anse Mitan. © **596/66-02-99.** Reservations recommended. Main courses 16€–21€ ($21–$28). DC, MC, V. Tues–Sat noon–2:30pm and Mon–Sat 7–10:30pm.

Pignon sur Mer CREOLE Simple and unpretentious, with a décor and a menu that has remained the same for the past 20 years, this is an intimate Creole restaurant containing about 15 tables, set within a rustically dilapidated building beside the sea. (It's a 12-min. drive from Pointe du Bout.) Menu items are island-inspired, and might include a platter of shellfish, or whatever grilled fish was hauled in that day. *Lambi* (conch), shrimp, and crayfish are usually available, and brochettes of chicken are flavorful. A specialty is a well-flavored filet of beef with a choice of green-peppercorn sauce or Roquefort sauce.

Anse-a-l'Ane, Trois Ilets. © **596/68-38-37.** Main courses 9€–32€ ($12–$42). MC, V. Tues–Sun 12:15–2:15pm; Tues–Sat 7–9:30pm.

HITTING THE BEACH

The clean white-sand beaches of **Pointe du Bout,** site of the major hotels of Martinique, were created by developers and tend to be rather small. Most of the tourists head here, so the narrow beaches are among the island's most crowded. It doesn't help that Pointe du Bout also has several marinas lining the shore and serves as the docking point for the ferry from Fort-de-France. Even if you don't find a lot of space on the beach, with its semi-clear waters, you will find toilets, phones, restaurants, and cafes galore. The waters suffer from industrial usage, although apparently the pollution is not severe enough to prevent people from going in. You'll often see the French standing deep in the water, smoking cigarettes—perhaps not your idea of an idyllic beach vacation.

To the south, however, the golden-sand beaches at **Anse Mitan** are far less crowded and more inviting, with cleaner waters. However, the steepness of Martinique's shoreline leaves much to be desired by its swimmers and snorkelers. The water declines steeply into depths, no reefs ring the shores, and fish are rarely visible. Nonetheless, beaches here are good for sunbathing. The neighboring beach is **Anse-à-l'Ane,** an ideal place for a picnic.

SPORTS & OTHER OUTDOOR PURSUITS

GOLF Robert Trent Jones, Sr., designed the 18-hole **Golf de l'Impératrice-Joséphine,** at Trois-Ilets (© **596/68-32-81**), a 5-minute drive from Pointe du Bout and about 30km (20 miles) from Fort-de-France. The only golf course on Martinique has greens that slope from the birthplace of Empress Joséphine across rolling hills with scenic vistas down to the sea. Amenities include a pro shop, a bar, and a restaurant. Greens fees are 46€ ($60) for 18 holes. There are also three rather battered tennis courts, which cost 13€ ($17) per hour to use.

HORSEBACK RIDING The premier riding facility on Martinique is **Ranch Jack,** Esperanze, Trois-Ilets (© **596/68-37-69**). It offers morning horseback rides for both experienced and novice riders, at a cost of 52€ to 60€ ($68–$78) for a 4-hour ride (either 8:30am–12:30pm or 2:30–6:30pm). Jacques and Marlene Guinchard make daily treks across the beaches and fields of Martinique, with a running (English-language) explanation of the history, fauna, and botany of the island. Cold drinks are included in the price, and transportation is usually free to and from the hotels of nearby Pointe du Bout. Four to 15 participants are needed to book a tour. This is an ideal way to discover both the botany and geography of Martinique.

SCUBA DIVING & SNORKELING   The beachfront of **The Hotel Carayou** is the headquarters for the island's best dive outfit, **Espace Plongée Martinique** (© 596/66-01-79), which welcomes anyone who shows up, regardless of where they happen to be staying. Daily dive trips, depending on demand, leave from Le Kalenda's pier every day at 8am, returning at noon, and departing again at 2pm, returning at 5pm. Popular dive sites within a reasonable boat ride, with enough diversity and variation in depth to appeal to divers of all levels of proficiency, include *La Baleine* (The Whale) and Cap Salomon. A dive shop stocks everything you'll need to take the plunge, from weight belts and tanks to wet suits and underwater cameras. Uncertified divers pay 60€ ($78) for a *baptême* ("baptism"), which consists of instruction and practice time in the hotel's swimming pool followed by a brief experience with a scuba tank in open water.

Certified divers pay 50€ ($65) for a one-tank dive, or around 125€ ($163) for a full-day excursion from Kalenda Resort to Baie de St-Pierre (St. Peter's Bay) on Martinique's northern coast. Here, the excursion includes two dives (morning and afternoon, in different spots), excursions in a minibus or minivan to sites of natural beauty along the north coast, and both continental breakfast and a picnic lunch. It departs whenever at least five participants show sufficient interest, at 8am. Participants return to the Kalenda the same day at 5:30pm.

Coral, fish, and ferns abound in the semi-clear waters around the Pointe du Bout hotels, and snorkeling equipment is usually available free to hotel guests.

JET SKIING   Also on the grounds of the Carayou Hotel is an outfit specializing in jet-skiing, **Jet Caraibes** (© 596/66-09-31). A 30-minute rental of a jet ski costs 60€ ($78).

WINDSURFING   An enduringly popular sport in the French West Indies, *la planche à voile* (windsurfing) is available at most of the large-scale hotels. One of the best equipped (and longest-lived) of Martinique's windsurfing centers is **Windsurf Club Martinique,** which occupies a site directly on the beachfront of the Hotel Carayou (© 596/66-19-06). Lessons cost 40€ ($52) per hour, and boards, depending on their make and model, rent for 20€ ($26) per hour. A 10-hour rental costs 185€ ($241).

A VISIT TO LES TROIS-ILETS

Marie-Josephe-Rose Tascher de la Pagerie was born here in 1763. As Joséphine, she was to become the wife of Napoleon I and empress of France from 1804 to 1809. Six years older than Napoleon, she pretended that she'd lost her birth certificate so he wouldn't find out her true age. Although many historians call her ruthless and selfish, she is still revered by some on Martinique as an uncommonly gracious lady. Others have less kind words for her—Napoleon is said by some historians to have "reinvented" slavery and they cite Joséphine's influence.

Thirty kilometers (20 miles) south of Fort-de-France, you reach Les Trois-Ilets, a charming little village. Two kilometers (1¼ miles) outside the village, turn left to La Pagerie, where the small **Musée de La Pagerie** (© 596/68-34-55) has been installed in the former estate kitchen, where Joséphine gossiped with her slaves and played the guitar. Regrettably most of the other buildings associated with this once-thriving plantation were destroyed in a hurricane. Visitors today can see mementos of Josephine's childhood, including the bed she slept in as a teenager and a passionate letter from Napoléon. The collection was compiled by Dr. Robert Rose-Rosette. Still remaining are the partially restored ruins of the Pagerie sugar mill and the church (in the village itself) where she was christened in 1763. The museum is open Tuesday to Friday from 9am to 5:30pm, Saturday and Sunday 9:30am to 12:30pm and 3 to 5pm. Admission is 5€ ($7) for adults, 1.50€ ($1.95) for children 5 to 12.

Modern artists and local potters banded together in 2005 to form a cooperative of shops, galleries, and studios at **Trois-Ilets Pottery** (© 596/63-03-44), at La Pagerie, next to the Musée de La Pagerie. You can shop for one-of-a-kind items such as a clay lamp hand painted in Creole colors.

Maison de la Canne, Pointe Vatable (© 596/68-32-04), is on the road to Trois-Ilets. Located on the premises of an 18th-century distillery, its permanent exhibitions tell the story of sugar cane and the sweeping role it played in the economic and cultural development of Martinique. It's open Tuesday to Sunday 9am to 5pm, charging an admission of 3€ ($3.90) for adults, .75€ ($1) for children 5 to 12, and free for children under 5.

The Marina complex has a number of interesting boutiques; several sell handicrafts and curios from Martinique. They're sometimes of good quality, but are quite expensive, particularly the enameled jewel boxes and some of the batiks of natural silk.

POINTE DU BOUT AFTER DARK

For such a popular resort area, nightlife is mostly confined to bars. Other entertainment options are sporadic, including offerings at the **Havana Café,** Village Créole, Pointe du Bout (© 596/66-15-93). Live entertainment is also featured on occasion at **La Casa de Da Paulette,** Village Créole, Pointe du Bout (© 596/66-15-15). This bar is set in a typical old Creole cottage and can be a lot of fun if the crowd is right. **L'Amphore,** a piano and karaoke bar, is found at the rear of Sofitel Bakoua, Pointe du Bout (© 596/66-03-09).

At presstime, Martinique had one of the dullest casinos in the Caribbean, **Casino des Trois-Ilets.** It's positioned on the lobby level of a grim, hulking building that once functioned as the centerpiece of a resort that was otherwise closed (Le Kalenda Resort, Trois-Ilets, Pointe du Bout; © 596/66-00-30). Slot machines, for which entrance is free, are available daily 10am to 3am. Roulette and *les grands jeux* (roulette and blackjack), for which there's an entrance charge of 11€ ($14), and for which a visitor must present ID or a passport, are open nightly from 9pm to 3am.

Look for a replacement of this casino, perhaps during the lifetime of this edition. At the time of writing, a new venue was under construction as a self-contained outbuilding of the Le Kalenda resort, but no official opening date had been announced either for the casino or the resort that contains it.

4 The South Loop

South of Pointe du Bout you can find sun and beaches. Resort centers here include Le Diamant and Ste-Anne.

From Trois-Ilets, you can follow a small curved road that brings you to **Anse-à-l'Ane, Grande Anse,** and **Anses-d'Arlets.** At any of these places you'll find small beaches, which are quite safe and usually not crowded.

ANSES-D'ARLETS

The scenery is beautiful here. Brightly painted fishing boats known as *gommiers* draw up on the white-sand beach, and the nets are spread out to dry in the sun. Children swim and adults fish from the good-size pier. The waters off Anses-d'Arlets are a playground for divers, with a wide variety of small tropical fish and colorful corals.

The area itself has been a choice spot for weekend second homes for many years, and is now becoming a destination for tourists. The little village features a pretty steepled church, a bandstand for holiday concerts, and a smattering of modest little dining spots. Aficionados of Martinique come here to see "the way it used to be" on the island. Unspoiled and folkloric, the hamlet still retains its *charm typique Martiniquaise*.

From Anses-d'Arlets, panoramic Route D37 takes you to Le Diamant.

LE DIAMANT

Set on the island's southwestern coast, about 40 minutes by taxi from the airport, this village offers a good beach, open to the prevailing southern winds. The village is named after one of Martinique's best-known geological oddities, **Le Rocher du Diamant (Diamond Rock),** a barren offshore island that juts upward from the sea to a height of 172m (564 ft.). Sometimes referred to as the Gibraltar of the Caribbean, it figured prominently in a daring British invasion in 1804, when British mariners carried a formidable amount of ammunition and 110 sailors to the top. Despite frequent artillery bombardments from the French-held coastline, the garrison held out for 18 months, completely dominating the passageway between the rock and the coast of Martinique. Intrepid foreigners sometimes visit Diamond Rock, but the access across the strong currents of the channel is risky.

Diamond Beach 𝕲𝕲𝕲, on the Martinique mainland, offers a sandy bottom, verdant groves of swaying palms, and many different surf and sunbathing possibilities. The entire district has developed in recent years into a resort, scattered with generally small hotels.

ACCOMMODATIONS

Hotel Diamant Les Bains This is an unpretentious, family-style hotel with direct access to a sandy beach. From the edge of the resort's pool, you can enjoy a view of the offshore island of Diamond Rock. Twenty units are in outlying motel-style bungalows set either in a garden or beside the beach; the others are in the resort's main building, which also houses the restaurant and bar. Accommodations have furnished terraces or patios, white-tile floors, small fridges, and built-in furniture made from polished fruitwood. Most rooms are medium in size except for the small units on the second floor of the main building, which are often rented to business travelers from the French mainland. The best are the 10 rustic bungalows directly above the beach. Bathrooms are accented with blue tiles and equipped with such extras as bidets; each has a shower stall.

The cuisine at the hotel restaurant is for the most part Creole, with some French dishes thrown in.

97223 Le Diamant, Martinique, F.W.I. © **596/76-40-14.** Fax 596/76-27-00. diamantlesbains@wanadoo.fr. 27 units. Winter 94€ ($122) double, 110€ ($143) bungalow; off season 60€ ($78) double, 70€ ($91) bungalow. Rates include continental breakfast. MAP (breakfast and dinner) 19€ ($25) per person extra. MC, V. Closed 1st week of June and Sept. **Amenities:** Restaurant; bar; outdoor pool; laundry service; dry cleaning; rooms for those w/limited mobility. *In room:* A/C, TV, fridge, safe.

Hotel Diamond-Rock On 2 hectares (5 acres) of forested land, 3km (2 miles) outside the village and 29km (18 miles) south of Fort-de-France, this low-rise building is in one of the most beautiful districts on Martinique. It's the ultimate in laissez-faire management—guests, often tour groups from France, are basically left to fend for themselves. Guest rooms, housed in four three-story wings, face either the pool or the coast, with its view of Diamond Rock. The inviting units have tropical decor, white-tile floors, whitewashed walls, roomy closets, and rattan furnishings, plus adequate desk space. Bathrooms have tub/shower combos and full-length mirrors.

Outside the hotel, the neighboring beaches aren't too crowded. They consist of white sand but are rather narrow. Two casual restaurants serve lunch, while more formal dinners are available at Le Flaboyant, a French and Creole restaurant.

97223 Le Diamant, Martinique, F.W.I. ℂ 596/76-42-42. Fax 596/76-22-87. 181 units. Year-round 250€ ($325) double; 327€ ($425) suite. Rates are all-inclusive. AE, MC, V. **Amenities:** 2 restaurants; bar; large outdoor pool; 2 tennis courts; diving; watersports; laundry service; dry cleaning; rooms for those w/limited mobility. *In room:* A/C, TV, hair dryer, safe.

STE-LUCE

Between Le Diamant and Ste-Anne lies this sleepy fishing village, which is known for its fine beaches of white sand. Scuba divers flock to the waters at Pointe Figuier to the east of Ste-Luce. Most visitors come here to lodge at the hotel below or just to enjoy the beaches.

You can also visit **Ecomusée de Martinique,** Anse Figuier (ℂ 596/62-79-14), which exhibits artifacts unearthed from the days of the earliest settlers, the Carib and Arawak Indians. Entrance is 3€ ($3.90) for adults, .75€ ($1) children 5 to 12, and hours are Tuesday to Friday 9am to 5pm, Saturday and Sunday 9am to 1pm and 2 to 5pm.

ACCOMMODATIONS

Karibéa Amandiers Resort   This is our favorite of three interrelated, side-by-side resorts, each of which is managed by the France-based Karibea Hotel Group. Opening directly onto the sea and a beach, it's a winning choice and imbued with a tropical ambience and a welcoming staff. In the south, this property enjoys a scenic location on a natural cove with a beach. Accommodations are found in buildings rising three floors, the upper levels reached by stairs in lieu of an elevator. The main feature of the hotel is its lovely pool, and the entire complex is set in well-landscaped tropical gardens. Many units open onto balconies, and are equipped with full kitchenettes. Cane furniture and West Indian decorative motifs are used throughout. Each room comes with two bathrooms with shower. The on-site restaurant's not bad, although not something you need to seek out if you're not a guest. The names of this hotel's two sister resorts include the **Karibéa Amyris** and the **Karibéa Caribéa.** Each is within walking distance of the other, and clients at one tend to mingle around the amenities of each of the three. When their room count is combined, the three hotels have a total of 300 units.

Quartier Désert 97228 Ste-Luce, Martinique, F.W.I. ℂ 596/62-12-00. Fax 596/62-12-12. www.karibea.com. 100 units. Winter 171€–186€ ($222–$242) double; off season 117€–170€ ($152–$221) double. AE, MC, V. **Amenities:** 2 restaurants; 2 bars; 3 outdoor pools; 2 tennis courts; snorkeling; children's programs (ages 4–12); car rentals; non-smoking rooms; rooms for those w/limited mobility. *In room:* A/C, TV, kitchenettes (in some), hair dryer, safe.

LE MARIN

This is the yachting capital of Martinique lying between Ste-Luce and Ste-Anne, about an hour south from the capital of Fort-de-France. There is a Jesuit church from 1766 crowning the hill overlooking town with a stone ruin next to it. But most visitors come for the yachting, with pleasure boats filling the protected harbor.

From Le Marin a signposted narrow road leads to **Cap Chevalier** (Cape Knight), one of the most panoramic lookout points on Martinique, lying about 1.5km (1 mile) from town. Waterfront restaurants specializing in seafood and clubs fill the town of Le Marin itself.

ACCOMMODATIONS

Club Med Buccaneer's Creek 🍴   Set on a tranquil cove at the southernmost tip of Martinique, Club Med reopened in December of 2005 after a long closing for a major and much-needed restoration. The resort is designed as a series of scattered out-buildings evocative of a Creole village. It is set on a 22-hectare (55-acre) former pirate's hideaway at Buccaneer's Creek, amid a forest of coconut palms.

Originally opened in 1969, the property fronts a beach of white sand with views of Diamond Rock off shore. After spending $60 million, the resort was vastly upgraded and expanded, including the addition of a modern spa with five treatment rooms. Other features include an "infinity edge" pool and a beach palapa for yoga and fitness classes.

Bedrooms are midsize and furnished tastefully and comfortably but far from lav-ishly. The hotel staff provides an activity-filled agenda for its guests and a respectable cuisine of Antillean and French dishes. Its dance club stays open until the wee hours. Because of the influx of families in summer, prices are slightly higher then.

Regarding pricing at this resort: Club Med tells us that getting North American clients to Martinique because of the lack of nonstop flights from North America is extremely tricky. Therefore, they price all winter U.S. sales at this place to include chartered roundtrip flights from Atlanta, with supplements charged for flights wing-ing in from other parts of the country to hook up with the Atlanta-based flights. In the off season, the equivalent per person rate does not include airfare. What compli-cates matters is that in the off season, no flights from Atlanta are offered at all. Many flights can be arranged from cities such as New York, for an add-on fee.

Pointe Marin, 97227 Ste-Anne, Martinique, F.W.I. ⓒ **800/258-2633** in the U.S., or 596/76-72-72. Fax 596/76-83-36. www.clubmed.com. 293 units. Winter 1,771€–2,337€ ($2,300–$3,035) per person, based on double occupancy for 1 week. Rates all-inclusive, including roundtrip passage from Atlanta. Off season 936€–1,381€ ($1,215–$1,793) all-inclusive per person double occupancy per week. AE, DC, MC, V. **Amenities:** 2 restaurants; 3 bars; 2 outdoor pools; dance club; tennis court; water sports; laundry service; nightly entertainment. *In room:* A/C, TV.

DINING

Le Zanzibar 🍴 *Finds* FRENCH/SEAFOOD/NORTH AFRICAN   There's nothing finer in the south of Martinique than sitting on the second-floor veranda of this restaurant, drinking a tropical punch and overseeing the yacht-clogged harbor. Din-ing is also on a terrace overlooking the sea. The restaurant is built in the courtyard style of a Moroccan *riad.* Also in the North African style, both the bar and restaurant are a series of alcoves for intimate dining and drinking. In the background, a DJ spins lounge music as you study the menu. The chef spins his magic with sea bass, sea urchins, and a tagine of lamb, each with a savory sauce. We especially like the roast duck with mango. If you didn't go for the chicken tagine, you can also order fish tagines Morocco style. Saffron-flavored cod filets on a bed of leeks or Indian chicken tikka are other main dish specialties.

Comptoir des boucaniers, 11 bd. Allègre, Le Marin. ⓒ **596/74-08-46.** Reservations required. Main courses 15€–25€ ($20–$33); lunch plat du jour 10€–12€ ($13–$16). DISC, MC, V. Mon–Fri noon–2:30pm and daily 7:30–11pm.

STE-ANNE

From Le Marin, an 8km (5-mile) drive brings you to Ste-Anne, at the extreme south-ern tip of Martinique. This sleepy little area is known for the white-sand beaches of

Les Salines (those to the north are more grayish in color). In many ways, these are Martinique's finest. The climate is arid like parts of Arizona, and the beaches are almost always sunny, perhaps too much so at midday. The name comes from Etang des Salines, a large salt pond forming a backdrop to the strip of sand. Manchineel trees are found at the southeastern end of the beach. **Warning:** Under no circumstances should you go under these trees for protection in a rainfall. When it's sunny you can seek shade here, but when it rains, drops falling from the poisonous tree will be like acid on your skin.

Holidays and weekends tend to be crowded, as many islanders and their families flock to this beach, which is just not big enough to handle the hordes.

Les Salines is also the site of Martinique's only real gay beach. Drive to the far end of the parking lot, near the sign labeled PETITE ANSE DES SALINES. Here you'll find a trail leading through thick woods to a sun-flooded beach often populated by naked gay men, with an occasional lesbian couple or two. Technically, there are no legal nudist beaches on Martinique, so it's possible you could be arrested for going nude, although authorities don't seem to enforce this law. (Throughout the island, however, the European custom of topless bathing is not uncommon on any of the beaches or even around hotel pools.)

Ste-Anne opens onto views of the Sainte Lucia Canal, and nearby is the Petrified Savanna Forest, which the French call **Savane des Petrifications.** It's a field of petrified volcanic boulders in the shape of logs. The eerie, desertlike site is studded with cacti.

ACCOMMODATIONS

La Dunette *(Value* A three-story motel-like stucco structure directly beside the sea, this hotel draws guests who appreciate its simplicity and its isolation from the more built-up resort areas of other parts of Martinique. An unpretentious seaside inn with summery decor and basic bedrooms painted in bright tropical colors, the hotel is accented with a garden filled with flowers and tropical plants. The furnishings are casual and modern, although some rooms are quite small. The private shower-only bathrooms, though cramped, are well maintained.

97227 Ste-Anne, Martinique, F.W.I. (C) 596/76-73-90. Fax 596/76-76-05. www.ladunette.com. 18 units. Winter 88€ ($114) double; off season 75€ ($98) double. Rates include continental breakfast. AE, MC, V. **Amenities:** Restaurant; bar; watersports; laundry service; dry cleaning. *In room:* A/C, TV, hair dryer.

Manoir de Beauregard *(★★* One of the most venerable and historic hotels on Martinique lies within the massive walls of a manor house that once administered many acres of surrounding sugar-cane fields. It was originally built between 1720 and 1800 by a prominent French family, and almost resembles a medieval church. A fire in 1990 completely gutted the building's interior and led to 4 years of restoration. Today, there are three bedrooms on the upper floors of the original house, and another eight within a modern, less inspired one-story annex. Rooms within the annex, although not as dignified, have antique West Indian beds and direct views over the garden. Most units are roomy with double or twin beds, plus a compact tiled bathroom with a combination tub/shower. A truly superb beach, Plage des Salines, is a 5-minute drive to the south, and a slightly less appealing beach, Plage de Ste-Anne, is within a 15-minute walk.

Meals here are conservative, traditional, tried-and-true Creole cuisine, with dishes like codfish fritters, *boudin Créole* (blood sausage), grilled fish in Creole sauce, curries, and fresh lobster.

Chemin des Salines (a 10-min. walk south of Ste-Anne), 97227 Ste-Anne, Martinique, F.W.I. © **596/76-73-40.** Fax 596/76-93-24. 11 units. Winter 90€–140€ ($117–$182) double; off season 78€–120€ ($101–$156) double. Rates include breakfast. AE, MC, V. **Amenities:** Restaurant; bar; outdoor pool. *In room:* A/C, TV, fridge.

5 The North Loop

As we swing north from Fort-de-France, our main targets are **Le Carbet, St-Pierre, Montagne Pelée,** and **Leyritz.** However, we'll sandwich in many stopovers along the way.

From Fort-de-France, there are three ways to head north to Montagne Pelée. The first is to follow Route N4 up to St-Joseph. From there take the left fork for 5km (3 miles) and then turn onto Route D15 toward Le Marigot.

Another option is to take Route N3 through the vegetation-rich *mornes* (hills) to Le Morne Rouge. This road is known as "Route de la Trace" and is now the center of the Parc Naturel de la Martinique.

Yet a third route to Montagne Pelée is via Route N2 along the coast. This is the route we'll follow, and the order in which we'll list the towns along the way is as follows. Near Fort-de-France, the first town you reach is **Schoelcher.** Farther along Route N2 is **Case-Pilote,** and then Bellefontaine. This portion, along the most popular drive in Martinique—from Fort-de-France to St-Pierre—is very reminiscent of the way the French Riviera used to look. **Bellefontaine** is a small fishing village, with boats stretched along the beach. Note the many houses also built in the shape of boats.

LE CARBET

Leaving Bellefontaine, an 8km (5-mile) drive north will deliver you to Le Carbet. Columbus landed here in 1502, and the first French settlers arrived in 1635. In 1887, Gauguin lived here for 4 months before going to Tahiti. You can stop for a swim at an Olympic-size pool set into the hills, or watch the locals scrubbing clothes in a stream. The town lies on the bus route from Fort-de-France to St-Pierre.

Centre d'Art Musée Paul-Gauguin, Anse Turin, Le Carbet (© **596/78-22-66**), is near the beach represented in the artist's *Bord de Mer.* The landscape hasn't changed in 100 years. The museum, housed in a five-room building, commemorates the French artist's stay on Martinique in 1887, with books, prints, letters, and other memorabilia. There are also paintings by René Corail, sculpture by Hector Charpentier, and examples of the paintings of Zaffanella. Of special interest are faience mosaics made of once-white pieces that turned pink, maroon, blue, and black in 1902 when the fires of Montagne Pelée devastated St-Pierre. There are also changing exhibits of works by local artists. Hours are daily from 9am to 5:30pm; admission is 4€ ($5.20) for adults, 2€ ($2.60) for students, and 1€ ($1.30) for children under 8.

ST-PIERRE ✪

At the beginning of this century, St-Pierre was known as the "Little Paris of the West Indies." Home to 30,000 inhabitants, it was the cultural and economic capital of Martinique. On May 7, 1902, the citizens read in their daily newspaper that "Montagne Pelée does not present any more risk to the population than Vesuvius does to the Neapolitans."

However, on May 8, at 8am, the southwest side of Montagne Pelée exploded into fire and lava. At 8:02am, all 30,000 inhabitants were dead—that is, all except one. A convict in his underground cell was saved by the thickness of the walls. When islanders reached the site, the convict was paroled and left Martinique to tour in Barnum and Bailey's circus.

Fun Fact **Photo Ops**

Martinique is a photographer's dream—certainly the French fashion magazines know it, because crews are always around on shoots. The most picturesque sites are **La Savane,** in Fort-de-France; **St-Pierre,** the best place to photograph towering Mount Pelée; **La Pagerie,** with its decaying ruins of a sugar factory; and the panoramic overlooks along **La Trace,** a serpentine road winding through the entire rainforest.

St-Pierre never recovered its former splendor. It could now be called the Pompeii of the West Indies. Ruins of the church, the theater, and some other buildings can be seen along the coast.

Musée Volcanologique, rue Victor-Hugo, St-Pierre (© **596/78-15-16**), was created by the American volcanologist Franck Alvard Perret, who turned the museum over to the city in 1933. Here, in pictures and relics dug from the debris, you can trace the story of what happened to St-Pierre. Dug from the lava is a clock that stopped at the moment the volcano erupted. The museum is open daily from 9am to 5pm; admission is 2.50€ ($3.25), free for children 7 and under. About a kilometer (⅔ miles) away, higher up the mountain, and clearly signposted, is a modern-looking museum, **Le Centre Decouverte des Sciences de la Terre** (© **596/52-82-42**), containing exhibits about the region's seismology and geology, replete with public service warnings about what to do in the event of another explosion. It's open Wednesday to Sunday 9am to 5pm. Admission is 5€ ($6.50) for adults over 26; 3.50€ ($4.55) ages 13 to 25, 2.50€ ($3.25) ages 6 to 12, and free for children 5 and under.

DINING

Le Fromager *(Finds* CREOLE/FRENCH   Set less than 1km (½ mile) east of the center of St-Pierre, this indoor-outdoor villa, owned by the René Dement family, welcomes luncheon guests with a humor and charm that's part French, part Martiniquais. The restaurant, which resembles a covered open-air pavilion, has a sweeping view of the town. Recommended dishes include marinated octopus, grilled conch or lobster, curried goat or chicken, and whatever grilled fish is available that day. This is a good lunch stopover during your tour of the island.

Route de Fonds–St-Denis, Quartier St. James, St-Pierre. © **596/78-19-07.** Reservations recommended on Sun. Main courses 11€–25€ ($14–$33); fixed-price Sun menu 24€ ($31). MC, V. Daily noon–2:30pm.

LE PRECHEUR

From St-Pierre, you can continue along the coast north to Le Prêcheur. Once the home of Madame de Maintenon, the mistress of Louis XIV, it's the last village along the northern coast of Martinique. Here you can see hot springs of volcanic origin and the *Tombeau des Caraïbes* (**Tomb of the Caribs**), where, according to legend, the collective suicide of many West Indian natives took place after they returned from a fishing expedition and found their homes pillaged by the French.

MONTAGNE PELEE

A panoramic and winding road (Rte. N2) takes you through a tropical rainforest. The curves are of the hairpin variety, and the road is not always kept in good shape. However, you're rewarded with tropical flowers, baby ferns, plumed bamboo, and valleys so deeply green you'll think you're wearing cheap sunglasses.

The village of **Morne Rouge,** right at the foot of Montagne Pelée, is a popular vacation spot for Martiniquais. From here on, a narrow and unreliable road brings you to a level of 750m (2,460 ft.) above sea level, 480m (1,575 ft.) under the round summit of the volcano that destroyed St-Pierre. Montagne Pelée itself rises 1,373m (4,503 ft.) above sea level.

If you're a serious mountain climber and you don't mind 4 or 5 hours of hiking, you can scale the peak, though you should hire an experienced guide to accompany you. Remember, this is a real mountain, rain is frequent, and temperatures drop very low. Tropical growth often hides deep crevices in the earth, and there are other dangers. The park service maintains more than 150km (100 miles) of trails. Although the hikes up from Grand-Rivière or Le Prêcheur are generally the less arduous of the three options leading to the top, most visitors opt for departures from Morne Rouge because it doesn't take as long to finish the trip. It's steeper, rockier, and more exhausting, but you can make it in just 2½ hours versus the 5 hours it takes from the other two towns. There are no facilities other than these villages, so it's vital to bring water and food with you. Your arduous journey will be rewarded at the summit with sweeping views over the sea and panoramas that sometimes stretch as far as mountainous Dominica to the south. As for the volcano, its deathly eruption in 1902 apparently satisfied it—for the time being.

Upon your descent from Montagne Pelée, drive down to **Ajoupa-Bouillon,** one of the most beautiful towns on Martinique. Abounding in flowers and shrubbery with bright yellow-and-red leaves, this little village is the site of the remarkable **Gorges de la Falaise.** These are minicanyons on the Falaise River, up which you can travel to reach a waterfall. Ajoupa-Bouillon also makes a good lunch stop.

GRAND-RIVIÈRE

After Basse-Pointe, the town you reach on your northward trek is Grand-Rivière. From here you must turn back, but before doing so, you may want to stop at Yva Chez Vava, a good restaurant right at the entrance to the town.

DINING

Yva Chez Vava ⟨ℛ⟩ ⟨*Finds*⟩ FRENCH/CREOLE   Directly west of Basse-Pointe, in a low-slung building painted the peachy-orange of a paw-paw fruit, Yva Chez Vava is a combination private home and restaurant. It represents the hard labor of three generations of Creole women. Infused with a simple country-inn style, it was established in 1979 by a well-remembered, long-departed matron, Vava, whose daughter, Yva, is now assisted by her own daughter, Rosy. Family recipes are the mainstay of this modest and very ethnic bistro. A la carte items include Creole soup, lobster, shark steak, and various *colombos* (curries). Local delicacies include *z'habitants* (crayfish), *vivaneau* (red snapper), *tazard* (kingfish), *accras de morue* (codfish beignets), roasted or curried goat, and court bouillon of fish. Occasionally available, but only during certain periods, are the very ethnic, and not-to-everyone's taste *aceras de titiris,* composed of hundreds of tiny, barely visible fish (*des titiris*) which are caught with nets as they swarm in the nearby river. These, heads, skeletons and all, are mixed with flour, herbs, and spices, and deep-fried in oil into *aceras* (fritters).

Before or after their meal, clients can bathe in the nearby river, or walk to an unnamed strip of sand, the nearest beach, which lies about .4km (¼ mile) from the restaurant.

Blvd. Charles-de-Gaulle. ⟨©⟩ **596/55-72-72.** Reservations recommended. Main courses 12€–30€ ($16–$39); prix-fixe menu 16€ ($21). MC, V. Dec–Apr daily noon–5pm; off season Thurs–Tues noon–5pm.

LE MARIGOT

After passing back through Basse-Pointe and Le Lorrain, you come to a small village that was relatively ignored by tourists until hotelier Jean-Louis de Lucy used France's tax-shelter laws to restore a landmark plantation and turn it into one of the finest hotels on the island. True, the nearest good beach is at Trinité, a 30-minute drive, but guests of the Habitation LaGrange don't seem to mind.

ACCOMMODATIONS & DINING

Habitation LaGrange ⭐⭐⭐   One of the most unusual and historic properties of Martinique, this hotel lies in isolation about 2km (1¼ miles) north of the village of Le Marigot. It's set on 2 hectares (5 acres) of land whose edges are engulfed by acres of banana fields. About 2km (1¼ miles) inland from the coast, it was originally built in 1928 as part of the last sugar plantation and rum distillery on Martinique. Today, the ruins of that distillery rise a short distance from the Louisiana-style main house. This hotel is superior in style and class to Leyritz, to which it bears some resemblance.

Rooms are either in the main house or in what used to be the stables. We actually prefer these rooms, photographs of which have appeared in architectural magazines. Each unit is different, and contains antique or reproduction furniture crafted from mahogany, baldachin-style (canopy) beds, and French colonial–style accessories. All units have verandas or patios, with views over a tropical landscape of gardens and banana groves. As part of an effort to preserve the quiet, units contain no TVs or radios. Bathrooms are among the island's finest, with wood paneling, four-footed tubs equipped with showers, and pedestal sinks. Meals are prepared in the Creole style by local chefs, then served in an open-sided pavilion in the garden.

97225 Le Marigot, Martinique, F.W.I. ℂ 596/53-60-60. Fax 596/53-50-58. www.habitationlagrange.com. 11 units. Year-round 190€–214€ ($247–$278) double, 300€ ($390) suite. Rates include breakfast. AE, MC, V. **Amenities:** Restaurant; bar; outdoor pool; library. *In room:* A/C, hair dryer (in some), safe (in some).

STE-MARIE

Heading south along the coastal road, you'll pass Le Marigot en route to the little town of Ste-Marie. **Musée du Rhum Saint-James,** route de l'Union at the Saint James Distillery (ℂ **596/69-30-02**), displays engravings, antique tools and machines, and other exhibits tracing the history of sugar cane and rum from 1765 to the present. When inventories of rum are low and the distillery is functioning (only 4 months of the year, from early Mar–late June or mid-July), guided tours of the distillery are offered daily, whenever clients show up, between 9am and 5pm. Tours cost 5€ ($6.50) per person. Admission to the museum (open daily year-round 9am–5pm, regardless of whether the distillery is functioning) is free. Rum is available for purchase on-site.

From here you can head out the north end of town and loop inland a bit for a stop at Morne des Esses, or continue heading south straight to Trinité.

TRINITÉ

Passing through Morne des Esses, continue south, then turn east, or from Ste-Marie head south along the coastal route (N1), to reach Trinité. The town is the gateway to the Caravelle peninsula, where the **Caravelle Nature Preserve,** a well-protected peninsula jutting into the Atlantic Ocean from the town of Trinité, has safe beaches and well-marked trails through tropical wetlands and to the ruins of historic Château Debuc. It offers excellent hiking and one of the only safe beaches for swimming on the Atlantic coast. It would hardly merit an actual stop, however, were it not for the Domaine Saint Aubin.

ACCOMMODATIONS

Saint-Aubin Hôtel ⟨ *Finds*   This restored three-story Victorian house is architecturally one of the loveliest inns in the Caribbean. With fancy gingerbread, the hotel was originally built in 1920 of brick and poured concrete as a replacement for a much older wood-sided house, which served as the seat of a large plantation. It sits on a hillside above sugar-cane fields and the bay, 3km (2 miles) from the village of Trinité itself. The nearest beach is Plage Cosmy, lying 1.5km (1 mile) from the hotel. The bedrooms are spacious and modern, with 19th-century furnishings. There are some family rooms as well. All of the bedrooms have only showers. New owners have made major changes to this place, breaking down walls between existing rooms to create larger bedrooms, upgrading the plumbing and electricity, and bringing in classier antiques. Although there were only 11 rooms in operation at presstime, during the life of this edition, they were developing an annex, hoping for an eventual room count of 30 units.

97220 Trinité, Martinique, F.W.I. ⓒ **596/69-34-77.** Fax 596/69-41-14. www.ledomainesaintaubin.com. 11 units. Winter 189€ ($246) double; off season 116€ ($151) double. MC, V. **Amenities:** Outdoor pool; fitness center; laundry service. *In room:* A/C.

DINING

La Table de Mamy Nounou FRENCH/ANTILLEAN   Set less than 1km (½ mile) east of the fishing village of Tartane, this is the most easterly restaurant in the most easterly hotel on La Caravelle peninsula. The setting, as created and maintained by a team of English-speaking expatriates from the French mainland, is idyllic, a renovated complex perched within a hill-hugging compound of veranda-fronted buildings overlooking the sea. The restaurant, which was rechristened La Table de Mamy Nounou in 2004, is the main allure of the well-managed and carefully maintained Hotel Caravelle.

Lunches are faster, and less elaborately orchestrated, than the candlelit dinners, where guests linger longer within an ambience that falls midway between what you'd expect on the French mainland and what you find in Fort-de-France. Menu items change frequently, but might include a *colombo* (spicy Creole stew) concocted from shark meat, fish, shellfish, or chicken; braised filets of red mullet with tropical fruits; or, depending on the mood of the chef, classic dishes such as boeuf bourguignon. Desserts might feature a semi-moist version of chocolate cake, or perhaps a rum-and-orange-flavored soufflé. There's dining on the veranda, easy access to a garden, and from virtually all points, a sweeping view of the sea.

On-site are 15 studio apartments, each with telephone, air-conditioning, ceiling fans, a kitchenette, plus TV. Accommodations rent for 55€ to 84€ ($72–$109) double.

In the Hotel Caravelle, Route du Château Dubuc, L'Anse l'Etang, 97720 Tartane (Trinité). ⓒ **596/58-07-32.** Fax 596/58-07-90. www.hotel-la-caravelle-martinique.com. Reservations recommended for nonresidents of the hotel. Lunch platters and salads 5€–20€ ($6.50–$26). Fixed-price dinner 25€ ($33). MC, V. Daily noon–2:30pm and 7–9:30pm. Closed Tues from mid-May to mid-Nov.

LE FRANÇOIS

Continuing your exploration of the east coast of Martinique, you can stop over in Le François to visit the **Musée Rhum Clement** at the Domaine de l'Acajou (ⓒ **596/54-62-07**), about 2km (1¼ miles) south of the village center. The setting for this museum is an outmoded distillery in the cellar of an 18th-century mansion with period furnishings that the Clement Rum Company closed in the early 1990s, when it shifted its production to a newer plant 6km (3.6 miles) away (which cannot be visited). A

Columbus exhibit is set up in caves, and other exhibits trace the institution of slavery in the islands. Products of the Clement rum distillery are prominently displayed for purchase, and tastings of some of the rums are available. The museum is in a botanic park; you could easily spend 2 or 3 hours exploring the exhibits and grounds. It's open daily from 9am to 5:30pm. Admission is 7€ ($9.10) for adults, or 4€ ($5.20) for ages 7 to 18. Free for ages 6 and under.

ACCOMMODATIONS

Rooms can also be rented at La Maison de L'Ilet Oscar and Le Plein Soleil (see "Dining" below).

Cap Est Lagoon Resort & Spa ✲✲✲

Set on the island's east coast between the fishing hamlets of Vauclin and Le François—5km (3 miles) from either of them—this is the poshest and most cutting-edge hotel on Martinique. Scattered across nearly 3.5 hectares (8½ acres) of gently sloping palm-studded beachfront, it's composed of 18 veranda-fronted, one- and two-story villas housing 50 well-designed suites. This is as top-of-the-line as you'll find in the French West Indies outside of St. Barts. It's the only government-rated five-star hotel on Martinique, and the only Relais & Château in either Martinique or Guadeloupe. Clients include a string of celebrities, the most impressive of which was the Queen of Denmark.

The venue is very French, artfully permissive, and luxurious. No one will mind if you simply vegetate, recovering from the stresses of urban life. Topless sunbathing for women is permitted on the beach or beside any of the pools, but not in the other public areas. Views throughout the resort extend outward over a coral reef to the wide blue seas. Construction and design emulates Creole models elsewhere, making full use of open access to sea breezes, with ample use of louvered doors, exotic tropical hardwoods, and exterior color schemes of blue, salmon, and pale pink. Public areas contain unusual artwork, including a large-scale triptych titled *Serenity.* It was choreographed by Didier Lefort, who's well known within Gallic circles for his award-winning designs of hotels in French-speaking Tahiti and Mauritius. Each unit has a landscaped terrace or balcony, and separate bathtubs and showers. Besides the showpiece public pool, there are 36 plunge pools, some of them specifically associated with individual suites. Live music emanates many evenings from one of the two in-house bars throughout the dinner hour, and overall, the ambience is lighthearted, agreeable, and fun. The restaurants, Le Bélem and Le Campêche, are recommended in "Dining," below.

Quartier Cap Est, 97240 Le François. (© **800/633-7411** in the U.S. and Canada, or 596/54-80-50. Fax 596/54-96-00. www.capest.com. 50 units. Winter 500€–1,200€ ($650–$1,560) suite; off season 400€–1,000€ ($520–$1,300) suite. Rates include buffet or American breakfast. AE, DC, MC, V. **Amenities:** 2 restaurants; bar; outdoor pool; 36 plunge pools; lit tennis court; health club; spa; dock for mooring of private yachts and sailboats; fishing; library; car rental; salon; room service; helipad. *In room:* A/C, plasma TV, minibar, beverage maker, hair dryer, safe.

Frégate Bleue ✲ *Finds*

This is the closest thing to a European B&B on the island. It's a calm and quiet choice with touches of personal, old-fashioned charm. It's not the place for vacationers looking for nightlife and lots of activities—it's for escapists who don't mind the 10-minute drive to the beaches of St-François or the prevailing sense of isolation. Much of this ambience is the work of owner Yveline de Lucy de Fossarieu, an experienced veteran of the hotel industry. Her house is a 5-minute drive inland from the sea, and it overlooks several chains of deserted offshore islands (including Les Ilets de St-François and Les Ilets de l'Impératrice). Bedrooms are small but cozy, each with a compact bathroom with a shower. The site is perched in a quiet residential neighborhood high on a hill. Each room has either a terrace or a balcony with sweeping views over the coast. The hotel has opened a Creole and French restaurant on site.

Route de Vauclin, 97240 Le François, Martinique, F.W.I. © **800/633-7411** in the U.S., or 596/54-54-66. Fax 596/54-78-48. www.fregatebleue.com. 10 units. Winter 122€–290€ ($159–$377) double; off season 84€–156€ ($109–$203) double. Rates include breakfast. AE, MC, V. **Amenities:** Restaurant; outdoor pool; laundry. *In room:* A/C, ceiling fan, TV, kitchenette.

DINING

La Maison de L'Ilet Oscar ☆ *(Finds)* INTERNATIONAL/FRENCH   Inside an antique Creole house, this establishment lies on a nearly adjacent island off the southeast coast of Martinique; you access it by motorboat from the marina at Le François. If you make advance reservations, you'll be taken on a 12-minute boat ride to the island, stopping at an emerald-colored tidal pool where legend says that Joséphine, wife of Napoleon I, once went swimming. You'll then head to the island's only dwelling, a one-story wood-sided house that was originally built in 1898 on nearby Ilet Thierry, and disassembled and floated, beam by beam, across to Ilet Oscar and reassembled there in 1935. Menu items focus on Creole specialties like an all-fish menu, an all-shrimp menu, or an all-lobster menu, but if you desire food inspired by the traditions of mainland France, Brittany-born Jean-Louis de Lussy and his staff will whip you up avocados stuffed with crayfish, magret of duckling, or whatever else happens to be in the larder. If you want to overnight, the four bedrooms (all with shower, toilet, and double sinks) rent for 135€ ($176) per person, with half-board included, and 165€ ($215) with full board included. None has TV, phone, or air-conditioning.

L'Ilet Oscar, B.P. 12, 97240 Le François, Martinique. © **596/45-33-30.** Reservations essential 1 day in advance. Fixed-price menu 45€–60€ ($59–$78). Round-trip transport from Le Marina du François 55€ ($72) for up to 6 passengers. AE, MC, V. Daily 11am–3pm and 6–9:30pm (dinner only for hotel guests).

Le Bélem/Le Campêche ☆☆ FRENCH/ANTILLEAN   Two of the best-recommended dining spots in Martinique lie on the Atlantic coastline. If you arrive for lunch, you'll be steered toward the less expensive, and less formal, of the two restaurants, Le Campêche, an ocean-fronting outdoor bistro where good-looking people in teeny bathing suits are not at all out of the ordinary. Menu items focus on tried-and-true Creole specialties, as well as salads, buffets, pastas, and well-prepared versions of grilled fish and meats.

Dinners are more elaborate and more formal, served within Le Bélem, a romantic eatery noted for its wine list and its "gastronomic" interpretation of all things French and Antillean. Begin with a tarte tatin of foie gras with caramelized yellow bananas, shallots, and a confit of limes; or perhaps ravioli stuffed with herb-seasoned rabbit. You might also enjoy a succulent version of magret of duckling with green papaya and *christophene* (Caribbean squash). Main courses include a filet of red snapper served with a fondue of leeks and truffled fava beans. Another artful dish is spiny lobster prepared three different ways: roasted with vanilla-flavored butter; as lobster ravioli; and served cold, in gelatin, with caviar.

In the Cap Est Lagoon Resort & Spa, Quartier Cap Est. © **596/54-80-80.** Reservations strongly recommended for nonresidents. Main courses in Le Bélem 25€–55€ ($33–$72); main courses in Le Campêche 15€–30€ ($20–$39). AE, DC, MC, V. Le Bélem daily 7:30–10:30pm; Le Campêche daily noon–3pm and 7–10:30pm.

Le Plein Soleil ☆ *(Finds)* INTERNATIONAL   With the noteworthy exception of the Cap Est Lagoon Resort and Spa (above), this is the most upscale and elegant hotel in this part of Martinique. Meals here are taken on the wide veranda of a 1880s French colonial–style house that sits on a hillside about 90m (300 ft.) from the seafront. Your hosts are entrepreneurs José Saint-Rose and Jean-Christophe Yo-Yo, who will welcome you, organize your meal (only if you phone in your intentions a day in advance), and cook sublime food. Menu items combine the aesthetics of France and the Antilles. Among the best examples are a terrine of foie gras with a compote of apples; an herb-enriched combination of scallops and dorado (mahimahi) in puff pastry; and a well-prepared filet of beef served with red-butter sauce.

There are also 16 units, each with private bathroom. In 2006, the owners spent lots of money reworking the layouts, upgrading the accommodations and the restaurant, and adding four all-new suites, each with its private small-scale swimming pool. In winter season, doubles cost 181€ to 219€ ($235–$285); suites 292€ to 316€ ($380–$411); off-season, doubles go for 135€ to 152€ ($175–$198); suites 204€ to 221€ ($265–$287). Rates include breakfast. There's a beach within a walk of about 275m (900 ft.), and a formal-looking, rectangular swimming pool, but in most cases, whatever distractions and diversions appeal to you, you'll have to organize on your own.

Villa Lagon S.A.R.L., Pointe Thalemont, 97240 Le François. © 596/38-07-77. www.pleinsoleil.mq. Reservations required 1 day in advance. Fixed-price lunches 34€ ($44); prix-fixe dinners 40€ ($52). MC, V. Daily noon–2pm; Mon–Sat 7:30–9pm. 5km (3 miles) north from Le François; follow signs first to Le Robert, then veer eastward when you see the signs to Thalemont, Mansarde, and Plein Soleil.

17

Puerto Rico

No one has ever suffered from boredom on Puerto Rico. It has hundreds of beaches, a mind-boggling array of watersports, miles of golf courses, acres of tennis courts, a huge variety of resorts, and casinos galore. It has more dance clubs than any other place in the Caribbean and shopping bargains to equal St. Thomas. Better yet, all this fun and variety comes with a much more reasonable price tag than on many of the other islands.

Lush, verdant Puerto Rico is half the size of New Jersey and is located some 1,600km (1,000 miles) southeast of the tip of Florida. With 438km (272 miles) of Atlantic and Caribbean coastline and a culture some 2,000 years old, Puerto Rico is packed with attractions. Old San Juan (aka Old Town) is its greatest historic center, with 500 years of history, as reflected in its restored Spanish colonial architecture.

It's also a land of contrasts. There are 79 cities and towns on Puerto Rico, each with a unique charm and flavor. The countryside is dotted with centuries-old coffee plantations, working sugar estates, a fascinating tropical rainforest, and forbidding caves and enormous boulders with mysterious petroglyphs carved by the Taíno peoples, the original settlers.

Dorado Beach, Cerromar Beach, and Palmas del Mar are the chief centers for those who have come for golf, tennis, and beaches. San Juan's hotels on the Condado/Isla Verde coast have, for the most part, a complete array of watersports. The continental shelf, which surrounds Puerto Rico on three sides, contributes to an abundance of coral reefs, caves, sea walls, and trenches for scuba diving and snorkeling.

San Juan is the world's second-largest home port for cruise ships.

You can base yourself at one resort and still do a lot of exploring elsewhere, if you don't mind driving for a couple hours. It's possible to branch out and see a lot of the island even if you're staying in San Juan.

For even more comprehensive coverage, consider getting yourself a copy of *Frommer's Puerto Rico* (Wiley Publishing, Inc.).

1 Essentials

VISITOR INFORMATION

For information before you leave home, visit **www.gotopuertorico.com** or contact one of the following **Puerto Rico Tourism Company** offices: 666 Fifth Ave., New York, NY 10013 (© **800/223-6530** or 212/586-6262); 3575 W. Cahuenga Blvd., Suite 405, Los Angeles, CA 90068 (© **800/874-1230** or 323/874-5991); or 901 Ponce de León Blvd., Suite 101, Coral Gables, FL 33134 (© **800/815-7391** or 305/445-9112). In **Canada,** contact the company at 6-295 Queen St. E., Suite 465, Brampton, ON L6W 4S6 (© **416/580-6287**).

Puerto Rico

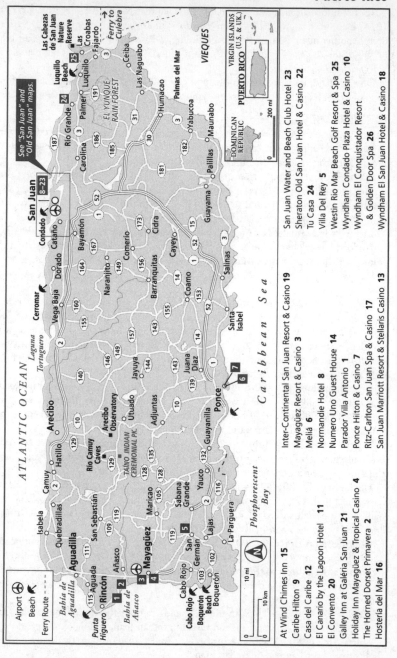

San Juan Water and Beach Club Hotel **23**

Sheraton Old San Juan Hotel & Casino **22**

Tu Casa **24**

Villa Del Rey **5**

Westin Rio Mar Beach Golf Resort & Spa **25**

Wyndham Condado Plaza Hotel & Casino **10**

Wyndham El Conquistador Resort
& Golden Door Spa **26**

Wyndham El San Juan Hotel & Casino **18**

Inter-Continental San Juan Resort & Casino **19**

Mayagüez Resort & Casino **3**

Meliá **6**

Normandie Hotel **8**

Numero Uno Guest House **14**

Parador Villa Antonio **1**

Ponce Hilton & Casino **7**

Ritz-Carlton San Juan Spa & Casino **17**

San Juan Marriott Resort & Stellaris Casino **13**

At Wind Chimes Inn **15**

Caribe Hilton **9**

Casa del Caribe **12**

El Canario by the Lagoon Hotel **11**

El Convento **20**

Galley Inn at Galéria San Juan **21**

Holiday Inn Mayagüez & Tropical Casino **4**

The Horned Dorset Primavera **2**

Hostería del Mar **16**

Tourist information is available at the **Luís Muñoz Marín Airport** (© 787/791-1014) December to April daily from 9am to 10pm, May to November daily 9am to 8pm. Another office is at La Princesa building, 2 Paseo La Princesa in Old San Juan (© **800/866-7827** or 787/721-2400), open Monday to Friday 8am to noon and 1 to 4:30pm.

On the island, it's best to go to the local city hall for tourist information. Ask for a copy of *Qué Pasa,* the official visitors' guide.

GETTING THERE

Before you book your own airfare, read the section "Packages for the Independent Traveler" in chapter 2—it can save you a bundle. There are more package deals to Puerto Rico than almost any other island except for Jamaica.

Puerto Rico is the major transportation hub of the Caribbean, with the best connections for getting anywhere in the islands. With San Juan as its hub for the entire Caribbean, **American Airlines** (© 800/433-7300 in the U.S. and Canada; www.aa.com) flies nonstop daily to San Juan from Baltimore; Boston; Chicago; Dallas–Fort Worth; Fort Lauderdale; Los Angeles; Miami; Newark; New Haven; New York (JFK); Orlando; Philadelphia; Tampa; and Washington (Dulles), plus flights to San Juan from both Montréal and Toronto with changes in Chicago or Miami. There are also at least two daily flights from Los Angeles to San Juan that touch down in Dallas or Miami.

Delta (© 800/221-1212 in the U.S. and Canada; www.delta.com) has four daily nonstop flights from Atlanta Monday to Friday, six nonstop on Saturday, and four nonstop on Sunday. Flights into Atlanta from around the world are frequent, with excellent connections from points throughout Delta's network in the South and Southwest. In addition, Delta also flies nonstop three times daily from New York's JFK and two times daily from Orlando.

United Airlines (© 800/864-8331 in the U.S. and Canada; www.united.com) flies nonstop daily from Chicago to San Juan. United also offers flights to San Juan, some of them nonstop, from both Memphis and Minneapolis, with a schedule that varies according to the season and the day of the week.

Northwest/KLM (© 800/225-2525 in the U.S. and Canada; www.nwa.com) has one daily nonstop flight to San Juan from Detroit, as well as at least one (and sometimes more) connecting flights to San Juan from Detroit.

US Airways (© 800/428-4322 in the U.S. and Canada; www.usairways.com) has daily direct flights between Charlotte, N.C., and San Juan. The airline also offers three daily nonstop flights to San Juan from Philadelphia, and one daily nonstop Saturday and Sunday flight to San Juan from Pittsburgh.

Continental Airlines (© 800/523-3273 in the U.S. and Canada; www.continental.com) flies nonstop daily from Newark, Houston, and Cleveland. The airline also flies five times a week direct to the northwestern airport outside Aguadilla should you wish to begin your tour of Puerto Rico in the west. In winter, service is increased to daily flights.

JetBlue (© 800/538-2583 in the U.S. and Canada) flies four times a day from New York's JFK airport, Boston, and Orlando to San Juan, and daily to Aguadilla.

Spirit Air (© 800/772-7117 in the U.S. and Canada) offers two daily nonstop flights from Fort Lauderdale to San Juan.

Canadians can fly **Air Canada** (© 888/247-2262 in the U.S. and Canada; www.aircanada.com) from either Montréal or Toronto to San Juan.

In addition to American Eagle (see American Airlines, above), **Cape Air** (© 800/ 352-0714 in the U.S. and Canada; www.flycapeair.com) links the two major islands in the U.S. Virgins, St. Croix and St. Thomas, as well as Tortola in the B.V.I., with San Juan.

Seaborne Airlines (© 888/359-8687 in the U.S. and Canada; www.seaborne online.com) offers daily links between St. Croix and St. Thomas with San Juan. The one-way cost from the U.S. Virgin Islands to Puerto Rico is $135 per person. The planes are small and frequent, carrying 15 to 19 passengers. Often there are more than 50 flights a day.

LIAT (© 888/844-5428 in the U.S. and Canada; www.liatairline.com) provides an air link to the Lesser Antilles islands.

British travelers can take a **British Airways** (© 0870/850-9850 in the U.K., or 800/247-9297 in the U.S. and Canada) weekly flight nonstop from London to San Juan on Sunday. **Lufthansa** (© 01/805-83-84-26 in Germany, or 800/399-5838 in the U.S. and Canada) passengers can fly on Saturday (one weekly flight) from Frankfurt to San Juan via Condor (a subsidiary operating the flight). And **Iberia** (© 902/ 400-500 in Spain, or 800/772-4642 in the U.S. and Canada; www.iberia.com) has two weekly flights from Madrid to San Juan, leaving on Thursday and Saturday.

GETTING AROUND

Cape Air (© 800/352-0714 in the U.S. and Canada; www.flycapeair.com) flies from Luis Muñoz Marín International Airport to Mayagüez, which can be your gateway to western Puerto Rico. Round-trip fares are $180.

BY RENTAL CAR   To really explore the island, a car is necessary. But we do not recommend renting a car in San Juan because of the city's heavy traffic and difficult parking. Some local car-rental agencies may tempt you with slashed prices, but you won't find any local branches to help you should you run into car trouble elsewhere on the island. Plus, some of the agencies advertising low-cost deals don't take credit cards and want cash in advance. You also have to watch out for hidden extras and insurance problems with smaller and not-very-well-known firms.

If you do rent a vehicle, it's best to stick with the old reliables: **Avis** (© 800/331-1212 in the U.S. and Canada, or 787/253-5926; www.avis.com), **Budget** (© 800/ 527-0700 in the U.S. and Canada, or 787/791-0600; www.budget.com), or **Hertz** (© 800/654-3131 in the U.S. and Canada, or 787/791-0840; www.hertz.com). Each of these companies offers minivan transport to its office and car depot. Be alert to the minimum-age requirements for car rentals in Puerto Rico. Avis, Hertz, and Budget require renters must be 21 or older, but those between the ages of 21 and 24 pay a $10 to $37 daily surcharge to the agreed-upon rental fee.

Added security comes from an antitheft double-locking mechanism that has been installed in most of the rental cars available in Puerto Rico. Car theft is common in Puerto Rico, so extra precautions are always needed.

Distances are often posted in kilometers rather than miles (1 mile = 1.61km), but speed limits are displayed in miles per hour.

BY PUBLIC TRANSPORTATION   *Públicos* are cars or minibuses that provide low-cost transportation and are designated with the letters *P* or *PD* following the numbers on their license plates. They usually operate only during daylight hours, carry up to six passengers at a time, and charge rates that are loosely governed by the

---

(Fun Fact **Special Events**

The annual **Casals Festival,** staged the first 2 weeks of March, is the Caribbean's most celebrated cultural event. The bill at San Juan's Performing Arts Center includes an array of international guest conductors, orchestras, and soloists who come to honor the memory of Pablo Casals, the renowned cellist who was born in Spain to a Puerto Rican mother, and who died in Puerto Rico in 1973. Tickets range from $20 to $100; a 50% discount is offered to students, seniors, and persons with disabilities. Call ℭ **787/620-4444** for tickets.

The island's **Carnival** celebrations feature float parades, dancing, and street parties in the week leading up to Ash Wednesday. The festivities in **Ponce** are marked by masqueraders wearing brightly painted horned masks, the crowning of a Carnival queen, and the closing "burial of the sardine." Hotel rates go up at this time of year, sometimes considerably. For more information, call the Ponce City Hall at ℭ **787/284-4141.** Ash Wednesday falls on February 6 in 2008.

Public Service Commission. Although prices are low, this option is slow and inconvenient, with frequent stops, and often erratic routing.

Locals are adept at figuring out their routes along rural highways, and in some cases, they simply wave at a moving *público* that they suspect might be headed in their direction. Unless you're fluent in Spanish and feeling adventurous, we suggest that you phone either of the numbers below, describe where and when you want to go, and agree to the prearranged price between specific points. Then, be prepared to wait. Although, at least in theory, a *público* might be arranged between most of the towns and villages of Puerto Rico, by far the most popular routes are between San Juan and Ponce and San Juan and Mayagüez. Fares vary according to whether a *público* will make a detour to pick up or drop off a passenger at a specific locale. If you want to deviate from the predetermined routes, you'll pay more than if you wait for a *público* at vaguely designated points beside the main highway, or at predefined points that include airports and, in some cases, the main plaza (central square) of a town.

Information about *público* routes between San Juan and Mayagüez is available from **Lineas Sultana,** Calle Esteban González 898, Urbanización Santa Rita, Rio Piedras (ℭ 787/765-9377). Information about *público* routes between San Juan and Ponce is available from **Choferes Unidos de Ponce,** Terminal de Carros Públicos, Calle Vive in Ponce (ℭ 787/721-2400 or 787/764-0540). Fares from San Juan to Ponce cost $30 to $50, from San Juan to Mayagüez $30.

SIGHTSEEING TOURS   Puerto Rico Tours, Condo Inter-Suite, Suite 5M, on Isla Verde in San Juan (ℭ 787/791-5479; www.puertorico-tours.com), offers specially conducted private sightseeing tours of Puerto Rico, including trips to the rainforest, Luquillo Beach, the caves of Camuy, and other attractions, such as a restored Taíno Indian village.

Backstage Partners (ℭ 787/791-0099; fax 787/791-2760; www.backstagepartners. com) offers customized tours that take in a wide range of island attractions, including eco-tours, deep-sea fishing, scuba diving and snorkeling, safaris, and golf packages.

Other leading escorted tour operators include **Atlantic San Juan Tours** (ℭ 787/ 644-9841; www.puertoricoexcursions.com), which covers all the major sights of the island from Ponce to El Yunque, and **Sunshine Tours** (© 866/785-3636; www. puerto-rico-sunshinetours.com), which encompasses much the same ground as the others.

If you'd like to explore Puerto Rico as part of a horseback-riding tour package, consult **PRwest Vacation Services** (© 888/779-3788; www.vacationpuertorico.com). A dozen well-trained Paso Fino horses are available to accommodate both advanced and novice riders. In northwest Puerto Rico, you can explore cavernous cliffs and tropical forests—all on horseback. Tours are customized.

Several other tour operators cater to special tastes, including **Castillo Tours & Travel Service,** 2413 Laurel St., Punta Las Marias, Santurce (© 787/791-6195; www.castillo tours.com), which is known for some of the best deep-sea fishing tours.

AdvenTours, Luquillo (© 787/530-8311), features customized private tours that include such activities as bird-watching, hiking, camping, visits to coffee plantations, and kayaking.

Eco Xcursion Aquatica, Route 191, Km 1.7, Rio Grande, Fajardo (© 787/888-2887), offers some of the best rainforest hikes and mountain-bike tours for both individuals and groups.

FAST FACTS: Puerto Rico

Banks Most major U.S. banks have branches with ATMs in the cities, and are open Monday to Friday from 8:30am to 4pm. Bank branches in malls are also open on Saturday from 8:30am to 6pm and Sunday from 9am to 3pm.

Currency The **U.S. dollar** is the coin of the realm. Canadian currency is accepted by some big hotels in San Juan, although reluctantly. *Prices in this chapter are quoted in U.S. dollars.*

Documents Since Puerto Rico is part of the United States, American citizens do not need a passport or visa. Canadians, however, should carry some form of identification, such as a birth certificate and photo ID, though we always recommend carrying your passport. Citizens of the United Kingdom should have a passport.

Electricity The electricity is 110-volt AC (60 cycles), the same as in the United States and Canada.

Emergencies Call © 911.

Language English is understood at the big resorts and in most of San Juan, though it's polite to at least greet people in Spanish and ask if they speak English before you make assumptions. Out in the island, Spanish is still *número uno.*

Safety Use common sense and take precautions. Muggings are commonly reported on the Condado and Isla Verde beaches in San Juan, so you might want to confine your moonlit-beach nights to the fenced-in and guarded areas around some of the major hotels. The countryside of Puerto Rico is safer than San Juan, but caution is always the rule. Avoid narrow little country roads and isolated beaches day or night.

Taxes There's a government tax of 9% in regular hotels or 11% in hotels with casinos. The airport departure tax is included in the price of your ticket.

Telephone Puerto Rico is on the North American telephone system; the area code is **787**. Place a call to or from Puerto Rico just as you would from within the United States or Canada.

Time Puerto Rico is on Atlantic Standard Time year-round, putting it 1 hour ahead of U.S. Eastern Standard Time. In winter, when it's noon in Miami, it's 1pm in San Juan. But during daylight saving time on the U.S. East Coast, Puerto Rico and the East Coast keep the same time.

Tipping Some hotels add a 10% service charge to your bill. If they don't, you're expected to tip for services rendered. Tip as you would in the United States (15%–20%).

Water The water in Puerto Rico is generally safe to drink, although you may prefer bottled water.

Weather Puerto Rico is cooler than most of the other Caribbean islands because of its northeast trade winds. Sea, land, and mountain breezes also help keep the temperatures at a comfortable level. The climate is fairly stable all year, with an average temperature of 76°F (24°C). The only variants are found in the mountain regions, where the temperature fluctuates between 66°F and 76°F (19°C–24°C), and on the north coast, where the temperature ranges from 70°F to 80°F (21°C–27°C). There is no real rainy season, but August is the wettest month.

2 San Juan ⋆⋆⋆

Puerto Rico's capital is a major city—actually an urban sprawl of several municipalities that lies along the island's north coast. Its architecture ranges from classic colonial buildings that recall the Spanish empire to modern beachfront hotels reminiscent of Miami Beach.

SAN JUAN ESSENTIALS

ARRIVING   Dozens of taxis line up outside the airport to meet arriving flights, so you rarely have to wait. The island's **Public Service Commission** (© 787/756-1401) sets flat rates between the Luís Muñoz Marín Airport and major tourist zones as follows: From the airport to any hotel in Isla Verde, $10; to any hotel in the Condado district, $13; and to any hotel in Old San Juan, $16. Tips of between 10% and 15% of that fare are expected.

For limousine service, **Bracero Limousine** (© 787/253-5466) offers cars with drivers that will meet you and your entourage at the arrivals terminal for luxurious, private transportation to your hotel. Transport to virtually anywhere in San Juan ranges from $85 to $125; transport to points throughout the island varies from $55 per hour in a sedan carrying four passengers to $75 per hour in a limousine with six passengers. Ideally, transport should be arranged in advance, so that a car and driver can be waiting for you near the arrivals terminal.

VISITOR INFORMATION   Tourist information is available at the **Luís Muñoz Marín Airport** (© 787/791-1014) December to April daily from 9am to 10pm, and May to November daily 9am to 8pm. Another office is at **La Casita**, Pier 1, Old San

Juan (℃ 787/722-1739), open Saturday to Wednesday 9am to 8pm, and Thursday and Friday 9am to 5:30pm.

ORIENTATION   The city center is on **San Juan Island,** connected to the rest of the metropolitan area by causeways. The western half of San Juan Island contains the walled city of **Old San Juan.** The eastern half is known as **Puerto de Tierra,** and contains many government buildings. Across the causeways is the neighborhood of **Miramar,** which fronts the Laguna del Condado. **Condado** is the narrow peninsula that loops around the top of Miramar almost all the way back to San Juan Island. It's where you'll find many of the best beaches. Just east of Condado is the residential neighborhood of **Ocean Park.** South of Condado and Ocean Park is **Santurce.** To the east is the International Airport, and even farther east is **Isla Verde,** home of some of the Caribbean's most upscale resort hotels, connected to the rest of San Juan by an isthmus.

GETTING AROUND   Walking is the best way to get around Old San Juan. The historic core of the old city is very compact. If your feet tire of the old cobblestone streets, board one of the free open-air trolleys that slowly make their way through the old city. You can board a trolley at any point along its route (either side of the Calle Fortaleza or Calle San José are good bets), or you can go to either the Marina or La Puntilla for departures.

The rest of the city is not so pedestrian-friendly. You'll want to take buses, taxis, or your own car to get around the rest of San Juan, including Condado and Isla Verde. The **Metropolitan Bus Authority** (℃ 787/767-7979) operates buses in the greater San Juan area. Bus stops are marked by upright metal signs or yellow posts that say PARADA. Bus terminals in San Juan are in the dock area and at Plaza de Colón. A typical fare is 25¢ to 50¢. The higher fee is for the faster buses that make fewer stops; call for more information about routes and schedules.

Taxis are metered; tips between 10% and 15% are customary. The initial charge for destinations in the city is $2, plus 10¢ for each ⅒ mile and 50¢ for every suitcase, with a minimum fare of $3. Taxis are invariably lined up outside the entrance to most of the island's hotels, and if not, a staff member can almost always call one for you. If you want to arrange a taxi on your own, call the **Cooperative Major Taxi** (℃ 787/723-2460). If you want to take a cab to a destination outside the city, you must negotiate a flat fee with the driver. For complaints or questions, contact the **Public Service Commission** (℃ 787/756-1401), which regulates cabs.

Tren Urbano, the first mass-transit project in the history of Puerto Rico, opened in 2005, linking San Juan to its suburbs such as Santurce, Bayamón, and Guaynabo. Costing $1.55 billion, the system provides an easy mode of transportation to the most congested areas of metropolitan San Juan. During rush hour (5–9am and 3–6pm), the train operates every 5 minutes; otherwise, it runs every 10 minutes. There is no service daily from 11pm to 5am. The fare is $1.50 one way. From the airport, it's possible to take the AMA-B40 bus to Tren Urbano, a 30-minute ride. For more information, call **787/765-0927.**

FAST FACTS   One of the most centrally located **pharmacies** is the **Puerto Rico Drug Co.,** Calle San Francisco 157 (℃ 787/725-2202), in Old San Juan; open Monday to Friday from 7:30am to 9:30pm, Saturday from 8am to 9:30pm, and Sunday from 7:30am to 9:30pm. **Walgreens,** 1130 Ashford Ave., Condado (℃ 787/725-1510), is a 24-hour pharmacy.

San Juan

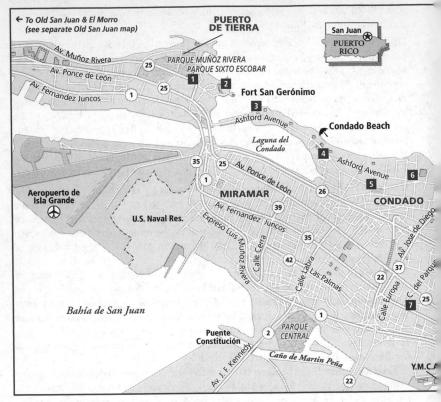

In a **medical emergency,** call ℂ **911. Ashford Memorial Community Hospital,** 1451 Ashford Ave. (ℂ **787/721-2160**), maintains a 24-hour emergency room.

ACCOMMODATIONS

All hotel rooms on Puerto Rico are subject to a 9% to 11% tax, which is not included in the rates listed in this chapter. Most hotels also impose a 10% service charge. Before you book a hotel, refer back to the section "Packages for the Independent Traveler" in chapter 2. Packages can save you a lot of money, especially if you want to stay at one of the big resorts.

IN OLD SAN JUAN

El Convento ✮ El Convento offers one of the most charming and historic hotel experiences anywhere in the Caribbean. Built in 1651, this hotel in the heart of the old city was once the New World's first Carmelite convent. Over the years El Convento has been everything from a flophouse to a parking lot. It opened as a hotel in 1962, thanks to backing by the Woolworth family.

Furnishings are traditionally Spanish in style, with mahogany beams, elaborate dark-stained paneling, and handmade Andalusian-style terra-cotta tile floors. Each unit contains extras like VCRs, stereos, and comfortable robes and slippers. The small marble-floored bathrooms have scales, second phones, and tub/shower combinations. The

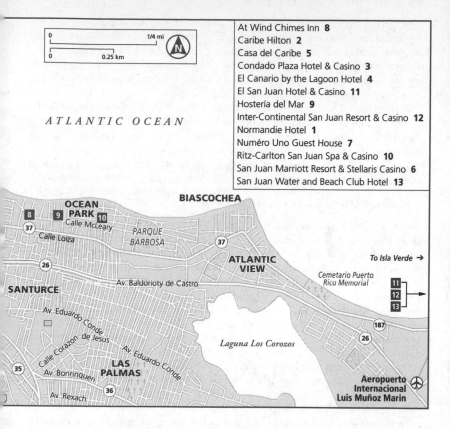

To Isla Verde →

interior courtyard is the focal point of the hotel. Of course, you won't have the same resort facilities here that you'd find in a blockbuster hotel on the Condado or in Isla Verde. The lower two floors house shops, bars, and restaurants.

The restaurants and bars are among the best in town. Delightful El Picoteo has terrific tapas, Patio del Nispero serves elegant alfresco meals, and hip Café Bohemio has great homemade desserts. El Convento is also affiliated with Il Perugino across the street. The so-called pool here is accessible via the fourth floor, but it measures only about 2m×3m (6×10 ft.)—very small, but charming and endearing because of its view over the facade of the nearby cathedral. There's a Jacuzzi immediately adjacent to the pool, and a big sun terrace.

Calle de Cristo 100, San Juan, PR 00901. ✆ 800/468-2779 or 787/723-9020. Fax 787/721-2877. www.elconvento. com. 68 units. Winter $325–$420 double, $600–$750 suite; off season $235–$295 double, $600–$750 suite. Rates include continental breakfast. AE, DC, DISC, MC, V. Parking $10. Bus: Old Town Trolley. **Amenities:** 4 restaurants; 3 bars; small rooftop plunge pool; fitness center; Jacuzzi; massage; laundry service; nonsmoking rooms; rooms for those w/limited mobility. *In room:* A/C, TV, dataport, beverage maker, hair dryer, iron, safe, Wi-Fi.

Gallery Inn at Galería San Juan ⭐ (Finds

This hotel's location and ambience are unbeatable, though the nearest beach is a 15-minute ride away. Set on a hilltop in Old Town, with a sweeping sea view, this unusual hotel contains a maze of verdant courtyards. In the 1700s it was the home of an aristocratic Spanish family. Today it's the most whimsically bohemian hotel in the Caribbean. Jan D'Esopo and Manuco Gandia created this inn out of their art studio. They cast bronze in their studio when not attending to their collection of birds, including macaws and cockatoos. The entire inn is covered with clay and bronze figures as well as other original art. We suggest booking one of the least expensive doubles; even the cheapest units are fairly roomy and attractively furnished, with good beds.

Note to lovers: The honeymoon suite has a Jacuzzi on a private balcony with a panoramic view of El Morro. From the rooftop terrace, there is a 360-degree view of the historic Old Town and the port. This is the highest point in San Juan and the most idyllic place to enjoy a breeze at twilight and a glass of wine.

Calle Norzagaray 204–206, San Juan, PR 00901. (***℃*** 787/722-1808. Fax 787/724-7360. www.thegalleryinn.com. 22 units (some with shower only). Year-round $225–$310 double; $410 suite (excluding honeymoon suite). Rates include continental breakfast. AE, DC, MC, V. There are 6 free parking spaces, plus parking on the street. Bus: Old Town Trolley. **Amenities:** Breakfast room. *In room:* A/C, dataport, hair dryer.

Sheraton Old San Juan Hotel & Casino ℛ   Opened in 1997, this dignified, nine-story, waterfront hotel was part of a $100-million renovation of San Juan's cruise-port facilities. The hotel has an unusual and desirable position between buildings erected by the Spanish monarchs in the 19th century and the city's busiest and most modern cruise-ship terminals. Most of the major cruise ships dock nearby, making this a worthwhile choice if you want to spend time in San Juan before boarding a ship. On days when cruise ships pull into port, the hotel's lobby and bars are likely to be jammed with passengers stretching their legs after a few days at sea.

Although the pastel building is modern, iron railings and exterior detailing convey a sense of colonial San Juan. The triangular shape of the building encircles an inner courtyard that floods light into the tasteful and comfortable bedrooms, each of which has two phone lines and a modem connection for laptop computers. Other than that, the smallish rooms lack character. Each room has a compact bathroom with a shower stall. Think of a Holiday Inn geared for business travelers. If you want Old Town character and atmosphere, head for El Convento (see above) instead. Most of the lobby level here is devoted to a mammoth casino. The upscale dining room serves perfectly fine, if unremarkable, international cuisine, with some regional specialties.

Calle Brumbaugh 100, San Juan, PR 00902. (***℃*** 787/721-5100. Fax 787/721-1111. www.sheraton.com. 240 units. Winter $240–$365 double; $315–$420 suite; off season $150–$220 double, $200–$330 suite. AE, DC, DISC, MC, V. Free self-parking; valet parking $12. Bus: A7. **Amenities:** Restaurant; 3 bars; outdoor pool; casino; fitness center; Jacuzzi; car-rental desk; business center; 24-hr. room service; nonsmoking rooms; rooms for those w/limited mobility. *In room:* A/C, TV, dataport, minibar, beverage maker, hair dryer, iron, safe, Wi-Fi.

IN PUERTO DE TIERRA

Caribe Hilton ℛ   Thanks to rivers of money poured into its radical, ongoing renovation, this deluxe hotel is one of the most up-to-date spa and convention hotels in San Juan. Because of an unusual configuration of natural barriers and legal maneuverings, the hotel has the only private beach on the island (and the only garden incorporating an antique naval installation: the semi-ruined colonial Fort San Gerónimo). Because this beachfront hotel was the first Hilton ever built outside the U.S. mainland (in 1949), the chain considers it its most historic property. The Caribe's size (7 hectares/17 acres of parks and gardens) and sprawling facilities often attract conventions and tour groups.

Rooms have been substantially upgraded. Variations in price are related to the views outside and the amenities within. Each room has a larger-than-expected bathroom with a tub/shower combo as well as comfortable, tropical-inspired furniture. In the Caribe Terrace Bar, you can order the bartender's celebrated piña colada, which was once enjoyed by movie legends Joan Crawford and Errol Flynn. An oceanfront spa and fitness center is the only beachside spa in Puerto Rico. It features such tantalizing delights as couples massages, body wraps, hydrotherapy tub treatments, and soothing cucumber sun therapies.

Next to the main hotel a cluster of luxurious Condado Lagoon Villas have been completed at the new Paseo Caribe, which makes the Hilton the largest conglomerate of bedrooms on island. These villas have a master bedroom, kitchen, dining room, and lots of storage space. In development for 2008 is a mini-mall with restaurants, boutiques, and a cinema lounge.

Calle Los Rosales, San Juan, PR 00901. © 800/HILTONS or 787/721-0303. Fax 787/725-8849. www.caribe.hilton. com. 812 units. Winter $385–$400 double; off season $275–$305 double; year-round $500–$1,220 suite. Children 16 and under stay free in parent's room (maximum 4 people per room). AE; DC, DISC, MC, V. Self-parking $15; valet parking $20. Bus: B21. **Amenities:** 5 restaurants; 2 bars; outdoor pool; health club; spa; children's activities and playground; business center (6am–3am); limited room service; babysitting; laundry service; dry cleaning; nonsmoking rooms; rooms for those w/limited mobility. *In room:* A/C, TV, dataport, minibar, hair dryer, iron, safe, Wi-Fi.

Normandie Hotel It isn't as well accessorized as its nearby competitor the Hilton, but for a clientele of mostly business travelers, it doesn't really matter. One guest, however, found the Hilton bright and festive, the Normandie "dark and haunting." The hotel first opened in 1939 and remains one of the purest examples of Art Deco architecture in Puerto Rico. Originally built for a Parisian cancan dancer by her tycoon husband, the building has a curve-sided design that was inspired by the famous French ocean liner, *Le Normandie.* The gardens are not particularly extensive, and the beach is unexceptional. But several multimillion-dollar renovations have given the place a conservative, vaguely historic charm. Bedrooms are tastefully outfitted, each with a neatly tiled tub-and-shower bathroom. The lobby retains its original Art Deco zest, soaring upward into an atrium whose centerpiece is a bubbling aquarium.

Av. Muñoz-Rivera, San Juan, PR 00919. © 877/987-2929 or 787/729-2929. Fax 787/729-3083. www.normandiepr. com. 173 units. Winter $195–$250 double, $500 suite; off season $145–$205 double, $450 suite. AE, DC, DISC, MC, V. Parking $10. Bus: A5 or B21. **Amenities:** Restaurant; bar; cafe; pool; health club; 24-hr. room service; babysitting; laundry service; rooms for those w/limited mobility. *In room:* A/C, TV, dataport, coffeemaker, hair dryer, iron/ironing board, safe, Wi-Fi.

IN CONDADO

Once this was a wealthy residential area, but with the recent construction of El Centro, the Puerto Rico Convention Center, all that has changed. Private villas were torn down to make way for high-rise hotels, restaurants, and nightclubs. The Condado shopping area, along Ashford and Magdalena avenues, became the center of a huge number of boutiques. There are bus connections into Old San Juan, or you can take a taxi.

Very Expensive

Condado Plaza Hotel & Casino (★ (Kids)   This is one of the busiest hotels on Puerto Rico, with enough facilities and restaurants to keep a visitor occupied for weeks. It's a favorite of business travelers, tour groups, and conventions, but it also attracts independent travelers. Families appreciate the extensive children's programs, some of the best on the island. The Caribe Hilton at Puerto de Tierra is its major rival, and we prefer that hotel's style and flair. The Condado has two minor and rather unattractive swimming pools, and lots of security-related tension between the sunbathing area around those two pools and the narrow sands of a not-so-great beach that the hotel shares with the public. Because the beach is small the pools tend to be overcrowded with hotel guests. The rooms, however, all have private terraces and are spacious, bright, and airy, fitted with deluxe beds and mattresses, either king-size or doubles, but most often twins. The good-size bathrooms contain tub/shower combinations. The complex's best section, the Plaza Club, has 80 units (including five duplex suites), a VIP lounge for guests, and private check-in/checkout.

Only Hotel El San Juan has a larger choice of dining options. This place is known for creating restaurants with culinary diversity. The hotel's premier restaurant, a hot ticket on San Juan's dining scene, is Cobia, winner of several culinary awards.

Av. Ashford 999, San Juan, PR 00907. ℂ 787/721-1000. Fax 787/721-1260. www.condadoplaza.com. 570 units. Winter $369–$560 double, $729–$1,200 suite; off season $239–$449 double, $399–$1,200 suite. AE, DC, DISC, MC, V. Valet parking $15; self-parking $10. Bus: C10 or B21. **Amenities:** 5 restaurants; 3 bars; 2 outdoor pools; 2 tennis courts; health club; spa; 3 Jacuzzis; watersports equipment; children's programs; car-rental desk; business center; salon; room service (7am-11pm); laundry service; dry cleaning; nonsmoking rooms; rooms for those w/limited mobility. *In room:* A/C, TV, minibar, beverage maker, hair dryer, iron, safe, Wi-Fi.

San Juan Marriott Resort & Stellaris Casino ☆

It's the tallest building on the Condado, a 21-story landmark that Marriott spent staggering sums to renovate after a deadly fire gutted the premises in 1989. The current building packs lots of postmodern style, and one of the best beaches on the Condado is right outside. Furnishings in the soaring lobby were inspired by Chippendale. If there's a flaw, it's the decor of the comfortable but bland bedrooms, with pastel colors that look washed out when compared to the rich mahoganies and jewel tones of the rooms in the rival Condado Plaza (see above). The units are generally spacious, with good views of the water, and each comes with a tiled bathroom with a tub/shower combination.

Av. Ashford 1309, San Juan, PR 00907. ℂ 800/228-9290 or 787/722-7000. Fax 787/722-6800. www.marriottpr.com. 525 units. Winter $420–$640 double, $830 suite; off season $225–$280 double, $385 suite. Suite rate includes breakfast. AE, DC, DISC, MC, V. Self-parking $14; valet parking $18. Bus: B21. **Amenities:** 3 restaurants; 3 bars; 2 pools; casino; 2 tennis courts; health club; Jacuzzi; sauna; tour desk; car-rental desk; business center; 24-hr. room service; babysitting; laundry service; dry cleaning; rooms for those w/limited mobility. *In room:* A/C, TV, dataport, minibar, beverage maker, hair dryer, iron, safe, Wi-Fi.

Moderate

El Canario by the Lagoon Hotel

A relaxing, informal European-style hotel, El Canario is in a quiet residential neighborhood just a short block from Condado Beach. This is one of the better B&Bs in the area. The hotel is very much in the Condado styling, which evokes Miami Beach in the 1960s. The bedrooms are generous in size and have balconies. All are nonsmoking and most have twin beds and sleek and contemporary bathrooms, with shower stalls and enough space to spread out your stuff. If the hotel doesn't have room for you, it can book you into its sibling properties, either El Canario Inn or El Canario by the Sea.

Calle Clemenceau 4, Condado, San Juan, PR 00907. ℂ 800/533-2649 or 787/722-5058. Fax 787/723-8590. www.canariohotels.com. 44 units. Winter $120–$135 double; off season $95–$105 double. Rates include continental breakfast. AE, DC, DISC, MC, V. Bus: B21 or C10. **Amenities:** Tour desk; coin-operated laundry. *In room:* A/C, TV, safe, Wi-Fi.

Inexpensive

At Wind Chimes Inn ☆

This restored and renovated Spanish manor, 1 short block from the beach and 5.5km (3½) miles from the airport, is one of the best guesthouses on the Condado. Upon entering a tropical patio, you'll find tile tables surrounded by palm trees and bougainvillea. There's plenty of space on the deck and a covered lounge for relaxing, socializing, and eating breakfast. Dozens of decorative wind chimes add melody to the daily breezes. The good-size rooms offer a choice of size, beds, and kitchens; all contain ceiling fans and air-conditioning. Beds are comfortable and come in four sizes, ranging from twin to king-size. The shower-only bathrooms, though small, are efficiently laid out. Families like this place not only because of the accommodations and the affordable prices but because they can also prepare light meals here, cutting down on food costs.

Av. McLeary 1750, Condado, San Juan, PR 00911. (℃) **800/946-3244** or 787/727-4153. Fax 787/728-0671. www.at windchimesinn.com. 22 units (shower only). Winter $99–$140 double, $135–$150 suite; off season $75–$125 double, $125 suite. AE, DISC, MC, V. Parking $5. Bus: B21 or A5. **Amenities:** Bar; outdoor pool; limited room service; rooms for those w/limited mobility. *In room:* A/C, ceiling fan, TV, dataport, kitchen (in some).

Casa del Caribe *Value*   Don't expect the Ritz, but if you're looking for a bargain on the Condado, this is it. This renovated guesthouse was built in the 1940s, later expanded, and then totally refurbished with tropical decor. A very Puerto Rican ambience has been created, with emphasis on Latin hospitality and comfort. On a shady side street just off Ashford Avenue, behind a wall and garden, you'll discover Casa del Caribe's wraparound veranda. The small but cozy guest rooms have ceiling fans and air conditioners, and most feature original Puerto Rican art. All are nonsmoking. The bedrooms are inviting, with comfortable furnishings and efficiently organized bathrooms. The front porch is a social center for guests, and you can also cook out at a barbecue area. The beach is a 2-minute walk away, and the hotel is also within walking distance of some megaresorts, with their glittering casinos.

Calle Caribe 57, El Condado, San Juan, PR 00907. (℃) **787/722-7139.** Fax 787/723-2575. www.casadelcaribe.net. 13 units. Winter $85–$125 double; off season $65–$99 double. Rates include continental breakfast. AE, DISC, MC, V. Parking $5. Bus: B21. **Amenities:** 1 room for those w/limited mobility. *In room:* A/C, TV, kitchen (in some).

IN OCEAN PARK

Hostería del Mar *六*   Lying a few blocks from the Condado casinos and right on the beach are the white walls of this distinctive landmark. It's in a residential seaside community that's popular with locals looking for beach action on weekends. The hotel boasts medium-size ocean-view rooms. Those on the second floor have balconies; those on the first floor open onto patios. The decor is invitingly tropical, with wicker furniture, good beds, pastel prints, and ceiling fans. The bathrooms are small but efficient, some with shower, some with tub only. The most popular unit is no. 201, with a king-size bed, private balcony, kitchenette, and a view of the beach; it's idyllic for a honeymoon. There's no pool, but a full-service restaurant here is known for its vegetarian, macrobiotic, and Puerto Rican plates, all freshly made. The place is simple, yet with its own elegance and warm hospitality.

Calle Tapía 1, Ocean Park, San Juan, PR 00911. (℃) **877/727-3302** or 787/727-3302. Fax 787/268-0772. www.hosteria delmarpr.com. 27 units. Winter $86–$143 double without ocean view, $189–$260 double with ocean view, $275–$289 apt; off season $69–$100 double without ocean view, $130–$165 double with ocean view, $216–$230 apt. Children 11 and under stay free in parent's room. AE, DISC, MC, V. Bus: A5. **Amenities:** Restaurant. *In room:* A/C, TV, dataport, kitchenette, beverage maker (in some).

Número 1 Guest House *六六 Finds*   As a translation of its name implies, this is the best of the small-scale, low-rise guesthouses in Ocean Park. It was originally built in the 1950s as a private beach house in a prestigious residential neighborhood adjacent to the wide sands of Ocean Park Beach. A massive renovation transformed the place into the closest thing in Ocean Park to the kind of stylish boutique hotel you might find in an upscale California neighborhood. Much of this is thanks to the hardworking owner, Esther Feliciano, who cultivates within her walled compound a verdant garden replete with splashing fountains, a small swimming pool, and manicured shrubbery and palms. Stylish-looking bedrooms (all of which are nonsmoking) contain tile floors, wicker or rattan furniture, comfortable beds, and tiled, shower-only bathrooms. Some repeat clients, many of whom are gay, refer to it as their fantasy version of a private villa beside a superb and usually convivial beach. The staff can direct you to watersports emporiums nearby for virtually any tropical watersport. Although it lacks the staggering diversity of the big hotels of the nearby Condado or Isla Verde, some guests value its sense of intimacy and small-scale charm.

Calle Santa Ana 1, Ocean Park, San Juan, PR 00911. © 866/726-5010 or 787/726-5010. Fax 787/727-5482. www. numero1guesthouse.com. 13 units. Winter $115–$225 double, $265 junior suite, $225 apt; off season $60–$145 double, $165 junior suite, $165 apt. $20 each additional occupant of a double room. Rates include continental breakfast. AE, MC, V. Bus: A5. **Amenities:** Restaurant; bar; outdoor pool; limited room service; rooms for those w/limited mobility. *In room:* A/C, ceiling fan, TV, dataport, minibar, hair dryer, iron/ironing board, safe.

IN ISLA VERDE

Isla Verde, right on the beach, is closer to the airport than the other sections of San Juan, but it's farther from Old Town. Some of the Caribbean's most upscale hotels are here. If you plan to spend most of your time on the beach rather than exploring the city, consider one of the following hotels.

El San Juan Hotel & Casino ☆ *Kids* This hotel is no longer the dazzler it once was. The Ritz-Carlton has taken the truly elite business, and The Water Club is even more sophisticated. Nonetheless, El San Juan Hotel is still a good choice for (well-to-do) families, with lots of activities for children. The beachfront hotel is surrounded by 350 palms, century-old banyans, and gardens. Its 630m (2,100-foot) sandy beach is the finest in the San Juan area. The hotel's river pool, with currents, cascades, and lagoons, evokes a jungle stream, and the lobby is the most opulent and memorable in the Caribbean. Entirely sheathed in red marble and hand-carved mahogany paneling, the public rooms stretch on almost endlessly.

The large, well-decorated rooms have intriguing touches of high-tech; each contains three phones and a VCR. Bedrooms are imbued with honey-hued woods and rattans and king-size or double beds. Bathrooms have all the amenities and tub/shower combos; a few feature Jacuzzis. About 150 of the units, designed as comfortable bungalows, are in the outer reaches of the garden. Known as casitas, they include Roman tubs, atrium showers, and access to the fern-lined paths of a tropical jungle a few steps away. A 17-story ultraluxury tower features 103 one- or two-bedroom units, 8 garden suites, 5 governor's suites, and 4 presidential suites.

No other hotel in the Caribbean offers such a rich diversity of dining options and such high-quality food. Japanese, Italian, Mexican, and 24-hour American/Caribbean restaurants are just a few of the options.

Note: In recent years, readers have occasionally complained about maintenance in some of the bedrooms. If possible, ask to see your room before you check in.

Av. Isla Verde 6063, San Juan, PR 00979. © 866/317-8935 or 787/791-1000. Fax 787/791-0390. www.elsanjuan hotel.com. 382 units. Winter $359–$819 double, from $1,200 suite; off season $219–$499 double, from $1,099 suite. AE, DC, DISC, MC, V. Self-parking $10; valet parking $20. Bus: A5. **Amenities:** 8 restaurants; 4 bars; 2 outdoor pools; casino; tennis; health club; spa; sauna and steam room; watersports equipment/rentals; children's programs; business center; 24-hr. room service; massage; babysitting; laundry service; dry cleaning; rooms for those w/limited mobility. *In room:* A/C, TV/VCR, minibar, beverage maker, hair dryer, iron, safe, Wi-Fi.

Inter-Continental San Juan Resort & Casino ✪ This resort competes with El San Juan Hotel & Casino (see above) next door, but here you'll get a better sense of living in a sophisticated beach resort. Most of the comfortable, medium-size rooms have balconies and terraces and tastefully conservative furnishings. Top-floor rooms are the most expensive, even though they lack balconies. Many bathrooms have power showerheads, deep tubs, and scales. Especially desirable units are in the Plaza Club, a minihotel within the hotel that sports a private entrance, concierge service, complimentary food and beverage buffets, and suite/spa and beach facilities. Dining within any of this hotel's five restaurants merits attention; during a day at the beach, refreshments at Ciao Mediterranean Café are especially good.

Av. Isla Verde 5961, Isla Verde, PR 00979. ✆ 888/424-6835 or 787/791-6100. Fax 787/253-2510. www.ichotelsgroup. com. 402 units. Winter $299–$699 double, $799–$1,099 suite; off season $279–$379 double, $399–$1,099 suite. Children 15 and under stay free in parent's room. AE, DC, DISC, MC, V. Self-parking $12; valet parking $22. Bus: A7, M7, or T1. **Amenities:** 5 restaurants; lounge; the Caribbean's largest free-form pool; whirlpool; health club; sauna; scuba diving; limo service; business center; 24-hr. room service; massage; babysitting; laundry service; dry cleaning; rooms for those w/limited mobility. *In room:* A/C, TV, dataport, minibar, beverage maker, hair dryer, iron, safe, Wi-Fi.

Ritz-Carlton San Juan Spa & Casino ✪✪✪ The Ritz-Carlton is one of the most spectacular deluxe hotels in the Caribbean. Set on over 3 hectares (8 acres) of prime beachfront, within a 5-minute drive from the airport, it appeals to both business travelers and vacationers. The hotel decor reflects Caribbean flavor and the Hispanic culture of the island, with artwork by prominent local artists. More visible, however, is an emphasis on Continental elegance. Some of the most opulent public areas feature wrought-iron balustrades and crystal chandeliers.

Beautifully furnished guest rooms open onto ocean views or the gardens of nearby condos. Rooms are very large, with excellent furnishings, fine linens, and dataports. The bathrooms are exceptionally plush, with tub/shower combinations, scales, bathrobes, and deluxe toiletries. Preferred accommodations are in the ninth-floor Ritz-Carlton Club, which has a private lounge and personal concierge staff.

As for top-shelf dining venues, Prime 787 is one of the finest restaurants in San Juan. The hotel also houses the Caribbean's largest casino (see "Casinos," later in this chapter).

Av. de los Gobernadores (State Rd.) 6961, no. 187, Isla Verde, PR 00979. ✆ 800/241-3333 or 787/253-1700. Fax 787/253-0700. www.ritzcarlton.com. 416 units. Winter $589–$819 double; off season $299–$549 double; year-round from $1,500 suite. AE, DC, DISC, MC, V. Self-parking $15; valet parking $20. Bus: A5, B40, or C45. **Amenities:** 5 restaurants; 3 bars; large pool; Caribbean's largest casino; 2 tennis courts; health club; spa; children's program; salon; 24-hr. room service; babysitting; laundry service; dry cleaning; nightclub; rooms for those w/limited mobility. *In room:* A/C, TV, dataport, minibar, hair dryer, safe.

San Juan Water and Beach Club Hotel ✪✪✪ A refreshing change from the megachain resorts of San Juan, this ultrachic hotel is hip and contemporary. It's the city's only "boutique hotel" on a beach. We find much to praise at this small and exclusive hotel because of its highly personalized and well-trained staff. Although avant-garde, the design is not daringly provocative. Behind glass are "waterfalls," even on the elevators, and inventive theatrical-style lighting is used to bring the outdoors inside. The one-of-a-kind glass art doors are from Murano, the famed center of glass-making outside Venice. Overlooking Isla Verde's best beach area, all the bedrooms are spacious and contain custom-designed beds positioned to face the ocean. Bathrooms are tiled and elegant, with tub/shower combinations. Unique features are the open-air

11th-floor exotic bar with the Caribbean's only rooftop fireplace. The pool is a level above; it's like swimming in an ocean in the sky.

Calle José M. Tartak 2, Isla Verde, Puerto Rico 00979. (✆ **888/265-6699** or 787/253-3666. Fax 787/728-3610. www. waterclubsanjuan.com. 84 units. Winter $269–$330 double, $695 suite; off season $179–$239 double, $695 suite. AE, DC, DISC, MC, V. Bus: T1 or A5. **Amenities:** Restaurant; 2 bars; outdoor rooftop pool; fitness center; Jacuzzi; limited room service; dry cleaning; nonsmoking rooms; rooms for those w/limited mobility. *In room:* A/C, TV, dataport, minibar, hair dryer, safe, iron-Wi-Fi.

DINING
IN OLD SAN JUAN
Expensive
Aquaviva 🏵🏵 LATINO/SEAFOOD   The location is at the bottom of Calle Fortaleza, in Old San Juan, within a cool, turquoise-colored environment. Presiding above the sometimes frenetic bar action and dining room hubbub of this place are replicas of three *aquaviva* (jellyfish), quivering with illumination, each painstakingly manufactured from stained glass specifically for this site. Its owners spend a small fortune on publicity and promotion, making it one of the hottest restaurant tickets in Old San Juan.

Oysters and stiff drinks are served at the bar. Flowing from the open-to-view kitchens come dishes whose ingredients derive from the watery turquoise world that inspired this restaurant's color scheme. The best examples include six different ceviches, including one made with mahimahi, mango juice, and lemons; and a different version from marlin and garlic. You might opt for a heaping tower composed of fried oysters, coco-flavored shrimp, fried octopus, and calamari. The best main courses include grilled fresh mahimahi with smoky shrimp, salsa, and coconut-poached yucca; seared medallions of halibut with a fondue of spinach and crabmeat; and a succulent version of paella garnished with seafood and pork sausage.

364 Calle Fortaleza. (✆ **787/722-0665.** Reservations not accepted. Main courses $16–$42. AE, MC, V. Mon–Wed 6–11pm; Thurs–Sat 6pm–midnight; Sun 4–10pm. Bus: Old Town Trolley.

Barú 🏵 CARIBBEAN/MEDITERRANEAN   This is one of the most fashionable and popular of the imaginative new restaurants of Old San Juan, with an attractive and hard-playing clientele, some of whom might effectively compete for roles on the Hispanic soap operas. Named after an unspoiled island off the north coast of Colombia, a personal favorite of its Colombian-born owner, it occupies a stately looking high-ceilinged space capped with massive timbers, fronted with a convivial mahogany bar, and decorated with paintings by such Colombia-born artistic luminaries as Botéro.

Many dishes are deliberately conceived as something midway between an appetizer and a main-course platter, so it's hard to know how much, or how many courses, to order. If unsure, ask your waitperson to guide you. Menu items include an unusual choice of five different kinds of carpaccio (tuna, halibut, salmon, beef, or Serrano ham), presented in paper-thin and very small portions that are spread out like a few sheets of tissue paper on a pretentiously large plate. Ceviche of mahimahi is appropriately tart, appealingly permeated with citrus; and the marinated lamb chops with a paprika and pineapple mojo sauce is flavorful. Other culinary creations include almond-encrusted goat cheese with Jamaican jerk mango dip and yucca chips, and sliced filet mignon. Regrettably, the place is not cheap, and service is well intentioned but disorganized as the youthful staff maneuvers as best it can through the packed-in crowd.

Calle San Sebastián 150. (✆ **787/977-7107.** Reservations recommended. Main courses $15–$28. AE, MC, V. Sun–Wed 6pm–midnight; Thurs–Sat 6pm–2am. Bus: Old Town Trolley.

Carli Café Concierto ✪ INTERNATIONAL   This stylish restaurant is owned by Carli Muñoz. The gold disc hanging on the wall attests to Carli's success in his previous role as a pianist for The Beach Boys. Nowadays, Carli entertains his dinner guests nightly with a combination of standards, romantic jazz, and original material on his grand piano. Diners can sit outside on the Plazoleta, where they can enjoy a panoramic view of the bay, or they can eat inside against a backdrop of a tasteful decor of terra-cotta walls and black marble tables. The chef tempts visitors with an imaginative international menu, including such delights as quail rockettes stuffed with dried fruits and sage. The filet of salmon and a mouthwatering rack of lamb are among the finest main dishes. The bar, with its mahogany and brass fittings, is an ideal spot to chill out.

Edificio Banco Popular, Calle Tetuán 206, off Plazoleta Rafael Carrión. © **787/725-4927.** Reservations recommended. Main courses $16–$34. AE, V. Mon–Fri 3:30–11pm; Sat 4–11:30pm. Bus: M2 or M3.

Il Perugino ✪✪ ITALIAN   Affiliated with the previously recommended El Convento Hotel, this is Puerto Rico's finest Italian restaurant, serving a cuisine that at times seems inspired. Located across from the hotel, the restaurant specializes in the cuisine of Umbria, that province of Italy adjoining Tuscany.

The chef and owner, Franco Seccarelli, hails from Umbria and insists that the classic dishes be authentic to his homeland. A special architectural feature of the restaurant is a converted dry well in the center which serves as a wine cellar. Service is impeccable and friendly.

Our favorite homemade pastas include black fettuccine with a shellfish ragout, or ricotta and spinach gnocchetti with fresh tomatoes. For a starter, opt for the shrimp salad with grilled zucchini, a sublime dish, as is another salad made with scallops and porcini mushrooms. Among the meat and poultry dishes, Seccarelli shines with his pheasant breast alla Cacciatora and his pork filets flavored with an unusual combination of thyme and blueberries. Another dish we recently raved about was the rack of lamb with fresh herbs and a rich red wine sauce. Desserts are also succulent and homemade.

105 Cristo St. © **787/722-5481.** Reservations recommended. Main courses $18–$36. AE, DISC, MC, V. Thurs–Sat noon–3pm; daily 6:30–11pm. Old Town trolley.

Trois Cent Onze (311) ✪✪ FRENCH   When the French and Puerto Rican owners of this place renovated this building in 1999, they discovered some of the most beautiful Moorish-Andalusian tilework in San Juan's Old Town buried beneath layers of later coverings. Because of those tiles, and because of the delicate Andalusian-style iron rosette above the door, they wisely decided to retain the area's Moorish embellishments during the reconfiguration of their restaurant's decor. What you'll get today is the premier French restaurant of San Juan, replete with a zinc bar near the entrance, a soaring and richly beamed ceiling, and a decor reminiscent of the Casbah of old Tangiers. Your hosts are Christophe Gourdain and Zylma Perez, who are proud to recite the building's former use as the photography studio that developed many of Puerto Rico's earliest movies. Colors, textures, and flavors combine here to produce an irresistible array of dishes. Menu items include a carpaccio of salmon marinated in citrus; sautéed sea scallops served with an almond-flavored butter sauce; mango and crabmeat salad; magret of duckling roasted with honey; and pork medallions served with caramelized onions, stewed white beans, and spicy *merguez* sausage.

Calle Fortaleza 311. © **787/725-7959.** Reservations recommended. Main courses $19–$35. AE, DISC, MC, V. Mon–Fri noon–3pm; Mon–Sat 6–11pm. Closed Sun. Bus: Old Town Trolley, T2, or 2.

Moderate

Amadeus ⭐ CARIBBEAN   Housed in a brick-and-stone building that was constructed in the 18th century by a wealthy merchant, Amadeus offers Caribbean ingredients with a nouvelle twist. The appetizers alone are worth the trip here, especially the Amadeus dumplings with guava sauce and arrowroot fritters. And try the smoked-salmon-and-caviar pizza. One zesty specialty is pork scaloppine with sweet-and-sour sauce.

Calle San Sebastián 106 (across from the Iglesia de San José). ℂ 787/722-8635. Reservations recommended. Main courses $8–$25. AE, DISC, MC, V. Mon 6-10pm; Tues–Sun noon–11pm. Bus: Old Town Trolley, M2, M3, or A5.

Dragonfly ⭐⭐⭐ LATIN/ASIAN FUSION   At one of San Juan's hottest restaurants, the decor has been compared to that of a bordello in Old San Francisco. You pass through the beaded curtains into a world of red ceilings, fringed lamps, and gilded mirrors. The restaurant lies right across the street from the Parrot Club, and these two dining enclaves have put the newly named SoFo district (south of Calle Fortaleza in Old Town) on the culinary map. In the bar, the preferred cigarette is Marlboro and the most popular drink, a lethal "Dragon Punch." Night after night Dragonfly is the fun party place in town. Along with the latest gossip, you can enjoy live Latin jazz as background music.

This new-generation San Juan restaurant offers sexy cookery, such as seafood ceviche scooped up with yucca, and plantain chips, *chicharrónes* (pork rinds), spicy crab cakes, and a host of other dishes, such as marinated grilled meats. We applaud the chefs for their use of root vegetables such as yucca. The red snapper and grouper are excellent, and we love the pumpkin and beans of every type. The barbecued lamb shanks are very hearty and filling. Ravioli, timbales, confits, cassoulets—it's a dizzy array of taste temptations.

Calle Fortaleza 364. ℂ 787/977-3886. Reservations not accepted. Main courses $8–$25. AE, MC, V. Mon–Wed 6–11pm; Thurs–Sat 6pm–midnight. Bus: A5 or T1.

Ostra Cosa ⭐⭐ *(Finds)* ECLECTIC/SEAFOOD   This artfully promoted restaurant has a growing clientele that calls its ambience one of the most sensual and romantic in Old San Juan. Former advertising executive Alberto Nazario, a lifestyle guru who mingles New Age thinking with culinary techniques to promote love, devotion, and a heightened sexuality, created Ostra Cosa. Couples dine beneath a massive quenepe tree—waiters will tell you to hug the tree and make a wish—in a colonial courtyard surrounded by a 16th-century building that was once the home of the colony's governor. The atmosphere, enhanced by domesticated quail and chirping tree frogs, will make you feel far removed from the cares of the city. Featured foods are high in phosphorus, zinc, and flavor, designed to promote an "eat-up, dress-down experience." The ceviche is superb, as are the grilled prawns. But it is the conch, known as Caribbean Viagra, that rates "Wow!!" or "Ay Ay Ay!!!"

Calle del Cristo 154. ℂ 787/722-2672. Reservations recommended. Main courses $11–$32. AE, MC, V. Sun–Wed noon–10pm; Fri–Sat noon–11pm. Bus: Old Town Trolley.

Tantra ⭐ *(Value)* INDO-LATINO   Set in the heart of "restaurant row" on Calle Fortaleza, it has become famous for a sophisticated fusion of Latino with South Indian cuisine. Its chef and owner, Indian-born Ramesh Pillai, oversees a blend of slow-cooked tandoori cuisine from South India with Puerto Rico–derived spices, flavors, and ingredients. All of this occurs within a warm, candlelit environment that focuses on Indian handicrafts and Hindu and Buddhist symbols.

An appropriate way to begin a meal here is to order one of the best martinis we've ever had—a concoction flavored with cinnamon and cloves. Menu highlights include sesame masala-crusted sushi tuna with peanut sauce; fried coconut sesame jumbo shrimp with Indian noodles; chicken tikka masala with nan (flat bread); and rice and chicken rolls with passion-fruit sauce. One of the establishment's bestsellers is an absolutely brilliant version of tandoori chicken that combines the traditional Indian recipe with manchego and mozzarella cheese, guayaba fruit, guava-flavored dip, and nan.

356 Calle Fortaleza. © 787/977-8141. Reservations recommended. Main courses $13–$19. AE, MC, V. Mon–Sat noon–3am; Sun noon–12:30am. Bus: T1 or 2.

Inexpensive
Café Puerto Rico CREOLE/PUERTO RICAN   On the Plaza de Colón, this restaurant offers balconies overlooking one of the most charming of Old Town squares. The setting is colonial, with beamed ceilings and tile floors, and with ceiling fans whirling overhead. The menu features hearty regional fare. Tasty options include fried fish filet, paella, and lobster cooked as you like it. Eggplant parmigiana is an excellent vegetarian option, and you might also order eye round stuffed with ham in Creole sauce. Of course, if you're getting hungry during a day of strolling Old San Juan's windy streets, don't wait for dinner—you'll enjoy a lunch break here, too.

Calle O'Donnell 208. © 787/724-2281. Main courses $9–$21. AE, MC, V. Daily 11:30am–11pm. Bus: Old Town Trolley.

Fatty's JAMAICAN/WEST INDIAN   Amazingly, Puerto Rico didn't have a Jamaican restaurant until this dive opened. You'll know it's Jamaican when you see a picture of Bob Marley and the Jamaican flag displayed. Not only that, but reggae music plays in the background. The welcoming owner, "Fatty," is a great cook, turning out marvelous jerk dishes, especially chicken, fish, and shrimp. The chef is also known for curry chicken or a rice dish flavored with coconut milk. Chicken balls with curry sauce is another local favorite. Fried red snapper and conch in garlic sauce also win our praise.

Calle O'Donnell 102. © 787/586-6925. Reservations not required. Main courses $7–$12. No credit cards. Fri–Wed noon–9pm; Thurs noon–3pm. Bus: Old Town Trolley.

La Bombonera ⋆⋆ (Value PUERTO RICAN   This place offers exceptional value in its homemade pastries, well-stuffed sandwiches, and endless cups of coffee—and it has done so since 1902. Its atmosphere evokes turn-of-the-20th-century Castille transplanted to the New World. The food is authentically Puerto Rican, homemade, and inexpensive, with regional dishes such as rice with squid, roast leg of pork, and seafood *asopao* (a thick rice soup). For dessert, you might select an apple, pineapple, or prune pie, or one of many types of flan. Service is polite, if a bit rushed, and the place fills up quickly at lunchtime.

Calle San Francisco 259. © 787/722-0658. Reservations recommended. American breakfast $4–$10; main courses $6–$20. AE, DC, MC, V. Daily 7:30am–8pm. Bus: Old Town Trolley.

PUERTA DE TIERRA
Madrid-San Juan ⋆ SPANISH   This restaurant lies within the mega-compound known as the Caribe Hilton. Its décor, especially that of its baronial-looking dining room in back, emulates that of a gracious and rather formal tasca in Spain, replete with Serrano hams hanging above the bar, a roster of oil paintings (many of which are for sale), a scarlet-covered dining room which you might have imagined as a *tableaux*

within a still-life by Goya, and rack upon rack of wine. There's something big, gener-ous, and well-mannered about this place, as a quick perusal of the list of tapas (both hot and cold) and the conventional lunch or dinner menu will quickly show. High-lights include piquillo peppers stuffed with pulverized codfish; fried plantain with smoked salmon; codfish fritters; *fabada asturianas* (a well-seasoned and soupy version of stew that combines fava beans, sausages, and ham); fried fresh anchovies; and chorizo sausages in red-wine sauce. Main courses include breast of chicken in garlic sauce; filet mignon with Manchego cheese and Serrano ham; thin-sliced filet of beef with onions; *asopao de mariscos;* mofongo stuffed with shrimp; and halibut steak gar-nished with shrimp, mushrooms, and raisin sauce.

In the Caribe Hilton, Calle Los Rosales. © 787/721-0303. Reservations recommended. Tapas $6.50–$12; main courses $21-$35. AE, DC, DISC, MC, V. Sun–Thurs noon–midnight, Fri noon–1am, Sat 6pm–midnight. Bus: B21.

Morton's of Chicago 🐟🐟   When it comes to steaks, Ruth's Chris Steak House in Isla Verde enjoys a slight edge, but otherwise Morton's is king of the steaks and other choice meats. The chain of gourmet steakhouses was founded in 1978 by Arnie Mor-ton, former executive vice president of the *Playboy* empire. Beef lovers know they'll get quality meats perfectly cooked at Morton's. Carts laden with your selection, ranging from prime Midwestern beefsteaks to succulent lamb or veal chops, are wheeled around for your selection. And Morton's has the island's best prime rib. This is a place where the bartenders make stiff drinks, and the waiters tempt you with their fresh fish, lobster, and chicken dishes. The vegetables here are among the freshest in the area. The house specialty is a 24-ounce porterhouse. Appetizers include perfectly cooked jumbo shrimp with cocktail sauce and smoked Pacific salmon. For dessert, we always gravi-tate to one of the soufflés, such as raspberry or Grand Marnier.

In the Caribe Hilton, Calle Los Rosales. © 787/977-6262. Reservations required. Main courses $26–$52. AE, DC, DISC, MC, V. Mon-Sat 5–11pm, Sun 5–10pm. Bus: B21.

IN CONDADO
Very Expensive
Pikayo 🐟🐟🐟 PUERTO RICAN/CAJUN   This is an ideal place to go for the next generation of Puerto Rican fusion cuisine. Pikayo not only keeps up with the latest culinary trends, it often sets them, thanks to the inspired guidance of owner and celebrity chef Wilo Benet. Formal but not stuffy, and winner of more culinary awards than virtually any other restaurant in Puerto Rico, Pikayo is a specialist in the *criolla cuisine* of the colonial age, emphasizing the Spanish, Indian, and African elements in its unusual recipes. Appetizers include a dazzling array of taste explosions: Try shrimp spring rolls with peanut sofrito sauce; crab cake with aioli; or perhaps a ripe plantain, goat-cheese, and onion tart. Main-course delights feature charred rare yellowfin tuna with onion *escabeche* and red-snapper filet with sweet-potato purée served with foie gras butter. Our favorite remains the grilled shrimp with polenta and barbecue sauce made with guava.

Museum of Art of Puerto Rico, Av. José de Diego 299. © 787/721-6194. Reservations recommended. Main courses $28–$54; fixed-price menus $85. AE, DC, MC, V. Tues–Sun noon–3pm; Tues–Sat 6–11pm. Bus: M2, A7, or T1.

Expensive
Ajili Mójili 🐟🐟 PUERTO RICAN/CREOLE   This restaurant serves *la cucina criolla,* the starchy, down-home cuisine that developed on the island a century ago. Though the building is quite modern, look for replicas of the crumbling brick walls

you'd expect in Old San Juan and a bar that evokes Old Spain. Locals come here for a taste of the food they enjoyed at their mother's knee, like *mofongos* (green plantains stuffed with veal, chicken, shrimp, or pork), *medallones de cerdo encebollado* (pork loin sautéed with onions), *carne mechada* (beef rib-eye stuffed with ham), and *lechon asado con maposteado* (roast pork with rice and beans). Wash it all down with an ice-cold bottle of local beer. The staff will eagerly describe menu items in colloquial English.

Av. Ashford 1006. ℂ 787/725-9195. Reservations recommended. Main courses $16–$30; lunch $12–$26. AE, DISC, MC, V. Mon–Fri noon–3pm; Mon–Thurs 6–10pm; Sat 11:45am–3:30pm; Fri-Sat 6–11pm; Sun 12:30–4pm and 6–10pm. Bus: B21.

Chayote's ⊛ PUERTO RICAN/INTERNATIONAL   Chayote's serves some of San Juan's most innovative cuisine. It attracts local business leaders, government officials, and the occasional celebrity. It's an artsy, modern, basement-level bistro in a surprisingly obscure hotel (the Olimpo). The restaurant changes its menu every 3 months, but you might find appetizers like a yucca turnover stuffed with crabmeat and served with a mango and papaya chutney, or a ripe plantain stuffed with chicken and served with a fresh tomato sauce. For a main dish, you might try a red snapper filet with a citrus vinaigrette made of passion fruit, orange, and lemon. An exotic touch appears in the pork filet seasoned with dried fruits and spices in a tamarind sauce and served with a green banana and taro root timbale. To finish off your meal, there's nothing better than the mango flan served with macerated strawberries.

In the Olimpo Hotel, Av. Miramar 603. ℂ 787/722-9385. Reservations recommended. Main courses $24–$48. AE, MC, V. Tues–Fri 11:30am–3pm; Tues–Sat 6:30–10:30pm. Bus: B5.

La Compostela ⊛ INTERNATIONAL/SPANISH   Established by a Galician-born family, this pine-trimmed restaurant has gained a reputation as one of the best in the capital. The chef made his name on the roast peppers stuffed with salmon mousse. Equally delectable is duck with orange-and-ginger sauce or baby rack of lamb with fresh herbs. Any shellfish grilled in a brandy sauce is a sure winner. The chef also makes two savory versions of paella. The wine cellar, comprising some 10,000 bottles, is one of the most impressive in San Juan. A battalion of well-dressed waiters offers formal service.

Av. Condado 106. ℂ 787/724-6088. Reservations required. Main courses $24–$39. AE, DC, MC, V. Mon–Fri noon–3pm; Mon–Sat 6:30–10:30pm. Bus: M2.

Zabó ⊛ AMERICAN/PUERTO RICAN/INTERNATIONAL   This restaurant enjoys citywide fame, thanks to its blend of bucolic charm and superb innovative food. It's set in a dignified villa that provides some low-rise dignity in a sea of skyscraping condos. The creative force here is owner and chef/culinary director Paul Carroll, who built the place from its origins as a simple deli into one of the most sought-after restaurants on the Condado. Menu items fuse the cuisines of the Mediterranean, the Pacific Rim, and the Caribbean into a collection that includes dishes such as blini stuffed with medallions of lobster with ginger, thyme, and beurre blanc; carpaccio of salmon with mesclun salad and balsamic vinegar; and baked chorizo stuffed with mushrooms, sherry, paprika, and cheddar. The black-bean soup is among the very best in Puerto Rico, served with parboiled cloves of garlic marinated in olive oil that melt in your mouth like candy.

Calle Candina 14 (entrance via alleyway leading from Av. Ashford between avenidas Washington and Cervantes). ℂ 787/725-9494. Reservations recommended. Snacks $6; main courses $15–$35. AE, MC, V. Mon–Fri 11am–3pm; Tues–Fri 6–10pm; Sat 7–11pm. Bus: A7.

IN SANTURCE

La Casona ✮ SPANISH/INTERNATIONAL   In a turn-of-the-20th-century mansion surrounded by gardens, La Casona offers the kind of dining usually found in Madrid, complete with a strolling guitarist. The much-renovated but still charming place draws some of the most fashionable diners in Puerto Rico. Paella marinara, prepared for two or more, is a specialty, as is *zarzuela de mariscos* (seafood medley). Or you might select filet of grouper in Basque sauce, octopus vinaigrette, *osso buco*, or rack of lamb. Grilled red snapper is a specialty, and you can order it with almost any sauce you want, although the chef recommends one made from olive oil, herbs, lemon, and toasted garlic. The cuisine here has both flair and flavor.

Calle San Jorge 609 (at the corner of Av. Fernández Juncos). ✆ **787/727-2717.** Reservations required. Main courses $25–$35. AE, DC, MC, V. Mon–Fri noon–3pm; Mon–Sat 6–11:30pm. Bus: 1.

IN OCEAN PARK

Pamela's ✮ CARIBBEAN FUSION/VEGETARIAN   A sense of cachet and style is very pronounced at this restaurant, a fact that's somewhat surprising considering its out-of-the-way location. Part of its allure derives from a sophisticated blend of Caribbean cuisines that combines local ingredients with Puerto Rican flair and a sense of New York style. Menu items include a salad that marries vine-ripened and oven-roasted tomatoes, each drizzled with a roasted-garlic-and-cilantro vinaigrette; club sandwiches stuffed with barbecued shrimp and cilantro-flavored mayonnaise; plantain-encrusted crab cakes with a spicy tomato-herb emulsion; and grilled island-spiced pork loin served with guava glaze and fresh local fruits. Beer and any of a wide array of party-colored drinks go well with this food.

In the Número 1 Guest House, Calle Santa Ana 1, Ocean Park. ✆ **787/726-5010.** Reservations recommended. Sandwiches and salads at lunch $10–$16; main course platters $22–$29. AE, MC, V. Daily noon–3pm and 6–10pm; tapas daily 3–7pm. Bus: A5.

IN ISLA VERDE

Expensive

La Piccola Fontana ✮ NORTHERN ITALIAN   Right off the luxurious Palm Court in the El San Juan Hotel, this restaurant delivers plate after plate of delectable food nightly. From its white linen to its classically formal service, it enjoys a fine reputation. The food is straightforward, generous, and extremely well prepared. You'll dine in one of two neo-Palladian rooms whose wall frescoes depict Italy's ruins and landscapes. Menu items range from the appealingly simple (grilled filets of fish or grilled veal chops) to more elaborate dishes such as *tortellini San Daniele*, made with veal, prosciutto, cream, and sage; or *linguine scogliere*, with shrimp, clams, and seafood. Grilled medallions of filet mignon are served with braised arugula, Parmesan cheese, and balsamic vinegar.

In El San Juan Hotel & Casino, Av. Isla Verde 6063. ✆ **787/791-0966.** Reservations required. Main courses $20–$40. AE, MC, V. Daily 6–10:30pm. Bus: A5.

Tangerine ✮✮ EURO-ASIAN   This is the ultimate in chic Isla Verde dining, and it just happens to lie adjacent to the street-level reception area of The Water Club (see "Accommodations," earlier in this chapter). Hailed by many international food critics, it glows in its much-deserved praise. Minimalist, postmodern, and angular, and outfitted in monochromatic colors that include steel gray and navy blue, it has a prominent bar area in back, bubbling waterfalls, big-windowed views of the tropical landscapes outside, and an occasional and rather whimsical reference to the orange-colored fruit that gave the place its name. Lighting radiates gently outward from the kind of ultraglam fixtures that make ordinary-looking people look good and beautiful people look fabulous. Menu items include such appetizers (the restaurant rather coyly refers to them as "foreplay") as crispy Vietnamese lobster rolls with mango-based sweet chile and avocado-minted melon relish; or citrus-cured yellowfin tuna tartare. For a main course try the cassia-smoked breast of chicken with sweet-garlic potato purée or Asian-herbed crusted Colorado lamb chops with garlic-flavored mashed potatoes and a sauce made from goat cheese, pulverized cucumbers, plum-flavored sake, and yogurt. Dessert might be a lemon-lime crème brûlée.

Tartak St. 2. ℭ 787/728-3666. Reservations required. Main courses $23–$42. AE, DC, MC, V. Daily 6:30–11pm. Bus: T1 or A5.

Moderate
Metropol CUBAN/PUERTO RICAN/INTERNATIONAL This is part of a restaurant chain known for serving the island's best Cuban food, although the chefs prepare a much wider range of dishes. Metropol is the happiest blend of Cuban and Puerto Rican cuisine we've ever had. The black-bean soup is among the island's finest, served in the classic Havana style with a side dish of rice and chopped onions. End-less garlic bread accompanies most dinners, including Cornish game hen stuffed with Cuban rice and beans or perhaps marinated steak topped with a fried egg (reportedly Castro's favorite). Smoked chicken and chicken-fried steak are also heartily recommended; portions are huge. Plantains, yucca, and all that good stuff accompany most dishes. Finish with a choice of thin or firm custard. Most dishes are at the low end of the price scale.

Club Gallistico, Av. Isla Verde. ℭ 787/791-4046. Main courses $10–$30. AE, MC, V. Daily 11:30am–10pm. Bus: C41, B42, or A5.

HITTING THE BEACH
Some public stretches of shoreline around San Juan are overcrowded, especially on Saturday and Sunday; others are practically deserted. If you find that secluded, hidden beach of your dreams, proceed with caution. On unguarded beaches you'll have no way to protect yourself or your valuables should you be approached by a robber or mugger, which has been known to happen. For more information about the island's many beaches, call the **Department of Sports and Recreation** at ℭ 787/728-5668.

All beaches on Puerto Rico, even those fronting the top hotels, are open to the public. Public bathing beaches are called *balnearios* and charge for parking and for use of facilities, such as lockers and showers. Beach hours in general are 9am to 5pm in winter, to 6pm summer. Major public beaches in the San Juan area have changing rooms and showers.

Famous with beach buffs since the 1920s, **Condado Beach** ⭐⭐ put San Juan on the map as a tourist resort. Backed up by high-rise hotels, it seems more like Miami Beach than any other beach in the Caribbean. From parasailing to sailing, all sorts of watersports can be booked at kiosks along the beach or at the activities desk of the hotels. There are also plenty of outdoor bars and restaurants. People-watching is a favorite sport along these golden strands.

At the end of Puente Dos Hermanos, the westernmost corner of the Condado is the most popular strip. This section of the beach is small and shaded by palms, and a natural rock barrier calms the turbulence of the waters rushing in, making for protected, safe swimming in gin-clear waters. The lagoon on the other side of the beach is ideal for windsurfing and kayaking.

Tips **Let the Swimmer Beware**

You have to pick your spots carefully if you want to swim along Condado Beach. The waters along the Condado Plaza Hotel are calmer than in other areas because of a coral breakwater. However, the beach near the Marriott is not good for swimming because of rocks and an undertow. Proceed with caution.

A favorite of San Juaneros themselves, golden-sand **Isla Verde Beach** is ideal for swimming, and it, too, is lined with high-rise resorts and luxury condos. Isla Verde has picnic tables, so you can pick up lunch and make it a day at the beach. This strip is also good for snorkeling because of its calm, clear waters; many kiosks will rent you equipment. Isla Verde Beach extends from the end of Ocean Park to the beginning of a section called Boca Cangrejos. The best beach at Isla Verde is in front of the Hotel El San Juan. Most sections of this long strip have separate names, such as El Alambique, which is often the site of beach parties, and Punta El Medio, bordering the new Ritz-Carlton, which is also a great beach and very popular even with the locals. If you go past the luxury hotels and expensive condos behind the Luís Muñoz Marín International Airport, you arrive at the major public beach at Isla Verde. Here you'll find a *balneario* with parking, showers, fast-food joints, and watersports equipment. The sands here are whiter than the golden sands of the Condado, and are lined with coconut palms, sea-grape trees, and even almond trees, all of which provide shade from the fierce noonday sun.

One of the most attractive beaches in the Greater San Juan area is **Ocean Park Beach** ★★, a mile of fine gold sand in a neighborhood east of Condado. This beach attracts both young people and a big gay crowd. Access to the beach at Ocean Park has been limited recently, but the best place to enter is from a section called El Ultimo Trolley. This area is ideal for volleyball, paddleball, and other games. The easternmost portion, known as Punta Las Marias, is best for windsurfing. The waters at Ocean Park are usually fine for swimming, although they can get rough at times.

Rivaling Condado and Isla Verde beaches, **Luquillo Beach** is the grandest in Puerto Rico and one of the most popular. It's about 50km (30 miles) east of San Juan, near the town of Luquillo. Here you'll find a mile-long half-moon bay set against a backdrop of coconut palms. Saturday and Sunday are the worst times to go, as hordes of San Juaneros head here for fun in the sun. Watersports kiosks are available, offering everything from windsurfing to sailing. Facilities include lifeguards, an emergency first-aid station, ample parking, showers, and toilets. You can easily grab lunch here at one of the beach shacks offering cod fritters and tacos.

SPORTS & OTHER OUTDOOR PURSUITS

DEEP-SEA FISHING ★ Deep-sea fishing is top-notch here. Allison tuna, white and blue marlin, sailfish, wahoo, dolphin (mahimahi), mackerel, and tarpon are some of the fish that can be caught in Puerto Rican waters, where 30 world records have been broken. Charter arrangements can be made through most major hotels and resorts.

Benitez Fishing Charters can be contacted directly at P.O. Box 9066541, Puerto de Tierra, San Juan, PR 00906 (© 787/723-2292 until 9pm). The captain offers a 45-foot air-conditioned deluxe Hatteras called the *Sea Born*. Fishing tours for parties of up to six cost $585 for a half-day excursion, $758 for a 6-hour excursion, and $968 for a full day, with beverages and all equipment included. (See "Scuba Diving," below, for another deep-sea fishing option.)

HORSE RACING Great thoroughbreds and outstanding jockeys compete year-round at **El Comandante,** Calle 65 de Infantería, Route 3, Km 15.3, at Canovanas (© 787/724-6060), Puerto Rico's only racetrack, a 20-minute drive east of the center of San Juan. Post time varies from 2:15 to 5:30pm on Monday, Wednesday, Friday, Saturday, and Sunday. Entrance to the clubhouse costs $3; no admission is charged for the grandstand.

SCUBA DIVING In San Juan, the best outfitter is **Caribe Aquatic Adventures,** Normandie Hotel San Juan, 1062 Calle 19, Villa Nevarez (© 787/281-8858). Its dive shop is open daily from 9am to 9pm. This outfitter will take you to the best local dive sites in the Greater San Juan area. Dives begin at $125 per person and a resort course for first-time divers also costs $135. Escorted dive jaunts to the eastern shore are also offered. Snorkeling lessons or tours lasting 1 hour and including basic equipment go for $50. Other activities include **deep-sea fishing trips,** costing $490 per half-day with a maximum of 6 fishermen.

SNORKELING Snorkeling is better in the outlying portions of the island than in overcrowded San Juan. But if you don't have time to explore greater Puerto Rico, you'll find that most of the popular beaches, such as Luquillo and Isla Verde, have pretty good visibility and kiosks that rent equipment. Snorkeling equipment generally rents for $15. If you're on your own in the San Juan area, one of the best places is the San Juan Bay marina near the Caribe Hilton.

Watersports desks at the big San Juan hotels at Isla Verde and Condado can generally make arrangements for instruction and equipment rental and can also lead you to the best places for snorkeling, depending on where you are in the sprawling metropolis. If your hotel doesn't offer such services, you can contact **Caribe Aquatic Adventures** (see "Scuba Diving," above), which caters to both snorkelers and scuba divers. You can also rent equipment from **Caribbean School of Aquatics,** Taft No. 1, Suite 10F, San Juan (© 787/728-6606).

TENNIS Most of the big resorts have their own tennis courts for the use of guests. There are 12 public courts, lit at night, at **San Juan Central Municipal Park,** at Calle Cerra (exit on Rte. 2; © 787/722-1646), open daily. Fees are $3 per hour from 7am to 6pm, and $4 per hour from 6 to 10pm.

WINDSURFING The savviest windsurfing advice and equipment rental are available at **Velauno,** Calle Loíza 2430, Punta Las Marías in San Juan (© 787/728-8716). A 1-day rental costs $75, 3 days $150, and 1 week $225. This is the second-biggest full-service headquarters for windsurfing in the United States. The staff here will guide you to the best windsurfing, which is likely to be the Punta Las Marías in the greater San Juan metropolitan area. Office hours are Monday to Friday 10am to 7pm, Saturday 11am to 7pm. Other spots on the island for windsurfing include Santa Isabel, Guánica, and La Parguera in the south; Jobos and Shacks in the northwest; and the island of Culebra off the eastern coast.

STEPPING BACK IN TIME: EXPLORING THE HISTORIC SITES OF SAN JUAN

The Spanish moved to Old San Juan in 1521, and the city played an important role as Spain's bastion of defense in the Caribbean. Today, the streets are narrow and teeming

Finds A Side Trip to Mona Island

Known locally as "the Galápagos of the Caribbean," **Mona Island** enjoys many legends of pirate treasure and is known for its white-sand beaches and marine life. The island is virtually uninhabited, except for two policemen and the director of the Institute of Natural Resources. Although the island is closer to Mayagüez than to San Juan, most boat tours of the island leave from the capital.

The island attracts hunters seeking pigs and wild goats, along with big-game fishers. But mostly it's intriguing to anyone who wants to escape civilization. **Playa Sardinera** on Mona Island was a base for pirates. On one side of the island, at **Playa de Pajaros,** are caves where the Taíno people left their mysterious hieroglyphs. Everything needed, including water, must be brought in, and everything, including garbage, must be taken out. For further information, call the **Departamento de Reservas Forestales** (📞 787/723-1616).

with traffic, but a walk through El Viejo San Juan makes for a good stroll. Some visitors have likened it to a "Disney park with an old-world theme." Fast food and junk stores mar a lot of the beauty. Nonetheless, it's the biggest and best collection of historic buildings, stretching back 5 centuries, in all the Caribbean. You can do it in less than a day. In a 7-square-block landmark area in the westernmost part of the city, you can see many of Puerto Rico's chief historical attractions, and do some shopping along the way.

CHURCHES

Capilla de Cristo   The chapel was built to commemorate what legend calls a miracle. In 1753, a young rider lost control of his horse in a race down this very street during the fiesta of St. John's Day, plunging over the precipice. Moved by the accident, the secretary of the city, Don Mateo Pratts, invoked Christ to save the youth, and had the chapel built when his prayers were answered. Today, it's a landmark in the old city and one of its best-known monuments. The chapel's gold-and-silver altar can be seen through its glass doors. Since the chapel is open only on Tuesdays, most visitors have to settle for a view of its exterior.

Calle del Cristo (directly west of Paseo de la Princesa). 📞 787/724-0700. Free admission. Tues 8am–5pm. Bus: Old Town Trolley.

Catedral de San Juan   San Juan Cathedral was begun in 1540 and has had a rough life. Looting, lacking funds, and hurricanes have continually hampered its construction and reconstruction. Over the years, a circular staircase and two adjoining vaulted Gothic chambers have been added. Many beautiful stained-glass windows escaped pillagers and natural disasters. In 1908, the body of Ponce de León was disinterred from the nearby Iglesia de San José and placed here in a marble tomb near the transept, where it remains. Since 1862, the cathedral has contained the wax-covered mummy of St. Pio, a Roman martyr persecuted and killed for his Christian faith. To the right of the mummy is a bizarre wooden statue of Mary with four swords stuck in her bosom. The cathedral faces Plaza de las Monjas (the Nuns' Square), a shady spot where you can rest and cool off.

Calle del Cristo 151 (at Caleta San Juan). 📞 787/722-0861. Free admission. Daily 8am–5pm. Bus: Old Town Trolley.

Old San Juan

ATLANTIC OCEAN

ACCOMMODATIONS ■
El Convento **8**
Gallery Inn at Galería San Juan **15**
Sheraton Old San Juan Hotel & Casino **14**

San Juan
PUERTO RICO

Castillo San Felipe del Morro **1**

EL CAMPO DEL MORRO

Cementerio de San Juan

Murallas de San Juan

Calle del Morro

Murallas de San Juan

Fort San Cristóbal

Norzagaray
Plaza San José
Del Cristo
Calle San José
Calle San Sebastian
Calle Sol
Calle Luna
Calle San Justo
Calle Cruz
Calle San Francisco
Plaza de Armas
Calle Fortaleza
Calle San Francisco
Paseo Princesa
Parque de las Palomas

Norzagaray
Plaza Colón
Calle O'Donell
C. Tamarindo
C. Capilla
Calle Tanca
Acosta
C. J. J.

Calle Harding
Calle Gen. Pershing
Calle Braumbaugh

Av. Muñoz Rivera
Av. Ponce de León
Paseo de Covadonga
Calle San Augustín
Av. Fernandez Juncos
C. de Contreras
Calle Muelle
Calle Allen
Calle Marina

Marina

Calle Recinto
Calle Tetuan
Calle Puntilla
Calle Presidio

El Arsenal
La Puntilla

Muralles de San Juan

Muralles de San Juan — Murallas de San Juan

ATTRACTIONS ●
Capilla de Cristo **12**
Casa Blanca **3**
Castillo de San Felipe del Morro **1**
Catedral de San Juan **9**
City Walls (Murallas de San Juan) **2**
El Arsenal **13**
Fort San Cristóbal **16**
Iglesia de San José **6**
La Fortaleza **11**
Museo de Arte **17**
Museo de San Juan **5**
Museo de las Américas **4**
Museo Pablo de Casals **7**
San Juan Gate **10**

0   1/10 mile
0   100 meters

(Moments Jogger's Trail or Romantic Walk

El Morro Trail, a jogger's paradise, provides Old Town's most scenic views across the harbor. The first part of the trail extends to the San Juan Gate. The walk then goes by El Morro, a 16th-century fort, and eventually reaches a scenic area known as Bastion de Santa Barbara. The walk passes El Morro's well-preserved walls, and the trail ends at the entrance to the fortress. The walkway is designed to follow the undulating movement of the ocean, and sea grapes and tropical vegetation surround benches. The trail is romantic at night, when the walls of the fortress are illuminated. Stop in at the tourist office for a map and set off, but be sure to stay alert, especially at night, as some muggings have been reported here.

FORTS

Castillo de San Felipe del Morro *(Kids)*   Called "El Morro," this fort stands on a rocky promontory dominating the entrance to San Juan Bay. In 1992 the parklike grounds around El Morro were restored to their 18th-century appearance and are ideal for walks.

Constructed in 1540, the original fort was a round tower, which can still be seen deep inside the lower levels of the castle. More walls and cannon-firing positions were added, and by 1787, the fortification attained the complex design you see today. This fortress was attacked repeatedly by both the English and the Dutch.

The U.S. National Park Service protects the fortifications of Old San Juan, which have been declared a World Heritage Site by the United Nations. With some of the most dramatic views in the Caribbean, you'll find El Morro an intriguing labyrinth of dungeons, barracks, vaults, lookouts, and ramps. Historical and background information is provided in a video in English and Spanish. The nearest parking is the underground facility beneath the Quincentennial Plaza at the Cuartel de Ballajá (Ballajá barracks) on Calle Norzagaray. Sometimes park rangers lead hour-long tours for free, although you can also visit on your own. With the purchase of a ticket here, you don't have to pay the admission for Fort San Cristóbal (see below) if you visit during the same day.

Before going into the citadel, you can visit the new $2-million San Juan National Historic Site (© 787/729-6960), which is open daily from 9am to 5pm, charging $3 for adults, $2 for seniors, and $1 for children 13 to 17 (free for 12 and under). The center is connected via two tunnels to Fort San Cristóbal, and was created from a strategic military base used in World War II. Visitors view a 12-minute film about the fortifications. A photo exhibit, a gift shop, and other exhibits are of interest.

At the end of Calle Norzagaray. © 787/729-6960. Admission $3 adults, $2 seniors, $1 children 13–17, free for children 12 and under. Daily 9am–5pm. Bus: A5, B21, or B40.

Fort San Cristóbal *(Kids)*   This huge fortress, begun in 1634 and reengineered in the 1770s, is one of the largest the Spanish ever built in the Americas. Its walls rise more than 45m (150 ft.) above the sea. Together San Cristóbal and El Morro, which are linked by nearly 1km (½ mile) of monumental walls and bastions filled with cannon-firing positions, protected San Juan against attackers coming by land. A complex system of tunnels and dry moats connects the center of San Cristóbal to its "outworks," defensive elements arranged layer after layer over an 11-hectare (27-acre) site. You'll get the idea if you look at the scale model on display. The fort is administered and maintained by the National Park Service.

Be sure to see the **Garita del Diablo,** or the Devil's Sentry Box, one of the oldest parts of San Cristóbal's defenses, and famous in Puerto Rican legend. The devil himself, it is said, would snatch away sentinels at this lonely post at the edge of the sea. In 1898, the first shots of the Spanish-American War in Puerto Rico were fired by cannons on top of San Cristóbal during an artillery duel with a U.S. Navy fleet. Sometimes park rangers lead hour-long tours for free, although you can visit on your own.

In the northeast corner of Old San Juan (uphill from Plaza de Colón on Calle Norzagaray). ℂ 787/729-6960. Admission $3 adults, $2 seniors, $1 children 13–17, free for children 12 and under. Daily 9am–5pm. Bus: A5, B21, or B40; then the free trolley from Covadonga station to the top of the hill.

OTHER HISTORIC SITES

The **city walls** around San Juan *(murallas de San Juan)* were built in 1630 to protect the town against both European invaders and Caribbean pirates, and indeed were part of one of the most impregnable fortresses in the New World. Even today, they're an engineering marvel. At their top, notice the balconied buildings that served for centuries as hospitals and also residences of the island's various governors. The thickness of the walls averages 6m (20 ft.) at the base and 3.5m (12 ft.) at the top, with an average height of 12m (40 ft.). Between Fort San Cristóbal and El Morro, bastions were erected at frequent intervals. The walls come into view as you approach from San Cristóbal on your way to El Morro. To get here, take the C45 or A5 bus.

San Juan Gate, Calle San Francisco and Calle Recinto Oeste, built around 1635, just north of La Fortaleza, several blocks downhill from the cathedral, was the main gate and entry point into San Juan—that is, if you arrived by ship in the 18th century. The gate is the only one remaining of the several that once pierced the fortifications of the old walled city. To get here, take the C45 and A5 bus.

Casa Blanca Ponce de León never lived here, although construction of the house (built in 1521) is sometimes attributed to him. The house was erected 2 years after the explorer's death, by the order of his son-in-law, Juan García Troche. The parcel of land was given to Ponce de León as a reward for services rendered to the Crown. His descendants lived in the house for about 2½ centuries, until the Spanish government took it over in 1779 for use as a residence for military commanders. The U.S. government also used it as a home for army commanders. On the first floor, the Juan Ponce de León Museum is furnished with antiques, paintings, and artifacts from the 16th through the 18th centuries. In back is a garden with spraying fountains, offering an intimate and verdant respite from the monumental buildings of Old San Juan.

Calle San Sebastián 1. ℂ 787/724-4102. Admission $2. Tues–Sat 9am–noon and 1–4:30pm. Bus: Old Town Trolley.

El Arsenal The Spaniards used shallow craft to patrol the lagoons and mangroves in and around San Juan. Needing a base for these vessels, they constructed El Arsenal in the 19th century. It was at this base that they staged their last stand, flying the Spanish colors until the final Spaniard was removed in 1898, at the end of the Spanish-American War. Changing art exhibitions are held in the building's three galleries.

La Puntilla. ℂ 787/723-3068. Free admission. Wed–Sun 8:30am–4:30pm. Bus: Old Town Trolley.

La Fortaleza The office and residence of the governor of Puerto Rico is the oldest executive mansion in continuous use in the Western Hemisphere, and has served as the island's seat of government for more than 3 centuries. Yet its history goes back even further, to 1533, when construction began on a fortress to protect San Juan's Spanish settlers during raids by Carib tribesmen and pirates. The original medieval towers remain, but as the edifice was subsequently enlarged into a palace, other modes of architecture and ornamentation were also incorporated, including baroque, Gothic, neoclassical, and Arabian. La Fortaleza has been designated a national historic site by the U.S. government. Thirty-minute tours of the gardens and building are conducted in English and Spanish. Informal but proper attire is required.

Calle Fortaleza #52, overlooking San Juan Harbor. © 787/721-7000, ext. 2358. Free admission. Tours of the gardens and building (given every half-hour and conducted in English and Spanish) Mon–Fri 9am–4pm. Bus: Old Town Trolley.

MUSEUMS

Museo de Arte 👁👁   Puerto Rico's most important gallery, which opened in 2000 and was constructed at a cost of $55 million, is a state-of-the-art showcase for the island nation's rich cultural heritage as reflected mainly by its painters. Housed in a former city hospital in Santurce, the museum features a permanent collection and temporary exhibitions. All the important modern island artists are represented, including the best known, the late Angel Botello, but also such contemporaries as Rafael Tufiño and Arnaldo Roche Rabell. Prominent local artists from the past also star—for example, Francisco Oller (1833–1917), who brought a touch of Cézanne or Camille Pissarro to Puerto Rico. (Oller actually studied in France with both of these Impressionists.) Another leading star of the permanent collection is José Campéche, a late-18th-century classical painter. The museum is like a living textbook of Puerto Rican art, beginning with its early development and going on to showcase camp aspects such as the poster art created here in the mid–20th century.

299 Av. Jose de Diego, Santurce. © 787/977-6277. www.mapr.org. Admission $6 adults, $3 children under 12 and seniors; seniors 75 plus free. Tues and Thurs–Sat 10am–5pm; Wed 10am–8pm; Sun 11am–6pm. Bus: A5 or B21.

Museo de las Américas 👁   This museum showcases the artisans of North, South, and Central America, featuring everything from carved figureheads from New England whaling ships to dugout canoes carved by Carib Indians in Dominica. It is unique in Puerto Rico and well worth a visit. Also on display is a changing collection of paintings by artists from throughout the Spanish-speaking world, some of which are for sale, and a permanent collection called "Puerto Rican *Santos*," donated by Dr. Ricardo Alegría.

Cuartel de Ballajá. © 787/724-5052. Free admission. Tues–Sun 10am–4pm. Bus: Old Town Trolley.

Museo de Pablo Casals   This museum is devoted to the memorabilia left to the people of Puerto Rico by the musician Pablo Casals. The maestro's cello is here, along with a library of videotapes (which can be played upon request) of some of his festival concerts. This small 18th-century house also contains manuscripts and photographs of Casals. The annual Casals Festival draws worldwide interest and internationally known performing artists; it's held during the first 2 weeks of June.

Plaza San José, Calle San Sebastián 101. © 787/723-9185. Admission $1 adults, 50¢ students, children 5–15, and seniors over 60. Tues–Sat 9:30am–5:30pm. Bus: Old Town Trolley.

Museo de San Juan   Located in a Spanish colonial building at the corner of Calle MacArthur, this cultural center was the city's main marketplace in the mid–19th century. Local art is displayed in the east and west galleries, and audiovisual materials reveal the history of the city. Sometimes major cultural events are staged in the

> ### (Moments) El Yunque Tropical Rainforest
>
> Some 40km (25 miles) east of San Juan lies the **Caribbean National Forest** 𝒜𝒜𝒜, known as El Yunque, the only tropical forest in the U.S. National Forest Service system. It was given its status by former president Theodore Roosevelt. Within its 11,200 hectares (28,000 acres) are some 240 tree species (only half a dozen of which are found on the mainland U.S.). In this world of cedars and satinwood, draped in tangles of vines, you'll hear chirping birds, see wild orchids, and perhaps hear the song of the tree frog, the *coquí*. The entire forest is a bird sanctuary and may be the last retreat of the rare Puerto Rican parrot.
>
> El Yunque offers a number of **walking and hiking trails,** high above sea level. The most scenic is the rugged El Toro Trail, which passes through four different forest systems en route to the 1,057m (3,523-ft.) Pico El Toro, the highest peak in the forest. The signposted El Yunque Trail leads to three of the recreation area's most spectacular lookouts. The Big Tree Trail is an easy walk to panoramic La Mina Falls. Just off the main road is La Coca Falls, a sheet of water cascading down mossy cliffs. You can be fairly sure you'll encounter rain—more than 100 billion gallons of rain falls here annually—but showers are usually brief, and there are plenty of shelters in the park.
>
> Nearby, the Sierra Palm Interpretive Service Center has maps and information and arranges for guided tours. A 45-minute drive southeast from San Juan (near the intersection of Rte. 3 and Rte. 191), El Yunque is a popular half-day or full-day outing. Major hotels provide guided tours.
>
> **El Portal Tropical Forest Center,** Route 191, Rio Grande (© **787/888-1880**), an $18-million exhibition and information center, has 930 sq. m (10,000 sq. ft.) of exhibition space. Three pavilions offer exhibits and bilingual displays. The actor Jimmy Smits narrates a documentary called *Understanding the Forest.* The center is open daily from 9am to 5pm, and it charges an admission of $3 for adults and $1.50 for children under 12.

museum's large courtyard. English- and Spanish-language audiovisual shows are presented Tuesday to Friday every hour on the hour from 9am to 4pm.

Calle Norzagaray 150. © **787/724-1875.** Free admission, but donations accepted. Tues–Sun 9am–noon and 1–4pm. Bus: B21 to Old San Juan terminal; then a trolley from the terminal to the museum.

SHOPPING 𝒜𝒜

U.S. citizens don't pay duty on items they purchase in Puerto Rico and bring back to the United States. And you can find great bargains on Puerto Rico, where the competition among shopkeepers is fierce.

The streets of **Old Town,** such as Calle San Francisco and Calle del Cristo, are the major venues for shopping. Note, however, that most stores in Old San Juan are closed on Sunday.

Local handicrafts can be good buys, including needlework, straw work, ceramics, hammocks, papier-mâché fruits and vegetables, and paintings and sculptures by Puerto Rican artists. Puerto Rican *santos* (saints) are sought by collectors. These carved wooden religious idols vary greatly in shape and size, and devout locals believe they have healing powers—often the ability to perform *milagros,* or miracles.

The biggest and most up-to-date shopping plaza in the Caribbean Basin is **Plaza Las Americas,** in the financial district of Hato Rey, right off the Las Americas Expressway. The complex, with its fountains and advanced architecture, has more than 200 mostly upscale shops. The stores (and their wares) are about what you'd find in a mall back home. Prices are comparable to those stateside.

ART

If you're interested in acquiring Puerto Rican art, there are many possibilities. **Galería Botello** (*, Calle del Cristo 208 (© 787/723-9987), is a contemporary Latin American gallery, a living tribute to the late Angel Botello, one of Puerto Rico's most outstanding artists. His paintings and bronze sculptures, evocative of his colorful background, are done in a style uniquely his own. On display are his and other local artists' paintings and sculptures, as well as a large collection of antique Puerto Rican *santos* (saints).

Galería Exodo, Calle del Cristo 200B (© 787/725-4252), is a specialty gallery, displaying unique art pieces from limestone and coral that may have existed at the time of the dinosaurs. The work is the creation of Radamés Rivera. One of the gallery's most noted artists is Yolanda Velasquez, who paints in an abstract style. The gallery also showcases the work of some 40 other artists.

Galería San Juan, at the Gallery Inn, Calle Norzagaray 204–206 (© 787/722-1808), specializes in the sculpture and paintings of Jan D'Esopo, a Connecticut-born artist who has spent much of her time in Puerto Rico. Many of her fine pieces are in bronze.

BOOKS

For travel guides, maps, and just something to read on the beach, there are two good bookstores. Try **Bell, Book & Candle,** 102 de Diego Ave., Santurce (© 787/728-5000), a large general-interest bookstore that carries fiction and classics in both Spanish and English, plus a huge selection of postcards. **Libreria Cronopios,** Calle San José 255 (© 787/724-1815), is the leading choice in the Old Town. It sells a number of books on Puerto Rican culture as well as good maps of the island.

COFFEE & SPICES

Spicy Caribbee, Calle del Cristo 154 (© 787/725-4690), offers the best selection of Puerto Rican coffee, which has a good reputation among aficionados. It also has the Old Town's best array of hot spicy sauces of the Caribbean.

FASHION

Nono Maldonado, 1051 Ashford Ave. (midway between the Condado Plaza and the Ramada Hotel; © 787/721-0456), is named after its owner, a Puerto Rican designer who worked for many years as the fashion editor of *Esquire* magazine. This is one of the most fashionable and upscale haberdashers in the Caribbean. Selling both men's and women's clothing, it has everything from socks to dinner jackets, as well as ready-to-wear versions of Maldonado's twice-a-year collections. **Polo Ralph Lauren Factory Store,** Calle del Cristo 201 (© 787/722-2136), has prices that are often 35% to 40% less than what you'd find on the U.S. mainland. You can get even greater discounts on irregular or slightly damaged garments. One upstairs room is devoted to home furnishings.

GIFTS, ARTS & CRAFTS

Butterfly People ✿, Calle Cruz 152, 2nd Floor (© 787/723-2432), is a gallery/cafe in a handsomely restored building in Old San Juan. Butterflies, preserved forever in artfully arranged boxes, range from $20 for a single mounting to thousands of dollars for whole-wall murals. Most of these butterflies come from farms around the world, some of the most beautiful from Indonesia, Malaysia, and New Guinea.

Barrachina's, Calle Fortaleza 104, between Calle del Cristo and Calle San José (© 787/725-7912), is more than a jewelry store. This is also the birthplace, in 1963, of the piña colada. It's a favorite of cruise-ship passengers, offering one of the largest selections of jewelry, perfume, cigars, and gifts in San Juan. There's a patio for drinks, plus a Bacardi rum outlet selling bottles cheaper than stateside, but at the same prices as the Bacardi distillery. You'll also find a costume-jewelry department, a gift shop, a restaurant, and a section for authentic silver jewelry.

Xian Imports, Calle de la Cruz 153 (© 787/723-2214), is a jumbled, slightly claustrophobic shop where you'll find compactly arranged porcelain, sculptures, paintings, and Chinese furniture, much of it antique. It's favored by the island's decorators as a source for unusual art objects.

El Artesano, Calle Fortaleza 314 (© 787/721-6483), is a curiosity. You'll find Mexican and Peruvian icons of the Virgin Mary; charming depictions of fish and Latin American birds in terra cotta and brass; all kinds of woven goods; painted cupboards, chests, and boxes; mirrors; and Latin dolls.

Bóveda, Calle del Cristo 209 (© 787/725-0263), is a long narrow space crammed with exotic jewelry, clothing, greeting cards of images of life in Puerto Rico, some 100 handmade lamps, antiques, Mexican punched tin and glass, and Art Nouveau reproductions, among other items.

Olé, Calle Fortaleza 105 (© 787/724-2445), deserves an *olé*. Browsing this store is a learning experience. Practically everything comes from Puerto Rico or Latin America. If you want a straw hat from Ecuador, hand-beaten Chilean silver, Christmas ornaments, or Puerto Rican *santos* (saints), this is the place.

Puerto Rican Arts & Crafts ✿, Calle Fortaleza 204 (© 787/725-5596), set in a 200-year-old colonial building, is one of the premier outlets on the island for authentic artifacts. Of particular interest are papier-mâché carnival masks from Ponce. Taíno designs inspired by ancient petroglyphs are incorporated into most of the sterling silver jewelry sold here. There's an art gallery in back, with silk-screened serigraphs by local artists, and a gourmet Puerto Rican food section with such items as coffee, rum, and hot sauces. The store also exhibits and sells small, carved *santos* (saints), laboriously carved by artisans in private studios around the island.

Centro Nacional de Artes Populares y Artesanías, Casa de los Contrafuertes, Plaza San Jose (© 787/721-6866), now located at the Museum of Raices Africanas, is a superb repository of high-quality native crafts. Centro Nacional scans the islands for artisans who still practice time-treasured crafts and do so with considerable skill. The prices aren't cheap, but the work merits the tab.

JEWELRY

Bared & Sons ✿, Calle Fortaleza 206 (at the corner of Calle San Justo; © 787/724-4811), now in its 4th decade, is the main outlet of a chain of at least 20 upscale jewelry stores on Puerto Rico. On the ground floor are gemstones, gold, diamonds, and watches. One floor up, there's a monumental collection of porcelain and crystal. It's a great source for hard-to-get and discontinued patterns from Christofle, Royal Doulton,

Wedgwood, Limoges, Royal Copenhagen, Lalique, Lladró, Herend, Baccarat, and Daum.

Joyería Riviera, Calle Fortaleza 257 (© 787/725-4000), is an emporium of 18-karat gold and diamonds, and the island's leading jeweler. Adjacent to Plaza de Armas, the shop has an impeccable reputation. This is the major distributor of Rolex watches on Puerto Rico.

Eduardo Barquet, Calle Fortaleza 200, at the corner of Calle La Cruz (© 787/723-1989), is known as a leading value-priced place to buy fine jewelry in Old San Juan. **Mounts and Gems,** Calle Fortaleza 205, sells convincing, glittering fake diamonds for those who don't want to wear or can't afford the real thing. It also stocks real diamond chips, emeralds, sapphires, and rubies, too.

Joseph Manchini, Calle Fortaleza 101 (© 787/722-7698), displays the works of its namesake and the shop's owner. He conceives almost anything you'd want in gold, silver, and bronze. Some of Old Town's most imaginative rings, bracelets, and chains are displayed here. If you don't like what's on sale, you can design your own, including pieces made with sapphire, emerald, and rubies.

LACE & LINENS

Linen House, Calle Fortaleza 250 (© 787/721-4219), has the island's best selection of napery, bed linens, and lace. Some of the more delicate pieces are expensive, but most are moderate in price. Inventories include embroidered shower curtains and lace doilies, bun warmers, placemats, and tablecloths that took workers weeks to complete. Some astonishingly lovely items are available for as little as $30. The aluminum/pewter serving dishes have beautiful Spanish-colonial designs. Prices here are sometimes 40% lower than those on the North American mainland.

SAN JUAN AFTER DARK
THE PERFORMING ARTS

Qué Pasa, the official visitor's guide to Puerto Rico, lists cultural events, including music, dance, theater, film, and art exhibits. It's distributed free by the tourist office.

A major cultural venue in San Juan is **Teatro Tapía,** Avenida Ponce de León (© 787/721-0180), across from Plaza de Colón, one of the oldest theaters in the Western Hemisphere (built around 1832). Much of Puerto Rican theater history is connected with the Tapía, named after the island's first prominent playwright, Alejandro Tapía y Rivera. Various productions, some musical, are staged here throughout the year and include drama, dance, and cultural events. You'll have to call the box office (open Mon–Fri 9am–6pm) for specific information. Tickets generally start at $20 to $30.

THE CLUB & MUSIC SCENE

Modeled after an artist's rendition of the once-notorious city of Mesopotamia, **Babylon,** in El San Juan Hotel & Casino, Av. Isla Verde 6063, Isla Verde (© 787/791-1000), is circular, with a central dance floor and a wraparound balcony where onlookers can scope out the action below. The crowd is usually in the 25-to-45 age group; you must be 21 to enter. This place has one of the best sound systems in the Caribbean. You might want to make a night of it, stopping into the El San Juan's bars and casino en route. The club is open from Thursday to Saturday from 10pm to 3am. Guests of the hotel enter free; otherwise, there's a $15 cover (bus no. A5).

Rumba, 152 Calle San Sebastian (© 787/725-4407), is small and cramped, but so photogenically hip that it was selected as the site for the filming of many of the crowd scenes within *Dirty Dancing: Havana Nights.* Set immediately adjacent to the also-recommended restaurant Barú (p. 468), with which it's not associated, it's known within San Juan's underground nightlife circuit as one of the places to hang. Expect beautiful people, a sense of cutting-edge Hispanic hip, and a cover charge of up to $15 whenever there's live music. It's open Thursday to Saturday 8pm to 4am (bus no. M2, M3, or A5).

Club Laser, Calle del Cruz 251 (✆ 787/725-7581), is set in the heart of Old Town near the corner of Calle Fortaleza. This dance club is especially crowded when cruise ships pull into town. Once inside, you can wander over the three floors, listening to whatever generic dance music happens to be hot, with lots of additional merengue and salsa thrown in as well. Depending on the night, the age of the crowd varies. It's open Thursday to Saturday from 9pm to 4am. It's also open on Monday and Tuesday when the cruise ships dock. Women enter free before midnight on Friday and Saturday. The cover ranges from $10 to $15 (bus: Old Town Trolley).

THE BAR SCENE

Two of the most dramatic bars in San Juan are at **El San Juan Hotel & Casino,** Av. Isla Verde 6063, Isla Verde (✆ 787/791-1000). There is no more beautiful bar in the Caribbean than the **Palm Court,** open daily 11am to 3am. Set in an oval wrapped around a sunken bar area, amid marble and burnished mahogany, it offers a view of one of the world's largest chandeliers. After 9pm Tuesday to Saturday, live music, often salsa and merengue, emanates from an adjoining room (the El Chico Bar). There's also the chic **Cigar Bar,** with a magnificent repository of the finest cigars in the world. Some of the most fashionable women in San Juan—and men, too—can be seen puffing away while sipping a cognac. It's open daily 6pm to 3am.

Ireland and its stouts and ales meet the Tropics at **Shannon's Irish Pub,** Calle Bori 496, Río Piedras (✆ 787/281-8466). A sports bar, it's the regular watering hole of many university students, who come to play pool, listen to a constant supplier of high-energy rock 'n' roll, or watch one of the 10 TV monitors. There's live music Tuesday to Sunday—everything from rock to jazz to Latin. A simple cafe serves inexpensive food daily from 11:30am to 8pm. A $3 cover is imposed after 9pm. It closes at 2:30am on Friday and at 3am on Saturday.

We're not so keen on the food served here any more (and neither are our readers), but we still like to visit Old Town's **El Patio de Sam,** Calle San Sebastian 102 (✆ 787/723-1149), one of the most popular late-night joints with a good selection of beers. Live entertainment is presented here Friday to Sunday. This is one of the most enduring of the Old Town eateries and it remains a fun joint—that is, if you dine somewhere else before coming here.

HOT NIGHTS IN GAY SAN JUAN

The Beach Bar, on the ground floor of the Atlantic Beach Hotel, 1 Calle Vendig (✆ 787/721-6900), is the site of a hugely popular Sunday afternoon gathering that gets really crowded beginning around 4pm, and which stretches into the wee hours. There's an occasional drag show on a dais at one end of the outdoor terrace on Sunday nights. There's also an open-air rectangular bar. The Beach Bar is open daily from 10am to at least 2am (bus no. 21).

Cups, Calle San Mateo 1708, Santurce (✆ 787/268-3570), is the only place in San Juan that caters almost exclusively to lesbians. Men (gay or straight) aren't particularly welcome. Although the club is open Wednesday through Saturday from 7pm to

4am, entertainment such as live music or cabaret is presented only on Wednesday at 9pm and Friday at 10pm.

Eros, 1257 Av. Ponce de León, Santurce (© **787/722-1131**), is one of the town's most popular gay dance clubs, with strippers and shows. Most of the crowd is in its late 20s. Rum-based drinks, merengue, and the latest dance tunes are on tap; the place really gets going after around 10:30pm. It's open Wednesday to Saturday from 10pm to 5am. The cover is $5.

CASINOS

Gambling is big in Puerto Rico. Many people come here to do little more than that. As a result, there are plenty of options. Unlike European casinos, visitors don't need to flash passports or pay admission to enter.

The casino generating all the excitement today is the 1,720-sq.-m (18,500-sq.-ft.) **Ritz-Carlton Casino,** Avenue of Governors, Isla Verde (© **787/253-1700**), the largest casino in Puerto Rico. It combines the elegant decor of the 1940s with tropical fabrics and patterns. This is one of the plushest and most exclusive entertainment complexes in the Caribbean. You almost expect to see Joan Crawford—beautifully frocked, of course—arrive on the arm of Clark Gable. It features traditional games such as blackjack, roulette, baccarat, craps, and slot machines.

One of the splashiest of San Juan's casinos is at the **Sheraton Old San Juan Hotel & Casino,** Calle Brumbaugh 100 (© **787/721-5100**), where five-card stud competes with some 240 slot machines and roulette tables. You can also try your luck at the **El San Juan Hotel & Casino** (one of the most grand), Av. Isla Verde 6063 (© **787/791-1000**), or the **Condado Plaza Hotel & Casino,** Av. Ashford 999 (© **787/721-1000**).

3 Rincón (★

At the westernmost point of the island—about 10km (6 miles) north of Mayagüez and a little over 150km (100 miles) west of San Juan—Rincón has one of the most exotic beaches on the island, drawing surfers from around the world. In and around this small fishing village are some unique accommodations.

GETTING THERE

If you rent a car at the San Juan airport, it will take approximately 2½ hours to drive here via the busy northern Route 2, or 3 hours via the scenic mountain route (no. 52) through Ponce to the south. We recommend the southern route.

In addition, there are two flights daily from San Juan to Mayagüez on **Cape Air** (© **800/352-0714;** www.flycapeair.com). These flights take 40 minutes, and round-trip fare is $180. From the Mayagüez airport, Rincón is a 30-minute drive to the north on Route 2 (go left or west at the intersection with Rte. 115).

ACCOMMODATIONS

The Horned Dorset Primavera   This is the most sophisticated hotel on Puerto Rico and one of the most exclusive and elegant small properties anywhere in the Caribbean. Set on 3 hectares (8 acres), it opens onto a secluded semiprivate beach, and it was built on the massive breakwaters and seawalls erected by a local railroad many years ago. The hacienda evokes an aristocratic Spanish villa, with wicker armchairs, hand-painted tiles, ceiling fans, seaside terraces, and cascades of flowers. Accommodations are in a series of suites that ramble amid lush gardens. The decor is tasteful, with four-poster beds and brass-footed tubs in marble-sheathed bathrooms, with showers as well. Rooms are spacious and luxurious, with Persian rugs over tile floors, queen-size sofa beds in the sitting areas, and fine linen and tasteful fabrics on the elegant beds.

The eight-suite Casa Escondida villa, set at the edge of the property, adjacent to the sea, is decorated with an accent on teakwood and marble. Some of the units have private plunge pools; others offer private verandas or sun decks. Each contains high-quality reproductions of colonial furniture by Baker.

The hotel's restaurant, also called Horned Dorset Primavera, is one of the finest on Puerto Rico (see "Dining," below).

Apartado 1132, Rincón, PR 00677. (C) **800/633-1857** or 787/823-4030. Fax 787/823-5580. www.horneddorset.com. 39 units. Winter $1,377–$1,865 suite for 2; off season $717–$1,023 suite for 2. Rates include MAP (breakfast and dinner). AE, MC, V. Children under 12 not allowed. **Amenities:** 1 restaurant; bar; 3 outdoor pools (1 infinity); fitness center; kayaking (free); library; limited room service; massage; laundry service. In room: A/C, hair dryer, safe.

Parador Villa Antonio   Ilia and Hector Ruíz offer apartments by the sea in this privately owned and run *parador* (inn). The beach outside is nice, but the local authorities don't keep it as clean as they ought to. Surfing and fishing can be enjoyed just outside your front door, and you can bring your catch right into your cottage and prepare a fresh seafood dinner in your own kitchenette. (There's no restaurant.) This is a popular destination with families from Puerto Rico who crowd in on the weekends, occupying the motel-like rooms with balconies or terraces. Furnishings are well used but reasonably comfortable, and bathrooms are small with shower stalls.

Rte. 115, Km 12.3 (P.O. Box 68), Rincón, PR 00677. (C) **787/823-2645.** Fax 787/823-3380. www.villa-antonio.com. 61 units (shower only). Year-round $96–$128 studio (up to 2 people); $125–$144 2-bedroom apt (holds up to 4 people); $120 junior suite; $128 suite. AE, DISC, MC, V. **Amenities:** 2 outdoor pools; 2 tennis courts; playground; babysitting; laundry service; nonsmoking rooms; rooms for those w/limited mobility. In room: A/C, TV, beverage maker, iron, safe, Wi-Fi.

DINING

Horned Dorset Primavera FRENCH/CARIBBEAN   This is the finest restaurant in western Puerto Rico, so romantic that people sometimes come from San Juan just for an intimate dinner. A masonry staircase sweeps from the garden to the second floor, where soaring ceilings and an atmosphere similar to that within a private villa await you.

The menu, which changes virtually every night based on the inspiration of the chef, might include chilled parsnip soup, a fricassee of wahoo with wild mushrooms, grilled loin of beef with peppercorns, and medallions of lobster in an orange-flavored beurre blanc sauce. The grilled breast of duckling with bay leaves and raspberry sauce is also delectable. Dorado (mahimahi) is grilled and served with a ginger-cream sauce on a bed of braised Chinese cabbage. It's delicious, as is the grilled squab with tarragon sauce.

In The Horned Dorset Primavera Hotel, Rte. 429. (C) **787/823-4030.** Reservations recommended. Fixed-price dinner $76 for 5 dishes, $110 for 9 dishes. AE, MC, V. Daily 7–9:30pm.

HITTING THE BEACH & THE LINKS

One of Puerto Rico's most outstanding surfing beaches is at **Punta Higuero,** on Route 413 near Rincón. During winter, uninterrupted swells from the North Atlantic form perfect waves, averaging 1.5 to 2m (5–6 ft.) in height, with ridable rollers sometimes reaching 4.5 to 7.5m (15–25 ft.).

Punta Borinquén Golf Club, Route 107 ((C) **787/890-2987**), 3km (2 miles) north of Aquadilla's center, across the highway from the city's airport, was originally built by the U.S. government as part of Ramey Air Force Base. Today, it is a public 18-hole golf course, open daily from 6:30am to 6:30pm. Greens fees are $20 per round; a golf cart that can carry two passengers rents for $34 for 18 holes. A set of clubs can be rented for $15. The clubhouse has a bar and a simple restaurant.

4 Mayagüez

The port city Mayagüez, not architecturally remarkable, is the third-largest city on Puerto Rico; it lies about 150km (100 miles) southwest of San Juan. It was once the needlework capital of the island, and there are still craftspeople who sew fine embroidery. Mayagüez is also the honeymoon capital of Puerto Rico for certain tradition-minded Puerto Rican couples. If we were honeymooning, we'd rather stay in the greater San Juan area or at one of the posh north-coast resorts, but this island tradition dates from the 16th century. It's said that when local fathers needed husbands for their daughters, they kidnapped young Spanish sailors who were en route to Latin America.

GETTING THERE

Cape Air (© **800/352-0714;** www.flycapeair.com) flies from San Juan to Mayagüez twice daily (flying time: 40 min.). Round-trip passage is $180 per person.

If you rent a car at the San Juan airport and want to **drive** to Mayagüez, it's fastest and most efficient to take the northern route that combines sections of the newly widened Route 22 with the older Route 2. Estimated driving time for a local resident is about 90 minutes, although newcomers usually take about 30 minutes longer. The southern route, which combines the modern Route 52 with transit across the outskirts of historic Ponce, and final access into Mayagüez via the southern section of Route 2, requires a total of about 3 hours and affords some worthwhile scenery across the island's mountainous interior.

ACCOMMODATIONS

Holiday Inn Mayagüez & Tropical Casino   This six-story hotel competes with the Mayagüez Resort & Casino, though we like the latter better. The Holiday Inn is well maintained, contemporary, and comfortable. It has a marble-floored, high-ceilinged lobby, an outdoor pool with a waterside bar, and a big casino, but its lawn simply isn't as dramatically landscaped as the Mayagüez resort's surrounding acreage. Bedrooms here are comfortably but functionally outfitted in motel style; they've recently been refurbished. Each unit is equipped with a tiled bathroom with a tub/shower combination.

2701 Rte. 2, Km 149.9, Mayagüez, PR 00680-6328. © **888/465-4329** or 787/833-1100. Fax 787/833-1300. www.holiday-inn.com. 142 units. Year-round $113–$147 double; $197 suite. AE, DC, DISC, MC, V. **Amenities:** Restaurant; 2 bars; outdoor pool; casino; gym; business center; limited room service; laundry service; rooms for those w/limited mobility. *In room:* A/C, TV, dataport, beverage maker, hair dryer, iron/ironing board, safe.

Mayagüez Resort & Casino   Except for the ritzy Horned Dorset Primavera (p. 488), this is the largest and best general hotel resort in western Puerto Rico, appealing equally to business travelers and vacationers. In 1995 local investors took over what was then a sagging Hilton and radically renovated it to the tune of $5 million. The hotel still benefits from its redesigned casino, country-club format, and 8 hectares (20 acres) of tropical gardens. The landscaped grounds have been designated an adjunct to the nearby Tropical Agriculture Research Station. Five species of palm trees, eight kinds of bougainvillea, and numerous species of rare flora are set adjacent to the institute's collection of tropical plants, which range from a pink torch ginger to a Sri Lankan cinnamon tree.

The hotel's well-designed bedrooms open onto views of the swimming pool, and many units have private balconies. Guest rooms tend to be small, but they have good beds. The restored bathrooms are well equipped with makeup mirrors, scales, and tub/shower combinations.

For details about El Castillo, the hotel's restaurant, see "Dining," below. The hotel is the major entertainment center of Mayagüez. Its casino has free admission and is open 24 hours a day. You can also drink and dance at the Victoria Lounge.

Rte. 104, Km 0.3 (P.O. Box 3781), Mayagüez, PR 00680. ℂ 877/784-6835 or 787/832-3030. Fax 787/265-3020. www. mayaguezresort.com. 140 units. Year-round $185–$250 double; $325 suite. AE, DC, DISC, MC, V. Parking $4.50. **Amenities:** Restaurant; 3 bars; Olympic-size pool; children's pool; casino; 3 tennis courts; small fitness room; Jacuzzi; steam room; playground; 24-hr. room service; massage; babysitting; laundry service; rooms for those w/limited mobility. *In room:* A/C, TV, minibar, beverage maker, iron, Wi-Fi.

DINING

El Castillo INTERNATIONAL/PUERTO RICAN This is the best-managed large-scale dining room in western Puerto Rico, as well as the main restaurant for the largest hotel and casino in the area. The food has real flavor and flair, unlike the typical bland hotel fare so often dished up. Known for its generous lunch buffets, El Castillo serves only a la carte items at dinner, including seafood stew served on a bed of linguine with marinara sauce, grilled salmon with a mango-flavored Grand Marnier sauce, and filets of sea bass with a cilantro, white wine, and butter sauce. Steak and lobster are served on the same platter, if you want it.

In the Mayagüez Resort & Casino, Rte. 104, Km 0.3. ℂ 787/832-3030. Breakfast buffet $14; Mon–Fri lunch buffet $17; Sun brunch buffet $25; main courses $14–$34. AE, MC, V. Daily 6:30am–midnight.

EXPLORING THE AREA: BEACHES & TROPICAL GARDENS

Along the western coastal bends of Route 2, north of Mayagüez, lie the best surfing **beaches** in the Caribbean. Surfers from as far away as New Zealand come to ride the waves. You can also check out panoramic **Punta Higuero** beach, nearby on Route 413, near Rincón (see above).

The chief sight in Mayagüez is the **Tropical Agriculture Research Station** (ℂ 787/ 831-3435), located at the corner of roads 65 and 108, adjacent to the University of Puerto Rico at Mayagüez campus and across the street from the **Parque de los Próceres (Patriots' Park).** At the administration office, ask for a free map of the tropical gardens, which contain a huge collection of tropical species useful to people, including cacao, fruit trees, spices, timbers, and ornamentals. The grounds are open Monday to Friday from 7am to 4pm, and there is no admission charge.

5 San Germán

An hour's drive from Ponce or Mayagüez and the beaches of the southern coast—and just over 2 hours from San Juan—San Germán, Puerto Rico's second-oldest town, has been compared to a small-scale outdoor museum. It was founded in 1512 and destroyed by the French in 1528. Rebuilt in 1570, it was named after Germain de Foix, the second wife of King Ferdinand of Spain. Once the rival of San Juan, but without the benefit of Old San Juan's lavish restoration budgets, San Germán harbored many pirates, who pillaged the ships that sailed off the nearby coastline. Many of today's residents are descended from the smugglers, poets, priests, and politicians who lived here.

Although the pirates and sugar plantations are long gone and the city has settled into a slumber, it still retains some colorful reminders of the Spanish colonial era. Flowers brighten some of the patios here as they do in Seville. Also as in a small Spanish town, many of the inhabitants stroll through the small but choice historic zone in early evening. Nicknamed "Ciudad de las Lomas," or City of the Hills, San Germán boasts verdant scenery that provides a pleasant backdrop to a variety of architectural styles—Spanish colonial (1850s), Creole (1880s), neoclassical (1910s), Art Deco (1930s), and international (1960s)—depicted in the gracious old-world-style buildings that line some of its streets. So significant are these buildings that San Germán is the only city other than San Juan to be included in the National Register of Historic Places.

ACCOMMODATIONS

Villa Del Rey   This is the best place to stay in historic San Germán, although you'll have to drive 15 minutes west to a good beach. The fine country inn is completely modernized and attractively furnished, mostly with picture windows. You're offered a choice of midsize to spacious and well-furnished accommodations—single, doubles, or suites. Both the doubles and suites are suitable for families with two children under 12 years old. Each unit comes with a private bathroom with tub and shower. Light meals can be prepared in the suites, each equipped with a kitchenette. Guests meet fellow guests at La Veranda, sheltered but in the open air, featuring three meals a day, with a focus on regional dishes.

Rte. 361 Cain Alto Ward, Km 0.8, San Germán, PR 00683. ℂ 787/642-2627. Fax 787/264-1579. www.villadelrey.net. 19 units. Year-round $90 double; $110 suite. $15 per child in parent's room. MC, V. **Amenities:** Restaurant; bar; outdoor pool; business center. *In room:* A/C, TV, coffeemaker.

SEEING THE SIGHTS

The city's 249 noteworthy historical treasures are within easy walking distance of one another, though you'll only see most of them from the outside. If some of them are actually open, consider yourself fortunate, as they have no phones, keep no regular hours, and are staffed by volunteers who rarely show up. Also, be aware that most of the city's architectural treasures lie uphill from the impossibly congested main thoroughfare (Calle Luna), that streets in the old town tend to run only one-way (usually the way you don't want to go), and that you're likely to be confused by the bad signs and dilapidated condition of many of the historic buildings. We usually try to park on the town's main street (Carretera 102, which changes its name within the border of San Germán to Calle Luna), and then proceed on foot through the city's grimy-looking commercial core before reaching the architectural highlights described below.

One of the most noteworthy churches in Puerto Rico is **Iglesia Porta Coeli (Gate of Heaven)** (ℂ 787/892-0160), which sits atop a knoll at the eastern end of a cobble-covered square, the Parque de Santo Domingo. Dating from 1606 and built in a style inspired by the Romanesque architecture of northern Spain, this is one of the oldest churches in the New World. Restored by the Institute of Puerto Rican Culture, and sheathed in a layer of salmon-colored stucco, it contains a museum of religious art with a collection of ancient *santos,* the carved figures of saints that have long been a major part of Puerto Rican folk art. Look for the 17th-century portrait of St. Nicholas de Bari, the French Santa Claus. Inside, the original palm-wood ceiling and tough ausobo-wood beams draw the eye upward. Other treasures include early choral books from Santo Domingo, a primitive carving of Jesus, and 19th-century Señora de la Monserrate Black Madonna and Child statues. Admission is $1. The church is open Wednesday through Sunday from 8:30am to noon and 1 to 4:30pm.

Less than 30m (100 ft.) downhill from Iglesia Porta Coeli, at the bottom of the steps that lead from its front door down to the plaza below, is the **Casa Morales** (also called the **Tomás Vivoni House** after its architect), San Germán's most photographed and widely recognized house. Designed in the Edwardian style, with wraparound porches, elaborate gables, and elements that might remind you of a Swiss chalet, it was built in 1913, reflecting the region's turn-of-the-20th-century agrarian prosperity. (Note that it is a private residence and can be admired only from the outside.)

The long and narrow, gently sloping plaza that prefaces Iglesia Porta Coeli is the **Parque de Santo Domingo,** one of San Germán's two main plazas. Street signs also identify the plaza as the **Calle Ruiz Belvis.** Originally a marketplace, the plaza is paved with red and black cobblestones, and it's bordered with cast-iron benches and portrait busts of prominent figures in the town's history. This plaza merges gracefully with a second plaza, which street signs and maps identify as **Plaza Francisco Mariano Quiñones, Calle José Julian Acosta,** and **Plaza Principal.** Separating the two plazas is the unused (and closed to the public) **Viejo Alcaldía (Old Town Hall).** Built late in the 19th century, it's awaiting a new vision, perhaps as a museum or public building.

San Germán's most impressive church—and the most monumental building in the region—is **San Germán de Auxerre** (© **787/892-1027**), which rises majestically above the western end of the Plaza Francisco Mariano Quiñones. Designed in the Spanish baroque style, it was built in 1573 in the form of a simple chapel with a low-slung thatch roof. Its present grandeur is the result of at least five subsequent enlargements and renovations. Much of what you see today is the result of a rebuilding in 1688 and a restoration in 1737 that followed a disastrous earthquake. Inside are 3 naves, 10 altars, 3 chapels, and a belfry that was rebuilt in 1939, following an earthquake in 1918. The central chandelier, made from rock crystal and imported from Barcelona in 1866, is the largest in the Caribbean. The pride of the church is the *trompe l'oeil* ceiling, which was elaborately restored in 1993. A series of stained-glass windows with contemporary designs were inserted during a 1999 restoration. The church can be visited daily from 8 to 11am and 1 to 3pm.

6 Ponce ⊀

Puerto Rico's second-largest city, Ponce ("The Pearl of the South"), was named after Loíza Ponce de León, grandson of Ponce de León. Today it's Puerto Rico's principal shipping port on the Caribbean Sea, located 120km (75 miles) southwest of San Juan. The city is well kept and attractive, with many plazas, parks, and public buildings. It has the air of a provincial Mediterranean town. Look for the *rejas* (framed balconies) of the handsome colonial mansions. Ponce is a city, not a beach resort, and should be visited mainly for its sights.

ESSENTIALS

GETTING THERE   Flying from San Juan to Ponce five times a day, **Cape Air** (© **800/352-0714;** www.flycapeair.com), a small regional carrier, offers flights for between $115 and $150 round-trip. Flight time is 25 minutes.

VISITOR INFORMATION   Maps and information can be found at the **tourist office,** Edificio Jose Dapena (© **787/841-8160**). It's open daily from 9am to 5pm.

ACCOMMODATIONS

Meliá   A city hotel with southern hospitality, the Meliá, which has no connection with the international hotel chain, attracts businesspeople. The location is a few steps away from the Cathedral of Our Lady of Guadalupe and from the Parque de Bombas (the red-and-black firehouse). Although the more expensive Hilton long ago outclassed this old and somewhat tattered hotel, many people who can afford more upscale accommodations still prefer to stay here for its old-time atmosphere. The lobby floor and all stairs are covered with Spanish tiles of Moorish design. The desk clerks speak English. The small rooms are comfortably furnished and pleasant enough, and most have a balcony facing either busy Calle Cristina or the old plaza. Bathrooms are tiny, each with a shower stall. Breakfast is served on a rooftop terrace with a good view of Ponce, and Mark's at the Meliá thrives under separate management (see "Dining," below). You can park your car in the lot nearby.

Calle Cristina 2, Ponce, PR 00731. © **800/448-8355** or 787/842-0260. Fax 787/841-3602. www.hotelmeliapr.com. 73 units (shower only). Year-round $95–$120 double; $130 suite. Rates include continental breakfast. AE, MC, V. Parking $3. **Amenities:** Restaurant; bar; outdoor pool; limited room service; rooms for those w/limited mobility. *In room:* A/C, TV, dataport, hair dryer, iron/ironing board, safe.

Ponce Hilton & Casino   On a 30-hectare (80-acre) tract of land right on the beach, this is the most glamorous hotel in southern Puerto Rico. At the western end of Avenida Santiago de los Caballeros, it's about a 10-minute drive from the center of Ponce. Designed like a miniature village, with turquoise-blue roofs, white walls, and lots of tropical plants, ornamental waterfalls, and gardens, it welcomes both conventioneers and individual travelers. Accommodations contain tropically inspired furnishings, ceiling fans, and terraces or balconies. All the rooms are medium to spacious, with adequate desk and storage space, tasteful fabrics, good upholstery, and fine linen. The ground-floor rooms are the most expensive. Each is equipped with a generous tiled bathroom with a tub/shower combination.

The food is the most sophisticated and refined on the south coast of Puerto Rico. All the waiters seem to have an extensive knowledge of the menu and will guide you through some exotic dishes—of course, you'll find familiar fare, too.

Av. Caribe 1150 (P.O. Box 7419), Ponce, PR 00716. © **800/445-8667** or 787/259-7676. Fax 787/259-7674. www. hilton.com. 153 units. Year-round $205–$345 double; $450 suite. AE, DC, DISC, MC, V. Self-parking $4.50; valet parking $10. **Amenities:** 2 restaurants; 2 bars; lagoon-shaped pool ringed w/gardens; casino; 2 tennis courts; fitness center; bike rentals; playground; children's program; business center; room service (7am–midnight); babysitting; laundry service; dry cleaning; night club; rooms for those w/limited mobility. *In room:* A/C, TV, dataport, minibar, beverage maker, hair dryer, iron, safe.

DINING

El Ancla PUERTO RICAN/SEAFOOD   Motorists who wish to escape from the city drive about 3km (2 miles) south of the city center to this spot for its especially good seafood. Lying in a commercial port area, the restaurant serves fresh and well-prepared Puerto Rican dishes and makes a good outing from Ponce.

Menu items are prepared with real Puerto Rican zest and flavor. A favorite here is red snapper stuffed with lobster and shrimp, served either with fried plantains or mashed potatoes. Other specialties are filet of salmon in caper sauce, and a seafood medley of lobster, shrimp, octopus, and conch. Most of the dishes are reasonably priced, especially the chicken and conch. Lobster tops the price scale. The side orders, including crabmeat rice and yucca in garlic, are delectable.

Av. Hostos Final, Playa Ponce. (C) **787/840-2450**. Main courses $13–$36. AE, DC, DISC, MC, V. Sun–Thurs 11am–10pm; Fri–Sat 11am–11pm.

La Cava INTERNATIONAL   This hive of venerable rooms within a 19th-century coffee plantation is the most appealing and elaborate restaurant in Ponce. There's a well-trained staff, old-fashioned charm, well-prepared cuisine, and a champagne-and-cigar bar where the bubbly sells for around $6 a glass. Menu items change every 6 weeks, but might include duck foie gras with toasted brioche, Parma ham with mango, cold poached scallops with mustard sauce, a fricassee of lobster and mushrooms in a pastry shell, and grilled lamb sausage with mustard sauce on a bed of couscous. Dessert could be a black-and-white soufflé or a trio of tropical sorbets.

In the Ponce Hilton, Av. Caribe 1150. (C) **787/259-7676**. Reservations recommended. Main courses $26–$30. AE, DC, DISC, MC, V. Mon–Sat 6:30–10:30pm.

La Montserrate PUERTO RICAN/SEAFOOD   Beside the seafront, in a residential area about 6.5km (4 miles) west of the town center, this restaurant draws a loyal following from the surrounding neighborhood. A culinary institution in Ponce since it was established 20 years ago, it occupies a large, airy, modern building divided into two different dining areas. The first of these is slightly more formal than the other. Most visitors head for the less formal, large room in back, where windows on three sides encompass a view of some offshore islands. Specialties, concocted from the catch of the day, might include octopus salad, several different kinds of asopao, a whole red snapper in Creole sauce, or a selection of steaks and grills. Nothing is innovative, but the cuisine is typical of the south of Puerto Rico, and it's a family favorite. The fish dishes are better than the meat selections.

Sector Las Cucharas, Rte. 2. (C) **787/841-2740**. Main courses $17–$29. AE, MC, V. Daily 11am–10pm.

Mark's at the Meliá INTERNATIONAL   Mark French (Isn't that a great name for a chef?) elevates Puerto Rican dishes into haute cuisine at this eatery. You'd think he'd been entertaining the celebs in San Juan instead of cooking at what is somewhat of a Caribbean backwater. French was hailed as "Chef of the Caribbean 2000" in Fort Lauderdale. With his constantly changing menus and his insistence that everything be fresh, he's still a winner. You'll fall in love with this guy when you taste his tamarind barbecued lamb with yucca mojo. Go on to sample the grilled lobster with tomato-and-chive salad or the freshly made sausage with pumpkin, cilantro, and chicken. All over Puerto Rico you get fried green plantains, but here they come topped with sour cream and a dollop of caviar. The corn-crusted red snapper with yucca purée and tempura jumbo shrimp with Asian salad are incredible. The desserts are spectacular, notably the vanilla flan layered with rum sponge cake and topped with a caramelized banana, as well as the award-winning bread pudding soufflé with coconut vanilla sauce.

In the Meliá Hotel, Calle Cristina. (C) **787/284-6275**. Reservations recommended. Main courses $16–$30. AE, MC, V. Tues–Sat noon–3pm and 6–10:30pm.

BEACHES & OTHER OUTDOOR PURSUITS

A 10-minute drive west of Ponce will take you to **Playa de Ponce,** a long strip of white sand opening onto the tranquil waters of the Caribbean. This beach is usually better for swimming than the Condado in San Juan. There's little in the way of organized sports here, however.

The city owns two **tennis complexes,** one at Poly Deportivos, with nine hard courts, and another at Rambla, with six courts. Both are open 5am to 9pm Sunday to Friday and 8am to noon on Saturday, and are lit for night play. You can play for free, but you must call to make a reservation. For information, including directions on how to get there, call the Secretary of Sports at © **787/840-4400.**

One of Puerto Rico's finest and newest courses is the **Costa Caribe Golf & Country Club** (© **787/812-2650**), on the site of the previously recommended Ponce Hilton & Casino (see above). This 27-hole course charges from $60 to $85 for guests to play 18 holes. The beautifully landscaped holes—with commanding views of the ocean and mountain—are laid out in former sugar-cane fields. The no. 12 hole, one of the most dramatic, calls for a 188-yard carry over water from the back tees. Trade winds add to the challenge. The three 9s can be played in 18-hole combinations, as conceived by golf architect Bruce Besse. The greens are undulating and moderate in speed, averaging 560 sq. m (6,000 sq. ft.). Golf carts are included in the greens fees, and both gas and electric carts are available.

SEEING THE SIGHTS

A $40-million, turn-of-the-millenium project has restored more than 1,000 buildings in town to their original turn-of-the-20th-century charm. Architectural styles that combine neoclassical with "Ponce Creole" and Art Deco give the town a distinctive ambience.

Any Ponceño will direct you to the **Museo de Arte de Ponce,** Av. de las Americas 23–25 (© **787/848-0505**), which has a fine collection of European and Latin American art, the best on the island. Among the nearly 400 paintings, sculptures, and artworks on display are exceptional pre-Raphaelite and Italian baroque paintings. The building was designed by Edward Durell Stone and has been called the "Parthenon of the Caribbean." It's open daily from 10am to 5pm. Adults pay $5; children age 12 and under are charged $2.50.

Most visitors head for the **Parque de Bombas,** Plaza de las Delicias (© **787/284-4141**), the main plaza of Ponce. This fantastic old black-and-red firehouse was built for a fair in 1883. It's open daily 9:30am to 5pm; admission is free.

Around the corner from the firehouse, a trail will lead you to the **Cathedral of Our Lady of Guadalupe,** Calle Concordia/Calle Union, Plaza de las Delicias (© **787/842-0134**). Designed by architects Francisco Porrata Doría and Francisco Trublard in 1931, and featuring a pipe organ installed in 1934, it remains an important place for prayer. It's open Monday to Friday from 6am to 12:30pm, Saturday and Sunday from 6am to noon and 3 to 8pm.

El Museo Castillo Serrallés, El Vigía 17 (© **787/259-1774**), the largest and most imposing building in Ponce, was constructed high on a hilltop above town by the Serrallés family (owners of a local rum distillery) in the 1930s. This is one of the architectural gems of Puerto Rico and the best evidence of the wealth produced by the turn-of-the-20th-century sugar boom. Guides will escort you through the Spanish Revival house, where Moorish and Andalusian details include panoramic courtyards, a baronial dining room, and a small cafe and souvenir shop. Hours are Tuesday to Sunday 9:30am to 5pm. Admission is $6 for adults, $3 for seniors over age 62 and children 15 and under. From the Plaza las Delicias de Ponce, a free trolley bus runs frequently throughout the day, taking visitors to the museum.

The oldest cemetery in the Antilles, excavated in 1975, is near Ponce on Route 503 at Km 2.7. The **Tibes Indian Ceremonial Center** (© **787/840-2255**) contains some

186 skeletons, dating from A.D. 300, as well as pre-Taíno plazas from A.D. 700. Guided tours in English and Spanish are conducted through the grounds. Shaded by trees are seven rectangular ball courts and two dance areas. The arrangements of stone points on the dance grounds, in line with the solstices and equinoxes, suggest a pre-Columbian Stonehenge. A re-created Taíno village includes not only the museum but also an exhibition hall where you can see a documentary about Tibes; you can also visit the souvenir shop. The museum is open Tuesday to Sunday from 9am to 4pm. Admission is $3 for adults and $2 for children.

Hacienda Buena Vista, Route 10, Km 16.8 (© **787/812-5027** or 787/722-5882), is a 30-minute drive north of Ponce. Built in 1833, it preserves an old way of life, with its whirring waterwheels and artifacts of 19th-century farm production. Once it was one of the most successful plantations on Puerto Rico, producing coffee, corn, and citrus. It was a working coffee plantation until the 1950s, and 34 hectares (86 acres) of the original 200 hectares (500 acres) are still part of the estate. The rooms of the hacienda have been furnished with authentic pieces from the 1850s. Tours, lasting 1½ hours, are conducted Wednesday to Sunday at 8:30am, 10:30am, 1:30pm, and 3:30pm. *Note:* Only the 1:30pm tour is in English. Reservations are required. Tours cost $7 for adults, $4 for children 5–11. Kids 4 and under are admitted free. The hacienda lies in the town of Barrio Magüeyes, on Route 123 (Km 16.8) between Ponce and Adjuntas.

If you feel a yen for **shopping,** head for the **Fox Delicias Mall,** at the intersection of Calle Reina Isabel and Plaza de Las Delicias de Ponce, the city's most innovative shopping center.

7 Las Croabas

From San Juan, Route 3 leads east toward the fishing town of Fajardo, where you'll turn north to Las Croabas, about 50km (30 miles) from the capital.

You'll be near **Luquillo Beach,** one of the island's best and most popular public stretches of sand. From here, you can also easily explore **El Yunque Rainforest.** See the section "San Juan," earlier in this chapter, for details on both.

GETTING THERE

El Conquistador staff members greet all guests at the San Juan airport and transport them to the resort. Guests at the resort can take a taxi or a hotel courtesy car, or they can drive a rental car to Luquillo Beach. The cost of a taxi from the San Juan airport averages around $60.

If you're driving from San Juan, head east on Route 3 toward Fajardo. At the intersection, cut northeast on Route 195 and continue to the intersection with Route 987, at which point you turn north.

ACCOMMODATIONS

El Conquistador Resort & Golden Door Spa El Conquistador is a destination unto itself. Its array of facilities sits on 200 hectares (500 acres) of forested hills sloping down to the sea. Accommodations are divided into five separate sections united by their Mediterranean architecture and lush landscaping. Most lie several hundred feet above the sea. At the same altitude, a bit off to the side, is a replica of an Andalusian hamlet, Las Casitas Village, which seems straight out of the south of Spain. These pricey units, each with a full kitchen, form a self-contained enclave.

A short walk downhill takes you to a circular cluster of tastefully modern accommodations, Las Olas Village. And at sea level, adjacent to an armada of pleasure craft bobbing at anchor, is La Marina Village, whose balconies seem to hang directly over the water. The accommodations are outfitted with comfortable furniture, tropical colors, and robes. All the far-flung elements of the resort are connected by serpentine, landscaped walkways, and by a railroad-style funicular that makes frequent trips up and down the hillside.

One of the most comprehensive spas in the Caribbean, the Golden Door, maintains a branch in this resort. The hotel is sole owner of a "fantasy island" (Palomino Island), with caverns, nature trails, horseback riding, and watersports such as scuba diving, windsurfing, and snorkeling. Free private ferries at frequent intervals connect the island, which is less than a kilometer (½ mile) offshore, to the main hotel. There's also a 25-slip marina. The hotel operates an excellently run Kids Club with activities planned daily.

Av. Conquistador 1000, Las Croabas, Fajardo, PR 00738. © 800/468-5228 or 787/863-1000. Fax 787/863-6500. www.luxuryresort.com. 918 units. Winter $364–$1,098 double, from $1,700 casita with kitchen for 1–6; off season $317–$630 double, $640–$1,379 casita with kitchen for 1–6. MAP (breakfast and dinner) $96 extra per adult per day, $45 extra per child 16 and under. Children 16 and under stay free in parent's room. AE, DC, DISC, MC, V. Self-parking $10 per day; valet parking $20. **Amenities:** 9 restaurants; 7 bars; 7 pools; casino; golf course; 7 Har-Tru tennis courts; health club; spa; 25-slip marina; dive shop; fishing; sailing; children's programs; tour desk; business center; limited room service; massage; laundry service; dry cleaning; nightclub; nonsmoking rooms; rooms for those w/limited mobility. *In room:* A/C, TV, minibar, fridge, beverage maker, hair dryer, iron, safe.

Westin Rio Mar Beach Golf Resort & Spa

Marking Westin's debut in the Caribbean, this $180-million, 190-hectare (480-acre) resort lies on relatively uncrowded Rio Mar Beach, a 5-minute drive from massively popular Luquillo Beach. It was designed to compete with the El Conquistador, with which it's frequently compared. It's the best property in the area.

Landscaping includes several artificial lakes situated amid tropical gardens. More than 60% of the guest rooms look out over palm trees to the Atlantic. Other units open onto the mountains and forests of nearby El Yunque National Park (just a 15-min. drive away). The style is Spanish hacienda with nods to the surrounding jungle; unusual art and sculpture alternate with dark woods, deep colors, rounded archways, big windows, and tile floors. In the bedrooms, muted earth tones, wicker, rattan, and painted wood furniture add to the ambience. Bedrooms are spacious, with balconies or terraces, and good mattresses, plus tub/shower combinations in the large bathrooms.

The resort encompasses the **Rio Mar Country Club,** site of two important golf courses. The older of the two, the Ocean Course, was designed by George and Tom Fazio as part of the original resort, and has been a staple on Puerto Rico's professional golf circuit since the 1960s. In 1997, Westin opened the property's second 18-holer, the slightly more challenging River Course, the first Greg Norman–designed course in the Caribbean. The resort also has a 600-sq.-m (6,500-square-ft.) casino.

The only hotel in Puerto Rico with more diverse cuisine is El Conquistador (see above).

6000 Rio Mar Blvd. (30km/19 miles east of Luís Muñoz Marín International Airport, with entrance off Puerto Rico Hwy. 3), Rio Grande, PR 00745. © 800/627-8556 or 787/888-6000. Fax 787/888-6320. www.westinriomar.com. 600 units. Winter $399–$599 double; off season $224–$429 double; year-round from $549 suite. Children 5–17 staying in parent's room $85, including meals and activities; free for children 4 and under. AE, DC, DISC, MC, V. **Amenities:** 8 restaurants; 4 bars; outdoor pool; casino; 2 golf courses; 13 tennis courts; health club; spa; deep-sea fishing; sailing;

horseback riding nearby; kid's club; 24-hr. room service; laundry; dry cleaning; nonsmoking rooms; rooms for those w/limited mobility. *In room:* A/C, TV, dataport, beverage maker, minibar, hair dryer, iron, safe.

DINING

Otello's NORTHERN ITALIAN   Here you can dine by candlelight either indoors or out. The decor is neo-Palladian. You might begin with one of the soups, perhaps pasta fagioli, or select one of the zesty Italian appetizers, such as an excellently prepared clams Posillipo. Pastas can be ordered as a half portion for an appetizer or as a main dish, and they include homemade gnocchi and fettuccine with shrimp. The chef is known for his superb veal dishes. A selection of poultry and vegetarian food is offered nightly, along with several shrimp and fish dishes. The salmon filet in champagne sauce has beautiful accents, as does the veal chop in an aromatic herb sauce.

In El Conquistador Resort. © 787/863-1000. Reservations required in winter, recommended off season. Main courses $26–$42. AE, MC, V. Daily 6–10:30pm.

Striphouse STEAKHOUSE   Of all the restaurants in El Conquistador Resort, this is the most American. If Ike were to miraculously return, he'd feel comfortable with this 1950s menu. The severely dignified baroque room was inspired by an aristocratic monastery in Spain. The massive gates are among the most spectacular pieces of wrought iron on Puerto Rico. The service is impeccable, the steaks tender, and the seafood fresh.

Special care is taken with the beef dishes, even though the meat is imported frozen. You can begin with the lobster bisque or Caesar salad, then move on to the thick cut of veal chop or the perfectly prepared rack of lamb. Prime rib of beef is a feature, as are the succulent steaks; try the New York strip or the porterhouse.

In the El Conquistador Resort. © 787/863-1000. Reservations required. Main courses $28–$41. AE, DISC, MC, V. Daily 6–10:30pm.

TO THE LIGHTHOUSE: EXPLORING LAS CABEZAS DE SAN JUAN NATURE RESERVE

Better known as El Faro or "The Lighthouse," this preserve in the northeastern corner of the island, north of Fajardo off Route 987, is one of the most beautiful and important areas on Puerto Rico. A number of different ecosystems flourish in the vicinity. Surrounded on three sides by the Atlantic Ocean, the 126-hectare (316-acre) site encompasses forestland, mangroves, lagoons, beaches, cliffs, offshore cays, and coral reefs. El Faro serves as a research center for the scientific community. It's home to a vast array of flora and fauna, including sea turtles and other endangered species.

The nature reserve is open Wednesday to Sunday; reservations are required, so call before going. For reservations throughout the week, call © **787/722-5882;** for reservations on Saturday and Sunday, call © **787/860-2560** (reservations on weekends can be made only on the day of your intended visit). Admission is $7 for adults, $4 for seniors and children 12 and under. Guided tours are conducted in Spanish at 9:30am, 10am, 10:30am, and in English at 2pm.

18

Saba

An extinct volcano with no beaches or flat land, cone-shaped Saba is 13 sq. km (5¾ sq. miles) of rock carpeted with lush foliage-like orchids, giant elephant ears, and Eucharist lilies. At its zenith, Mount Scenery, it measures 870m (2,854 ft.). Under the sea, the volcanic walls continue a sheer drop to great depths, making for some of the most panoramic diving in the Caribbean.

Unless you're a serious hiker or diver, you might confine your look at Saba to a day trip from St. Maarten. If you're a self-sufficient type who demands almost no artificial amusement, then sleepy Saba might be your hideaway.

One of the smallest islands of the Netherlands Antilles, Saba is 240km (150 miles) east of Puerto Rico and 145km (90 miles) east of St. Croix. Most visitors fly from St. Maarten, 45km (28 miles) to the north.

The official language of Saba is Dutch, but because so many English missionaries and Scottish seamen from the Shetland Islands settled here, Saba has always been English-speaking. All those European settlers have resulted in a population that is 60% Caucasian, many with red hair and freckled fair skin.

1 Essentials

VISITOR INFORMATION

The **Saba Tourist Board** is located in the heart of Windwardside (© **599/416-2231;** fax 599/416-2350). It's open Monday to Friday 8am to noon and 1 to 5pm. Saba is on the Web at **www.sabatourism.com**.

GETTING THERE

BY PLANE You'll have to get to St. Maarten before you can get to Saba. **American Airlines** (© **800/433-7300** in the U.S. and Canada; www.aa.com) flies nonstop from New York's JFK; **Continental Airlines** (© **800/523-3273** in the U.S. and Canada; www.continental.com) flies out of Newark, New Jersey. From Queen Juliana Airport on St. Maarten, you can take the 12-minute hop to Saba on **Winair** (© **866/466-0410** in the U.S. and Canada, or 599/545-4237; www.fly-winair.com). There are at least five flights per day, depending on volume; fares are $151 (£79) round-trip in the winter, $149 (£78) round-trip in the summer.

Saba's **Juancho Yrausquin Airport** (© **599/416-2255**) is one of the shortest landing strips in the world, stretching only 394m (1,292 ft.) along the aptly named Flat Point, one of the few level areas on the island.

Many guests at hotels on St. Maarten fly over to Saba on the morning flight, spend the day sightseeing, and then return to St. Maarten on the afternoon flight. Winair connections can also be made on Saba to both St. Kitts and St. Eustatius.

The Cottage Club **4**
Ecolodge Rendez-Vous **3**
The Gate House **1**
Juliana's **5**
Queen's Gardens Resort **2**
Scout's Place **6**
Willard's of Saba **7**

BY BOAT   You can also take a high-speed ferry from St. Maarten's Pelican Marina at Simpson Bay to Fort Bay on Saba; you'll arrive in about an hour. *The Edge* (© 599/ 544-2640) departs Wednesday through Sunday at 9am, returning at 5pm, making a day trip to Saba possible. Sometimes the waters are turbulent, making passengers seasick. The round-trip fare is $65 (£34) per person or $45 (£23) one way if returning on a different day from your departure.

GETTING AROUND

BY TAXI   Taxis meet every flight. Up to four people are allowed to share a cab. The fare from the airport to Windwardside is $10 (£5.20), or $16 (£8.30) to The Bottom. A taxi from Windwardside to The Bottom costs $8 (£4.15). There is no central number to call for service. Taking a taxi ride on Saba is likely to involve you in local life— it's decidedly informal here. Don't be surprised if your driver interrupts the trip to rush a sick child to a plane to be flown to a hospital or pick up an old man to take him up the hill because he'd fallen and hurt himself.

BY RENTAL CAR   None of the major U.S. firms operates on Saba, partly because most visitors opt to get around by taxi. In the unlikely event that you should dare to drive a car on Saba, locally operated companies include **Caja's Car Rental,** The Bottom (© 599/416-2388), starting at $50 (£26) per day and including a full tank of gas and unlimited mileage. Some insurance is included in the rates, but you might be held partly responsible in the event of an accident. Because of the very narrow roads and dozens of cliffs, it's crucial to exercise caution when driving on Saba. Note that traffic moves on the right.

BY HITCHHIKING   Hitchhiking has long been an acceptable means of transport on Saba, where everybody seemingly knows everybody else. And if you hitchhike, you'll probably get to know everybody else, too.

ON FOOT   The traditional means of getting around on Saba—walking—is still much in evidence. Just don't do the walk from The Bottom up to Windwardside unless you're fairly fit and have shoes with good traction, particularly after a recent rain.

FAST FACTS: Saba

Banks The main bank on the island is **First Caribbean International,** Windwardside (© **599/416-2216**), open Monday to Friday from 8:30am to 3:30pm. The **Royal Bank of Trinidad and Tobago** is another option. It's located at Windwardside (© **599/416-2454** or 599/416-2453), and is open Monday to Friday 8:30am to 3:30pm.

Currency Saba, like the other islands of the Netherlands Antilles, uses the **Netherlands Antilles guilder (NAf),** valued at 1.77 NAf to US$1 (1 NAf = US56¢). However, U.S. money is accepted by almost everybody here. *Unless otherwise specified, prices in this chapter are quoted in U.S. dollars and British pounds.*

Customs You don't have to go through Customs in Saba; it's a free port.

Documents The government requires that all visitors have a passport, plus a return or ongoing ticket.

Electricity Saba uses 110-volt AC (60 cycles), so U.S.-made appliances don't need transformers or adapters.

Emergencies Call © **599/416-2410** in case of fire and © **599/416-3289** for an ambulance. The police can be reached by calling © **599/416-3237.**

Hospital Saba's hospital complex is the **A. M. Edwards Medical Centre,** The Bottom (© **599/416-3239** or 599/416-3289).

Language The official language on Saba is Dutch, but English is widely spoken.

Pharmacies Try **The Pharmacy,** The Bottom (© **599/416-3289**), open Monday to Friday 8am to noon and 2 to 5pm.

Safety Crime on this island, where everyone knows everyone else, is practically nonexistent. But who knows? A tourist might rob you. It is always wise to safeguard your valuables.

Taxes The government imposes a 5% tourist tax on hotel rooms, plus a $3 (£1.55) "turnover tax" on all rooms. If you're returning to St. Maarten or flying over to Statia, you must pay a $6 (£3.10) departure tax. If you're going anywhere else, a $20 (£10) tax is imposed. A service charge of 10% to 15% will be added to your restaurant bill.

Telephone To call Saba from the United States, dial **011** (the international access code), then **599** (the country code for the Netherlands Antilles), and finally **416** (the area code for all of Saba) and the four-digit local number. To make a call within Saba, only the four-digit local number is necessary.

Time Saba is on Atlantic Standard Time year-round, 1 hour earlier than Eastern Standard Time. When the United States is on daylight saving time, clocks on Saba and the U.S. East Coast read the same.

Water The water on Saba is generally safe to drink.

Weather Temperatures from January to April average 69°F to 83°F (21°C–28°C). The rest of the year temperatures range from 70°F to 88°F (21°C–31°C).

2 Accommodations

If you're looking for a hotel on the beach, you've come to the wrong island. Saba's only beach, Well's Bay Beach, is tiny and can be reached from most hotels only via a $10 (£5.20) taxi ride.

The Cottage Club ✿   Small, intimate, and immersed in Saba's architectural and aesthetic traditions, this hotel complex occupies about .2 hectares (½ acre) of steeply sloping and carefully landscaped terrain, a 2-minute walk from the center of the island's capital. Designed of local stone, and set at an altitude above the other buildings of the complex, the lobby is filled with a collection of island antiques and lace curtains.

Each medium-size studio apartment has a semiprivate patio, a living-room area, and a queen-size bed. Bathrooms have showers and are well maintained. These units are housed in clapboard replicas of antique cottages—two studios per cottage—with red roofs, green shutters, white walls, and yellow trim. The interiors are breezy, airy, and comfortable. If you'd like a room with an ocean view, request no. 1 or 2. There's no bar or restaurant on the premises, but a nearby supermarket will deliver supplies on request. The owners of the establishment are three Saban brothers (Gary, Mark, and Dean), whose families all seem to help out.

Windwardside, Saba, N.A. ℂ **599/416-2486** or 599/416-2386. Fax 599/416-2476. www.cottage-club.com. 10 cottages. Winter $118 (£61) studio apt for 2; off season $105 (£55) studio apt for 2. 3rd and 4th person $25 (£13) each. Children 12 and under stay free in parent's room. Dive packages available. DISC, MC, V. **Amenities:** Outdoor pool; coin-operated laundry. *In room:* Ceiling fan, TV, kitchenette, beverage maker.

Ecolodge Rendez-Vous   This nature lover's retreat is buried deep in the rainforest off the Crispeen Trail. A small, family-operated eco-resort, it is enveloped by lush vegetation and is the perfect hideaway, especially since its accommodations can be kept mosquito free. The owners prefer to say that they are not a hotel but a lifestyle based on a close encounter with nature, with an aim of "rediscovery of a sense of self." A lofty goal indeed.

Accommodations are spread across nearly a dozen small Saban-style cottages, each with a private deck, hammock, and shower-only bathroom. Local artist Heleen Cornet decorated each unit with an individual theme. You live as Sabans did in the 19th century—that is, by candlelight after dark. The lodge is solar-powered, coming with "sun showers." Most of the vegetables served in the restaurant and certainly the herbs are home grown, as well as the fruits such as Surinam cherries and bitter skin oranges.

Crispeen Track, Windwardside, Saba. © 877/416-3888 or 599/416-3348. Fax 599/416-3299. www.ecolodge-saba. com. 11 units. Winter $95 (£49) double; off-season $75 (£39) double. Add $10 (£5.20) for kitchenette. Dive packages available. MC, V. **Amenities:** Restaurant; bar; outdoor pool; hot tub. *In room:* Kitchenette (in some), no phone.

The Gate House ★ *Finds*   In an amusingly named village, Hell's Gate, Lyliane and Michel Job welcome you to their bright little guesthouse. All of their comfortably and tastefully furnished rooms are in a bright West Indian motif, and have a well-maintained private bath. Families may prefer the Gate House Cottage, which can house a couple with a child and even includes a fully equipped kitchen and its own pool. Balconies surrounding the house open onto scenic views. Yet another rental is a luxurious four-bedroom villa with spacious rooms, three bathrooms, a fully equipped kitchen, and a private pool along with deck, balconies, and patios galore. The Gate House also has one of the finest chefs on island; see the review on p 506.

Hell's Gate, Saba, N.A. © 877/456-5198 in the U.S., or 599/416-2416. Fax 599/416-2550. www.sabagatehouse. com. 7 units. Winter $135 (£70) double, $155 (£81) cottage, $325 (£169) villa for up to 4; off season $125 (£65) double, $145 (£75) cottage, $305 (£159) villa for up to 4. Rates include continental breakfast. DISC, MC, V. **Amenities:** Restaurant; 2 outdoor pools; laundry service. *In room:* Ceiling fan, TV (in villa), kitchen/kitchenette (in some), hair dryer, no phone.

Juliana's   This hostelry is set on a hillside and each guest room is modern, immaculate, and simply but comfortably furnished. All have access to a sun deck and balconies opening onto beautiful views of the Caribbean, except nos. 1, 2, and 3, which are in the rear. Opt for one of the upper-level rooms (nos. 7, 8, or 9), as they offer the best views. The shower-only bathrooms are small but adequate, and housekeeping wins high marks here. Also available are a 2½-room apartment, complete with kitchenette; and a renovated original Saban cottage, with two bedrooms, a spacious living room, a dining room, a TV, and a fully equipped kitchen.

Windwardside, Saba, N.A. © 599/416-2269. Fax 599/416-2389. www.julianas-hotel.com. 12 units. Winter $125–$135 (£65–£70) double, $160 (£83) apt, $185 (£96) cottage; off season $110–$120 (£57–£62) double, $145 (£75) apt, $165 (£86) cottage. Extra person $30 (£16). Dive packages available. DISC, MC, V. **Amenities:** Restaurant; bar; outdoor pool; recreation room; babysitting. *In room:* Ceiling fan, TV, kitchen/kitchenette (in some), minibar, fridge, beverage maker (in some), hair dryer, iron (in some), no phone.

Queen's Gardens Resort ★   It's still outclassed by Willard's of Saba (see below), but this is a classy joint as well. One of the most massive engineering projects in Saba's recent memory included the placement of a rock-sided terrace on this plot of forested, steeply sloping land 360m (1,180 ft.) above the sea. The result is a well-conceived cluster of white-walled, red-roofed bungalows angled for sweeping views, and clustered around the semicircular edges of the largest pool on Saba, with north-facing views over the island's capital and the sea. From a distance, the compound evokes a fortified village in Iberia; close-up, it's charming and comfortable. Accommodations are simple, modern, airy, and clean, with dark-wood furniture. Most units are split-level, with large living rooms; all have kitchenettes and fine king-size or queen-size beds. Bathrooms are large but have showers only, with the exception of a few suites that have their own Jacuzzi overlooking the coast and sea.

Troy Hill, Drive 1 (P.O. Box 4), The Bottom, Saba, N.A. © 599/416-3494. Fax 599/416-3495. www.queensaba.com. 12 units. Winter $350 (£182) double, $395 (£205) 1-bedroom suite for 2, $495 (£257) 2-bedroom suite for up to 4; off season $275 (£143) double, $325 (£169) 1-bedroom suite for 2, $425 (£221) 2-bedroom suite for up to 4. AE, MC,

V. **Amenities:** Restaurant; bar; outdoor pool; dive shop; babysitting. *In room:* Ceiling fan, TV, kitchen, minibar, beverage maker, safe.

Scout's Place   Right in the center of Windwardside, funky Scout's Place, a dive resort, is hidden from the street and set on the ledge of a hill. With only 13 rooms, it's still the second-largest inn on the island. The old house has a large, covered, open-air dining room, where every table has a view of the sea. It's informal, with a decor ranging from Surinam hand-carvings to red-and-black wicker peacock chairs to silver samovars. Guest rooms open onto an interior courtyard filled with flowers, and each has a view of the sea. The rooms are small and rather plain, except for the four-poster beds; many have linoleum floors and tiny TVs. The best units are on the lower floor, as they have French doors opening onto balconies fronting the ocean. Furniture is haphazard. Bathrooms are small, with showers only. The apartment with kitchenette is suitable for up to four.

Windwardside, Saba, N.A. ⓒ **866/656-7222** in the U.S., or 599/416-2740. Fax 599/416-2741. www.sabadivers.com. 14 units. Winter $83–$109 (£43–£57) double, $128 (£67) cottage; off season $83–$94 (£43–£49) double, $128 (£67) cottage. Rates include continental breakfast. MC, V. **Amenities:** Restaurant; bar; outdoor pool; dive shop; laundry service. *In room:* Ceiling fan, TV, fridge, beverage maker (in some), Wi-Fi.

Willard's of Saba ✸✸   This is Saba's only luxurious hotel. Until Brad Willard arrived, there was nothing remotely comparable here. The hotel opened in 1994 and immediately began to attract large numbers of visitors, among them celebrities who might not have set foot on the island before. Guest rooms have *Casablanca*-like ceiling fans; furnishings are not of the highest standard, but are still comfortable. Because the hotel is in a garden high on a hill overlooking the island's southwestern coastline, each room has sweeping views and almost constant ocean breezes. Much care went into the design, making use of everything from cedar from the U.S. Northwest to original island paintings.

The least expensive units are the two rooms in the main building, which are quite spacious. The other five units are in a concrete building designed in the island's distinctive style, with red roofs, white walls, and green shutters. For the most luxurious living, ask for the VIP Room overlooking the pool, with its own large balcony. Lower cliffside units are the smallest, but have good views from their private balconies. Honeymooners prefer the Room in the Sky. Bathrooms are small, shower-only affairs.

The hotel restaurant and its bar are recommended in "Dining," below.

Booby Hill, Saba, N.A. ⓒ **800/504-9861** in the U.S., or 599/416-2498. Fax 599/416-2482. www.willardsofsaba.com. 7 units. Winter $400 (£208) double, $700 (£364) honeymoon suite or VIP room; off season $350 (£182) double, $500 (£260) honeymoon suite or VIP room. AE, DISC, MC, V. Children 12 and under not allowed. **Amenities:** Restaurant; bar; outdoor pool; tennis court; fitness center; Jacuzzi; room service; laundry service. *In room:* Ceiling fan, no phone.

3 Dining

Brigadoon Pub & Eatery ✸ CARIBBEAN/AMERICAN   The island's best restaurant is in this century-old colonial building with an open front. Your hosts, Trish Chammaa, and her husband, Michael (he labors over the hot stove), are virtual legends on the island. Whenever possible, local ingredients are used, including herbs, spices, fruits, and farm-fresh vegetables. Fresh local fish and lobster (prices vary) are generally the best things to order. Steaks are flown in weekly. Other recommended dishes include mahimahi (dolphin) with citrus-butter sauce and Thai shrimp in a coconut-curry sauce. The closing time listed below is not hard and fast. The owner closes the joint "whenever all the customers leave," even if it's really late.

Windwardside. ⓒ **599/416-2380.** Main courses $10–$30 (£5.20–£16). AE, DC, MC, V. Wed–Mon 6:30–9:30pm.

The Gate House Café ★ *Finds* FRENCH/SABAN   Saba has never been known for its cuisine, but the chefs who run this place are masters. Michel Job, a self-taught cook, obtains fresh vegetables and seafood from local vendors, but 90% of the food items are imported from France. The menu changes regularly but we recommend the bisque appetizer made from fresh Saban lobster and flambéed with cognac. A classic French soup is served with Swiss cheese, and a coconut soup is made from onions, leeks, and tania (a locally grown root vegetable). Seafood gets top priority here, especially the grilled mahimahi and the tuna steak coated in mild pepper. Savory meat offerings include chicken breast sausage in a mushroom sauce and aged beef tenderloin generously coated with Jamaican cracked black pepper and flambéed in cognac. Ask about the freshly made dessert of the day. There is also an impressive wine list.

Hell's Gate. © 599/416-2416. Reservations required. Main courses $17–$33 (£8.85–£17). DISC, MC, V. Daily 6:30–8:30pm.

My Kitchen ★ *Finds* INTERNATIONAL/MEDITERRANEAN   Near the office of Saba Divers in the center of Windwardside, this rooftop restaurant prepares and serves food with considerable skill. The atmosphere is one of the more inviting on island, with tropical plants, and a rustic deck overlooking the valley, the vegetable garden, a gazebo, and the mountains in the distance. A bakery is attached, and many islanders visit during the day for coffee and some of the more delectable baked goods in Saba. At night, tasty dishes emerge from the kitchen's grills, ovens, and pots, including pastas, chicken, steaks, and burgers. The latest owner, a Zealander from the Netherlands, wants to retain the loyalty of the former patrons of YIIK, which stood on this spot. He is retaining much of the old menu but also adding a number of fusion dishes, many from the Mediterranean.

Windwardside. © 599/416-2539. Reservations recommended. Main courses $7.50–$30 (£3.90–£16). MC, V. Mon–Sat noon–2pm and 6–8:30pm.

Saba Chinese Bar & Restaurant (Moo Goo Gai Pan) CANTONESE/INDONESIAN   Amid a cluster of residential buildings on a hillside above Windwardside, this place is operated by a family from Hong Kong. It offers some 120 dishes, an unpretentious decor of plastic tablecloths and folding chairs, and food so popular that many residents claim this is the restaurant they eat at most often. Meals include an array of Cantonese and Indonesian specialties—lobster Cantonese, Chinese chicken with mushrooms, sweet-and-sour fish, conch chop suey, several curry dishes, roast duck, and *nasi goreng* (fried rice with vegetables and meat). It doesn't rank with the great Chinese restaurants of New York, San Francisco, and Hong Kong, but it's good, change-of-pace fare.

Windwardside. © 599/416-2353. Main courses $8–$25 (£4.15–£13). MC, V. Tues–Sun 11am–9:30pm.

Scout's Place INTERNATIONAL/CARIBBEAN   This is a popular dining spot among day-trippers to the island, so you should have your driver stop by early to make a reservation for you. Lunch is simple, good, and filling, and the prices are low. The sandwiches are the island's best, made with fresh-baked bread. Locals come from all over the island to sample them. Dinner is more elaborate, with tables placed on an open-sided terrace, the ideal spot for a drink at sundown. Fresh seafood is a specialty, as is curried goat. Each day, a selection of homemade soups is also offered, perhaps pumpkin or pigeon pea. Scout's chef is proud of his ribs as well. Fresh local fruits and vegetables are used whenever possible. Even if you don't like the food, it's the best place on the island to catch up on the latest gossip.

In the Scout's Place hotel, Windwardside. © 599/416-2740. Reservations recommended. Lunch $10–$18 (£5.20–£9.35); fixed-price dinner $10–$25 (£5.20–£13). MC, V. Daily 7:30am–11pm.

Willard's of Saba ✿ ANTILLEAN/ASIAN/INTERNATIONAL   This restaurant features a breezy island decor, a sweeping high-altitude view of Saba's southeastern coastline, and some of the freshest fish and lobster on the island. Most of the catch featured on the "island-inspired" menu comes from the boats of local fisherfolk. Entrees change with the availability of the ingredients, although grouper, snapper Florentine, and lobster thermidor are usually featured, as are pork loin with a champagne-and-caper sauce, and Chinese-style beef with oyster sauce. You can cool down with a crepe stuffed with banana and jackfruit, then fried and served with homemade ice cream. The restaurant is nearly always referred to as Corazon's, taking this nickname from Corazon de Johnson, manager and chef. Although born in the Philippines, she doesn't limit her inspiration to her homeland, but roams the world for ideas for her fusion cuisine. There's a pleasant bar where you can enjoy a round of before-dinner drinks.

In the Willard's of Saba hotel, Booby Hill. © 599/416-2498. Reservations required. Main courses $22–$35 (£11–£18). AE, DISC, MC, V. Daily 11:30am–3pm and 6:30–9:30pm.

4 Sports & Other Outdoor Pursuits

If it's beaches you're seeking, forget it. It's better to remain on St. Maarten. Sports here are limited primarily to diving and hiking.

DIVING & SNORKELING ✿✿

Circling the entire island and including four offshore underwater mountains (seamounts), the **Saba Marine Park,** Fort Bay (© **599/416-3295**), preserves the island's coral reefs and marine life. The park is zoned for various pursuits. The all-purpose recreational zone includes **Well's Bay Beach,** Saba's only beach, but it's seasonal, disappearing with the winter seas only to reappear in late spring. There are two anchorage zones for visiting yachts and Saba's only harbor. The five dive zones include a coastal area and four seamounts, 2km (1¼ miles) offshore. In these zones are more than two dozen marked and buoyed dive sites and a snorkeling trail. You'll plunge into a world of coral and sponges, swimming with parrotfish, doctorfish, and damselfish.

The **snorkel trail** is not for the neophyte. It can be approached from Well's Bay Beach but only from May to October. Depths of more than 450m (1,475 ft.) are found between the island and the seamounts, which reach a minimum depth of 27m (89 ft.). There's a $3 (£1.55) per-dive visitor fee. Funds are also raised through souvenir sales and donations. The park office at Fort Bay is open Monday to Friday from 8am to 4pm, Saturday from 8am to noon, and Sunday from 10am to 2pm. There's a fully operational decompression chamber/hyperbaric facility in the Fort Bay harbor.

Sea Saba Dive Center, Windwardside (© **599/416-2246**), has nine experienced instructors eager to share their knowledge of Saba Marine Park and its famous deep and medium-depth pinnacles, walls, spur-and-groove formations, and giant boulder gardens. Their two 12m (39-ft.), uncrowded boats are best suited for a comfortable day on Saba's waters. Daily boat dives are made between 9:30am and 1:30pm, allowing a relaxing interval for snorkeling. Courses range from resort through dive master.

(*Moments* **A Roller-Coaster Road**

Regardless of what road you travel in the Caribbean, there's nothing to compare with 31km-long (19-mile) **"The Road."** Its hairpin curves climb from the little airport up the steep, steep hillside to the lush interior of Saba. In days of yore, engineer after engineer came to the island and told Sabans they'd have to forget ever having a road on their volcanic mountain. However, Josephus Lambert Hassell, a local, had high hopes. In the 1930s he began to take a correspondence course in engineering while he plotted and planned The Road. Under his guidance, his fellow islanders built The Road over the next 2 decades or so. In recent years, it's been necessary to reconstruct The Road, but it's there waiting to thrill you. At the top of The Road stands Windwardside at 541m (1,774 ft.), Saba's second-largest settlement and the island's midpoint.

Extra day and night dives can be arranged. A one-tank dive costs $60 (£31), a two-tank dive $110 (£57).

Saba Deep Dive Center, P.O. Box 22, Fort Bay, Saba, N.A. (© **599/416-3347;** www.sabadeep.com), is a full-service dive center that offers scuba diving, snorkeling, equipment rental/repair, and tank fills. Mike Myers and his staff of NAUI and PADI instructors and dive masters make an effort to provide personalized service and great diving, whether you're an old pro or a first-timer. A certification course goes for $450 (£234). A single-tank dive costs $60 (£31); a two-tank dive, $110 (£57). Night dives are $75 (£39). The center is open daily from 8am to 5pm. On the same property, the **In Two Deep Restaurant** and the **Deep Boutique** offer air-conditioned comfort, a view of the harbor area and the Caribbean Sea, good food and drink, and a wide selection of clothes, swimwear, lotions, and sunglasses. The restaurant is open for breakfast and lunch.

HIKING 🐾

Saba is as beautiful above the water as it is below. It offers many trails, both for beginners and more experienced hikers, all reached by paths leading off from "The Road." There's nothing more dramatic than the hike to the top of **Mount Scenery,** a volcano that erupted 5,000 years ago. Allow at least 3 hours and take your time climbing the 1,064 sometimes-slippery chiseled-rock and concrete steps up to the cloud-reefed, 857m (2,811-ft.) mountain. You'll pass through a lush rainforest of palms, bromeliads, elephant ears, heliconia, mountain raspberries, lianas, and tree ferns. Queen Beatrix of the Netherlands climbed these steps in her pumps and, upon reaching the summit, declared: "This is the smallest and highest place in my kingdom." On a clear day, you can see the neighboring islands of St. Kitts, St. Eustatius, St. Maarten, and even St. Barts. Ask your inn to pack you a picnic lunch, and bring water. The higher you climb, the cooler it grows, a drop of about 1°F (.5°C) every 98m (321 ft.); on a hot day this can be quite an incentive.

One of our favorite hikes—with some of Saba's most panoramic views—is the **Crispeen Track,** reached from Windwardside as the main road descends to the hamlet of St. John's. Once at St. John's, the track heads northeast going through a narrow but dramatic gorge covered in thick tropical foliage. The vegetation grows lusher and lusher, taking in banana and citrus fields. As you reach the higher points of a section of the island called **Rendezvous,** the fields are no longer cultivated and begin to resemble a rainforest, covered with such flora as philodendron, anthurium, and the wild mammee. Hiking time to Rendezvous is about an hour.

If you don't want to explore the natural attractions of the island on your own, the **Saba Tourist Office,** P.O. Box 527, Windwardside (© **599/416-2231**), can arrange tours of the tropical rainforests. Jim Johnson (© **599/416-2630**), a fit, 40-ish Saban guide, conducts most of these tours, and knows the terrain better than anyone else on the island. (He's sometimes difficult to reach, however.) Johnson will point out orchids, golden heliconia, and other flora and fauna, as well as the rock formations and bromeliads you're likely to see. Tours can accommodate one to eight hikers and usually last about half a day; depending on your particular route and number of participants, the cost can be anywhere from $50 to $90 (£26–£47). Actual prices, of course, are negotiated.

5 Exploring the Island

Tidy white houses cling to the mountainside, and small family cemeteries adjoin each dwelling. Lace-curtained, gingerbread-trimmed cottages give a Disneyland aura.

The first jeep arrived on Saba in 1947. Before that, Sabans went about on foot, climbing from village to village. Hundreds of steps had been chiseled out of the rock by the early Dutch settlers in the 1640s.

Past storybook villages, "The Road" goes over the crest to **The Bottom.** Derived from the Dutch word *botte,* which means "bowl-shaped," this village is nestled on a plateau 240m (790 ft.) above the sea, which is surrounded by rocky volcanic domes. It's also the official capital of Saba, a charming Dutch village of chimneys, gabled roofs, and gardens.

From The Bottom, you can take a taxi up the hill to the mountain village of **Windwardside,** perched on the crest of two ravines about 541m (1,774 ft.) above sea level. This village of red-roofed houses, the second most important on Saba, is the site of the two biggest inns and most of the shops.

From Windwardside, you can climb steep steps cut in the rock to yet another village, **Hell's Gate,** teetering on the edge of a mountain. There's also a serpentine road from the airport to Hell's Gate, where you'll find the island's largest church. Only the most athletic climb from here to the lip of the volcanic crater.

6 Saba After Dark

If you want to do a lot of partying on your vacation, you might want to consider another island. Saba is known for its tucked-away, relaxed, and calm atmosphere. However, don't be too dismayed; there's still something to do at night.

Scout's Place, Windwardside (© **599/416-2740**), is the place to hang out if you want to relax, enjoy a drink, and have a laugh, especially on weeknights. A hotel and restaurant, Scout's Place moonlights as a local watering hole, entertaining tourists and locals with a distinct Saban/Caribbean atmosphere. You won't do much dancing (well, that actually depends on how much you've had to drink), but it's much better than the weeknight alternative: nothing. It's open daily from 7am to around 11pm (but actual closing hours depend on business or the lack thereof). There's no cover.

A British-style pub with a nautical motif, **Saba's Treasure,** Windwardside (© **599/ 416-2819**), is the new social center of the island. Robbie Lynn, a local artist, designed and built the structure himself. He decorated the walls with old magazine articles about Saba's maritime past. Expats and visitors alike flock here at night, mainly for the beer but also for the well-stuffed sandwiches and stone-oven pizzas.

If you'd like to combine the ambience of a British pub with a saloon that might have been found in the Arizona Badlands, head for **Swinging Doors,** Windwardside (© **599/416-2506**). Saba's good ol' boy watering hole, where locals start consuming the brew at 9am and keep drinking until late at night (no set closing hour). If you get hungry along the way, go for the jalapeño poppers.

19

St. Barthélemy

For luxury with minimum hassle, albeit at a high price tag, St. Barts is rivaled only by Anguilla. It's the ultimate in sophistication in the tropics: chic, rich, and very Parisian. Forget historic sites or ambitious watersports programs. You go to St. Barts for the relaxation, the French cuisine, the white-sand beaches, and the ultimate in comfort.

New friends call it "St. Barts," while old-time visitors prefer "St. Barths." Either way, it's short for St. Barthélemy (San Bar-te-le-*mee*), named by its discoverer Columbus in 1493. For the most part, St. Bartians are descendants of Breton and Norman fisherfolk. Many are of French and Swedish ancestry, the latter evident in their fair skin, blond hair, and blue eyes. The mostly Caucasian population is small, about 6,500 living in some 21 sq. km (8¼ sq. miles), 24km (15 miles) southeast of St. Martin and 225km (140 miles) north of Guadeloupe.

Occasionally you'll see St. Bartians dressed in the provincial costumes of Normandy and speaking Norman French. In little **Corossol,** more than anywhere else, people sometimes follow customs brought from 17th-century France. You might see elderly women wearing the traditional starched white bonnets, at least on special occasions. The bonnets, known as *quiche-nottes* (a corruption of "kiss-me-not"), served as protection from the close attentions of English or Swedish men on the island. The bonneted women can also be

spotted at local celebrations, particularly on August 25, **St. Louis's Day.** Many of these women are camera-shy, but they offer their homemade baskets and hats for sale to visitors.

For a long time, the island was a paradise for a few millionaires, such as David Rockefeller, who had a hideaway on the northwest shore, and Edmond de Rothschild, who occupies some fabulous acres at the "other end" of the island. Nowadays, however, St. Barts is developing a broader base of tourism as it opens more hotels. Nevertheless, the island continues to be a favorite of celebrities, attracting the likes of Tom Cruise, Harrison Ford, and Mikhail Baryshnikov.

St. Barts also attracts a lot of star-seeking paparazzi, who stalk celebrities not only at their private villas, but also at the beach, including Grand Saline beach, where the late John F. Kennedy, Jr., was photographed bathing in the nude (which is common and legal at this beach). On another occasion, the paparazzi caught Brad Pitt sunning in the nude at his private villa, with then-girlfriend Gwyneth Paltrow. In February, the island guest list reads like a roster from *Lifestyles of the Rich and Famous.*

The island's capital is **Gustavia,** named after a Swedish king. It's St. Barts's only town and seaport. A sheltered harbor, it has the appearance of a dollhouse-scale port.

1 Essentials

VISITOR INFORMATION

For information before you go, contact the **French Government Tourist Office** (© **202/659-7779;** www.franceguide.com). There are offices at 444 Madison Ave., New York, NY 10022 (© **212/745-0960**); 9454 Wilshire Blvd., Suite 210, Beverly Hills, CA 90212 (© **310/271-6665**); and 205 N. Michigan Ave., Suite 3770, Chicago, IL 60601 (© **312/327-0290**).

On the island, go to the **Office du Tourisme,** in the commercial heart of Gustavia, adjacent to La Capitanerie (the Port Authority Headquarters), quai du Général-de-Gaulle (© **590/27-87-27;** www.st-barths.com).

GETTING THERE

BY PLANE   Before you book your own airfare, read the section on "Packages for the Independent Traveler" in chapter 2—it can save you a bundle!

The makeshift landing strip on St. Barts has been the butt of many jokes. It's short and accommodates only small aircraft; the biggest plane it can land is a 19-seater. And even on these small planes, landing on St. Barts has often been compared (and not favorably) to touching down on an aircraft carrier. No landings or departures are permitted after dark.

There are no nonstop flights from North America. From the United States, the principal gateways are St. Maarten, St. Thomas of the U.S. Virgin Islands, and Guadeloupe (see the individual chapters on these islands). At any of these islands, you can connect to St. Barts via interisland carriers.

From St. Maarten, your best bet is **Windward Islands Airways International** (known by everybody as **Winair;** © **866/466-0410** in the U.S. and Canada, or 590/27-61-01; www.fly-winair.com), which usually offers 22 to 27 daily flights to St. Barts. One-way passage costs 58€ to 72€ ($76–$93); flight duration is a mere 15 minutes.

Air Caraïbes (© **877/772-1005** in the U.S. and Canada, or 590/82-64-51; www. aircaraibes.com) flights depart four or five times a day from Pointe-à-Pitre's Le Raizet Airport in Guadeloupe. One-way passage to St. Barts costs 139€ ($181); trip time is 45 minutes. The airline also flies 10 times a day from St. Martin, costing 71€ ($92) one-way.

BY BOAT   The *Voyager* vessels (© **590/87-10-68;** www.voyager-st-barths.com), which operate from a base in Gustavia harbor, make frequent (usually daily, sometimes twice a day) runs between St. Barts and either side of St. Maarten/St. Martin. The schedule varies according to the season and the whim of the proprietors, but the

---

⌒Tips Airline Advice

Always reconfirm your return flight from St. Barts with your interisland airline. If you don't, your reservation will be canceled. Also, don't check your luggage all the way through to St. Barts, or you may not see it for a few days. Instead, check your bags to your gateway destination (whatever island you're connecting through, most often St. Maarten), and then take your luggage to your interisland carrier and recheck your bags to St. Barts.

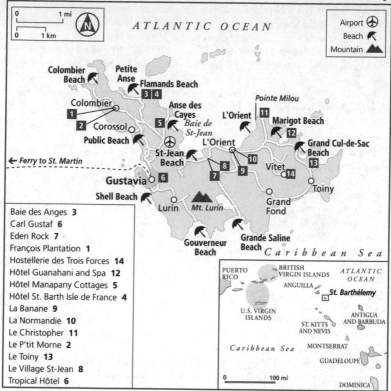

Baie des Anges **3**
Carl Gustaf **6**
Eden Rock **7**
François Plantation **1**
Hostellerie des Trois Forces **14**
Hôtel Guanahani and Spa **12**
Hôtel Manapany Cottages **5**
Hôtel St. Barth Isle de France **4**
La Banane **9**
La Normandie **10**
Le Christopher **11**
Le P'tit Morne **2**
Le Toiny **13**
Le Village St-Jean **8**
Tropical Hôtel **6**

Voyager II (a catamaran with room for 154 passengers) usually departs Marigot Harbor for St. Barts every morning at 9:15am, arriving in Gustavia at 10:45am, and at 6:45pm, arriving at 8:15pm. *Voyager I,* a single-hulled sailboat with room for 117 passengers, travels from Oyster Pond to Gustavia Wednesday and Sunday at 9am and 6:45pm, arriving 45 minutes later in Gustavia. Both vessels charge 52€ ($68) round-trip on the same day or 71€ ($92) round-trip on different days, with a one-way passage going for 44€ ($57). Fares for children under 12 are reduced in half. Advance reservations are a good idea.

GETTING AROUND

BY TAXI Taxis meet all flights and are not very expensive, mostly because destinations aren't far from one another. Dial ⓒ **590/27-75-81** for taxi service. A typical rate, from the airport to Cul-de-Sac, is 22€ ($29). Night fares between 8pm and 6am are 50% higher. Taxi service must be arranged between midnight and 6am—call ahead.

Virtually every cab driver is aware of the official prices that the island government imposes on **tours by taxi.** Many travelers simply approach a likely looking taxi driver and ask him to show them around. The official rates for one to three passengers are 42€ ($55) for 45 minutes, 46€ ($60) for 60 minutes, and 62€ ($81) for 90 minutes. For four or more passengers, add 8€ ($10) to each of the above-mentioned prices.

BY RENTAL CAR Nowhere will you see so many open-sided Mitsubishi Mini-Mokes and Suzuki Samurais as on St. Barts. You'll enjoy driving one, too, as long as you're handy with a stick shift and don't care about your coiffure.

Budget (© 800/472-3325 in the U.S., or 590/29-62-40; www.budget.com) offers the least stringent terms for its midwinter rentals, and some of the most favorable rates. It rents Suzuki Samurais for 62€ ($81) a day or 403€ ($524) a week, with unlimited mileage. A collision-damage waiver (CDW; in French, *une assurance tous-risques*), absolving renters of all but 500€ ($650) of responsibility in the event of an accident, costs 11€ ($14) a day. For the lowest rate, you should reserve at least 3 business days before your arrival.

Hertz (© 800/654-3131 in the U.S. and Canada; www.hertz.com) operates on St. Barts through a local dealership, **Henry's Car Rental,** with branches at the airport and in St-Jean (© 590/27-71-14). It offers open-sided Suzuki Samurais for 65€ ($85) a day, and more substantial Suzuki for 75€ to 90€ ($98–$117) per day. The CDW is about 10€ to 15€ ($13–$20) per day (with a 534€–840€/$694–$1,092 deductible).

At **Avis** (© 800/331-1212 in the U.S. and Canada, or 590/27-71-43; www.avis.com or www.avis-stbarth.com), you'll need to make a reservation a full month in advance during high season. In the winter, cars range from 57€ to 75€ ($74–$98) a day. In the off season, rentals are 43€ ($56) a day. The CDW costs 10€ to 14€ ($13–$18) extra per day (with a 500€–1,500€/$650–$1,950 deductible).

Driving is on the right. Never drive with less than half a tank of gas on St. Barts. There are only two gas stations on the island, and they're closed on Sunday and open only from 7:30am to noon and 2 to 7pm on other days of the week. (Remarkably, though, you can pay at the pump during business hours if you have a Visa card.) One gas station is near the airport; the other is near L'Orient. All valid foreign driver's licenses are honored. *Warning:* Honk your horn furiously while going around the island's blind corners to avoid having your fenders sideswiped.

BY MOTORBIKE & SCOOTER Denis Dufau operates two affiliates (© **590/27-54-83**). A helmet is provided, and renters must leave an imprint of a valid credit card. Rental fees vary from 25€ to 35€ ($33–$46) per day, depending on the size of the bike. For all but the smallest models, presentation of a valid driver's license is required and you must be 21 or older.

FAST FACTS: St. Barthélemy

Banks The two main banks, which both have **ATMs,** are in Gustavia. The **Banque Francaise Commerciale,** rue du General-de-Gaulle (© 590/27-65-88), is open Monday to Friday from 7:45am to 12:30pm and 1:35 to 4pm. The **Banque Nationale de Paris,** rue du Bord-de-Mer (© 590/27-63-70), is open Monday to Friday 8am to noon and 2 to 3:30pm, and closes at noon on Wednesday.

Currency Both euros and U.S. dollars are accepted currency. Under the current exchange, 1 euro equals US$1.30. Just before you leave home, you can check the current exchange rate on the Web at **www.xe.com**. *Prices in this chapter are quoted in U.S. dollars and euros.*

Documents U.S., British, and Canadian citizens need a passport to enter St. Barts. If you're flying in, you'll need to present your return or ongoing ticket.

Electricity The electricity is 220-volt AC (50 cycles); U.S.-made appliances will require adapter plugs and transformers.

Emergencies Dial ℂ **17** for **police** or **medical** emergencies, ℂ **18** for **fire** emergencies.

Hospital St. Barts is not the greatest place to find yourself in a medical emergency. Except for vacationing doctors escaping their own practices in other parts of the world, it has only seven resident doctors and about a dozen on-call specialists. The island's only hospital, with the only emergency facilities, is the **Hôpital de Bruyn,** rue Jean-Bart (ℂ **590/27-60-35**), about .4km (¼ mile) north of Gustavia. Serious medical cases are often flown to St. Maarten, Martinique, Miami, or wherever the person or his/her family specifies.

Language The official language is French, but English is widely spoken.

Pharmacies The **Pharmacie de Saint-Barth** is on quai de la Republique, Gustavia (ℂ **590/27-61-82**). Its only competitor is the **Pharmacie de l'Aeroport,** adjacent to the airport (ℂ **590/27-66-61**). Both are open Monday through Saturday from 8am to 8pm; on Sunday, one or the other remains open for at least part of the day.

Safety Although crime is rare, it's wise to protect your valuables. Don't leave them unguarded on the beach or in parked cars, even if locked in the trunk.

Taxes You're assessed a $5 departure tax if you're heading for another French island. Otherwise, you'll pay $10. Taxes are included in your airline ticket.

Telephone St. Barts is linked to the Guadeloupe telephone system. To call St. Barts from the United States, dial **011** (the international access code), then **590** (the country code for Guadeloupe), then **590** again, and finally the six-digit local number. To make a call within St. Barts, dial only the six-digit local number, and ignore the prefix 590. To reach an AT&T operator from anywhere on the island, dial ℂ **0800-99-00-11.** To reach **MCI,** dial ℂ **0800-99-00-19,** and to reach **Sprint,** dial ℂ **0800-99-00-87.**

Time When standard time is in effect in the United States and Canada, St. Barts is 1 hour ahead of the U.S. East Coast. When daylight saving time is in effect in the United States, clocks in New York and St. Barts show the same time.

Tipping Hotels usually add a service charge of 10% to 15%; always ask if this is included in the price you're quoted. Restaurants typically add a service charge, too. Taxi drivers expect a tip of 10% of the fare.

Water The water on St. Barts is generally safe to drink.

Weather The climate of St. Barts is ideal: dry with an average temperature of 72°F to 86°F (22°C–30°C).

2 Accommodations

Excluding a few of the really expensive hotels, most places here are homey, comfortable, and casual. Everything is small, as tiny St. Barts is hardly in the mainstream of tourism. In March, it's often difficult to stay on St. Barts unless you've made reservations far in advance. Accommodations throughout the island, with some exceptions, tend to be remarkably expensive, and a service charge of between 10% and 15% is usually added to your bill.

St. Barts has a sizable number of villas, beach houses, and apartments for rent by the week or month. Villas are dotted around the island's hills—very few are on the beach. Instead of an oceanfront bedroom, you get a panoramic view. One of the best agencies to contact for villa, apartment, or condo rentals is **St. Barth Properties,** 12 Washington St., Suite 201, Franklin, MA 02038 (© **800/421-3396** or 508/528-7727 in the U.S. and Canada; www.stbarth.com). Peg Walsh, a longtime aficionado of St. Barts, and her capable son, Tom Smyth, will let you know what's available. She can also make arrangements for car rentals and air travel to St. Barts. When you arrive, she can book babysitters and restaurant reservations. Rentals can range from a one-room "studio" villa away from the beach for $1,270 per week off season, up to $50,000 per week for a minipalace at Christmas. Yes, that $50,000 is right, but it's for a very unusual, antique-furnished luxury home. Most rentals average between $2,500 and $4,000 a week between mid-December and mid-April, with discounts of 30% to 50% the rest of the year. In addition to villas, Ms. Walsh can also arrange accommodations in all categories of St. Barts's hotels.

VERY EXPENSIVE

Carl Gustaf 🏵🏵🏵 The most glamorous hotel in Gustavia rises above the town's harbor from a steep hillside. Each state-of-the-art unit is in one of 14 red-roofed villas whose facilities include a private kitchenette, two phones, a fax machine, a stereo system, a private terrace, a private plunge pool, two TVs, and comfortably plush rattan furniture. Access to each building is via a central staircase, which tests the stamina of even the most active guests. The wood-frame units are angled for maximum views of the boats bobbing far below in the bay and panoramic sunsets. Bedrooms aren't as large as might be expected at such prices, but they are exceedingly well furnished, especially suites nos. 30 through 33. You'll walk across Italian marble floors under a pitched ceiling to reach your luxurious bed fitted with elegant fabrics. Bathrooms are also well equipped with mosaic-clad showers (no tubs) and makeup mirrors. Beach facilities are within a 10-minute walk. The mood is French, not unlike what you'd find on the coast of Provence.

The cuisine is French and Creole. Often a well-known chef from Paris appears in winter.

Rue des Normands, 97099 Gustavia, St. Barthélemy, F.W.I. © 800/322-2223 in the U.S., or 590/29-79-00. Fax 590/27-82-37. www.hotelcarlgustaf.com. 14 units. Winter 1,050€ ($1,365) 1-bedroom suite, 1,545€ ($2,009) 2-bedroom suite; off season 580€ ($696) 1-bedroom suite, 760€ ($912) 2-bedroom suite. Rates include continental breakfast. AE, MC, V. **Amenities:** Restaurant; bar; outdoor pool; health club; sauna; deep-sea fishing; sailing; scuba diving; water-skiing; windsurfing; helicopter rides; room service; massage; laundry service; dry cleaning. *In room:* A/C, TV, fax, kitchenette, minibar, fridge, hair dryer, iron, safe.

Eden Rock 🏵🏵 Greta Garbo checked out long ago, but this legendary hotel still occupies the most spectacular site on St. Barts, flanked by two perfect beaches. Years ago, when the island's former mayor, Remy de Haenen, bought the quartzite promontory this hotel sits on from an old woman, she laughed at him for paying too much. Today, the story is part of island lore. Offering the best panoramas on the island, it's surrounded on three sides by the waters of St. Jean Bay.

The building atop the pinnacle looks like an idealized version of a Provençal farmhouse. The stone house contains a collection of French antiques and paintings left over from the de Haenen family, plus English antiques and paintings. The decor in each guest room includes a stylish mixture of tasteful antiques and reproductions; the fabrics and accessories are pulled together with flair. Some rooms are right on the beach, with their own access to the sand. The best and most expensive are the ocean suites with private balconies. The least expensive are the small and cozy cabins. Bathrooms are compact and most have only showers. Named in honor of former guest Howard Hughes, a rooftop loft suite opened in 2005 with verandas on three sides and a panoramic view of St. Jean Bay. In addition, Eden Rock took over a neighboring beachfront resort, redoing all the bedrooms and increasing its room count. The new units include eight suites with decks opening onto the beach as well as five beachfront rooms. Five of the new suites have outdoor Jacuzzis, and two units come with private pools.

There's great emphasis on the quality and elegance of the cuisine at Eden Rock's three restaurants. There's a casual beachfront bar for lunch. Dinner is served at On-The-Rocks Restaurant—a stylish and swanky French joint—as well as at the Sand Bar.

Baiede, 97133 St-Jean, St. Barthélemy, F.W.I. (C) **877/563-7105** in the U.S., or 590/29-79-99. Fax 590/27-88-37. www.edenrockhotel.com. 32 units. Winter 650€–2,175€ ($845–$2,828) double; off season 475€–1,615€ ($617–$2,100) double. Extra person 105€ ($137). Rates include buffet breakfast. AE, MC, V. **Amenities:** 2 restaurants; bar; fitness center; snorkeling; windsurfing; room service; babysitting; laundry service; dry cleaning. *In room:* A/C, TV, minibar, hair dryer, safe.

François Plantation 𝐀𝐀

On a steep hill with panoramic views of the beach below, this complex recreates the plantation era. Fourteen bungalows, each decorated in an elegant West Indian style, surround a tropical garden. Eight of the units have sea views, and the others look out over a garden. Spacious bedrooms contain mahogany four-posters, ceiling fans, and Moroccan rugs on marble or tile floors that make the places extra cozy. Marble bathrooms come with bidets, open showers, and dual basins.

The hotel has an exceptional restaurant, François Plantation (see below).

Colombier, 97133 St. Barthélemy, F.W.I. (C) **590/29-80-22.** Fax 800/207-8071 in the U.S., or 590/27-61-26. www.francois-plantation.com. 14 units. Winter 450€–875€ ($585–$1,138) bungalow for 2; off season 320€–750€ ($416–$975) bungalow for 2. Rates include continental breakfast. AE, MC, V. Closed Sept–Oct. **Amenities:** Restaurant; bar; outdoor pool; babysitting; laundry service; dry cleaning. *In room:* A/C, TV, minibar, beverage maker, hair dryer, safe.

Hôtel Guanahani and Spa 𝐀𝐀 *Kids*

Better equipped than its nearest rival, Hôtel Manapany Cottages (see below), this is the largest hotel on St. Barts, opening onto two scenic beaches. It and the Sofitel Christopher (see below) are the most commercial properties on island. Isolated in the northeast part of the island, this hotel on its own peninsula is spread over 6.4 steeply sloping hectares (16 acres), dotted with a network of 68 Lilliputian cottages trimmed in gingerbread and painted in bold tropical colors. Don't consider this place if you have mobility problems or just don't relish the idea of huffing up and down steep slopes. But if that's not a problem, the views over the sea from each unit are broad and sweeping. Most units, at least those on the resort's upper slopes, are self-contained in their own individual cottages. Some of the bungalows closest to the beach, a private white-sand strip on a reef-protected bay, contain two units each. Traditional and contemporary-style desks and tables, tasteful upholstery, and four-poster king-size beds spell deluxe living, as do the fine linen and comfortable beds. Bathrooms are brightly tiled with showers only. Each of the accommodations has a private patio. In 2005 the resort underwent major restoration, blossoming out in a trendy lime-and-plum theme. An eight-room spa facility was integrated discreetly into the bungalow village. A hammam, lily pond, Indonesian-style daybed, and swimming pool were added to the spa's package of goodies.

Light lunches are served at Indigo, an airy venue positioned between the swimming pool and the sea. More formal dinners are available at Bartoloméo Restaurant. In summertime both lunch and dinner are served at Indigo.

Grand Cul-de-Sac, 97133 St. Barthélemy, F.W.I. ℂ **800/223-6800** in the U.S., or 590/27-66-60. Fax 590/27-70-70. www.leguanahani.com. 68 units. Winter 565€–905€ ($735–$1,177) double, from 1,025€ ($1,333) suite; off season 340€–565€ ($442–$735) double, from 685€ ($891) suite. Rates include American breakfast and round-trip airport transfers. AE, MC, V. **Amenities:** 2 restaurants; 3 bars; 2 outdoor pools; tennis court; fitness center; spa; Jacuzzi; boat rental; catamaran; fishing; sailing; scuba; windsurfing; horseback riding; children's programs (ages 2–6); car rental; salon; room service; massage; babysitting; laundry service; dry cleaning. *In room:* A/C, ceiling fan, TV, minibar, hair dryer, safe.

Hôtel Manapany Cottages ⚡

This resort climbs a steep, well-landscaped hillside on the northwestern side of the island, a 10-minute taxi ride north of the airport. This is one of the most stylish hotels on St. Barts, although not in the league of Carl Gustaf (see above) or Sofitel Christopher (see below). It's small, intimate, and accommodating; the name, translated from Malagese, means "small paradise." The place was designed as a minivillage of gingerbread-trimmed Antillean cottages set either on a steeply sloping hillside or beside the water. The rambling verandas and open-sided living rooms allow you to enjoy the trade winds, while the bedrooms have air-conditioning in case it gets too hot. The furnishings include both white rattan and Caribbean colonial pieces carved from mahogany and imported from the Dominican Republic. Mosquito netting covers most of the four-poster beds for a romantic touch. Rooms come with large-screen TVs with in-house videos, and kitchenettes. Bathrooms are quite luxurious, most with tub/shower combinations.

Le Fellini serves well-prepared Italian and French food at lunch and dinner.

Anse des Cayes, 97098 St. Barthélemy, F.W.I. ℂ **590/27-66-55.** Fax 590/27-75-28. www.lemanapany.com. 42 units. Winter 420€–450€ ($546–$585) double, 520€–850€ ($676–$1,105) junior suite, 800€–1,250€ ($1,040–$1,625) cottage; off season 240€–270€ ($312–$351) double, 320€–470€ ($416–$611) junior suite, 455€–695€ ($592–$904) cottage. AE, MC, V. **Amenities:** Restaurant; bar; outdoor pool; tennis court; fitness room; small spa; room service; laundry service; dry cleaning. *In room:* A/C, TV, fridge, hair dryer, safe.

Hôtel St. Barth Isle de France ⚡

Like François Plantation (see above), this resort evokes colonial era charm, though François does it more elegantly. This small, family-run hotel has unusually spacious guest rooms for St. Barts. Each top-notch unit contains a private patio or terrace, and an individual decor with antique mahogany and rattan furniture and engravings collected from neighboring islands. Beds are luxurious, fitted with fine linen. Clad in marble, bathrooms are spacious and well equipped with dual basins, large tubs (in some cases with whirlpool jets) and showers.

Meals are charming and sophisticated (with strong French overtones), despite their informality.

97098 Baie des Flamands, St. Barthélemy, F.W.I. ℂ **800/810-4691** in the U.S., or 590/27-61-81. Fax 590/27-86-83. www.isle-de-france.com. 33 units. Winter 720€–1,095€ ($936–$1,424) double, from 1,325€ ($1,723) suite; off season 510€–770€ ($663–$1,001) double, from 995€ ($1,294) suite. Rates include continental breakfast. AE, MC, V. **Amenities:** Restaurant; bar; 2 outdoor pools; tennis court; exercise room; spa; car rental; room service; babysitting; laundry service. *In room:* A/C, TV, minibar, fridge, beverage maker, hair dryer, safe.

La Banane ⚡

On the outskirts of the village of L'Orient lies this intimate and well-furnished hotel. Because of La Banane's small size and carefully restricted access, it seems like a private hideaway. The Brussels-born owner, De Nys Philippe, uses such accents as Artemide lighting, Casa Milano canopy beds, and Belgian linens to effect a change of pace from Creole designs.

The hotel is elegant and harmonious. Nine bungalows are scattered around a minimalist two-tiered pool. Bathrooms open onto patios or private gardens so that taking a shower becomes a perfumed ritual in a setting of such plants as frangipani, jasmine, and hibiscus. Set on flat, low-lying grounds, the gardens are richly planted with bananas, flowering shrubs, and palms, and are just a 3-minute walk from the beach.

Baie de L'Orient, 97133 St. Barthélemy, F.W.I. ⓒ 590/52-03-00. Fax 590/27-68-44. www.labanane.com. 9 units. Winter 450€ ($585) double; off season 320€ ($416) double. Rates include breakfast. AE, MC, V. **Amenities:** Bar; 2 outdoor pools; lounge; room service; massage; babysitting; laundry service; dry cleaning. *In room:* A/C, ceiling fan, TV, minibar, hair dryer, safe.

Le Christopher 🏛🏛   Set on a dramatic promontory above the ocean, this full-service hotel offers views of St. Martin and nearby islets. It has a French-colonial decor and a low-rise design that incorporates four slate-roofed, white-sided buildings arranged in a semicircle above a rocky coastline. The hotel is not adjacent to the water; guests must drive about 10 minutes to reach a good beach, Plage de l'Orient. Most of the resort's activities revolve around the swimming pool. The roomy accommodations, with king-size and twin beds, fall into two categories: deluxe oceanfront with patio or deluxe ocean view with terrace. All are furnished in a West Indian style and have ceiling fans. The differences between the two categories of rooms are most pronounced in the bathrooms. The oceanfront rooms have separate tub/shower combinations, while the rooms opening onto the gardens contain showers only. The resort's pool, a 370-sq.-m (4,359-sq.-ft.) pair of interconnected ovals with a bridge, is the largest on the island.

Le Mango, a poolside daytime restaurant, specializes in light fare. In the evening, more formal French and Creole meals are served at Taïno.

9 Pointe Milou (B.P. 571), 97133 St. Barthélemy, F.W.I. ⓒ 800/221-4542 in the U.S., or 590/27-63-63. Fax 590/27-92-92. www.hotelchristopherstbarth.com. 41 units. Winter 450€–564€ ($585–$733) double, 928€ ($1,206) suite; off season 289€–399€ ($376–$519) double, from 630€ ($819) suite. Rates include American breakfast. 1 child under 12 can stay free in parent's room. AE, MC, V. Closed Sept–Oct 25. **Amenities:** 2 restaurants; bar; outdoor pool; gym; scuba; snorkeling; room service; massage; babysitting; laundry service; dry cleaning; nonsmoking rooms; rooms for those w/limited mobility. *In room:* A/C, ceiling fan, TV, minibar, beverage maker, hair dryer, safe.

Le Toiny 🏛🏛🏛   This posh retreat is about equal to Carl Gustaf (see above). One of the most glamorous and chillingly expensive resorts on St. Barts, it contains only 15 suites, scattered among a half-dozen buildings clinging to a gently sloping hillside near Plage des Gouverneurs. The nearest swimming beach is a 5-minute drive away at Grande Saline, the only sanctioned nude beach on the island. All the suites have floors made of wide planks or terra-cotta tiles, kitchenettes, bathrooms with tub/shower combinations, and mahogany four-posters draped with mosquito netting. Each provides plenty of privacy, with lots of space and shrubbery between units. The hotel restaurant is reviewed in "Dining," below.

Anse de Toiny, 97133 St. Barthélemy, F.W.I. ⓒ 800/278-6469 in the U.S., or 590/27-88-88. Fax 590/27-89-30. www.hotelletoiny.com. 15 units. Winter 1,600€ ($2,080) 1-bedroom suite for 2, 2,650€ ($3,445) 3-bedroom suite for up to 6; off season 800€–830€ ($1,040–$1,079) 1-bedroom suite for 2, 1,500€–1,530€ ($1,950–$1,989) 3-bedroom suite for up to 6. AE, DC, MC, V. Closed Sept 1–Oct 25. **Amenities:** Restaurant; bar; outdoor pool; bike rental; car rental; room service; babysitting; laundry service; dry cleaning; rooms for those w/limited mobility. *In room:* A/C, TV, kitchenette, minibar, beverage maker, iron, hair dryer, safe.

EXPENSIVE

Baie des Anges ✦   Opening right onto the white sands of Flamands beach, this retreat is cooled by trade winds and has a laid-back, carefree atmosphere, as opposed to the more snooty and pricey French inns on the island. Surrounded by gardens, the two-story, ocean-fronting property is relatively simple but has its own style and charm. You can opt for a room opening onto the sea or the courtyard with its pool, where guests can be found when the Atlantic waves get too rough for swimming. All units have a kitchenette, plus a balcony with chaise longues. The accommodations are in sea colors of blue and green. For such a small place, the inn has a sophisticated, first-class restaurant, La Langouste, where nonguests are invited to drop in for lunch and dinner. Feast off the Creole or French specialties such as Caribbean lobsters selected from a tank.

Baie des Anges, Flamands, 97133 St. Barthélemy, FWI. ✆ 590/27-63-61. Fax 590/27-83-44. www.hotelbaiedes anges.fr. 10 units. Winter 300€–415€ ($390–$539) double, 170€–230€ ($334–$457) triple; off season 154€–242€ ($200–$315) double, 177€–273€ ($230–$355) triple. MC, V. **Amenities:** Restaurant; bar; outdoor pool; room service; laundry service; babysitting. *In room:* A/C, ceiling fan, TV, kitchenette, hair dryer, safe.

MODERATE

Hostellerie des Trois Forces ✦ *Finds*   The domain of St. Barts's astrologer emeritus might be called a New Age holistic retreat, but it's much more than that. It welcomes all patrons of whatever persuasion to one of its gingerbread cottages or its fine restaurant. The heart and soul of the place is Hubert Delamotte, who arrived from Brittany with his wife to create a hotel where happiness, good food, comfort, and conversation are a way of life. Each cottage is named for a sign of the zodiac and is decorated with the appropriate color scheme, such as red for the sign of Leo. Holistic services include massage therapy, osteopathy, and yoga. High on a hilltop, the inn occupies panoramic grounds in Vitet, above the freshwater ponds of Cul-de-Sac and about a 5-minute drive from the Cul-de-Sac beaches and L'Orient. As for the view, Hubert says, "There's not a soul between us and Africa."

Morne Viet, 97133 St. Barthélemy, F.W.I. ✆ 590/27-61-25. Fax 590/27-81-38. www.3forces.net. 7 cottages. Winter 184€ ($240) double; off season 107€ ($140) double. AE, MC, V. **Amenities:** Restaurant; bar; outdoor pool; laundry service. *In room:* A/C, kitchenette (in 2 units), minibar, safe.

Le P'tit Morne ✦ *Finds*   This is hardly the most luxurious or stylish lodging on an island that's legendary for its glamour and its five-star hotels. But the hotel's three-star format, its relatively low rates, and the warm welcome extended by its island-born owners, Mr. and Mrs. Felix and their daughter Marie-Joëlle, make it a worthy vacation site. It's a 10-minute drive from the beach. The colonial-designed guest rooms are filled with completely unpretentious furniture and comfortable king-size beds. A modern room was added in 2004. Called "New Moon," it offers a panoramic deck and a private pergola. There's plenty of elbowroom and units were built to catch the trade winds. Bathrooms are compact and have shower stalls.

Colombier (P.O. Box 14), 97095 St. Barthélemy, F.W.I. ✆ 590/52-95-50. Fax 590/27-84-63. www.timorne.com. 14 units. Winter 170€–230€ ($221–$299) double; off season 80€–170€ ($104–$221) double. AE, MC, V. Closed Sept. **Amenities:** Room service; babysitting. *In room:* A/C, TV, kitchen, fridge, beverage maker, iron.

Le Village St-Jean ✦ *Value*   This family-owned cottage colony hideaway, 2km (1¼ miles) from the airport toward St-Jean, attracts a distinguished clientele. Lying in the center of St. Barts, a 5-minute drive uphill from Saint-Jean Beach, it offers one of the best values on this high-priced resort island. Despite that, you may see a media headliner here; after all, some of them like to save money, too. The cottages contain kitchens, sun decks or gardens, terraced living rooms, balconies, and ceiling fans. Furnishings are modest but comfortable, and the living space is generous. The tiled shower-only bathrooms are spacious, and some have bidets. The complex has a well-managed restaurant and bar, La Terrazza, with a sprawling terrace on a platform above the sloping terrain (see "Dining," below).

Colline de Saint-Jean (B.P. 623), 97133 St. Barthélemy, F.W.I. ✆ **590/27-61-39.** Fax 590/27-77-96. www.villagestjean hotel.com. 30 units. Winter 195€ ($254) double, 250€–440€ ($325–$572) 1-bedroom cottage, 600€ ($780) 2-bedroom cottage; off season 120€ ($156) double, 150€–290€ ($195–$377) 1-bedroom cottage, 350€ ($455) 2-bedroom cottage. Extra person 40€–70€ ($52–$91). AE, MC, V. **Amenities:** Restaurant; bar; outdoor pool; Jacuzzi; car rental; room service; babysitting; laundry service; dry cleaning. *In room:* A/C, ceiling fan, kitchen, fridge, hair dryer, safe.

Tropical Hôtel   The facade of this small, unpretentious hotel looks like a picture-postcard Caribbean colonial inn. Originally built in 1981 and restored in 1997, it's perched on a hillside about 40m (130 ft.) above St-Jean Beach. Each room contains a private shower-only bathroom, a king-size bed with a good mattress, tile floors, and a fridge. Nine units have sea views and balconies; no. 11 has a porch that opens onto a garden that's so lush it looks like a miniature jungle.

The hotel has a hospitality center where guests read, listen to music, or order drinks and snacks at a paneled bar surrounded by antiques. The pool is small, but watersports are available on the beach.

St-Jean (B.P. 147), 97133 St. Barthélemy, F.W.I. ✆ **800/223-9815** in the U.S., or 590/27-64-87. Fax 590/27-81-74. www.tropical-hotel.com. 21 units. Winter 205€–230€ ($267–$299) double; off season 120€–144€ ($156–$187) double. Rates include continental breakfast. AE, MC, V. Closed June to mid-July. **Amenities:** Outdoor pool; car rental; babysitting; laundry service. *In room:* A/C, TV, ceiling fan, fridge, hair dryer.

INEXPENSIVE

La Normandie   This modest, unassuming, family-owned hotel offers no facilities other than its clean, though somewhat dreary, accommodations. But what do you expect for this kind of money on St. Barts? This is what the French call an *auberge antillaise* (Antillean inn). Set near the intersection of two major roads, about 200m (660 ft.) from L'Orient Beach, it offers motel-inspired bedrooms of casual comfort. The more expensive, larger units lie adjacent to the hotel's modest pool and contain TVs. The less expensive, smaller rooms are next to the highway. The shower-only bathrooms are really too small, but they're well kept.

97133 L'Orient, St. Barthélemy, F.W.I. ✆ 590/27-61-66. Fax 590/27-98-83. 8 units. Winter 60€ ($78) double, 70€ ($91) triple; off season 55€ ($72) double, 60€ ($78) triple. DC, MC, V. **Amenities:** Outdoor pool. *In room:* A/C, TV (in some), fridge, beverage maker.

3 Dining

IN GUSTAVIA

Au Port FRENCH/CREOLE   This restaurant is one of the culinary staples of the island, having survived for many years, thanks to a straightforward and unpretentious ambience that focuses on good cooking, generous portions, and an utter lack of snobbery. Set one floor above street level, in the center of town, it features a neocolonial decor with models of sailboats, antique accessories, and flavorful cuisine. Appetizers are a delight, featuring such treats as creamy Caribbean pumpkin soup with a vanilla flavor or a tarte with nuts and honey. A homemade duck foie gras adds an elegant touch. Fresh seafood is always a good choice; specialties include sautéed scallops in a lime sauce and shrimp dumplings with Caribbean vegetables. Meat and poultry are also treated with tender loving care, especially the breast of honey-roasted duck and the very typical island dish—goat stew with bananas au gratin.

Rue Sadi-Carnot. ⓒ **590/27-62-36.** Reservations recommended, especially for veranda tables. Main courses 18€–34€ ($23–$44); fixed-price menu 35€ ($46). AE, MC, V. Mon–Sat 6:30–10pm. Closed June 15–July 31.

La Mandala 🔍🔍 *(Finds* THAI/EUROPEAN   This is one of the most exciting restaurants on St. Barts. It occupies a house on the steepest street in Gustavia, high above the harbor, with a dining deck overlooking a swimming pool. The owners and chefs are partners Kiki and Boubou (Christophe Barjetta and Olivier Megnin), whose nicknames belie their formidable training at some of the grandest restaurants of France. Some recommended dishes are tempura of snapper or mahimahi with mango salad and coriander sauce; a traditional Thai dish, *tataki,* composed of deliberately undercooked tuna with a ginger-flavored vinaigrette, shallots, and sesame oil; grilled beef with teriyaki sauce; or duck with soy sauce and caramel. Try the warm chocolate tart for dessert.

Rue de la Sous Prefecture. ⓒ **590/27-96-96.** www.lamandala.com. Reservations recommended. Main courses 19€–32€ ($25–$42). AE, MC, V. Daily 7–11pm; sushi and cocktails 5pm–1am.

La Route des Boucaniers 🔍 *(Finds* FRENCH/CREOLE   What a discovery! Near the harbor, this bistro is the domain of Francis and Christiane Delage. Having written a five-volume primer, Francis is said to be the definitive authority on Creole cuisine. Wonderful ingredients turn up here, and they are concocted into a medley of local dishes whose flavors are not found elsewhere on this island and have attracted the likes of Cameron Diaz and Steven Segal. The decor evokes a rum shack—there's even a boat wreck—but these artifacts belie the sophistication of the cuisine. Our avocado salad was reason to return the following night. It was given added zest by chewy flakes of dried cod in a hot Creole sauce. For the main course, the chef's pride and joy is a large bowl of fresh fish, shellfish, and octopus huddled together in red-bean purée, everything blended into a smooth texture that is properly seasoned and delicious. Other surprises await, especially the Cajun mahimahi with conch gratin. What makes everything taste so good? Maybe you don't want to know. It's *beurre rouge* (lobster butter) and *lardons* (strips of salt pork) that have been heavily spiced. Not what your doctor ordered, but irresistible.

Rue de Bord de Mer, Gustavia. ⓒ **590/27-73-00.** Reservations required in winter. Main courses $22–$55. AE, MC, V. Daily 10am–10pm.

Le Gaïac 🔍 FRENCH   This restaurant is for folks who want to dine among the rich and jaded at Le Toiny—St. Barts's most expensive hotel—but aren't willing to mortgage their futures for a room. Your meal is served in an open-air pavilion adjacent to the resort's pool, with a view that sweeps out over the wide blue sea. The emphasis is French, casually stylish, and offhanded in a way that might remind you of a particularly rich version of bohemian Paris. At lunchtime, menu items might include ravioli with red pepper and goat cheese, marinated tuna or shrimp, and chicken fettuccini with soy sauce and vegetables. After dark, choices are even more exquisite. The best examples include rack and saddle of lamb, Chilean sea bass, and crayfish served under waffle pasta. The cuisine, the setting, and the first-rate ingredients make for a memorable meal.

> ## ⌐Finds⌐ Picnic Fare on St. Barts
>
> St. Barts is so expensive that many visitors opt to buy at least one of their meals (perhaps a "gourmet lunch to go" package) from a takeout deli. The most centrally located of the island's epicurean delis is **La Rôtisserie**, rue Oskar-II (ⓒ 590/27-63-13), which is proud of its endorsement by Fauchon, the world-famous food store in Paris. On display are bottles of wine, crocks of mustard, pâté, herbs, caviar, chocolate, and exotic oils and vinegars, as well as takeout (and very French) platters sold by the gram. *Plats du jour* cost around 5€ to 15€ ($6.50–$20) for a portion suitable for one. Set on a narrow street behind the eastern edge of Gustavia's harbor, the place is open Monday through Saturday from 7am to 7pm, Sunday from 7am to 1pm. American Express, MasterCard, and Visa are accepted.

In Le Toiny Hotel, Anse de Toiny. ⓒ 590/27-88-88. Reservations recommended in winter. Main courses lunch 20€–30€ ($26–$39), dinner 30€–45€ ($39–$59). AE, DC, MC, V. Daily noon–2:30pm and 7–10pm; Sun 11am–2:30pm. Closed Sept 1–Oct 23.

Le Rivage ⭐ FRENCH/CARIBBEAN

This restaurant offers the kind of offhanded charm and oversize Gallic egos that you'd expect in a chic but somewhat disorganized beach resort in the south of France. It's set on a covered veranda built on piers above the waters of the lagoon. About half the tables are open to views of the stars. During the day, no one objects to bathing suits at the table; at night, fashionably casual is the preferred dress. With a rapidly changing menu, items that merit raves include carpaccio of beef and a tempting roster of "supersalads," the most popular of which combines shrimp with smoked salmon and melted goat cheese. There's also a seafood platter of raw shellfish (scallops, clams, and crayfish), artfully arranged on a bed of seaweed; grilled crayfish, *daurade* (bream), snapper, and tuna; and a full complement of such Creole specialties as *boudin noir* (blood sausage) and *accras de morue* (beignets of codfish).

In the St. Barth Beach Hotel, Grand Cul-de-Sac. ⓒ 590/27-82-42. Reservations recommended in winter. Main courses 18€–28€ ($23–$36). AE, DISC, MC, V. Daily noon–10pm.

Le Sapotillier ⭐⭐ FRENCH/SEAFOOD

Le Sapotillier is near the top of the list for every visiting gourmet. This West Indian house beside the less frequented part of the harbor is the domain of Austrian-born Adam Rajner, who runs one of the best-known restaurants in Gustavia. Dine outside on the candlelit patio or inside the clapboard-covered Antillean bungalow that was transported from the outlying village of Corossol.

Chef Rajner pays strict attention to the quality and presentation of his food. Your meal might begin with snails in lasagna with a Provençal sauce, or a slice of fried duck liver served with caramelized pineapples and a zesty sprinkling of Szechuan pepper. From here, you can proceed to such perfectly prepared main courses as sole meunière with spinach. Two French specialties you'd be hard pressed to find anywhere else on St. Barts are based on chicken and pigeon flown in fresh from Bresse, a city known throughout Europe for its poultry. The chicken is served *en cocotte* (in a stew) and the pigeon with snow peas and spaetzle (egg noodles).

Rue Sadi-Carnot. (C) **590/27-60-28.** Reservations required. Main courses 30€–38€ ($39–$49). MC, V. Nov–Apr daily 6:30–10:30pm. Closed May–Oct.

IN THE ST-JEAN BEACH AREA

La Plage 😺😺 FRENCH/SEAFOOD   At a chic little boutique hotel, this beach-front restaurant has made waves in St. Barts—in fact, it's the hottest dining address in town. Tables spill out on the sands, just the way the host, Thierry de Bradereau, dreamed they would when he envisioned it. La Plage is the best restaurant on the island for a late-night party after dinner, and the music plays deep into the night. The theme for such a party is likely to be Bay Watch, La Cage Aux Folles, and even Santa arriving on jet skis (but only at Christmas). Singers and live bands are presented in the evening. The owner even offers Cine-Plage, or cinema on the beach, showing such old movies as Bogie's *Casablanca*. The decorator wasn't afraid of color, using mauve, pink, violet, and turquoise, a rampant fantasy of the Caribbean. Grilled fish and seafood are the highlights of the menu, which centers around barbecue on Sunday nights. Start perhaps with a spicy avocado salad. The menu changes every season, and even the desserts are homemade. Regardless of what will be on the menu at the time of your visit, expect fresh food exploding with flair and perfect seasonings. A warm welcome and attentive service are extras.

In Le Tom Beach Hotel. Plage St-Jean. (C) **590/27-53-13.** Reservations recommended. Main courses 12€–46€ ($16–$60). AE, MC, V. Daily 11:30am–3pm and 5:30–10pm.

La Terrazza (Value) ITALIAN/INTERNATIONAL   Proudly positioned as the centerpiece of a charming and not particularly expensive hotel (see "Accommodations," earlier in this chapter), La Terrazza has a deserved reputation for well-conceived food, such as a bowl of fish soup, based on the catch of the day, with pesto and homemade croutons. Other examples include spaghetti with squid ink and eggplant, ravioli stuffed with spiny crayfish meat, *saltimbocca* (veal and ham) alla Romana, an unusual version of spaghetti *en papillote* (cooked in parchment paper) with fresh vegetable sauce, and one of our personal favorites, chicken breast with rosemary potatoes. Dessert usually includes a homemade tiramisu.

In Le Village St-Jean hotel, St-Jean Hill. (C) **590/27-70-67.** Reservations required in winter. Main courses 18€–40€ ($23–$52). AE, MC, V. Thurs–Tues 7–10:30pm.

AT MORNE LURIN

Francois Plantation Restaurant 😺😺 FRENCH   This longtime favorite enjoys one of the best romantic settings on the island. On a beautiful white veranda, opening onto views, this restaurant is for serious foodies. Filled with casual redwood furniture and opening onto a garden, it is a citadel of fine wines and grand cuisine. Chefs treat their products with sensitivity and care, fashioning them into such appetizers as a flower-poached egg with chorizo and date marmalade or steamed tiger shrimp with passion-fruit-flavored ratatouille. For a main course, expect such delights as mahimahi with white coco beans and a foie gras puree or pan-roasted red snapper accompanied by a black sesame coulis with tangerine milk.

In the François Plantation, Colombier. (C) **590/29-80-22.** Reservations required. Main courses 39€–60€ ($51–$78). AE, MC, V. Tues–Sun 7–10:30pm. Closed June–Oct.

Santa Fe FRENCH   This informal restaurant opens for dinner at 5pm so visitors can come here to see the legendary sunsets from the best perspective on island. But be prepared: The kitchen doesn't get going until 7pm. For decades this place was known as a good burger joint. However, it is now much more upmarket, specializing in French dishes along with barbecued meats and fish, which are executed extremely well. Santa Fe is set inland atop one of the highest points on the island. It contains wraparound decks with bar tops constructed of teakwood that give the place a kind of nautical flair. In addition to the catch of the day, you can order other signature dishes such as lobster medallions in Creole sauce.

Morne Lurin. © 590/27-61-04. Burgers $20–$26; platters $15–$26. MC, V. Winter daily noon–3pm and 6–10:30pm; May–Nov Wed–Mon 11am–3pm and Wed–Sat 5–10pm.

IN THE GRANDE SALINE BEACH AREA

Le Tamarin ⍟ FRENCH/CREOLE   One of the island's genuinely offbeat restaurants is Le Tamarin, a deliberately informal bistro that caters to a clientele from the nearby Plage de Saline. It's isolated amid rocky hills and forests east of Gustavia, in a low-slung cottage whose eaves are accented with gingerbread. Inside, a teak-and-bamboo motif prevails. Lunch is the more popular and animated meal here, with most customers dining in T-shirts and bathing suits. If you have to wait, you can order an aperitif in one of the hammocks stretched under a tamarind tree. The menu focuses on light, summery meals that go well with the streaming sunlight and tropical heat. Examples include gazpacho, grilled tuna with Creole sauce, a carpaccio of fish that includes very fresh portions of marinated salmon and tuna, and chicken roasted with soy sauce, lemon, and ginger. There's a broadly based wine list, plus a chocolate cake dessert specialty that appeals to chocoholics. Service can be erratic, but if you're in a rush, you shouldn't be here. It's the perfect place for a lazy afternoon on the beach.

Plage de Saline. © 590/27-72-12. Reservations required for dinner. Main courses $28–$45. AE, MC, V. Nov 16–Apr 30 daily noon–5pm; Tues–Sun 7–9pm. Closed May 1–Nov 15.

IN THE GRAND CUL-DE-SAC BEACH AREA

Bartoloméo ⍟ FRENCH/MEDITERRANEAN   Although this deluxe dining choice is located at one of the island's most exclusive and expensive hotels, Bartoloméo works hard to be nonthreatening, informally sophisticated, and gracefully upscale. A pianist plays soothing music while diners choose from a frequently changing menu. Appetizers are a delight, especially the pan-fried escalope of foie gras. Main courses are prepared with skill and flair as evidenced by the Chilean sea bass with ratatouille or the roast duck of Landes with turnips, spinach, and fondue. The chefs are imaginative in their choice of ingredients, as exemplified by their sautéed cod with goat cheese and black truffles or their saddle of lamb with zesty black peppercorns and oranges. Wednesday features a sweeping array of cold antipasti, and the chef will prepare any pasta you want from an artfully arranged display of seafood, meats, herbs, wines, and cream.

In the Hôtel Guanahani, Grand Cul-de-Sac. © 590/27-66-60. Reservations recommended. Main courses 32€–55€ ($41–$72). AE, DC, MC, V. Daily 7:30–10pm. Closed Sept.

IN VITET

Cap au Sud ⍟ *Finds* FRENCH/PROVENÇAL   Isolated from the bulk of St. Barts's tourism, this restaurant lies midway up Morne Vitet, the island's highest mountain. The place has a French provincial decor, terraces accented with gingerbread, and food that the locals return for time and time again. Although the same menu is available throughout the day and evening, dinners are more formal than lunches, and might include escargot in garlic butter, crayfish grilled over charcoal and served with a garlic-flavored butter, filet of beef in pepper sauce, or magret of duckling with red berries and ginger. "Each dish takes time," says the owner, who believes in freshly preparing everything. Count on a leisurely meal and a well-informed host who has spent years studying astrology.

Vitet. ℂ 590/27-61-25. Reservations recommended. Main courses 27€–52€ ($35–$67). AE, MC, V. Mon–Sat 11:30am–3pm and 6–10:30pm.

IN THE PUBLIC BEACH AREA

Maya's 🌟 *Finds* CREOLE/THAI/FRENCH   This is the most surprising restaurant on St. Barts, thanks to its artful simplicity and glamorous clients. The much-rebuilt Antillean house with almost no architectural charm attracts crowds of luminaries from the worlds of media, fashion, and entertainment. It's the kind of place you might find on Martinique, where its French Creole chef, Maya Beuzelin-Gurley, grew up. Maya stresses "clean, simple" food with few adornments other than a sprinkling of island herbs and lime juice. You might begin with the salad of tomatoes, arugula, and endive, and then follow with grilled fish in sauce *chien* (hot), or a grilled filet of beef. Maya also prepares what she calls "sailor's chicken," a marinated version made with fresh chives, lime juice, and hot peppers. Almost no cream is used in any dish, a fact that makes the place beloved by the fashion models and actors who hang out here. You'll find the place directly west of Gustavia, close to the island's densest collection of factories and warehouses. Views face west and south, ensuring glorious sunset watching.

Public Beach. ℂ 590/27-75-73. Reservations required in winter. Main courses 30€–36€ ($39–$47). AE, MC, V. Mon–Sat 6:30–10pm. Closed Sept–Oct.

AT POINTE MILOU

Le Ti St. Barth FRENCH/CARIBBEAN   You'll either love or hate this place, depending on how you fit into an environment that manages to be frenetic, stylishly permissive, and Franco-chauvinistic all at the same time. From a point near the summit of a low-rise hill, Thierry de Bradereau—who assists his partner, Carole Gruson—defines stylized service rituals and cuisine among a jazzy and theatrical decor. Menu items range from the affordable and practical (platters of locally smoked fish, barbecued ribs, grilled beefsteaks and filet mignons, wahoo or red snapper in Creole sauce, grilled filet of duck with cranberry sauce) to the overpriced. An example includes local lobster garnished with truffles—definitely not a bargain. Events that can, however, be a lot of fun here involve erratically scheduled late-night parties, some of them held in honor of the full moon or high tides.

Pointe Milou. ℂ 590/27-97-71. Reservations required. Main courses 25€–36€ ($33–$47). AE, MC, V. Daily 7:30pm to around midnight or later, depending on business.

4 Beaches

St. Barts has 14 white-sand beaches. Few are ever crowded, even in winter; all are public and free. Topless sunbathing is quite common. The best known is **St-Jean Beach** 🌟🌟, which is actually two beaches divided by the Eden Rock promontory. It offers watersports, restaurants, and a few hotels, as well as some shady areas. **Flamands Beach,** to the west, is a very wide, long beach with a few small hotels and some areas shaded by lantana palms. In winter, the surf here can be a bit rough, although it is rarely hazardous. **L'Orient Beach,** on the north shore, is quiet and calm, with shady areas. It's popular with surfers and swimmers who like rolling waves. **Marigot Beach,** also on the north shore, is narrow but offers good swimming and snorkeling.

For a beach with hotels, restaurants, and watersports, **Grand Cul-de-Sac Beach,** on the northeast shore, fits the bill. It's narrow and protected by a reef.

North of the commercial port at Gustavia, the rather unromantic-sounding **Public Beach** is a combination of sand and pebbles. This beach is more popular with boaters than swimmers—it's also the location of the St. Barts Sailing School. There is no more beautiful place on the island, however, to watch the boats at sunset. Located near a small fishing village, **Corossol Beach** offers a typical glimpse of French life, St. Barts style. This is a calm, protected beach, with a charming little **seashell museum.**

South of Gustavia, **Shell Beach** or **Grand Galet** is awash with seashells. Rocky outcroppings protect this beach from strong waves. It's also the scene of many a weekend party.

Gouverneurs Beach, on the southern coast, can be reached by driving south from Gustavia to Lurin. Turn at the Santa Fe restaurant (see "Dining," earlier) and head down a narrow road. The beach is gorgeous and uncrowded, but there's no shade. **Grande Saline Beach,** to the east of Gouverneurs Beach, is reached by driving up the road from the commercial center in St-Jean; a short walk over the sand dune and you're here. Like Gouverneurs Beach, Grande Saline Beach offers some waves but no shade. This beach is full of beautiful sunbathers, all nude.

Colombier Beach is difficult to get to but well worth the effort. It can only be reached by boat or by taking a rugged goat path from Petite Anse past Flamands Beach, a 30-minute walk. Shade and snorkeling are found here, and you can pack a lunch and spend the day. Locals call it Rockefeller's Beach because for many years David Rockefeller owned the property surrounding it.

5 Sports & Other Outdoor Pursuits

FISHING Anglers are fond of the waters around St. Barts. From March to July, they catch mahimahi; in September, wahoo. Atlantic bonito, barracuda, and marlin also turn up frequently. **Marine Service,** quai du Yacht-Club, Gustavia (© **590/27-70-34**), rents a 9m (30-ft.) Phoenix specifically outfitted for big-game fishing. A full day for four costs 1,200€ ($1,560), which includes a captain and first mate. The outfitter also offers shore fishing on a 29-ft. day cruiser, which tends to remain close to the island's shoreline, searching for tuna, barracuda, and other fish. A full-day excursion, with fishing for up to four, costs 800€ ($1,040).

SCUBA DIVING **Marine Service,** quai du Yacht-Club, in Gustavia (© **590/27-70-34**), is the most complete watersports facility on the island. It operates from a one-story building set directly on the water at the edge of a marina, on the opposite side of the harbor from the more congested part of Gustavia. Tailoring its dives for both beginners and advanced divers, the outfit is familiar with at least 20 unusual sites scattered at various points offshore. The most interesting of these include the **Grouper,** a remote reef west of St. Barts, close to the rich reef life surrounding the uninhabited cay known as Ile Forchue. The island has only one relatively safe wreck dive, the rusting hulk of *Kayali,* a trawler that sank offshore in 1994. Set in deep waters, it's recommended only for experienced divers. A resort course, including four open-water dives, costs 300€ ($390). A "scuba review," for certified divers who are out of practice, also goes for 75€ ($98), while a one-tank dive for certified divers begins at 60€ ($78). Multidive packages are available.

SNORKELING   You can test your luck at hundreds of points offshore, simply by donning a mask, fins, and a snorkel. **Marine Services,** quai du Yacht-Club, Gustavia (© **590/27-70-34**), runs daily snorkeling expeditions. An 7-hour excursion (9am to 4pm), including a full French-style picnic, open bar, all equipment, and exploration of two separate snorkeling sites, costs 110€ ($143). They can also rent snorkeling gear and tell you where to go on your own.

6 Shopping

You don't pay any duty on St. Barts, so it's a good place to buy liquor and French perfumes, at some of the lowest prices in the Caribbean—often cheaper than in France itself. You'll find good buys in sportswear, crystal, porcelain, watches, and other luxuries. The only trouble is that selections are limited. If you're in the market for **island crafts,** try to find the fine straw hats St. Bartians like to wear. You may also see some interesting block-printed resort clothing in cotton.

Diamond Genesis, 12 rue du General-de-Gaulle/Les Suites du Roi-Oskar-II (© **590/ 27-66-94**), a well-respected gold, gemstone, and diamond shop, maintains an inventory of designs strongly influenced by European tastes. Although the prices can go as high as 10,000€ ($13,000), a particularly appealing and more affordable bestseller is an 18-karat-gold depiction of St. Barts, which sells for around 195€ ($254). It's one of the few shops on the island where jewelry is handcrafted on the premises. You can also peruse the selection of watches by Jaeger Lecoultre, available only through this store, as well as Breitling, Chanel, and Tag Heuer.

For handicrafts, **Made in St-Barth,** Villa Creole (© **590/27-56-57**), is the best place to shop. The women of the hamlet of Corossol sell their intricate straw work, including those ever-so-fashionable wide-brim beach hats at this outlet. Other crafts include local paintings, pottery, and decorative ornaments.

Gold Fingers (✪, rue de la France (© **590/27-64-66**), is the largest purveyor of luxury goods on St. Barts. The entire second floor is devoted to perfumes and crystal, the street level to jewelry and watches. Prices are usually 15% to 20% less than equivalent retail goods sold stateside. Ask about sales when you visit.

The elegant, upscale **Le Comptoir du Cigare,** 6 rue du Général-de-Gaulle (© **590/ 27-50-62;** www.comptoirducigare.com), caters to the December-to-April crowd of villa and yacht owners. It's sheathed in exotic hardwood, and enhanced with a glass-sided, walk-in humidor for the storage of thousands of cigars from Cuba and the Dominican Republic. Smoke the Cubans on the island—it's illegal to bring them back to the United States. There's also a worthy collection of silver ornaments, lighters, pens suitable for adorning the desk of a CEO, artisan-quality Panama hats from Ecuador, and the most beautiful collection of cigar boxes and humidors in the Caribbean.

Laurent Eiffel, rue du Général-de-Gaulle (© **590/27-54-02**), is faux fashion. Despite the elegance of this store and the tact of its employees, nothing sold here is original—everything is either "inspired by" or crafted "in imitation of" designer models that usually cost 10 times as much. Look for belts, shoes, bags, and accessories that are copies of Versace, Prada, Hermès, Gucci, and Chanel, sold at prices much lower than what you'd pay in Paris.

St. Barts Style, rue Lafayette, near rue du Port (© **590/27-76-17**), offers racks of beachwear and shoes by such makers as Banana Moon and Claire Mercier in citrus colors like lemon, lime, grapefruit, and orange, and psychedelic-looking T-shirts from about a dozen different manufacturers.

Sud, Sud, Galerie du Commerce (adjacent to the airport), St-Jean (© **590/ 27-98-75**), is known for its stylish clothing, both day and evening wear. The inventory is solely for women. If you're a high-fashion model, or an heiress who's trying to look like one, chances are this boutique will have something that appeals to you.

7 St. Barts After Dark

Most visitors consider a French Creole dinner under the stars enough of a nocturnal adventure. Beyond that, there isn't a lot of excitement here.

In Gustavia, the most popular gathering place is **Le Select** ⊀, rue de la France (© **590/27-86-87**), apparently named after its more famous granddaddy in the Montparnasse section of Paris. It's utterly simple: Tables are set on the gravel in the open-air garden, near the port, and a game of dominoes might be under way as you walk in. You never know who might show up here—perhaps Mick Jagger. Beer costs from $3 to $5; and a cheeseburger goes for $5 to $10. The place is open Monday to Thursday 10am to 10pm, and Friday to Saturday 10am to 11pm. There's live entertainment weekly, but no one knows in advance which particular night of the week it will appear. The locals like it here a lot; they allow outsiders, but don't necessarily embrace you until they get to know you a bit. If you want to start a rumor and have it travel fast across the island, do so here.

La Cantina, rue du Bord-de-Mer (© **590/27-55-66**), is one of the more self-consciously hip watering holes in Gustavia, where you're likely to hear rapid, idiomatic French like it's spoken, argot and all, in cutting-edge Paris, and where the art objects and sculptures scattered throughout the premises are likely to include conversation-inducing depictinos of phalluses and vaginas. Set beside Gustavia's harborfront, the mood is post-millennium Côte d'Azur, with a casual mix of pretentiousness and permissiveness that's artful and very very French. The menu includes party-colored drinks, meal-sized salads, sandwiches, including a hefty version of a club sandwich; and platters, each priced from 10€ to 18€ ($13–$23) each. La Cantina is open Monday to Saturday 7:15am to 11:30pm, and Sunday 4:30 to 10:30pm.

Bar de l'Oubli, 5 rue de la Republique (© **590/27-70-06**), occupies the most prominent corner in Gustavia, at the intersection of streets that are so well known that most local residents don't even know their names—they refer to it simply as "Centre-Ville." The setting is hip and Gallic, the color scheme is marine blue and white, and the background music might be the Rolling Stones. Sandwiches and salads are served. It's open daily from 7am (when breakfast is served to clients recovering from various stages of their hangovers) to midnight or later, depending on business.

20

St. Eustatius

Called "Statia," this Dutch-held island, a mere 21 sq. km (8¼-sq.-mile) pinpoint in the Netherlands Antilles, still basks in its 18th-century heritage as the "Golden Rock." One of the true backwaters of the West Indies, it's slowly awakening to tourism.

You might want to visit first on a day trip from St. Maarten to see if you'd like it for an extended stay. The volcanic, black-sand beaches aren't especially alluring, and as Caribbean islands go, it's rather dull here, with no nightlife. Some pleasant strips of beach exist on the Atlantic side, but the surf is dangerous for swimming.

However, if you're a hiker or a diver, the outlook on Statia improves considerably for you. You can hike around the base of the Quill, an extinct volcano on the southern end of the island. Wandering through a tropical forest, you'll encounter wild orchids, philodendron, heliconia, anthurium, fruit trees, ferns, wildlife, and birds, along with the inevitable oleander, hibiscus, and bougainvillea.

The island's reefs are covered with corals and enveloped by marine life. At one dive site, known as "Crack in the Wall" or sometimes "the Grand Canyon," pinnacle coral shoots up from the floor of the ocean. Darting among the reefs are barracudas, eagle rays, black-tip sharks, and other large fish.

Statia is about 240km (150 miles) east of Puerto Rico, 60km (40 miles) south of

St. Maarten, and 30km (20 miles) southeast of Saba. A sloping agricultural plain known as De Cultuurvlakte—where yams and sweet potatoes grow—links Statia's two extinct volcanoes, the Quill and Little Mountain.

Overlooking the Caribbean on the western edge of the plain, **Oranjestad (Orange City)** is the capital and the only village, consisting of both an Upper and Lower town, connected by stone-paved, dogleg Fort Road.

Columbus sighted Statia in 1493, on his second voyage, and Jan Snouck claimed the island for the Netherlands in 1640. The island's history was turbulent before it settled down to peaceful slumber under Dutch protection; from 1650 to 1816, Statia changed flags 22 times! Once the trading hub of the Caribbean, Statia was a thriving market, both for goods and for slaves.

Before the American Revolution, the population of Statia did not exceed 1,200, most of whom were slaves engaged in raising sugar cane. When war came and Britain blockaded the North American coast, Europe's trade was diverted to the Caribbean. Dutch neutrality lured many traders, leading to the construction of 2km (1¾ miles) of warehouses in Lower Town. The American revolutionaries obtained gunpowder and ammunition through Statia—perhaps one of the first places anywhere to recognize the United States of America as a new nation.

1 Essentials

VISITOR INFORMATION

On the island, the **Tourist Bureau** is located at Fort Oranje (℃ **599/318-2433**), open Monday to Friday 8am to noon and 1 to 5pm (Fri till 4:30pm). Statia's official website is **www.statiatourism.com**.

GETTING THERE

St. Eustatius can be reached from Dutch St. Maarten's Queen Juliana Airport via the 20-seat planes of **Windward Islands Airways International (Winair;** ℃ **888/975-7888** in the U.S. and Canada, or 599/318-2333). The little airline, launched in 1961, has an excellent safety record. Always reconfirm your return passage once you're on Statia. The seven flights a day take only 16 minutes to hop the waters to Statia's Franklin Delano Roosevelt Airport (℃ **599/318-2887**). There are usually three flights a day between Statia and Saba, and two per week between Statia and St. Kitts, but schedules are irregular. To be sure of getting to another island from Statia, you'll want to go to St. Maarten first.

GETTING AROUND

BY TAXI   Taxis meet all incoming flights. Taxi rates are low, probably no more than $10 (£5.20) from the airport to your hotel. On the way to the hotel your driver may offer himself as a guide. If you book a 2- to 3-hour tour (long enough to cover all the sights on Statia), the cost is about $80 (£42) per vehicle. To summon a taxi, call **Rainbow Taxis** (℃ **599/318-2811**) or **Josser Daniel** (℃ **599/318-2358**).

BY RENTAL CAR   **Rainbow Car Rental** (℃ **599/318-2811**) or **Walter's** (℃ **599/318-2719**) are your best bets if you want to reserve a car in advance. Drivers must be 21 years old and present a valid license and credit or charge card. Walter's rents only cars.

FAST FACTS: St. Eustatius

Banks **Barclays Bank,** Upper Town (℃ 599/318-2392), is open Monday to Friday 8:30am to 3:30pm. The **Post Office Bank** (℃ 599/318-2207), Post Spaarbank, is open Monday to Friday 7:30am to 4pm. The **Windward Island Bank,** Upper Town (℃ 599/318-2846), is open Monday to Friday 8:30am to noon and 1:30 to 3:30pm. The banks have **ATMs.**

Currency The official unit of currency is the **Netherlands Antilles guilder (NAf)**, at NAf 1.77 to each US$1 (1 NAf = US56¢), but nearly all places will quote you prices in U.S. dollars. *Unless otherwise specified, prices in this chapter are quoted in U.S. dollars and British pounds.*

Customs There are no Customs duties since the island is a free port.

Documents U.S. and Canadian citizens need proof of citizenship, such as a passport or a birth certificate with a raised seal and a government-authorized photo ID, along with an ongoing ticket. British subjects need valid passports. All visitors need an ongoing or return ticket. Frommer's urges all travelers to be in possession of a valid passport when traveling in the Caribbean, even though it may not be required.

Electricity It's 110-volt AC (60 cycles), the same as in the United States.

Emergencies For the police call ℂ **911,** for an ambulance call ℂ **913,** in case of fire call ℂ **912.**

Hospital A licensed physician is on duty at the **Queen Beatrix Medical Center,** 25 Princessweg, in Oranjestad (ℂ **599/318-2211** or 599/318-2371).

Language Dutch is the official language, but English is commonly spoken.

Safety Although crime is rare, it's wise to secure your valuables and take the kind of discreet precautions you would anywhere. Don't leave valuables unguarded on the beach.

Taxes & Service Charges There's a $5.65 (£2.95) tax if you're returning to the Dutch-held islands of St. Maarten or Saba; if you're going elsewhere, the tax is $12 (£6.25). Hotels on Statia collect a 7% government tax, plus a 3% turnover tax. Most hotels, guesthouses, and restaurants add a 10% to 15% service charge.

Telephone To access **AT&T Direct** for calls to the United States from Statia, call ℂ **001-800/872-2881.**

To call Statia from the U.S., dial **011** (the international access code), then **599** (the country code for the Netherlands Antilles), and finally **318** (the area code for Statia) and the four-digit local number. To make a call within Statia, only the four-digit local number is necessary.

Time St. Eustatius operates on Atlantic Standard Time year-round. Between November and March, when it's 6pm in Oranjestad it's 5pm in New York. During daylight saving time (April to October) the island keeps the same time as the U.S. East Coast.

Water The water here is safe to drink.

Weather The average daytime temperature ranges from 78°F to 82°F (26°C–28°C). The annual rainfall is 1.1m (45 in.).

2 Accommodations

Don't expect deluxe hotels or high rises—Statia is strictly for escapists. Guests are sometimes placed in private homes. A 10% to 15% service charge and 7% government tax are added to hotel bills.

Golden Era Hotel   Set directly on the water, this 1960s hotel is clean, serviceable, and comfortable. Twelve units offer full or partial sea views (the most stunning panorama is from no. 205). All accommodations are spacious, with king-size or queen-size beds, although the look is that of a rather dated motel room. Regrettably, the shower-only bathrooms are so tiny that it's hard to maneuver. You can, if you wish, sit on the toilet and wash your face at the same time. Lunch and dinner are served daily in the simply decorated bar and dining room.

Bay Rd., Lower Town, Oranjestad, St. Eustatius, N.A. ℂ 800/223-9815 or 599/318-2455. Fax 599/318-2445. golden erahotel@gmail.com. 18 units. Winter $88–$95 (£46–£49) single or double; off season $88 (£46) single or double. AE, DISC, MC, V. **Amenities:** Restaurant; bar; outdoor pool; laundry service. *In room:* A/C, ceiling fan, TV, fridge.

King's Well Resort ⍟   This small resort is the best address on Statia, surpassing The Old Gin House (see below). Set on the Caribbean side of the island, less than

Golden Era Hotel **3**
King's Well Resort **1**
The Old Gin House **2**

0   1 mi
0   1 km

Airport
Beach
Mountain

Venus Bay

Jenkins Bay

Zeelandia Beach

Little Mountain
Zeelandia

Concordia Bay

ATLANTIC OCEAN

Franklin D. Roosevelt Airport

Compagnie Bay

Signal Hill

Golden Rock

Lynch Bay Beach

Lynch Plantation Museum

Orange Beach **1**

Upper Town

Corre Corre Bay

Oranjestad

2 Fort Oranje

Lower Town **3**

Crooks Castle Beach

The Quill

Key Bay

PUERTO RICO

BRITISH VIRGIN ISLANDS

ANGUILLA

LESSER ANTILLES
LEEWARD ISLANDS

ATLANTIC OCEAN

Buccaneers Bay

U.S. VIRGIN ISLANDS

St. Eustatius

ST. KITTS AND NEVIS

ANTIGUA AND BARBUDA

Caribbean Sea

Caribbean Sea

MONTSERRAT

GUADELOUPE

0   100 mi

1km (½ mile) north of Oranjestad, this secluded choice occupies about .3 hectare (¾ acre) on an oceanfront cliff, 20m (60 ft.) above the surf. If you're looking for a laid-back, escapist vacation, this is your place. (Your nearest neighbors are in the local cemetery.) Most views look to the southwest, ensuring colorful sunsets that tend to be enhanced by drinks served from the bar at the King's Well Restaurant (see "Dining," below). Just below the hotel is a breeding bay for fish and octopus. The owner has several friendly pet dogs on the property.

There are no room keys, so don't expect much security. The accommodations are small and rather sparsely furnished, and each is unique. Room no. 4 contains a waterbed. The rooms in the rear are larger and face the sea, and those in front open onto a shared sea-view balcony. Bathrooms are small, with showers only. This resort might not be suitable for very young children, as there is no guard around the pool. The inn has a catamaran and will ferry guests on day trips to St. Kitts or Saba.

Oranje Bay Rd-1, Oranjestad, St. Eustatius, N.A. ⓒ/fax **599/318-2538.** www.kingswellstatia.com. 14 units. Year-round $110–$140 (£57–£73) double. Rates include breakfast. DISC, MC, V. **Amenities:** Restaurant; outdoor pool; Jacuzzi; boating; fishing; laundry service. *In room:* A/C (in some), ceiling fan, TV, fridge.

The Old Gin House ⋆

For years the premier resort of Statia, The Old Gin House is a historic landmark. The inn is a faithful reconstruction of an 18th-century building that once housed a cotton gin. The bricks that went into the construction were once used by sailing ships as ballast. Surrounded by tropical gardens, including palms and bougainvillea, the hotel enjoys a central but tranquil location. All the good-size bedrooms are comfortably furnished, with queen-size beds, direct-dial phones, and restored shower-only bathrooms.

Oranjebaai 1, St. Eustatius, N.A. (C) 800/634-4907 or 599/318-2319. Fax 599/318-2135. www.oldginhouse.com. 18 units. Year-round $135–$165 (£70–£86) double; $275 (£143) suite. Rates include breakfast. AE, DISC, MC, V. **Amenities:** 2 restaurants; 2 bars; outdoor pool; dive shop; babysitting; laundry service. In room: A/C, TV, fridge (in some).

3 Dining

Blue Bead Restaurant & Bar ⋆ Finds FRENCH/WEST INDIAN   Across from the waterfront, in relatively simple surroundings, this little eatery serves some of the best homemade food on the island. Set at 18th-century ruins at Gallows Bay, it's decorated in bright Caribbean colors. Try to get a table on the veranda with its potted palms. Dig into such local delights as mussels with French fries. Salt cod fritters, and tasty ones at that, are a specialty. If you drop in for lunch, you can choose from a selection of well-made sandwiches among other offerings, and the pizza oven is kept piping hot at night. Locals end their meal with a taste of the house special, homemade vanilla rum. On Friday nights fresh seafood is a feature. Island families frequent the place on Saturday night.

Bay Rd., Lower Town, Oranjestad. (C) 599/318-2873. Reservations recommended. Main courses $16–$28 (£8.30–£15). No credit cards. Daily 11am–9:30pm.

Chinese Bar & Restaurant ASIAN/CARIBBEAN   This place caters to locals and serves standard Chinese-restaurant fare with a bit of local flavor—the curried shrimp, for example. The atmosphere is very laid-back. For instance, even though the terrace isn't set up for dining, you can request to have your table moved there for an alfresco meal. The portions are hearty and range from the typical sweet-and-sour pork and a variety of shrimp dishes to chop suey and chow mein. This is the best place on the island for vegetarian food.

Princessweg, Oranjestad. (C) 599/318-2929 or 599/318-2389. Main courses $8–$16 (£4.15–£8.30). No credit cards. Daily 11am–midnight.

King's Well Restaurant INTERNATIONAL   The restaurant here is more successful than the simple hotel in which it's housed (see "Accommodations," above). Set less than 1km (½ mile) north of Oranjestad, and perched on a cliff about 20m (60 ft.) above the surf, it features an open kitchen and great sunset panoramas. Enjoy a fruity drink from the rustic bar before your meal. Lunches feature deli-style sandwiches and a selection of platters form the dinner menu, which is more elaborate. Dishes might include veal *cordon bleu* (thin slices of ham and Swiss cheese sandwiched between scallops of veal, then breaded and sautéed), fresh lobster, pan-fried grouper or snapper with parsley-butter sauce, plus a few German dishes like Jaeger schnitzel (veal sautéed in burgundy with mushrooms). Be sure to finish with the homemade apple strudel.

Oranje Bay Rd., Oranjestad. (C) 599/318-2538. Reservations required. Main courses $10–$20 (£5.20–£10). DISC, MC, V. Daily 6–8pm.

Ocean View Terrace ⋆ Finds CARIBBEAN/SEAFOOD   This pleasant restaurant is set within a billowing, open-sided tent, inside the courtyard of the government's guesthouse, part of historic Fort Oranje. Diners sit amidst dozens of hanging plants and historical artifacts and get a sweeping view of the sea. Menu items are firmly grounded in local culinary traditions, but usually include well-prepared versions of local seafood, especially dishes made from shrimp and lobster. Specific examples, based on the whim of the chef, might include shrimp in either a garlic- or a curry-flavored sauce; teriyaki fish; a medley of chicken dishes; and if you want to go native, several versions of goat and oxtail, including curried and stewed. Lunches, which include a range of salads and sandwiches, tend to be simpler than the more elaborate food featured at dinner.

In Fort Oranje. ℂ 599/318-2934. Reservations recommended. Main courses lunch $5–$8 (£2.60–£4.15), dinner $16–$27 (£8.30–£14). DISC, MC, V. Mon–Sat 8am–2pm and 7–9pm.

The Old Gin House Restaurant ⓖ INTERNATIONAL/FRENCH/ASIAN   Escape here for some of the more imaginative, exotic dishes on an island that tends to be devoted to a basic Antillean cuisine. It's a popular spot for divers, who can usually be found at the bar (Mooshay Pub) watching Winston prepare their favorite drinks. This beautiful old bar is in the main building, a former warehouse that once housed sugar, cotton, and indigo. The dining room and kitchen are also here. You can enjoy a candlelit dinner by the pool if the weather cooperates. Fresh lobster appears almost daily on the menu in winter, and the catch of the day, which can be grilled, typically includes red snapper, mahimahi, and kingfish. Fishermen bring their catch right to the door of the kitchen to sell.

Oranjebaai 1. ℂ 599/318-2319. Reservations required. Main courses $10–$29 (£5.20–£15). AE, DISC, MC, V. Daily 7:30–10:30am, 11:30am–1:30pm, and 6:30–9pm.

4 Beaches

Most of Statia's beaches are small, narrow strips of sand, either volcanic black or a dull mudlike gray. Regrettably, the best beaches are not on the tranquil Caribbean side, but on the turbulent Atlantic side, where the waters are often too rough for swimming.

Beachcombers delight, however, in their search for the fabled **blue-glass beads,** which were manufactured in the 1600s by a Dutch West Indies Company. They were used as money for the trading of such products as tobacco, cotton, rum—and even slaves. These beads, which are real collector's items, are often unearthed after a heavy rainfall or tropical storm.

Orange Beach, also called Smoke Alley Beach, lies on the Caribbean side of the island directly off Lower Town. This is one of the small volcanic beaches on the southwest shore, with beige or black sands and waters suitable for a leisurely swim. You virtually have the beach to yourself until late afternoon, when locals start to arrive for a dip.

Also on the leeward, or Caribbean, side is **Crooks Castle Beach,** south of Oranjestad. The waters, filled with giant yellow sea fans, sea whips, and pillar coral, attract snorkelers, while beachcombers are drawn to the many blue beads that have been unearthed here.

On the southeast Atlantic side of the island, **Corre Corre Bay** has a strip of dark golden sand. It's about half an hour down Mountain Road and is worth the trip to get here, although the waters are often too churned up for comfortable swimming. Two bends north of this beach, the light-brown-sand **Lynch Bay Beach** is more sheltered from the wild swells of the Atlantic. Nonetheless, the surf here is still almost always rough, plus there's a dangerous undertow; this beach is better for sunbathing than swimming.

Also on the Atlantic side, **Zeelandia Beach** is 3km (2 miles) long and filled with very dark beige and volcanic-black sand. One tourist promotion speaks of its "exciting Atlantic surf and invigorating trade winds," but fails to warn of the dangerous undertow.

Moments **Catching Crabs Means Something Different Here**

We're perfectly serious: If you're interested, you can join Statians in a crab hunt. The Quill's crater is the breeding ground for these large crustaceans. At night they emerge from their holes to forage, and that's when they're caught. Either with flashlights or relying on moonlight, crab hunters climb the Quill, catch crabs, and take them home to prepare the local delicacy, stuffed crab. Your hotel can usually hook you up with this activity.

Only one small, designated section is safe for swimming. The beach is suitable, however, for wading, hiking, and sunbathing. It's almost always deserted.

5 Sports & Other Outdoor Pursuits

HIKING　Hiking is the most popular outdoor activity on the island. Those with enough stamina can climb the slopes of the **Quill,** the highest point on Statia. Its extinct volcanic cone harbors a crater filled with a dense tropical rainforest, containing towering kapok trees and a dozen or more species of wild orchids, some quite rare. It's also home to at least 50 species of bird life, including the rare blue pigeon, known to frequent the breadfruit and cottonwood trees here. Islanders once grew cocoa, coffee, and cinnamon in the crater's soil, but today bananas are the only crop. The **tourist office** (© **599/318-2433**) will supply you with a list of a dozen trails of varying degrees of difficulty and can also arrange for a guide. You'll have to negotiate the fee; it's usually $10 (£5.20) and up.

WATERSPORTS　**Dive Statia** is a full PADI diving center on Fishermen's Beach in Lower Town (© **599/318-2435**), offering everything from beginning instruction to dive master certification, costing $450 (£234). Its professional staff guides divers of all experience levels to spectacular walls, untouched coral reefs, and historic shipwrecks. Dive Statia offers one- and two-tank boat dives, costing $40 to $75 (£21–£39). Equipment is $10 (£5.20) extra. Night dives and snorkel trips are also available.

Statia is mostly a divers' island, but there is some decent **snorkeling** on the Caribbean side. You can explore the remnants of an 18th-century man-of-war and the walls of warehouses, taverns, and ships that sank below the surface of Oranje Bay more than 200 years ago. The best place to go is **Crooks Castle Beach,** southwest of Lower Town. Any dive shop can rent you snorkeling gear.

Water-skiing is expensive on Statia. **Dive Statia** (see above) will outfit you for around $90 (£47) per hour.

6 Exploring the Island

Oranjestad stands on a cliff looking out on a beach and the island's calm anchorage, where in the 18th century you might have seen 200 vessels offshore. **Fort Oranje** was built in 1636 and restored in honor of the U.S. bicentennial celebration of 1976. Perched atop the cliffs, its terraced rampart is lined with the old cannons.

St. Eustatius Historical Foundation Museum, Upper Town (© **599/318-2288**), is also called the Donker House in honor of its former tenant, Simon Donker. After British Admiral Rodney sacked Statia for cooperating with the United States, he installed his own headquarters here. Today, the 18th-century house and museum stands in a garden, with a 20th-century wing crafted from 17th-century bricks. There are exhibits on the process of sugar refining and shipping and commerce, a section devoted to the pre-Columbian period, archaeological artifacts from the colonial period, and a pair of beautiful rooms furnished with 18th-century antiques. In the annex is a massive piece of needlework by American Catherine Mary Williams, showing the flowers of Statia. The museum is open Monday to Friday from 9am to 5pm, and Saturday and Sunday from 9am to noon; admission is $3 (£1.55) for adults, $1 (50p) for children.

A few steps away, a cluster of 18th-century buildings surrounding a quiet courtyard is called **Three Widows' Corner.**

Nearby are the partially restored ruins of the first **Dutch Reformed church,** on Kerk-weg ("Church Way"). To reach it, turn west from Three Widows' Corner onto Kerkweg. Tilting headstones record the names of the characters in the island's past. The St. Eustatius Historical Foundation recently completed restoration of the church. You can climb to the top level of the tower and see the bay as lookouts did many years before.

Statia once had a large colony of Jewish traders, and you can explore the ruins of **Honen Dalim,** the second-oldest Jewish synagogue in the Western Hemisphere (see p. 152 for information on the oldest). Built around 1740 and damaged by a hurricane in 1772, the synagogue stands beside Synagogpad, a narrow lane whose entrance faces Madam Theatre on the square.

The walls of a *mikvah* (ritual bath) rise beside the **Jewish burial ground** on the edge of town. Most poignant is the memorial of David Haim Hezeciah de Lion, who died in 1760 at the age of 2 years, 8 months, 26 days; carved into the baroque surface is an angel releasing a tiny songbird from its cage.

You can also visit **Lynch Plantation Museum** at Lynch Bay (© **599/318-2338**), but you'll have to call to arrange a tour. Donations are accepted; otherwise, admission is free. Locals still call this place the Berkel Family Plantation; although today it's a museum depicting life on Statia a century ago, through antiques, fishing and farming equipment, pictures, and old Bibles. Usually Ismael Berkel is on hand to show you around. This is still very much a residence, rather than some dead, dull museum.

7 Shopping

At **Mazinga Giftshop,** Fort Oranje Straat, Upper Town (© **599/318-2245**), you'll find an array of souvenirs—T-shirts, liquor, costume jewelry, 14-karat-gold jewelry, cards, drugstore items, beachwear, office supplies, children's books, handbags, and paperback romances. You may have seen more exciting stores in your life, but this is without parallel for Statia. You can buy books, office supplies, and stationery at the **Paper Corner,** Van Tonningenweg, Upper Town (© **599/318-2208**).

8 St. Eustatius After Dark

As for after-dark fun, Statia ain't Las Vegas. Nightlife pickings here are among the slimmest in the Caribbean. Weekends are the best—maybe the only—time to go out. **Smoke Alley Bar & Grill,** Lower Town, Gallows Bay (© **599/318-2002**), is an open-air beach bar with live music on Friday night; it's open Monday to Saturday 6 to 10pm. **The Stone Oven,** 16A Feaschweg, Upper Town, Oranjestad (© **599/318-24809**), often has dancing and local bands on weekends; you can also enjoy simple West Indian fare. For local flavor, try **Cool Corner** (© **599/318-2523**), across from the St. Eustatius Historical Foundation Museum, in the center of town. Another option is **Largo Heights,** Chapel Piece (© **599/318-2811**).

21

St. Kitts & Nevis

The two islands of St. Kitts and Nevis (*Nee*-vis) were British possessions until 1983, when they became a tiny, independent two-island nation (a ministate, really), complete with U.N. membership. British traditions remain in evidence, however. Cricket is still fiercely popular and motorists drive on the left.

St. Kitts and Nevis slumbered as backwaters of the Caribbean for decades. The country's economy was dependent entirely on sugar cane, making it especially vulnerable to the ravages of hurricanes. (Hurricane Hugo, in 1990, caused particularly serious damage.) But in recent years, tourists, especially celebrities, have discovered the islands' average year-round temperature of 79°F (26°C), low humidity, white-sand beaches, and unspoiled natural beauty.

This doesn't mean that St. Kitts and Nevis are playgrounds for the rich and famous—not yet. But people who can go anywhere have been spotted here in the near past: Britney Spears, Oprah Winfrey, Catherine Zeta-Jones, Michael Douglas, Sarah Jessica Parker, Sylvester Stallone, Danny Glover, Michael J. Fox, and Gerald and Betty Ford, to name a few.

Of the two islands, Nevis is the sleepier. It has fewer nonstop flights from North America, fewer luxury hotels, and almost no nightlife to speak of. It also has a reputation as being a money-laundering haven for drug traffickers and other suspicious businesses (despite adamant denials by Nevis officials). The tiny island has some 9,000 offshore businesses—about one business per inhabitant—registered and operating under strict secrecy laws.

In fact, disagreements about controls over offshore banking activities triggered a rift between the two islands that almost led to Nevis's secession. In the most recent referendum on the issue, in 1998, a majority of Nevisians (but not the two-thirds required) voted for independence from St. Kitts.

1 Essentials

VISITOR INFORMATION

Information is available from the **tourist board**'s stateside offices at 414 E. 75th St., New York, NY 10021 (© **800/582-6208** or 212/535-1234).

In **Canada,** an office is located at 133 Richmond St., Suite 311, Toronto, ON M5H 2L3 (© **416/368-6707**), and in the **United Kingdom** at 10 Kensington Court, London, W8 5DL (© **020/7376-0881**).

The website for both St. Kitts and Nevis is **www.stkittsnevis.net**.

FAST FACTS: St. Kitts & Nevis

Banks The most convenient bank, with **ATM** services, is the **St. Kitts-Nevis-Anguilla National Bank** on Central Street in Basseterre (© **869/465-2204**).

Currency The local currency is the **Eastern Caribbean dollar (EC$)**, pegged at EC$2.70 to the U.S. dollar (EC$1 = US37¢). Many prices, however, including those of hotels, are quoted in U.S. dollars. *Unless otherwise specified, prices in this chapter are quoted in U.S. dollars and British pounds.* Always determine which "dollar" locals are talking about.

Customs You are allowed in duty-free with your personal belongings. Sometimes luggage is subjected to a drug check. If you clear customs in one of the islands, you don't have to do it again if you visit the other.

Documents U.S., British, and Canadian citizens need a passport. A return or ongoing ticket is mandatory.

Electricity Electricity on St. Kitts is 230-volt AC (60 cycles), so you'll need an adapter and a transformer for U.S.-made appliances. However, most hotels on the islands have outlets that will accept North American appliances. Check with your hotel to see if it has converted its voltage and outlets.

Emergencies Dial © **911** for emergencies, © **311** for fire department.

Language English is the language of both islands, and it is spoken with a decided West Indian lilt; patois is commonly spoken as well.

Safety This is still a fairly safe place to travel. Most crimes against tourists—and there aren't a lot—are robberies on Conaree Beach on St. Kitts, so exercise the usual precautions. It's wise to safeguard your valuables, and women should not go jogging alone along deserted roads. Crime is rare on Nevis.

Taxes The government imposes a 7% tax on rooms and meals, plus another US$22 (£11) airport departure tax. (You don't pay the departure tax when you travel between St. Kitts and Nevis.)

Telephone The area code for St. Kitts and Nevis is **869**. You can make calls to or from the United States as you would for any other area code in North America. To access **AT&T Direct**, call © **800/225-5288**; to reach **MCI**, dial © **800/888-8000**.

Time St. Kitts and Nevis are on Atlantic Standard Time year-round. This means that in winter, when it's 6am in Basseterre, it's 5am in New York. When the United States goes on daylight saving time, St. Kitts and Nevis are on the same time as the East Coast of the United States.

Tipping Most hotels and restaurants add a service charge of 10% to cover tipping. If not, tip 10% to 15%.

Water The water on St. Kitts and Nevis is so good that Baron de Rothschild's chemists selected St. Kitts as their only site in the Caribbean to distill and produce CSR (Cane Sugar Rothschild), a pure sugar-cane liqueur. In the 1700s, Lord Nelson regularly brought his fleet to Nevis just to collect water, and Nevis still boasts of having Nelson spring water.

Weather St. Kitts and Nevis are tropical, and the warm climate is tempered by the trade winds. The average air temperature is 79°F (26°C); the average water temperature, 80°F (27°C). Dry, mild weather is usually experienced from November to April; May to October is hotter and rainier.

2 St. Kitts

St. Kitts has become a resort mecca in recent years. Its major crop is sugar, a tradition dating from the 17th century. But tourism may overwhelm it in the years to come, as its southeastern peninsula, site of the best white-sand beaches, has been set aside for massive resort development. Most of the island's other beaches are of gray or black volcanic sand.

The Caribs, the early settlers, called the island Liamuiga, or "fertile isle." Its mountain ranges reach up to nearly 1,200m (3,940 ft.), and its interior contains virgin rainforests, alive with hummingbirds and wild green vervet monkeys. The monkeys were brought in as pets by the early French settlers but were set free when the British took control of the island in 1783. These native African animals have proliferated and can be seen at the Estridge Estate Behavioral Research Institute. The British brought in mongooses to control rats in the sugar-cane fields, only to discover that the predators slept during the rats' most active forays. Wild deer are found in the mountains.

The capital of St. Kitts, **Basseterre,** lies on the Caribbean shore near the southern end of the island, about 2km (1¼ miles) from the airport. Its white colonial houses with toothpick balconies look like a Hollywood version of a West Indian port.

ST. KITTS
ESSENTIALS
GETTING THERE   There is only one nonstop flight a week to St. Kitts from North America: **US Airways** (© 800/428-4322 in the U.S. and Canada; www.usairways.com) flies nonstop on Saturday from both Philadelphia and Charlotte to St. Kitts. Otherwise, you have to connect through Antigua, St. Maarten, or Puerto Rico. **American Airlines** (© 800/433-7300 in the U.S. and Canada; www.aa.com) has dozens of daily flights to San Juan. From here, American's commuter partner, **American Eagle,** makes four daily nonstop flights into St. Kitts.

Windward Islands Airways International (known to everybody as **Winair;** © 888/255-6889 in the U.S. and Canada, or 869/465-8010; www.fly-winair.com) flies to St. Kitts from St. Maarten. The Antigua-based carrier, **LIAT** (© 888/844-5428; www.liatairline.com), flies to St. Kitts from Antigua, Puerto Rico, and St. Maarten. Winair has two daily flights between Nevis and St. Kitts.

Moments **Sweet Treat**

At some point during your visit you should eat sugar directly from the cane—any farmer will sell you a huge stalk. Ask your taxi driver to take you to one of the sugarcane plantations that dot the island. Strip off the hard exterior of the stalk, bite into it, chew on the tasty reeds, and swallow the juice. It's best with a glass of rum.

Air Canada (*©* **888/247-2262** in the U.S. and Canada, or 514/422-5000; www.aircanada.ca) flies from Toronto to Antigua, and **British Airways** (*©* **800/247-9297** in the U.S. and Canada; www.britishairways.com) flies from London to Antigua. From Antigua, you can make connections on LIAT or Winair (see above).

You can also use the **interisland ferry service** between St. Kitts and Nevis. Ferry schedules follow no obvious patterns and are subject to change without notice. The **MV *Sea Hustler*** makes at least three trips per day, and sometimes four. There is usually one morning crossing and one afternoon crossing from each island. Travel time is 1 hour. The **MV *Caribe Queen*** makes the crossing in 45 minutes, but it doesn't run on Thursdays or Sundays. Its schedule is also different every day—it generally makes one round-trip in the morning (usually 7 or 7:30am) and at least one trip each way in the afternoon (at 4, 5, or 6pm, depending on the island). The fare is US$8 (£4.20) round-trip for either ferry. The best vessel of all is the air-conditioned 110-passenger ferry **MV *Caribe Breeze,*** which makes the run in only 30 minutes. The regular fare is US$12 (£6.25) per passenger one-way (or US$15 (£7.80) in first class). There are only two runs per day on Thursday and Sunday but more frequent runs on other days, depending on demand. Call *©* **869/466-6734** for scheduling information on the *Sea Hustler,* and *©* **869/469-0304** for information on the *Caribe Breeze* and *Caribe Queen.*

Fun Fact **Party Times in St. Kitts**

Carnival in St. Kitts is celebrated not in the days leading up to Ash Wednesday, but from Christmas Eve to January 2. The festivities include parties, dancing, talent shows, and the crowning of the Carnival Queen. The final day of the celebration is known as "Last Lap," and features a repeat of many of the activities, including a multitude of bands jamming in the streets of Basseterre.

Another popular party time is the **St. Kitts Music Festival,** held the last weekend in June (Thurs–Sun). The Soca/Calypso night is usually the festival's opening event, and its most popular. You can also hear reggae, jazz, rhythm and blues, and gospel performances over the 4 days. For more information, call the Department of Tourism at ℰ **869/465-1999.**

GETTING AROUND   Since most **taxi** drivers are also guides, this is the best means of getting around. You don't even have to find a driver at the airport—one will find you. Drivers also wait outside the major hotels. First, however, you must agree on the price, since taxis aren't metered. Also, ask if the rates quoted to you are in U.S. or Eastern Caribbean dollars. The fare from the airport to Basseterre is about EC$20 (US$7.40/£3.85); to Sandy Point, EC$40 (US$15/£7.80) and up. For more information, call the **St. Kitts Taxi Association** (ℰ **869/465-8487**).

Avis, South Independence Square, Bay Road (ℰ **800/331-1212** in the U.S. and Canada, or 869/465-6507; www.avis.com), charges from US$40 to US$80 (£21–£42) per day, US$260 to US$480 (£135–£250) per week, plus US$15 (£7.80) per day for collision damage, with a US$950 (£494) deductible and a US$1.50 (80p) per day surcharge. The company offers free delivery service to either the airport or to any of the island's hotels; drivers must be between ages 25 and 75. Avis will arrange for a rental exchange if you also go to Nevis.

Delisle Walwyn & Co., Liverpool Row, Basseterre (ℰ **869/465-8449**), is a local company offering cars and jeeps starting at US$40 to US$60 (£21–£31) per day. Tax and insurance are extra ($10/£5.20 per day for collision damage, US$750/£390 deductible). This might be your best deal on the island.

Remember: Driving is on the left! You'll need a local driver's license, which can be obtained at the **Traffic Department,** on Cayon Street in Basseterre, for US$24 (£13). Usually a member of the staff at your car-rental agency will drive you to the Traffic Department to get one.

FAST FACTS   **Banks** on St. Kitts are open Monday to Thursday from 8am to 2pm, Friday from 8am to 4pm, and Saturday from 8:30 to 11am. You can place **international telephone calls,** including collect calls, at **Cable and Wireless,** Cayon Street, Basseterre (ℰ **869/465-1000**), Monday to Wednesday from 8am to 5pm, Thursday and Friday 8am to 4pm, and Saturday from 9am to noon.

The most centrally located pharmacy is **City Drug,** Fort Street in Basseterre (ℰ **869/465-2156**), open Monday to Wednesday and Friday to Saturday from 8am to 7pm, Thursday from 8am to 5pm, and Sunday from 8 to 11am.

There's a 24-hour **emergency room** in Basseterre at **Joseph N. France General Hospital,** Buckley's Site (ℰ **869/465-2551**).

The **St. Kitts tourist board** operates at Pelican Mall, Bay Road in Basseterre (© **869/465-4040**). It's open Monday to Tuesday 8am to 4:30pm, Wednesday to Friday 8am to 5pm.

ACCOMMODATIONS
VERY EXPENSIVE

Golden Lemon Inn & Villas ✷✷✷   Sophisticated and elegant describe both the Golden Lemon and its clientele. Arthur Leaman, one-time decorating editor of *House & Garden* magazine, used his taste and background to create a hotel of great charm in this once-busy shipping port. The 1610 French manor house with an 18th-century Georgian upper story is set back from a coconut grove and a black volcanic-sand beach, on the northwest coast of St. Kitts. Flanking the great house are the Lemon Court and Lemon Grove Condominiums, where you can rent luxuriously furnished suites surrounded by manicured gardens; most have private pools.

The spacious rooms are furnished with antiques and always contain fresh flowers, but are not air-conditioned. Bedrooms have been redecorated with new fabrics, rugs, and accessories. Many beds are raised four-posters draped in mosquito netting in the old plantation style; each is equipped with fine linen. Most of the tiled bathrooms are huge; they contain deluxe toiletries, tub/shower combinations, and dressing areas. The larger villas even have sunken tubs, kitchens, and dishwashers. The Golden Lemon restaurant serves fine Continental and Caribbean cuisine (see "Dining," below).

Dieppe Bay, St. Kitts, W.I. © **800/633-7411** in the U.S., or 869/465-7260. Fax 869/465-4019. www.goldenlemon. com. 26 units. Winter US$220–US$360 (£114–£187) double, from US$545 (£283) villa; off season US$145–US$275 (£75–£143) double, from US$400 (£208) villa. Rates include American breakfast. Extra person US$150 (£78). 4-night minimum stay required in winter. Honeymoon packages available. AE, MC, V. Closed Sept to mid-Oct. Children 18 and under not usually accepted. **Amenities:** Restaurant; outdoor pool; tennis court; catamarans; scuba diving; snorkeling; horseback riding; island tours; car rental; room service; massage; laundry; rooms for those w/limited mobility. *In room:* A/C (in 2); ceiling fan, kitchenette, fridge, hair dryer.

Ottley's Plantation Inn ✷✷✷   This is the island's finest place to stay, outdoing even the more mellow and time-seasoned Golden Lemon. Ten kilometers (6¼ miles) north of the airport, and near a rainforest, it occupies a 14-hectare (35-acre) site on a former 17th-century West Indian plantation. Those seeking charm and tranquility will like the nine rooms in an 1832 great house. Other units are divided among three cottages, with air-conditioning and overhead fans. Each has modern amenities, including private pools and panoramic views. The suites are truly deluxe, with their own Jacuzzis. Rooms are elegantly appointed and very spacious with queen- or king-size beds; the bathrooms have tub/shower combinations and deluxe toiletries. Guests enjoy body polishing or body wraps at the trendy Mango Orchard Spa set in a replica of a traditional wood-framed Antillean cottage called a chattel house.

The plantation operates one of the best restaurants on the island, The Royal Palm (see "Dining," below), which serves a Sunday champagne brunch.

Ottley's Village (P.O. Box 345), St. Kitts, W.I. © **800/772-3039** in the U.S., or 869/465-7234. Fax 869/465-4760. www. ottleys.com. 24 units. Winter US$318–US$518 (£165–£269) double, US$778 (£405) suite, US$998–US$1,498 (£519–£779) villa; off season US$208–US$394 (£108–£205) double, US$508 (£264) suite, US$724–US$1,048 (£377–£545) villa. US$72 (£37) per person daily for half-board (breakfast and dinner). Wedding, honeymoon, and other packages available. AE, DISC, MC, V. Children under 10 discouraged. **Amenities:** Restaurant; 2 bars; outdoor pool; tennis court; spa; Jacuzzi; bikes; croquet; shuttle to beach; room service; massage; babysitting; laundry service. *In room:* A/C, ceiling fan, TV (by advance request), minibar, beverage maker, hair dryer, iron, safe.

Rawlins Plantation Inn ⭐⭐   This hotel near Dieppe Bay is situated among the remains of a muscovado sugar factory on the northeast coast, with a good sandy beach just a short drive away. The rather isolated former plantation is 105m (344 ft.) above sea level and enjoys cool breezes from both ocean and mountains. Behind the 5 hectares (12 acres) of manicured grounds, the land rises to a rainforest and Mount Liamuiga.

A 17th-century windmill has been converted into charming accommodations, complete with private bathroom and sitting room; the boiling houses, formerly used to distill cauldrons of molasses, have been turned into a cool courtyard, where guests dine amid flowers and tropical birds. Other accommodations are in pleasantly decorated cottages equipped with modern facilities. There's no air-conditioning, but ceiling fans and cross-ventilation keep the place comfortable. Each unit, generous in size, is decorated in a Caribbean country-house style with antiques, stone or white walls, floral prints, local art, and rattan furnishings. Many bedrooms have mahogany four-posters; all have fine linen. Bathrooms are superb, with plenty of shelf space, toiletries, and tub/shower combinations.

Mount Pleasant (P.O. Box 340), St. Kitts, W.I. © 800/346-5358 in the U.S., 0208/874-9534 in the U.K., or 869/465-6221. Fax 869/465-4954. www.rawlinsplantation.com. 10 units. Winter US$375–US$1,150 (£195–£598) double; off season US$200–US$735 (£104–£382) double. Wedding packages available. Rates include breakfast, dinner, afternoon tea, and laundry service. MC, V. Closed Aug–Oct. No children under 12 allowed. **Amenities:** Restaurant; bar; outdoor pool; tennis court; croquet; laundry service. *In room:* Ceiling fan, hair dryer, no phone.

EXPENSIVE

St. Kitts Marriott Royal Beach Resort & Spa ⭐⭐⭐ *Kids*   The sprawling resort evokes the Mediterranean with its tile roofs and lush landscaping. In the center is a replica of Columbus's *Santa Maria,* complete with waterfalls. The location, with its adjacent Royal Beach Casino, is near the narrowest part of St. Kitts, close to Atlantic-fronting beaches. Its 9 hectares (22 acres) include an 18-hole golf course designed by Canadian-born Tom McBroom and one of the largest casinos in the Caribbean Basin. Architectural surprises include a ceiling in the casino that reflects the heavens, the stars, and meteors in electronic patterns.

The decor is self-tabbed as "Euro-Caribbean," with vague references to the Italian Renaissance within its pastel-colored compound of artfully landscaped buildings. Most of the tasteful, comfortable, and elegant accommodations are within a five-story central core. Bubbling Jacuzzis, a lagoon-shaped pool, sprawling gardens, deluxe bathrooms, and a bevy of restaurants and bars ensure you'll never have to leave the grounds.

858 Frigate Bay Rd., Frigate Bay, St. Kitts, W.I. © 800/228-9290 in the U.S., or 869/466-1200. Fax 869/466-1201. www.marriott.com. 636 units. Winter US$263–US$529 (£137–£275) double, US$718 (£373) suite; off season US$128–US$369 (£67–£192) double, US$369 (£192) suite. AE, DC, DISC, MC, V. **Amenities:** 8 restaurants; 6 bars; 3 outdoor pools; whirlpool; 18-hole golf course; 4 tennis courts; health club; full-service spa; sauna; children's programs; business center; salon; room service; babysitting; laundry service (also self-serve); casino; night club; nonsmoking rooms; rooms for those w/limited mobility. *In room:* A/C, TV, fridge, beverage maker, hair dryer, iron, safe.

MODERATE

Bird Rock Beach Hotel   Set on a secluded, half-moon-shaped beach 3km (2 miles) southeast of Basseterre, this small resort is uncomplicated and easygoing. Views from most bedroom balconies are of either the Bay of Basseterre and the capital, or of the water stretching toward Nevis. All units have private patios or balconies and rather bland furniture inspired by the Tropics. Bedrooms carry out the Caribbean motif with flowery fabrics and paintings of birds. The tub/shower combination bathrooms are small but adequate. Each superior room has one king-size or two double beds, and each studio suite offers a queen-size bed plus a sofa bed and a kitchenette. Apartments have full kitchens.

P.O. Box 227, Basseterre, St. Kitts, W.I. © 800/621-1270 in the U.S., or 869/465-8914. Fax 869/465-1675. www.bird rockbeach.com. 46 units. Winter US$105 (£55) double, US$135 (£70) studio suite for 2, US$225 (£117) 2-bedroom suite, US$300 (£156) 3-bedroom suite; off season US$90 (£47) double, US$105 (£55) studio suite for 2, US$165 (£86) 2-bedroom suite, US$215 (£112) 3-bedroom suite. AE, MC, V. **Amenities:** 2 restaurants; 2 bars; outdoor pool; dive shop; snorkeling; room service; laundry service; nonsmoking rooms. *In room:* A/C, TV, kitchenette (in some), fridge (in some), beverage maker (in some), hair dryer.

Ocean Terrace Inn ⚐ This inn is affectionately known as the "OTI" by its mainly business clients. If you want to be near Basseterre, it's the best hotel around the port, with oceanfront verandas and a view of the harbor and the capital. It's so compact that a stay here is like a house party on a great liner. Terraced into a landscaped hillside above the edge of Basseterre, the hotel also has gardens and well-kept grounds. All the handsomely decorated rooms have a light, tropical feel and overlook a well-planted terrace. Bedrooms are a wide variety of sizes, and bathrooms, with tub/shower combinations, are small and tidily maintained. The hotel also offers apartments at the Fisherman's Wharf and Village, a few steps from the nearby harbor. These units are filled with most of the comforts of home.

Wigley Ave. (P.O. Box 65), Fortlands, St. Kitts, W.I. © 869/465-2754. Fax 869/465-1057. www.oceanterraceinn.com. 71 units. Winter US$195–US$460 (£101–£239) double; off season US$170–US$410 (£88–£213) double. Dive, honeymoon, and eco-safari packages available. Extra person US$40 (£21) per night. AE, DC, MC, V. Go west along Basseterre Bay Rd. past the Cenotaph. **Amenities:** 3 restaurants; 3 bars; 3 outdoor pools; fitness center; Jacuzzi; sauna; water-skiing; windsurfing; dive shop; horseback riding; business center; room service; laundry service; nonsmoking rooms. *In room:* A/C, ceiling fan (in some), TV, kitchenette (in some), fridge, beverage maker, hair dryer, safe, Wi-Fi.

INEXPENSIVE
Morgan Heights Condo Resort Morgan Heights is more of a condo complex than a resort, and its staff is of minimal assistance. But each of the small to medium-size units is well maintained and fairly inviting. Most units have good beds and tub/shower combination bathrooms. The two-bedroom condos have wicker furniture, covered patios overlooking the Atlantic Ocean, and a kitchen. The suites are a more recent addition. All rooms are nonsmoking. Although there's a view of the water, the beach is a 10-minute drive away.

Canada Estate (P.O. Box 735), Basseterre, St. Kitts, W.I. © 869/465-8633 or 869/465-9828. Fax 869/465-9272. 15 units. Winter US$125 (£65) 1-bedroom condo, US$186 (£97) 2-bedroom condo; off season US$95 (£49) 1-bedroom condo, US$105 (£55) 2-bedroom condo. Extra person US$25 (£13) in winter, US$15 (£7.80) off season. AE, DISC, MC, V. **Amenities:** Restaurant; outdoor pool; babysitting; laundry service. *In room:* A/C, TV, kitchenette, beverage maker, iron.

Timothy Beach Resort ⚐Kids Located at the foot of a green mountain, 5km (3 miles) east of Basseterre, this condo resort is a family favorite. Though short on atmosphere, it's on one of St. Kitts' finest beaches. Naturally, the most sought-after units are those opening directly onto the beach, which offers swimming, sailing, and watersports. There's also a pool, and an 18-hole golf course is just a short drive away. The rooms are furnished in a Caribbean motif, and the larger accommodations have kitchens. Units here are timeshares, so there are no routine extras. All rooms have medium-size bathrooms with tub/shower combinations.

Frigate Bay (P.O. Box 1198), Basseterre, St. Kitts, W.I. © 800/288-7991 in the U.S. and Canada, or 869/465-8597. Fax 869/466-7085. www.timothybeach.com. 60 units. Winter US$138–US$180 (£72–£94)double, US$190 (£99) studio suite, US$210 (£109) 1-bedroom apt, US$315 (£164) 2-bedroom apt for up to 4; off season US$99–US$125 (£52–£65) double, US$135 (£70) studio suite, US$150 (£78) 1-bedroom apt, US$215 (£112) 2-bedroom apt for up to

4. AE, MC, V. **Amenities:** Restaurant; bar; outdoor pool; golf (nearby); babysitting; laundry service; nonsmoking rooms. *In room:* A/C, TV, kitchenette (in some), fridge, beverage maker, hair dryer, safe.

DINING
VERY EXPENSIVE
The Royal Palm ⟨⟨ CARIBBEAN FUSION   On the grounds of Ottley's Planta-tion Inn, the Royal Palm is a favorite, serving St. Kitts's most creative and best cuisine. It also has a colorful setting: Gaze through the ancient stone arches to the ocean on one side, and Mount Liamuiga and the inn's great house on the other. The menu changes daily. If they're available, you might start with roasted vegetable torte or chile-flavored shrimp corn cakes. The lobster quesadillas, made with local lobster, are worth crossing the island to sample. Main courses are impeccably prepared, especially the French roast of lamb and the breast of chicken Molyneux with almonds, country ham, mozzarella, and mushroom stuffing.

In Ottley's Plantation Inn, north of Basseterre, on the east coast. ⟨ **869/465-7234.** Reservations required. Lunch main courses US$13–US$27 (£6.75–£14); Sun champagne brunch US$35 (£18); prix-fixe dinner US$65 (£34). AE, MC, V. Daily 8am–10pm.

EXPENSIVE
Ballahoo Restaurant ⟨ CARIBBEAN   Overlooking the town center's Circus Clock, the Ballahoo is about a block from the sea, on the second story of a traditional stone building. Its open-air dining area is one of the coolest places in town on a hot afternoon, thanks to the sea breezes. One of the best and most reliable dishes is blue parrotfish filet, but the house special is sexy, succulent conch in garlic butter. The chef also makes some of the best chili and baby back ribs in town. Seafood platters, such as chile shrimp or fresh lobster, are served with coconut salad and rice. For more ele-gant fare, there's Italian-style chicken breast topped with pesto, tomatoes, and cheese and served with pasta and salad or the salade niçoise (anchovies, eggs, and potatoes topped with fresh fish). The service is casual. Because of its central location, this restaurant draws the cruise-ship crowd.

The Circus, Fort St., Basseterre. ⟨ **869/465-4197.** Reservations recommended. Main courses EC$25–EC$75 ($9.25–US$28/£4.80–£14). MC, V. Mon–Sat 8am–10pm.

Fisherman's Wharf Seafood Restaurant and Bar ⟨ SEAFOOD/CARIBBEAN At the west end of Basseterre Bay Road, the Fisherman's Wharf is between the sea and the white picket fence of the Ocean Terrace Inn. Near the busy buffet grill, hardwork-ing chefs prepare fresh seafood. An employee will take your drink order, but you per-sonally place your food order at the grill. It's a bit like eating at picnic tables, but the fresh-fish selection is excellent, caught locally and grilled to order over St. Kitts char-coal. Spicy conch chowder is a good starter; grilled lobster is an elegant main course choice, or you may prefer the grilled catch of the day, often snapper. Grilled swordfish is always good, as is the combination platter, which includes lobster, barbecued shrimp kabob, and calypso chicken breast.

Fortlands, Basseterre. ⟨ **869/465-2754.** Reservations recommended. Main courses US$8–US$40 (£4.15–£21). AE, MC, V. Daily 6:30–11pm.

The Golden Lemon ⟨ CONTINENTAL/CREOLE   The food is very good, and the service polite in this fine hotel on the northern coast (see "Accommodations," above). It makes a great lunch stop on a tour of the island. Dinner is served in an ele-gant, candlelit dining room, in the garden, or on the gallery. The hotel's sophisticated owner created many of the recipes. The menu changes daily, but is likely to include baked Cornish hen with ginger, fresh fish of the day, and Creole sirloin steak with a spicy rum sauce. Vegetarian dishes are also available. Dress is casually chic.

In the Golden Lemon Inn, Dieppe Bay. © 869/465-7260. Reservations usually required; walk-ins accepted if space available. Main courses lunch US$10–US$25 (£5.20–£13); fixed-price dinner US$35–US$65 (£18–£34); Sun brunch US$15–US$35 (£7.80–£18). AE, MC, V. Mon–Sat 7:30–10am, noon–3pm, and 7–11pm; Sun noon–3pm and 7–10pm.

Manhattan Gardens ⊛ CARIBBEAN/INTERNATIONAL This 18th-century island home is painted in flamboyant colors and extends a hearty welcome. Try to eat in the rear garden, which opens onto a view of the water. Chef/owner Rosalind Warner has some real local dishes such as conch fritters or curried mutton, although you might opt for the fresh catch of the day, which may be mahimahi in a lemon-and-thyme sauce. We're fond of her shrimp with white wine or garlic butter. Her boneless chicken stuffed with Monterey Jack cheese is another winner, as are her homemade soups, especially the pumpkin.

Main St., Old Road Town. © 869/465-9121. Reservations required. Main courses EC$40–EC$70 (US$15–US$26/ £7.80–£14). No credit cards. Mon–Sat 11am–3pm and 7–11pm.

Marshall's ⊛ *Finds* JAMAICAN/INTERNATIONAL Jamaica-born chef Verral Marshall infuses the island's local cuisine with his own spice and flair. Installed around the pool area of Horizons Villa Resort and built on the foundations of a long-gone fort, his restaurant overlooks Frigate Bay. It's quite romantic at night, with beautifully laid tables. You'll get a warm welcome, excellent service, and good food. Fresh shrimp in a tomato-and-basil sauce is perfectly prepared and a tasty choice. Even more exotic is the house signature dish of conch cutlets (pounded like a veal cutlet) and served with a rum-laced lime sauce. The fish depends on the catch of the day. Our party recently took delight in the grilled mahimahi and the grilled lobster. Prices are a bit steep but overall it's worth it for an evening out on the island.

Horizons Villa Resort. Frigate Bay. © 869/466-8245. Reservations required. Main courses US$24–US$46 (£13–£24). AE, DISC, MC, V. Mon–Sat 6–10pm.

Stonewalls ⊛ *Finds* CARIBBEAN/INTERNATIONAL This open-air bar in a tropical garden in Basseterre's historical zone is cozy and casual. It's the type of Caribbean bar that you hope exists but can rarely find. In a garden setting of banana, plantain, and bamboo trees, Wendy and Garry Steckles present an innovative and constantly changing menu. The fare might be Caribbean, with fresh kingfish or tuna and a zesty gumbo, or an authentic, spicy Dhansak-style curry. Hot-off-the-wok stir-fries are served along with sizzling grilled chicken breast in a teriyaki glaze. Appetizers might include piquant conch fritters. A small but carefully chosen wine list is available. The bar here is one of the most convivial places on the island for a drink.

Princes St. © 869/465-5248. Reservations recommended. Main courses EC$45–EC$76 (US$17–US$28/£8.65–£15). AE, MC, V. Mon–Fri 5–11pm.

Turtle Beach Bar & Grill ⊛ SEAFOOD/INTERNATIONAL Set directly on the sands above Turtle Beach, this airy, sun-flooded restaurant is one of the most popular lunch stops for those doing the whirlwind tour of St. Kitts. Many guests spend an hour before their meal swimming or snorkeling beside the offshore reef; others simply relax on the verandas or in hammocks under the shade trees, perhaps with a drink in hand. Scuba diving, ocean kayaking, windsurfing, and volleyball are available, and rental sailboats are moored nearby. Menu specialties are familiar, but extremely flavorful. Typical dishes are stuffed broiled lobster, conch fritters, grilled fish, pasta salads, and barbecued honey-mustard spareribs.

Southeastern Peninsula. © 869/469-9086. Main courses EC$26-EC$90 (US$9.60–US$33/£5–£17). AE, MC, V. Daily 10am–6pm (Fri–Sat buffet 6–10pm). Follow the Kennedy Simmonds Hwy. over Basseterre's Southeastern Peninsula; then follow the signs.

The Waterfalls Restaurant ☆ CARIBBEAN/INTERNATIONAL   Some of the finest cuisine in Basseterre is found here. The views from the open-air veranda—especially at night when the harbor is lit up—are also some of the best around. We prefer the real down-home island dishes; international specialties tend to be blander. Dinner might include tasty fish cakes, accompanied by breaded carrot slices, creamed spinach, a stuffed potato, a cornmeal dumpling known as a johnnycake, and a green banana in a lime-butter sauce, topped off by a tropical fruit pie and coffee. The less daring can stick with chateaubriand. Friday night is Caribbean night with an all-you-can-eat buffet and a steel band at a cost of EC$70 ($26/£14).

Ocean Terrace Inn, Fortlands. © 869/465-2754. Reservations recommended. Main courses EC$45-EC$97(US$17–US$36/£8.65–£19); fixed-price lunch EC$35–EC$75 (US$13–US$28/£6.75–£15), dinner EC$60–EC$125 (US$22–US$46/£12–£24). AE, MC, V. Daily 7–10pm. Drive west on Basseterre Bay Rd. to Fortlands.

INEXPENSIVE

Glimbara Diner CARIBBEAN   Don't expect grand cuisine from this everyday eatery. Established in 1998 in a simple family-run guesthouse in the heart of Basseterre, it has become a local favorite, thanks to the hardworking staff and down-to-earth food. Small and cozy, and painted in shades of blue, white, and gray, it serves Creole cuisine that varies with the mood and inspiration of the cook. Examples might include large or small portions of the stewlike goat water, pumpkin or bean soup, and several kinds of fried or grilled fish, which might be accompanied by coleslaw or green salad. American-style platters, including hamburgers and hot dogs, are usually served with fries and soda. Ask for a local fruit punch known as *fairling* or the bottled sugary grapefruit drink called Ting.

In the Glimbara Guesthouse, Cayon St., Basseterre. © 869/465-1786. Main courses EC$15–EC$20 (US$5.55–US$7.40/£2.90–£3.85). AE, MC, V. Daily 7am–11pm.

BEACHES

Most visitors to St. Kitts are primarily concerned with its beaches. The narrow peninsula in the southeast that contains the island's salt ponds also boasts the best white-sand beaches. All beaches, even those that border hotels, are open to the public. However, to use the beach facilities of a hotel, you must first obtain permission and will probably have to pay a small fee.

Until the Dr. Kennedy Simmonds Highway (named for the nation's first prime minister)—a 10km (6¼-mile) road beginning in the Frigate Bay area—opened to the public in 1989, it was necessary to take a boat to enjoy the beautiful, unspoiled beaches of the southeast peninsula. To travel this road is one of the pleasures of a visit to St. Kitts. Not only will you see some of the island's most beautiful scenery, but you'll also pass lagoonlike coves and fields of tall guinea grass. If the day is clear (and it usually is), you'll have a panoramic vista of Nevis. The best beaches along the peninsula are **Frigate Bay, Friar's Bay, Sand Bank Bay, White House Bay, Cockleshell Bay,** and **Banana Bay.** Of all these, **Sand Bank Bay** ☆ gets our nod as the finest strip of sand.

Both **Cockleshell Bay** and **Banana Bay** also have their devotees. Together these two beaches run a distance of 3km (2 miles), all with powder-white sands. So far, in spite of several attempts, this area hasn't filled with high-rise resorts.

A live steel band plays on Sundays from 12:30 to 3pm at the **Turtle Beach Bar and Grill,** Turtle Bay, making this the place for afternoon cocktails on the beach.

For excellent **snorkeling,** head to somewhat rocky **White House Bay,** which opens onto reefs. Schools of rainbow-hued fish swim around a tugboat sunken long ago—a stunning sight.

South Friar's Bay is lovely and many locals consider it their favorite. **Frigate Bay,** with its powder-white sand, is ideal for swimming as well as windsurfing and water-skiing.

You may also want to visit **Great Salt Pond** at the southeastern end of St. Kitts. This is an inland beach of soft white sand, opening onto the Atlantic Ocean in the north and the more tranquil Caribbean Sea in the south.

The beaches in the north of St. Kitts are numerous but are of gray volcanic sand and much less frequented than those of the southeast peninsula. Beachcombers like to visit them, and they can be ideal for sunbathing, but swimming is much better in the southeast, as waters in the north, sweeping in from the Atlantic, can often be turbulent.

The best beach on the Atlantic side is **Conaree Bay,** with a narrow strip of gray-black sand. Bodysurfing is popular here. **Dieppe Bay,** another black-sand beach on the north coast, is good for snorkeling and windsurfing but not for swimming. This is the site of the island's most famous inn, the Golden Lemon, which you might want to visit for lunch. *Beware:* If you should be on this beach during a tropical shower, do not seek shelter under the dreaded manchineel trees, which are poisonous. Rain falling off the leaves will feel like acid on your skin.

SPORTS & OTHER OUTDOOR PURSUITS

GOLF   The **Royal St. Kitts Golf Course,** Frigate Bay (© **869/466-2700**), is an 18-hole championship course that covers 64 hectares (158 acres). It features 10 water hazards, not including the Caribbean Sea and the Atlantic Ocean, which border it. It's open daily from 7am to 6pm. Greens fees are US$170 (£88) for 18 holes. Carts are free for 18 holes, but US$50 (£26) for clubs. A bar and an on-site restaurant open daily at 7am. The course is part of the St. Kitts Marriott Resort.

HIKING   **Kris Tours** (© **869/465-4042**) takes small groups into the crater of Mount Liamuiga (see "Into the Volcano," below), through a rainforest to enjoy the lushness of the island. A full-day tour costs US$62(£32) per person and includes lunch and drinks.

HORSEBACK RIDING   **Trinity Stables** (© **869/465-3226**) charges US$55 (£29) for a half-day tour through a rainforest. You might also get to see the wild lushness of the North Frigate Bay area and the rather desolate Conaree Beach. You must call for a reservation; you'll then be told where to meet and offered advice, including what to wear.

SCUBA DIVING, SNORKELING & OTHER WATERSPORTS   Some of the best dive spots include **Nag's Head,** at the south tip of St. Kitts. This is an excellent shallow-water dive starting at 3m (10 ft.) and extending to 21m (69 ft.). A variety of tropical fish, eagle rays, and lobster is found here. The site is ideal for certified divers. Another good spot for diving is **Booby Shoals,** off the southeast Atlantic coast near Cockleshell Bay. Booby Shoals has abundant sea life, including nurse sharks, lobster, and stingrays. Dives are up to 9m (30 ft.) in depth, ideal for both certified and resort divers.

A variety of activities is offered by **Pro-Divers,** at Turtle Beach (© **869/466-3483**). You can swim, float, paddle, or go on scuba-diving and snorkeling expeditions from here. A two-tank dive costs US$90 (£47); night dives are US$70 (£36). A PADI certification is available for US$350 (£182), and a resort course costs US$90 (£47). Three-hour snorkeling trips are US$35 (£18).

Pro-Divers also rent snorkeling gear and can tell you the best places to go **snorkeling.** We like **Dieppe Bay** at the northern tip of St. Kitts.

EXPLORING THE ISLAND

The British colonial town of **Basseterre** is built around a so-called **Circus,** the town's round square. A tall green Victorian clock stands in the center of the Circus. After Brimstone Hill Fortress, **Berkeley Memorial Clock** is the most photographed landmark of St. Kitts. In the old days, wealthy plantation owners and their families used to promenade here.

At some point, try to visit the **marketplace,** especially on a Saturday morning. Here, country people bring baskets brimming with mangos, guavas, soursop, mammee apples, and wild strawberries and cherries just picked in the fields. Tropical flowers abound.

Another major landmark is **Independence Square.** Once an active slave market, it's surrounded by private homes of Georgian architecture.

You can negotiate with a taxi driver to take you on a tour of the island for about US$80 (£42) for a 3-hour trip; most drivers are well versed in the lore of the island. You might want to make lunch reservations at either the Rawlins Plantation Inn or the Golden Lemon. For more information, call the **St. Kitts Taxi Association,** the Circus, Basseterre (© **869/465-8487** until 10pm).

The island's latest attraction is the **St. Kitts Scenic Railway** ✵ (© **869/465-7263**). In double-decker and air-conditioned railcars, you're taken on a panoramic tour of the most spectacular scenery the island has to offer. The upper level features a spacious, open-air observation deck. The narrow-gauge railway follows the old sugar-cane train tracks, taking in the best vistas of mountains and the Caribbean Sea. There is a service bar, and passengers can also enjoy live musical entertainment. The train is boarded at Needsmust Station. This is certainly the quickest and easiest way to see "St. Kitts in a nutshell," especially if you're a cruise-ship passenger with limited time. The 50km (30-mile) ride costs US$89 (£46) for adults, half price for children, and lasts 3½ hours. The first departure is daily at 8:10am. Sometimes a second tour, if demand warrants it, leaves at 11:50am.

Brimstone Hill Fortress ✵ (© **869/465-6211**), 14km (8¾ miles) west of Basseterre, is a major stop. This historic monument, among the largest and best preserved in the Caribbean, is a complex of bastions, barracks, and other structures ingeniously adapted to the top and upper slopes of a steep-sided 240m (790-ft.) hill. The fortress dates from 1690, when the British attempted to recapture Fort Charles from the French. Admission is US$8 (£4.15) for adults, US$4 (£2.10) for children.

Today, the fortress is the centerpiece of a national park with nature trails and a diverse range of plant and animal life, including the **green vervet monkey.** It's also a photographer's paradise, with views of mountains, fields, and the Caribbean Sea. On a clear day, you can see six neighboring islands.

Visitors can enjoy self-guided tours among many ruins and restored structures, including the barrack rooms at Fort George, which contain an interesting museum. The gift shop stocks prints of rare maps and paintings of the Caribbean. Admission is US$8 (£4.15), half price for children. The Brimstone Hill Fortress National Park is open daily from 9:30am to 5:30pm.

You can visit the site where a large tamarind tree in the hamlet of **Half-Way Tree** once marked the boundary between the British- and French-held sectors.

It was near the hamlet of **Old Road Town** that Sir Thomas Warner landed with the first band of settlers and established the first permanent colony to the northwest at Sandy Point. Sir Thomas's grave is in the cemetery of St. Thomas Church.

A sign in the middle of Old Road Town points the way to **Carib Rock Drawings,** all the evidence that remains of the former inhabitants. The markings are on black boulders, and the pictographs date from prehistoric days.

INTO THE VOLCANO

Mount Liamuiga was dubbed "Mount Misery" long ago, but it sputtered its last gasp around 1692. This dormant volcano on the northeast coast is today one of the major highlights for hikers on St. Kitts. The peak of the mountain often lies under cloud cover.

The ascent to the volcano is usually made from the north end of St. Kitts at Belmont Estate. The trail winds through a rainforest and travels along deep ravines up to the rim of the crater at 788m (2,585 ft.). The actual peak is at 1,138m (3,733 ft.). Figure on 5 hours of rigorous hiking to complete the round-trip walk.

The caldera itself is some 120m (390 ft.) from its rim to the crater floor. Many hikers climb or crawl down into the dormant volcano. However, the trail is steep and slippery, so be careful. At the crater floor is a tiny lake along with volcanic rocks and various vegetation.

Greg's Safaris (© 869/465-4121), offers guided hikes to the crater, including breakfast and a picnic at the crater's rim, for US$85 (£44) per person with a minimum of six people. The same outfit also offers half-day rainforest explorations for US$50 (£26) per person. **Kris Tours** (© 869/465-4042) offers similar tours for US$62 (£32), but with no breakfast and a far less luxurious picnic spread.

SHOPPING

The good buys here are local handicrafts, including leather (goatskin) items, baskets, and coconut shells. Some good values can also be found in clothing and fabrics, especially Sea Island cottons. Store hours vary, but are likely to be Monday to Saturday from 8am to noon and 1 to 4pm.

If your time is limited, head first for the **Pelican Shopping Mall,** Bay Road, which contains some two dozen shops. Opened in 1991, it also offers banking services, a restaurant, and a philatelic bureau. Some major retail outlets in the Caribbean, including Little Switzerland, have branches here. Also check out the offerings along the quaintly named **Liverpool Row,** which has some unusual merchandise, and **Fort Street.**

Linen and Gold, in the Pelican Mall (© 869/465-9766), offers a limited selection of gold and silver jewelry, usually in bold modern designs. But the real appeal of this shop is the tablecloths, doilies, and napkins, laboriously handcrafted in China from cotton, linen, and polyester. The workmanship is as intricate as anything you'll find in the Caribbean.

Ashburry's, the Circus/Liverpool Row, Basseterre (© 869/465-8175), is a local branch of a chain of luxury-goods stores based on St. Maarten. This well-respected emporium sells fragrances, fine porcelain, Baccarat crystal, designer handbags, watches, and jewelry at prices 25% to 30% below what you might pay in retail stores in North America; the selection is similar to dozens of equivalent stores throughout the Caribbean.

Spencer Cameron Gallery, 10 N. Independence Sq., Basseterre (© **869/465-1617**), is a leading art gallery. On display are scenes of St. Kitts and Nevis by Brit Rosie Cameron-Smith, along with works by 10 to 15 other artists. Rosey is well known on the island for her paintings of Kittitian Carnival clowns, monkeys, and figurative work, and she also produces greeting cards, postcards, calendars, and lithographs.

The finest gallery on St. Kitts is **Kate Design,** Mount Pleasant (© **869/465-7740**), set in an impeccably restored West Indian house, on a hillside below the Rawlins Plantation. Virtually all the works on display are by English-born Kate Spencer, who is well known throughout North America and Europe. Her paintings of island scenes range in price from US$200 to US$6,000 (£104–£3,120) and have received critical acclaim. Also for sale is a series of Ms. Spencer's silk-screened scarves, each crafted from extra-heavy stonewashed silk.

Island Fever, in the Palms Arcade, Basseterre (© **869/465-2599**), specializes in island things, including handicrafts and perfumes. Also available are tropical clothing and a wealth of souvenirs.

Island Hopper (known as "The Big Shop of the Little Island"), the Circus, below the popular Ballahoo Restaurant, Basseterre (© **869/465-1640**), is one of St. Kitts's most patronized shops, with the biggest inventory of any store on the island. Notice the all-silk, shift-style dresses from China and the array of batiks made on St. Kitts. About half of the merchandise is from the islands.

Caribelle Batik at Romney Manor, Old Road, about 15km (10 miles) west of Basseterre (© **869/465-6253**), is the most unusual factory in St. Kitts. It was built around 1625 as a manor house for sugar baron Lord Romney. For years, it has been used as the headquarters and manufacturing center for a local clothier, Caribelle Batik, whose tropical cottons sell widely to cruise-ship passengers and tourists from at least three outlets in the eastern Caribbean. The merchandise ranges from scarves to dresses, along with an extensive collection of wall hangings and cushions. In 1995, a tragic fire and hurricane completely gutted the historic building. The manor has now been rebuilt and extended. Consider a stopover here if only to admire the 2 hectares (5 acres) of lavish gardens, where 30 varieties of hibiscus, rare orchids, huge ferns, and a 250-year-old saman tree still draw horticultural enthusiasts. Entrance to the gardens is free.

ST. KITTS AFTER DARK

The **Ocean Terrace Inn's Fisherman's Wharf,** Fortlands (© **869/465-2754**), has a live band every Friday from 8 to 10pm. It's not "after dark," but the **Turtle Beach Bar and Grill,** Turtle Bay (© **869/465-9086**), on the southeast peninsula, offers a live steel band daily from 12:30 to 3pm; on Saturday, it's beach disco time. There's no cover at either place.

A favorite watering hole is **Bambu's,** Bank Street, right off the Circus in Basseterre (© **869/466-5280**), which is filled with lots of bamboo and bright colors. There's a big-screen TV for those who want to watch the games, but also spaces for those who want to retreat. On Friday happy hour is from 5 to 7pm.

A few other nightspots come and go (mostly go). Currently, islanders hang out at **Bobsy's,** Bay Road (© **869/466-6133**), in Basseterre. Another local dive, **Henry's Night Spot,** Dunn's Cottage, Main Street, Cayon (© **869/465-3508**), has a loyal following. At the Marriott Resort at Frigate Bay, the **Royal Beach Casino** (© 869/466-5555) lures gamblers to its large casino with slot machines and games of chance with croupiers. For the high roller, there are private salons.

3 Nevis

A local once said that the best reason to go to Nevis was to practice the fine art of *limin'*. To him, that meant doing nothing in particular. Limin' might still be the best reason to venture over to Nevis. Once here, you can relax and experience this small, calm volcanic island. If you want to lie out in the sun, head for reef-protected Pinney's Beach, a 5km (3-mile) strip of dark-gold sand set against a backdrop of palm trees with panoramic views of St. Kitts.

Columbus sighted Nevis in 1493. The explorer called it *Nuestra Señora de Las Nieves*—"Our Lady of the Snows"—because its peak is often shrouded in clouds, making it look snow-capped. From St. Kitts, the island appears to be a perfect cone, rising gradually to a height of 970m (3,182 ft.). A saddle joins the tallest mountain to two smaller peaks, Saddle Hill (375m/1,230 ft.) in the south and Hurricane Hill (only 75m/246 ft.) in the north.

Centuries before the British settled the island in 1628, Nevis was a habitat for the friendly Arawaks and later the fierece Carib Indians. These native populations were replaced with the arrival of the British, who established both sugar and tobacco plantations beginning in the mid-1600s. In the ensuing decades both the Spanish and the French battled the British for control of the island, the British finally winning out in this tug-of-war in 1783 when both Nevis and St. Kitts came under British control. The two-island nation would remain under British control until independence was achieved in 1983.

Nevis' beauty has remained relatively unspoiled. Coral reefs rim the shoreline, and there's mile after mile of palm-shaded white-sand beaches. Natives of Nevis, for the most part, are descendants of African slaves.

The volcanic island is famous as the birthplace of Alexander Hamilton, the American statesman who wrote many of the articles contained in *The Federalist Papers* and was George Washington's treasury secretary. Nevis is also the island on which Admiral Horatio Lord Nelson married Frances Nisbet, a local woman, in 1787, an episode described in James Michener's *Caribbean* (the historical facts are romanticized, of course).

In the 18th century, Nevis's hot mineral springs made it the leading spa of the West Indies. The island was also once peppered with prosperous sugar-cane estates, but they're gone now—many have been converted into some of the most intriguing hotels in the Caribbean. Sea Island cotton is the chief crop today.

On the Caribbean side, **Charlestown,** the capital of Nevis, was fashionable in the 18th century, when sugar planters were carried around in carriages and sedan chairs. A town of wide, quiet streets, this port only gets busy when its major link to the world, the ferry from St. Kitts, docks at the harbor.

NEVIS ESSENTIALS

GETTING THERE   There are no nonstop flights to Nevis from North America. To get here, you'll have to stop or change planes in Antigua, St. Maarten, or Puerto Rico. **American Airlines** (© 800/433-7300 in the U.S.; www.aa.com) has dozens of daily flights to San Juan. From here, you can catch a propeller plane to Nevis, arriving on

Nevis at the **Vance W. Armory International Airport,** which has a single runway. You can also fly into Nevis from San Juan on two daily flights operated by **American Eagle** (© **800/433-7300** or 869/465-2273). The airport is located on the north side of the island—just 15 minutes outside the capital of Charlestown and less than 30 minutes from all the major resorts, hotels, and plantation inns on the island.

For information on traveling to Nevis by ferry, please see "Getting There," on p. 540 earlier.

GETTING AROUND **Taxi** drivers double as guides, and you'll find them waiting at the airport or the ferry dock. The fare between Newcastle Airport and Charlestown is US$15 (£7.80); between Charlestown and Old Manor Estate, US$13 (£6.75); and from Charlestown to Pinney's Beach, US$5 (£2.60). Between 10pm and 6am, 50% is added to the prices. Call © **869/469-1042** for more information.

You can arrange for a **rental car** from a local firm through your hotel. Or you can check with **Nevis Car Rental,** Newcastle, near the airport (© **869/469-9837**). Another reliable firm is **Noel's Courtesy Garage,** Farms Estate (© **869/469-5199**), which is convenient to guests in hotels east of Charlestown, including Hermitage, Montpelier, Old Manor, and Golden Rock. To drive on Nevis, you must obtain a permit from the traffic department, which costs US$24 (£13) and is valid for 3 months. Car-rental companies will handle this for you. *Remember:* Drive on the left side of the road. About 2/3 of the road that encircles Nevis has been improved and resurfaced post-millennium; the remaining stretch of road continues to be bumpy and pot-holed but passable for either 2- or 4-wheel-drive vehicles.

FAST FACTS **Banks** are usually open Monday to Thursday from 8am to 3pm, Friday 8am to 5pm, and some on Saturday 8 to 11am. Normal **store hours** are Monday to Saturday from 8am to noon and 1 to 4pm. Some places close Thursday afternoon; most are closed Sunday. Many bank branches in Charletown have ATMs dispensing Eastern Caribbean dollars.

The **post office** is on Main Street in Charlestown. It's open Monday to Friday from 8am to 3pm. You can make **international phone calls,** including collect calls, from the **Cable & Wireless office,** Main Street, Charlestown (© **869/469-5000**). Open Monday to Wednesday 8am to 5pm, Thursday and Friday 8am to 4pm.

If you need a pharmacy, try **Evelyn's Drugstore,** Charlestown (© **869/469-5278**), open Monday to Friday from 8am to 6pm, Saturday from 8am to 7pm, and Sunday for only 1 hour, from 7 to 8pm, to serve emergency needs.

There's a 24-hour **emergency room** at **Alexandra Hospital,** Government Road, in Charlestown (© **869/469-5473**).

The **Nevis Tourist Authority** is on Main Street in Charlestown (© **866/556-3847** in the U.S., or 869/469-7550).

For more information search **www.nevisisland.com**.

ACCOMMODATIONS
VERY EXPENSIVE
Four Seasons Resort Nevis ★★ (Kids)   This hotel is hands-down the best choice on the island. Even so, discerning travelers have detected a problem or two, especially when conventions dominate or raucous families check in. Located on Nevis's west coast, it's set in a palm grove beside Pinney's Beach, the finest sandy beach on Nevis. On an island known for its small and intimate inns, this low-rise resort built in 1991

Nevis

Legend:
- Airport
- Beach
- Ferry
- Mountain

Four Seasons Resort Nevis **1**
Golden Rock Plantation Inn **6**
Hermitage Beach Club **8**
Hurricane Cove Bungalows **3**
Montpelier Plantation Inn **9**
Mount Nevis Hotel
  & Beach Club **4**
Nisbet Plantation Beach Club **5**
Old Manor Hotel **7**
Oualie Beach Hotel **2**

↑ To 'St. Kitts
The Narrows
ATLANTIC OCEAN
Vance W. Amory International Airport
Newcastle
Newcastle Beach
Mosquito Bay
Oualie Beach
Long Haul Bay
Fort Ashby
Cotton Ground
Pinney's Beach
Nelson's Spring
Eden Brown Estate
Huggins Bay
Mount Nevis
Charlestown
New River
Caribbean Cove
Hermitage Village
White Bay
Fig Tree
Bath
Gingerland
Montpelier
Saddle Hill
White Bay Beach
Caribbean Sea
Botanical Garden
Indian Castle Beach

PUERTO RICO
BRITISH VIRGIN ISLANDS
ATLANTIC OCEAN
LESSER ANTILLES
LEEWARD ISLANDS
ANGUILLA
U.S. VIRGIN ISLANDS
ST. KITTS AND NEVIS
Nevis
ANTIGUA AND BARBUDA
Caribbean Sea
MONTSERRAT
GUADELOUPE
0   100 mi

0   2 mi
0   2 km
N

stands out as the largest and best-managed hotel, with the most complete sports facilities (including a fabulous golf course), and even the best children's program. Designed in harmony with the surrounding landscape, the accommodations offer rich but conservative mahogany furniture, touches of marble, carpeting, and wide patios or verandas overlooking the beach, the golf course, or Mount Nevis. Public rooms are a bit garish, but the spacious guest rooms have generous closet space, full-length mirrors, luxurious upholstery and fabrics, and king-size or double beds. The roomy bathrooms have tub/shower combos, double sinks, makeup mirrors, and Bulgari toiletries. As part of the hotel's most recent renovation, two suites were added for history buffs: the Alexander Hamilton and the Horatio Nelson suites, which are filled with antiques and memorabilia of these two figures.

Guests have the largest choice of bars and dining venues on Nevis. The resort's centerpiece is the plantation-inspired great house, which contains the most formal restaurant, the Four Seasons Dining Room (see "Dining," below). A special feature is an elegant spa, featuring beachside massages and hydrotherapy. Ever had a mango–sea salt exfoliation and a heavenly hot-stone massage? Even though the beach in front is open to the public, staffers have been known to try to shoo visitors away. If you're shopping for crafts in the on-site gift shop, check the labels—often the merchandise is not made in Nevis but in such faraway places as Kenya or China.

Pinney's Beach (P.O. Box 565), Charlestown, Nevis, W.I. ☎ **800/332-3442** in the U.S., 800/268-6282 in Canada, or 869/469-1111. Fax 869/469-1112. www.fourseasons.com/nevis. 196 units. Winter US$655–US$995 (£341–£517) double, from US$1,625 (£845) suite; off season US$325–US$725 (£169–£377) double, from US$725 (£377) suite. Up to 2 children under 18 stay free in parent's room. AE, DC, MC, V. **Amenities:** 4 restaurants; 2 bars; 3 pools; 18-hole golf course; 10 tennis courts; health club; spa; Jacuzzi; sauna; fishing; windsurfing; scuba diving; horseback riding; children's programs; business services; room service; massage; babysitting; laundry service; dry cleaning; nonsmoking rooms; rooms for those w/limited mobility. *In room:* A/C, TV, minibar, beverage maker, hair dryer, iron, safe, Wi-Fi.

Hermitage Beach Club ☆☆

This much-photographed, frequently copied historians' delight is said to be the oldest all-wood house in the Antilles, and was built amid the high-altitude plantations of Gingerland in 1740. Some say it once hosted Alexander Hamilton and Horatio Nelson. Today, former Philadelphian Richard Lupinacci and his wife, Maureen, have assembled one of the best collections of antiques on Nevis here. Wide-plank floors, intricate latticework, and high ceilings add to the hotel's beauty. The accommodations are in 12 glamorous buildings designed like small plantation houses. Many contain huge four-poster beds, antique accessories, and colonial louvered windows. The spotlessly maintained private bathrooms contain tub/shower combos. The most luxurious and expensive unit is a yellow manor house on .2 hectares (½ acre) of private gardens with its own ceramic-tile pool, three large bedrooms furnished with antique canopy beds, oversize bathrooms with dressing rooms, a comfortable living room, dining room, and a full kitchen.

Complimentary beach transportation is provided because the best nearby beach is a 15-minute drive away. The on-site restaurant is one of the finest hotel dining rooms on island (see "Dining," below).

St. John's Parish, Nevis, W.I. ☎ **800/682-4025** in the U.S., or 869/469-3477. Fax 869/469-2481. www.hermitage nevis.com. 15 units. Winter US$325 (£169) double, US$390–US$450 (£203–£234) cottage, US$790 (£411) manor house villa; off-season US$170 (£88) double, US$205–US$265 (£107–£138) cottage, US$650 (£338) manor house villa. AE, MC, V. Take the main island road 6km (3¾ miles) from Charlestown. **Amenities:** Restaurant; bar; outdoor pool; tennis court; horseback riding; car rental; room service; laundry service. *In room:* Ceiling fan, TV (in some), kitchen/kitchenette (in some), fridge, beverage maker, hair dryer, iron, safe.

Montpelier Plantation Inn ☆☆

One of the Plantation Inns of Nevis, the Montpelier stands in the hills, 210m (689 ft.) high, with grandstand views of the ocean. The 18th-century plantation is in the center of its own 12-hectare (30-acre) estate, which contains 4 hectares (10 acres) of ornamental gardens surrounding the cottage units. Admiral Horatio Nelson married Frances Nisbet at this historic sugar plantation back in 1787. Accommodations are generally spacious and brightened with fresh flowers and luxuries like comfortable chairs and dressing tables. Tasteful fabrics in contemporary colors—such as blue- or sage-green accents on camel-colored or coral linen—are used. The guest rooms contain bamboo tables and chairs, as well as rich mahogany writing desks and cedar and mahogany wall closets. Bathrooms, with glass-enclosed tub/shower combinations, are sparkling clean. Today the look is one of minimalist chic as befits the 21st century. Most of the elegant bedrooms have four-posters. Service is among the best on island. The staff will even unpack your clothing, press your garments, and put them away for you.

Montpelier prides itself on its food, wine, and service. At the restaurant that shares the name of the resort, much use is made of fresh local produce (see "Dining," below). Montpelier by the Sea is the hotel's private .8-hectare (2-acre) beach, featuring waterfront dining and beverages in an old Nevisian house.

St. John Figtree (P.O. Box 474), Montpelier, Nevis, W.I. ☎ **869/469-3462.** Fax 869/469-2932. www.montpeliernevis. com. 17 units. Winter US$480 (£250) double, US$555 (£289) suite, US$747 (£388) 2-bedroom suite; off season

US$280–US$380 (£146–£198) double, US$355–US$455 (£185–£237) suite, US$467–US$607 (£243–£316) 2-bed-room suite. Rates include breakfast and afternoon tea. AE, MC, V. Closed Aug–Sept. Children under 8 not allowed. **Amenities:** 3 restaurants; 2 bars; outdoor pool; tennis court; spa; snorkeling; windsurfing; horseback riding; library; transport to private beach; room service (breakfast only); babysitting; laundry service. *In room:* A/C, ceiling fan, fridge, beverage maker, hair dryer, safe.

Mount Nevis Hotel & Beach Club ★ *Kids*

This family-owned and -run resort—built on the site of a lime plantation—is on the slopes of Mount Nevis, a 5-minute drive southwest of the Vance Amory International Airport. It's known for the quality of its accommodations, for its panoramic views, and for serving some of the best food on Nevis. Near the historic fishing village of Newcastle, it offers standard rooms, junior suites, and supervisor suites—the latter with fully equipped kitchens and enough space for at least four guests, making it an ideal family choice. The rooms have such amenities as ceiling fans, and are furnished in a tropical motif, with wicker and colorful island prints. The tidily maintained private bathrooms are well equipped and contain shower stalls.

The Mount Nevis Beach Club offers a site on Newcastle Bay and features a beach pavilion, bar, and restaurant. It pretty much introduced pizza to the island.

Newcastle (P.O. Box 494), Charlestown, Nevis, W.I. © **800/756-3847** in the U.S. and Canada, or 869/469-9373. Fax 869/469-9375. www.mountnevishotel.com. 32 units. Winter US$350 (£182) double, US$400 (£208) suite, US$675 (£351) 2-bedroom; off season US$250 (£130) double, US$300 (£156) suite, US$500 (£260) 2-bedroom. Rates include breakfast. Extra person US$35 (£18). Children stay free in parent's room. AE, MC, V. **Amenities:** 2 restaurants; bar; outdoor pool; exercise room; beach shuttle; business services; room service; massage; babysitting; laundry service; nonsmoking rooms. *In room:* A/C, ceiling fan, TV, kitchen (in some), fridge, beverage maker (in some), hair dryer, iron.

Nisbet Plantation Beach Club ★★

A respect for fine living prevails in this gracious estate house on a coconut plantation, which is the only plantation-style house that lives up to the grace notes of Montpelier Plantation Inn. This is the former home of Frances Nisbet, who, at the age of 22, married Lord Nelson. Although enamored of Miss Nisbet when he married her, Lord Nelson later fell in love with Lady Hamilton (as detailed in the classic film *That Hamilton Woman*). This is the only plantation hotel in Nevis that opens directly onto the beach—a kilometer or so (½ mile) of pulverized coral sand against a backdrop of palm trees.

The present main building was rebuilt on the foundations of the original 18th-century great house. The ruins of a circular sugar mill stand at the entrance, covered with bougainvillea, hibiscus, and poinciana. Guest cottages are set in the palm grove. All rooms are brightly decorated and beautifully appointed, with king-size beds and firm mattresses. The bathrooms, with tub/shower combos, are tidily maintained. In 2006 the Nisbet completed a US$2 million renovation that included the guest rooms, the facilities at the beach, the fitness center, and the Great House. They also added a hot tub next to the pool at the beach.

In addition to two casual beachfront eateries, the Great House Restaurant serves some of the most elegant and best dinners on the island, a delightful combination of Caribbean and international cuisine.

Newcastle, St. James's Parish, Nevis, W.I. © **800/742-6008** in the U.S. and Canada, or 869/469-9325. Fax 869/469-9864. www.nisbetplantation.com. 38 units. Winter US$550 (£286) double, US$650–US$680 (£338–£354) suite; off season US$300–US$350 (£156–£182) double, US$400–US$480 (£208–£250) suite. Rates include MAP (breakfast and dinner) and afternoon tea. Additional person US$85–US$125 (£44–£65). AE, MC, V. Turn left out of the airport and go 2km (1¼ miles). **Amenities:** 2 restaurants; 2 bars; outdoor pool; fitness center; golf at Four Seasons; tennis court; snorkeling; horseback riding; massage; spa; babysitting; laundry service; car rental; nonsmoking rooms. *In room:* A/C, ceiling fan, minibar, beverage maker, hair dryer, iron, safe.

EXPENSIVE

Golden Rock Plantation Inn ☆ This place doesn't have the polish and glaze of such choices as the Hermitage (see above), but it has down-home qualities and quiet charm. This former sugar estate, built in 1815, is set in the lush hills only a 15-minute drive east of Charlestown. Set on 40 tropical hectares (100 acres), it fronts a 10-hectare (25-acre) garden. Guests live in fairly spacious surroundings, in a setting of pineapple friezes, island crafts, family heirlooms, and tile flowers. Fabrics are island-made, with tropical flower designs. The shower-only bathrooms are a bit small. Cottages are scattered about the garden, and each has a four-poster king-size bed made of bamboo or mahogany. Rooms have large porches with views of the sea as well. The original stone tower windmill has been turned into a duplex honeymoon suite (or accommodations for a family of four).

The hotel lies at the beginning of a rainforest walk; it takes about 3 to 4 hours to follow the trail round-trip (the hotel provides a map). For the equestrian, horseback riding can be arranged. If you want to go to the beach, the complimentary hotel shuttle will take you to either Pinney's Beach (on the leeward side) or White Bay Beach (aka Windward Beach), which has good surfing. The shuttle also stops in Charlestown if requested. Caribbean-style meals are served at the 175-year-old "long house." The inn also maintains a lunch-only restaurant (open daily 11am–3pm) with changing facilities at Pinney's Beach. In 2007 substantial renovations were made, including an overhaul of the public rooms and the addition of a new dining room and library area. Incidentally, the Golden Rock is one of the best places to spot the island's colony of Vervet monkeys, introduced here in the 17th century.

P.O. Box 493, Gingerland, Nevis, W.I. © 869/469-3346. Fax 869/469-2113. www.golden-rock.com. 12 units. Winter US$220–US$285 (£114–£148) double; off season US$160–US$195 (£83–£101) double. Children under age 2 stay free in parent's room. AE, MC, V. **Amenities:** 2 restaurants; bar; outdoor pool; sailing; scuba diving; snorkeling; windsurfing; horseback riding; beach shuttle; babysitting; laundry service. *In room:* Ceiling fan, hair dryer, no phone.

Hurricane Cove Bungalows This cluster of self-contained bungalows is set on a hillside with a world-class ocean view, a far better sight than the complex's rather ramshackle facade. It's located on the northernmost point of Nevis, a 5-minute drive west of the airport. Each bungalow is wood-sided and vaguely Scandinavian in design, with a tile roof and a massive foundation that anchors it into the rocky hillside. No meals are served, but each unit has a full kitchen and there's a poolside barbecue grill. Each bungalow has a queen-size bed, a covered porch, and a ceiling fan. The small, compact bathrooms are efficiently organized, with adequate shelf space and a shower stall. A freshwater pool is built into the foundation of a 250-year-old fortification, and the beach lies at the bottom of a steep hillside. The three-bedroom villa has its own small, but private, pool.

Oualie Beach, Nevis, W.I. ©/fax 869/469-9462. www.hurricanecove.com. 12 units. Winter US$245–US$410 (£127–£213) 1-bedroom bungalow, US$375–US$435 (£195–£226) 2-bedroom bungalow, US$685 (£356) 3-bedroom villa; off season US$165–US$325 (£86–£169) 1-bedroom bungalow, US$255–US$330 (£133–£172) 2-bedroom bungalow, US$495 (£258) 3-bedroom villa. MC, V. **Amenities:** Outdoor pool; snorkeling; babysitting; nonsmoking rooms. *In room:* Ceiling fan, kitchen, fridge, beverage maker, safe, no phone (in most).

Old Manor Hotel ☆ The least elaborate of the plantation-style inns of Nevis, this hotel is the most evocative of a *Gone With the Wind* Nevisian life. East of Charlestown and north of Gingerland, at a cool and comfortable elevation of 240m (787 ft.), the Old Manor Hotel has an old-world grace. The forested plot of land on which the hotel sits was granted to the Croney family in 1690 by the king of England. The estate thrived as a working sugar plantation until 1936. Today, the stately ruins of its great house, once described by British historians as "the best example of Georgian domestic architecture in the Caribbean," complement the hotel's outbuildings. The hotel has been renovated and now has a far more cheerful, tropical appearance. Accommodations contain wide-plank floors of tropical hardwoods, reproduction furniture, and high ceilings. Bathrooms come neat and tidy; some are shower only.

The Old Manor runs a complimentary shuttle to Pinney's Beach, 15 to 20 minutes away.

P.O. Box 70, Gingerland, Nevis, W.I. *(C)* 800/892-7093 in the U.S., or 869/469-3445. Fax 869/469-3388. www.oldmanor nevis.com. 13 units. Winter US$290 (£151) double, US$380 (£198) suite; off season US$220 (£114) double, US$280 (£146) suite. Rates include full breakfast. Extra person US$50–US$70 (£26–£36). Children under age 2 stay free. AE, MC, V. **Amenities:** Restaurant; bar; outdoor pool; Jacuzzi; sauna; beach shuttle; babysitting; laundry service. *In room:* Ceiling fan, kitchenette (in some), minibar, beverage maker, hair dryer, iron, safe.

Oualie Beach Hotel

This complex of gingerbread cottages is often fully booked several months in advance by European sun-worshippers. The Oualie Beach Hotel is set on flatlands adjacent to the white sands of its namesake, the island's second-most-famous beach. Each medium-size unit is clean and simple, with tiled floors and small fridges; a few have kitchenettes. Extras include full-length mirrors, mahogany furnishings, and double or four-poster queen-size beds. Bathrooms are small and have showers only. The resort's centerpiece is its well-recommended restaurant and bar, where doors open directly onto a view of the beach (see "Dining," below).

Oualie Beach, Nevis, W.I. *(C)* 869/469-9735. Fax 869/469-9176. www.oualiebeach.com. 32 units. Winter US$270–US$325 (£140–£169) double; off season US$215–US$270 (£112–£140) double. Children under 16 stay free in parent's room. Extra person US$35 (£18). AE, DC, DISC, MC, V. **Amenities:** Restaurant; bar; dive shop; fishing; kayaks; sailing; snorkeling; windsurfing; bikes; horseback riding; massage; babysitting; laundry service; nonsmoking rooms. *In room:* A/C, TV, kitchen (in studios), fridge, minibar, beverage maker, hair dryer, iron, safe, Wi-Fi.

DINING
VERY EXPENSIVE
Four Seasons Dining Room 🖈🖈 INTERNATIONAL/CARIBBEAN/ASIAN
Set beneath a soaring, elaborately trussed ceiling, this is the largest and most formal dining room on Nevis, and the island's best and most expensive restaurant. Decorated in a Caribbean interpretation of French Empire design, it offers rows of beveled-glass windows on three sides, massive bouquets of flowers, hurricane lamps with candles, a fireplace, a collection of unusual paintings, and impeccable service.

The fusion cuisine, with lots of nouvelle touches, roams the world for inspiration. Only quality ingredients are used, and some dishes are low in fat and calories. The menu changes nightly, but appearing frequently are a savory herb-scented pork loin with vegetable spring roll or grilled local wahoo with coconut dumplings. For a marvelous change of pace, opt for a baked baby pumpkin filled with charred pineapple couscous. The grilled spiny Caribbean lobster tail comes with steamed jasmine rice and wok-fried vegetables. The *coup de grace* is the star anise butter. Dessert might be a coconut or mango soufflé. The service and the wine selection are the island's best.

In the Four Seasons Resort Nevis, Pinney's Beach. *(C)* 869/469-1111. Reservations required. Main courses US$40–US$55 (£21–£29). AE, DC, MC, V. Mon-Sat 6–10pm.

Hermitage Plantation 🖈 INTERNATIONAL
At this restaurant, you can combine an excellent dinner with a visit to the oldest house on Nevis, now one of the island's most unusual hotels (see "Accommodations," above). Meals are served on the

latticed porch of the main house, amid candles and good cheer. Maureen Lupinacci, who runs the place with her husband, Richard, combines Continental recipes with local ingredients. Enjoy a before-dinner drink in the colonial-style living room, then move on to the likes of snapper steamed in banana leaves, carrot-and-tarragon soup, marinated shrimp on black-bean cakes, and a delectable version of cold rum soufflé. Many people turn up on Wednesday for the roast-pig dinner (in season).

In the Hermitage Plantation hotel, St. John's Parish. © **869/469-3477**. Reservations required. Lunch US$5–US$20 (£2.60–£10); dinner US$30–US$55 (£16–£29). AE, MC, V. Daily 8–10:30am, noon–2:30pm, and 6:30–8:30pm. Go south on the main island road from Charlestown.

Miss June's 𝒦𝒦 *Finds* CARIBBEAN/INTERNATIONAL   This charming venue, midway between the Four Seasons Resort and the airport, is the private home of June Mestier, a Trinidad-born grande dame, and probably wouldn't exist if it had not been for Oprah Winfrey's enthusiasm. While visiting Nevis, Oprah heard that Ms. Mestier was the finest cook on the island and arranged a private dinner; after being served an excellent meal, Oprah urged her to open a restaurant.

A dinner in Mestier's West Indian house, which is adorned with latticework, requires advance reservations; some visitors call before they even arrive on Nevis. Guests at these dinner parties assemble for canapés and drinks in an airy living room, then sit down for soup and sherry. The tables hold from four to eight diners, and the silver and porcelain are quaintly elegant and charmingly mismatched. Fish and wine follow. All this is followed with samples of about 20 to 40 buffet dishes that hail from Trinidad, New Orleans, India, and the French isles. Mestier's comments on the food are one of the evening's most delightful aspects. After dinner, guests retire to a lounge for coffee, chocolates, and port. Many visitors find a meal here to be one of the highlights of their visit to Nevis.

Jones Bay. © **869/469-5330**. Reservations required. Fixed-price meal US$85 (£44). MC, V. 2 evenings a week, depending on business, beginning around 7pm. Dinner served at 8pm.

Montpelier Plantation Inn 𝒦 INTERNATIONAL   This hotel (see above), 2km (1¼ miles) off the main island road to Gingerland, provides some of the finest dining on the island. You sit by candlelight on the verandas of a grand old West Indian mansion, overlooking floodlit gardens, the lights of Charlestown, and the ocean. Lobster and fish are served the day the catch comes in, and the foreign and Nevisian chefs conspire to produce delectable tropical dishes. On a recent visit the best menu items started with a crispy seafood cake, followed by five-spice duck with a honey flavor and a vegetable-filled mandarin pancake. Other members of our party enjoyed the seared filet of mahimahi with sauce vert and garlic cream potatoes. Cape Brandy pudding with Chantilly cream was everybody's favorite dessert. There's limited seating for dinner, so try to show up on time. An excellent and well-balanced wine list is available. An even more elegant dining choice is the Sugar Mill, open only certain nights a week. Torches line your pathway as you head up to the elegantly decorated mill, with its mahogany antiques and crystal sconces. Some of the finest meals on island are served here.

In the Montpelier Plantation Inn, Montpelier. © **869/469-3462**. Reservations required. Main courses lunch US$5–US$25 (£2.60–£13); fixed-price dinner US$75 (£39). AE, MC, V. Daily 8–10:30am, 11:30am–2:30pm, and 7–8:30pm or 9pm. Closed Aug to Sept.

EXPENSIVE
Coconut Grove 𝒦𝒦 FRENCH/PACIFIC RIM/FUSION   The building itself looks like a hut from Tahiti. It was the creation of restaurateur Gary Colt and his wife,

Karin. You dine under a roof of thatched palm leaf fronds in a rough timbered structure. A crying Buddha emerges from the root of a teak tree. All this is but a backdrop for one of the best cuisines on island. Quality ingredients and first-rate dishes emerge from the kitchen of Francis Knight, a chef who graduated from the Culinary Institute of America. His prowess in the kitchen is demonstrated by such dishes as a seafood Napoléon with shrimp and lobster in a Madras curry sauce or his sliced flank steak in a Cabernet Sauvignon butter sauce with a side of truffle-laced mashed potatoes. You might also sample his chicken breast with a pistachio dressing, a divine marriage. Finish off with crème brûlée, his dessert specialty, although the chocolate almond tart is also sublime.

Main Island Rd., Nelson's Spring (off Pinney's Beach). ℂ 869/469-1020. Reservations required. Main courses US$25–US$29 (£13–£15). MC, V. Daily 6-10pm.

The Cooperage ✦ INTERNATIONAL/CARIBBEAN

Directly east of Charlestown and north of Gingerland, The Cooperage is set in a reconstructed 17th-century building where coopers once made barrels for the sugar mill. The dining room has a high raftered ceiling and stonewalls. The food doesn't even try to compete with that at the Four Seasons, but it's good and reliable. Some of the appetizers are those 1950s favorites: green-pepper soup or shrimp cocktail. For a main course, you can order a 12-ounce New York strip steak or charcoal-grilled filet mignon with a mushroom sauce. The grilled Caribbean lobster is also appealing, as is the jerk pork. Main dishes are served with fresh vegetables of the day and your choice of a twice-baked potato, rice, or pasta. Few leave hungry, especially after finishing with Old Manor's cheesecake, which has been sampled by all the movers and shakers on the island. The ginger pudding is also recommended.

In the Old Manor Estate, Gingerland. ℂ 869/469-3445. Reservations recommended, especially for nonguests. Main courses US$19–US$33 (£9.90–£17). AE, MC, V. Daily 8am–3pm and 6:30–9:15pm.

Oualie Beach Hotel INTERNATIONAL/NEVISIAN

This restaurant is the centerpiece of the Oualie Beach Hotel (see above), the only lodging adjacent to Oualie Beach. The airy building contains a bar area and a screened-in veranda just a few steps from the ocean. Every day the chef prepares a creative menu with real Caribbean flair, so you may want to study it closely before ordering. The pleasant staff can also make recommendations. The chef prepares several lobster dishes, and the Creole conch stew is the island's best. Pastas appear frequently, along with some fairly bland international dishes such as chicken breast with rice, fries, or salad. Special nights are Tuesday, which features a barbecue surf-and-turf buffet along with a live band; Friday and Saturday nights with another band; and Super Sunday (the last Sunday of the month) with steel pan music and beach activities such as the greasy pole. An array of brightly colored rum drinks is available, and you can get a reasonably priced breakfast or lunch here, too.

In the Oualie Beach Hotel. ℂ 869/469-9735. Reservations required for dinner. Breakfast US$6–US$12 (£3.10–£6.25); lunch US$10–US$15 (£5.20–£7.80); dinner main courses US$19–US$26 (£9.90–£14). Tuesday night buffet US$45 (£23). AE, MC, V. Daily 7–10am, noon–3pm, and 6:30–9:30pm.

INEXPENSIVE

Le Bistro INTERNATIONAL

This is one of the tiniest restaurants on island, but its Friday-night happy hour makes it the most popular. Locals call this place "Matt's," for Matt Lloyd, who sharpened his skills cooking at Montpelier. All the dishes are familiar but full of flavor, including the ground beef lasagna, coconut chicken, and the spicy curried chicken. In the British tradition, you can also order fish and chips. A savory kettle of mussels flavored with lemon butter is another good choice. The fish is especially recommended, as Matt catches them himself in his boat, *Deep Venture*. The chef's specialty is lobster served in a coconut sauce.

Chapel St. (©) 869/469-5110. Reservations recommended. Main courses EC$18–EC$40 (US$6.65–US$15/£3.45–£7.70). AE, MC, V. Daily 10am–3pm and 6–10pm.

Caribbean Kitchen *Value* ENGLISH/CREOLE   Most of the business within this cozy and very local restaurant transpires on the big concrete patio in front, where battered chairs and a large bar seem to satisfy the alchohol-fueled chill-out cravings of much of the downtown area's commercial zone. Don't expect a street number here, as there aren't any: You'll find the place because of its location immediately adjacent to the **Panache Gift Shop** (© 869/469-7382), a purveyor of cut glass and crystal from Eastern Europe, that's under the same management. And if you want, you can migrate into this restaurant's concrete-block interior, where white walls, white curtains, and photos and paintings of Caribbean landscapes add tropical touches. Anglo-Jamaican owner Peter James and his St-Kitts-born wife, Jean, are the owners of this place, dispensing a mixture of Anglo-Caribbean food that includes homemade soups (vegetable, mutton, or fish soups are usually on the menu); hot and spicy chicken; stewed creole-style chicken (in a tomato-pepper-and-onion base); and escovitch of the day made from "potfish," which in this case means whatever fresh fish arrived that morning from local fishermen. You'll be happiest here, frankly, if you don't expect *haute* designer cuisine, but it's all in good fun, and you'll never know who you'll be likely to meet or the gossip you're likely to hear.

Prince William Street (without number), Charlestown. (©) 869/469-0572. Reservations not necessary. Lunch main courses EC$25–EC$40 (US$9.25–US$15/£4.80–£7.70); dinner main courses EC$30–EC$50 (US$11–US$19/£5.75–£9.60). MC, V. Mon–Thurs 8am–5pm; Fri 8am–10pm; Sat 9am–10pm.

The Gallipot CARIBBEAN   The oldest part of this yellow-and-blue wood-sided building dates from 1960: the newer parts were added by British expatriates Julian and Tracy Rigby, who had sailed around the Caribbean for a while before establishing this place within a palm grove. Today, within a roofed-over but open-to-the-breezes beachfront venue that includes lots of lattices and a sophisticated wine list, you'll find a dining room that's often completely full on the 4 nights a week that they're open. Celebrities might be discreetly in attendance, including frequent visits from Meryl Streep, who owns a private house in the nearby hills. Menu items feature a wide variety of fish that's smoked in-house according to whatever comes in fresh that week. Angus steaks, some of the best on Nevis, arrive regularly from the U.S. and are prepared any way you want them. There's also a selection of curries, beef, chicken, and vegetarian. Desserts made fresh daily include tiramisu, mocha-chocolate torte, pastries, and cheesecakes. The restaurant's name, incidentally, is a corruption of a word the Rigby's developed during their years as yachtspeople, "The Galley Pot."

Tamarind Bay, Charlestown. (©) 869/469-8230. Reservations recommended for dinner. Lunch main courses EC$25–EC$35 (US$9.25–US$13/£4.80–£6.75); dinner main courses EC$35–EC$70 (US$13–US$26/£6.75–£14). AE, MC, V. Thurs–Sun noon–2:30pm; Thurs–Sat 6–9pm. Closed: July–Oct.

Pizza Beach INTERNATIONAL   This open-air restaurant on the water, housed in a concrete-block building with cathedral ceilings, is part of the Mount Nevis Beach Club. From the deck, you can take in a panoramic sea view. The informal cuisine is usually prepared with flair by the hardworking chef. Examples are a roster of meal-size pizzas big enough for two (try the one with seafood) as well as chicken parmigiana with pasta, shrimp with salsa verde, and Mexican platters piled high with quesadillas, tacos, flautas, and spicy beef. The best way to begin a meal is with one of the colorful margaritas.

Newcastle Marina, Charlestown. (€) **869/469-9395.** Reservations recommended for large groups. Main courses EC$20–EC$50 (US$7.40–US$19/£3.85–£9.60); pizzas for 2 EC$40–EC$60 (US$15–US$22/£7.70–£12). AE, MC, V. Thurs–Tues 6–10pm.

BEACHES

There are several fabulous public beaches on the island as well. The best one—in fact, one of the best in the Caribbean—is the reef-protected **Pinney's Beach** ★★, which has crystal-clear water, golden sands, and a gradual slope. It's no accident that the Four Seasons chose this location for its chic and superexpensive Nevis resort. Beaches are public on Nevis and hotels are forbidden to restrict access. However, hotels can protect their private grounds from trespassers.

Pinney's is just a short walk north of Charlestown on the west coast. You'll have 5km (3 miles) of sand (often virtually to yourself) that culminates in a sleepy lagoon, set against a backdrop of coconut palms. It's almost never crowded, and its calm, shallow waters are perfect for swimming and wading, which makes it a family favorite. It's best to bring your own sports equipment; the hotels along this beach have only limited gear that may be in use by its guests. You can go snorkeling or scuba diving here among damselfish, tangs, grunts, blue-headed wrasses, parrot fish, and other species. The beach is especially beautiful in the late afternoon, when flocks of cattle egrets fly into its north end to roost at the freshwater pond at **Nelson's Spring.**

If you're going to be around for a few days you might want to search out the other beaches as well, notably beige-sand **Oualie Beach,** known especially for its diving and snorkeling. The location is north of Pinney's and just south of Mosquito Bay. The beach is well maintained and rarely crowded; you can purchase food and drink, as well as rent watersports equipment, at the Oualie Beach Hotel.

Indian Castle Beach, at the southern end of Nevis, has active surf and a swath of fine-gray sand. Indian Castle is definitely for escapists—chances are you'll have the beach all to yourself except for an indigenous goat or two, who may be very social and interested in sharing your picnic lunch.

Newcastle Beach is by the Nisbet Plantation, at the northernmost tip of the island on the channel that separates St. Kitts and Nevis. Snorkelers flock to this strip of soft, beige sand set against a backdrop of coconut palms.

The beaches along the east coast aren't desirable. They front Long Haul Bay in the north and White Bay in the south. These bays spill into the Atlantic Ocean and are rocky and too rough for swimming, although they're rather dramatic to visit if you're sightseeing. Of them all, **White Bay Beach** (sometimes called Windward Beach), in the southeastern section, east of Gingerland, is the best (especially for surfers). But be careful, as the waters can become turbulent suddenly.

SPORTS & OTHER OUTDOOR PURSUITS

BOATING   Scuba Safaris, an outfit that operates independently on the premises of the Oualie Beach Hotel (€) **869/469-9518;** www.scubanevis.com), offers boat charters to Turtle Beach, which can make for a great day's outing; it costs US$60 (£31) round-trip (minimum of four people). Although it gives preference to guests of the

Four Seasons, another good boat outfitter is **Leeward Island Charters** (© 869/465-8494). The captain, Lennox, also built the boat, a 49-foot catamaran called *Caona.* A typical cruise is across the 2-mile passage to St. Kitts, where the snorkeling is better than it is on the western side of Nevis.

FISHING **Nevis Water Sports** (© 869/469-9060; www.fishnevis.com) offers the best deep-sea fishing aboard its custom 9m (30-ft.) fishing boat. The boat holds up to six; a 4-hour trip costs US$400 (£208), while an 8-hour trip is US$800 (£416). Snorkeling trips are available for US$45 (£23) per person, including equipment.

GOLF The **Four Seasons Golf Course** ★★★, Pinney's Beach (© 869/469-1111), has one of the most challenging and visually dramatic golf courses in the world. Designed by Robert Trent Jones, Jr. (who called it "the most scenic golf course I've ever designed"), this 18-hole championship course wraps around the resort and offers panoramic ocean and mountain views at every turn. From the first tee (which begins just steps from the sports pavilion), through the 660-yard, par-5 18th green at the ocean's edge, the course is, in the words of one avid golfer, "reason enough to go to Nevis." Nonguests of the hotel pay US$195 (£101) for 18 holes. Rental clubs are available at US$35 (£18) for 9 holes, or US$65 (£34) for 18 holes.

HIKING & MOUNTAIN CLIMBING Hikers can climb **Mount Nevis,** 970m (3,182 ft.) up to the extinct volcanic crater, and enjoy a trek to the rainforest to watch for wild monkeys. This hike is strenuous and is recommended only for those in good shape. Ask your hotel to pack a picnic lunch and arrange a guide (who will charge about US$35/£18 per person). The hike takes about 5 hours; at the summit you'll be rewarded with views of Antigua, Saba, Statia, St. Kitts, Guadeloupe, and Montserrat. Reaching the summit means scrambling up near-vertical sections of the trail requiring handholds on not-always-reliable vines and roots. It's definitely not for acrophobes! Information on guides can also be obtained at the **Nevis Historical and Conservation Society,** based at the Museum of Nevis History, Main Street, Charlestown (© 869/469-5786; www.nevis-nhcs.org). **Sunrise Tours,** Gingerland (© 869/469-2758; www.nevisnaturetours.com), is run by a husband-and-wife team, Lynell and Earla Liburd, who offers an unusual assortment of hikes, not just the usual climbs around the slopes of Mount Nevis. They'll take you to little-known areas such as Devil's Copper, New River Spring, and three magnificent waterfalls. Rainforest and hidden ruins are also part of their hikes, which also include trips to rarely visited local villages.

SCUBA DIVING & SNORKELING Some of the best dive sites on Nevis include **Monkey Shoals,** 3km (2 miles) west of the Four Seasons. This is a beautiful reef, starting at 12m (39 ft.), with dives up to 30m (100 ft.) in depth. Angelfish, turtles, nurse sharks, and extensive soft coral can be found here. **The Caves** are on the south tip of Nevis, a 20-minute boat ride from the Four Seasons. A series of coral grottoes with numerous squirrelfish, turtles, and needlefish make this ideal for both certified and resort divers. **Champagne Garden,** a 5-minute boat ride from the Four Seasons, gets its name from bubbles created from an underwater sulfur vent. Because of the warm water temperature, large numbers of tropical fish are found here. Finally, **Coral Garden,** 3km (2 miles) west of the Four Seasons, is another beautiful coral reef with schools of Atlantic spadefish and large sea fans. The reef is at a maximum depth of 21m (69 ft.) and is suitable for both certified and resort divers.

Snorkelers should head for Pinney's Beach. You might also try the waters of Fort Ashby, where the settlement of Jamestown is said to have slid into the sea; legend has it that the church bells can still be heard, and the underwater town can still be seen when conditions are just right. So far, no diver, to our knowledge, has ever found the conditions just right.

Scuba Safaris, Oualie Beach (© **869/469-9518;** www.scubanevis.com), on the island's north end, offers PADI scuba diving and snorkeling in an area rich in dive sites. It also offers resort and certification courses, dive packages, and equipment rental. A one-tank scuba dive costs US$65 (£34); a two-tank dive, US$95 (£50). Full certification courses cost US$450 (£234) per person. Snorkeling trips cost US$45 (£23) per person (minimum of four people).

TENNIS   There are no public courts on Nevis. Guests at the big hotels play on their courts for free. Nonguests can play on the courts at the **Hermitage Plantation** (© **869/ 469-3477**) for US$15 (£7.80) per hour.

WINDSURFING   The waters here are often ideal for this sport, especially for beginners and intermediates. **Windsurfing Nevis** at the Oualie Beach Hotel (© **869/ 469-9682**) offers the best equipment, costing US$20 (£10) for 1 hour.

EXPLORING THE ISLAND

It's a good idea to negotiate with a taxi driver to take you around Nevis. The distance is only 58km (36 miles), but you may find yourself taking a long time if you stop to see specific sights and talk to all the people who will want to chat with you. A 3-hour sightseeing tour around the island will cost US$65 (£34); the average taxi holds up to four people. No sightseeing bus companies operate on Nevis, but a number of individuals own buses that they use for taxi service. Call **Nevis Taxi Service** (© **869/ 469-5631**) for information.

The major attraction is the **Museum of Nevis History,** in the house where Alexander Hamilton was born, on Main Street in Charlestown (© **869/469-5786;** www. nevis-nhcs.org), overlooking the bay. The lava-stone house by the shore has been restored. The museum, dedicated to the history and culture of Nevis, houses the island's archives. Hours are Monday to Friday from 9am to 4pm, Saturday from 9am to noon. Admission is US$5 (£2.60) for adults, US$2 (£1.05) for children.

Eden Brown Estate, East Coast Rd. about 2km (1¼ miles) from New River, is said to be haunted. It was once the home of a wealthy planter whose daughter was to be married, but her husband-to-be was killed in a duel at the prenuptial feast. The mansion was then closed forever and left to the ravages of nature. Only the most adventurous come here on a moonlit night.

At one time, Sephardic Jews from Brazil made up a quarter of the island's population, and it's believed that Jews introduced sugar production to the Leeward Islands. Outside the center of Charlestown, at the lower end of Government Road, the **Jewish Cemetery** has been restored and is the resting place of many of the early shopkeepers of Nevis. Most of the tombstones date from 1690 to 1710.

One of the island's best attractions is the 4-hectare (10-acre) **Botanical Garden of Nevis** (© **869/469-3509;** www.botanicalgardennevis.com), 5km (3 miles) south of Charlestown on the Montpelier Estate. Rainforest plants grow in re-created Mayan ruins on a hillside site overlooking the Caribbean. A retired Philadelphia businessman, Joseph Murphy, has spent some US$8 million on these gardens, containing, among other treasures of nature, 100 species of palms from Madagascar, Asia, and Hawaii, along with 70 varieties of orchids. In the Kew Gardens–like greenhouse, you can see rainforest flora and waterfalls. The on-site restaurant, **Martha's Tea House,** serves an English tea with scones and double Devon cream. You can also order a ploughman's lunch (French bread, pickled onions, and cheese), barbecue chicken breast, mahimahi, or tuna salad. If you patronize the restaurant or gift shop, you don't have to pay the admission of US$10 (£5.20) adults, US$7 (£3.65) children ages 6 to 12, free children under 6, to the gardens. The garden is open Monday to Friday from 9am to 4pm.

Nevis Jockey Club organizes and sponsors thoroughbred races every month. Local horses as well as some brought over from other islands fill out a typical five-race card. If you want to have a glimpse at what horse racing must have been like a century or more ago, you'll find the Nevis races a memorable experience. For information, contact Richard Lupinacci, a Jockey Club officer and owner and operator of the Hermitage Plantation (© **869/469-3477**).

Father Gill's Nevisian Heritage Village (© **869/469-5521**), is a collection of historic structures moved to this site, with an old sugar mill as its centerpiece. Among the attractions are a blacksmith's workshop, a rum store, and a cobbler's outpost, along with replicas of buildings ranging from African-styled slave huts to thatched shelters once inhabited by the Caribs. The village is open Monday to Saturday 9am to 3:30pm, charging an admission of EC$8 (US$2.95/£1.55).

SHOPPING

For original art, visit **Eva Wilkin Gallery,** Clay Ghaut, Gingerland (© **869/469-2673**). Wilkin was the island's most famous artist; even Prince Charles showed up to look at her work. Until her death in 1989, she painted island people, local flowers, and scenes of Nevis life. Prints are available in some of the local shops, but originals sell for US$100 (£52) and up. You can visit her former atelier, on the grounds of an old sugar-mill plantation near Montpelier.

In a stone building about 60m (200 ft.) from the wharf, near the marketplace, **Nevis Handicraft Cooperative Society,** Cotton House, Charlestown (© **869/469-1746**), contains locally made gift items, including unusual objects of goatskin, local wines made from a variety of fruits grown on the island, hot-pepper sauce, guava cheese, jams, and jellies.

Hand-painted, tie-dyed, and batik clothing are featured at **Island Hopper,** in the TDC Shopping Mall, Main Street, Charlestown (© **869/469-0893**), which also has locations on St. Kitts and Antigua. From beach wraps to souvenirs, a wide selection of products is available.

Island Fever, Main Street in Charlestown (© **869/469-9613**), has a tasteful and varied selection of items that might range from puppets and batiks from Indonesia to caftans, informal ware, steel drums, painted fish, or handmade jewelry. It's closed in September.

Those interested in stamp collecting can see a wide range of colorful stamps at the **Nevis Philatelic Bureau,** Head Post Office, Market Street (next to the public market), Charlestown (© **869/469-5535**). It features butterflies, shells, birds, flowers, and fish.

A craftsperson worthy of mention is Kennedy Tyrell (© **869/469-3442**), who sells handcarved wooden figures of monkeys, birds, pineapples, and other objects from his workshop along the road in New River Estate on the eastern side of Nevis.

NEVIS AFTER DARK

Nightlife is not the reason to visit Nevis. Summer nights are quiet, but there's organized entertainment in winter, often steel bands performing at the major hotels.

Most action takes place at the **Four Seasons Resort,** Pinney's Beach (© **869/469-1111**), on Friday and Saturday nights.

Oualie Beach Hotel, Oualie Beach (© **869/469-9735**), offers a live string band entertaining guests.

If you're on Nevis on a Friday night, the place to be for happy hour (4–6pm) is **Le Bistro** (p. 561). Islanders flock here for the reduced drink prices, the good company, and the fun atmosphere.

Another Friday night "jump-up" is at **The Water Department Barbecue,** Pump Road, Charlestown (no phone), to help raise money for the department. Tents go up in the late afternoon and meat goes on the grill. Some of the best barbecue chicken and ribs on island are served here.

Wednesday night is all the rage at **Eddy's Bar & Restaurant,** Main Street in Charlestown (© **869/469-5958**), which serves the best conch fritters in town. Karaoke and dancing to music spun by an island DJ lasts way past midnight.

22

St. Lucia

St. Lucia (*Loo*-sha) is one of the most popular destinations in the Caribbean, with some of its finest resorts. The heaviest tourist development is concentrated in the northwest, between the capital, Castries, and the northern end of the island, where there's a string of white-sand beaches.

The rest of St. Lucia remains relatively unspoiled, a checkerboard of green-mantled mountains, valleys, banana plantations, a bubbling volcano, wild orchids, and fishing villages. The island has a mixed French and British heritage, but there's a hint of the South Pacific about it as well.

A mountainous island of some 623 sq. km (243 sq. miles), St. Lucia has about 160,000 inhabitants. The capital, Castries, is built on the southern shore of a large harbor surrounded by hills.

Writer Derek Walcott was born in Castries. His father was an unpublished poet who died when Walcott was just a year old, and his mother was a former headmistress at the Methodist school on St. Lucia. In 1992, Walcott won the Nobel Prize for literature. He prefers, however, not to tout the charms of St. Lucia, telling the press, "I don't want everyone to go there and overrun the place." Alas, his warning has come too late.

Rising out of the relative obscurity in which it languished for most of the 20th century, St. Lucia is becoming—post-millennium—one of the biggest players in Caribbean tourism. Since the dawn of the new century, *World Travel Awards* has named it "the world's leading honeymoon destination." Local authorities estimate that 36% of the island's business comes from visitors either getting married or else on a honeymoon here. At the same time, *Natural History Magazine* has honored St. Lucia as one of the 50 top ecotourism destinations in the world.

1 Essentials

VISITOR INFORMATION

In the **United States,** the St. Lucia Tourist Board office is located at 800 Second Ave., Suite 910, New York, NY 10017 (© **800/456-3984** or 212/867-2950). In **Canada,** information is provided at the tourist board at 8 King St. East, Suite 709, Toronto, ON M5C 1B5 (© **416/362-4242**).

On the island, the main tourist office is at Sureline Building, Vive Boutielle, Castries (© **758/452-4094**). In **Soufrière,** there's a branch on Bay Street (© **758/ 459-7419**). St. Lucia information is on the Web at **www.stlucia.org**.

GETTING THERE

Before you book your own airfare, read the section "Packages for the Independent Traveler," in chapter 2—it can save you a bundle.

The island maintains two separate airports, whose different locations cause endless confusion to many newcomers. Most international long-distance flights land at

St. Lucia

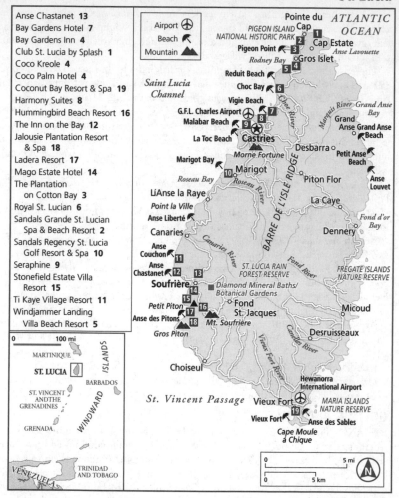

Anse Chastanet **13**
Bay Gardens Hotel **7**
Bay Gardens Inn **4**
Club St. Lucia by Splash **1**
Coco Kreole **4**
Coco Palm Hotel **4**
Coconut Bay Resort & Spa **19**
Harmony Suites **8**
Hummingbird Beach Resort **16**
The Inn on the Bay **12**
Jalousie Plantation Resort
& Spa **18**
Ladera Resort **17**
Mago Estate Hotel **14**
The Plantation
on Cotton Bay **3**
Royal St. Lucian **6**
Sandals Grande St. Lucian
Spa & Beach Resort **2**
Sandals Regency St. Lucia
Golf Resort & Spa **10**
Seraphine **9**
Stonefield Estate Villa
Resort **15**
Ti Kaye Village Resort **11**
Windjammer Landing
Villa Beach Resort **5**

Hewanorra International Airport (© **758/454-6355**) in the south, 72km (45 miles) from Castries. If you arrive here and you're booked into a hotel in the north, you'll spend about an hour and a half traveling along the potholed East Coast Highway. Many hotels arrange transfers to and from the airport, but if not, taxis are available; the average fare is US$65 (£34) for up to four passengers. Many visitors now prefer to take helicopter flights from Hewanorra International Airport to their resorts rather than endure the long, stomach-churning car ride. **St. Lucia Helicopters** (© **758/453-6950;** www.stluciahelicopters.com) offers flights between Castries and Hewanorra Airport or Soufrière, costing US$105 (£55) per person one-way. Flights can also be arranged to the Jalousie Plantation (p. 574), which has its own helicopter pad.

Flights from other parts of the Caribbean usually land at the smaller, somewhat antiquated **George F. L. Charles Airport** (formerly known as Vigie; © **758/452-1156**), in the northeast. Its location just outside Castries affords much more convenient access to the capital and many of the island's hotels. It is a long (about an hour and a half) twisting drive to lodging in and around Soufrière, but you'll pass through beautiful terrain and quaint fishing villages along the way.

There are now nonstop flights from the United States to St. Lucia. **Delta** (© 800/221-1212; www.delta.com) flies once daily from Friday to Tuesday from Atlanta; and **American** (© 800/433-7300; www.aa.com) flies daily from Miami to the island.

American Eagle (© 800/433-7300 in the U.S. and Canada, or 758/452-1820; www.aa.com) serves George F. L. Charles Airport with nonstop flights from San Juan. Connections from all parts of the North American mainland to the airline's enormous hub in San Juan are frequent and convenient. American also offers some good package deals.

US Airways (© 800/428-4322; www.usairways.com) flies two times a week from Philadelphia to St. Lucia's Hewanorra Airport.

Air Canada (© 888/247-2262; www.aircanada.ca) has two nonstop weekly flights to St. Lucia's Hewanorra Airport that depart from Toronto.

British Airways (© 800/247-9297 in the U.S.; www.britishairways.com) offers two flights a week from London's Gatwick Airport to St. Lucia's Hewanorra Airport.

LIAT (© 758/452-3051; www.liatairline.com) has small planes flying from many points throughout the Caribbean into George F. L. Charles Airport. Points of origin include such islands as Barbados, Antigua, St. Thomas, St. Maarten, and Martinique. On some LIAT flights, you may visit all these islands before arriving in St. Lucia.

Air Jamaica (© 800/523-5585 in the U.S. and Canada; www.airjamaica.com) serves the Hewanorra Airport with nonstop service from New York's JFK 4 days a week.

Another option is **BWIA** (© 800/538-2942 in the U.S. and Canada; www.bwee.com), which offers two weekly flights on Sunday and Tuesday from London's Heathrow to St. Lucia's Hewanorra Airport. All flights make a quick stopover in Barbados.

GETTING AROUND

BY TAXI Since driving St. Lucia's unmarked, bad roads is rather difficult, a taxi is recommended for all but the most adventurous. Taxis are ubiquitous and most drivers are eager to please. The drivers have special training that allows them to serve as guides. Their cabs are unmetered, but the government fixes tariffs for all standard trips. From Castries, the fare to Marigot Bay should be US$25 to US$30 (£13–£16); to Rodney Bay, the fare is US$18 to US$20 (£9.35–£10). Always ask if the driver is quoting a rate in U.S. dollars or Eastern Caribbean dollars (EC$). For more information, call the **Taxi Associatino** at © 758/454-6136.

BY RENTAL CAR **Avis** (© 800/331-1212 in the U.S. and Canada, or 758/452-2046 or 758/454-6325; www.avis.com), **Traders Auto Rentals** (© 758/452-0233), and **Hertz** (© 800/654-3131 in the U.S. and Canada, or 758/454-9636; www.hertz.com) have offices at (or will deliver cars to) both of the island's airports. Each also has an office in Castries and, in some cases, at some of the island's major hotels.

Avis' rates begin at US$82 (£43) per day, and Hertz's begin at US$91 (£47) per day. You can sometimes save money by booking through one of the local car-rental agencies, where rates begin at US$60 (£31) per day, depending on size. Try **C.T.L. Rent-a-Car,** Grosislet Highway, Rodney Bay Marina (© 758/452-0732). **Cool Breeze Car Rental,** New Development, Soufrière (© 758/459-7729), is also a good bet if you're staying in the south. Prices are US$50 (£26) and up.

Remember: Drive on the left, and try to avoid some of the island's more obvious potholes. Drive carefully and honk your horn while going around the blind hairpin turns. You'll need a St. Lucia driver's license ($20/£10), which you can purchase at either airport when you pick up your rental car.

BY BUS   **Minibuses** (with names like "Lucian Love") and **jitneys** connect Castries with such main towns as Soufrière for EC$7 (US$2.60/£1.40) and Vieux Fort EC$5 (US$1.85/£1). They're cheap but they're generally overcrowded and often filled with produce on its way to market. Buses for Cap Estate, in the northern part of the island, leave from Jeremy Street in Castries, near the market. Buses going to Vieux Fort and Soufrière depart from Bridge Street in front of the department store.

BY HELICOPTER   In addition to providing the fastest mode of transport on this island (preferred by such visitors as Harrison Ford), **St. Lucia Helicopters** (© 758/ 453-6950; www.stluciahelicopters.com) offers the island's most dramatic sightseeing. The 10-minute North Trip, costing US$70 (£36) per person, flies you over Castries, the major resort hotels, the elegant Cap Estate homes, Pigeon Point, Rodney Bay, Rat Island, and the more turbulent Atlantic coast. The longer 20-minute South Tour, costing US$120 (£62) per passenger, flies over Castries, the banana plantations, beautiful Marigot Bay, fishing villages, the lush rainforest, the Pitons, the Soufrière volcano, and even remote waterfalls, rivers, and lush valleys. Another tour, combining both the north and south, costs US$155 (£81) per person.

FAST FACTS: St. Lucia

Banks   Banks are open Monday to Thursday from 8am to 3pm, Friday from 8am to 5pm, and Saturday 8am to noon. **ATMs** can be found at all bank branches, transportation centers, and shopping malls.

Currency   The official monetary unit is the **Eastern Caribbean dollar (EC$)**, which is pegged at EC$2.70 per U.S. dollar (EC$1 = 37¢/20p). Nearly all hotels, restaurants, and shops accept U.S dollars. Always ascertain which dollar prices are listed. *Unless otherwise specified, prices in this chapter are quoted in U.S. dollars and British pounds.*

Customs   At either airport, Customs may be a hassle if there's the slightest suspicion, regardless of how ill-founded, that you're carrying illegal drugs.

Documents   U.S., British, and Canadian citizens need valid passports, plus an ongoing or return ticket.

Electricity   St. Lucia runs on 220- to 230-volt AC (50 cycles), so bring an adapter if you plan to use U.S. appliances. Some hotels are wired for U.S. appliances. Ask when you book.

Emergencies   Call the police at © 999. For an ambulance or in case of fire call © 911.

Hospitals   There are 24-hour emergency rooms at **St. Jude's Hospital,** Vieux Fort (© 758/454-6041), and **Victoria Hospital,** Hospital Road, Castries (© 758/452-2421).

Language   English is the official tongue, but islanders often speak a French-Creole patois similar to that heard on Martinique.

Pharmacies The best is **M&C Drugstore,** Bridge Street, in Castries (© **758/458-8146**), open Monday to Friday 8am to 5pm, and Saturday 8am to 1pm.

Safety St. Lucia has its share of crime, like every other place these days. Use common sense and protect yourself and your valuables. If you've got it, don't flaunt it! Don't pick up hitchhikers if you're driving around the island. The use of narcotic drugs is illegal, and their possession or sale could lead to stiff fines or jail.

Taxes The government imposes an 8% occupancy tax on hotel rooms, and there's a US$21 (£10) departure tax for both airports. Children under 12 don't pay departure tax.

Telephone The area code for St. Lucia is **758**. Make calls to or from St. Lucia just as you would with any other area code in North America. On the island, dial all seven digits of the local number. If your hotel won't send a fax for you, try **Cable & Wireless,** in the SMC Building on the waterfront in Castries (© **758/453-9922**). To access **AT&T Direct,** call © **800/225-5288**; to reach **MCI,** dial © **800/888-8000**.

Time St. Lucia is on Atlantic Standard Time year-round, placing it 1 hour ahead of New York. However, when the United States is on daylight saving time, St. Lucia matches the clocks of the U.S. East Coast.

Tipping Most hotels and restaurants add a 10% service charge. (Ask if it's been included in the initial hotel rate you're quoted.) If you're pleased with the service in a restaurant, by all means, supplement with an extra 5%. Taxi drivers expect 10% of the fare.

Water Water here is generally considered safe to drink; if you're unsure or have a delicate constitution, stick to bottled water.

Weather This little island, lying in the path of the trade winds, has year-round temperatures of 70°F to 90°F (21°C–32°C).

2 Accommodations

Most of the leading hotels on this island are pretty pricey; you have to really search for the bargains. However, many of the big resorts here are frequently featured in packages (see the section "Packages for the Independent Traveler," in chapter 2). Once you reach your hotel, chances are you'll feel pretty isolated, which is exactly what most guests want. Many St. Lucian hostelries have kitchenettes where you can prepare simple meals. Prices are usually quoted in U.S. dollars. An 8% hotel tax is added to your bill. Most hotels also add a 10% service charge. (Ask if it's been included in the initial hotel rate you're quoted.)

VERY EXPENSIVE

Anse Chastanet ✹✹✹   One of the few places that merits the cliché "tropical paradise," this is not only St. Lucia's premier dive resort, but also an exceptional Caribbean inn. It offers warm service, excellent food, a beach location, and first-class facilities. It lies 29km (18 miles) north of Hewanorra International Airport (a 50-min. taxi ride), 3km (2 miles) north of Soufrière on a forested hill, and a 103-step climb above palm-fringed Anse Chastanet Beach. The main building—surrounded by coffee trees, mangos, papayas, banana plants, breadfruit, grapefruit, coconut palms, and hibiscus—is decorated in a typical island style, with a relaxing bar and dining room. Guests can book first-rate spa treatments at the on-site Kai Belte Spa.

Guests can stay on the beach in spacious accommodations styled like West Indian plantation villas. Other units, constructed like octagonal gazebos and cooled by ceiling fans, have views of the Pitons. The large rooms are comfortably appointed with locally made furniture crafted from island woods. They have tropical hardwood floors, wooden jalousie louvers, king-size beds, and roomy private bathrooms with shower stalls and dual sinks. The cluster of suites has its own concierge desk and a communication room with phones and computers. A freshwater pool is found on the resort's 18th-century French Colonial plantation, along the Jungle Biking trail. Late in 2005, the resort opened two dozen exclusive "infinity suites." These form a "resort within a resort," with their own reception area, concierge services, and the Jade Mountain Club restaurant. Located at the highest point on Anse Chastanet Hill, every suite has a personal "infinity pool." Rooms have only three walls to allow for an unobstructed view of the Pitons and the Caribbean.

You can dine or drink on a wind-cooled terrace, built like a tree house over the tropical landscape, in the Pitons Bar and Restaurant. Even if you're not a guest of the hotel, consider stopping at the beachside restaurant, Trou au Diable, which offers West Indian cuisine and a grill, plus a twice-weekly Creole dinner buffet. The resort's excellent staff has few equals in the Caribbean.

Anse Chastanet Beach (P.O. Box 7000), Soufrière, St. Lucia, W.I. © **800/223-1108** in the U.S., or 758/459-7000. Fax 758/459-7700. www.ansechastanet.com. 49 units. Winter US$405–US$665 (£211–£346) double, from US$775 (£403) suite; off season US$265–US$465 (£138–£242) double, US$575 (£299) suite. Winter rates include breakfast and dinner. AE, MC, V. **Amenities:** 2 restaurants; 2 bars; outdoor pool; tennis court; gym; spa; dive shop; kayaks; sailboat rentals; snorkeling; windsurfing; bikes; airport transfers; laundry service; nonsmoking rooms. *In room:* Ceiling fan, minibar, fridge, beverage maker, hair dryer, safe, no phone.

Coconut Bay Resort & Spa ✦✦✦ (Kids)
On the southern shore, on the site of a now defunct Club Med, and close to Hewanorra Airport, this sprawling oceanfront resort has burst on the scene with a splash. Splash is the right word, as this all-inclusive features a water park with two 4-story high waterslides, and even an activity pool with massage jets and waterfalls. Not only that, but a lazy 230m (750-ft.) stream runs sleepily through the property.

Unlike some resorts, Coconut Bay welcomes singles, couples (of all persuasions), and families. When not frolicking in the water park, you can take your vows in an Oceanside gazebo, or else enjoy oceanfront treatment rooms, even water aerobics. This is not a sleepy retreat: there is an array of constant activities, including nightly entertainment from local bands.

Spanning 34 lushly planted hectares (85 acres), Coconut Bay is aptly named, as it is fringed with coconut palms, opening onto Savannes Bay. Rooms are among the finest on island, each with at least a partial ocean view (those on the fourth floor have unobstructed vistas). Units come with separate sitting areas and a private balcony. The cuisine is among the most varied on island, including Asian and Italian specialties and buffets for three meals a day. There's even a beachside grill, and tropical drinks and fruit juices are served all over the property, even at a swim-up bar.

Vieux Fort, St. Lucia, W.I. © **758/459-6000.** Fax 758/456-9900. www.coconutbayresortandspa.com. 254 units. Winter US$380–US$610 (£198–£317) double; off season US$310–US$470 (£161–£244) double. Extra adult US$100 (£52); extra child under 18 US$55–US$75 (£29–£39). Rates are inclusive. AE, DC, MC, V. **Amenities:** 3 restaurants; 4

bars; 3 outdoor pools; water park; 4 tennis courts; fitness center; spa; children's activity center; evening entertainment and theme nights; dance club. *In room:* A/C, TV, dataport (in some), beverage makers (in some), hair dryer, iron, safe.

Jalousie Plantation Resort & Spa ★★★   This unusual and elegant resort is for visitors to St. Lucia's southwest coast who are looking for privacy, a sense of isolation, and greater degrees of luxury than what's available at Ladera or Anse Chastanet. It originated in the late 1990s, when an already-existing hotel, positioned on the fertile tropical plain midway between the two Pitons, was radically upgraded with an infusion of more than US$6 million in cash. Sprawling across one of the best building sites in St. Lucia, the property is so large (130 hectares/321 acres) that vans constantly circulate to shuttle guests around. Most of the resort's accommodations are in individual villas or villa suites (slightly larger, with separate sitting rooms) that dot the hillside. All the tile-floored villa rooms have four-star luxuries, including remote-controlled air-conditioning, foldout sofas, and tub/shower combinations. All villas and suites also have private plunge pools. Our only complaint is that the degree of privacy is not always enough to allow, say, nude sunbathing. In addition to the villas, 12 Sugar Mill double rooms are in two buildings; they're slightly smaller than the other rooms, but they still have private terraces. The staff here is especially friendly and helpful.

The chef's inventive cuisine is ambitious but best when it concentrates on flavorful, local ingredients.

P.O. Box 251, Soufrière, St. Lucia, W.I. Ⓒ **800/544-2883** in the U.S. for reservations only, or 758/456-8000. Fax 758/459-7667. www.jalousieplantation.com. 112 units. Winter US$450–US$505 (£234–£263) double, US$570–US$605 (£296–£315) suite; off season US$230–US$295 (£120–£153) double, US$360–US$395 (£187–£205) suite. MAP (breakfast and dinner) US$75 (£39) per person extra. Honeymoon, dive, and spa packages available. AE, MC, V. Small pets allowed. **Amenities:** 2 restaurants; 4 bars; outdoor pool; par-3 executive golf course; 4 lit Laykold tennis courts; health club; squash court; spa; fitness classes; Jacuzzi; sauna; dive shop; fishing; scuba diving; snorkeling; water-skiing; children's programs; tour desk; car rental; business center; salon; 24-hr. room service; babysitting; laundry service; dry cleaning; nonsmoking rooms; night club. *In room:* A/C, TV/VCR, dataport, minibar, beverage maker, hair dryer, iron, safe, bathrobes.

Ladera Resort ★★★   The Ladera is an exercise in luxurious simplicity on St. Lucia's southwest end, frequently a retreat for the rich and famous who seek total privacy from the outside world: There are no phones or TVs in the rooms. Outside the town of Soufrière, this hideaway is perched on a hillside 330m (1,080 ft.) above sea level. Sandwiched between the Pitons, the resort has views of Jalousie Bay—perhaps the most stunning vistas you'll find on St. Lucia. The villas and suites are completely open to the views of the Pitons. You don't come here for the beach—it's a 15- to 20-minute complimentary shuttle ride away—but for the lovely setting, gracious service, and privacy. Ladera's new spa, Ti Kai Pose, was recently added to the premises with a full-line of spa treatments to help you further relax.

Accommodations are constructed of tropical hardwoods, stone, and tile, and are furnished with 19th-century French furniture, wicker, and accessories built by local craftspeople. You'll find interesting touches in all the rooms: sinks made of shells, or open, rock-walled showers. All units afford total privacy and have indoor gardens and plunge pools, plus showers. Many rooms have four-poster queen-size beds draped in mosquito netting, and all have fridges. Breezes cool the rooms, which are not air-conditioned. To get a room here in the winter, reserve 4 months in advance. We're not kidding.

The Dasheene Restaurant & Bar offers fine dining and specializes in Creole and Continental cuisine. The seafood is caught fresh daily. Guests enjoy high tea in Ladera's botanical garden.

P.O. Box 225, Soufrière, St. Lucia, W.I. © 800/738-4752 in the U.S. and Canada, or 758/459-7323. Fax 758/459-5156. www.ladera-stlucia.com. 27 units. Winter US$495–US$740 (£257–£385) suite, US$980 (£510) 2-bedroom villa; off season US$310–US$560 (£161–£291) double, US$860 (£447) 2-bedroom villa. Extra person in villa US$100–US$125 (£52–£65). 7-night minimum Dec 23–29; 3-night minimum Jan 3–Apr 16. AE, MC, V. Closed mid-Sept to mid-Oct. **Amenities:** Restaurant; bar; outdoor pool; spa; fishing charters; sailing; scuba diving; snorkeling; horseback riding; shuttle service to the beach; limited room service; laundry service. *In room:* Fridge, beverage maker, hair dryer, safe, plunge pool, no phone.

The Plantation on Cotton Bay ★★ *Kids*

On the northeast of St. Lucia, 18km (11 miles) north of Castries, this property was launched in 2006, with a series of luxury suites, town houses, and villas. Some of its larger units are available with a pool cottage. Almost immediately it became one of the swankiest properties on island, attracting luxury-minded guests. Furnished in an eclectic style, the plantation features units with designer kitchens and living rooms, even state-of-the-art entertainment systems. Town houses or villas come with their own private pool and spa. The resort would be ideal for honeymooners, but also caters to children 3 to 14 with its Humming Bird Kids Club. Its Casuarina Spa and Fitness Center features an outdoor treatment gazebo and even a rooftop restaurant, Heaven. This facility features light lunches, but also a champagne and seafood bar. The cuisine is first rate with a varied menu so guests don't get bored eating all their meals on site. The main restaurant, with the curious name of 14° 61°, opens on the beach with entertainment nightly.

Cap Estate, Cotton Bay, St. Lucia, W.I. © 758/450-8551. Fax 758/450-8999. www.plantationoncottonbay.com. 74 units. Winter US$475–US$550 (£247–£286) double suite; from US$650 (£338) 2-bedroom suite; from US$1,225 3-bedroom townhouse. Off-season US$275–US$450 (£143–£234) double suite; from US$375 (£195) 2-bedroom suite; from US$950 (£494) 3-bedroom townhouse. AE, MC, V. **Amenities:** 2 restaurants; 2 bars; outdoor pool; private pool in villas; golf club privileges; fitness center; water sports; sunset catamaran cruises; kids' club; limited room service; massage; laundry service; nonsmoking rooms; rooms for those w/limited mobility. *In room:* A/C, TV, dataport, kitchen (in suites), beverage maker.

Royal St. Lucian ★★ *Kids*

A fine resort with a deluxe spa, the Royal St. Lucian lies north of Castries. Standing in its own gardens of royal palms and tropical foliage, it opens onto a dramatic lobby. All the accommodations are luxury suites, the best of which have sea views and balconies. There are eight even more spacious suites right at beachfront, each with a private terrace. Some of the units are split-level, with spacious bathrooms containing tubs and jet showers, cream-colored tile floors, rattan furniture, and woven rugs. Everywhere you look, the setting is lush. The food is among the best hotel cuisine on the island, and candlelit beach dinners are featured. The chefs are also known for West Indian and Italian buffets. Jazz can be heard in the chic cocktail lounge, and the spa offers everything from hydrotherapy to herbal body wraps.

Rodney Bay (P.O. Box 977), Castries, St. Lucia, W.I. © 800/255-5859 in the U.S., or 758/452-9999. Fax 758/452-9639. www.rexcaribbean.com. 96 units. Winter US$500–US$730 (£260–£382) double; off season US$390–US$630 (£203–£328) double. Children under 3 stay free in parent's room; children 3–12 US$30 (£16) extra per night (50% discount on meals). AE, DC, DISC, MC, V. **Amenities:** 3 restaurants; 2 bars; outdoor pool; 2 tennis courts; health club; fitness center; spa; sauna; dive shop; fishing; snorkeling; Sunfish sailboats; water-skiing; windsurfing; children's programs; business services; room service (7am–11pm); babysitting; laundry service/dry cleaning; rooms for those w/limited mobility. *In room:* A/C, TV, minibar, beverage maker (in some), hair dryer, safe.

Sandals Grande St. Lucian Spa & Beach Resort ★★★

The popular chain, Sandals, is leaving its footprints all over the sands of the island. In the summer of 2002, Jamaican hotelier Butch Stewart opened his third couples-only all-inclusive on St. Lucia. Its former policy of barring same-sex couples was rescinded in 2004. This one is the best Sandals of the lot. The luxury resort lies at the causeway on the northern tip of St. Lucia, linking the "mainland" with Pigeon Island, with the tranquil Caribbean Sea on one side and the often more turbulent Atlantic Ocean on the other side. Set on a landscaped 1-hectare (2½-acre) lagoon, the megaresort took over the already existing property of the Hyatt Regency, at a point 10km (6¼ miles) northwest of Castries at Rodney Bay. With a private golden sandy beach, the most lavish lagoon-style swimming pool on the island, a state-of-the-art spa, and a choice of restaurants, many find it hard to tear themselves away from the grounds.

Even the standard bedrooms are spacious, with antique reproductions in a plantation style. Local art brightens the walls, and the bathrooms are full and luxurious. The fourth-floor rooms have better views, service, and space, and are more comfortable overall. For the ultimate in luxury, ask for one of the two-dozen "swim-up" units with their own free-form pools and terraces. Inquire about the "stay at one, play at three" program where you stay at one Sandals and are able to use facilities at other properties as well.

Pigeon Island Causeway, Gros Islet, St. Lucia. W.I. © **800/726-3257** or 758/455-2000. Fax 758/455-2001. www.sandals. com. 193 units. Winter US$360–US$595 (£187–£309) double, from US$645 (£335) suite; off season US$345–US$545 (£180–£283) double, from US$630 (£328) suite. Rates are per person and all-inclusive. AE, DISC, MC, V. Children not accepted. **Amenities:** 6 restaurants; 6 bars; 5 outdoor pools; 4 whirlpools; night club; golf privileges; 4 tennis courts; health club; spa; fitness center; sauna; deep-sea fishing; dive shop; kayaks; sailing; snorkeling; water-skiing; windsurfing; airport shuttle; business services; limited room service; laundry service; nonsmoking rooms; rooms for those w/limited mobility. *In room:* A/C, TV, beverage maker, hair dryer, iron, safe.

Sandals Regency St. Lucia Golf Resort & Spa ⭓⭓   The Sandals chain opened this clone on a forested 85-hectare (210-acre) site that slopes steeply down to the sea. This is larger and more upscale than the Sandals Grande St. Lucian, but not as spiffy as the newest Sandals Grande St. Lucian Beach Resort. Catering to couples regardless of sexual preference, the hotel is near Castries, on the island's northwestern coast. The center of the resort is a gazebo-capped pool that incorporates two waterfalls, a swim-up bar, and a dining pavilion. Larger-than-expected guest rooms contain king-size four-poster beds with mahogany headboards, balconies or patios, and a pastel tropical decor. Bathrooms are spacious, with tub/shower combinations.

The resort's six restaurants are infinitely superior to the cuisine served at Sandals Grande St. Lucian (see above). The most upscale, La Toc, features French cuisine. Kimonos offers Japanese food cooked on a heated table top, teppanyaki style. The Arizona Restaurant, as befits its name, features the cuisine of the U.S. Southwest. After dark, guests gravitate to Jaime's, the nightclub/disco, or to Herbie's Piano Bar. Inquire about the "stay at one, play at three" program where you stay at one Sandals property but are able to use the other properties as well.

La Toc Rd. (P.O. Box 399), Castries, St. Lucia, W.I. © **800/726-3257** in the U.S. and Canada, or 758/452-3081. Fax 758/ 452-1012. www.sandals.com. 327 units. Winter US$360–US$510 (£187–£265) double, from US$550 (£286) suite; off season US$350–US$470 (£182–£244) double, from US$510 (£265) suite. All-inclusive rates per person. AE, DISC, MC, V. Children under 18 not allowed. **Amenities:** 7 restaurants; 10 bars (2 swim-up); 4 outdoor pools; 9-hole golf course; 5 lit tennis courts; health club; spa; 4 Jacuzzis; dive shop; kayaks; sailing; snorkeling; windsurfing; business services; salon; limited room service; massage; laundry service; night club. *In room:* A/C, TV, beverage maker, hair dryer, iron, safe.

EXPENSIVE

Club St. Lucia by Splash ⭓ *Kids*   Beefed up by a US$6-million renovation, this all-inclusive resort sits in Cap Estate on a 26-hectare (65-acre) site, with two beaches in the area. It's 13km (8 miles) north of George F. L. Charles Airport at the northern tip of the island. Very sports- and entertainment-oriented, with a well-organized children's club, the hotel opens onto a curved bay where smugglers used to bring in brandies,

cognacs, and cigars from Martinique. The club's core is a wooden building with decks overlooking a free-form pool. The accommodations are in simple bungalows scattered over landscaped grounds. Each features one king-size or two twin beds, air-conditioning and/or ceiling fans, and patios or terraces. Bathrooms have recently been upgraded, with makeup mirrors, marble vanities, and excellent tub/shower combinations.

The inclusive package is impressive, offering all meals, even snacks, along with unlimited beer, wine, and mixed drinks, both day and night. The food is standard resort fare, but you'll never go hungry. To break the monotony, guests are often transported to the Great House (p. 583), a restaurant at Cap Estate, where they receive a discount on meals.

Cap Estate (P.O. Box 915), St. Lucia, W.I. ℂ 877/927-7527 or 758/450-0551. Fax 758/450-0281. 372 units. Winter US$270–US$350 (£140–£182) double, from US$380 (£198) suite; off season US$270–US$330 (£140–£172) double, from US$310 (£161) suite. Rates are all-inclusive per person. AE, DC, MC, V. **Amenities:** 4 restaurants; 4 bars; 5 outdoor pools; 9 lit tennis courts; squash court; fitness center; kayaks; sailing; scuba lessons; snorkeling; water-skiing; windsurfing; children's club; airport shuttle; Internet cafe; babysitting; laundry service; dance club. In room: A/C, TV, beverage maker, hair dryer, safe.

Stonefield Estate Villa Resort ⋆ (Finds)

Nestled at the base of Petit Piton, this place is for escapists. In the southwestern part of the island, it stands on its own 10 hectares (24½ acres), complete with a nature trail and some of the island's most striking panoramas. Removed from the overrun resort areas, it lies near the little fishing village of Soufrière and close enough to the Jalousie Hilton that Stonefield guests can use the beach there, a free 5-minute shuttle ride away. The estate's plantation houses are surrounded by tropical greenery, and each of the cottages available for rent has its own character and privacy. The estate here has one of the island's oldest sites, a well-preserved petroglyph dating from pre-Columbian times. All the accommodations come with antiques, high ceilings, verandas, bedrooms, full bathrooms with intimate outdoor garden showers, and fully furnished kitchens. Villas range in size from one to three bedrooms.

Stonefield Villas (P.O. Box 228), Soufrière, St. Lucia, W.I. ℂ 758/459-7586. Fax 758/459-5550. www.stonefieldvillas. com. 20 units. Winter US$190–US$300 (£99–£156) 1-bedroom villa, US$260–US$500 (£135–£260) 2-bedroom villa, US$600–US$780 (£312–£406) 3-bedroom villa; off season US$140–US$250 (£73–£130) 1-bedroom villa, US$200–US$400 (£104–£208) 2-bedroom villa, US$400–US$550 (£208–£286) 3-bedroom villa. MC, V. **Amenities:** Restaurant; bar; outdoor pool; snorkeling; library; car rental; Internet service; babysitting; laundry service; nonsmoking rooms. In room: Ceiling fan, kitchen, beverage maker, iron, safe, no phone.

Ti Kaye Village Resort ⋆⋆

It's special, it's fun, and there's nothing like it on St. Lucia. An elite retreat, it sprawls across a cliff overlooking the Caribbean and evokes a little laid-back village. A hideaway for those seeking a tranquil getaway, it was designed by Wayne Brown, one of the founders of Anse Chastanet. Standing on over 6 hectares (16 acres) of lushly planted grounds, it offers beautifully furnished and comfortable bedrooms in individual cottages trimmed in gingerbread or else a dozen units in duplex cottages. Each of the accommodations comes with a spacious porch with a hammock. Bedrooms are furnished with four-posters along with a private open-air garden shower, and some have their own plunge pool. A wooden staircase, 166 steps down, leads to a secluded cove of white sands. An on-site restaurant, House of Food (Kai M'jame, in Creole patois) serves excellent fresh meals overlooking the sea.

Anse Cochon, St. Lucia, W.I. ℂ 758/456-8101. Fax 758/456-8105. www.tikaye.com. 33 units. Winter US$200–US$380 (£104–£198) double; off season US$160–US$300 (£83–£156) double. Rates include full breakfast. AE, DC, MC, V. **Amenities:** Restaurant; bar; outdoor pool; fitness center; kayaks; scuba diving; snorkeling; massage; laundry service. In room: A/C, fridge, beverage maker, hair dryer, safe.

Windjammer Landing Villa Beach Resort ★★★ *Kids*   Windjammer, set on 22 tropical hectares (60 acres) north of Reduit Beach, about a 15-minute drive from Castries, is a quiet, luxurious retreat, one of the most glamorous in the West Indies. The resort was designed with a vaguely Moorish motif, heavily influenced by Caribbean themes; tropical colors predominate. It's composed of a cluster of white villas climbing a forested hillside above a desirable beach. This is an all-suite/villa resort (the villas have private plunge pools), making it a good choice for families or anyone who likes a lot of space. Standard features include ceiling fans, fridges, and queen-size, king-size, or paired twin beds. The roomy villas offer separate living and dining rooms, full kitchens, CD players, and VCRs upon request. All bedrooms adjoin private bathrooms and open onto sun terraces. Some bathrooms have showers only.

The resort contains more restaurants per capita than most of its competitors. Papa Don's is an Italian trattoria specializing in pizza and pasta. Jammer's restaurant and bar is a nautically styled, informal bar/steakhouse/grill. Dragonfly serves Asian and West Indian food.

Labrelotte Bay (P.O. Box 1504), Castries, St. Lucia, W.I. © **800/958-7376** in the U.S., or 758/456-9000. Fax 758/452-9454. www.windjammer-landing.com. 234 units. Winter US$250–US$400 (£130–£208) double, from US$675 (£351) 2-bedroom villa; off season US$175–US$355 (£91–£185) double, from US$495 (£257) 2-bedroom villa. MAP US$70 (£36) per person. AE, DISC, MC, V. **Amenities:** 5 restaurants; 4 bars; 4 outdoor pools; 2 lit tennis courts; fitness center; Jacuzzi; dive shop; sailing; snorkeling; water-skiing; windsurfing; children's programs; car rental; limited room service; massage; babysitting; laundry service; nonsmoking rooms; rooms for those w/limited mobility. *In room:* A/C, ceiling fan, TV, dataport, kitchen, minibar, fridge, beverage maker, hair dryer, iron, safe.

MODERATE

Bay Gardens Hotel ★ *Value*   This hotel offers one of the best values, as well as some of the best service, on the island. It's not right on the sands, but Reduit Beach, one of St. Lucia's finest, is a 5-minute walk or a complimentary 2-minute shuttle ride away. One of the newest and most up-to-date hotels on the island, Bay Gardens opens onto a large atrium lobby with a designer fountain pool and bamboo furnishings. Joyce and Desmond Destang are among the most hospitable hosts on the island. Their medium-size bedrooms in vivid florals contain a terrace or balcony, and tropical art and accessories. Bathrooms are tiled with a combination tub/shower. Families might want to consider one of the eight apartments, each a self-contained unit with a kitchenette. One child is accommodated without charge. Its international restaurant, Spices, serves some of the island's best hotel food. Look for weekly rum punches, barbecues, Caribbean buffets, and live music on occasion. Did we mention the ice-cream shop?

Rodney Bay (P.O. Box 1892), Castries, St. Lucia. W.I. © **877/620-3200** in the U.S., or 758/452-8060. Fax 758/452-8059. www.baygardenshotel.com. 71 units, 8 apts. Winter US$120–US$140 (£62–£73) double, US$170–US$305 (£88–£159) suite; off season US$115–US$130 (£60–£68) double, US$155–US$250 (£81–£130) suite. 1 child (2–12 years old) stays free in parent's room. MAP (breakfast and dinner) US$45 (£23). AE, MC, V. **Amenities:** Restaurant; 2 bars; 2 outdoor pools; Jacuzzi; library; car rental; shuttle to beach; business services; room service (7:30am–10pm); babysitting; laundry service; dry cleaning; nonsmoking rooms; rooms for those w/limited mobility. *In room:* A/C, ceiling fan, TV, dataport, kitchenette, minibar, fridge, beverage maker, hair dryer, iron, safe.

Coco Palm Hotel ★   In the center of the heavily built-up Rodney Bay Village, Coco Palm is affordable chic. It's the latest creation of Caribbean guru, Allen Chastanet, who co-founded the Island Outpost group that also operates Coco Kreole (see below). Rooms are spread across a three-story building in candy colors. The special feature here is seven "swim-up rooms," where testing the waters means simply stepping from your terrace onto the hotel's serpentine pool. The bedrooms and suites are decorated with plantation-style furniture, local paintings, and glass-walled showers. The top floor suites open onto roof decks with views of the village restaurants.

Reduit Beach Ave., Rodney Bay Village. St. Lucia, W.I. ℂ **758/456-2800**. Fax 758/452-0713. www.coco-resorts.com. 84 units. Winter US$185–US$285 (£96–£148) double, US$300–US$330 (£156–£171) suite; off season US$145–US$245 (£75–£127) double, US$260–US$290 (£135–£150) suite. AE, MC, V. **Amenities:** Restaurant; bar; outdoor pool. *In room:* A/C, TV, dataport, fridge, beverage maker, hair dryer.

Harmony Suites 𝔊 This complex of two-story buildings offers well-maintained accommodations at reasonable rates, a short walk from one of the island's finest beaches at Reduit. The suites—decorated in rattan, wicker, and florals—sit adjacent to a saltwater lagoon. Each unit offers a patio or balcony with views of moored yachts, the lagoon, and surrounding hills. Those on the top floor have more privacy. All suites, except the VIP/honeymoon units, have sofa beds. Each VIP suite features a double Jacuzzi, a four-poster queen-size bed on a pedestal, a sun deck, white rattan furnishings, and a bidet. Eight of the suites contain kitchenettes, complete with beverage makers, fridges, and wet bars—ideal for families on a budget. Tub/shower combination bathrooms are small, of the routine motel variety, but are tidily maintained.

Rodney Bay Lagoon (P.O. Box 155), Castries, St. Lucia, W.I. ℂ **758/452-8756**. Fax 758/452-8677. www.harmony suites.com. 30 units. Winter US$120–US$233 (£62–£121) double; off season US$100–US$155 (£52–£81) double. Extra person US$35 (£18) per night. AE, MC, V. **Amenities:** Restaurant; bar; outdoor pool; limited room service; laundry service; rooms for those w/limited mobility. *In room:* A/C, TV, kitchenette (in some), minibar, beverage maker; hair dryer, iron/ironing board, safe.

The Inn on the Bay This small-scale inn perched 90m (300 ft.) above the waters of Marigot Bay makes for a great romantic escape. It's the creative statement of Montreal-born Normand Viau and his wife, Louise Boucher. Abandoning careers as a lawyer and social worker, respectively, they designed the hotel themselves, modeling its blue roof and veranda-ringed style on the island's plantation-house tradition. Today, the centerpiece of their establishment is an open-air terrace, site of a small pool and semiprivate dinners available only to hotel guests. Bedrooms, with 3m (10-ft.) ceilings, are spacious, comfortably furnished, and airy. Each has a ceiling fan and ample windows for cross-ventilation. Some bathrooms are shower only.

Seaview Ave., Marigot Bay (P.O. Box RB2377), Castries, St. Lucia, W.I. ℂ **758/451-4260**. Fax 928/438-3828. www.saint-lucia.com. 5 units. Winter US$155 (£81) double; off season US$125 (£65) double. Rates include breakfast. MC, V. Children under 18 not allowed. **Amenities:** Breakfast room; outdoor pool; limited room service; nonsmoking rooms. *In room:* Ceiling fan, kitchenette, fridge, hair dryer, iron, no phone.

Mago Estate Hotel 𝔊 *Finds* This is a true Caribbean Shangri-La, ideal for a honeymoon. Just above the fishing village of Soufrière and overlooking the Pitons, German-born Peter Gloger runs this glamorous little inn. A 5-minute walk from the beach, this property is surrounded by tropical trees, including *mago* (patois for mango), mahogany, papaya, *maracuya* (passion fruit), and banana. Each of the accommodations has only three walls; the other side of the room is open to a view of the mountains and sea. Guests sleep in four-poster beds underneath ceilings of painted clouds, with mosquito netting for protection from insects. Each unit comes with a small shower-only bathroom and a spacious private terrace. The most recently built units are four large bedrooms with teakwood furnishings or handcrafted antiques along with plunge pools, hammocks, and large sliding doors opening to the terrace and pool. The food is excellent, and it's served at communal tables surrounded by carved African chairs.

Palm Mist, Soufrière, St. Lucia, W.I. ⓒ 758/459-5880. Fax 758/459-7352. www.magohotel.com. 10 units. Winter US$200–US$500 (£104–£260) double; off season US$150–US$400 (£78–£208) double. Rates include breakfast and beach shuttle service. MAP (Caribbean breakfast and dinner) US$40 (£21) per person extra. AE, MC, V. **Amenities:** Dining room; bar; outdoor pool; limited room service; massage; laundry service. *In room:* A/C (in some), ceiling fan, minibar, fridge, beverage maker, iron/ironing board, no phone.

Seraphine This two-story concrete-sided building painted cerulean blue and white is a 15-minute walk from Vigie Beach, overlooking the marina and the harbor of Castries. Owned and operated by the St. Lucia–born Joseph family, whose hotel skills were honed during a long sojourn in England, the hotel offers well-maintained, but very simple, accommodations. They're generally spacious and often decorated with bright colors and tropical prints. The bathrooms, though small, are clean and have tiled showers. Most activities surround an open terrace whose surface is sheathed with terra-cotta tiles ringing a small round-sided pool. Don't expect too many extras, as the place's charm derives from its simplicity.

Vigie Cove (Box 390), Castries, St. Lucia, W.I. ⓒ **758/453-2073.** Fax 758/451-7001. 28 units. Year-round US$115 (£60) double; US$135 (£70) suite for 2. AE, MC, V. **Amenities:** Restaurant; bar; outdoor pool; room service; laundry service; nonsmoking rooms. *In room:* A/C, TV, beverage maker, hair dryer, iron.

INEXPENSIVE

The Green Parrot (see "Dining," below) also offers inexpensive rooms.

Bay Gardens Inn *⟨Value⟩* In the heart of Rodney Bay, near Reduit Beach, this inn enjoys a prime location. Its proximity to Rodney Bay Marina puts it at the heart of the action. The inn is small and modern, with a 1.2m-deep (4-ft.) freshwater pool. Rooms are divided into four categories across two floors. The most desirable are called Bay View Superior, each with a spacious queen-size bed. Rooms open onto a private balcony or terrace, and each comes with a tiled bathroom with shower.

Rodney Bay, St. Lucia, W.I. ⓒ **758/452-8200.** Fax 758/452-8002. www.baygardensinn.com. 33 units. Winter US$110–US$130 (£57–£68) double; off season US$105–US$120 (£55–£62) double. AE, DC, DISC, MC, V. **Amenities:** Restaurant; bar; outdoor pool; car rental; beach shuttle; Internet cafe; business services; salon; babysitting; laundry service; rooms for those w/limited mobility. *In room:* A/C, TV, fridge, beverage maker, hair dryer, iron, Wi-Fi.

Coco Kreole *⟨Value⟩* At Rodney Bay, one of the most scenic parts of St. Lucia, this hotel is the more affordable alternative to its newer sibling, Coco Palm (see above). A St. Lucian, Allen Chastanet, operates this informal, laid-back resort. Reduit Beach, one of the best on island, lies only a 5-minute walk from the property. Bedrooms are done in a rather lackluster and clichéd Caribbean style—think motel—but are completely comfortable and well-maintained. Bedrooms are a bit small, and bathrooms come with showers. The least expensive rooms face the street, the better units opening poolside. Breakfast is taken poolside, and all of Rodney Bay's restaurants and bars lie close at hand.

Rodney Bay, St. Lucia, W.I. ⓒ **758/452-0712.** Fax 758/452-0773. www.cocokreole.com. 20 units. Winter US$95–US$105 (£49–£54); off season US$85–US$95 (£44–£49). Rates include continental breakfast. AE, DC, MC, V. **Amenities:** Bar; outdoor pool; Internet cafe; limited room service. *In room:* A/C, TV, fridge, beverage maker, hair dryer.

Hummingbird Beach Resort *⟨Finds⟩* Set on .3 hectare (¾ acre) of verdantly landscaped grounds, this is a small, charming, and carefully maintained inn that enjoys direct access to a sandy strip of beachfront, on the northern edge of Soufrière on St. Lucia's southwest coast. Bedrooms are sheathed in white stucco and accented with varnished hardwoods like mahogany. Views are of the water or the soaring nearby heights of Petit Titon and the rugged landscape of southern St. Lucia. Each has a ceiling fan and mosquito netting that's artfully draped over the sometimes elaborately carved bedsteads. Regrettably, the low wattage in the bedside lamps makes nighttime reading difficult. Bathrooms are very compact but have tub/shower combinations and adequate shelf space. Standard units share a bath. There's a restaurant, Lifeline, on the premises (see "Dining," below).

P.O. Box 280, Soufrière, St. Lucia, W.I. (☎) 758/459-7232. Fax 758/459-7033. www.istlucia.co.uk. 7 units. Winter US$165–US$170 (£86–£88); from US$170 (£88) suite. Off-season US$95–US$110 (£49–£57) double; from US$110 (£57) suite. Extra person US$25–US$35 (£13–£18). AE, DISC, MC, V. **Amenities:** Restaurant; bar; outdoor pool; access to nearby health club; car rental; room service (7am–10pm); babysitting; laundry service; nonsmoking rooms. *In room:* A/C (in some), ceiling fan, TV, safe.

3 Dining

IN CASTRIES

Green Parrot ⍟ CONTINENTAL/CARIBBEAN   About 2km (1¼ miles) east of the center of town, Green Parrot overlooks Castries Harbour and remains the local hot spot for visitors, expatriates, and locals. It takes about 12 minutes to walk here from downtown, but the effort is worth it. Chef Harry, who runs this elegant place, had many years of training in prestigious restaurants and hotels in London, including Claridge's. Guests take their time and make an evening of it, many enjoying a before-dinner drink in the Victorian-style salon. Try a Grass Parrot (made from coconut cream, crème de menthe, bananas, and white rum). An evening in the English-colonial dining room usually includes free entertainment on Wednesday and Saturday nights, which might be a limbo contest or a fire-eating show.

All this may sound gimmicky, but the food doesn't suffer. There's an emphasis on St. Lucian specialties and homegrown produce. Try the *christophene* au gratin (a Caribbean squash with cheese) or the Creole soup made with callaloo and pumpkin. There are five kinds of curry with chutney, as well as a selection of omelets and sandwiches at lunch.

Green Parrot also offers some of the island's least expensive lodging; rooms have air-conditioning and phones. In winter, doubles are US$100 (£52); in off season, US$80 (£41). Rates include breakfast.

Chef Harry Drive, Morne Fortune. (☎) 758/452-3399. Reservations recommended. Lunch main courses EC$45–EC$70 (US$17–US$26/£9–£14); fixed-price dinner EC$90–EC$110 (US$33–US$41/£18–£22). AE, MC, V. Daily 7am–midnight.

Jacques Waterfront Dining ⍟⍟ SEAFOOD/CARIBBEAN   Chef Jacky Rioux has traveled the world, picking up ideas for a fusion cuisine that combines market-fresh ingredients with French cooking methods. Local fishermen are always bringing him unusual catches from the sea, which he shapes into such dishes as conch in a curried coconut sauce. Among our favorite of his main courses are boneless chicken breast stuffed with smoked salmon in a citrus butter sauce or oven-baked kingfish with a white wine and sweet pepper sauce. The chef mixes his own spices and seasonings and is a talented sauce maker. He even smokes his own fish and meat. The chef's knowledge and love of wine are reflected in his carefully chosen *carte*. His open-air garden restaurant overlooks Vigie Cove.

Vigie Marina. (☎) 758/458-1900. Reservations required. Main courses at lunch EC$32–EC$65 (US$12–US$24/£6.40–£13); at dinner EC$50–EC$80 (US$19–US$30/£10–£16). AE, MC, V. Mon–Sat 11:30am–2:30pm and 7–11pm.

AT MARIGOT

J.J.'s Paradise *(Finds)* SEAFOOD/ST LUCIAN   Chef/owner Gerard (J.J.) Felix is one of the island's best cooks and most welcoming hosts. In lush foliage, the restaurant frames the edge of Marigot Bay. The fish and seafood are freshly caught and seasoned with locally grown herbs and fruits from island gardens. J.J. has sailed the world on his vessel, *Vendredi 13,* learning new recipes and different languages. Wednesday night is devoted to his finger-licking callaloo crab feast as local bands play. He also serves Creole style lobster, shrimp, and other treats, including prime meats and chicken dishes. Chances are J.J. makes a better curried octopus than your mother did.

Marigot Bay Rd., Marigot. (758/451-4076. Reservations recommended. Main courses EC$38–EC$110 (US$14–US$41/£7.60–£22). MC, V. Daily 8pm–midnight.

IN THE SOUFRIERE AREA

Camilla's Restaurant & Bar WEST INDIAN/CREOLE   Set a block inland from the waterfront, one floor above street level, this is a decent Caribbean-style restaurant with simple, unpretentious food. Local matriarch Camilla Alcindor will welcome you for coffee, a soda, or Perrier. The food is straightforward but flavorful. Opt for the fish and shellfish (Caribbean fish Creole or lobster thermidor) rather than the beef; chicken curry is another savory choice. Lunches are considerably less elaborate and include an array of sandwiches, salads, omelets, and burgers. Our favorite tables are the pair sitting on a balcony overlooking the energetic activities in the street below. The inside tables can get a bit steamy on a hot night as there's no air-conditioning.

7 Bridge St., Soufrière. (758/459-5379. Main courses EC$29–EC$72 (US$11–US$27/£5.80–£14). AE, MC, V. Tues–Sun 8am–midnight.

Dasheene Restaurant & Bar *(Finds)* CARIBBEAN/INTERNATIONAL   This is one of the most widely heralded restaurants on St. Lucia and it has the most dramatic setting. Inspired by the best of the Caribbean/Creole kitchen and the innovations of California, this mountaintop hideaway offers some of the island's most refined and creative cuisine. Start with such tantalizing appetizers as St. Lucia fish pot consommé, or the green-papaya-and-pumpkin fritters served with a lettuce rémoulade dressing. Another favorite is the fried green tomato and plantain tart with a goat-cheese salad. Moving on to the main dishes, we tend to prefer the fisherman's catch of the day, often red snapper or kingfish. It's served with your choice of a mild jerk butter or else lemon-caviar butter. A local way of preparing steak, called Mojo steak, is marinated in a lime-and-pepper seasoning before it's pan seared. The chocolate rum mousse for dessert makes for a festive evening.

In the Ladera Resort, between Gros and Petit Piton. (758/459-7323. Reservations recommended. Main courses EC$43–EC$85 (US$16–US$31/£8.60–£17). AE, MC, V. Daily 7:30–10am, noon–2:30pm, and 6:30–10pm.

Lifeline Restaurant at the Hummingbird CARIBBEAN/INTERNATIONAL   This restaurant is the best part of the Hummingbird Beach Resort complex. Tables are set on a stylish veranda adjacent to the sands of Hummingbird Beach. The cuisine focuses on such West Indian dishes as Creole-style conch, lobster, burgers, steaks, and filets of both snapper and grouper, punctuated with such American staples as burgers and BLTs. A tiny gift shop on the premises sells batik items crafted by staff members.

At the Hummingbird Beach Resort, on the waterfront just north of the main wharf at Soufrière. (758/459-7232. Platters EC$55–EC$100 (US$20–US$37/£11–£20). AE, DISC, MC, V. Daily 7am–11pm.

The Still 🐟 *Finds* CREOLE   This is the most authentic and atmospheric place for lunch in the southern Soufrière area. The first thing you'll see as you drive up the hill from the harbor is a very old rum distillery set on a platform of thick timbers. The site is a working cocoa and citrus plantation that has been in the same St. Lucian family for four generations. The front blossoms with avocado and breadfruit trees, and a mahogany forest is just steps away. The bar near the front veranda is furnished with tables cut from cross-sections of mahogany tree trunks. In the more formal and spacious dining room, you can feast on excellently prepared St. Lucian specialties, depending on what's fresh at the market that day. Try to avoid the place when it's overrun with cruise-ship passengers or tour groups.

Soufrière. © 758/459-7224. Main courses EC$22–EC$60 (US$8.15–US$22/£4.40–£12). AE, DC, DISC, MC, V. Daily 8am–4pm.

IN RODNEY BAY

The Charthouse AMERICAN/CREOLE   In a large building with a sky-lit ceiling and a mahogany bar, The Charthouse is one of the oldest restaurants in the area and one of the island's most popular. It was built several feet above the bobbing yachts of the lagoon, without walls, to allow an optimal view of the water. The helpful staff serves simple, honest, good food in large portions. The specialties might include pumpkin soup, St. Lucian crab backs, baby back ribs, and fresh local lobster. (From Sept–Apr, you can often witness the live lobster being delivered from the boat at around 5pm.) If you fancy a well-cooked charcoal-broiled steak, you'll see why this dish made the restaurant famous. Of course, traditionalists visit The Charthouse for one reason—its roast prime rib of beef, which is good, but never better here than in the U.S.

Reduit Beach, Rodney Bay. © 758/452-8115. Reservations required. Main courses EC$55–EC$105 (US$20–US$38/£11–£21). AE, MC, V. Daily 6–10:30pm.

The Lime 🐟 AMERICAN/CREOLE   This bistro stands north of Reduit Beach in an area that's known as restaurant row. Some of these places are rather expensive, but The Lime continues to keep its prices low, its food good and plentiful, and its service among the finest on the island. Both locals and visitors come here for *limin'*, or hanging out. West Indian in feeling and open-air in setting, the restaurant features a "lime special" drink. Specialties include grilled lobster, and fish-steak Creole, as well as shrimp, steaks, lamb, pork chops, and *rotis* (Caribbean burritos). The steaks are done over a charcoal grill. Nothing is fancy, nothing is innovative, and nothing is nouvelle—just like the savvy local foodies like it. It's less expensive and less touristy than Capone's.

Rodney Bay. © 758/452-0761. Reservations not necessary. Main courses EC$28–EC$75 (US$10–US$28/£5.60–£15). MC, V. Daily 11am–1am.

IN GROS ISLET

Great House 🐟 FRENCH/CREOLE/INTERNATIONAL   Built on the foundation stones of the original plantation house of Cap Estate, this restaurant lies under a canopy of cedar trees. The inviting ambience extends to the formal dining room, which opens onto a tranquil patio overlooking the sea. French cuisine is served here with Caribbean flair. The service, food, and wine are first-rate. The menu is adjusted frequently to take advantage of the freshest ingredients. Begin with an appetizer such as shrimp and scallop gratinée (with a cheese sauce) and proceed to sample the delectable duck breast in a honey-and-balsamic-vinegar sauce, grilled lobster sautéed in a butter sauce, savory chicken, or a St. Lucian beef dish. Finish with the velvety smooth passion-fruit cheesecake.

Cap Estate. © **758/450-0450**. Reservations required. Main courses EC$59–EC$103 (US$22–US$38/£12–£20). AE, DC, DISC, MC, V. Tues–Sun 6:30–10pm.

4 Beaches

Since most of the island hotels are built right on the beach, you won't have to go far to swim. All beaches are open to the public, even those along hotel properties. However, if you use any of the hotel's beach equipment, you must pay for it. We prefer the beaches along the western coast, as the rough surf on the windward (east) side makes swimming potentially dangerous. The best hotels are all on the western coast for good reason.

One of the best beaches is **Pigeon Point Beach** ⊛ off the north shore, part of the **Pigeon Island National Historic Park** (see below). The small beach here has white sand and is an ideal place for a picnic. Pigeon Island is joined to the mainland of St. Lucia by a causeway, so it's easy to reach.

The most frequented beach is **Reduit Beach** ⊛⊛ at Rodney Bay, 2km (1¼ miles) of soft beige sand fronting very clear waters. Many watersports kiosks can be found along the strip bordering Royal St. Lucian Hotel. With all its restaurants and bars, you'll find plenty of refueling stops.

Choc Bay is a long stretch of sand and palm trees on the northwestern coast, convenient to Castries and the big resorts. Its tranquil waters lure swimmers and especially families (including locals) with small children.

The 3km (2-mile) white-sand **Malabar Beach** runs parallel to the George F. L. Charles Airport runway, in Castries, to the Rendezvous resort. **Vigie Beach,** north of Castries Harbour, is also popular. It has fine beige sands, sloping gently into crystalline water. **La Toc Beach,** just south of Castries, opens onto a crescent-shaped bay containing golden sand.

Marigot Bay is the quintessential Caribbean cove, framed on three sides by steep emerald hills and skirted by palm trees. There are some small but secluded beaches here. Some of the Caribbean's most expensive yachts anchor in this bay.

One of the most charming and hidden beaches of St. Lucia is the idyllic cove of **Anse Chastanet,** north of Soufrière. This is a beach connoisseur's delight. Towering palms provide shade from the fierce noonday sun, and lush hills are a refreshing contrast to the dark sandy strip.

The dramatic crescent-shaped bay of **Anse des Pitons** is at the foot of and between the twin peaks of the Pitons, south of Soufrière. The Jalousie Plantation transformed the natural black-sand beach by covering it with white sand; you walk through the resort to get to it. It's popular with divers and snorkelers. While here, you can ask about a very special beach reached only by boat, the black volcanic sands and tranquil waters of **Anse Couchon.** With its shallow reefs, excellent snorkeling, and picture-postcard charm, this beach has become a hideaway for lovers. It's south of Anse-le-Raye.

You'll find miles of white sand at the beach at **Vieux Fort,** at the southern end of the island. Reefs protect the crystal-clear waters here, rendering them tranquil and ideal for swimming. At the southern end of the windward side of the island is **Anse des Sables,** which opens onto a shallow bay swept by trade winds that are great for windsurfing.

5 Sports & Other Outdoor Pursuits

BOATING   The most dramatic trip offered is aboard the 42m (138-ft.) **brig** *Unicorn* (© **758/452-8644**), used in the filming of the TV miniseries, *Roots*. Passengers sail from Rodney Bay in Castries to Soufrière and the twin peaks of the Pitons, among other natural attractions of the island. A full-day sail costs US$90 (£47) for adults, US$45 (£23) for children.

CAMPING   Camping is now possible on St. Lucia courtesy of the **Environmental Educational Centre,** a division of the St. Lucia National Trust (© **758/452-5005**). This reserve features 12 campsites along a beautiful stretch of beach on historic Anse Liberté, in the fishing town of Canaries, 40km (25 miles) southwest of Castries and 13km (8 miles) north of Soufrière. At present you must bring your own tent, paying US$15 (£7.80) per night to rent the site. There are nearby community bathrooms and community cooking areas. The reserve has 8km (5 miles) of hiking trails; staff members give tours of the area and explain the rich history of the Anse Liberté, which literally translated means "freedom harbor."

DEEP-SEA FISHING   The waters around St. Lucia are known for their game fish, including blue marlin, sailfish, mako sharks, and barracuda, with tuna and kingfish among the edible catches. Most hotels can arrange fishing expeditions. Call **Mako Watersports** (© **758/452-0412**), which offers half-day fishing trips from US$450 (£234) or full-day trips from US$750 (£390). **Captain Mike's** (© **758/452-7044**) also conducts fishing trips, renting boats by the half-day for US$450 to US$550 (£234–£286), or a whole day in the US$750 to US$900 (£390–£468) price range.

GOLF   St. Lucia has an 18-hole golf course (6,815 yards, par 71) at the **St. Lucia's Golf and Country Club,** Cap Estate, at the northern end of the island (© **758/450-9905**). Greens fees are US$110 (£57) for 18 holes, US$85 (£44) for 9 holes; there are no caddies. Carts are included, and clubs can be rented for US$20 (£11). Hours are from 7am to 6pm daily. Reservations are needed.

HIKING   A tropical rainforest covers a large area in the southern half of St. Lucia, and the St. Lucia Forest and Lands Department manages it wisely. This forest reserve divides the western and eastern halves of the island. There are several trails, the most popular of which is the **Barre de l'Isle Trail,** located almost in the center of St. Lucia, southeast of Marigot Bay; it's a fairly easy trail that even children can handle. There are four panoramic lookout points with dramatic views of the sea where the Atlantic and the Caribbean meet. It takes about an hour to walk this 2km-long (1.2-mile) trail, which lies about a 30-minute ride from Castries. Guided hikes can usually be arranged through the major hotels or through the **Forest and Lands Department** (© **758/450-2078**).

HORSEBACK RIDING   North of Castries is the island's oldest riding establishment—**Trim's National Riding Stable,** Cas-en-Bas, Gros Islet (© **758/450-8139**). Its activities range from trail rides to beach tours, and the stable even offers horse-drawn carriage tours of Pigeon Island. Rides are US$45 (£23) for an hour, US$70 (£36) for 2 hours, or US$88 (£46) for a 3-hour beach ride with a barbecue.

SCUBA DIVING   In Soufrière, **Scuba St. Lucia,** in the Anse Chastanet Hotel (© **758/459-7000**), offers one of the world's top dive locations at a five-star PADI dive center. At the southern end of Anse Chastanet's .4km-long (¼-mile) secluded beach, it features premier diving and comprehensive facilities for divers of all levels. Some of the most spectacular coral reefs of St. Lucia, many only 3 to 6m (10–20 ft.) below the surface, lie a short distance from the beach.

Many PADI instructors offer five dive programs a day. Photographic equipment is available for rent (film can be processed on the premises), and instruction is offered in picture taking. Experienced divers can rent any equipment they need. PADI certification courses are available for US$480 (£250). A 2- to 3-hour introductory lesson costs US$85 (£44) and includes a short theory session, equipment familiarization, development of skills in shallow water, a tour of the reef, and all equipment. Single dives cost US$40 (£21). Hours are from 8am to 6pm daily.

Another full-service scuba center is available on St. Lucia's southwest coast at the **Jalousie Plantation,** at Soufrière (© **758/456-8000**). The PADI center offers dives in St. Lucia's National Marine Park; there are numerous shallow reefs near the shore. The diver certification program is available to hotel guests and other visitors ages 12 and up. Prices range from a single dive for US$60 (£31) to a certification course for US$535 (£278). There's a daily resort course for noncertified divers that includes a supervised dive from the beach; it costs US$85 (£44). A 10-dive package is US$347 (£180); a six-dive package is US$237 (£123). All prices include equipment, tax, and service charges.

TENNIS   The best place for tennis on the island is the **St. Lucia Racquet Club,** adjacent to Club St. Lucia (© **758/450-0551**). It's one of the finest tennis facilities in the Lesser Antilles. Its seven illuminated courts are maintained in state-of-the-art condition, and there's also a good pro shop on-site. You must reserve 24 hours in advance. Guests of the hotel play for free; nonguests are charged EC$54 (US$20/£11) for a full-day pass. Tennis racquets rent for EC$21 (US$7.75/£4.20) per hour.

The **Jalousie Plantation,** at Soufrière (© **758/456-8000**), has a good program. Vernon Lewis, the top-ranked player in St. Lucia, is the pro. You'll find four brand-new Laykold tennis courts (three lit for night play). Hotel guests play for free (though they pay for lessons). Nonguests can play for US$20 (£10) per hour.

OTHER WATERSPORTS   The best all-around watersports center is **St. Lucian Watersports,** at the Rex St. Lucian Hotel (© **758/452-8351**). Water-skiing costs US$17 (£8.85) for a 10- to 15-minute ride (three rounds). Windsurfers can be rented for US$45 (£23) per half-hour. Snorkeling is free for guests of the hotel; nonguests pay US$10 (£5.20) per hour for equipment.

6 Exploring the Island

With lovely little towns, beautiful beaches and bays, mineral baths, and banana plantations, you won't tire of exploring St. Lucia. You can even visit a volcano.

Most hotel front desks will make arrangements for tours that take in all the major sights of St. Lucia. For example, **Sunlink Tours,** Reduit Beach Avenue (© **758/456-9100** or 758/452-8232), offers many island tours, including full-day boat trips along the west coast of Soufrière, the Pitons, and the volcano; the cost is US$90 (£47) per person. Jeep safaris can be arranged for US$50 to US$120 (£26–£62) apiece, depending on the tour. One of the most popular jaunts is a rainforest ramble for US$85 (£44) by jeep. There's also a daily shopping tour for US$25 (£13). The company has tour desks and/or representatives at most of the major hotels.

CASTRIES

The capital city has grown up around its **harbor,** which occupies the crater of an extinct volcano. Charter captains and the yachting set drift in here, and large cruise-ship wharves welcome vessels from around the world. Because several devastating fires (most recently in 1948) destroyed almost all the old buildings, the town today looks new, with glass-and-concrete (or steel) buildings rather than the French colonial or Victorian look typical of many West Indian capitals.

Castries may be architecturally dull, but its **public market** is one of the most fascinating in the West Indies, and our favorite people-watching site on the island. It goes full blast every day of the week except Sunday, and is most active on Friday and Saturday mornings. The market stalls are a block from Columbus Square along Peynier Street, running down toward the water. The local women dress traditionally, with cotton headdresses; the number of knotted points on top reveals their marital status. (Ask one of the locals to explain it to you.) The luscious fruits and vegetables of St. Lucia may be new to you; the array of colors alone is astonishing. Sample one of the numerous varieties of bananas: On St. Lucia, they're allowed to ripen on the tree, and taste completely different from those picked green and sold at supermarkets in the United States. You can also pick up St. Lucian handicrafts such as baskets and unglazed pottery here.

To the south of Castries looms **Morne Fortune,** the inappropriately named "Hill of Good Luck." In the 18th century, some of the most savage Caribbean battles between the French and the British took place here. You can visit the military cemetery, a small museum, the old powder magazine, and the "Four Apostles Battery" (a quartet of grim muzzle-loading cannons). Government House, now the official residence of the governor-general of St. Lucia, is one of the few examples of Victorian architecture that escaped destruction by fire. The private gardens are beautifully planted, aflame with scarlet and purple bougainvillea. Morne Fortune also offers what many consider the most **scenic lookout** perch in the Caribbean. The view of the harbor of Castries is panoramic: You can see north to Pigeon Island or south to the Pitons; on a clear day, you may even spot Martinique. To reach Morne Fortune, head east on Bridge Street.

PIGEON ISLAND NATIONAL HISTORIC PARK ⟨⟩

St. Lucia's first **national park** is joined to the mainland by a causeway. On its west coast are two white-sand beaches (see "Beaches," above). There's also a restaurant, Jambe de Bois, named after a wooden-legged pirate who once used the island as a hideout.

Pigeon Island offers an **Interpretation Centre,** equipped with artifacts and a multimedia display on local history, ranging from the Amerindian occupation of A.D. 1000 to the Battle of the Saints, when Admiral Rodney's fleet set out from Pigeon Island and defeated Admiral De Grasse in 1782. The Captain's Cellar Olde English Pub lies under the center and is evocative of an 18th-century English bar.

Pigeon Island, only 18 hectares (44 acres), got its name from the red-neck pigeon, or ramier, that once colonized this island in huge numbers. Now the site of a Sandals Hotel and interconnected to the St. Lucian "mainland" with a causeway, the island offers pleasant panoramas but no longer the sense of isolated privacy that reigned here prior to its development. Parts of it, those far from the hotel on the premises, seem appropriate for nature walks. For more information, call ⟨⟩ **758/452-2231.**

RODNEY BAY ⊛

This scenic bay is a 15-minute drive north of Castries. Set on a man-made lagoon, it has become a chic center for nightlife, hotels, and restaurants—in fact, it's the most active place on the island at night. Its marina is one of the top watersports centers in the Caribbean, and a destination every December for the Atlantic Rally for Cruisers, when yachties cross the Atlantic to meet and compare stories.

MARIGOT BAY ⊛

Movie crews, including those for Sophia Loren's *Fire Power*, have used this bay, one of the most beautiful in the Caribbean, for background shots. Thirteen kilometers (8 miles) south of Castries, it's narrow yet navigable by yachts of any size. Here Admiral Rodney camouflaged his ships with palm leaves while lying in wait for French frigates. The shore, lined with palm trees, remains relatively unspoiled, although some building sites have been sold. It's a delightful spot for a picnic. A 24-hour ferry connects the bay's two sides.

SOUFRIERE

This little fishing port, St. Lucia's second-largest settlement, is dominated by two pointed hills called **Petit Piton** and **Gros Piton** ⊛⊛⊛. The Pitons, two volcanic cones rising to 738m and 696m (2,421 ft. and 2,283 ft.), have become the very symbol of St. Lucia. Formed of lava and rock, and once actively volcanic, they are now covered in green vegetation. Their sheer rise from the sea makes them a landmark visible for miles around, and waves crash at their bases. It's recommended that you attempt to climb only Gros Piton, but doing so requires the permission of the **Forest and Lands Department** (© 758/450-2078) and the company of a knowledgeable guide.

Near Soufrière lies the famous "drive-in" volcano, **Mount Soufrière** ⊛⊛, a rocky lunar landscape of bubbling mud and craters seething with sulfur. You literally drive your car into a millions-of-years-old crater and walk between the sulfur springs and pools of hissing steam. Entrance costs EC$7 (US$2.60/£1.40) per person and includes the services of your guide, who will point out the blackened waters, among the few of their kind in the Caribbean. Hours are daily from 9am to 5pm; for more information, call © 758/459-7200.

Nearby are the **Diamond Mineral Baths** (© 758/452-4759) in the **Diamond Botanical Gardens** ⊛. Deep in the lush tropical gardens is the Diamond Waterfall, one of the geological attractions of the island. Created from water bubbling up from sulfur springs, the waterfall changes colors (from yellow to black to green to gray) several times a day. The baths were constructed in 1784 on the orders of Louis XVI, whose doctors told him these waters were similar in mineral content to the waters at Aix-les-Bains; they were intended to provide recuperative effects for French soldiers fighting in the West Indies. The baths have an average temperature of 106°F (41°C). For EC$15 (US$5.55/£3), you can bathe and try out the recuperative effects for yourself. There is a EC$11 (US$4/£2) entrance fee.

From Soufrière in the southwest, the road winds toward Fond St-Jacques, where you'll have a good view of mountains and villages as you cut through St. Lucia's Cape Moule-Chique tropical rainforest. You'll also see the Barre de l'Isle divide.

NATURE RESERVES

The fertile volcanic soil of St. Lucia sustains a rich diversity of bird and animal life. Some of the richest troves for ornithologists are in protected precincts off the

(Finds) Discovering "Forgotten" Grande Anse

The northeast coast is the least visited and least accessible part of St. Lucia, but it contains dramatic rockbound shores interspersed with secret sandy coves. The government has set Grand Anse aside as a **nature reserve** so that it will never be developed. The terrain is arid and can be unwelcoming, but it is fascinating nonetheless. Grande Anse is home to some **rare bird** species, notably the white-breasted thrasher, as well as the fer-de-lance, the only poisonous snake on the island (but visitors report rarely seeing them). Its beaches—Grande Anse, Petite Anse, and Anse Louvet—are nesting grounds for **endangered sea turtles,** including the hawksbill, the green turtle, the leatherback, and the loggerhead. Nesting season lasts from February to October. Many locals tackle the poor road in a four-wheel-drive vehicle, especially the bumpiest part from Desbarra to Grande Anse.

St. Lucian coast, in either of two national parks, Fregate Islands Nature Reserve and the Maria Islands Nature Reserve.

The **Fregate Islands** are a cluster of rocks a short distance offshore from Praslin Bay, midway up St. Lucia's eastern coastline. Barren except for tall grasses that seem to thrive in the salt spray, the islands were named after the scissor-tailed frigate birds *(Fregata magnificens)* that breed here. Between May and July, large colonies of the graceful birds fly in well-choreographed formations over islands that you can only visit under the closely supervised permission of government authorities. Many visitors believe that the best way to admire the Fregate Islands (and to respect their fragile ecosystems) is to walk along the nature trail that the St. Lucian government has hacked along the cliff top of the St. Lucian mainland, about 45m (150 ft.) inland from the shoreline. Even without binoculars, you'll be able to see the frigates wheeling overhead. You'll also enjoy eagle's-eye views of the unusual geology of the St. Lucian coast, which includes sea caves, dry ravines, a waterfall (during the rainy season), and a strip of mangrove swamp.

Maria Islands are larger and more arid and are almost constantly exposed to salt-laden winds blowing up from the equator. Set to the east of St. Lucia's southernmost tip, off the town of Vieux Fort, their biodiversity is strictly protected. The approximately 12 hectares (30 acres) of cactus-dotted land that make up the two largest islands (Maria Major and Maria Minor) are home to more than 120 species of plants, lizards, butterflies, and snakes that are believed to be extinct in other parts of the world. These include the large ground lizard *(Zandolite)* and the nocturnal, nonvenomous kouwes snake *(Dromicus ornatus).*

The Marias are also a bird refuge, populated by such species as the sooty tern, the bridled tern, the Caribbean martin, the red-billed tropicbird, and the brown noddy, which usually nests under the protective thorns of prickly pear cactus.

Tours to either island must be arranged through the staff of the **St. Lucia National Trust (© 758/454-5014).** Full-day excursions, including the boat ride to the refuge and the guided tour, cost US$70 (£36) for the Fregates and US$85 (£44) for the Marias (the Marias jaunt includes lunch).

7 Shopping

Most of the shopping is in **Castries,** where the principal streets are William Peter Boulevard and Bridge Street. Many stores will sell you goods at duty-free prices (providing you don't take the merchandise with you but have it delivered to the airport or cruise dock). There are some good (but not remarkable) buys in bone china, jewelry, perfume, watches, liquor, and crystal.

Built for the cruise-ship passenger, **Pointe Seraphine,** in Castries, has the best collection of shops on the island, along with offices for car rentals, organized taxi service (for sightseeing), a bureau de change, a philatelic bureau, an information center, and international phones. Cruise ships berth right at the shopping center. Under red roofs in a Spanish-style setting, the complex requires that you present a cruise pass or an airline ticket to the shopkeeper when purchasing goods. Visitors can take away their purchases, except liquor and tobacco, which will be delivered to the airport. The center is open in winter Monday to Friday from 8am to 5pm and Saturday from 8am to 2pm; off season, Monday to Saturday from 9am to 4pm. It has extended hours when cruise ships are in port.

On Gros Islet Highway, 3km (2 miles) north of Castries, **Gablewoods Mall** contains three restaurants and one of the island's densest concentrations of shops.

8 St. Lucia After Dark

Friday-night "jump-ups" are weekly street parties where islanders let it rip. For reggae and hot times, head for the gatherings at **Gros Islet,** attracting both St. Lucians and the visiting yachties from Rodney Bay. You won't go hungry: stall after stall hawks barbecued meats along with such sides as rice 'n' beans and a tuber called dasheen, as seafood sizzles over hot coals and the smell of barbecued chicken whets appetites. More jump-ups take place at **Anse la Raye** on St. Lucia's western shore. Rum and reggae flow from about six in the evening to midnight or beyond. Stalls along the Anse la Raye waterfront often sell fresher and better seafood than you get in the upmarket dining rooms of the all-inclusives—conch, lobster, mahimahi, and even "potfish." Islanders claim that if you drink a "sea-moss shake" (seaweed, milk, sugar, and fruit), you'll keep jumping up throughout the night. In the winter, at least one hotel has a steel band or calypso music every night of the week. Otherwise, check to see what's happening at the **Green Parrot** (✆ 758/452-3399), in Castries.

If you'd like to go barhopping, begin at **Shamrocks Pub,** Rodney Bay (✆ 758/ 452-8725). This Irish-style pub is especially popular among boaters and gets really lively on weekends.

St. Lucia Jazz 2008

Amazingly, the **St. Lucia Jazz Festival** ✦✦✦ is now ranked as number two in the Caribbean, eclipsed only by Trinidad's Carnival. It's slated for May 5 through 14 in 2008. Leading jazz artists from all over the world descend on St. Lucia at this time, offering varied shows that range from new age jazz to rhythm and blues. Shows range from formal performances to late-night open-air venues. The tourist office has complete details of the festival, and information is also available online at www.stluciajazz.org. There's a downside to all this: many hotels take advantage of all these arrivals to jack up room prices.

Among the dance clubs, islanders and visitors favor **Late Lime,** Reduit Beach (© **758/452-0761**). A DJ plays dance music on Saturday.

At Marigot Bay, where the 1967 version of *Doctor Doolittle* starring Rex Harrison was filmed, the memory is perpetuated at **Doolittle's,** part of the Marigot Beach Club Hotel (© **758/451-4974**), lying 14km (8¾ miles) south of Castries. The Marigot Bay ferry takes you to the palm-studded peninsula of the resort; tickets cost EC$5 (US$1.85/£1). On Saturday nights—when Doolittle's offers a lavish seafood and barbeque buffet along with a steel band—this is the best place to be on the island. You can come here for drinks (try the Singapore Slings) or dishes like chunky pumpkin soup, jerk chicken, or lobster and coconut shrimp Creole.

Other island choices include the **Captain's Cellar** on Pigeon Island, Rodney Bay (© **758/450-0253**), which evokes an old British pub, with live jazz New Orleans style featured on Friday and Saturday nights. Live music or karaoke is often heard at **The Wharf,** Choc Bay (© **758/450-4844**).

23

St. Maarten/St. Martin

For an island with a big reputation for restaurants, hotels, and energetic nightlife, St. Maarten is small—only 96 sq. km (37 sq. miles), about half the area of Washington, D.C. An island divided between the Netherlands and France, St. Maarten (Sint Maarten) is the Dutch half, and St. Martin is French. Legend has it that a gin-drinking Dutchman and a wine-guzzling Frenchman walked around the island to see how much territory each could earmark for his country in a day; the Frenchman walked farther, but the canny Dutchman got the more valuable piece of property.

The divided island is the smallest territory in the world shared by two sovereign states. The only way you'll know you're crossing an international border is when you see the sign BIENVENUE PARTIE FRANCAISE, attesting to the peaceful co-existence between the two nations. The island was officially split in 1648, and many visitors still ascend Mount Concordia, near the border, where the agreement was reached. Even so, St. Maarten changed hands 16 times before it became permanently Dutch.

Returning visitors who haven't been to the island for a while are often shocked when they see today's St. Maarten. No longer a sleepy Caribbean backwater, now it's a boomtown. Duty-free shopping has turned the island into a virtual mall, and the Dutch capital, Philipsburg, is often bustling with cruise-ship hordes.

Although the island's 39 white-sand beaches remain unspoiled, much has been lost to the bulldozer on St. Maarten. This is not a place for people who don't like crowds, so if you want to get away from it all, head to the nearby Dutch islands of St. Eustatius (Statia) and Saba, or choose another getaway, such as the British Virgin Islands. Even the French side of the island would suit you better. Nevertheless, despite problems like crime, occasional storms, traffic congestion, and corruption, St. Maarten continues to attract massive numbers of visitors who want a Caribbean island vacation with a splash of Las Vegas.

The Dutch capital, **Philipsburg,** curves like a toy village along Great Bay. The town lies on a narrow sand isthmus separating Great Bay and the Great Salt Pond. Commander John Philips, a Scot in Dutch employ, founded the capital in 1763. To protect Great Bay, Fort Amsterdam was built in 1737.

The French side of the island has a slightly different character. It's been undergoing a building boom of late, with lots of new hotels opening, but for now at least, it's still sleepier than the Dutch side. Most hotels tend to be quieter and more secluded than their Dutch counterparts, and you won't be overwhelmed with cruise-ship crowds. There are no dazzling sights, and there's no spectacular nightlife. Even the sports scene on St. Martin isn't as well organized as on many Caribbean islands (though the Dutch side has golf and other diversions). Most people come to St. Martin to relax on its many white-sand beaches and to experience "France in the Tropics."

French St. Martin has a distinctly French air. Police officers, for example, wear *képis*. The towns have names like Colombier and Orléans, the streets are *rues,* and the French flag flies over the *gendarmerie* in **Marigot,** the capital. It also has some of the best cuisine in the Caribbean, with an extraordinary number of good bistros and restaurants. Advocates cite French St. Martin as distinctly more sophisticated, prosperous, stylish, and cosmopolitan than its neighboring *départements d'outre-mer,* Guadeloupe and Martinique.

French St. Martin is governed from Guadeloupe and has direct representation in the government in Paris. The principal town on the French side is Marigot, the seat of the subprefect and municipal council.

Marigot is not quite the same size as its counterpart, Philipsburg, in the Dutch sector. It has none of the frenzied pace of Philipsburg, which is often overrun with cruise-ship passengers. In fact, Marigot looks like a French village transplanted to the Caribbean. If you climb the hill over this tiny port, you'll be rewarded with a view from the old fort.

About 20 minutes by car beyond Marigot is **Grand-Case,** a small fishing village that's an outpost of French civilization, with many good restaurants and a few places to stay.

1 Essentials

VISITOR INFORMATION

If you're going to either **Dutch St. Maarten** or **French St Martin,** contact the St. Maarten/St Martin Tourist Office, 675 Third Ave., Suite 1807, New York, NY 10017 (© **800/786-2278** or 212/953-2084 for the department servicing the Dutch side, and © **877/956-1234** or 212/475-8970 for the department servicing the French side). In Canada, the office for information about the Dutch side of the island is located at 703 Evans Ave., Suite 106, Toronto, ON M9C 5E9 (© **416/622-4300**). For information about the French side of the island, contact 1981 Ave. McGill College, Suite 490, in Montréal (© **514/288-4264**). Once on the island, go to the **Tourist Information Bureau,** Vineyard Office Park, 33 W. G. Buncamper Rd., Philipsburg, St. Maarten, N.A. (© **599/54-22337**), open Monday to Friday from 9am to 5pm.

The tourist board on French St. Martin, called the **Office du Tourisme,** is at Route de Sandy Ground, Marigot, 97150 St. Martin (© **590/87-57-21**), open Monday to Friday from 8am to 1pm and 2:30 to 5:30pm.

For information on the Web about the French side, go to **www.st-martin.org**. For information about the island's Dutch side, search out **www.st-maarten.com**.

GETTING THERE

There are two airports on the island. St. Maarten's **Princess Juliana International Airport** (© **599/54-54211**) is the second-busiest airport in the Caribbean, topped only by San Juan, Puerto Rico. You can also fly to the smaller **L'Espérance Airport,** in Grand-Case on French St. Martin (© **590/87-10-36**).

American Airlines (© **800/433-7300** in the U.S. and Canada; www.aa.com) offers more options and more frequent service into St. Maarten than any other airline—two daily nonstop flights from New York's JFK and one from Miami. Additional nonstop daily flights into St. Maarten are offered by American and its local affiliate, **American Eagle** (same number), from San Juan. Ask about American's package tours, which can save you a bundle.

St. Maarten/St. Martin

ST. MAARTEN
ACCOMMODATIONS
Belair Beach Hotel **40**
Caravanserai Beach Resort **11**
Divi Little Bay Beach Resort **39**
The Horny Toad Guesthouse **13**
La Vista **18**
Mary's Boon Beach Plantation **15**
Oyster Bay Beach Resort **33**
Pasanggrahan Royal Inn **37**
The Pelican **17**
Princess Heights **34**
Sonesta Maho Beach Hotel & Casino **9**

DINING
Antoine's **35**
The Boathouse **16**
Cheri's Café **10**
The Greenhouse **38**
Kangaroo Court **36**
Rare **8**
Saratoga **14**
Temptation **8**
Turtle Bar Pier & Restaurant **12**

ST. MARTIN
ACCOMMODATIONS
Alamanda Resort **32**
Club Orient Naturist Resort **30**
Esmeralda Resort **27**
Hotel Beach Plaza **2**
Hotel L'Esplanade Caraïbes **19**
Hotel St-Tropez des Caraïbes **29**
La Plantation Orient Bay Resort **31**
La Samanna **7**
Le Casy **3**
Le Petit Hotel **20**
Mercure Coralia Simpson Beach **1**

DINING
Claude Mini Club **6**
Il Nettuno **21**
Kakao **28**
La Marine **22**
La Vie en Rose **5**
Le Cottage **23**
Le Pressoir **24**
L'Oizeau Rare **4**
Rainbow Café **25**
Sunset Café **26**

Pointe Arago

Pointe du Bluff

Baie de Marigot

Baie Nettlé

Marigo

Nettlé Beach

Pointe du Plum
Baie aux Prunes

Baie Rouge

Marigot Fort

Baie Longue

Simpson Bay Lagoon

Cupecoy Bay Beach

Mullet Bay Beach

Queen Juliana International Airport

Border Monumen

Maho Bay Beach

Simpson Bay Beach

Caribbean Sea

Koolbaai

Cole Bay

Schrijnwerkersteeg

C. A. Cannegieter St.
Back St.
Front St.
Walter Nisbet Rd.
Back St.
Front St.
St. Jansteeg
Kerksteeg

Great Bay Beach

Philipsburg

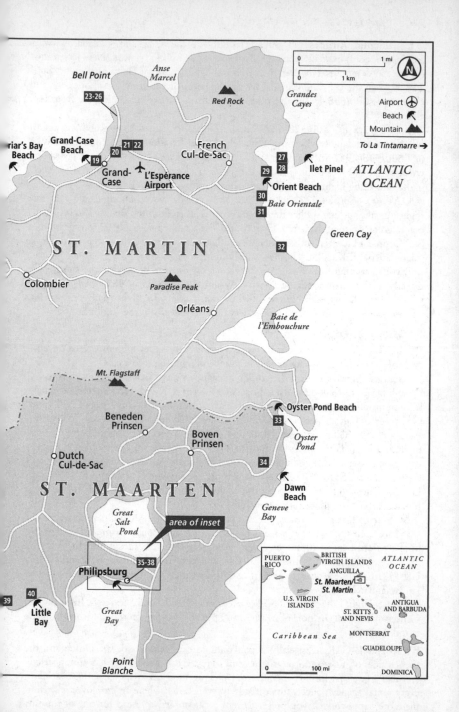

Continental Airlines (© 800/231-0856 in the U.S. and Canada; www.fly continental.com) has daily nonstop flights out of its hub in Newark, New Jersey, during the winter months. However, in low season flight times vary. **Delta Airlines** (© 800/241-4141 in the U.S. and Canada; www.delta.com) flies in from New York City, and **United** (© 800/538-2929) also offers flights from New York. Both leave from JFK airport.

US Airways (© 800/428-4322 in the U.S. and Canada; www.usairways.com) offers nonstop daily service from Philadelphia and Charlotte to St. Maarten. **BWIA** (© 800/538-2942 in the U.S. and Canada, or 599/54-54646 on St. Maarten; www.bwee.com) flies from Trinidad and Jamaica to Antigua, Barbados, and St. Lucia with connecting flights to St. Maarten offered by partner LIAT.

LIAT (© 868/624-4727 in the U.S. and Canada; www.liatairline.com) has one flight out of San Juan. Other flights stop first at Tortola in the British Virgin Islands before going on to St. Maarten. Even so, the trip usually takes only 90 minutes. From St. Martin, LIAT, often with connections, offers ongoing service to Antigua, St. Croix, Puerto Rico, St. Kitts, St. Thomas, and Dominica.

If you're coming from St. Barts, there's at least one airline serving the short route directly to French-speaking St. Martin. **Winair** (© 888/255-6889 in the U.S. and Canada, or 599/54-54237; www.fly-winair.com) offers 15 flights daily between St. Maarten and St. Barts, as well as a variety of other islands in the Caribbean.

GETTING AROUND

BY TAXI   Most visitors use taxis to get around. Since they are unmetered on both sides of the island, always agree on the rate before getting into a cab.

Rates are slightly different depending on which side of the island the taxi is based, though both Dutch and French cabs service the entire island. **St. Maarten taxis** have minimum fares for two passengers, and each additional passenger pays US$4 extra. One piece of luggage per person is allowed free; each additional piece is US$1 extra. Fares are 25% higher between 10pm and midnight, and 50% higher between midnight and 6am. Typical fares around the island are as follows: Queen Juliana Airport to Grand-Case: US$25 for up to two passengers and all their luggage; Marigot to Grand Case, US$15; Queen Juliana airport to anywhere in Marigot, US$15 to US$20; Queen Juliana Airport to the Maho Beach Hotel, US$6; and from Queen Juliana Airport to Philipsburg, about US$15.

St. Martin taxi fares are also for two passengers, but you should plan to add about US$1 for each suitcase or valise and US$2 for each additional person. These fares are in effect from 6am to 10pm; after that, they go up by 25% until midnight, rising by 50% after midnight. On the French side, the fare from Marigot to Grand-Case is US$15, from Queen Juliana Airport to Marigot and from Queen Juliana Airport to La Samanna, US$15.

For late-night cab service on St. Maarten, call © 147. **Taxi Service & Information Center** operates at the port of Marigot (© 590/87-56-54) on the French side of the island.

BY RENTAL CAR   Especially if you want to experience both the Dutch and the French sides of the island, you might want to rent a car. The taxi drivers' union strictly enforces a law that forbids anyone from picking up a car at the airport. As a result, every rental agency delivers cars directly to your hotel, where an employee will complete the paperwork. If you prefer to rent a car on arrival, head for one of the tiny rental kiosks across the road from the airport, but beware of long lines.

Avis maintains offices on both sides of the island (© **800/331-1212** in the U.S. and Canada, 599/54-52847 on the Dutch side, or 590/87-50-60 on the French side; www. avis.com). **National** (© **800/328-4567** in the U.S.; www.nationalcar.com) is downtown on Airport Road, or at Queen Juliana Airport (© **599/54-54415**). **Budget** (© **800/472-3325** in the U.S. and Canada; www.budget.com) has offices at the airport (© **599/54-54030**), and at the cruise-ship terminal (© **599/54-30431**). All these companies charge roughly equivalent rates.

All four major car-rental agencies require that renters be at least 25 years old. Your credit card issuer may provide insurance coverage, so check before your trip; otherwise, it may be wise to buy the fairly cheap collision-damage waiver (CDW) when you rent.

Drive on the right-hand side of both the French and Dutch roads, and expect traffic jams near the major towns. International road signs are observed, and there are no Customs formalities at the border between the two sides of the island.

BY MINIBUS   Minibus is a reasonable means of transport on St. Maarten/St. Martin if you don't mind some inconvenience and overcrowding. Buses run daily from 6am to midnight and serve most of the major locations on both sides of the island. The most popular run is from Philipsburg on the Dutch side to Marigot on the French side. Privately owned and operated, minibuses tend to follow specific routes, with fares as follows: Grand Case to Marigot US$1; Philipsburg to Marigot US$1.50.

FAST FACTS: St. Maarten/St. Martin

Banks On the Dutch side, most banks are open Monday to Friday from 8am to 4:30pm, Saturday from 9am to 1pm. On the French side, they are usually open Monday to Friday 8am to noon. It's easy to find ATMs. On the Dutch side, several banks are clustered along Front Street in Philipsburg. On the French side, most banks are along rue de la République in Marigot.

Currency Despite the dominance of the euro since January 2002 within the mother country, Holland, the legal tender on the Dutch side is still the **Netherlands Antilles florin (NAf)**; the official exchange rate is NAf 1.77 for each US$1. U.S. dollars are widely accepted, and prices in hotels and most restaurants and shops are most often designated in dollars as well. On the French side, the official monetary unit is the **euro,** with most establishments widely quoting and accepting either dollars or NAf guilders as well. At press time, the U.S. dollar was trading at US$1.30 to the euro. (Just before you leave home, you can check the current exchange rates on the Web at **www.x-rates.com.**) *Prices throughout this chapter are given in U.S. dollars for establishments on the Dutch side, and in either euros or U.S. dollars for establishments on the French side.*

Documents U.S., British, and Canadian citizens should have a passport, plus an ongoing or return ticket and a confirmed hotel reservation.

Electricity Dutch St. Maarten uses the same voltage (110-volt AC, 60 cycles) with the same electrical configurations as the United States, so adapters and transformers are not necessary. However, on French St. Martin, you'll usually need transformers and adapters. To simplify things, many hotels on both sides of the island have installed sockets suitable for both European and North American appliances.

Emergencies On the **Dutch** side, call the **police** at ⓒ **599/54-22222** or an **ambulance** at ⓒ **599/54-22111;** to report a **fire,** call ⓒ **911** or ⓒ **120.** On the **French** side, you can reach the **police** by dialing ⓒ **17** or 590/87-88-33. In case of **fire,** dial ⓒ **18.** For an **ambulance** dial ⓒ **15.**

Hospitals On the Dutch side, go to the **Medical Center,** Welegen Road, Cay Hill (ⓒ **599/54-31111**). On the French side, the local hospital is **Hôpital Concordia Mont Accords,** near Marigot in Concordia (ⓒ **590/52-25-25**).

Language The language on the St. Maarten side is officially Dutch, and it's officially French on St. Martin. But most people speak English. A French-based patois is spoken by a small segment of the local populace, as are French Creole, Spanish, and Papiamento.

Liquor Laws On both sides of the island, liquor is sold in grocery and liquor stores on any day of the week. It's legal to have an open container in public, though the authorities are very strict about littering, disorderly behavior, and drunk driving.

Safety If possible, avoid night driving—it's particularly unwise to drive on remote, unlit, back roads at night due to carjackings. Also, let that deserted, isolated beach remain so. You're safer in a crowd, although under no circumstances should you ever leave anything unguarded on the beach.

Taxes & Service Charges There is 3€ (US$3.90) departure tax for departures from Espérance Airport on the French side. However, for departures from Princess Juliana Airport on the Dutch side, there's a tax of US$30 (US$10 if you're leaving the island for St. Eustatius or Saba; if you're leaving by ferry from Marigot Pier to Anguilla, the departure tax is US$4).

On the Dutch side, a government tax of between 5% and 8%, depending on the category of hotel you stay in, is added to hotel bills. On the French side, hotels must levy a *taxe de séjour* (hotel tax); this differs from hotel to hotel, depending on its classification, but is often 5% a day. In addition to these taxes, most hotels add a (mandatory) service charge of around 10% to 15% to your hotel bill.

Telephone To call Dutch St. Maarten from the United States, dial **011** (the international access code), then **599** (the country code for the Netherlands Antilles), followed by **54** and then the five-digit local number. To make a local call on Dutch St. Maarten, dial **54,** then the five-digit local number. But if you're calling "long distance" from the Dutch side of the island to the French side of the island, dial **00,** followed by **590590** (the most prevalent international access code for French St. Martin) or for cellular phones **590690,** followed by the six-digit local number.

If you're on the French side of the island and want to call anyone on the Dutch side, dial **00,** followed by **599,** then **54,** and the five-digit local number. Know in advance that calls between the French and Dutch sides are considered long-distance calls and are much, much more expensive than you might have imagined, considering the relatively short distance.

French St. Martin is linked to the Guadeloupe telephone system. To call French St. Martin from the United States, dial **011** (the international access code), then **590** (the country code for Guadeloupe), then **590** again, and the six-digit local number. To make a call from French St. Martin to any point within French St. Martin, no codes are necessary; just dial the local six-digit French number.

To call the United States from the island, dial **AT&T Direct** at ℂ **001-800/872-2881.** To reach **MCI,** dial ℂ **0800/99-00-19,** and to reach **Sprint,** dial ℂ **0800/99-00-87.** On the Dutch side there are facilities for overseas calls, but from the French side you cannot make collect calls to the States and there are no coin-operated phones. At the Marigot post office you can purchase a *Telecarte,* giving you 40 units. A typical 5-minute call to the States takes up to 120 units. There are two public phones at the Marigot tourist office from which it's possible to make credit card calls. There are six public phones at the post office.

Time St. Maarten and St. Martin operate on Atlantic Standard Time year-round. Thus, in winter, if it's 6pm in Philipsburg, it's 5pm in New York. During daylight saving time in the United States, the island and the U.S. East Coast are on the same time.

Tipping Most hotels on both sides on the island add a 10% or 15% service charge to your bill; make sure you're clear on whether or not it's already included in the original price quoted to you. Most restaurants automatically add a service charge to your bill. If service has not been added (unlikely), it's customary to tip around 15%. Taxi drivers also expect a 15% tip.

Water The water on the island is safe to drink. In fact, most hotels serve desalinated water.

Weather The island has a year-round temperature of about 80°F (27°C).

2 Accommodations

IN DUTCH ST. MAARTEN

Remember, a government tax of between 5% and 8%, plus a service charge of 10% to 15% will be added to your hotel bill. Ask whether it's included in the original rates you're quoted to save yourself a shock when you check out.

VERY EXPENSIVE

Belair Beach Hotel 🌟 *(Kids* Families, who appreciate the kitchens and the fact that children stay free, find this timeshare a good value. Originally built in 1980, a 10-minute drive from the airport, this hotel has lasted because of excellent management, good maintenance, and a reputation for quality and good value. The resort rises above a smallish swimming pool and beach. The units are one- and two-bedroom suites, each with a rather large master bedroom, two full bathrooms with tub/shower combinations, a fully equipped kitchenette (there's an on-site grocery store), and a 6m (20-ft.) terrace with a sweeping view of the sea. The suites are either timeshares or privately owned condos that are rented to visitors when their owners are not on the island.

Belair (P.O. Box 940), Philipsburg, St. Maarten, N.A. ℂ **800/480-8555** in the U.S., or 599/54-23366. Fax 599/54-26017. www.belairbeach.com. 68 units. Winter US$299–US$389 1-bedroom suite, US$349–US$419 2-bedroom suite; off season US$249 1-bedroom suite, US$279 2-bedroom suite. Children 17 and under stay free in parent's suite (subject to availability). AE, DC, DISC, MC, V. **Amenities:** Restaurant; bar; outdoor pool; tennis court; jet skis; kayaks; sailing; scuba diving; snorkeling; windsurfing; activities desk; car rental; business center; babysitting; laundry service;

coin-operated laundry; dry cleaning; rooms for those w/limited mobility. *In room:* A/C, TV, kitchen, beverage maker, hair dryer, iron, safe.

Divi Little Bay Beach Resort 🕏

Built on a desirable peninsula about a 10-minute drive east of the airport, this hotel sits on a sandy beach that's rocky in places. It originated as a simple guesthouse in 1955, and it soon became famous as the vacation home of the Netherlands' Queen Juliana, Prince Bernhard, and Queen Beatrix. It was severely damaged during the hurricanes of the early 1990s, and then it was rebuilt in 1997 as the flagship of the Divi chain. Its design evokes a European seaside village, with pastel stucco walls and terra-cotta roofs, with some Dutch colonial touches. In the upper reaches of the property are the ruins of Fort Amsterdam, once Dutch St. Maarten's most prized military stronghold and today a decorative historical site. Gardens are carefully landscaped, and Divi improved the nearby beach after it suffered massive erosion.

This hotel development is larger than its 265 units imply, since part of it is devoted to the maintenance and marketing of timeshare units. It evokes a large residential apartment complex that's enhanced with hotel-style amenities and services. Accommodations are airy, accented with ceramic tiles and pastel colors; deluxe units have kitchenettes. Bathrooms tend to be small and compact, but have adequate shelf space and a tub/shower combination.

Little Bay (P.O. Box 961), Philipsburg, St. Maarten, N.A. 🕻 **800/367-3484** in the U.S., or 599/54-22333. Fax 599/54-24336. www.divilittlebay.com. 265 units. Winter US$277–US$288 double, US$286–US$328 1-bedroom apt, US$475 2-bedroom apt; off season US$206–US$218 double, US$296–US$308 1-bedroom apt, US$355 2-bedroom apt. MAP (breakfast and dinner) US$42 per day adult, US$25 per day child (3–12). Children under 15 stay free in parent's room. AE, DC, MC, V. **Amenities:** 3 restaurants; bar; 3 outdoor pools; 2 lit tennis courts; gym; spa; watersports center; dive shop; jet skis; kayaks; sailing; snorkeling; water-skiing; windsurfing; activities coordinator; car rental; salon; laundry service; coin-operated laundry; nonsmoking rooms. *In room:* A/C, TV, kitchenette, beverage maker, hair dryer, iron, safe, Jacuzzi (in some).

Princess Heights 🕏 *Finds*

In the hills above Dawn Beach, which is just across the road, this is a luxury boutique hotel and an intimate hideaway. Condo accommodations showcase views of the water, and it's reached after a 10-minute drive from Philipsburg. Opening onto St. Barts in the distance, the suites are elegantly and tastefully furnished, each unit containing 1 or 2 bedrooms, with separate living rooms opening onto balconies. Granite-topped counters, clay-tiled terraces, lots of marble, and well-crafted kitchens make for fine living, and the hillside location spells privacy.

156 Oyster Pond Rd., Oyster Pond, St. Maarten, N.A. 🕻 **599/54-36906.** Fax 599/54-36007. www.princessheights.com. 15 units. Winter US$350–US$500 double; off season US$225–US$375 double. AE, DISC, MC, V. **Amenities:** Outdoor pool; fitness room; car rental; limited room service; massage; babysitting; laundry service; dry cleaning. *In room:* A/C, TV, minibar, kitchen, safe, washer/dryer (in some).

Sonesta Maho Beach Hotel & Casino 🕏

Separated into three distinct sections, each built over an 8-year period beginning in the mid-1980s, this megaresort, with its sprawling convention facilities, is the largest hotel on the island. Even with its failings, it's the closest thing on either side of the island to a Las Vegas–style blockbuster resort. It has a rather anonymous feeling (it's always full of conventioneers and giant tour groups), but it is completely modern and up-to-date, with lots of facilities that were enhanced after a US$30-million upgrade in 2001. Set on a 4-hectare (10-acre) tract that straddles the busy, and often congested, coastal road adjacent to the crescent-shaped Maho Beach, the hotel's scattered structures are painted a trademark cream and white.

The rooms are fairly spacious and conservatively but comfortably furnished. Each has wicker furniture, Italian tiles, a large TV, comfortable upholstered pieces, a walk-in closet, and good soundproofing (which is important, since you hear the thundering noise of planes landing at the nearby airport several times a day when you're on the hotel's beach). Bathrooms are spacious, with bidets and tub/shower combinations.

Because of its size, the hotel contains three separate restaurants that are managed directly by the hotel, with another half-dozen on-site that are independently managed. The Casino Royale, across the street from the hotel's accommodations, is the largest casino on the island, with a cabaret theater for shows loaded with girls, razzmatazz, and glitter. The Q-Club, attached to the Casino Royale, is the island's splashiest late-night spot for drinking and dancing, complete with sophisticated light shows and cat-walks looking down on the action below.

Maho Beach, 1 Rhine Rd., St. Maarten, N.A. © **800/223-0757** in the U.S., or 599/54-52115. Fax 599/54-53180. www.mahobeach.com. 600 units. Winter US$290–US$390 double, US$425–US$590 suite, from US$780 2-bedroom unit; off season US$225–US$295 double, US$330–US$400 suite, from US$660 2-bedroom unit. AE, DC, DISC, MC, V. **Amenities:** 3 restaurants; 2 outdoor pools; casino; dance club; golf (nearby); 4 tennis courts; fitness center; spa; business services; babysitting; laundry service; rooms for those w/limited mobility. *In room:* A/C, TV, dataport, beverage maker (in some), fridge (in some), hair dryer, safe.

EXPENSIVE

Caravanserai Beach Resort 🏵 This long-time favorite at the airport keeps getting blown away by hurricanes, but always bounces back to reclaim its place as one of the island's leading hostelries. It fronts a small beach where the hotel has erected a sea wall for protection. Grounds feature palms, waterfalls, and rock pools. Accommodations are spacious and tastefully furnished, with tub/shower combinations in the suites, showers in the doubles, a mixture of pastel colors and dark-stained wood trim, and much comfort. You can choose between ocean-view rooms and units opening onto the gardens or pools, as well as one-bedroom suites.

2 Beacon Hill Rd., St. Maarten, N.A. © **877/796-1002** in the U.S., or 599/54-54000. Fax 599/54-54001. www. caravanseraibeachresort.com. 75 units. Winter US$210–US$270 double, US$395 1-bedroom apt; off season US$160–US$220 double, US$350 1-bedroom apt. AE, MC, V. **Amenities:** 4 restaurants; 4 bars; 4 outdoor pools; casino; tennis court; fitness center; diving; fishing; snorkeling; tour desk; minimarket; boutique; babysitting; laundry service; nonsmoking rooms. *In room:* A/C, TV, fax, fridge, hair dryer, iron, safe.

The Horny Toad Guesthouse 🏵 *(Value)* This homey, welcoming place is run by an expatriate from Maine, Betty Vaughan. Unfortunately, the hotel is near the airport, but the roar of jumbo jets is heard only a few times a day for a few moments. Children 7 and under are not allowed, but families with older children often come here to avoid the megaresorts, and second-timers quickly become "part of the family."

Seven well-maintained units are in an amply proportioned beachside house originally built in the 1950s as a private home by the island's former governor. The eighth room is in half of an octagonal "round house," with large windows and views of the sea. Guest rooms range from medium-size to spacious, and each has a fully equipped kitchen, and a small but well-kept shower-only bathroom. There's no pool, no restaurant, and no organized activities of any kind. However, the beach is a few steps away, and there are often impromptu get-togethers around the pair of gas-fired barbecues.

2 Vlaun Dr., Simpson Bay, St. Maarten, N.A. © **800/417-9361** in the U.S., or 599/54-54323. Fax 599/54-53316. www.thehornytoadguesthouse.com. 8 units. Winter US$198 double; off season US$107 double. Extra person US$40 in winter, US$25 off season. MC, V. No children under 7 allowed. **Amenities:** Laundry service; nonsmoking rooms. *In room:* A/C (in some), ceiling fan, kitchen, fridge, safe, no phone.

Oyster Bay Beach Resort ⭐ At the end of a twisting, scenic road, a 1-minute walk from Dawn Beach, this elegant retreat was originally designed for vacationers who don't like overly commercialized megaresorts, like Maho Beach Hotel. Once an intimate inn, it's been growing by leaps and bounds, having witnessed a five-fold increase in size since it was established as an isolated inn in the 1960s. It can't be considered intimate anymore, but it's still not overwhelming. On a circular harbor on the eastern shore, near the French border, the fortresslike structure stands guard over a 14-hectare (35-acre) protected marina. There's a central courtyard and an alfresco lobby, with brown wicker and fine paintings. There's an intense focus here on marketing some of the units as timeshares.

More than half the units have kitchens, and most have West Indian decor with lots of rattan and wicker. The bedrooms offer balconies overlooking the pond or sea; the deluxe and superior rooms are preferable to the tower suites. Rooms are airy and fairly spacious, and suites have a bathroom with a tub and a shower.

The resort's restaurant, Jade, serves international and Asian (mostly Indonesian) food for breakfast, lunch, and dinner. Beaubeau's, on the beach, serves seafood and international fare at lunch and dinner.

10 Emerald Merit Rd., Oyster Pond (P.O. Box 239), St. Maarten, N.A. © **866/978-0212** in the U.S., or 599/54-36040. Fax 599/54-36695. www.oysterbaybeachresort.com. 178 units (of those, 153 are timeshares). Winter US$225–US$300 double, US$325–US$675 suite; off season US$150–US$250 double, US$250–US$520 suite. Extra person US$50–US$60. Children under 12 stay free in parent's room. AE, DISC, MC, V. **Amenities:** 2 restaurants; 2 bars; outdoor pool; 4 tennis courts; fitness center; car rental; activities desk; babysitting; coin-operated laundry; 1 room for those w/limited mobility. *In room:* A/C, TV, dataport, kitchen (in most), fridge, beverage maker, hair dryer, iron, safe.

MODERATE/INEXPENSIVE

La Vista ⭐ This small West Antillean–style complex lies at the foot of Pelican Cay. For a fee, guests can use the more elaborate facilities of the nearby Pelican Resort, with its casino, shops, and spa. The resort consists of two parts—La Vista Resort, a 2-minute walk from a good sandy beach, and La Vista Beach Resort, whose units open directly on the beach with studios and 2-bedroom apartments. Rooms with a view come in seven different categories, including a junior suite, deluxe suite, penthouse, or cottage. Accommodations feature fully equipped kitchenettes and medium-size bathrooms with shower. Our preference is the one-bedroom Antillean cottage with its front porch (suitable for occupancy by four).

The Hideaway serves well-prepared French cuisine adjacent to the pool, with live entertainment several nights a week.

53 Billy Folly Rd., Pelican Cay (P.O. Box 2086), Simpson Bay, St. Maarten, NA © **599/54-43005.** Fax 599/54-43010. www.lavistaresort.com. 50 suites. Winter US$180 double, US$210–US$330 suites for 4; off season US$140 double, US$160–US$225 suites for 4. Children under 12 stay free when sharing with 2 adults. AE, DISC, MC, V. **Amenities:** Restaurant; bar; large outdoor pool; coin-operated laundry. *In room:* A/C, TV, kitchenette, fridge, beverage maker, hair dryer, iron, safe.

Mary's Boon Beach Plantation ⭐⭐ *(Finds)* This is the most charming and well-managed small inn on Dutch St. Maarten. It's very near the airport (so you do get the sounds of jets taking off and landing a few times a day), but it's also only minutes from casinos, shops, and restaurants. Mary's Boon draws a loyal repeat clientele that appreciates its sense of intimacy and understated elegance. Everything's relaxed and informal, though the service is alert and attentive.

Accommodations have verandas or terraces, but each varies architecturally. Those facing the sea directly are breezy, high-ceilinged, and comfortably unpretentious, with furnishings like what you'd expect in a 1970s-era Florida motel. Try to get one of the newer units set within the garden; they're very stylish, showing the deft touch of a professional decorator. Done in jewel tones, they usually contain four-poster cherrywood beds and Balinese woodcarvings. Regardless of their age, most units have king-size beds. The inn enjoys direct access to one of the best beaches on St. Maarten, with white sands. The family-style restaurant offers good-value fixed-price dinners (with seconds included).

117 Simpson Bay Rd., St. Maarten, N.A. (or P.O. Box 523882, Miami, FL 33152). (C) **599/54-57000.** Fax 599/54-53403. www.marysboon.com. 26 units. Winter US$175–US$275 double; off season US$75–US$200 double. AE, MC, V. Take the first right-hand turn as you head from the airport toward Philipsburg, then follow the signs to Mary's Boon. **Amenities:** Restaurant; bar; outdoor pool; limited room service; babysitting. *In room:* A/C, ceiling fan, TV, dataport, kitchenette, fridge, beverage maker, hair dryer, iron, safe.

Pasanggrahan Royal Inn ⭐ *(Value* *Pasanggrahan* is the Indonesian word for guesthouse, and this West Indian–style guesthouse lies 15m (50 ft.) from a private beach. A small, informal place, it's right on the busy, narrow main street of Philipsburg, toward the end of the mountainside of Front Street. It's set back under tall trees, with a white wooden veranda. The interior has peacock bamboo chairs, Indian spool tables, and a gilt-framed oil portrait of Queen Wilhelmina. The small- to medium-size renovated bedrooms have queen-size, double, or king-size beds with good mattresses and four-poster designs; some are in the main building and others are in an adjoining annex. Bathrooms are small but tidy, and all have tub/shower combinations.

Set among the wild jungle of palms and shrubbery is the Pasanggrahan Restaurant, which specializes in freshly caught fish, lobster being the house specialty.

19 Front St. (P.O. Box 151), Philipsburg, St. Maarten, N.A. (C) **599/54-23588.** Fax 599/54-22885. www.pasanhotel. com. 30 units. Winter US$158–US$250 double; off season US$125–US$165 double. Extra person winter US$75, off-season US$55. DISC, MC, V. Closed Sept. **Amenities:** Restaurant; 2 bars; laundry service. *In room:* A/C, ceiling fan, TV, dataport, kitchenette (in some), fridge, beverage maker (in some), safe (in some).

The Pelican *(Value* *(Kids* This resort, built in 1979 on 5 hectares (12 acres) of land near the airport, is the largest timeshare facility on St. Maarten, and the staff appears at times more interested in hawking these properties than in running a hotel. Nevertheless, it's a good value, with lots of amenities, and it's a decent backup choice if the other resorts are full. Although many of the suites are leased for predesignated periods throughout the year, others are rented by the on-site managers as they become available. Accommodations, which contain ceiling fans, tub/shower bathrooms, and full kitchens, are arranged into village-style clusters separated from other units by lattices, hibiscus hedges, and bougainvillea. Each unit is fairly spacious, equipped with straightforward furnishings and comfortable king-size or double beds, and most units have patios or verandas. Scattered around the property are many small waterways and an orchid garden, not to mention the beachfront.

Simpson Bay (P.O. Box 431), Philipsburg, St. Maarten, N.A. (C) **800/550-7088** in the U.S., or 599/54-42503. Fax 599/54-42133. www.pelicanresort.com. 342 units. Winter US$135-US$170 studio, US$215 1-bedroom suite, US$336 2-bedroom suite, US$400 3-bedroom suite. Off-season US$90-US$115 studio, US$170 1-bedroom suite, US$235 2-bedroom suite, US$295 3-bedroom suite. AE, DISC, MC, V. **Amenities:** 2 restaurants; 5 bars; 5 outdoor pools; casino; 4 lit tennis courts; gym; spa; dive shop; windsurfing; children's center; car rental; babysitting; laundry service; dry cleaning; rooms for those w/limited mobility. *In room:* A/C, ceiling fan, TV, kitchen, fridge, beverage maker, hair dryer (in some), safe.

IN FRENCH ST. MARTIN

Hotels on French St. Martin add a 10% service charge and a *taxe de séjour.* This visitors' tax on rooms differs from hotel to hotel, depending on its classification, but is often US$4 a day.

VERY EXPENSIVE

Alamanda Resort ⓕ★   Small and intimate, like a European beachfront inn, the Alamanda is a sort of boutique resort opening onto Orient Bay's beautiful beach. The resort is a cluster of Creole *cazes* or little houses surrounding a lushly landscaped outdoor pool quite near the beach. Not all rooms have ocean views but that's one of the few drawbacks. Bedrooms are spacious and decorated with Caribbean fabrics and bold colors, ranging from sunflower yellow to tomato red or "ocean turquoise." Framed lanatana weavings and throw pillows in pineapple patterns are just some of the decorative accents used, and the beds are elegantly carved, often a four-poster. The best accommodations are the 2-bedroom duplexes with a second bathroom. Our favorite place to dine here is at Kakao Beach restaurant, featuring both Creole and European specialties in a laid-back Caribbean atmosphere. A less expensive choice is the Alamanda Café, with an inventive tropical cuisine served at poolside.

Baie Orientale, St. Martin, F.W.I. ⓒ **800/622-7836** in the U.S. or 590/52-87-40. Fax 590/52-87-41. www.alamanda. resort.com. 42 units. Winter US$330–US$495 double, US$495–US$605 suite. Off season US$240–US$330 double, US$330–US$420 suite. AE, MC, V. Closed Sept. **Amenities:** 2 restaurants; 2 bars; outdoor pool; gym; car rental; limited room service; massage; babysitting; laundry service/dry cleaning; Wi-Fi access. *In room:* A/C, ceiling fan, TV, kitchenettes, dataport, hair dryer, iron, safe.

Esmeralda Resort ⓕ★   Originally conceived as a site for a single private villa, and then for a semiprivate club, this hillside housing development gives the appearance of a well-maintained compound of Creole-inspired villas on sloping terrain that's interspersed with lush gardens. It lies within a 25-minute taxi ride northeast of Queen Juliana Airport. Opening onto Orient Beach, the Esmeralda blossomed into a full-scale resort in the early 1990s, offering views over Orient Bay and a decidedly French focus. Each of the 18 Spanish mission–style, tile-roofed villas can be configured into four separate units by locking or unlocking the doors between rooms. Each individual unit contains a king-size or two double beds, a kitchenette, a shower or tub bathroom, a terrace, and a private entrance. Each villa has a communal pool, which creates the feeling of a private club.

L'Astrolabe serves French food at breakfast and dinner daily. At lunch, the hotel issues an ID card that can be used for discounts at any of a half-dozen restaurants along the nearby beach.

Parc de la Baie Orientale (B.P. 5141), 97071 St. Martin, F.W.I. ⓒ **590/87-36-36.** Fax 590/87-35-18. www.esmeralda-resort.com. 65 units. Winter US$330–US$495 double, US$605–US$715 suite; off season US$240–US$320 double, US$370-US$440 suite. AE, MC, V. Closed Sept. **Amenities:** 2 restaurants; bar; 18 outdoor pools; 2 tennis courts; parasailing; scuba diving; snorkeling; water-skiing; horseback riding (nearby); car rental; limited room service; massage; babysitting; laundry service. *In room:* A/C, ceiling fan, TV, dataport, kitchenette, fridge, beverage maker, hair dryer, safe.

Hôtel L'Esplanade Caraïbe ⓕ★   This elegant collection of suites lies on a steeply sloping hillside above the road leading into the village of Grand-Case from Marigot. Covered with cascades of bougainvillea, and accented with a vaguely Hispanic overlay of white walls, hand-painted tiles, and light-blue-colored roofs, the resort's various elements are connected by a network of concrete steps that add to the layout's drama. There's a pool, a series of gorgeous terraced gardens, and access to a beach via a 6-minute walk on a winding, stair-dotted pathway. There's no restaurant (only a bar that's open in midwinter), but the village of Grand-Case is known for its restaurants.

All views from the guest rooms and their terraces angle out toward the sea and the sunset. Each unit contains a kitchen with a large fridge, up-to-date cookware, mahogany and wicker furniture, and very comfortable queen-size or king-size beds. Bathrooms are beautifully equipped right down to elegant toiletries baskets, and showers. The loft suites on the upper floors are worth the extra charge, as they include a sofa bed that can sleep extra guests, an upstairs master bedroom with a king-size bed, and a partial bathroom downstairs.

Grand-Case (B.P. 5007), 97150 St. Martin, F.W.I. ℂ **866/596-8365** in the U.S., or 590/87-06-55. Fax 590/87-29-15. www. lesplanade.com. 24 units. Winter US$320–US$370 double studio, US$420 suite; off season US$220-US$270 double studio, US$320 suite. Extra person winter US$70, off season US$50. AE, MC, V. **Amenities:** Bar (winter season); outdoor pool; car rental; babysitting; laundry service; rooms for those w/limited mobility. *In room:* A/C, ceiling fan, TV, dataport, kitchen, fridge, beverage maker, hair dryer, iron, safe.

La Samanna ★★★ Luxurious, sybaritic, and spectacularly expensive, this world-class resort features Mediterranean-style architecture on a 2km (1¼-mile) stretch of one of St. Martin's finest beaches. The resort was acquired by Orient Express Hotels and made especially competitive with regular and massive infusions of cash. Since then, the resort has earned a reputation as a sleek, sexy, and stylish complex where celebrities sometimes come to hide out and unwind. Despite the price tag, La Samanna isn't stuffy, and in fact reminds us in some ways of the French Riviera.

Rows of mature royal palms enhance the 22-hectare (54-acre) property's front entrance. As you enter, you see lavish art objects from Morocco and Thailand. Regardless of their size, most units have private terraces. Suites and villas have spacious bedrooms with luxurious beds, fully equipped kitchens, living and dining rooms, and large patios. The bathrooms are simpler than might be expected, but they're well designed nonetheless, with bidets, hand-painted Mexican tiles, and tub/shower combinations. The fourth floor of the main building is the site of one of the grandest suites in the Caribbean. In 2005 the resort became even more luxurious when it upgraded the interiors of five of its deluxe suites, adding rooftop terraces and plunge pools.

Guests enjoy superb French cuisine alfresco, on a candlelit terrace overlooking Baie Longue. After dinner, the bar becomes a dance club. At the poolside grill, waiters serve food, St-Tropez style, on the beach.

Baie Longue (B.P. 4077), 97064 St. Martin CEDEX, F.W.I. ℂ **800/237-1236** in the U.S., or 590/87-64-00. Fax 590/87-87-86. www.lasamanna.com. 81 units. Winter US$950 double, from US$1,750 suite or villa; off season US$450–US$680 double, from US$850 suite or villa. Rates include breakfast. AE, MC, V. Closed late Aug–late Oct. **Amenities:** Restaurant; 2 bars; outdoor pool; 3 tennis courts; fitness center; spa; sailing; snorkeling; water-skiing; windsurfing; library; 24-hr. room service; babysitting; laundry service; dry cleaning; nonsmoking rooms. *In room:* A/C, ceiling fan, TV, minibar, beverage maker, hair dryer, iron, safe, plunge pool (in some).

Le Petit Hotel ★ *Finds* This is a stylish, well-managed, thoughtfully designed hotel, set on a small parcel of property that's squeezed between other buildings, with direct access to the sands of Grand-Case Beach. Much of its appeal derives from its hardworking manager, Miriam Staley, who offers advice on any of the two dozen restaurants in nearby Grand-Case (since there's no restaurant on-site). Nine of the spacious units are studios, while the 10th is a one-bedroom apartment. Each has a well-equipped kitchenette with a microwave, fridge, and a two-burner stovetop, but no oven. All units have balconies or outdoor terraces, plus durable, comfortable furniture. The small bathrooms come with shower stalls.

248 bd. de Grand-Case, Grand-Case, 97150 St. Martin, F.W.I. ℂ **590/29-09-65.** Fax 590/87-09-19. www.lepetithotel. com. 10 units. Winter US$340–US$380 studio for 2, US$450 1-bedroom apt for up to 4; off season US$240–US$280 studio for 2, US$350 1-bedroom apt for up to 4. Extra person US$70. Children under 7 stay free in parent's room. AE, MC, V. **Amenities:** Activities desk; babysitting; laundry service; 1 room for those w/limited mobility. *In room:* A/C, ceiling fan, TV, kitchenette, fridge, beverage maker, hair dryer, iron, safe, Wi-Fi.

EXPENSIVE

Club Orient Naturist Resort ⚡ *Finds* Occupying an isolated spot, this is the only true nudist resort in the French West Indies. Established in the late 1970s by a Dutch-born family, it welcomes a European and North American clientele. This is definitely *not* a wild, swinging, party place. It's very clean, decent, middle-class, and even family friendly. Very few single guests check in, so if you're looking for partners to play with, don't plan on meeting someone here. Despite their lack of clothing, many of the guests are very conservative—looking for a quiet, reclusive getaway with like-minded nudists. There's no pool on the premises, but the chalets are right on an excellent beach. Accommodations, set in red-pine chalets imported from Finland, are utterly plain and simple; all have outside showers and most have both front and back porches. At Papagayo you can dine alfresco (literally). However, most guests opt to cook their own meals, as each unit has a kitchenette and there's a minimarket on-site.

Baie Orientale, 97150 St. Martin, F.W.I. © **800/690-0199** in the U.S., or 590/87-33-85. Fax 590/87-33-76. www.club orient.com. 137 units. Winter 215€–270€ (US$280–US$351) studio and mini-suites; 330€–395€ (US$429–US$514) chalet; 1,000€ (US$1,300) villa. Off-season 125€–200€ (US$163–US$260) studio and suites, 185€–250€ (US$241–US$325) chalet, 600€–800€ (US$780–US$1,040) villa. AE, DC, DISC, MC, V. **Amenities:** Restaurant; 2 bars; gym; library; massage; babysitting; laundry service; coin-operated laundry; 1 room for those w/limited mobility. *In room:* A/C, ceiling fan, kitchen, beverage maker, safe.

Hotel Beach Plaza ⚡ This is our favorite hotel within a reasonable distance of Marigot's commercial heart. A three-story building that centers on a soaring atrium festooned with live banana trees and climbing vines, it's within a cluster of buildings mostly composed of condominiums. Built in 1996, and painted in shades of blue and white, it's set midway between the open sea and the lagoon, giving all rooms water views. Inside, the decor is pure white, accented with varnished, dark-tinted woods and an inviting tropical motif. Each room contains a balcony, tile floors, native art, and simple hardwood furniture, including a writing desk and comfortable beds. Bathrooms have tub/shower combinations and generous shelf space.

The hotel's restaurant, Le Corsaire, serves French food except for the all-you-can-eat buffets on Tuesday and Friday nights, which feature Creole and seafood, respectively.

Baie de Marigot, 97150 St. Martin, F.W.I. © **590/87-87-00.** Fax 590/87-18-87. www.hotelbeachplazasxm.com. 144 units. Winter US$238–US$381 double, from US$547 suite; off season US$193–US$270 double, from US$438 suite. Rates higher between Christmas and New Year's. Rates include buffet breakfast. AE, MC, V. **Amenities:** Restaurant; 2 bars; outdoor pool; jet skis; kayaks; scuba diving; snorkeling; bike rental; car rental; limited room service; babysitting; laundry service; nonsmoking rooms; rooms for those w/limited mobility. *In room:* A/C, TV, minibar, fridge, hair dryer, safe.

Mercure Coralia Simpson Beach *Value* This is one of the most stylish hotels in its price bracket on the French side of the island. The complex occupies a flat, sandy stretch of land between a saltwater lagoon and the beach, 8km (5 miles) west of Princess Juliana Airport. Decorated throughout in ocean-inspired pastels, its five three-story buildings are each evocative of a large, many-balconied Antillean house. In its center, a pool serves as the focal point for a bar built out over the lagoon, an indoor/outdoor restaurant, and a flagstone terrace that hosts steel bands and evening cocktail parties. Each unit offers, in addition to the kitchenette, simple, durable wicker furniture, plus a tiled, shower-only bathroom. The most desirable accommodations, on the third (top) floor, contain sloping ceilings sheltering sleeping lofts, and two bathrooms.

Baie Nettlé (B.P. 172), Marigot, 97052 St. Martin, F.W.I. © **800/221-4542** in the U.S., or 590/87-54-54. Fax 590/87-92-11. 168 units. Winter US$294 studio for 2, from US$323 duplex; off season US$205 studio for 2, US$244 duplex. Rates include buffet breakfast. AE, DC, MC, V. **Amenities:** Restaurant; bar; outdoor pool; tennis court; dive center;

kayaking; snorkeling; water-skiing; windsurfing; bikes; car rental; babysitting; laundry service; dry cleaning; rooms for those w/limited mobility. *In room:* A/C, TV, dataport, minibar, beverage maker (in some), hair dryer (in some), safe.

MODERATE/INEXPENSIVE

Hôtel St.-Tropez des Caraïbes

In the early 1990s, a much larger hotel on this spot split up after its managers dissolved their partnership. This hotel is one of the two separate entities, and the background explains why it's flanked on either side by very similar-looking properties. The St.-Tropez des Caraïbes is the better maintained of the two. Don't expect too many hotel-style amenities here, as there's no bar, and very little to do on-site—but with the sweeping sands of Orient Beach at your disposal, you may not care. Three of the units have a kitchen, but many bars and restaurants are within walking distance. Seven units lie within each of eight neo-Romanesque buff- and pink-colored buildings. Rooms are genuinely appealing, each with bright but soft tones of pink and green, floral upholsteries, a balcony, and a bathroom with a shower. The best accommodations, with the highest ceilings and the greatest sense of space, lie on the top (third) floor of each of the eight buildings. A 7-day minimum stay is required.

Baie Orientale (B.P. 5137), 97070 St. Martin, F.W.I. ✆ **590/87-42-01.** Fax 590/87-41-69. www.st-tropez-caraibes. com. 28 units. Winter US$185-US$280 per week double; off-season US$135-US$185 double. Extra person US$44 per day. AE, DISC, MC, V. **Amenities:** Outdoor pool; laundry service; 1 room for those w/limited mobility. *In room:* A/C, ceiling fan, TV, kitchenette (in some), fridge, beverage maker, hair dryer, safe.

La Plantation Orient Bay Resort ✶

Although it requires a few minutes walk to reach the gorgeous white-sand beach, this is one of the most attractive and appealing hotels at Orient Bay. It's set on a steep, carefully landscaped slope, and designed like an upscale and rather charming condo complex. Seventeen colonial-style villas are scattered around the tropically landscaped grounds and pool; each villa contains a suite and two studios, which can be rented separately or combined. The spacious units are stylishly furnished in a South Seas/Polynesian/Creole theme, complete with hand-painted or hand-stenciled murals, and each sports its own ocean-view terrace. Studios have kitchenettes and queen-size or twin beds; the suites have separate bedrooms with king-size beds, spacious living rooms, full kitchens, and beautifully tiled full bathrooms.

Café Plantation serves French and Creole dinners. At lunch, clients use an in-house ID card to buy French/Creole/international meals at any of five beachfront restaurants loosely associated with the resort.

C 5 Parc de la Baie Orientale, Orient Bay, 97150 St. Martin, F.W.I. ✆ **590/29-58-00.** Fax 590/29-58-08. www.la-plantation.com. 52 units. Winter US$245 studio for 2, from US$360 suite; off season US$160–US$185 studio, from US$245 suite. Rates include breakfast. DISC, MC, V. Closed Sept 1 to mid-Oct. **Amenities:** Restaurant; beach bar and grill; outdoor pool; 2 tennis courts; health club; diving; jet ski; parasailing; windsurfing; bike rental; horseback riding; boutiques; massage. *In room:* A/C, ceiling fan, TV, kitchen, fridge, beverage maker, hair dryer, safe.

Le Cosy

In the commercial center of Marigot (and favored by business travelers for its location), Le Cosy's concrete facade is enlivened with neo-Victorian gingerbread fretwork. A bar with a soaring tent serves drinks to guests relaxing on wicker and bentwood furniture. The small bedrooms are arranged around a landscaped central courtyard with a fish-shaped fountain. Each room is minimally decorated, and all but a few are duplexes with mahogany-trimmed stairs climbing to a sleeping loft. Bathrooms are also small, with shower stalls.

The simple restaurant serves dinner only. The staff rather defines meals as French *cuisine gastronomique,* but we think they're more prosaic than that.

Rue du Général-de-Gaulle (B.P. 679), Marigot, 97150 St. Martin, F.W.I. ✆ **590/87-63-93.** Fax 590/87-43-95. www.lecosy hotel.com 15 units. Year-round 78€–90€ ($94–$108) double. MC, V. **Amenities:** Restaurant. *In room:* A/C, TV, minibar.

3 Dining

IN DUTCH ST. MAARTEN
EXPENSIVE

Antoine's ✦ FRENCH/ITALIAN   In a lovely setting by the sea, Antoine's serves fine food with sophistication and style. The service is first-class and the wine list impressive. Start off with a cocktail in the bar while you peruse the menu. The Gallic specialties with Creole overtones are among the best on the island, and as good as those in the better restaurants in the French zone. However, Da Livio (see below) serves better Italian food. We always start with the chef's savory kettle of fish soup or his home-made pâté. If it's featured, try the baked red snapper filet delicately flavored with white wine, lemon, shallots, and a butter sauce, or lobster thermidor. Although the veal and beef are shipped in frozen, they're used in some rather good dishes—try the veal scaloppini with its smooth, perfectly balanced mushroom, lemon, and butter sauce.

119 Front St., Philipsburg. ✆ 599/54-22964. Reservations recommended. Main courses lunch US$8–US$20, dinner US$16–US$37. AE, DISC, MC, V. Daily 11am–9:30pm.

Rare ✦✦ STEAK   We'll go out on a limb here, and claim this Dino Jagtiani's steak-house is the best and most classic "chophouse" in the Caribbean. He selects only the choice cuts, which he ages to perfection. The meat is hung in large sterile refrigerators for 21 days during its "ripening" period. The chefs here are the only ones in the Caribbean to offer certified Angus prime beef. The house specialty is a 16-ounce dry aged Angus strip steak—hand cut, robust in flavor, and grilled to your liking. The fork-tender veal chop, weighing 12 ounces, bursts with flavor. Perhaps the ultimate for steak lovers is the "de-constructed porterhouse," a 16-ounce dry aged strip. If you don't like steak (perhaps you should eat elsewhere), the menu also features a succulent Maine lobster and even Dover sole in lemon butter. To get you going, appetizers are some of the best on island, especially the Prince Edward oysters Rockefeller and the jumbo lump crab cake. Vegetarians can come here just for the side dishes, especially those truffled mashed potatoes or the Vidalia onion rings with chipotle catsup.

Atlantis Casino, Cupecoy. ✆ 599/54-55714. www.dare-to-be-rare.com. Reservations required. Main courses US$20–US$54. AE, DISC, MC, V. Daily 6-10:30pm.

Saratoga ✦ INTERNATIONAL/SEAFOOD   This is the most creative and cut-ting-edge restaurant in St. Maarten; it's laid-back and intensely choreographed at the same time. It's a beautiful setting, resembling a Spanish colonial structure from the out-side, and lined with rich mahogany inside. You might like a predinner drink ("ultra-premium margaritas" and vodka martinis are the house specialties) in the bar. Seating is either indoors or on a marina-side veranda. The menu changes every 2 days, but there's always an artfully contrived low-fat selection like onion-crusted salmon served on a compote of lentils and sweet corn. Yellowfin tuna might be grilled with basmati rice or wasabi-flavored butter and daikon leaves. Another dish is crispy-fried black sea bass with an Asian-style sauce of fermented black beans and scallions. Rack of veni-son is often featured with port sauce or some other sauce concocted by owner/chef John Jackson, who hails from Saratoga Springs, New York.

Simpson Bay Yacht Club, Airport Rd. ✆ 599/54-42421. Reservations recommended. Main courses US$24–US$37. AE, MC, V. Mon–Sat 6:30–10pm. Closed Aug–Sept.

Temptation ✦✦✦ NOUVELLE CARIBBEAN   Owner-chef Dino Jagtiani not only brings us Rare (see above) at the Atlantis Casino, but he also tempts our palates with

Temptation. Chances are you'll be seduced by his inventive menu that bursts with flavor and freshness. Each dish is an original such as the grilled peach salad that uses hydroponic garden greens tossed with rosemary-flavored fresh peaches, candied pecans, and blue cheese. How about a hot and cold soup in the same bowl—chilled avocado gazpacho and Cuban-style black bean soup? Tandoori "quack quack" may have a silly name but is actually a delectable wedding of ingredients—tandoori-spiced duck breast with a coconut chile chutney along with a candied tamarind sauce and a vegetable biryani. An audacious dish is the caramelized onion-crusted Atlantic salmon with eggplant fondue and Italian sausage. If all this weren't enough, the chef also offers the island's best wine list and to-die-for desserts such as cheesecake featuring white chocolate ganache and toasted coconut/peanut ice cream, or a wet chocolate cobbler with macadamias and homemade pistachio ice cream.

Atlantis Casino, Cupecoy. ℂ 599/54-52254. www.nouveaucaribbean.com. Main courses US$25-US$37. AE, MC, V. Tues-Sun 6:30-10:30pm.

MODERATE

The Boathouse AMERICAN/INTERNATIONAL   Funky, irreverent, and friendly, this is one of the Dutch side's most enduringly popular bars/restaurants. The seafaring theme of the interior includes a soaring network of heavy timbers accented with soft yellows, blues, greens, and lots of nautical accessories. Come here for the bar, a wraparound affair that attracts good-natured expatriates and locals alike, and for the generous portions dished up by the hardworking kitchen staff. Lunches consist of sandwiches, pastas, and salads. (Especially good are the shrimp salad and the grilled chicken Caesar salad.) Main courses at dinner are more substantial, including filet mignon, pepper steak, surf and turf, and red snapper either charcoal-grilled or stuffed with shrimp and crabmeat and served with a white-wine cream sauce.

74 Airport Rd., Simpson Bay. ℂ 599/54-45409. Reservations not required. Main courses lunch US$6–US$18, dinner US$15–US$22. DISC, MC, V. Mon–Sat 11:30am–3pm; daily 5:30–10:30pm.

Cheri's Café ☞ INTERNATIONAL/AMERICAN   American expatriate Cheri Batson's island hot spot is the best bar on the island. Touristy but fun and sassy, a great place to meet people, it's outfitted in an irrepressible color scheme of hot pink and white. This open-air cafe, serving some 400 meals a night, is really only a roof without walls, and it's not even on a beach. But people flock to it anyway, devouring 18-ounce steaks, the ever-popular burgers, and grilled fresh-fish platters. The clientele represents everybody from rock bands to movie stars, from high rollers at the casino to beach bums. Some come for the cheap eats, others for the potent drinks, many to dance and flirt. The bartender's special is a frozen Straw Hat made with vodka, coconut, tequila, pineapple and orange juices, and strawberry liqueur. (We suspect yet another ingredient, but nobody's talking.) There's live music every night beginning at 8pm, and ending around midnight.

45 Cinnamon Grove Shopping Centre, Maho Beach. ℂ 599/54-53361. www.cheriscafe.com. Reservations recommended. Main courses US$11–US$33. DISC, MC, V. Wed–Mon 11am–midnight. Closed Sept.

The Greenhouse AMERICAN/INTERNATIONAL   Breezes filter through this plant-filled, open-air eatery with a view of the harbor. The menu features the catch of the day as well as burgers, and salads. Dinner specials might include fresh lobster thermidor, Jamaican jerk pork, or salmon in light dill sauce. Some of the island's best steaks are served here, each cut certified Angus beef, including New York strip, T-bone, porterhouse, or filet mignon. The chef specializes in chicken, ranging from mango chicken to chicken parmigiana. Happy hour is daily from 4:30 to 7pm and features discounted appetizers and two-for-one drinks. If entertainment is what you're after, then show up on Tuesday nights, when a DJ not only spins tunes but also gives prizes to bingo champs and trivia experts. Other nights, you can occupy yourself with pool tables and video games.

Bobby's Marina (off Front St.), Philipsburg. ℭ 599/54-22941. www.thegreenhouserestaurant.com. Main courses US$10–US$28. DISC, MC, V. Daily 11am–1am.

Turtle Pier Bar & Restaurant ★ *(Finds)* AMERICAN/SEAFOOD   Although turtles swim in a large protected pool in the nearby lagoon, they're not destined for the stew pot, but are released when they become adults. This restaurant does, however, offer one of the island's best menus of fresh seafood, much of which is caught in waters off neighboring islands. The location across from the Juliana airport is not its greatest asset, but once inside, you forget all about jets. Located on a pier beside the water, the place evokes a small zoo, with chattering parrots, even rabbits, and monkeys. On Wednesday, lobster prepared many different ways is the specialty. Because they're shipped in containers of seawater by air or sea, they're the freshest-tasting on the island. At night, you can start with the Creole-style conch soup. Fish such as mahimahi, snapper, tuna, or grouper can be grilled, poached, served meunière, or blackened. Duck is also a specialty. Our favorite is pan-seared duck breast in a sauce made from local guavaberry liqueur. Chops and steaks round out the menu.

Turtle Pier, Simpson Bay. 116 Airport Rd. ℭ 599/54-52562. www.turtlepier.com. Main courses lunch US$12–US$18, dinner US$19–US$30. AE, DISC, MC, V. Daily 7:30am–11pm.

INEXPENSIVE
Kangaroo Court SANDWICHES/SALADS   Simple and unpretentious, this cafe and sandwich shop is set on a side street between Front and Back streets, adjacent to the courthouse. The thick 200-year-old walls that shelter it are among the oldest in town, crafted of black stone that has withstood many a hurricane. Within an interior that's brightly painted in vibrant Creole colors, you'll find display racks loaded with fresh-baked pastries and espresso machines that chug out endless cups of caffeine. Salads (including versions with sesame chicken, or shrimp, avocado, and papaya) and sandwiches (beef, turkey, tuna, and grilled chicken) are sold at a roaring pace, mostly to passengers from the nearby cruise-ship docks, throughout the day.

Hendrick's Straat 6, Philipsburg. ℭ 599/54-27557. Sandwiches and salads US$8–US$14. DISC, MC, V. Mon–Sat 7:30am–5pm.

IN FRENCH ST. MARTIN
No other town in the Caribbean features as many restaurants, per capita, as the village of Grand-Case, set near French St. Martin's northernmost tip. Don't be put off by the town's ramshackle appearance: Behind the slowly decaying clapboards are French-, Italian-, and American-style restaurants managed by some extremely canny entrepreneurs, many of whom are very sophisticated cooks. If you're a real foodie and you want a decadent vacation, check into one of Grand-Case's hotels, go to a topless beach every day, and dine at a different restaurant every night.

EXPENSIVE
La Vie en Rose ★★ CLASSIC FRENCH   The dining room in this balconied second-floor restaurant evokes a tropical version of Paris in the 1920s, thanks to ceiling fans, candlelight, and some well-developed culinary showmanship. The menu is classic

French, although Caribbean flavors and overtones often creep in. Lunches are relatively simple affairs, with an emphasis on fresh, meal-size salads, simple grills like beefsteak with shallot sauce, brochettes of fresh fish, pastas, sandwiches, and salads. Dinners are more elaborate, and might begin with a lobster salad with passion-fruit dressing. Main courses include grilled filet of red snapper in puff pastry with fresh basil sauce; breast of duck with an orange-walnut sauce; fresh medallions of smoked lobster with fresh-made pasta and herbs; boneless breast of duck with raspberry sauce and fried bananas; and an unusual version of roasted rack of lamb with mushrooms. A particularly worthwhile beginner at either lunch or dinner is the house version of lobster bisque.

Bd. de France at rue de la République, Marigot. © 590/87-54-42. www.lavieenrosestmartin.com. Reservations recommended as far in advance as possible, especially in winter. Main courses lunch 9€–18€ (US$12–US$23), dinner 19€–35€ (US$25–US$46). AE, DC, DISC, MC, V. Mon–Sat 11:30am–3pm; daily 6:30–10pm.

Le Pressoir ☆ FRENCH   This bistro occupies a charming, old-fashioned Creole house painted yellow and blue. Favored by locals, it presents a combination of old and new French cuisine that includes sliced foie gras terrine, grilled beef tenderloin with camembert sauce, filet of snapper in vanilla sauce, and roasted rack of lamb with sweet-onion port sauce. Fresh products are deftly handled, their natural flavors enhanced by the use of imaginative flavorings. The restaurant's signature dish combines very fresh grilled shellfish and fish in a stew pot with beurre blanc.

30 bd. de Grand-Case, Grand-Case. © 590/87-76-62. Reservations recommended. Main courses 28€–35€ (US$36–US$46). AE, MC, V. Daily 6–10:30pm.

Rainbow Café FRENCH/INTERNATIONAL   Set on the northeastern end of the row of restaurants that line Grand-Case's main road, this little bistro thrives under the direction of Dutch-born Fleur Radd, and Buffalo, New York–born David Hendricks. The house containing the cafe opens onto views over the sea. Meals are served in an artfully simple dining room outfitted in shades of dark blue and white. Menu items evolve almost every evening—we've enjoyed chopped lamb with mashed potatoes and an onion-garlic marmalade; snapper in Parmesan-onion crust with tomato-flavored vinaigrette; and chicken breast marinated in lemon grass and ginger, with grilled balsamic-glazed vegetables. There's also salmon in puff pastry with spinach and citrus-dill butter sauce, and fricassee of scallops and shrimp served with Caribbean pineapple chutney.

176 bd. de Grand-Case, Grand-Case. © 590/87-55-80. Reservations recommended. Main courses 22€–36€ US($29–US$47). MC, V. Mon–Sat 6:30–10:30pm.

MODERATE

Claude Mini-Club ☆ (Finds) CREOLE/FRENCH   For a real Caribbean aura, head for this little discovery overlooking the harbor at Marigot. For more than 3 decades, this has been a long-enduring favorite with in-the-know locals and discerning visitors. The setting has a certain charm as it was constructed to resemble a tree house around the trunks of old palms. The decor is Haitian, capturing much of the vibrancy of that troubled island. A big terrace opens onto the sea.

The cuisine features a judicious treatment of fine products, including crab *farci* (stuffed) served with a Creole sauce. The grilled crayfish is succulent and tender. One of our favorite dishes, and certainly one of the most authentic Creole offerings, is a *lambi* (conch) stew in a zesty tomato sauce with hot spices. Other more classical dishes include a filet of beef in a green-peppercorn sauce, and veal escalope with fresh morels.

Such classic desserts as banana flambé and crème brûlée are offered. This place is busiest on Wednesday and Saturday nights, as the restaurant stages the island's best buffets, featuring such crowd pleasers as roast suckling pig, roast beef, quail, chicken, red snapper, and Caribbean lobster.

Bd. de la Mer, Marigot. ✆ **590/87-50-69.** Reservations required. Main courses 18€–30€ (US$23–US$39); fixed-price menu 26€ (US$34); buffet 42€ (US$55). AE, MC, V. Mon–Sat 11am–3pm and 6–10pm. Closed Sept.

Il Nettuno ✿ ITALIAN

This is the most elaborate, best-managed, and most appealing Italian restaurant on either side of the island, coping gracefully with a cosmopolitan, international crowd. It was established by a seasoned Italian restaurateur, Raymon Losito, whose career included a 25-year stint at a French restaurant in Washington, D.C., where he developed a deep attachment to the Washington Redskins football team, whose banners and memorabilia decorate the walls of the restaurant's bar. It's a great watering hole, outfitted in the colors of the Italian flag, and drawing a fervent crowd of fans for U.S. football games.

Meals are served on a large, rambling wooden veranda that the owners bravely refurbish after hurricanes. It serves the best blackened tuna we've ever had, as well as grilled portobello mushrooms, mussels in white-wine sauce, filet of sea wolf cooked in parchment, filet of grouper encrusted with pistachio nuts, and a worthy version of lobster risotto. The pastas are superb. There's an especially worthwhile version of sea bass baked in rock salt, prepared for a minimum of two diners.

70 bd. de Grand-Case, Grand-Case. ✆ **590/87-77-38.** www.ilnettuno.com. Reservations recommended. Main courses 21€–27€ (US$27–US$35). AE, DC, DISC, MC, V. Daily noon–2:30pm and 6–10:30pm. Closed for lunch Apr–Oct; closed Aug 30–Oct 15.

La Marine ✿ *Finds* FRENCH

Many other restaurants have occupied this blue-and-white clapboard-sided house that's set on the seaward side of the main road running through Grand-Case. Under its current management, it's one of the most laid-back restaurants in town, with the kind of insouciance you might associate with the French Riviera, and an otherwise charming staff that's sometimes a wee bit distracted. If you happen to just walk into this place, you'll be offered a roster of well-prepared but relatively uncomplicated food. These will include at least three kinds of fish fast-frozen and flown in from the French mainland, including sea bass, snapper, and salmon, each prepared as grills or "in the French style" (*à la meunière*). There are also lamb cutlets, steaks, quail, and chicken. Many locals who find this menu too limited phone in their orders a day or two in advance. If you have a hankering for duck with cocoa-and-black-pepper sauce, or fresh local seafood, it's wise to do likewise. (You might be asked to pay a deposit if your gastronomic demands are too esoteric.)

158 bd. de Grand-Case, Grand-Case. ✆ **590/87-02-31.** Reservations recommended. Main courses 18€–27€ (US$23–US$35). AE, DC, MC, V. Daily 11am–11pm.

Le Cottage ✿ FRENCH/CREOLE

One of our favorite restaurants in a town that's loaded with worthy contenders is set in what looks like a private house on the inland side of the main road running through Grand-Case. Its atmosphere is at least partly influenced by Burgundy-born wine steward, Stephane Émorine, who shows a canny ability to recommend the perfect wine by the glass to complement the French and Caribbean cuisine. Meals tend to begin dramatically with such dishes as a casserole of crayfish and avocados with a citrus sauce, or foie gras. Mains include both rustic *cuisine du terroir* (such as roasted rack of lamb with either a rosemary or a cream-based *pistou* sauce) and Creole dishes, including a filet of local dorado (mahimahi) served with a reduction of crayfish.

97 bd. de Grand-Case, Grand-Case. ✆ 590/29-03-30. www.restaurantlecottage.com. Reservations recommended. Main courses 24€–59€ (US$31–US$77). AE, DC, MC, V. Daily 6–11pm.

Sunset Café FRENCH/INTERNATIONAL   Set on the sands at the Grand-Case Beach Club, this open-air restaurant and bar wraps around the rocky peninsula that divides Grand-Case Beach from Petite Plage. Tables are strewn along a narrow veranda-style terrace that affords sweeping views of the setting sun. A planter's punch will make the fish soup, locally smoked fish, snails with Roquefort sauce, Chilean sea bass with Provençal sauce, or red snapper filet with vanilla sauce taste even better. Lunch items are simpler, with emphasis on sandwiches, burgers, pastas, and salads. The hotel here tends to be a little staid, so this place is better suited to a quiet, romantic dinner than a wild party.

In the Grand-Case Beach Club, rue de Petit-Plage, Grand-Case. ✆ 590/87-51-87. Reservations recommended for weekend dinners in winter. Main courses lunch 10€–22€ (US$12–US$29), dinner 18€–30€ (US$23–US$39). AE, MC, V. Daily 7am–midnight.

INEXPENSIVE

Kakao *Finds* *Kids* INTERNATIONAL   This French Polynesian–style open-air pavilion beside the sands of Orient Beach is always hopping. Amid dark-stained timbers, thatch-covered roofs, and nautical pieces that include the artifacts from several demolished or sunken yachts, you can drink, eat, sun, lie on lounge chairs, or simply gossip with the Euro-Caribbean crowd that hangs out here. If you're hungry, the menu lists pizzas, grilled steaks and fish, burgers, ice cream, and banana splits. This place is a bit more family friendly, and a bit less irreverent and raunchy, than Kon Tiki next door.

Orient Beach. ✆ 590/87-43-26. Pizzas 10€–14€ (US$13–US$18); main courses 17€–22€ (US$22–US$29). AE, DISC, MC, V. Daily 11:30am–5pm.

L'Oizeau Rare *Finds* *Value* FRENCH/INTERNATIONAL   This rather grand, upscale restaurant is reminiscent of a stylish eatery along the Côte d'Azur. French cuisine is served in a blue-and-ivory-colored antique house with a view of three artfully landscaped waterfalls in the garden. The tables are dressed with snowy cloths and Limoges china. At lunch, served on the covered terrace, you can choose from a number of salads and pizzas, as well as fish and meat courses. Dinner choices include fresh fish, such as snapper, salmon, and roasted rack lamb with Provençal herbs. Duck with sweet-and-sour sauce has always been a specialty, as has bouillabaisse. The cooking is grounded firmly in France, but there are Caribbean twists and flavors, which come as delightful surprises. The wine list has an extensive selection of imported French options at moderate prices. Many guests come here at sundown to enjoy the harbor view.

Bd. de France, Marigot. ✆ 590/87-56-38. Reservations recommended. Main courses lunch 15€–24€ (US$20–US$31), dinner 18€–30€ (US$23–US$39). AE, MC, V. Mon–Sat 11:30am-3pm and 6:30-10:30pm. Closed May to mid-June.

4 Beaches ★★

The island has 39 beautiful white-sand beaches, so it's fairly easy to find a place to park your towel. *Warning:* If it's too secluded, be careful. It's unwise to carry valuables to the beach; there have been robberies on some remote strips.

Regardless of where you stay, you're never far from the water. If you're a beach sampler, you can often use the changing facilities at some of the bigger resorts for a small fee. Nudists should head for the French side of the island, although the Dutch side is getting more liberal about such things. Here's a rundown of the best, starting on the Dutch side of the island.

Popular **Cupecoy Bay Beach** is very close to the Dutch-French border, on the western side of the island. It's a string of three white-sand beaches set against a backdrop of caves, beautiful rock formations, and cliffs that provide morning shade. There are no restaurants, bars, or other facilities, but locals come around with coolers of cold beer and soda for sale. The beach has two parking lots, one near Cupecoy and Sapphire beach clubs, the other a short distance to the west. Parking costs US$2. You must descend stone-carved steps to reach the sands. Cupecoy is also the island's major gay beach. Clothing is optional toward the northwest side of the beach.

Also on the west side of the island, west of the airport, white-sand **Mullet Bay Beach** is shaded by palm trees. Once it was the most crowded beach on the island, but St. Maarten's largest resort, Mullet Bay, remained closed at press time, so the crowds aren't so bad anymore. Weekdays are best, as many locals flock here on weekends. Watersports equipment can be rented at a local kiosk.

Another lovely spot near the airport, **Maho Bay Beach,** at the Maho Beach Hotel and Casino, is shaded by palms and is ideal in many ways, if you don't mind the planes taking off and landing nearby. This is one of the island's busiest beaches, buzzing with windsurfers. Food and drink can be purchased at the hotel.

Stretching the length of Simpson Bay Village are the 2km-long (1¼-mile) white sands of crescent-shaped **Simpson Bay Beach,** west of Philipsburg before you reach the airport. This beach is an ideal place for a stroll or a swim. Watersports equipment rentals are available, but there are no changing rooms or other facilities.

Great Bay Beach ⚓ is best if you're staying along Front Street in Philipsburg. This 2km-long (1¼-mile) beach is sandy, but since it borders the busy capital, it may not be as clean as some of the more remote choices. On a clear day, you'll have a view of Saba. Immediately to the west, at the foot of Fort Amsterdam, is picturesque **Little Bay Beach,** but it, too, can be overrun with tourists. When you tire of the sands here, you can climb up to the site of Fort Amsterdam itself. Built in 1631, it was the first Dutch military outpost in the Caribbean. The Spanish captured it 2 years later, making it their most important bastion east of Puerto Rico. Only a few of the fort's walls remain, but the view is panoramic.

On the east side of the island, **Dawn Beach** is noted for its underwater life, with some of the island's most beautiful reefs immediately offshore. Visitors talk ecstatically of its incredible sunrises. Dawn is suitable for swimming and offers year-round activities such as sand-castle-building contests and crab races. There's plenty of wave action for both surfers and windsurfers. The road to this beach is bumpy, but worth the effort. Nearby are the pearly white sands of **Oyster Pond Beach,** near the Oyster Bay Beach Resort. Bodysurfers like the rolling waves here.

Top rating on French St. Martin goes to **Baie Longue** ⚓ on the west side of the island, a beautiful beach that's rarely overcrowded. Chic, expensive La Samanna opens onto this beachfront. Its reef-protected waters are ideal for snorkeling, but there is a strong undertow. Baie Longue is to the north of Cupecoy Bay Beach, reached via the Lowlands Road. Don't leave any valuables in your car, as many break-ins have been reported along this occasionally dangerous stretch of highway.

Isolated **Friar's Bay Beach** lies at the end of a winding country road; its clearly sign-posted entrance intersects with the main highway between Grand-Case and Marigot. Although you certainly won't be alone here, this is a less-visited beach with ample parking. There's some topless sunbathing, depending on who happens to show up. Friar's Bay is known for its "dueling" drink shacks including an outpost called **Friar's Bay Beach Café** (no phone) where you can purchase a painting on display or order one of Laurent's platter of stuffed mussels. The competitor is **Kali's Beach Bar** (© 590/49-06-81), where Kali himself serves some of the island's best burgers and barbecue. Ask Kali about one of his "full moon parties," featuring reggae bands on the beach along with a bonfire and plenty of drink. *Tip:* Have one of the staff here point you in the direction of Happy Bay, where you avoid the crowds and discover a beach of natural, sandy beauty set against a backdrop of palms. You can snorkel around the rocks, or order the makings of a picnic at one of the bars.

White-sand **Grand-Case Beach** is right in the middle of Grand-Case and is likely to be crowded, especially on weekends. The waters are very calm, so swimming is excellent and it's a good choice for kids. A small but select beach, it has its own charm, with none of the carnival-like atmosphere found elsewhere.

To the east of Grand-Case, follow the winding road up and over Pigeon Pea Hill. The spectacular setting of **Anse Marcel** comes into view. If you'd like to anchor here, check out **Caraibes Watersports** (© 590/29-57-64), offering snorkel gear, bike rentals, parasailing, or kayaks. You can swim here or else take a hike for 1½ hours north over a hill and down to our favorite and most pristine beach on island, **Baie de Petites Cayes.** This is also the most idyllic spot on St. Martin for a picnic. A ribbon of brilliant white sand beckons, and the waters always seem to be a shade of turquoise. Part of the fun of coming here is the hike itself, with panoramic views stretching all the way to Anguilla.

On the eastern side of the island, **Orient Beach** is the island's only official nudist beach. There's steady action here: bouncy Caribbean bands, refreshments of all kinds (Dom Perignon to Beluga caviar), watersports, and clothing, crafts, and jewelry vendors. Everyone comes to enjoy this stretch of velvety white sands. The coral reef off the beach teems with marine life, making for great snorkeling. Club Orient, the nude resort, is at the end of the beach; voyeurs from cruise ships can always be spotted here. This is also a haven for windsurfers. When you tear your eyes away from the topless French beauties showing their wares, or the sunscreen-slathered Lotharios parading their endowments, you can turn to food. **Kon Tiki** (© 590/87-43-27) is your best bet, serving everything from jerk chicken to sushi. **Bikini Beach** (© 590/87-43-25), which also stays open for dinner, serves every food item from American styled hamburgers to Spanish-influenced platters of paella studded with lobster.

Finally, for the most isolated and secluded beach of all, you have to leave St. Martin. **Ilet Pinel,** off the coast at Cul-de-Sac, is reached by a ferry ride off the northeast coast. Ferries, costing US$6 per passenger, run from Cul de Sac to Pinel daily on the hour from 10am to 4pm. Watch for the last return trip at 4:30pm. You can hop aboard a CNS Watersports catamaran from Orient Beach for US$45 per person. The island has no residents (except wild goats), phones, or electricity. You will find fine white-sand beaches, idyllic reefs with great snorkeling, and waters ideal for bodysurfing. Once on Pinel, head for **Karibuni** (© 590/-39-67-00), the longest running beach bar in this country. This waterside restaurant and bar is famous for its fresh lobster lunches. At **Pinel Watersports,** a hut on the beach, you can rent pedal boats, water bikes, kayaks, and snorkeling gear.

5 Sports & Other Outdoor Activities

DEEP-SEA FISHING **Pelican Watersports,** on the Dutch side, at the Pelican Resort and Casino, Simpson Bay (© **599/54-42640**), is part of one of the island's most comprehensive resorts. Their 12m (39-ft.) *Kratuna* is available for deep-sea-fishing expeditions priced at US$125 per person for a half-day (7:30–11:30am) or US$250 per person for a full-day (7:30am–3pm) excursion. In high season, reservations must be made 1 week in advance.

GOLF The **Mullet Bay Resort** (© **599/54-53069**), on the Dutch side, has the island's only golf course. It's a slightly battered, slightly dusty 18-hole Joseph Lee–designed course, whose fate has hung in the balance, based on some ongoing court battles, for years. Although the resort itself is closed, the golf course is still operational. Mullet Pond and Simpson Bay Lagoon provide both beauty and hazards. Greens fees are US$60 for 9 holes or US$88 for 18 holes, for players who opt to walk instead of ride. Renting a two-person electric cart will cost an additional US$8 to US$18 depending on how many holes you play. Club rentals cost US$21 for 9 holes or US$26 for 18 holes.

HORSEBACK RIDING Horseback riding is available at **Bayside Riding Club,** Route Galion Beach, Orientale (© **590/87-36-64**). Beach rides are a highlight, and prices start at US$70 for 2 hours per person, US$50 for 1 hour.

SCUBA DIVING Scuba diving is excellent around **St. Martin,** with reef, wreck, night, cave, and drift diving; the depth of dives is 6 to 21m (20–69 ft.). Off the northeastern coast on the French side, dive sites include Ilet Pinel, for shallow diving; Green Key, a barrier reef; and Tintamarre, for sheltered coves and geologic faults. To the north, Anse Marcel and neighboring Anguilla are good choices. Most hotels will arrange scuba excursions on request.

The island's premier dive operation is **Scuba Fun,** whose offices are immediately adjacent to the West Indies Mall, Chemin du Port, Marigot (© **590/87-36-13;** www. scubafun.com), it offers morning and afternoon dives in deep and shallow water, wreck dives, and reef dives, at a cost of US$45 per dive (certified divers only). A resort course for first-time divers with reasonable swimming skills costs US$75 and includes instruction in a swimming pool and a one-tank shallow dive above a coral reef. Full PADI certification costs US$350, an experience that requires 5 days and includes classroom training, sessions with a scuba tank within the safety of a swimming pool, and three open-water dives. Snorkeling trips cost US$30 for a half-day, plus US$10 for equipment rental.

St. Maarten's crystal-clear bays and countless coves make for good scuba diving as well as snorkeling. Underwater visibility runs from 23 to 38m (75–125 ft.). The biggest attraction for divers is the 1801 British man-of-war, **HMS *Proselyte,*** which came to a watery grave on a reef 2km (1¼ miles) off the coast. Most of the big resorts have facilities for scuba diving and can provide information about underwater tours, photography, and night diving.

SNORKELING 🐠🐠 The calm waters ringing the shallow reefs and tiny coves found throughout the island make it a snorkeler's heaven. The waters off the northeastern shores of French St. Martin have been classified as a regional underwater nature reserve, **Réserve Sous-Marine Régionale,** which protects the area around Flat Island (also known as Tintamarre), Ilet Pinel, Green Key, Proselyte, and Petite Clef.

Equipment can be rented at almost any hotel, and most beaches have watersports kiosks.

One of St. Martin's best sources for snorkeling and other beach diversions is **Carib Watersports** (© 590/87-51-87), a clothing store, art gallery, and watersports kiosk on the beachfront of the Grand-Case Beach Club. Its French and U.S. staff provides information on island activities and rents kayaks for US$20 an hour, paddleboats for US$20 an hour, and snorkeling equipment for US$10 a day. The main allure, however, are the guided snorkeling trips to St. Martin's teeming offshore reefs, including Creole Rock, an offshore clump of reef-ringed boulders rich in underwater fauna. The 2-hour trips depart daily at 10am, noon, and 2pm, and cost US$30, with all equipment included. Reservations are recommended.

TENNIS You can try the courts at most of the large resorts, but you must call first for a reservation. Preference, of course, is given to hotel guests.

On the Dutch side, there are four courts at the **Maho Beach Hotel,** Maho Bay (© 599/54-52115). **The Pelican,** Simpson Bay (© 599/54-42503) has four courts, and the **Divi Little Bay Beach Resort,** Little Bay Road (© 599/54-22333), has one court, but they are for guest play only. On the French side, the **Privilège Resort & Spa,** Anse Marcel (© 590/87-46-15), offers four lit tennis courts and two squash courts.

WATER-SKIING & PARASAILING Most of French St. Martin's large beachfront hotels maintain facilities for water-skiing and parasailing, often from kiosks that operate on the beach.

An independent operator on Orient Bay, close to the cluster of hotels near the Esmeralda Hotel, is **Kon Tiki Watersports** (© 590/87-46-89). It rents jet skis for around US$45 per half-hour, US$80 per hour; parasailing costs US$50 for 10 minutes or US$90 if two go together.

Jet-skiing and water-skiing are also especially popular in Dutch St. Maarten. The unruffled waters of Simpson Bay Lagoon, the largest lagoon in the West Indies, are ideal for these sports, and outfitters have facilities right on the sands.

WINDSURFING Most windsurfers gravitate to the eastern part of the island, most notably Coconut Grove Beach, Orient Beach, and to a lesser extent, Dawn Beach, all in French St. Martin. The best of the several outfitters here is **Tropical Wave,** Coconut Grove, Le Galion Beach, Baie de l'Embouchure (© 590/87-37-25). Set midway between Orient Beach and Oyster Pond, it has an ideal combination of wind and calm waters. Tropical Wave is the island's leading sales agent for Mistral windsurfers. They rent for 20€ (US$26) an hour, with instruction offered at 30€ (US$39) an hour. In St. Maarten, visitors usually head to Simpson Bay Lagoon for windsurfing.

6 Shopping ⟨⋆⟨⋆⟨⋆

IN DUTCH ST. MAARTEN

Not only is St. Maarten a free port, but it also has no local sales taxes. Prices are sometimes lower here than anywhere else in the Caribbean, except possibly St. Thomas. On some items (fine liqueurs, cigarettes, Irish linen, German cameras, French perfumes), we've found prices 30% to 50% lower than in the United States or Canada. Many well-known shops on Curaçao have branches here.

Except for the boutiques at resort hotels, the main shopping area is in the center of **Philipsburg.** Most of the shops are on **Voorstraat (Front Street),** which stretches for about 2km (1¼ miles) and is lined with stores. More shops are along the little lanes, known as *steegjes,* that connect Front Street with **Achterstraat (Back Street),** another shoppers' haven.

In general, the prices marked on the merchandise are firm, though at some small, very personally run shops, where the owner is on-site, some bargaining might be in order.

Antillean Liquors, Queen Juliana Airport (② **599/54-54267**), has a complete assortment of liquor and liqueurs, cigarettes, and cigars. Prices are generally lower here than in other stores on the island, and the selection is larger. Locally produced guavaberry liqueur is also for sale.

Del Sol St-Maarten, 23 Front St. (② **599/54-28784**), sells men's and women's sportswear. Embedded into the mostly black-and-white designs are organic crystals that react to ultraviolet light, which transforms the fabric into a rainbow of colors. Step back into the shadows, and your T-shirt will revert to its original black-and-white design. The same technology is applied to yo-yos, which shimmer psychedelically when you bob them up and down.

Colombian Emeralds International, Old Street Shopping Center (② **599/54-23933**), sells unmounted emeralds from Colombia, as well as emerald, gold, diamond, ruby, and sapphire jewelry. Prices are approximately the same as in other outlets of this famous Caribbean chain. There are some huckster vendors around the island pawning fakes off on unsuspecting tourists; if you're seriously shopping for emerald, this is the place.

Belgian Chocolate Shop, 109 Old St. (② **599/54-28863**), is the best of its kind on island. Contrary to popular rumor, only *some* of the velvety chocolates sold in this upscale shop are pornographic, portraying parts of the human anatomy. It's always busy here, especially when cruise ships are berthed at the nearby piers.

Guavaberry Company, 8–10 Front St. (② **599/54-22965**), sells the rare "island folk liqueur" of St. Maarten, which for centuries was made only in private homes. Sold in square bottles, this rum-based liqueur is flavored with rare guavaberries, usually grown on the hills in the center of the island. (Don't confuse guavaberries with guavas—they're very different.) The liqueur has a fruity, woody, almost bittersweet flavor. You can blend it with coconut for a guavaberry colada or pour a splash into a glass of icy champagne. They also sell mango liqueur, spices, and various types of hot sauces.

Greenwich Galleries, 35 Front St. (② **599/54-23842**), is the most interesting and sophisticated art gallery on either side of the island, with Bajan pottery in tones of sea greens and blues, replicas of Taíno artifacts from the Dominican Republic, enameled metal cutouts that are both quirky and perplexing, and a range of paintings and lithographs from artists as far away as Holland and Britain.

Little Switzerland, 52 Front St. (② **599/54-22523**), is part of a chain of stores spread throughout the Caribbean. These fine-quality European imports are made even more attractive by the prices, often 25% (or more) lower than stateside. Elegant famous-name watches, china, crystal, and jewelry are for sale, plus Tiffany perfumes and accessories. Little Switzerland has the best overall selection of these items of any shop on the Dutch side.

IN FRENCH ST. MARTIN

Many day-trippers come over to Marigot from the Dutch side of the island just to visit the French-inspired boutiques and shopping arcades. Because St. Martin is also a duty-free port, you'll find some of the best shopping in the Caribbean here as well. There's a wide selection of European merchandise, much of it luxury items such as crystal, fashions, fine liqueurs, and cigars, sometimes at 25% to 50% less than in the United States and Canada. Whether you're seeking jewelry, perfume, or St. Tropez bikinis, you'll find it in one of the boutiques along **rue de la République** and **rue de la Liberté** in Marigot. Look especially for French luxury items, such as Lalique crystal, Vuitton bags, and Chanel perfume.

Prices are often quoted in U.S. dollars, and salespeople frequently speak English. Credit cards and traveler's checks are generally accepted. When cruise ships are in port on Sundays and holidays, some of the larger shops stay open.

At harborside in Marigot, there's a lively **morning market** on Wednesday and Saturday with vendors selling spices, fruit, shells, and handicrafts. Shops here tend to be rather upscale, catering to passengers of the small but choice cruise ships that dock offshore.

At bustling **Port La Royale,** mornings are even more active: Schooners unload produce from the neighboring islands, boats board guests for picnics on deserted beaches, a brigantine sets out on a sightseeing sail, and a dozen different little restaurants are readying for the lunch crowd. One of the largest shopping arcades on St. Martin, Port La Royale has lots of boutiques.

Havane Boutique, 50 Marina Port La Royale (© **590/87-70-39**), is a hyper-stylish menswear store, more couture than ready-to-wear. **Serge Blanco "15" Boutique,** Marina Port La Royale (© **590/29-65-49**), is a relatively unknown name in North America, but in France Blanco is revered as one of the most successful rugby players of all time. His menswear is sporty, fun, and elegant. Clothes include polo shirts, shorts, shoes, and truly wonderful latex jackets.

Another complex, the **Galerie Périgourdine,** facing the post office, also has a cluster of boutiques. Here you can pick up designer wear for both men and women, including items from the collection of Ted Lapidus.

Act III, 3 rue du Général-de-Gaulle (© **590/29-28-43**), is perhaps the most glamorous women's boutique in St. Martin. It prides itself on its evening gowns and chic cocktail dresses. If you've been invited to a reception aboard a private yacht, this is the place to find the right outfit. Designers include Alaïa, Gianni Versace, Christian Lacroix, Cavalli, Armani, Lanvin, and Gaultier. The bilingual staff is accommodating, tactful, and charming.

Roland Richardson Paintings and Prints, 6 rue de la République (© **590/87-84-08**), has a beautiful gallery. A native of St. Martin, Mr. Richardson is one of the Caribbean's premier artists, working in oil, watercolors, pastels, and charcoal. Called a "modern-day Gauguin," he is known for his landscapes, portraits, and colorful still lifes. His work has been exhibited in more than 70 one-man and group exhibitions in museums and galleries around the world.

7 St. Maarten/St. Martin After Dark ★★

After-dark activities begin early here, as guests start off with a sundowner, perhaps on the garden patio of **Pasanggrahan Royal Inn** (p. 603). The most popular bar on the island is **Cheri's Café** (p. 609).

Many hotels sponsor **beachside barbecues** (particularly in season) with steel bands, native music, and folk dancing. Outsiders are welcomed at most of these events, but call ahead to see if it's a private affair.

(*Moments* **Spectacular Sunsets**

Each evening, visitors watch for the legendary **green flash,** an atmospheric phenomenon described by Hemingway that sometimes occurs in these latitudes
just as the sun drops below the horizon. The best place to view this is from the
Santa Fe Restaurant, the highest point of St. Martin.

One of the island's most visited **casinos,** the **Oasis,** is at the Caravanserai on Beacon Hill Road (© **599/54-54000**). Gamblers start pouring in here at 3pm daily, some
staying until 4 the next morning.

Atlantis World Casino ✮, Rhine Road 106, Cupecoy (© **599/54-54601;** www.
atlantisworld.com), is St. Maarten's version of Las Vegas, with some of the best of the
island restaurants (Rare and Temptation, see above), but also a posh interior with all
the big table games along with 500 slot and video poker machines.

Pelican Resort Club, Simpson Bay (© **599/54-44463**), has a popular Vegas-style
casino with a panoramic view of the bay. It offers 3 roulette tables, 8 blackjack tables,
2 stud-poker tables, and 120 slot machines. The Pelican also features horse racing,
bingo, and sports nights with events broadcast via satellite, plus nightly dancing on
the Pelican Reef Terrace and island shows featuring Caribbean bands. It's open daily
from 2pm to 4am.

Right in the heart of Philipsburg's shopping-crazed Front Street, **Rouge et Noir**
(© **599/54-22952**) has a futuristic design. It offers slot machines, roulette, blackjack,
and video poker. It opens Monday to Saturday at 9am and Sunday at 11am to snag
cruise-ship passengers and stays open until 4am.

Casino Royale ✮, at the Sonesta Maho Beach Hotel on Maho Bay (© **599/54-
52590**), has 16 blackjack tables, 6 roulette wheels, and 2 craps and 2 Caribbean stud-
poker tables. The casino offers baccarat, minibaccarat, and more than 200 slot machines.
It's open daily from 1pm to 6am. The **Showroom Royale** is the largest and most tech-
nologically sophisticated theater on either side of St Maarten/St. Martin; its glittery
shows change according to whatever act has been booked. Within the same building
is the island's loudest dance club, the **Q-Club.** Containing wraparound catwalks that
look down on the dance floor, multiple bars, and colored lights, it's open nightly from
around 10pm, attracting dancers from both sides of the island. A cover charge of
between US$5 and US$10 is sometimes imposed, depending on the season and the
night of the week. Wednesday is ladies night.

Sunset Beach Bar, 2 Beacon Hill Rd., Airport Beach (© **599/54-53998**), is directly
on the sands of the beach, and resembles an oversize gazebo. This place is mobbed
most afternoons and evenings with office workers, off-duty airline pilots, beach people, and sometimes celebs like Sandra Bullock. No one seems to mind the whine of
airplane engines, or the fumes that filter down from aircraft that seem to fly just a few
dozen feet overhead. Drinks are cheap, and you can order burgers, sandwiches, steaks,
fish, chicken, shrimp, and hot dogs from an outdoor charcoal grill. Many local residents time their arrival here for sundown (usually beginning around 6:30pm), when
"shooters of the day" cost only US$1 each.

In Grand-Case, **Calmos Café,** bd. de Grand Case no. 40 (© **590/29-01-85;** www.
calmoscafe.com), is funky and low-key. This beachfront shack draws a young, hip
crowd, with an occasional pop icon like Linda Evangelista dropping in. Management

posts a sign that says NO SNOBS near the entrance. On Tuesday and Sunday, there's sometimes live music from 8 to 11pm. Most people come just to flirt, gossip, and drink, but there's also good, affordable food, such as a Greek salad, a tuna salad, and "New Wave burgers" that are slathered with goat cheese. There is also jazz and lounge music to accompany your food. Also popular is the Ocean Salad, combining salad greens with three kinds of grilled fish plus shrimp. The house special drink is a Ti-Punch that's a local variation on an old-fashioned rum punch. It's open daily from 10am to midnight.

From the Orient Beach parking lot, **Kon Tiki** (© 590/87-43-27) is the most distant of the several bars that flank the sands of Orient Bay. Inside, you'll find everything you'll need to amuse yourself for a day at the beach. Facilities include two bars, a watersports facility, volleyball courts, and a bandstand where there's often live music. Chaise longues with mattresses rent for US$6 for a full day's use, and there's a staff member who'll bring you drinks like Sex on the Beach (US$5). If you opt to spend part of a day here, you won't be alone. Open daily 9am to 6pm.

24

St. Vincent & The Grenadines

One of the major British Windward Islands, sleepy St. Vincent is just beginning to awaken to tourism. Sailors and the yachting set have long known of St. Vincent and the Grenadines, but until recently it was a well-kept vacation secret. Even if you've not been here, you may have seen its scenery in *Pirates of the Caribbean,* starring Johnny Depp.

You visit St. Vincent for its lush beauty, and the Grenadines for the best sailing waters in the Caribbean. Don't come for nightlife, grand cuisine, or spectacular beaches. There are some white-sand beaches near Kingstown on St. Vincent, but most of the other beaches ringing the island are black sand. The yachting crowd seems to view St. Vincent merely as a launching pad for the 65km (40-mile) string of the Grenadines, but the island still has a few attractions that make it worth exploring on its own.

Unspoiled by the fallout that mass tourism sometimes brings, islanders treat visitors courteously. British customs predominate, along with traces of Gallic cultural influences, but all with a distinct West Indian fláir.

South of St. Vincent, the islands forming the small chain called the Grenadines have such romantic-sounding names as Bequia, Mustique, Canouan, and Petit St. Vincent. We'll explore Union and Palm Islands, and Mayreau as well. A few of the islands have accommodations, but many are so small and undeveloped that they attract only beachcombers and stray boaters.

Populated by the descendants of African slaves and administered by St. Vincent, the Grenadines collectively add up to a landmass of about 80 sq. km (30 sq. miles). These specks of land may lack natural resources, but they're blessed with white-sand beaches, coral reefs, and their own sleepy beauty. If you don't stay overnight in the Grenadines, at least try to visit one on a day trip, and enjoy a picnic lunch (which your hotel will pack for you) on your own quiet stretch of sand.

1 Essentials

VISITOR INFORMATION

In the United States, you can get information at the **St. Vincent and Grenadines Tourist Office,** 801 Second Ave., 21st Floor, New York, NY 10017 (© **800/729-1726** or 212/687-4981). The website for St. Vincent and the Grenadines is **www.svg tourism.com**.

On St. Vincent, the local **Department of Tourism** is on Upper Bay Street, Government Administrative Centre, Kingstown (© **784/457-1502**). Hours are Monday to Friday from 8am to 4pm.

GETTING THERE

In the eastern Caribbean, St. Vincent—the "gateway to the Grenadines" (the individual islands are discussed later in this chapter)—lies about 160km (100 miles) west of

Barbados. There are no direct flights. The best connections are through Barbados and Antigua. From Barbados you can take **LIAT** (© **784/458-4841**), which connects the islands of Grenada and St. Lucia with St. Vincent, Bequia, and Union Island. From Antigua, **Caribbean Star** (© **866/864-6272** in the U.S. and Canada; www.fly caribbeanstar.com) flies twice daily to St. Vincent.

There are other links as well. **American Eagle** (© **800/433-7300** in the U.S. and Canada, or 784/456-5555; www.aa.com) flies nonstop from San Juan, Puerto Rico to Canouan, one of the most visited of the Grenadine islands.

Dependable **Grenadine Airways** (© **784/457-5124;** www.grenadine-airways. com) makes daily shuttle runs from St. Vincent to the satellite islands of Mustique, Union, and Canouan, with per-person fares ranging from US$40–US$60 (£21–£31) one-way. With advance warning, Grenadine Airways will arrange reasonably priced special charters to and from many of the surrounding islands and inner islands (including Grenada, Aruba, St. Lucia, Antigua, Barbados, Trinidad, and any others in the southern Caribbean). The price of these chartered flights is less than you might expect and often matches the fares on conventional Caribbean airlines.

GETTING AROUND ST. VINCENT

BY TAXI   Because of the bad roads, most visitors use taxis to get around. The government sets the rates, but taxis are unmetered, so be sure to agree on the fare before getting in. Figure on spending US$15–US$20 (£7.80–£10) or more to go from the airport to your hotel. You should tip about 12% of the fare.

You can also hire taxis to take you to the island's major attractions. Most drivers seem to be well-informed guides. (It won't take you long to learn everything you need to know about St. Vincent.) You'll spend from US$20 (£10) per hour for a car holding two to four passengers.

BY RENTAL CAR   Driving on St. Vincent is a bit of an adventure because of the narrow, twisting roads (sound your horn as you make the sharp hairpin turns). *Most importantly:* Drive on the left. If you present your valid driver's license from home at the police department, on Bay Street in Kingstown, and pay an EC$76 (US$28/£15) fee, you'll get a temporary permit to drive.

Avis (© **800/331-1212** in the U.S. and Canada; www.avis.com) has a branch at the airport. One local rental firm is **Star Garage,** on Grenville Street in Kingstown (© **784/ 456-1743**). Make sure your car has a spare tire because the roads are full of potholes.

BY BUS   Flamboyantly painted "alfresco" buses travel the principal roads of St. Vincent, linking the major towns and villages. The price is low, depending on where you're going, and the experience will connect you with the locals. The central departure point is the bus terminal at the New Kingstown Fish Market. Fares range from EC$.95–EC$6 (35¢–US$2.25/20p–£1.20).

⸉Fun Fact Special Events

Late June brings St. Vincent's weeklong **Carnival,** one of the largest such celebrations in the eastern Caribbean. The festivities include steel-band and calypso competitions, parades, costumes, and the crowning of the king and queen of the carnival. The fun extends through the first 2 weeks in July, culminating in a huge street party.

FAST FACTS: St. Vincent & The Grenadines

Banks Most banks are open Monday to Thursday from 8am to either 1 or 3pm, and Friday from either 8am to 5pm or 8am to 1pm and 3 to 5pm. There are a few banks with ATMs on Halifax Street in Kingstown on St. Vincent (plus one at the airport), and there are also a few on Bequia and Union Island.

Currency The official currency of St. Vincent is the **Eastern Caribbean dollar (EC$)**, pegged at about US$2.70 per U.S. dollar (EC$1 = US37¢/20p). Most restaurants, shops, and hotels will accept payment in U.S. dollars or traveler's checks. *Unless otherwise specified, prices in this chapter are quoted in U.S. dollars and British pounds.*

Documents British, Canadian, and U.S. citizens should have a passport and a return or ongoing airplane ticket.

Electricity Electricity is 220-volt AC (50 cycles), so if you're traveling with U.S. appliances, you'll need an adapter and a transformer. Some hotels have transformers, but it's best to bring your own.

Emergencies In an emergency, dial ℭ **999** or 911.

Hospitals There is one hospital on St. Vincent in Kingstown: **Milton Cato Memorial General Hospital** (ℭ **784/456-1185**), Hospital Road.

Language English is the official language.

Liquor Laws Liquor can be sold on any day of the week. It's legal to have an open container on the beach as long as you don't get rowdy or litter.

Pharmacies On St. Vincent, try **The People's Pharmacy,** Greenville Street, Kingstown (ℭ **784/456-1170**), open Monday to Saturday from 8am to 8pm. There are a few other drugstores in Kingstown as well.

Post Office The **General Post Office,** on Halifax Street in Kingstown (ℭ **784/456-1111**), is open Monday to Friday from 8am to 4:15pm and Saturday from 8 to 11:30am. There are smaller post offices in 56 districts throughout the country, including offices on the Grenadine islands of Bequia, Mustique, Canouan, Mayreau, and Union Island.

Safety St. Vincent and its neighboring islands of the Grenadines are quite safe. Even in Kingstown, the capital of St. Vincent, chances are you'll encounter little serious crime. However, take the usual precautions and never leave valuables unguarded.

Taxes & Service Charges The government imposes an airport departure tax of EC$40 (US$15/£8) per person. A 10% government occupancy tax is charged for all hotel accommodations. Hotels and restaurants almost always add a 10% to 15% service charge. Ask whether or not it's included in the initial hotel rates you're quoted. If it's not already added at a restaurant, tip at that rate.

Telephone To call St. Vincent or the Grenadines from the United States, dial **1**, then **784** (the area code for St. Vincent), and then the local seven-digit number. Once on St. Vincent, you can access **AT&T Direct** at ℭ **800/225-5288**. To reach **MCI**, dial ℭ **800/888-8000**.

Time Both St. Vincent and the Grenadines operate on Atlantic Standard Time year-round: When it's 6am on St. Vincent, it's 5am in New York. During daylight saving time in the United States, St. Vincent keeps the same time as the U.S. East Coast.

Water In St. Vincent and the Grenadines, stick to bottled water.

Weather The climate of St. Vincent and the Grenadines is pleasantly cooled by the trade winds year-round. The tropical temperature is in the 78°F to 82°F (26°C–28°C) range. The rainy season is July to October.

2 St. Vincent Accommodations

Don't expect high-rise resorts here. The places are small and comfortable, not fancy, and you usually get a lot of personal attention from the staff.

If you want a luxurious resort, head for the Grenadines. Except for Young Island, most resorts here are fairly simple affairs, and since most people are only in St. Vincent for a night or two, you may prefer to be located directly in the center in the capital of Kingstown.

VERY EXPENSIVE

Young Island Resort On its own private island off Villa Beach, this resort is as good as it gets in St. Vincent. It's far more stylish and comfortable than its nearest competitor, Grand View Beach Hotel. This 14-hectare (35-acre) resort, its grounds full of lush fruit trees, white ginger, hibiscus, and ferns, is supposedly where a Carib tribal chieftain kept his harem. It lies just 180m (600 ft.) off the south shore of St. Vincent; a ferry makes the 5-minute run from the pier right on Villa Beach. Hammocks are hung under thatched roofs, and the beach has brilliant white sand. Set in a tropical garden are romantic wood-and-stone Tahitian cottages (all for couples), with bamboo decor and outdoor showers in little rock grottoes (open but hidden from public view). Floors are of tile and terrazzo, covered with rush rugs. The spacious accommodations come with queen- or king-size beds (rarely a twin) and generous storage. Some units open onto the beach; others are on a hillside. Some guests have complained of hearing noises from the rooms adjoining them.

Dining is by candlelight, and dress is informal. Sometimes a steel band plays for after-dinner dancing, and strolling singers serenade diners.

Young Island (P.O. Box 211), St. Vincent, W.I. ✆ 800/223-1108 in the U.S. and Canada, or 784/458-4826. Fax 784/457-4567. www.youngisland.com. 29 units. Winter US$440–US$955 (£228–£496) double; off season US$370–US$775 (£192–£403). Extra person US$100 (£52). Rates include breakfast and dinner. Ask about packages. AE, MC, V. **Amenities:** Restaurant; 2 bars; outdoor pool; tennis court; spa; access to nearby health club; boating; snorkeling; windsurfing; car rental; airport shuttle; babysitting; laundry service; dry cleaning. *In room:* Ceiling fan, fridge, beverage maker (in some), hair dryer, safe, no phone.

EXPENSIVE

Grand View Beach Hotel Owner/manager F. A. (Tony) Sardine named this place well: The "grand view" promised is of islets, bays, yachts, Young Island, headlands, lagoons, and sailing craft. On well-manicured grounds, this resort is set on 3 hectares (7½ acres) of gardens, just steps from the beach. The 19th-century plantation house is a large, white, two-story mansion. Most bedrooms are medium-size and comfortable, opening onto views. The most luxurious and spacious rooms, some of which have wide terraces and faraway views of the Grenadines, are in the Mediterranean-style modern wing. The other units are on the upper level of a former great house and have a B&B feel. Most of the bathrooms have showers only. The West Indian fare served here is average.

Villa Point (P.O. Box 173), St. Vincent, W.I. ⓒ **800/223-6510** in the U.S., or 784/458-4811. Fax 784/457-4174. www. grandviewhotel.com. 19 units. Winter US$175–US$215 (£91–£112) double; off season US$130–US$170 (£68–£88) double. MAP (breakfast and dinner) US$55 (£29) per person extra. AE, MC, V. **Amenities:** 2 restaurants; 2 bars; outdoor pool; tennis court; fitness center; squash court; sauna; bike rental; car rental; limited room service; massage; laundry service. *In room:* A/C, TV, dataport, hair dryer, safe.

MODERATE

Lagoon Marina & Hotel   A two-story group of rambling modern buildings crafted from local wood and stone, this hotel lies 6km (3¾ miles) from the airport on the main island road, opening onto a narrow, curved, black-sand beach. There's a pleasantly breezy bar that's often filled with sailors and yachties. As you relax, you'll overlook a moored armada of boats tied up at a nearby marina. A lagoon-shaped pool is terraced into a nearby hillside. Snorkeling, windsurfing, and daily departures on sailboats to Mustique and Bequia can be arranged through the hotel. Each of the recently refurbished medium-size, high-ceilinged guest rooms has a balcony. The bedrooms have ceramic-tile floors and good furnishings. Bathrooms are in the standard motel style, with tub/shower combinations. The simple, airy ground-floor restaurant serves international and West Indian food.

Blue Lagoon (P.O. Box 133), St. Vincent, W.I. ⓒ **784/458-4308.** Fax 784/456-8928. www.lagoonmarina.com. 19 units. Winter US$125 (£65) double; off season US$100 (£52) double. MC, V. **Amenities:** Restaurant; bar; 2 outdoor pools; boating; snorkeling; bike rental; babysitting; car rental; laundry service; limited room service. *In room:* A/C, TV, hair dryer.

Villa Lodge Hotel   Set on a residential hillside a few minutes southeast of the center of Kingstown and the airport, this place is a favorite of visiting businesspeople. Because of its access to a beach and its well-mannered staff, it evokes the feeling of a modern villa. It's ringed with tropical, flowering trees and shrubs growing in the gardens. The air-conditioned rooms have ceiling fans, king-size beds, comfortable rattan and local mahogany furniture, and small bathrooms equipped with tub/shower combinations. The hotel also rents eight apartments in its Breezeville Apartments complex next door, charging US$145 (£75) for a double in winter and US$130 (£68) for a double in summer. The restaurant serves straightforward West Indian and international dishes.

Indian Bay (P.O. Box 1191), St. Vincent, W.I. ⓒ **800/448-8355** in the U.S., or 784/458-4641. Fax 784/457-4468. www. villalodge.com. 19 units. Winter US$130 (£68) double, US$150 (£78) apt; off season US$115 (£60) double, US$135 (£70) apt. MAP (breakfast and dinner) US$40 (£21) per person extra. AE, DISC, MC, V. **Amenities:** Restaurant; bar; outdoor pool; limited room service (noon–2pm and 7–9pm); babysitting; laundry service; nonsmoking rooms. *In room:* A/C, ceiling fan, TV, kitchenette (in some), fridge, hair dryer, safe.

INEXPENSIVE

Beachcombers Hotel 𝒢 *Value*   Richard and Flora Gunn operate this B&B in a tropical garden right on the beach. Three chaletlike buildings house the small to medium-size accommodations, all with private bathrooms and tasteful decor. All have ceiling fans; a few rooms have air-conditioning as well. The rooms are spotless and well maintained. Try for nos. 1, 2, or 3, as they open onto the water. Two units have small kitchenettes. Bathrooms are a bit cramped, with showers only. The hotel has a health spa (Mrs. Gunn is a massage and beauty therapist) with a steam room, sauna,

St. Vincent

Beachcombers Hotel **7**
The Cobblestone Inn **1**
Grand View Beach Hotel **6**
Heron Hotel **3**
Lagoon Marina & Hotel **9**
New Montrose Hotel **2**
Roy's Inn **4**
Villa Lodge Hotel **5**
Young Island Resort **8**

Airport
Beach
Mountain

facials, and aromatherapy. The Beachbar & Restaurant, a favorite gathering place for locals, fronts an open terrace and has excellent food. Curtis Chas, who mastered his cooking skills in the Caribbean, is the chef.

Villa Beach (P.O. Box 126), St. Vincent, W.I. ☎ **784/458-4283**. Fax 784/458-4385. www.beachcombershotel.com. 31 units. Year-round US$90–US$270 (£47–£140) double. Rates include a complimentary breakfast. AE, MC, V. **Amenities:** Restaurant; bar; outdoor pool; spa; sauna; library; babysitting; laundry service. *In room:* A/C, ceiling fan, TV, dataport, kitchenette (in some), fridge (in some), beverage maker (in some), safe (in some).

The Cobblestone Inn

Originally built as a warehouse for sugar and arrowroot in 1814, the core of this historic hotel is made of stone and brick. Today, it's one of the most famous hotels on St. Vincent, known for its labyrinth of passages, arches, and upper hallways. To reach the high-ceilinged reception area, you pass from the waterfront through a stone tunnel into a chiseled courtyard. At the top of a massive sloping stone staircase, you're shown to one of the simple, old-fashioned bedrooms. Most of the small units contain TVs, and some have windows opening over the rooftops of town. The most spacious is no. 5, but it opens onto a noisy street. Furnishings are comfortable, but bathrooms are tiny, with tub/shower combinations. Meals are served on a third-floor aerie, high above the hotel's central courtyard. The bar here is one of the most popular in town. The hotel is convenient to town, but it's a 5km (3-mile) drive to the nearest beach.

Bax St. (P.O. Box 867), Kingstown, St. Vincent, W.I. (©) **784/456-1937**. Fax 784/456-1938. www.thecobblestoneinn.com. 19 units. Year-round US$70 (£36) double; US$85 (£44) triple; US$90 (£47) suite. AE, MC, V. **Amenities:** 2 restaurants; 2 bars; limited room service; laundry service. *In room:* A/C, TV.

Heron Hotel   This hotel—renovated in 2006—is in one of St. Vincent's historic buildings. In spite of modern improvements, it still exudes a sense of old-fashioned timelessness you simply won't find in modern resorts. Built of local stone and tropical hardwoods, it served as a warehouse in the late 18th century, and then later provided lodgings for colonial planters doing business along the wharves of Kingstown. Some of the simple and rather small rooms overlook an inner courtyard; others face the street. Room no. 15 is the largest. Accommodations have renewed furnishings, single beds, and cramped bathrooms with shower stalls. Although you don't get grand comfort here, the price is hard to beat, and the staff is hospitable. The hotel attracts a variety of guests: Some conduct business in the heart of the island's capital, others want to be near the docks for early morning departures. The on-site restaurant is busiest at lunch. (It may close after dusk, so dinner reservations are important.)

Upper Middle St. (P.O. Box 226), Kingstown, St. Vincent, W.I. (©) **784/457-1631**. Fax 784/457-1189. 8 units. Year-round US$80 (£42) double. AE, MC, V. **Amenities:** Restaurant; bar; nonsmoking rooms. *In room:* A/C, TV, dataport, fridge, minibar, beverage maker.

New Montrose Hotel (© *Finds*   A real discovery, this bright, sunflower-yellow hotel lies on the northern fringe of town. The beach is a short ride away and there is no on-site pool, but what you will find is a handsomely furnished and comfortable room at an affordable price in a tranquil location. Accommodations have such extras as a full-length mirror closet, smoke detector, and good lighting. Some of the units have refrigerators or even a fully equipped kitchenette. The best rooms, even more expensive than the two-bedroom family apartments, are the deluxe executive suites with a complete kitchen and a vista balcony. The Caribbean/International dishes are good so you can eat in if you don't want to wander the streets of Kingstown at night.

New Montrose (P.O. Box 215), Kingstown, St. Vincent, W.I. (©) **784/457-0172**. Fax 784/457-0213. www.newmontrose hotel.com. 25 units. Year-round US$70–US$100 (£36–£52) double; US$120 (£62) 2-bedroom family apt. Additional person US$15 (£7.80). AE, MC, V. **Amenities:** Restaurant; bar; spa; room service; laundry service; nonsmoking rooms. *In room:* A/C, kitchenette, fridge, beverage maker (in some).

Roy's Inn (© *Value*   A 5-minute ride by taxi from the center of town, this stylish inn grew out of the 1781 home of the first French governor. Much modified and changed over the years, it is today a heavily favored destination for collectors of Caribbean inns, those visitors who don't want to be part of activity-packed resort activities. Its midsize bedrooms are elegantly appointed and comfortably furnished, opening onto garden, mountain, ocean, and city views. The wide porches of the inn open onto views of the harbor. The hotel also offers good food, most often served on its open-air terrace.

Kingstown Park (P.O. Box 2500), Kingstown, St. Vincent W.I. (©) **784/456-2100**. Fax 784/456-2233. www.roysinnsvg. com. 22 units. Year-round US$110–US$120 (£57–£62) double; US$130–US$150 (£68–£78) suite. Additional person US$15 (£7.80). AE, MC, V. **Amenities:** 2 restaurants; 2 bars; outdoor pool; gym; sauna; airport shuttle; business services; limited room service; massage; laundry service. *In room:* A/C, ceiling fan, TV, safe.

3 St. Vincent Dining

Most guests eat at their hotels on the Modified American Plan (breakfast and dinner), and many Vincentian hostelries serve authentic West Indian cuisine. There are also a few independent restaurants, but not many.

Basil's Bar & Restaurant ⊕ SEAFOOD/INTERNATIONAL   This enclave is set beneath the previously recommended Cobblestone Inn, a former sugar warehouse. The air-conditioned interior is accented with exposed stone and brick, soaring arches, and a rambling mahogany bar, which remains open throughout the day. The food is quite acceptable, but nowhere near as good as that enjoyed by Princess Margaret or Mick Jagger at Basil's more famous bar on Mustique. The menu might include lobster salad, shrimp in garlic butter, sandwiches, hamburgers, and barbecued chicken. Dinners feature grilled lobster, shrimp cocktail, grilled red snapper, and grilled filet mignon, all fairly standard dishes of the international repertoire. You can order meals here throughout the day and late into the evening.

Bay St., Kingstown. ⓒ 784/457-2713. Reservations recommended. Main courses EC$43–EC$68 (US$16–US$25/ £8.60–£14). AE, MC, V. Mon–Sat 8am–10pm.

Bounty AMERICAN/WEST INDIAN   In the redbrick Troutman Building in the center of Kingstown, you'll find the extremely affordable Bounty serving the local workers. (The true power-lunch venue is Basil's, recommended above.) Fill up on pastries, *rotis* (Caribbean burrito), sandwiches, homemade soups, pastas, quiche, and pizza. The cooking is as simple as the surroundings. An interesting collection of juices includes passion fruit. An on-site gallery and gift shop sells works by local artists.

Egmont St., Kingstown. ⓒ 784/456-1776. Snacks and sandwiches EC$9–EC$15 (US$3.35–US$5.55/£1.80–£3); main courses EC$9–EC$30 (US$3.35–US$11/£1.80–£6). No credit cards. Mon–Fri 7:30am–5pm; Sat 7:30am–1:30pm.

The French Verandah ⊕ FRENCH/INTERNATIONAL   The island's finest dining is at one of the candlelit tables on the waterfront terrace of Mariners Hotel, overlooking Villa Beach. There is an elegance to the service and setting, the cuisine is well crafted, and the ingredients first rate. There is a harmonious blending of regional dishes and French favorites, such as a choice between Vincentian calaloo and conch soup or else snails in garlic butter. Many international dishes also appear in the chef's repertoire, including lobster crepes or fish salad Tahitian style. Our favorite main courses are the grilled yellow fin tuna or the shrimp in a mango and coconut salsa, the latter with real island flavor. Classic French main courses also appear on the menu, including grilled beef tenderloin with a black pepper sauce.

Villa Bay. ⓒ 784/453-1111. Reservations required. Main courses EC$50–EC$70 (US$19–US$26/£10–£14). AE, MC, V. Daily 7am–11pm.

L'Aubergine des Grenadines ⊕ FRENCH/CARIBBEAN   On the waterfront opening onto Admiralty Bay, this expat operation is popular with yachties, locals, and visitors alike. With its wood tables and high ceilings, it offers as a special feature a lobster tank. With your guaranteed fresh catch, the lobster can be grilled to your specifications. The couple who runs the place consistently turn out excellent fare, including appetizers such as salads made with fresh conch or goat cheese. The mussels come all the way from New Zealand, and they are awash in garlic and butter. For a main course, we go for the lobster flamed with old dark rum or the seafood platter with the likes of shrimp, mussels, fresh white fish, and lobster. The seafood curry has mussels, shrimp, and lobster cooked delectably in coconut milk.

Belmont Walkway, Belmont. ⓒ 784/458-3201. Reservations required in winter. Main courses EC$55–EC$150 (US$20–US$56/£11–£30); prix-fixe menu EC$70–EC$100 (US$26–US$37/£14–£20). MC, V. Daily 11:30am–9:30pm.

Lime N' Pub Restaurant ⊛ (Value WEST CARIBBEAN/INDIAN/INTERNATIONAL
Opposite super expensive Young Island Hotel on Young Island Channel sits one of the island's most popular restaurants. It's the most congenial pub on St. Vincent, with a wide selection of pub grub, including pizza. In the more formal section of this indoor and alfresco restaurant, you can partake of some good West Indian food, along with dishes from India or the international kitchen. The *rotis* (Caribbean burritos) win high praise, but we always order fresh fish and lobster (from the live lobster pond). Don't faint when you see the highest price of a main course listed below. That's actually the superexpensive cost of lobster, but the meal is big enough for two dinners. The coconut shrimp is usually excellent. Service is among the most hospitable on the island.

Opposite Young Island at Villa Beach. © **784/458-4227.** Main courses EC$50–EC$200 (US$19–US$74/£10–£40); pub grub EC$8–EC$40 (US$2.95–US$15/£1.60–£8). AE, MC, V. Daily 9am–midnight.

Rooftop Restaurant & Bar WEST INDIAN/INTERNATIONAL This restaurant does a thriving business, thanks to its well-prepared food and its location three stories above the center of Kingstown. After you climb some flights of stairs, you'll see a bar near the entrance, an indoor area decorated in earth tones, and a patio open to the prevailing breezes. Lunches stress traditional Creole recipes using fresh fish, chicken, mutton, beef, and goat. Dinners are more international, and may include lobster, excellent snapper with lemon-butter and garlic sauce, steaks with onions and mushrooms, and several savory preparations of pork. Every Wednesday and Friday, there's a karaoke singalong; Saturday is family night, with a barbecue and a steel band after 6pm. In addition, 60 different drinks are featured at the bar.

Bay St., Kingstown. © **784/457-2845.** Reservations recommended for dinner. Lunch platters EC$29 (US$11/£5.80); dinner main courses EC$25–EC$42 (US$9.25–US$16/£5–£8.40). AE, MC, V. Daily 10am-10pm.

Young Island Resort Restaurant ⊛⊛ CARIBBEAN/CONTINENTAL St. Vincent's best dining is on this 14-hectare (35-acre) private island lying off Villa Beach that's reached by a 5-minute scenic ride on the hotel's launch. Even if you're not staying here, we recommend one dinner. An evening at this restaurant, under thatched kiosks near the beach and surrounded by tropical gardens, will be your most romantic night on St. Vincent. If you drop in for a predinner drink, try one of the exotic rum punches. Patrons are treated to lavish and elegant buffets twice a week.

Whenever possible, fresh local fish, fruit, and vegetables are served. We always enjoy their freshly baked bread—banana, raisin, cinnamon, wheat, coconut, or just plain white with lots of butter. The lunch menu changes frequently but is likely to feature the catch of the day served on rice with roasted garlic and thyme sauce.

Go in the evening for the most glamorous experience and order the five-course dinner, which changes nightly. On our most recent visit we were enthralled by the roasted-red-pepper soup dusted with Parmesan, followed by oven-roasted baby quail on a tropical sweet-potato purée or grilled local lobster with a timbale of pine-nut couscous. A delightful memory lingers of the chocolate espresso torte with caramel sauce.

Young Island. © **784/458-4826.** Reservations required. Main courses lunch EC$22–EC$35 (US$8.15–US$13/£4.40–£7), dinner EC$30–EC$112 (US$11–US$41/£6–£22); Sun lunch buffet EC$53 (US$20/£11); Sat barbecue buffet EC$100 (US$37/£20). AE, MC, V. Daily 7:30–10am, 12:30–2:30pm, and 7–10pm.

4 Exploring St. Vincent

BEACHES

All beaches on mainland St. Vincent are public, and many of the best border hotels, where you can order drinks or lunch. Most of the resorts are in the south, where the beaches have golden-yellow sand. The only real white-sand beach is on Young Island, which is private. (See "St. Vincent Accommodations," earlier in this chapter, for a review of this resort.) Many of the beaches in the north have sands of a lava-ash color. The safest swimming is on the leeward beaches; the surf on the windward or eastern beaches is often rough and can be quite dangerous.

The island's most popular strip is narrow **Villa Beach,** only a 10-minute drive from Kingstown. Its tranquil waters make swimming safe, and there are numerous simple cafes and watersports stands. Unfortunately this beach can barely accommodate the crowds who flock here; weekends can be particularly bad.

Nearby **Indian Bay Beach** is similar to Villa Beach and also attracts lots of Vincentians on weekends. Monday to Thursday, however, you'll probably have plenty of room on this narrow strip. The sand is slightly golden, but tends to be rocky. The reef-protected tranquil waters are ideal for both swimming and snorkeling. You'll find both bars and restaurants here.

Heading north from Kingstown, you'll reach **Buccament Bay Beach,** where the waters are clean, clear, and tranquil enough for swimming. This beach is very tiny, however, and it has black volcanic sand. In the same area, **Questelle's Bay Beach** (pronounced Keet-*ells*) is also on the leeward, tranquil Caribbean side of the island. This black-sand beach, next to Camden Park, is very similar to Buccament Bay.

Only die-hards head for the beaches on the east coast, or windward side, where the big breakers roll in from the Atlantic. Don't plan to go swimming in these rough waters; you might just enjoy a beach picnic instead. The best beaches, all with black volcanic sand, are found at **Kearton's Bay, Richmond Beach,** and **Peter's Hope,** all reached along the leeward highway running up the west coast of St. Vincent.

SPORTS & OTHER OUTDOOR PURSUITS

FISHING   It's best to go to a local fisherman for advice, but your hotel can also arrange a trip for you. It's sometimes possible to accompany a fisherman on a trip, perhaps 6 or 8km (4 or 5 miles) from shore. A modest fee should suffice. The fishing fleet leaves from the leeward coast at Barrouallie. People have been known to return to shore with everything from a 6-inch redfish to a 6m (20-ft.) pilot whale. Visitors don't need a fishing license.

HIKING   Exploring St. Vincent's hot volcano, **La Soufrière,** is an intriguing adventure. As you travel the island, you can't miss its cloud-capped splendor. The most recent eruption was back in 1979, when it spewed ashes, lava, and hot mud that covered the vegetation on its slopes. Belching rocks and black curling smoke filled the

---

All This & Johnny Depp, Too

While scouting a location for its *Pirates of the Caribbean* movie series, Disney officials settled on St. Vincent for its virtually untouched coastline that seemingly belongs back in the 1800s.

blue Caribbean sky. About 17,000 people were evacuated from a 15km (10-mile) ring around the volcano.

At the rim of the crater, you'll be rewarded with one of the most panoramic views in the Caribbean—that is, if the wind doesn't blow too hard and make you topple over into the crater itself! *Warning:* Use extreme caution. Looking inside, you can see the steam rising from the crater.

Even if you're an experienced hiker, don't attempt to explore the volcano without a guide. Wear suitable hiking clothes and be sure that you're in the best of health before making the arduous journey. The easiest route is the 5km-long (3-mile) eastern approach from Rabacca. The more arduous trail, longer by 2km (1¼ miles), is the western trail from Chateaubelair. The round-trip to the crater takes about 5 hours.

St. Vincent Forestry Headquarters, in the village of Campden Park, about 5km (3 miles) from Kingstown along the west coast (© 784/457-8594), offers a pamphlet on hiking to La Soufrière. It's open Monday to Friday from 8am to noon and 1 to 4pm. **HazEco Tours** (© 784/457-8634) offers guided hikes up to La Soufrière, costing US$140 per couple, including drinks and lunch.

If you don't want to face Soufrière, the best hikes are the **Vermont Nature Trails.** These marked trails (get a map at the tourist office) take you through a rainforest and pass long-ago plantations reclaimed by nature. If it's your lucky day, you might even see the rare St. Vincent parrot with its flamboyant plumage. Wear good hiking shoes and lots of mosquito repellent.

SAILING & YACHTING ⟨⟨ St. Vincent and the Grenadines are one of the great sailing centers of the Caribbean. If you want to go bareboating, you can obtain a fully provisioned yacht. If you're a well-heeled novice, you can hire a captain and a crew. Rentals are available for a half-day, a full day, overnight, or even longer.

The longest established yacht-chartering company in St. Vincent, **Barefoot Yacht Charters,** Blue Lagoon (© 784/456-9526; www.barefootyachts.com), is better than ever, and is now granting substantial discounts for last-minute or walk-in bookings. The outfitter has a fleet of 25 yachts run by the American Sailing Association and offers charters with or without a crew. Its operation is at its own custom-built marina with docks and moorings, along with a restaurant opening onto a panoramic vista of Bequia. There's even an Internet cafe. In winter, and depending on the vessel rented, rates range from US$350 to US$855 (£182–£445), with off-season prices going from US$210 to US$640 (£110–£333). We'd also suggest **Nicholson Yacht Charters** ⟨⟨ (© 800/662-6066 in the U.S.). Prices at Nicholson are roughly comparable to those at Barefoot Yacht Charters.

SNORKELING & SCUBA DIVING ⟨⟨ St. Vincent's 30 or so dive sites are sprinkled along its leeward shore, where you might spot seahorses and frogfish. The best area for snorkeling and scuba diving is the Villa/Young Island section on the southern end of the island.

Dive St. Vincent, on the Young Island Cut (© 784/457-4928; www.divestvincent. com), has been owned and operated by a transplanted Texan, Bill Tewes, for more than a decade. St. Vincent's oldest and best dive company, it now has an additional shop, **Grenadines Dive,** at the Sunny Grenadines Hotel on Union Island (© 784/ 458-8138). Also try **Dive Canouan,** at the Tamarind Beach Hotel on Canouan Island (© 784/482-0820). The shops have a total of one instructor and four dive masters, as well as three dive boats. They offer dive/snorkel trips as well as sightseeing day-trips and dive instruction. Single-tank dives cost US$60 (£31) and two-tank dives go for US$95 (£49), including all equipment and instructors and/or dive-master guides. Dive packages are also available.

EXPLORING KINGSTOWN

Though lush and tropical, the capital isn't as architecturally significant as Grenada's St. George's. There are some English-style houses, many of which look as though they belonged in Penzance or Cornwall rather than the Caribbean. This is a chief port and gateway to the Grenadines, and you can see the small boats and yachts that have dropped anchor here. On Saturday morning, the **market** at the south end of town is at its most active.

At the top of a winding road on the north side of Kingstown, **Fort Charlotte** was built on Johnson Point around the time of the American Revolution. The ruins aren't much—the reason to come here is the view. The fort sits atop a steep promontory some 190m (630 ft.) above the sea. From its citadel, you'll have a sweeping view of the leeward shores to the north, Kingstown to the south, and the Grenadines beyond. On a clear day, you can even see Grenada. Three cannons used to fight off French troops are still in place and there's a series of oil murals depicting the history of black Caribs. Admission is free, and the fort is open daily 6am to 6pm.

The second major sight is the **Botanic Gardens** 🛪, on the north side of Kingstown at Montrose (© **784/457-1003**). Founded in 1765 by Gov. George Melville, these are the oldest botanic gardens in the West Indies. You'll see 8 hectares (20 acres) of such tropical exotics as teak, almond, cinnamon, nutmeg, cannonball, and mahogany; some of the trees are more than 200 years old. One of the breadfruit trees was reputedly among those original seedlings brought to this island by Captain Bligh in 1793. There's also a large *Spachea perforata* (the Soufrière tree), a species believed to be unique to St. Vincent and not found in the wild since 1812. The gardens are open daily from 8am to 4pm; admission is US$3(£1.55)

THE LEEWARD HIGHWAY 🛪🛪

The leeward, or sheltered, west side of the island has the most dramatic scenery. North of Kingstown, you rise into lofty terrain before descending to the water again. There are views in all directions. Here you can see one of the finest petroglyphs in the Caribbean: the massive **Carib Rock,** with a human face carving dating from A.D. 600.

Continuing north, you reach **Barrouallie,** where there's a Carib stone altar. Even if you're not into fishing, you might want to spend some time in this village, where whalers still occasionally set out in brightly painted boats armed with harpoons. While Barrouallie may be one of the few outposts in the world where whaling is legal, Vincentians claim that it doesn't endanger an already endangered species, as so few are caught each year. If one is caught, it's an occasion for festivities.

The highway continues to **Chateaubelair,** the end of the line. Here you can swim at attractive **Richmond Beach** before heading back to Kingstown. In the distance, the volcano, La Soufrière, looms menacingly.

The adventurous set out from here to see the **Falls of Baleine,** 12km (7½ miles) north of Richmond Beach on the northern tip of the island, accessible only by boat. Baleine is a freshwater falls that comes from a stream in the volcanic hills. If you're interested in making the trip, check with the tourist office in Kingstown for tour information.

MARRIQUA VALLEY ⊛

Sometimes known as the Mesopotamia Valley, the Marriqua Valley is one of the lushest cultivated valleys in the eastern Caribbean. Surrounded by mountain ridges, the drive takes you through a landscape planted with nutmeg, cocoa, coconut, breadfruit, and bananas. The road begins at the Vigie Highway, east of the airport. Surrounded by mountain ridges, it opens onto a panoramic view of Grand Bonhomme Mountain, rising 954m (3,129 ft.). At Montréal, you'll come upon natural mineral springs where you can have lunch and take a dip. Only rugged vehicles should make this trip.

Around Kingstown, you can also enjoy the **Queen's Drive,** a scenic loop into the high hills to the east of the capital. From here, the view is panoramic over Kingstown and its yacht-clogged harbor to the Grenadines in the distance.

SHOPPING

St. Vincent isn't a shopping destination, but while you're here, you might pick up some of the Sea Island cotton fabrics and clothing that are local specialties. Vincentian artisans also make pottery, jewelry, and baskets.

Since Kingstown consists of about 12 small blocks, you can walk, browse, and see about everything in a single morning. Try to be in town for the colorful, noisy **Friday-morning market.** You might not purchase anything, but you'll enjoy the riot of color.

At **Sprott Brothers,** Homeworks, Bay Street (© 784/457-1121), you can buy clothing designed by Vincentians, along with an array of fabrics, linens, and silk-screened T-shirts, and even Caribbean-made furniture.

St. Vincent Philatelic Services, Dee's Service Building, Bay Street (© 784/457-1911), is the largest operating bureau in the Caribbean, and its issues are highly acclaimed by stamp collectors around the world.

ST. VINCENT AFTER DARK

Most nightlife centers on the hotels, where activities usually include barbecues and dancing to steel bands. In season, at least one hotel seems to have something planned every night. Beer is extremely cheap at all the places noted.

Aquatic Club, adjacent to the departure point of the ferryboat from St. Vincent to Young Island (© 784/458-4205), is the loudest and most raucous nightspot on St. Vincent; it often features live reggae, soca, or calypso. It's a source of giddy fun to its fans and a bone of contention to nearby hotel guests, who claim they can't sleep because of the noise. On Friday and Saturday nights, things heat up by 11pm and continue to the wee hours. Other nights of the week the place functions as a bar. Centered on an open-sided veranda and an outdoor deck, it's open every night from 10pm to 2 or 3am. There's no cover.

The hotel with the best entertainment is predictably **Young Island Resort,** Young Island (© 784/458-4826), which in winter hosts live musical entertainment on Wednesday nights. A West Indian band is brought in on Friday night for the manager's sunset cocktail party. Local musicians play on instruments made of bottles, gourds, and bamboo. The week's events are climaxed on Saturday with steel band music and a barbecue dinner.

Vee Jay's Rooftop Diner & Pub, Upper Bay Street in Kingstown (© 784/457-2845), is across from the Cobblestone Inn. Come here for vegetable *rotis* and curried goat, consumed with the bittersweet *mauby,* a local drink made from tree bark. Come here on a Wednesday or Friday night, and you're treated to karaoke along with a panoramic view of the harbor.

5 The Grenadines

GETTING THERE

BY PLANE   Four of the Grenadines—Bequia, Mustique, Union Island, and Canouan—have small airports. Service from St. Vincent is by small inter-island carriers. **SVG Air** (© **784/457-5124;** www.svgair.com), one of the longest-established airlines in the region, will fly you in modern five- to nine-seaters to any island within the Eastern Caribbean. The one-way fare from E. T. Joshua Airport on St. Vincent is EC$52 (US$19/£10) per person to Mustique, and EC$80 (US$30/£16) per person to Canouan or Union Island.

BY BOAT   The ideal way to go, of course, is to hire your own yacht, as many wealthy visitors do. A far less expensive option is to take a mail, cargo, or passenger boat, as the locals do, but you'll need time and patience. The **government mail boat,** MV *Barracuda* (© **784/457-1502,** St. Vincent's tourist office), leaves on Monday, Tuesday, Thursday, Friday, and Saturday at 10:30am, stops at Bequia, Canouan, and Mayreau, and arrives at Union Island at about 3:45pm. On Tuesday, the boat leaves Union Island at about 6:30am, stops at Mayreau and Canouan, reaches Bequia at about 10:45am, and makes port at St. Vincent at noon. One-way fares from St. Vincent to Bequia are EC$15 (US$5.55/£3). To Canouan, it's EC$20 (US$7.40/£4); Mayreau; EC$25 (US$9.25/£5); and Union Island, EC$30 (US$11/£6).

You can also reach Bequia daily on the *Admiral I* and *II* for EC$25 (US$9.25/£5). For information on these sea trips, inquire at the **Tourist Board,** Upper Bay Street, in Kingstown (© **784/457-1502**).

BEQUIA 𝒢𝒢

Only 18 sq. km (7 sq. miles) of land, Bequia (*Beck*-wee) is the largest of the Grenadines. It's the northernmost island in the chain (only 14km/8¾ miles south of St. Vincent), offering quiet lagoons, reefs, and long stretches of nearly deserted beaches. Its friendly population of some 6,000 is descended from seafarers and other early adventurers. Some 10% are of Scottish ancestry, living mostly in the Mount Pleasant region. A feeling of relaxation and informality prevails.

ESSENTIALS

VISITOR INFORMATION   The **Tourist Information Centre,** is at Port Elizabeth (© **784/458-3286;** www.bequiatourism.com).

GETTING AROUND   Most visitors find it unnecessary to rent a car as roads are atrocious. Those wanting to see more of the island might consider a taxi guide. Before going to your hotel, drop in at the **Tourist Information Centre** and ask for a driver who's familiar with the attractions of the island (all of them are). You should negotiate the fare in advance. **Rental cars,** owned by locals, are available at the port, or you can hire a **taxi** at the dock to take you around the island or to your hotel. Taxis are reasonably priced, but an even better bet are the so-called **dollar cabs,** which take you anywhere on the island for a small fee. They don't seem to have a regular schedule—you just flag one down.

BANKS   There are a few bank branches on Bequia, mostly in Port Elizabeth. All have ATMs.

ACCOMMODATIONS

The Frangipani 𝒢𝒢   This local favorite of yachties is a great hangout, its ambience created by James Mitchell, longtime prime minister of the island chain. The core of

Special Events

The **Easter Regatta** is held over Easter weekend, with boat races, food, and music. Bequia's **Carnival** celebrations are a 4-day affair, held just before St. Vincent's party in late June.

this pleasant guesthouse originated as the home of a 19th-century sea captain. Since it was transformed into a hotel, it has added accommodations that border a sloping tropical garden in back. The complex overlooks the island's historic harbor, Admiralty Bay, and draws many return visitors. The five rooms in the original house are smaller and much less glamorous (and less expensive) than the better-outfitted accommodations in the garden. The garden units are handcrafted from local stone and hardwoods, and have tile floors, carpets of woven hemp, wooden furniture (some made on St. Vincent), and balconies. Most of the rooms have a small private bathroom with a shower; otherwise, corridor bathrooms are adequate and tidily maintained.

The open-sided restaurant, Frangipani, overlooks the yacht harbor (see "Dining," below). Guests can play tennis or arrange scuba dives, sailboat rides, or other watersports nearby. The nearest scuba outfitter, Dive Adventures, is fully accredited by PADI (© **784/458-3826;** www.bequiadiveadventures.com). In winter there is an outdoor barbecue, with a steel band, every Thursday night.

Admiralty Bay (P.O. Box 1), Bequia, The Grenadines, St. Vincent, W.I. © **784/458-3255.** Fax 784/458-3824. www.frangipanibequia.com. 10 units. Winter US$60 (£31) double without bathroom, US$150–US$175 (£78–£91) double w/bathroom; off season US$45 (£23) double without bathroom, US$90–US$120 (£47–£62) double w/bathroom. AE, MC, V. **Amenities:** Restaurant; bar; tennis court; boating; nearby dive shop; private yacht charter; limited room service; babysitting; laundry service. *In room:* Ceiling fan, fridge (in some), beverage maker (in some), safe (in some), no phone.

Friendship Bay Resort 𝒢

More comfortable and stylish than Frangipani, this beachfront resort offers well-decorated rooms with private verandas, nestled in 5 hectares (12 acres) of tropical gardens. The complex stands on a sloping hillside above one of the best white-sand beaches on the island, at Friendship Cove. Guests have a view of the sea and neighboring islands. Brightly colored curtains, handmade wall hangings, and grass rugs decorate the rooms, which are cooled by the trade winds and ceiling fans (in lieu of air-conditioning). Driftwood and various flotsam art, along with sponge-painted walls, evoke the sea. The accommodations have generous storage space, beds draped in mosquito netting, and small, shower-only bathrooms. The most requested units are those set directly on the ocean. The owners have added a beach bar and offer a local string band on Tuesday, Wednesday, Friday, and every other Sunday. The food is good, and the menu features many island specialties.

Friendship Cove (P.O. Box 9), Bequia, The Grenadines, St. Vincent, W.I. © **784/458-3222.** Fax 784/458-3840. www.friendshipbayhotel.com. 28 units. Winter US$165–US$199 (£86–£104) double, US$350–US$375 (£182–£195) suite; off season US$140–US$199 (£73–£103) double, US$299 (£156) suite. Rates include continental breakfast. MC, V. **Amenities:** 2 restaurants; 2 bars; tennis court; boating; dive shop; windsurfing; babysitting; laundry service. *In room:* A/C (in some), ceiling fan, no phone.

Spring on Bequia 𝒢 *Finds*

Fashioned from beautifully textured honey-colored stone, the hotel has a flattened hip roof inspired by the old plantation houses of Martinique. Constructed on the 18th-century foundations of a West Indian homestead, it sits in the middle of 11 hectares (28 acres) of hillside orchards, producing oranges, grapefruit, bananas, breadfruit, plums, and mangos. Thanks to the almost constant

BEQUIA
The Frangipani **2**
Friendship Bay Resort **3**
Spring on Bequia **1**

MUSTIQUE
The Cotton House **5**
Firefly Hotel **4**

CANOUAN
Raffles Resort **7**
Tamarind Beach Hotel
& Yacht Club **6**

MAYREAU
Saltwhistle Bay Club **8**

UNION ISLAND
Anchorage Yacht Club **9**
Lambi's Guest House
& Restaurant **10**

PALM ISLAND
Palm Island **11**

PETIT ST. VINCENT
Petit St. Vincent Resort **12**

Airport
Ferry Route

To St. Vincent
Bequia
Port Elizabeth
Mt. Pleasant
Petit Nevis
Battowia
Quatre
Baliceaux
Dovers
Mustique
Petit Mustique
Petit Canouan
Savan
Canouan
Petit St. Vincent
Mayreau
Tobago Cays
Sail Rock
Clifton
Palm Island
Union Island
Caribbean Sea
Carriacou
Petit Martinique

MARTINIQUE
ST. LUCIA
ST. VINCENT
BARBADOS
THE GRENADINES
GRENADA
WINDWARD ISLANDS
VENEZUELA
TRINIDAD AND TOBAGO

blossoming of one crop or another, it always feels like spring (hence the name). From the main building's stone bar and open-air dining room, you might hear the lowing of a herd of cows.

All rooms have terraces; the three units in the main building are smaller and darker than the others. Each room is ringed with stone and contains Japanese-style screens to filter the sun. The high pyramidal ceilings and the constant trade winds keep things cool. The king-size or double platform beds are draped in mosquito netting, and the bathrooms have stone-grotto-like showers that use solar-heated water. The overall feeling is quiet and tranquil. The sandy beach is a 3-minute walk away through a coconut grove, but it's too shallow for good swimming.

Spring Bay, Bequia, The Grenadines, St. Vincent, W.I. © 784/458-3414 or 612/823-1202 in the U.S. Fax 784/457-3305. www.springonbequia.com. 9 units. Winter US$130–US$220 (£68–£114) double; off season US$70–US$140

(£36–£73) double. Extra person US$50 (£26). MAP (breakfast and dinner) US$45 (£23) per person extra. AE, DISC, MC, V. Closed late June–Oct. **Amenities:** Restaurant; bar; outdoor pool; tennis court; snorkeling; laundry service. *In room:* Ceiling fan (in some), fridge, no phone.

DINING

The food here is good and healthy—lobster, chicken, and steaks from such fish as mahimahi, kingfish, and grouper, plus tropical fruits, fried plantains, and coconut and guava puddings made fresh daily. Even the beach bars are kept spotless.

Frangipani ⚑ CARIBBEAN/INTERNATIONAL   This waterside dining room, always full of yachties, is one of the best restaurants on the island. With the exception of the juicy steaks imported for barbecues, only local food is used in the specialties. Lunches, served throughout the day, include sandwiches, salads, and seafood platters. Dinner specialties include homemade soup, conch chowder, baked chicken with rice-and-coconut stuffing, lobster, and an array of fresh fish. A Thursday-night barbecue with live entertainment is an island event.

In the Frangipani Hotel, Port Elizabeth. ✆ 784/458-3255. Reservations required for dinner. Breakfast EC$8.50–EC$25 (US$3.15–US$9.25/£1.70–£5); lunch EC$10–EC$65 (US$3.70–US$24/£2–£13); dinner main courses EC$27–EC$88 (US$10–US$33/£5.40–£18); fixed-price dinner EC$55–EC$135 (US$20–US$52/£11–£27). AE, MC, V. Daily 7:30am–3pm and 6:30–10pm. Closed Sept.

Friendship Bay Resort INTERNATIONAL/WEST INDIAN   Guests dine in a candlelit room high above a sweeping expanse of seafront on a hillside rich with the scent of frangipani and hibiscus. Lunch is served at the Spicy 'n Herby beach bar, but dinner is more elaborate. Meals, based on fresh ingredients, might include grilled lobster in season, curried beef, grilled or broiled fish (served Creole style with a spicy sauce), shrimp curry, and charcoal-grilled steak flambé. Dishes are flavorful and well prepared. Special barbecues are held on Wednesday and Sunday nights.

Port Elizabeth. ✆ 784/458-3222. Reservations required for dinner. Fixed-price lunch EC$30–EC$58 (US$11–US$21/£6–£12); fixed-price dinner EC$75 (US$28/£15). MC, V. Daily 8am–9:30pm. Closed Sept to mid–Oct.

Le Petit Jardin ⚑ INTERNATIONAL   Set in a varnished wooden house behind the post office, this restaurant is the slow-moving but likable creation of the Belmar family, who use as many fresh ingredients as the vagaries of the local fishing fleet will allow. You'll dine within view of a garden, in a likable ambience inspired by both the British and French West Indies. Menu items include grilled swordfish with lemon sauce; grilled lobster; shrimp and vegetable kabobs; chipped steak in cream sauce; and conventional grilled sirloin.

Backstreet, Port Elizabeth. ✆ 784/458-3318. Reservations recommended. Main courses EC$70–EC$89 (US$26–US$33/£14–£18). AE, MC, V. Daily 6:30–10pm.

Whaleboner Inn WEST INDIAN/SEAFOOD/INTERNATIONAL   An enduring favorite, the Whaleboner is still going strong, serving Bequia's most authentic local dishes. Inside, the bar is carved from the jawbone of a giant whale, and the barstools are made from the vertebrae. The owners serve the best pizza on the island, along with a selection of fish and chips and well-made sandwiches for lunch. At night, you choose among lobster, fish, chicken, or steak. We prefer the curried-conch dinner beginning with the callaloo soup. The bar often stays open later than 10:30pm, depending on the crowd. On Monday, Friday, and Saturday there is live music.

Next to the Frangipani Hotel, Port Elizabeth. ✆ 784/458-3233. Reservations recommended. Main courses EC$46–EC$89 (US$17–US$33/£9.20–£18). MC, V. Daily 8am–9pm.

EXPLORING BEQUIA

Obviously, the secluded beaches are at the top of everyone's list of Bequia's attractions. As you walk along the beaches, especially near Port Elizabeth, you'll see craftspeople building boats by hand, a method passed on by their ancestors. Whalers sometimes still set out from here in wooden boats with harpoons. Some beaches require a taxi ride. You might check out the uncrowded, pristine white sands at **Friendship Bay,** where you can rent watersports equipment or order a drink from the bar at the hotel. **Industry Bay** and **Lower Bay** are both gorgeous beaches shaded by palm trees, offering good swimming and snorkeling.

Dive Bequia, Gingerbread House, Admiralty Bay (P.O. Box 199), Bequia (© 784/458-3504), specializes in diving and snorkeling on the lush reefs of Bequia, where you might spot manta rays. Scuba dives cost US$60 (£31) for one, US$90 (£47) for two in the same day, and US$450 (£234) for a 10-dive package. A four-dive open-water certification course is US$495 (£258). Snorkeling trips are US$20 (£10) per person, and these prices include all the necessary equipment.

The main harbor village, **Port Elizabeth,** is known for its safe anchorage, Admiralty Bay. The bay was a haven in the 17th century for the British, French, and Spanish navies, as well as for pirates. Descendants of Captain Kydd (or Kidd) still live on the island. Today, the yachting set anchors here.

SHOPPING

The **Crab Hole,** next door to the Plantation House, Admiralty Bay (© 784/458-3290), is the best of the shops scattered along the water, selling sterling-silver and 14-karat-gold jewelry.

Anyone on the island can show you the way to the workshops of **Sargeant's Model Boatshop Bequia,** Front Street, Port Elizabeth (© 784/458-3344), west of the pier past the oil-storage facility. Sought out by yacht owners looking for a scale-model reproduction of their favorite vessel, Lawson Sargeant is the self-taught wood carver who established this business. The models are carved from white pine and mahogany, and then painted brilliant colors. When a scale model of the royal family's yacht, *Britannia,* was commissioned in 1985, it required 5 weeks of work. You can pick up a model of a Bequia whaling boat for much less.

MUSTIQUE ✻✻✻

This island of luxury villas, which someone once called "Georgian West Indian," is so remote and small that it would be unknown—if it didn't attract the likes of Princess Margaret, Paul Newman, Mick Jagger, Raquel Welch, Richard Avedon, Tommy Hilfiger, and Prince Andrew, many of whom have cottages here.

The island, privately owned by a consortium of businesspeople, is only 5km (3 miles) long and 2km (1¼-mile) wide, and it has only one major hotel (the Cotton House). It's located 24km (15 miles) south of St. Vincent. After settling in, you'll find many good white-sand beaches against a backdrop of luxuriant foliage. Our favorite is **Macaroni Beach,** where the water is turquoise, the sands are pure white, and a few trees shade the picnic tables. If you've come over on a day trip, you might go to **Britannia Bay,** which is next to the jetty and close to Basil's Bar.

On the northern reef of Mustique lies the wreck of the French liner *Antilles,* which ran aground on the Pillories in 1971. Its massive hulk, now gutted, can be seen cracked and rusting a few yards offshore—an eerie sight.

If you want to tour the small island, you can rent a **Mini-Moke** (a small golf cart-like car) to see some of the most elegant homes in the Caribbean, including the late Princess Margaret's place, **Les Jolies Eaux (Pretty Waters).**

GETTING THERE & GETTING AROUND

This posh island is serviced by **Mustique Airways,** which runs only private charter flights. For information and reservations, call **Grenadine Airways** at ℭ **784/456-6793.**

Once here, you can call a taxi (ℭ **784/488-8000,** ext. 448), but chances are someone at the Cotton House will already have seen you land.

ACCOMMODATIONS

The Cotton House 𝕽𝕽𝕽   The Caribbean's most exclusive hotel is as casually elegant and sophisticated as its clientele. The 18th-century main house is built of coral and stone, and it was painstakingly restored, reconstructed, and redecorated by Oliver Messel, uncle by marriage to Princess Margaret. The antique loggia, arched louvered doors, and cedar shutters set the style. The decor includes everything from Lady Bateman's steamer trunks to a scallop-shell fountain on a quartz base, where guests sit and enjoy their sundowners, perhaps after an afternoon on the tennis court or in the pool. Guests go between two beaches, each only a couple of minutes away on foot—Endeavour Bay, on the leeward side, with calmer waters, and L'Ansecoy, on the other side.

Guest rooms are in five fully restored Georgian houses, a trio of cottages, a newer block of four rooms, and a five-room beach house, all of which open onto windswept balconies or patios. Extras include king-size beds dressed in Egyptian cotton and swathed in netted canopies, robes, slippers, and toiletries from Floris in London. Some of the more romantic units have wrought-iron four-posters, and some of the bathrooms offer private outdoor showers. The Tower Suite is one of the most luxurious of the accommodations, filling the entire second floor. The most expensive residence is Cotton Hill, a 2-bedroom villa with a private pool.

The hotel enjoys an outstanding reputation for its Caribbean/Continental food and service. Nonguests are welcome to dine here but must make reservations. The hotel also has three bars—you might find Mick Jagger at one of them.

Endeavour Bay, Mustique (P.O. Box 349), The Grenadines, St. Vincent, W.I. ℭ 888/452-8380 from U.S. or 784/456-4777. Fax 784/456-5887. www.cottonhouse.net. 20 units. US$850–US$1,305 (£442–£679) double; from US$1,305 (£679) suite. Off season US$610–US$1,150 (£317–£598) double; from US$1,150 (£598) suite. Rates include MAP (breakfast and dinner). AE, MC, V. **Amenities:** 2 restaurants; 3 bars; outdoor pool; 2 tennis courts; exercise room; spa; boating; deep-sea fishing; dive shop; snorkeling; windsurfing; horseback riding; limited room service; babysitting; laundry service. In room: A/C, ceiling fan, dataport, minibar, beverage maker (in some), hair dryer, safe.

Firefly Hotel 𝕽 *(Finds*   This stone house, constructed in 1972, is one of the first homes ever built by an expatriate English or North American on Mustique. It functioned as a simple, not particularly glamorous B&B until the late 1990s, when Sussex-born Elizabeth Clayton spent huge sums of money to upgrade and enlarge the hotel and its restaurant. Although it contains only four bedrooms, it thrives as one of the most consistently popular and animated bars and restaurants (see "Dining," below) on an island where lots of the expatriate residents enjoy partying 'til the wee hours. Each of the rooms has Caribbean decor, ceiling fans, mahogany furniture, an antique four-poster bed, and a bathroom with a plunge pool, plus showers and countertops crafted from smooth-worn pebbles set into beds of mortar. The ambience is more like a private home than a hotel.

Britannia Bay (P.O. Box 349), Mustique, The Grenadines, W.I. © **784/488-8414.** Fax 784/488-8514. www.firefly mustique.com. 4 units. Winter US$850–US$1,050 (£442–£546) double; off season US$750–US$950 (£390–£494) double. Rates are all-inclusive. AE, MC, V. Children under 12 not allowed. **Amenities:** Restaurant; bar; 2 outdoor pools; tennis (nearby); snorkeling; limited room service; laundry service; nonsmoking rooms. *In room:* Ceiling fan, minibar, hair dryer, safe.

DINING

Basil's Beach Bar ☆ SEAFOOD/CARIBBEAN   Nobody ever visits this island of indigenous farmers and fisherfolk without spending a night at Basil's, which looks straight out of the South Seas with its wooden deck, open-air dance floor, and thatched roof. Built on piers above the sea, the beach bar is a popular gathering place for yachties sailing the Grenadines. Some people come for drinks and the panoramic view, but Basil's also has a reputation as one of the finest seafood restaurants in the Caribbean. Everything is simple, but well prepared. You can dine under the open-air sunscreens or in the sun. On Wednesday night in winter you can "jump-up" at a barbecue, and there's live music on Mondays. A boutique is also on the premises.

13 Britannia Bay. © **784/488-8000.** Reservations recommended. Main courses EC$80–EC$110 (US$30–US$41/ £16–£22). AE, MC, V. Daily 8am–10pm. Bar daily 8am until "very late."

The Restaurant at Firefly ☆ FRENCH/INTERNATIONAL   This is one of the island's most consistently popular restaurants, characterized by its bright tropical colors and open-air terraces, a busy bar area where you're likely to see Mustique's glitterati at play, and a menu that's the byproduct of a European-trained chef whose earlier venues were very grand and very prestigious. Some of the establishment's tried-and-true dishes include spicy Caribbean crab cakes and pineapple-shrimp curry with rice. Other entrees change with the season and the inspiration of the chef. The drink associated with this place is the Firefly Special, made with coconut cream, two kinds of rum, fresh papaya, and nutmeg. Don't miss the banana flambé.

In the Firefly Hotel, Britannia Bay. © **784/488-8414.** Reservations recommended for dinner. Main courses EC$75– EC$105 (US$28–US$39/£15–£21). AE, MC, V. Daily 8:30am–9:30pm. Bar daily 8am–midnight.

CANOUAN ☆☆
In the shape of a half circle, Canouan rises from its sandy beaches to the 240m (787-ft.) high peak of Mount Royal in the north, where you'll find unspoiled forests of white cedar. Twenty-three kilometers (14 miles) south of St. Vincent and 32km (20 miles) north of Grenada, Canouan has a population of fewer than 2,000 people, many of whom fish for a living and live in **Retreat Village,** the island's only village.

Only 6×2km (3¾×1¼ miles), Canouan is surrounded by long ribbons of absolutely gorgeous powdery white-sand beaches and blue lagoons. The surrounding coral reefs teem with life, making for great diving. As for snorkeling, it's the best this side of the Maldives.

GETTING THERE
Reaching Canouan by air is slightly different from traveling to the other islands of the Grenadines. **American Eagle** (© **800/433-7300** in the U.S. and Canada, or 784/ 456-5555) flies nonstop from San Juan to Canouan. **SVG Air** in St. Vincent (© **784/ 457-5124**) makes two daily flights to Canouan at a cost of US$330 (£172) round-trip.

ACCOMMODATIONS
Raffles Resort ☆☆   Named after the famous hotel of Singapore, this villa-studded resort opens onto a beautiful white-sand beach set on 120 hectares (300 acres). It is

the latest reincarnation of the Carenage Bay Club, which was once hailed as one of the grandest and most luxurious resorts in the southern Caribbean. The Raffles incarnation has even better facilities and more comfortable bedrooms. Opening onto Carenage Bay, each of the accommodations is a villa suite set near the beach. The golf course has been extended to a full 18 holes, and a deluxe European-style casino has been added. Each suite comes with its own private terrace. Decorated in pastels, the bedrooms have a light, airy, tropical feel. Rooms come in a variety of categories from deluxe through luxurious suites. The Caribbean's largest hotel pool is one of the allures, lying at the edge of the beach. Top chefs, often Italian, have been imported to turn out a first-rate cuisine that begins with an opulent breakfast buffet and ends with late-night Continental dining.

Carenage Bay, Canouan, St. Vincent, W.I. (C) **784/458-8000.** Fax 784/458-8885. www.raffles-canouanisland.com. 156 units. Winter from US$785 (£408) double; off season from US$545 (£283) double. AE, MC, V. **Amenities:** 4 restaurants; 4 bars; giant outdoor pool; children's pool; casino; 18-hole golf course; 4 tennis courts; fitness center; 929-sq.-m (10,000-sq.-ft.) spa; boat excursions; 24-hr. room service; laundry service; kids club. *In room:* A/C, TV, dataport, kitchenette (in some), minibar, hair dryer, safe, Wi-Fi.

Tamarind Beach Hotel & Yacht Club 𝒢   Italian-owned and -managed, this idyllic inn opens onto the long white sands of Grand Bay Beach. Thatched-roof bungalow-style hideaways, each enveloped by tropical gardens, are called seaside hideaways here—and so they are. Rooms have private balconies or patios, wicker furnishings, louvered wooden doors, and wood walls. Whirling ceiling fans go night and day. The staff provides several thoughtful touches, such as leaving a tropical fruit basket in your bedroom. The staff will help you arrange "island safaris" to such neighboring sandy strips as the Tobago Cays. Although everything is imported, the food is good and is served at water's edge on an open terrace with a view of the boats.

Charlestown, Canouan, St. Vincent, W.I. (C) **784/458-8044.** Fax 784/458-8851. www.tamarindbeachhotel.com. 60 units. Winter US$335–US$500 (£174–£260) double, US$610 (£317) suite; off season US$250–US$395 (£130–£205) double, US$480 (£250) suite. MAP (breakfast and dinner) US$70 (£36) per person extra, US$35 (£18) for children. Children under 12 stay free in parent's room. AE, MC, V. **Amenities:** 2 restaurants; 2 bars; dive shop; sailing; scuba diving; windsurfing; travel services; car rental; babysitting; laundry service. *In room:* A/C, ceiling fan, minibar, fridge, beverage maker (in some), hair dryer, safe.

DINING

Jambu's 𝒢 CHINESE/ASIAN   The best Chinese and Asian food in this tiny archipelago nation is served here at the chic Raffles Resort. Many of the dishes have flavors familiar to Singaporeans. With these Far East flavors, regional ingredients are often used as well, making for some intriguing combinations. It's a true East-meets-West kitchen. The Chinese "tapas" alone would make a meal unto themselves—coconut seafood *tom yam* soup, pan-seared marinated duck with hoisin sauce in rice paper rolls, or delectable soft-shell crab and lobster wontons. The barracuda served comes from the Caribbean but the red chili curry paste is from the Pacific. Lemon-grass crusted lamb chops are another celestial delight. Opt for a beach-bordering table where candles flicker in the trade winds at the island's most romantic spot.

Carenage Bay in the Raffles Resort. (C) **784/458-8000.** Reservations required. Breakfast buffet US$8–US$17 (£4–£9); main courses lunch US$14–US$30 (£7.30–£16), dinner US$28–US$42 (£15–£22). AE, MC, V. Daily 7–10:30am, 11:30am–2:30pm, and 7–11pm.

MAYREAU 𝒢

A tiny cay, 4 sq. km (1½ sq. miles) of land, Mayreau is a privately owned island shared by a hotel and a little hilltop village of about 250 inhabitants. It's on the route of the mail boat that plies the seas to and from St. Vincent. (See "Getting There" at the beginning of this section.) It's completely sleepy unless a cruise ship anchors offshore and hustles its passengers over for a lobster barbecue on the beach.

ACCOMMODATIONS & DINING

Saltwhistle Bay Club *Finds* Slightly less formal and expensive than the Petit St. Vincent Resort on Petit St. Vincent (see below), to which it's frequently compared, Saltwhistle Bay Club caters to escapists with money. You can spend your days lolling in one of the hammocks strung among the trees in the 8-hectare (20-acre) tropical garden, perhaps taking a swim off the expanse of white-sand beaches that curve along both the leeward and windward sides of the island, or the staff will take you to a little uninhabited island nearby for a Robinson Crusoe–style picnic.

Set back from the beach, the accommodations were built by local craftspeople, using local stone and tropical woods like purpleheart and greenheart. All units have ceiling fans. Inside, the spacious cottages have an almost medieval feel, with thick stone walls and dark wood furnishings. Bathrooms are large, with cylindrical stone showers.

The dining room is made up of circular stone booths topped by thatch canopies, where you can enjoy seafood fresh from the waters around Mayreau: lobster, curried conch, and grouper. Since there are no room phones, room service has to be requested at the reception desk.

Mayreau Island, The Grenadines, St. Vincent, W.I. © 784/458-8444. Fax 784/458-8944. www.saltwhistlebay.com. 10 units. Winter US$480 (£250) double; off season US$360 (£187) double. Children under 18 pay half. Rates include MAP (breakfast and dinner). AE, MC, V. Closed Sept–Oct. Take the private hotel launch from the airport on Union Island (US$60/£31 per person round-trip). **Amenities:** Restaurant; bar; boating; scuba diving; snorkeling; limited room service; babysitting; laundry service. *In room:* Ceiling fan, hair dryer, no phone.

UNION ISLAND

Midway between Grenada and St. Vincent, Union Island is one of the southernmost of the Grenadines. It's known for its dramatic 270m (886-ft.) peak, Mount Parnassus, which yachters can see from miles away. For those cruising in the area, Union is the port of entry for St. Vincent. Yachters are required to check in with Customs upon entry.

ESSENTIALS

GETTING THERE The island is reached by chartered or scheduled aircraft, cargo boat, private yacht, or mail boat. (See "Getting There," at the beginning of this section.)

ACCOMMODATIONS & DINING

Anchorage Yacht Club Although at least two other hotels are nearby, this club is among the best. It has a threefold function as a hotel, a restaurant, and a bar, with a busy marine-service facility in the same compound under different management.

It occupies a prominent position a few steps from the bumpy landing strip that services at least two nearby resorts (Petit St. Vincent and Palm Island) and about a

---

Fun Fact **Special Events**

Over Easter weekend, **Easterval** features boat races, a calypso competition, and the Big Drum Dance, a festive cultural show that highlights the islanders' African heritage.

half-dozen small islands nearby. Something of an airline-hub aura permeates the place, as passengers shuttle between their planes, boats, and the yacht club's bar and restaurant.

Each of the small guest rooms, set between a pair of airy verandas, has white-tile floors and simple, somewhat sun-bleached modern furniture. Shower-only bathrooms are very small and the towels a bit thin, but in this remote part of the world, you're grateful for hot water. The better units are the bungalows and cabanas beside the beach.

The yachting set meets in the wood-and-stone bar, which serves breakfast, lunch, and dinner daily.

Clifton, Union Island, The Grenadines, St. Vincent, W.I. ☏ 784/458-8221. Fax 784/458-8365. 15 units. Winter US$90 (£47) double, US$120 (£62) cabana; off season US$80 (£42) double, US$80 (£42) cabana. Extra person US$30–US$40 (£16–£21). Rates include continental breakfast. MC, V. **Amenities:** Restaurant; bar; marina; snorkeling; babysitting; laundry service. *In room:* A/C (in some), ceiling fan, beverage maker (in some).

Lambi's Guest House & Restaurant *(Value* CREOLE/SEAFOOD *Lambi* means conch in Creole patois, and if you've never tried this shellfish before, this is a good place to do so. Built partially on stilts on the waterfront in Clifton, this is also the best place to sample the local cuisine. You can order various fresh fish platters depending on the catch of the day, and lobster is frequently available. You can also order chicken, steak, lamb, or pork chops, but all this is shipped in frozen. Fresh vegetables are used whenever possible. In winter a steel band entertains nightly in the bar. Other entertainment includes limbo dancers or fire dancing.

Upstairs are 41 dormitory-style rooms for rent, each with two double beds, ceiling fans, and a tiny, tiny bathroom. Year-round, they go for EC$70 (US$26/£14) single, EC$90 (US$33/£18) double, and EC$120 (US$44/£24) triple.

Clifton Harbour, Union Island, The Grenadines, St. Vincent, W.I. ☏ 784/458-8549. Main courses EC$33–EC$62 (US$12–US$23/£6.60–£12); buffet EC$45 (US$17/£9). MC, V. Daily 7am–11pm.

PALM ISLAND ⚓

Is this island a resort or is the resort the island? Casual elegance prevails on these 52 hectares (128 acres) in the southern Grenadines. Surrounded by five white-sand beaches, this private island is sometimes called "Prune," so we can easily understand the more appealing name change. This little islet offers complete peace and quiet with plenty of sea, sand, sun, and sailing.

To get to Palm Island, you must first fly to Union Island. From Union Island, a hotel launch will take you to Palm Island.

ACCOMMODATIONS

Palm Island ⚓⚓⚓ Tranquility reigns at this all-inclusive resort with its five white-sand beaches. The old Palm Island Beach Club was completely razed to the ground and rebuilt in 1999. This exclusive and remote retreat has come a long way since its founder, John Caldwell ("Coconut Johnny"), began planting palms here to give the island a lush, tropical look. Now under new developers, the posh retreat consists of a cluster of 37 units contained in 22 Caribbean cottages. Bedrooms capture the spirit of the Grenadines, occupying both standard guest rooms and "tree houses," each with ceiling fans, custom-designed bamboo and rattan furnishings, colorful balconies or patios opening onto the view, shower-and-tub bathrooms, and bathrobes. The romantic tree houses have high-peaked ceilings, breezy balconies, and four-poster bamboo beds. In addition to the regular accommodations, the Plantation House boasts four bedrooms, each with queen-size beds. Children are allowed April 2 to January 2.

Good-quality cuisine is served in the Sunset Grill and Bar and the Royal Palm Restaurant with specialties from the Caribbean, the U.S., and Europe. One guest wrote, "If you don't dig the vittles here, you can rent a boat for the night to take you over to Union Island or else crack open a coconut." Chances are you won't have to do either, as the cuisine is great. From the pink grapefruit with honey-rum sauce that begins breakfast to the coconut mousse that completes dinner, you dine "high on the hog," as the chef says. Room service must be scheduled 24 hours in advance at the front desk since there are no phones in the room.

Palm Island, The Grenadines, St. Vincent, W.I. ⓒ **800/858-4618** in the U.S., or 784/458-8824. Fax 784/458-8804. www.eliteislandresorts.com. 37 units. Winter US$775–US$850 (£403–£442) double, US$920–US$1,010 (£478–£525) cottages and suites; off season US$650 (£338) double, US$795–US$875 (£413–£455) cottages and suites. Rates are all-inclusive. AE, MC, V. **Amenities:** 2 restaurants; 2 bars; outdoor pool; tennis court; fitness room; fishing; marina; snorkeling; windsurfing; bikes; laundry service; nonsmoking rooms. *In room:* A/C, minibar, beverage maker, hair dryer, safe, no phone.

PETIT ST. VINCENT ⚓

A private island 6km (3¾ miles) from Union Island in the southern Grenadines, this speck of land is rimmed with white-sand beaches. On 45 hectares (111 acres), it's an out-of-this-world corner of the Caribbean that's only for self-sufficient types who want to escape just about everything.

The easiest way to get to Petit St. Vincent is to fly to Union Island via St. Vincent. Make arrangements with the hotel to have its "PSV boat" pick you up on Union Island. This is the southernmost of St. Vincent's Grenadines.

ACCOMMODATIONS
Petit St. Vincent Resort ⚓⚓⚓   This nautical-chic resort was conceived by Hazen K. Richardson, who did everything from planting trees to laying cables on the 45-hectare (111-acre) property. It's the only place to stay on the island. Open to the trade winds, this self-contained cottage colony was designed by a Swedish architect, Arne Hasselquist, who used purpleheart wood and the local stone, blue bitch (yes, that's right), for the walls.

Some cottages are built on a hillside, with great views, and some are set conveniently close to the beach. Cottages open onto big outdoor patios and are cooled by trade winds and ceiling fans. Each of the spacious accommodations has an ample living area, two daybeds, a good-size bedroom with two queen-size beds, a shower-only bathroom, a dressing room, Caribbean-style wicker and rattan furnishings, and a large patio with a hammock for lying back and taking it easy. For payment, personal checks are accepted and preferred. When you need something (perhaps a picnic lunch made up for your day on the beach), you simply write out your request, place it in a slot in a bamboo flagpole, and run up the yellow flag. A staff member will arrive on a motorized cart to take your order.

This resort has a top-notch chef, and menus are changed daily. Although the food has to be shipped in, the fine U.S. and Continental dishes taste fresh and are very well prepared. The chefs are sensitive to special requests and special diets.

Petit St. Vincent, The Grenadines, St. Vincent, W.I. ⓒ **954/963-7401**. Fax 954/963-7402. www.psvresort.com. 22 units. Winter US$770–US$940 (£400–£489) cottage for 2; off season US$605–US$770 (£315–£400) cottage for 2. Rates are all-inclusive. AE, MC, V. Closed Sept–Oct. **Amenities:** Dining room; bar; tennis court; kayaks; sailing; snorkeling; windsurfing; limited room service; babysitting; laundry service; fitness trail. *In room:* Ceiling fan, minibar, hair dryer, iron/ironing board, robes, no phone.

25

Trinidad & Tobago

Trinidad, which is about the size of Delaware, and even tinier Tobago, some 30km (20 miles) to the northeast, form a nation popularly known as "T&T." South African Bishop Desmond Tutu once dubbed it "The Rainbow Country," for its abundance of floral growth and the diversity of its population. The islands are the southernmost outposts of the West Indies. Trinidad lies only 11km (6¾ miles) from the Paria Peninsula of Venezuela, to which it was physically connected in prehistoric times.

Trinidad—the birthplace of calypso, steel drum music, and the limbo—used to be visited only by business travelers in Port-of-Spain. The island was more interested in its oil, natural gas, and steel industries than in its potential for tourism. But that has changed. Trinidad is now a serious vacation destination, with a spruced-up capital and a renovated airport. The island's sophistication and cultural mélange, far greater than that of any other island in the southern Caribbean, is also a factor in increased tourism.

Conversely, Tobago, its sibling island, is just as drowsy as ever—but that's its charm. Through the years, immigrants from almost every corner of the world have come here, and today the island is a fascinating mixture of cultures, races, and creeds.

The Spanish founded Trinidad in 1592 and held it longer than they did any of their other real estate in the Caribbean. The English settled Tobago in 1642 and captured Trinidad in 1797. Both islands remained in British hands until the two-island nation declared its independence in 1962. The British influence remains visible today, apparent through the British dialect and the islanders' fondness for cricket.

1 Essentials

VISITOR INFORMATION

There is no Trinidadian tourism office that can be visited in the U.S., but you can call the **Trinidad & Tobago Tourism Office** (② 868/675-7034) for information. The islands are also on the Web at **www.visittnt.com**.

Canadians can get information from **RMR Group,** 512 Duplex Ave., Toronto, Ontario M4R 2E3 (② **888/535-5617** in Canada, or 416/485-8724).

There's also an office in **England** at **Albany House,** Albany Crescent, Claygate, Surrey KTIO OPF (② **0800/804-8787**).

Once you're on Trinidad, you can stop by **Maritime Plaza 29,** 10th Ave., Barataria, Trinidad (② **868/675-7034**). There's also an information desk at Piarco Airport (② 868/669-5196).

On Tobago, go to the **Tobago Division of Tourism,** N.I.B. Mall, Level 3, Scarborough (② **868/639-2125**), or the information desk at Crown Point Airport (② **868/639-0509**).

FAST FACTS: Trinidad & Tobago

Currency The official currency is the **Trinidad and Tobago dollar (TT$)**, which at press time was trading at US$1 = TT$6.24 (or, stated differently, TT$1 = US16¢), and at UK£ = TT$12.26 (or, stated differently, TT$1 = 8.15pence). Ask what currency is being referred to when rates are quoted. We've used both in this chapter, depending on the establishment. U.S. and Canadian dollars are often accepted, particularly in Port-of-Spain. However, you'll usually do better by converting your Canadian or U.S. dollars into local currency. British pounds should be converted into the local currency. *Unless otherwise specified, prices in this chapter are quoted in U.S. dollars and British pounds.*

Customs To avoid the long delays inherent in clearing Trinidad's Customs (reportedly, the worst delays in the southern Caribbean), it helps to arrive during the day. Visitors may bring in 200 cigarettes or 50 cigars plus 1 quart of spirits.

Documents Citizens of the United States, Britain, and Canada need passports and an ongoing or return ticket to enter Trinidad and Tobago. A visa is not required for tourist or business stays of 90 days or less. Save the carbon copy of the immigration card you'll fill out when you arrive. You'll have to return it to immigration officials when you depart.

Electricity The electricity is either 110- or 230-volt AC, so ask when making your hotel reservations if you'll need transformers and/or adapters.

Embassies & High Commissions In Port-of-Spain on Trinidad, the **U.S. Embassy** is at 7–9 Marli St., 15 Queen's Park West (© **868/622-6371;** Monday to Fri 7:30am–noon and 1–4pm); the **Canadian High Commission** is situated at Maple House, 3-3A Sweet Briar Rd., St. Clair (© **868/622-6232**); and the **British High Commission** is found at 19 St. Clair Ave., St. Clair (© **868/628-1234**).

Emergencies On both Trinidad and Tobago, call the **police** at © **999;** to report a **fire** or summon an **ambulance,** dial © **990.**

Language English is the official language, although you'll hear it spoken with many different accents, especially British. Chinese, French, Spanish, Hindi, and Trinibagianese—a local dialect—are also spoken.

Safety Like neighboring countries such as Colombia and Venezuela, Trinidad is importing a dangerous kidnapping culture. High unemployment and easy money lure newcomers to the kidnapping industry. No one, including tourists, is immune. There is no sure way to prevent kidnappings, but do take the usual precautions—avoid lonely beaches and walking alone at night.

As a general rule, Tobago is safer than Trinidad. Crime does exist on Tobago, but it's not of raging dimensions. If you can, avoid the downtown streets of Port-of-Spain at night, especially those around Independence Square, where muggings have been reported. Evening jaunts down Wilson Street and the Market of Scarborough are also discouraged. Visitors are open prey for pickpockets during Carnival, so be alert during large street parties. It is wise to safeguard your valuables; never leave them unattended at the beach or even in a locked car.

Taxes & Service Charges The government imposes a 15% value-added tax (VAT) on room rates. It also imposes a departure tax of TT$100 (US$16/£8.15) on every passenger over 5 years old, and it must be paid in local currency. The big hotels and restaurants add a 10% to 15% service charge to your final tab.

Telephone The area code for Trinidad and Tobago is **868**. Make calls to or from the islands as you would to any other area code in North America. On either island, just dial the local seven-digit number. For **MCI** call 🕾 **800/888-8000**, for **Sprint** 🕾 **800/877-8000**, and for **AT&T** 🕾 **800/872-2881**.

Time Trinidad and Tobago are in the Eastern Time zone, but don't follow daylight saving time; from November through March, time here is the same as the U.S. East Coast. During daylight saving time in the United States, T&T will be 1 hour behind (when it's 6am on the East Coast, it's 5am in T&T).

Tipping Tip taxi drivers 10% to 15% of the fare, and tip waiters 10% to 15% of the cost of a meal. Tip skycaps and bellboys US$1 (50p) per bag.

Water On Trinidad and Tobago, stick to bottled water.

Weather Trinidad has a tropical climate all year, with constant trade winds maintaining mean temperatures of 84°F (29°C) during the day and 74°F (23°C) at night. It rarely gets above 90°F (32°C) or below 70°F (21°C). The rainy season runs from May to November, but it shouldn't deter you from visiting; the rain usually lasts no more than 2 hours before the sun comes out again. However, carry along plenty of insect repellent if you visit then.

2 Trinidad

Trinidad is completely different from the other Caribbean islands, which is part of its charm and appeal. It's not for everyone, though. Because **Port-of-Spain,** the capital, is one of the most bustling commercial centers in the Caribbean, more business travelers than tourists are drawn here. The island—approximately 80km (50 miles) long and 65km (40 miles) wide—does have beaches, but the best of them are far away from the capital. The city itself, with a population of about 120,000, is hot, humid, and somewhat dirty. With the opening of its US$2-million cruise-ship complex, Port-of-Spain has become a major port of call for Caribbean cruise lines.

Although Port-of-Spain, with its shopping centers, fast-food joints, modern hotels, and active nightlife, draws mixed reviews, the countryside is calmer. Far removed from the traffic jams of the capital, you can explore the fauna and flora of the island. It's estimated that there are some 700 varieties of orchids alone, plus 400 species of birds.

Prices on Trinidad are often lower than on many other islands in the West Indies. Port-of-Spain abounds in inexpensive inns and guesthouses. Since most of the restaurants cater to locals, dining prices reflect the low wages.

The people are part of the attraction on Trinidad, the most cosmopolitan island in the Caribbean. The island's polyglot population includes Syrians, Chinese, Americans, Europeans, East Indians, Parsees, Madrasis, Venezuelans, and the last of the original Amerindian settlers of the island. You'll also find Hindustanis, Javanese, Lebanese, African descendants, and Creole mixes. The main religions are Christianity, Hinduism, and Islam. In all, there are about 1.2 million inhabitants, whose language is English, although you may also hear the local dialect, Trinibagianese.

One of the most industrialized nations in the Caribbean, and one of the biggest exporters of oil in the Western Hemisphere, Trinidad is also blessed with the huge

Trinidad

Asa Wright Nature Centre & Lodge **9**
Carnetta's Inn **6**
The Chancellor Hotel **5**
Coblentz Inn **1**
Crowne Plaza Hotel Trinidad **4**
Hilton Trinidad & Conference Centre **3**
Kapok Hotel & Restaurant **2**
Maracas Bay Hotel **8**
Monique's Guest House **7**

46-hectare (114-acre) Pitch Lake, the source of most of the world's asphalt. It's also the home of Angostura Bitters, the recipe for which is a closely guarded secret.

TRINIDAD ESSENTIALS

GETTING THERE From North America, Trinidad is one of the most distant islands in the Caribbean. **Caribbean Star** (© 866/864-6272 in the U.S. and Canada; www.flycaribbeanstar.com) services Trinidad from Antigua, Barbados, Curaçao, Grenada, St. Kitts, St. Maarten, and St. Vincent.

In addition, **Air Canada** (© 888/247-2262 in the U.S. and Canada, or 868/669-4065; www.aircanada.ca) flies Tuesday, Thursday, Saturday and Sunday nonstop from Toronto to Trinidad, and **British Airways** (© 800/247-9297 in the U.S. and Canada; www.britishairways.com) has three flights a week (Wednesday, Thursday, and Saturday), leaving year-round from London's Gatwick Airport. Most passengers from eastern North America fly **American Airlines** (© 800/433-7300 in the U.S. and Canada, or 868/627-7013; www.aa.com), which has one daily flight from New York and another from Miami.

Caribbean Airlines (© 800/538-2942 in the U.S. and Canada, or 868/625-7200; www.caribbean-airlines.com), the national carrier, offers service from New York,

Miami, and Philadelphia, to Port-of-Spain. The airline also flies from Toronto in Canada and from London in the U.K.

Trinidad is the transfer point for many passengers to Tobago. For information about getting to Tobago, see the section "Tobago," later in this chapter.

Arrivals are at Trinidad's Piarco International Airport, which is about a 30-minute drive east of Port-of-Spain.

GETTING AROUND Trinidad **taxis** are unmetered, and they're identified by their license plates, which begin with the letter *H*. There are also "pirate taxis" as well: private cars that cruise around like regular taxis and pick up passengers. Whether you take an official taxi or a pirate taxi, make sure you agree on the fare beforehand; otherwise, you're likely to get ripped off. **Maxi Taxis,** or **vans,** can also be hailed on the street. A fare from Piarco Airport into Port-of-Spain generally costs TT$95 (US$15/ £7.75). Call **Phone-A-Taxi** ② **868/627-8294** for taxi information or to order a cab.

To avoid the anxiety of driving, you can **hire a local driver** for your sightseeing jaunts. Although it costs more than doing it yourself, it alleviates the hassles of badly marked (or unmarked) roads and the sometimes-bizarre local driving patterns. Most drivers will serve as guides. Their rates, however, are based on route distances, so get an overall quotation and agree on the actual fare before setting off.

If you're brave enough to set out via **rental car,** arm yourself with a good map and **never forget to drive on the left.** Visitors with a valid international driver's license or a license from the United States, Canada, France, or the United Kingdom may drive without extra documentation for up to 3 months.

Since the island is one of the world's largest exporters of asphalt, Trinidad's some 7,245km (4,492 miles) of roads are well paved. However, outback roads should be avoided during the rainy season, as they're often narrow, twisting, and prone to washouts. Inquire about conditions, particularly if you're headed for the north coast. The fierce traffic jams of Port-of-Spain are legendary, and night driving anywhere on the island is rather hazardous.

The major U.S.-based car-rental firms currently have no franchises on the island, so you'll have to make arrangements with a local firm (go over the terms and insurance agreements carefully). Count on spending about US$50 to US$100 per day or more, with unlimited mileage included. Your best bet is one of the firms maintaining offices at Piarco Airport. These include **Econo-Car Rentals** (② **868/669-2342**), **Thrifty** (② **800/847-4389** in the U.S. and Canada, or 868/669-0602), and the simply named **Auto Rentals** (② **868/669-2277**). *Warning:* Although these local car-rental firms technically accept reservations, a car may not be waiting for you even if you reserve ahead of time.

All the towns of Trinidad are linked by regular **bus service** from Port-of-Spain. Fares are low (about US$1 for runs within the capital). However, the old buses are likely to be very overcrowded. Try to avoid them at rush hours and beware of pickpockets.

FAST FACTS Most **banks** are open Monday to Thursday from 8am to 2pm and Friday from 9am to noon and 3 to 5pm. **Citibank** has offices at 12 Queen's Park East, Port-of-Spain (② **868/625-1046** or 868/625-1049), and 18–30 High St., San Fernando (② **868/652-3691**). **Republic Bank Ltd.** (9–11 Park St.; ② **868/623-1056**) and **Royal Bank of Trinidad & Tobago Ltd.** (Royal Court, 19–21 Park St.; ② **868/ 625-7288**) are two of the many banks in Port-of-Spain with **ATMs.** You'll also find ATMs at some big supermarkets.

Fun Fact **The Carnival of Trinidad**

Called "the world's most colorful festival," the **Carnival of Trinidad** is a spectacle of dazzling costumes and gaiety. Hundreds of bands of masqueraders parade through the cities on the Monday and Tuesday preceding Ash Wednesday, bringing traffic to a standstill. The island seems to explode with music, fun, and dancing.

Some of the **Carnival costumes** cost hundreds of dollars. "Bands" might depict the birds of Trinidad, such as the scarlet ibis and the keskidee, or a bevy of women might come out in the streets dressed as cats. Costumes are often satirical and comical.

Trinidad, of course, is the land of **calypso,** which grew out of the folk songs of the African–West Indian immigrants. The lyrics command great attention, as they're rich in satire and innuendo. The calypsonian is a poet-musician, and lyrics have often toppled politicians from office. In banter and bravado, the calypsonian gives voice to the sufferings and aspirations of his people. At Carnival time, the artist sings his compositions to spectators in tents. There's one show a night at each of the calypso tents around town, from 8pm to midnight. Tickets for these are sold in the afternoon at most record shops.

You can attend rehearsals of **steel bands** at their headquarters, called panyards, beginning about 7pm. Preliminary band competitions are held at the grandstand of Queen's Park Savannah in Port-of-Spain and at Skinner Park in San Fernando, beginning 2 weeks before Carnival.

Carnival parties, or fetes, with three or four orchestras at each one, are public and are advertised in the newspaper. For a really wild time, attend a party on Sunday night before Carnival Monday. To reserve tickets, contact the **National Carnival Committee,** Queen's Park Savannah, Port-of-Spain, Trinidad (© **868/627-1358**). Hotels are booked months in advance, and most inns raise their prices—often considerably—over Carnival.

There is no 24-hour **pharmacy.** In Port-of-Spain, **Star Lite Drugs** at Four Roads (© **868/632-0516**) is open Monday to Saturday from 8:30am to 9:30pm.

The **Port-of-Spain General Hospital** is located at 169 Charlotte St. (© **868/623-2951**). Medical care is sometimes limited, and physicians and health-care facilities expect immediate cash payment for services.

The main **post office** (© **868/625-4784**) is on Wrightson Road, Port-of-Spain, and is open Monday to Friday from 7:30am to 5pm.

ACCOMMODATIONS

The number of hotels on Trinidad is limited, and you shouldn't expect your Port-of-Spain room to open directly onto a white-sand beach. The nearest beach is a long, costly taxi ride away. Hotels are booked months in advance of Carnival (the week before Ash Wednesday) and they raise their rates, often considerably, at this time.

EXPENSIVE

Asa Wright Nature Centre & Lodge 🐸 *Finds*   There really isn't anything else like this in the Caribbean. Known to bird-watchers throughout the world, this center sits on 74 remote hectares (183 acres) of protected land at an elevation of 360m (1,180 ft.) in the rainforested northern mountain range of Trinidad, 15km (10 miles) north of Arima, beside Blanchisseuse Road. Hummingbirds, toucans, bellbirds, manakins, several varieties of tanagers, and the rare oilbird are all on the property. Back–to-basics accommodations are available in the lodge, in the 1908 Edwardian main house, and in the cottages on elevated ground above the main house. Even though they offer less privacy, we prefer the two rooms in the main house, which are more atmospheric and are outfitted with dark-wood antiques and two king-size beds each. Furnishings in the cottages are rather plain but comfortable. Shower-only bathrooms are a bit cramped, but you generally get hot water—count yourself lucky.

Guided tours are available on the nature center's grounds, which contain several well-maintained trails and a natural waterfall with a pool in which guests can swim (getting to the beach involves a 90-min. drive to the coast).

The kitchen prepares Caribbean food, based for the most part on the catch of the day. Some regional meat dishes, such as stewed goat, are also offered.

Spring Hill Estate, Arima, Trinidad, W.I. (For information or reservations, call the toll-free number or write Caligo Ventures, P.O. Box 6356, Key West, FL 33041.) © **800/426-7781** in the U.S., or 868/667-4655. Fax 868/667-4540. www. asawright.org. 24 units. Winter US$360 (£187) double; off season US$250–US$280 (£130–£146) double. Rates include all meals, afternoon tea, and a welcoming rum punch on arrival. MC, V. No children under 8 allowed. **Amenities:** Dining room; swimming pond; laundry service; nonsmoking rooms; rooms for those w/limited mobility. *In room:* Ceiling fan, safe, no phone.

Crowne Plaza Hotel Trinidad 🐸   This bland but modern 14-story hotel is a favorite with business travelers, who tolerate the noise and congestion for the convenient location, a 5-minute walk from the city center. The renovated bedrooms, tastefully decorated in pastels, contain private balconies and two double beds. The hotel has two executive floors and such luxuries as trouser presses, magnifying mirrors, mahogany furniture, and brass lamps. The bathrooms have tub/shower combinations and dual basins in faux marble or granite. An on-site restaurant, 360°, is the only revolving restaurant on island, providing a striking view of the city.

Wrightson Rd. at London St. (P.O. Box 1017), Port-of-Spain, Trinidad, W.I. © **877/227-6963** in the U.S. and Canada, or 868/625-3366. Fax 868/625-4166. www.crowneplaza.com. 245 units. Year-round US$230 (£120) double; US$420 (£218) suite. Rates include breakfast. AE, MC, V. **Amenities:** 2 restaurants; bar; outdoor pool; fitness center; rental-car service; business center; room service; babysitting; laundry service; dry cleaning; nonsmoking rooms. *In room:* A/C, TV, beverage maker, hair dryer, iron, safe, trouser press.

Hilton Trinidad & Conference Centre 🐸🐸 *Kids*   This is the most dramatic and architecturally sophisticated hotel on Trinidad, and will be receiving guests during an ongoing renovation program that will be completed in 2010. The lobby is on the uppermost floor, while the guest rooms are staggered in rocky but verdant terraces that sweep down the steep hillside. The location just above Queen's Park Savannah affords most of its rooms a view of the sea and mountains. The higher rooms are cheaper than lower ones. This is not the greatest Hilton in the world, or even in the Caribbean, but all rooms still meet international first-class standards, with queen-size or twin beds, balconies, generous closet space, and modern tiled bathrooms with combination tub/showers. Accommodations in the main wing are the most sought after, as they have good views over Queen's Park Savannah. Executive Floor rooms have upgraded services and amenities.

Lady Young Rd. (P.O. Box 442), Port-of-Spain, Trinidad, W.I. © 800/445-8667 in the U.S. and Canada, or 868/624-3211. Fax 868/624-4485. www.hilton.com. 420 units. Year-round US$170–US$235 (£88–£122) double; US$225–US$375 (£117–£195) suite. AE, DC, MC, V. **Amenities:** 2 restaurants; 4 bars; 2 outdoor pools; 2 tennis courts; fitness center; sauna; children's activities; car rental; business center; salon; room service; massage; babysitting; laundry service; nonsmoking rooms; rooms for those w/limited mobility. *In room:* A/C, TV, minibar, hair dryer, safe, iron.

MODERATE

The Chancellor Hotel *Value*
Designed for the business traveler, this lovely little inn is also ideal for vacationers. In the valley of St. Ann's, the hotel sits in lush landscaped gardens studded with palms. An Iberian-style courtyard filled with sculptures and a cascading waterfall emptying into a swimming pool is one of the hotel's more attractive features. Each of the accommodations is tastefully and comfortably furnished with batik quilts, wall hangings, and teakwood desks. All units come with a small tiled bathroom with shower. The beds are Victorian style.

The chef prepares both Caribbean and international dishes, and locals often come here for the fresh fish of the day. The chef is known for game specials such as stewed deer. More standard meats like grilled lamb chops and grilled pork chops are also often served.

5A St. Ann's Ave., St. Ann's, Trinidad. © 868/623-0883. Fax 868/623-0883. www.thechancellorhotel.com. 22 units. Year-round US$182–US$218 (£95–£113) double; US$205–US$302 (£107–£157) suite. AE, MC, V. **Amenities:** Restaurant; 2 bars; outdoor pool; business center; room service; laundry service; nonsmoking rooms; rooms for those w/limited mobility. *In room:* A/C, TV, beverage maker, hair dryer, iron, safe.

Coblentz Inn *Finds*
In the residential suburb of Cascade, right outside Port-of-Spain, stands this little boutique hotel of charm and a certain grace. Each accommodation is decorated in an individual and whimsical theme—the Central Room evokes the opulence of Indian palaces and the colorful marketplaces of Asia; the Government House room pays tributes to past governor generals and visiting royalty, and the Cocoa House is inspired by the amber and gold leaves of the cocoa tree. A complimentary, fully stocked minibar is part of the deal, and the on-site restaurant, Baltimamzelle, is one of Port-of-Spain's best (see below).

44 Coblentz Ave., Cascade. © 868/621-0541. Fax 868/624-7566. www.coblentzinn.com. 16 units. Year round US$179–US$189 (£93–£98) double. Rates include continental breakfast. AE, MC, V. **Amenities:** Restaurant; business services; room service; massage; laundry service/dry cleaning; nonsmoking rooms. *In room:* A/C, TV, minibar, Wi-Fi.

Kapok Hotel & Restaurant *Value*
This modern but unpretentious nine-floor hotel, in the residential suburb of St. Clair, is an efficient, well-maintained operation run by the Chan family. It's located away from the worst traffic of the city, near the zoo, the Presidential Palace, and just north of Queen's Park Savannah. From its lounge, you'll have panoramic views of the Savannah and the Gulf of Paria. The comfortably appointed, spacious rooms have wicker furnishings and private bathrooms with combination tub/showers. For a hotel of this price range, it comes as a surprise to find phones with voice mail and dataports, and even room service until 10pm. The rooftop restaurant, Tiki Village, serves Chinese and Polynesian food. In the back is an expanded pool area with a bistro/bar, waterfall, garden, menagerie, and sun deck.

16–18 Cotton Hill, St. Clair, Trinidad, W.I. © 868/622-5765. Fax 868/622-9677. www.kapokhotel.com. 94 units. Year-round US$181–US$201 (£94–£105) double; US$234 (£122) suite. Additional person US$16(£8.30) per night. Rates include continental breakfast. AE, MC, V. **Amenities:** 2 restaurants; outdoor pool; fitness center; business services;

room service; laundry service; self-service laundry; nonsmoking rooms. *In room:* A/C, TV, kitchenette (in some), beverage maker, hair dryer, safe.

INEXPENSIVE

Carnetta's Inn *(*Finds*)*   This home is in the suburb of Andalusia in the cool and scenic Maraval neighborhood, about a 15-minute ride from the central business district and a 45-minute ride to Maracas Beach, the most popular sand strip on island. It's owned by Winston and Carnetta Borrell—both have a wealth of information about touring the island (he was a former director of tourism) and both are keen naturalists. Winston is a gardener, filling his property with orchids, ginger lilies, and anthuriums, among other plant life. Carnetta grows her own herbs to produce some of the finest meals around. The rooms have floral themes and are furnished in a tropical style. For the most privacy, request a guest room on the upper floor. Our preferred nest is Le Flamboyant, opening onto the little inn's patio. Most of the rooms are medium in size, and each has a small and immaculately maintained bathroom with shower.

99 Saddle Rd., Maraval, Trinidad, W.I. © 868/628-2732. Fax 868/628-7717. www.carnettasinn.com. 14 units. Year-round US$81 (£42) double; US$94 (£71) triple. Rates include breakfast. MC, V. **Amenities:** Restaurant; bar; limited room service; laundry service; nonsmoking rooms. *In room:* A/C, TV, kitchenette (in some), safe (in some).

Maracas Bay Hotel   If you'd like to sightsee in Trinidad and also be on the beach, Maracas Bay Hotel is a decent choice. It's the only beachfront hotel in all of Trinidad, and even here, you'll have to walk across the coastal road to reach the sands. Owned and operated by a local family, it's nestled in a valley on sloping terrain across the road from Maracas Bay. It's only 11km (6¾ miles) north of Port-of-Spain, but dense traffic and a winding road mean at least a 45-minute drive from the commercial center of the capital. There's a bar/lounge accented with Hindu art and an unpretentious dining room. Bedrooms contain simple furnishings, white-and-blue walls, and terra-cotta tile floors. Each unit has two queen-size beds and a tiled bathroom with a tub/shower combination. The beach, a wide strip of white sand bordered by palm trees, is a lovely oasis from the bustle of Port-of-Spain. The inn provides chaises and beach umbrellas for its guests, though nobody will be taking your drink order on the sands.

Maracas Bay, Trinidad, W.I. © 868/669-1914. Fax 868/669-1643. www.maracasbay.com. 32 units. Winter US$88 (£45), off season US$72 (£37). AE, MC, V. **Amenities:** Restaurant; bar; room service. *In room:* A/C, TV (in some), safe.

Monique's Guest House *(*Kids*)*   In the lush Maraval Valley just an 8-minute (5km/3-mile) drive north of the center of Port-of-Spain, Monique's offers 20 bungalow-style rooms. Some are large enough to accommodate up to four people, and 10 rooms offer kitchenettes with their own porches. The biggest are nos. 25 and 26, which can sleep up to six, though everyone would feel a bit crowded. Families are fond of booking rooms here because of the kitchenettes. Accommodations have open balconies so you can enjoy the tropical breezes and scenic hills. The bathrooms are well organized and spotless, each with a shower. The air-conditioned dining room and bar offers a medley of local and international dishes, and Maracas Beach is only a 25-minute drive away.

114–116 Saddle Rd., Maraval, Trinidad, W.I. © 868/628-3334. Fax 868/622-3232. www.moniquestrinidad.com. 20 units. Year-round US$65–US$75 (£34–£39) double, US$90 (£47) triple. AE, DC, DISC, MC, V. **Amenities:** Restaurant; bar; babysitting; laundry service; rooms for those w/limited mobility. *In room:* A/C, TV, kitchenette (in some), iron.

DINING

The food in Trinidad should be better, considering all the different culinary backgrounds that shaped the island. But being as it is, we recommend sticking to local specials like stuffed crabs and *chip-chip* (tiny clamlike shellfish). Skip the armadillo and opossum stews. Spicy *rotis* filled with vegetables or ground meat seems to be everyone's favorite lunch, and the drink of choice is a fresh rum punch flavored with Angostura Bitters. Except for a few fancy places, dress tends to be very casual.

EXPENSIVE

A La Bastille 🗗🗗 FRENCH   Housed in a one-story, cream-colored house, built in the 1960s, this grand restaurant of Port-of-Spain is a short walk from the sea and about a mile west from the center of Port-of-Spain. Menu items usually reflect classical and conservative French cuisine at its most traditional, as shown by the foie gras (cold and in aspic, and served with warm toast); the *escargots* (snails) in garlic butter; and the roasted rack of lamb with a tapenade of black olives and coated with an herb crust. Slightly more reflective of the Creole traditions of Trinidad is a warm version of an upscale goat meat salad, served with red wine and herbs; and a spicy version of "Provençale" gumbo made with clams, shrimp, oysters, fish, and shellfish.

84A Ariapita Ave., Woodbrook, Port-of-Spain. 🕐 **868/622-1789.** Reservations required. Prix-fixe lunch TT$129–TT$149 (US$21–$24/£11–£12), dinner main courses TT$148–TT$286 (US$24–$46/£12–£23). AE, MC, V. Tues-Sat 11:30am-3pm and 6:30-10pm.

Apsara 🗗 NORTHERN INDIAN   Marie Kavanagh welcomes you graciously to her restaurant, the name of which translates as "heavenly dancer." An island painter, Sarah Beckett, has decorated the place with her contemporary take on Moghul art. The skilled chefs are from India, bringing with them their exotic palette of spices. The menu is widely varied—almost too large—but the dishes are a delight, especially tandoori specialties like jumbo shrimp marinated in yogurt, fresh lime juice, and Indian spices. We're also fond of the tender lamb cooked in a rich curry sauce. Many dishes will please vegetarians. Some of the main courses emerge from the oven on a sizzling platter—try *machi masala*, a hot and spicy fish cooked in a rich and aromatic sauce. Most meals end with the masala tea flavored with clove, cardamom, and cinnamon.

13 Queen's Park East, Port-of-Spain. 🕐 **868/623-7659.** Reservations required. Main courses US$30–US$60 (£16–£31). AE, MC, V. Mon–Sat 11am–11pm.

Battimamzelle 🗗 *Finds* *Kids* CARIBBEAN/INTERNATIONAL   The name of this restaurant, which means "dragonfly" in the local dialect, sets the whimsical tone for this joint. Its decor—red and yellow walls adorned with flower paintings and red lampshades with imprints of *battimamzelles* on them—is often called "Mexicanish." For his inspiration, the chef roams the world, offering Greek-style lamb (but stuffed with Moroccan sausage) served with fruits, nuts, and couscous. The barbecued kingfish is brushed with fresh guava and served with pumpkin. The delightful Cornish hens come with a fricassee of wild mushrooms, and the 22-ounce "cowboy" rib-eye steak is tantalizingly provided with hash browns and sizzling onions. A kiddie menu is also offered on request. Most dishes are priced at the lower end of the scale.

In the Coblentz Inn, 44 Coblentz Ave., Cascade. 🕐 **868/621-0591.** Reservations required. Main courses TT$175–TT$275 (US$28–$44/£14–£22). AE, MC, V. Daily 11am–3pm and 6–10:30pm. Closed Dec 22–29.

Plantation House Restaurant 🗗 ITALIAN   This 1920s gingerbread colonial building makes an elegant setting for the excellent cuisine here. The chefs search for quality ingredients and allow their natural flavors to shine. The restaurant was long known for its Caribbean cuisine before switching to Italian specialties in 2007. However, it will still prepare Caribbean dishes but only by request. Otherwise, it features an ever-changing menu filled with succulent pastas, fresh seafood, and meat dishes such as tender veal along with sumptuous Italian desserts.

38 Ariapita Ave., Woodbrook. ⓒ 868/628-5551. Reservations recommended. Main courses TT$85–TT$220 (US$14–$35/£6.95–£18). AE, MC, V. Mon–Fri 11:30am–2:30pm and 6:30–10:30pm; Sat 6:30–10:30pm.

Solimar ⓡ INTERNATIONAL   Some think this restaurant offers the most creative cuisine in Trinidad and Tobago. Established by Joe Brown, an English-born chef who worked for many years in the kitchens of Hilton hotels around the world, it occupies a garden-style building cooled by open walls and ceiling fans. As you dine, you'll hear the sound of an artificial waterfall that cascades into a series of fishponds.

The menu, which changes every 3 months, presents local ingredients inspired by the cuisines of the world. The results are usually very compelling. Dishes might include an English-motivated combination of grilled breast of chicken and jumbo shrimp dressed with a lobster sauce, and a Sri Lankan dish of herb-flavored chicken vindaloo. The restaurant's double-chocolate mousse is the highlight of any meal here.

6 Nook Ave. (next to the Normandie Hotel, 6km/3¾ miles northwest of the city center), St. Ann's. ⓒ 868/624-6267. Reservations recommended. Main courses TT$130–TT$160 (US$21–US$26/£11–£13). AE, MC, V. Mon–Sat 6–10:30pm (Fri opening at 11:30am).

Tamnak Thai ⓡⓡ THAI/ASIAN   In the landmark center at Queen's Park Savannah, this upmarket restaurant in a restored colonial home is the island nation's finest Asian restaurant, specializing in the regional fare of Thailand. Refined dishes are beautifully served in an elegant, luxuriant, and tasteful setting, especially if you select a table on the patio. The kitchen makes the most of excellent ingredients, fashioning them into subtle dishes like red-curry chicken in coconut milk or stir-fried lobster with spring onions. Our favorite dish is the steamed mussels in a clay pot with fresh herbs such as lemon grass. If you're with a large party, you can order a selection of hors d'oeuvres that are full of zest and flavor. Many dishes are very spicy, filled with fiery chiles, but there are also milder choices.

13 Queen's Park East, Port-of-Spain. ⓒ 868/625-9715. Reservations required. Main courses TT$45–TT$195 (US$7.20–$31/£3.70–£16); set lunch TT$99 (US$16/£7.95). AE, MC, V. Tues–Fri 11am–3pm; daily 6–11pm.

MODERATE
La Trattoria Guiliano's ⓡ ITALIAN   This is a an intimate Italian-style bistro with an extensive wine list that is a cherished address for local foodies. Offering marvelous change-of-pace dining, it makes the best pizzas in town (with a thin crust) and also turns out an array of succulent pastas served with either creamy or meaty sauces. There is also an extensive list of fresh fish, which is beautifully prepared and cooked to perfection in an open kitchen where customers can see what's going on. No secrets here! To begin your meal, order a fresh and very tasty antipasto. Owner/chef Dwayne Henderson and his wife are the welcoming hosts.

63 Abercromby St. ⓒ 868/624-1236. Reservations recommended. Main courses TT$30–TT$150 (US$4.80–$24/£2.45–£12). MC, V. Mon–Fri 11:30am–10pm, Sat 11:30am–2pm.

Restaurant Singho CHINESE   This restaurant, with an almost mystically illuminated bar and aquarium, is on the second floor of one of the capital's largest shopping malls, midway between the commercial center of Port-of-Spain and the Queen's Park

Savannah. For Trinidad, the food isn't bad. In fact, it's better than your typical chop suey and chow mein joint; many of the dishes are quite tasty and spicy. A la carte choices include shrimp with oyster sauce, stewed or curried beef, almond pork, and spareribs with black-bean sauce. The to-go service is one of the best in town. The Wednesday-night buffet offers an enormous selection of main dishes, along with heaps of rice and fresh vegetables, and dessert.

Long Circular Mall, Level 3, Port-of-Spain. © 868/628-2077. Main courses TT$250–TT$300 (US$40–$48/£20–£24); Wed night buffet TT$127 (US$20/£10). AE, MC, V. Daily 11am–11pm.

Veni Mangé ★★ _Finds_ CREOLE/INTERNATIONAL Originally built in the 1930s and set about 2km (1¼ miles) west of Port-of-Spain's center, Veni Mangé (which means "come and eat") is painted in coral tones and has louvered windows on hinges that ventilate the masses of potted plants. It was established by two of the best-known women in Trinidad, Allyson Hennessy and her sister, Rosemary Hezekiah. Allyson, the Julia Child of Trinidad, hosts a daily TV talk show that's broadcast throughout the island.

Start with the bartender's special, a coral-colored fruit punch that's a rich, luscious mixture of papaya, guava, orange, and passion fruit juices. The authentic callaloo soup, according to Trinidadian legend, can make a man propose marriage. With a menu that changes daily, the main courses might be curried crab, a West Indian hot pot (a variety of meats cooked Creole style), or perhaps a vegetable lentil loaf. The helpings are large, but if you still have room, order the pineapple upside-down cake.

67A Ariapita Ave., Port-of-Spain. © 868/624-4597. Reservations recommended. Main courses TT$70–TT$130 (US$11–$21/£5.70–£11). AE, MC, V. Mon–Fri 11:30am–3pm; Wed and Fri 7:30–9:30pm.

HITTING THE BEACH

Trinidad isn't thought of as beach country, yet it has more beach frontage than any other island in the West Indies. The only problem is that most of its beaches are undeveloped and in distant, remote places, far removed from Port-of-Spain. The closest of the better beaches, **Maracas Bay,** is a full 29km (18 miles) from Port-of-Spain on the North Coast Road. It's a delight to visitors, with its protected cove and quaint fishing village. The crowds and the strong current are the only drawbacks. Facilities include restrooms and snack bars.

Farther up the North Coast Road is **Las Cuevas Bay,** which is far less crowded. The narrow beach is set against a backdrop of palm trees. There are changing rooms and vendors selling luscious tropical fruit juices.

To reach the other beaches, you'll have to go a bit farther, perhaps to **Blanchisseuse Bay** on the North Coast Road. This narrow strip of sand set against palms is an excellent spot for a picnic, although there are no facilities.

Bodysurfers frequent **Balandra Bay** on the northeast coast, but the waters generally aren't good for more pedestrian swimming.

Manzanilla Beach, along the east coast of Trinidad, north of Cocos Bay and south of Matura Bay, is not ideal for swimming either. Nonetheless, it has some picnic facilities, and the view of the water is dramatic.

SPORTS & OTHER OUTDOOR PURSUITS

For serious golf and tennis, we recommend that you try another island.

DEEP-SEA FISHING Some of the best fishing in the Caribbean is possible in the waters off the northwest coast of Trinidad—or at least Franklin D. Roosevelt used to think so. Try **Hard Play Fishing Charters,** 13 The Evergreen, Auchenskeoch, Buccoo (© **868/639-7108** or 868/682-3474). Your skipper is "Frothy" De Silva, who charges US$350(£182) for 4-hour trips on his 12m (39-ft.) vessel, *Hard Play.* Another good possibility is **Dillon's Fishing Charter,** Crown Point (© **868/639-8765**), offering 4-hour trips costing US$350 (£182) or full-day trips for US$600 (£312), including drinks and lunch. Along with record catches in blue marlin, fishermen also pursue wahoo, mahimahi, kingfish, and barracuda.

GOLF　The oldest golf club on the island, **St. Andrew's Golf Course,** Moka Estate (© **868/629-2314**), is in Maraval, about 3km (2 miles) from Port-of-Spain. This 18-hole course has been internationally acclaimed ever since it hosted the 1976 Hoerman Cup Golf Tournament. There's a full-service clubhouse on the premises. Greens fees are TT$400 (US$64/£33) for 18 holes. Club rental costs TT$100 (US$16/£8.15). Hours are daily 6am to 6pm.

TENNIS　At the **Trinidad Country Club,** Champs-Elysées, Maraval (© **868/622-3470**), six courts are lit at night. One session of 1 to 2 hours costs TT$40 (US$6.40/ £3.25). There are public courts in Port-of-Spain on the grounds of the Prince's Building (ask at your hotel for directions).

EXPLORING TRINIDAD
ORGANIZED TOURS

Sightseeing tours are offered by **Trinidad & Tobago Sightseeing Tours,** 12 Western Main Rd., St. James (© **868/628-1051;** www.trintours.com), in late-model sedans with a trained driver/guide. Several different tours are offered, including a daily city tour that takes you past (but not inside) the main points of interest of Port-of-Spain. The 3-hour tour costs US$30 (£16) per person for two.

You'll see tropical splendor at its best on a Port-of-Spain/Maracas Bay/Saddle Road jaunt, tours lasting 3½ hours. The tour begins with a drive around Port-of-Spain, passing the main points of interest in town and then going on through mountain scenery. The cost is US$40 (£21) per person.

PORT-OF-SPAIN ⊙

One of the busiest harbors in the Caribbean, Trinidad's capital, Port-of-Spain, can be explored on foot. Start out at **Queen's Park Savannah** ⊙, on the northern edge of the city. "The Savannah" consists of 80 hectares (200 acres), complete with soccer, cricket, and rugby fields, and vendors hawking coconut water and *rotis* (Caribbean burritos). This area was once a sugar plantation, but a fire in 1808 swept it and destroyed hundreds of homes.

Among the Savannah's outstanding buildings is pink-and-blue **Queen's Royal College** ⊙, containing a clock tower with Westminster chimes. Today a school for boys, it stands on Maraval Road at the corner of St. Clair Avenue. The Roodal clan's family home—affectionately called **"the gingerbread house"** by Trinidadians—is on the same road. It was built in the baroque style of the French Second Empire.

Nearby stands **Whitehall,** a former private mansion turned into the office of the prime minister of Trinidad and Tobago. In the Moorish style, it was erected in 1905 and served as the U.S. Army headquarters here during World War II. These houses, including Hayes Court, the residence of the Anglican bishop of Trinidad, and others, form what is known as the **"Magnificent Seven"** ⊙ big mansions standing in a row.

On the south side of Memorial Park, a short distance from the Savannah and within walking distance of the major hotels, stands the **National Museum and Art Gallery,** 117 Frederick St. (✆ **868/623-5941**), open Tuesday to Saturday from 10am to 6pm, Sunday from 2 to 6pm. The free museum contains a representative exhibition of Trinidad artists, including an entire gallery devoted to Jean Michel Cazabon (1813–1888); permanent collections of artifacts giving a general overview of the island's history and culture; examples of Amerindian archaeology; British historical documents; and a small natural-history exhibition including geology, corals, and insect collections. There's also a large display filled with costumes dedicated to the colorful culture of Carnival.

At the southern end of Frederick Street, the main artery of Port-of-Spain's shopping district, stands **Woodford Square.** The gaudy **Red House,** a large neo-Renaissance structure built in 1906, is the seat of the government of Trinidad and Tobago. Nearby stands **Holy Trinity Cathedral,** with a Gothic look reminiscent of the churches of England.

Another of the town's important landmarks is **Independence Square,** dating from Spanish days. Now mainly a parking lot, it stretches across the southern part of the capital from Wrightson Road to the **Cathedral of the Immaculate Conception.** This Roman Catholic church was built in 1815 in the neo-Gothic style and consecrated in 1832.

The cathedral has an outlet that leads to the **Central Market,** on Beetham Highway on the outskirts of Port-of-Spain. Here you can see all the spices and fruits for which Trinidad is known. It's one of the island's most colorful sights, made all the more so by the wide diversity of people who sell wares here.

North of the Savannah, the **Royal Botanical Gardens** (✆ **868/622-4221**) cover 28 hectares (69 acres) and are open daily from 6am to 6pm; admission is free. The park is filled with flowering plants, shrubs, and rare and beautiful trees, including an orchid house. Seek out the raw beef tree: An incision made in its bark is said to resemble rare, bleeding roast beef. Guides will take you through and explain the luxuriant foliage. In the gardens is the **President's House,** official residence of the president of Trinidad and Tobago. Victorian in style, it was built in 1875.

Part of the gardens is the **Emperor Valley Zoo** (✆ **868/622-3530**), in St. Clair, which shows a good selection of the fauna of Trinidad as well as some exotic animals from around the world. The star attractions are a family of mandrills, a reptile house, and open bird parks. You can take shady jungle walks through tropical vegetation. Admission is TT$10 (US$1.60/85p) for adults, TT$5 (80¢/40p) for children 3 to 12, and free for children under 3. It's open daily from 9:30am to 6pm.

AROUND THE ISLAND

One of the most popular attractions in the area is the **Asa Wright Nature Centre** ✿ (✆ **800/426-7781** in the U.S., or 868/667-4655; www.asawright.org; see "Accommodations," earlier in this chapter). If you're not a guest of the hotel, you can call and reserve a space for its noonday lunch for TT$85 (US$14/£6.95) Monday to Saturday or TT$120 (US$19/£9.80) on Sunday. It's also possible to reserve one of the daily guided tours of its sanctuary at 10:30am or 1:30pm, which costs TT$60 (US$9.60/£4.90).

On a peak 330m (1,082 ft.) above Port-of-Spain, **Fort George** was built by Governor Sir Thomas Hislop in 1804 as a signal station in the days of the sailing ships. Once reached only by hikers, today it's accessible by an asphalt road. From its citadel, you can see the mountains of Venezuela. Locals refer to the climb up the winding road as

Finds **Evocative of India**

Visiting the little town of Chaguanas—located south of Port-of-Spain and the Parco International Airport—is like taking a shopping trip to India. To get there, drive out Uriah Butler Highway and look for the turn-off sign to **Chaguanas.** This was the birthplace of the Nobel Prize–winning novelist V. S. Naipaul.

As you come in on Main Road you'll think you've miraculously arrived in Calcutta. A hodgepodge of shops sell Indian clothing, jars of spicy chutney, and Bollywood music. The gem of shops is **Radika's Pottery,** 183 Edinburgh Village (© **868/665-4267**), run for three generations by the Pickal family, which is acclaimed around the world for its exquisite pottery—jugs, pots, candle holders, and more. Even Naipaul is a fan of this pottery, which is exhibited at international art fairs.

If you're in town for lunch, head for the very simple but good **Indo-Chinese Vegetarian Restaurant** on Main Road (© **868/665-6928**). Main courses cost from US$1 to US$5 (50p–£2.60).

"traveling up to heaven." The drive is only 15km (10 miles), but to play it safe, allow about 2 hours.

Pointe-à-Pierre Wild Fowl Trust, Le Riene Town House, Flagstaff Hill, Long Circular Road (© **868/658-4230,** ext. 2512), is a 10-hectare (25-acre) bird sanctuary, 2 hours by car south of Port-of-Spain. The setting is unlikely, near an industrial area of the state-owned Petrotrin oil refinery, with flames spouting from flare stacks in the sky. However, in this seemingly inhospitable clime, wildfowl flourish amid such luxuriant vegetation as crape myrtle, flamboyant soursop, mango trees, and even black sage bushes said to be good for high blood pressure. You can spot the yellow-billed jacana, plenty of Muscovies, and, if you're lucky, such endangered species as the toucan or the purple gallinule. Admission is TT$10 (US$1.60/83p) or TT$3 (US50¢/26p) for kids under 12. Hours are Monday to Friday 8am to 5pm, Saturday and Sunday by appointment only from 10am to 5pm.

Enhanced by the blue and purple hues of the sky at sunset, clouds of scarlet ibis, the national bird of Trinidad and Tobago, fly in from their feeding grounds to roost at the 104-sq.-km (41-sq.-mile) **Caroni Bird Sanctuary** ⊕ (© **868/645-1305**), a big mangrove swamp interlaced with waterways. The setting couldn't be more idyllic, with blue, mauve, and white lilies; oysters growing on mangrove roots; and caimans resting on mud banks. Visitors are taken on a tour through these swamps to see the birds (bring along insect repellent). The most reliable tour operator is **James Meddoo,** Bamboo Grove Settlement, 1 Butler Hwy. (© **868/662-7356**), who has explored the swamps for some 25 years. His 2 1/2 -hour excursion leaves daily at 4pm and costs US$10 (£5.20) per person, or US$5 (£2.60) for kids ages 5 to 11. The sanctuary is about a half-hour drive (11km/6¾ miles) south of Port-of-Spain.

Pitch Lake ⊕ is on the west coast of Trinidad, with the village of Le Brea on its north shore. To reach it from Port-of-Spain, take the Solomon Hocoy Highway. It's about a 2-hour drive, depending on traffic. One of the wonders of the world, with a surface like elephant skin, the lake is 90m (295 ft.) deep at its center. It's possible to walk on its rough side, but we don't recommend that you proceed far. Legend has it that the lake devoured a tribe of Chayma Amerindians, punishing them for eating hummingbirds in which the souls of their ancestors reposed. The lake was formed millions of years ago, and it's believed that at one time it was a huge mud volcano into which muddy asphaltic oil seeped. Churned up and down by underground gases, the oil and mud eventually formed asphalt. According to legend, Sir Walter Raleigh discovered the lake in 1595 and used the asphalt to caulk his ships. Today, the bitumen mined here is used to pave highways throughout the world. You can tour Pitch Lake on your own, paying an admission of US$5 (£2.60) per person. **Trinidad & Tobago Tours** (© 868/628-1051) runs guided tours of the lake for US$55 (£29) per person. You'll find some bars and restaurants at Le Brea.

The **Saddle** ✿ is a humped pass on a ridge dividing the Maraval and the Santa Cruz valleys. Along this circular run, you'll see luxuriant grapefruit, papaya, cassava, and cocoa trees. Leaving Port-of-Spain by Saddle Road, going past the Trinidad Country Club, you pass through Maraval Village and St. Andrew's Golf Course. The road rises to cross the ridge at the spot from which the Saddle gets its name. After going over the hump, you descend through Santa Cruz Valley (rich with giant bamboo), into San Juan, and back to the capital along Eastern Main Road or Beetham Highway. You'll see panoramic views in every direction; the 29km (18-mile) tour takes about 2 hours.

Nearly all cruise-ship passengers are hauled along Trinidad's "Skyline Highway," the **North Coast Road.** Starting at the Saddle, it winds for 11km (6¾ miles) across the Northern Range and down to Maracas Bay. At one point, 30m (100 ft.) above the Caribbean, you'll see on a clear day as far as Venezuela to the west or Tobago in the east—a sweep of some 160km (100 miles).

Most visitors take this route to the beach at **Maracas Bay,** the most splendid beach on Trinidad. Enclosed by mountains, it has the charm of a Caribbean fantasy: white sands, swaying coconut palms, and crystal-clear water (see "Hitting the Beach," above).

SHOPPING

One of the largest **bazaars** of the Caribbean, Port-of-Spain has luxury items from all over the globe, including Irish linens, English china, Scandinavian crystal, French perfumes, Swiss watches, and Japanese cameras. Even more interesting are the Asian bazaars, where you can pick up items in brass. Reflecting the island's culture are calypso shirts, sisal goods, woodwork, cascadura bracelets (made from the scales of the cascadura fish), silver jewelry in local motifs, and saris. For souvenirs, visitors often like to bring back figurines of limbo dancers, carnival masqueraders, or calypso singers.

Stecher's, Gulf City Complex (© 868/657-6993), is the best bet for luxury items—crystal, watches, jewelry, perfumes, Georg Jensen silver, Lladró, Wedgwood, Royal Doulton, Limoges, and Royal Albert. You can find other branches at Long Circular Mall and West Mall. You can also pay a last-minute call at their tax-free airport branches or at the cruise-ship complex at the Port-of-Spain docks.

Y. De Lima, 83 Queen St. (© 868/623-1364), is a good store for watches, but the main focus is local jewelry. Its third-floor workroom will make whatever you want in jewelry or bronze. You might emerge with anything from steel drum earrings to a hibiscus-blossom brooch.

Art Creators and Suppliers, Apt. 402, Aldegonda Park, 7 St. Ann's Rd., St. Ann's (© 868/624-4369), is in a banal apartment complex, but the paintings and sculptures here are among the finest in the Caribbean. Among the artistic giants displayed are Glasgow, Sundiata, Keith Ward, Jackie Hinkson, and many others.

Lovers of Caribbean art also flock to the **101 Art Gallery,** 101 Tragarete Rd. (© **868/ 628-4081**), in Port-of-Spain. This is the best showcase for the hottest local talent. Some of local artist Sarah Beckett's work is viewed so highly that her abstract oils appear on regional stamps. Often you can meet some of the artists here, especially on Tuesday evenings during openings. The gallery is closed on Sunday and Monday.

The Market, 10 Nook Ave., St. Ann's (© **868/624-1181**), is one of the most fashionable shopping complexes on Trinidad. Some 20 boutiques represent the best jewelers, designers, and art dealers on the island. You'll find a wide assortment of clothing, cosmetics, bags, shoes, china, tableware, handicrafts, and accessories. The complex forms an interconnected bridge among the Normandie Hotel and Restaurant, and the restaurant Vidalia.

TRINIDAD AFTER DARK

The most popular spot on the weekends, although busy any night, is **Trotters,** at Maraval and Sweet Briar roads, St. Clair (© **868/627-8768**). This is a rustic, earthy, and multilevel English-style sports bar and pub with an eatery on the upper level. The bartenders stock more than 25 beers from around the world, and the pub has 30 TV monitors blaring at all times. There's pub grub, of course, such as barbecue ribs and chicken. Friday night a DJ is brought in for your listening pleasure. There is no cover.

Known for its pop-rock nights, **HiRpm,** Gulf City Mall, South Trunk Road, La Romain (© **868/652-3760**), is located slightly out of town, reached by heading south of Port-of-Spain, following the South Trunk Road to the mall. Attracting mostly a 21-to-35 age group, it features different entertainment on different nights—for example, techno night on Tuesday and rock bands on Wednesday. Club nights are on weekends when there is a great mix of music and a gyrating dance party. On Saturday the action begins at noon and doesn't stop until Sunday morning.

You can catch us having a beer at **Mas Camp Pub,** corner of French Street and Avenue Ariapata in Woodbrook (© **868/627-4042**). This place has a big stage where some of the best live bands in Trinidad frequently appear (or a DJ rules the night). There's also a reliable kitchen dishing up local specialties.

Local joints come and go with alarming frequency, but locals continue to flock to the live music at **The Base,** Main Street (no phone), at Chaguaramas, a 20-minute drive or taxi ride west of Port-of-Spain. This nightclub takes its name from its former role as a World War II air base, and is open Friday and Saturday night (no set hours). Also on this former airfield is The Base's competitor, **Anchorage,** Point Gourde Road (© **868/634-4334**), a popular gathering spot for "sundowners." Later on groups head across the base to **Pier 1,** Williams Bay (© **868/634-4426**), for dancing. Back in town, British pub-style **Pelican,** 2–4 Coblentz Ave., St. Ann's (© **868/624-7486**), is a hot drinking spot, especially on the weekend. It draws a very mixed crowd, including singles and businessmen (who wish they were single, at least for the night), plus a colony of Trinidadian gays.

3 Tobago

Tobago is 30km (20 miles) northeast of Trinidad, to which it's connected by frequent flights. Long known as a honeymooner's paradise, Tobago's idyllic natural beauty makes it one of the greatest escapes in the Caribbean. It has forests of breadfruit,

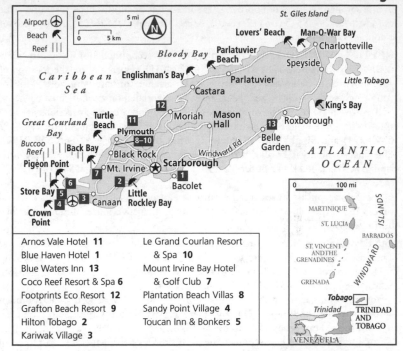

Airport ✈
Beach 🏖
Reef ‖‖‖

0   5 mi
0   5 km

St. Giles Island

Lovers' Beach   Man-O-War Bay
Charlotteville

Bloody Bay   Parlatuvier
Beach   Speyside

Caribbean
Sea   Englishman's Bay
Parlatuvier   Little Tobago

Castara

12   Moriah   Mason   King's Bay
Hall

Turtle   11
Beach
Great Courland   Plymouth   13   Roxborough
Bay   8–10
Buccoo   Black Rock   Belle
Reef ‖‖‖ Back Bay   Windward Rd.   Garden   ATLANTIC
Pigeon Point   Scarborough   OCEAN
7   Mt. Irvine ★
Store Bay   2   Bacolet   0   100 mi
6
5   3   Little
4   Canaan   Rockley Bay   MARTINIQUE
Crown   ST. LUCIA   WINDWARD ISLANDS
Point   BARBADOS
ST. VINCENT
AND THE
GRENADINES

GRENADA

Tobago
Trinidad   TRINIDAD
AND
TOBAGO
VENEZUELA

Arnos Vale Hotel **11**   Le Grand Courlan Resort
Blue Haven Hotel **1**   & Spa **10**
Blue Waters Inn **13**   Mount Irvine Bay Hotel
Coco Reef Resort & Spa **6**   & Golf Club **7**
Footprints Eco Resort **12**   Plantation Beach Villas **8**
Grafton Beach Resort **9**   Sandy Point Village **4**
Hilton Tobago **2**   Toucan Inn & Bonkers **5**
Kariwak Village **3**

mango, cocoa, and citrus through which a chartreuse-colored iguana will suddenly dart. It's for those who like a generous dose of sand, sun, and solitude in a mellow atmosphere. Snorkelers especially will find plenty to entertain them.

Unlike bustling Trinidad, Tobago is sleepy, and Trinidadians come here, especially on weekends, to enjoy the wide, sandy beaches. The legendary home of Daniel Defoe's Robinson Crusoe, Tobago is only 43km (27 miles) long and 12km (7½ miles) wide. The people are hospitable and their tiny villages seem to blend in with the landscape.

The island's villagelike capital and main port, **Scarborough,** lies on the southern coast. Surrounded by mountains, its bay provides a scenic setting, but the town itself is rather plain. Most of the shops are clustered in streets around the local market.

TOBAGO ESSENTIALS
GETTING THERE   Combining services with BWIA, **LIAT** (© **868/625-9451**) offers direct service to Tobago from either Barbados or Grenada. There are also regular flights from Trinidad to Tobago on **Tobago Express** (© **868/627-5160**) and **Caribbean Star** (© **800/723-1111** in the U.S. and Canada; www.flycaribbeanstar. com). **British Airways** (© **800/247-9297** in the U.S. and Canada; www.britishairways. com) flies weekly from London to Tobago.

Tobago's small **airport** at Crown Point (© **868/639-8547**) is near the island's southwestern tip.

It's possible to travel between Trinidad and Tobago by **ferry service,** although the trip takes 5½ to 6 hours. Call the **Port Authority of Trinidad and Tobago** (© **868/639-2417** in Scarborough, Tobago, or 868/625-3055 in Port-of-Spain) for departure times. The roundtrip fare is TT$75 (US$12/£6.10), or else TT$160 (US$26/£13) round–trip for a double occupancy cabin.

GETTING AROUND   From the airport to your accommodations, you can take a **taxi,** which will cost US$10 to US$60 (£5.20–£31), depending on the location of your hotel (taxis are unmetered). You can also arrange (or have your hotel do it for you) a **sightseeing tour** by taxi. Rates must be negotiated on an individual basis.

If you want to do extensive touring, we recommend a car as attractions are very spread out. Options include **Rattan's Car Rentals** at Crown Point Airport (© 868/639-8271) and **Singh's Auto Rentals,** Grafton Beach Resort (© 868/639-0191). One final possibility is **Thrifty,** at the airport or at the Rex Turtle Beach Hotel, Courtland Bay, Black Rock (© 868/639-8507). Charges range from US$50 to US$70 (£26–£36) a day.

Inexpensive **public buses** travel from one end of the island to the other several times a day. Expect an unscheduled stop at any passenger's doorstep and never be in a hurry. Fares are TT$6 (95¢/50p).

FAST FACTS   Most **banks** are open Monday to Wednesday from 8am to 2pm and Thursday and Friday from 8am to 1pm and 3 to 5pm. **RBTT Bank Limited** (Main St. in Scarborough; © 868/639-2404) and **Republic Bank Ltd.** (Carrington St., Scarborough; © 868/639-2811) both have **ATMs.**

You can send mail from the island post offices: **Tobago Post Office,** Scarborough Wilser Road (© 868/660-7377), and the **TT Post Office,** Cruise Ship Complex, Milford Road, Scarborough (© 868/800-7678).

For **tourist information,** contact the Tourism Division of the Tobago House of Assembly at the airport office (© 868/639-0509), or at the main office on Mount Marie Road in Scarborough (© 868/639-2125; www.visittobago.gov.tt).

Scarborough Regional Hospital is on Fort George Street, Scarborough (© 868/639-2551). Medical care is sometimes limited, and physicians and health-care facilities expect immediate cash payment for services.

ACCOMMODATIONS

To save money, it may be best to take the breakfast and dinner (MAP) plan when reserving a room. There's a 10% value-added tax (VAT) on all hotel bills, and often a service charge of about 10%. In addition, there is a 15% service charge on other hotel charges (other than the room rate) and on restaurant bills. Don't forget to ask if the VAT and service charge are included in the prices quoted to you.

VERY EXPENSIVE

Blue Haven Hotel *Finds*   It's made a comeback. In the 1950s, it was the hottest ticket in town. Rita Hayworth and Robert Mitchum even stayed here when they made *Fire Down Below* in 1957. In romantic legend, the inn stands at the place where Robinson Crusoe was stranded in 1659 in the Defoe novel. Elegantly furnished bedrooms open onto panoramic views of the water—the inn is, in fact, surrounded on three sides by the sea and opens onto a secluded beach of fine white sands. Guests walk on wooden floors, and there's a glass wall separating the bedrooms from the sleekly modern bathrooms. Guests have several options for lodging, ranging from standard doubles to deluxe suites, plus 2-bedroom villas with a private pool. All accommodations come with private balconies with ocean views. Even the pool overlooks the ocean. Honeymooners take special delight in this little charmer. In the winter, live entertainment—such as folklore shows, calypso, soca, and steel bands—is brought in to amuse the guests.

Bacolet Bay, Scarborough, Tobago, W.I. © 868/660-7400. Fax 868/660-7900. www.bluehavenhotel.com. 55 units. Winter US$238–US$275 (£124–£143) double, US$355 (£185) suite, US$585 (£304) 2-bedroom villa; off season US$181–US$220 (£94–£114) double, US$275 (£143) suite, US$425 (£221) 2-bedroom villa. Children under 3 stay free in parent's room. AE, DISC, MC, V. **Amenities:** Restaurant; 2 bars; outdoor pool; tennis court; fitness center; sauna; watersports by special arrangement; children's playground; limited room service; babysitting; laundry service. In room: A/C, minibar, TV, hair dryer, iron, safe.

Le Grand Courlan Resort & Spa ✪✪✪

Operated by the same owners as the Grafton Beach Resort (see below), this pricey hotel is definitely five-star and definitely deluxe. For those who want to live in style but don't want a megaresort like the Hilton, the Courlan is a good choice. It's named for the bay on the western edge of the island on which it sits. A soft, sandy beach is at its door and everything is set against a backdrop of bougainvillea, white frangipani, and hibiscus. Constructed to fit in with its natural surroundings, the hotel was built of stone and teak harvested from farms on Trinidad, then furnished with handcrafted mahogany pieces and decorated with original artwork. The floors are covered in Italian porcelain tile, and the ceilings are made from Guyanan hardwood. The bedrooms are handsomely tropical in decor, with two phones, king-size beds, and large balconies. Bathrooms are small, but equipped with robes, scales, phones, and tub/shower combinations.

The hotel offers a Caribbean-style bistro and an international a la carte restaurant. The food is among the best on the island. There's also nightly entertainment.

The spa specializes in cell therapy. It has a koi pond and aerobics and offers consultations in nutrition, fitness coaching, and ozone and steam detoxing, and even fresh-fruit facials and full-body compression "release" massages.

Black Rock (P.O. Box 25), Scarborough, Tobago, W.I. © 868/639-9667. Fax 868/639-0030. www.legrandcourlan-resort.com. 86 units. Winter US$318–US$402 (£165–£209) per person double, US$510 (£265) per person suite; off season US$172–US$276 (£89–£144) per person double, US$330 (£172) per person suite. Extra person US$80 (£42). Includes all meals and beverages, 1 spa treatment or scuba dive daily. AE, MC, V. **Amenities:** 2 restaurants; bar; outdoor pool; golf privileges; 2 tennis courts; spa; sauna; steam room; dive shop; fishing; massage; laundry service; non-smoking rooms. In room: A/C, TV, minibar, fridge, hair dryer, iron, safe.

Plantation Beach Villas ✪

At the edge of a tropical rainforest, between a bird sanctuary and the Caribbean, this pink-and-white cottage complex stands above a palm-fringed beach. The resort is reminiscent of the plantation era, with its British colonial architecture, rocking chairs on the front porch, four-poster beds, and louvered doors. Two sailing buddies and native Tobagonians, Jennifer Avey and Brenda Farfan, created this little gem, furnishing it with handmade pieces and original art work. Each spacious villa has three bedrooms, a trio of baths with showers, and a teak-covered front porch with a sea view. It's like living in your own private vacation retreat. A staff member will even prepare breakfast and lunch or come back to make dinner, but that costs US$20 (£10) extra. The site is a 15-minute drive from the airport.

Stonehaven Bay Rd., Black Rock (P.O. Box 435), Scarborough, Tobago, W.I. © 800/633-7411 in the U.S., or 868/639-9377. Fax 868/639-0455. www.plantationbeachvillas.com. 6 units. Winter US$560–US$680 (£291–£354) for up to 4 persons, US$640–US$735 (£333–£382) for up to 5 or 6 persons; off season US$385 (£200) for 4 persons, US$480 (£250) for up to 5 or 6 persons. AE, MC, V. **Amenities:** Restaurant; bar; outdoor pool; babysitting; laundry service. In room: A/C, TV, kitchenette, beverage maker, hair dryer, iron, safe, washing machine/dryer.

EXPENSIVE

Arnos Vale Hotel 𝒦 This inn—one of the first hotels of Tobago's modern tourist age—sprawls over 180 hectares (445 acres) of very private land. It's named after a township in England, although tour groups from Italy often fill up its chambers. This place was once a closely guarded secret, but it was a long time ago that the late Princess Margaret honeymooned here. The other celebs who used to flock here are off in Anguilla these days. Rooms, each with a private patio or veranda, are furnished with a wide spectrum of furniture, including some pieces dating back to the early 1960s, retained because many clients appreciate their slightly battered charm. Only a few of the units are actually on the beach. Suites are in a handful of individual bungalows. Not all bathrooms have tubs. Most of the socializing occurs at the likable bar, where you'll find a TV, strong drinks, and a loyal clientele that returns year after year.

Arnos Vale Rd. (P.O. Box 208), Scarborough, Tobago, W.I. 𝒸 **868/639-2881.** Fax 868/639-4629. www.arnosvale hotel.com. 19 units. Winter US$209 (£109) double, US$267–US$320 (£139–£166) suite; off season US$145 (£75) double, US$202–US$279 (£105–£145) suite. MAP (breakfast and dinner) US$66 (£34) per person extra. AE, MC, V. **Amenities:** 2 restaurants; 2 bars (1 swim-up); outdoor pool; tennis court; babysitting; laundry service; dry cleaning. *In room:* A/C, minibar (in some), beverage maker.

Coco Reef Resort & Spa 𝒦𝒦 This is one of the largest beachfront hotels on the island and it has a certain South Florida pizzazz. It's on Tobago's northern shore, near the airport. Most accommodations are in the two- and three-story main building, although about a half-dozen villas are scattered over the surrounding acreage. The designer incorporated a number of environmentally friendly features and used some recycled materials. The bedrooms are spacious and airy, filled with wicker furniture, and the big bathrooms are tiled in white with tub/shower combinations. Most rooms have an intricately trimmed balcony. In 1998, the hotel added 15 new suites with large balconies and patios overlooking the Caribbean and lush tropical gardens. These suites contain marble bathrooms equipped with tub/shower combinations and are embellished with hand-painted murals and custom-designed wicker furniture. The complex is near a trio of the island's best beaches—Store Bay, Pigeon Point, and Coconut Beach itself, just steps from your room.

Tamara's, the resort's most formal restaurant, offers some of the most sophisticated food in Trinidad and Tobago (see "Dining," below).

Coconut Bay (P.O. Box 434), Scarborough Tobago, W.I. 𝒸 **800/221-1294** in the U.S., or 868/639-8571. Fax 868/639-8574. www.cocoreef.com. 137 units. Winter US$384–US$434 (£200–£226) double, from US$682 (£355) suite or villa; off season US$296–US$378 (£154–£197) double, from US$560 (£291) suite or villa. MAP (breakfast and dinner) US$72 (£37) per person extra, US$46(£24) for children 5–12. Extra person US$60(£31) per day. AE, MC, V. **Amenities:** 2 restaurants; 2 bars; outdoor pool; tennis court; health club; spa; dive shop; snorkeling; horseback riding; car rental; salon; room service; babysitting; laundry service. *In room:* A/C, TV, minibar, hair dryer, iron, safe.

Footprints Eco Resort 𝒦 *Finds* The island's first "eco-resort" sprawls across some 24 hectares (60 acres) on Culloden Bay. A local doctor and his daughter carved this "environmentally responsible" resort out of a dense forest of cocoa and fruit trees in 1997. The result is a rustic and charming compound of wood-sided, thatch-roofed cottages. Each unit is artfully built of recycled lumber with an emphasis on native termite-resistant hardwoods such as wallaba and teak. Accommodations are rough-hewn but comfortable, with a hammock for classic island lounging, wooden floors, and a lot of idiosyncratic charm. Rooms range from standard doubles to king superior units with fridges. Some rooms have garden showers, and others have two full bathrooms with tub/shower combinations, as well as a small private pool and Jacuzzi. On-site luxuries include the excellent Cocoa House restaurant (see "Dining," below), a network of nature trails that fan out across the nearby hills, and a minimuseum that contains Amerindian artifacts uncovered during the excavations on the property. You can practice your yoga here with on-site instruction, and there's a library to satisfy your cravings for the written word. Good beaches, including Courland Bay and Castara Bay, are only a 15-minute drive away.

Golden Lane, Culloden Bay Rd., Tobago, W.I. © 868/660-0118. Fax 868/660-0027. www.footprintseco-resort.com. 15 units. Winter US$115–US$140 (£60–£73) double, US$225–US$300 (£117–£156) villa; off season US$95–US$115 (£49–£60) double, US$185–US$250 (£96–£130) villa. AE, MC, V. **Amenities:** Restaurant; bar; 2 pools; spa; fitness center; yoga; Jacuzzi; rainforest tours; room service; massage; babysitting; laundry service. *In room:* A/C, TV (in some), ceiling fan, kitchenette (in some), minibar (in some), beverage maker (in some).

Grafton Beach Resort ☆

Still going strong although it's now outclassed by many others, this complex sprawls across a beach shoreline set against a backdrop of palms. It draws the most European clientele on the island, and is under the same ownership as the neighboring and superior Le Grand Courlan Resort (Grafton guests can use Courlan's spa). Rooms are in three- and four-story buildings scattered over 2 hectares (5 acres) descending to a nice white-sand beach. The well-furnished units contain ceiling fans, sliding-glass doors opening onto balconies, and handcrafted teak furniture. Most bathrooms are small but well appointed, with combination tub/showers, mirrored closets, and retractable laundry lines.

The resort's pool is ringed with cafe/restaurant tables, and there is a swim-up bar. Fine regional and international cuisines are served in the Ocean View and Neptune's Restaurant. Limbo dancing and calypso, or some other form of entertainment, is featured nightly.

Black Rock (P.O. Box 25), Scarborough, Tobago, W.I. © 868/639-0191. Fax 868/639-0030. www.grafton-resort.com. 105 units. Year round US$152–US$162 (£79–£84) per person. Rates are all-inclusive. AE, MC, V. **Amenities:** 2 restaurants; 3 bars (1 swim-up); outdoor pool; golf privileges; boating; dive shop; snorkeling; windsurfing; car rental; laundry service; 1 room for those w/limited mobility. *In room:* A/C, ceiling fan, TV, fridge, hair dryer, iron/ironing board, safe.

Mount Irvine Bay Hotel & Golf Club ☆☆

This 6-hectare (15-acre) resort, established in 1972, stands on the site of an 18th-century sugar plantation. The surrounding Mount Irvine Golf Course is one of the finest courses in the Caribbean. Although Mount Irvine retains a loyal clientele, Le Grand Courlan Resort and the Hilton surpassed it long ago. The center of the resort is a luxurious oval pool and the ruins of a stone sugar mill. The grounds slope down to a good sandy beach. On the hill leading to the beach are the newer and better-maintained cottage suites, covered with heliconia. Most accommodations are in the main building, a two-story, hacienda-inspired wing of rather large but standard guest rooms, each with a view of green lawns and flowering shrubbery. Some of the better units have Queen Anne–style furniture with two- and four-posters. Bathrooms have tub/shower combos. The hotel serves good international food. There's dancing almost every evening, and often calypso singers. There is also a resident piano player.

Mount Irvine (P.O. Box 222), Scarborough, Tobago, W.I. © 868/639-8871. Fax 868/639-8800. www.mtirvine.com. 105 units. Winter US$195 (£101) double, US$300 (£156) cottage, US$460 (£239) 1-bedroom suite; off season US$182 (£95) double, US$300 (£156) cottage, US$460 (£239) 1-bedroom suite. MAP (breakfast and dinner) US$45 (£23) per person extra. AE, MC, V. 8km (5 miles) northwest of the airport. **Amenities:** 3 restaurants; 6 bars; outdoor pool; 18-hole golf course; 2 tennis courts; fitness center; sauna; fishing; snorkeling; water-skiing; windsurfing; Internet cafe; salon; room service; massage; babysitting; laundry service; nonsmoking rooms. *In room:* A/C, TV, hair dryer, fridge (in some).

MODERATE

Blue Waters Inn ⚡ *Kids*   Attracting nature lovers, this family-run property on the northeastern coast of Tobago is nestled along the shore of Batteaux Bay, where a private 300m-long (1,000-ft.) beach beckons guests. This charming and rustic retreat extends onto acres of tropical rainforest with myriad exotic birds, butterflies, and other wildlife. The building's entrance almost appears to drop over a cliff, and birds may actually fly through the open windows of the driftwood-adorned dining room. It's a very informal place, so leave your fancy resort wear at home. The inn now offers several units with kitchenettes, suitable for families. A few are wheelchair accessible, and all of the basic, no-frills accommodations have ceiling fans and small private showers; all are air-conditioned as well. The second-floor rooms offer lovely views of the water. The inn is about 40km (25 miles) from the airport, a 75-minute drive along narrow, winding country roads.

Tobago's local food is mixed with international dishes on the menu here. The emphasis in on fresh fish caught daily, and the chef also offers leaner dishes with reduced fats.

Batteaux Bay, Speyside, Tobago, W.I. ⓒ 800/448-8355 in the U.S., or 868/660-4341. Fax 868/660-5195. www.blue watersinn.com. 38 units. Winter US$175–US$203 (£91–£106) double, US$225 (£117) efficiency, US$400–US$430 (£208–£224) 2-bedroom efficiency; off season US$95–US$120 (£50–£62) double, US$130 (£68) efficiency, US$225–US$250 (£117–£130) 2-bedroom efficiency. MAP (breakfast and dinner) US$40 (£21) per person extra. AE, MC, V. **Amenities:** Restaurant; bar; boating; dive shop; kayaks; snorkeling; windsurfing; car rental; babysitting; non-smoking rooms; rooms for those w/limited mobility. *In room:* A/C, ceiling fan, hair dryer.

Hilton Tobago Golf and Spa Resort ⚡⚡⚡   On an 8-hectare (20-acre) site 4km (2½ miles) east of the airport is Tobago's first international hotel and the island's market leader. This five-star luxury resort rests on a 1,500m (4,900-ft.) beach with a mangrove forest in the background. The hotel is on the island's southwest coast and is part of a 300-hectare (740-acre) development that embraces a 36-hectare (89-acre) lagoon. With an 18-hole, par-72 championship PGA golf course, the hotel lures golfers from Mount Irvine Bay (see review below). The Hilton also lies in the heart of some of the best scuba-diving waters in the southern Caribbean. Rooms are tastefully and luxuriously furnished, and every suite has a Jacuzzi. Each unit opens onto ocean views and has a tub/shower combination.

The food is the finest on the island in terms of quality, although we still prefer our favorite local eateries, some mere dives. The best local bands are brought in and, overall, the Hilton has more activities than all its rivals.

Lowlands, Scarborough, Tobago, W.I. ⓒ 800/445-8667 in the U.S., or 868/660-8500. Fax 868/660-8503. www. hilton.com. 200 units. Year round US$140 (£73) double, US$340 (£177) suite. AE, DC, MC, V. **Amenities:** 3 restaurants; 3 bars; 3 outdoor pools; 18-hole golf course; 2 tennis courts; gym; sauna; deep-sea fishing; glass-bottom boat tours; scuba diving; snorkeling; children's learning center; room service; massage; babysitting; laundry service; dry cleaning; nonsmoking rooms; rooms for those w/limited mobility. *In room:* A/C, TV, minibar, beverage maker, hair dryer, iron, safe, Wi-Fi.

Kariwak Village ⚡ *Finds*   This cluster of cottages evoking the South Pacific is about a 6-minute walk from the beach on the island's west end and a 2-minute drive from the airport. The name is a combination of the two native tribes that originally inhabited Tobago, the Caribs and the Arawaks. In this "village" Cynthia and Allan Clovis run a "holistic" haven as well as an inn. Come here, among other reasons, for Hatha Yoga, Qi Gong, and various stretching and relaxing exercises. Two on-site massage therapists give you all your favorite massages. If you're a vegetarian headed for Tobago, this is the place for you. You can even walk through Cynthia's garden, where she grows fresh herbs and vegetables for the meals served here. Nine of the accommodations are hexagonal cabanas with two rooms each, opening onto the pool. The units are quite spacious, with king-size beds, and the shower-only bathrooms are bright and well maintained.

Live entertainment is provided on Friday and Saturday year-round. The food served in the Kariwak Village Restaurant (see "Dining," below) is among the best on the island, and you may want to come by for a bite even if you aren't staying here.

Local Rd., Store Bay (P.O. Box 27), Scarborough, Tobago, W.I. ℂ 868/639-8442. Fax 868/639-8441. www.kariwak. com. 24 units. Winter US$125 (£65) double; off season US$90 (£47) double. Children 12 and under stay free in parent's room. MAP (breakfast and dinner) US$40 (£21) per person extra. AE, MC, V. **Amenities:** Restaurant; bar; outdoor pool; yoga; Jacuzzi; massage; laundry service; nonsmoking rooms. *In room:* A/C, hair dryer, iron, safe.

INEXPENSIVE

Sandy Point Village   This miniature vacation village resembles a Riviera condominium complex. It's just a 5-minute ride from the airport, but its shoreside position on the island's southwestern coast makes it seem remote. Airport noise, however, can be a problem. The little village of peaked and gabled roofs is landscaped all the way down to the sandy beach, where the rustic Steak and Lobster Grill serves meals throughout the day and evening. The fully equipped accommodations have patios that open toward the sea, living and dining areas with Jamaican wicker furniture, and satellite TV. All but six of the units (those at poolside) contain kitchenettes, and each has a shower-only bathroom. Some of the studios have a rustic open stairway leading to a loft with bunk beds, with a twin-bedded room on the lower level as well.

Crown Point, Tobago, W.I. ℂ 868/639-8533. Fax 868/639-8496. www.sandypt.net. 45 units. Winter US$70–US$90 (£36–£47) double, US$100 (£52) 2-bedroom apt; off season US$50–US$60 (£26–£31) double, US$70 (£36) 2-bedroom apt. Children 11 and under US$15 (£7.80) extra. AE, MC, V. **Amenities:** Restaurant; bar; outdoor pool; fitness center; dive shop; Jacuzzi; sauna; bike rental; car rental. *In room:* A/C, TV, kitchenette (in most), safe.

Toucan Inn & Bonkers ⍟ *Value*   This combination restaurant and hotel is one of Tobago's best values. An inn of charm and grace, it is close to the airport and surrounded by attractively landscaped gardens. If you stay here, you'll be just a short drive from some of the island's best sandy beaches. The staff is helpful in directing you. Bedrooms are done in a modern style with comfortable though streamlined furniture; rooms come in various shapes and sizes, each with a queen-size or two twins and a small but efficiently organized private bathroom with shower. The hotel offers an option of well-furnished bedrooms with tiled shower bathrooms. The cluster of rooms facing the garden is more secluded, but even so, many guests prefer the cabanas around the pool. Teak furnishings predominate in the bedrooms. On-site Bonkers is one of the most frequented restaurants and bars in Tobago. Live entertainment is presented about 4 nights a week, and savory regional fare includes the likes of sweet curried lamb or sizzling blackened shrimp.

Store Bay Local Rd. (Box 452), Crown Point, Tobago, W.I. ℂ 868/639-7173. Fax 868/639-8933. www.toucan-inn. com. 20 units. Winter US$100–US$120 (£52–£62) double; off season US$80–US$100 (£41–£52) double. AE, MC, V. **Amenities:** Restaurant; bar; outdoor pool; babysitting; nonsmoking rooms. *In room:* A/C, hair dryer, iron, safe.

DINING
EXPENSIVE

Dillon's ⍟ INTERNATIONAL   Set in a simple house near the Coco Reef Resort and the airport, this restaurant is run by one of Tobago's leading operators of a deep-sea-fishing boat. Consequently, the fish is sure to be fresh. There's both an indoor, air-conditioned room with framed memorabilia of the island's tradition of steel-pan music, and an outdoor terrace with views over the garden. Menu items include fresh snapper with lemon-butter sauce; tenderloin steak with a spinach-bacon ragout; pan-fried or grilled shrimp served with grilled Parmesan polenta, basmati rice, and a tomato/basil sauce; curried shrimp in coconut sauce and mango chutney; and a lobster crepe with white-wine sauce and fresh herbs.

Milford Rd., near Crown Point. © 868/639-8765. Reservations recommended. Main courses TT$120–TT$275 (US$19–$44/£9.80–£22). AE, DISC, MC, V. Mon–Sat 6–10pm. Closed 6 weeks May–June.

Tamara's ⚑ CREOLE/INTERNATIONAL   One of the most appealing restaurants on Tobago occupies a two–tiered, stone-and–timber gazebo whose curved edges are open on all sides for maximum exposure to cool breezes and views of the nearby sea. It serves some of Trinidad and Tobago's most sophisticated food, based on West Indian traditions with lots of international touches. Start, perhaps, with homemade veal-and-bacon terrine or pan-fried shrimp with wilted greens and wasabi sauce. Try the lamb loin on couscous, the charcoal-grilled ocean snapper with a cream mushroom-and-lemon-grass sauce, or most definitely the pork tenderloin garnished with a lima-bean ragout. The menu changes every 2 days.

In the Coco Reef Resort, Coconut Beach. © 868/639-8571. Reservations recommended. Breakfast TT$87 (US$14/£7.10); lunch buffet TT$160 (US$26/£13); fixed-price dinner TT$300 (US$48/£24). AE, DISC, MC, V. Daily 7am–10pm.

MODERATE TO INEXPENSIVE

Arnos Vale Water Wheel Restaurant INTERNATIONAL   This restaurant occupies the weathered premises of a former 19th-century water mill used to crush sugar cane. You'll dine in the wheelhouse, with an antique oven and the wheel's original machinery still in place, while overlooking the verdant banks of the Franklin River. Menu items include Cornish hen, shaved pear and Parmesan salad, deviled chicken, honey-roasted duck breast, caramelized breast of chicken with polenta and callaloo sauce, grilled fish served with a medley of sauces, and at least three different shrimp and lobster dishes. Three times a week, there's a performance of live Trinidadian/Tobagan music and dance; the animated sounds perk up the otherwise calm and quiet landscape of chirping tree frogs and splashing water.

Arnos Vale Rd., Plymouth. © 868/660-0815 or 868/639-2881. Reservations recommended. Main courses TT$160–TT$200 (US$26–$32/£13–£16). AE, MC, V. Daily 8am–10pm. The restaurant is a 5-min. drive from the Arnos Vale Hotel.

The Blue Crab ⚑ *Finds* CARIBBEAN/INTERNATIONAL   One of our favorite restaurants in the capital, this family-run spot occupies an Edwardian-era house with an oversize veranda. The menu makes the most of local ingredients and regional spices, and is dictated by whatever is available that day in the marketplace. The good, homemade food includes fresh conch, stuffed crab backs, an array of Creole meat dishes grilled over coconut husks, flying fish in a mild curry-flavored batter, shrimp with garlic butter or cream, and a vegetable rice dish of the day. Lobster sometimes appears on the menu.

Robinson St., Scarborough. © 868/639-2737. Dinner reservations required 24 hr. in advance. Lunch TT$45–TT$65 (US$7.20–$10/£3.65–£5.30). AE, MC, V. Mon–Fri noon–3pm.

The Cocoa House ⚑ WEST INDIAN/TOBAGONIAN   Proud of its eco-sensitivity (waste water and paper trash are recycled here), this restaurant is a worthy choice for its allegiance to tried-and–true Tobagonian food that's prepared in a style endorsed by many of the island's matriarchs and grandmothers. Its name comes from its unusual roof, made from the fronds of the timit palm. On balmy evenings, the roof retracts (just as it might at an old-fashioned cocoa pod drying room), allowing views of the setting sun and, a bit later, of the moon and stars. Well-flavored dishes include jerk versions of shrimp, chicken, and pork; duck with either orange or pineapple sauce; and *pelau,* a French-inspired dish that combines chicken and beef bound together with rice. For a dish that many Tobagonians remember from their childhood, try pork and dumplings.

In Footprints Eco Resort, Golden Lane, Culloden Bay Rd. © 868/660-0118. Dinner reservations required. Breakfast TT$31–TT$50 (US$4.95–US$8/£2.55–£4.05); main courses lunch TT$45–TT$65 (US$7.20–US$10/£3.65–£5.30), dinner TT$75–TT$105 (US$12–US$17/£6.25–£8.75). AE, MC, V. Daily 8am–9pm.

Jemma's Seaview Kitchen ★ *Finds* TOBAGONIAN A short walk north of the hamlet of Speyside, on Tobago's northeastern coast, this is one of the very few restaurants in the Caribbean designed as a tree house. Although the simple kitchen is firmly anchored to the shoreline, the dining area is set on a platform nailed to the massive branches of a 200-year-old almond tree that leans out over the water. Some 50 tables are available on a wooden deck that provides a rooflike structure for shelter from the rain. The charming staff serves up good main courses that come with soup or salad. Lunch platters include shrimp, fish, and chicken, while dinners feature more elaborate portions of each, as well as steaks, curried lamb, grilled or curried kingfish, lamb chops, and lobster served grilled or thermidor style. No liquor is served.

Speyside. © 868/660-4066. Reservations recommended. Lunch main courses TT$60–TT$250 (US$9.60–US$40/£4.90–£20). Dinner main courses TT$80–TT$250 (US$13–US$40/£6.50–£20). MC, V. Sun–Thurs 8am–9pm; Fri 8am–4pm.

Kariwak Village Restaurant ★ *Value* CARIBBEAN Even if you're not a guest here, consider visiting at dinnertime. The chefs prepare one of the choicest menus on the island, a four-course repast that changes nightly, based on what's best and freshest at the market. On our latest rounds, we began with creamy breadfruit soup, followed by freshly grilled fish, rice, stuffed butternut pumpkin, and *christophene* (Caribbean squash). The price even includes dessert and coffee. In an open-air setting, you can enjoy recorded music from Trinidadian steel bands. The owner, Cynthia Clovis, grows herbs and vegetables in an on-site organic garden. The Friday- or Saturday-evening buffet is one of the best spreads on the island, with live music to boot. Shrimp and steak are favorites, but save room for the green-banana salad seasoned with fresh herbs.

In the Kariwak Village hotel, Local Rd., Store Bay. © 868/639-8442. Reservations recommended. Breakfast US$11 (£5.70); lunch US$14 (£7.25); 4-course dinner US$24 (£13). AE, MC, V. Daily 7am–11pm.

La Belle Creole ★ *Finds* CAJUN/INTERNATIONAL This unusual and noteworthy restaurant occupies an Edwardian house .8km (½ mile) south of Scarborough. The restaurant serves freshly made fruit drinks laced with the local rum. We highly recommend the delectable "mammy's golden apple chutney," and the locally caught crayfish shaped into cakes and served with a tangy sauce. The kitchen also prepares Cajun dishes such as blackened chicken and shrimp jambalaya along with seared tuna. To begin your meal, you can do no better than the callaloo soup with tender crabmeat (the secret is in the tender, young dasheen leaves). A house specialty is piña colada mahimahi marinated in herbs and coconut milk along with a honey-pineapple purée.

In the Half-Moon Blue Hotel, 73 Bacolet St., Scarborough. © 868/639-3551. Fax 868/639-6124. Reservations required. Main courses TT$100–TT$350 (US$16–US$56/£8.15–£29). MC, V. Daily 8am–9pm.

La Tartaruga *Finds* ITALIAN/SEAFOOD/VEGETARIAN Born in Milan, Lombardian Gabriele de Gaetano has brought the flavors of his homeland to remote Tobago and has infused the island with marvelous change-of-pace dining. The eatery is casual yet elegant, with lots of color used along with local artwork. The island's most gracious host, Gaetano "table hops," always concerned about your welfare and whether or not you like his food. Diners almost invariably tell him how tasty and flavorful his Italian-inspired cuisine is. Perhaps he can't find all the authentic ingredients needed for his food, but he succeeds admirably nonetheless. His ravioli won our hearts until we tasted his tagliatelle with lobster, made all the tastier with the use of Trinidadian capers in wine and fresh cream. For a main course, we heartily endorse the mixed seafood grill of lobster, shrimp, and calamari among other delights. Many of the dishes will appeal to the vegetarian in all of us. Desserts are homemade fresh daily and are luscious. Everything is backed up by the best wine *carte* on the island.

Buccoo Rd., Buccoo. (© 868/639-0940. Reservations recommended. TT$55–TT$145 (US$8.80–US$23/£4.50–£12). AE, MC, V. Mon–Sat 6:30–10pm.

HITTING THE BEACH

On Tobago, you can still feel like Robinson Crusoe in a solitary sandy cove—at least until Saturday, when the Trinidadians fly over for a weekend on the beach.

Pigeon Point, on the northwestern shore, is the best-known bathing area, with a long coral beach. It's public, but to reach it you must enter a former coconut estate, which charges a fee of TT$10 (US$1.60/80p). Set against a backdrop of royal palms, this beach is becoming increasingly commercial. Facilities include food kiosks, crafts shops, a diving concession, paddleboat rentals, changing rooms in thatched shelters, and picnic tables. Pigeon Point is also the jumping off point for snorkeling cruises to **Buccoo Reef.**

Another good beach, **Back Bay,** is an 8-minute walk from the Mount Irvine Bay Hotel on Mount Irvine Bay. Along the way, you'll pass a coconut plantation and an old cannon emplacement. Snorkeling is generally excellent, even in winter. There are sometimes dangerous currents, but you can always explore Rocky Point Beach and its brilliantly colored parrotfish. In July and August, the surfing is the finest in Tobago; it's also likely to be good in January and April. Stop in Scarborough for picnic fixings, which you can enjoy at the picnic tables here; a snack bar sells cold beer and drinks.

Great Courland Bay is known for its calm, gin-clear waters, and is flanked by **Turtle Beach,** named for the turtles that nest here. Near Fort Bennett and south of Plymouth, Great Courland Bay is one of the longest sandy beaches on the island and the site of several hotels and a marina.

The locals and the fishing boats make the setting at half-moon-shaped **Parlatuvier Beach** (on the north side of the island) more bucolic than the swimming. If you can't stand crowds, head for **Englishman's Bay,** on the north coast just west of Parlatuvier. We don't know why this beach is virtually deserted: It's charming, secluded, good for swimming, and there have been no reports of muggings despite the seclusion.

Near the little fishing village of Charlotteville, **Man-O-War Bay** is one of the finest natural harbors in the West Indies. It has a long, sandy beach and a government-run rest house. Sometimes local fishermen will hawk the day's catch (and clean it for you as well). Nearby **Lovers' Beach** is accessible only by boat and is famous for its pink sand, formed long ago from crushed sea shells. Negotiate a fee with one of the local boatmen; expect to pay around US$25 (£13).

The true beach buff will head for **King's Bay** in the northeast, south of the town of Speyside near Delaford. Against a backdrop of towering green hills, the crescent-shaped grayish-sand beach is one of the best places for swimming.

SPORTS & OTHER OUTDOOR PURSUITS

GOLF Tobago is the proud possessor of an 18-hole, 6,800-yard course at Mount Irvine. Called the **Tobago Golf Club** at the Mount Irvine Estates (© 868/639-8871), it covers 60 breeze-swept hectares (150 acres) and was featured in the *Wonderful World of Golf* TV series. Even beginners agree the course is friendly to duffers. Guests of the Mount Irvine Bay Hotel are granted temporary membership, use of the clubhouse and facilities, and a 15% discount on greens fees. The course is also open to nonguests, who pay US$55 (£29) for 18 holes or US$35 (£18) for 9 holes. Cart rentals are US$42 (£22) for 18 holes or US$23 (£12) for 9 holes. **Tobago Plantations Golf & Country Club,** Hampden Road, Lowlands (© 868/631-0875), lies on a 303-hectare (748-acre) estate that was previously a sugar-cane plantation. It adjoins the grounds of the Hilton Tobago. Some holes on this par-72, 7,000-yard course follow the coastline. Greens fees, including golf cart, are US$100 (£52) for 18 holes, US$68 (£35) for 9 holes.

SCUBA DIVING, SNORKELING 🐟🐟 **& OTHER WATERSPORTS** The unspoiled reefs off Tobago teem with a great variety of marine life. Divers can swim through rocky canyons 18 to 39m (59–128 ft.) deep, underwater photographers can shoot pictures they won't find anywhere else, and snorkelers can explore the celebrated **Buccoo Reef** (off Pigeon Point), which teems with gardens of coral and hundreds of fish in the waist-deep water. Even nonswimmers can wade knee-deep in the waters. Remember to protect your head and body from the sun and to guard your feet against the sharp coral. Nearly all the major hotels arrange boat trips here. After about half an hour at the reef, passengers reboard their boats and go over to **Nylon Pool,** with its crystal-clear waters. Here in this white-sand-bottom spot, about 2km (1¼ mile) off-shore, you can enjoy a dip in water only 1m (3¼-ft.) deep.

Wreck divers have a new adventure to enjoy with the sinking of the former ferryboat *Maverick,* in 30m (100 ft.) of water near Mount Irvine Bay Hotel on Tobago's southwest coast.

Dive Tobago, Pigeon Point (© 868/639-0202; www.divetobago.com), is the oldest and most established operation on Tobago, run by Jay Young, a certified PADI instructor. It offers easy resort courses, single dives, and dive packages, along with equipment rentals. A basic resort course costs US$75 (£39), although for certification you must pay US$450 (£234). A one–tank dive goes for US$45 (£23).

Tobago Dive Experience, at the Manta Lodge, Speyside (© 868/660-4888; www.tobagodiveexperience.com), offers scuba dives, snorkeling, and boat trips. All dives are guided, with a boat following. Exciting drift dives are available for experienced divers. A one–tank dive costs US$48 (£25) without equipment; a two–tank dive starts at US$75 (£39); and a resort course costs US$70 (£36).

Frank's Glass Bottom Boat Tours, Blue Waters Inn, Bateaux Bay, Speyside (© 868/660-5438), takes visitors on trips to Angel Reef to see a collection of the largest brain coral in the world. Combined with a snorkeling trip, the cost is US$20 (£10) per person. A glass-bottom boat tour and snorkeling tour plus a guided tour of the Little Tobago Bird Sanctuary, costs only US$20 (£10), and is the most popular jaunt.

TENNIS   The best courts on the island are at the **Mount Irvine Bay Hotel** (© **868/ 639-8871**). Nonguests may use one of the two courts here for TT$35 (US$5.60/ £2.90) per hour. There is an additional TT$25 (US$4/£2) light fee on request.

EXPLORING TOBAGO

If you'd like a close-up view of Tobago's many rare and exotic tropical birds, as well as a range of other island wildlife and lush tropical flora, naturalist-led field trips are the answer. Each 5-hour trip leads you to forest trails and coconut plantations, along rivers and past waterfalls; one excursion even goes to two nearby islands. Trips cost US$50 to US$65 (£26–£34). For details, contact **Newton George,** Speyside (© **868/ 660-5463** or 868/754-7881).

Tobago's capital, **Scarborough,** need claim your attention only briefly before you climb up the hill to **Fort King George,** about 130m (425 ft.) above the town. Built by the English in 1779, it was later captured by the French, then was tossed back and forth among various conquerors until nature decided to end it all in 1847, blowing off the roofs of its buildings. You can view the ruins of a military hospital, and also see artifacts displayed at the **Tobago Museum** (© **868/639-3970**), in the fort's old barracks. Admission is US$1 (50p), and hours are Monday to Friday 9am to 4:30pm.

From Scarborough, you can drive northwest to **Plymouth,** Tobago's other town. Perched on a point at Plymouth is **Fort James,** which dates from 1768. Now it's mainly in ruins.

From Speyside in the north, you can make arrangements with a local fisher to go to **Little Tobago** ⨶, a 180-hectare (445-acre) offshore island whose bird sanctuary attracts ornithologists. The 20-minute crossing is likely to be rough, but the effort is worth it. Threatened with extinction in New Guinea, many birds—perhaps 50 species—were brought over to this little island in the early part of last century. The islet is arid and hilly, with a network of marked trails.

Off Pigeon Point in the south is **Buccoo Reef** ⨶⨶, where sea gardens of coral and hundreds of fish can be seen in waist-deep water (see "Scuba Diving, Snorkeling & Other Watersports," above). This is the natural aquarium of Tobago, offering the island's best **snorkeling** and **scuba diving.** Nearly all the major hotels arrange boat trips here.

SHOPPING

In Tobago's capital, Scarborough, you can visit the local **market** Monday to Saturday mornings. Scarborough's stores have a limited range of merchandise, more to tempt the browser than the serious shopper.

Farro's, Wilson Road (no phone), across from the marketplace, offers the tastiest condiments on the island, packed into little straw baskets for you to carry back home. Sample the delectable lime marmalade, any of the hot sauces, the guava jelly, and most definitely the homemade tamarind chutney.

If you're seeking handicrafts, especially straw baskets, head for the **Shaadijas Souvenir & Gift Shop,** Port Mall (© **868/660-1000**), also in Scarborough.

Cotton House Fashion Studio, Old Windward Road, in Bacolet (© **868/639- 2727**), is the island's best choice for "hands-on" appreciation of the fine art of batik. In the Indonesian tradition, melted wax is brushed onto fabric, resisting dyes and creating unusual colors and designs. This outlet contains the largest collection of batik clothing and wall hangings on Tobago. Dying techniques are demonstrated to visitors, who can then try their skills.

The Art Gallery, Hibiscus Drive, Lowlands (© 868/639-0457; www.tobagoart gallery.com), across from the Tobago Hilton, features the works of at least 10 artists. On permanent exhibit upstairs is a collection of island watercolors by Rachel Superville and her husband, Martin. Sculptures and a number of handicrafts are also sold here.

TOBAGO AFTER DARK

Your best bet for entertainment is at the **Mount Irvine Bay Hotel** at Mount Irvine Bay (© 868/639-8871), where you might find some dance action or a steel band performing by the beach or pool.

Grafton Beach Resort at Black Rock owns one of the island's most charming bars, **Buccaneer's Beach Bar** (© 868/639-0191), across from the resort. Here you'll find a wide wood terrace sheltered by a grove of almond trees. Daily specials written up on a surfboard include burgers, fried fish, and the like (don't expect the elegant beachside Creole cooking of Martinique). The resort itself offers cabaret-like entertainment nightly. Try to catch the local troupe, Les Couteaux Cultural Group, which performs a version of Tobagonian history set to dance.

Want some local action? Try **Bonkers** ⚘, Store Bay Road at Crown Point (© 868/639-7173), a lively bar where you'll hear the best soca, reggae, or jazz on the island. If you've been "bad," the DJ might order you to walk the gangplank into the pool.

26

Turks & Caicos

With the pre- and post-millennium growth of Turks and Caicos (*Kayk*-us) Islands, people no longer ask, Turks and Who? A Gallup poll in the late 1990s found that the small island nation of Turks and Caicos had the least name recognition in the world. That is no longer true. Since sun worshippers discovered the islands, especially Providenciales—nicknamed "Provo" in the early '90s—more and more vacationers are flocking to the islands. A "second Bahamas" in the making is clearly becoming a reality. Provo since 2000 has become the fastest growing destination in the Caribbean. The islands are part of the Bahamian archipelago, and once in their history, they were governed by The Bahamas. Lying to the east of the southernmost islands of The Bahamas, Turks and Caicos are self-governing today, although under the protection of Great Britain.

Directly north of Haiti and the Dominican Republic, the islands lie at the crossroads of the Caribbean and the Americas. Technically, this obscure outpost is not in Caribbean waters, but on the fringe of the Atlantic.

Grand Turk and Salt Cay (which constitute the Turks Islands) and Cockburn Harbour (South Caicos) are ports of entry, while the major island to visit is Provo.

The Turks and Caicos Islands (TCI) are a coral-reef paradise, largely shut off from the world, free of pollution and crowds. Even with the advent of real tourist development and the bustle of construction, particularly in Provo, the beauty and tranquility of this little island chain remain intact. They're still off the beaten track, and they're not right for travelers who want lots of glitzy facilities or nightlife. You won't find the highly refined tourist infrastructure that exists in the Bahamas, but that's the appeal for some travelers.

What's beginning to put Turks and Caicos on the map is an incredible array of beaches—362km (224 miles) worth, to be precise. Some stretches of soft white sand run for miles; others are small, hidden in secluded coves. The islands are also home to some of the world's most magnificent underwater life. For years, divers and snorkelers have enjoyed the countless varieties of brilliant coral and colorful fish that thrive within TCI's nearly 800km (500-mile) pristine reef system.

Turks and Caicos are mainly self-governing today. Queen Elizabeth selects a governor to be her representative in island affairs, and this governor appoints the chief minister who, in turn, appoints minor ministers.

1 Essentials

VISITOR INFORMATION

The Turks & Caicos Sales and Information Office, Front Street, Cockburn Town, Grand Turk, B.W.I. (© **800/241-0824** in the U.S., or 649/946-2321), is open Monday to Friday 8am to 5pm. The website for Turks and Caicos is **www.turksandcaicos**

The Turks & Caicos Islands

tourism.com. In the United States, the Turks & Caicos Island Tourist Board Office is at 60 E. 42nd St., Suite 2817, New York, NY 10165 (© **800/241-0824** in the U.S., or 646/375-8830).

FAST FACTS: Turks & Caicos Islands

Banks Branches of **First Caribbean International Bank** (© **649/946-4245**) and **Scotiabank** (© **649/946-4750**) are at convenient and central locations on both Provo and Grand Turk. There is an **ATM** at the Bank of Novia Scotia on Cherokee Road in Providenciales (© **649/946-4750**), open Monday to Thursday 9am to 3pm and Friday 9am to 4:30pm.

Currency The **U.S. dollar** is the official currency. *Prices in this chapter are quoted in U.S. dollars.*

Customs On arriving, you may bring in 1 quart of liquor, 200 cigarettes, 50 cigars, or 8 ounces of tobacco duty-free. There are no restrictions on cameras, film, sports equipment, or personal items, provided they aren't for resale. Absolutely no spear guns or Hawaiian slings are allowed, and the importation of firearms without a permit is also prohibited. Illegal imported drugs bring heavy fines and lengthy terms of imprisonment.

Documents U.S. and Canadian citizens must have a passport or a combination of a birth certificate and photo ID, plus a return or ongoing ticket, to enter the country. Citizens of the United Kingdom, Commonwealth countries of the Caribbean, the Republic of Ireland, and E.U. countries must ALSO have a current passport.

Electricity The electric current on the islands is 120 volts, 60 cycles, AC. European appliances will need adapters.

Emergencies Call © **911** or **999** for an **ambulance,** to report a **fire,** or to contact the **police.**

Language The official language is English.

Safety Although crime is minimal in the islands, petty theft does take place, so protect your valuables, money, and cameras. Don't leave luggage or parcels in an unattended car. Beaches are also vulnerable to thievery.

Taxes There is a departure tax of $35, payable when you leave the islands. Also, the government collects a 10% occupancy tax, applicable to all hotels, guesthouses, and restaurants in the 40-island chain. Hotels add a 10% to 15% service charge on top of the government tax.

Telephone To call Turks and Caicos, dial **1** and then the number. To call a phone carrier in the U.S., dial **0,** then **1,** and then the number. The international-operator telephone service is available 24 hours a day.

Time The islands are in the Eastern Standard Time zone, and daylight saving time is observed.

Tipping Hotels usually add 10% to 15% to your bill automatically, to cover service. If individual staff members perform various services for you, it is customary to tip them something extra. In restaurants, 10% to 20% is appropriate unless a service charge has already been added. If in doubt, ask. Taxi drivers like at least a 10% tip.

Water Government officials insist that the water in Turks & Caicos is safe to drink. Nonetheless, stick to bottled water, especially if you have a delicate stomach.

Weather The average temperature here is 82°F (28°C), dropping to 77°F (25°C) at night. The cooling breezes of the prevailing trade winds prevent the climate from being oppressive. The islands receive approximately 21 inches of rainfall annually.

2 Providenciales (Provo) ★★★

Affectionately known as **Provo,** Providenciales has white-sand beaches that stretch for 19km (12 miles) along the northeast coast. It also has peaceful rolling hills, flowering cactus, clear water, a natural deep harbor, and a barrier reef that attracts swimmers, divers, and boaters. The island is served by an airport (capable of handling wide-body jets), four marinas, and diving facilities.

Provo is the most developed island in the Turks and Caicos chain. Once known mainly to a group of millionaires headed by Dick du Pont, Provo has now developed a broader base of tourism.

The island is undergoing a major growth spurt, and you're sure to see lots of construction around the island from the minute you land at the airport. New resorts are being built, and the real-estate market is booming. Once you reach your hotel, however, it's easy to feel that you've gotten away from it all.

ESSENTIALS

GETTING THERE   Before you book your flight, read "Packages for the Independent Traveler" in chapter 2—it could save you a bundle. Even if you don't book a package, you should check that chapter's tips on finding the best airfare. Provo is the most easily reached island in the nation because of frequency of flights.

American Airlines (© 800/433-7300 in the U.S. and Canada; www.aa.com) flies twice daily from Miami to Provo with direct flights from New York's JFK. In winter only, there are also Saturday and Sunday flights from Boston to Provo. **US Airways** (© 800/428-4322 in the U.S. and Canada; www.usairways.com) also flies to Provo, daily from Charlotte and on Saturday from Philadelphia. **Delta Airlines** (© 800/221-1212 in the U.S. and Canada; www.delta.com) flies daily from Charlotte to Provo and from Atlanta Wednesday to Sunday. **Air Canada** (© 888/247-2262 in the U.S. and Canada; www.aircanada.ca) flies from Toronto to Provo on Saturday and Wednesday, and **British Airways** (© 800/247-9297 in the U.S. and Canada, or 0870/850-9850 in the U.K.; www.britishairways.com) flies Sunday from Heathrow to Provo. **Bahamasair** (© 800/222-4262 in the U.S. and Canada; www.bahamasair.com) flies Sunday, Tuesday, and Thursday from Nassau to Provo. **Spirit Airlines** (© 800/772-7117) flies from Fort Lauderdale, Florida, to Provo on Saturday and Sunday. Spirit also flies from Fort Lauderdale to Grand Turk on Sunday.

GETTING AROUND   Taxis meet arriving flights; otherwise, call the **Provo Taxi Association** (© 649/946-5481). Cabs are metered and rates are set by the government.

Provo

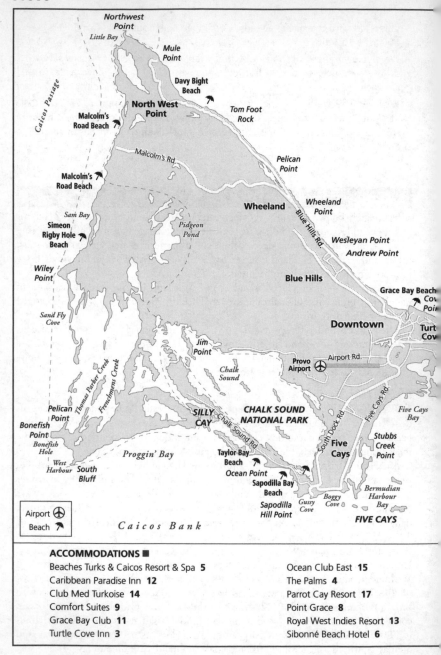

Northwest Point
Little Bay
Mule Point
Davy Bight Beach
North West Point
Tom Foot Rock
Caicos Passage
Malcolm's Road Beach
Malcolm's Rd.
Pelican Point
Malcolm's Road Beach
Wheeland
Wheeland Point
Sam Bay
Pidgeon Pond
Simeon Rigby Hole Beach
Wesleyan Point
Andrew Point
Wiley Point
Blue Hills
Sand Fly Cove
Grace Bay Beach
Cove
Poi
Downtown
Turt
Cove
Jim Point
Thomas Parker Creek
Frenchmens Creek
Chalk Sound
Provo Airport
Airport Rd.
Pelican Point
SILLY CAY
CHALK SOUND NATIONAL PARK
Five Cays Bay
Bonefish Point
Bonefish Hole
Chalk Sound Rd.
South Dock Rd.
Five Cays Rd.
Stubbs Creek Point
West Harbour
South Bluff
Proggin' Bay
Taylor Bay Beach
Ocean Point
Five Cays
Sapodilla Bay Beach
Bermudian Harbour Bay
Sapodilla Hill Point
Gussy Cove
Boggy Cove
FIVE CAYS

Airport
Beach

Caicos Bank

ACCOMMODATIONS ◼

Beaches Turks & Caicos Resort & Spa **5**
Caribbean Paradise Inn **12**
Club Med Turkoise **14**
Comfort Suites **9**
Grace Bay Club **11**
Turtle Cove Inn **3**

Ocean Club East **15**
The Palms **4**
Parrot Cay Resort **17**
Point Grace **8**
Royal West Indies Resort **13**
Sibonné Beach Hotel **6**

ATLANTIC OCEAN

WATER CAY

To Parrot Cay ↗

Grace Bay

LITTLE WATER CAY

Donna Cut

DONNA CAY

Done Bobbin'

Leeward-Going-Through Point

Stubbs Creek

MANGROVE CAY

Grace Bay Beach

Thomas Stubbs Point

Dolphin Ave.

Governor's Rd.

16

15

Heaving Down Rock

Caicos Conch Farm

Crist Point

PRINCESS ALEXANDRA NATIONAL MARINE PARK

Leeward

8 **8**

11

11 **14**

13

12

Forbes Point

Grace Bight

Provo Golf Club

7

6

The Bight

9 **10**

Leeward Hwy.

Stubbs Cove

3

3

Long Point

Grace Bay Beach

5

2

4

Richmond Hills

1

Lower Bight Rd.

Leeward-Going-Through Rd.

Kingston

Cheshire Hall Circle

Long Bay Beach

Bay Hwy.

Seasage Hill Rd.

Flamingo Rd.

Long Bay Hwy.

Long Bay Beach Dr.

Discovery Bay

Turtle Creek Dr.

Venetian Dr.

Flamingo Lake

Ocean Dr.

Bristol Hill Dr.

Turtle Lake

Jim Hill Bight

Bristol Hill Point

Turtle Tail Dr.

Juba Point Salina

Long Bay Hwy.

Long Bay Beach Extreme Point

Cooper Jack Bight

Cooper Jack Point

FIVE LITTLE CAYS

Juba Point

| 0 | 1 mi |
| 0 | 1 km |

N

ATLANTIC OCEAN

PROVO (PROVIDENCIALES)

CAICOS ISLANDS

TURKS ISLANDS

0   15 mi

DINING◆

Anacaona **11**	Grace's Cottage **8**
Aqua Restaurant **3**	Hemingway's Beachfront Restaurant **7**
Baci Ristorante **2**	Hey José Cantina **1**
Banana Boat Restaurant **3**	
Coco Bistro **10**	
Coyaba Restaurant **16**	

Because the island is so large and its hotels and restaurants are so far-flung, you might find a car useful on Providenciales. A major U.S.-based car-rental agency with a franchise in the Turks and Caicos Islands is **Budget** on Providenciales. It's located in Butterfield Square, near the airport (© **800/472-3325** in the U.S., or 649/946-4079; www.budgetrentacar.com). Cars rent for $52 to $75 a day; collision-damage insurance costs $10 to $12 a day. The local government will collect $15 tax for each rental contract, regardless of the number of days you keep the car. Because the company's main office lies in the commercial center of the island, a short drive from the airport, a representative will come to meet your flight at the airport if you notify them in advance of your arrival.

Charging comparable prices, **Avis** (© **800/331-1212** in the U.S. and Canada, or 649/946-4705; www.avis.com) has a branch at the airport.

If you'd like to try your luck with a local agency, call one of the following: **Rent A Buggy** (© **649/946-4158;** www.rentabuggy.tc), **Turks & Caicos National** (© **649/946-4701**), or **Provo Rent-a-Car** (© **649/946-4404;** www.provo.net). Rates average from $40 to $90 per day, plus a $15 government tax.

Note: In the British tradition, cars throughout the country drive on the left.

VISITOR INFORMATION   There's a branch of the **Turks & Caicos Islands Tourist Board** at Stubbs Diamond Place, The Bite, Providenciales (© **649/946-4970**), open Monday to Friday 8am to 5pm.

FAST FACTS   Head for **First Caribbean International Bank,** Butterfield Town Square (© **649/946-4245**), for cashing traveler's checks and other banking services on Provo. **Scotia Bank** is at Leeward Highway, Cherokee Road (© **649/946-4752**).

Grace Bay Medical Center, Neptune Plaza, Grace Bay (© **649/941-5252**), takes care of most needs. Anyone critically ill or requiring advanced medical care might be flown to Miami.

Call © **649/946-4259** if you need the **police.**

There's a **post office** in the Town Square (© **649/946-4676**), open Monday to Thursday from 8:30am to 4pm, Friday from 8:30am to 12:30pm.

ACCOMMODATIONS
VERY EXPENSIVE
Beaches Turks & Caicos Resort & Spa 🛇🛇 *Kids*   This resort is part of the Sandals chain of all-inclusive hotels, though unlike most Sandals, families with kids are welcome here. This is a luxurious, pampering place, opening onto the luscious sands of 19km-long (12-mile) Grace Bay Beach. The $30-million resort's Bermuda-style bungalows, with lovely pink-and-yellow exteriors, are gorgeous. The price tag is high, but you get a lot for your money; there's a fine spa, excellent watersports, and good service. Actors dressed as characters from Sesame Street—Elmo and his friends Cookie Monster, Grover, and Zoe—are on hand to interact with children. The resort's success is reflected in its $70 million expansion that will include nearly 170 family suites, a water park, and a gigantic swimming pool in its new "Italian Village," that should be up and running by the time you read this.

Catering to travelers from Europe and North America, the property features guest rooms that are finely decorated, though they could use more warmth; the one- and two-bedroom villa suites are veritable pockets of posh. All accommodations have panoramic ocean views from private balconies, king-size or double beds, individual climate control, and full bathrooms. Villa suites also have butler service, a spacious living room, a kitchenette, and two bathrooms (one with a Roman tub and separate shower).

The restaurant Reflections serves casual fare for breakfast, lunch, and dinner. Its weekend breakfast buffet is the island's best. Other restaurants offer seafood, Southwestern cuisine, and Japanese food. The Turtles and Iguanas is the spot for an after-dinner drink, and there's another bar and lounge at poolside. The resort's showcase restaurant, Sapodilla's, features Caribbean-influenced international cuisine.

Lower Bight Rd. (P.O. Box 186), Providenciales, Turks and Caicos, B.W.I. © **800/232-2437** in the U.S., or 649/946-8000. Fax 649/946-8001. www.beaches.com. 453 units. Prices based on 2-night minimum stay: winter $425–$525 double, $695 1-bedroom suite, $1,235 2-bedroom suite for 4, $1,720 3-bedroom family suite; off season $410–$475 double, $625 1-bedroom suite, $1,125 2-bedroom suite for 4, $1,570 3-bedroom family suite. Rates are all-inclusive. AE, DISC, MC, V. **Amenities:** 11 restaurants; 7 bars; 6 outdoor pools; golf course (nearby); 4 lit tennis courts; fitness center; spa; 2 saunas; kayaks; windsurfing; children's center; game room; massage; babysitting; laundry service; dry cleaning; nonsmoking rooms; rooms for those w/limited mobility; dance club. *In room:* A/C, TV, dataport, kitchenettes (in some), beverage maker, hair dryer, iron, safe, Wi-Fi.

Club Med Turkoise 𝒢 Set on 28 hectares (69 acres) of sun-blasted scrubland, on a white strip of beachfront overlooking Grace Bay, 18km (11 miles) from the airport, this is one of the most popular and successful Club Meds in the Americas. This was the first major resort built on Provo, and although more recent newcomers have pulled out in front, it remains an appealing oasis of charm and communal fun. Unlike some Club Meds, this one does not allow children under 18. Its ambience is also among the most casual of any Club Med, a fact that seems to appeal to the laid-back French and North American clientele.

The village-style cluster of two- and three-story, basic accommodations is capped with cedar shingles imported from Sweden. The resort contains simple rooms with twin or king-size beds, all designed with beachfront living in mind. Each has a mid-size, shower-only bathroom.

Most meals are served buffet-style and consumed at long communal tables. Table wine and beer are free at mealtime. Two specialty restaurants have waiter/waitress service and include a pizzeria and a beachfront eatery (the Grill) that specializes in late breakfasts, late lunches, and late suppers. A dance club keeps residents active, if they wish, from 11:30pm to at least 2am nightly. All meals are included; drinks, which cost extra, are paid for with bar tickets.

Grace Bay, Providenciales, Turks and Caicos, B.W.I. © **800/258-2633** in the U.S., or 649/946-5500. Fax 649/946-5497. www.clubmed.com. 297 units. Winter $1,545–$1,722 per person weekly; off season $1,300–$1,600 per person weekly. Rates include all meals, wine and beer at meals, and most activities except for scuba diving. AE, DISC, MC, V. No children under 18 allowed. **Amenities:** 3 restaurants; 2 bars; outdoor pool; 8 lit tennis courts; gym; sailing; scuba diving; snorkeling; windsurfing; laundry service; coin-operated laundry; dry cleaning; nonsmoking rooms; nightclub. *In room:* A/C, TV, minifridge, beverage maker, hair dryer, iron, safe, Wi-Fi.

Grace Bay Club 𝒢𝒢𝒢 This tasteful American-owned and -managed development is one of the island's top hotels, sitting in a desirable spot on a white-sand beach. Ringed with about 200 palm trees imported from Florida and Nevis, it lies on 2 landscaped hectares (5 acres) of what used to be barren scrubland on Provo's North Shore. Designed in the spirit of a Spanish seaside village at the edge of a white-sand beach, the hotel is capped with terra-cotta tiles and partially sheathed in sculpted coral stone, and it was built around a courtyard with a splashing fountain in the center. The price is high, but if you can afford it, you'll get a lot of pampering and superb food for your money.

Each of the accommodations has an eclectic kind of elegance, with views that extend out either over the sea or over the gardens. Each contains a king-size bed with carved headboards imported from Mexico, carpets and art objects from India and/or Turkey, tables and armoires from Mexico or Guatemala, and artwork from Haiti and/or Brazil. Suites and penthouses each have their own kitchens, washing machines, and dryers. Full-size bathrooms throughout the resort contain tub/shower combinations, hand-painted Mexican tiles, and lots of mirrors.

The resort was massively expanded in 2005 after the expenditure of more than $45 million, some of which went into upgrades of the interior decor of the existing rooms, and some of which went into new construction that more than doubled its number of accommodations in the form of 38 luxurious new condos positioned within four separate "villas," each positioned directly on the beach. These condos are privately owned but are available for guest bookings. Even the beach benefited from the massive upgrade of 2005, more than doubling in length after the acquisition of additional footage. In March 2007, the original 22-suite adults-only hotel reopened after a substantial upgrade.

The hotel's restaurant, Anacaona, is recommended separately in "Dining" below, and part of the expansion included the opening of the casual-dining Grill restaurant. The beachfront lounge, with its Hamptons-style white–cushion seating and glowing fire pit, is one of the best spots on the island to have a cocktail and watch the sunset on Grace Bay. A program called Kids Town offers a full menu of kid-friendly eco-activties and half- or full-day excursions.

Grace Bay Rd. (P.O. Box 128), Providenciales, Turks and Caicos, B.W.I. ℂ 800/946-5757 in the U.S., or 649/946-5050. Fax 649/946-5758. www.gracebayclub.com. 59 units. Winter $785–$955 junior suite, $1,025–$1,435 1-bedroom suite, $1,745–$2,165 2-bedroom suite, $5,000–$7,000 penthouse; off season $455–$705 junior suite, $615–$1,075 1-bedroom suite, $1,045–$1,625 2-bedroom suite, $2,995–$5,525 penthouse. Rates include continental breakfast. MAP (breakfast and dinner) $70 per person extra. AE, MC, V. **Amenities:** 2 restaurants; 2 bars; 2 outdoor pools; 2 lit tennis courts; fitness center; 4,000-sq.-ft. spa; Jacuzzi; boating excursions; deep-sea fishing; kayaks; sailing; windsurfing; bikes; car rental; business services; room service (7am–9pm daily); massage; laundry service. *In room:* A/C, ceiling fan, TV, kitchen (in some), hair dryer, safe, washer/dryer (in some), Wi-Fi.

The Palms 🃏🃏🃏 *Kids* This boutique resort, which challenges the Grace Bay Club, opened in 2005 amid landscaped gardens, immediately adjacent to the white sands of Provo's best beach, Grace Bay.

Although a few are conventional, well-decorated large double rooms, the majority of the units here are one-, two-, and three-bedroom suites. Their numbers are equally divided among five separate buildings, each with five stories. The buildings form a horseshoe-shaped curve that encompasses a view of the beach, a showcase $1.8-million swimming pool with an "infinity edge" that gives the optical illusion that it's an extension of the sea, and "The Mansion"—a neo-Palladian replica of a manor house, designed by Oliver Messel (decorator to, among others, the late Princess Margaret in Mustique and the Sandy Lane in Barbados).

The so-called mansion doubles as the check-in area and headquarters of the more elegant of the resort's two restaurants. The major restaurant offers an open kitchen with a wood-burning oven, sushi bar, wok station, and a tandoori oven.

Accommodations are big, airy, and stylish, featuring dark-grained (usually mahogany) furniture imported from South Africa, white marble trim, and ample use of crisp white linens and white and off-white color tones. Many units contain four-poster beds, vaulted ceilings, wide-screen TVs, and marble floors. Bathrooms are luxurious retreats clad in elegant marble with state-of-the-art plumbing, including large hydro-massage tubs and power showers.

Grace Bay Rd. (P.O. Box 681), Providenciales, Turks and Caicos, B.W.I. © **866/877-7256** or 649/946-8666. Fax 649/946-5189. www.thepalmstc.com. 72 units. Winter $575–$750 double, $1,200–$1,700 1-bedroom suite, $1,775–$2,275 2-bedroom suite, $2,350–$2,850 3-bedroom suite, $3,950–$5,000 penthouse; off season $300–$400 double, $650–$775 1-bedroom suite, $950–$1,075 2-bedroom suite, $1,250–$1,375 3-bedroom suite, $2,750–$3,750 penthouse. Children under 12 stay free in parent's room. Rates include breakfast and free transfers from the airport. AE, MC, V. **Amenities:** 2 restaurants; conventional bar; pool bar and pool restaurant; "showcase" outdoor pool; exercise equipment; full (25,000-ft.) spa facility w/manicure, pedicure, massage, beauty, and fitness regimes; Jacuzzi; sauna; motorized watersports; salon; 24-hr. room service; babysitting/nanny service; children's clubs. *In room:* A/C, ceiling fan, TV, free use of an iPod during tenure at the hotel, private kitchen (in penthouses), minibar, hair dryer, safe, Wi-Fi.

Parrot Cay Resort 🐦🐦

This laid-back hideaway, a favorite of celebrities and honeymooners, is on an isolated and very private 400-hectare (988-acre) island with a white-sand beach that lies north of Provo. The compound features 8 white- or peach-colored buildings, each with a terra-cotta roof and a design by Keith Hobbs, creator of such London landmarks as the Clarence Hotel and the Metropolitan Hotel. What he's created is a leave-your-jewelry-at-home kind of place, where a mostly neutral decor enhances the intense sunlight, turquoise waters, sands, and greenery.

Spacious rooms have louvered doors that open onto private terraces or verandas, stark white walls with dark wooden trim, terra-cotta tiles, and mosquito netting artfully draped over four-poster beds. The large tiled bathrooms are beautifully appointed with tub/shower combos and deluxe toiletries.

There's a rectangular swimming pool—the largest in the Turks and Caicos—onsite. Watersports facilities include access to scuba diving, Hobie Cats, snorkeling, canoes, and water-skiing. A holistic spa, the finest in The Bahamas or the Caribbean, has a trio of pavilions with treatment salons where Eastern-influenced healing and rejuvenating therapies are applied, everything from yoga to meditation. The resort is riddled with nature trails, which guests can explore at their leisure. However, the beach is the real draw. There's a shuttle that will take you to the restaurants and diversions on the "mainland" of Provo.

The kitchen produces elegant and wholesome meals; they are served in the stylish main dining room or your room.

Parrot Cay (P.O. Box 164), Providenciales, Turks and Caicos, B.W.I. © **877/754-0726** in the U.S., or 649/946-7788. Fax 649/946-7789. www.parrotcay.como.bz. 60 units. Winter $680–$865 double, $1,075–$1,580 1-bedroom suite, from $2,220 1-bedroom beach house; off season $450–$627 double, $755–$1,075 1-bedroom suite, $1,640–$1,780 1-bedroom beach house. Rates include breakfast and round-trip airport transfers by car and hotel boat. AE, MC, V. Reached by a 35-min. private boat ride north from Provo, leaving from Leeward Marina. **Amenities:** 2 restaurants; 2 bars; outdoor pool; 2 tennis courts; spa; Jacuzzi; sauna; fishing; kayaks; snorkeling; limited room service; babysitting; laundry service; nonsmoking rooms. *In room:* A/C, ceiling fan, TV, dataport, kitchenette (in some), minibar, beverage maker, hair dryer, safe.

Point Grace 🐦🐦🐦

Opened in 2000 on one of the best beaches in the Western Hemisphere, this boutique hotel is the most charming and atmospheric on the island. From exceptional suites to panoramic penthouses, its accommodations are the finest in the country. The motif is British colonial–inspired, and the services and amenities are first-rate, ranging from complimentary Indonesian sarongs to scented oil lamps. The complex features one-, two-, and three-bedroom suites, furnished with Indonesian hardwood and teak, and brightened by Indonesian silk fabrics. Hand-painted tile and mahogany grace the bedrooms and each suite has a full kitchen. Point Grace is set in the Princess Alexandra Park, a protected marine reserve on the north coast. The hotel is named for Grace Hutchings, who spent her honeymoon here in a small cottage a century ago. Four replicas of Grace's original honeymoon cottage sit poolside. A very contemporary Caribbean cuisine with Asian touches is served here.

Point Grace (P.O. Box 700), Providenciales, Turks and Caicos, B.W.I. © **866/924-7223** in the U.S., or 649/946-5096. Fax 649/946-5097. www.pointgrace.com. 32 units. Winter $595–$935 double, $1,140–$2,730 2-bedroom suite; off season $425–$750 double, $695–$2,185 2-bedroom suite. Rates include continental breakfast. AE, MC, V. **Amenities:** 2 restaurants; 2 bars; outdoor pool; golf (nearby); oceanfront spa; fishing; kayaks; sailing; bikes; limited room service; babysitting; nonsmoking rooms. *In room:* A/C, TV, kitchenette, minibar, beverage maker, hair dryer, iron, safe, washer/dryer.

EXPENSIVE

Ocean Club East *Kids*

Across from the Provo Golf Club, this luxury condo complex—the best of its type on the island—opens onto Grace Bay, site of the finest beach. This resort community has accommodations available for sale or rent, all spread across a 3-hectare (7½-acre) piece of landscaped property.

The resort consists of studio suites, deluxe studio suites, and one-, two-, or three-bedroom deluxe suites, all with ocean views and tub/shower combination bathrooms, plus fully equipped kitchens (studios have kitchenettes only). Each suite is equipped with both ceiling fans and central air-conditioning. Except for the studio suite (the cheapest rental), accommodations are spacious and comfortable, with large screened balconies.

The hotel has a grill restaurant that serves international food, plus a cabana bar. There is a dive shop that is an annex for Art Pickering's Provo Turtle Divers Ltd. (See the section "Snorkeling & Scuba Diving," later.) Dive classes are available at the hotel, but for diving and rental equipment, you'll have to take a shuttle bus to the company's headquarters in Turtle Cove. There's also a daily shuttle-bus service for dining in the evenings and a part-time shuttle bus for daytime shopping, both for a small fee.

Grace Bay Beach (P.O. Box 240), Providenciales, Turks and Caicos, B.W.I. © **800/457-8787** in the U.S., or 649/946-5880. Fax 649/946-5845. www.oceanclubresorts.com. 86 units. Winter $240–$295 studio suite, $435–$545 1-bedroom suite, $595–$705 2-bedroom suite; off season $180–$225 studio suite, $300–$335 1-bedroom suite, $415–$485 2-bedroom suite. AE, DISC, MC, V. **Amenities:** 2 restaurants; 2 bars; 2 outdoor pools; golf; tennis court; fitness room; sauna; dive shop; fishing; bikes; Rolls Royce airport transfers; babysitting; children's clubs. *In room:* A/C, ceiling fan, TV, dataport, kitchen or kitchenette, fridge, beverage maker, hair dryer, iron, safe, washer/dryer.

Royal West Indies Resort

This is one of the most luxurious condo resorts along Grace Bay, offering first-class style and a hint of British colonial architecture. Lying on one of the best parts of the sandy beach, this elegant retreat is between Grace Bay Club and Club Med. Surrounding the property are well-manicured gardens, the centerpiece of which is a 24m-long (79-ft.) pool set against a backdrop of tropical fruit trees. Guests have a choice of oceanfront, ocean-view, studio, or garden-view one- and two-bedroom suites. Suites are large and have balconies and kitchenettes with different bedding configurations to suit various groups or families. Two-bedroom suites can be subdivided into one-bedroom accommodations or self-sufficient units. The interiors are furnished in an eclectic blend of woods and fabrics from South America and other locales. Even if you're not a guest, consider a meal at Mango Reef, the casual on-site Caribbean restaurant at poolside.

Grace Bay (P.O. Box 482), Providenciales, Turks and Caicos, B.W.I. © **800/332-4203** in the U.S., or 649/946-5004. Fax 649/946-5008. www.royalwestindies.com. 99 units. Winter $245–$375 studio, $340–$540 1-bedroom, $490–$720 2-bedroom suite; off season $180–$275 studio, $260–$410 1-bedroom, $360–$495 2-bedroom suite. AE, MC, V. **Amenities:** Restaurant; bar; 2 outdoor pools; golf (nearby); Jacuzzi; kayaks; sailing; scuba diving; snorkeling; bike rental; massage; babysitting. *In room:* A/C, ceiling fan, TV, kitchenette, fridge, hair dryer, iron, safe, Wi-Fi, washer/dryer.

MODERATE

Caribbean Paradise Inn   This intimate, cozy inn is a short walk to Grace Bay Beach, which is visible from the balconies of the second-floor units. In the summer of 2007, the rooms were upgraded with better furnishings and given a fresh coat of paint, making them more inviting than ever. The bathrooms were also refreshed, and each comes with a shower (no tub). Rooms open onto the pool or else a tropical garden. Most of them have a combined bedroom and sitting area, with a private patio or balcony. For families, the best deal is the hotel's suite, which has a separate living room and kitchenette.   For dining, one of Provo's best restaurants, Coyaba, with chef Paul Newman (not the movie star, of course), moved here in the autumn of 2007 (see separate recommendation).

Grace Bay (P.O. Box 673), Providenciales, Turks and Caicos, B.W.I. © 649/946-5020. Fax 649/946-5022. www. paradise.tc. 17 units. Winter $162–$184 double, $230 suite; off season $130–$150 double, $160 suite. Extra person $35. MC, V. Rates include breakfast. **Amenities:** Restaurant; bar; outdoor pool; golf; watersports; babysitting; laundry service. *In room:* A/C, ceiling fan, TV, dataport, minibar, beverage maker, hair dryer, safe.

Comfort Suites   This is the first franchise hotel ever to open on Provo. As a Comfort Suites hotel, it is far superior to the standard format, and the welcome and hospitality provided by the staff is exceptional. The handsomely landscaped property lies across the road from Grace Bay Beach, and is within an easy walk of many attractions, including the casino. Guests stay here in one of the spacious junior suites, with either a king-size or two double beds, or else in one of the so-called honeymoon suites (you don't have to be a honeymooner to book one of these). Accommodations are spread across two three-floor structures, enveloping an Olympic-size swimming pool and courtyard.

Grace Bay (P.O. Box 590), Providenciales, Turks and Caicos, B.W.I. © 888/678-3483 in the U.S., or 649/946-8888. Fax 649/946-5444. www.comfortsuitesci.com. 99 units. Winter $160–$170 double, $180 suite; off season $145–$160 double, $170 suite. Rates include breakfast. Children under 16 stay free in parent's room. Extra person $30. AE, MC, V. **Amenities:** Bar; outdoor pool; nonsmoking rooms. *In room:* A/C, TV, dataport, fridge, beverage maker, hair dryer, iron, safe.

Sibonné Beach Hotel ⭐ *Value*   This was the first hotel constructed on the fabulous sands of Grace Bay Beach. If you prefer an intimate inn of charm and a certain grace, this is a good bet. The hotel is informal and laid-back, and its courtyard gardens are especially alluring. Each of the accommodations has a light, breezy decor with an emphasis on comfort. The best unit is a beach-bordering one-bedroom suite, detached from the actual hotel. Even if you're not a guest, consider a visit to the Grace Bay Bistro, one of only a few on the beach itself. The restaurant excels at offering a creative menu that features fresh local seafood along with a selection of international dishes. Honeymooners like the seclusion of the place, as do more mature visitors. Possibilities for spas, casinos, shopping, and nightlife are close at hand.

Grace Bay (P.O. Box 144), Providenciales, Turks and Caicos, B.W.I. © 800/528-1905 in the U.S., or 649/946-5547. Fax 649/946-5770. www.sibonne.com. 30 units. $125–$235 double, $375 apt; off season $110–$205 double, $285 apt. Extra person $45. AE, MC, V. **Amenities:** Restaurant; bar; outdoor pool; babysitting; laundry service. *In room:* A/C, ceiling fan, TV, dataport, fridge, beverage maker, hair dryer, iron, safe.

Turtle Cove Inn ⭐ *Value*   This two-story hotel, built in a U shape around a freshwater swimming pool, is a favorite with divers and boaters. A few feet away, boats dock at the hotel's pier, which juts into Seller's Pond amid the many yachts floating at anchor. Each bedroom is simply but comfortably furnished, with views over either the pool or the marina. All units are equipped with a small bathroom containing a shower stall. The on-site Aqua Restaurant is reviewed in "Dining," below.

Turtle Cove Marina, Suzie Turn Rd. (P.O. Box 131), Providenciales, Turks and Caicos, B.W.I. © **800/887-0477** in the U.S., or 649/946-4203. Fax 649/946-4141. www.turtlecoveinn.com. 29 units. Winter $105–$180 double; off season $85–$155 double. Extra person $30. AE, MC, V. **Amenities:** Restaurant; bar; outdoor pool; scooter and bike rental; car rental; babysitting; laundry service; nonsmoking rooms. *In room:* A/C, TV, fridge, safe.

DINING

In addition to the restaurants below, you may want to check out the options at Beaches Turks & Caicos Resort & Spa (recommended earlier). The resort's showcase restaurant, **Sapodilla's** (© **649/946-8000**), can be visited by outsiders who purchase a day pass (9am–5pm) for $120, or an evening pass (6pm–midnight) for $140. The price of the pass covers meals and drinks anywhere at the resort.

Be aware that restaurants do come and go. Have your hotel call ahead for you if you're venturing off the beaten path.

EXPENSIVE

Anacaona ✦✦ MEDITERRANEAN/CARIBBEAN   Set in three thatched-roof outbuildings at the Grace Bay Club, this place is lighthearted, fun, and elegant. It's as good as hotel restaurants get in Provo. You might enjoy a frothy drink in the bar before crossing over a fountain stream to the restaurant. French recipes are combined effectively with Caribbean produce—not always an easy marriage, but here the result is successful. In the evening the atmosphere becomes more romantic, with flickering light from the torches and candlelight on the tables. The chef's grilled lobster tail is among the island's finest dishes. He also does fresh fish dishes extremely well. A local specialty is the conch chowder flavored with dark rum. Creative dishes with successful flavor combinations include grilled magret of duck with a corn pancake and a raspberry-ginger reduction, and seared filet of snapper with roasted Belgian endives stuffed with mashed sweet potatoes. Another tantalizing dish is roast Cornish hen marinated in honey and soy sauce and served with wasabi mashed potatoes and grilled eggplant.

In the Grace Bay Club, Grace Bay Rd. © **649/946-5050**. Reservations required. Lunch salads, sandwiches, and platters $25–$35; dinner main courses $28–$40. AE, DC, MC, V. Daily noon–10pm.

Aqua Restaurant ✦ CARIBBEAN/SEAFOOD   Divers, boaters, and couples have turned this convivial place into Provo's trendiest spot. Trendy would mean little if the food wasn't good; fortunately, it is. The setting, an enclosed outdoor bar and terrace overlooking the marina, also helps. The menu changes weekly. The chef's classic, home-smoked conch, appears with a wasabi-laced mayonnaise. The best of the signature dishes include pan-seared wahoo on a bed of sweet coconut hummus with mango salsa and grilled local lobster with lemon-garlic butter. One of the most enticing conch dishes sampled in the islands is pecan-encrusted conch with a spicy orange-butter sauce.

In the Turtle Cove Inn, Suzie Turn Rd., North Shore. © **649/946-4763**. www.provo.net. Reservations recommended. Main courses $19–$38. AE, MC, V. Daily 7am–10pm.

Baci Ristorante ✦ ITALIAN/MEDITERRANEAN   At a waterside table here you can imagine you're dining on the Mediterranean. The affordable and tasty cuisine, the romantic patio, the stone floors and wrought iron, and the whirling *Casablanca*-style overhead fans conspire to make this an agreeable stopover. Since 1999, this has been one of the preferred dining choices at Provo. The chef specializes in veal, serving it five different ways that include fork-tender filets in a zesty lemon-butter sauce. Pasta dishes are usually superb, and we also like the well-flavored breast of chicken with shrimp. If you want a particular dish that's not on the limited but varied menu, the chef will often prepare it for you if he has the ingredients. For dessert, we recommend the tiramisu, the best on the island.

Turtle Cove Marina, Harbour Town. $\textcircled{C}$ **649/941-3044**. Reservations recommended. Lunch main courses $10–$12; dinner main courses $17–$30. AE, MC, V. Mon–Fri noon–2pm and 6–10pm, Sat 6–10pm. Closed Sun.

Coyaba Restaurant *★★* CONTINENTAL/CARIBBEAN   Chef Paul Newman (no, not that one) shows off his culinary flair in this deluxe restaurant. A helpful staff serves some of the island's freshest and best seafood against a background of pleasant music. Many local recipes have a strong Continental influence. Start your meal with tempura shrimp in Barcelo honey–rum sauce, a freshly made ceviche, or a platter of smoked fish. The truffle mousse with sherry and the New England–style fish chowder are also delightful. For a main course, try the French-trimmed rack of lamb or *osso buco* (veal shank) with a porcini risotto. A first for many diners is the baked spiny lobster (with vanilla extract, chèvre, toasted coconut, and threads of saffron). For dessert, nothing tops the made-to-order upside-down apple pie accompanied by Blue Mountain coffee from Jamaica.

Grace Bay Rd. (adjacent to Caribbean Paradise Inn). $\textcircled{C}$ **649/946-5186**. www.provo.net. Reservations required. Main courses $32–$45. AE, DC, MC, V. Wed-Mon 6-10pm.

Grace's Cottage *★★* CARIBBEAN/ASIAN   An elegant restaurant seating 62, Grace's Cottage is a little architectural gem with bright white gingerbread trim that features outdoor seating under gazebos on a terrace. Inside you can enjoy an aperitif at the mahogany bar before taking a chair at one of the teak tables covered with Egyptian cotton tablecloths set with Villeroy Boch china, Italian glasses, and Sambonet cutlery. The light, sophisticated cuisine changes daily, taking advantage of exotic ingredients. Begin with the smoked duck quesadilla or baby chicken and young coconut soup with ginger and scallions. For a main course you might sample Caribbean baked grouper with mustard mayonnaise and a banana-infused risotto. Or else try jerk-marinated mahimahi on a coconut rice cake. Desserts are sumptuous and include our favorite: chocolate, strawberry, and rum soufflé with a vanilla-bean crème Anglaise.

In the Point Grace Hotel, Grace Bay. $\textcircled{C}$ **649/946-5096**. www.pointgrace.com. Main courses $30–$40. AE, MC, V. Daily 6:30–11pm.

MODERATE

Banana Boat Restaurant SEAFOOD/CARIBBEAN   The Banana Boat is the most popular restaurant on the island that's not in a hotel. It's not the best, but it's certainly the most convivial. Since 1981, there's not a yachtie on Provo who hasn't moored here to enjoy an island meal and a potent tropical drink. For a main course, you might try T-bone steak, cracked conch, or some freshly caught local fish. At lunch, favorites include lobster salad or a half-pound burger. Dessert might be cheesecake or Key lime pie. No one in the kitchen fusses too much with these dishes, but they are good and flavorful. A choice seat is on the timber-and-plank veranda that juts out over piers on Turtle Cove. *Note:* Shellfish such as lobster could make this reasonably priced restaurant very expensive.

Turtle Cove Marina. $\textcircled{C}$ **649/941-5706**. www.turksandcaicos.tc. Reservations recommended. Main courses $16–$30; lunch $6.50–$15. AE, MC, V. Daily 11am–11pm.

Coco Bistro ☆ *Finds* FRENCH/CARIBBEAN   The most attractive and appealing French restaurant on Provo lies on a plot of land that was a plant nursery in the 1980s, which has since grown into the largest palm grove on the island. The vaguely Mexican/vaguely Moroccan-looking restaurant is run by owners from Montreal. Most meals are enjoyed in the garden, under the palms. Menu items, often Mediterranean in origin, include penne pasta with chicken and basil-infused sun-dried tomatoes; spaghetti in a lobster-flavored cream sauce; grouper in puff pastry; *tagine* (stew) of lamb or lamb kabobs; or snapper baked in a crust of sea salt, served with a sauce of olive oil, basil, and sage. Desserts are all French and homemade. We especially recommend the banana tempura.

Grace Bay Rd. © 649/946-5369. Reservations recommended. Main courses $25–$38. DISC, MC, V. Daily 6–10pm.

Hemingway's Beachfront Restaurant CARIBBEAN/INTERNATIONAL   An instant island hot spot, Hemingway's beachside locale attracts international travelers as well as locals. The selections are inviting. Fresh grouper is lightly spiced and pan-seared, served with a tequila-spiked veggie salsa with charred onions, black beans, corn, red and green peppers, and carrots. Shrimp is lightly sautéed with a scrumptious pesto cream over penne, and filet mignon is exquisitely grilled with a fragrant red wine-mushroom sauce. Hemingway's is also a good lunch choice, serving gourmet sandwiches, hearty salads, soft fish tacos, or fresh vegetable pitas. Finish with crème brûlée or deep-fried ice cream. At night torches and candlelight lend a hint of romance. Tuesday is "Caribbean night," when barbecue ribs and grilled fish are featured, along with seafood shish kabobs.

At The Sands at Grace Bay. © 649/946-5199. Reservations required. Lunch main courses $9–$11; dinner main courses $20–$53. AE, MC, V. Daily 8am–10pm.

INEXPENSIVE

Hey José Cantina MEXICAN/PIZZA/AMERICAN   One of the focal points of a small shopping center in the center of the island, this lighthearted place is run by James Folice. Here you can enjoy the best margaritas in Provo. The parade of burritos, tacos, quesadillas, chimichangas, and grilled steaks and chicken will make you think you've been transplanted to some fiery little eatery along the Tex-Mex border. Also popular, especially with expatriate North Americans who have had their fill of grouper and cracked conch, are the richly topped pizzas. Available in three sizes, they culminate with a variety known as "the kitchen sink," with virtually everything you can think of thrown into the mix.

Central Square, Leeward Hwy. © 649/946-4812. Pizzas $9–$30; main courses $12–$22. No credit cards. Mon–Fri noon–11:30pm (bar until midnight), Sat 5pm–1am.

HITTING THE BEACH

Starting at Leeward and running all the way to Thompson Cove, **Grace Bay Beach** ☆☆☆ is Provo's finest beach, stretching for 19km (12 miles) of spectacular, powdery-soft white sand. The gin-clear, crystal-blue waters are extremely tranquil and there are no rocks, making it ideal for kids. Many resorts, such as Club Med, have developed along its edge, so you won't have these sands all to yourself. Though there are no public facilities on the beach, the hotels themselves come in handy, because all of them have restrooms and bars serving tropical drinks. The folks at *Condé Nast* rated Grace Bay the "number-one beach on the planet."

Grace Bay Beach is so stunning that you might not want to venture anywhere else, but there are a few other beaches on the island. They're less spectacular, but also less crowded. In the east, **Long Bay Beach** lies on the opposite shore from Grace Bay, opening onto Long Bay itself. It begins around Juba Point and extends east to Stubbs Cove, and is essentially free of hotels. The sand here isn't as powdery fine as that of Grace Bay, but you'll have more privacy. The waters here are very sheltered and there are virtually no waves.

If you want to flee the hordes, you can rent a four-wheel-drive vehicle and follow Malcolm's Road west to **Malcolm's Road Beach.** Figure a 30-minute drive to reach this beach from Grace Bay, and the last 5km (3 miles) of the road are very rocky. But once you reach this beach, it is stunningly lovely, with fine white sands, and nearly always empty. There's good snorkeling, though you'll have to bring your own gear. There are no facilities.

A final choice worth exploring is **Sapodilla Bay Beach** in the west, opening on Proggin's Bay, south of the airport. It's a gem of a white-sand beach with crystal-clear waters. It lies between two 9m (30-ft.) cliffs at Gussy Cove, stretching all the way west to Ocean Point. This is such a well-protected beach—with fine sands and clear shallow water (even 30m/100 ft. out)—that the locals often refer to it as "the children's beach."

WATERSPORTS & OTHER OUTDOOR PURSUITS

FISHING   **Silver Deep** (© 649/941-5441; www.silverdeep.com) offers the best fishing excursions, with both half- and full-day expeditions, usually for bonefishing or bottom fishing. Tackle and bait are thrown in.

For those who'd like to venture farther afield—and pay a lot more money—half- and full-day deep-sea fishing expeditions are available, with all equipment included. Catches turn up wahoo, tuna, kingfish, marlin, and even shark.

GOLF   **Provo Golf Club** ⛳ at Grace Bay Road (© **649/946-5991;** www.provogolfclub.com), is the only golf course in the country. It was rated as one of the top-10 golf courses in the Caribbean by *Caribbean Travel and Life*. The 6,560-yard, par-72, 18-hole course was designed by Karl Litten of Boca Raton, Florida, and is owned by the Turks and Caicos Water Company. It is powerfully green and—because Provo is one of the driest spots on the globe—it takes an extraordinary amount of water to keep it that way. Young palms and bougainvillea, as well as rocky outcroppings and powdery sand traps, help make the course a challenge to the serious golfer or a lovely day on the links for the beginner or novice. Four sets of tees allow golfers to tailor a game to their level of expertise. A driving range and putting greens are also available. The clubhouse contains a bar and a restaurant open Monday to Saturday from 7am to 10pm, Sunday 7am to 6pm. Greens fees are $160 per person for 18 holes. The price includes the use of a golf cart, which is mandatory. Golf clubs can be rented for $20 to $40 per set.

PARASAILING   Your best bet is to call on **Captain Marvin's Parasailing,** Grace Bay (© **649/231-0643;** www.captainmarvinsparasail.com). A 15-minute flight over beautiful Grace Bay costs $75. You can also go on banana boat rides at $25 per person or enjoy water-skiing at $225 per hour.

SAILING   Sailing excursions are offered by many charter groups, notably **Sail Provo** (© **649/946-4783;** www.sailprovo.com). It sails 14 or 15m (48- or 52-ft.) catamarans on half-day or full-day excursions. One of the most frequented is a sailing and snorkeling trip for $63 on Monday, Wednesday, and Saturday to Iguana Island, called a Mini Jurassic Park. Iguanas await you. A full-day cruise Tuesday to Friday costs $124, including a lunch buffet served aboard. A retired rumrunner, *Atabeyra,* is owned by **Sun Charters** (© **649/231-0624;** www.suncharters.tc). Full-day trips, costing $975 with a 12-person minimum, including an afternoon buffet, take you down the chain of Caicos Cays, perhaps following an ocean trail blazed by Columbus.

SNORKELING & SCUBA DIVING   Dive experts, including the late Jacques Cousteau, have cited Provo as one of the 10 best sites in the world, because of a barrier reef that runs the full length of the island's 27km (17-mile) north coast. At Northwest Point there is a vertical drop-off to 2,100m (6,900 ft.).

From the shore at **Grace Bay** ⑀, visitors can see where the sea breaks along 23km (14 miles) of barrier reef, the teeming undersea home to sea life that ranges from swarms of colorful schools of fish to barracuda to rotund grouper.

Off the northwest corner of the island of Provo is **Smith's Reef** ⑀, a walk-in dive to a seascape of brain and fan corals, purple gorgonians, anemones, sea cucumbers, sergeant majors, green parrot fish, long-nosed trumpet fish, the ominous-looking green moray, an occasional southern ray, and a visiting hawksbill turtle or two. Smith's Reef has a total of 13 underwater signs that describe the coral reef ecosystem and the diversity of life that thrives there. Snorkelers can learn about the various creatures camouflaged within the reef, the importance of sea-grass beds, and the ways that parrotfish contribute to the environment. The trail follows the perimeter of the reef starting inshore in about 1 to 2m (3¼–6½ ft.) of water, increasing to 7 to 9m (23–30 ft.) deep. The depth marks a spectacular display of coral creations, colorful schooling fish, and spotted eagle rays; even resident turtles can be found.

Bight Reef is located in the Grace Bay area known as the Bight, just offshore from a large white house. A public footpath leads to the beach, and two marker buoys indicate both ends of the snorkel trail. The Bight Reef Snorkel Trail has a total of 11 underwater trail signs that describe corals and how they grow. Water depth ranges from 1 to 5m (3¼–16 ft.), and visitors can view mobile species like yellow-tailed snappers, big jolthead porgies, and sand-sifting mojarras.

Art Pickering's Provo Turtle Divers Ltd., Turtle Cove (© **800/833-1341** in the U.S. for reservations, or 649/946-4232; www.provoturtledivers.com), with headquarters directly in front of the Miramar Resort on the water, is the oldest and best dive operation in the islands, offering personalized service. There are scuba tanks for rent, plus ample backpacks and weight belts. A single-tank dive costs $75, a night dive goes for $79, and a morning two-tank dive is $114. Prices include all equipment. Provo Turtle is a PADI training facility, with full instruction and resort courses. An open-water PADI referral course goes for $415.

TENNIS   The best courts are at the all-inclusive **Club Med Turkoise** (see "Accommodations," earlier in this chapter), but these are usually set aside for guests. Non-guests can play at many other courts, however, including **Miramar Resort** (© **649/ 946-4240**) for a $10 per-hour fee.

EXPLORING THE ISLAND

Chalk Sound, a landlocked lagoon west of Five Cays Settlement, has been turned into a public park. The hamlet of Five Cays itself has a small harbor and a modern airport.

Caicos Conch Farm, Leeward Highway (© **649/946-5330;** www.caicosconch farm.com), is on the isolated eastern end of the island, amid a flat and sun-baked terrain of scrub and sand. This is the only place in the West Indies where the conch is commercially produced. Though its techniques are not economically viable, this conch farm could spark breeding techniques that could change the way conch is cultivated worldwide. Its staff will give visitors a walking tour of the breeding basins. Admission of $6 for adults and $3 for children includes a tour of the hatchery and the laboratories. In the gift shop, you can buy rare conch pearls, shell jewelry, and T-shirts. The farm is open Monday through Friday 9am to 4pm, Saturday 9am to 2pm.

SHOPPING

You might enjoy browsing through the **Bamboo Gallery,** Leeward Highway (© 649/ 946-4748; www.provo.net), one of the island's leading art galleries. Its inventories include woodcarvings, ceramic sculptures, and the kinds of colorful oil paintings that, if they don't come directly from Haiti, were at least inspired by that island's traditions. The most unusual pieces—to look at if not to buy—are some of the locally made metal sculptures, sometimes created from oil drums or old car wrecks.

Caicos Wear & Gear Boutique, La Petite Place, Grace Bay Rd., Grace Bay (© 649/ 941-3346), sells the best in casual wear, including South American bathing suits and Caribbean print shirts in florid colors as well as "beach jewelry."

For the best duty-free shopping, head to **Royal Jewels,** Leeward Highway (© 649/ 946-4699). It has good stocks in gold jewelry and designer watches, and French and international perfumes—all that standard showcase stuff found on other islands in the Caribbean.

PROVO AFTER DARK

Ripsaw music can be heard at an Irish pub, **Danny Buoy's,** Grace Bay Rd. (© 649/ 946-5921), which has Cuban cigars (illegal in the United States), whisky tastings, and Guinness on tap. Bangers and mash and Irish stew appear on the menu, and there are darts and pool tables as in Ireland. The bar at the lovely **Gecko Grille,** Ocean Plaza, in the Ocean Club, Grace Bay Beach (© 649/946-5880), stays open until 11pm.

Dora's, Leeward Highway (no phone), is an island hot spot, with casual dining, cold beer, island-style drinks, and a good jukebox. On Thursday and Friday nights, you might catch a local band. The best sports bar is **Club Sodax,** Leeward Highway, Grace Bay (© 649/941-4540), which also offers food in a hurry, including fish fingers and jerk pork Jamaican style. Another place for watching sports events is **Bonnie's,** Lower Bight Rd., Grace Bay (© 649/941-8452; www.bonniesrestaurant.com).

3 Grand Turk ✦

Grand Turk is the capital of the Turks and Caicos Islands, although it is no longer the financial and business hub of the island nation, having lost that position to Provo. It is no longer the transportation hub either, as Provo receives 95% of the international airplane landings. The island is rather barren and windswept, and there is little vegetation. Don't come here looking for lush tropical foliage. Do consider Grand Turk, however, if you want a real bargain destination that's excellent for snorkeling and diving, with luscious white-sand beaches.

Many scholars believe that Grand Turk was the site of Columbus's first landfall in 1492. They maintain he set foot on the western shores of the island late on the day of October 12. The native Arawaks were here to welcome him to their island of "Guanahani," although they were later to pay a terrible price for that hospitality, because they were sold into slavery in the Caribbean.

Cockburn Town (*Coe*-burn) is the financial and business center of this tiny island. You'll find **Governor's Beach** near—you guessed it—the governor's residence on the west coast of the island. It's the best place for swimming. If you are on your way to another island, at least take time to tour Cockburn Town's **historic section,** particularly Duke and Front streets, where some houses built of wood and limestone stand along the waterfront. The 12-sq.-km (4¾-sq.-mile) island of Grand Turk has several protected historical buildings, one of which is a hotel, Turks Head Inn. The other landmark buildings include the police station and Government House.

ESSENTIALS

GETTING THERE   Once on Provo (see "Getting There" in section 2, earlier in this chapter), you can fly **Sky King Airlines** (© 649/941-5464) to Grand Turk. Sky King has nine daily flights from Providenciales to South Caicos and Grand Turk. The fare to Grand Turk is $88 one-way or $151 round-trip.

VISITOR INFORMATION   The **Turks & Caicos Islands Tourist Board Information Office,** Front Street, Cockburn Town, Grand Turk, B.W.I. (© 649/946-2321), is open Monday to Friday from 8am to 5pm. At this office, the National Parks of Turks and Caicos produces a guide to the marine parks, nature reserves, sanctuaries, and historic sites of the island nation.

GETTING AROUND   Many visitors walk where they are going, or check with **Yellow Man Car Rental** (© 649/231-0167) if they need a car. Rental prices start at $65 per day. *Remember:* Drive on the left.

Used mainly by the islanders themselves, a public **bus** system was launched, but service is patchy, with fares costing 50¢ one-way.

Taxis are available, but there is no central agency to call. Your hotel can summon you one, or you can find them at the airport when you arrive. The fare is $5 to $7 from the airport to most major hotels.

FAST FACTS   For cashing traveler's checks and other transactions, try **First Caribbean International,** Front Street (© 649/946-2831), or the **Scotia,** also on Front Street (© 649/946-2506). Both banks have ATMs.

Grand Turk Hospital, Hospital Road (© 649/946-2040), can fill prescriptions and provide simple medical assistance. The hospital itself has 35 beds, X-ray facilities, an operating theater, and a pathology laboratory.

Call © 649/946-2299 if you need the **police.**

The **General Post Office** (© 649/946-1334) is open Monday to Friday from 8am to 4pm. There's also a Philatelic Bureau, operated separately from the post office, but with the same hours.

ACCOMMODATIONS

The Arches of Grand Turk Island ✦ *Kids*   Atop the island's North Ridge, these modern town houses—a short walk from beautiful beaches—are the most deluxe way to live on Grand Turk. Bedrooms open onto island or ocean views. Two-story townhouse units, each linked together, contain two bedrooms and two baths with tub/shower combinations and balconies for taking in those sunsets. Families and couples are especially fond of the complex, and accommodations contain two double beds or one queen-size bed. Two-bedroom units with a fully equipped kitchen are suitable for six guests. Maid service is available upon request. All rooms are nonsmoking.

Lighthouse Road (P.O. Box 226), Grand Turk, Turks and Caicos, B.W.I. © **649/946-2941**. Fax 649/946-1312. www. grandturkarches.com. 4 units. Winter $210 double, $270 for 4 people; off season $190 double, $250 for 4 people. DISC, MC, V. **Amenities:** Outdoor pool; bikes; coin-operated laundry. *In room:* A/C, TV, ceiling fan, kitchen, fridge, beverage maker, hair dryer, iron/ironing board, no phone.

Island House *❋ Finds*   On a breezy site overlooking North Creek, this inn is the creation of Colin Brooker, an English expat, and his Grand Turk–born wife, Lucy. The complex's architectural style evokes the Mediterranean, with rooms opening onto water views. The studios and one-bedroom suites all have kitchens, bathrooms with tub and shower, and balconies overlooking the water and the well-planted gardens. The location is 2km (1¼ miles) from the center of town, which can be reached by a gas-powered golf cart. The idyllic spot here is a pool set against a backdrop of palms. Activities such as fishing and scuba diving can be arranged. Divers often book here because of the inn's location near fabulous reefs and "walls" only minutes from shore. The hotel offers its own dock on North Creek, featuring sailing, canoeing, and windsurfing. A vehicle is provided for every guest—either a van or a pickup truck.

Lighthouse Rd. (P.O. Box 36), Grand Turk, Turks and Caicos, B.W.I. © **649/946-1519**. Fax 649/946-2646. www.island house-tci.com. 9 units. Winter $104–$120 per person nondiver, $179–$195 per person diver; off season $95–$112 per person nondiver, $170–$187 per person diver. Dive rates include 2 morning boat dives. Children under 12 stay free in parent's room. AE, MC, V. **Amenities:** Outdoor pool; dock; fishing; sailing; snorkeling; windsurfing; bikes; babysitting; laundry; Wi-Fi. *In room:* A/C, ceiling fan, TV, dataport, kitchen, fridge, beverage maker, hair dryer, safe.

Osprey Beach Hotel *Kids*   This landmark hotel has a white-sand beach that offers good swimming and snorkeling. A family favorite, its bedrooms occupy modern two-story town houses, each with a ceiling crafted from varnished pine. Some rooms have kitchenettes, but all contain ceiling fans and verandas with a view of the sea, plus small bathrooms with tub/shower combinations. The rooms on the upper floors are larger and have higher ceilings. Across the street in the older wing of the hotel is Michael's Atrium, open for breakfast and lunch. Dinner is served at the Osprey Pool bar.

Duke St., P.O. Box 216, Grand Turk, Turks and Caicos, B.W.I. © **649/946-2666**. Fax 649/946-2817. www.ospreybeach hotel.com. 27 units. Winter $125–$145 per person double occupancy; off season $105–$140 2-night minimum stay. Dive packages available. AE, MC, V. **Amenities:** Restaurant/cafe; bar; outdoor pool; laundry service; rooms for those w/limited mobility. *In room:* A/C, TV, dataport, kitchenette (in some), fridge.

The Salt Raker Inn   Once the home of a shipwright who immigrated here from Bermuda, this inn—one of the most historic on the islands—dates from the early 1800s. Today it's been converted into a modernized, small inn as well as a well-recommended restaurant. (See the Secret Garden review, below.) The hotel stands right across the street from a good beach of golden sands. Casual and laid back, it offers midsize bedrooms each with a private bath, containing a shower stall. Furnishings are unpretentious but comfortable. The original pine floors are still intact here. The best units are upstairs suites, each with small balconies opening onto vistas of the water. A ground floor suite has a private patio. Guests meet fellow guests relaxing on the oceanfront terrace. A street vendor selling "peanuts rhythms pills" (actually conch fritters) is likely to pass by.

1 Duke St., Grand Turks (P.O. Box 1), Turks & Caicos, B.W.I. © **649/946-2260**. Fax 649/946-2263. www.hotelsalt raker.com. 13 units. Winter $110–$124 double, $155 suite; off season $95–$112 double, $139 suite. MC, V. **Amenities:** Restaurant; babysitting; laundry service. *In room:* A/C, TV, beverage maker (in suites).

DINING
Secret Garden SEAFOOD/CARIBBEAN   In the previously recommended Salt Raker Inn, this casual eatery is an island favorite, serving only breakfast and lunch. Try

for a seat in the garden of the covered patio. The day begins early as locals and visitors alike pile in for breakfast, delighting in the fish and grits or the three-egg omelet. Lunch specials are also tasty, including a different curry every day or homemade fish-cakes. Sandwiches are always available, including one made with grouper. The menu is larger and tastier in the evening. Try beginning with the yummy conch salad, then going on to a main course such as a fresh fish platter featuring the catch of the day. Top off your meal with Key lime pie or a slice of rum cake.

1 Duke St. ℂ **649/946-2260.** Reservations recommended in winter. English breakfast $5–$13; lunch specials $10–$19. MC, V. Mon, Tues & Thurs-Sun 7:30am–2:30pm. Closed Wed.

Water's Edge BAHAMIAN/AMERICAN   Set directly on the sands, close to the center of town, this newly renovated and enlarged restaurant manages to transform the simple conch into a surprising number of dishes. Come here for views of the sea, an engaging informality, a short list of standard fish and chicken dishes, as well as "conch burgers," pizzas, curried conch platters, and overstuffed sandwiches.

Duke St. ℂ **649/946-1680.** Main courses $15–$26. MC, V. Daily 11am–9:30pm. Bar until 2am.

SCUBA DIVING & SNORKELING ✪

Some of the finest diving in the archipelago is around Grand Turk. Here you can enjoy one of the underwater world's great experiences: a night dive on a wall where, due to bioluminescence, the colors of the day become the phosphorescent illumination of the night.

Divers can explore the wreck of the **HMS** *Endymion* ✪ off **Salt Cay,** which went down in a storm in 1790. Two centuries later, Brian Sheedy, a local diver and inn oper-ator, discovered the wreck. Today, while the reef has reclaimed the hull and all else that was biodegradable, divers can still get a close-up look at its cannons and four huge anchors lying about.

But Salt Cay is more than the resting place of a ghost ship. Between January and March, humpback whales come here to play. Visitors can watch their antics from shore, boat out among them, or don dive equipment and go below. The dive shops below all also rent snorkel gear.

Blue Water Diver, Front Street (ℂ/fax **649/946-1226;** www.grandturkscuba.com), offers single dives, PADI registration and dive packages, and even runs trips to Salt Cay. These people are top rate and will tell you many facts and legends about diving in their country (like the fact that the highest mountain in the Turks and Caicos is 2,400m/7,872 ft. tall, but only the top 42m/138 ft. are above sea level!). Scuba divers flock here to enjoy panoramic "wall dives" on the vertical sides of the reefs. A single-tank dive costs $45, with a two-tank dive going for $80; a night dive costs $50. A PADI-instruction resort course is priced at $125. Full PADI certification is $400.

Sea Eye Diving, Duke Street or Front Street (ℂ **649/946-1407;** www.seaeyediving.com), is convenient to most hotels in town. It offers two-tank morning dives at $75. An afternoon single-tank dive costs $45, and a single-tank night dive goes for $50. Rental equipment is also available. NAUI and PADI courses at all levels are offered. A full-certification course goes for $400, including training equipment and boat check-out dives. Dive packages that include accommodations can be arranged at a hotel of your choice. Snorkeling and cay trips are available for nondivers. The owners and operators are among the more experienced divers on the island, and they know where to find marine life in a kaleidoscope of colors.

EXPLORING THE ISLAND

People go to Grand Turk mainly to swim, snorkel, dive, or do nothing but soak up the sun. Other activities include bird-watching, horseback riding, heritage walks, and golf. You might also want to stroll over to the lighthouse that was brought in pieces from the United Kingdom, where it had been constructed in 1852. It has been restored and still works, guarding the northern tip of the island.

Turks & Caicos National Museum ⚓ This is the country's first (and only) museum. It occupies a 150-year-old residence, Guinep House, originally built by Bermudan wreckers from timbers they salvaged from ships that crashed on nearby reefs. Today, about half of its display areas are devoted to the remains of the most complete archaeological excavation ever performed in the West Indies, the wreck of a Spanish caravel (sailing ship) that sank in shallow offshore water sometime before 1513. Used to transport local Arawaks who had been enslaved, the boat was designed solely for exploration purposes and is similar to vessels built in Spain and Portugal during the 1400s.

Treasure hunters found the wreck and announced that it was Columbus's *Pinta,* in order to attract financial backers for their salvage—to guarantee a value to the otherwise-valueless iron artifacts, in case there proved to be no gold on board. There is no proof, however, that the *Pinta* ever came back to the New World after returning to Spain from the first voyage. Researchers from the Institute of Nautical Archaeology at Texas A&M University began excavations in 1982, although staff members never assumed that the wreck was the *Pinta*. Today, the remains are referred to simply as the Wreck of Molasses Reef.

Today, although only 2% of the hull remains intact, the exhibits contain a rich legacy of the everyday (nonbiodegradable) objects used by the crews and officers.

The remainder of the museum is devoted to exhibits about the island's salt industries, its plantation economy, the pre-Columbian inhabitants of the island, and its natural history. The natural-history exhibit features a 2×6m (6½×20-ft.), three-dimensional reproduction of a section of the Grand Turk Wall, the famous vertical reef. You'll also find displays on the geology of the islands and information on the reef and coral growth.

Guinep House, Front St., Cockburn Town, Grand Turk. ⓒ 649/946-2160. www.tcmuseum.org. Admission $5 nonresidents, free for full-time island residents. Mon–Tues and Thurs–Fri 9am–4pm; Wed 9am–5pm; Sat 9am–1pm.

GRAND TURK AFTER DARK

In search of action? **Nookie Hill Club,** Nookie Hill (no phone), offers dancing and late-night drinking. A "rake-and-scrape" band plays on Friday at the previously recommended **Salt Raker Inn,** 1 Duke St., Cockburn Town (ⓒ 649/946-2260). The previously recommended **Osprey Beach Hotel,** Duke St. (ⓒ 649/946-2666), hosts "rake-and-scrape" music on Wednesday and Sunday.

27

The U.S. Virgin Islands

The U.S. Virgin Islands are known for their sugar-white beaches, among the finest in the world, and also for duty-free shopping. The most developed island in the chain is **St. Thomas,** whose capital, Charlotte Amalie, is the shopping mecca of the Caribbean. With a population of some 50,000 and thousands more cruise-ship passengers arriving on any given day, tiny St. Thomas isn't exactly a secluded tropical retreat; you won't have its beautiful beaches to yourself. It abounds in bars and restaurants, including fast-food joints, and has a vast selection of hotels at all prices.

St. Croix is bigger and more tranquil than St. Thomas. Another favorite with cruise-ship passengers, St. Croix touts its shopping and has more stores than most islands in the Caribbean, especially in and around Christiansted, although it's not as dense with stores as Charlotte Amalie. Its major attraction is Buck Island, a U.S. National Park that lies offshore. St. Croix is peppered with inns and hotels and is condo heaven.

St. John, the smallest of the three islands, is also the most beautiful and the least developed. It has only two big hotels. Some two-thirds of this island is set aside as a U.S. National Park. Even if you visit only for the day while based on St. Thomas, you'll want to see the island's dreamy beach, Trunk Bay.

The U.S. Virgin Islands lie in two bodies of water: St. John is entirely in the Atlantic Ocean, St. Croix is entirely in the Caribbean Sea, and St. Thomas spans the Atlantic and the Caribbean. Directly in the belt of the subtropical, easterly trade winds, these islands enjoy one of the most perfect year-round climates in the world. The U.S. Virgins are some 60 miles east of Puerto Rico and 1,100 miles southeast of Miami.

1 Essentials

VISITOR INFORMATION

Before you go, contact the **U.S. Virgin Islands Division of Tourism,** at One Penn Plaza, Suite 3525, New York, NY 10019 (© **212/502-5300**). Branch offices are located at: 245 Peachtree Center Ave., Marriott 1 Tower, Suite MB-05, Atlanta, GA 30303 (© 404/688-0906); 500 N. Michigan Ave., Suite 2030, Chicago, IL 60611 (© 312/670-8784); 2655 Le Jeune Rd., Suite 907, Coral Gables, FL 33134 (© 305/442-7200); 3460 Wilshire Blvd., Suite 412, Los Angeles, CA 90010 (© 213/739-0138); and 444 North Capital St., Suite 305, Washington, D.C. 20009 (© 202/624-3590).

In Canada, there's an office at 2810 Matheson Blvd. E., Suite 200, Mississauga, ON L4W 4X7, Canada (© **416/622-7600**). In Britain, contact the office at 114 Power Rd., Chiswick, London W45PY (© **020/8994-0978**).

On the Web, you can get information at **www.usvi.net**.

GETTING THERE

Before you book your airline ticket, refer to the section "Packages for the Independent Traveler," in chapter 2. You might save a bundle.

It's possible to fly from the mainland of the U.S. directly to St. Thomas and St. Croix, but the only way to get to St. John is by a ferry from St. Thomas, or from Jost Van Dyke or Tortola in the British Virgin Islands.

TO ST. THOMAS OR ST. CROIX **American Airlines** (© 800/433-7300 in the U.S. and Canada; www.aa.com) offers frequent service to St. Thomas and St. Croix from the U.S. mainland, with three daily flights from New York to St. Thomas in high season. Passengers originating in other parts of the world are usually routed to St. Thomas through American's hubs in Miami or San Juan, both of which offer nonstop service (often several times a day) to St. Thomas. (American Eagle has 12 nonstop flights daily from San Juan to St. Thomas.)

Delta (© 800/241-4141 in the U.S. and Canada; www.delta.com) offers two daily nonstop flights between Atlanta and St. Thomas in winter. In 2005 it also launched nonstop three times weekly flights between Atlanta and St. Croix. **US Airways** (© 800/428-4322 in the U.S. and Canada; www.usairways.com) has one nonstop daily flight from Philadelphia to St. Thomas, and an additional flight on Saturday.

Cape Air (© 800/352-0714 in the U.S. and Canada; www.flycapeair.com) has service between St. Thomas and Puerto Rico. This Massachusetts-based airline offers 5 to 12 flights daily. Cape Air has expanded its service to include flights from San Juan to St. Croix and flights between St. Croix and St. Thomas.

United Airlines (© 800/538-2929 in the U.S. and Canada; www.united.com) has nonstop service on Saturday to St. Thomas from Chicago and Washington, D.C.

Continental Airlines (© 800/231-0856 in the U.S. and Canada; www.continental. com) has daily flights from Newark International Airport in New Jersey to St. Thomas.

Launched in 2004, **Caribbean Sun Airlines** (© 866/864-6272 in the U.S. and Canada; www.flycsa.com) flies from San Juan to both St. Thomas and St. Croix.

A **ferry** service between Charlotte Amalie in St. Thomas and Puerto Rico, with a stop in St. John, is available about once every 2 weeks. The trip takes about 2 hours, costing $70 one-way or $100 round-trip. For more information, call © 340/776-6282 or 787/863-0582.

TO ST. CROIX FROM ST. THOMAS **American Eagle** (© 800/433-7300 in the U.S. and Canada; www.aa.com) has eight flights a day, costing $304 one-way between St. Thomas and St. Croix, with a stopover in San Juan. In addition, **Seaborne Airlines** (© 888/359-8687 in the U.S. and Canada, or 340/773-6442; www.seaborne airlines.com) offers 21 round-trip flights daily, going for $85 one-way and $168 round-trip. Flight time is 25 minutes.

TO ST. JOHN The easiest and most common way to get to St. John is by **ferry** (© 340/776-6282), which leaves from the Red Hook landing pier on St. Thomas's eastern tip; the trip takes about 20 minutes each way. Beginning at 6:30am, boats depart more or less every hour. The last ferry back to Red Hook departs from St. John's Cruz Bay at noon. The service is frequent and efficient enough that even cruise-ship passengers temporarily anchored in Charlotte Amalie can visit St. John for a quick island tour. The one-way fare is $5 for adults, $1 for children 12 and under. Schedules change without notice, so call in advance.

To reach the ferry, take the **Vitran** bus from a point near Market Square (in Charlotte Amalie) directly to Red Hook. The cost is $1 per person each way. In addition, privately owned taxis will negotiate a price to carry you from virtually anywhere to the docks at Red Hook.

If you've just landed on St. Thomas and want to go straight to the ferry dock, your best bet is to take a cab from the airport (Vitran buses run from Charlotte Amalie but don't serve the airport area). After disembarking from the ferry on St. John, you'll have to get another cab to your hotel. Depending on the traffic, the cab ride on St. Thomas could take 30 to 45 minutes, at a fare between $20 and $22.

It's also possible to board a **boat** for St. John directly at the Charlotte Amalie waterfront for a cost of $10 each way. The ride takes 45 minutes. The boats depart from Charlotte Amalie at 7:15am and continue every 2 hours, until the last boat departs around 5:30pm. (The last boat to leave St. John's Cruz Bay for Charlotte Amalie departs at 3:45pm.) Call ⓒ **340/776-6282** for more information.

FAST FACTS: The U.S. Virgin Islands

Banks Banks are generally open Monday to Thursday from 9am to 3pm, and Friday from 9am to 6pm. It's not hard to find a bank with an ATM on St. Thomas or St. Croix.

Currency The **U.S. dollar** is the unit of currency in the Virgin Islands. *Prices in this chapter are quoted in U.S. dollars.*

Customs Every U.S. resident can bring home $1,600 worth of duty-free purchases, including 2 cases of liquor per adult. If you go over the $1,600 limit, you pay a flat 5% duty, up to $1,000. You can also mail home gifts valued at up to $100 per day, which you don't have to declare. (At other spots in the Caribbean, U.S. citizens are limited to $400 or $600 worth of merchandise and a single bottle of liquor.)

Documents U.S. and Canadian citizens are required to present some proof of citizenship to enter the Virgin Islands, such as a birth certificate with a raised seal along with a government-issued photo ID. A passport is not strictly required, but carrying one is a good idea. The requirements for other citizens are the same as for foreigners entering the U.S. mainland; travelers from the United Kingdom, Australia, and New Zealand need valid passports, but not visas.

Electricity It's the same as on the U.S. mainland: 120-volt AC (60 cycles). No transformer, adapter, or converter is needed for U.S. appliances.

Emergencies In an emergency, dial ⓒ **911**.

Liquor Laws Liquor is sold 7 days a week, but it is not permitted on beaches.

Safety The U.S. Virgin Islands have more than their share of crime. Travelers should exercise extreme caution both day and night, especially in the back streets of Charlotte Amalie on St. Thomas, and in Christiansted and Frederiksted on St. Croix. Muggings are commonplace. Avoid strolling at night, especially on the beaches.

Taxes There is no departure tax for the U.S. Virgin Islands. Hotels add on a 10% tax. (Always ask if it's included in the original price you're quoted.)

Telephone The phone system for the U.S. Virgin Islands is the same as on the U.S. mainland. The area code is **340**. To reach **Sprint** dial Ⓒ **800/877-8000**, and to reach **MCI** dial Ⓒ **800/950-5555**.

Time The U.S. Virgins are on Atlantic Standard Time, which is 1 hour ahead of Eastern Standard Time. However, the islands do not observe daylight saving time, so in the summer during daylight saving time, the Virgin Islands and the U.S. East Coast are on the same time. In winter, when it's 6am in Charlotte Amalie, it's 5am in Miami.

Tipping Tip as you would on the U.S. mainland (15% in restaurants, 10%–15% to taxi drivers, $2 per round to bartenders, at least $1 or $2 per day for chambermaids). Some hotels add a 10% to 15% surcharge to cover service, so check before you wind up paying twice.

Water Most visitors drink the local tap water with no harmful aftereffects. Those with more delicate stomachs might want to stick to bottled water.

Weather From November to February, temperatures average about 77°F (25°C). Sometimes in August the temperature peaks in the high 90s (mid-30s Celsius), but the subtropical breezes keep it comfortably cool in the shade. The temperature in winter may drop into the low 60s (mid-teens Celsius), but this rarely happens.

2 St. Thomas ⭑⭑⭑

St. Thomas, the busiest cruise-ship destination in the West Indies, is not the largest of the U.S. Virgins. (St. Croix holds that distinction.) But bustling Charlotte Amalie is the capital of the U.S. Virgin Islands, and the shopping hub of the Caribbean. The beaches on this island are renowned for their white sand and calm, turquoise waters, including the very best of them all, **Magens Bay.** Despite all the development, *National Geographic* rated St. Thomas as one of the top destinations in the world for sailing, scuba diving, and fishing.

Charlotte Amalie, with its white houses and bright red roofs glistening in the sun, is one of the most beautiful towns in the Caribbean. In addition to its shopping, the town is also filled with historic sights, like Fort Christian, an intriguing 17th-century building constructed by the Danes. The town's architecture reflects the island's culturally diverse past. You'll pass Dutch doors, Danish red-tile roofs, French iron grillwork, and Spanish-style patios.

Because of St. Thomas's thriving commercial activity, as well as its lingering drug and crime problems, the island is often referred to as the most "unvirgin" of the Virgin Islands. Charlotte Amalie's Main Street is virtually a 3- to 4-block-long shopping center. But while this area tends to be overcrowded, for the most part, the island's beaches, major hotels, restaurants, and entertainment facilities are removed from the cruise-ship chaos. And you can always find a secluded resort in the more remote sections of the island. Hotels on the north side of St. Thomas look out at the Atlantic; those on the south side front the calmer Caribbean Sea.

Fun Fact **Carnival**

The annual **Carnival** celebration, held after Easter, is a spectacular event, with echoes of the islanders' African heritage. "Mocko Jumbies," people dressed as spirits, parade through the streets on stilts nearly 6m (20 ft.) high. Steel and fungi bands, "jump-ups" (Caribbean hoedowns), and parades bring the event to life. Events take place islandwide, but most of the action is on the streets of Charlotte Amalie. Contact the visitor center in St. Thomas for a schedule of events.

ST. THOMAS ESSENTIALS

VISITOR INFORMATION   At 78 1-2-3 Estate Constant, across from the Nisky Shopping Center, on the waterfront in downtown Charlotte Amalie, the **visitor center** (© 340/774-8784) is open Monday to Friday from 9am to 5pm and Saturday 8am to 2pm. There's also an information desk at the cruise-ship terminal.

GETTING AROUND   Taxis are unmetered, but fares are controlled and widely posted; however, we still recommend that you negotiate a fare with the driver before you get into the car. A typical fare—say, from Havensight Mall to Magens Bay for a day at the beach—runs to $8.50 per person or $6 per person in a shared cab. Surcharges, one-third of the price of the excursion, are added after midnight. You'll pay $2 to $4 per bag for luggage. For 24-hour radio-dispatch taxi service, call © 340/774-7457. If you want to hire a taxi and a driver (who just may be a great tour guide) for a day, expect to pay about $25 per person for 2 hours of sightseeing in a shared car, or $50 per hour for two to four people.

Taxi vans transport 8 to 12 passengers to multiple destinations on the island. It's cheaper to take a van instead of a taxi if you're going between your hotel and the airport. The cost for luggage ranges from $1 to $2 per bag.

Buses, called **Vitrans,** leave from street-side stops in the center of Charlotte Amalie, fanning out east and west along all the most important highways. They run between 5:30am and 9pm daily, but waits can be very long and this is a difficult way to get about. A ride within Charlotte Amalie is 75¢, and anywhere else, $1. For schedule and bus-stop information, call © 340/774-5678.

St. Thomas has many leading North American **car-rental firms** at the airport, and competition is stiff. Before you go, compare the rates of the "big three": **Avis** (© 800/331-1212 in the U.S. and Canada, or 340/774-1468; www.avis.com); **Budget** (© 800/472-3325 in the U.S. and Canada, or 340/776-5774; www.budgetstt.com); and **Hertz** (© 800/654-3131 in the U.S. and Canada, or 340/774-1879; www.hertz.com). You can often save money by renting from a local agency, although vehicles aren't always as well maintained. Try **Dependable Car Rental,** 3901 B Altona, Welgunst, behind the Bank of Nova Scotia and the Medical Arts Complex (© 800/522-3076 or 340/774-2253; www.dependablecar.com), which will pick up renters at the airport or their hotel; or the aptly named **Discount Car Rental,** 14 Harwood Hwy., outside the airport on the main highway (© 877/478-2833 or 340/776-4858; www.discountcar.vi), which grants drivers a 12% discount on rivals' rates. There is no tax on car rentals in the Virgin Islands.

St. Thomas

Bolongo Bay Beach Club **6**
Elysian Beach Resort **12**
Galleon House **1**
The Green Iguana **2**
Hotel 1829 **4**
The Inn at Blackbeard's Castle **2**
Pavilions and Pools **9**

Point Pleasant Resort **7**
Ritz-Carlton, St. Thomas **10**
Secret Harbour Beach Resort **11**
Villa Blanca **5**
Villa Santana **3**
Wyndham Sugar Bay Beach Resort & Spa **8**

⚠ *Warning* Drivers Beware

Remember: Drive on the left. This comes as a surprise to many U.S. visitors, who expect that U.S. driving practices will hold here. Speed limits are 20 mph in towns, 35 mph outside towns. St. Thomas has a high accident rate, as tourists are not used to driving on the left, the hilly terrain hides blind curves and entrance ramps, roads are narrow and poorly lit, and drivers often get behind the wheel after too many drinks. Double-check whether your own car insurance will cover you on the island, or whether your credit card will provide coverage. If not, to be on the safe side, consider getting **collision-damage insurance,** which usually costs an extra $19 to $34 per day. Be aware that even with this insurance, you could still get hit with a whopping deductible: The Hertz deductible is the full value of the car; at Avis and Budget, it's $500.

FAST FACTS   The local **American Express** representative on St. Thomas is **Caribbean Travel Agency/Tropic Tours,** 14AB The Guardian Building (© **800/ 524-4334** or 340/774-1855), a 5-minute drive east of Charlotte Amalie's center, opposite Havensight shopping mall; it's open Monday to Friday from 8:30am to 5pm and Saturday from 10:30am to 2pm.

Roy Lester Schneider Hospital, 9048 Sugar Estate, Charlotte Amalie (© **340/ 776-8311**), a 5-minute drive east of the town's commercial center, is the largest hospital with the best-equipped emergency room.

ACCOMMODATIONS

Nearly every beach on St. Thomas has its own hotel, and the island also has more quaint inns than anyplace else in the Caribbean. If you want to stay here on the cheap, consider one of the guesthouses in the Charlotte Amalie area. All the glittering, expensive properties lie in the east end.

Remember that hotels in the Virgin Islands slash their prices in summer by 20% to 60%. Unless otherwise noted, the rates listed below do *not* include the 8% government tax.

VERY EXPENSIVE

Ritz-Carlton, St. Thomas ✶✶✶ *Kids*   Fronted by white-sand beaches, its architecture evokes a *palazzo* in Venice. It stands on 12 hectares (30 acres) of an oceanfront estate at the island's southeastern tip, 6.5km (4 miles) from Charlotte Amalie. The Ritz is set amid landscaped gardens, with bubbling fountains and hidden courtyards evoking the feel of a sprawling villa.

In the summer of 2006, the hotel underwent a $40 million renovation, making it better than ever. Its most outstanding new feature is a key-activated Club Lounge featuring 55 guestrooms, 16 executive suites, 4 presidential suites, and two exclusive villas, each opening onto views of the Caribbean. Regardless of your room assignment, each accommodation has been fully renovated and painted in light pastel colors. Some of the units also contain separate tubs and "rainshower stalls," and each room comes with a private balcony. Most of the accommodations are in half a dozen three-story villas designed with Italian Renaissance motifs. Rooms are spacious with mahogany furniture, as well as marble-clad bathrooms with deep soaking tubs.

Both the landscaping and the public rooms have been considerably upgraded, including a spa that saw the addition of eight new luxurious treatment rooms and more open-air cabanas. A wide variety of cardiovascular and weight-training equipment was also added.

One of the most notable changes has been in the quality of the dining and an improvement in the service. Of the restaurants, most of which serve a Caribbean cuisine, Sails is at water's edge with a sailing ship roof cover, offering all-day dining. The Ritz Kids program is one of the best on the island, with such features as iguana feeding.

6900 Great Bay, St. Thomas, U.S.V.I. 00802. (C) **800/241-3333** or 340/775-3333. Fax 340/775-4444. www.ritzcarlton. com. 204 units. Winter $759–$859 double; from $1,300 suite; off season $559–$669 double, from $819 suite. AE, DC, DISC, MC, V. **Amenities:** 4 restaurants; 3 bars; 2 outdoor pools; 2 tennis courts; health club; spa; Jacuzzi; nonmotorized watersports equipment rental; children's programs; 24-hr. room service; massage; babysitting; laundry service; dry cleaning. *In room:* A/C, TV, minibar, beverage maker, safe, Wi-Fi.

Wyndham Sugar Bay Beach Resort & Spa ⋆⋆

At the east end of the island, a 5-minute ride from Red Hook, this all-inclusive hotel is much improved. It has panoramic views, although its secluded beach is really too small for a resort of this size. Many of the attractive rooms are decorated with rattan pieces and pastels, and they have roomy marble bathrooms with shower stalls. After a $15-million renovation in 2006, guest rooms have modern carpeting, Balinesian furnishings, electronics, wall treatments, and state-of-the-art plumbing. The hotel's spa, Journeys, is the largest full-service spa in the U.S. Virgins, and the first to offer hydrotherapy treatments. Nonguests can call for an appointment at the spa.

6500 Estate Smith Bay, St. Thomas, U.S.V.I. 00802. (C) **800/996-3426** or 340/777-7100. Fax 340/777-7200. www. wyndham.com. 294 units. Winter $296–$345 double, from $680 suite; off season $215–$304 double, from $600 suite. AE, DC, DISC, MC, V. **Amenities:** 3 restaurants; 2 bars; 3 outdoor pools; 4 lit Laykold tennis courts; fitness center; spa; sauna; dive shop; kayaks; sailing; snorkeling; windsurfing; children's club; secretarial services; babysitting; laundry service; dry cleaning; nonsmoking rooms; rooms for those w/limited mobility. *In room:* A/C, ceiling fan, TV, dataport, fridge, beverage maker, hair dryer, iron, safe, Wi-Fi.

EXPENSIVE

Bolongo Bay Beach Club ⋆ (Value)

This is an unpretentious, barefoot kind of place. You'll find a half-moon-shaped, 300m (1,000-ft.) white-sand beach—a bit rocky—and a cluster of pink two- and three-story buildings, plus some motel-like units closer to the sands. There's also a social center consisting of a smallish pool and a beachfront bar, replete with palm fronds. It's a relatively small property, but it offers all the facilities of a big resort. Many guests check in on the continental plan, which includes breakfast; others opt for plans that include all meals, drinks, a sailboat excursion to St. John, and use of scuba equipment. Rooms are simple, summery, and filled with unremarkable but comfortable furniture. Each unit has its own balcony or patio, a refrigerator, and one king-size or two double beds, plus tiled, shower-only bathrooms. Some of the units on the beach come with kitchenettes. Villas, in a three-story building, are apartment-style condos with full kitchens.

The best and most formal dining is at the Beach House, known especially for its fresh seafood. Iggies Beach Bar and Grill is more fun and casual.

7150 Bolongo, St. Thomas, U.S.V.I. 00802. (C) **800/524-4746** or 340/775-1800. Fax 340/775-3208. www.bolongobay. com. 65 units. EP (room only): winter $270–$300 double, off season $195–$244 double. AP (all-inclusive): winter $514–$544 double, off season $414–$475 double. Ask about other packages and various meal plans. AE, MC, V. **Amenities:** 2 restaurants; 2 bars; 2 outdoor pools; 2 tennis courts; fitness center; basketball courts; sauna; boating; deep-sea fishing; dive shop; scuba diving; snorkeling; windsurfing; children's programs (ages 4–12); babysitting. *In room:* A/C, ceiling fan, TV, kitchenette (in some), fridge, beverage maker, hair dryer, iron, safe.

Tips **Renting a Condo, Apartment, or Villa**

Sometimes you can get a deal on a moderately priced condo, apartment, or villa. In our experience, **Calypso Realty** (© **800/747-4858** or 340/774-1620; www.calypsorealty.com) has the best offers, especially on rentals from April to mid-December. A condo goes for $2,400 per week, with a 7-day minimum stay.

Another source is **McLaughlin Anderson Luxury Villas** (© **800/666-6246,** 800/537-6246, or 340/776-0635; www.mclaughlinanderson.com), which has rentals not only on St. Thomas, but on St. John and St. Croix as well. A two-bedroom villa begins at $2,700 per week in winter, with off-season rates beginning at $1,800.

You can also contact **Paradise Properties of St. Thomas** (© **800/524-2038** or 340/779-1540; fax 340/779-6109; www.st-thomas.com/paradiseproperties), which currently represents two condo complexes. Rental units range from studio apartments to two-bedroom villas suitable for up to six people; each has a fully equipped kitchen. A minimum stay of 3 days is required in any season, and 7 nights around Christmas. The prices range from $160 to $400 per day in winter and from $120 to $260 per day in the off season.

Elysian Beach Resort ☆   This timeshare resort on Cowpet Bay in the east end, a 30-minute drive from Charlotte Amalie, is imbued with a certain European resort chic. The beautiful white-sand beach is the most compelling reason to stay, but you might also come if you're looking for tranquility and seclusion without the razzle-dazzle of other east-end resorts. The thoughtfully planned bedrooms contain balconies, and 4 offer sleeping lofts reached by a spiral staircase. The decor is tropical, with rattan and bamboo furnishings, ceiling fans, and natural-wood ceilings. The rooms are in a bevy of four-story buildings connected to landscaped gardens. All units are one- or two-bedroom suites. Designer fabrics and white ceramic-tile floors make the tropical living quite grand. Try to avoid rooms in buildings V through Z, as they are some distance from the beach. Each unit has a full, tiled bathroom.

Robert's American Grill serves American food, while less formal Bonnie's by the Sea features cocktails and West Indian and international food.

6800 Estate Nazareth, Cowpet Bay, St. Thomas, U.S.V.I. 00802. © **800/438-6499** or 340/775-1000. Fax 340/776-0910. www.equivest.com. 182 units. Winter $252–$376 double, $399 suite; off season $196–$267 double, $319 suite. AE, DC, DISC, MC, V. **Amenities:** 2 restaurants; 2 bars; outdoor pool; tennis court; fitness center; volleyball; sauna; snorkeling gear; Sunfish sailboats; open-air shuttle to town; massage; laundry service; dry cleaning; nonsmoking rooms; rooms for those w/limited mobility. *In room:* A/C, TV, kitchenette, beverage maker, hair dryer, iron, safe.

Pavilions and Pools ☆ *Finds*   At this resort, which is ideal for those who want to run around as nude as Adam and Eve, Eve and Eve, or Adam and Adam, you stay in your own villa with floor-to-ceiling glass doors that open onto a private swimming pool. After checking in and following a wooden pathway to your attached villa, you don't have to see another soul until you leave, if you so desire—the fence and gate around your space are that high. Your swimming pool is encircled by a deck and plenty of tropical greenery. The resort, 11km (7 miles) east of Charlotte Amalie, is a string of condominium units, tastefully rebuilt and furnished. However, the place is not posh, and an average good motel in the States will have better-quality furniture. Inside, a room divider screens a full, well-equipped kitchen. The bathroom has an outdoor garden shower where you can rinse off after a swim or trip to the beach. The resort adjoins Sapphire Bay, which has one of the island's best beaches and many watersports concessions. Honeymooning couples should ask about packages.

Clients can head for any of a half-dozen lunch (independently operated) kiosks on the nearby beach. Dinners are simple and focus on steaks and seafood.

6400 Estate Smith Bay, St. Thomas, U.S.V.I. 00802. ℂ 800/524-2001 or 340/775-6110. Fax 340/775-6110. www. pavilionsandpools.com. 25 units. Winter $250–$350 double; off season $190–$265 double. Rates include continental breakfast. AE, MC, V. **Amenities:** Restaurant; 25 outdoor pools; day sails; snorkeling gear; laundry service; nonsmoking rooms; rooms for those w/limited mobility. *In room:* A/C, ceiling fan, TV, dataport, kitchen, fridge, beverage maker, hair dryer, iron, safe.

Point Pleasant Resort ⍟

This is a very private, unique resort on Water Bay, on the northeastern tip of St. Thomas, just a 5-minute walk from lovely Stouffer's Beach. These condo units, which are rented when their owners are not in residence, are set on a 6-hectare (15-acre) bluff with flowering shrubbery, century plants, frangipani trees, secluded nature trails, old rock formations, and lookout points. The villa-style accommodations have light and airy furnishings, mostly rattan and floral fabrics. They all have full bathrooms and full kitchens with microwaves. Beds are very comfortable with fine linens. From your living room, you'll have a gorgeous view over Tortola, St. John, and Jost Van Dyke.

The restaurant, Agavé Terrace (p. 712), is one of the finest on the island. The cuisine, featuring seafood, is a blend of nouvelle American dishes and Caribbean specialties. Local entertainment is provided Tuesday and Thursday nights, and you can brush up on your salsa and samba with a complimentary lesson.

6600 Estate Smith Bay, St. Thomas, U.S.V.I. 00802. ℂ 800/524-2300 or 340/775-7200. Fax 340/776-5694. www. pointpleasantresort.com. 128 units. Winter $255–$275 junior or superior suite, $355 deluxe suite, $525 2-bedroom suite; off season $180–$195 junior or superior suite, $255 deluxe suite, $355 2-bedroom suite. Ask about package deals. Children under 12 stay free in parent's room. AF, DC, DISC, MC, V. **Amenities:** 2 restaurants; 2 bars; 3 outdoor pools; fitness center; snorkeling; coin-operated laundry; nonsmoking rooms. *In room:* A/C, ceiling fan, TV, kitchen, beverage maker, iron, safe.

Secret Harbour Beach Resort ⍟

This all-suites combo resort is on the stunning white-sand beach at Nazareth Bay, just outside Red Hook Marina. All four contemporary buildings have southwestern exposure (great for sunsets), and each unit has a private deck or patio. You'll be just steps from the sand, and great snorkeling is right offshore. There are three types of accommodations: studio apartments, one-bedroom suites, and two-bedroom suites. Each studio apartment has a bedroom/sitting-room area, patio, and dressing-room area; each one-bedroom suite has a living/dining area, a separate bedroom, and a sun deck; and each luxurious two-bedroom suite has two bathrooms with tub/shower combinations and a private living room. Honeymooners are likely to show up in the winter months.

The Blue Moon Café (see "Dining," below) serves simple American dishes at lunch. At dinner look for some of the best steaks on the island and the fresh catch of the day.

6280 Estate Nazareth, Charlotte Amalie, St. Thomas, U.S.V.I. 00802-1104. ℂ 800/524-2250 or 340/775-6550. Fax 340/775-1501. www.secretharbourvi.com. 60 units. Winter $275–$345 studio double, $295–$465 1-bedroom suite, $485–$619 2-bedroom suite; off season $159–$190 studio double, $189–$305 1-bedroom suite, $295–$349 2-bedroom suite. Children under 13 stay free in parent's room. AE, MC, V. **Amenities:** Restaurant; bar; outdoor pool; 3 tennis courts; fitness center; Jacuzzi; dive shop; snorkeling; windsurfing; scuba; massage; rooms for those w/limited mobility. *In room:* A/C, TV, kitchen, fridge, beverage maker, iron, hair dryer, safe.

MODERATE

Villa Blanca *Value*   Small, intimate, and charming, this hotel lies east of Charlotte Amalie on 1.2 secluded hectares (3 acres) of hilltop land, among the most panoramic areas on the island, with views over the harbor and the green rolling hills. The hotel's main building served as the private home of its present owner, Blanca Terrasa Smith, between 1973 and 1985. After the death of her husband, Mrs. Smith added a 12-room annex in the garden and opened her grounds to paying guests. Today, a homey, caring ambience prevails. Each room contains tile floors, a ceiling fan and/or air-conditioning, a shower-only tiled bathroom, a well-equipped kitchenette, and a private balcony or terrace with sweeping views either eastward to St. John or westward to Puerto Rico and the harbor of Charlotte Amalie. On the premises are a freshwater pool and a large covered patio where you can enjoy the sunset. The closest beach is Morning Star Bay, about a 6.5km (4-mile) drive away. Other than a continental breakfast, no meals are served.

4 Raphune Hill, Rte. 38, Charlotte Amalie, St. Thomas, U.S.V.I. 00801. © 800/231-0034 or 340/776-0749. Fax 340/779-2661. www.villablancahotel.com. 14 units. Winter $135–$155 double; off season $95–$125 double. Rates include continental breakfast. AE, DISC, MC, V. **Amenities:** Outdoor pool; sport-fishing; nonsmoking rooms. *In room:* A/C and/or ceiling fan, TV, kitchenette, beverage maker, hair dryer.

Villa Santana *Value*   This unique country villa is an all-suites property. It was originally built by Gen. Antonio Lopez de Santa Anna of Mexico in the 1850s, and has a panoramic view of Charlotte Amalie and the St. Thomas harbor. The shopping district in Charlotte Amalie is just a 5-minute walk away, and Magens Beach is a 10-minute drive. Guest rooms are at La Mansion, the former library of the general; La Terraza, originally the wine cellar; La Cocina de Santa Anna, once the central kitchen for the entire estate; La Casa de Piedra, once the bedroom of the general's most trusted attaché; and La Torre, the old pump house converted into a modern lookout tower. All rooms have fully equipped kitchens and tiled shower-only bathrooms. The Mexican decor features clay tiles, rattan furniture, and stonework. The property has a pool, sun deck, and small garden with hibiscus and bougainvillea.

2602 Bjerre Gade #2D, Denmark Hill, Charlotte Amalie, St. Thomas, U.S.V.I. 00802. ©/fax 340/776-1311. www.villa santana.com. 6 units. Winter $125–$195 suite for 2; off season $85–$135 suite for 2. AE, MC, V. **Amenities:** Outdoor pool. *In room:* Ceiling fan, TV, kitchen, beverage maker, iron, no phone.

INEXPENSIVE

Galleon House *Value*   The rates at Galleon House are among the most competitive around, and the resident managers are especially helpful. You walk up a long flight of stairs to reach a concrete terrace that doubles as the reception area. The small rooms are in scattered hillside buildings, each with a ceiling fan and air-conditioning, plus a well-maintained shower-only bath. The best accommodations have panoramic views from private verandas. Breakfast is served on a veranda overlooking the harbor, and Magens Beach is a 15-minute drive from the hotel.

Government Hill (P.O. Box 6577), Charlotte Amalie, St. Thomas, U.S.V.I. 00804. © 800/524-2052 or 340/774-6952. Fax 340/774-6952. www.galleonhouse.com. 12 units, 11 with bathroom. Winter $83 double without bathroom, $103–$145 double w/bathroom; off season $73 double without bathroom, $83–$103 double w/bathroom. Rates include full breakfast. AE, MC, V. **Amenities:** Outdoor pool; snorkeling equipment. *In room:* A/C, ceiling fan, TV, dataport.

The Green Iguana *Value*   Sitting on Blackbeard's Hill, in the center of Charlotte Amalie, this is one of the best run and most comfortable B&Bs to open in town in a long time. The bedrooms have panoramic views of the harbor, the constantly arriving cruise ships, and the other Virgin Islands. The little inn lies only a 5-minute walk from the town's shops, restaurants, and bars, and Magens Beach is a 10-minute drive over the hill. Bedrooms are midsize and done in a tropical motif with wicker. You have a choice of a king-size, queen-size, or twin-size bed, and each comes with a tiled bathroom with shower. The helpful managers live on the property.

37B Blackbeard's Hill, Charlotte Amalie, St. Thomas, U.S.V.I. 00802. © **800/484-8825** or 340/776-7654. Fax 340/777-4312. www.thegreeniguana.com. 9 units. Winter $135–$165 double; off season $95–$125 double. Extra person $20. AE, MC, V. **Amenities:** Laundry facilities; nonsmoking rooms. *In room:* A/C, ceiling fan, kitchenette, fridge, coffeemaker, iron, hair dryer, safe.

Hotel 1829 ☞   This national historic site is one of the leading small hotels in the Caribbean. It was designed in a Spanish motif, with French grillwork, Danish bricks, and sturdy Dutch doors. Danish and African labor completed the structure in 1829 (hence the name), and since then it has entertained the likes of Edna St. Vincent Millay and Mikhail Baryshnikov. The place stands right in the heart of town, on a hillside 3 minutes from Government House. Magens Bay Beach is about a 10-minute drive. It's a bit of a climb to the top of this multitiered structure—there are many steps, but no elevator. Amid a cascade of flowering bougainvillea are the upper rooms, which overlook a central courtyard with a miniature pool. The rooms in the main house are well designed and attractive, and most face the water. All have wood beams and stone walls. The smallest units, in the former slave quarters, are the least comfortable. Each unit has a small, tiled bathroom with a shower stall. One of the most historic restaurants on St. Thomas, **Hervé Restaurant & Wine Bar,** is located here (see "Dining," below).

Kongens Gade (P.O. Box 1567), Charlotte Amalie, St. Thomas, U.S.V.I. 00804. © **800/524-2002** or 340/776-1829. Fax 340/776-4313. www.hotel1829.com. 15 units. Winter $125–$220 double, from $260 suite; off season $90–$165 double, from $190 suite. Rates include continental breakfast. DISC, MC, V. Children under 12 not allowed. **Amenities:** Bar; small outdoor pool; laundry service; nonsmoking rooms. *In room:* A/C, TV, fridge, hair dryer, iron, no phone.

DINING

The St. Thomas dining scene is among the best in the West Indies; however, meals tend to be expensive, and the best spots (with a few exceptions) are outside Charlotte Amalie, and can only be reached by taxi or car.

IN CHARLOTTE AMALIE

Banana Tree Grille INTERNATIONAL   This place serves up candlelit dinners, sweeping views over the busy harbor, and a decor that includes genuine banana plants artfully scattered through the two dining rooms. The cuisine is creative, the patrons often hip and laid-back. Start with one of the aptly named "fabulous firsts," such as bacon-wrapped horseradish shrimp grilled and dancing over mango glaze. The house specialties, lobster-tail tempura with orange-sambal sauce and mango-mustard-glazed salmon, are particularly good. If it's offered, try the aioli lamb shank, another specialty: The meat is slowly braised in Chianti and served with aioli sauce over vegetables and garlic mashed potatoes. The desserts are truly decadent. The bar opens at 5pm.

In Bluebeard's Castle, Bluebeard's Hill. © 340/776-4050. www.bananatreegrille.com. Reservations required. Main courses $20–$47. AE, MC, V. Tues–Sun 6–9:30pm.

Beni Iguana's Sushi Bar JAPANESE   The only sushi restaurant on St. Thomas makes a nice change of pace from the Caribbean, steak, and seafood choices nearby. Along with a handful of shops, it occupies the sheltered courtyard and an old cistern across from Emancipation Square Park. You can eat outside or pass through wide

Danish colonial doors into a red-and-black-lacquered interior devoted to a sushi bar and a handful of simple tables. A perennial favorite is the "13" roll, stuffed with spicy crabmeat, salmon, lettuce, cucumbers, and scallions.

In the Grand Hotel Court, Veteran's Dr. © 340/777-8744. www.beniiguanas.com. Reservations recommended. Sushi $5–$16 per portion (2 pieces); main courses $8–$20; combo plates for 4–5 diners $16–$35 each. AE, DC, MC, V. Daily 11:30am–3pm and 5–9:30pm.

Blue Moon Café CREATIVE AMERICAN

For idyllic dining in an open-air setting, this beachfront restaurant claims, with some degree of accuracy, one of the most memorable settings for panoramic sunset views. *The Wine Spectator* twice recognized the Blue Moon Café as having the most romantic setting in St. Thomas. The menu, based on market-fresh ingredients, is changed twice seasonally. The list of food is geared to appeal to a wide range of palates, beginning with such tropical starters as coconut-honey shrimp with a guava dipping sauce or a portobello mushroom-and-goat cheese tart with field onions. Tiptop foodstuffs are handled with imagination and appear in zestful combinations like mahimahi with pecans, bananas, and a coconut-rum sauce, and grilled scallops with a tomato-basil risotto with fresh asparagus. For lunch, you can enjoy burgers, wraps, salads, and sandwiches.

In the Secret Harbour Beach Resort, 6280 Estate Nazareth Bay. © 340/779-2262. www.bluemooncafevi.com. Reservations required. Main courses $14–$30. AE, DC, DISC, MC, V. Daily 8am–3pm, and 6–10pm.

Hervé Restaurant & Wine Bar ⨁ AMERICAN/CARIBBEAN/FRENCH

This is the hottest restaurant on St. Thomas. A panoramic view of Charlotte Amalie and a historic setting are side benefits—it's the cuisine that matters. Hervé Paul Chassin is a restaurateur with a vast classical background. In an unpretentious setting, he offers high-quality food at reasonable prices. There are two dining areas: a large open-air terrace and a more intimate wine room. Start with the pistachio-encrusted brie, shrimp in a stuffed crab shell, or conch fritters with mango chutney. For a main course, try the house special bouillabaisse, or a delectable black-sesame-crusted tuna with a ginger/raspberry sauce. There are also nightly specials of game, fish, and pasta. Desserts are divine—you'll rarely taste a creamier crème caramel or a lighter, fluffier mango or raspberry cheesecake.

Next to Hotel 1829, Government Hill. © 340/777-9703. www.herverestaurant.com. Reservations required. Main courses lunch $9–$36, dinner $22–$38. AE, MC, V. Mon–Fri 11am–2:30pm; daily 6–10pm.

Tavern on the Waterfront ⨁ *Finds* CARIBBEAN/FRENCH

Celebrities visiting the island often come here. The setting is relatively simple but elegant, with African mahogany vaulted ceilings. Original artwork hangs on the white walls. The chefs present their inventive dishes attractively. Start with the St. Thomas conch fritters or the coconut shrimp with mango chutney. Main dishes include award-winning barbecue pork ribs that take 120 hours—from marinade to cooking—to prepare. We also enjoy the exotic pork platter, with espresso-and-cinnamon-encrusted pork medallions with a passion fruit demi-glace. The blackened seafood linguini, another winner, comes with mahimahi, jumbo sea scallops, New Zealand mussels, and shrimp blended with a Cajun cream sauce. There's often live entertainment on Friday, which you can enjoy while taking in harbor views. There's a happy hour, plus a children's menu.

Waterfront at Royal Dane Mall. © 340/776-4328. www.tavernonthewaterfront.com. Reservations required. Main courses $14–$53. AE, DISC, MC, V. Mon–Sat 11am–3pm; Mon–Thurs 5–9pm, Fri–Sat 5–10pm.

Virgilio's ⓕ NORTHERN ITALIAN   Virgilio's is the best northern Italian restaurant in the Virgin Islands. Its neobaroque interior is sheltered under heavy ceiling beams and brick vaulting. A well-trained staff serves meals against a backdrop of stained-glass windows, crystal chandeliers, and soft Italian music. The *cinco peche* (clams, mussels, scallops, oysters, and crayfish simmered in a saffron broth) is delicious, and the Alfredo fettuccine is one of the best we've tasted. Classic dishes are served with a distinctive flair—the lamb shank, for example, is filled with a porcini-mushroom stuffing and glazed with a roasted garlic aioli. The marinated grilled duck is served chilled. You can also order individual pizzas.

18 Dronningens Gade (entrance on a narrow alley running between Main and Back sts.). ⓒ 340/776-4920. Reservations recommended. Main courses lunch $14–$33, dinner $22–$44. AE, MC, V. Mon–Sat 11:30am–10:30pm, Sun 5-10:30pm.

IN FRENCHTOWN

Bella Blu ⓕ MEDITERRANEAN/SEAFOOD   West of Charlotte Amalie, this restaurant's 14 tables overlook the harbor. For years Bella Blue enjoyed fame throughout the Caribbean under the name Alexander's, serving a rather heavy (for the Tropics) Austrian cuisine. Under new owners, the fare is much lighter and focuses on the sunny flavors of the Mediterranean. To begin with, you might try the tuna tartare or one of the Moroccan dishes. The cooks are a whiz at concocting superb creations from lamb, veal, and seafood. The menu changes based on seasonal shopping and what's good and fresh at the marketplace.

French Town Mall. ⓒ 340/774-4349. Reservations recommended. Main courses lunch $7–$28, dinner $16–$34. AE, MC, V. Mon–Sat 11:30am–10pm.

Craig & Sally's ⓕ ECLECTIC/INTERNATIONAL   This Caribbean cafe is set in an airy, open-sided pavilion, with views of the sea and sky. Dishes range from pasta to seafood, with influences from Europe and Asia. You can try such light dishes as filet of salmon with a lemon grass–flavored mayonnaise, or perhaps the pan-seared trout with fresh mushrooms. The lobster-stuffed, twice-baked potatoes are inspired, and the wine list is the most extensive and sophisticated on St. Thomas. The menu changes daily.

3525 Honduras. ⓒ 340/777-9949. Reservations recommended. Main courses $16–$45. MC, V. Wed–Fri 11:30am–2:30pm; Wed–Sun 5:30–10pm.

Oceana INTERNATIONAL/SEAFOOD   The upscale restaurant is a hip and stylish enclave popular with locals. It occupies what was during the Danish occupation the Russian consulate. Outfitted with slabs of carefully oiled paneling, and painted in bright blues and greens inspired by the ocean, it offers two distinctly different venues. The street level has a wine-cum-singles bar where small platters of food (blini, crostinis, and cheese platters) specifically designed to go with the changing array of wines help foster convivial after-work chitchat. Upstairs, within a relaxed but relatively formal dining room, candles and oil lamps flicker amid bouquets of flowers. Menu items focus mainly on fish, but a fair number of beef and lamb dishes appear as well. Our favorites include spicy shrimp served with a cup of Andalusian-style gazpacho; house-marinated salmon (gravlax); mussels in white-wine sauce; pan-fried freshwater trout from Idaho; oven-roasted sea bass with a white wine, thyme, and olive oil sauce; grilled sirloin of lamb; several different preparations of Caribbean lobster; and New York strip, porterhouse, and filet mignon steaks. For sheer delight, visit the "tasting table," a long bar that offers an array of such concoctions as portobellos topped with bacon bits and goat cheese or smoked oyster, crab, and avocado salad—even a wild rice and lamb manchego. You can dine on either floor.

In the Villa Olga, 8 Honduras. © 340/774-4262. www.oceana.vi. Reservations recommended. Tapas $12–$16; main courses $25–$45. AE, DC, MC, V. Mon–Sat 5:30–10pm. Bar Mon–Sat 5pm–midnight, daily Jan–Apr.

ON THE NORTH COAST

The Old Stone Farmhouse AMERICAN/INTERNATIONAL   Set in a wooded valley close to the 11th hole of the Mahogany Run Golf Course, this restaurant dates from the 1750s. Once it was a stable for a nearby Danish sugar plantation. Ceiling fans and breezes blowing through the valley keep the place cool. For more than a quarter of a century, it has been feeding golfers and those who love them from an eclectic menu that takes advantage of the best seasonal produce. The fresh fish dishes are always the best option. Begin, perhaps, with grilled portobello mushrooms with Asian duck. Many regulars come here for the well-prepared steak.

Mahogany Run. © 340/777-6277. www.oldstone.rummi.com. Reservations recommended. Main courses $19–$32. AE, MC, V. Tues–Sun 5:30–9:30pm.

Romanos Restaurant ITALIAN   Located near Coral World, this hideaway is owned by New Jersey chef Tony Romano, who specializes in a flavorful and herb-laden cuisine that makes a nice change from Caribbean food. House favorites include *linguine con pesto,* four-cheese lasagna, a tender and well-flavored *osso buco* (veal shanks), scaloppine Marsala, and broiled salmon. All desserts are made on the premises. With exposed brick and well-stocked wine racks, this restaurant always seems full of happy, lively diners.

66–97 Smith Bay Rd. © 340/775-0045. www.romanosrestaurant.com. Reservations recommended. Main courses $27–$40; pastas $22–$24. MC, V. Mon–Sat. 6–10:30pm. Closed Sept, 4 days in Apr for Carnival, and 4 days in Dec and New Year's Day.

IN & AROUND RED HOOK BAY (THE EAST END)

The Agavé Terrace ✿ CARIBBEAN   Perched high above a steep and heavily forested hillside on the eastern tip of St. Thomas, one of the island's best restaurants offers a sweeping panorama and unparalleled romance. The house drink is Desmond Delight, a combination of Midori, rum, pineapple juice, and a secret ingredient. After a few Delights, try the house appetizer, an Agavé sampler for two, which includes portions of crabmeat, conch fritters, and shrimp cocktail. The catch of the day features three different fish, which can be prepared in any of seven different ways with a choice of nine sauces. Some of our favorite meals here include Chef Nakata's Jerk Chicken, and Coral Bay Crab Cakes served with rémoulade. There are also vegetarian selections. The wine list is extensive. A live steel-drum band draws listeners Tuesday and Thursday nights.

In the Point Pleasant Resort, 6600 Estate Smith Bay. © 340/775-4142. Reservations recommended. Main courses $24–$52. AE, DC, MC, V. Daily 6–10pm.

Duffy's Love Shack ✿ *Finds* AMERICAN/CARIBBEAN   You can mingle with locals at this fun, happening place. As the evening wears on, the customers become the entertainment, often dancing on tables or forming conga lines. Yes, Duffy's also serves food, standard American dishes with Caribbean flavors. The restaurant is open-air, with lots of bamboo and a thatched roof over the bar. Even the menu appears on a bamboo stick, like an old-fashioned fan. Start with honey-barbecued ribs, then move on to pork Cuban. After midnight, a late-night menu (mainly sandwiches) appears. The bar business is huge, and the bartender is known for his lethal rum drinks. Ask about the Lobster Lunacy parties.

6501 Red Hook Plaza, Rte. 38. © **340/779-2080**. www.duffysloveshack.com. Main courses $9–$17. No credit cards. Daily 11am–2am.

Fungi's on the Beach CARIBBEAN   This funky native bar opens onto Pineapple Beach. It's a lot of fun and the burgers are some of the juiciest on the island. You can also order Caribbean specialties like conch in butter sauce, Yellowtail Snapper Creole, johnnycakes, plantains, rice and beans, and callaloo soup. Stewed chicken is a local favorite. The place has an outdoorsy atmosphere with a reggae theme. Nightly entertainment—reggae and more reggae—is also a feature.

Point Pleasant Rd, East End. © **340/775-4142**. Main courses $6.50–$29. AE, MC, V. Daily 11:30am–10pm.

Havana Blue ⟲⟲ CUBAN/PACIFIC RIM/FUSION   This chic venue at a resort hotel enjoys a beachfront ambience and a sophisticated menu that is the island's most inspired. An inventive crew is in the kitchen, running wild in their culinary imagination. Cool cigars, hip drinks (mango mojitos), and a chic decor draw serious foodies to this cutting-edge restaurant, where chef Jose Rodriguez intoxicates with his aromas and flavors. After launching yourself with the black bean hummus or the tuna tartare with a soy lime vinaigrette, it's on to such delights as breaded chicken breast stuffed with manchego cheese and diced jalapeños or a miso-crusted sea bass. What about ancho chile–rubbed beef filet with espresso sauce? Desserts are worth crossing the island for if it means Cuban chocolate cake with coconut ice cream or a warm banana and macadamia spring rolls with a strawberry balsamic purée.

In the Marriott Frenchman's Reef and Morning Star Beach Resort, 5 Estate Bakkeroe. © **340/715-2583**. www.havanabluerestaurant.com. Reservations required. Main courses $28–$48. AE, DC, MC, V. Daily 5:30–10pm.

Molly Malone's IRISH/CARIBBEAN   At the Red Hook American Yacht Harbor, you can join the good ol' boys and dig into the best baby back ribs on the island. No one can drink more brew than the boisterous crowd that assembles here every night to let the good times roll. If you're nostalgic for the Emerald Isle, go for the shepherd's pie. The conch fritters are the best in the east end, and an Irish/Caribbean stew is a nightly feature. You can dine outdoors under a canopy on the dock at the eastern end of Red Hook where the ferry from St. John pulls in.

6100 Red Hook Quarters. © **340/775-1270**. Main courses $10–$25. AE, MC, V. Daily 7am–midnight.

Off the Hook ⟲ ASIAN/CARIBBEAN   Using some of the West Indies' freshest and finest ingredients, the chefs here concoct an eclectic medley of Asian-inspired dishes. In an open-air dining room near the American Yacht Harbor, close to the departure point for the ferry to St. John, the fresh catch of the day—hauled off the little fishing boats just pulling in—is delivered to the kitchen, where it's grilled perfectly. The yellowfin tuna keeps us coming back and the tuna and salmon sushi platter is also excellent. The black Angus steak is always a pure delight. The decor is rustic, with outdoor dining and wooden tables.

6300 Estate Smith Bay. © **340/775-6350**. Reservations required. Main courses $16–$30. AE, MC, V. Daily 6–10pm. Closed Sept 15–Oct 15.

HITTING THE BEACH

Chances are your hotel will be right on the beach, or very close to one. All the beaches in St. Thomas are public, and most lie anywhere from 3 to 8km (2–5 miles) from Charlotte Amalie.

Moments **Two Great Escapes**

Water Island, 1km (¾ mile) off the coast from the harbor of Charlotte Amalie, is the fourth-largest island of the U.S. Virgins, with 200 hectares (500 acres) of land. At palm-shaded **Honeymoon Beach,** you can swim, snorkel, sail, water-ski, or sunbathe, then order lunch or a drink from the beach bar (Sat–Sun only). A ferry runs between Crown Bay Marina and Water Island several times a day; it's $5 for a one-way ticket. (Crown Bay Marina, © **340/774-2255,** is part of the St. Thomas submarine base.)

In the same bay, and even closer to shore, is **Hassel Island.** It's almost completely deserted, and it is protected as part of a U.S. National Park. There are no hotels or services of any kind here, and swimming is limited to narrow, rocky beaches. Even so, many visitors hire a boat to drop them off for an hour or two. A hike along part of the shoreline is a welcome relief from the cruise-ship congestion of Charlotte Amalie. Bring water and food if you plan to spend more than 3 hours here.

THE NORTH SIDE   The gorgeous white sands of **Magens Bay** ★★ lie between two mountains 5km (3 miles) north of the capital. *Condé Nast Traveler* named this beach one of the world's 10 most beautiful. The turquoise waters here are calm and ideal for swimming, and the snorkeling is also good. The beach is no secret, and it's usually terribly overcrowded, though it gets better in the midafternoon. Changing facilities, snorkeling gear, lounge chairs, paddleboats, and kayaks are available. There is no public transportation to get here (though some hotels provide shuttle buses) from Charlotte Amalie; take Route 35 north all the way. The gates to the beach are open daily from 5am to 6pm (After 4pm, you'll need insect repellent.) Admission is $3 per person. Don't bring valuables, and certainly don't leave anything essential in your parked car.

A marked trail leads to **Little Magens Bay,** a separate, clothing-optional beach that is especially popular with gay and lesbian visitors. This is also former president Clinton's preferred beach on St. Thomas. (No, he doesn't go nude.)

Coki Point Beach, in the northeast near Coral World, is good but often very crowded. It's noted for its warm, crystal-clear water, ideal for swimming and snorkeling. (You'll see thousands of rainbow-hued fish swimming among the beautiful corals.) Locals even sell small bags of fish food, so you can feed the sea creatures while you're snorkeling. The beach is said to have put the fun in funky. Informal shacks serve fresh food, including just-caught fish, at ramshackle picnic tables. Kiosks rent beach chairs and snorkel gear, and there are outdoor showers as well as toilets. Of course, there are the inevitable hair braiders. From the beach, there's a panoramic view of offshore Thatch Cay. Concessions can arrange everything from water-skiing to parasailing. An east-end bus runs to Smith Bay and lets you off at the gate to Coral World and Coki. Watch out for pickpockets.

Also on the north side is luscious **Grand Beach,** one of the island's most beautiful. It opens onto Smith Bay and is near Coral World. Many watersports are available here. The beach is right off Route 38.

THE EAST END   Small and special, **Secret Harbour** is near a collection of condos. With its white sand and coconut palms, it's the epitome of Caribbean charm. The snorkeling near the rocks is some of the best on the island and it is likely you'll spot a hawksbill turtle foraging for some sea anemones for lunch. Kiosks rent gear for watersports, and a beachside restaurant offers snacks and drinks. No public transportation stops here, but it's an easy taxi ride east of Charlotte Amalie heading toward Red Hook.

Sapphire Beach is set against the backdrop of the Sapphire Beach Resort and Marina, where you can have lunch or order drinks. There are good views of offshore cays and St. John, a large reef is close to the shore, and windsurfers enjoy this beach. The all-day beach party that goes on here is the best on island. Snorkel gear, beach chairs, Sunfish, and kayaks can be rented from various kiosks, and there is also a bar, plus a restaurant, toilets, and an outdoor shower. Just off the beach there is good snorkeling over a shallow reef populated by conch, eagle rays, and starfish among other species. The best place for snorkeling here is at Prettyklip Point. Take the east-end bus from Charlotte Amalie, going via Red Hook. Ask to be let off at the entrance to Sapphire Bay; it's not too far to walk from here to the water.

White-sand **Lindquist Beach** isn't a long strip, but it's one of the island's prettiest. It's between Wyndham Sugar Bay Beach Club and the Sapphire Beach Resort. Many films and TV commercials have used this photogenic beach as a backdrop. It's not likely to be crowded, as it's not very well known.

THE SOUTH SIDE Morning Star Beach (also known as Frenchman's Bay Beach) is near the Marriott Frenchman's Reef Beach Resort, about 3km (2 miles) east of Charlotte Amalie. Here, among the often-young crowds of visitors (many of whom are gay), you can don your skimpiest bikini. Sailboats, snorkeling equipment, and lounge chairs are available for rent. The beach is easily reached by a cliff-front elevator at Frenchman's Reef.

Limetree Beach, set against a backdrop of sea-grape trees and shady palms, lures those who want a serene spread of sand where they can bask in the sun and even feed hibiscus blossoms to iguanas. Snorkeling gear, lounge and beach chairs, towels, and drinks are available. There's no public transportation, but the beach can easily be reached by taxi from Charlotte Amalie.

WEST OF CHARLOTTE AMALIE Near the University of the Virgin Islands in the southwest, **Brewer's Bay** is one of the island's most popular beaches. The strip of

---

Finds Hidden Beach Discoveries

At this point you'd think all the beaches in overrun St. Thomas had been discovered. But there are two less-trampled strands of sand we recently came upon. A sparkling beach of white sand, **Vessup Bay,** is at the end of Bluebeard's Road (Rte. 322) as it branches off Route 30 near the hamlet of Red Hook. Against a rocky backdrop, the beach curves around a pristine bay studded with vegetation including cacti, agave plants, and sea grape. One end of the beach is less populated than the other. A watersports concessionaire operates here. Another find is **Hull Bay,** on the north shore, just west of overcrowded Magens Bay. Surfers are attracted to the waves along the western tip of Hull Bay, and local St. Thomas fishermen anchor in the more tranquil strands. Part of the beach is in shade. Don't expect much in the way of watersports, but there is a combined restaurant and open-air bar.

white coral sand is almost as long as the beach at Magens Bay. Unfortunately, this isn't the place for snorkeling. Vendors sell light meals and drinks. From Charlotte Amalie, take the Fortuna bus heading west; get off at the edge of Brewer's Bay, across from the Reichhold Center.

Lindbergh Beach, which has a lifeguard, restrooms, and a bathhouse, lies at the Island Beachcomber Hotel and is used almost exclusively by locals, who sometimes stage political rallies here, as well as Carnival parties. It's not good for snorkeling. Drinks are served on the beach. Take the Fortuna bus route west from Charlotte Amalie.

SPORTS & OTHER OUTDOOR PURSUITS

DEEP-SEA FISHING   The U.S. Virgins have excellent deep-sea fishing—some 19 world records (8 for blue marlin) have been set in these waters. Outfitters abound at the major marinas like Red Hook. We recommend angling off the *Fish Hawk* (© 340/775-9058), which Captain Al Petrosky sails out of Fish Hawk Marina Lagoon on the east end. His 15m (48-ft.) diesel-powered craft is fully equipped with rods and reels. For all equipment (as well as sodas and beers, but not meals) you'll pay $650 per half-day for up to six passengers. Full-day excursions start at $1,300.

GOLF   Mahogany Run, on the north shore at Mahogany Run Road (© 800/253-7103), is an 18-hole, par-70 course. This beautiful course rises and drops like a roller coaster on its journey to the sea; cliffs and crashing sea waves are the ultimate hazards at the 13th, 14th, and 15th holes. Former president Bill Clinton called this course very challenging. Greens fees are $130 to $150 for 18 holes, reduced to $95 to $110 in the late afternoon. Carts are included. Club rental costs $40.

SAILING 🎖🎖   **American Yacht Harbor** 🎖🎖, Red Hook (© 340/775-6454), can refer both bareboat and fully crewed charters. It leaves from the east end of St. Thomas in Vessup Bay. The harbor is home to numerous boat companies, including day-trippers, fishing boats, and sailing charters. There are also five restaurants on the property, serving everything from Continental to Caribbean cuisine. Another reliable outfitter is **Charteryacht League** 🎖🎖, at Gregory East (© 800/524-2061 in the U.S., or 340/774-3944; www.vicl.org).

Sailors may want to check out the *Yachtsman's Guide to the Virgin Islands,* available at major marine outlets, at bookstores, through catalog merchandisers, or directly from **Tropical Publishers,** P.O. Box 12, Adelphia, NJ 07710 (© 877/923-9653; www.yachtsmansguide.com). This annual guide, which costs $16, is supplemented by sketch charts, photographs, and landfall sketches and charts showing harbors and harbor entrances, anchorages, channels, and landmarks, plus information on preparations necessary for cruising the islands.

SCUBA DIVING   The best scuba diving site off St. Thomas, especially for novices, has to be **Cow and Calf Rocks,** off the southeast end (45 min. from Charlotte Amalie by boat); here you'll discover a network of coral tunnels riddled with caves, reefs, and ancient boulders encrusted with coral. The *Cartanser Sr.,* a sunken World War II cargo ship that lies in about 11m (35 ft.) of water, is beautifully encrusted with coral and now home to a myriad of colorful fish. Another popular wreck dive is the *Maj. General Rogers,* the stripped-down hull of a former Coast Guard cutter.

Experienced divers may want to dive at exposed sheer rock pinnacles like **Sail Rock** and **French Cap Pinnacle,** which are encrusted with hard and soft corals and frequented

Moments **Bringing Out the Sir Francis Drake in You**

Tired of escorted tours? **Nauti Nymph Magic Moments,** American Yacht Harbor, Red Hook ((© **800/734-7345** in the U.S., or 340/775-5066; www.yachtmagic moments.com), reaches out to the independent traveler and adventurer. The knowing staff assists in designing a personal itinerary for a bareboat rental, or can hook you up with a captained day trip. A choice of Coast Guard–approved and fully equipped vessels ranging in size from 7.5m to 9m (25–31 ft.) are available. Boats are kept in top condition. On your own you can explore the British Virgin Islands, including such little-known islands as Jost van Dyke and Norman Island, in the tradition of Sir Francis Drake. Norman Island, incidentally, was the inspiration for Robert Louis Stevenson's *Treasure Island.* Boat rentals without captain are $315 to $510 depending on the size of the boat; with captain costs $115 extra.

by lobsters and green and hawksbill turtles. They are also exposed to open-ocean currents that can make these very challenging dives.

St. Thomas Diving Club, 7147 Bolongo Bay (© **877/538-8734** in the U.S., or 340/776-2381; www.stthomasdivingclub.com), is a full-service, PADI five-star IDC center, the best on the island. An open-water certification course, including four scuba dives, costs $429. An advanced open-water certification course, including five dives that can be accomplished in 2 days, goes for $308. You can also enjoy local snorkeling for $40.

DIVE IN!, in the Sapphire Beach Resort & Marina, Smith Bay Road, Route 36 (© **866/434-8346,** ext. 2144, in the U.S., or 340/777-5255), is a well-recommended, complete diving center that offers some of the finest services in the U.S. Virgin Islands, including professional instruction (beginner to advanced), daily beach and boat dives, custom dive packages, snorkeling trips, and a full-service PADI dive center. An introductory resort course costs $90, with a one-tank dive going for $75 and two-tank dives for $90. A six-dive pass costs $255.

SEA KAYAKING   Virgin Island Ecotours/Mangrove Adventures (© **340/779-2155;** www.viecotours.com) offers half-day kayak trips through a mangrove lagoon on the southern coastline. The cost is $65 per person. The professional naturalists who lead the tour allow for 30 to 40 minutes of snorkeling.

SNORKELING ⋒⋒   With 30 spectacular reefs just off St. Thomas, this is a terrific destination for snorkeling. We like the waters off **Coki Point** ⋒⋒, on the northeast shore of St. Thomas; the coral ledges near Coral World's underwater tower are especially enticing. **Magens Bay** also has great snorkeling year-round. If your hotel doesn't provide snorkel gear, it's easy to rent on most of the island's popular beaches.

You may also want to take a snorkeling cruise. Many leave from the Red Hook and Yacht Haven marinas. The 15m (50-ft.) yacht *Nightwind,* Sapphire Marina (© **340/ 775-4110,** 24 hr. a day), offers full-day sails to St. John and the outer islands. The $120 price includes free snorkeling equipment and instruction, plus a continental breakfast, a buffet lunch, and an open bar.

New Horizons, 6501 Red Hook Plaza, Suite 16, Red Hook (© **800/808-7604** or 340/775-1171), offers windborne excursions amid the cays and reefs of the Virgin Islands. The two-masted, 20m (65-ft.) sloop has circumnavigated the globe and has

⎧ *Tips*   **Getting to the Bottom of It**

The air-conditioned *Atlantis* submarine will take you on a 50-minute voyage (the whole experience is really 2 hr., when you include transportation to and from the sub) to depths of 30m (90 ft.), where an amazing world of exotic marine life unfolds. You'll have up-close views of coral reefs and sponge gardens through the sub's .5m (2-ft.) windows. On some voyages, *Atlantis* divers swim with the fish and bring them close to the windows for photos.

Passengers take a surface boat from the West Indies Dock, right outside Charlotte Amalie, to the submarine, which is near Buck Island (the St. Thomas version, not the more-famous Buck Island near St. Croix). The fare is $89 for adults, $45 for children 12 and under; children under 36 inches not allowed. The *Atlantis* operates daily. Reservations are suggested. (The sub carries only 48 passengers.) For tickets, go to the Havensight shopping mall, building 6, or call ℭ **866/546-7820** or 340/776-5650.

---

been used as a design prototype for other boats. Owned and operated by Canadian Tim Krygsveld, it contains a hot-water shower, serves a specialty drink called a New Horizons Nooner (with a melon-liqueur base), and carries a complete line of snorkeling equipment for adults and children. A full-day excursion, with continental breakfast, an Italian buffet lunch, and an open bar, costs $110 per person. Children ages 2 to 12, when accompanied by an adult, pay $55. Excursions depart daily, weather permitting, from the Sapphire Beach Resort & Marina. Call ahead for reservations and information. Another vessel, *New Horizons II,* a 13m (44-ft.) custom-made speedboat, runs full-day trips to some of the most scenic highlights of the British Virgin Islands, costing $135 for adults or $95 for children ages 2 to 12. You will need your passport and will have to pay an additional $25 per person customs fee.

You can avoid the crowds by sailing aboard the *Fantasy,* Red Hook (ℭ **340/775-5652;** fax 340/775-6256), which departs from the American Yacht Harbor at Red Hook at 9:30am daily. It takes a maximum of six passengers to St. John and nearby islands for swimming, snorkeling, beachcombing, and trolling. Snorkel gear with expert instruction is provided, as is a champagne lunch. The full-day trip costs $125 per person in the summer. A full-day sail for six people costs $750.

TENNIS   The best tennis on the island is at the **Wyndham Sugar Bay Beach Club** 𝕽𝕽, 6500 Estate Smith Bay (ℭ **340/777-7100**), with four Laykold courts lit at night. Nonguests pay $8 per hour.

Another good resort for tennis is the **Bolongo Bay Beach Resort,** Bolongo Bay (ℭ **340/775-1800**), which has two courts that are lit until 6pm. They're free to members and hotel guests, but cost $10 per hour for nonguests.

Marriott Frenchman's Reef Tennis Courts, Flamboyant Point (ℭ **340/776-8500**), has two courts. Again, nonguests are charged $10 per hour per court. Lights stay on until 10pm.

EXPLORING ST. THOMAS
CHARLOTTE AMALIE 𝕽
The capital, Charlotte Amalie, where most visitors begin their sightseeing, has all the color and charm of an authentic Caribbean waterfront town. In days of yore, seafarers

from all over the globe flocked here, as did pirates and members of the Confederacy, who used the port during the American Civil War. (Sadly, St. Thomas was the biggest slave market in the world.)

The old warehouses once used for storing pirate goods still stand; today, many of them house shops. In fact, the main streets are now a virtual shopping mall and are usually packed. (See "Shopping," below, for our specific recommendations.) Sandwiched among these shops are a few historic buildings, most of which can be seen on foot in about 2 hours.

Fort Christian This imposing structure, which dates from 1671, dominates the center of town, and underwent a complete renovation with many improvements in 2006. It was named after the Danish king Christian V and has been everything from a fort to a governor's residence to a jail. It became a national historic landmark in 1977, but functioned as a police station, court, and jail until 1983. Now a museum, the fort houses displays on the island's history and culture. Cultural workshops and turn-of-the-20th-century furnishings are just some of the exhibits. A museum shop features local crafts, maps, and prints.

In the town center. © 340/776-8605. Admission $4 adults, free for children 16 and under. Mon–Fri 9am–4pm.

St. Thomas Skyride This contraption affords visitors a dramatic view of Charlotte Amalie harbor, with a ride to a 200m (700-ft.) peak. The tramway, similar to those used at ski resorts, operates six cars, each with a 8-person capacity, for the 15-minute round-trip ride. It transports customers from the Havensight area to Paradise Point, where they can disembark to visit shops and the popular restaurant and bar.

© 340/774-9809. www.stthomasskyride.com. Round-trip $18 adults, $9 children 6–12. Daily 9am–5pm.

Seven Arches Museum Browsers love checking out the private home of longtime residents Philibert Fluck and Barbara Demaras. This is an 18th-century Danish house, restored to its original condition and furnished with West Indian antiques. You can walk through the yellow ballast arches and visit the great room, with its wonderful view of the busiest harbor in the Caribbean. Night-blooming cacti and iguanas are on the roof of some of the quarters.

Government Hill. © 340/774-9295. Admission $5. Daily 10am–4pm.

Synagogue of Beracha Veshalom Vegmiluth Hasidim ᚜ This is the oldest synagogue in continuous use under the American flag. It was erected in 1833 by Sephardic Jews, and it maintains the tradition of having sand on the floor, commemorating the exodus from Egypt. The structure was built of local stone, along with ballast brick from Denmark and mortar made of molasses and sand. Next door, the **Weibel Museum** showcases 300 years of Jewish history. It keeps the same hours as the synagogue.

16 Crystal Gade. © 340/774-4312. Free admission. Mon–Fri 9am–4pm.

ELSEWHERE ON THE ISLAND

Route 30 (Veterans Dr.) will take you west of Charlotte Amalie to **Frenchtown.** (Turn left at the sign to the Admiral's Inn.) Early French-speaking settlers arrived on St. Thomas from St. Bart's after the Swedes uprooted them. Some island residents today are the direct descendants of those long-ago immigrants, who were known for speaking a distinctive French patois. This colorful village contains a number of restaurants and taverns and a reputation as a nightclubbing destination. Because Charlotte Amalie

---

(Moments Into the Deep for Nondivers

Nondivers can experience some of the thrills familiar to scuba aficionados by participating in **Sea Trek at the Coral World Marine Park & Underwater Observatory** (© **340/775-1555**). For $68, or $59 for children, you get a full immersion undersea. No experience is needed. Participants are given a helmet and a tube to breathe through. The tube is attached to an air source at the observatory tower. You then enjoy a 20-minute stroll in water 5.5m (18 ft.) deep. You're on the sea floor taking in the rainbow-hued tropical fish and the coral reefs as you go along. It's a marvelous way to experience the world through the eyes of a fish.

---

has become somewhat dangerous at night, Frenchtown has picked up its after-dark business and is the best spot for dancing and other local entertainment.

Coral World Marine Park & Underwater Observatory ⍟   This marine complex features a three-story underwater observation tower 30m (100 ft.) offshore. Inside, you'll see sponges, fish, coral, and other aquatic creatures in their natural state. An 80,000-gallon reef tank features exotic marine life of the Caribbean; another tank is devoted to sea predators, with circling sharks and giant moray eels. Activities include daily fish and shark feedings. The latest attraction is a Nautilus semi-submarine going 2m (6 ft.) below the surface of the water. On board, passengers can enjoy close encounters with a sea of coral gardens and rainbow-hued fish outside their portholes.

Coral World's guests can take advantage of adjacent **Coki Beach** for snorkel rentals, scuba lessons, or simply swimming and relaxing. Lockers and showers are available. Also at the marine park are a bar and a nature trail.

6450 Estates Smith Bay, a 20-min. drive from Charlotte Amalie off Rte. 38. © 340/775-1555. www.coralworldvi. com. Admission $18 adults, $9 children 3–12. Daily 9am–5pm.

Estate St. Peter Greathouse Botanical Gardens ⍟   This estate consists of 11 acres at the foot of volcanic peaks on the northern rim of the island. The grounds are laced with self-guided nature walks that identify some 200 varieties of West Indian plants and trees, including an umbrella plant from Madagascar. From a panoramic deck in the gardens, you can see some 20 of the Virgin Islands, including Hans Lollick, an uninhabited island between Thatched Cay and Madahl Point. The house itself, filled with local art, is worth a visit.

At the corner of Rte. 40 (6A St. Peter Mountain Rd.) and Barrett Hill Rd. © 340/774-4999. Admission $12 adults, $6 children under 12. Daily 8am–4pm.

French Heritage Museum   Lying in historic Frenchtown, this museum houses artifacts such as wooden tools, original fishing nets, mahogany antiques, musical instruments, pictures, and memorabilia that document the lives of the people of French descent who lived on St. Thomas.

Frenchtown. © 340/714-2583. Free admission. Mon–Fri 9am–noon and 1-6pm.

SHOPPING ⍟⍟⍟

The discounted, duty-free shopping in the Virgin Islands makes St. Thomas a mecca for consumers. It's possible to find well-known brand names here at savings of up to 60% off mainland U.S. prices. But be warned—not all savings are so good. Before you leave home, check prices in your local stores if you think you might want to make a major purchase, so you can be sure that you are in fact getting a good deal. Having said that, we'll recommend some shops where we have found really good buys.

The best deals include china, crystal, perfume, jewelry (especially emeralds), Haitian art, fashion, watches, and items made of wood. Cameras and electronic items, based on our experience, are not the good buys they're reputed to be. St. Thomas is also the best place in the Caribbean for discounts on porcelain, but remember that U.S. brands may often be purchased for 25% off the retail price on the U.S. mainland. Look for the imported patterns for the biggest savings.

Most shops, some of which occupy former pirate warehouses, are open Monday to Saturday from 9am to 5pm. Some stores open Sunday and holidays if a cruise ship is in port. *Note:* Friday is the biggest cruise-ship day at Charlotte Amalie (we once counted eight ships in port at once), so try to avoid shopping then. It's a zoo.

Nearly all the major shopping is along the harbor of Charlotte Amalie. Cruise-ship passengers mainly shop at the **Havensight Mall** at the eastern edge of town. The principal shopping street is **Main Street,** or Dronningens Gade (its old Danish name). To the north is another merchandise-loaded street called **Back Street,** or Vimmelskaft. Many shops are also spread along the **Waterfront Highway (Kyst Vejen).** Between these major streets is a series of side streets, walkways, and alleys, all filled with shops. You might also browse along Tolbod Gade, Raadets Gade, Royal Dane Mall, Palm Passage, Storetvaer Gade, and Strand Gade.

It's illegal for most street vendors (food vendors are about the only exception) to ply their trades outside the designated area called **Vendors Plaza,** at the corner of Veterans Drive and Tolbod Gade. Monday to Saturday, hundreds of vendors converge here at 8am; they usually pack up around 5pm.

When you completely tire of French perfumes and Swiss watches, head for **Market Square,** also called Rothschild Francis Square. Under a Victorian tin roof, locals with machetes slice open fresh coconuts, while women wearing bandanas sell akee, cassava, and breadfruit.

All the major stores in St. Thomas are located by number on an excellent map in the publication *St. Thomas This Week,* distributed free to all arriving plane and boat passengers and at the visitor center. A lot of the stores on the island don't have street numbers, or don't display them, so look for their signs instead.

Diamonds International ☠, 31 Main St. (☏ **800/444-4025** or 340/774-1516), stocks the biggest inventory of diamonds in the Virgin Islands. A wide selection of loose diamonds and fine jewelry is on display, although not necessarily living up to the outlet's boast of "the best deals on the planet." There are ten stores in Charlotte Amalie.

Crystal Shoppe ☠, 14 Main St. (☏ **340/777-9835**), is a family-run store offering a dazzling array of crystal from around the world. All the big names in glass—Wedgwood, Hummel, Royal Copenhagen, Swarovski, and Rosenthal—are on parade, along with some particularly good pieces from the Swedish firm of Kosta Boda. Their porcelain Lladró figurines from Spain are also a fast-moving item.

Fabric in Motion, Storetvaer Gade (☏ **340/774-2006**), culls the globe for fabrics, and has a wonderful selection of silky cottons from Liberty's of London, the best Italian linens, and flamboyant batiks from Indonesia. Other tempting items include leather handbags and fun beach bags.

Boolchand's ☠☠, 31 Main St. (☏ **340/776-0794**), is the place to go when you're in the market for a camera. Famous throughout the Caribbean, this is the major retailer of not only cameras but electronics and digital products throughout the West Indies. Now into its 8th decade, it sells all the big names from Kodak to Leica, from Nikon to Fuji. In the electronics divisions are the latest in DVDs, minidiscs, and other items. There is also a jewelry department and a wide selection of watches.

Bernard K. Passman 𝕬𝕬𝕬, 38A Main St. (© 340/777-4580), is the world's leading sculptor of black-coral art and jewelry. He's famous for his *Can Can Girl* and his four statues of Charlie Chaplin. After being polished and embellished with gold and diamonds, some of Passman's work has been treasured by royalty. There are also simpler and more affordable pieces for sale.

Gallery Camille Pissarro, 14 Main St. (© 340/774-4621), is located in the house where Pissarro was born in 1830. In three high-ceilinged and airy rooms, you can view many prints of local artists, and the gallery also sells original batiks, alive in vibrant colors.

Mango Tango Art Gallery, Al Cohen's Plaza, Raphune Hill, Route 38 (© 340/777-3060), is one of the largest galleries on island, closely connected with a half-dozen internationally recognized artists who spend at least part of the year in the Virgin Islands. Original works begin at $500; prints and posters are cheaper.

Gallery St. Thomas, 1 Main St. (© 877/797-6363 or 340/777-6363; www.gallery stthomas.com), showcases the works of Virgin Island painters, notably Lucinda Schutt, best known for her Caribbean land and seascapes. At this gallery Schutt sells artwork beginning at $150 and prints for $18, and teaches painting with watercolors.

Native Arts and Crafts Cooperative 𝕬, Tolbod Gade 1 (© 340/777-1153), is the largest arts-and-crafts emporium in the U.S. Virgin Islands, offering the output of 80 different artisans. It specializes in items small enough to be packed into a suitcase or trunk, such as spice racks, lamps crafted from conch shells, salad bowls, crocheted goods, and straw goods.

Caribbean Marketplace, Havensight Mall, building 3 (© 340/776-5400), carries a selection of spices including the Sunny Caribbee line, a vast array of condiments, and botanical products. Don't expect very attentive service.

Aromatic **Down Island Traders,** Waterfront (© 340/776-4641), has Charlotte Amalie's most attractive array of spices, teas, candies, jellies, jams, and condiments, most of which are packaged in natural Caribbean products. There are also local cookbooks, and silk-screened T-shirts and bags.

The clutter and eclecticism of **Carson Company Antiques,** Royal Dane Mall, off Main Street (© 340/774-6175), may appeal to you. The shop is loaded with merchandise, tasteless and otherwise, from virtually everywhere. Bakelite jewelry is cheap and cheerful, and the African artifacts are often interesting.

A. H. Riise Gift 𝕬, 37 Main St. (© 800/524-2037 or 340/776-2303), is St. Thomas's oldest outlet for luxury items, and offers the best liquor selection on the island. The store carries fine jewelry and watches from Europe's leading craftspeople, including Bulgari, Omega, Rolex, and Gucci, as well as a wide selection of gold, platinum, and precious gemstone jewelry. Imported cigars are stored in a climate-controlled walk-in humidor. Waterford, Lalique, Baccarat, and Rosenthal are featured in the china and crystal department. Specialty shops in the complex sell Caribbean gifts, books, T-shirts, food, prints, note cards, and designer sunglasses.

One of the island's most famous outlets, **Al Cohen's Discount Liquors,** Havensight Mall (© 340/774-3690), occupies a big warehouse at Havensight with a huge selection of liquor and wine. The wine department is especially impressive. You can also purchase T-shirts and souvenirs.

Royal Caribbean (R), 33 Main St. ((C) **340/776-4110**), is one of the largest camera and electronics stores in the Caribbean. It carries Nikon, Minolta, Pentax, Canon, and Panasonic products, plus watches by Seiko, Movado, Corum, Fendi, Philippe Charriol, and Zodiac. There are also leather bags, Mikimoto pearls, and 14- and 18-karat jewelry. Another branch is located at the Havensight Mall ((C) **340/776-8890**).

Often called the Tiffany's of the Caribbean, **Cardow Jewelers** (RR), 39 Main St. ((C) **340/776-1140**), stocks the largest selection of fine jewelry in the world. This fabulous shop, where more than 20,000 rings are displayed, offers savings because of its worldwide direct buying, large turnover, and duty-free prices. Unusual and traditional designs are offered in diamonds, emeralds, rubies, sapphires, and pearls. The Treasure Cove has cases of fine gold jewelry priced under $400.

Cardow's leading competitor is **H. Stern Jewellers,** Havensight Mall ((C) **800/524-2024** or 340/776-1223), an international chain with some 175 outlets. Besides this branch, there are two more on Main Street. Stern gives worldwide guaranteed service, including a 60-day exchange privilege.

Azura, Havensight Mall ((C) **340/774-2442**), is renowned throughout the Caribbean for its collection of Colombian emeralds, both set and unset. Here you buy direct from the source, which can mean significant savings. The shop also stocks fine watches.

Another good place to browse for gemstones is **Pierre's,** 24 Palm Passage ((C) **800/300-0634** or 340/776-5130), one of the most impressive repositories of collector's items in the Caribbean. Look for alexandrites (garnets in three shades of green); spinels (pink and red); sphenes (yellow-green sparklers from Madagascar that are as reflective as high-quality diamonds); and tsavorites (green stones from Tanzania).

The most comprehensive and the best showcase for Caribbean music in all the Virgin Islands is **Parrot Fish Music,** Back Street at Store Tvaer Gade ((C) **340/776-4514;** www.parrotfishmusic.com). With the selection available here, you can dance all night to the sounds of calypso, reggae, soca, and the music of steel bands.

Mr. Tablecloth, 6 Main St. ((C) **340/774-4343;** www.mrtablecloth-vi.com), receives shipments of top-quality linens from the Republic of China. It has the best selection of tablecloths, doilies, place mats, aprons, and runners in Charlotte Amalie.

If you are shopping for a simple souvenir, stop in at **Captain's Corner,** Main Street across from H. Stern ((C) **340/774-8435**), the oldest and biggest souvenir outlet in town. Its most popular item is the Caribbean "map watch," but there is countless other merchandise, including voodoo masks and other island crafts such as handmade items crafted from wood.

Virgin Islands Brewing Company, across from Happy Buzzard at Royal Dane Mall ((C) **340/714-1683**), was founded on St. Croix but has invaded St. Thomas with one local beer, Blackbeard Ale. At the company store, you're given free samples and can purchase six-packs of the home-brewed suds along with T-shirts, caps, and polo shirts.

Outside of Charlotte Amalie, another noteworthy destination is **Tillett Gardens,** a virtual oasis of arts and crafts—pottery, silk-screened fabrics, candles, watercolors, jewelry, and more. It's on the highway across from Four Winds Shopping Center (take Rte. 38 east from Charlotte Amalie). A major island attraction is the **Jim Tillett Art Gallery and Silk Screen Print Studio** (RR) ((C) **340/775-1929;** www.tillettgardens. com), which displays the best work of local artists, including originals in oils, watercolors, and acrylics. The prints are all one of a kind, and prices start as low as $20. The famous Tillett maps on fine canvas are priced from $45.

ST. THOMAS AFTER DARK 👀

St. Thomas has more nightlife than any other island in the Virgins, U.S. and British, but not as much as you might think. Charlotte Amalie is no longer the swinging town it used to be. Many of the streets are dangerous after dark, so visitors have abandoned all but a few places in town. Most of the action is in **Frenchtown,** which has some great restaurants and bars. However, just as in Charlotte Amalie, some of these little hot spots are along dark, badly lit roads.

Note: Sexual harassment can be a problem in certain bars in Charlotte Amalie, where few single women would want to be alone at night anyway. Any of the major resort hotels are generally safe.

The big hotels, such as Marriott's Frenchman's Reef Beach Resort and Bluebeard's, have the liveliest after-dark scenes. After a day of sightseeing and shopping in the hot West Indies sun, sometimes your best bet is just to stay at your hotel in the evening, perhaps listening to a local calypso band. You might also call the **Reichhold Center for the Arts,** University of the Virgin Islands, 2 John Brewer's Bay (© **340/693-1559;** www.reicholdcenter.com), or check with the tourist office to see what's on during your visit. Its Japanese-inspired amphitheater is set into a natural valley, with seating for 1,196. Several different repertory companies of music, dance, and drama perform here. Performances usually begin at 8pm. Tickets range from $18 to $45, but depending on the attraction, this could vary greatly.

In Charlotte Amalie, head to the **Bar at Paradise Point** (© **340/777-4540**) at sunset. It's 200m (700 ft.) above sea level, across from the cruise-ship dock, and provides excellent photo ops and panoramic views. A tram takes you up the hill. (See the review of St. Thomas Skyride in "Exploring St. Thomas," earlier.) Get the bartender to serve you their specialty, a Bushwacker. Sometimes a one-man steel band is on hand to serenade the sunset watchers. You can also order inexpensive food, such as pizza, hot dogs, and hamburgers.

We recommend only a few other places in Charlotte Amalie. They include **Greenhouse,** Veterans Drive (© **340/774-7998;** www.thegreenhouserestaurant.com), a bar/restaurant that's directly on the waterfront and features live entertainment Friday night, ranging from reggae to disco. There's a $5 charge.

Attracting a wide age group, **Happy Buzzard,** 26A Royal Dane Mall (© **340/777-8676**), once known as Fat Tuesday, is also along the waterfront in the center of Charlotte Amalie. The bartenders offer a wide variety of beer, highballs, and shooters. Special events are often presented. Open daily from 10am to 8pm, later on Friday and Saturday.

The scenic **Banana Bar,** Bluebeard's Hill (© **340/774-1600**), overlooking the yacht harbor, hosts piano-bar entertainment on Thursday, Saturday, and Sunday from 7 to 10pm. It's a popular gathering spot for both locals and visitors. Entertainment varies from month to month, but a steel band comes in some nights, while others are devoted to reggae and salsa. It's open daily 5 to 10pm. There's no cover.

During the day **Iggie's Bolongo,** in the Bolongo Beach Resort, 7150 Bolongo (© **340/693-2600;** www.iggiesbeachbar.com), is an informal, open-air restaurant, serving hamburgers, sandwiches, and salads. After dark, it presents karaoke and offers night volleyball. It's also one of the most active sports bars on island.

West of Charlotte Amalie, in Frenchtown, **Epernay,** rue de St. Barthélemy (© **340/ 774-5348**), next to Bella Blu, is a stylish watering hole with an ocean view. You can order vintage wines and at least six different brands of champagne by the glass. Also available are appetizers, including sushi, main courses ($15–$33), and tempting desserts like chocolate-dipped strawberries.

The popular **Turtle Rock Bar** lies in the Mangrove Restaurant at the Wyndham Sugar Bay Beach Club, 6500 Estate Smith Bay (© **340/777-7100**). Sunday night is karaoke. Burgers, salads, steaks, and grilled fish are available at the Iguana Grill a few steps away. There's no cover.

3 St. Croix ★★★

With 218 sq. km (84 sq. miles), St. Croix is the largest of the U.S. Virgin Islands. At the east end (actually the easternmost point of the United States), the terrain is rocky and arid. The west end is lusher, and even includes a small "Rain Forest" of mango, mahogany, tree ferns, and dangling lianas. Between the two extremes are beautiful beaches, rolling hills, pastures, and, increasingly, miles of condos.

Columbus named the island Santa Cruz (Holy Cross) when he landed here on November 14, 1493. He anchored his ship off the north shore but was quickly driven away by the spears, arrows, and axes of the Carib Indians. The French laid claim to the island in 1650, and the Danes purchased it from them in 1773. Under Danish rule, slave labor and sugar-cane fields proliferated during a golden era for both planters and pirates, which came to an end in the latter half of the 19th century. Danish influence still permeates the island today.

ESSENTIALS

See "Getting There" at the beginning of the chapter for details on flights to St. Croix.

VISITOR INFORMATION   You can begin your explorations at the **visitor bureau,** 53A Company St., in Christiansted (© **340/773-0495**), a yellow building across from the open-air market. It's open Monday to Friday 8am to 5pm.

GETTING AROUND   At Henry E. Rohlsen International Airport, official taxi rates are posted. From the airport, expect to pay about $16 to $32 to Christiansted and about $12 to $24 to Frederiksted. Cabs are unmetered, so agree on the rate before you get in. The **St. Croix Taxicab Association** (© **340/778-1088**) offers door-to-door service.

Air-conditioned **buses** run between Christiansted and Frederiksted about every 45 minutes daily between 5:30am and 8pm. They start at Tide Village, to the east of Christiansted, and go along Route 75 to the Golden Rock Shopping Center. They

---

⟨Fun Fact⟩ Special Holiday Events

Christmas is celebrated in a big way on St. Croix. A 12-day celebration includes Christmas Day, the legal holiday on December 26, New Year's Eve (called "Old Year's Day"), and New Year's Day. It ends January 5 with a children's parade, and January 6 with an adult parade for the Feast of the Three Kings, a parade of flamboyantly attired merrymakers. For information, call the **tourism office** in Christiansted (© **340/773-0495**).

transfer along Route 70, with stopovers at the Sunny Isle Shopping Center, La Reine Shopping Center, St. George Village Botanical Garden, and Whim Plantation Museum, before reaching Frederiksted. The fare is $1, or 55¢ for seniors. For more information, call © **340/778-0898.**

If your hotel is in Christiansted, and you don't plan to do extensive touring around the island, you can manage without a car. But if you plan to get out and explore, a car is the way to go. Many of the roads are quite good. St. Croix offers moderately priced car rentals, even on cars with automatic transmission and air-conditioning. However, because of the island's higher-than-normal accident rate, insurance costs are a bit higher than usual. If you're not covered under your existing insurance policies or by your credit card, you should consider paying for the collision damage waiver.

Avis (© **340/778-9355;** www.avis.com), **Budget** (© **800/472-3325** in U.S. and Canada, or 340/778-9636; www.budgetrentacar.com), and **Hertz** (© **800/654-3131** in the U.S. and Canada, or 340/778-1402; www.hertz.com) all maintain headquarters at the airport; look for their kiosks near the baggage-claim areas. In most rural areas, the speed limit is 35 mph; certain parts of the major artery, Route 66, are 55 mph. In towns and urban areas, the speed limit is 20 mph. If you're going into the "bush country," you'll find the roads very difficult. Sometimes the government smoothes the roads out before the rainy season begins (often in Oct or Nov), but they deteriorate rapidly. *Be warned:* Driving is on the left.

FAST FACTS   The local **American Express** representative is Southerland Tours, Queens Cross Street, Carvelle Arcade Building (© **800/260-2603** or 340/773-9500).

If you need medical assistance, go to the **Governor Juan F. Luis Hospital & Medical Center,** 4007 Diamond Ruby, Christiansted (© **340/778-6311**).

ACCOMMODATIONS

All rooms are subject to an 8% hotel room tax, which is not included in the rates below. If you're interested in a villa or condo rental, contact the places reviewed below or **Century 21 Island Villas,** Property Management Rentals, 340 Strand St., Frederiksted, St. Croix, U.S.V.I. 00840 (© **800/626-4512** or 340/772-0420; fax 340/772-2958; www.stcroixislandvillas.com), which offers some of the best accommodations on the island. Some are private residences with pools; many are on the beach. They range from one-bedroom units to seven-bedroom villas, with prices from $1,050 to $10,000 per week year-round. The minimum stay is 7 nights.

VERY EXPENSIVE

The Buccaneer 🏵🏵🏵 🄺ids   This large, luxurious, family-owned resort has three of the island's best beaches, and the best sports program on St. Croix. The property was once a cattle ranch and a sugar plantation; its first estate house, which dates from the mid–17th century, stands near a freshwater pool. Accommodations are either in the main building or in one of the beachside properties. The baronially arched main building has a lobby opening onto landscaped terraces, with a sea vista on two sides and Christiansted to the west. The rooms are fresh and comfortable, though some of the standard units are a bit small. All have wicker or mahogany furnishings and full bathrooms. The best bathrooms are in the Beachside Doubloons, and come complete with whirlpool tubs. A free Kid's Camp is available year-round.

This resort serves the best cuisine of any hotel on the island—a Caribbean and international repertoire of first-class dishes.

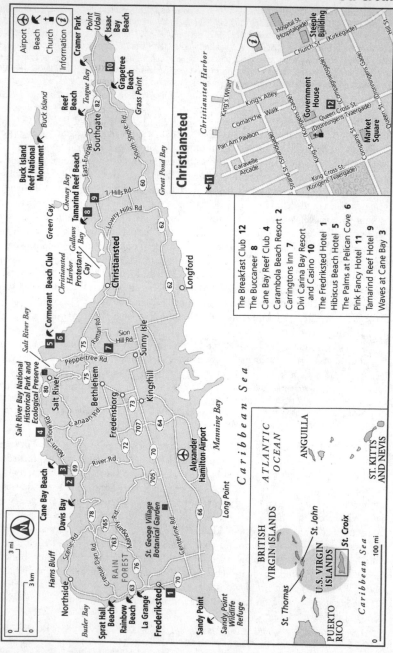

St. Croix

Christiansted

Christiansted Harbor

Hospital St. (Hospitalgade)
Church St. (Kirkegade)

Steeple Building

Government House

Market Square

King's Wharf
King's Alley
Comanche Walk
Pan Am Pavilion
Caravelle Arcade

Queen Cross St. (Dronningens Tvaergade)
King Cross St. (Kongens Tvaergade)

Strand St. (Strandgade)
King St. (Kongens Gade)
Company St. (Companiesgade)
Queen St. (Dronningens Gade)
Hill St.

10
12
11

The Breakfast Club **12**
The Buccaneer **8**
Cane Bay Reef Club **4**
Carambola Beach Resort **2**
Carringtons Inn **7**
Divi Carina Bay Resort and Casino **10**
The Fredriksted Hotel **1**
Hibiscus Beach Hotel **5**
The Palms at Pelican Cove **6**
Pink Fancy Hotel **11**
Tamarind Reef Hotel **9**
Waves at Cane Bay **3**

Point Udall
Cramer Park
Isaac Bay Beach
Grapetree Beach **10**
Reef Beach
Grass Point
Southgate **82**
Chenay Bay
Tamarind Reef Beach **9**
Buck Island
Buck Island Reef National Monument
Green Cay
Cormorant Beach Club **5 6**
Salt River Bay
Protestant Cay
Gallows Bay
Christiansted Harbor
East End Rd.
7 Hills Rd. **60**
Lowry Hills Rd.
8
Great Pond Bay
Longford
62
62

Salt River Bay National Historical Park and Ecological Preserve
North Shore Rd.
4
Salt River
Bethlehem **80**
Peppertree Rd.
Sion Hill Rd.
7
Sunny Isle
Kingshill
Fredensborg
Canaan Rd.
75
73
707
64
Rattan Rd.
75

Cane Bay Beach
Davis Bay **3**
2 69
78
765
763
River Rd.
72
70
705
Centerline Rd.
St. George Village Botanical Garden
Alexander Hamilton Airport
Manning Bay
Long Point
66

Hams Bluff
Northside
Butler Bay
Scenic Rd.
Creque Dam Rd.
Mahogany Rd.
RAIN FOREST
76
63
La Grange
Frederiksted **1**
Sprat Hall Beach
Rainbow Beach
Sandy Point
Sandy Point Wildlife Refuge
70

Caribbean Sea

Legend
Airport
Beach
Church
Information

N
0   3 mi
0   3 km

ATLANTIC OCEAN
ANGUILLA
ST. KITTS AND NEVIS
BRITISH VIRGIN ISLANDS
St. John
St. Thomas
U.S. VIRGIN ISLANDS
St. Croix
PUERTO RICO
Caribbean Sea
0   100 mi

P.O. Box 25200, Gallows Bay (3km/2 miles east of Christiansted on Rte. 82), Christiansted, St. Croix, U.S.V.I. 00824.
🕿 800/255-3881 in the U.S., or 340/773-2100. Fax 340/712-2104. www.thebuccaneer.com. 138 units. Winter $310–
$630 double, $580–$900 suite; off season $265–$420 double, $400–$660 suite. Children under 18 stay free. Rates
include American breakfast. AE, DISC, MC, V. **Amenities:** 4 restaurants; bar; 2 outdoor pools; 18-hole golf course; 8
tennis courts (2 lit); fitness center; spa; kayaks; scuba; snorkeling; Sunfish sailboats; children's program; limited room
service; massage; babysitting; laundry service; nonsmoking rooms; rooms for those w/limited mobility. *In room:* A/C,
TV, dataport, fridge, beverage maker, hair dryer, iron, safe.

EXPENSIVE

Carambola Beach Resort   This hotel is set on 11 hectares (28 acres) above Davis
Bay, about a 30-minute drive from Christiansted. It's one of the largest hotels on St.
Croix, and it lies adjacent to an outstanding golf course, in a lovely, lush setting on a
white-sand beach whose turquoise waters provide fine snorkeling. Despite its spectacular physical location, this resort doesn't match The Buccaneer's class and style. Originally built as a Rock Resort, it has suffered hurricanes and management changes.
Maintenance could definitely improve, but it is still a good choice if you don't come
looking for problems. Guests are housed in red-roofed, two-story buildings, each of
which contains six units. The accommodations are furnished in mahogany, with Danish design; each has a balcony partially concealed from outside view, overlooking either
the garden or the sea. Rooms have an upscale flair, with louvered doors, tile floors,
mahogany trim, and sometimes extras like screened-in porches with rocking chairs.
Bathrooms are luxurious and roomy, with oversize showers (with seats) and tiled vanities. If you want the very finest room, ask for the Davis Bay Suite, which was a former
Rockefeller private beach home. Its veranda alone is capable of entertaining 50 people,
should that many drop in.

The resort is known for its excellent cuisine, especially the Caribbean and international dishes served at the formal Mahogany Restaurant.

Estate Davis Bay (P.O. Box 3031), Kingshill, St. Croix, U.S.V.I. 00851. 🕿 888/503-8760 in the U.S., or 340/778-3800.
Fax 340/778-1682. www.carambolabeach.com. 151 units. Winter $219–$372 suite; off season $199–$330 suite. AE,
DISC, MC, V. **Amenities:** 2 restaurants; bar; outdoor pool; whirlpool; golf course; 2 tennis courts; fitness center; dive
shop; fishing; snorkeling; game room; car rental; massage; laundry service; dry cleaning; nonsmoking rooms; rooms
for those w/limited mobility. *In room:* A/C, TV, kitchenette (in some), fridge, beverage maker, hair dryer, iron, safe.

Divi Carina Bay Resort and Casino ✦   Opening onto 300m (1,000 ft.) of sugar-
white beach, this resort brought gambling to the U.S. Virgin Islands. That fact seems
to obscure its success as a place of barefoot elegance and a top resort property. The
complex was built on the ruins of the former Grapetree Shores, which was destroyed
by Hurricane Hugo. Accommodations feature oceanfront guest rooms and villa suites
with views of the Caribbean. Rooms are good size and well equipped with
computer/fax lines, VCRs, a small kitchen, full bathrooms, and balconies. We prefer
the accommodations on the ground floor as they are closer to the water's edge. The 20
villas across the street are about a 3-minute walk from the sands. The latest building
to open on the grounds made its debut in 2005, with 50 oceanfront accommodations
with balconies. You can simply go upstairs for a massage at the spa on the top floor.

The kitchen is strong on fresh seafood and serves the island's best Sunday brunch
($35) in its Starlite Grille.

5025 Estate Turner Hole, Christiansted, St. Croix, U.S.V.I. 00820. 🕿 800/823-9352 in the U.S., or 340/773-9700. Fax
340/773-6802. www.diviresorts.com. 200 units. Winter $250–$470 double, $460–$645 suite; off season $189–$258
double, $347 suite. Children 15 and under stay free in parent's room. AE, MC, V. **Amenities:** 3 restaurants; 2 bars; 2
outdoor pools; 2 outdoor whirlpools; casino; lit tennis court; health club; spa services; dive center; snorkeling; limited

room service; massage; babysitting; laundry service; nonsmoking rooms; rooms for those w/limited mobility. *In room:* A/C, TV, dataport, kitchen (in some), wet bar, fridge, beverage maker, hair dryer, safe.

Hibiscus Beach Hotel 𝕽

This hotel, on one of the island's best beaches, attracts a lively clientele. The accommodations are in six two-story white-and-blue buildings. Each guest room is a retreat unto itself, with a private patio or balcony and a view of the Caribbean, plus tasteful Caribbean furnishings and floral prints. Shower-only bathrooms are small but well maintained. The on-site restaurant serves standard American food—competent, but nothing exciting.

4131 La Grande Princesse (about 5km/3 miles northwest of Christiansted, beside Rte. 75, next to the Cormorant), St. Croix, U.S.V.I. 00820. © 800/442-0121 in. the U.S., or 340/773-4042. Fax 340/773-7668. www.1hibiscus.com. 38 units. Winter $190–$200 double; off season $140–$150 double. Honeymoon, dive, and golf packages available. AE, DISC, MC, V. **Amenities:** Restaurant; bar; outdoor pool; snorkeling; babysitting; nonsmoking rooms. *In room:* A/C, ceiling fan, TV, dataport, minibar, beverage maker, hair dryer, iron, safe.

Tamarind Reef Hotel

A sandy beach at the Tamarind Reef's doorstep and good snorkeling along the reef highlight this property. And with new renovations, completed in January of 2007, the resort exudes a fresh, bright new look. Each motel-style room features a garden patio or private balcony, affording guests a view of the blue Caribbean. In addition, 18 of the suites provide fully equipped kitchenettes and accommodate up to four people. All units have well-maintained bathrooms with shower stalls. Guests can relax by the pool and enjoy cocktails, light lunches, and snacks from the poolside bar and grill. For those who want to explore St. Croix underwater, the hotel offers complimentary watersports equipment. Adjoining the hotel is the Green Cay Marina, where guests can charter boats for deep-sea fishing or sailing expeditions.

On-site a restaurant serves burgers, sandwiches, fries, and pasta. For more formal dining, the hotel's restaurant, Galleon, at the adjacent Green Cay Marina, serves French and northern Italian cuisine.

5000 Estate Southgate, St. Croix, U.S.V.I. 00820. © 800/619-0014 in the U.S., or 340/773-4455. Fax 340/773-3989. www.usvi.net/hotel/tamarind. 39 units. Winter $232–$292 double; off season $210–$228 double. Extra person $31. Children under 7 stay free in parent's room. Ask about dive, golf, and honeymoon packages. AE, DC, MC, V. **Amenities:** 2 restaurants; bar; outdoor pool; 4 lit tennis courts; kayaks; snorkeling; windsurfing; laundry; nonsmoking rooms; rooms for those w/limited mobility. *In room:* A/C, ceiling fan, TV, dataport, kitchenette (in some), fridge, beverage maker, hair dryer, iron, safe.

The Palms at Pelican Cove 𝕽

For years this property was operated as the Cormorant Beach Club, attracting a gay clientele from all over the world. It is no longer gay owned, but still attracts a large number of gay men, and "commitment ceremony packages" are still offered. Even so, the resort is much more diverse today and has been improved with new furnishings and an upgraded decor. The 2.5-hectare (6-acre) property is designed in a boxy, modern-looking series of rectangles, with outcroppings of exposed natural stone. It strikes a pleasant balance between seclusion and accessibility. Long Reef lies a few hundred feet offshore from the resort's sandy beachfront. Bedrooms contain a restrained decor of cane and wicker furniture, spacious bathrooms with tubs and showers, and sliding-glass doors that flood the interior with sunlight.

The social life revolves around an open-air clubhouse, with views of the sea. Off the central core is a bar (see "St. Croix After Dark," later in this chapter) and an airy dining room.

4126 La Grande Princesse (about 5km/3 miles northwest of Christiansted, beside Rte. 75), St. Croix, U.S.V.I. 00820. © 800/548-4460 in the U.S., or 340/778-8920. Fax 340/778-9218. www.palmspelicancove.com. 40 units. Winter $180–$210 double, $265 suite; off season $130–$160 double, $225 suite. Extra bed $25. AE, MC, V. Dive, golf, snorkeling, and "commitment ceremony" packages available. **Amenities:** 2 restaurants; bar; outdoor pool; 2 tennis courts; snorkeling; Internet cafe; massage; nonsmoking rooms; rooms for those w/limited mobility. *In room:* A/C, ceiling fan, TV, kitchenette (in some), wet bar (in some), fridge, beverage maker, safe.

MODERATE

Cane Bay Reef Club *Finds*   This is one of the little gems of the island, offering large suites, each with a living room, a full kitchen, and a balcony overlooking the water. It's on the north shore, about a 20-minute taxi ride from Christiansted, fronting the rocky Cane Bay Beach near the Waves at Cane Bay. Sunsets are beautiful, and the snorkeling's great. The decor is breezily tropical, with cathedral ceilings, overhead fans, and Chilean tiles. Bedrooms are spacious, cool, and airy, with comfortable beds; living rooms also contain futons. The shower-only bathrooms are medium in size and excellently maintained. There's a golf course nearby, and there's a dive shop within walking distance. You can cook in your own kitchen, barbecue, or dine at the in-house restaurant, Bogey's.

P.O. Box 1407, Kingshill, St. Croix, U.S.V.I. 00851. (C) **800/253-8534** in the U.S., or 340/778-2966. Fax 340/778-2966. www.canebay.com. 9 units. Winter double $150–$250 daily, $970–$1,600 weekly; off season double $110–$160 daily, $700–$990 weekly. Extra person $20. AE, DC, DISC, MC, V. **Amenities:** Restaurant; bar; outdoor pool; laundry service; rooms for those w/limited mobility. *In room:* A/C, ceiling fan, TV, kitchen, minibar, fridge, beverage maker, phone (in some).

Carringtons Inn *Finds*   If you've read stories about celebrities such as screen legend Maureen O'Hara, who own villas on St. Croix, and you wonder what life is like in them, here's your chance to experience one firsthand. This grandly elegant B&B was once the home of a wealthy family who spent winters here. Much evidence of their former lifestyle remains. This is an intimate B&B with personalized attention and five spacious and beautifully furnished guest rooms with first-class private bathrooms. Some rooms have a king-size canopy bed, and wicker furnishings are in tasteful abundance. When guests gather around the pool, a house-party atmosphere prevails. Even your breakfast of such delights as rum-flavored French toast can be served poolside. The staff delivers thoughtful touches such as a full concierge service, bathrobes, and even freshly baked cookies in the evening.

4001 Estate Hermon Hill (1.5km/1 mile west of Christiansted), St. Croix, U.S.V.I. 00820. (C) **877/658-0508** in the U.S., or 340/713-0508. Fax 340/719-0841. www.carringtonsinn.com. 5 units. Winter $120–$150 double; off season $100–$120 double. Rates include breakfast. AE, MC, V. **Amenities:** Breakfast room; outdoor pool; tennis courts (nearby); health club (nearby). *In room:* A/C, ceiling fan, kitchenette (in some), hair dryer, iron.

Waves at Cane Bay   This intimate and tasteful condo property is about 13km (8 miles) from the airport, midway between the island's two biggest towns. It's set on a well-landscaped plot of oceanfront property on Cane Bay, the heart of the best scuba and snorkeling at Cane Bay Beach. New owners in 2006 brought many changes and improvements, and each accommodation is gradually being renovated. Accommodations are within a pair of two-story cement-sided buildings, each directly on the beach. Each of the accommodations is high-ceilinged and relatively large, with a well-equipped kitchenette, a selection of reading material, tiled floors, a shower-only bathroom, and a very private veranda that's partially or fully concealed from the views of any of the other verandas. Attached to one of the buildings is an open-sided pavilion that functions as a bar and restaurant, open every Monday to Saturday for dinner.

Cane Bay (P.O. Box 1749), Kingshill, St. Croix, U.S.V.I. 00851. (C) **800/545-0603** in the U.S., or 340/778-1805. Fax 340/778-4945. www.canebaystcroix.com. 12 units. Winter $140–$155 double; off season $89–$99 double. Extra person $20. AE, MC, V. From the airport, go left on Rte. 64; after 1.5km/1 mile, turn right on Rte. 70; after another 1.5km/1 mile, go left at the junction with Rte. 75; after 3km/2 miles, turn left at the junction with Rte. 80; follow for 8km/5 miles. **Amenities:** Restaurant; bar; saltwater outdoor pool; dive shop; snorkeling; nonsmoking rooms. *In room:* A/C, ceiling fan, TV, kitchen, beverage maker, safe.

INEXPENSIVE

The Breakfast Club *Value* Here you'll get the best value of any bed-and-breakfast on St. Croix. This comfortable place combines a 1950s compound of efficiency apartments with a traditional-looking stone house that was rebuilt from a ruin in the 1930s. Each of the units has a cypress-sheathed ceiling, off-white walls, a beige-tile floor, and summery furniture. Shower-only bathrooms are small and adequately maintained. Adiel Israel, a native-born Caribbean took over ownership in 2006 and began to make many improvements. An on-site chef specializes in banana pancakes and will prepare lunch or dinner on request. When there is a full house count, occasional "party nights" are staged, featuring recorded music.

18 Queen Cross St., Christiansted, St. Croix, U.S.V.I. 00820. (2) 340/773-7383. Fax 340/773-8642. www.nav.to/the breakfastclub. 10 units. Year-round $75 double. Rates include breakfast. AE, V. *In room:* A/C (in some), TV, fridge, no phone.

The Frederiksted Hotel This contemporary four-story inn is a good choice for the heart of historic Frederiksted. It's in the center of town, about a 10-minute ride from the airport. Much of the activity takes place in the outdoor tiled courtyard, where guests enjoy drinks. The cheery rooms are like those of a motel on the U.S. mainland, perhaps showing a bit of wear, and with good ventilation but bad lighting. They're done in a tropical motif of pastels and are equipped with small fridges. The best (and most expensive) rooms are those with ocean views; they're subject to street noise but have the best light. Accommodations come with a small, tiled, shower-only bathroom. The nearest beach is Fort Frederik, a 3-minute walk away.

442 Strand St., Frederiksted, St. Croix, U.S.V.I. 00840. (2) 800/595-9519 in the U.S., or 340/772-0500. Fax 340/772-0500. www.frederikstedhotel.com. 40 units. Winter $100–$110 double; off season $90–$100 double. Extra person $10. AE, DISC, MC, V. **Amenities:** Restaurant; bar; outdoor pool. *In room:* A/C, TV, fridge, microwave.

Pink Fancy Hotel *Finds* This small, unique hotel is a block from the Annapolis Sailing School. You get more atmosphere here than anywhere else in town. The oldest part of the four-building complex is a historic 1780 Danish town house. In the 1950s, the hotel became a mecca for writers and artists, including Noël Coward. The owners have made major renovations, installing more antiques and fine furnishings. Guest rooms have a bright, tropical feel, with ceiling fans, floral prints, and rattan furnishings. The deluxe rooms are furnished with canopy or iron beds, as well as antiques and artwork. The medium-size bathrooms have combination tub/showers. A 3-minute boat ride takes guests to the beach on the Cay, a sandy islet in Christiansted's harbor.

27 Prince St., Christiansted, St. Croix, U.S.V.I. 00820. (2) 800/524-2045 in the U.S., or 340/773-8460. Fax 340/773-6448. www.pinkfancy.com. 11 units. Winter $120–$165 double; off season $99–$145 double. Rate includes continental breakfast. Ask about packages and weekly rates. AE, MC, V. **Amenities:** Outdoor pool; nonsmoking rooms. *In room:* A/C, ceiling fan, TV, kitchenette.

DINING
IN CHRISTIANSTED

Bacchus *STEAKHOUSE/CONTINENTAL* In a restaurant dedicated to the god of wine, it's no surprise that the wine *carte* receives as much attention as the food. Both *Wine Spectator* and *Food & Wine* have praised the cellar here. The decor, the fine service, and the presentation of the dishes make for a fine evening out. The kitchen uses first-class ingredients, many imported, to craft a number of dishes that combine flavor and finesse. The rib-eye steak Florentine is a local favorite. To finish, it doesn't get any better than the rum-infused sourdough bread pudding. Most dishes, except lobster, are at the lower end of the price scale.

Queen Cross St., off King St. ℂ 340/692-9922. www.restaurantbacchus.com. Reservations requested. Main courses $18–$42. AE, DC, DISC, MC, V. Tues–Sun 6–10pm.

Comanche Club CARIBBEAN/CONTINENTAL   Relaxed yet elegant, Comanche is one of the island's most popular restaurants. It's not the best, but the specialties are eclectic—everything from fresh fish to shark cakes. Each night, a different special and a different local dish are featured. Other choices include salads, curries, fish sautéed with lemon butter and capers, and typical West Indian dishes such as conch Creole with fungi. There are also standard international dishes like New York strip.

1 Strand St. ℂ 340/773-0210. Reservations recommended. Main courses dinner $16–$35; lunch $12–$15. AE, MC, V. Mon–Sat 11am–3pm and 5–10pm.

Kendricks 🍴🍴 FRENCH/CONTINENTAL   Kendricks, the island's toniest restaurant, lies in the historic Quin House complex at King Cross and Company streets. Some of its recipes have been featured in *Bon Appétit,* and deservedly so. You'll immediately warm to specialties like roasted pecan-crusted pork loin with ginger mayonnaise or grilled filet mignon with a port-wine demi-glace and red-onion confit. The signature appetizer is king-crab cakes with lemon-pepper aioli. Another great choice is the pecan-crusted roast pork loin with ginger mayonnaise.

King Cross St. ℂ 340/773-9199. Reservations recommended. Main courses $24–$35. AE, MC, V. Mon–Sat 6–9:30pm. Closed Mon Sept–Oct .

Luncheria Mexican Food *Value* MEXICAN/CUBAN/PUERTO RICAN   This restaurant is a bargain. You get the usual tacos, tostadas, burritos, nachos, and enchiladas, as well as chicken fajitas, enchiladas verde, and *arroz con pollo* (spiced chicken with brown rice). Daily specials feature both low-calorie and vegetarian choices (the chef's refried beans are lard-free), and whole-wheat tortillas are offered. The complimentary salsa bar has mild to hot sauces, plus jalapeños. Some Cuban and Puerto Rican dishes appear on the menu; these include a zesty chicken curry, black-bean soup, and roast pork. The bartender makes the island's best margaritas.

In the historic Apothecary Hall Courtyard, 2111 Company St. ℂ 340/773-4247. Main courses $3–$10. No credit cards. Mon–Sat 11am–9pm.

Paradise Café *Value* DELI/AMERICAN   This neighborhood favorite draws locals seeking good food and great value. Its brick walls and beamed ceiling were originally part of an 18th-century great house. New York–style deli fare is served during the day. The homemade soups are savory, and you can add grilled chicken or fish to the freshly made salads. At breakfast, you can select from an assortment of omelets, or try the steak and eggs. Dinners are more elaborate. The 12-ounce New York strip steak and the freshly made pasta specialties are good choices. Appetizers include mango chicken quesadillas and crab cakes.

53B Company St. (at Queen Cross St., across from Government House). ℂ 340/773-2985. Breakfast $5:50–$10; lunch $7–$10; dinner $18–$24. No credit cards. Mon–Sat 7:30am–9pm.

Rum Runners *Kids* CARIBBEAN   This open-air restaurant sits right on the boardwalk and offers some fabulous views to accompany the excellent dining. The ambience reeks of the Caribbean and the sound of waves in the background can put even the tensest of people at ease. Excellent choices here include the New York strip steak, the fresh, broiled whole lobster, the Caribbean pork tenderloin served with a grilled banana, and one of the house specials, baby back ribs slow cooked in island spices and Guinness. The younger vacationers can pick from the children's menu.

Hotel Caravelle, on the boardwalk at Queen's Cross St. ⓒ 340/773-6585. Reservations recommended. Main courses $12–$28. AE, MC, V. Mon–Sat 7–10:30am, 11:30am–3pm, and 5:30–9:30pm; Sun 8am–2pm and 5:30–9:30pm.

Savant ⓡ Finds CARIBBEAN/THAI/MEXICAN   The spicy fusion cuisine here provides a marvelous burst of palate-awakening flavors. The bistro atmosphere is stylish, yet fun and laid-back. Black-and-white photos and other original artwork line the walls of the restaurant. Fresh fish is deftly handled. We gravitate to the tantalizing Thai curries, most of which are mildly spiced. You can ask the chef to "go nuclear" if you prefer hotter food. The red-coconut-curry sauce is one of the best we've ever had on the island. If you're craving an enchilada, try the one stuffed with seafood. The maple-teriyaki pork tenderloin, one of the chef's specialties, is terrific, as are the steak choices. There are only 20 candlelit tables, so call for a reservation as far in advance as you can.

4C Hospital St. ⓒ 340/713-8666. Reservations required. Main courses $16–$33. AE, MC, V. Mon–Sat 6–10pm.

IN FREDERIKSTED

Blue Moon INTERNATIONAL/CAJUN   The best little bistro in Frederiksted becomes a hot, hip spot during Sunday brunch and on Friday nights, when it offers entertainment. The 200-year-old stone house on the waterfront is a favorite of visiting jazz musicians, and visitors have discovered (but not ruined) it. It's decorated with funky, homemade art from the U.S., including a trashcan-lid restaurant sign. The atmosphere is casual and cafelike. Begin with the "lunar pie," with feta, cream cheese, onions, mushrooms, and celery in phyllo pastry, or the artichoke-and-spinach dip. Main courses include the catch of the day and, on occasion, Maine lobster. The clams served in garlic sauce are also from Maine. There's also the usual array of steak and chicken dishes. Save room for the brownie ice cream.

7 Strand St. ⓒ 340/772-2222. Reservations recommended. Main courses $23–$28. AE, MC, V. Tues–Fri 11:30am–2pm; Tues–Sat 6–9pm; Sun 11am–2pm.

Le St. Tropez FRENCH/MEDITERRANEAN   This is the most popular bistro in Frederiksted. It's small, so call ahead for a table. If you're visiting for the day, make this bright little cafe your lunch stop, and enjoy crepes, quiches, soups, or salads in the sunlit courtyard. At night, the atmosphere glows with candlelight and becomes more festive. Try the pâté de champagne and escargots Provençal, or one of the freshly made soups. Main dishes are likely to include rack of lamb with mushrooms, the fish of the day, or a magret of duck. Ingredients are always fresh and well prepared.

Limetree Court, 227 King St. ⓒ 340/772-3000. Reservations recommended. Main courses $17–$36. AE, MC, V. Mon–Fri 11:30am–2:30pm; Mon–Sat 6–10pm.

Villa Morales PUERTO RICAN   This inland spot is one of the best Puerto Rican restaurants on St. Croix. You can choose between indoor and outdoor seating areas. No one will mind if you come here just to drink; the cozy bar is lined with the memorabilia collected by several generations of the family who maintains the place. Look for a broad cross-section of Hispanic dishes, including many that Puerto Ricans remember from their childhood. These include fried snapper with white rice and beans, stewed conch, roasted or stewed goat, and stewed beef. Meal platters are garnished with beans and rice. Most of the dishes are inexpensive. On special occasions, the owners transform the place into a dance hall, bringing in live salsa and merengue bands.

Plot 82C, Estate Whim (off Rte. 70 about 3km/2 miles from Frederiksted). ℂ 340/772-0556. Reservations recommended. Main courses lunch $8–$15, dinner $8–$35. MC, V. Thurs–Sat 10am–10pm.

AROUND THE ISLAND

Duggan's Reef CONTINENTAL/CARIBBEAN   This is one of the most popular restaurants on St. Croix. It's only a few feet from the still waters of Reef Beach and makes an ideal perch for watching windsurfers and Hobie Cats. At lunch, an array of salads, crepes, and sandwiches is offered. The more elaborate night menu features the popular house specialties: Duggan's Caribbean lobster pasta and Irish whiskey lobster. Begin with fried calamari or conch chowder. Main dishes include New York strip steak, fish, and pastas. The local catch of the day can be baked, grilled, blackened Cajun style, or served island style (with tomato, pepper, and onion sauce).

East End Rd., Teague Bay. ℂ 340/773-9800. Reservations required for dinner in winter. Main courses $20–$40; pastas $19–$27. MC, V. Daily noon–3pm and 6–9:30pm; Sun brunch 11am–2:30pm. Bar daily noon–11:30pm. Closed for lunch in summer.

Elizabeth's at the Palms 𝒦 INTERNATIONAL   Both the restaurant and its bar are a mecca for gay or gay-friendly people who appreciate its relaxed atmosphere, well-prepared food, and gracefully arched premises overlooking the sea. The menu changes nightly. Lunch specialties may include meal-size salads, club sandwiches, burgers, and fresh fish. To begin, sample the chef's classic Caesar salad. In the evening expect such dishes as roast rack of lamb served with a pecan-and-Parmesan-herb crust or grilled local mahimahi, its flavor enhanced with fresh cilantro and lime-butter sauce. Desserts are sumptuous, especially the Cruzan rum cake with bananas, chocolate, or coconut and the chocolate rum torte with layers of mousse and rum cake sealed in chocolate.

In the Palms at Pelican Cove, 4126 La Grande Princesse. ℂ 340/719-0735. Reservations recommended. Main courses lunch $8–$16, dinner $19–$30. AE, DC, MC, V. Daily 7:30am–9pm.

The Galleon FRENCH/NORTHERN ITALIAN   This restaurant, which overlooks the ocean, is a local favorite, and deservedly so. It serves northern Italian and French cuisine, including *osso buco,* just as good as that dished up in Milan. Freshly baked bread, two fresh vegetables, and rice or potatoes accompany main dishes. The menu always includes at least one local fish, such as wahoo, tuna, swordfish, mahimahi, or even fresh Caribbean lobster. You can order a perfectly done rack of lamb, which will be carved right at your table. There's an extensive wine list, including many sold by the glass. Music from a baby grand accompanies your dinner several nights a week and you can enjoy guitar music on Thursday and Saturday.

East End Rd., Green Cay Marina, 5000 Estate Southgate. ℂ 340/773-9949. www.galleonrestaurant.com. Reservations recommended. Main courses $25–$70; lunch main courses $8–$17. MC, V. Daily 11am–4pm and 6–10pm. Happy hour 4–6pm. Go east on Rte. 82 from Christiansted for 5 min.; after going 1.5km/1 mile past The Buccaneer, turn left into Green Cay Marina.

Sunset Grill 𝒦 (Finds CARIBBEAN/AMERICAN   This informal spot is on the west coast, near Sprat Hall Plantation. It's the best place on the island to combine lunch and a swim. The restaurant has been in business since 1948, feeding both locals and visitors. Try such local dishes as seafood chowder and the fried fish of the day. These dishes have authentic island flavor, perhaps more so than any other place on St. Croix. You can also get salads and burgers. The bread is baked fresh daily. The owners allow free use of the showers and changing rooms.

Rte. 63 (1.5km/1 mile north of Frederiksted). (C) 340/772-5855. Sandwiches $5–$13; main courses $16–$30. MC, V. Daily 11am–9pm, Sun brunch 10:30am.

HITTING THE BEACH

The most celebrated beach is offshore **Buck Island,** part of the U.S. National Park Service network. Buck Island is actually a volcanic islet surrounded by some of the most stunning underwater coral gardens in the Caribbean. The white-sand beaches on the southwest and west coasts are beautiful, but the snorkeling is even better. Buck Island is home to three kinds of sea turtles and more than 250 species of fish. The islet's interior is filled with such plants as cactus, wild frangipani, and pigeonwood. There are picnic areas for those who want to make a day of it. Boat departures are from Kings Wharf in Christiansted; the ride takes half an hour. John F. Kennedy visited the island as a young man in the 1950s, calling it "one of the finest marine gardens in the Caribbean Sea." When he became president, he proclaimed it a national monument. For more information, see the section "Buck Island," later in this chapter.

Your best choice for a beach in Christiansted is the one at the **Hotel on the Cay.** This white-sand strip is on a palm-shaded island. Lying in only 1m (3 ft.) of water, the artificial reef here consists of old car parts and conch shells, and has an array of small tropical reef fish, including sergeant majors and French grunts. If you're a more advanced snorkeler, you can head out a bit to where the reef drops off about 4.5m (15 ft.). Here you can encounter squid, octopus, and eagle rays. To get here, take the ferry from the fort at Christiansted; it runs daily from 7am to midnight. The 4-minute trip costs $3 round-trip, free for guests of the Hotel on the Cay. Eight kilometers (5 miles) west of Christiansted is **The Palms at Pelican Cove,** where some 360m (1,200 ft.) of white sand shaded by palm trees attracts a gay and mixed crowd. Since a reef lies just off the shore, snorkeling conditions are ideal.

We highly recommend **Davis Bay** and **Cane Bay,** with swaying palms, white sand, and good swimming. Because they're on the north shore, these beaches are often windy, and their waters are not always tranquil. The snorkeling at Cane Bay is truly spectacular; you'll see elkhorn and brain corals, all some 225m (750 ft.) off the "Cane Bay Wall." Cane Bay adjoins Route 80 on the north shore. Davis Bay doesn't have a reef; it's more popular among bodysurfers than snorkelers. There are no changing facilities. It's near Carambola Beach Resort.

On Route 63, a short ride north of Frederiksted, lies **Rainbow Beach,** which has white sand and ideal snorkeling conditions. Nearby, also on Route 63, about 5 minutes north of Frederiksted, is another good beach, called **La Grange.** Lounge chairs can be rented here, and there's a bar nearby.

Sandy Point, directly south of Frederiksted, is the largest beach in all the U.S. Virgin Islands. Its waters are shallow and calm, perfect for swimming. Try to concentrate on the sands and not the unattractive zigzagging fences that line the beach. Continue west from the western terminus of the Melvin Evans Highway (Rte. 66).

There's an array of beaches at the east end of the island; they're somewhat difficult to get to, but much less crowded. At **Isaac Bay Beach,** you come upon a tropical paradise, with shallow, calm waters protected by an offshore reef. Snorkelers encounter schools of blue tang, trunkfish, trumpetfish, and other species swimming through forests of sea fans, elkhorn coral, staghorn coral, and other types. If you packed a picnic lunch, this is the spot at which to enjoy it. Windsurfers like **Reef Beach,** which opens onto Teague Bay along Route 82, East End Road, a half-hour ride from Christiansted. You can get food at Duggan's Reef (see the review, above). **Cramer Park** is a special public park operated by the Department of Agriculture. It's lined with sea-grape trees and has a picnic area, a restaurant, and a bar. **Grapetree Beach** is off Route 60 (the South Shore Rd.). Watersports are popular here.

SPORTS & OTHER OUTDOOR PURSUITS

Some of the best snorkeling, diving, and hiking are found on Buck Island. See the section "Buck Island," below.

FISHING   The fishing grounds at **Lang Bank** are about 15km (10 miles) from St. Croix. Here you'll find kingfish, dolphin fish, and wahoo. Using light-tackle boats to glide along the reef, you'll probably turn up jack or bonefish. At **Clover Crest,** in Frederiksted, local anglers fish right from the rocks.

Serious sportfishers can board the *Fantasy,* an 11m (38-ft.) Bertram special. It's anchored at King's Alley Hotel at 59 Kings Wharf in Christiansted. Reservations can be made by calling © **340/773-2628** during the day. The cost for up to six passengers is $500 for 4 hours, $600 for 6 hours, and $800 for 8 hours with bait and tackle, and drinks included.

GOLF   St. Croix has the best golf in the U.S. Virgins. Guests staying on St. John and St. Thomas often fly over for a round on one of the island's three courses.

Robert Trent Jones, Sr., created the **Carambola Golf Course,** on the northeast side of St. Croix (© **340/778-5638;** www.golfcarambola.com), calling it "the loveliest course I ever designed." It's been likened to a botanical garden. Golfing authorities consider the par-3 holes here the best in the Tropics. The greens fees of $95 in winter, or $65 in summer, allow you to play as many holes as you like. Carts are included.

The Buccaneer, Gallows Bay (© **340/712-2144**), 5km (3 miles) east of Christiansted, has a challenging 5,685-yard, 18-hole course with panoramic vistas. Nonguests of this deluxe resort pay $100 in winter or $60 off season, which includes use of a cart.

The **Reef,** on the east end of the island at Teague Bay (© **340/773-8844**), is a 3,100-yard, 9-hole course, charging greens fees of $20 for 9 holes and $35 for 18 holes. Golf carts can also be rented at an additional $12 for 9 holes or $18 for 18 holes. The longest hole here is a 465-yard par 5.

HIKING   Scrub-covered hills make up much of St. Croix's landscape. The island's western district, however, includes a dense, 6-hectare (15-acre) forest known as the **"Rain Forest"** (though technically it's not a rainforest). The network of footpaths here provides some of the best nature walks in the Caribbean. For more details on hiking in this area, see the section, "The 'Rain Forest,'" below. **Buck Island** (see the section "Buck Island," below), just off St. Croix, also offers some wonderful nature trails.

The **St. Croix Environmental Association,** Arawak Building, Suite 3, Gallows Bay (© **340/773-1989;** www.stxenvironmental.org), has scheduled hikes costing $10 per person.

HORSEBACK RIDING   **Paul and Jill's Equestrian Stables,** 2 Sprat Hall Estate, Route 58 (© **340/772-2880**), the largest equestrian stable in the Virgin Islands, is known throughout the Caribbean for its horses. It's set on the sprawling grounds of the island's oldest plantation great house. The operators lead scenic trail rides through the forests, along the beach, and past ruins of abandoned 18th-century plantations and sugar mills, to the tops of the hills of St. Croix's western end. Beginners and experienced riders alike are welcome. A 2-hour trail ride costs $60. Tours usually depart daily in winter at 10:30am and 3pm, and in the off season at 4pm, with slight variations according to demand. Reserve at least a day in advance.

KAYAKING   The beauty of St. Croix is best seen on a kayak tour such as those offered by **Caribbean Adventure Tours** (© 340/778-1522). You use stable, sit-on-top ocean kayaks, which are a blast. These enable you to traverse the tranquil waters of Salt River of Columbus landfall fame and enjoy the park's ecology and wildlife. You also go into secluded estuaries and mangrove thickets. Some of the landscape was used as ancient Indian burial grounds. Highlights are snorkeling on a pristine beach and paddling to where Christopher Columbus and his crew came ashore some 500 years ago. The tour, lasting 3 hours, costs $45 per person and includes water and a light snack.

SAFARI TOURS   The best are run by **St. Croix Safari Tours** (© 340/773-6700) in a 25-passenger open-air bus tour led by a hip tour guide who knows all about the botany, cuisine, and history of the island. Tours crisscross the island with stops at plantation houses, historic Frederiksted, the Salt River landfall of Columbus, and a drive through the rainforest, with a stop for lunch. There are lots of photo ops. The cost of the tour is $38 per person, including admission fees to the botanical garden, rum factory, and museum.

SNORKELING & SCUBA DIVING ☆☆   Sponge life, black coral (the finest in the West Indies), and steep drop-offs near the shoreline make St. Croix a snorkeling and diving paradise. The island is home to the largest living reef in the Caribbean, including the fabled north-shore wall that begins in 9m (30 ft.) of water and drops to 4,000m (13,000 ft.), sometimes straight down. See "Hitting the Beach," above, for information on good snorkeling beaches. The **St. Croix Water Sports Center** (see "Windsurfing," below) rents snorkeling equipment for $20 per day if your hotel doesn't supply it.

Buck Island ☆☆ is a major scuba-diving site, with a visibility of some 30m (100 ft.). It also has an underwater snorkeling trail. All the outfitters offer scuba and snorkeling tours to Buck Island. See the section "Buck Island," below.

Other favorite dive sites include the historic **Salt River Canyon** (northwest of Christiansted at Salt River Bay), which is for advanced divers. Submerged canyon walls are covered with purple tube sponges, deep-water gorgonians, and black coral saplings. You'll see schools of yellowtail snapper, turtles, and spotted eagle rays. We also like the gorgeous coral gardens of **Scotch Banks** (north of Christiansted), and **Eagle Ray** (also north of Christiansted), the latter so named because of the rays that cruise along the wall there. **Cane Bay** ☆☆ is known for its coral canyons.

Davis Bay is the site of the 3,600m-deep (12,000-ft.) Puerto Rico Trench. **Northstar Reef,** at the east end of Davis Bay, is a spectacular wall dive, recommended for intermediate or experienced divers only. The wall here is covered with stunning brain corals and staghorn thickets. At some 15m (50 ft.) down, a sandy shelf leads to a cave where giant green moray eels hang out.

At **Butler Bay,** to the north of the pier on the west shore, three ships were wrecked: the *Suffolk Maid,* the *Northwind,* and the *Rosaomaira,* the last sitting in 30m (100 ft.) of water. These wrecks form the major part of an artificial reef system that also contains abandoned trucks and cars. This site is recommended for intermediate or experienced divers.

Anchor Dive, Salt River National Park (© **800/523-3483** in the U.S., or 340/778-1522; www.anchordivestcroix.com), is located within the most popular dive destination in St. Croix. It operates two boats. The staff offers complete instruction, from resort courses through full certification, as well as night dives. A resort course is $90, with a two-tank dive going for $80. Dive packages begin at $215 for six dives.

Another recommended outfitter is the **Cane Bay Dive Shop** (© 340/773-9913).

TENNIS   Some authorities rate the tennis at **The Buccaneer** ⚓⚓, Gallows Bay (© 340/773-3036), as the best in the Caribbean. This resort offers a choice of eight courts, two lit for night play, all open to the public. Nonguests pay $8 daytime, $10 nighttime per person per hour; you must call to reserve a court at least a day in advance. A tennis pro is available for lessons, and there's also a pro shop.

WINDSURFING   Head for the **St. Croix Water Sports Center** (© 340/773-7060), on a small offshore island in Christiansted Harbor and part of the Hotel on the Cay. It's open daily from 9am to 5pm. Here you can rent snorkeling equipment for $20 per day and Yamahas that seat two for $60 per half-hour.

EXPLORING ST. CROIX

Taxi tours are the ideal way to explore the island. The cost is around $80 for 2 hours or $100 for 3 hours for up to 3 passengers. All prices should be negotiated in advance. For more information, call the **St. Croix Taxi Association** at © 340/778-1088; www.stcroixtaxi.com.

CHRISTIANSTED

One of the most picturesque towns in the Caribbean, **Christiansted** is an old, handsomely restored (or at least in the process of being restored) Danish port. On the northeastern shore of the island, on a coral-bound bay, the town is filled with Danish buildings erected by prosperous merchants in the booming 18th century. These red-roofed structures are often washed in pink, ocher, or yellow. Arcades over the sidewalks provide shade for shoppers. The whole area around the harbor front has been designated a historic site, including **Government House** (© 340/773-1404), which is looked after by the U.S. National Park Service.

Fort Christiansvaern   This fortress overlooking the harbor is the best-preserved colonial fortification in the Virgin Islands. It's maintained as a historic monument by the U.S. National Park Service. Its original four-pronged, star-shaped design was in accordance with the most advanced military planning of its era. The fort is now the site of a military museum, which has exhibits on local Danish military history on the island from the late 1800s to 1917.

On the waterfront. © 340/773-1460. Admission $3 (also includes admission to the Steeple Building). Mon–Fri 8am–4:45pm, Sat–Sun 9am–4:45pm.

Steeple Building   This building's full name is the Church of Lord God of Sabaoth. It was built in 1753 as St. Croix's first Lutheran church, and it was deconsecrated in 1831; the building subsequently served as a bakery, a hospital, and a school. Today, it houses exhibits relating to island history and culture.

On the waterfront off Hospital St. © 340/773-1460. Admission $3 (also includes admission to Fort Christiansvaern). Daily 8am–4:45pm.

FREDERIKSTED

This former Danish settlement at the western end of the island, about 27km (17 miles) from Christiansted, is a sleepy port town that comes to life only when a cruise ship docks at its shoreline. Frederiksted was destroyed by a fire in 1879. Its citizens

The St. Croix Heritage Trail

A trail that leads into the past, **St. Croix Heritage Trail** (© **340/772-0598**; www.stcroixheritagetrail.com), launched at the millennium, helps visitors relive the Danish colonial history of the island. All you need are a brochure and map, available at the tourist office in Christiansted (p. 725). This 116-km (72-mile) itinerary consists mainly of existing roadways and includes a combination of asphalt-covered roads suitable for driving, and narrow woodland trails which must be navigated on foot. The brochure will identify everything you're seeing. Many aficionados opt to drive along the route whenever practical, descending onto the footpaths wherever indicated, then returning to their cars for the continuation of the tour. En route, you'll be exposed to one of the Caribbean's densest concentrations of historical and cultural sites.

The route connects the two major towns of Christiansted and Frederiksted, going past the sites of former sugar plantations. It traverses the entire 45km (28-mile) length of St. Croix, passing cattle farms, suburban communities, even industrial complexes and resorts. It's not all manicured and pretty, but much is scenic and worth the drive. Allow at least a day for this trail, with stops along the way.

Nearly everyone gets out of the car at **Point Udall**, the easternmost point under the U.S. flag in the Caribbean. You'll pass an eclectic mix of churches and even a prison.

The highlight of the trail is the **Estate Mount Washington Plantation** (p. 742), a strikingly well-preserved sugar plantation. Another highlight is **Estate Whim Plantation** (p. 742), one of the best of the restored great houses with a museum and gift shop. Another stop is along **Salt River Bay**, which cuts into the northern shoreline. This is the site of Columbus's landfall in 1493.

Of course, you'll want to stop and get to know the locals. We recommend a refreshment break at **Smithens Market.** Lying off Queen Mary Highway, vendors here offer freshly squeezed sugar-cane juice and sell locally grown fruits and homemade chutneys.

subsequently rebuilt it with wood frames and clapboards on top of the old Danish stone and yellow-brick foundations.

Most visitors begin their tour at russet-colored **Fort Frederik,** at the northern end of Frederiksted next to the cruise-ship pier (© **340/772-2021**). This fort, completed in 1760, is said to have been the first to salute the flag of the new United States. When a U.S. brigantine anchored at port in Frederiksted hoisted a homemade Old Glory, the fort returned the salute with cannon fire, violating the rules of neutrality. It was also here on July 3, 1848, that Governor-General Peter von Scholten emancipated the slaves in the Danish West Indies in response to a slave uprising led by a young man named Moses "Buddhoe" Gottlieb. A bust of Buddhoe now stands here. The fort has been restored to its 1840 appearance and is today a national historic landmark. You can explore the courtyard and stables. A **local history museum** has been installed in what was once the Garrison Room. Admission is $3 or free for children 15 and under. It's open Monday to Friday from 8:30am to 3:30pm.

The **Customs House,** just east of the fort, is an 18th-century building with a 19th-century two-story gallery. On the ground floor is the **visitor bureau** (© **340/772-0357**), where you can pick up a free map of the town.

BUCK ISLAND 🐟🐟🐟

The crystal-clear water and white-coral sand of **Buck Island,** a satellite of St. Croix, are legendary. Some call this island the single most important attraction of the Caribbean. Only .5km (⅓ mile) wide and 1.5km (1 mile) long, Buck Island lies 2.5km (1½ miles) off the northeastern coast of St. Croix. A barrier reef here shelters many reef fish, including queen angelfish and smooth trunkfish. In years past, Morgan, Blackbeard, and Captain Kidd frequented the island.

Buck Island's greatest attraction is its **underwater snorkeling trails,** which ring part of the island and provide some of the most beautiful underwater views in the Caribbean. Plan on spending at least two-thirds of a day at this famous ecological site maintained by the U.S. National Park Service. There are also many **labyrinths and grottoes for scuba divers.** The sandy **beach** has picnic tables and barbecue pits, as well as restrooms and a small changing room.

You can follow **hiking trails** through the tropical vegetation that covers the island. Circumnavigating the island on foot takes about 2 hours. Buck Island's trails meander from several points along its coastline to its sunny summit, affording views over nearby St. Croix. *A couple of warnings:* Wear lots of sunscreen. Even more important, don't touch every plant you see. The island's western edge has groves of poisonous manchineel trees, whose leaves, bark, and fruit cause extreme irritation to human skin that comes into contact with them.

Small boats run between St. Croix and Buck Island. Nearly all charters provide snorkeling equipment and allow for 1½ hours of snorkeling and swimming. **Caribbean Sea Adventures,** in the King Christian Hotel, 59 King's Wharf, Christiansted (© **340/773-2628**), conducts two different types of tours. The first option is a half-day tour aboard a glass-bottom boat departing from the King Christian Hotel, daily from 9:30am to 1pm and 1:30 to 5pm; it costs $40 per person. The second is a full-day tour, offered daily from 10:30am to 4pm on a 12m (40-ft.) trimaran for $60. Included in this excursion is a box lunch.

Captain Heinz (© **340/773-3161** or 340/773-4041) is an Austrian-born skipper with more than 25 years of sailing experience. His trimaran, *Teroro II,* leaves the Green Cay Marina "H" Dock at 9am and 2pm, never filled with more than 23 passengers. This snorkeling trip costs $60 for adults, $40 for children 11 and under. The captain is not only a skilled sailor but also a considerate host. He will even take you around the outer reef, which the other guides do not, for an unforgettable underwater experience.

THE "RAIN FOREST" 🐟

The island's western district contains a dense, 6-hectare (15-acre) forest, called the "Rain Forest" (though it's not a real one). The area is thick with mahogany trees, *kapok* (silk-cotton) trees, turpentine (red-birch) trees, *samaan* (rain) trees, and all kinds of ferns and vines. Sweet limes, mangoes, hog plums, and breadfruit trees, all of which have grown in the wild since the days of the plantations, are also interspersed among the larger trees. Crested hummingbirds, pearly eyed thrashers, green-throated caribs, yellow warblers, and perky but drably camouflaged banana quits nest here. The 45m-high (150-ft.) Creque Dam is the major man-made sight in the area.

The "Rain Forest" is private property, but the owner lets visitors go inside to explore. To experience its charm, some people opt to drive along Route 76 (also known as Mahogany Rd.), stopping beside the footpaths that meander off on either side of the highway into dry riverbeds and glens. Stick to the most worn footpaths. You can also hike along some of the little-traveled four-wheel-drive roads in the area. Three of the best for hiking are the **Creque Dam Road** (routes 58/78), the **Scenic Road** (Rte. 78), and the **Western Scenic Road** (routes 63/78).

Our favorite trail in this area takes about 2½ hours one-way. From Frederiksted, drive north on Route 63 until you reach Creque Dam Road, where you turn right, park the car, and start walking. About .5km (1 mile) past the Creque Dam, you'll be deep within the forest's magnificent flora and fauna. Continue along the trail until you come to the Western Scenic Road. Eventually, you reach Mahogany Road (Rte. 76), near St. Croix Leap Project. Hikers rate this trail moderate in difficulty.

You could also begin near the junction of Creque Dam Road and Scenic Road. From here, your trek will cover a broad triangular swath, heading north and then west along Scenic Road. First, the road will rise, and then descend toward the coastal lighthouse of the island's extreme northwestern tip, **Hams Bluff.** Most trekkers decide to retrace their steps after about 45 minutes of northwesterly hiking. Real die-hards, however, will continue all the way to the coastline, then head south along the coastal road (Butler Bay Rd.), and finally head east along Creque Dam Road to their starting point at the junction of Creque Dam Road and Scenic Road. Embark on this longer expedition only if you're really prepared for a hike lasting about 5 hours.

SANDY POINT WILDLIFE REFUGE ✦

St. Croix's rarely visited southwestern tip is composed of salt marshes, tidal pools, and low vegetation inhabited by birds, turtles, and other wildlife. More than 5km (3 miles) of ecologically protected coastline lie between Sandy Point (the island's westernmost tip) and the shallow waters of the Westend Saltpond. The area is home to colonies of green, leatherback, and hawksbill turtles. It's one of only two such places in U.S. waters. It's also home to thousands of birds, including herons, brown pelicans, Caribbean martins, black-necked stilts, and white-crowned pigeons. As for flora, Sandy Point gave its name to a rare form of orchids, a brown/purple variety.

This wildlife refuge is only open on Saturday and Sunday from 10am to 4pm. To get here, drive to the end of Route 66 (Melvin Evans Hwy.) and continue down a gravel road. For guided weekend visits, call ✆ **340/773-4554.**

AROUND THE ISLAND

North of Frederiksted, you can drop in at **Sprat Hall,** the island's oldest plantation, or continue along to the "Rain Forest" (see above). Most visitors come to the area to see the jagged estuary of the northern coastline's **Salt River.** The Salt River was where Columbus landed on November 14, 1493. Marking the 500th anniversary of Columbus's arrival, Congress created the 365-hectare (912-acre) **Salt River Bay National Historical Park and Ecological Preserve.** The park contains the site of the original Carib village explored by Columbus and his men, including the only ceremonial ball court ever discovered in the Lesser Antilles. Also within the park is the largest mangrove forest in the Virgin Islands, sheltering many endangered animals and plants, plus an underwater canyon attracting divers from around the world.

Estate Mount Washington Plantation is the island's best-preserved sugar plantation and a highlight along the St. Croix Heritage Trail. It flourished from 1780 to 1820 when St. Croix was the second-largest producer of sugar in the West Indies. The on-site private residence is closed to the public, but you can arrange to go on a self-guided tour of the 5 hectares (13 acres). There is no admission charge, although donations are appreciated. Know that this is one of St. Croix's more loosely organized cultural attractions, but if you phone in advance (© **340/772-1026**), someone might give you permission. The plantation site lies at the very southwestern tip of the island, off Route 63, 1.5km (1 mile) inland from the highway that runs along the Frederiksted coast.

Cruzan Rum Factory   This factory distills the famous Virgin Islands rum, which some consider the finest in the world. Guided tours depart from the visitors' pavilion; call for reservations and information. There's also a gift shop.

Estate Diamond W. Airport Rd., Rte. 64, Frederiksted. © 340/692-2280. Admission $4. Tours given Mon–Fri 9–11:30am and 1–4:15pm.

Estate Whim Plantation Museum   This restored great house is unique among the many sugar plantations whose ruins dot the island. It's comprised of only three rooms. With 1m-thick (3-ft.) walls made of stone, coral, and molasses, the house resembles a luxurious European château. A division of Baker Furniture Company used the Whim Plantation's collection of models for one of its most successful reproductions, the "Whim Museum–West Indies Collection." Upscale reproductions of some of the furniture on display within the Whim Plantation, plus others from the Caribbean, are for sale on-site. Slightly different inventories are available from an associated store in downtown Christiansted: **St. Croix Landmarks Museum Store,** 6 Company St. (© **340/713-8102**). For more information, refer to "Shopping," below.

The ruins of the plantation's sugar-processing plant, complete with a restored windmill, also remain.

Centerline Rd. (3km/2 miles east of Frederiksted). © 340/772-0598. Admission $8 adults, $4 children. Mon–Sat 10am–4pm.

St. George Village Botanical Garden   This is a 6.5-hectare (16-acre) Eden of tropical trees, shrubs, vines, and flowers. The garden is a feast for the eye and the camera, from the entrance drive bordered by royal palms and bougainvillea to the towering kapok and tamarind trees. It was built around the ruins of a 19th-century

---

⌒Moments   The Easternmost Point of the Caribbean

The rocky promontory of **Point Udall,** jutting into the Caribbean Sea, is the easternmost point under the U.S flag in the Caribbean. Die-hards go out to see the sunrise, but considering the climb is via a rutted dirt road, you may want to wait until there's more light before heading here. Once at the top, you'll be rewarded with one of the best views in the U.S. Virgin Islands. On the way to the lookout point, you'll see **"The Castle,"** a local architectural oddity, owned by the island's most prominent socialite, the Contessa Nadia Farbo Navarro. Point Udall is signposted along Route 82.

sugar-cane workers' village. Self-guided walking-tour maps are available at the entrance to the garden's great hall. Facilities include restrooms and a gift shop.

127 Estate St., 1 St. George, Frederiksted (just north of Centerline Rd., 6km/4 miles east of Frederiksted). © 340/692-2874. www.sgvbg.org. Admission $6 adults, $1 children 12 and under; donations welcome. Daily 9am–5pm.

SHOPPING ☆☆☆

In **Christiansted,** the emphasis is on hole-in-the-wall boutiques selling one-of-a-kind merchandise. The selection of handmade items is especially strong. Knowing that it can't compete with the volume of Charlotte Amalie on St. Thomas, Christiansted has forged its own identity as the chic spot for merchandise in the Caribbean. All its shops are within about a half-mile of each other. **King's Alley Complex** is a pink-sided compound filled with the densest concentration of shops on St. Croix.

Frederiksted has also become a popular shopping destination. Its urban mall appeals to cruise-ship passengers arriving at Frederiksted Pier. The mall is on a 15m (50-ft.) strip of land between Strand and King streets, the town's bustling main thoroughfare.

Below are our favorite shops in Christiansted.

The operators of **Folk Art Traders** ☆, 1B Queen Cross St. (© **340/773-1900**), travel throughout the Caribbean ("in the bush") to add to their unique collection of local art and folk-art treasures: Carnival masks, pottery, ceramics, original paintings, and hand-wrought jewelry. There's nothing else like it in the Virgin Islands.

At the hip and eclectic **From the Gecko,** 1233 Queen Cross St. (© **340/778-9433**), you can find anything from hand-painted local cottons and silks to that old West Indian staple, batiks. We found the Indonesian collection here among the most imaginative in the U.S. Virgin Islands—everything from glass jewelry to hemp linens.

Many Hands, 102 Strand St. (© **340/773-1990**), sells locally made pottery, art, and handmade jewelry. The collection of local paintings is intriguing, as is the year-round "Christmas tree."

For an upscale insight into the 19th-century aesthetics of plantation life on St. Croix, head to the well-organized and genteel **St. Croix Landmarks Museum Store** ☆, 6 Company St. (© **340/713-8102**). It focuses on reproductions of some of the antiques on display at the Whim Plantation, recommended above. Also available are framed engravings of the kind of botany you'd expect on St. Croix, paperweights, books, brass candlesticks, and gift items redolent with memories and references to the West Indies.

Purple Papaya, 39 Strand St., Pan Am Pavilion (© **340/713-9412**), is the best place to go for inexpensive island gifts. It has the biggest array of embroidered T-shirts and sweatshirts on island. Although you're in the Caribbean and not Hawaii, there is a large selection of Hawaiian shirts and dresses, along with beachwear for the whole family, plus island souvenirs.

Royal Poinciana, 1111 Strand St. (© **340/773-9892**), looks like an antique apothecary. You'll find hot sauces, seasoning blends for gumbos, island herbal teas, Antillean coffees, and a scented array of soaps, toiletries, lotions, and shampoos. There's also a selection of museum-reproduction greeting cards and calendars, plus educational but fun gifts for children.

About 60% of the merchandise at **Gone Tropical,** 5 Company St. (© **340/773-4696;** www.gonetropical.com), is made in Indonesia (usually Bali). Prices of new, semiantique, or antique sofas, beds, chests, tables, mirrors, and decorative carvings are the same as (and sometimes less than) those of new furniture in conventional stores. Gone Tropical also sells art objects, jewelry, batiks, candles, and baskets.

The small West Indian cottage of **Crucian Gold,** 59 Kings Wharf (© 877/773-5241; www.cruciangold.com), holds the gold and silver creations of island-born Brian Bishop. His most popular item is the Crucian bracelet, which contains a "True Lovers' Knot" in its design. The shop also sells hand-tied knots (bound in gold wire), rings, pendants, and earrings.

Sonya Hough of **Sonya Ltd.,** 1 Company St. (© 340/778-8605; www.sonyaltd. com), has a group of loyal local fans who wouldn't leave home without wearing one of her bracelets. She's most famous for the sterling silver and gold versions of her C-clasp bracelet. Locals say that if the cup of the "C" is turned toward your heart, you're taken; if the cup is turned outward, you're available. Prices range from $30 to $3,100.

Coconut Vine, Strand Street (© 340/773-1991), is one of the most colorful and popular little boutiques on the island. Hand-painted batiks for both men and women are the specialty.

ST. CROIX AFTER DARK

St. Croix doesn't have the nightlife of St. Thomas. To find the action, you might have to consult the publication *St. Croix This Week,* which is distributed free to cruise-ship and air passengers and is also available at the tourist office.

Try, if it's taking place, to catch a performance of one of the **Quadrille Dances** 🏝🏝 performed by either of two independent, part-time dance troupes based on St. Croix. Hours, performance details, and organization of these dance groups vary widely from season to season, but the basic steps associated with *La Quadrille* have changed little since the plantation days. The women wear long dresses, white gloves, and turbans, while the men wear flamboyant shirts, sashes, and tight black trousers. At one of these performances, after you've learned the (relatively basic) steps, you might be invited to join the dancers on the floor. Ask at your hotel if and when one of these loosely organized dance troupes might be performing, if at all, during your visit.

If you enjoy gambling, visit the **Divi Carina Bay Casino,** 35 Estate Turner Hole (© 340/773-7529; www.carinabay.com). Set on the grounds of the Divi Carina Bay Resort, with which its management is not associated, it's sheltered from the glaring Caribbean sunlight with a glistening white dome inspired by the architecture of the North African desert. Inside, within a decor inspired by the Moroccan casbah, you'll find the only casino in the U.S. Virgin Islands, with 3,000m (10,000 ft.) of gaming space, a cafe-style bistro and bar, at least 20 gaming tables, and 300 jangling slot machines. Entrance is free. It's open Monday to Thursday from noon to 4am; from Friday to Sunday, 24 hours a day.

If you're looking to hear some live music, try **Blue Moon,** 7 Strand St. (© 340/772-2222), a hip little dive and a good bistro. It's currently the hottest spot in Frederiksted on Fridays, when a five-piece ensemble entertains. On Sunday a live jazz trio performs. There's no cover.

The **Terrace Lounge,** in The Buccaneer, Route 82, Estate Shoys (© 340/773-2100), off the main dining room of one of St. Croix's most upscale hotels, welcomes some of the Caribbean's finest entertainers every night, often including a full band.

2 Plus 2 Disco, at the La Grande Princess (© 340/773-3710), is a real Caribbean dance club. It features the regional sounds of the islands, not only calypso and reggae but also salsa and soca (a hybrid of calypso and reggae). Usually there's a DJ, except on weekends when local bands are brought in. The place isn't fancy or large. Hours are Thursday and Sunday from 10pm to 1am and Friday and Saturday from 9pm to either 4 or 5am. The cover is $10 when there's a live band.

Elizabeth's at the Palms, 4126 La Grande Princesse (© **340/719-0735**), is set in a resort about 5km (3 miles) northwest of Christiansted. It caters both to straight guests as well as gays and lesbians. You can sit at tables overlooking the ocean or around an open-centered mahogany bar, adjacent to a gazebo. Excellent tropical drinks are mixed here. It is open daily from 7pm until the last customer leaves.

4 St. John ★★★

A few miles east of St. Thomas, across a glistening, turquoise channel known as Pillsbury Sound, lies St. John, the smallest and least densely populated of the three main U.S. Virgin Islands.

St. John is a wonder of unspoiled beauty. Along its rocky coastline are beautiful crescent-shaped bays and white-sand beaches, and the interior is no less impressive. The variety of wildlife here fascinates naturalists around the world. And there are miles of serpentine hiking trails, leading past the ruins of 18th-century Danish plantations to magnificent panoramic views. At scattered intervals along the trails, you can even find mysteriously geometric petroglyphs, of unknown age and origin, incised into boulders and cliffs.

Today, St. John (unlike the other U.S. islands) remains truly pristine, its preservation rigidly enforced by the U.S. Park Service. Thanks to the efforts of Laurance Rockefeller, who purchased acres of land here and donated them to the United States, the island's shoreline waters, as well as more than half its surface area, make up the **Virgin Islands National Park.** The hundreds of coral gardens that surround St. John are protected rigorously—any attempt to damage or remove coral from the water is punishable with substantial and strictly enforced fines.

Despite the unspoiled beauty of much of St. John, the island manages to provide visitors with modern amenities and travel services, including a sampling of restaurants, car-rental kiosks, yacht-supply facilities, hotels, and campgrounds. **Cinnamon Bay,** founded by the U.S. National Park Service in 1964, is the most famous campsite in the Caribbean. In addition, the roads are well maintained, and there's even a small commercial center, **Cruz Bay,** on the island's western tip. Don't come here for nightlife; St. John is sleepy, and that's why people love it.

ST. JOHN ESSENTIALS

GETTING THERE   To get to St. John, you take a ferry from St. Thomas. (There are also ferries from the British Virgin Islands.) See the "Getting There" section at the beginning of this chapter for information on how to get to St. Thomas, and for details about the ferry to St. John.

VISITOR INFORMATION   The **tourist office** (© **340/776-6450**) is located near the Battery, a 1735 fort that's a short walk from the St. Thomas ferry dock. It's open Monday to Friday from 8am to 5pm. A **National Park visitor center** (© **340/776-6201**) is also found at Cruz Bay, offering two floors of information and wall-mounted wildlife displays, plus a video presentation about the culture of the Virgin Islands. Open daily 8am to 4:30pm.

GETTING AROUND   The most popular way to get around is via the local **Vitran** (© **340/774-0165**) service, the same company that runs the buses on St. Thomas. Buses run between Cruz Bay and Coral Bay, costing $1 for adults and 75¢ for children.

An open-air **surrey-style taxi** is more fun, however. Typical fares are $9 to Trunk Bay, $11 to Cinnamon Bay, or $14 to Maho Bay. Between midnight and 6am, fares are increased by 50%. Call © **340/693-7530** for more information.

The island's undeveloped roads offer some of the best views anywhere. Because of this, many people opt to rent a vehicle (sometimes with four-wheel drive) to tour the island. Most visitors need a car for only a day or two. *Remember:* Drive on the left and follow posted speed limits, which are generally very low.

Unless you need to carry luggage, which should probably be locked away in a trunk, you might consider one of the sturdy, open-sided, jeeplike vehicles that offer the best view of the surroundings and are the most fun way to tour St. John. Note that most of these vehicles have manual transmission, which can be especially tricky in a car built to drive on the left side of the road. They cost $76 to $84 a day.

The largest car-rental agency on St. John is **Hertz** (© **800/654-3131** in the U.S. and Canada, or 340/776-6171; www.hertz.com). If you want a local firm, try **St. John Car Rental,** across from the Catholic church in Cruz Bay (© **340/776-6103;** www. stjohncarrental.com).

FAST FACTS   If you need a **pharmacy,** or want to purchase film, books, and other daily necessities, try **Chelsea Drug Store,** in the Marketplace Shopping Center, Route 104, Cruz Bay (© **340/776-4888**). It's open Monday to Saturday from 8:30am to 6pm, and Sunday 10am to 4:30pm.

If you need a **hospital,** go to **St. John Myrah Keating Smith Community Health Clinic,** 3B Sussanaberg (© **340/693-8900**), which can be reached along Route 10, about 3km (2 miles) east of Cruz Bay.

ACCOMMODATIONS

There are actually more villa and condo beds available on St. John than there are hotel beds. These units are spacious and comfortable, as well as private, and they often come with fully equipped kitchens, dining areas, bedrooms, and such amenities as VCRs and patio grills. Rentals range from large multiroom resort homes to simply decorated one-bedroom condos. In addition to the condo and villa complexes reviewed below, **Caribbean Villas & Resorts** (© **800/338-0987**; fax 207/510-6308, www.caribbean villa.com), the island's biggest real-estate agency, is an excellent choice. Villa Rentals begin at $1,950 weekly in winter, $1,350 weekly off-season, though private homes are more expensive.

VERY EXPENSIVE

Caneel Bay 🌴🌴🌴   Conceived by megamillionaire Laurance S. Rockefeller in 1956, this is the Caribbean's first eco-resort. Though long one of the Caribbean's premier resorts, Caneel Bay is definitely not one of the most luxurious. A devoted fan once told us, "It's like living at summer camp." That means no phones or TVs in the rooms. Nevertheless, the movers and shakers of the world continue to come here, though younger people tend to head elsewhere. To attract more families, young children are now allowed. Go to Westin St. John Resort (see below) for glitz and glitter; head here for a touch of class.

The resort lies on a 68-hectare (170-acre) portion of the National Park, offering a choice of seven beaches. Surrounded by lush greenery, the main buildings are strung along the bays, with a Caribbean lounge and dining room at the core. Other buildings housing guest rooms stand along the beaches. Try to get one of the five rooms in cottage no. 7, overlooking two of the most idyllic beaches, Scott and Paradise. This

St. John

Caneel Bay **5**
Cinnamon Bay
Campground **6**
Concordia Eco-Tents **10**
Estate Concordia
Studios **9**
Estate Lindholm
Bed & Breakfast **9**
Garden by the Sea
Bed & Breakfast **3**
Harmony Studios **8**
The Inn at Tamarind
Court **2**
Maho Bay Camps **7**
Westin St. John Resort
& Villas **1**

was the former beach house owned and occupied by Laurance R. himself. Now it's a cluster of five different accommodations, the most upscale at the entire resort. Most rooms, however, are set back on low cliffs or headlands. The decor within is understated, with Indonesian wicker furniture, hand-woven fabrics, sisal mats, and plantation fans. All have neatly kept bathrooms with showers.

The resort has consistently maintained a high level of cuisine, often quite formal for the laid-back Caribbean. See "Dining," below for more information on the Equator.

Virgin Islands National Park, St. John, U.S.V.I. 00831. © **888/767-3966** in the U.S., or 340/776-6111. Fax 340/693-8280. www.caneelbay.com. 166 units. Winter $450–$1,400 double; off season $375–$1,100 double. MAP (breakfast and dinner) $90 per person, per day extra. 1 child under 13 can stay free in parent's room. AE, MC, V. **Amenities:** 4 restaurants; 2 bars; outdoor pool; 11 tennis courts; fitness center; spa; boating; deep-sea fishing; dive shop; kayaks; snorkeling; Sunfish sailboats; windsurfing; children's center; business center; limited room service; babysitting; laundry service; dry cleaning; nonsmoking rooms; rooms for those w/limited mobility; afternoon tea. *In room:* A/C, ceiling fan; minibar, beverage maker, hair dryer, iron, safe, no phone.

Westin St. John Resort & Villas ★★★ (Kids)   Come here if you like megaresort flash and glitter as opposed to the "old-school ties" of Caneel Bay (see above). This is the most architecturally dramatic and visually appealing hotel on St. John. The complex is set on 14 hectares (34 acres) of gently sloping, intricately landscaped grounds on the southwest side of the island. It consists of 21 cedar-roofed postmodern buildings, each with ziggurat-shaped angles, soaring ceilings, and large windows. Herringbone-patterned brick walkways connect the gardens (with 400 palms imported from Puerto Rico) to the 360m (1,200-ft.) white-sand beach and one of the largest pools in the Virgin Islands. Some of the stylish accommodations contain fan-shaped windows and curved ceilings. Most units open onto private balconies, and some have their own whirlpools. All bedrooms have full, deluxe bathrooms. In 2006 and 2007, Westin converted 108 of their guest rooms into villas, the latter offering more space and coming with a full kitchenette.

Cuisine is more versatile here than at Caneel Bay, but not always as good. Expect nouvelle cuisine, buffets, and even New York–deli sandwiches.

Great Cruz Bay, St. John, U.S.V.I. 00831. © **888/627-7206** in the U.S., or 340/693-8000. Fax 340/779-4500. www.westinresortstjohn.com. 266 units. Winter $1,399 1-bedroom suite, $1,849 2-bedroom townhouse, $769 studio villa, $1,449 1-bedroom villa, $1,969 2-bedroom villa, $2,389 3-bedroom villa; Off-season $1,209 1-bedroom suite, $1,259 2-bedroom townhouse, $579 studio villa, $1,259 1-bedroom villa, $1,779 2-bedroom villa, $2,199 3-bedroom villa. AE, DC, DISC, MC, V. Round-trip shuttle and private ferryboat transfers from St. Thomas airport $85 per adult, $65 per child. **Amenities:** 4 restaurants; 2 bars; outdoor pool; nearby golf; 6 lit tennis courts; fitness center; sauna; dive shop; fishing; sailboats; snorkeling; windsurfing; hiking; children's programs; business center; 24-hr. room service; babysitting; laundry service; nonsmoking rooms; rooms for those w/limited mobility. *In room:* A/C, TV, dataport, minibar, kitchenette (in some), Jacuzzi (in some), beverage maker, hair dryer, iron, safe.

MODERATE/EXPENSIVE

Estate Concordia Studios   This environmentally sensitive 20-hectare (50-acre) development has been widely praised for its integration with the local ecosystem. Its elevated structures were designed to coexist with the stunning southern edge of St. John. The secluded property is nestled on a low cliff above a salt pond, surrounded by hundreds of pristine National Park acres. It's best for those with rental vehicles. Each building was designed to protect mature trees and is connected to its neighbors with boardwalks. The nine studios are contained in five postmodern cottages. Each unit has a kitchen, a shower-only bathroom, a balcony, and a ceiling fan; some have an extra bedroom. On-site management assists with activity suggestions. For information on the on-site **Eco-Tents,** refer to "Campgrounds," below.

20–27 Estate Concordia, Coral Bay, St. John, U.S.V.I. 00830. © **800/392-9004** in the U.S. and Canada, 212/472-9453 or 340/776-6226. Fax 340/776-6504. www.maho.org. 9 units. Winter $140–$215 studio for 2; off season $100–$155 studio for 2. Extra person $25 winter, $15 off season. MC, V. **Amenities:** Outdoor pool; coin-operated laundry. *In room:* Ceiling fan, kitchen, no phone.

Estate Lindholm Bed & Breakfast ✦ *Finds*

The island's best B&B grew out of an estate originally settled by Dutch planters in the 1720s. Set amongst the Danish ruins, Estate Lindholm is a charming guesthouse on a hill overlooking Cruz Bay, each of its nonsmoking bedrooms opening onto a view. The spacious bedrooms are attractively and comfortably furnished, many resting under ceiling beams. Guests can enjoy private balconies as well. On the property is the Asolare restaurant, one of the island's best (see recommendation below). The staff is helpful in hooking you up with any number of outdoor activities, including everything from sea kayaking to windsurfing.

Cruz Bay, 0831 St. John, U.S.V.I. © **800/322-6335** in the U.S., or 340/776-6121. www.estatelindholm.com. 10 units. Winter $320–$370 double; off-season $170–$270 double. Rates include continental breakfast. AE, DISC, MC, V. **Amenities:** Restaurant; outdoor pool; fitness room. *In room:* A/C, TV, fridge, beverage maker, microwave.

Garden by the Sea Bed & Breakfast ✦ *Finds*

Overlooking the ocean, this B&B lies a 10-minute walk south of the little port Cruz Bay. It has easy access to the north shore beaches and lies between Frank and Turner bays. From the gardens of the house, a short path along Audubon Pond leads to Frank Bay Beach. Be sure to reserve a room ahead, as it offers only three bedrooms. Artifacts from around the world have been used to furnish the units. Each bedroom features elephant bamboo canopy beds, Japanese fountains, hardwood floors, and well-kept bathrooms with shower stalls. Don't expect phones or TVs, as this is a getaway, not a communications center. The 1970s house is designed in a Caribbean gingerbread style with cathedral beamed ceilings. Breakfast is served on the veranda (try the homemade muffins and quiche).

P.O. Box 37, Cruz Bay, St. John, U.S.V.I. 00831 © **340/779-4731**. www.gardenbythesea.com. 3 units. Winter $250–$275 double; off season $160–$200 double. No credit cards. **Amenities:** Nonsmoking rooms. *In room:* A/C, ceiling fan, hair dryer, no phone.

Harmony Studios ✦

Built on a hillside above the Maho Bay Camps, this is a small-scale cluster of 12 luxury studios in six two-story houses with views sweeping down to the sea. The complex is designed to combine both ecological technology and comfort; it's one of the few resorts in the Caribbean to operate exclusively on sun and wind power. Most of the building materials are derived from recycled materials, including reconstituted plastic and glass containers, newsprint, old tires, and scrap lumber. The managers and staff are committed to offering educational experiences, as well as the services of a small-scale resort. The studios contain tiled shower-only bathrooms, kitchenettes, dining areas, and outdoor terraces. Guests can walk a short distance downhill to use the restaurant, grocery store, and watersports facilities at the Maho Bay Camps.

P.O. Box 310, Cruz Bay, St. John, U.S.V.I. 00831. © **800/392-9004** in the U.S. and Canada, or 340/776-6226. Fax 340/776-6504. www.maho.org. 12 units. Winter $205–$230 studio for 2; off season $125–$150 studio for 2. Extra person $25. MC, V. **Amenities:** Sailing; snorkeling; scuba diving, windsurfing. *In room:* Ceiling fan, kitchenette, no phone.

INEXPENSIVE

The following places offer just the basics, but they're fine if you're not too finicky.

The Inn at Tamarind Court

Right outside Cruz Bay but still within walking distance of the ferryboat dock, this modest place consists of a small hotel and an eve simpler West Indian inn. Bedrooms are small, evoking those in a little country motel. Most have twin beds. Shower-only bathrooms in the inn are shared among the single rooms; units in the hotel have small private bathrooms. The social life here revolves around its courtyard bar and the in-house restaurant under the same name. From the hotel, you can walk to shuttles that take you to the beaches.

South Shore Rd. (P.O. Box 350), Cruz Bay, St. John, U.S.V.I. 00831. ℂ 800/221-1637 in the U.S., or 340/776-6378. Fax 340/776-6722. www.tamarindcourt.com. 20 units, 14 w/bathroom. Winter $75 single without bathroom, $148 double w/bathroom, $240 apt, $240 suite; off season $60–$65 single without bathroom, $110–$120 double w/bathroom, $170–$190 apt, $190 suite. Rates include continental breakfast. AE, DISC, MC, V. **Amenities:** Restaurant; bar. *In room:* A/C, ceiling fan, TV, fridge, no phone.

CAMPGROUNDS

Cinnamon Bay Campground ⊛ This National Park Service campground is the
most complete in the Caribbean. The site is directly on the beach, surrounded by thousands of acres of tropical vegetation. Life is simple here: You have a choice of a tent, a cottage, or a bare site. At the bare campsites, you get just the site, with no fancy extras. Each canvas tent is 10×14 feet and has a floor as well as a number of extras, including all cooking equipment; your linens are even changed weekly. Each cottage is 15×15 feet, consisting of a room with two concrete walls and two screen walls. Each cottage contains cooking facilities and four twin beds with thin mattresses; one cot can be added. Lavatories and cool-water showers are in separate buildings nearby. In winter, guests can camp for a maximum of 2 weeks; the rest of the year camping is limited to 30 days, closed September.

P.O. Box 720, Cruz Bay, St. John, U.S.V.I. 00831. ℂ 340/776-6330. Fax 340/776-6458. www.cinnamonbay.com. 126 units, none with bathroom. Winter $110–$140 cottage for 2, $80 tent site, $27 bare site; off season $70–$90 cottage for 2, $58 tent site, $27 bare site. Extra person $7–$17. AE, MC, V. **Amenities:** Restaurant; kayaks; sailing; snorkeling; windsurfing; grocery store; message center; lockers; safe deposit boxes; grill. *In room:* No phone.

Concordia Eco-Tents   This is the newest addition to Stanley Selengut's celebrated
Concordia development project on the southern tip of St. John, overlooking Salt Pond Bay and Ram Head Point. These solar- and wind-powered tent-cottages combine sustainable technology with some of the most spectacular views on the island. The light framing, fabric walls, and large screened-in windows lend a tree-house atmosphere to guests' experience. Set on the windward side of the island, the tent-cottages enjoy natural ventilation from the cooling trade winds. Inside, each has two twin beds with rather thin mattresses in each bedroom, one or two twin mattresses on a loft platform, and a queen-size futon in the living-room area. (Each unit can sleep up to six people comfortably.) Each kitchen is equipped with a running-water sink, propane stove, and cooler. In addition, each Eco-Tent has a small solar-powered private shower, rather meager towels, and a composting toilet. The secluded hillside location, surrounded by hundreds of acres of pristine National Park land, requires guests to arrange for a rental vehicle. Beaches, hikes, and the shops and restaurants of Coral Bay are only a 10-minute drive from the property. (If you're interested in regular on-site studios, see Estate Concordia Studios, above.)

20–27 Estate Concordia, Coral Bay, St. John, U.S.V.I. 00830. ℂ 800/392-9004 in the U.S., or 212/472-9453. Fax 212/861-6210. www.maho.org. 18 tent-cottages (4 are wheelchair accessible). Winter $155–$175 tent for 2; off season $105 tent for 2. Extra person $15. MC, V. **Amenities:** Outdoor pool. *In room:* No phone.

Maho Bay Camps ⊛ Right on Maho Bay, this is an interesting concept in ecology
vacationing, where you camp close to nature, but with considerable comfort. It's set

on a hillside above the beach surrounded by the Virgin Islands National Park. To preserve the existing ground cover, all 114 tent-cottages are on platforms, above a thickly wooded slope. Utility lines and pipes are hidden under wooden boardwalks and stairs. Each tent-cottage, covered with canvas and screens, has two twin beds with thin mattresses, a couch, electric lamps and outlets, a dining table, chairs, a propane stove, an ice chest (cooler), linens, thin towels, and cooking and eating utensils. Guests share communal bathhouses. Maho Bay Camps is more intimate and slightly more luxurious than its nearest competitor, Cinnamon Bay.

P.O. Box 310, Cruz Bay, St. John, U.S.V.I. 00830. ℂ 800/392-9004 in the U.S., or 340/715-0501. Fax 340/776-6504 or 212/861-6210. www.maho.org. 114 tent-cottages, none with bathroom. Winter $130 tent-cottage for 2 (minimum stay of 7 nights); off season $80 tent-cottage for 2. Extra person winter $15, off season $12. MC, V. **Amenities:** Restaurant; sailing; snorkeling; scuba; kayaking; windsurfing.

DINING

St. John has some posh dining, particularly at the luxury resorts like Caneel Bay, but it also has West Indian establishments with plenty of local color and flavor. Many of the restaurants here command high prices, but you can lunch almost anywhere more reasonably. Dinner is often an event on St. John, since it's about the only form of nightlife the island has.

EXPENSIVE

Asolare ✿ INTERNATIONAL/ASIAN   This is the most beautiful and elegant restaurant on St. John, with the hippest and best-looking staff. It sits on a hill overlooking Cruz Bay and some of the British Virgin Islands. *Asolare* translates as "the leisurely passing of time without purpose," and that's what many diners do here. The chef uses some of the best and freshest ingredients available on island. To begin, try the grilled Asian barbecued shrimp or the squid-and-shrimp medley. For a main course, try the ginger lamb or the peppercorn-dusted filet of beef. Two other truly excellent dishes are the chicken Kiev and sashimi tuna on a sizzling plate with plum-passion fruit-sake vinaigrette. For dessert, we like the fresh berry dishes and the chocolate pyramid cake.

Cruz Bay. ℂ 340/779-4747. Reservations required. Main courses $30–$50. AE, MC, V. Daily 5:30–8:45pm.

Equator ✿ CARIBBEAN/INTERNATIONAL   This restaurant lies behind the tower of an 18th-century sugar mill, where ponds with water lilies fill former crystallization pits for hot molasses. A flight of stairs leads to a monumental circular dining room, with a wraparound veranda and sweeping views of a park. In the center rises the stone column that horses and mules once circled to crush sugar-cane stalks. In its center the restaurant grows a giant poinciana-like Asian tree of the *Albizia lebbeck* species. Islanders call it "woman's tongue tree."

For the most part, the chefs pull off their intriguing flavor combinations. A spicy and tantalizing opener is lemon grass-and-ginger-cured salmon salad. A classic Caribbean callaloo soup is offered, and the salads use fresh ingredients such as Roma tomatoes and endive. Daily Caribbean selections are offered, or you can opt for such fine dishes as seared Caribbean tuna, or penne pasta with shiitake mushrooms and roasted tomatoes in an herb-garlic-cream sauce. There's always a dry, aged Angus steak or a grilled veal chop for the more traditional palate.

In the Caneel Bay hotel, Caneel Bay. ℂ 340/776-6111. Reservations required. Main courses $28–$42. AE, MC, V. Days vary 6–9pm.

Paradiso ✻✻ ITALIAN   This is the most talked-about restaurant on St. John, other than Asolare (see above), and it's the only one that's air-conditioned. The interior has lots of brass, glowing hardwoods, and nautical antiques, not to mention the most beautiful bar on the island, crafted from mahogany, purpleheart, and angelique.

Try such appetizers as grilled chicken spring rolls with roasted sweet peppers. Roasted garlic Caesar salad with sun-dried tomatoes and Parmesan grissini is a new twist on this classic dish. But the main dishes truly shine, especially a pan-seared local yellowfin tuna with baby arugula, fennel, pear, and radicchio, and a grilled Kansas City sirloin marinated in garlic and fresh herbs. Another enticing choice is oven-roasted free-range chicken breast with roasted potatoes, carrots, and butternut squash.

Mongoose Junction. ✆ 340/693-8899. Reservations recommended. Main courses $19–$39. AE, MC, V. Daily 6–9pm; bar daily 6–10:30pm.

Tage ✻✻✻ AMERICAN/INTERNATIONAL   Karrl Foster, the island's best chef, a devotee of the "Alice Waters Northern California" approach to cuisine, walks the beach every morning with his dogs, dreaming up the night's five or six food specials that he plans to offer. Perhaps it will be ahi and carambola with a mango Key lime salsa, or a maple bourbon glazed smoked tenderloin panini with a roasted tomato aioli. He recently won the hearts of our dinner party with such dishes as pan-seared fennel-pollen-dusted yellowfin tuna with a champagne truffle vinaigrette. Locally grown organic produce is used whenever possible. His menu is elegant, as is the ambience of his restaurant, but Foster claims he likes to "keep it simple." (He doesn't even own a pair of shoes.) Other highlights of his ever-changing menu include shiitake-filled porcini ravioli with arugula oil or pan-roasted duck breast with roasted sweet potato, prosciutto, smoked almonds, and rum vinaigrette. There's no doubt about it: Tage is the "hot" dining ticket on St. John.

Cruz Bay. ✆ 340/715-4270. Reservations required. Main courses $29–$39. AE, MC, V. Daily 6–9:30pm.

Zozo's Ristorante ITALIAN   An in-the-know crowd of locals and visitors flocks to this charming Italian trattoria, with an open-air terrace and a sweeping panoramic view over the sea. It's the kind of place that locals would book to the rafters on holidays such as New Year's Eve or private celebrations such as birthdays or anniversaries. First-rate ingredients, style, and fresh seasonings contribute to such winning dishes as an eggplant tower (layers of eggplant, fontina, ricotta, and red peppers); little neck clams in white wine, garlic, and plum tomatoes; and lump crab cakes with a roasted-pepper aioli. The pastas are the island's best, especially the lobster ravioli with wild mushrooms and toasted pine nuts, and the basil-infused linguine. Tuck into such fish dishes as a grilled sea bass with an eggplant tapenade in a roasted garlic–shrimp sauce or pan-seared black grouper with a sauce flavored with orange and fresh basil. Their *osso buco* (veal shank) is slowly simmered in red wine, tomato, and veal stock and is a tasty main course.

Gallows Point. ✆ 340/693-9200. www.zozos.net. Reservations recommended. Main courses $29–$36. AE, MC, V. Nov–May daily 5:30–9pm; off season Mon–Sat 5:30–9pm.

MODERATE
Café Roma ITALIAN   This restaurant in the center of Cruz Bay is not a place for great cooking finesse, but it's a longtime favorite, and has pleased many who just want a casual meal. To enter, you have to climb a flight of stairs. You might arrive early and have a strawberry colada, then enjoy a standard pasta, veal, seafood, or chicken dish.

There are usually 30 to 40 vegetarian items on the menu. The owner claims, with justification, that his pizzas are the best on the island; try the white pizza (served only at the bar). Italian wines are sold by the glass or bottle, and you can end the evening with an espresso.

Cruz Bay. ℂ 340/776-6524. Main courses $15–$27. MC, V. Daily 5–10pm.

La Tapa INTERNATIONAL/MEDITERRANEAN   There's a tiny bar with no more than five stools, a two-tiered dining room, and lots of original paintings. (The establishment doubles as an art gallery.) Menu items are thoughtful and well conceived, and include fast-seared tuna with a Basque-inspired relish of onions, peppers, garlic, and herbs; filet *poivre,* a steak soaked with rum and served with a cracked-pepper sauce and mashed potatoes; and linguine with shrimp, red peppers, and leeks in peanut sauce. Live jazz is offered on Mondays.

Centerline Rd. (across from First Bank), Cruz Bay. ℂ 340/693-7755. Reservations recommended. Main courses $29–$36. AE, MC, V. Wed–Mon 5:30–10pm.

Morgan's Mango CARIBBEAN   The chefs here roam the Caribbean for tantalizing flavors, which they adapt for their ever-changing menu. The restaurant is easy to spot, with its big canopy, the only protection from the elements. The bar wraps around the main dining room and offers some 30 frozen drinks. Some think the kitchen tries to do too much with the nightly menu, but it does produce some zesty fare—everything from Anegada lobster cakes to spicy Jamaican pickapepper steak. Try flying fish served as an appetizer, followed by Haitian voodoo snapper pressed in Cajun spices, then grilled and served with fresh-fruit salsa. Equally delectable is mahimahi in Cruzan rum-and-mango sauce. The knockout dessert is the mango-banana pie.

Cruz Bay (across from the National Park dock). ℂ 340/693-8141. Reservations recommended. Main courses $12–$29. AE, MC, V. Daily 5:30–10pm.

Shipwreck Landing SEAFOOD/CONTINENTAL   Thirteen kilometers (8 miles) east of Cruz Bay on the road to Salt Pond Beach, Shipwreck Landing has palms and tropical plants on a veranda overlooking the sea. The intimate bar specializes in tropical frozen drinks. Lunch features a lot more than just sandwiches, salads, and burgers—try pan-seared blackened snapper in Cajun spices, or the conch fritters. The chef shines at night, offering a pasta of the day along with such specialties as tantalizing Caribbean blackened shrimp. A lot of the fare is routine, including New York strip steak and fish and chips, but the grilled mahimahi in lime butter is worth the trip. Entertainment, mainly jazz, is featured Thursday and Sunday nights, with no cover.

34 Freeman's Ground, Rte. 107, Coral Bay. ℂ 340/693-5640. Reservations requested. Lunch $7.50–$16; main courses $17–$24. AE, DISC, MC, V. Daily 11am–9pm (bar until 11pm).

INEXPENSIVE

Vie's Snack Shack *(Finds* WEST INDIAN   Vie's looks like little more than a plywood-sided hut, but its charming and gregarious owner is known as one of the best local chefs on St. John. Her garlic chicken is famous. She also serves conch fritters, johnnycakes, island-style beans and rice with meat sauce, and coconut and pineapple tarts. Don't leave without a glass of homemade limeade. The place is open most days, but as Vie says, "Some days, we might not be here at all"—so you'd better call before you head out.

East End Rd., Rte. 10 (21km/13 miles east of Cruz Bay). ℂ 340/693-5033. Main courses $7–$12. No credit cards. Tues–Sat 10am–5pm (but call first!).

HITTING THE BEACH

The best beach, hands down, is **Trunk Bay** 𝕲𝕲, the biggest attraction on St. John. To miss its picture-perfect shoreline of white sand would be like touring Paris and skipping the Eiffel Tower. One of the loveliest beaches in the Caribbean, it offers ideal conditions for diving, snorkeling, swimming, and sailing. The only drawback is the crowds (watch for pickpockets). The only way to avoid these hordes is to arrive early in the morning or late in the afternoon. Beginning snorkelers in particular are attracted to the underwater trail near the shore (see "Sports & Other Outdoor Pursuits," below); you can rent snorkeling gear here. Lifeguards are on duty. Admission is $4 per person for those over age 16. If you're coming from St. Thomas, both taxis and safari buses to Trunk Bay meet the ferry from Red Hook when it docks at Cruz Bay.

Caneel Bay, the stamping ground of the rich and famous, has seven beautiful beaches on its 68 hectares (170 acres), and all are open to the public. **Caneel Bay Beach** is easy to reach from the main entrance of the Caneel Bay resort. A staff member at the gatehouse will provide directions. **Hawksnest Beach** is one of the most beautiful beaches near the Caneel Bay properties. It's not wide, but it's choice. Since it's near Cruz Bay, where the ferry docks, it is the most crowded, especially when cruise-ship passengers come over from St. Thomas. Safari buses and taxis from Cruz Bay will take you along Northshore Road.

The campgrounds of **Cinnamon Bay** have their own beach, where forest rangers sometimes have to remind visitors to put their swim trunks back on. This is our particular favorite, a beautiful strip of white sand with hiking trails, great windsurfing, ruins, and wild donkeys. (Don't feed or pet them!) Changing rooms and showers are available, and you can rent watersports equipment. Snorkeling is especially popular; you'll often see big schools of purple triggerfish. This beach is best in the morning and at midday, as afternoons are likely to be windy. A marked **nature trail,** with signs identifying the flora, loops through a tropical forest on even turf before leading up to Centerline Road.

Maho Bay Beach is immediately to the east of Cinnamon Bay, and it also borders campgrounds. As you lie on the sand, you can see a whole hillside of pitched tents. This is also a popular beach, often with the campers themselves.

Francis Bay Beach and **Watermelon Cay Beach** are just a couple more of the beaches you'll encounter traveling eastward along St. John's gently curving coastline. Watermelon is actually an island in Sir Francis Drake Channel, and it's far from a melon, with a reef of rainbow-hued fish surrounding it. It lies right offshore, and you can easily swim across to it along with the starfish gliding through turtle-grass beds. To reach Watermelon, follow the Leinster Bay Trail for 1.2km (¾ mile) along the Sir Francis Drake Channel, which is studded with islands. Francis Bay Beach lies near the Annaberg Plantation. Locals come here for Sunday barbecues, and snorkelers explore its shallow reef washing up on the bay's rock-strewn northern shore. Swimming among the algae-covered rocks are the territorial damselfish, French grunts, and even "Christmas tree worms" with their feathery tentacles. The beach at **Leinster Bay** is another haven for those seeking the solace of a private sunny retreat. You can swim in the bay's shallow water or snorkel over the spectacular and colorful coral reef, perhaps in the company of an occasional turtle or stingray.

The remote **Salt Pond Bay** is known to locals but often missed by visitors. It's on the beautiful coast in the southeast, adjacent to **Coral Bay.** The bay is tranquil, but the beach is somewhat rocky. It's a short walk down the hill from a parking lot. (**Warning:** A few cars have been broken into here.) The snorkeling is good, and the bay has some fascinating tidal pools. The Ram Head Trail begins here and, winding for about 1.5km (1 mile), leads to a belvedere overlooking the bay. Facilities are meager but include an outhouse and a few tattered picnic tables.

If you want to escape the crowds, head for **Lameshur Bay Beach,** along the rugged south coast, west of Salt Pond Bay and accessible only via a bumpy dirt road. The sands are beautiful and the snorkeling is excellent. You can also take a 5-minute stroll down the road past the beach to explore the nearby ruins of an old plantation estate that was destroyed in a slave revolt.

Does St. John have a nude beach? Not officially, but lovely **Solomon Bay Beach** is a contender, although park rangers sometimes ask people to put their swimwear back on. Leave Cruz Bay on Route 20 and turn left at the park service sign, about .5km (¼ mile) past the visitor center. Park at the end of a cul-de-sac, then walk along the trail for about 15 minutes. Go early, and you'll practically have the beach to yourself. The beach interests snorkelers of all levels of experience. Also on the north shore and to the immediate south of Salomon is the aptly named **Honeymoon Beach,** where couples often openly display their affection.

SPORTS & OTHER OUTDOOR PURSUITS ⭐⭐

St. John offers some of the best snorkeling, scuba diving, swimming, fishing, hiking, sailing, and underwater photography in the Caribbean. The island is known for the Virgin Islands National Park, as well as for its coral-sand beaches, winding mountain roads, hidden coves, and trails that lead past old, bush-covered sugar-cane plantations. Just don't visit St. John expecting to play golf.

The most complete line of watersports equipment available, including rentals for windsurfing, snorkeling, kayaking, and sailing, is offered at the **Cinnamon Bay Watersports Center,** on Cinnamon Bay Beach (© 340/776-6330). One- and two-person sit-on-top kayaks rent for $15 to $25 per hour. You can also sail away in a 4 or 5m (14- or 16-ft.) Hobie monohull **sailboat,** for $30 to $140 per hour.

BOAT EXCURSIONS   You can take half- and full-day boat trips, including a full-day excursion to The Baths at Virgin Gorda. **Cruz Bay Watersports** (© 340/776-6234) offers trips to the British Virgin Islands for $150, including food and beverages. **Note:** Be sure and bring your passport for any excursions to the British Virgin Islands.

FISHING   Outfitters located on St. Thomas offer sport-fishing trips here—they'll come over and pick you up. Call the **Charter Boat Center** (© 340/775-7990) at Red Hook. Count on spending from $450 to $600 per party for a half-day of fishing.

HIKING   St. John has the most rewarding hiking in the Virgin Islands. The terrain ranges from arid and dry (in the east) to moist and semitropical (in the northwest). The island has more than 800 species of plants, 160 species of birds, and more than 20 trails maintained beautifully by the island's crew of park rangers. Much of the land on the island is designated as **Virgin Islands National Park.** Visitors must stop by the **Cruz Bay Visitor Center,** where you can pick up the park brochure, which includes a map of the park, and the *Virgin Islands National Park News,* which has the latest information on park activities. It's important to carry a lot of water and wear sunscreen and insect repellent when you hike.

St. John is laced with a wide choice of clearly marked walking paths. At least 20 of these originate from Northshore Road (Rte. 20) or from the island's main east-west artery, Centerline Road (Rte. 10). Each is marked at its starting point with a pre-planned itinerary; the walks can last anywhere from 10 minutes to 2 hours. Maps are available from the national park headquarters at Cruz Bay.

One of our favorite hikes, the **Annaberg Historic Trail** (identified by the U.S. National Park Service as trail no. 10), requires only about a 1km (½-mile) stroll. It departs from a clearly marked point along the island's north coast, near the junction of routes 10 and 20. This self-guided tour passes the partially restored ruins of a manor house built during the 1700s. Signs along the way give historical and botanical data. Visiting the ruins is free. If you want to prolong your hiking experience, take the **Leinster Bay Trail** (trail no. 11), which begins near the point where trail no. 10 ends. It leads past mangrove swamps and coral inlets rich with plant and marine life; markers identify some of the plants and animals.

Near the beach at **Cinnamon Bay,** there's a marked nature trail, with signs identifying the flora. It's a relatively flat walk through a tropical forest, eventually leading straight up to Centerline Road.

The **National Park Service** (© 340/776-6201) provides a number of ranger-led activities. One of the most popular is the guided 4km (2.5-mile) **Reef Bay Hike.** Included is a stop at the only known petroglyphs on the island and a tour of the sugar-mill ruins. A park ranger discusses the area's natural and cultural history along the way. The hike starts at 9:30am on Monday, Tuesday, Thursday, and Friday and costs $21 per person. Reservations are required and can be made by phone (at least 2–3 weeks in advance).

SCUBA DIVING & SNORKELING 𝕲𝕲 **Cruz Bay Watersports,** P.O. Box 252, Cruz Bay, St. John (© 340/776-6234; www.divestjohn.com), is a PADI and NAUI five-star diving center. Certifications can be arranged through a dive master, for $385. Beginner scuba lessons start at $110. Two-tank reef dives with all dive gear cost $95, and wreck dives, night dives, and dive packages are available. In addition, snorkel tours are offered daily for $65.

Divers can ask about scuba packages at **Low Key Watersports,** Wharfside Village (© 800/835-7718 in the U.S., or 340/693-8999; www.divelowkey.com). All wreck dives offered are two-tank/two-location dives and cost $88, with night dives going for $75. Snorkel tours are also available at $50 per person. The center also rents watersports gear, including masks, fins, snorkels, and dive skins, and arranges day sailing trips, kayaking tours, and deep-sea fishing.

The best place for snorkeling is **Trunk Bay** (see "Hitting the Beach," above). Snorkeling gear can be rented from the Cinnamon Bay Watersports Center (see above) for $5, plus a $25 deposit. Two other choice **snorkeling spots** around St. John are **Leinster Bay** 𝕲𝕲 and **Haulover Bay** 𝕲𝕲. Usually uncrowded Leinster Bay offers some of the best snorkeling in the U.S. Virgins. The water is calm, clear, and filled with brilliantly hued tropical fish. Haulover Bay is a favorite among locals. It's often deserted, and the waters are often clearer than in other spots around St. John. The ledges, walls, and nooks here are set very close together, making the bay a lot of fun for anyone with a little bit of experience.

SEA KAYAKING **Arawak Expeditions,** based in Cruz Bay (© 800/238-8687 in the U.S., or 340/693-8312; www.arawakexp.com), provides kayaking gear, healthful

---

(Moments   Underwater Wonderful

At Trunk Bay, divers and snorkelers can follow the **National Park Underwater Trail** (© **340/776-6201**), which stretches for 200m (650 ft.) and helps you identify what you see—everything from false coral to colonial anemones. You'll pass lavender sea fans and schools of silversides. Rangers are on hand to provide information. There is a $4 admission fee to access the beach.

---

meals, and experienced guides for full- and half-day outings. Trips cost $90 and $50, respectively. Multiday excursions with camping are also available; call their toll-free number if you'd like to arrange an entire vacation with them. These 5-day trips range in price from $1,100.

WINDSURFING   The windsurfing at Cinnamon Bay is some of the best anywhere, for either the beginner or the expert. The **Cinnamon Bay Watersports Center** (see above) rents high-quality equipment for all levels, even for kids. Boards cost $25 to $65 an hour; a 2-hour introductory lesson costs $80.

EXPLORING ST. JOHN

The best way to see St. John quickly, especially if you're on a cruise-ship layover, is to take a 2-hour **taxi tour.** The cost is $50 for one or two passengers, or $25 per person for three or more. Almost any taxi at Cruz Bay will take you on these tours, or you can call the **St. John Taxi Association** (© **340/693-7530;** www.stjohntaxi.com).

Many visitors spend time at **Cruz Bay,** where the ferry docks. This village has interesting bars, restaurants, boutiques, and pastel-painted houses. It's a bit sleepy, but relaxing after the fast pace of St. Thomas.

Most cruise-ship passengers dart through Cruz Bay and head for the island's biggest attraction, **Virgin Islands National Park** 𝒢𝒢 (© **340/776-6201**). The park totals 5,050 hectares (12,624 acres), including submerged lands and water adjacent to St. John, and has more than 30km (20 miles) of hiking trails to explore. See "Sports & Other Outdoor Pursuits," above, for information on trails and organized park activities.

Other major sights on the island include **Trunk Bay** (see "Hitting the Beach," above), one of the world's most beautiful beaches, and **Fort Berg** (also called Fortsberg), at Coral Bay, which served as the base for the soldiers who brutally crushed the 1733 slave revolt. Finally, try to make time for the **Annaberg Ruins** on Leinster Bay Road, where the Danes maintained a thriving plantation and sugar mill after 1718. It's located off Northshore Road, east of Trunk Bay. Admission is free. On certain days of the week (dates vary), park rangers lead guided walks of the area. For information on the **Annaberg Historic Trail,** see "Sports & Other Outdoor Pursuits," above.

SHOPPING 𝒢𝒢

Compared to St. Thomas, St. John's shopping isn't much, but what's here is interesting. The boutiques and shops of Cruz Bay are individualized and quite special. Most of the shops are clustered at **Mongoose Junction,** in a woodsy area beside the roadway, about a 5-minute walk from the ferry dock.

Before you leave the island, you'll want to visit the recently expanded **Wharfside Village** (© **340/693-8210;** www.wharfsidevillage.com), just a few steps from the ferry-departure point. In this complex of courtyards, alleys, and shady patios is a mish-mash of all sorts of boutiques, along with some restaurants, fast-food joints, and bars.

Bamboula, Mongoose Junction (© **340/693-8699;** www.bamboulastjohn.com), has an exotic and very appealing collection of gifts from St. John, the Caribbean, India, Indonesia, and Central Africa. The store also has clothing for both men and women under its own label—hand-batiked soft cottons and rayons made for comfort in a hot climate.

Sun Angels, Mongoose Junction (© **340/779-6274**), sells handpainted clothing created in Costa Rica. This fine tropical clothing is designed for women only.

Coconut Coast Studios, Frank Bay (© **340/776-6944;** www.coconutcoaststudios.com), is the studio of Elaine Estern, best known for her Caribbean landscapes. It's 5 minutes from Cruz Bay; walk along the waterfront, bypassing Gallows Point. The outlet also sells calendars, gifts, limited edition prints, and lithographs. From December to May, the studio hosts a free sunset cocktail party Wednesday 5:30 to 7pm.

At the **Donald Schnell Studio,** Mongoose Junction (© **340/776-6420;** www.donaldschnell.com), Mr. Schnell and his assistants have created one of the finest collections of handmade pottery, sculpture, and blown glass in the Caribbean. The staff can be seen working daily. They're known for their rough-textured coral work. Water fountains are a specialty item, as are house signs and coral-pottery dinnerware.

The **Fabric Mill,** Mongoose Junction (© **340/776-6194**), features batik fabrics from around the world. Vibrant rugs and bed, bathroom, and table linens, sarongs, scarves, and handbags are all made here.

R and I Patton Goldsmithing, Mongoose Junction (© **340/776-6548**), is one of the oldest businesses on the island. Three-quarters of the merchandise here is made on St. John. There's a large selection of jewelry in sterling silver, gold, and precious stones. Also featured are the works of goldsmiths from outstanding American studios, as well as Spanish coins.

ST. JOHN AFTER DARK

Bring a good book. When it comes to nightlife, St. John is no St. Thomas. Most people are content to have a leisurely dinner and then head for bed.

Woody's Seafood Saloon, Cruz Bay (© **340/779-4625**), is the local dive and hangout at Cruz Bay, right by the ferry dock. It draws both expats and a cross-section of island life from taxi drivers to fishermen. You can come here to eat or drink. The place is particularly popular during happy hour from 3 to 6pm, featuring dollar beers. It's about the only place on island you can order food as late as 1am. Try the blackened-fish sandwich or the "biggest, baddest cheeseburger on island." The joint's hosts are Chad and Todd Beaty, identical twins. They hire bartenders who are willing to pour alcohol in navels or spray whipped cream "anywhere," and we do mean that literally. The joint jumps Sunday to Thursday 11am to 1am, Friday and Saturday 11am to 2am.

The **Caneel Bay Bar,** at the Caneel Bay resort (© **340/776-6111**), has live music Tuesday to Sunday 8:30 to 10:30pm. The most popular drinks are the Cool Caneel (local rum with sugar, lime, and anisette) and the trademark Plantation Punch (lime and orange juice with three different kinds of rum, bitters, and nutmeg).

The two places above are very touristy. If you'd like to drink and gossip with the locals, try **JJ's Texas Coast Café,** Cruz Bay (© **340/776-6908**), a real dive, across the park from the ferry dock. The margaritas here are lethal. Also at Cruz Bay, check out the action at **Fred's** (© **340/776-6363**), across from the Lime Inn. Fred's brings in bands and has dancing on Friday nights. It's just a little hole-in-the-wall and can get crowded fast.

The best sports bar on the island is **Skinny Legs,** Emmaus, Coral Bay, beyond the fire station (© **340/779-4982**). This shack made of tin and wood happens to have the best burgers in St. John. (The chili dogs aren't bad, either.) The yachting crowd likes to hang out here, though you wouldn't know it at first glance—it often seems that the richer they are, the scruffier they dress. The bar has a satellite dish, dartboard, and horseshoe pits. Live music is presented on Friday and Saturday nights during high season.

Morgan's Mango (© **340/693-8141**) is one of the hottest watering holes on the island (see "Dining," earlier in this chapter). It's in Cruz Bay, across from the National Park dock. Count yourself lucky if you get in on a crowded night in winter. The place became famous locally when it turned away Harrison Ford, who was vacationing at Caneel Bay. Thursday is Margarita Night, and Tuesday night is Lobster Night.

Index

A Guide for Every Type of Traveler

Frommer's Complete Guides

For those who value complete coverage, candid advice, and lots of choices in all price ranges.

Pauline Frommer's Guides

For those who want to experience a culture, meet locals, and save money along the way.

MTV Guides

For hip, youthful travelers who want a fresh perspective on today's hottest cities and destinations.

Day by Day Guides

For leisure or business travelers who want to organize their time to get the most out of a trip.

Frommer's With Kids Guides

For families traveling with children ages 2 to 14 seeking kid-friendly hotels, restaurants, and activities.

Unofficial Guides

For honeymooners, families, business travelers, and others who value no-nonsense, *Consumer Reports*–style advice.

For Dummies Travel Guides

For curious, independent travelers looking for a fun and easy way to plan a trip.

Visit Frommers.com

Now you know.

FROMMER'S® CRUISE GUIDES

Alaska Cruises & Ports of Call

Cruises & Ports of Call

European Cruises & Ports of Call

FROMMER'S® NATIONAL PARK GUIDES

Algonquin Provincial Park
Banff & Jasper
Grand Canyon

National Parks of the American West
Rocky Mountain
Yellowstone & Grand Teton

Yosemite and Sequoia & Kings
  Canyon
Zion & Bryce Canyon

FROMMER'S® MEMORABLE WALKS

London
New York

Paris
Rome

San Francisco

FROMMER'S® WITH KIDS GUIDES

Chicago
Hawaii
Las Vegas
London

National Parks
New York City
San Francisco

Toronto
Walt Disney World® & Orlando
Washington, D.C.

SUZY GERSHMAN'S BORN TO SHOP GUIDES

France
Hong Kong, Shanghai & Beijing
Italy

London
New York

Paris
San Francisco

FROMMER'S® IRREVERENT GUIDES

Amsterdam
Boston
Chicago
Las Vegas

London
Los Angeles
Manhattan
Paris

Rome
San Francisco
Walt Disney World®
Washington, D.C.

FROMMER'S® BEST-LOVED DRIVING TOURS

Austria
Britain
California
France

Germany
Ireland
Italy
New England

Northern Italy
Scotland
Spain
Tuscany & Umbria

THE UNOFFICIAL GUIDES®

Adventure Travel in Alaska
Beyond Disney
California with Kids
Central Italy
Chicago
Cruises
Disneyland®
England
Florida
Florida with Kids

Hawaii
Ireland
Las Vegas
London
Maui
Mexico's Best Beach Resorts
Mini Mickey
New Orleans
New York City

Paris
San Francisco
South Florida including Miami &
  the Keys
Walt Disney World®
Walt Disney World® for
  Grown-ups
Walt Disney World® with Kids
Washington, D.C.

SPECIAL-INTEREST TITLES

Athens Past & Present
Best Places to Raise Your Family
Cities Ranked & Rated
500 Places to Take Your Kids Before They Grow Up
Frommer's Best Day Trips from London
Frommer's Best RV & Tent Campgrounds
  in the U.S.A.

Frommer's Exploring America by RV
Frommer's NYC Free & Dirt Cheap
Frommer's Road Atlas Europe
Frommer's Road Atlas Ireland
Great Escapes From NYC Without Wheels
Retirement Places Rated

FROMMER'S® PHRASEFINDER DICTIONARY GUIDES

French

Italian

Spanish

THE NEW TRAVELOCITY GUARANTEE

EVERYTHING YOU BOOK WILL BE RIGHT, OR WE'LL WORK WITH OUR TRAVEL PARTNERS TO MAKE IT RIGHT, RIGHT AWAY.

To drive home the point,
we're going to use the word "right" in every single sentence.

Let's get right to it. Right to the meat! Only Travelocity guarantees everything about your booking will be right, or we'll work with our travel partners to make it right, right away. Right on!

Here's a picture taken smack dab right in the middle of Antigua, where the guarantee also covers you.

The guarantee covers all but one of the items pictured to the right.

For example, what if the ocean view you booked actually looks out at a downright ugly parking lot? You'd be right to call – we're there for you. And no one in their right mind would be pleased to learn the rental car place has closed and left them stranded. Call Travelocity and we'll help get you back on the right track.

Now, you may be thinking, "Yeah, right, I'm so sure." That's OK; you have the right to remain skeptical. That is until we mention help is always right around the corner. Call us right off the bat, knowing that our customer service reps are there for you 24/7. Righting wrongs. Left and right.

Now if you're guessing there are some things we can't control, like the weather, well you're right. But we can help you with most things – to get all the details in righting,* visit **travelocity.com/guarantee**.

*Sorry, spelling things right is one of the few things not covered under the guarantee.

I'd give my right arm for a guarantee like this, although I'm glad I don't have to.

You'll never roam alone.

IF YOU BOOK IT, IT SHOULD BE THERE.

Only Travelocity guarantees it will be, or we'll work
with our travel partners to make it right, right away.
So if you're missing a balcony or anything else you
booked, just call us 24/7. 1-888-TRAVELOCITY.

travelocity
You'll never roam alone.